ABOUT THE AUTHOR

Alton Hornsby, Jr., has been a professor at Morehouse College since 1968 where he is currently the Fuller E. Callaway professor of History and Chairman of the History Department.

Often recognized for his scholarly achievements, Dr. Hornsby counts among his awards and fellowships the 1995 Georgia Governor's Award in the Humanities, the 1990 Georgia Association of Historians Distinguished Service Award, the 1989 WEB DuBois Distinguished Scholar Award presented by the Association of Social and Behavioral Scientists, a 1981–82 National Endowment for the Humanities Fellow, and 1977–78 Rockefeller Humanities Fellow.

In addition to the *Chronology of African American History* 1st and 2nd editions, his publications include *In the Cage: Eyewitness Accounts of the Freed Negro in Southern Society* (1971), *The Negro in Revolutionary Georgia* (1976), *The Black Almanac*, 4th rev. ed. (1977), and *Milestones in Twentieth Century African-American History* (1993).

Since 1976 Dr. Hornsby has served as editor for *The Journal of Negro History*.

Chronology
OF AFRICAN
AMERICAN HISTORY

HIGHLIGHTS

The Chronology of African American History is a reference source designed for users seeking information on important people, places, and events in the history of African American people from the arrival of Christopher Columbus in 1492 to the present. Chronologically arranged entries cover numerous topics including:

- Agriculture
- Anthropology
- Art & Architecture
- Civil Rights & Discrimination
- Economics
- Education
- Film & Theater
- Labor
- Literature
- Media
- Music
- Politics & Law
- Religion
- Science & Medicine
- Sports

The Chronology of African American History provides an abundance of information, and its orderly format makes it easy to use. Special features include:

- Historical timeline
- Short biographical sketches of prominent African Americans
- Bibliography
- Historical documents
- Subject index
- Over 180 photos

Chronology

OF AFRICAN AMERICAN HISTORY

SECOND EDITION

FROM 1492 TO THE PRESENT

ALTON HORNSBY, JR.

GALE

DETROIT · NEW YORK · TORONTO · LONDON

Cover Illustration: *The Congregation,* painted in 1990 by Jonathan Green, Naples, Florida. Original Work: Oil on Canvas 72" x 55."

Back cover illustrations: Selma to Montgomery March. Photo provided by United Press International. Slave Catcher Handbill. Photo courtesy of Library of Congress.

Library of Congress Cataloging-in-Publication Data

Hornsby, Jr., Alton
Chronology of African American History/Alton Hornsby, Jr.
    p. cm.
  Includes bibliographical references and index.
  ISBN 0-8103-8573-2
  1. Afro-Americans—History—Chronology.
E185.H64 1997
973'.0496073'00202—dc21   97-10558
                                                                                      CIP

While every effort has been made to ensure the reliability of the information presented in this publication, Gale Research does not guarantee the accuracy of the data contained herein. Gale accepts no payment for listing; and inclusion in the publication of any organization, agency, institution, publication, service, or individual does not imply endorsement of the editors or publishers. Errors brought to the attention of the publisher and verified to the satisfaction of the publisher will be corrected in future editions.

This book is printed on acid-free paper that meets the minimum requirements of American National Standard for Information Sciences—Permanence Paper for Printed Library Materials, ANSI Z39.48-1984.

ISBN 0-8103-8573-2
Printed in the United States of America by Gale Research

10 9 8 7 6 5 4 3 2 1

TO the memory of my parents,
Alton Parker and Lillie Newton Hornsby, and

TO the future of my children,
Alton Hornsby, III, and Angela Mandee Hornsby;
and my students.

TABLE OF CONTENTS

PREFACE

This second edition of *Chronology of African American History* extends the historical time line to the end of 1996. It also includes many additional entries for the years prior to 1991, particularly the period from 1492 to 1940. There is also a revised section on selected documents and a revised and updated bibliography. Furthermore, this volume contains a list of references that supported the research.

As in the first edition, the second edition of *Chronology of African American History* is a selective compilation of those events in black American history that have had significant effects, impacts, and influences—politically, economically, socially, and culturally. They reflect appropriate diversities in region, gender, and class.

Several persons have assisted me in the production of this new volume, and I wish here to express my deepest appreciation. They include:

Angela Hornsby, Hasan Kwame Jeffries, and Hajj Malik Womack, graduate assistants; Willie Griffin and Max Hull, undergraduate assistants; and Mozell Powell, typist. Also, the librarians at the Auburn Avenue Research Library of the Atlanta-Fulton County Public Library and at the Robert W. Woodruff Library of the Atlanta University Center. Additionally, Anne R. Hornsby, who performed numerous detailed chores, as well as my meticulous editors at Gale Research—Larry Baker and Camille Killens. Finally, much gratitude is extended to all of the readers of the first edition of *Chronology of African American History* and particularly to those who provided valuable suggestions for improving this revised volume.

Alton Hornsby, Jr.
Atlanta, Georgia
February 28, 1997

INTRODUCTION

OUT OF AFRICA

The ancestors of most black Americans came from the area of the continent of Africa known as the Western Sudan. This area extended from the Atlantic Ocean in the west to Lake Chad in the east, and from the Sahara desert in the north to the Gulf of Guinea in the south.

From about 300 A.D. to the late 1500s, three powerful empires dominated the Western Sudan in succession. The empires were Ghana, Mali and Songhai. Each originated as a small, generally peaceful kingdom but subsequently expanded and gained dominance over the entire region. The economies of the Sudan empires were based on farming and mining gold. Although the topography of the Sahara provided an often frustrating barrier, there was continuous trade between the Western Sudanese and the then-known world through the Muslims of North Africa.

The cultivation of crops was most prominent in the savanna, the rain forests of the Guinea Coast south of the savanna, and in the Sahara north of the savanna. West African agriculture was conducted under a system which combined private enterprise and communitarianism. Farm land was owned collectively by the descendants of the first occupant. Individual descendants of the elder were given parcels of land to cultivate, but once cultivation ended, the land reverted back to the collective community. The administrator of the land, the

Master of the Ground, determined the usages of the soil.

While agriculture and gold mining were the principal occupations of blacks living in the Western Sudan, others supported themselves by undertaking numerous crafts, including basketry, pottery, and woodwork.

The first of the great Sudanic empires to gain control of the Western Sudan was Ghana. The Ghanians were mostly black Soninke people who spoke a language in the Manda branch of the Sudanic language group. While Ghana's economy was centered on agricultural pursuits in the various villages, its people also engaged in a lucrative trade from their principal commercial center at Koumbi (Kumbi). The Ghanaians served as middlemen in the trade between North and West Africa, obtaining gold from the mines in Wangara, a forest region south of Ghana, which they exchanged for salt mined by the Berbers and later the Arabs in the northern Sahara. While gold was plentiful in the Sudan, salt was a scarce commodity. Consequently, salt became extremely valuable and was often bartered for gold. The Ghanaians also traded ivory and slaves for textiles and beads which were brought in from North Africa. The government of Ghana levied taxes on all caravans, merchants, and commercial transactions. Once the kingdom expanded, it increased its wealth further by exacting tribute from other peoples whom it had conquered and brought under its control. Because of its vast wealth, many of the residents of Ghanaian cities constructed homes of wood and stone.

Once the Arabs occupied North Africa in the seventh and eighth centuries, Islamic missionaries moved into the Western Sudan and quickly became an important cultural force in the region. At about the same time, the Ghanaians began to raise large armies to subjugate many of their neighbors. Since they were the first West Africans to learn how to smelt iron ore, the Ghanaians were able to make arrows, swords, and other weapons which they used to easily conquer less technologically advanced peoples. One of the more noted kings of Ghana, Tenkhamenen, reportedly had 200,000 warriors in his army in 1067.

Following a drought, compounded by religious divisions, the Ghanaian empire began to decline in the twelfth century. The weakening of Ghana opened the way for many of its former subject kingdoms to increase their strength and influence in the area. Two of the principal candidates to replace Ghana as the superior power in West Africa were Koniaga, inhabited by the Soso people, and Mali, occupied by the Malians. Led by Sundiata Keita, Mali defeated Koniaga in the battle of Karina in 1235 and five years later, subdued the once dominant Ghanaians.

The Malians were also a Sudanic-speaking people who lived principally as farmers and traders. They constructed a prosperous capital city at Niani on the Niger River. The chief administrator of the nation was the emperor. He ruled, however, through a decentralized system of regional and local officials, which included *ferbas,* or governors of provinces, and *mochrifts,* or mayors of important cities. One of the most fabled Malian emperors was Mansa Musa, who ruled the empire from 1309 to 1332.

Much of Musa's notoriety stemmed from descriptions of his famous pilgrimage to Mecca in 1324. A contemporary picture drawn by the Arab traveler, Ibn Batuta, in his *Travels in Asia and Africa, 1325–1354,* depicts the emperor

being sent on his journey to the sound of drums, trumpets, and bugles. In addition, John Hope Franklin commented in his *From Slavery to Freedom* that Musa's entourage "was composed of 60,000 persons." Franklin reported: "Books, baggagemen, and royal secretaries there were in abundance. To finance the pilgrimage, the king carried eighty camels to bear more than 24,000 pounds of gold." The exact amount of the gold carried on the journey totaled more than $5 million.

Once Mansa Musa arrived in the Middle East, he spent so much money, according to Edgar Allan Toppin in his book *A Biographical History of Blacks in America Since 1528,* that he "depressed the price of gold in the great commercial center of Cairo." After running low on funds, however, Musa had to borrow money from local gold merchants. Following the grand pilgrimage of 1324, the Malian kingdom and its emperor were placed on many of the maps of the medieval world, and Musa was given the title "Rex Melle (Mali), King of the Gold Mines."

In addition to Mali's great wealth, Ibn Batuta also observed that the kingdom was virtually free of crime an astonishing feat for any nation, then as now. But the Malians were not strangers to violence, for they had achieved their control of the Western Sudan through the subjugation of their neighbors. Eventually, the Malians had to defend their hegemony against the growing power of other rivals.

After 1332, Mali was ruled by an increasingly inept group of monarchs. Spending continued to be lavish, and local officials often threatened secession from the central government. The people of Songhai were more unified and were led by stronger rulers. Songhai, then, emerged as Mali's strongest rival for supremacy in the Western Sudan.

The Sunni dynasty of Songhai, which was established in 1335, contested Mali for control of the Western Sudan for more than a century. The empire emerged victorious during the reign of King Sunni Ali Ber in 1473. The Sunni dynasty remained in power through Ali Ber and his son until it was overthrown by Askia Muhammad Touré, one of Ali Ber's generals, in 1492. Askia Muhammad expanded Songhai's boundaries to the salt mines of the Sahara, the Hansa states of the Lake Chad region, and the Mossi of the Volta region.

Askia Muhammad established a government which included an efficient central administration as well as appointed local officials. He also made a great pilgrimage to Mecca between 1495 and 1497. Unlike Mansa Musa, however, Askia had a much smaller entourage and spent his money more wisely. Instead of depleting his funds on lavish goods, Askia engaged the services of several Arabic scholars and physicians. The scholars were employed to teach in the empire's two major universities at Timbuktu and Jenne. Because of these and other accomplishments, Edgar Allan Toppin called Askia Muhammad "the greatest of the emperors of West Africa."

Even before Christopher Columbus sailed for the New World, Songhai had become the largest and richest country in Africa. Much of its wealth and the products of that affluence could be seen in the city of Timbuktu, which became a principal center of learning and trade in the Muslim world. An Arab traveler, Al-Hasan Ibn Muhammad, observed in 1526 that all of the houses in Timbuktu were built of "chalke, and covered thatch." There was also "a stately temple" and a "princely palace" built "by a most excellent workman of Granada." All of the inhabitants, especially the "strangers" residing there, "seemed exceeding[ly] rich."

Timbuktu was best known for its multitude of educational institutions. Boys and men studied history, medicine, astronomy, mathematics, and literature. The scholars who taught in the schools and universities were well maintained at the king's expense.

While Askia Muhammad ruled Songhai effectively and efficiently for more than forty years, the empire began to weaken after his sons deposed the aging emperor in 1528. As Askia

neared death, warfare over his succession disrupted the kingdom. Both Askia Ishak I and Askia Dared made valiant but unsuccessful efforts between 1539 and 1582 to restore the efficient, centralized rule which had existed under the great Askia Muhammad. Thus, when a smaller Moroccan army equipped with cannons and gunpowder invaded the empire in 1590, they were able, in the words of Benjamin Da Silva, et al. in their book, *The Afro-American in United States History,* to "cut Songhai to pieces. The days of the great black kingdoms of West Africa were over."

But these great Western Sudanic kingdoms, which served as an ancestral home for African Americans, had demonstrated sophisticated economic activities, a capacity for government which was highly developed, and a complex social structure.

Political life in these African nations consisted of local rule at the tribal and village level, but also a combination of hereditary monarchy and aspects of representative government, particularly at the national or central levels. In some instances, councilors elected their leaders. More typically, however, West African kingdoms were governed by three hereditary families: royal, electing, and enthroning. The monarch was generally selected from the hereditary royal family, but the hereditary electing family made the selection from among those considered the quintessential members of the royal family. Hence, it was not always a matter of primogeniture, where the deceased king's eldest son ascended to the throne. In many situations, the hereditary enthroning family exercised the right to confirm the choice in installing the new ruler. The character of the monarchs and their influence on their subjects ranged from tyrannical to benevolent, from great nation builders to inept and corrupt charlatans. A common characteristic was that, particularly after the eighth century, almost all of them were Muslim.

While Islamic influence became pervasive in West African life and directly affected governance, economic, social, and intellectual activities among the Sudanese, animistic worship, which advocated the propitiation of the spirit of the ancestors, also persisted. Animism was often practiced through chants, sacred songs, and ceremonial dancing. The oldest living relative or descendant of a common ancestor served as the local priest for this form of religion.

The priest of the more ancient, indigenous religions was also known as the Master of the Ground in the extended family, the most common form of social organization. The extended family was composed of several generations of people who were descended from a common ancestor. They all lived in a common village or similar residential area. Individuals who were not obviously related to the group could often become a part of the family in return for performing services for the actual members of the family. Because of its size, both the usual as well as any extraordinary needs of any member of the family, either legitimate or adopted, could normally be supported within the extended family itself. Most disputes could be settled by the Master of the Ground.

Aside from family, work, and worship, there were African cultural expressions in song, instrumental music, dance, art, and literature. Singing took the form of chants, festive tunes, and lullabies as well as sacred songs. Traditional musical instruments included the flute, guitar, harp, and violin. Dancing was used for ritualistic and recreational purposes as well as religious ones. Because of the multitude of languages within a single empire, writing was limited; most of the surviving literature is, understandably, written in Arabic. However, a rich oral traditionwhich included such literary forms as fables, legends, and mythsflourished. By the fourteenth century, the Griot, a professional storyteller, appeared. This elder usually collected and recited tales for a living. In art, utilitarian, ceremonial, and religious themes were prevalent. Cookware, eating utensils, latches, and pulleys were often decorated. Carvers produced masks, dolls, and statuettes. Generally, Edgar Allan Toppin contends, African art was "non-

representational, distorting natural shapes, such as the human figure, with marvelous plasticity to achieve a truer artistic reality."

Yet, despite the existence of complex political and social systems and highly developed intellectual and cultural activities, the West Africans were not above participating in the ancient practice of owning other human beings.

Slavery developed along with civilization in ancient Europe, Asia, and Africa. Normally, an individual became the slave of another through birth (the child of a slave often was consigned to slavery himself), through capture (such as a prisoner of war), through kidnapping (particularly as a result of pirate attacks on ships), through sale by a relative or another person, and as a result of capture and sale by slave traders.

African slaves were generally treated as lesser members of the extended family, but were, for the most part, treated humanely and could share in some of the privileges afforded other members of the family. But they could also be sold as chattel by their owners. The largest category of sales was probably the result of monarchs disposing of surplus prisoners who had become slaves.

In ancient times West Africans sold their slaves to Arab traders from northern Africa. By the early 1500s, however, after they had established colonies in Latin America and in the West Indies, Portugal and Spain became increasingly involved in the African slave trade. Portugal placed African slaves on the sugar plantations which its colonists developed in Brazil. Spain used Africans on its sugar plantations in the West Indies. After 1600, England, France, and the Netherlands also began to import African slaves into their colonies in North America.

Many of the African slaves obtained by Europeans were sold or traded by other Africans for cloth, rum, and other items, especially weapons. Guns were a precious commodity in the interminable warfare between neighboring African peoples. Other black slaves were captured by traders on the continent, pirated from ships, or kidnapped elsewhere, including Europe.

The nefarious European slave trade took several triangular routes. One of the routes guided ships from Europe transporting manufactured products to the west coast of Africa, where traders exchanged the goods for slaves. Then, on the infamous "Middle Passage," the blacks were carried across the Atlantic Ocean to the West Indies and sold for huge profits. The slave traders then purchased coffee, sugar, and tobacco in the West Indies to be sold in Europe. Over another route, ships from New England colonies took rum and other products to Africa, where they were exchanged for slaves. These blacks were also transported to the West Indies to be sold. Some of the profits were used to purchase molasses and sugar, which was returned to New England and sold to rum producers.

Most of the slave voyages across the Atlantic took several months. Since the slave trade was conducted for profit, the captains of slave ships tried to deliver as many blacks as possible. Some captains used a system called "loose packing" to deliver their cargo. This meant that fewer slaves than the ships could carry would be transported in the hope that sickness and death among them could be reduced. Other captains, seeking larger profits and believing that many blacks would die on the voyage nonetheless, carried as many slaves as their ships could hold. The blacks were generally chained together below deck all day and night except for brief periods of exercise. These crowded and filthy conditions resulted in stench, diseases, and death. This system was called "tight packing." Approximately twelve percent of all slaves died during the crossings of the Atlantic. Thus, the story of the "Middle Passage" is a tale of horrors.

The Euro-American slave trade continued from the 1500s to the 1800s. Although the exact number of Africans who were enslaved during these four centuries is unknown, the most reliable estimates range from ten million to twenty million blacks. Between 400,000 and 1,200,000 of this total arrived in North America.

Slaver[…] Caribbean [̲…] land. The [̲…] ment of Sa[…] European s[…] employed s[…] first Africa[…] After the S[…] Carib India[…] larger numl[…] that blacks [̲…] peans in tl[…] placed restr[…]

of three republics at P[…] a government, enact[…] Their economy [̲…] trade, althoug[…] was attaine[…] nally, in [̲…] the M[…] m[…]

Bishop Bartholomew Las Casas and others persuaded King Charles I of Spain to rescind the restrictions in order for Africans to augment the dwindling supply of Indian labor. Subsequently, in 1518 large numbers of blacks were imported directly from Africa. Those newly-arrived slaves were known as *bozal* Negroes, which distinguished them from the group of Africans who were initially transported to Europe and Christianized before being sent to the Caribbean.

The Spanish, Portuguese, and eventually the English developed great plantations in the West Indies where cocoa, coffee, tobacco, and sugar were produced. Slaves grew and processed all of these crops, but most were employed in the furious labor of producing sugar. The Europeans also maintained several colonies on the South American mainland, in such places as Brazil and the territory that now comprises Columbia. Here, in addition to agricultural labor, the slaves worked in mines.

As the black population increased, there was always fear among the settlers that the slaves would rebel against their captivity. Thus, harsh slave codes which mandated severe punishments for insurgency were enacted. These codes served to deter large scale violence, but did not prevent another common form of rebellion escape. Large numbers of black runaways, known as Maroons, formed camps called *quilombos* (cabins). One of the large's" *quilombos* was at Palmares, in the northeastern section of Brazil. Between 1630 and 1697, the Maroons established a succession

almares, which contained
ed laws, and elected a king.
as based upon agriculture and
much of their food and supplies
by raiding nearby plantations. Fi-
697, an army of settlers broke through
aroon fortifications and destroyed the com-
nity. Several of the republic's leaders committed suicide rather than be returned to slavery.

The patterns of black enslavement which
developed in Latin America, including the
Christianization of Africans, provided ready examples and precedents for the establishment of
an even larger "slavocracy" in the English colonies to the north. There, beginning in the first
half of the seventeenth century, millions of Africans would begin the long cultural process of
becoming African Americans.

INVOLUNTARY SERVITUDE

The beginning of the history of African
Americans in the United States is that period of
involuntary servitude from 1619 to 1860, when the
large majority of blacks were chattels. Although
blacks are known to have accompanied the early
explorers to the New World, the first permanent
settlers were the twenty blacks deposited at Jamestown, Virginia in 1619. These blacks, who had
been captured in Africa and sold to the highest
bidders (as many lower-class whites had been
similarly captured or kidnapped and sold in Europe) were not slaves, but indentured servants.

African Americans were probably indentured servants in the American colonies until
1640, and perhaps as late as 1650. After serving
their period of indenture, (normally seven years),
some of these blacks became property holders and
politically active citizens. Throughout the seventeenth century, however, the numbers of blacks-
servants, slaves, or free-were still relatively small. There
were about 300 blacks in the colonies by 1650. The
first rapid increase in their number occurred during the close of the seventeenth century. By the
time of the American Revolution, almost half of

the population in several Southern states was black.
Virginia and Maryland, for example, had a total
population of approximately 480,000 at the time
of the Revolutionary War, about 206,000 of these
people were black. South Carolina's black population was larger than the white one. However,
slavery was not confined to the South. The first
black slaves arrived in New England probably in
1638. By 1700, there were about 1,000 blacks out
of a population of 90,000 in the New England
colonies, and at the time of the American Revolution there were 16,000 slaves in the region. Massachusetts and Rhode Island became great slave-
trading colonies, while Connecticut was the leading New England slave colony. On the eve of the
American Revolution, there were about half a
million black slaves in the American colonies.

In the South, the slaves were principally
employed in producing the staple crops that were
the basis of the Southern economy. By 1700 they
had proved to be the most reliable form of cheap
labor for the Southern planters. The typical slave,
however, did not work on a large plantation. He
would be found more likely on a small farm, with
one or two other blacks, where he worked alongside the master and his family. The majority of
blacks were field slaves who worked under one of
two systems-the Gang Plan or the Task System.
Under the Gang Plan, large groups of blacks,
especially on the larger plantations, worked long
hours in the fields. In the Task System, individual
blacks were given various specific chores to perform. Most urban slaves worked under the Task
System in such occupations as messengers, domestic servants, and craftsmen. A smaller group of
favored slaves (selected principally because of their
light skin color, loyalty, or old age) worked in and
around the master's house as domestic servants.

The climate and soil in New England prevented huge profits from agriculture, but skilled
and unskilled labor was in much demand on small
farms and in homes, ships, factories, and ship-
yards, as well as on fishing and trading ships. Since
Indians and indentured servants proved to be
insufficient laborers, black slaves were a welcome
supplement. In the Middle Colonies and later

states, black slaves were employed in similar occupations and in larger numbers.

Since English law did not define the status of a slave, the colonies were left to adopt their own regulations. Essentially, all the colonies and states aimed first to protect the property rights of the master, and, secondly, to protect white society from what was considered an alien and savage race. The codes grew out of laws regulating indentured servitude, but the slave had practically no rights, while the servant had many.

The first statutory recognition of slavery came from Massachusetts in 1641. Rhode Island passed a law regulating slavery in 1652. Virginia's regulations, which were to set the standards for the South, were passed in 1661. The status of the mother would determine whether a child was slave or free. Children born to slave mothers would become slaves. Most interracial unions and unions of slaves and free persons were of black women and white men, so the products of such unions would be classified as slaves. This practice ran counter to the English tradition which determined the status of a child according to that of his father.

Generally speaking, the slave codes prohibited the assembling or the wandering of blacks without permission from masters. Slaves could not, for instance, own weapons, testify against white persons, and received harsher punishment for some crimes, lesser for others. An attack, for example, on a white person usually meant severe punishment, while petty theft often went unpunished. A master or any white man could not kill a slave with impunity, but was likely to receive less punishment than for killing a free man. Cases involving relations between slave and master could be tried in special courts without juries. Justices of the Peace and a selected group of planters heard such cases and passed judgment. The strictness of enforcement of slave codes varied from region to region, from colony to colony, from state to state, and even from one plantation to another. The Massachusetts code was less restrictive than the Mississippi one, for example, where blacks could be emancipated or manumitted only with legal approval. Urban slaves were less restricted than

rural ones. Slaves on small farms enjoyed more freedom than those on huge plantations.

Physical cruelties were inflicted upon some slaves, primarily for insubordination, refusal to work, slave plots or revolts, and for running away. The cruelest punishment was likely to be seen on large plantations and was received at the hands of foremen or slave drivers. Modern historians tend to indict American slavery not so much for physical cruelty and the psychological effects of the slave system, but because of the harshness of the slave codes, wherein the blacks had little legal protection. In the view of many, the slave system almost completely distorted the African American's personality.

Early historians disagreed vehemently on the question of the slaves' acceptance or rejection of his status and on many related matters, such as whether or not religion stifled resistance or served as a vehicle for leadership and protest. One school, commonly associated with the Southern-born historian Ulrich B. Phillips, portrayed a docile, contented African, naturally pliable, and logically a slave. Another school, taking its name from the New England historian Stanley Elkins, assessed the psychological consequences of slavery and concluded that the blacks' personalities were so distorted by the harshness of the system that they assumed a docile "Sambo," character. Still another school, which includes such liberal historians as Kenneth Stampp and the Marxist scholar Herbert Aptheker, saw the slave as rebellious and troublesome to his master. Contemporary historians widely agree that the slave community was a complex environment. Many, perhaps most slaves accommodated themselves to their immediate surroundings, with the realization that open rebellion was futile and suicidal. Others were openly rebellious. Many others sought any means available, other than violent insurrection, to show their displeasure with their bondage. This "day to day resistance" was carefully documented as early as 1943 by historians Alice and Raymond Bauer.

Slaves did, in fact, protest their enslavement from the very beginning. Aside from daily acts of rebellion, which took such forms as escape, destruction of property, feigned illness, and disloyalty, there were a number of plots and at least one major mutiny and one major revolt. Black slaves joined with white servants in a conspiracy in Gloucester County, Virginia in 1663; fifty-five whites were killed in the slave rebellion led by Nat Turner in Southhampton County, Virginia in 1831; and slaves mutineered on the *Amistad* off the coast of Long Island in 1839. In the final analysis, African American slave plots, mutinies, and revolts resulted in the freeing of only a few blacks, although vicious reprisals often followed such acts. Many more slaves secured freedom by escape and by manumission or emancipation.

The origins of a large free black population in America came after the Revolutionary War. In appreciation of the service of approximately 5,000 blacks in the War for Independence, and as a result of the libertarian and egalitarian spirit inspired by the Declaration of Independence and the war, many masters, especially Northerners, manumitted their slaves. Soon individual states in the North decreed the gradual abolition of the institution, beginning with Vermont's action in 1777. In 1776, the population of the United States was about two and one-half million, with more than 500,000 black slaves and approximately 40,000 free blacks. More than one-half of these free blacks lived in the South. The Revolutionary leaders, including George Washington and Thomas Jefferson, anticipated a continuation of this trend toward manumission and emancipation until eventually slavery would disappear from the land. This expectation was to be drowned, almost literally, by the whirling noise of Eli Whitney's cotton gin. The invention of this native of Massachusetts made cotton production increasingly profitable and caused rapid and substantial increases in the slave population. On the eve of the Civil War, there were four million black slaves in the South.

Free blacks in the rural South worked primarily as farm workers or as independent farmers. In the urban areas, North and South, free blacks were employed in factories, such as tobacco plants and

textile mills, and also worked in ship yards and in railroad construction. There were some independent merchants and many personal servants and artisans. The principal professional occupation was preaching, hence the first black leader of national stature was Bishop Richard Allen of Philadelphia, one of the founders of the African Methodist Episcopal (A.M.E.) Church.

Prior to the American Revolution, free blacks were so small in number that they did not pose a threat to whites in most of the states. Then, during the Revolutionary era, thousands of slaves were freed from Delaware to the North. This rapid increase in the free black population resulted in more severe restrictions. By 1790, free blacks faced regulations similar to those governing slaves. In the early history of New England, blacks could not serve in the militias as combatants (the black military hero, Peter Salem, had to beg his master's permission to serve during the American Revolution), although they could be called upon to work on the roads and other menial tasks. Free blacks could not walk on the streets at night without a pass or visit a town other than the one in which they lived without passes. They could not entertain black or Indian slaves without permission. In the South, they ran the risk of being enslaved themselves if caught without proof of their status. In early Rhode Island history, free blacks were not allowed to keep horses, sheep, or any other domestic animals. In Boston, they could not own hogs. The possession of weapons was severely restricted. In one New England state, blacks could not possess walking sticks or canes unless demonstrably required for the actual support of the person. There was constant conflict in places like New York as free blacks and whites competed for jobs.

By 1840, the free black population in the United States was almost completely disfranchised. More than ninety percent of the American free black population lived in states which totally, or in part, restricted their right to vote. On the eve of the Civil War, blacks voted with relative freedom and safety only in Massachusetts, Vermont, New Hampshire, and Maine.

Restrictions on the political and civil rights of free blacks were motivated by racial prejudice and, additionally, in the South by beliefs that the group had a disquieting influence on the institution of slavery. Free blacks were implicated in a number of the slave plots and uprisings and their very existence pointed to a different life, although not a very radical one, for black men in America. In the final analysis, a free black in pre-Civil War America was little better off than a slave. The inferior status of this group has led historians to classify them appropriately as quasi-free African Americans.

Despite the inferior civil, social, and political status of quasi-free blacks, many managed to achieve considerable distinction in American society. Although discriminated against in employment and in other economic endeavors, a number of free blacks acquired substantial wealth. Even in the pre-Civil War era, there were prosperous free black communities in Philadelphia, Baltimore, Charleston, New Orleans, and elsewhere. Such black individuals as John Jones and Paul Cuffe acquired considerable fortunes. In the military, the arts and sciences, and in religion there were free blacks who distinguished themselves and won recognition even from White America. The free black communities, especially in the North, were vociferous opponents of slavery and discrimination, and the abolition movement of the 1830s and the convention movement of the 1840s and 1850s were interrelated vehicles used by blacks to protest their status in America, whether slave or quasi-free.

THE CIVIL WAR AND RECONSTRUCTION YEARS

Momentous changes in the lives of black Americans occurred in the years between 1861 and 1876. These were the years of the American Civil War, Emancipation, and Reconstruction. Four million African Americans were freed as a result of a war in which many of them participated. Then, for the first time, large numbers of blacks had an opportunity to direct their own social and economic destinies; and some, during the Reconstruction era, were able to assert political leadership. Despite the war and the resulting freedom, however, these were still very difficult years for the black masses as they struggled to survive in a hostile environment, and even the gains made during Black Reconstruction failed to provide lasting security.

After the Confederate attack on Fort Sumter, South Carolina on April 12, 1861 and President Abraham Lincoln's call for 75,000 volunteers to "defend the Union," many Northern blacks rushed to answer the president's appeal. The blacks erroneously interpreted the unfolding conflict as a war against slavery. They soon discovered that Lincoln's war aims did not include interference with slavery where it already existed and that they were not to be permitted combat roles. Abraham Lincoln judged that a war against slavery would drive additional Southern and Border states into the Confederacy and that such a program, along with the employment of black troops, would anger most Northern whites. Blacks and their white abolitionist supporters, in and out of Congress, clearly expressed their opposition to a war whose aims did not include the abolition of slavery, as well as the refusal to employ blacks as troops.

The first year of the Civil War was for the most part a frustrating one for Abraham Lincoln and the Union. In addition to inept military commanders, he had to contend with apathy and even disloyalty in the North; the possibility of an alliance between the Confederacy and cotton-seeking European nations; abolitionist and African American agitation; runaway slaves crossing into Union lines; unauthorized slave emancipation by military leaders; and the employment of blacks in fatigue duties by the Confederacy. There was also the continuous matter of preventing the secession of additional slave states. By the summer of 1862, President Lincoln concluded that the emancipation of certain slaves and the eventual employment of black troops had become military necessities. There were risks involved in such an act: the Border states might join the Confederacy; many

Northern whites might become alienated; and morale in the Union Army might be lowered. On the other hand, England and the rest of Europe would not likely oppose a war against slavery; abolitionist sentiment in the North would enthusiastically support the effort; and thousands of blacks would be lost to the Confederacy while thousands more could be drawn to the Union.

The Emancipation Proclamation specifically excluded all slave states and areas loyal to the Union, hence preserving the Border States for the North and having little immediate effect in most of the South, which the Confederate Army controlled. At the same time, the Proclamation and the employment of African American troops convinced blacks and abolitionists that the "Day of Jubilee" was at hand. Bells rang from the spires of Northern black churches and blacks rejoiced when the emancipation edict took effect on January 1, 1863.

The moral crusade known as abolitionism had sprung up during the 1830s. This new, militant movement resulted from the efforts of such New England and Midwestern reformers as William Lloyd Garrison, James Finney, Lewis Tappan, and Theodore Dwight Weld. The talents of former slaves like Frederick Douglass, Henry Highland Garnett, and Harriet Tubman, as well as members of the free black communities in the North, were joined by the efforts of white reformers. These people were successors to the Quaker protectors of earlier centuries, the moderate abolitionists of the eighteenth and early nineteenth centuries, and the colonizationists of the early 1800s, who would rid the land of the African American problem by shipping blacks back to Africa or to other foreign lands. In 1863, the abolitionists' long and painful efforts finally received political sanction at the highest level when emancipation became a war objective, even though prompted not by moral suasion or moral right, but by military necessity.

Almost 200,000 blacks fought for the Union during the Civil War. Although they faced discrimination of one type or another throughout the conflict, many rendered distinguished service and won commendations from the Commander-in-Chief himself. A few rose to the ranks of officers. About 40,000 blacks died in the fight for freedom—most of these deaths were disease-related, reflecting the poor medical attention received by black soldiers as well as the disproportionate number of blacks on the front line and other hazardous duties. The Confederacy debated the use of black troops until 1864, but when the decision to employ them was grudgingly made, the war was nearing its end. Blacks never saw combat duty for the Confederacy.

The generous terms of surrender which General Ulysses S. Grant offered the Confederates on April 9, 1865 were symptomatic of much of Northern white opinion at the close of the Civil War. It certainly reflected the attitude of President Lincoln toward the seceded states which should, in his view, be returned to the Union as expeditiously as possible in a spirit of leniency and reconciliation. Lincoln's mild Reconstruction program was aborted by an assassin's bullet on April 14, 1865, but his successor, Andrew Johnson, a Southerner, continued the lenient policies toward the white South. Following Lincoln's example, Johnson (who did not believe in African American equality) supported ratification of the Thirteenth Amendment abolishing slavery, but did not push African American enfranchisement or the protection of civil rights. He tolerated anti-black violence in Louisiana, Tennessee, and Mississippi, as well as the Black Codes enacted by the Southern white or "Johnson" governments in 1865 and 1866. These codes, reminiscent of the ante-bellum slave codes, proscribed the African American to an inferior status once again in Southern society.

Republican leaders in Congress correctly viewed the Johnson program as a motivation to restore white Democratic supremacy in the South. Some of these leaders, motivated by a desire to institute Republican party supremacy in the region, and others motivated by a sincere interest in protecting African American civil rights, combined to form a solid front of opposition to the president's programs. The "Radical Republicans" favored a harsh program of Southern Reconstruction, one which would delay the reentrance of the Southern states until Republican strength could be garnered; until the blacks could be enfranchised with the premise that they would form a bloc of Southern Republican votes; and one which would guarantee civil rights for African Americans. In addition, the Republicans believed that Southern white Democratic agriculturists should not be allowed to regain economic and political ascendancy in the nation.

In 1866 and 1867 the Republican leadership, using the party's majorities in Congress, took the Reconstruction of the South from President Johnson's control and instituted their own program. Their plans included an extension of the Freedmen's Bureau (originally proposed by Lincoln) to help freed blacks and poor whites eat, attain clothing and shelter, secure job protection, receive medical attention and some education. African Americans were to be made citizens of the United States and granted all rights and privileges enjoyed by other American citizens. This was accomplished through the Civil Rights Act of 1866 and the Fourteenth Amendment (ratified in 1868). The blacks' right to vote was to be insured through the Fifteenth Amendment (ratified in 1870).

The Radical Republican Reconstruction program that was guided through the House by the Pennsylvania egalitarian Thaddeus Stevens and through the Senate by Charles Sumner, a Massachusetts humanitarian, paved the way for the first large scale participation by blacks in the state conventions in the South. These conventions were called in 1867 and 1868 to establish new fundamental laws to replace the pro-Democratic, antiblack documents instituted by the Johnson governments. In South Carolina, more blacks than whites attended these conventions, and in Louisiana the races attended in equal numbers. Elsewhere, Northern whites ("carpetbaggers"), some of them economic and political opportunists, and Southern whites ("scalawags"), political and economic allies of the Northern Republicans, dominated the conventions. The latter group had exercised the greatest influence in the new Southern

governments, except in South Carolina, where blacks had a majority in the Legislature throughout the early years of Radical or Black Reconstruction.

Although blacks never really controlled any part of the Southern governments (with the exception of South Carolina) during the whole Reconstruction era (1865–1877), they voted in large numbers and elected, members of their own race and sympathetic whites to offices ranging from city councilman to United States Senator. There were, for example, four black lieutenant governors, twenty U.S. congressmen, two U.S. senators, three secretaries of state, a state supreme court justice, two state treasurers, and numerous other minor black officials. P.B.S. Pinchback served briefly as acting governor of Louisiana.

Black voters and elected officials tended to pursue an attitude of charity and reconciliation toward their former slave masters and their descendants. They refrained from passing or supporting vindictive legislation and insisted that Southern whites reap equal benefits from the reformist acts which they passed. The Black Reconstruction governments, despite examples of waste and corruption, made great strides in the physical reconstruction of the South: in providing free public schools; in eliminating anachronistic penal institutions; and in guaranteeing civil rights. In these matters, black and white alike could look for a better life.

THE POST-RECONSTRUCTION, "NADIR" YEARS

The growing Republican strength in the Northwest, economic ties between Northern and Southern capitalists, anti-African American intimidation and violence by the Ku Klux Klan and other hate groups, and the economic helplessness of black Americans eventually caused the waning of Northern Republican enthusiasm for Black Reconstruction. The nadir came with the disputed election of 1876. In return for Republican pledges of federal aid for internal improvements in the

South and the withdrawal of the remaining federal troops supporting Radical Reconstruction, Southern Democratic leaders allowed Congress to proceed in certifying Rutherford B. Hayes as president of the United States instead of the Democratic contender, Samuel Tilden. Following his inauguration, Hayes removed the last federal troops from the South, and the remaining Radical or Black Reconstruction governments in Florida, Louisiana, and South Carolina toppled.

Historian Rayford Logan of Howard University and others have called the period between 1877 and 1900 the nadir in African American life and history. Following the disputed election of 1876 and the so-called Compromise of 1877 which settled it, the Republican party abandoned the Negro and left him in the hands of Southern "redeemers," those native whites who reasserted white supremacy. From Hayes through William McKinley, the national government exhibited a "hands off" policy toward the "Southern problem." With little or no relief to be expected from state and local authorities, blacks faced an environment reminiscent of slavery. Legalized segregation, discrimination, and political disfranchisement became the order of the day. The United States Supreme Court in 1883 and 1896 conclusively stamped legality on racial separation. In the Civil Rights cases of 1883, the Court struck down the Civil Rights Act of 1875, which, among other things, had guaranteed blacks equal access to public accommodations. In 1896, in the historic *Plessy v. Ferguson* decision, the Court sanctioned the principle of separate-but-equal facilities for blacks and whites. In practice, however, the facilities were separate and unequal. Beginning with a Mississippi law in 1890, one Southern state after another adopted ingenious devices for denying the ballot to blacks. These ranged from literacy tests to the infamous white primary, in which blacks were excluded from the most important state and local elections. Ku Klux Klan-type violence, of which the most notorious form was lynching, continued to augment the legal oppression. Out of this nadir, however, were to come two outstanding voices who would leave large imprints upon African

American historyBooker T. Washington and W.E.B. DuBois.

THE AGE OF BOOKER T. WASHINGTON

Booker T. Washington was the only black American invited to speak at the 1895 Cotton States International Exposition in Atlanta. Most prominent Southern whites were aware of the significant work he was performing at Tuskegee Institute in Alabama, where as principal since 1881, Washington was producing trained black agriculturists, artisans, and teachers. He also encouraged cleanliness, respect for hard labor, and fostered racial harmony. In his address at the Exposition, latter dubbed "the Atlanta Compromise," Washington admonished blacks for agitating for political power and social equality, and called on whites to assist them in education, principally agricultural-industrial training, and economic advancement.

The formula for racial peace and progress which Washington outlined at the Exposition met wide approval from Southern and Northern whites. The *Atlanta Constitution* called it the greatest speech ever delivered in the South, and President Grover Cleveland sent Washington a congratulatory telegram. While many blacks supported Washington's ideas, others, particularly publisher William Monroe Trotter and scholar W.E.B. DuBois, disagreed with Washington's remarks and launched attacks against him. Although Trotter was his first and most vociferous antagonist, the best known opposition to Washington was W.E.B. DuBois.

The publication of DuBois' *The Souls of Black Folk* in 1903 crystallized the opposition to the "accommodationist" philosophy of Booker T. Washington. A group of black "radicals" led by DuBois and Trotter met at Niagara Falls, Canada, in June of 1905 and adopted resolutions calling for aggressive action to end racial discrimination in the United States. The lynchings, riots, intimidation, and disfranchisement of the previous decade had taught them that temporizing would not guarantee security to black Americans. The Niagara group held other meetings in the United States, recruiting black intellectuals in nearly every major city. The protest group has become known to history as the Niagara Movement.

Following the anti-black riots in Brownsville, Texas, Atlanta, Georgia, and Springfield, Illinois between 1906 and 1908, the Niagara Movement, with the exception of Trotter (who was suspicious of white people), merged in 1909 with a group of white progressives and founded the National Association for the Advancement of Colored People (NAACP). The NAACP became the most militant civil rights organization in the United States, as it sought to obtain racial equality for all Americans.

Despite the activities of the Niagara "radicals" and the NAACP, the policies and practices of Booker T. Washington and his "Tuskegee Machine" remained in vogue, and continued to garner substantial financial subsidies from wealthy white Americans as well as political endorsements from the White House to state and local authorities. The Niagara "radicals" were hard put in their efforts against Washington. Indeed, the period in African American history following the "Atlanta Compromise" to the death of "the wizard of Tuskegee" in 1915 was the Age of Booker T. Washington.

BETWEEN WAR AND DEPRESSION

After the death of Booker T. Washington, several members of the NAACP and other individuals gained the ascendancy in black leadership, for there could really be no one successor to the Tuskegee "king pin." White America, however, was resistant in accepting these militant demands, and racial oppression continued to be commonplace. Legal and extra-legal discrimination in employment, housing, education, and political disfranchisement were combined with police brutality and atrocious lynchings. Tuskegee Institute kept a running count of lynchings in the United

States and published annual reportsas many as eighty-three were recorded in one yearand it was 1952 before none was recorded. When the United States intervened in World War I, some seemed to believe that the participation of blacks in the conflict would prick the conscience of white Americans and lead to concessions for blacks. Such precedents, in fact, existed in the War for Independence and in the Civil War. The contemporary story, however, turned out to be one of harassment of black soldiers, even while in uniform at home and abroad, and the war itself was followed by one of the worst series of racial clashes in American history. During the summer of 1919, at least twenty-five cities witnessed racial disturbances in what the poet and civil rights reader James Weldon Johnson called "the Red Summer."

The "Red Summer," a product of the postwar depression and the growing black migration to large urban areas, produced a wave of disillusionment in black America. This disenchantment had positive as well as negative effects. In the early 1920s, for example, scores of black intellectuals, centered in Harlem, began producing literary and artistic works depicting Negro life in the ghettoes and often crying for relief from oppression. The Harlem Renaissance, as the new movement was called, came of age in 1922 with the publication of Claude McKay's volume of poetry, *Harlem Shadows*. His poem "If We Must Die" was a militant protest against white attacks in the North and lynchers in the South and urged blacks to resist physical assaults against them. Other notable literary works from this period include Jean Toomer's *Canc*, Jessie Fauset's *There Is Confusion*, Countee Cullen's *Color*, Walter White's *Flight*, and Langston Hughes' *The Weary Blues*. The era was synthesized in Alain Locke's anthology, *The New Negro*.

In this same period, such singers as Marian Anderson, Roland Hayes, and Paul Robeson carried performances of African American spirituals to new heights while black musicians and composers, including Louis Armstrong, Fletcher Henderson, Duke Ellington, Scott Joplin, King Oliver, and Bessie Smith brought jazz and blues from

Southern "honky tonks" to the major cities of the North.

Black nationalism was revived in the movement of Marcus Garvey. The West Indian immigrant taught race pride and urged large-scale emigration of blacks to Africa. Garvey's would-be African empire collapsed behind the cell doors of the Atlanta Federal Penitentiary, where he was incarcerated after being convicted of mail fraud.

The Great Depression that hit the country in 1929 stung the African American. Most blacks were already on the lowest rung of the economic ladder, now they were in serious danger of touching ground. The Depression, of course, stifled much of the growing militancy among the race while doing little to relieve discontent. Blacks contended that even in the midst of common woes, they were still singled out and made the victims of discrimination. Their plight in the area of employment, for instance, was depicted by the slogan "the last hired and the first fired." When Franklin D. Roosevelt took office as president in 1933, American blacks were certainly ready for a New Deal.

A NEW DEAL A NEW LIFE?

Such New Deal measures as the Civilian Conservation Corps (CCC), the National Youth Administration (NYA), and the Works Progress Administration (WPA) lifted blacks as well as whites out of the depths of the Depression, but some blacks felt that they did not receive their fair share of the benefits. Since many of the recovery and reform programs were administered by the state and local governments, this meant all-white control, especially in the South. Discriminatory handling of the measures for relief, in many instances, would not be difficult to imagine. In any case, the New Deal Administration was a segregated one. Nonetheless, President Roosevelt established his so-called "Black Cabinet," black advisers on African American affairs. These individuals included Mary McCleod Bethune, an educator, Ralph Bunche, a political scientist, William

Hastie, an attorney, and Robert Weaver, an economist. In the end, the New Deal, despite its imperfections, was viewed by blacks as well as whites as an era of progress certainly a marked advance over the Depression years."

WAR AGAIN

The outbreak of the Second World War in Europe, like its predecessor, encouraged a new wave of black emigration to the North. As the nation entered a state of defense-readiness, blacks sought to obtain a share of the increasing number of jobs in defense industries. Again, they met a good deal of frustration resulting from discrimination. Finally, after blacks threatened to stage a massive protest march in Washington, D. C., President Franklin D. Roosevelt issued an executive order forbidding discrimination in defense related industries. Once the United States entered the world war, hundreds of thousands of black Americans served with distinction. This service, along with the growing black populations in the urban centers, a rise in the literacy rate among blacks, and increasing economic opportunities appeared to foster a new determination to end racial discrimination in American life. The NAACP, bolstered by the records of black servicemen, an increased membership, a new corp of brilliant young lawyers, and steady financial support from white philanthropists, led the way toward freedom.

THE ATTACK AGAINST SEGREGATION

The existence of segregation and discrimination in the most democratic nation in the world constituted an American dilemma, according to the Swedish social scientist Gunnar Myrdal, who in 1944 had concluded a year-long study of the race problem entitled *An American Dilemma*. The NAACP had long been aware of the dilemma and was determined to resolve it by eliminating segregation and discrimination from American society. The NAACP leaders, like most Americans, revered the constitutional structure of the United States and thus sought to implement its program through legal channels. Prior to World War II, the organization's legal minds were chipping away at the foundations of segregation and discrimination by winning important decisions before the United States Supreme Court. After the war, there was a virtual avalanche. From 1945 to 1954, the NAACP attacked legalized segregation and discrimination in almost every domain and its foundations slowly crumbled. Ingenious devices for denying blacks the right to vote, discrimination in housing, bias in transportation, and segregation in recreation and educational facilities fell victim to NAACP-sponsored law suits. The Supreme Court decisions on school segregation, which are highlighted by the Brown case in 1954, were so far-reaching and portended so much for the future that they inaugurated a whole new era in African American history, the era of civil rights.

"THE SECOND RECONSTRUCTION"

The schoolhouse had long been considered an integral part of the democratic process. It was, in fact, a bulwark of American society. Indeed, its ability to socialize individuals made it an almost sacred institution. The destruction of segregation and discrimination in the schools could then bring the day closer when America would boast of an integrated society. The school decisions inspired a literal stampede for equality. Court decisions quickly knocked down the remaining vestiges of legalized segregation, Congress, in the face of skillful lobbying by black organizations and increasing black voter registrants in the North, began passing laws designed to insure Negro voting rights against extra-legal trickery in the South. President Harry S. Truman issued an executive order banning segregation in the armed forces; several years later, President Dwight Eisenhower signed a bill that prohibited discrimination in housing assistance by the FHA and the Veterans' Administration. Civil rights committees were established to investigate and report injustices. Boycotts, such as the famous

one in Montgomery, Alabama in 1955–56, broke down Jim Crowism on local buses. With segregation and discrimination by law a dead letter, black groups turned to overt and covert bias in the private sector. Centering their attention on the humiliating separate lunch counters and restaurants, the sit-in technique (aided by the boycott) was revived and used frequently to wipe out discrimination in restaurants and other public accommodations from hotels to cemeteries. The Civil Rights Act of 1964 acknowledged the correctness of sit-ins by, among other things, outlawing discrimination in public accommodations. The American dilemma seemed to be over, all citizens would be free in "the land of the free." The dream which Martin Luther King, Jr. had so eloquently described at the March on Washington in August 1963 seemed near fulfillment.

In assessing the gains in civil rights and human freedoms which blacks had made in a single decade, 1954–1964, it was easy for some to see them as a continuation of the progress aborted by the end of Reconstruction in the 1870s and 1880s. The achievements and the prospects seemed so significant that many felt that the era could properly be called "The Second Reconstruction."

"THE SECOND RECONSTRUCTION" WANES

President Lyndon B. Johnson's signature on the Civil Rights Act of 1964 had barely become law when a serious racial disturbance erupted in Harlem. That same summer several other Northern ghettoes were the scenes of violence. Then in August, 1965, the black ghetto of Watts in Los Angeles exploded, leaving many dead and injured, and property losses in the millions of dollars. For the next two summers, peaking with the equally destructive Detroit riot of 1967, scores of major racial outbursts, often times sparked by clashes between blacks and white police officers, occurred. The nation sought an answer to these eruptions, particularly at a time when the millennium appeared at hand. The Presidential Commission on

Civil Disorders (Kerner Commission) offered its findings in March 1968. In spite of all the court decisions, the sit-ins, marches and boycotts, the average black American was disillusioned with his status in American society, for he still found himself ill-housed, ill-clothed, poorly paid, (if at all), segregated, and discriminated against (through covert and extra-legal means) in all walks of American life. Ingrained white racism, the Commission reasoned, blocked the legitimate aspirations of black people. The slaying of Martin Luther King, Jr., the nation's leading apostle of non-violent resistance to racism and bias, in April of 1968 increased the disillusionment and, in fact, led to some outright despair. New cries of black nationalism, black separatism, and violent resistance were heard in African-America.

In three and one-half centuries of life in America, the African race has seen momentous changes in the legal and social structures of the country which relate directly to its own status. The legal foundations of segregation and discrimination which kept it in a straitjacket were toppled in the last decade. The attainment of these goals involved a long, painful, often times frustrating and disillusioning struggle. Yet, as the Kerner Commission Report so dramatically depicted, the long fight for dignity and justice was by no means completed, for the real victory would have to involve the repression of white racism. White Americans would have to confront its ingrained and often unconscious bias on the subject of race, and work consciously to erase its effects from the land.

"THE SECOND RECONSTRUCTION" BETRAYED

The landslide proportions of Richard Nixon's re-election as president in 1972 cast a dark cloud over black America. During his first term, the president had consistently reaffirmed his commitment to racial equality and justice, but at the end of his term many of the most prominent leaders in black America found Nixon's record on civil rights seriously wanting. Some even claimed that there had been an erosion of the gains made under the two previous Democratic administrations. They cited, for example, the president's failure to appoint blacks to top level positions in the federal government (i.e., under Nixon, the cabinet returned to an all-white status); his nominations of G. Harold Carswell and Clement Haynsworth, both "conservative" Southerners, for seats on the United States Supreme Court; his vehement opposition to busing to achieve school desegregation; and his indifference towards desegregated housing and support of black institutions of higher education. The United States Commission on Civil Rights joined its voice with that of the black leaders, charging that the Nixon administration was derelict in its enforcement of existing civil rights laws.

President Nixon used several occasions, including press conferences and meetings with blacks inside and outside of government, to express concern with the disillusionment and disenchantment with his administration within black America. Yet he refused to alter his course. Nixon was prone to cite the phenomenal progress of black Americans in the past decade in the areas of civil rights, economic opportunity, and political development. He seemed to suggest that the remaining problems of blacks were less a matter of race and more of initiative, self-reliance, and economic development, and discussed the need for "black capitalism" and black entrepreneurship. As Nixon approached the election campaign of 1972, he predicted substantial black support for his candidacy and did, in fact, win endorsement from several prominent blacks in his bid for re-election. However, the leaders of most of the major black civil rights organizations in the country urged Nixon's defeat, and on election day he amassed only about thirty percent of the total black vote.

The president began his second administration amid the aura of the greatest election victory in American history, while the growing cancer of Watergate still only slowly creeping into his political life. The "Watergate" scandal, whose discovery was attributed to a black security guard, Frank

Wills, would soon bring down the presidency of Richard Nixon. Meanwhile, the president continued his policies of "benign neglect" toward black America.

The indifference of a national administration toward the peculiar problems of black Americans, combined with a growing economic recession, created a certain amount of confusion among blacks. Ironically, this was also a time of substantial political progress at the local level, particularly in the South. The problem, however, in large measure, was that the local political prowess which blacks were gaining could not be transformed or translated into influence at the national level, and could not halt the growing spiral of black unemployment and underemployment. The indifference manifested by the national administration had its impact in other facets of black American life. The drive for "affirmative action" in recruiting blacks to higher paying jobs seemed to lose some of its furor, as did the preferential recruiting of black students to previously all-white or majority-white schools and colleges. The economic decline was a part of the explanation; the cry by some whites of "reverse discrimination" was another, but the complacent tone set in Washington was also of great significance. What should blacks, still the most ill-fed, ill-housed, poorly trained segment of the American population, do now? Would the disillusionment of the past become outright despair? Would there be new Wattses, Detroits, and Atlantas? Would the black masses again take to the streets to vent their frustrations at still not being able to share fully in the American Dream? There were, as always, voices in the black community urging such a course of action, but they were, as in the past, on the fringe of the black mainstream without a substantial following.

During the Nixon nadir, the black mainstream would continue to look to the leadership of the black middle class, as exemplified in the major civil rights organizationsthe NAACP, the Southern Christian Leadership Council (SCLC), Operation PUSH (People United to Save Humanity), the Urban League for the right path to the Promised Land. That leadership, faced with the

political and economic realities of the 1970s and the growing displays of overt racism in the North, could only sprout the old shibboleths of the Civil Rights era and espouse similar strategies. In fact, black American leaders were now faced with problems, policies, and practices that defied simple solutions; such previous tactics as marches, court edicts, or even a brick thrown through a plate-glass window seemed to be less than effective. Black America needed influence at the highest levels of political and economic decision-making, and that it did not have.

While the Nixon administration undoubtedly exaggerated the extent of black progress in America in the 1960s, it was nevertheless true that all indexes relating to income, education, housing, and the like revealed numerical and often percentage gains for black Americans during the 1960s. In many respects, black America was still a colonized nation, but its colonial status was closer to that of America in the 1760s than to Rhodesia in the 1970s. These facts, together with the apparent futility of violent outbursts, seemed to suggest to black America, the masses as well as the elite, that after a decade of disillusionment, a return to the mainstream would best promote physical and psychological well-being. The mood of black America suggested a harvesting of gains to prevent further erosions; to place education above demonstration; to seek whatever securities that were inherent in the middle-class society in America; and to acknowledge the fact that America was still a nation of two societiesone black, one white separate and unequal.

The "Watergate" scandal of the early 1970s, in which President Richard Nixon was recorded on tape as allegedly condoning criminal conspiracy, did what black voters had been unable to do in 1972remove him from office. Nixon's successor, Vice President Gerald R. Ford, a "more moderate" Republican, came into the White House under the major constraint of not having been elected to the Oval Office. The next presidential campaign was less than two years away.

Given the constraints under which he assumed office, Ford, who eventually pardoned former President Nixon, acted in the manner of a caretaker. He continued many of his predecessor's policies while trying "to heal the nation" in the aftermath of Watergate. President Ford made no new major civil rights initiatives and generally opposed "forced busing" to achieve school desegregation. One of his cabinet members, Agriculture Secretary Earl Butz, was forced to resign after uttering a racial slur against blacks.

Ford's propensity for simplicity, particularly in foreign affairs, a continued downturn in the economy, and the "stain" which Watergate left on the Republican party, particularly its "conservative wing," left the president particularly vulnerable as the 1976 elections approached. Jimmy Carter, a relatively unknown peanut farmer and the former governor of Georgia, emerged from the close race victorious.

Carter had sprung on the nation during the Democratic primaries as a populist who would strengthen the economy so that both farmers and laborers could reap a better harvest. As a former Southern governor, he was suspect among blacks, particularly in the North. Although the Southerner from the small town of Plains had captured the Georgia governor's office as a segregationist, he declared in his inaugural address that the time for racial bigotry in his state was over. Carter won the allegiance of many of Georgia's black leaders, particularly in the capital city of Atlanta. Since Atlanta was the headquarters of the Civil Rights Movement, the Atlanta black leadership cadre, including the father and widow of slain civil rights leader Martin Luther King, Jr. as well as such civil rights veterans as John Lewis and Andrew Young, was highly respected throughout the nation. The Atlanta group was thus able to win over other influential blacks in other parts of the nation to join them in their support of Carter's candidacy. Even when Carter stumbled in a speech in Gary, Indiana, in which he discussed "the ethnic purity" of neighborhoods, the Atlanta leadership group stuck with him and helped save him from disaster in black America. The strong showing which Carter made among blacks in the South, particu-

larly, gave him, according to several journalists and political analysts, his margin of victory over President Ford.

Many blacks apparently believed that they had put Carter in the White House and placed great expectations on him when he took the oath of office in January, 1977. There were predictions of several black Cabinet officers, increased financial support of black institutions, and greater sensitivity toward other special aspirations and needs of black America. But even after Carter, in an unprecedented and unexpected move, named the black Georgia congressman Andrew Young U. S. Ambassador to the United Nations and appointed Patricia Roberts Harris, a former Howard University law professor, Secretary of Housing and Urban Affairs, some blacks began to grumble that the president had made too few high level black appointments. There were even some complaints that Mrs. Harris, a fair-complexioned, middle class African American, was "not black enough " in her racial consciousness. Harris, a former civil liberties lawyer, bristled at the suggestion.

As President Carter developed his financial policies in the midst of a continuing economic downturn in the nation, Vernon Jordan, the head of the National Urban League, began a chorus of protests that the president was not doing enough to help the most depressed segment of the nation, black America. In the beginning, Jordan's comments drew few adherents, but shortly thereafter only Carter's staunchest supporters among America's black leadership establishment were withholding criticisms. Carter himself vacillated between bristling and appeasing his black critics. On one occasion, he noted that he was under no compulsion to have a "quota" of blacks in his cabinet; on another, he expressed disappointment that he had not been able to recruit more highly qualified, high-level black appointees. On some occasions, Carter extolled the progress that his administration had made in civil rights and in other major issues of concern to blacks; on other occasions, he admitted that much remained to be done.

Yet it was the soaring inflation which brought higher gasoline prices and diminished supplies, and the Iran hostage crisis of 1979 that crippled the Carter presidency. Carter's inability to restore a full, healthy economy and to secure the release of American citizens from Iran brought accusations of a "malaise" at the White House. Finally, when Ronald Reagan, the former Hollywood star and governor of California, who ran an unsuccessful campaign for the Republican presidential nomination in 1976, told voters in the 1980 elections that he would restore the economy and make Americans proud of their nation again, the American electorate turned Jimmy Carter out of the White House. Although black voters still provided Carter with the heaviest support of any segment of the American population, there was less enthusiasm for him in the 1980 election. Many blacks apparently agreed that the president was not forceful enough in solving the problems of the economy or in dealing with terrorists. Others seemed to believe that he had still done too little to advance the major concerns of black America: fuller employment, better education, and enhancement of civil rights.

In the end, Jimmy Carter, by any fair assessment, was the strongest supporter of black America's "Agenda" than any American president since Lyndon Baines Johnson. While only two blacks served in his Cabinet, others were generously sprinkled throughout other high levels of government. They included Clifford Alexander, Secretary of the Army; Mary Frances Berry, Assistant Secretary of Education; and Drew Days, Assistant Attorney General. Carter appointed more black federal judges than all of his predecessors combined. He consulted with such black leaders as Jesse L. Jackson, Martin Luther King, Sr., and Benjamin Mays to a degree much larger than Johnson, and took more initiatives to support black colleges than any of his predecessors. But President Carter's gestures toward black America were not only hampered by a slow economy, but also by a growing white backlash against affirmative action and other preferential and compensatory programs for African Americans as well as continued opposition to school desegregation. In a similar fashion, if not outright overtly, Ronald Reagan had also appealed to such sentiments in his 1980 campaign, while et the same time declaring himself a proponent of "equal opportunity."

Exponents of one version of a cyclical theory of history relate the nature and character of events of certain periods to the policies and practices of the presidential party or administration in power. Often, such an analysis takes into account the personality of the president himself. For example, both Lyndon Johnson and Jimmy Carter were Southerners of somewhat humble origins who later achieved considerable wealth. Even after rising to social and political prominence, however, they tended to eschew lavishness and elitism. Both were raised among substantial black populations in the segregated South. Both overcame their backgrounds to become proponents of racial equality and racial justice. Reagan, on the other hand, emerged from modest means to fame and fortune as a Hollywood star. During his acting career and later as governor of California, Reagan associated primarily with his peers, whose lifestyles reflected glamor and power. Although he later referred to his appointments of blacks to high positions in the California state government, Reagan rarely, if ever, identified with the black masses or their particular circumstances, aspirations, and needs.

While one can make too much of the relationships between the cycles of party and administration policies and practices, and the differing characters of chief executives, it was, nevertheless, true that the "Second Reconstruction" blossomed under Democratic administrations, whose leaders, although men of substantial wealth, exhibited a special sensitivity to all of black America. The new era of progress and hope first waned under Republican presidents, one of whom allowed arrogance to place him outside of the law. The "Second Reconstruction" gained new life under a Southern Democrat who once made a living producing peanuts with poor blacks. This interlude was ended when the Republican governor of California occupied the White House.

TOWARD A BLACK AGENDA

Ronald Reagan appointed only one black person, Samuel R. Pierce, a "conservative" lawyer, to his Cabinet. When Pierce left the White House, he was being investigated by Congress for possible corruption in office. Another Reagan black appointee was William Allen, another "conservative" who left his post as head of the U.S. Civil Rights Commission in disgrace under clouds of mismanagement and buffoonery. President Reagan rarely consulted with members of the black leadership establishment largely because he felt that they were partisan (almost all of them were either Democrats or Independents) and because they continuously complained that he was insensitive to their "Black Agenda." While Reagan did not sway in his opposition to such "Black Agenda" items as affirmative action and mandatory busing to achieve desegregation, he boasted of strengthening the economy and its subsequent benefits to all Americans, including black ones. President Reagan also took offense at any suggestion that he was a racist. However, as he prepared to leave the White House in 1989 after serving two terms, Reagan suggested on network television that some of the black leadership establishment deliberately continued to fan the fires of racism for self-gain, while distorting the declining significance of race in American life as well as his own record in behalf of civil rights and equal opportunity.

While Reagan did sign a bill extending the provisions of the historic Civil Rights Act of 1965 and the legislation creating the Martin Luther King, Jr. federal holiday (both with some initial reluctance), he advocated tax exemptions for segregated private schools and opposed two civil rights bills designed to strengthen the provisions of the Civil Rights Act of 1964. These protections were struck down by a Supreme Court dominated by Reagan appointees. The "Reagan Court" emerged after the president appointed three justices and elevated another to Chief Justice, jurists who were widely suspected of being "conservative idelogues." One of his nominees, Robert Bork, was rejected by the United States Senate. Reagan appointed only two blacks to federal judgeships.

Indeed, it was Reagan's appointments to the judiciary, particularly the United States Supreme Court, which highlighted the "betrayal of the Second Reconstruction." After all, the new era of human and civil rights for blacks, women, other ethnic minorities, and dissidents had begun with the high Court's decision in *Brown v. Board of Education of Topeka, Kansas* in 1954. Then, after blacks took control of their own destinies beginning with the Montgomery Bus Boycott of 1955, the Supreme Court remained steadfast in guarding and protecting their liberties under constitutional guarantees. When Reagan appointees joined the "conservative" minority on the high Court, however, affirmative action and other preferential and compensatory programs to readdress past discrimination, as well as mandatory busing to achieve school desegregation, were rebuffed time and time again. The concept of "reverse discrimination" gained new prominence as the Court frequently agreed with the complaints of white males, particularly, that they were the victims of bias because of their race or sex.

While the policies of the Reagan administration and the rulings of the Supreme Court may have accurately reflected the current mood of White America, i.e., that the "Second Reconstruction" had achieved its objectives in granting full constitutional rights to black Americans, many blacks continued to blame President Reagan for "rolling back the [civil rights] clock." Some even suggested that despite what opinion polls might say about race conscious policies, the president had a constitutional and moral duty to promote such ideas and programs until the "Second Reconstruction" was, in fact, completed. They often enlisted in their assessments the history of the first Reconstruction which ended when another Republican president, Rutherford B. Hayes, made a "corrupt bargain" with racism in 1876.

During what some black and white leaders, scholars, and other individuals came to call "the Reagan Nadir," a number of proponents of the "Black Agenda" turned their focus away from traditional politics into independent parties, apolitical postures, or new structures of political activity.

Others chose to remain within the traditional structure. Some placed their hopes on the shoulders of the Reverend Jesse Louis Jackson, a veteran African American minister and civil rights leader. The former SCLC leader, through his organizations Operation PUSH and the Rainbow Coalition, emerged in the 1980s as the most popular national black leader since the late Martin Luther King, Jr. In 1984, Jackson sought the Democratic nomination for president and was promptly hailed as the first major black figure to seek that office. But Jackson's candidacy seriously divided the black leadership establishment. Several contended that his candidacy would further polarize the races in the United States, while others believed that it would undermine the solidarity which the Democratic presidential nominee would need in the general election to defeat Ronald Reagan. Furthermore, the black leadership establishment insisted that Jackson had absolutely no chance of capturing his party" nomination, let alone the White House.

Jackson persisted, however, insisting that he could win both the nomination and the presidency by galvanizing black Americans, bringing additional minorities (a rainbow coalition) into his ranks, and winning the support of whites "of goodwill." Although his campaign did inspire a significant increase in new black voters, particularly in the South, Jackson stumbled with other minorities and whites when he became associated with the Nation of Islam leader Louis Farrakhan, and after making allegedly anti-Semitic remarks himself.

Louis Farrakhan had long been accused of harboring anti-Semitic views. He allegedly called Judaism "a gutter religion" and Adolph Hitler, the Nazi dictator, "wickedly great." At the time these comments were made, Farrakhan was a strong supporter of Jesse Jackson. There were loud outcries from Jews, gentiles, and even some African Americans, particularly when Jackson procrastinated in disassociating himself from Farrakhan. However, Jackson himself created his most crucial political mistake when he was quoted as having privately referred to Jews by the epithet "hymie."

After initial denials and vacillations, the presidential candidate apologized, but severe, perhaps irreparable damage had been done to his quest to broaden his Rainbow Coalition beyond black people.

The black opposition to the Jackson candidacy took on more strident tones after the "hymie" remark. There were more assertions that the Jackson campaign represented divisiveness and futility. At the Democratic National Convention in San Francisco, Andrew Young, the mayor of Atlanta, Georgia, and a colleague of Jackson's in the Civil Rights Movement, publicly severed ties with the African American candidate and seconded the nomination of the leading contender, former Vice President Walter Mondale. Young was roundly jeered by Jackson delegates and supporters and open warfare between pro and anti-Jackson blacks seemed a real possibility in the Golden Gate city. With deep divisions among blacks and barely five percent of support from whites, the Jackson campaign of 1984 was doomed.

No matter what the outcomes were in 1984, the candidacy of Jesse Jackson for the Democratic nomination inspired thousands of blacks to enter or reenter the traditional political process and to pin their hopes on a candidate who espoused, for the most part, a "Black Agenda." Jackson's showing among whites, while not very impressive, was the best ever attained by a black presidential candidate. Furthermore, the barrier against a major African American candidate for a major party's nomination was shattered.

By 1988, even amidst continuing racial divisions, blacks were mayors in almost all of the nation's larger cities. Other American cities were on the verge of electing blacks to high office and even smaller municipalities, some with minority black populations, had elected black mayors. Black representation in state legislatures, school boards, and state courts were increasing, especially in the South. There was a black lieutenant-governor in Virginia. These trends were encouraging to Jesse Jackson and his hard-core supporters. Despite the results of 1984, they decided that the preacher-politician should make a new effort for the White House in 1988.

The lessons to be learned from the Jackson campaign of 1984 included the imperative to solidify African Americans, particularly the black leadership establishment, to avoid the appearance of being an exclusive "Black Agenda" candidate, and to avoid such embarrassing episodes as the Farrakhan affair and the "hymie" remark so as not to alienate white voters. In the 1988 campaign Jackson succeeded remarkably well in unifying blacks; almost all of the nation's prominent black Democrats rallied around his candidacy or remained neutral. He kept arm's length from Farrakhan and made overtures to Jewish leaders (Jackson had begun these gestures during his address at the 1984 Democratic Convention). Jackson carried his populist theme to urban black ghettos as well as rural hamlets, and courted the white working class laborer as well as the Midwestern and Southern farmer. He said he wanted to give hope to the hopeless and make America a better place for all people. Black voters gave him ringing endorsements and Jackson increased his white support at least threefold, but far short of enough to win the Democratic nomination for president of the United States.

Nevertheless, Jackson's primary successes, which resulted in him finishing second with more than 1,200 delegates at the 1988 Democratic Convention, had some immediate and long-range results. It helped to reduce the alienation felt among the black masses and gave them new hope that their agenda could become reality through the traditional political process. Jackson helped to shape his party's platform and secured new high-ranking positions for African Americans in the Democratic party; one of his campaign managers, Ron Brown, was subsequently elected Chairman of the Democratic National Committee. Most importantly, Jackson helped reduce white antipathy to the election of blacks to high offices. Within months of the end of Jackson's campaign, L. Douglas Wilder was elected governor of Virginia and David Dinkins mayor of New York City with substantial white support. However, many be-

lieved that Jackson had driven the Democratic party "too far to the left," which contributed to its defeat in the 1988 presidential election. Also, despite his populist appeals, many still viewed Jackson as the candidate of the "Black Agenda." Indeed, several commentators suggested that while Jackson's efforts may have helped to pave the way for Wilder in Virginia and Dinkins in New York City, these triumphs were only secured by an abandonment of a "Black Agenda" in favor of one which suited "mainstream" White America. Such an agenda deemphasized "race conscious" policies and practices.

To be sure, even in the euphoria among most blacks over the Jackson candidacies, others, including academicians Thomas Sowell and Robert Woodson, contended that such an adherence to a "Black Agenda" would impair efforts to promote equal opportunity for African Americans. They deplored "race conscious" policies and practices, including affirmative action programs, which they implied lowered black self-esteem and increased racial animosity. Instead, they argued, the black leadership establishment should encourage initiative and enterprise among blacks and focus their attention on the serious internal problems of African American communities: the disproportionate number of unwed mothers and school drop-outs, drug abuse, crime and violence, poverty, and other social ills. While many in the black leadership establishment had acknowledged such problems, they all too often, the black "conservatives" asserted, placed blame upon white racism and were too dependent on relief from the federal government. The black "conservatives" would have middle income blacks promote their agenda to the black masses which could lead to solutions. Smaller numbers of blacks during the "betrayal of the Second Reconstruction" shunned the traditional political processes altogether and sought refuge in African national parties, the Nation of Islam and other such groups, or withdrew entirely from structured political involvement. They had apparently abandoned all hope of achieving a "Black Agenda," however defined, in any variation of the American political process. Many of these people were leaders or promoters of a new wave of Afro-centricity, which gained momentum, particularly among intellectuals and students.

The new Afro-centricity, which was by no means confined to non-traditional partisans or apolitical blacks, was in reality a continuation of the Black Consciousness Movement of the 1960s and 1970s, whose political anthem was "Black Power" and whose cultural themes were "Black Is Beautiful" and "I'm Black and I'm Proud." The earlier movement led to many changes in the students, faculties, and curricula of the nation's institutions of higher education. Hand-in-glove with affirmative action programs, the movement changed the physical and intellectual complexion of many educational facilities and even made an impact in libraries, museums, the media, and other institutions. The Black Consciousness Movement was the mother of the Black Studies or Afro-American Studies programs, inspired the epic television production "Roots" in 1977, and was instrumental in establishing African and African American history as important areas of scholarly research and study. In literature, its progenitors and leading practitioners included such poets as Gwendolyn Brooks and Dudley Randall; novelists Margaret Walker Alexander, Ernest Gaines, and James Baldwin; dramatists Imanu Amiri Baraka (LeRoi Jones) and Ron Milner; and literary critics Houston A. Baker, Jerry Ward, and Larry Neal. In art, its promoters included David Driskill, Jacob Lawrence, and Elizabeth Prophet. In music, Bernice Johnson Reagon and Quincy Jones were among the leading exponents of the Movement, while Ossie Davis and Ruby Dee were the leaders on the Broadway stage. Among historians, Vincent Harding, Lawrence Reddick, and Lenore Bennett emerged as vocal and prolific adherents. Former SNCC leader Stokely Carmichael and Black Panther founders Huey P. Newton and Bobby Seale were among its political pioneers. Culturally and politically, the older movement was far from monolithic. Although some partisans might argue vigorously for their concept of Afro-centricity, the tenets and practices actually ranged from infusion into Euro-centered scholarship and

institutions to distinct and separate emphases and institutions.

The earlier Afro-centric or Black Consciousness Movement began to wane during the Nixon presidency. There appeared to be increased apathy, disillusionment, and some return to the mainstream. Enrollment in Black Studies courses decreased as did the demand for them, and new questions were even raised about the academic legitimacy of the discipline. Then, during the "Reagan Nadir," there appeared what some called "a resurgence of racism" in the United States. Black men were assaulted and killed by whites in New York City when they "intruded" into all-white neighborhoods. Blacks in Miami, Florida rioted at least three times during the 1980s after alleged racially motivated killings of black men by white and Hispanic police officers. Nonviolent demonstrators were assaulted in Forsyth County, Georgia in 1986 by Ku Klux Klansmen and other white supremacists on the eve of the first Martin Luther King, Jr. national holiday. Black students were subjected to verbal and physical abuse on hundreds of high school and college campuses throughout the nation.

This "resurgence" of racism led to new demands that colleges and universities increase the diversity of their student bodies and faculties and that there be a greater infusion of ethnic studies, particularly African and African American curricula. But some African American youths decided to turn inward, electing instead to attend or to transfer to all-black or majority black colleges in order to "escape" the throes of academic racism while immersing themselves in their own culture. Meanwhile, on the nation's black campuses, there were, in addition to demands that such institutions should become "blacker," i. e., a greater infusion of Black Studies and black administrative control, there was a new insistence that these historical institutions be reformed internally, in terms of physical facilities, efficiency, and effectiveness.

As in the Black Consciousness Movement, exponents of the new Afro-centricity espoused a levelling of African American society. They challenged the black social and economic elite to move away from any attempt at assimilating into the white world and to identify with their black "brothers and sisters," regardless of class. Indeed, like the black "conservatives," the Afro-centrists contended that the black elite had an obligation to help pull the black underclass out of its quagmire of poverty, illiteracy, drug abuse, crime, and despair.

The new Afro-centrists tended to be boldly nationalistic in their orientation. They identified closely with the continent of Africa. Many came to reject the racial designation Negro, as their predecessors had done, and even the term black itself, preferring instead to be known as African American. Some took African names and wore African dress, as in the 1960s movement. New slogans, often proudly worn on tee shirts and other clothing, proclaimed "Black Is Back" and "It's a Black Thing; You Wouldn't Understand" (an apparent taunt to whites). While Martin Luther King, Jr. remained a revered martyr, other civil rights heroes and heroines slipped in esteem among the new Afrocentrists. The black "radicals" of earlier periods: W. E. B. DuBois, Paul Robeson, Angela Davis, and Malcolm X, were elevated to new heights of respect and admiration. The suggestion was that aggressive, nationalist strategies, not non-violent assimilationist or integrationist attitudes, were the key to achieving the "Black Agenda."

The intellectual foundation for the new Afro-centricity was laid by black scholars, including Molefi Kete-Asante of Temple University, Maulena Karenga of the University of California, and Ronald Bailey of the University of Mississippi. These scholars were also leaders in the National Council of Black Studies, which had emerged during the earlier movement as a major coordinator, along with the older Association for the Study of Afro-American Life and History and the Association of Social and Behavioral Scientists, of the changing scholarship. Kete-Asante and others wrote that black culture, even human civilization itself (because of its African origins) must be studied and understood with African history, folkways, philosophy, geography, diaspora, etc. at the center.

The Afro-centrist scholars, however, faced strong challenges not only from white intellectuals, but from some black ones as well. Historians, including Nell Painter of Princeton University and Armstead Robinson of the University of Virginia, argued that African American experiences could not be fully understood from a narrow, internally-centered focus. They contended that such matters as class and gender must be strongly considered and, indeed, that these factors may well emerge as more central to the understanding of issues than race. In fact, the research and publication of the peculiar roles of black women in American and African American societies became one of the major fields of scholarship in the 1980s.

Other cultural manifestations in African American life during "the betrayal" included new motion pictures and new musical forms delineating the black experience. A young black filmmaker, Spike Lee, emerged in the 1980s with new media presentations of black people. Lee began his career with a racy comedy, She's Gotta Have It, and later established himself in the film industry with School Daze, a film about fraternity antics and color consciousness on a black college campus. Do the Right Thing, Lee's third film, was probably the best of these productions. With its theme of violent racial confrontation set in the Bedford-Stuyvesant section of Brooklyn, New York, it was certainly Lee's most controversial effort to date. Some critics even suggested that the film risked provoking the "race war" that it had so graphically depicted. Nonetheless, Lee's work in Do the Right Thing garnered an Academy Award nomination for Best Original Screenplay in 1990.

While gospel, jazz, blues, and soul music remained staples of the African American musical diet in the 1980s, "rap," a new form, appeared. Although rap music could be used for nearly any purpose from comedy to sex to politicsit was often employed to express a description of, and offer an opinion on, life in the black ghetto. Some of the messages presented as musical essays in verse, addressed such problems as drug abuse, violence against women, inferior education, and gang-related crime. Leading rappers of the period included 2 Live Crew, Run DMC, M.C. Hammer, and Public Enemy.

It should be clear that the new Afro-centrists did not represent a majority view in black America during "the betrayal." African American aesthetics continued to run the gamut from assimilationist to nationalist. Still, there were variations among all people, so that an "assimilationist" and a "nationalist" could both condemn the racist South African system of apartheid and celebrate the release of African National Congress leader Nelson Mandela in February of 1990. Both camps could also find common ground in supporting the retention of black colleges and other race institutions. A more definitive line between them came on the issue of full participation in the American political process and on social relations with white people. Many of the more zealous Afrocentrists, however, tended to reject both ideals.

Many of those African Americans who still believed that the "Black Agenda" could be achieved through traditional political avenues had their spirits dampened in the election of another Republican president, George Bush, in 1988. They had voted overwhelmingly for the Democratic candidate, Massachusetts governor Michael Dukakis. But despite minimal black support, once in office, Bush promised, without criticizing his predecessor Ronald Reagan, "a kinder and gentler nation." He pledged his commitment to equal opportunity and justice and invited black establishment leaders to the White House for consultation. Such early gestures raised some hope that "the betrayal" might be reversed and that the "Second Reconstruction" could be resurrected once again.

Amid signs of hope that "the betrayal" might be reversed and that the "Second Reconstruction" resurrected once again, George Walker Bush was inaugurated as President of the United States in January, 1989. His appointments of General Colin Powell as head of the military Joint Chiefs of Staff and Dr. Louis W. Sullivan as Secretary of Health and Human Services, although controversial, found favor with many African Americans. He continued to support the concept and ideals of the Martin Luther King, Jr. national holiday, sending high-ranking officials to the annual celebrations and speaking of the significance of King and his

legacy. He received, in 1990, the African National Congress leader Nelson Mandela at the White House during his American "freedom tour," even deferring to the wishes of African-American leaders that he not see South African prime minister Nelson de Klerk during the same period. But by the middle of 1990 many African Americans soon became suspicious of the President's sympathy with their longings for a renewed Second Reconstruction.

Although the President welcomed Mandela in July of 1990, black leaders soon complained that Bush was too quick to push for a lifting of sanctions against the "reformist" white minority government in South Africa and that he, like Prime Minister de Klerk, exaggerated the pace of reforms. Domestically, many blacks angrily denounced the President's veto of the 1991 Civil Rights Bill, which sought to strengthen employment guarantees. The President's cry that the bill contained unconstitutional "quotas" rang hollow in much of black America.

The American participation in the 1991 Gulf War, Bush's appointment of controversial black judge Clarence Thomas to the U.S. Supreme Court, his public statements on the Rodney King police brutality incident, and the disturbances that followed the acquittal of the white officers accused of beating King further widened the level of trust between the President and black America.

African Americans were deeply divided over American involvement in the Gulf War, with almost 50 percent of those polled opposing it. Yet nearly a third of all combat troops in the war were African Americans. Similarly, more than 30 percent of black Americans opposed the elevation of Judge Thomas to the Supreme Court, and many also opposed the televised spectacle that was made of attorney Anita Hill's accusations of sexual harassment.

But the 1991 police beating of Rodney King in Los Angeles, which was captured on videotape, and the subsequent acquittal of the officers involved awakened African Americans to new fury and outrage. Not since the Civil Rights Era of the

1950s and 1960s and the urban rebellions of the 1960s had there been so much protest, both organized and sporadic, non-violent and violent.

President Bush's outrage at the King beating (he said it "sickened" him) and the acquittal were comforting to many. His summoning of black leaders to the White House in the early hours of the Los Angeles rioting, which followed the verdict, was generally applauded. But when he began to seemingly emphasize the "lawlessness" of the rebellion and the need to suppress it over the precipitating acquittal by an all-white jury, several black spokespersons, including Los Angeles congresswoman Maxine Waters, suggested that his priorities and attitudes were misguided. Whatever one's views, however, the Los Angeles disturbance and smaller ones throughout the country did serve to bring the depressed condition of urban black Americans, albeit temporarily, back to the forefront of national attention.

Yet the problems of blacks and other inner city minorities could not upstage the continuing economic recession that the country was currently facing. These financial woes cut across ethnic, class, gender, and party lines. So by the time of the 1992 presidential elections in November, a sizeable number of white Americans were ready to join with an overwhelming majority of black voters to seek a change. The change came on November 3, when George Bush was turned out of the White House after only one term, and the nation decided to trust its fortunes with Democratic Governor William "Bill" Clinton of Arkansas.

Interestingly enough, however, many black Americans, including some in the leadership cadre and the scholarly community, questioned the sincerity of Clinton's commitment to a Black Agenda. They pointed to his heavy courting of middle-class whites in his presidential campaign, his shunning of the Reverend Jesse L. Jackson and other more aggressive black leaders, and his ill-defined prescriptions for peculiarly black social ills. Others, disappointed with the efforts of previous national administrations in addressing the Black Agenda, cautioned against holding any great expectations that the Clinton record would be any

better. They again sought and urged solutions through black nationalistic and self-help programs. Nevertheless, as of January 20, 1993, the United States will, for the first time in twelve years, enter a new and different cycle of presidential party leadership. Certainly as all watch its directions, Black America, especially, can be counted upon to place its agenda early and often on the presidential and congressional tables.

A DEMOCRAT IS BACK IN THE WHITE HOUSE

The preinaugural and inaugural activities for the new administration of Bill Clinton were full of promising and encouraging signs for black America. Clinton appointed four African Americans to his cabinet, the largest number in American history. Two of the four, Ronald Brown and Michael Espy, occupied the "non-traditional black positions" of Secretary of Commerce and Secretary of Agriculture, respectively. Blacks were prominent at the inauguration itself, including Maya Angelou, who read one of her own poems aloud. It seemed clear, after having been marginalized at the highest levels of political influence for the past twelve years, that blacks would now have a new place at the table of national decision making.

Yet barely halfway through the new administration, it became apparent that the president's liberal views toward minority and other social issues were not shared by many of the Republicans in Congress. Even moderate and conservative members of his own party were lukewarm, if not outright opposed, to reform and progressive measures. And many African Americans found themselves questioning the sincerity of the president in promoting their agenda after he abandoned Lani Guinier, an African American law professor, as his nominee for assistant attorney general for civil rights. Influential members of both parties alleged that her views on civil and political rights were "too radical."

But it was the "Republican Revolution" in the congressional elections of 1994, in which the

GOP captured both houses of Congress, that posed a new and serious threat to the administration's support for the "Black Agenda." The election results, which also led to the placing of Newt Gingrich, a conservative Georgia Republican, as Speaker of the House, were widely interpreted as a rebellion of white males against "liberal" political and social policies, particularly preferences for women and minorities. It was also generally believed that this voting bloc wanted a reduction in government spending, especially on such "entitlements" as welfare. Meanwhile, African American officials in the Clinton administration became the targets of ethics investigations and were attacked for their policy statements. Commerce Secretary Brown and Agriculture Secretary Espy faced congressional probes; Espy eventually resigned. Surgeon General Joycelyn Elders was forced out of office for her "liberal" views on abortion and sexuality, and Energy Secretary Hazel O'Leary faced constant criticism for alleged excessive spending, particularly on travel.

Then, as attacks on affirmative action heightened in the public and private sectors, the president, while staunchly defending the concept, did allow that some programs needed "review." And just before the 1996 presidential election, he signed a welfare reform bill that many black leaders opposed. Nevertheless, black America had little choice but to support Clinton for re-election. Again they voted for him by large majorities and he was returned to the White House for a second term.

As African Americans pondered whether the Clinton administration would move back toward the left or more toward the right in its last term, whether the "Black Agenda" would be promoted, marginalized, or opposed, black America, itself, continued to be torn politically and culturally, between hip-hoppers and traditionalists. The hip-hop culture, epitomized by rap music, was still attracting and maintaining many adherents, particularly among young blacks. And many of them were still maintaining that revolution, rather than reform, was the answer to black political and social needs. In speeches, writings, and songs, they tended to decry traditional politics, and withdraw

from the process. At least, in rhetoric, they still disdained non-violent, direct action as well. Traditionalists, on the other hand, continued to deplore the "pernicious effects" of "gangsta rap," contending that it glorified violence and drugs and was sexist. It did little to solve the rampant epidemic of crime, violence, illegitimate births, and drug abuse that they believed to be threatening the very existence of African America.

There began to appear, however, a major sign of a possible common ground between the hip-hop and the traditional cultures in black America. Some rappers emerged as principal proponents of pietist living in such groups as the Five Percent Nation of Islam, an offshoot of Elijah Muhammad's Nation of Islam. Mega-urban black churches sprang up in large cities across the country, and thousands of young blacks particularly supported these churches in which the worship services increasingly included contemporary gospel, jazz, and even rap. Ministries, on black college campuses particularly, drew new adherents, and such ministries, including gospel choirs, even appeared on mostly white campuses.

Still, as the new millennium approaches, the state of African America remains much the same as it has been for the past fifty years. It has been a half-century since the Second Reconstruction dismantled "de jure" segregation and struck at legal and extra-legal discrimination. But it has not led to the "promised land" of freedom, equality, and justice. Most troubling are the continuing high rates of semi-literacy and the low rates of higher education; the staggering rates of illegitimate births, drug abuse, domestic and other violence; and the assaults on young black males through injustices in the criminal justice system. These have resulted in extraordinarily high rates of incarcerations much greater than college enrollments among the same people. Many of these ills are the result of stagnant levels of poverty, and many have exacerbated the prevalence of poverty. Through it all, no new Black Messiah appeared, and the strategies for solutions remain floating in a sea of division, which often reflects class and gender as well as generational differences. Except during major racial crises such as an urban riot, the beating of Rodney King, or the trial of popular black hero and football star O. J. Simpson, these differences have prevented the unity necessary to achieve impact and influence on policies and actions as was accomplished most effectively during the Second Reconstruction. And so the search continues, not only to achieve the "Black Agenda," but indeed to define that agenda.

Historical Timeline

1492 Black sailor arrived in the New World with Christopher Columbus on the *Santa Maria*.

1501 Queen Isabella of Spain authorized the transport of slaves from southern Spain to the New World.

1510 Spain's Ferdinand II ordered the transport of two-hundred and fifty slaves to Hispaniola to work the gold mines.

1513 Slave trade became a source of profit for Spain as she began to require licenses to import slaves into her colonies.

1514 Slave importation to Hispaniola was regulated as their numbers were increasing at an alarming rate.

1516 Cardinal Ximenes suspended the importation of slaves after Ferdinand II of Spain died.

1518–1526 King of Spain Charles V, granted permission to ship 4,000 blacks to Spanish colonies on Hispaniola, Cuba, Jamaica, and Puerto Rico.

1518 As Spain's profits from the slave trade grew, England entered into slave trade competition by granting commercial licenses to ship slaves to the Spanish colonies free of customs duties.

1525 After the Lucas-Vásques de Ayllón expeditions of 1525–1527 some rebellious African slaves were left along the Carolina coast. These blacks became the first permanent, non-Indian residents of what is now the United States.

1527 Estevanico, an African slave from Morocco, accompanied Andres de Dorantes on an expedition to conquer Florida.

1530 Spain's Charles V issued a royal edict to control the purchase and supply of slaves.

1531 A second royal decree was issued reiterating the ban on importation of North African slaves into the New World.

1550 Charles V issued another royal decree prohibiting the importation of Wolof blacks

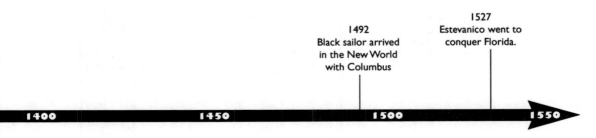

1492
Black sailor arrived
in the New World
with Columbus

1527
Estevanico went to
conquer Florida.

1400   1450   1500   1550

from the Senegal River area to the West Indian islands.

1562 England joined the slave trade when English navigator John Hawkins hijacked a Portuguese ship carrying African slaves to Brazil.

1581 First slaves arrived in North America when Philip II of Spain sent some of his black slaves to St. Augustine, Florida, the oldest permanent city founded by Europeans in America.

1595 Philip II, the king of Spain, granted a slave import monopoly to a slave trader to ship 4,250 slaves to the Americas each year.

1599 Black slave population estimated in the New World at 900,000.

1619 Twenty Africans arrived in Jamestown, Virginia, aboard a Dutch ship. They are the first blacks to be forcibly settled as involuntary laborers in the North American British Colonies.

1626 Eleven blacks were brought to New York as indentured or bonded servants.

1639 The colony of Virginia passed a regulation prohibiting blacks from bearing firearms.

1641 Massachusetts is the first colony to legalize slavery by statute.

1655 Anthony Johnson, a black man, qualified for a 200-acre land grant after importing five servants to North Hampton, Virginia. Other blacks joined Johnson and began an African community.

1663 The first documented attempt at a rebellion by slaves took place in Gloucester County, Virginia.

1688 The Quakers of Germantown, Pennsylvania, passed the first formal antislavery resolution.

1690 According to South Carolina law, slaves were freehold property except in payment of the master's debts.

1690 Colonial Connecticut passed a law that forbade black and Indian servants from wandering beyond town limits without a ticket or pass from a master or other person in position of authority.

1691 The colony of Virginia outlawed the practice of freeing blacks unless those freed were to leave the colony within six months.

1693 A Pennsylvania provincial council expressed concern regarding the tumultuous gatherings of the blacks in the town.

1696 Statutes in the colony of South Carolina stated that slaves needed written permission to leave their masters' residences.

1698 The colony of Massachusetts changed the tax laws by declaring that "all Indian, mulatto and Negro servants be estimated as other personal estate."

1700 A monthly meeting for blacks was established with the help of William Penn and the Quakers.

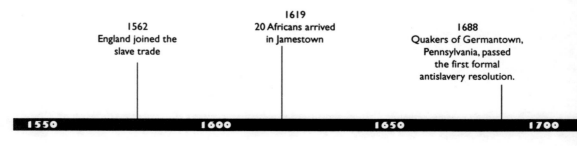

1562
England joined the
slave trade

1619
20 Africans arrived
in Jamestown

1688
Quakers of Germantown,
Pennsylvania, passed
the first formal
antislavery resolution.

1550   1600   1650   1700

1700 The Pennsylvania colonial assembly enacted two laws regarding the African American: one for regulating "Negroes in their Morals, and Marriages," and the other regarding "Negroes and their trials."

1703 The colony of Massachusetts required every slave master to post a bond as security to support each freed slave to decrease the financial cost of indigents on a town.

1704 A mulatto slave, Abda, sued his owner, Thomas Richards, for illegally detaining him in bondage. A court declared Abda free. The General Assembly reversed the decision upon appeal and he was returned to Richards.

1705 The colony of Massachusetts prohibited interracial marriages.

1706 New York colonial law prohibited a slave from testifying for or against a freeman in either civil or criminal cases.

1707 Colonial Massachusetts passed a law prohibiting free blacks from harboring or entertaining nonwhite servants in their homes without the approval of the masters.

1712 South Carolina slave regulations provided that no white person would be punished for injuring or killing a slave if that slave was resisting lawful punishment and that a fine was required of a white person who murdered a slave.

1712 A slave revolt in New York City ended with nine whites slain and twenty-one blacks executed as participants of the revolt.

1714 Colonial Rhode Island passed a law forbidding ferrymen from transporting or conveying any slaves out of the colony without a certificate from their master or mistress or official person.

1717 England authorized the importation of slaves by the South Sea Company.

1727 Between 1718 and 1727 slightly over 17,000 Africans were imported to Virginia in 76 vessels.

1728 Colonial Massachusetts forbade black, Indian, and mulatto servants or slaves from buying provisions directly from country people.

1729 The colony of Rhode Island required every master to post a bond of one hundred pounds to guarantee that the emancipated slave would not become a public charge "through sickness, lameness" or other cause.

1730 The Connecticut colony passed a law forbidding any black, Indian, or mulatto from slandering or libeling a white person.

1732 The British Parliament prohibited the colonies from placing taxes on slaves.

1735 The colony of Georgia prohibited the importation of blacks.

1739 The Stono Rebellion began when a large group of slaves stole guns and ammunition from a store in South Carolina. The escaped slaves killed 21 whites and burned a number of plantation homes before a battle with the militia.

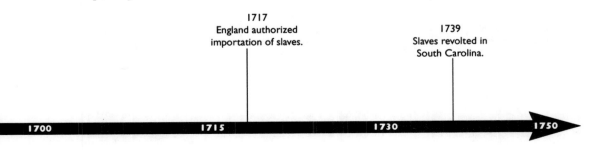

1717
England authorized
importation of slaves.

1739
Slaves revolted in
South Carolina.

1700   1715   1730   1750

1741 New Yorkers blamed Roman Catholic priests for inciting slaves to burn the town on orders from Spain. Eighteen blacks and four whites were hanged for the conspiracy.

1750 The colony of Georgia authorized the importation of slaves.

1761 Black poet Jupiter Hammon published his poem, *Salvation by Christ with Penitential Cries.*

1763 Between 1753 and 1763, thirteen New England vessels transported 869 slaves to Virginia.

1769 California was occupied by Spanish African residents when members of the Portolá Expedition moved to the area.

1770 Quaker philanthropist Anthony Benezet established a free school for blacks in Philadelphia.

1773 Jean Baptiste Pointe duSable became the first permanent settler in Chicago.

1775 Free blacks fought with the Minutemen in the initial skirmishes of the Revolutionary War at Lexington and Concord, Massachusetts.

1777 Vermont became the first state to abolish slavery.

1777 George Washington reversed previous policy and allowed the recruitment of black soldiers. Some 5,000 participated in the Revolutionary War.

1783 A Massachusetts slave successfully sued her master on the grounds that all men were born free and equal.

1787 The Continental Congress passed the Northwest Ordinance, forbidding slavery northwest of the Ohio River.

1787 Moses Sash led Shays Rebellion in Massachusetts.

1787 Richard Allen and Absalom Jones established the Free African Society.

1787 The U.S. Constitution provided for a male slave to count as 3/5 of a man in determining representation.

1791 Free blacks in South Carolina petitioned the state legislature protesting laws restricting their freedom.

1793 Congress passed the first Fugitive Slave Law.

1804 The Ohio legislature passed "Black Laws" designed to restrict the legal rights of free blacks—a trend in both the North and the South before the Civil War.

1808 The federal law prohibiting the importation of African slaves went into effect. It was largely circumvented.

1816 The African Methodist Episcopal Church was organized as the first independent black denomination in the U.S.

1822 The Denmark Vesey conspiracy was betrayed in Charleston, South Carolina. It was claimed that some 5,000 blacks were prepared to rise in July.

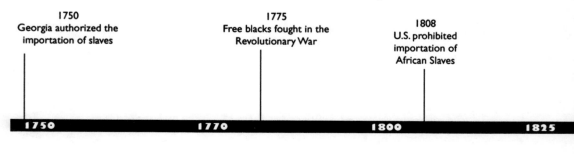

1750
Georgia authorized the
importation of slaves

1775
Free blacks fought in the
Revolutionary War

1808
U.S. prohibited
importation of
African Slaves

1750   1770   1800   1825

1829 David Walker's militant antislavery pamphlet, *An Appeal to the Colored People of the World*, was in circulation in the South. This work was the first of its kind written by a black person.

1829 The first National Negro Convention met in Philadelphia.

1831 The Nat Turner revolt ran its course in Southampton County, Virginia.

1839 The slaves on the Spanish ship *Amistad* took over the vessel and sailed it to Montauk, Long Island. They eventually won their freedom in a case taken to the Supreme Court.

1849 Harriet Tubman escaped from slavery. She returned to the South at least 20 times, leading more than 300 slaves to freedom.

1854 *Ashmun* Institute, the precursor of Lincoln University, was chartered at Oxford, Pennsylvania.

1855 John Mercer Langston was elected clerk of Brownhelm Township in Lorain County, Ohio, making him the first African American to win elective office.

1855 Massachusetts Supreme Court integrated public schools in the commonwealth.

1857 The Dred Scott decision of the Supreme Court denied blacks U.S. citizenship and denied the power of Congress to restrict slavery in any federal territory.

1859 John Brown led the raid on the U.S. arsenal at Harpers Ferry, Virginia.

1859 The U.S. Supreme Court overruled an act by a Wisconsin state court that declared the Fugitive Slave Act of 1850 unconstitutional.

1862 Congress allowed the enlistment of blacks in the Union Army. More than 186,000 blacks served in the army during the Civil War; 38,000 died in service.

1863 The Emancipation Proclamation freed the slaves in those states rebelling against the Union.

1865 The 13th Amendment, which outlaws slavery in the U.S., was ratified.

1868 The 14th Amendment, validating citizenship rights for all persons born or naturalized in the U.S., was ratified.

1868 The South Carolina House became the first and only legislature to boast a black majority, having 87 black legislators and 40 whites. A white majority was reestablished in 1874.

1870 The ratification of the 15th Amendment secured voting rights for all male U.S. citizens.

1875 Congress passed a civil rights bill that banned discrimination in places of public accommodation. The Supreme Court overturned the bill in 1883.

1876 Meharry Medical College, the first all-black medical school, was established in Nashville, Tennessee.

1881 Tuskegee Institute was founded in Alabama.

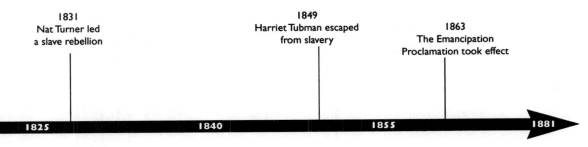

1831	1849	1863
Nat Turner led a slave rebellion	Harriet Tubman escaped from slavery	The Emancipation Proclamation took effect

| 1825 | 1840 | 1855 | 1881 |

1883 The U.S. Supreme Court ruled that the Civil Rights Act of 1875 was unconstitutional.

1890 The Land Grant Act required states to provide educational training for black youths.

1895 Booker T. Washington delivered his "Atlanta Compromise" speech to the Cotton States International Exposition in Atlanta.

1895 Frederick Douglass died.

1896 The Supreme Court's decision in *Plessy v. Ferguson* affirmed the concept of "separate but equal" public facilities.

1897 The Supreme Court upheld literacy and poll tax voting requirements established by the Mississippi state constitution.

1898 Four black regiments participated in fighting around Santiago, Cuba, during the Spanish-American War, including the 9th and 10th Cavalry Squadrons.

1900 A race riot broke out in New Orleans. Black schools and homes were destroyed during the disturbance.

1903 W. E. B. Du Bois's *The Souls of Black Folk* was published.

1904 The U.S. Supreme Court decided that the exclusion of African Americans from juries was a violation of the equal protection clause.

1905 The Niagara Movement (the forerunner of the National Association for the Advancement of Colored People (NAACP), was es-

tablished. Among its leaders were W. E. B. Du Bois and William Monroe Trotter.

1906 The first African American fraternity, Alpha Phi Alpha, was established at Cornell University.

1907 Alain Locke, a prominent African American intellectual, received a Rhodes Scholarship.

1909 The National Association for the Advancement of Colored People (NAACP) was founded in New York City.

1909 Matthew H. Henson, a black servant, accompanied Commodore Robert E. Peary to the North Pole.

1910 The National Urban League was founded.

1912 *The Autobiography of an Ex-Colored Man* was published anonymously by James Weldon Johnson.

1913 Harriet Tubman died.

1915 Carter G. Woodson established the Association for the Study of Negro Life and History.

1917 The U.S. Supreme Court unanimously decided that residential racial zoning laws were in violation of the 14th Amendment.

1917 About 370,000 African Americans served during World War I.

1918 W. E. B. Du Bois led the first Pan-African Congress which was held in Paris while the Paris Peace Conference was convening.

1881 Tuskegee Institute was founded	1895 Booker T. Washington delivered his "Atlanta Compromise" speech		1909 NAACP founded	
1881	**1900**		**1905**	**1920**

1919 Archibald Grimké received the Spingarn Award from the NAACP.

1919 The U.S. Supreme Court ruled that African Americans should be admitted to juries.

1920 Marcus Garvey's national convention of the Universal Negro Improvement Association (UNIA) met in New York City.

1922 The Harlem Renaissance, a golden age of black literature and art in the U.S., began, lasting until 1929.

1923 Garrett A. Morgan, a black inventor, was awarded a U.S. Patent for the automatic traffic light.

1923 George Washington Carver was awarded the Spingarn Medal from the NAACP

1925 A. Philip Randolph organized the Brotherhood of Sleeping Car Porters.

1936 Jesse Owens won four gold medals at the Summer Olympics in Berlin, Germany.

1937 Joe Louis defeated James J. Braddock, becoming heavyweight boxing champion of the world.

1940 Benjamin 0. Davis, Sr., was named the first black general in the U.S. Army.

1944 The United Negro College Fund was founded.

1947 Jackie Robinson joined the Brooklyn Dodgers, becoming the first black player in major league baseball.

1950 Ralph J. Bunche won the Nobel Peace Prize for his work as a mediator in Palestine.

1952 After keeping statistics for 71 years, Tuskegee Institute reported that this was the first year with no lynchings.

1954 In *Brown v. Board of Education* of Topeka, Kansas, the Supreme Court ruled unanimously that racial segregation in public schools is unconstitutional, overruling *Plessy v. Ferguson.*

1954 Rosa Parks refused to change seats on a Montgomery, Alabama, bus. On December 5, blacks began a boycott of the bus system, which continued until shortly after December 13, 1956, when the U.S. Supreme Court outlawed bus segregation in the city.

1956 The U.S. Supreme Court upheld the decision of a lower court, outlawing the segregation of buses in Montgomery, Alabama.

1957 The Southern Christian Leadership Conference (SCLC) was formed with Martin Luther King, Jr., as president.

1957 Congress passed the Voting Rights Bill of 1957, the first major civil rights legislation in more than 75 years.

1960 Sit-ins in Greensboro, North Carolina, initiated a wave of similar protests throughout the South.

1960 The Student Non-Violent Coordinating Committee (SNCC) was founded in Raleigh, North Carolina.

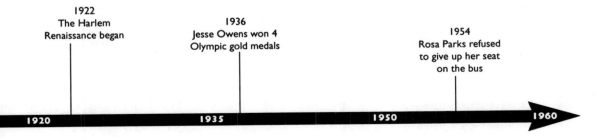

1922
The Harlem
Renaissance began

1936
Jesse Owens won 4
Olympic gold medals

1954
Rosa Parks refused
to give up her seat
on the bus

1920   1935   1950   1960

1963 Racial tensions were renewed in Birmingham, Alabama, when four black girls died in the bombing of the 16th Street Baptist Church.

1963 The March on Washington was the largest civil rights demonstration to date. Martin Luther King, Jr., delivered a speech entitled "I Have a Dream."

1964 Beginning in Harlem, serious racial disturbances occurred in more than six major cities.

1964 The 24th Amendment forbade the use of the poll tax to prevent voting.

1965 Malcolm X was assassinated, 11 months after his split from Elijah Muhammad's Nation of Islam.

1965 The SCLC launched a voter drive in Selma, Alabama, which escalated into a nationwide protest movement.

1965 The Watts riots resulted in 34 deaths, more than 3,500 arrests, and property damage of about 225 million dollars.

1966 CORE (Congress of Racial Equality) endorsed the concept of "Black Power." SNCC also adopted it. SCLC did not, and the NAACP emphatically did not.

1966 The Black Panther Party was founded by Huey P. Newton and Bobby Seale in Oakland, California

1967 In the worst summer for racial disturbances in U.S. history, more than 40 riots and 100 other disturbances occurred.

1968 Martin Luther King, Jr., was assassinated in Memphis, Tennessee. In the following week riots occurred in at least 125 places throughout the country.

1969 The Supreme Court ruled that school districts must end racial segregation at once, and must operate only unitary school systems.

1969 Kenneth Gibson became the first black mayor of a large eastern city—Newark, New Jersey.

1970 Implicated in a shootout during an attempted escape in a San Rafael, California courthouse, Angela Davis went into hiding to avoid arrest. Davis was acquitted of all charges on June 4, 1972.

1973 Thomas Bradley was elected the first black mayor of Los Angeles. On October 16, Maynard H. Jackson was elected the first black mayor of Atlanta. On November 6, Coleman A. Young was elected the first black mayor of Detroit.

1974 Henry Aaron hit his 715th home run, breaking Babe Ruth's long-standing record.

1977 For eight consecutive nights, ABC-TV broadcasts an epic miniseries based on Alex Haley's *Roots*. The final episode received the highest ratings to date.

1980 Racial disturbances began on May 17 resulting in 15 deaths in Miami, Florida.

1982 Lee P. Brown was named the first black police commissioner of Houston, Texas.

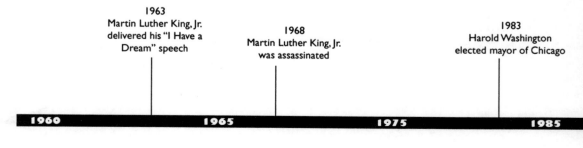

1983 Harold Washington was elected the first black mayor of Chicago.

1983 The state legislature of Louisiana repealed the last racial classification law in the U.S. The criterion for being classified as black was having 1/32nd "Negro" blood.

1986 A bronze bust of Martin Luther King, Jr., was the first of any black American placed in the Capitol. The first national Martin Luther King, Jr. holiday was celebrated on January 20.

1988 Jesse L. Jackson received 1,218.5 delegate votes at the Democratic National Convention. The number needed for the nomination, which went to Michael Dukakis, was 2,082.

1989 Barbara Harris was elected the first woman bishop of the Episcopal Church.

1989 General Colin L. Powell was named chair of the U.S. joint chiefs of staff.

1989 David Dinkins was elected the first black mayor of New York, and L. Douglas Wilder, the first black governor of Virginia.

1990 George Augustus Stallings became the first bishop of the African-American Catholic Church, a breakaway group from the Roman Catholic Church.

1991 Roland Burris became the first black attorney general of Illinois.

1992 Jackie Joyner-Kersee was the first woman to repeat as Olympic heptathlon champion.

1992 Carol Moseley Braun of Illinois was the first black woman elected to the U.S. Senate.

1993 M. Joycelyn Elders became the first black and the first woman U.S. surgeon general.

1993 Toni Morrison became the first black woman to win the Nobel Prize in Literature.

1994 The U.S. Postal Service issued stamps honoring jazz and blues greats.

1994 The Supreme Court ruled that the Civil Rights Act of 1991 could not be applied retroactively.

1995 Nation of Islam leader Louis Farrakhan hosted the Million Man March on Capitol Hill in Washington, D.C.

1995 The U.S. Court of Appeals for the Ninth Circuit ruled that African Americans could not sue the federal government for damages or an apology for racial discrimination and slavery.

1996 A statue was dedicated to Arthur Ashe in Richmond, Virginia.

1996 Colin Powell spoke at the Republican National Convention while Jesse Jackson spoke at the Democratic National Convention.

1996 The Connecticut Supreme Court ruled that racial segregation in public schools near Hartford violated the state constitution.

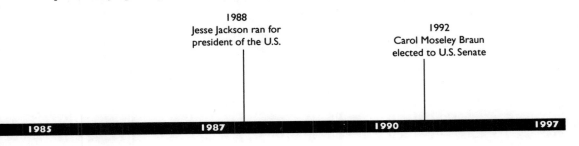

1988
Jesse Jackson ran for
president of the U.S.

1992
Carol Moseley Braun
elected to U.S. Senate

1985   1987   1990   1997

Part 1

OUT OF AFRICA
1492–1769

1492 to 1769

1492 Black Sailor Arrived with Columbus.
Pedro Alonzo Niño, a black sailor, arrived in
the New World on Christopher Columbus's
Santa Maria.

**SEPTEMBER 3, 1501 Spain Authorized Slave
Importation.** Spain's Queen Isabella authorized the transport of slaves from southern Spain
to the New World. Spanish colonists in Hispaniola
had appealed to the Crown, asking for laborers
to help work the mines. Gold-hungry Spain
was inclined to approve, however only a handful slaves were actually shipped to the New
World in this decade.

1510 Slave Traffic to New World Began.
Spain's Ferdinand II ordered the transport of
two-hundred and fifty slaves to Hispaniola to
work the gold mines. These slaves were purchased in Lisbon, Portugal, where they had
been converted to Christianity. A system of
shipping slaves directly to the New World
colonies from Africa was in the works.

1513 Slave Importation Licensed. Slave trade
became a source of profit for Spain as she began
to require licenses to import slaves into her
colonies. Ferdinand II granted permission to
import blacks for two ducats a head. Colonists

in Hispaniola, Cuba, and Santo Domingo were
requesting slaves.

1514 Hispaniola Slave Import Regulated. Slave
importation to Hispaniola was regulated as
their numbers were increasing at an alarming
rate. The population of blacks on the island
increased drastically after their importation came
to be licensed only one year earlier.

1516 Hispaniola Slave Import Suspended.
Spain's Ferdinand II died and the slave importation he had been licensing was suspended by
Cardinal Ximenes. It is not clear whether the
cardinal opposed slavery itself, or the loose
method of import licensing that was causing
the colonies' black populations to grow almost
out of control. The suspension had little effect,
though, as the new Spanish king, Charles V,
immediately resumed the issuance of licenses.

1517 Colonial Slave Import Encouraged.
Spanish Bishop Bartoloméo de las Casas persuaded Charles V, the king of Spain, to grant
Spanish colonists permission to import twelve
African slaves each. The Bishop also requested
that these slaves be Spanish or Christian blacks.
Charles V agreed as a means of encouraging
emigration to the New World colonies in this
time when European countries were in heavy
competition for land claims and the rights to
the riches that were being discovered.

1518   England Undercut Slave Imports to Colonies. As Spain's profits from the slave trade grew, England entered into competition by granting asientos. These were commercial licenses to ship slaves to the Spanish colonies free of customs duties, thereby making the English-shipped slaves cheaper.

1518–1526   Thousands of Slaves Shipped to Colonies. Charles V, the king of Spain, granted the governor of Brese, Lorenzo de Gomenot, permission to ship 4,000 blacks to Spanish colonies on Hispaniola, Cuba, Jamaica, and Puerto Rico. As a favorite of Charles V, Gomenot was also able to secure a virtual monopoly on slave trade to the Spanish colonies. Other licenses were granted, but primarily only to those who were importing domestic slaves in small numbers and were not trafficking them.

1525   Blacks Abandoned in New World. Some rebellious African slaves were left behind by Spanish explorers during the Lucas-Vásques de Ayllón expeditions of 1525–1527. The Spaniards had attempted to found a colony along the Carolina coast, but the expeditions were plagued by fever and Indian hostility. The slaves were left behind in the wake of the fleeing Europeans. Nearly a century before Jamestown was founded, these blacks became the first permanent, non-Indian residents of what is now the United States.

1527   African Slave Accompanied Expedition. Estevanico, an African slave from Morocco, accompanied his master, Andres de Dorantes, on an expedition to conquer Florida. Estevanico, born around 1503 in Azemmour, Morocco, had probably been sold into slavery by the Portuguese, who had captured Morocco in 1513 and started selling its people after a drought in 1520.

When Estevanico and the explorers arrived in Florida on April 12, 1528, they fought with the native population and lost. The survivors, Estevanico among them, served as slaves and medicine men until 1535 when Estevanico, Cabez de Vaca, Dorantes, de Carranza, and Alonso del Castillo Maldonado escaped and headed up the Rio Grande toward the Northwest. In March of 1536, the five-man party met up with a Spanish patrol on the Rio Sinaloa and followed it back to a Spanish outpost. Later that year the group made its way to Mexico where the Viceroy of Mexico asked if they would lead an expedition into Arizona and New Mexico. Estevanico was the only one to accept and, in February of 1539, he led a party to northwest New Mexico. Later that year, however, he was captured by the Zuni tribe and killed as a spy.

1527   Puerto Rican Slave Revolt. Black and Indian slaves in Puerto Rico revolted and caused such great economic losses that many whites left the island.

1530   Spanish Slave Supply Restricted. Spain's Charles V issued a royal edict to the *Casa de Contratación*, the Spanish House of Commerce which controlled the purchase and supply of slaves. The edict intended to prevent the introduction of North African blacks, such as the Berbers and Wolofs, into Spanish colonies because they were thought to have created the 1527 uprising in Puerto Rico. Those found guilty of the offense were fined 100,000 maravedís.

OCTOBER 23, 1530   Black Caribs. Carib Indian warriors raided some of the Windward Islands and looted the islands' Spanish plantations. Many of the black slaves were carried off the plantations by the Caribs. The blacks later married some of the Caribs and the children of these unions were known as "Black Caribs."

1531   North African Slaves Banned. A second royal decree was issued reiterating the ban on importation of North African slaves into the New World.

1550   Ban on North African Slaves Enforced. Charles V issued another royal decree prohibit-

Colonial slaves being captured. (Courtesy of Library of Congress.)

ing the importation of Wolof blacks from the Senegal River area to the West Indian islands. According to the decree, "inasmuch as the black uprising in the island of San Juan and others were the result of the independence, disobedience, rebelliousness and incorrigibility of the Wolof slaves, they must not be transported to any part of the Indies without special license." These blacks were also undesirable in that they were descendants of the Moorish race and could pose a danger to the recently-planted Christianity in the colonies.

1562   England Joined Slave Trade. English navigator John Hawkins hijacked a Portuguese ship carrying African slaves to Brazil and, thus, English participation in the slave trade began. He traded the slaves at Hispaniola for a sizable profit. Queen Elizabeth also profited from Hawkins's slave trade despite having expressed outrage at the institution of slavery.

1581   First Slaves to Arrive in North America. The first slaves arrived on North America when Philip II of Spain sent some of his black slaves to St. Augustine, Florida, the oldest permanent city founded by Europeans in America.

1595   Slave Import Monopoly Granted. Philip II, the king of Spain, granted Gómez Reynal the most comprehensive slave trading agreement to the time. Reynal was to ship 38,250 slaves over a nine-year span. Of the 4,250 he was to take to the Americas each year, he had to ensure that 3,500 survived the trip. He agreed to bring slaves directly from Africa who were not mulattoes, mestizos, Turks, or Moors. Reynal paid 900,000 ducats for the deal, ten of which he had to forfeit for each slave short of the quota he fell.

1599   Black Slave Population Estimated. Estimates placed the New World slave population at 900,000. They were primarily in Latin America engaged in producing sugar, which was used as a fruit preservative.

AUGUST 20, 1619   Slaves Arrived at Jamestown. Twenty blacks who had been captured in Africa were sold to the highest bidders at Jamestown, Virginia. However, these were not the first of their race to arrive in North America. Blacks had traveled with Spanish, Portuguese, and French explorers in the Americas throughout the sixteenth century. The most noted black explorer, Estevanico, had arrived in Florida in 1528 with Andres de Dorantes on a conquering expedition. Diego el Negro was a crew member on the *Capitana* as part of Christopher Columbus's last voyage to the New World. And as many as thirty blacks, including Nuflo de Olano, were with Vasco Núñez de Balboa when the explorer discovered the Pacific Ocean.

The twenty blacks sold at Jamestown in 1619 were, nonetheless, the first permanent involuntary settlers of their race, hence the history of African Americans in what is now the United States began with their arrival.

1622   First Free Blacks. Anthony Johnson and his wife, Mary, were the first free blacks in the United States, according to court records in Accomack, later Northampton County, in the

First slave immigrants at Jamestown, Virginia. (Courtesy of Library of Congress.)

colony of Virginia. The Johnsons had two sons, John and Richard, whose names appeared in 1654 Northampton County land transaction records.

1626   Slaves Arrived in New York. Eleven blacks were brought to New York in 1626 as indentured or bonded servants. They first lived in lower Manhattan in the area of Fort Amsterdam and Wall Street. They were later freed of their bonds and eventually developed into a free black community in Manhattan and nearby Brooklyn. However, slavery was legal in New York for another two-hundred years.

1638   Slaves Brought to New England. Prior to this date, blacks had been sold in Boston, but it is not definitely known when the first black slaves were directly brought to the region. Authorities who claim that black slaves were first brought to New England in 1638 base their contention on an entry in John Winthrop's *Journal.* Winthrop recorded on December 12, 1638, the arrival of the ship *Desire* at Boston.

The cargo of the vessel, according to Winthrop, included salt, cotton, tobacco, and slaves. The statement of Governor Winthrop is the first recorded account of black slavery in New England.

1639   Blacks Regulated in Virginia. The colony of Virginia passed a regulation prohibiting blacks from bearing firearms.

1641   Massachusetts Legalized Slavery. Massachusetts recognized slavery as a legal institution, the first of the North American colonies to do so. Section ninety-one of the *Body of Liberties* of 1641 read: "There shall never be any bond slaverie, villinage or Captivities amongst us, unless it be lawful Captives taken in just warres, and such strangers as willingly sell themselves or are sold to us. And these shall have all the liberties and Christian usages which the law of God established in Israel. . . . This exempts none from servitude who shall be Judged thereto by Authoritie."

1643   New England Fugitive Laws. The New England Confederation declared that certification by a magistrate was sufficient evidence to convict runaway slaves.

1655   Black Settlement. Anthony Johnson, a black man, qualified for a 200-acre land grant after importing five servants to North Hampton, Virginia. Other blacks joined Johnson and began an African community. The settlement had twelve African homesteads at its height.

1661   Slavery Defined in Virginia. A Virginia statute recognized slavery and established the status of mixed-blood offspring as slave or free in accordance with the status of the mother. The slave codes of Virginia, and those that followed them, were motivated by the growth of the black population and the fears of slave uprisings. They were also specifically designed to protect the property in slaves. Generally, slaves were not allowed to leave the plantation, to wander, or to assemble without permission

from the master. They could not own weapons and could not testify against whites in court. Slaves found guilty of murder or rape were to be executed. For petty offenses, slaves were whipped, maimed, or branded. The slave codes grew out of the laws regulating indentured servitude, but the slaves, unlike the indentured servants, had practically no rights.

1663   Royal African Company Traded Slaves. The Royal African Company began its monopoly on the slave trade to the British-American colonies. The monopoly held strong until 1698 when the trade was opened to all English subjects.

SEPTEMBER 13, 1663   Slave Conspiracy Foiled. The first major conspiracy of people in servitude in colonial America was documented. But the plot of white servants and black slaves failed as it was betrayed by a servant in Gloucester County, Virginia.

SEPTEMBER 20, 1664   Interracial Marriage Banned. Maryland took the lead in passing laws against the marriage of English women to black men. The preamble of the statute justified the prohibition of intermarriage because "diverse freeborn English women, forgetful of their free condition, and to the disgrace of our nation, do intermarry with Negro slaves," causing, among other things, questions over the status of such blacks. The law was passed to remove this problem and to deter "such freeborn women from such shameful matches."

1667   Black Physician Rewarded for Services. Lucas Santomée was the first trained black physician in New Amsterdam. In reward for his services he received a land grant from the colony.

1670   Black Offspring Enslaved. The colony of Massachusetts revised slavery laws established in 1641 to permit the enslavement of a slave's offspring. The law gave children the same status as their mothers.

1671   Black Population of Virginia Colony. In 1671 the Virginia colony's 2,000 blacks made up less than five percent of the colony's population, according to the colony's governor. Virginia's black population tripled by 1700.

1672   Bounty for Maroons. The colony of Virginia passed a law providing a bounty on the heads of Maroons. The Maroons were black fugitives who formed communities in the mountains, swamps, and forests of Southern colonies. The law was passed in response to Maroon attacks on local communities.

OCTOBER 31, 1680   Black Codes in Massachusetts. The General Court of Massachusetts ordered that no ship was to sail from any port or harbor or to entertain on board "any servant or Negro" without a permit from the governor. Violators were charged twenty pounds.

1681   Slave Executed for Arson. The slave Maria was burned alive after having been convicted of burning her master's home and causing the death of a baby in the colony of Massachusetts.

FEBRUARY 18, 1688   Anti-slavery Resolution Adopted. Quakers at Germantown, Pennsylvania, adopted the first formal anti-slavery resolution in American history. The Society of Friends declared that slavery was in opposition to Christianity and the rights of man. The Quakers continued their anti-slavery protests throughout the seventeenth century.

1690   Connecticut Slave Codes. Colonial Connecticut passed a law that forbade black and Indian servants from wandering beyond town limits without a ticket or pass from a master or other person in position of authority. Violators were deemed runaways and would be returned to their masters. Ferrymen were fined twenty shillings for providing passage on their ferries for such persons.

1690   South Carolina Slave Statute. According to South Carolina law, slaves were freehold property except in payment of the master's debts. The statute provided that slaves, "as to the payment of debts, shall be deemed and taken as all other goods and chattels and that Negroes shall be accounted as freehold in all other cases, watsoever, and descent accordingly."

1691   Virginia Outlawed Manumission. The colony of Virginia outlawed the practice of freeing blacks unless those freed were to leave the colony within six months.

1693   Black Gatherings Caused Concern. A Pennsylvania provincial council expressed concern regarding the "tumultuous gatherings of the negroes in the towne of Philadelphia, of the first dayes of the weeke."

1693   Publication Opposed Owning Blacks. George Keith and a group of Quakers published *An Exhortation & Caution to Friends Concerning Buying or Keeping of Negroes.*

1696   South Carolina Ruled on Slave Conduct. Statutes in the colony of South Carolina stated that slaves needed written permission to leave their masters' residences. In addition, slave owners were required to make regular searches of slave quarters for weapons, and slaves who ran away or struck their masters faced severe penalties, including whipping, branding, slitting of the nose, and emasculation.

1698   Slave Taxes Changed. The colony of Massachusetts changed the tax laws by declaring that "all Indian, mulatto and Negro servants be estimated as other personal estate." Prior to this change slaves were listed as persons on the tax lists.

1700   Penn Established Monthly Meetings for Blacks. A monthly meeting for blacks was established with the help of William Penn and the Quakers.

1700   Pennsylvania Regulated Blacks. The Pennsylvania colonial assembly enacted two laws regarding the African American: one for regulating "Negroes in their Morals, and Mar-

Female slave being branded in Colonial America.

riages," and the other regarding "Negroes and their trials."

1700 *The Selling of Joseph* **Condemned Slavery.** Boston, Massachusetts, jurist Samuel Sewall condemned the business of slavery in *The Selling of Joseph*. Sewall is remembered for his public confession of error and guilt in the condemnation to death of nineteen alleged witches in Salem.

1703 **Massachusetts Regulated Blacks.** The colony of Massachusetts required every slave master to post a bond as security to support each freed slave to decrease the financial cost of indigents on a town. Connecticut and Massachusetts made it illegal for any Indian, black, or mulatto servant or slave to be on the streets after nine in the evening without the master's consent.

1704 **Abda Sued Richards.** A mulatto slave, Abda, ran away from his owner, Thomas Richards of Hartford, Connecticut. After Richards went to court to recover his "property," Abda filed a countersuit against Richards for illegally detaining him in bondage. Abda claimed that because of his "white" blood, there were no legal grounds to enslave him. A court declared Abda free. The General Assembly reversed the decision upon appeal and he was returned to Richards.

1704 **Nau Opened School for Slaves.** One of the first schools in the colonies to enroll slaves was opened by Elias Nau, a Frenchman, in New York City.

DECEMBER 1705 **Interracial Marriages Prohibited.** "An Act for the Better Preventing of a Spurious and Mist Issues" was passed in the colony of Massachusetts. The act prohibited both the marriage of a black or mulatto to any person of a "Christian nation" and illicit intercourse between blacks and whites. Prior to this law interracial marriages were not illegal. The law also imposed a four-pound duty on blacks imported into the colony. A later section of the

law stated that any black or mulatto who struck a white man would be "severely" whipped.

1706 **New York Slave Codes.** New York colonial law prohibited a slave from testifying for or against a freeman in either civil or criminal cases.

1707 **Massachusetts Slave Codes.** Colonial Massachusetts passed a law prohibiting free blacks from harboring or entertaining nonwhite servants in their homes without the approval of the masters. Penalties for the crime included repairing highways and cleaning streets.

1708 **White Colonists Outnumbered by Slaves in Carolina.** The Carolina colony had 2,900 black slaves and 1,100 Indian slaves, while adult whites numbered 2,400.

1708 **Connecticut Slave Codes.** According to colonial Connecticut law, a slave striking a white person was to be whipped thirty times.

1710 **Tanner Amos Fortune Born.** Amos Fortune was born a slave and purchased his freedom at age sixty. In 1779 Fortune purchased the freedom of his wife, Violet Baldwin, and his adopted daughter, Celyndia. After moving to Jaffrey, New Hampshire, Fortune opened a tannery that employed blacks and whites. He helped establish the Jaffrey Social Library in 1796. He bequeathed his estate, valued at nearly $800, to his wife, stipulating that funds remaining after her death be given to the local church and school.

1712 **South Carolina Regulated Slaves.** South Carolina slave regulations provided that no white person would be punished for injuring or killing a slave if that slave was resisting lawful punishment and that a fine was required of a white person who murdered a slave.

APRIL 7, 1712 **Slave Revolt in New York City.** Nine whites were slain and twenty-one blacks were executed as participants of a slave revolt in New York City. Six other alleged participants committed suicide. The insurrection was spearheaded by twenty-seven armed slaves who met in an orchard near the center of the city. A fire was set to an outhouse of a white man, and as other whites attempted to extinguish the blaze, they were shot by the blacks. The state militia was called to pursue and capture the black rebels, and New Yorkers responded to the uprising by strengthening their slave code. The number of slave crimes punishable by death was increased to include willful burning of property. Conspiracy to murder was also made a capital offense.

1713   Britain Slave Trade Participation Increased. Britain heightened its participation in the colonial slave trade with the South Sea Company, which imported 4,800 African slaves annually into Spain's New World colonies for the next 30 years. This began Britain's most active period of participation in the slave trade.

1714   Rhode Island Slave Codes. Colonial Rhode Island passed a law forbidding ferrymen from transporting or conveying any slaves out of the colony without a certificate from their master or mistress or official person. Violators paid all costs and charges were sustained by the master. The law did not prevent blacks from being carried away by privateersmen and other vessels. The law was amended in 1757, imposing a 500-pound fine upon any man-of-war commander or merchant ship master who knowingly carried any abducted slaves out of the colony.

1715   Blacks Counted in Census. According to the census there were 2,000 blacks in New England.

1715   Virginia Slave Population Grew. The black slave population in the Virginia colony rose to 24 percent, up from less than five percent in 1671.

1717   Cotton Mather Opened School. Cotton Mather, a white minister, began an evening school for Indians and blacks in Boston, Massachusetts.

1717   Importation of Slaves Authorized. The South Sea Company of England was authorized to import 144,000 African slaves to the Americas (4,800 per year) for the next thirty years.

1718–27   Blacks Imported to Virginia. More than 11,000 blacks were brought to Virginia aboard British vessels.

1720   Slave Population Estimated. The slave population of the Pennsylvania colony was estimated at 2,000.

1727   Blacks Educated in New Orleans. Blacks received instruction in New Orleans, Louisiana, from the Roman Catholic Ursuline Nuns.

1727   England Ships Slaves to Colonies. Between 1718 and 1727 slightly over 17,000 Africans were imported to Virginia in 76 vessels. Only six of those vessels were originally from Virginia; they carried a total of 649 African slaves. The remaining 70 ships, carrying 10,442 slaves, were from Bristol, Liverpool, and London.

1727–38   Slave Trade Statistics. Between 1727 and 1738, sixteen New England vessels brought 540 blacks into Virginia at an average of 45 per year. There were 447 ships from Africa and 85 ships from the West Indies.

1728   Pigott Founded School for Blacks. Nathaniel Pigott announced his plans to begin a school for the "instruction of Negroes in reading, catechizing, and writing."

JULY 1728   Slave Conduct Restricted. Colonial Massachusetts forbade black, Indian, and mulatto servants or slaves from buying provisions directly from country people. It was permissible for slaves to request their mistress or master to make the sale. Violators were fined five shillings.

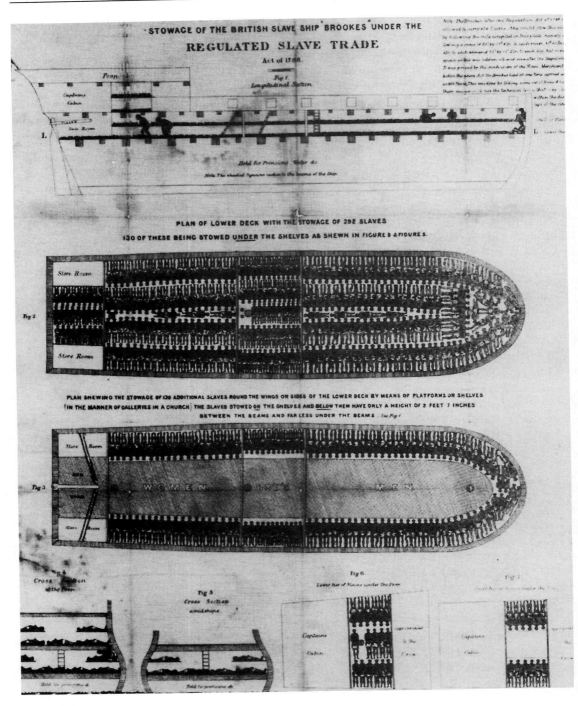

Diagram illustrating the layout of a slave ship. (Courtesy of Library of Congress.)

1729   Emancipated Slaves Required Bond. The colony of Rhode Island required every master to post a bond of one hundred pounds to guarantee that the slave would not become a public charge "through sickness, lameness" or other cause.

1730   Connecticut Slave Codes. The Connecticut colony passed a law forbidding any black, Indian, or mulatto from slandering or libeling a white person. If convicted by a justice of the peace, the accused was whipped with forty lashes.

1732   British Prohibited Taxes on Slaves. The British Parliament sent all of the colonial governors, including Jonathan Belcher, governor of Massachusetts, a directive stating: "Wheraas Acts have been bassed in some of our Plantations in America for laying Duties on the Importation and Exportation of Negroes to the Discouragement of the Merchants trading thither—from the Coast of Africa. . .It is our Will and Pleasure That you do not give your Assent to or pass any Law imposing Duties upon Negroes imported into Our Province of the Massachusetts Bay payable by the Importer or upon any slaves exported that have not been sold in Our said Province, and continued there for the Space of Twelve Months."

1735   Georgia Prohibited Importation of Blacks. The Georgia colony board, a governing entity, passed an act "for rendering the colony of Georgia more defensible by Prohibiting the Importation and use of Black Slaves or Negroes into the same." At the time, it was believed that Georgia would serve as a barrier against the Spanish. In an effort to circumvent the ban, many Georgia residents hired slaves from South Carolina. On January 1, 1750, after many of the settlers demonstrated through petitions, the ban against the importation of slaves was lifted.

SEPTEMBER 9–11, 1739   Stono Rebellion. The Stono Rebellion began near the village of Rantowles, about twelve miles west of Charleston, South Carolina. A large group of slaves stole guns and ammunition from a store. The slaves began a march toward the Spanish in St. Augustine because the king of Spain had issued a decree granting freedom to slaves escaping to Florida. The lieutenant governor, William Bull, and a group of men happened to meet the armed slaves. Bull alerted the militia and 44 of the escapees were killed. The escaping slaves killed 21 whites and burned a number of plantation homes before the battle with the militia.

MARCH 1741   Blacks Blamed for New York Fires. A "Negro conspiracy" was charged with a series of fires in New York. New Yorkers blamed Roman Catholic priests for inciting slaves to burn the town on orders from Spain. Eighteen blacks and four whites were hanged December 31, 1741, and thirteen blacks were burned at the stake.

APRIL 15, 1742   Slave Divorced Wife. A slave named Boston petitioned the General Court of Massachusetts for a divorce from his wife, Hagar. She was charged with "not having the fear of God before her eyes and being instigated by a white man has been guilty of the detestable sin of adultery and during the time of intermarriage was delivered of a mulatto bastard child begotten on her body." The court granted Boston a divorce.

1745   Abolitionist Vassa Born. Gustavus Vassa was born Olaudah Equiano in Nigeria. Vassa enjoyed a childhood filled with tribal unity. At the age of ten, he was kidnapped by nearby tribesmen and sold into slavery. He was brought to Virginia where he was purchased by a British sailor, Michael Pacal, who took him to England. There he began his formal education and was given the name Gustavus Vassa, after the sixteenth-century Swedish king. He traveled with his master across the seas, witnessing fighting between the French and the British. He was further educated in London and was baptized in St. Margaret's Church, Westminster, in February 1759. When Vassa requested

Slaves appearing before a judge for the insurrection of 1741. (Courtesy of Library of Congress.)

freedom, his master angrily sent him to the West Indies to be sold. Vassa's new master was a Philadelphia Quaker who taught him commercial arts. Vassa bought his freedom in 1766 and earned his living trading goods from the Caribbean. His interest in abolition was aroused by his exposure to the slave trade and inspired his autobiography, *Interesting Narrative*. Vassa died in 1794.

1749 "The Bar's Fight" Written. At age sixteen, Lucy Terry Prince wrote "The Bar's Fight," a poem about an Indian attack on Deerfield, Massachusetts, where she was a slave. The poem wasn't published until 1855, in Josiah Gilbert Holland's *History of Western Massachusetts*. Prince is considered by some to be the first black American female poet, though Phillis Wheatley published work in 1776. Born in Africa, Prince was kidnapped as a child and brought to Deerfield, where she became a slave to Ebenezer Wells. Prince was married in 1756 to Abijah Prince, a free man who bought his wife's freedom. Prince's past probably inspired her civil rights efforts. She succeeded in convincing the governor's council of Guilford, Vermont, where she was living, to order the protection of her family after their fence had been torn down by white neighbors. She also tried, but failed, to get one of her sons enrolled in Williams College. In 1821, Prince died on the family farm in Sunderland.

c. 1750 Minister George Liele Born. George Liele was born to slave parents in Virginia. He was introduced to the Baptist faith by a white minister in Burke County, Georgia, who preached to slaves. During Britain's occupation of Savannah, Liele began preaching to black Baptists, and when the British sailed from Savannah to Jamaica, Liele accompanied them as an indentured servant. In Jamaica, Liele began preaching in a private home but eventually was permitted to expand his ministry to rural areas, much to the dismay of the Anglican church. Liele built a church and a public school, and worked as a farmer and hauler of goods. In 1820 he died in

Jamaica and was buried there, survived by a wife and four children.

1750 Georgia Authorized Slave Importation. The colony of Georgia authorized the importation of slaves. The law required a ratio of four male slaves for each white servant. It also required that blacks be tried according to the laws of England and that slaves be taught the sanctity of marriage. The law also prohibited intermarriage of blacks and whites.

1752 Soldier Oliver Cromwell Born. Oliver Cromwell was reportedly born free in Columbus, Burlington County, New Jersey. He worked as a farmer before joining the 2nd New Jersey Regiment under the command of Colonel Israel Shreve. Cromwell recalled that he accompanied General George Washington when he crossed the Delaware in 1776 and also claimed to have fought in the battles of Princeton, Brandywine, Monmouth, and Yorktown. He received an honorable discharge from the Jersey Battalion—signed by General Washington at his headquarters—on June 5, 1783. Cromwell received a federal pension of ninety-six dollars a year. He died in January 1853.

1755 Author and Chaplain John Marrant Born. John Marrant was born in New York. He lived in St. Augustine, Florida, for a time before being captured by Cherokee Indians. Marrant was influenced by the Reverend George Whitefield, an English preacher who co-founded, with John Wesley, the Methodist Movement. He served with the British Royal Navy and was a Methodist missionary in Nova Scotia before becoming an author. His writings detailed the events of his own life that led him to his religious convictions. His most popular work, *A Narrative of the Lord's Wonderful Dealings with John Marrant*, describes Marrant's "dealings" with God. Historian Arthur Schomburg reprinted Marrant's Masonic Sermon in 1789 and described him as "undoubtedly one of the first, if not the first, Negro minister of the gospel in North America." Marrant rarely referred to racial matters in his works and thus was never cited in early collected works of African American biographies. He died in 1791.

1759   Soldier Agrippa Hull Born. Agrippa Hull was born free in Northampton, Massachusetts. Hull enlisted as a private in the brigade of the Massachusetts line on May 1, 1777, where he served for the duration of the Revolutionary War. He served his first two years as a private and the next four years as an orderly for General Tadeusz Kosciuszko, the Polish patriot. Hull received his discharge (signed by General George Washington) in July 1783 at West Point. Kosciuszko later met with Hull in New York when the general visited the United States in 1797. Hull married a fugitive slave, adopted another fugitive slave, and farmed a plot of land in Stockbridge, Massachusetts. He died in 1848.

c. 1760   Seaman Joseph Ranger Born. Joseph Ranger was born in Northumberland County, Virginia. Ranger was aboard the *Jefferson* when the British blew it up. He also served on the *Hero,* the *Dragon,* and the *Patriot* during the American Revolution. Ranger was part of the captured *Patriot* crew that was held by the British until the surrender at Yorktown. He served on the *Patriot* and the *Liberator* in the years following the Revolution. He reportedly received the benefits of the Federal Pension Act of 1832, an annual payment of $96 and 100 acres of land.

1760   Spy James Lafayette Armistead Born. James Lafayette Armistead was born a slave of William Armistead of New Kent County, Virginia. In March 1781 Armistead was granted permission to serve with General Lafayette during the war and infiltrated the headquarters of British general Charles Cornwallis. Armistead was noted for his written intelligence reports concerning the Yorktown campaign that ended the Revolutionary War.

Lafayette gave Armistead a certificate stating: "This is to certify that the bearer by the name of James had done essential services to me

while I had the honor to command in this State. His intelligences from the enemy's camp were industriously collected and more faithfully delivered. He properly acquitted himself with some important communications I gave him and appears to be entitled to every reward his situation can admit of. Done under my hand, Richmond, November 21st, 1784. LaFayette."

As a reward for his services, Armistead was granted his freedom by the Virginia legislature in 1786. Thirty years later, he purchased forty acres of land near New Kent County and raised a family. He was granted an annual pension of $40 in 1819 and in 1824 was personally greeted by General Lafayette upon the general's return to America. Armistead died in 1832.

c. 1760   Soldier Austin Dabney Born. Austin Dabney is believed to have been born to a Virginia white woman and a black father in North Carolina. Dabney was enlisted in the Georgia Militia by Richard Aycock. In February 1779, Dabney fought along with white men in the name of colonial independence. He was wounded in battle, ending his military career. Dabney was emancipated in 1786 by the Georgia legislature, and in 1821 he was granted 112 acres of choice farmland in Walton County. His prosperity grew from owning horses during the later years of his life. Dabney was, according to some, Georgia's only genuine black hero of the American Revolutionary War. Dabney died in Zebulon in 1834.

DECEMBER 15, 1761   Black Poet Published. Jupiter Hammon, born a slave October 17, 1711, published *Salvation by Christ with Penitential Cries,* the first known poetical work by a black. Hammon's masters had given him a rudimentary education, including religious instruction, and helped to publish his verse. Scholars do not accord much literary merit to Hammon's work, but he is an important figure because of his place in the chronology of black literature. Hammon is also known for his *Address to the Negroes of the State of New York*

(1787), in which he called upon blacks to be faithful and obedient to their masters. Hammon believed that the race should endure its bondage humbly and patiently until it earned its freedom by honest and good conduct.

1763   Slave Trade Grew. Between 1753 and 1763, thirteen New England vessels brought 869 slaves to Virginia.

1764   Brown University Founded. Brown University was founded in Providence, Rhode Island. The university was named for the wealthy New England shippers, the Brown Brothers, who made substantial profits from the African slave trade.

1766   Washington Traded Slave for Liquor. Virginia farmer and future president George Washington sent an unruly slave to the West Indies in exchange for rum and other commodities.

JULY 19, 1767   Clock Maker Peter Hill Born. Peter Hill was born into a slave family in a New Jersey Quaker household, where he learned the craft of clock making from his master. He worked in his master's clock shop until age 27, when he was manumitted. Hill received his manumission document May 1, 1795. On September 9, 1795, Hill married Tina Lewis, a free person of color. Hill went on to open clock shops of his own in Burlington Township and Mount Holly, New Jersey. Two of Hill's tall case clocks are known to still be in existence: one in Westtown (Pa.) School, the other in the National Museum of History and Technology of the Smithsonian Institution in Washington, D.C. Hill died in 1820.

1769   California Occupied by Spanish African Residents. When the Spanish Empire expanded into coastal California in 1769, the large population of Spanish-speaking residents of African descent was influential to the occupation. The Portolá Expedition in particular was known to have at least one mulatto soldier, Juan Antonio Coronel, and several mule drivers of Spanish African heritage.

Part 2

BUILDING A NATION
1770–1859

Chapter 2
1770 TO 1799

1770 to 1779

1770   Quakers Educated Blacks. Quaker philanthropist Anthony Benezet established a free school for blacks in Philadelphia. In 1784, when Benezet died, he left his fortune to the school known as the Binoxide House.

MARCH 5, 1770   Escaped Slave Died in Boston Massacre. Crispus Attucks of Framingham, Massachusetts, an escaped slave, died with four other Americans in the so-called Boston Massacre. He was in the forefront of the group that taunted British soldiers during the altercation and reportedly was the first to fall from their fire. Massachusetts later honored Attucks with a statue in Boston.

      Attucks was born a slave of Deacon William Brown in Framingham. In November 1750 he escaped slavery at the age of twenty-seven. In Boston, African Americans held an annual Crispus Attucks Day from 1858 to 1870.

1773   Black Baptist Church Organized. In Savannah, Georgia, George Liele and Andrew Bryan organized the American colonies' first Negro Baptist Church. Liele and Bryan were both former slaves with modest education. When they first began preaching (at very young ages) there were no black denominations. Liele and Bryan preached without compensation. Liele

Crispus Attucks. (Courtesy of Library of Congress.)

supported himself as a laborer-for-hire after being freed by his pious master. Opposition to black worship eventually forced Liele to flee to Jamaica. Bryan's master defended him against other whites who were alarmed over the growth of the black church, and although Bryan bought his wife's freedom, he did not purchase his own until after his master's death, because of the sense of gratitude Bryan had for his master's support of him.

1773   Phillis Wheatley Published Book. Phillis Wheatley, an African-born poet, published

---

First African Baptist Church in Savannah, Georgia.

Poems on Various Subjects, Religious and Moral. becoming the second American woman to publish a book. Wheatley was born in Senegal, circa 1753, and was sold as a slave in 1761 to Boston tailor John Wheatley, whose wife tutored young Phillis, enabling her to become literate. Wheatley began writing verse in her early teens. Manumitted in 1773, she travelled to London and was received by the Lord Mayor and other influential Londoners. On February 28, 1776, Wheatley had an audience with General George Washington at his Cambridge,

Massachusetts, headquarters, so that he might express his appreciation for her poem in his honor.

1773. DuSable Became First Permanent Settler in Chicago. Jean Baptiste Pointe duSable, the first permanent settler of Chicago, purchased the property of Jean Baptiste Millet at "Old Peoria Fort." DuSable was born in St. Marc, Haiti, in 1745, the son of a Frenchman who had emigrated to Haiti from Marseilles, France, and a black slave. DuSable was educat-

Phillis Wheatley.

1775 **Narrator Isaac Jefferson Born.** Isaac Jefferson was born to Usler and George, slaves of Thomas Jefferson, at Monticello in December 1775. He accompanied Thomas Jefferson to Philadelphia in 1790, where he learned the trade of tinning. After Thomas Jefferson's death in 1826, it is believed that Isaac Jefferson was a blacksmith in Petersburg, Virginia, in 1847. In 1951, his memories as a slave were published in *Memoirs of a Monticello Slave, As Dictated to Charles Campbell in the 1840s by Isaac, one of Thomas Jefferson's Slaves.* The book is valued mainly for its information about Thomas Jefferson.

MARCH 6, 1775 **Prince Hall Inducted to Masons.** Prince Hall and 14 other blacks were inducted into the British Army Masonic Lodge near Boston. This was the first formal fraternal organization of blacks. Hall, who ministered the gospel to his group, was refused when he asked the Massachusetts Grand Lodge for permission to establish a separate African lodge.

APRIL 14, 1775 **First Abolitionist Society Organized.** Known originally as the Pennsylvania Society for the Abolition of Slavery, this group included many active Quakers. The Society first worked toward obtaining an abolition law in Pennsylvania and protecting free blacks from being kidnapped and sold into slavery. After a successful campaign for adequate protective legislation, the Society helped enforce the new laws through committees of correspondence and by employing lawyers to secure the conviction of offenders. The Society suspended its operations during the Revolutionary War, although individual members continued active work. The group was reorganized in 1787 as the Pennsylvania Society for Promoting the Abolition of Slavery, the Relief of Free Negroes Unlawfully held in Bondage, and Improving the Condition of the African Race.

ed in France and later worked in his father's business in New Orleans in 1765. When the Spanish occupied Louisiana that same year, duSable and an associate, Jacques Clemorgan of Martinique, left for the French-settled areas of the upper Mississippi River. They stopped in St. Louis, where they carried on a successful fur trade with the Indians for two years. Later, duSable and Clemorgan moved farther north into Indian territory and lived with the Peoria and Potawatomie tribes. At the same time, duSable participated in fur trapping expeditions, which carried him to the present sites of Chicago, Detroit, and Ontario, Canada. In 1772, duSable decided to build a fur trading post on the Chicago river near Lake Michigan. A successful trading center grew around the post and the Chicago settlement developed. After Illinois came under the jurisdiction of the United States, duSable sold his property and returned to Missouri, where he died in 1818.

DECEMBER 1, 1774 **Importation of Slaves Prohibited.** George Washington signed the Fairfax Resolves, barring importation of slaves and threatening to halt all colonial exports to England.

APRIL 19, 1775 **Revolutionary War Began.** The War for Independence began at Lexington

Jean Baptiste Pointe duSable and the fur trading settlement he established.

and Concord, Massachusetts. Blacks were among the Minutemen who opposed the British.

JUNE 17, 1775   Black Soldiers Honored. Two blacks, Peter Salem and Salem Poor, were commended for their participation on the side of the Patriots at the Battle of Bunker Hill. Salem had been a slave in Framington, Massachusetts, but was manumitted so that he could serve in the Revolutionary Army. The Committee on Safety of the Continental Congress had decreed in May 1775 that only free blacks could serve in the American army. During the Battle of Bunker Hill, Salem killed the British commander, Major John Pitcairn. Although the Americans did not achieve victory at Bunker Hill, Pitcairn's death raised the rebels's morale at the time. The Massachusetts General Court later commended Salem for the act. Poor also won commendation from the Massachusetts Court and from his officers. He was described by his officers as an excellent soldier. On July 9, 1775, however, General George Washington announced that there would be no further enlistments of blacks. The Continental Congress sanctioned Washington's decree in October.

OCTOBER 23, 1775   Black Enlistment Prohibited. The Continental Congress prohibited black enlistment in the American army.

NOVEMBER 7, 1775   British Promised Slaves Freedom. Lord Dunmore, British royal governor of Virginia, issued a proclamation promising freedom to slaves who joined the British forces in the Revolutionary War. Southerners, especially Virginians, were alarmed and angered. Virginia responded by attempting to convince blacks that the British motives were purely selfish, and promised them good treatment if they remained loyal to the Patriot cause. On December 13, 1775, a Virginia Convention promised to pardon all slaves who returned to their masters within ten days. It is not clear how many slaves served with the British, but the war did have an unsettling effect on the institution of slavery. At least 100,000 blacks ran away from their masters during the conflict. The Dunmore Proclamation helped to bolster Southern support for the Patriots as the British threatened slavery.

DECEMBER 31, 1775   Black Enlistment Allowed. General George Washington, revising an earlier decision, ordered recruiting officers

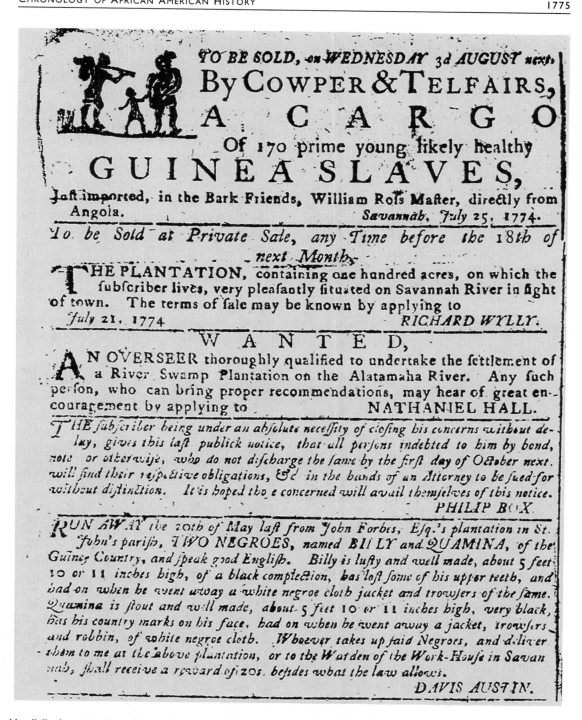

TO BE SOLD, on WEDNESDAY 3d AUGUST next.

By COWPER & TELFAIRS,

A CARGO

Of 170 prime young likely healthy

GUINEA SLAVES,

Just imported, in the Bark Friends, William Ross Master, directly from Angola.   Savannah, July 25, 1774.

To be Sold at Private Sale, any Time before the 18th of next Month,

THE PLANTATION, containing one hundred acres, on which the subscriber lives, very pleasantly situated on Savannah River in sight of town. The terms of sale may be known by applying to

July 21, 1774   RICHARD WYLLY.

WANTED,

AN OVERSEER thoroughly qualified to undertake the settlement of a River Swamp Plantation on the Alatamaha River. Any such person, who can bring proper recommendations, may hear of great encouragement by applying to   NATHANIEL HALL.

THE subscriber being under an absolute necessity of closing his concerns without delay, gives this last publick notice, that all persons indebted to him by bond, note or otherwise, who do not discharge the same by the first day of October next, will find their respective obligations, &c in the hands of an Attorney to be sued for without distinction. It is hoped those concerned will avail themselves of this notice.

PHILIP BOX

RUN AWAY the 20th of May last from John Forbes, Esq.'s plantation in St. John's parish, TWO NEGROES, named BILLY and QUAMINA, of the Guiney Country, and speak good English. Billy is lusty and well made, about 5 feet 10 or 11 inches high, of a black complexion, has lost some of his upper teeth, and had on when he went away a white negroe cloth jacket and trowsers of the same. Quamina is stout and well made, about 5 feet 10 or 11 inches high, very black, has his country marks on his face, had on when he went away a jacket, trowsers and robbin, of white negroe cloth. Whoever takes up said Negroes, and deliver them to me at the above plantation, or to the Warden of the Work-House in Savannah, shall receive a reward of 20s. besides what the law allows.

DAVIS AUSTIN.

Handbill advertising the sale of slaves in 1774. (Courtesy of Library of Congress.)

to accept free blacks in the American army. More than 5,000 blacks, mostly from the North, fought against the British. Georgia and South Carolina steadfastly opposed the enlistment of black soldiers. In 1770, the Continental Congress agreed to pay owners of slaves in Georgia and South Carolina $1,000 for each slave allowed to serve in the American army, but at the end of the war the blacks were to be freed and given fifty dollars. The two Southern states rejected the offer.

JULY 4, 1776   Declaration of Independence Signed. A section that alleged that King George III had forced the slave trade and slavery on the colonies was eliminated at the insistence of representatives from Georgia and South Carolina. Thomas Jefferson had charged King George with waging "cruel war against human nature itself, violating its most sacred rights of life and liberty in the persons of a distant people who never offended him, captivating and carrying them into slavery in another hemisphere, or to incur miserable death in their transportation thither." In the monarch's determination "to keep open a market where men should be bought and sold," Jefferson said he had suppressed "every legislative attempt to prohibit or to restrain this execrable commerce." Historians agree that this was one example of the American exaggerations in the list of grievances against King George III.

DECEMBER 25, 1776   Black Slave Accompanied Washington. Prince Whipple, a native of Amabou, Africa, accompanied George Washington across the Delaware River. Though Whipple was born free, he was sold into slavery en route to the colonies where he was sent by his parents to be educated. An 1819 painting by Thomas Sully and a later work by Emanuel Gottlieb Leutze depicted a black man as part of Washington's party. Whipple, whose surname was taken from his master, regained his freedom after serving in the Revolutionary War by petitioning to the council and House of New Hampshire in 1779.

1777   Early Segregation. New Jersey began educating whites and blacks separately.

JULY 1777   Black Soldier Captured Prescott. British Major-General Richard Prescott was captured at his Rhode Island headquarters by American revolutionary forces. Jack Sisson (c.1743–1821) was the leader of the troop that captured Prescott. Newspaper reports noted Sisson's pivotal role in the event.

JULY 2, 1777   Slavery Abolished in Vermont. By 1804, all the states north of Delaware had taken action leading to the gradual abolition of slavery. (Some slaves were seen in New Jersey as late as 1860, however.) Pennsylvania passed a law for gradual abolition in 1780. New Hampshire's law was passed in 1783. In 1784 Connecticut and Rhode Island took similar action. Manumission acts were passed in New York in 1785 and in New Jersey in 1786, though effective legislation stipulating gradual abolition was not achieved in the two states until 1799 and 1804, respectively. In 1783, the courts of Massachusetts upheld the contention of blacks that slavery in that state violated a section of the state constitution of 1780 that asserted that "all men are born free and equal." One immediate result of the Northern manumissions was the establishment of schools for free blacks by the early abolition and philanthropic societies. The African Free School in New York City, for example, was opened on November 1, 1787.

1780 to 1789

1781   Former Slave Spied on British. James Armistead (1760–1832), in the service of General Lafayette, infiltrated British general Cornwallis's camp and sent vital written reports back to the Americans and French. Acting on Armistead's information, the Revolutionary commanders sent a French fleet to Chesapeake Bay and forced Cornwallis's surrender. Armistead, a slave, was given leave by his master in 1881 to serve General Lafayette. For his contribution to the success of the war effort, the Virginia legislature granted him his freedom in 1786.

MAY 8, 1781   Convicted Slave Was Reprieved.
Known as Billy, Will, or William, the mulatto slave of John Tayloe of Virginia was sentenced to death by the Court of Oyer and Terminer, Prince William County, for aiding in the seizure of an armed vessel and "feloniously and traitorously" waging war against Virginia. Billy argued that his part in the attack was not of his own free will. Two justices, Henry Lee and William Carr, dissented with the court on grounds that, because Billy was a slave, he owed no allegiance and, therefore, could not be guilty of treason. Virginia governor Thomas Jefferson moved to pass a reprieve to June 30 through the state legislature. The reprieve was apparently granted, a move that may have evidenced a sense of justice in a slave-holding state, as well as Jefferson's hypothesized anti-slavery views.

1783   Freed Slave Opened Medical Practice.
James C. Derham bought his freedom from Doctor Robert Dove, who had educated Derham in pharmacy and therapeutics. Derham went to New Orleans and set up his own successful practice treating blacks and whites.

1783   Massachusetts Slave Sued Master and Won. Elizabeth (Mumbet) Freeman, born a slave around 1742, escaped a physically abusive master and appealed to a young lawyer, Theodore Sedgwick, to prevent re-enslavement. Freeman told the lawyer that she had overheard conversations about the Bill of Rights and the new constitution of Massachusetts, which claimed that all men were born free and equal. Sedgwick argued the case before the county court of Great Barrington, which freed Freeman and ordered her former master to pay her thirty shillings in damages. Freeman died on December 28, 1829.

MARCH 23, 1784   Boxer Tom Molineaux Born.
Tom Molineaux was one of four boys born a slave, in Georgetown, District of Columbia. As

Revolutionary War spy James Armistead.

a boy, Molineaux began to box, following in the footsteps of his father. His abilities as a boxer won him his freedom and a hundred-dollar prize when Molineaux defeated a slave from a nearby plantation on the bet of their masters. He used his prize money to go to London, where boxing was a popular and profitable sport, and he became the first American to fight with distinction abroad. Unfortunately, his success was short-lived; he lost two highly publicized matches with Tom Cribbs, the British champion. Molineaux then entered a downward spiral into poverty and alcoholism. He died penniless in Ireland on August 4, 1818.

MARCH 27, 1784   Businesswoman Elleanor Eldridge Born. Elleanor Eldridge was born in Warwick, Rhode Island. She began working for the Baker family at an early age, washing clothes for twenty-five cents a week. During her six years with the family, she became skilled at spinning, weaving, and arithmetic. In 1812 she and her sister began a business of weaving, washing, and soap boiling that enabled Elleanor to buy a lot and build a house, which she would later rent for $40 a year. By 1822 she had saved enough from her various business ventures to

Advertisement for the sale of slaves in 1780. (Courtesy of Library of Congress.)

build a large house. Over a period of years she added to the house and began making payments toward a second house. When Eldridge made a trip to visit relatives, it was mistakenly reported that she had died. Upon her return, all her property, valued at $4,000, had been sold. On the advice of friends, she entered a "trespass and ejectment" suit, which she won. However, she could recover her property only after payment of $2,700, which likely went unpaid. In 1838 Eldridge's memoirs were written by Frances Harriet Whipple Greene McDougall.

c. 1785 Sally Hemings and Thomas Jefferson at Monticello. Sally Hemings was believed to have captured the heart of Thomas Jefferson, who at the time was a forty-five-year-old widower. Born in 1773, Hemings had arrived at Jefferson's Monticello plantation in 1775 as a slave. She accompanied his daughter to join him in France and was apparently educated and financially compensated during the three-year stay. Soon after she returned to Monticello, in 1789, Hemings gave birth to a son. Writings by Jefferson, Hemings's children, and Virginia's *Richmond Recorder* evidenced their intimate relationship and Jefferson's paternity to this and probably six other of Hemings's children. Hemings was discreetly freed by Jefferson's daughter after his death in 1826. Hemmings died in 1835.

1787 African Free School Established. The Manumission Society established the New York African Free School, where enrollment averaged about 50 students. Another school for African Americans was built in Philadelphia, and six more were established in the next ten years.

JANUARY 20, 1787 Moses Sash Led Shays Rebellion. Moses Sash was indicted for taking up arms against the Commonwealth and encouraging others to do the same, according to a Suffolk County, Massachusetts, courthouse document. A second document showed he was indicted for stealing two guns. Reportedly Sash's indictments indicated he played a major role in

African Free School in New York. (Schomburg Center for Research in Black Culture.)

the rebellion, as the members of Shays's council of war and directors of the rebel strategy were excluded from the indemnity that was granted to less serious offenders. Governor John Hancock pardoned all participants.

Sash had been born to Sarah Sash and Samson Dunbar in Braintree, Massachusetts, in 1755. During the Revolutionary War, Sash enlisted as a private in Colonel Ruggles Woodbrige's Regiment in August 1777. In May 1781 he reenlisted as a private in the seventh Regiment.

APRIL 12, 1787 Free African Society Established. Richard Allen and Absalom Jones organized the Free African Society, a black self-help group, in Philadelphia. Allen was perhaps the most conspicuous African American leader in the country before the rise of Frederick Douglass. His stature rested upon his leadership in the establishment of such organizations as the Free African Society and the African Methodist Episcopal (A.M.E.) Church. Jones was a close associate of Allen for many years, but the two parted when Jones, who was attracted by Anglicanism, became rector of the first Protestant Episcopal congregation for

Rev. Richard Allen. (Courtesy of the National Portrait Gallery.)

Prince Hall. (Schomburg Center for Research in Black Culture.)

blacks. Jones was born a slave in Sussex, Delaware. His master took him to Philadelphia to work as a handyman in a store, where he was taught to write by one of the clerks. He later attended night school and completed his education. Saving money that visitors to his master's house had given him, together with his earnings, Jones purchased both his own freedom and that of his wife. He became a member of the St. George's Methodist Church in Philadelphia.

While attending services there one Sunday in 1786, Jones, Allen, and other worshippers, were pulled from their knees and ordered to move to the reserved worship area for blacks in the church's balcony. Out of this incident grew the Free African Society, a quasi-religious organization whose programs included a fund for mutual aid, burial assistance, relief for widows and orphans, strengthening of marriage ties and personal morality, cooperation with abolition societies, and correspondence with free blacks in other areas. It was probably the first stable, independent black social organization in the United States. Among the other joint efforts of Allen and Jones were the organi-

zation of relief measures for the black population in Philadelphia during the yellow-fever epidemic in 1793, and the raising of a company of black militia during the War of 1812.

JULY 13, 1787 Slavery Outlawed in Northwest. The Continental Congress prohibited slavery in the Northwest Territory under the famous Ordinance of 1787. Specifically, there could be neither slavery nor involuntary servitude in the region northwest of the Ohio River except as punishment for a crime.

SEPTEMBER 1787 Constitution Adopted. The "Three-fifths Compromise," which allowed the South to count three-fifths of the slave population in determining representation in the House of Representatives was incorporated. The Constitution also prohibited any legislation that might close the slave trade before 1808, but allowed a tax of ten dollars per head on each slave imported before that date and demanded that fugitive slaves be returned to their owners.

SEPTEMBER 12, 1787 Masonic Lodge for Blacks Chartered. Prince Hall, a veteran of the

War for Independence, received a charter for a Masonic Lodge for blacks. This group was chartered in England as African Lodge No. 459. Hall, the first master of the organization, set up additional African lodges in Pennsylvania and Rhode Island during 1797. Hall was born in Barbados, British West Indies, in 1735, the son of an Englishman and a free black woman. He was apprenticed as a leather worker but abandoned that training to emigrate to Boston. During the Revolutionary War, Hall and twelve other free blacks were inducted into a Masonic Lodge by a group of British soldiers stationed in Boston. When the British evacuated the area, Hall organized a Masonic Lodge for blacks. Hall, a self-educated clergyman, also championed the establishment of schools for black children in Boston, urged Massachusetts to legislatively oppose slavery, and proposed measures to protect free blacks from kidnapping and enslavement. Following his death in Boston on December 4, 1807, the African Grand Lodge became the Prince Hall Grand Lodge, which has become a major social institution in black America.

1789   Black Soldier Gained Freedom. Caesar Tarrant was freed by the Virginia legislature for having served with distinction in the American Revolution. Tarrant was instructed by his master, Carter Tarrant, on piloting ships. Tarrant was piloting the schooner *Patriot* when it captured a British brig headed for Boston with supplies. After his service, Tarrant acquired property which was willed to his family upon his death in 1798.

1790 to 1799

c. 1790   Abraham, Seminole Interpreter, Born. Abraham was born in slavery in Pensacola, Florida. His Seminole name was "Sohanac" or "Souanakke Tustenukle." By the early 1820s he was living in Florida with the slave-holding Seminole Indians, among whom runaway black slaves often sought refuge. In 1825 Abraham

accompanied Seminole chief Micanopy on an official visit to Washington, D.C., and was granted his freedom. Over the next several years, Abraham witnessed many Seminole treaties as an interpreter. During this period, the Seminole were being pressured by the U.S. government to move from Florida; Abraham secretly advised Micanopy to resist this pressure and encouraged the plantation slaves of the area to support the Seminole and the blacks associated with the Seminole. During the Third Seminole War, which began in 1835, Abraham negotiated for peace, eventually persuading Micanopy to surrender. Abraham's settlement provided that the African American allies of the Seminole be allowed to leave Florida with them. On February 25, 1839, Abraham was sent west, where he raised cattle near the Little River in Arkansas. Abraham had two sons, Renty and Washington, and one daughter by his wife, Hagar.

1791   Music School opened for African Americans. Newport Gardner, one of the first black music teachers in America, opened a music school in Newport, Massachusetts. Gardner, born in 1746, was a slave of Caleb Gardner, one of Newport's leading merchants. The slave taught himself to read, sing, and write music. One of his compositions, "Crooked Shanks," was included in the collection *A Number of Original Airs, Duettos and Tiros,* published in 1803. He was also active in religious affairs. He was a founder of the Newport Colored Union Church and Society and became a missionary in Africa in 1826, the estimated year of his death.

JANUARY 1791   Free Blacks Protested. Free blacks in Charleston, South Carolina, presented a petition to the state legislature protesting laws restricting their freedoms. The blacks pointed specifically to the Act of 1740, which deprived slaves and free blacks of the right to testify under oath in court and the right to trial by jury. The blacks reminded the legislators that they were taxpaying citizens of South Carolina and were considered free citizens of

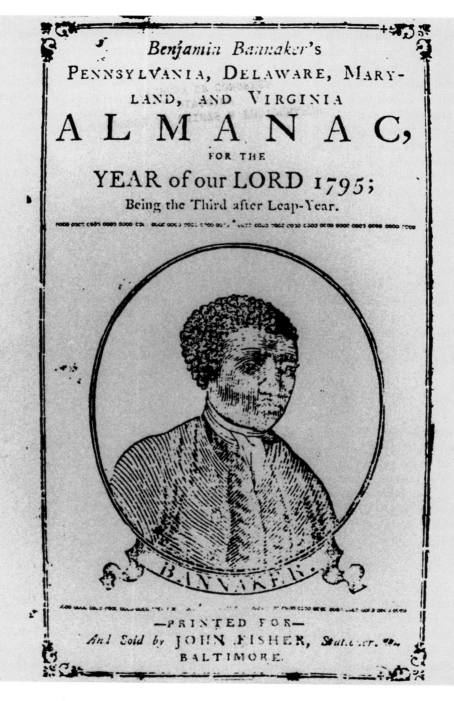

Benjamin Banneker's Almanac in 1795.

the state, and thus hoped to be treated as such. At the same time, the blacks acknowledged that they did not "presume to hope that they shall be put on an equal footing with the free white citizens of the state in general." The petitioners were seeking the repeal of the objectionable clauses of the Act of 1740.

NOVEMBER 9, 1791 Inventor and Mathematician Benjamin Banneker Born. Benjamin Benneker was born in Ellicott, Maryland, the grandson of a white woman. He secured a modest education from a school for free blacks near Joppa, Maryland, but received assistance in his study of science from George Ellicott, a Maryland Quaker, planter, and philanthropist. As a youth, Banneker made a wooden clock which is said to have remained accurate throughout his lifetime. Between 1791 and 1802, Banneker published a yearly almanac, which was widely read, and was also the first black man to publish astronomical materials in the United States. His other publications included a treatise on bees. Banneker is also credited with computing the cycle of the seventeen-year locust.

In 1791, Banneker was appointed upon the recommendation of Thomas Jefferson to serve as a member of a commission to survey plans for Washington, D.C. That August, he wrote a famous letter to Jefferson appealing for a more liberal attitude toward African Americans, using his own work as evidence of African American intellectual equality. Banneker said in part, "I apprehend you will embrace every opportunity to eradicate that train of absurd and false ideas and opinions which so generally prevail with respect to [blacks]; and that your sentiments are concurrent with mine which are: that one universal Father hath given being to us all; that He not only made us all of one flesh, but that He had also without partiality afforded us all with these same faculties and that, however diversified in situation or color, we are all the same family and stand in the same relation to Him." Jefferson accepted, then later rejected,

the notion of African American mental equality and even entertained doubts about Banneker's intellectual capabilities.

FEBRUARY 12, 1793 First Fugitive Slave Act Passed. Congress passed the first Fugitive Slave Act, making it a crime to harbor an escaped slave or to interfere with his or her arrest.

MARCH 14, 1793 Cotton Gin Patented. Eli Whitney of Massachusetts, a white inventor, obtained a patent for his cotton gin. The invention strengthened the institution of slavery, especially in the South.

JUNE 10, 1794 First American A.M.E. Church Founded. Richard Allen of Philadelphia founded the Bethel African Methodist Episcopal Church, the first A.M.E. church in the United States.

1795 Abolitionist John Malvin Born. John Malvin was born free to a free mother, Dalcus Malvin, and a slave father in Dumfries, Prince William County, Virginia. He was taught reading and spelling by an old slave who used the Bible as a teaching guide, and he learned carpentry from his father. He moved to Cincinnati, Ohio, in 1827 to remain free, and he became a community leader and helped with the underground railroad. Malvin married Harriet Dorsey in Cincinnati on March 8, 1829. After his arrests and brief imprisonment as a "fugitive slave" in 1831, Malvin became interested in emigration and migration. In 1832 he founded the School Education Society in Cleveland to provide a school for black children. Malvin purchased his father-in-law's freedom in 1833. He was a delegate to the National Convention of Colored Freemen in Cleveland in 1848. During the 1850s Malvin attended meetings of the influential Ohio State Conventions of Colored Citizens and was elected vice-president of the Ohio Anti-Slavery Society in 1858. Malvin worked to end the Black Laws of Ohio, which prohibited blacks from attending schools and imposed a five-hundred-dollar security bond on blacks entering the state.

At the start of the Civil War, Malvin urged African Americans in Cleveland to organize troops, although it would be several years before blacks would be allowed to serve. One year before his death, Malvin's autobiography was published in the *Cleveland Leader* as a forty-two page booklet entitled *Autobiography*. Malvin died July 30, 1880, in Cleveland and was buried in Erie Cemetery.

c. 1796 Colonizationist James Barbadoes Born. Little documentation of James Barbadoes's life remains, despite his activism and leadership among free Negroes in Boston. In 1930 Barbadoes's name appeared on a list of freed black heads of familes in Boston. He was a member of the Massachusetts General Colored Association and a delegate to the Convention of the People of Color in Philadelphia in 1831. Barbadoes was also a founding member of the American Anti-Slavery Society. At a May 1934 meeting of the New England Anti-Slavery Society, Barbadoes urged support for William Lloyd Garrison and his abolitionist newspaper, *The Liberator*. Barbadoes and three others extended an invitation to Garrison to attend a meeting of African American citizens after Garrison returned from England. In the 1830s, Barbadoes ran a barbershop and rented rooms in Boston. He died on June 22, 1841, of "West India Fever" after a doomed mission to settle a group of blacks in Jamaica.

Trader James Beckwourth. (Granger Collection.)

1797 Polish General Established School for Blacks. Polish General Tadeusz Kosciuszko was awarded a land grant in Ohio for his services during the Revolutionary War. Kosciuszko directed the land be sold and the proceeds be used to found a school for blacks.

1797 Poet George Horton Born. George Horton was born a plantation slave in Northampton County, North Carolina. He bargained with his slave masters for the "privilege" of earning money by selling love poems to students at the University of North Carolina. Not able to write

himself, Horton dictated his poems to the students. As a result, his earliest works have been forgotten or attributed to others. Horton was taught to write by Carolina Hentz, a writer, abolitionist, and wife of a professor. His first volume of poetry, *The Hope of Liberty* (1829), was not successful enough to pay for Horton's freedom, but it earned him some local fame and later promoted the cause of abolition with two reprintings under the title *Poems by a Slave* (1837, 1838). Horton published two more volumes of poetry in his lifetime: *The Poetical*

Works of George M. Horton, the Colored Bard of North Carolina (1845) and *Naked Genius* (1865). It is believed Horton died in 1883 in Philadelphia, Pennsylvania.

JANUARY 30, 1797 Anti-slavery Petition Presented. Blacks in North Carolina presented a petition to Congress protesting a state law that required slaves, although freed by their Quaker masters, to be returned to the state and to the status of slavery. This first recorded anti-slavery petition by blacks was rejected by the Congress.

AUGUST 30, 1797 Slave Uprising Thwarted. A slave uprising planned by Gabriel Prosser and Jack Bowler near Richmond, Virginia, was suspended because of bad weather and betrayal. Prosser was born in Virginia in 1776. In 1800, the young insurrectionist planned to seize an arsenal at Richmond, attack whites in the area, and free the slaves. It was hoped that the revolt would spread throughout the state. Perhaps as many as 1,000 slaves were prepared to participate in what would have been one of the largest slave revolts in U.S. history. Prosser had won such a large following by telling fellow blacks that he was their chosen leader, quoting Scripture to bolster his claim. The rebels had made or obtained swords, bayonets, and bullets in preparation for the uprising when a storm hit the area. Two slaves belonging to Mosby Sheppard betrayed Prosser's plot. Governor James Monroe declared martial law in Richmond and called up 600 members of the state militia. Prosser fled, but was captured in Norfolk on September 25. He was later convicted and, with fifteen others, sentenced to hang on October 7. Another thirty-five blacks were later executed. Although interviewed by Governor Monroe himself, Prosser refused to implicate others. The demeanor of the captured rebels led John Randolph of Virginia to declare that "the accused have exhibited a spirit, which if it becomes general, must deluge the southern country in blood. They manifested a sense of their rights, and a contempt of danger."

1798 Slave Narrative Published. A compilation of stories called *A Narrative of the Life and Adventures of Venture* detailed the life of the former Connecticut slave known as Venture (1729?–1805). A son of the prince of the Dukandarra tribe, Venture was born into slavery in Guinea, West Africa. His birth name, Broteer, was changed to Venture by the slaver who brought him to America. Nicknamed "Black Bunyan," Venture worked to purchase his own freedom at the age of thirty-six, and the freedom of his wife, daughter, two sons, and three other slaves. The *Narrative* described, and possibly exaggerated, the great feats of work that Venture performed, such as carrying a barrel of molasses on his shoulders for two miles. The depiction of the lives of enslaved and free blacks in eighteenth-century Connecticut was a key element in the *Narrative*.

1798 School for Blacks Founded. A white teacher in Boston started a school for black children in the home of Primus Hall, a prominent African American.

APRIL 6, 1798 Trader James Pierson Beckwourth Born. James Pierson Beckwourth was born to a white father and a black slave mother in Fredericksburg, Virginia, the third of thirteen children. Beckwourth signed up as a scout for General William Henry Ashley's Rock's Rocky Mountain Fur Company in 1823 and 1824. He worked as a "mountain man" for the next thirteen years. Beckwourth established his own trading post in St. Fernandez (now Taos, New Mexico) and later in Pueblo de Angles (now Los Angeles, California). In 1846 Beckwourth fought in the California revolution against Mexico and in 1846 in the war with Mexico. He served as chief scout for General John Charles Frémont on his exploring expedition in 1848. Beckwourth discovered a path in the Sierra Nevada Mountains between the California Feather and Truckee Rivers. This path became a major emigrant route to California. It was later named the Beckwourth Pass. Beckwourth died in 1866.

Chapter 3
1800 TO 1859

1800 to 1809

1800 Black School in Boston. Boston blacks requested a school for the education of their children. Upon refusal, they started one on their own with two Harvard alumni as instructors.

1800 Rumor of Slave Revolt Sparked Fear. Plans to send blacks to Africa were proposed when a conspiracy organized by the slave "General Gabriel" was reported. Gabriel's Insurrection was suppressed by Virginia governor James Monroe, who ordered in the federal militia. The ringleaders of the insurrection were executed.

AUGUST 30, 1800 Slave Insurrection Stifled. About 1000 slaves, organized by Gabriel Prosser, attempted an insurrection in Richmond, Virginia. The band made weapons in preparation and designed a plan to arrive in Richmond, seize an arsenal and a powder house, close off bridges, and kill countless whites. The attack might have succeeded were it not for two slaves who told their master of the plot. Governor James Monroe sent troops to counter the movement. Gabriel escaped that night but was found and tried within a month. Gabriel and forty other men were hanged for involvement in the revolt.

JANUARY 5, 1804 Free Blacks Restricted in the North. The Ohio legislature took the lead in passing "Black Laws" designed to restrict the rights and freedom of movement of free blacks in the North. The laws reflected the steady deterioration of the legal and social status of free blacks since the Revolutionary War. Although Northern blacks had endured severe restrictions in the Colonial period—in some areas of New England they faced curfews at night, could not visit another town without permission, and could not own certain types of property—these were somewhat relieved by the atmosphere of freedom that prevailed in the North after 1776. By 1835, however, several Northern states prohibited free black immigration and severely restricted or completely disfranchised black voters. By 1860, according to Professor John Hope Franklin, it was difficult to distinguish, in terms of legal status, between slaves and free blacks.

MAY 14, 1804 Slave Embarked on Lewis and Clark Expedition. The slave known as York set out as part of the Lewis and Clark expedition, officially as Clark's valet. York was the son of Old York and his wife, Rose, who were house slaves of the Clark family. During the two-year journey, however, York also served as a diplomat of sorts: he apparently acted as a French-Canadian interpreter for Clark and built friendships with Native Americans by dancing for them. According to some accounts, York returned to Kentucky with Clark and served as his valet until his death. Clark, however, claimed to have set York free in 1813 when he went to St. Louis as governor of the Missouri Territory.

c. 1806   Freed Slave Built Church. The freed slave Cato Gardner raised funds to build an African American church in Boston. William Lloyd Garrison started his New England Abolitionist Society in it, and a school operated out of its basement. The structure is the oldest extant black church building in the United States today.

1806   Abolitionist Sarah Mapps Douglass Born. Sarah Mapps Douglass was born into a prominent Quaker family in Philadelphia. Her maternal grandfather, Cyril Bustill, owned a bakeshop, was a schoolmaster, and was an early member of the Free African Society. Her mother ran a Quaker millinery store adjacent to the family bakeshop, and her father was a founding member of the First African Presbyterian Church of Philadelphia. Douglass was privately tutored, and in the 1820s she opened a school for African American children that would later receive support from the Philadelphia Female Anti-Slavery Society. It was through her involvement as corresponding secretary of this society that Douglass became acquainted with Sarah and Angelina Grimké, daughters of a prominent white judge. Their association spurred condemnation from whites, resulting in riots and mob violence in the 1830s and 1840s. Realizing the futility of her struggle against segregation, Douglass in 1853 took charge of the girls primary department of the Institute for Colored Youth in Philadelphia, a job she held until her retirement in 1877. After the Civil War she served as vice-chairperson of the Women's Pennsylvania Branch of the American Freedmen's Aid Commission. Douglass died on September 8, 1882, in Philadelphia.

1807   Escaped Slave Guided Expeditions. Edward Rose accompanied the Manuel Lisa trapping expedition as a guide, hunter, and interpreter. Rose, an escaped slave of black, white,

and Cherokee blood, was also part of the 1809 escort that took Mandan chief Big White back to his home after traveling with the Louis and Clark party. Rose's knowledge of the topography of the Upper Missouri region and of the languages and customs of Indian tribes made him invaluable to these and other exploration and trading ventures. In 1823, as part of William H. Ashley's second trapping venture, Rose distinguished himself by negotiating peace after a battle with the Arikara Indians; this secured a safe Missouri River passage to the Rockies. Rose was apparently also instrumental in taming a tribe of 600 Crow Indians during an 1825 treaty-making expedition into the Upper Missouri.

1807   First Black School in Washington, D.C. The first school for African American children was built in Washington, D.C., by George Bell, with the help of Nicholas Franklin and Moses Liverpool. This effort, by former slaves who still could not read or write, preceded Congressional establishment of public schools for blacks in the capital by 57 years. (Public education for whites was authorized in 1804, and two schools opened for them in 1806.) Though financial difficulties soon forced the closing of the school, Bell, with the help of his Resolute Beneficial Society, was able to reopen the facility in 1818. John Adams, the first black male teacher in the District of Columbia, was part of this second school, which had an average attendance of sixty-five students. By the time the Civil War began, an estimated 1,200 of the 3,172 school-age blacks were enrolled in some type of privately run school.

JUNE 1807   British Boarded *Chesapeake*. The U.S. Navy's *Chesapeake* was attacked by the British Navy boat *Leopard*, resulting in 21 American casualties. When the British boarded the vessel, they took into custody deserters of

William Leidesdorff's San Francisco hotel.

the British Navy, including three black men. U.S. sailors, both black and white, were also captured for Royal Navy service.

JANUARY 1, 1808 Law Prohibited Import of African Slaves. A federal law prohibiting the importation of African slaves into the United States went into effect. The law was passed in March 1807 and stipulated that persons convicted of violating it were to be fined anywhere from $800 (for knowingly buying illegally imported slaves) to $20,000 (for equipping a slave vessel), or imprisoned. Illegally imported slaves were to come under the jurisdiction of the state legislatures, which would decide their disposition. The coastwide trade of slaves was prohibited also if it was carried on in vessels of less than forty tons. The responsibility for the law's enforcement shifted among the Treasury Department, the secretary of the Navy, and the secretary of state. Some Southern states passed laws against the illegal importation of slaves, while other states took no action at all. Some of the newly-imported slaves were sold in these states with the proceeds going into the state treasury. Both Northern commercial interests

and Southern planters ignored the law with impunity.

1810 to 1819

1810 Hotelier William Leidesdorff Born. William Leidesdorff was born in Saint Croix, Virgin Islands, to an African mother and a Danish father. Leidesdorff moved to New Orleans, Louisiana, in 1834. After becoming a ship captain he piloted a voyage from New York to California around the southern tip of South America aboard the schooner *Julia Ann* in 1841. Leidesdorff settled in California and built a hotel, school, and steamboat. He served as U.S. vice-counsel for the port of San Francisco from 1845 to 1846. He died in 1848.

JANUARY 8–10, 1811 Slave Uprisings Suppressed. U.S. troops suppressed slave uprisings in two Louisiana parishes near New Orleans.

MAY 6, 1812 Birth of Physician, Colonizationist, and Union Army Officer. Born in Virginia, Martin R. Delany was educated in the African Free School of New York City, the Canaan Academy in New Hampshire, the Onei-

Major Martin Delany. (AP/Wide World Photos.)

da Institute in upper New York, and the Harvard University Medical School, where he received his medical degree in 1852. Delany attempted to practice medicine in Pittsburgh, but prejudice and poor profits drove him into other areas. He became a member of the British Association for the Promotion of Social Science and published two books, *The Condition, Elevation, Emigration and Destiny of the Colored People of the United States* (1852) and *Principle of Ethnology* (1879). In 1843, Delany published a newspaper, *Mystery,* and joined Frederick Douglass in the publication of *The North Star* in 1847. He was also a leader of the national convention movement of African Americans. Following the passage of the Compromise of 1850, with its new Fugitive Slave Act, Delany became convinced that the United States was too inhospitable for people of African descent and turned his attention to colonization. He helped organize an expedition to Nigeria in 1858, negotiated treaties with eight African chiefs who granted lands for prospective African American settlers, and began plans for the expanded production and exportation of cotton in the region. During the Civil War, Delany was a medical officer with the rank of major in the 104th Union Regiment in South Carolina. He settled in Charleston after the war, working with the Freedmen's Bureau, and later served as a justice of the peace there. He was defeated in a bid for lieutenant governor of South Carolina in 1874. Delany died in 1885.

1813   Civil Rights Activist Jermain Wesley Loguen Born. Jermain Wesley Loguen was born in Davidson County, Tennessee. His mother, Cherry, was born free in Ohio, kidnaped, and sold to David Logue, who fathered Jermain. Logue sold Jermain and his mother to a brutal master. After witnessing the constant whipping of his mother, the murder of a slave, and the sale of his sister, Loguen sought his freedom. With the help of Quakers, Loguen escaped on the Underground Railroad to Hamilton, Ontario, where he learned to read and worked as a lumberjack and farmer. He later settled in central New York. After opening a school for black children in Utica, Loguen and his wife moved to Syracuse, where he opened another school and managed the Underground Railroad station there. In 1842 he was ordained a minister of the New York Conference of the African Methodist Episcopal Zion church and went on to establish several churches between 1840 and 1850. He worked closely with Frederick Douglass on the Underground Railroad, and he wrote for Douglass's *North Star* and *Frederick Douglass' Paper*. The Fugitive Slave Act of 1850 threatened the freedom of Loguen and other runaway slaves, so in 1851 he escaped to Canada. Upon returning to Syracuse, he continued his work with the Underground Railroad, helping some 1,500 slaves escape, including Harriet Tubman, who stayed at his home. He was twice elected bishop of the A.M.E. Zion church and was about to begin mission work on the west coast when he died in 1872.

1814   First Sunday School Established. Catherine (Katy) Ferguson established the first modern Sunday School in the basement of a Manhattan, New York, church. She educated and found homes for street children—black and white—and unwed mothers. Ferguson was born a slave during a trip her mother was taking to New York City from Virginia around 1779. At the age of sixteen a benefactress purchased her freedom for two hundred dollars. She died of cholera in New York City on July 11, 1854.

1815   African American Enlisted. James Nickens enlisted in the navy at the start of the American Revolution. Nickens served on several vessels, including the *Norfolk Revenge* for over two years. Nickens performed land service at the Lancaster Court House for the remainder of the war. He was prevented from fighting at the battle of Eutaw Springs and instead was responsible for the baggage. Nickens returned to Virginia in 1818 where he received the standard veterans' pension of $96 per year. After Nickens's death in 1838, the state government awarded his son, James, Jr., a grant of 200 acres

of land in Ohio for his father's service in the Revolution.

1815   Insurrectionist Dangerfield Newby Born. Dangerfield Newby was born in Virginia to a slave mother and a Scotsman. His father granted all his children freedom upon his death. Newby married and had seven children. Desperate to free his enslaved family, Newby joined John Brown's group. He was killed in the Harpers Ferry raid the night of October 17, 1859; afterward, his body was beaten and mutilated by the town's citizens. His remains were buried in a shallow grave in Harpers Ferry and later moved to North Elba, New York, where they were laid to rest near the grave of John Brown.

1815   Missionary Promoted Efforts in Africa and Haiti. Vermont's Prince Saunders arrived in England seeking backers for education and missionary efforts in Africa. Saunders also supported emigration of American blacks to Africa. In England, however, Saunders' interest turned to Haiti when he met up with English reformers with the long-term goal, supported by Haitian king Henri Christophe, of changing the island's language and religion. Saunders joined them and taught in Haiti from 1816 to 1818. He then returned to Philadelphia to rekindle his colonization efforts, this time with Haiti in mind. He arrived again on the island in 1820, supposedly representing colonists-in-waiting. But when Christophe arranged passage to Haiti for them, his army rebelled and his regime collapsed, taking Saunders's plans down with it. Saunders published *Haytian Papers* while in London. The work was a translation of Haitian laws and the Code Henri— laws regulating agriculture, commerce, police, and social-political organizations in the kingdom.

Saunders had been born to Cuff and Phyllis Saunders. He was baptized on July 25, 1784. Saunders received his early education at Thetford, Connecticut. Later he taught at a school for blacks in Colchester. During 1807 and 1808 Saunders studied at Moor's Charity School at Dartmouth College. In 1811 he served as secretary of the African Masonic Lodge and organized the Belles Lettres Society, a group of literary white men. Saunders died in Port-au-Prince, Haiti, in 1839.

1816   Birth of John Jones, Businessman, Abolitionist. John Jones was born free in Green City, North Carolina. He was self-educated and became a tailor's apprentice in Memphis, Tennessee, before moving to Chicago in 1845. Jones opened a tailoring business there, from which he amassed a fortune. Using his wealth and influence, Jones led the successful fight against the prohibition of the immigration of free blacks into Illinois in 1853, the "Black Laws," and school segregation in Chicago. He was elected a Cook County, Illinois, commissioner in 1875 and served for two terms. Jones was also the first African American elected to the Chicago Board of Education. Prior to the Civil War, he was also active in the abolitionist movement, his home being used as a station on the Underground Railroad. Jones died in 1879, leaving an estate valued at more than $100,000.

JANUARY 3, 1816   Ex-Slave Prospered. Stephen Smith purchased his freedom from slavery for fifty dollars in January 1816 and, later that year, his release from indentured servitude. Smith had previous experience in the lumber business and soon established his own firm. Smith was born to a slave mother, Nancy Smith, in Paxtang, Pennsylvania. At the age of five he was indentured to a patriot of the Revolutionary War, Thomas Boude. Great success allowed Smith to dabble in coal, railroading, stocks, and real estate, and eventually brought him into ownership of more than fifty houses and $18,000 worth of stock in New York's Columbia Bank. But Smith still faced challenges because he was black. In 1834, envious whites attacked his office, and later that year, Smith was warned that he should leave his Columbia community. (Smith remained in Columbia until 1842 when he moved to Philadelphia.) Smith attended a national convention for free people of color in New York and Philadelphia, Pennsylvania.

The businessman was also an activist who participated in the operations of the Underground Railroad, the American Moral Reform Society, and the Pennsylvania Anti-Slavery Society, among many other abolitionist groups. Smith was a benefactor to the Institute for Colored Youth, the Home for Destitute Colored Children, the House of Refuge, and the Olive Cemetery. The House for Age and Infirm Colored Persons was renamed the Stephen Smith Home for the Aged, in recognition of the man who had donated $28,000 and the ground to build on and made the Home the principal beneficiary of his estate. Smith died in 1873.

APRIL 9, 1816   A.M.E. Church Formally Recognized in Philadelphia. The African Methodist Episcopal (A.M.E.) Church, the first all-black religious denomination in the United States, was formally organized in Philadelphia. Richard Allen was named the first bishop of the Church. Allen was born a slave in Philadelphia and was sold as a youth to a white man in Delaware. He became a preacher shortly thereafter and received permission to hold services in his master's home. Allen preached to both blacks and whites and was allowed, at the same time, to hire himself out. He bought his freedom by hauling salt, wood, and other products, and by laboring in a brickyard. After leading the A.M.E. Church for fifteen years, Allen died in 1831. He was succeeded by Morris Brown, an exile from South Carolina who had resided in Philadelphia since 1823.

DECEMBER 28, 1816   American Colonization Society Formed. The American Colonization Society, formed to ease American race problems by transporting free blacks to Africa, was organized in Washington, D.C. Representatives John C. Calhoun of South Carolina and Henry Clay of Kentucky were among its sponsors.

The Pennsylvania Anti-Slavery Society. (Courtesy of the National Portrait Gallery.)

1817   George De Baptiste, Abolitionist and Businessman, Born George De Baptiste was born free in Fredericksburg, Virginia, and worked as a barber in Madison, Wisconsin, for many years until 1866, when tensions between blacks and whites prompted him to move to Detroit, a more tolerant area. He became a member of a secret abolition society and a leader in the Underground Railroad. De Baptiste was instrumental in recruiting Michigan's black regiment during the Civil War. In 1870 he served on Detroit's first all-black jury. De Baptiste was elected a delegate to the local Republican senatorial convention and actively promoted integration of Detroit's public schools. One of Detroit's wealthiest African Americans, he died of stomach cancer on February 25, 1875, survived by his second wife and two of his ten children.

1817   Paul Cuffe, Shipbuilder and African Colonizer, Died. Paul Cuffe was born in New Bedford, Massachusetts, in 1758 as a free man. In 1797, he purchased a farm and built a school for the children in his hometown. An activist in the cause of civil rights, Cuffe and his brother John unsuccessfully sued the state of Massa-

chusetts for the right to vote. Disillusioned over the future of free blacks in America, Cuffe transported a group of thirty-eight blacks to Sierra Leone, a British colony on the West Coast of Africa, in 1811. Failing health and uncertainty about the colonization scheme caused him to withdraw from the venture shortly before his death. At his death, Cuffe left an estate valued at more than $20,000, making him one of the wealthiest African Americans in early American history.

JANUARY 1817   African Americans Protest Deportation. Philadelphia blacks, meeting at the Bethel A.M.E. Church, formally protested against the American Colonization Society's efforts to deport blacks from the United States to Africa.

1818   Elizabeth Keckley, Assistant to Mary Todd Lincoln, Born. Elizabeth Keckley was born a slave in Dinwiddie, Virginia, and was taken to St. Louis, Missouri, in her teens. She helped support her master's family and her own son through her dressmaking and seamstressing skills. Through loans from her customers, Keckley bought her freedom and that of her son on November 15, 1855, and moved to Wash-

Captain Paul Cuffe and his ship. (Courtesy of Library of Congress.)

ington. She became the dressmaker, personal maid, and confidante of first lady Mary Todd Lincoln in early 1861 and continued until 1868, when the publication of Keckley's memoirs ended their friendship. The book, *Behind the Scenes, or Thirty Years a Slave, and Four Years in the White House,* was highly controversial, as it relayed Mrs. Lincoln's personal opinions of government officials and her own family life. Keckley's dressmaking business declined after the public furor over the book, and she pursued a brief career as a school teacher. She died of a paralytic stroke in Washington on May 26, 1907.

1818   Soldier William Flora Dies. William Flora, born a free man, served under Lord Dunmore, governor of Virginia, at the Battle of the Great Bridge during the winter of 1775–76. Flora was remembered by Captain Thomas Nash, who was wounded in the engagement, for his stamina and courage. After the Revolution, Flora returned to his hometown of Portsmouth, Virginia, and was one of the first blacks to buy property there. Prospering, he bought the freedom of his wife and children. Shortly before his death, Flora applied for and was granted 100 acres of land in Virginia for his service during the war.

APRIL 18, 1818   First Seminole War Ended. A force of Indians and blacks was defeated in the Battle of Suwanne, Florida, ending the First Seminole War by U.S. troops under General Andrew Jackson. Jackson characterized the hostilities as a "savage and negro war."

1820 to 1829

1820   Albany African Church Organized. The Albany African Church Association was organized with the help of Nathaniel Paul, who, in 1822, became the first pastor of the African Baptist Church, the only black church in Albany at the time. The Wilberforce School, the only school for black youths in Albany at the

time, was also formed by Paul and met in his church. In 1831 Paul went to England to seek financial backing for a college-level manual labor school for blacks. He became involved with British abolitionists and decided to remain there to be a part of the worldwide abolitionist societies that were beginning to form there.

1820   Boston Opened School for Blacks. Boston opened an elementary school for blacks.

MARCH 3, 1820   Missouri Compromise Approved. The famous Missouri Compromise was approved by Congress. Slavery was prohibited north and west of the 36–30 parallel line within the Louisiana territory. Missouri itself entered the Union as a slave state, while Maine entered as a free state.

1821   African Americans Encouraged to Emigrate. The black Republic of Liberia was founded under the auspices of the American Colonization Society. African Americans were encouraged to emigrate to the West African country as a means of alleviating the race problem. In the end, only about 20,000 did so. The capital city, Monrovia, was named for President James Monroe.

MAY 30, 1822   Slave Conspiracy Betrayed. A slave conspiracy led by Denmark Vesey in Charleston, South Carolina, was betrayed. Vesey, a former slave, had been free since 1800 and had worked as a carpenter in Charleston. He plotted his slave uprising for several years, during which he carefully chose his associates, collected weapons, and sought assistance from Santo Domingo. Vesey's revolt, in which as many as 5,000 blacks were prepared to participate, was first set for the second Sunday in July 1822, but the authorities were alerted and thwarted their efforts. As a result of the plot, South Carolina and other states tightened their control of slaves and free blacks.

1823   Birth of Mary Smith Kelsick Peake, Teacher. Mary Peake was born in Norfolk

County, Virginia. In September of 1861, she opened the first school sponsored by the American Missionary Association. It was housed in a cottage on the Chesapeake Female College campus where she had arrived only one month before. Chesapeake had become her home after she fled Hampton as Confederates set the city aflame on August 7. In Hampton, Peake had founded the Daughters of Zion through which children and adults received education in Peake's home. Her motivation to teach others may have stemmed from her own opportunity as a free-born woman to receive a good education in Alexandria before the city was retroceded to Virginia in 1846 and its schools closed to blacks.

1823 Twilight First Black College Graduate.

Alexander Lucius Twilight received his B.A. degree from Vermont's Middlebury College in 1823, making him the first known African American to graduate from college. He then turned to educating African Americans, teaching in New York and Vermont. In 1829, Twilight became principal of the Orleans County Grammar School in Brownington, Vermont, where he also ministered to the congregation that worshiped in the same building. Under Twilight's administration, the school's expanding enrollment led to the construction of an additional three-story building. He left the school in 1847 to educate blacks in villages, but he returned as headmaster in 1852. During Twilight's tenure in Brownington, he also became one of the first African Americans to be elected to a state legislature, serving in the Vermont congress from 1836 to 1837.

Twilight was one of six children born to free blacks, Mary and Ichabod Twilight, in Bradford, Vermont. He was indentured to a neighboring farmer but purchased his freedom in 1815. Mary Ladd Merrill married him in 1926. Twilight died in June 1857.

1824 African Free Schools Gained Support.

African Free Schools succeeded in gaining the support of the New York Common Council.

NOVEMBER 1824 Voting System Changed.

American politics was becoming democratized as the elimination of the caucus system for choosing presidential candidates was accompanied by the removal of property qualifications for voting. The way was being paved for virtual universal male suffrage in the United States. At the same time, the Northern and Western states adopted measures denying African Americans the right to vote.

MARCH 16, 1827 Debut of First African American Newspaper.

Two African Americans, John Russwurm and Samuel Cornish, began publication of *Freedom's Journal*, the nation's pioneer African American newspaper, in New York City. The paper was not very successful, and two years later Cornish began a second publication, the militant *Rights of All*, which also was short-lived. In 1836, Cornish published *Weekly Advocate* and the following year co-edited the *Colored American*. Most of the African American newspapers founded before the Civil War were principally abolitionist propaganda sheets, with Frederick Douglass's *North Star* being the most successful.

1828 First Black Seminary Graduate.

Theodore Sedgwick Wright graduated from the Princeton Theological Seminary, making him the first black to graduate from an American theological seminary. He then took his lifelong post as pastor of the First Colored Presbyterian Church, also called the Shiloh Presbyterian Church. Wright constantly organized and promoted civil rights efforts. Throughout the 1830s, he lectured for active abolitionist movements and, in 1833, helped found the American Anti-Slavery Society. After withdrawing from the organization in 1840 over the growing trend toward Garrisonian radicalism, he helped form the American and Foreign Anti-Slavery Society. In addition to fighting for freedom, Wright pushed for jury trials in fugitive slave cases and black franchisement, including an 1840 push for suspension of the property requirement for black voters. Wright was also

active in the temperance movement and missions to evangelize African peoples.

Wright was born to R. P. G. Wright in
1797. He received his early education at the
New York African Free School. Wright died in
1847.

**MARCH 4, 1829 African Americans at Jack-
son's Inauguration.** African Americans attended the inaugural reception for President
Andrew Jackson at the White House.

**SEPTEMBER 28, 1829 Abolitionist Pamphlet
Discovered.** David Walker's militant anti-slavery pamphlet calling on blacks to revolt was
discovered in several areas of the country. Walker's *Appeal,* published in Boston, stirred
slaveholders in several Southern states. Walker
was a free black who had wandered across the
South before settling in Boston as the proprietor of a secondhand clothing store. He had
become widely acquainted with anti-slavery
and revolutionary literature. The *Appeal,* which
was probably smuggled into the South by black
sailors, called for mass slave uprisings, with
violent reprisals against slaveowners. Although
perhaps only a few literate blacks could read it,
Southern states took extreme precautions. The
mails were scrutinized, ships arriving in Southern ports were searched, and black seamen were
restricted. The circulation of the work became a
crime and a bounty was placed on Walker's life.
Walker died under mysterious circumstances in
1830.

1830 to 1839

**APRIL 6, 1830 Birth of First Black Catholic
Bishop in America.** James Augustine Healy
was the son of an Irish immigrant and a mulatto
slave. His father sent he and his brothers to the
North for their education, but after being rejected by several academies, the Healys entered
a Quaker school on Long Island, New York.
Later, they transferred to the College of the
Holy Cross in Worcester, Massachusetts, where

James was the most outstanding pupil. In 1852,
he entered the Sulpician Seminary in Paris, and
on June 10, 1854, he was ordained a priest in
Notre Dame Cathedral in Paris. Healy's first
assignment as a priest was in a white parish in
Boston. He became secretary to the bishop of
Boston, then became pastor of the New St.
James Church. Healy's stature in the New
England Catholic hierarchy continued to rise;
in 1874, he was appointed bishop of Maine and
was consecrated in the Cathedral at Portland
on June 2, 1875. Healy proved to be energetic
and devoted to duty. He ministered to an all-
white following, but only occasionally was subjected to racial abuse. Shortly before his death
on August 5, 1890, Healy was promoted to the
rank of assistant at the Papal Throne.

**SEPTEMBER 20–24, 1830 First National Ne-
gro Convention Met.** The initial National
Negro Convention met at Bethel A.M.E.
Church in Philadelphia. Delegates from Delaware, Maryland, New York, Pennsylvania, and
Virginia attended. The convention, under the
leadership of Richard Allen (other prominent
African American leaders present included abolitionist and shipmaker James Forten and journalist Samuel Cornish), adopted resolutions
calling for improvements in the social status of
African Americans. The delegates considered
projects to establish a black college and to
encourage blacks to emigrate to Canada. Neither of these proposals was adopted. Opposition even arose to the mere idea of an African
American convention. Yet these ad-hoc conventions continued to convene and occasionally
were attended by white abolitionists and reformers. In the ten years before the Civil War,
there was a rash of such conventions held in
Cleveland, Rochester, and New York City as
well as in Philadelphia. One of the most important meetings was in Rochester in 1853, when
the National Council of Colored People was
formed. This group issued a statement that
both denounced racial oppression in America
and cited instances of black progress. These

conventions were in the American tradition of assembling for redress of grievances and increased solidarity among African Americans.

JANUARY 1, 1831 *The Liberator* **Debuted.** William Lloyd Garrison published the first issue of the militant anti-slavery newspaper, the *Liberator*, with financial aid and moral support from such prominent African Americans as James Forten of Philadelphia.

AUGUST 21–22, 1831   Nat Turner Led Slave Revolt. The most momentous slave revolt in U.S. history occurred in Southhampton County, Virginia. It was led by black minister Nat Turner, who had run away from, then returned to, his master. Approximately sixty whites were slain in the revolt. Turner was captured on October 30 and hanged on November 11. Thirty other blacks were implicated, then executed. The revolt caused near pandemonium in the South. Slave codes were vigorously enforced, slave patrols were increased, and suspicious blacks were either incarcerated or killed. No other major slave revolt or conspiracy followed the Turner insurrection until John Brown's raid on the U.S. Arsenal at Harpers Ferry, Virginia, in 1859.

1834   Council Took Control of   Free Schools. The New York Common Council took control of the African Free Schools.

JUNE 1–5, 1835   Fifth National Negro Convention Met. The fifth National Negro Convention met in Philadelphia and urged blacks to abandon the use of the terms "African" and "colored" when referring to black institutions, organizations, and themselves.

DECEMBER 1835   John Caesar Organized Slave Rebellion. John Caesar led hundreds of slaves in the attack of the St. Johns River plantations on the eve of the second Seminole War. Near the end of the war, he organized a guerrilla campaign against plantations in the St. Augustine vicinity, recruiting black and Indian slaves.

On the night of January 17, 1837, Caesar was killed in a surprise attack. Nevertheless, his efforts at the beginning and end of the war led to the Treaty of Fort Dade, resulting in freedom for many runaway slaves who might otherwise have been reenslaved.

1836   "Gag Rule" Adopted. The infamous "gag rule" was adopted in the U.S. House of Representatives. Under the act, anti-slavery petitions were simply laid on the table without any further action. This denial of the right of petition angered former president John Quincy Adams, then a congressman from Massachusetts. Adams fought vigorously against the rule, helping to rouse public opinion in the North. Anti-slavery petitions began to pour into Washington, more than 200,000 of them in a single session. In 1844 the gag rule was rescinded. Its opponents saw it as an effort to deny white men their right of freedom of petition in an attempt to keep black men slaves.

1837   Cheyney University Founded. Cheyney University, originally known as the Institute for Colored Youth, was founded in Philadelphia, Pennsylvania, in 1837, by Quaker Richard Humphreys. The school moved to Cheyney, Pennsylvania, in 1902, and began offering postsecondary education in 1931.

1838   African American Bandleader Performed for Queen. Frank Johnson, one of America's first African American bandleaders, gave a command performance before Queen Victoria at Buckingham Palace. He was presented with a silver bugle. Johnson was born in 1792 and by 1820 had established himself as a versatile musician, playing with white bands in Philadelphia. When he organized his own band, principally a woodwind ensemble, it won national acclaim for its excellent performances at parades and dances. Frank Johnson's Colored Band, as it was called, even performed on plantations as far south as Virginia. Johnson became noted for his ability to "distort a song

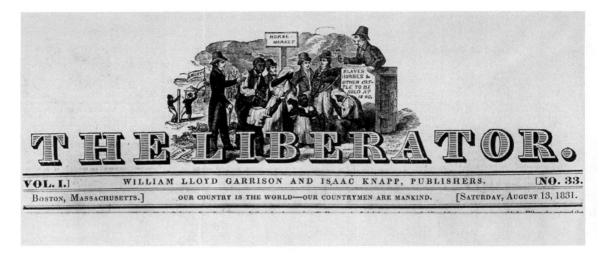

Masthead from *The Liberator* newspaper. (Courtesy of Library of Congress.)

into a reel, jig, or country dance." He also composed music, including the "Recognition March on the Independence of Hayti" in 1825. Johnson died in 1844.

1838   First Black Labor Union Founded. The Caulkers' Association formed as one of the first African American labor unions.

MARCH 14, 1838   African Americans Protested Voting Reform. African Americans held a mass meeting in Philadelphia to protest the action of the Pennsylvania Reform Convention of 1837, which denied them the right to vote. The Convention, acting on the basis of an 1837 state supreme court decision (*Fogg v. Hobbs*), held that blacks were not freemen and restricted suffrage to white males. Attendees, claiming to represent 40,000 blacks threatened with disfranchisement, said the denial of suffrage would make political rights dependent upon the "skin in which a man is born" and divide "what our fathers bled to unite, to wit, taxation and representation." They further argued that they were indeed citizens, having been recognized as such by article four of the Articles of Confederation, which stated: "The free inhabitants of each of these states, paupers, vaga-

bonds, and fugitives from justice excepted, shall be entitled to all privileges and immunities of free *citizens* in the several states." The Constitution of the United States, according to the black petition, made no changes as to their rights of citizenship. The petitioners asked the state court to reverse its decision in *Fogg v. Hobbs* and/or the people of Pennsylvania to reject the new Constitution. The court's action stood, however, and the new constitution's disfranchising clauses won popular approval.

JULY 1839   Slaves Captured *Amistad*. The most famous slave mutiny in U.S. history took place on the Spanish ship *Amistad*. A group of Africans, led by Joseph Cinque, brought the captured vessel into Montauk, Long Island, where they were arrested. Former president John Quincy Adams defended the rebels before the Supreme Court, which granted their freedom.

1840 to 1849

1840   Delaware Allowed Integrated Schooling. Blacks in Wilmington, Delaware, were permitted to attend schools with whites.

Mutineer Joseph Cinque. (Courtesy of the New York Public Library.)

1841   Abolitionist Sanderson Made His First Public Address. Jeremiah Burke Sanderson (1821–75) made his first public address at an abolitionists meeting in Nantucket, Massachusetts. (Frederick Douglass also gave his first public speech there.) Throughout the 1840s, the Scottish and African-blooded Sanderson, born and educated in New Bedford, Massachusetts, spoke out against slavery in his state as well as in New York, where, in 1853, he joined the National Council of the National Colored Convention. Although Sanderson did not promote immigration of blacks abroad, he did support the massive migration of blacks to California in 1854 by going there himself. There he helped many black religious, social, political, and educational organizations increase their status in American society.

Sanderson was elected to A.M.E. positions of secretary of the California conference and state delegate to the church's national conference, but died in a train accident on August 19, 1875, before he was able to serve.

AUGUST 22, 1843   National Convention of Black Men Held in Buffalo, New York. Black abolitionist and minister Henry Highland Garnet called for a slave revolt and a general strike to improve the lot of blacks in the United States. Many of the delegates, including Frederick Douglass, denounced the speech. Garnet had served as pastor to whites and blacks in Troy, New York.

DECEMBER 27, 1843   *Palladium of Liberty* Founded. Abolitionist and businessman David Jenkins founded the *Palladium of Liberty,* a weekly Columbus, Ohio, newspaper that advocated the abolition of slavery. Although the paper ran for little more than a year, it influenced future black-operated newspapers in the midwest.

1844   Birth of Henry Vinton Plummer. Henry Vinton Plummer was born a slave in Prince George's County, Maryland. At eighteen, Plummer escaped from slavery after having been sold at least twice. In 1864 he enlisted in the navy and taught himself to read during his year and a half of service. In 1867, Plummer married Julia Lomax; together they had six sons and two daughters. Plummer began ministering in Maryland congregations while preparing to attend Wayland Seminary in Washington D.C., from which he graduated in 1879. Upon the recommendation of Frederick Douglass, President Chester A. Arthur appointed Plummer chaplain of the 9th Cavalry in 1884. Championing temperance, Plummer formed the Loyal Temperance Legion for the children of the black troops at Fort Robinson, Nebraska. Although he was popular among the soldiers, his influence may have been viewed as a threat to the white-run army. In the months following Plummer's proposed plan for the colonization of central Africa by African American volunteer soldiers, he was accused and convicted of drunkenness. Upon his dismissal, Plummer moved to Kansas where his attempts to return to the service were unsuccessful. He spent the remainder of his life serving his churches. Plummer died in Wichita, Kansas, on Feburary 8, 1905.

JUNE 24, 1844 Boston Blacks Urged School Integration. At a mass meeting in Boston, African Americans adopted a resolution declaring that the city's segregated public schools violated the State Constitution. They urged the city's School Committee to abolish separate schools and to extend to African American citizens the right to send their children "to the schools established in the respective district" in which they resided. Their request was denied and the schools in Massachusetts remained segregated until 1855.

1845 First Anthology of African American Verse Published. The 215-page *Les Cenelles* was published as the first anthology of African American verse. Fourteen of the poems were written by Camille Thierry (1814–75), a New Orleans Creole who lived most of his life in France trying to escape racism. Thierry was asked to contribute to the compilation after he had published his first poem, *Les Idées,* which appeared in *L'Album Littéraire,* a collection of writings intended to promote racial equality.

AUGUST 1846 African American Inventor Patented Sugar-Refining Machine. Norbert Rillieux (1806–94) obtained his first patent for the revolutionary multiple-effect vacuum evaporation process, which made the refined sugar whiter and grainier. The technique became the basic manufacturing process in the sugar industry. Rillieux, born in New Orleans in 1806, was the son of a white engineer and a free mulatto woman. His father invented the steam-operated cotton-baling press.

JUNE 30, 1847 Dred Scott Filed Lawsuit. Dred Scott, a slave, filed suit in the St. Louis Circuit Court claiming that his temporary residence in a free territory should have made him a free man. Scott was a semi-literate man whose travels throughout the country—specifically into the free portions of the Louisiana territory, where slavery had been excluded by the Missouri Compromise of 1820, and into free Illinois—formed the basis for the case.

DECEMBER 3, 1847 Douglass Began Publication of *North Star*. African American abolitionist Frederick Douglass began publication of his own newspaper, the *North Star.* Douglass, a former slave, became the era's most well-known black anti-slavery speaker and writer. Born in Tuckahoe, Maryland, in 1817, Douglass was separated in infancy from his mother and had harsh masters as a child. While still very young, Douglass became a house servant in Baltimore, where white playmates taught him to read. His first attempt at escape was thwarted, but in 1838, while working as a ship calker, he managed a successful break from slavery. Further education by anti-slavery groups in the North made Douglass a very lucid speaker and writer. The publication of the *North Star* was one of the factors that led to Douglass's break with William Lloyd Garrison, the noted white abolitionist and publisher of the *Liberator.* Garrison saw no need for two major rival anti-slavery publications, but Douglass and other blacks had become convinced that they must play a more leading role in the abolitionist movement, and that included the printing of a newspaper. In later years Douglass was appointed to several political and diplomatic posts, including unofficial advisor to presidents Abraham Lincoln and Andrew Johnson, marshal of the District of Columbia, recorder of deeds of the District of Columbia, and minister to Haiti. He also served as president of the Freedmen's Bank in 1874.

FEBRUARY 1848 Slavery Debate Escalated with Treaty. The Treaty of Guadalupe Hidalgo was concluded between the United States and Mexico, ending two years of combat between the countries. Under the terms of the treaty, the present states of New Mexico and California were ceded to the United States. Many pro-slavery Southerners had supported the war, anticipating that new lands would be opened to slavery. Many anti-slavery Northerners had opposed the war, fearing that it was the result of a pro-slavery conspiracy designed to open new

$200 Reward.

RANAWAY from the subscriber, on the night of Thursday, the 30th of Sepember,

FIVE NEGRO SLAVES,

To-wit : one Negro man, his wife, and three children.

The man is a black negro, full height, very erect, his face a little thin. He is about forty years of age, and calls himself *Washington Reed*, and is known by the name of Washington. He is probably well dressed, possibly takes with him an ivory headed cane, and is of good address. Several of his teeth are gone.

Mary, his wife, is about thirty years of age, a bright mulatto woman, and quite stout and strong.

The oldest of the children is a boy, of the name of FIELDING, twelve years of age, a dark mulatto, with heavy eyelids. He probably wore a new cloth cap.

MATILDA, the second child, is a girl, six years of age, rather a dark mulatto, but a bright and smart looking child.

MALCOLM, the youngest, is a boy, four years old, a lighter mulatto than the last, and about equally as bright. He probably also wore a cloth cap. If examined, he will be found to have a swelling at the navel.

Washington and Mary have lived at or near St. Louis, with the subscriber, for about 15 years.

It is supposed that they are making their way to Chicago, and that a white man accompanies them, that they will travel chiefly at night, and most probably in a covered wagon.

A reward of $150 will be paid for their apprehension, so that I can get them, if taken within one hundred miles of St. Louis, and $200 if taken beyond that, and secured so that I can get them, and other reasonable additional charges, if delivered to the subscriber, or to THOMAS ALLEN, Esq., at St. Louis, Mo. The above negroes, for the last few years, have been in possession of Thomas Allen, Esq., of St. Louis.

WM. RUSSELL.

ST. LOUIS, Oct. 1, 1847.

Handbill offering a cash reward for the return of slaves. (Courtesy of Library of Congress.)

territory to slavery. Shortly after the war began in 1846, Democratic representative David Wilmot of Pennsylvania introduced an amendment to a pending bill in Congress—to become known as the "Wilmot Proviso—which sought to prohibit slavery in any territory acquired as a result of the Mexican War. The proviso passed in the House of Representatives, but was defeated in the Senate. The Mexican Cession and the status of slavery there precipitated bitter debate between North and South from 1848 to 1850. One proposed solution was offered by President Zachary Taylor, who suggested that California and New Mexico bypass the territorial stage of government and apply directly for statehood, thus nullifying the question of slavery in the Mexican Cession territories. This proposal was unacceptable to the South, for both New Mexico and California would enter the Union as free states, thus upsetting the precarious sectional balance in the U.S. Senate that now stood at fifteen states each. The grounds were laid for the famous Compromise of 1850.

1849 The Fugitive Blacksmith Published in London. The autobiography of James William Charles Pennington, who had escaped slavery when he was twenty-one, was written in 1849. Upon escape, he devoted himself to Christianity and abolition, using his story to gain support and expose the horrors of slavery. His work took him to London as Connecticut's representative at the World's Anti-Slavery Convention and to Paris, Brussels, Scotland, and Frankfurt as a lecturer. Though Pennington did not support emigration by African Americans to Africa, he did support the evangelization of Africa's indigenous peoples. In 1855 Pennington helped organize the New York Legal Rights Association, which worked to bring equality to the city's transportation system.

1849 South's First African American Pastor. Elder Peter Lowery became pastor of a black church in Nashville, Tennessee, making him probably the first African American pastor of a church in Tennessee. Lowery, who was born a slave, had managed to purchase his freedom and that of other members of his family, including his mother, brothers, and sisters, over a period of more than forty years. In his endeavor, he was substantially aided by his wife, Ruth, a free woman of color.

1849 Mammy Pleasant Prospered in California. Mary Ellen Pleasant, also referred to as Mammy Pleasant, moved to San Francisco from Boston where she had met William Lloyd Garrison. In California, Pleasant opened a restaurant and boarding house, managed estates, and made loans. She is believed to have rescued slaves who were being held illegally and to have worked to secure blacks' rights to testify in court and ride street cars. Pleasant was also said to have given money to John Brown to help his attack on Harpers Ferry. But Pleasant, believed to be of black and Indian blood, holds a more prominent name as the planner and operator of the House of Mystery, a brothel. She also admitted to helping one of her women forge a marriage contract in order to gain wealth through divorce.

1849 "Separate But Equal Doctrine" Established. Benjamin Roberts, a black parent in Boston, sued the city for denying his daughter admission to a white public school. The Massachusetts Supreme Court rejected the suit, *Roberts v. The City of Boston,* establishing the "separate but equal" doctrine instead. Charles Sumner unsuccessfully represented the plantiff's side.

MAY 25, 1849 Musical Prodigy Thomas Greene Bethune (Blind Tom) Born. By the time Thomas Greene Bethune was four, the blind child, who was born into slavery, was being exhibited as the "musical marvel" of the Bethune plantation in Georgia. The exhibition of Tom, however, soon turned into exploitation as his owners made several fortunes on his talent, including an estimated $100,000 from an 1866 European tour. Colonel James Bethune even used Tom's talent to benefit the Confederacy throughout the Civil War. When Tom was 15, Colonel Bethune gained guardianship of the boy, supposedly with his parents' consent. In 1865, with the end of the war, an attempt was made to liberate Tom from the guardianship that was akin to slavery. That, however, failed and Tom's "guardianship" was eventually passed on to the colonel's son, and later, the son's widow and her second husband who profited off the last fifteen years of Tom's life. Tom reportedly died penniless on June 13, 1908, in Hoboken, New Jersey. His accomplishments included performances before foreign dignitaries and President James Buchanan, the composition of over 100 piano and vocal pieces, and the mastery of over 700 pieces by European greats such as Beethoven and Bach.

JULY 1849 Harriet Tubman Escaped from Slavery in Maryland. Harriet Tubman, the best-known black female abolitionist, returned to Maryland and Virginia at least twenty times and is credited with freeing more than three

Harriet Tubman with some of the slaves she helped free. (Courtesy of Library of Congress.)

hundred slaves. The daring abolitionist was born in Dorchester County, Maryland, in 1823. While working as a field hand as a young girl, she suffered a severe head injury by a weight that an enraged overseer had thrown at another slave. The damage from that blow caused Tubman to suffer from "sleeping seizures" for the rest of her life. In 1844, she married a free black, John Tubman, but remained a slave. In 1849, her master died and rumors emerged that his slaves were to be sold into the Deep South. Tubman, along with two of her brothers, escaped. Fearing capture and punishment or death, the brothers returned to the plantation, but Tubman, using the North Star for directions, marched on until she reached Philadelphia. In 1850, Tubman returned to Maryland for a sister and a brother, and in the following year she led a party of eleven blacks from the South into Canada, leaving behind her husband, who had married another woman. In 1857, Tubman made one of her last trips into Maryland, rescuing her parents and three additional brothers and sisters. The family then settled in Auburn, New York. The family home, purchased from anti-slavery senator William H. Seward,

was later turned into a home for elderly and indigent African Americans. After serving in the Civil War as a nurse and a spy, Tubman devoted all of her energy and earnings to this home during the twilight of her life. Tubman, often called "the Moses of her People," died in Auburn in 1913.

1850 to 1859

SEPTEMBER 18, 1850 Compromise of 1850 Enacted. Congress enacted the famous Compromise of 1850. Senator Henry Clay of Kentucky and other "moderate" statesmen from both sections drew up this omnibus solution to the problem of slavery in the Mexican Cession as well as other outstanding differences between North and South. The provisions of the Compromise relating to slavery included the outlawing of the slave trade in Washington, D.C., but the retention of slavery itself; the passage of a new, tougher fugitive slave law to replace the poorly enforced act of 1793; and the admission of California as a free state.

1851 "Black Swan" Made Her Singing Debut. Elizabeth Taylor Greenfield, the "Black Swan," made her debut at a concert sponsored by the Buffalo Musical Association. Greenfield, a soprano, was born a slave in Natchez, Mississippi, in 1809. As an infant, she was taken to Philadelphia and adopted by a Quaker woman named Greenfield who arranged for her to study music and to sing at private parties. After her debut in Buffalo, Greenfield toured the Northern states between 1851 and 1853. She toured England in 1854 and gave a command performance before Queen Victoria in Buckingham Palace. A contemporary critic described her voice as one of "amazing power," "flexibility," and "ease of execution." America's leading historian of African American music, Eileen Southern, called Greenfield "the best known black concert artist of her time."

Josiah Henson, considered the model for character "Uncle Tom." (*Harper's Weekly.*)

MARCH 20, 1852 *Uncle Tom's Cabin* **Published.** *Uncle Tom's Cabin,* a novel by a Northern white woman, Harriet Beecher Stowe, was published in Boston. The book, which exaggerated the cruelties of slavery, evoked sympathy for the blacks in the North and greatly angered the South.

SEPTEMBER 15, 1852 Jan Earnst Matzeliger Born. Jan Earnst Matzeliger, was born in Paramaribo, Suriname, to a Holland-born engineer and a native African American mother. He began to apprentice at his father's machine shops when he was ten, an experience that would shape his future in machinery and mechanics. In 1871 he boarded an East Indian vessel to work as a sailor. He settled in Philadelphia two years later and by 1876 had made his home in Lynn, Massachusetts, where he found work in a shoe factory. After years of observing the production of shoes, Matzeliger began working on his own machine, a mechanical laster for the manufacture of shoes. On March 20, 1883, he was granted a patent for the "lasting machine." It proved to be a great success, turning out 100 to 600 more pairs of shoes a day than could be produced using the manual

method. Unfortunately, Matzeliger did not live to enjoy the financial rewards nor to see his invention's impact on shoe manufacture. He died of tuberculosis less than a month before his thirty-seventh birthday in 1889.

1853 First Novel by an African American Published. William Wells Brown, a former slave, abolitionist, historian, and physician, published *Clotel,* the first novel written by an African American, in London. The work, an account of the life of a black woman whose father was an American president, draws on the legend that Thomas Jefferson had fathered many children by his slave mistresses. Brown was born to a slave and a white slave-owner in Lexington, Kentucky, in 1816. He was educated in St. Louis, Missouri, where he served as an apprentice to the martyred abolitionist editor, Elijah P. Lovejoy. Brown also published *Three Years in Europe: or, Places I Have Seen and People I Have Met* (1852), in which he gave his impressions of such notables as Richard Cobden, Victor Hugo, and Alexis de Tocqueville. Brown was also a regular contributor to William Lloyd Garrison's *Liberator,* the *London Daily News,* and the *National Anti-Slavery Standard.* His

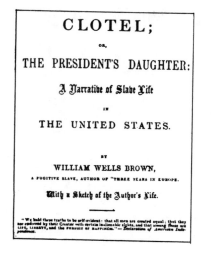

CLOTEL;

OR,

THE PRESIDENT'S DAUGHTER:

A Narrative of Slave Life

IN

THE UNITED STATES.

BY

WILLIAM WELLS BROWN,

A FUGITIVE SLAVE, AUTHOR OF "THREE YEARS IN EUROPE."

With a Sketch of the Author's Life.

"We hold these truths to be self-evident: that all men are created equal; that they are endowed by their Creator with certain inalienable rights, and that among these are LIFE, LIBERTY, and the PURSUIT of HAPPINESS."—*Declaration of American Independence.*

Cover of William Wells Brown's book, *Clotel.*

reputation as an historian rests largely upon such works as *The Black Man* (1863) and *The Negro in the American Rebellions* (1867). Brown's principal anti-slavery work was as a "conductor" on the Underground Railroad and as an anti-slavery lecturer. He died in 1884.

JULY 6–8, 1853 National Council of Colored People Founded. The National Council of Colored People was founded in Rochester, New York. An outgrowth of the antebellum Negro Convention Movement, the new organization was formed as a permanent body to advance the cause of African Americans. A notable feature of the Rochester convention was a proposal to erect a national industrial school for the race. The institution was to be financed by the issuance of $50,000 worth of stock in shares of ten dollars each, through the sale of scholarships "at judicious rates," and by the raising of a $100,000 endowment. The school was to be co-educational and was to be governed by a board of trustees, consisting of residents of the state wherein the institution was located. The sponsors of the measure, which was never implemented, hoped that the education of African American youths would

"give them means of success adapted to their struggling condition; and ere long, following the enterprise of the age . . . see them filling everywhere positions of responsibility and trust, and gliding on the triple tide of wealth, intelligence, and virtue, reach eventually to a sure resting place of distinction and happiness."

1854 Ashmun Institute Founded. The Ashmun Institute was founded in Pennsylvania in 1854. In 1866 it was renamed Lincoln University in honor of Abraham Lincoln. Lincoln graduated its first class of four black men and two white women in 1868. In 1873, ten students from Liberia came to study at Lincoln, making the university one of the first, if not the first, U.S. institutions of higher learning to accept African students. Lincoln claims to be the oldest college in the United States to have as its original purpose the higher education of youths of African decent.

1854 Deadwood Dick Born. Nat Love, later known as Deadwood Dick, was born a slave in Davidson County, Tennessee, where he learned to break horses as a teenager. A winning raffle ticket brought him enough money to travel west, where he found work as a cowboy. He excelled at roping, shooting, and the other skills of his trade, winning the championship title in 1876 in Deadwood, South Dakota. He used his meager writing abilities to pen an autobiography, *The Life and Adventures of Nat Love: Better Known in the Cattle Country as "Deadwood Dick."* After being captured by Indians and sustaining two bullet wounds, Love escaped and quit his work as a cowboy. He worked for the Pullman service until his death in Los Angeles in 1921.

MAY 30, 1854 Missouri Compromise Repealed by Kansas-Nebraska Act. The Kansas-Nebraska Act was approved by Congress and President Franklin Pierce. In addition to providing formal organization for the two territories of Kansas and Nebraska, the act repealed the Missouri Compromise of 1820, thus re-

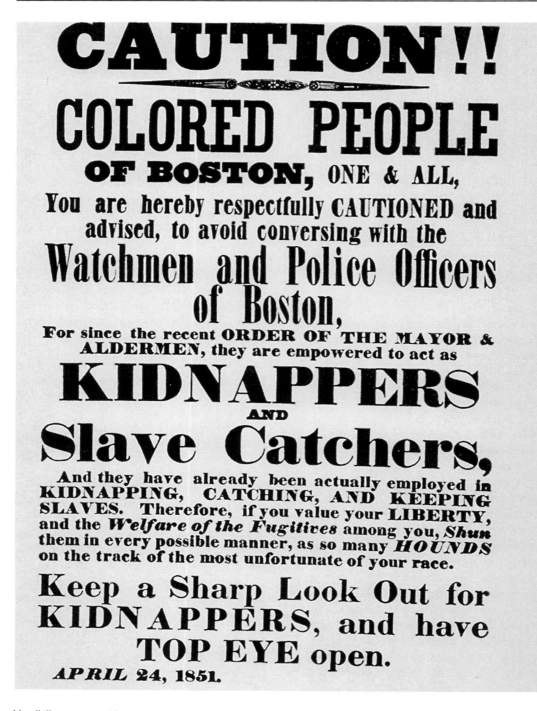

Handbill cautioning African Americans to be on the lookout for slave catchers. (Courtesy of Library of Congress.)

Author William Wells Brown. (Courtesy of Fisk University.)

Deadwood Dick.

moving anti-slavery restrictions north and west of the 36–30 parallel line in the Louisiana territory. According to the bill's author, Senator Stephen A. Douglas of Illinois, Congress, in the Compromise of 1850, had abandoned all efforts to protect or to prohibit slavery in the territories. Therefore, it was only consistent, Douglas reasoned, that the new principle be applied in the Louisiana territory as elsewhere.

Southerners viewed Kansas as ripe for slavery. Northern anti-slavery men opposed the prospects of a slave Kansas and the repeal of the Compromise of 1820. The contest for control of Kansas between the pro- and anti-slavery forces led to several years of bitter, often bloody, strife in the territory and in Congress. In fact, Kansas came to be known as "Bleeding Kansas." The most significant acts of violence were the sacking of the anti-slavery town of Lawrence, Kansas, in May 1856 and the subsequent retaliation by John Brown (who, with his followers, slaughtered five pro-slavery men at Pottawatomie Creek), and the beating of anti-slavery senator Charles Sumner of Massachusetts by congressman Preston S. Brooks of South Carolina on the floor of the U.S. Senate, also in the spring of 1856. Sumner had de-nounced the South and some of its representatives for the "crime against Kansas," the rape of a virgin territory by slaveholders. His remarks against Senator Andrew P. Butler of South Carolina led to the attack by Brooks, Butler's nephew. The acrimony and political confusion in Kansas prevented the territory from being admitted into the Union by Congress until just before the Civil War. On January 29, 1861, Kansas joined the Union as a free state, representing the will of the majority of the bona fide residents there.

JUNE 3, 1854   Fugitive Slave Arrested in Boston. Anthony Burns, a fugitive slave, was arrested in Boston. His master refused an offer of $1,200 made by Boston citizens for his freedom. Burns was escorted through the streets of Boston by U.S. troops as he returned to the South. The incident was indicative of a growing anti-slavery sentiment in the North, especially following the passage of the Kansas-Nebraska Act.

1855   First African American to Win Elective Office. John Mercer Langston was elected clerk of Brownhelm Township in Lorain County, Ohio, making him the first African American to win an elective political office in the United States. Langston was born to a white man and a black slave on a Virginia plantation in 1829. After his father's death, Langston was sent to Ohio, where he was reared by one of his father's friends. By 1854, Langston was engaged in an active law practice in Chillicothe, Ohio, and in 1855, as the only African American attorney in Brownhelm, he was elected clerk. Langston won a seat on the Brownhelm City Council the following year, a post he held until 1860. In 1865, he was named president of the National Equal Rights League and in 1867 he became a member of the Board of Education in Oberlin, Ohio. After his return to the South during Reconstruction, Langston served as inspector general to the Freedman's Bureau Schools (1868–69); teacher, law school dean, and acting vice-president of Howard University (1869–76); minister to Haiti (1877–85); president of the Virginia Normal and Collegiate Institute (1885–88); and congressman from Virginia (1889–91). Langston, who died in 1897, was one of the last African Americans elected to the U.S. Congress in the nineteenth century, and was the great-uncle of Harlem Renaissance poet Langston Hughes.

1855   Massachusetts Schools Integrated. Public opinion led the Massachusetts legislature to overturn an 1849 ruling by the state Supreme Court that upheld separate schooling for blacks.

Congressman John Mercer Langston. (Courtesy of Library of Congress.)

Public schools were thus integrated in Massachusetts.

1856   Wilberforce University Founded. Amidst a cry for the end of slavery, Wilberforce was founded in 1856 as Wilberforce University of the Methodist Episcopal Church and named after British abolitionist and philanthropist William Wilberforce. The school was part of a plan to establish education for blacks in Ohio. Wilberforce was sold to the A.M.E. Church in 1863 and awarded its first bachelor's degrees in

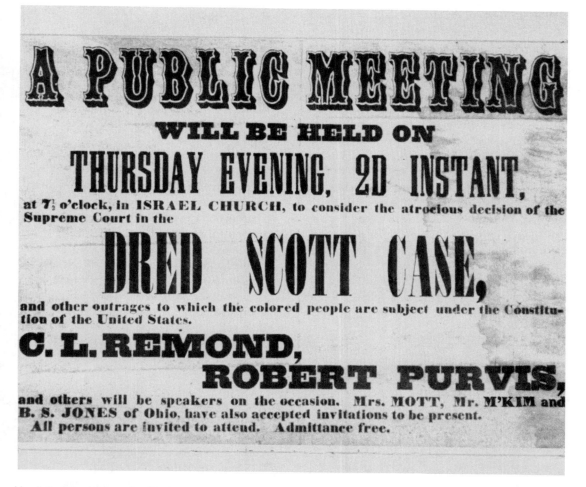

A PUBLIC MEETING

WILL BE HELD ON

THURSDAY EVENING, 2D INSTANT,

at 7½ o'clock, in ISRAEL CHURCH, to consider the atrocious decision of the Supreme Court in the

DRED SCOTT CASE,

and other outrages to which the colored people are subject under the Constitution of the United States.

C. L. REMOND,
ROBERT PURVIS,

and others will be speakers on the occasion. Mrs. MOTT, Mr. M'KIM and B. S. JONES of Ohio, have also accepted invitations to be present. All persons are invited to attend. Admittance free.

Handbill of *Dred Scott v. Sandford* case.

1867. Wilberforce was distinguished as the first black college and the first college with a black president.

MARCH 6, 1857 *Dred Scott* **Case Decided.** The Supreme Court rendered its decision in the case of *Dred Scott v. Sandford,* declaring that African Americans were not citizens of the United States and denying to Congress the power to prohibit slavery in any federal territory. Scott was eventually freed by new owners. Meanwhile, he remained a slave, albeit a fa-

mous one, in St. Louis where he worked as a porter. The Dred Scott decision, a clear-cut victory for the South, alarmed abolitionists in the North and fueled the fires leading to the Civil War.

JUNE 1857 **African Americans Denied Immigration into California.** The California legislature defeated by a narrow margin of thirty-two to thirty an attempt to prevent the immigration of blacks into the state. The opposition to the measure was lead by Representative G.

A. Hall. Despite the defeat, California blacks continued to protest instances of racial discrimination against them. An excerpt from a protest of two black businessmen in 1857 follows:

"During a residence of seven years in California, we, with hundreds of other colored men, have cheerfully paid city, state and county taxes on real estate and merchandise, as well as licenses to carry on business, and every other species of tax that has been levied from time to time for the support of the government, save only the 'poll tax' that we have persistently refused. On the day before yesterday, the Tax Collector called on us, and seized and lugged off twenty or thirty dollars' worth of goods, in payment, as he said, of this tax. . . . Now, while we cannot understand how a 'white' man can refuse to pay each and every tax for the support of government, under which he enjoys every privilege—from the right to rob a negro up to that of being Governor of the State—we can perceive and feel the flagrant injustices of compelling 'colored men' to pay a special tax for the enjoyment of a special privilege, and then break their heads if they attempt to exercise it. We believe that every voter should pay poll-tax, or every male resident who has the privilege of becoming a voter; but regard it as low and despicable, the very quintessence of meanness, to compel colored men to pay it, situated as they are politically. However, if there is no redress, the great State of California may come around annually, and rob us of twenty or thirty dollars' worth of goods, as we will never willingly pay three dollars as poll tax as long as we remain disfranchised, oath-denied, outlawed colored Americans."

1858 Judson Lyons Born. The African American man whose name would come to be printed on U.S. paper currency, Judson W. Lyons, was born in Georgia. He began his political career at the age of twenty when he became an elected delegate to a Congressional convention. Two years later he served in Georgia's internal revenue service and at the Republican National Convention as a delegate. The Augusta bar association admitted Lyons after he graduated from Howard University in 1884. American currency came to bear his name when he was appointed the Register of the Treasury in 1898.

APRIL 14, 1858 Archy Lee Won Slave Case. Archy Lee is remembered as the victor in California's most important fugitive-slave case. He was born a slave in Carroll County, Mississippi, where he remained until he was eighteen, when he was taken to Sacramento, California. Fearing that Lee would try to escape, his master made plans to return Lee to Mississippi. When Lee learned this, he fled, but soon was apprehended and jailed. Leaders of the Sacramento African American community became interested in his cause. After a series of contradictory court decisions, Lee was finally granted freedom and moved to Victoria, British Columbia. The court decision prompted a mass exodus of blacks from California to Victoria to escape further persecution.

1859 Fugitive Slave Act Upheld by Supreme Court. The U.S. Supreme Court, in *Ableman v. Booth*, overruled an act by a Wisconsin state court that declared the Fugitive Slave Act of 1850 unconstitutional. The Fugitive Slave Act and its methods of enforcement were increasingly opposed by Northern residents. Many Northern cities and states passed Personal Liberty Laws, denying the use of Northern jails for the housing of fugitive slaves and prohibiting local law enforcement officers from assisting in their capture, in an attempt to offset the Fugitive Slave Act. The Wisconsin case arose when a journalist was arrested for rousing a mob to free a captured runaway. The state court ordered him released on a writ of *habeas corpus* and declared the federal statute unconstitutional.

1859 Last Slave Ship Landed in Alabama. The *Clothilde*, the last slave ship to stop at an American port, landed at Mobile Bay, Alabama.

The slave market in Atlanta, Georgia. (Courtesy of Library of Congress.)

John Brown on his way to the gallows.

MARCH 7, 1859 African Americans Denied Land Rights. The acting commissioner of general lands for the United States, J. S. Wilson, stated that blacks were not citizens of the United States "as contemplated by the preemption law of September, 1841" and, therefore, were "not legally entitled to preempt public lands."

OCTOBER 16, 1859 John Brown Led Raid at Harpers Ferry. John Brown, a white abolitionist from Kansas, attacked the U.S. Arsenal at Harpers Ferry, Virginia. Brown, who had unsuccessfully sought the aid of leading abolitionists, including Frederick Douglass, was accompanied by a dozen white men and five blacks. The raid, which was to be a prelude to a general slave uprising, was foiled by local, state, and federal forces. Two blacks were killed for their part in the affair. Brown was executed on December 2.

Part 3

WAR AND FREEDOM
1860–1889

1860

1860 Pony Express Began Operations in the West. Eastern mails went by railroad to St. Joseph, Missouri, then were picked up by professional riders who, working in relays, delivered letters as far west as San Francisco. Two of the earliest black Pony Express riders were George Monroe and William Robinson.

JANUARY 1, 1860 Free Blacks Denied Employment on Arkansas Rivers. A law went into effect in Arkansas that prohibited the employment of free blacks on boats and ships navigating the rivers of that state.

NOVEMBER 6, 1860 Lincoln Elected President. Abraham Lincoln, viewed by Southerners as an abolitionist, was elected president of the United States on a platform opposed to the further expansion of slavery into the territories.

DECEMBER 17, 1860 South Carolina Secedes. South Carolina seceded from the Union, partly because of Lincoln's election as president.

1861

1861 Fremont Proclaimed Military Emancipation. General John C. Fremont proclaimed military emancipation in Missouri. President Abraham Lincoln countermanded the order.

Congressman Robert Smalls. (Courtesy of Library of Congress.)

APRIL 12, 1861 Civil War Began with Attack of Fort Sumter. The Confederates attacked Fort Sumter in South Carolina. President Abraham Lincoln called for 75,000 volunteers to defend the Union; thus the Civil War began. Many African Americans viewed the conflict as a war for freedom. Some rushed to join the Union forces, but were refused because of their race.

AUGUST 6, 1861 Confiscation Act. Congress passed the Confiscation Act, which said that any property used by the owner's consent and with his knowledge in aiding or abetting insurrection against the United States could be captured wherever found. When the property consisted of slaves, they were to be forever free. President Abraham Lincoln refused to order vigorous enforcement of the law.

AUGUST 23, 1861   Fugitive Slave Enlisted in Union Army. James Stone, a very light complexioned fugitive slave who was often mistaken for a white, enlisted in the First Fight Artillery of Ohio. Having fought for the Union in Kentucky, where he had been a slave, Stone died from a service-related illness in 1862. After his death his true racial identity was revealed. Thus, Stone was actually the first African American to fight for the Union during the Civil War—almost two full years before African Americans were authorized to join Union forces.

SEPTEMBER 25, 1861   Navy Authorized Enlistment of African Americans. The Secretary of the Navy authorized the enlistment of African Americans in this branch of the armed forces.

1862

1862   LeMoyne-Owen College Opened. Memphis, Tennessee's, LeMoyne-Owen College started as an elementary school for blacks, with the name Lincoln School for Negroes. The chapel that housed the school was destroyed by fire in the 1866 race riots, but it was soon rebuilt and reopened in 1867. In 1871 the school's name was changed to LeMoyne Normal and Commercial School, in honor of donor Dr. Francis J. LeMoyne. In 1868, LeMoyne College merged with Owen College and became LeMoyne-Owen College.

MARCH 6, 1862   Lincoln Proposed Emancipation of Slaves. President Abraham Lincoln proposed to Congress a plan for gradual, compensated emancipation of slaves. Lincoln urged the congressional delegations from Delaware, Kentucky, Maryland, Missouri, and West Virginia to support his proposal. They opposed it, as did Northern abolitionists who felt slaveholders should not be paid for property that they could not rightfully own. Congress, however, passed a joint resolution on April 10, 1862, endorsing the concept of gradual, compensated emancipation.

APRIL 16, 1862   Slavery Abolished in District of Columbia. The U.S. Senate passed a bill abolishing slavery in the District of Columbia. Slaveowners were to be compensated at the rate of $300 per slave. One hundred thousand dollars was also allocated for the voluntary emigration of these freedmen to Haiti or Liberia.

MAY 9, 1862   Slaves Named "Contrabands of War." General David Hunter issued a proclamation emancipating slaves in Georgia, Florida, and South Carolina as "contrabands of war." President Abraham Lincoln overruled Hunter's order.

MAY 13, 1862   Former Slave Captured Confederate Ship. Robert Smalls, an African American pilot, sailed the Confederate steamer *Planter* out of Charleston, South Carolina, and turned the ship over to the United States. Smalls, a former slave, had received some education through the indulgence of his master. He was a member of a crew in the Confederate Navy when he performed his Civil War heroics. Smalls' war deeds aided his rise in South Carolina politics and business endeavors during Reconstruction. He later served five terms in the U.S. House of Representatives.

JUNE 19, 1862   Slavery Abolished in Federal Territories. President Abraham Lincoln signed a bill abolishing slavery in the federal territories.

JULY 17, 1862   African Americans Allowed to Serve in Union Army. Congress authorized President Abraham Lincoln to accept African Americans for service in the Union Army. They were to receive less pay than white sol-

Former slaves serving in the Union army. (Courtesy of Library of Congress.)

diers. A white soldier was paid $13 a month and $3.50 for clothing, while African Americans of the same rank received $7 and $3, respectively. Eventually, more than 186,000 African Americans served in the Union Army; approximately 38,000 lost their lives. Many of the deaths were non-combat related, due principally to overwork and poor medical care.

AUGUST 14, 1862   Lincoln Addressed Group of African Americans. President Abraham Lincoln called in a group of African Americans for the first discussion by an American president with blacks on public policy. He urged them to emigrate to Africa or to Latin America. Many African Americans denounced the president's suggestion.

SEPTEMBER 22, 1862   Lincoln Issued Preliminary Emancipation Proclamation. President Abraham Lincoln issued a preliminary Emancipation Proclamation, giving rebellious states and territories until January 1, 1863, to abandon their hostilities or lose their slaves.

"Contrabands" on Mr. Follen's farm in Virginia. (Courtesy of Library of Congress.)

1863

1863 African American Regiment Protested Unfair Wages. The 54th Massachusetts Negro Regiment served a year without pay rather than accept discriminatory wages.

JANUARY 1, 1863 Lincoln Signed Emancipation Proclamation. President Abraham Lincoln signed the Emancipation Proclamation. Based upon military necessity, it declared slaves free in all states and territories then in rebellion against the United States.

MAY 1, 1863 Confederate Congress Condemned African American Troops. The Confederate Congress passed a resolution calling African American troops and their officers criminals, thus permitting captured black soldiers and their officers to be murdered or enslaved.

JULY 9, 1863 African American Sieged Port Hudson. Eight African American regiments played a vital role in the siege of Port Hudson, which, with the capture of Vicksburg, Mississippi, allowed the Union to control the Mississippi River.

JULY 13–16, 1863 Union Draft Law Prompted Riots. Four days of rioting ensued in New York City in protest of the Union's Draft Law. The disturbance left more than one thousand people, mostly African Americans, dead or wounded and resulted in approximately two million dollars in property damage. The riot grew out of the Civil War Draft Law's provision that allowed men to pay $300 for a substitute draftee. Since poor white laborers, many of them Irish and German immigrants, could not afford substitutes, they bore the brunt of the draft. African Americans were ineligible (at the time) for the draft. In venting their frustrations over the draft law, the poorer laborers turned on African Americans especially, who they regarded as the principal inheritors of the jobs they would have to leave behind to enter the Army. During this period of racial tension, similar riots occurred in Boston, where twenty people were killed or wounded, and in Troy, New York, where a ship with black servants aboard had to be diverted to avoid an attack.

JULY 30, 1863 Lincoln Issued Warning to Confederates. President Abraham Lincoln warned of retaliatory action if the Confederates

The Emancipation Proclamation.

continued to murder or enslave captured African American soldiers.

1864

1864 Protest Leader Executed. African American sergeant William Walker of the Third South Carolina Regiment was shot under order of a court martial for leading a protest against discriminatory pay for African American soldiers.

APRIL 12, 1864 Confederates Captured Fort Pillow. Confederate forces under General Nathan Bedford Forrest captured Fort Pillow, Tennessee. Following the surrender, the Union's African American troops were massacred.

JUNE 15, 1864 Congress Legislated Equal Pay for African American Troops. Congress passed a bill equalizing salaries and supplies for African American troops.

JUNE 19, 1864 African American Sailor Awarded Congressional Medal of Honor. An African American sailor, Joachim Pease, was awarded the Congressional Medal of Honor for his role in the famous naval battle between the *USS Kearsage* and the *USS Alabama* off the coast of France.

JULY 21, 1864 First Black Daily Paper. *La Tribune de la Nouvelle Orleans,* the first triweekly published in English and French and eventually the first black daily in the United States, published its first edition. The paper was headed by Louis Charles Roudanez (1823–90) and his brothers, who took over the financially failing *L'Union,* the first black paper published in Louisiana. The *Tribune* pushed for economic equality, abolition, and black suffrage. With emancipation, the paper supported the Freedman's Aid Association, an organization that attempted to establish cooperatives among, and secure suffrage and weekly wages for, former slaves. While Roudanez pushed for political rights for African Americans, he did not support social equality. This may be partly because Roudanez himself was half French and probably of very light skin since his baptismal records registered him as white. When the *Tribune* folded in 1869, he, too, faded from the spotlight of the equal rights movement.

1865

1865 Atlanta University Founded. Atlanta University was founded by the American Missionary Association in 1865 in Atlanta, Georgia. The school's undergraduate courses were discontinued in 1930 when it became a graduate and professional school. In 1988, Atlanta University merged with another historically black school, Clark College.

1865 "Black Codes" Restricted Rights of African Americans. All-white legislatures, under the Johnson Reconstruction program, began enacting "Black Codes" that restricted the rights and freedom of movement of African Americans. These codes were patterned after the antebellum slave codes. Newer aspects of the laws imposed heavy penalties for vagrancy, "seditious speeches," "insulting gestures," and curfew violations.

1865 "Black Laws" of Illinois Repealed. These laws, like similar ones in other Northern states, restricted the freedom of movement and limited the civil and political rights of free blacks. John Jones, one of the wealthiest African Americans in America, led the fight for repeal.

1865 Bluefield Colored Institute Founded. Bluefield Colored Institute was founded in Bluefield, West Virginia, to train black teachers. Bluefield offered its first bachelor's degree in 1932 and changed its name to Bluefield State College in 1943. The school is one of two historically black colleges in West Virginia, although the school's black population has now dropped below 10 percent.

1865 Bowie State University Founded. Originally known as Baltimore Normal School, Bowie State University was founded under the auspices of the Baltimore Association for the Moral and Educational Improvement of Colored People. With money bequeathed by black philanthropist Nelson Wells for the education of freed black children, the school moved to a 237-acre tract in Prince George's County, Marylan. The school's name changed several times between 1865 and 1988.

1865 Richmond Theological Institute Founded. Richmond Theological Institute was founded on a site that was once a slave jail in Richmond, Virginia. The name was changed to Virginia Union University in 1899 when the institute merged with Wayland Seminary. The school later merged with Hartshorn Memorial College of Richmond and Storer College of Harpers Ferry, West Virginia. The university's mission was to "free the mind of the newly emancipated through education in a humanistic environment."

JANUARY 11, 1865 Lee Recommended Drafting African Americans to Aid Confederate Forces. Robert E. Lee, with his armies depleted, recommended the employment of African Americans in Confederate forces because it was "not only expedient but necessary."

MARCH 3, 1865 Freedman's Bank Chartered. The U.S. government chartered the Freedmen's Bank in Washington, D.C., to encourage financial responsibility among the former slaves. On April 4, 1865, the headquarters of the Freedmen's Bank opened in New York. Shortly thereafter, branches were established in Louisville, Nashville, New Orleans, Vicksburg, and Washington. By 1872 there were thirty-four branches, all but two of which were located

in the South. Incompetency and inefficiency in the bank's operation appeared almost immediately. By the time Frederick Douglass became president in March 1874, the bank was already a failure. It closed on June 28, 1874.

MARCH 3, 1865 Freedmen's Bureau Established. Congress established, within the War Department, a Bureau of Freedmen, Refugees and Abandoned Lands. The Freedmen's Bureau sought to help freed blacks survive, as well as aiding them in their contractual relationships and education. In its five years of existence, the Bureau issued more than twenty million rations; established approximately fifty hospitals; resettled more than 30,000 people; set up 4,330 schools, enrolling 247,000 students; and aided in the establishment of such black colleges as Atlanta University, Fisk University, Hampton Institute, and Howard University.

MARCH 13, 1865 Confederate President Authorized Use of African American Soldiers. Confederate president Jefferson Davis signed a bill authorizing the employment of African Americans as soldiers in the Confederate Army. The law culminated a long period of dispute in the South over the use of African Americans as soldiers. While Southerners willingly used African Americans for fatigue duties and personal service, the idea of African American combat soldiers was generally repugnant to them. It seemed to invite slave violence and make a mockery of the concept of African American inferiority. The war ended before any African Americans faced combat.

APRIL 11, 1865 Lincoln Recommended African American Suffrage, with Provisions. President Abraham Lincoln again conceded that some African Americans might be given the right to vote. He had suggested in a letter to Governor Michael Hahn of Louisiana in 1864 that the "very intelligent" and those who had "fought gallantly in our ranks" should be considered for the franchise. At the time of Lin-

The Freedmen's Bureau sought to keep peace between white southerners and former slaves. (*Harper's Weekly*.)

coln's death, no serious efforts had been made to grant suffrage to freed blacks.

APRIL 14, 1865 Lincoln Shot by Booth. Abraham Lincoln was shot by John Wilkes Booth during a performance at Ford's Theater in the nation's capital. Lincoln died early the next morning.

MAY 29, 1865 Johnson Introduced Reconstruction Program. President Andrew Johnson announced his program of Reconstruction. It required ratification of the Thirteenth Amendment but did not guarantee African American suffrage.

OCTOBER 1865 Avery Institute Opened. Philanthropist Charles Avery founded the Avery Institute in Charleston, South Carolina. The first class numbered about 1,000 students, four-fifths of whom were freed slaves who had not received any prior education. The American Missionary Association of New York eventually took over the school's finances.

DECEMBER 18, 1865 Thirteenth Amendment Adopted. The Thirteenth Amendment, which prohibited slavery or involuntary servitude, except as punishment for a crime, was adopted.

1866

1866 Alabama State University Founded. Alabama State University was founded under the name Lincoln Normal School as a private school for blacks in Marion, Alabama. William Burns Paterson became president of the school in 1878, and through his efforts it became the first state-supported institution for the training of African American teachers in the United States. Paterson headed the school for 37 years, keeping it open despite great difficulties. The school moved to its present location in Montgomery in 1887 as a result of racial tensions in Marion. Alabama State University's name changed several times over the years. The school adopted its current name in 1969 when it earned university status.

1866 Edward Waters College Founded. Edward Waters College was founded in Jacksonville, Florida, as Brown Theological Institution. The school's mission was to train African American clergy for the A.M.E. Church. Edward Walters College succeeded despite many hardships, including a fire in 1904. The college is Florida's oldest independent institution of higher learning and its first institution established for the education of blacks.

1866   First African Americans Elected to Legislature. The first African Americans to sit in an American legislative assembly, Edward G. Walker and Charles L. Mitchell, were elected to the Massachusetts House of Representatives.

1866   Rust College Founded. The Freedmen's Aid Society of the Methodist Episcopal Church founded what is now Rust College as Shaw School. It is the oldest historically black college in Mississippi. The school, located in Holly Springs, originally provided elementary education; later, high school and college courses were added. The elementary and secondary programs were discontinued in 1930 and 1953, respectively. Rust's first president, Rev. A. C. McDonald, gave the school its motto, "By their fruits ye shall know them."

1866   Soldiers Donated Money to Education. After the Civil War, the soldiers and officers of the Sixty-second U.S. Colored Infantry donated $5,000 to create a school to educate the freed blacks of Missouri. The Sixty-ninth Colored Infantry contributed another $1,325. Now known as Lincoln University, the Lincoln Institute opened in Jefferson City, Missouri, in 1866.

JANUARY 9, 1866   Fisk University Opened. Fisk University, which became famous for its fund-raising Jubilee Singers, was founded in Nashville, Tennessee, as Fisk College. Fisk offered its first bachelor's degree in 1875 and in 1967 became the first black institution to be awarded university status. In 1976 Fisk's Jubilee Hall, the first permanent building of higher

education for southern blacks, was designated a national landmark.

APRIL 9, 1866   Congress Passed Civil Rights Bill. The Civil Rights Bill of 1866, granting African Americans the rights and privileges of American citizenship, was passed by Congress. The law formed the basis for the Fourteenth Amendment to the U.S. Constitution and was passed over the veto of President Andrew Johnson.

MAY 1–3, 1866   Forty-Eight Killed in Memphis Race Riot. A race riot took place in Memphis, Tennessee. Forty-eight people, mostly black, were killed. African American veterans were special targets, and at least five African American women were raped during the disturbances. Schools and churches were burned.

JUNE 30, 1866   Thirty-five Killed in New Orleans Race Riot. A race riot occurred in New Orleans, Louisiana. At least thirty-five people were killed; more than 100 were wounded. Anti-African American attitudes and actions on the part of police allegedly prompted the violence.

1867

1867   African Americans Excluded from Professional Baseball. The National Association of Baseball denied admission to any club with African American players. In a statement, the association said: "It is not presumed by your committee that any clubs who have applied are composed of persons of color, or any portion of them; and the recommendations of your committee in this report are based upon this view, and they unanimously report against the admission of any club which may be composed of one or more colored persons. . . . If colored clubs were admitted, there would be in all probability some division of feeling—whereas

First site of Atlanta University.

by excluding them, no injury could result to anybody."

1867 Atlanta University Chartered. Atlanta University, the first all-black American graduate school, received its charter. The university began as an undergraduate institution, but switched to post-baccalaureate studies in 1929.

1867 Fayetteville State University Opened. The school that would become Fayetteville State University began in 1867, when seven black men contributed $136 to buy land for a school for black children. Originally called the Howard School, Fayetteville took its present name in 1969.

1867 Johnson C. Smith University Opened. Biddle Memorial Institute opened as a school of higher learning for black men in 1867, and in 1872 the school awarded its first bachelor's degrees. Known since 1923 as Johnson C. Smith University, the school is affiliated with the Presbyterian Church.

The Fisk Jubilee Singers. (Courtesy of Library of Congress.)

1867   Morgan State University Opened. Founded as Centenary Biblical Institute, Morgan State University opened in 1867 in Baltimore, Maryland, for the purpose of preparing black men for the ministry.

1867   Saint Augustine's College Founded. Together, the Protestant Episcopal Church and the Episcopal Diocese of North Carolina founded Saint Augustine's College in Raleigh, North Carolina. This historically black college is a member school of the United Negro College Fund.

1867   Scotia Seminary Founded. Established by the Presbyterian Church, Scotia Seminary trained black women as social workers and teachers. Mary McLeod Bethune graduated from the school in 1894 and went on to found Bethune-Cookman College. In 1930 Scotia merged with Barber Memorial College; the name Barber-Scotia College was adopted in 1932. Barber-Scotia allowed men to enroll in

School children in the rural South. (Courtesy of Library of Congress.)

1954. The school is located in Concord, North Carolina.

1867 Talladega College Founded. Talladega College was founded by a group of former slaves in Talladega, Alabama. It was the first college open to blacks in Alabama, and until 1916, it was the only college there to award degrees without regard to race. The first Talladega bachelor's degree was awarded in 1895. The school is affiliated with the United Church of Christ. Three of the buildings on the school's 50-acre campus have been declared historic landmarks.

JANUARY 8, 1867 Suffrage Extended to African Americans in District of Columbia. Congress enacted a law giving the suffrage to African Americans in the District of Columbia.

FEBRUARY 7, 1867 African American Delegation Urged Suffrage. A delegation of blacks, led by Frederick Douglass, visited President Andrew Johnson and urged that suffrage be given to all qualified African Americans.

African American college students. (Courtesy of the United Negro College Fund.)

FEBRUARY 18, 1867 Morehouse College Founded. Morehouse College first opened in Augusta, Georgia, as the Augusta Institute. It was established to train freed slaves to read and write. The school moved to Atlanta in 1879, and adopted the name Morehouse College in 1913. Its mission was to train men with disciplined minds who will lead lives of leadership, service, and self-realization.

MARCH 2, 1867 Reconstruction Began. Congress began passing a series of Reconstruction Acts that laid the foundation for African American political participation in the South. The former Confederate states were required to ratify the Fourteenth Amendment, which guaranteed civil rights to African Americans, before being readmitted to the Union.

APRIL 1, 1867 KKK Held First National Convention. The first national convention of the Ku Klux Klan, a violent anti-African American group, was held in Nashville, Tennessee.

MAY 1, 1867 Howard University Established. The Howard Normal and Theological Institute was established as a training institution for

black teachers and ministers in 1867. Named for General Oliver Otis Howard, one of the founding members and commissioners of the Freedmen's Bureau, it became Howard University the same year. Howard awarded its first bachelor's degree in 1872 and became the only truly comprehensive, predominantly black institution of higher education in the world.

1868

1868 Menard Elected to Congress. John W. Menard was elected to the U.S. House of Representatives from Louisiana. However, the House Committee on Elections refused to seat him. On February 27, 1869, Menard became the first African American to speak on the House floor as he fought for his right to serve.

JANUARY 14, 1868 African American Delegates Promoted Cooperation. The new state constitutional conventions met in Charleston, South Carolina. African American delegates were in a decided majority. Louisiana had an equal number of blacks and whites in its convention, while all other Southern states had

Cartoon depicting an African American casting his ballot. (*Harper's Weekly.*)

white majorities. The magnanimity of the African American delegates at Charleston was reflected in the words of African American representative Beverly Nash: "I believe, my friends and fellow-citizens, we are not prepared for this suffrage. But we can learn. . . . We recognize the Southern white man as the true friend of the black man. . . . In these public affairs we must unite with our white fellow-citizens. They tell us that they have been disfranchised, yet we tell the North that we shall never let the halls of Congress be silent until we remove that

disability." The state constitutions drawn up by Southern constitutional conventions with black members in 1867 and 1868 sought to abolish property qualifications for voting and holding office, imprisonment for debt, and slavery.

APRIL 1868 Hampton Institute Opened. The Hampton Normal & Agricultural Institute opened in Hampton, Virginia, in 1868. Later renamed the Hampton Institute, this agricultural-industrial college for blacks sought to educate selected former slaves who would then teach and lead other newly-freed blacks. Samuel Chapman Armstrong, a former Union officer and an advocate of agricultural-industrial training for freed blacks, was a founder and first leader of the institution. Hampton University remains one of the most prestigious black colleges in the United States.

JUNE 13, 1868 Dunn Became First Black Lieutenant Governor. Oscar J. Dunn, a freedman, became lieutenant governor of Louisiana, the highest elective office held by an African American up to that time. Dunn was an apprentice to a plasterer and house painter until age fifteen, when he escaped. Born in New Orleans in 1826, Dunn took a job with the Freedman's Bureau there at the close of the Civil War. (He had served as a captain in the Union Army during the War). As a Bureau agent, Dunn checked the employment practices of planters who hired black laborers. He found that the freedmen were often cheated of their minimum $15-a-month earnings and thus reported these and other abuses of the Freedman's Bureau wage-contract system. Dunn was one of the forty-nine African Americans who attended the Louisiana Constitutional Convention in 1867–68. As lieutenant governor, Dunn presided over the state senate and signed some of the laws emanating from the new state constitution. In 1871, he was named chairman of the Republican State Convention. Since Dunn was a skillful politician, some considered nominating him for governor or U.S. senator before his untimely death in 1871.

JULY 6, 1868 South Carolina Legislature Had Black Majority. The South Carolina Legislature met in Columbia, the state's capital. More than half of the lawmakers were black (87 blacks and 40 whites), making South Carolina the only state legislature in American history to have a black majority. The whites, however, controlled the state senate, and by 1874 there was a white majority in the lower house. At all times there was a white governor. There were

Louisiana lieutenant governor Oscar Dunn. (*Harper's Weekly.*)

two African American lieutenant-governors, Alonzo J. Ransier in 1870 and Richard H. Gleaves in 1872. Two African Americans, Samuel J. Lee and Robert B. Elliott, served as speaker of the house between 1872 and 1874. One of the most accomplished black South Carolina officeholders was Francis L. Cardozo, who served as secretary of state (1868–72) and treasurer (1872–76).

JULY 28, 1868 Fourteenth Amendment Adopted. The Fourteenth Amendment, which provided blacks Americans with the protection and privileges of natural citizenship and gave them constitutional guarantees, was adopted. All persons born or naturalized in the United States were defined as American citizens as well as citizens of the states in which they resided. No state could make or enforce laws denying such persons the rights and privileges of citizens or to fail to give them the equal protection of the laws.

SEPTEMBER 22–OCTOBER 26, 1868 Racism Sparked Riots in Louisiana. A series of race riots developed in Louisiana. Such disturbances occurred in New Orleans on September 22; in

South Carolina congressman Robert Elliott. (*Harper's Weekly*.)

Opelousas on September 28; and in St. Bernard Parish on October 26.

1869

1869   Clark College Founded. In order to provide formal education to blacks in the south, Atlanta's Clark College was founded by the Freedman's Aid Society of the Methodist Episcopal Church in 1869 as Clark University. In 1877 Clark was chartered by the state of Georgia. Clark College merged with the historically black Atlanta University in 1988.

1869   Dillard University Founded. Union Normal School was founded in 1869 by the Methodist Episcopal Church. By the end of the century Union was renamed New Orleans University. On June 6, 1930, New Orleans University merged with another historically black school, Straight College, to become Dillard University.

1869   Tougaloo College Established. In 1869 the American Missionary Association of New

York bought 500 acres of a former plantation in Tougaloo, Mississippi, to train young people "irrespective of their religious tenets" and to educate with "the most liberal principles for the benefit of our citizens in general." Tougaloo College offered college courses starting in 1897.

1870

1870   Allen University Opened. The A.M.E. Church opened the Payne Institute in 1870 in Columbia, South Carolina. The school reopened in 1880 under the name Allen University in honor of A.M.E. founder Richard Allen. Allen University is the oldest traditionally black college in South Carolina.

1870   Benedict College Founded. Benedict College was founded as Benedict Institute in 1870 in Columbia, South Carolina. The school awarded its first degree and adopted its present name in 1984.

1870   Freedmen's Education Supported. The Western Freedmen's Aid Commission merged with the American Methodist Association. The commission was originally formed by clergy who withdrew from the Cincinnati Contraband Relief Association when their proposal to educate freedmen through the association was opposed.

FEBRUARY 2, 1870   Wright Became Associate Justice of South Carolina Supreme Court. Jonathan Jasper Wright, a well-educated Pennsylvanian, became associate justice of the South Carolina Supreme Court. Wright served for seven years as the highest black judicial officer in the nation. Although Wright was one of only three members of the court, he exercised no influence on behalf of African American rights. Yet white Democratic leaders sought constantly to have him removed on charges of corruption. Wright left the bench in 1877 as black reconstruction toppled in the state.

FEBRUARY 25, 1870 Revels Took Seat in U.S. Congress. Hiram R. Revels of Mississippi took Jefferson Davis' former seat in the U.S. Senate, becoming the only African American in Congress. Revels, a former barber and preacher, was a reluctant politician. It is said that his fervent prayer before the Mississippi legislature in 1870 persuaded many to vote for him. Many Democrats opposed his selection to the Senate and argued vainly that he could not legally be seated, not having been a citizen before the Civil War. (Constitutionally, senators must be U.S. citizens for at least nine years). After retiring from politics, leaving an undistinguished legislative record behind him, Revels became president of Alcorn College for Negroes in Mississippi.

MARCH 30, 1870 Fifteenth Amendment Ratified. The Fifteenth Amendment, forbidding the denial of the right to vote to American citizens, was ratified.

MAY 31, 1870–OCTOBER 17, 1871 Protection Extended to African American Voters. Congress and President Ulysses S. Grant made efforts to prevent intimidation of African American voters. The Enforcement Acts (Ku Klux Klan Acts) and a presidential proclamation were the most important measures.

DECEMBER 12, 1870 Rainey Elected to U.S. House. Joseph H. Rainey of South Carolina was seated in the U.S. House of Representatives. Rainey was born to slave parents in Georgetown, South Carolina, in 1832. His own freedom was purchased before the Civil War by his father, a barber. A well-educated mulatto, Rainey himself became a barber in Charleston. Even though he was a respected member of the Charleston black community, he was called to work on fortifications by the Confederates during the Civil War. Rainey refused and exiled himself in the West Indies, where he remained until the end of the Civil War. During Reconstruction, he returned to South Carolina and served as a delegate to the Constitutional Convention of 1868. In 1870 he was elected to the

South Carolina Supreme Court justice Jonathan Wright. (*Harper's Weekly.*)

state senate, but soon resigned to accept the House seat vacated by B. Franklin Whittimore. Rainey was then elected to the four succeeding congresses. As a House member, he frequently spoke in favor of education and other social advances for African Americans. The House's first black member was also a consultant to President Rutherford B. Hayes and once received the president's personal commendation for sobriety and attention to duty. After returning from Congress in 1879, Rainey served as an Internal Revenue Service (IRS) agent in South Carolina, then entered business in Washington, D.C. He returned to Georgetown in 1886 and died there a year later.

1871

1871 Alcorn University Established. The state of Mississippi purchased the defunct Oakland College in 1871 as a school for black men. Located in Lorman, Alcorn University, as it was then known, became a land grant institution in 1878. Alcorn State's first president, Hiram Revels, was the first black elected to the U.S. Senate.

Senator Hiram Revels. (*Harper's Weekly.*)

1871   Claflin College Founded. In 1871, Baker Biblical Institute, which was founded in 1866, merged with Claflin University, founded in 1869. The Orangeburg, South Carolina, school granted its first diploma in 1882. Claflin College is a traditionally black institution.

OCTOBER 1871   Octavius Catto Murdered. Octavius Catto, the headmaster of the Institute for Colored Youth in Philadelphia, Pennsylvania was shot and killed on the night of a city election.

1872

1872   Paul Quinn College Founded. A group of black circuit-riding A.M.E. ministers founded Paul Quinn College in Austin, Texas. The school moved to Waco in 1887 and Dallas in 1990.

1872   South Carolina State University Founded. South Carolina State University was founded as South Carolina Agricultural and Mechanical Institute in 1872 in Orangeburg. From 1872 to 1895 the school existed as part of

Claflin College; it opened independently in 1896 as a land grant institution.

DECEMBER 11, 1872   Pinchback Was First African American Governor. P. B. S. Pinchback, a former Union officer and lieutenant governor of Louisiana, was named temporary governor of the state, becoming the first African American to serve as a state governor. He served for forty-three days as incumbent Henry C. Warmoth was impeached. Pinchback was the son of a white Mississippi planter and army officer and a mulatto woman who bore nine other children. His father moved his children north for manumission. Young Pinchback was tutored at home and then formal schooled in Cincinnati, Ohio. After his father's death, he worked on Mississippi river boats. During the Civil War, Pinchback organized a company of Union volunteers at New Orleans and became their captain. He held many political offices during the Reconstruction of Louisiana, including U.S. senator. Pinchback earned a reputation as a shrewd, aggressive politician.

1873

1873   Bennett College Founded. Bennett Seminary was founded in Greensboro, North Carolina, by the United Methodist Church in 1873. It adopted the name Bennett College in 1889. Bennett is one of the few remaining four-year liberal arts colleges for women and one of only two historically black colleges for women.

1873   Slaughterhouse Cases. The Supreme Court's first interpretation of the Fourteenth Amendment was revealed in its ruling on the slaughterhouse cases. With only a five-to-four majority, the court came forth with a conservative precedent that defined the way the equal protection and due process clauses would be applied for the next decade. The court heard the case after a butchering company mainly comprised of blacks challenged a Louisiana statute that gave another slaughtering opera-

The first African American senator, Hiram Revels, and U.S. congressional representatives from Alabama, Florida, Georgia, and South Carolina. (Courtesy of Library of Congress.)

tion a twenty-five-year monopoly in New Orleans. The black firm argued that the law violated the Fourteenth Amendment in that it defied their equal protection of laws and their rights to the privileges and immunities of citizenship. The court rejected all of their claims.

1873 Wiley College Opened. Wiley College opened in two frame buildings just south of Marshall, Texas. The school, affiliated with the Methodist Church, was chartered in 1882 by the Freedmen's Aid Society to provide educational opportunities for newly freed men.

NOVEMBER 1873 University of South Carolina Appointed First Black Faculty Member. The first black graduate of Harvard University, Richard T. Greener, was appointed to the faculty of the University of South Carolina. Some of the university's white students and faculty left the college when it was integrated.

1874

JANUARY 24, 1874 Historian Schomburg Born. Bibliophile, curator, writer, and mason Arturo

Alfonso Schomburg was born to Carlos and Maria Schomburg in San Juan, Puerto Rico. He attended public schools in San Juan and graduated from the Instituto de Instrucción and the Instituto de Enseñanza Popular. Schomburg attended St. Thomas College in the Virgin Islands and began to collect books and photographs about Puerto Ricans of African descent. (The passion for collecting material sprang from an incident in grade school—a teacher asked him to write an essay on his heritage and he was unable to find any material.)

Schomburg expands his collection to include all people of African descent—by 1926 his collection included over 5,000 books, 3,000 manuscripts, 2,000 etchings, and several thousand pamphlets. In April 1891, he went to New York City and became a member of the Puerto Rico Revolutionary Party. He became a mason a year later. Schomburg wrote *Racial Integrity: A Plea for the Establishment of a Chair of Negro History in Our Schools, Colleges, etc.,* and magazine articles and brochures on masonry. In 1927, he received the William E. Harmon Award for his outstanding work. He served as curator in 1932 for the Division of Negro Literature, History, and Prints at the New York Public Library. Schomburg died June 10, 1938.

APRIL 4, 1874 Sculptor Hathaway Born. Isaac Scott Hathaway was born in Lexington, Kentucky. Hathaway, an African American sculptor, ceramist, and educator, studied at Chandler College, Pittsburgh College, and the New England Conservatory of Music. The U.S. Mint commissioned the noted ceramist to design the Booker T. Washington and George Washington Carver memorial coins. Hathaway's most famous works were portrait busts of Washington, Frederick Douglass, and Paul Lawrence Dunbar.

JULY 31, 1874 African American Priest Presided over Georgetown University. Father Patrick Francis Healy became president of Georgetown University, the oldest Catholic college in the United States. Healy, the brother of James Augustine Healy, the first African American to become a Roman Catholic bishop, headed the institution until 1883.

Historian Arthur Schomburg. (AP/Wide World Photos.)

1875

1875 Alabama A&M Founded. Alabama Agricultural & Mechanical University was founded as Huntsville Normal School in 1875. The first president was William Hooper Councill, a former slave. It became a land-grant institution with the passage of the Morrill Act in 1890 and moved to its present location in Normal, Alabama, a suburb of Huntsville. Alabama A&M achieved the status of junior college in 1919 and awarded its first bachelor's degree in 1941. In 1969, the school adopted its present name.

1875 Houston-Tillotson College Was Established. Historically black Tillotson College was established in 1875 in Austin, Texas. In 1952, it merged with another historically black college, Samuel Houston College, which was founded in 1876, to form Houston-Tillotson College.

1875 Knoxville College Founded. The McKee School for Negro Youth, founded in 1863 in Knoxville, Tennessee, became Knoxville College. Knoxville, founded by Presbyterian missionaries, was dedicated to the development of first-generation college students.

1875 Classes Began at the University of Arkansas at Pine Bluff. The first classes at the historically black University of Arkansas at Pine Bluff were taught to seven students in a rented building. In 1882 the state built the university a two-story brick building. From 1894 to 1929 the school, then known as Branch Normal College, operated as a junior college. University of Arkansas at Pine Bluff adopted its current name when it joined the University of Arkansas System in 1972.

MARCH 1, 1875 Bill Prohibited Discrimination in Accommodations. A Civil Rights Bill was passed by Congress that prohibited discrimination in places of public accommodation. Inns, public conveyances on land or water, theaters, "and other places of public amusement" were included among those accommodations to which "all persons within the jurisdiction of the United States" were entitled to enjoy, regardless of any previous condition of servitude. Because of economic deprivation and prickly legal arrangements, few African Americans were able to take advantage of the law's provisions. The U.S. Supreme Court overturned the law in 1883.

MARCH 15, 1875 Bruce Served as Mississippi's Second Black Senator. Mississippi's second black senator, thirty-five-year-old Blanche K. Bruce, took his seat in Congress. He was the only African American to serve a full term in the U.S. Senate until the mid-twentieth century. The native Virginian was born a slave and worked as a body servant for the son of a wealthy planter. When his young master took him to the Confederate Army as a valet, Bruce escaped in Missouri. There he established a school for blacks. Bruce later attended Oberlin College, where he studied for two years. After the Civil War, he became a modestly wealthy Mississippi planter, taught school occasionally, and held minor political offices as a Republican before being elected to the Senate. Bruce's good reputation even won him a few votes from white Democrats in the Mississippi legislature. However, when Bruce's fellow senator (a white) from Mississippi refused to escort him to be sworn in, as was the custom, Senator Roscoe Conkling of New York took Bruce's hand and led him to the front of the chamber. It was a well-publicized event and an historic moment.

APRIL 17, 1875 Nash Used Character to Impeach. A news article that appeared in *Harper's Weekly* described how black South Carolina statesman Beverly Nash aided in the removal of the state treasurer from office. The treasurer's supporters had apparently been jeered the investigators, calling them "Chadbands," a name derived from a character in a book. Nash reportedly read the description of Chadband from

Mississippi senator Blanche Bruce. (Courtesy of the U.S. Senate Historical Office.)

the book, then noted that the character more closely resembled the treasurer. The antic apparently won the popular support of the legislature and the treasurer was removed.

1876

1876 Bouchet Was First African American to Earn Ph.D. Reportedly, the first doctor of philosophy degree to be awarded to an African American by a major university was bestowed upon Edward A. Bouchet, a physicist, by Yale University.

1876 First All-Black Medical School Established. Meharry Medical College, the first all-black medical school in the United States (and still one of only three), was established in Nashville, Tennessee, in 1876, as the medical department of Central Tennessee College. Dentistry and pharmacy were added to the school's curriculum over the next few years. In 1915, it became its own institution. Currently, about 40 percent of all black physicians and dentists in the United States are graduates of Meharry.

1876   Stillman College Founded. Tuscaloosa Institute, which later came to be called Stillman College, was founded in Tuscaloosa, Alabama, as a theological training school for black men. The school's general assembly approved the enrollment of women in 1899. Stillman College became a four-year liberal arts institution in 1948. It is a private school affiliated with the Presbyterian Church.

MARCH 8, 1876   Pinchback Refused Congressional Seat. The U.S. Senate, following three years of debate and controversy, refused to seat P. B. S. Pinchback of Louisiana. In the fall of 1872, Pinchback was elected to the U.S. House of Representatives and later to the U.S. Senate in the winter of 1873. During the long debate over Pinchback's case, including nearly an entire extra session of Congress, the affable Pinchback became a national political figure as well as a prominent name in Washington society. Opponents of Pinchback argued that he had not been properly elected and was not qualified; others insisted that the opposition to Pinchback supposedly stemmed from senators' wives being against social intercourse with Pinchback's wife, thereby resulting in their husbands' negative votes.

MARCH 27, 1876   *United States v. Cruikshank.* In *United States v. Cruikshank,* the Supreme Court reversed the indictments and convictions of whites involved in the 1873 killings of 280 blacks in Colfax, Louisiana. The defendants had been convicted for violating the Civil Rights Enforcement Act of 1870 which prohibited the interference of civil rights due to race. The high court, however, ruled that the racial motivations behind the attack had not been specified, so the intent to deprive blacks of civil rights had not been proven. The charges were dropped.

MARCH 27, 1876   *United States v. Reese.* In its *United States v. Reese* ruling, the Supreme Court reversed a federal Civil Rights Enforcement Act that made illegal the obstruction of any person's vote. The issue went before the court when federal prosecutors charged a Kentucky voting official with violating the law when he refused to count an African American's vote. The Supreme Court, however, declared that control over suffrage rested in states' hands, and so, the federal Enforcement Act was unlawful as Congress had overextended its authority in enacting it.

JUNE 25, 1876   Battle of Little Big Horn. Angered by the advancing whites, Sioux tribesmen led by Sitting Bull massacred 264 U.S. cavalrymen. One of the casualties was a black army interpreter, Isaiah Dorman, who had briefly lived with the Sioux.

JULY 8–OCTOBER 26, 1876   Racial Unrest Swelled in South Carolina. Racial disturbances in South Carolina resulted in President Ulysses S. Grant's ordering federal troops in to restore order. In Hamburg, five blacks were killed in July.

SEPTEMBER 26, 1876   Educator William Jasper Hale Born. William Jasper Hale began his administrative work at a small African American elementary school and worked his way up to the role of principal of the African American St. Elmo secondary school in Chattanooga, Tennessee. In 1911 Hale was appointed principal of the Tennessee Agricultural and Industrial State Normal School, Tennessee's first and only African American state college. He later became its president. His administrative talents helped land the school a fully accredited four-year status in the 1920s. During Hale's thirty-one-year-tenure, enrollment grew from 200 to 3,000.

Hale was president of the Conference of the Negro Land Grant Colleges, and he founded and was president of the Tennessee Inter-Racial League. He received the Harmon Foundation Medal in 1930 for advancing black education in the South and was a member of the Nashville Board of Trade and of President Herbert Hoover's Negro Housing Committee.

Hale died on October 5, 1944, in New York City.

1877

1877 First Black West Point Graduated. Henry Ossian Flipper finished 50th in a class of 76, becoming West Point's first African American graduate. He was commissioned as a second lieutenant and assigned to the all-black 10th Cavalry Regiment in Texas. In 1878 he penned an autobiography, *The Colored Cadet at West Point.* Flipper served in Texas until 1881 when he was dismissed for allegedly embezzling funds, a charge he vehemently denied for the rest of his life. After his dismissal, Flipper worked as an engineer and a miner. He continued to write, publishing at least three books. He contributed articles to the *Old Santa Fe* and several newspapers.

His knowledge of law was impressive and made him a valuable commodity to employers. Between 1892 and 1903 he worked in the Court of Private Land Claims of the Department of Justice as a special agent. Flipper voluteered his services at the start of the Spanish-American War, and two legislators initiated bills to reinstitute Flipper's military rank. Both bills failed to garner support. In 1919 Flipper moved to Washington to work as a subcommittee translator and interpreter of Spanish. In 1923 he left the government in the wake of the Teapot Dome scandal (he was not implicated) and worked for an oil company in Venezuela. In 1930 he moved to Atlanta and lived with his brother, Joseph. Flipper died of a heart attack in 1940. He was exonerated posthumously by the military in 1976.

1877 Jackson State University Opened. The school that would become Jackson State University in 1974 opened in 1877 as the Natchez Seminary in Natchez, Mississippi. Established by the American Baptist Home Mission Society for the moral, religious, and intellectual improvement of the black leaders of Mississip-

West Point graduate Henry Flipper. (Courtesy of National Archives.)

pi, the Natchez Seminary moved to Jackson in 1882. The school operated as a private church-school until 1940 when it became a state institution for training rural and elementary school teachers.

FEBRUARY 26, 1877 Hayes Met with Southern Representatives. Representatives of presidential candidate Rutherford B. Hayes met with representatives from the South at the black-operated Wormely Hotel in Washington, D.C. A complicated agreement was reached that led to the election of Hayes as president and the removal of the last federal troops supporting black reconstruction in the South.

FEBRUARY 26, 1877 Mainstream Press Praised Progress. The network of benevolent institutions pulling together human and monetary resources for the purpose of educating blacks gained recognition from the mainstream press that typically ignored black topics. *The New York Times* praised the significant contributions to black education of the African Methodist Episcopal Church, the American Missionary Association, and the Freedmen's Aid Society of the Methodist Episcopal Church. The *Times*

Philanthropic institutions provided resources for schools such as this one in South Carolina. (Courtesy of Library of Congress.)

article asserted that most of the work by white churches was done by those in the North while those in the South "plead poverty as their excuse for not doing more. . . . If their work is not stopped by the White Leaguers, they will effect a great improvement in the intellectual and moral condition of the next generation of their people."

MARCH 18, 1877 Douglass Appointed Marshal for D.C. Despite Southern opposition—and opposition from within his own party—

President Rutherford Hayes appointed Frederick Douglass marshal for the District of Columbia.

1878

1878 *Hall v. Decuir.* The U.S. Supreme Court, in *Hall v. Decuir,* ruled that state anti-discrimination laws were not applicable to interstate carriers. The court heard the case of a steamboat operator who had appealed a Louisiana state court judgment against him for refusing transportation to a woman because of her race.

1878   Journalist Jesse Max Barber Born. Jesse Barber was born in Blackstock, South Carolina, to Jesse Max and Susan Barber, former slaves. Barber worked his way through school, earning a bachelor's degree from Virginia Union University in Richmond. Following graduation, he moved to Atlanta to help start a new publication, *The Voice of the Negro*. Barber worked his way up from managing editor to principal editor of the publication, which became a respected and popular magazine. As editor, Barber was an outspoken advocate of the early civil rights movement. In 1905 he was one of twenty-nine who answered W. E. B. Du Bois's call to form the Niagara Movement, a "radical" group that was the predecessor of the NAACP. When *The Voice* folded in 1907, Barber returned to school, earning a degree in dentistry. He began a professional practice in Philadelphia in 1912. Barber worked with the newly-formed NAACP, serving as president of its Philadelphia branch and as a member of its national board of directors for several years. Barber's final public activity was the founding of the John Brown Memorial Association, a group formed to raise funds for a statue honoring the famed abolitionist. The statue was erected in 1935 in North Elba, New York. Barber continued his dental practice until his death in Philadelphia in September 1949.

1878   Selma University Founded. Selma University was founded in Selma, Alabama, to train African Americans for careers as teachers and ministers. In 1881 the school was incorporated; the first class—11 coeds—graduated in 1884. The name Selma University was adopted in 1908 when the school was granted the right to confer degrees and grant diplomas. Selma is affiliated with the Alabama State Baptist Convention.

1878   State Supported Black School. Eight black men became the first blacks to enroll at a state-supported school in Texas when they enrolled at the Agricultural and Mechanical College of Texas for Colored Youths. The school, now known as Prairie View A&M University, is the second oldest institution of higher education in the state of Texas.

NOVEMBER 16, 1878   Violent Democrats Reprimanded. A *Harper's Weekly* article denounced the practices of the Red Shirts, an organization of Southern Democrats who were violently interrupting black-inclusive Republican meetings and, the article claimed, stifling the party. The writer asserted, "The Ku-Klux has been revived under the name of Red Shirts [and] this new form of the Ku-Klux has done more to justify the estimate of 'the South' as a nest of hopeless barbarism than any recent event."

1879

1879   "Exodus of 1879" Disappointed Southern Blacks. Large numbers of Southern blacks, frustrated with discrimination and poverty in the South, emigrated to the West. Most were disappointed in the "Exodus of 1879" as they met white and Indian hostility in the West. The most prominent leader of the exodus, which led principally to Kansas, was Benjamin "Pap" Singleton. He was a former mulatto slave who, after a number of unsuccessful attempts, made his way to freedom in Canada. Singleton favored racial separatism and encouraged industriousness among blacks. Many of the better educated blacks were hostile to Singleton's movement, especially to his concept of a black community apart from white influence.

1879   Livingstone College Founded. A.M.E. Zion ministers founded Zion Wesley Institute, now Livingstone College, in Salisbury, North Carolina. The college started in the parsonage of Bishop C. R. Harris and moved to a one-building, 40-acre site in 1882. Livingstone awarded its first bachelor's degree in 1887.

Pioneer Exodusers who started the colony Nicodemus in Kansas. (Courtesy of the Denver Public Library-Wester Collection.)

APRIL 26, 1879 Flight of Black Labor Addressed. An article in *Harper's Weekly* attempted to explain the migration of thousands of blacks from the South, Mississippi, and Louisiana in particular, to Kansas. The article refuted other claims that Southern blacks were not far behind whites with regard to education, wages, and civil rights: "If the colored people felt sure of fair wages and fair play at the polls in Mississippi, they would certainly not go by hundreds to Kansas. . . . Agents and knaves and demagogues may have promised mules and forty acres and a charming climate, but they would have been vain allurements against fair play at home."

1880

1880 Louisiana Supported Black Education. With support from the nation's first black governor, P. B. S. Pinchback, Louisiana legislators passed provisions for a school for blacks. Southern University was established as a result of this legislation, opening its doors to 12 students in 1881. Five years later the state appropriated $14,000 for new facilities for the

school. An agricultural and mechanical department was added in 1890 and within a year Southern became a land-grant institution.

1880 *Neal v. Delaware.* The Supreme Court, in *Neal v. Delaware,* reversed an African American's death sentence because of the admission, by the state attorney general, that blacks had purposefully been excluded from the trial jury.

1880 *Strauder v. West Virginia.* A West Virginia law that excluded blacks from jury service was declared unconstitutional by the U.S. Supreme Court in *Strauder v. West Virginia.* The case was heard by the court after Taylor Strauder, a black man found guilty of murder, petitioned to have his case heard by a federal court because, he claimed, he could not be tried fairly by West Virginia's all-white jury system.

MARCH 1, 1880 *Virginia v. Rives.* A challenge of jury selection practices failed in front of the U.S. Supreme Court with the *Virginia v. Rives* case. Two Virginia blacks accused of murdering a white man had petitioned for a new jury pool when the original one turned up all white. The state refused on grounds that the pool was selected in accordance with Virginia law, which did not exclude blacks. The high court upheld that decision, leaving states free to appoint state officials who would not choose blacks for the jury panels though they were legally able to participate.

APRIL 6, 1880 West Point Black Assaulted. Twenty-one year old Johnson Chesnutt Whittaker, the only African American at the U.S. Military Academy at West Point in 1880, was found unconscious in his room by a guard. Whittaker's hands were bound, his legs were tied to the bedposts, and his earlobes and hair were cut. Upon investigation, Whittaker said he had been assaulted by three masked attackers. However, he was found guilty of self-mutilation by a military court of inquiry. When another military court of inquiry sustained that decision, an unfavorable public reaction led

P. B. S. Pinchback, the first African American governor. (AP/Wide World Photos.)

President Rutherford B. Hayes to appoint a new superintendent to West Point. Whittaker was then granted a leave of absence and a court martial. According to news accounts in *Harper's Weekly* at the time, the facts demonstrated the Administration was not satisfied that Whittaker had received a fair opportunity at West Point. In 1881 a court martial found him guilty of self-mutilation. March 22, 1882 President Chester Arthur invalidated the trial on the recommendations of the judge-advocate of the army and the Secretary of War. Later that day, Whittaker was dismissed from the academy for failing an exam in June of 1880.

Whittaker was born a slave August 23, 1858 to James Whitaker, a free black and Maria Whitaker, a slave. Later he added the second "t" to his name. He attended the University of South Carolina and received a congressman's appointment to the U.S. Military Academy at West Point. After leaving the academy he taught at Avery Institute, in Charleston, South Carolina. He later practiced law in Sumpter. Page E. Harrison married him in 1890 and they had two sons. Whittaker died January 14, 1931 of a gastric ulcer. October 1995 Whittaker was

honored with a commission as second lieutenant by President Bill Clinton, who made the presentation to the cadet's granddaughter and great-grandson.

1881

1881   Army Dismissed Lieutenant Flipper. The U.S. Army dismissed Lieutenant Henry Ossian Flipper for allegedly having embezzled funds. Flipper, the first African American to graduate from West Point Military Academy, was the only black officer in the U.S. Army. He denied the charges to his dying day, blaming the dismissal on racism. Although a congressman and a senator attempted to clear Flipper's name through legislation, their bills died in committees. He was not exonerated until 1976, some thirty-six years after his death.

1881   Morris Brown College Opened. Morris Brown College opened with two teachers and 107 students. Affiliated with the A.M.E. Church, the school was founded "for the Christian education of negro boys and girls in Atlanta." Morris Brown operated as a primary, secondary, and normal school until 1894, when its college department was established.

1881   Tennessee Segregates Railroad Cars. Tennessee took the lead in requiring segregation in railroad cars. By 1907, all of the Southern states required segregation in public accommodations.

1881   Tuskegee University Founded. Tuskegee University was founded in Tuskegee, Alabama, as a school for rural black children. Booker T. Washington was the new school's first principal. Though it started in a one-room shack, the school expanded into an abandoned plantation that remains the heart of the present-day campus. Tuskegee established the first degree-granting nursing program in Alabama and was

Tuskegee Institute.

the first training ground for black military pilots. Tuskegee achieved university status in 1967.

APRIL 11, 1881   Spelman College Founded. Originally the Atlanta Baptist Female Academy, Spelman College was founded in Atlanta, Georgia, to provide education for newly-freed black women. Classes were first held in a damp church basement with eleven pupils who were determined to learn to read the Bible and write well enough to send letters to their families in the North. John D. Rockefeller, impressed by the school on a visit, became an early benefactor by paying off a $6,700 debt on buildings purchased for the school. It became "the Radcliffe and the Sarah Lawrence of Negro education."

MAY 17, 1881   Douglass Named Recorder of Deeds for D.C. President James A. Garfield appointed Frederick Douglass the recorder of deeds for the District of Columbia.

MAY 19, 1881   Bruce Appointed Register of the Treasury. President James A. Garfield appointed former Senator Blanche K. Bruce of Mississippi register of the treasury.

AUGUST 6, 1881   Garnett Appointed Minister to Liberia. Reverend Henry Highland Garnett was appointed minister to Liberia. In 1816, at the age of eight, Garnett freed himself from slavery after his master died. In 1839 he graduated from Oneida Collegiate Institute and, in 1842, from Troy Theological College.

1882

1882   CME Church Founded. After the Civil War, black members of the Methodist Episcopal Church South established the Colored (now Christian) Methodist Episcopal Church. Recognizing the need to train black ministers and teachers, the CME Church created the Paine Institute in Augusta, Georgia, within the year. Paine Institute was chartered in 1883 and adopted the name Paine College in 1903.

1882   Lane College Founded. The historically black Lane College was founded in 1882 as the Colored Methodist Episcopal High School. It became Lane College in 1896 and awarded its first bachelor's degree in 1899.

1882   Virginia Normal Founded. Virginia Normal and Collegiate Institute was founded in 1882, though a hostile lawsuit prevented from it from opening until 1883. The historically black college awarded its first bachelor's degrees in 1889. Now known as Virginia State University, the school is located in Petersburg, Virginia, and is one of Virginia's two land grant institutions.

1882   Philander Smith College Received Donation. Adeline Smith donated $10,500 to Walden Seminary in 1882, five years after the seminary was founded, to provide educational opportunities to freedmen west of the Mississippi River. In appreciation, the school changed its name to Philander Smith College, after Smith's husband. Located in Little Rock, Arkansas, the college was chartered as a four-year institution in 1883 and awarded its first bachelor's degree in 1888.

1882 United States v. Harris. The Supreme Court struck the third Enforcement Act (Ku Klux Act) of 1871, which made it illegal to block a state's execution of equal protection of the laws. Twenty whites, R. G. Harris among them, had been charged with violating this portion of the law when they attacked four black suspects in police custody. But the Enforcement Act was nulled because, the court said, it went beyond the boundaries of the Thirteenth and Fourteenth Amendments, which made punishable acts of discrimination by the state, not by private persons. The men were acquitted and private acts of discrimination were, in effect, legalized.

1883

1883 Pace v. Alabama. The Supreme Court, in *Pace v. Alabama,* unanimously upheld an Alabama law that provided a harsher sentence for interracial adulterers than for same-race offenders. The law was not discriminatory, the court ruled, because the same punishment was mandated for both offenders.

MARCH 20, 1883 African American Shoemaker Patented Machine. Jan E. Matzeliger, a Massachusetts shoemaker, invented a complicated machine that manufactured an entire shoe. The invention, which was sold to the United Shoe Company, revolutionized the industry. By 1880, machines were able to cut and stitch the leather, but not to shape and attach the upper portion of the shoe to the sole. This had to be done by hand, a slow and tedious process. Working in secret, Matzeliger tackled the "lasting" problem for ten years. In 1883, he received the patent for his perfected product, a "lasting machine," which could hold the shoe on the last, grip and pull the leather down around the heel, set and drive the nails, and discharge the completed shoe.

SEPTEMBER 27, 1883 Blacks Outlined Needs. The National Colored Convention met in Louisville, Kentucky, and presented an outline of societal changes desired by African Americans. The proclamation focused on the discrepancy between the rights that all citizens have by law and the rights that blacks, particularly in the South, felt did not exist for them. The address called for an end to the plantation, credit, and mortgage systems and segregation of schools and the armed forces. Conventioneers also called for reforms in the voting and justice systems.

OCTOBER 15, 1883 Civil Rights Act Ruled Unconstitutional. The U.S. Supreme Court ruled that the Civil Rights Act of 1875 was unconstitutional. The Reconstruction Amendments, the court reasoned, did not extend into the area of public accommodations.

NOVEMBER 26, 1883 Death of Sojourner Truth. Sojourner Truth died in Battle Creek, Michigan. Truth was born in 1797 as a slave, with the name Isabella, in Hurley, New York. The mother of five children, she was separated from her husband prior to gaining her freedom in 1827. After her statutory emancipation in New York in 1827, Truth went to work for a "religious fanatic" named Pierson in New York City. By 1843, she had become disillusioned with Pierson and left, proclaiming that her name was no longer Isabella, but Sojourner. She said that "the Lord gave [her] Truth, because [she] was to declare the truth to the people." She became a legendary "sojourner," as she traveled about espousing abolition, women's rights, and other reforms. She held steadfastly to the belief that she was a chosen messenger of God. Though illiterate, Truth made a substantial impression upon her audiences. On one occasion, when Frederick Douglass was speaking at Faneuil Hall in Boston, he said that blacks could not hope to find justice in America. Truth countered this pessimism by asking "Frederick, is God dead?" Truth also played a prominent role in the Second National Women's Suffrage Convention in Akron, Ohio, in

Sojourner Truth. (*Harper's Weekly.*)

1852. During the Civil War, she supported the arming of slaves and helped care for wounded soldiers and freedmen. During the Reconstruction era and until the end of her life, she urged property ownership and education as keys to black advancement.

1884

1884   Arkansas Baptist College. The Arkansas Baptist Consolidated Convention opened the

Minister's Institute in 1884. The school became Arkansas Baptist College the next year.

1884   Black Journalist Founded *New York Age*. T. Thomas Fortune founded the *New York Age*. Fortune, born in Florida in 1856 to mulatto parents, was the leading African American journalist until the World War I. After the Civil War, he attended a Freedmen's Bureau school. Fortune's father, a tanner and shoe merchant, served several terms in the Florida legislature during Reconstruction and secured for his son an appointment as page boy in the state senate. The family's political activities and close social contacts with some whites created racial animosity among other whites that eventually forced the family from the capital to Jacksonville, where Fortune's father became town marshal. Fortune himself went to Washington, where he attended Howard University, partly from earnings secured as a special customs agent in Delaware. After leaving Howard, he taught briefly in Florida but soon left for New York.

In 1879, Fortune began his long newspaper career in New York City. He first worked at the *New York Sun,* one of the city's leading newspapers. He published three books—the well-known *Black and White* (1884), a historical essay on land, labor, and politics in the South, as well as *The Negro in Politics* (1885) and *Dreams of Life* (1905). He was active in Republican politics after the Civil War and advocated civil rights for blacks. Fortune closely identified with Booker T. Washington and his ideas, but in later years edited some of Marcus Garvey's black nationalist publications. During World War I, Fortune helped establish the famous 369th black regiment. He died in 1928.

1884   Oscar Micheaux Born. Ficton writer Oscar Micheaux was born in 1884. Although his semiautobiographical stories were considered poor writing by some, Micheaux ensured their success with extensive promotional tours. His third book, *The Homesteader* (1917), attracted the interest of the black, independant Lincoln Motion Picture Company. When Micheaux stubbornly insisted on directing the film version, the company backed out, and Micheaux himself set about financing the film. He found support from the Oklahoma farmers who had funded his novels and thus organized the Oscar Micheaux Corporation in New York City. *The Homesteader* was its first product, released in 1919.

Micheaux went on to produce about thirty more pictures from 1919 to 1937, most suffering from quick production and low budgets. The plots were standard melodramas featuring light-skinned blacks who were often touted as African American versions of Hollywood stars. Micheaux was responsible for the screen debut of Paul Robeson in *Body and Soul* (1924). On April 1, 1951, Micheaux died in Charlotte, North Carolina.

JANUARY 3, 1884   Woods Received His First Patent. Granville T. Woods received his first patent for a steam boiler furnace. The invention, which used a more efficient method of combustion and therefore economized fuel, was the first of about thirty-five that he patented throughout his life. Though Woods dealt mainly with electricity as it pertained to telephone communications and telegraphy, he invented other items such as the incubator and an apparatus consisting of a series of tracks for amusement park rides. Woods retained about one-third of his patents for himself and sold or assigned the others to companies such as General Electric, American Engineering, and Westinghouse Electric and Manufacturing. Woods gained experience with machines at the age of ten when he worked in a machine shop and received instruction in the evenings. At 16 he worked as a fireman and engineer on a Missouri railroad.

1885

1885   Black Minister to Liberia. Reverend Moses A. Hopkins was appointed U.S. minister to Liberia. Hopkins had escaped slavery during the Civil War and joined the Union Army as a cook. He had attended Avery College, Lincoln University, and the Theological Seminary at Auburn, New York, before attaining his position as minister. He had also reportedly organized the Albion Academy in North Carolina with six students under him.

1885   Blues Legend Leadbelly Born. Famous bluesman Huddie Ledbetter was born near Mooringsport, Louisiana, the son of farmers. Taught music by his mother and uncles, Ledbetter earned a reputation as the best guitar player and singer in Louisiana by the time he was sixteen. Nicknamed "Leadbelly" because of his strong base voice, he was deeply influenced by the talented blues singers who played in the red-light district of nearby Shreveport. He switched to a twelve-string guitar immediately after hearing one played. Between 1918 and 1934 Ledbetter's womanizing and volatility landed him in prison several times, and three times he escaped. After serving four years of a ten-year sentence, he was reprieved, thanks to a heartfelt plea for mercy and a recording of his song, "Irene, Good Night." Ledbetter continued to sing and record until his death from Lou Gehrig's Disease in New York City.

JUNE 24, 1885   First Black Bishop Named. Reverend Samuel David Ferguson was named the first black bishop within the American House of Bishops. The Charleston, South Carolina, native had been teaching and ministering in the states for more than twenty years and decided to spread his word in Cape Palmas, Africa, as the fourth bishop to work there as a missionary.

1886

1886   Kentucky State University Opened. The State Normal School for Colored Persons, later Kentucky State University, opened as a teacher-training college. In 1890 the school became a land grant college.

1886   Shorter College Founded. Historically black Shorter College was founded in Little Rock, Arkansas, in 1886 as Bethel University. The name changed to Shorter College in 1903. Shorter was affiliated with the African Methodist Episcopal (A.M.E.) Church.

1886   University of Maryland Eastern Shore Opened. Despite opposition, Princess Anne College opened in Princess Anne, Maryland, as a school for blacks. The school was affiliated with the Methodist Episcopal Church and classes were held in the historic Onley House. The school, now part of the University of Maryland system and known as University of Maryland Eastern Shore, became a land grant institution in 1890.

JUNE 12, 1886   Former Slaveholder Bequeathed Fortune to Black Daughter. The Georgia state supreme court sustained the will of the late David Dickson, thus making Amanda Eubanks the wealthiest African American of her day. Dickson, a former slaveholder, willed more than a half million dollars to Eubanks. White relatives of Dickson, a bachelor, had contested the will on the grounds that it was illegal for a white man to leave property to his black illegitimate children. The court disagreed.

1887

1887   Central State University Founded. The Normal and Industrial Department, later Central State University, was founded by Wilberforce University in Wilberforce, Ohio. Central State is Ohio's only predominantly black public institution of higher education and is also one of

H. P. Cheatham. (*Harper's Weekly.*)

only a few black institutions located in the North.

1887   Florida A&M Opened. When Florida A&M University opened as the State Normal College for Colored Students in 1887, it had only two teachers and 15 students. The Tallahassee school became a land grant institution in 1890 and in 1905 offered post-secondary education for the first time. Florida A&M awarded its first bachelor's degree in 1910 and achieved university status in 1953 when it adopted its present name.

1888

1888   St. Paul's College Founded. Located in Lawrenceville, Virginia, St. Paul's Normal and Industrial School was founded by the Episcopal Church. This historically black school changed its name in 1957 to St. Paul's College.

NOVEMBER 1888   Monument to Crispus Attucks. Boston presented a monument in commemoration of Crispus Attucks, the leader of the 1770 Boston Massacre in which five Americans were slain by British soldiers. Attucks is believed to have been of African and Native American descent.

NOVEMBER 17, 1888   Funds Handed to Education. Businessman Daniel Hand donated one million dollars to the American Missionary Association for the purpose of educating blacks.

1889

C. 1889   Add Earned Fame as Cowboy. Celebrated rider and bronco buster known variously as Nigger Add, Old Add, and Old Negro Add was the only black range boss in the Southwest. He worked for the LFD brand owned by cattleman George Littlefield. Reportedly, Add could break any horse and was thrown only once in his life. His roping skills were also legendary. Add worked primarily in the Texas Panhandle and eastern New Mexico. By the end of the century, probably due to increasing racism, Add was no longer a range boss. Add died around 1906, a horseman all his life. The dates of his birth and death and his surname are still unknown.

JANUARY 1889   Death of Samuel Sewall. Harvard graduate Samuel E. Sewall died at the age of ninety. Sewall had counseled fugitive slaves and played a role in the cases of John Brown and Dred Scott. *Harper's Weekly* called him the oldest Free-Soiler in the country.

MARCH 1889   H. P. Cheatham Joined Congress. H. P. Cheatham took his seat in the U.S. House of Representatives, following his election the previous November. At the time, he was the only African American in Congress. Cheatham was born in Henderson, North Carolina, in 1857. He graduated from Shaw University in Raleigh, North Carolina. Cheatham served as superintendent for the Colored State Normal School in Plymouth, North Carolina, until 1885.

Part 4

1890

1890   Black Education Legislated. The 1890 Land Grant Act required states to provide educational training for black youths. The same year, Georgia State Industrial College for Colored Youth, later Savannah State College, was established in Savannah, Georgia, under the law. The school served as Georgia's land-grant school for blacks until 1947. Savannah State awarded its first baccalaureate degree in 1898.

1890   Colored Farmers' Alliance Numbered One Million. The Colored Farmers' Alliance, a socio-economic-political organization dedicated to improving the lot of the black farmer, reached a membership of one million. The Alliance, founded in 1886, included twelve state organizations and many local chapters formed wherever black farmers were sufficiently numerous. There was for a time cooperation between the black group and the white farmers alliance, but this was ruptured when the black group called for a strike by black cotton pickers. Leonidas L. Polk, president of the National Farmers' Alliance, accused the blacks of attempting to better their condition at the expense of whites.

1890   Harris-Stowe State College Opened. The St. Louis, Missouri, public school system opened Sumner Normal School in 1890 to train black elementary school teachers. In 1924, Sumner became a four-year degree-granting college and five years later changed its name to Stowe Teachers College, in honor of abolitionist Harriet Beecher Stowe. The St. Louis Board of Education created the current Harris-Stowe State College in 1954 by merging Stowe with another teaching college. This merger was one of the first steps taken by the board of education to integrate the St. Louis school system.

MARCH 3, 1890   Railway Segregation Upheld. In the case of *Louisville, New Orleans, and Texas Railway Company v. Mississippi,* the Supreme Court upheld a Mississippi law that required separate accommodations for blacks and whites. The railway that challenged the law had argued that separate accommodations placed a burden on interstate carriers, not that it violated civil rights.

JULY 1890   Black Land Purchase Opposed. African Americans looking to begin a vocational school for blacks bought the Kirkwood, Missouri, property on which Anna Sneed Cairns had been operating a female seminary. The wealthy, white community offered Cairns $27,000 for the land in an attempt to keep it from being sold to blacks. But Cairns had little reason to appease the Kirkwood community as her decision to relocate her school stemmed from a quarrel with the town board. Upon settling on a price of $32,000, she accepted a partial payment for the land from Henry Bridgewater, the proprietor of two large saloons for blacks that were reportedly raided frequently. Bridgewater, with his $10,000 donation, became the founder of the first manual training school for blacks.

AUGUST 12–NOVEMBER 1, 1890 Black Voters Disenfranchised by "Understanding" Tests. A constitutional convention in Mississippi adopted the literacy and "understanding" tests as devices to disfranchise black voters. A poll tax of two dollars and a provision excluding voters convicted of bribery, burglary, theft, arson, murder, bigamy, and perjury were also included in the amendment. Before the convention, black delegates from forty counties had met and protested to President Benjamin Harrison their impending disfranchisement. Harrison chose not to interfere. To avoid a fight over ratification, the white proponents of the disfranchising measures declared the amendment to be in effect after passage by the convention.

SEPTEMBER 14, 1890 Maryland Law School Refused Blacks. Blacks were refused admittance into the Maryland Law School after most of the white students of the law, medical, and dental departments petitioned to the school's faculty to implement the measure. Two black students had already graduated from the program with honors; the two who were enrolled at the time of the decision were told not to return.

SEPTEMBER 15, 1890 Writer Claude McKay Born. Writer Claude McKay was born in Jamaica, the son of a farmer. He began writing early in life and published two volumes of poetry shortly after his twentieth birthday. In 1913 he came to the United States to study agriculture, but his desire to write poetry prevailed, and he moved to New York City. He began publishing his work in small literary magazines, traveled abroad, and returned to New York to serve under Max Eastman as associate editor of *The Liberator*. In 1922 he

completed *Harlem Shadows,* a landmark work of the Harlem Renaissance. McKay continued to write, producing novels, poetry, and an autobiography. He died in 1948.

1891

1891 Black Jockey Won Third Kentucky Derby. Isaac Murphy, a black jockey riding "Kingman," became the first man to win three Kentucky Derbys. Murphy won his first Derby in 1884 on "Buchanan" and his second in 1890 on "Riley."

1891 Delaware State University Opened. The State College for Colored Students opened in Dover, Delaware. The school is now known as Delaware State University.

1891 Elizabeth City State University Opened. The Elizabeth State Colored Normal School opened in Elizabeth City, North Carolina, in 1891. It awarded its first bachelor's degree in 1939 and changed its name to Elizabeth City State University in 1969.

1891 North Carolina A&T State University Founded. Historically black North Carolina A&T State University got its start in 1891 as A&M College for the Colored Race, one of two land grant institutions in North Carolina.

1891 West Virginia State College Created. The Second Morrill Act of 1890 stipulated that no land grant institution may receive federal funds unless provisions are made for the education of black youth. To assure continued federal funds for the state's land grant university, the West Virginia Legislature created another school for blacks called the West Virginia Colored Institute. Today the school is known as West Virginia State College. It is located in Institute, West Virginia.

JANUARY 22, 1891 Voter Protection Bill Died in Senate. The Lodge Bill, aiming to prevent infringements on the African American's right to vote, failed in the U.S. Senate.

FEBRUARY 15, 1891   Black Population in the Capital. Census Office statistics showed that the black population in Washington, D.C., had increased 27.4 percent in ten years from 55,596 in 1880 to 75,927 in 1890. In the same decade the white population in the capital had increased 30.8 percent.

JULY 10, 1891   Black Jockey Won Six Straight Races. Black jockey "Monk" Overton won six straight horse races at the Washington Park race track in Chicago. In 1907, another black jockey, Jimmy Lee, also won six straight races at Churchill Downs in Louisville. Prior to 1907, only two other jockeys had equaled the achievements of Overton and Lee—Englishmen Fred Archer and George Fordham.

1892

1892   Mary Holmes College Opened. Mary Holmes Seminary, named for a woman who devoted her life to helping former slaves, opened in Jackson, Mississippi. The Board of Freedmen of the Presbyterian Church had founded the school to provide black females with a Christian education and instruction in the domestic arts. The school moved to West Point in 1897 and eventually changed its name to Mary Holmes College. Men were first admitted in 1932.

1892   Populist Party Gained Support in South. The Populist Party, which at first welcomed black support, became a viable political organization in the South.

1892   Soprano "Black Patti" Performed at White House. Sissieretta Jones, the "Black Patti," performed for President Benjamin Harrison at the White House. Jones, a soprano, was born in Virginia, spent her childhood in Providence, Rhode Island, and studied at the New England Conservatory. She first attracted the attention of critics in 1892 when she appeared at the Jubilee Spectacle and Cakewalk at Madison Square Garden in New York. One critic called her the "Black Patti," a comparison with the Italian prima donna Adelina Patti. According to some authorities, "Black Patti Jones" was sought for roles in *Aida* and *L'Africaine* by the Metropolitan Opera, but the project was dropped, reportedly because the "musical world was not ready to accept black prima donnas." Jones toured Europe in 1893. Upon her return to the United States, she organized an all-black company, "Black Patti's Troubadours," in which she was the featured soloist. Jones died in 1933.

1892   Winston-Salem State University Opened. Winston-Salem's Slater Industrial Academy opened in 1892 in a one-room building for 25 students. The school was known for its quality training of elementary school teachers and was rewarded by the General Assembly of North Carolina in 1925 with a new charter and the authority to confer degrees, making it the first black institution in the United States to grant elementary education degrees. In 1969 the school adopted its present name, Winston-Salem State University.

JUNE 7, 1892   Plessy Arrested. Homer Adolf Plessy purchased a first-class ticket from New Orleans to Covington on the East Louisiana Railway. Plessy, who is believed to have been a carpenter born in New Orleans, was seven-eighths Caucasian and one-eighth African. He boarded the train and took a seat in the coach reserved for whites. When the conductor ordered him to move to the coach reserved for blacks, Plessy refused. An officer removed Plessy from the train and took him to the parish jail of New Orleans where he was charged with criminally violating an 1890 Louisiana statute that required separate accommodations for blacks and whites. In *Plessy v. Ferguson*, Plessy petitioned the Louisiana State Supreme Court for a writ of prohibition and certiorari against John H. Ferguson, judge of the criminal district court for the Parish of Orleans, and he asked the higher courts to prohibit Ferguson from holding the trial. The Louisiana Supreme Court denied Plessy's requests on grounds that the law was constitutional, but his writ of error was passed on to the U.S. Supreme Court.

NOVEMBER 1892 Blacks Left Tennessee. Seven hundred African Americans left Chattanooga in one month. Possible causes were an overcrowded labor market due to the city's declining economy and the prospect of fairer treatment in Northern and Western states.

1893

1893 Lomax-Hannon Junior College Founded. The historically black Lomax-Hannon Junior College was founded in Greenville, Alabama. The idea for the school had been conceived four years earlier at the annual conference of the A.M.E. Zion Church in Montgomery, Alabama. At the time of its founding, Lomax-Hannon was both a high school and a junior college, but the high school department closed in 1975. The A.M.E. Zion Church continues to run the school.

1894

1894 Clinton Junior College Founded. In an attempt to eradicate illiteracy among the freedmen of South Carolina, the A.M.E. Zion Church established Clinton Junior College in Rock Hill.

1894 Painter Henry Tanner Gained Recognition. The Music Lesson, painted by Henry Ossawa Tanner (1859–1937) was accepted by the Société des Artistes for exhibition. Tanner,

originally from Pennsylvania, had moved to Paris in 1891 to escape racism and study art after several failed attempts to make a name for himself in the states. In 1896 Tanner turned to painting biblical themes. His *Daniel in the Lion's Den* was the first, followed by *The Raising of Lazarus*, which was purchased by the French government after winning a medal at the Paris Exhibition of 1897. His other biblical works included *Christ and Nicodemus*, which won a Lippincott prize, *Wise and Foolish Virgins*, and *The Two Disciples at the Tomb*, which won a Harris prize.

Tanner was awarded a gold medal at the Panama Pacific Exposition (1915); silver medals at the Exposition Universelle in Paris (1900), the Pan-American Exposition in Buffalo (1901), and the St. Louis Exposition (1904); and a bronze medal at the National Arts Club exhibition (1927). In 1905, Tanner became the first black artist to have work included in the Carnegie Institute's exhibition. The French government named Tanner the chevalier of the Legion of Honor in 1923.

Tanner was born the eldest of seven children of Benjamin Tucker and Sarah Elizabeth Tanner on June 21, 1859, in Pittsburgh, Pennsylvania. He married a white singer, Jessie Maculey Olssen, on December 14, 1899. The couple had one son, Jesse. Tanner died on May 25, 1937.

1894 Texas College Founded. Ministers of the Colored Methodist Church (now the Christian Methodist Church) founded Texas College in Tyler, Texas.

1895

1895 Fort Valley State College Established. Fort Valley High and Industrial School was established by leading black and white citizens of Fort Valley, Georgia, for the education of blacks in the South. During the 1920s and

1930s students at the school helped construct several of its buildings. In 1939 Fort Valley merged with the State Teachers and Agricultural College and the two schools became Fort Valley State College.

JANUARY 14, 1895 National Steamboat Company Organized by Blacks. Blacks organized the National Steamboat Company in Washington, D.C. The company sailed a steamboat, the *George Leary,* between Washington, D.C., and Norfolk, Virginia. The luxury boat held a capacity of 1,500 passengers and included three decks, sixty-four state rooms, one hundred berths, and a dining room.

FEBRUARY 20, 1895 Frederick Douglass Died. Frederick Douglass died in Anacostia Heights, in Washington, D.C.

JUNE 1895 Du Bois Earned Ph.D. from Harvard. W. E. B. Du Bois became the first African American to receive a Ph.D. from Harvard University. He immediately embarked upon a successful career of teaching and research, principally at Atlanta University.

SEPTEMBER 18, 1895 Washington Delivered "Atlanta Compromise" Speech. Book er T. Washington, the principal of Tuskegee Institute, delivered his controversial "Atlanta Compromise" speech to the Cotton States International Exposition in Atlanta. Washington asked for economic and educational progress for blacks aided by whites while playing down political power and social equality.

1896

1896 Du Bois Published Dissertation. W. E. B. Du Bois's *The Suppression of the African Slave Trade to America,* his Harvard dissertation, was published as the first volume in the Harvard Historical Studies Series. This work, along

Frederick Douglass. (Harper's Weekly.)

with *The Philadelphia Negro* (1899), *The Souls of Black Folk* (1903), and *The Atlanta University Publications* (1898–1914), helped to establish Du Bois's scholarly reputation.

1896 Oakwood College Opened. Oakwood Industrial School, later Oakwood College, opened in 1896. The school, affiliated with the Seventh-day Adventist Church, became a member of the United Negro College Fund in 1964.

MAY 18, 1896 *Plessy v. Ferguson.* The U.S. Supreme Court upheld separate but equal public facilities for blacks in the case of *Plessy v. Ferguson,* a case that stemmed from a dispute over transportation facilities in Louisiana. The plaintiff, Homer Adolph Plessy, contended that the 1890 Louisiana statute that required separate accommodations be used by blacks and whites violated the Thirteenth and Fourteenth Amendments. Plessy, who was seven-eighths Caucasian and one-eighth African, also argued that, because the "colored blood" in him was not detectable, he should have the same rights and privileges as white citizens. The Comité des Citoyens, an organization of blacks in New Orleans, aided Plessy and his lawyers. The Court majority, however, ruled that the Louisi-

Booker T. Washington. (Courtesy of Library of Congress.)

ana statute did not, in fact, violate either amendment. The segregation of the races thus won the sanction of the highest national tribunal. Justice John Harlan, in a prophetic dissent, asserted that segregation laws fostered ideas of racial inferiority and would increase attacks against the rights of blacks.

JUNE 1896   Washington Awarded Honorary Master Degree. Booker T. Washington received an honorary master of arts degree from Harvard University.

JULY 21, 1896   National Association of Colored Women Organized. The National Association of Colored Women, led by Mary Church Terrell, was organized in Washington, D.C. Terrell was born in Memphis, Tennessee, at the close of the Civil War, to wealthy and well-educated parents. Terrell inherited a substantial fortune and received an Oberlin education. She probably would have become a teacher, but her father considered the occupation beneath her. As Mary Church, she married Robert Terrell, a prominent Washington, D.C., educator, attorney, and judge. Terrell did become a feminist leader and a close associate of a number of white feminist leaders. She remained

wedded to the goal of racial integration despite numerous disappointments.

OCTOBER 31, 1896   Nursing School Opened. The Phyllis Wheatley Training School for Nurses opened its doors. The school, primarily for black women, was wholly funded and organized by African Americans.

1897

1897   Langston University Opened. The Colored Agricultural and Normal University, later Langston University, opened in Langston, Oklahoma, as a school for blacks to learn agricultural, mechanical, and industrial arts. Within a year of the passage of the territorial act that established the college, black settlers determined to provide higher education for their children had raised enough money through auctions, bake sales, and donations to purchase the land on which the school was built. The first bachelor's degree was awarded in 1901. The school adopted its present name in 1941.

1897   Southern States Disenfranchised Blacks. The Supreme Court, in *Williams v. Mississippi*, upheld voting requirements established by the Mississippi state constitution. Voters were to have paid a poll tax for at least the previous two years, and they had to prove either literacy or the ability to comprehend a section of the state constitution when read aloud. The literacy and comprehension tests were usually evaluated by white registration officials. The U.S. Supreme Court upheld the requirements because the constitution did not mention race, and the requirements, as written, were to be applied to blacks and whites equally. The court's interpretation found no violation of the Fifteenth Amendment.

1897   Voorhees College Opened. The Denmark Industrial School, later Voorhees College, opened in Denmark, South Carolina, with one teacher for its 14 students. The school was founded by Elizabeth Evelyn Wright and was affiliated with the Protestant Episcopal Church. The school's singing group toured the country in the 1920s to raise money for the financially strapped institution. In 1935, the school's St. Phillips Episcopal Chapel was built entirely by Voorhees students. Voorhees became a four-year college in 1962.

MAY 31, 1897 Shaw Memorial Unveiled. A ten-foot tall, eighteen-foot long relief depicting Col. Robert Gould Shaw and his 54th Massachusetts Regiment was unveiled at Boston Commons. The regiment, which was the first black regiment from a free state to be called to federal service, lost its leader in heavy battle while leading the charge against the Confederate line at Fort Wagner, South Carolina. Augustus St.-Gaudens sculpted the life-size memorial.

1898

1898 "Black Opera" Opened on Broadway. Will Marion Cook directed the sensational musical-comedy sketch *Clorindy, the Origin of the Cakewalk* on Broadway. Disregarding warnings that Broadway audiences would not listen to African Americans singing black opera, Cook composed music to lyrics written by famed black poet Paul Laurence Dunbar and assembled a company of twenty-six black performers. The performances of the first African American musical-comedy sketch in New York were held at the Casino Roof Garden.

Cook was born in Washington, D.C., in 1869. The son of a Howard University law professor, he was sent at age thirteen to the Oberlin Conservatory to study the violin. Cook later studied with violinist Joseph Joachim in Berlin and with John White and Antonin Dvorák at the National Conservatory of Music. Cook made additional theatrical history when *In Dahomey* (1902), his satire on the American Colonization Movement's efforts to promote

black emigration to Africa, opened on Times Square on Broadway. Other Cook successes were *In Abyssinia* (1906) and *In Bandana Land* (1907). Cook's lively shows left his audiences whistling and tapping their feet and helped popularize the "cakewalk" both in the United States and Europe. Cook died in 1944.

1898 Hampton Institute Expanded. Virginia's Hampton Institute, in its thirty-first year of operation, began using a newly constructed building for its agricultural and domestic science program. The building included laboratories, laundry facilities, and a creamery.

1898 Monument Dedicated to Douglass. A monument was dedicated to black civil rights leader Frederick Douglass. The tone of the ceremony was set by T. Thomas Fortune, president of the Afro-American League. "The management of the colored race in the South has been a conspicuous failure," he said. "I see other black and yellow peoples about to come under the care of this government. If you rule [them] . . . as the South has been and is being ruled, you will have revolution upon revolution, and you ought to have it."

MARCH 17, 1898 Blanche K. Bruce Died. Former U.S. senator Blanche K. Bruce died in Washington, D.C. After leaving the Senate, Bruce had served as register of the U.S. Treasury and had been a successful banker.

JULY 1, 1898 Black Soldiers Participated at San Jan Hill. At least twenty-five black soldiers, members of the U.S. Tenth Colored Cavalry, participated in the famous charge up San Juan Hill in Cuba. The assault was a major engagement of the Spanish-American War.

JULY 1, 1898 Black Regiments Involvement in Spanish-American War. Four black regiments participated in fighting around Santiago, Cuba, during the Spanish-American War, including the 9th and 10th Cavalry Squadrons. Approximately twenty African American regiments served in the conflict. Most of the black

The 10th Calvary in action during the Battle of San Juan Hill.

outfits had been activated shortly after the end of the Civil War for action against the Indians in the West. In the present conflict, blacks, like many of their white counterparts, were ill prepared in terms of experience, equipment, and training for combat in a tropical zone. Yet in the end, the blacks won the praises of almost all their officers. At the beginning of the Spanish-American War, there was only one black commissioned officer, Captain Charles Young. At the close of the war there were more than one hundred black officers, including Young, now a Brevet Major and commander of the Ninth Ohio regiment.

DECEMBER 16, 1898 Presidential Visit to Tuskegee Institute. Upon visiting Alabama's Tuskegee Institute, President William McKinley paid tribute to the institution's successes and to its founder, Booker T. Washington. The students and faculty welcomed the presidential party with a display of floats that illustrated the phases of the school and its teachings throughout its seventeen years of existence. In his speech, McKinley said, "An evidence of the soundness of the purposes of this institution is that those in charge of its management evident-

ly don't believe in attempting the unattainable, and their instruction in self-reliance and practical industry is most valuable."

1899

1899 Carter v. Texas. The U.S. Supreme Court ruled that Texas resident Seth Carter was entitled to a new trial because the state had purposefully excluded blacks from the jury that convicted him for murder.

1899 Chesnutt Published *The Conjure Woman*. Charles Waddell Chesnutt published a volume of tales called *The Conjure Woman*, which helped establish him as the foremost African American novelist of his time. *The Conjure Woman*, based upon the superstitions of North Carolina blacks, was probably his best work.

Chesnutt was born in North Carolina in 1858, but spent much of his adult life in Ohio. After the Civil War, he taught in the public schools of North Carolina, then was principal of the Fayetteville State Teachers College. As segregation and discrimination intensified in the South in the 1880s, Chesnutt returned to the North, first to New York, where he worked as a journalist, then Cleveland, where he was a clerk and an attorney.

Prior to the publication of *The Conjure Woman*, Chesnutt had contributed several short stories to American periodicals, including the *Atlantic Monthly*. Following the highly successful *Conjure Woman*, Chesnutt published *The Wife of His Youth* and *The House behind the Cedars*, both in 1900; *The Marrow of Tradition* (1901); and *The Colonel's Dream* (1905). In recognition of his literary and other achievements, the NAACP awarded him its prestigious Spingarn Medal in 1928. Chesnutt died in 1932.

1899 Cumming v. Richmond County Board of Education. The U.S. Supreme Court, in *Cumming v. Richmond County Board of Education*, upheld the "equal" of the separate but equal policy. The case came out of Richmond County, Georgia, where sixty black high school students' facility was taken away to alleviate the black elementaries that were overcrowded. The trial court had granted parental requests to suspend operations of the white high school until a black facility was reinstated. The order, however, was suspended until the case could be heard by the state Supreme Court which, upon review, reversed the decision. The U.S. Supreme Court restored the trial court's decision, but Richmond County reportedly defied it and continued to provide secondary schooling for whites but not blacks.

MAY 20, 1899 Women Protested Lynching. Boston women met to protest the lynching of African Americans in the South. It was reported that the women's main concerns were the indifference of Northerners concerning the rights of Southern blacks, the refusal to count the votes of blacks, and the false pretense that lynchings were necessary for the protection of Southern women when, in fact, a majority of

the lynchings were for reasons not concerning women.

1900

1900 Population Counted. According to the United States Bureau of Census 8,833,994 blacks, 237,196 Native Americans, and 66,809,196 whites were living in the country.

APRIL 30, 1900 "Casey Jones Created." The famed steam locomotive driven by John "Casey" Jones collided with another train. Two black men, Wallace Saunders and Sim Webb, were members of the crew. At the time of the collision, Jones ordered Webb to jump to safety while he remained with his train. When Jones's body was recovered, it was discovered that he had kept one hand on the airbrake and the other on the whistle. The incident inspired Saunders to write "Casey Jones," the song that immortalized the noted engineer and his train.

JULY 24–27, 1900 New Orleans Riots. Another race riot broke out in New Orleans. Black schools and homes were destroyed during the disturbance.

AUGUST 23–24, 1900 National Negro Business League Formed. The National Negro Business League, sponsored by Booker T. Washington, formed in Boston. More than four hundred delegates from thirty-four states had answered Washington's call to stimulate black businesses. Washington himself was elected the first president of the organization, and after only one year of the League's existence, he reported a large number of new black businesses. By 1907 the national organization had 320 branches. Though service-oriented businesses were the most numerous, blacks engaged in various types and sizes of business enterprises. The North Carolina Mutual Insurance Company, founded in 1898, became the largest black-owned firm.

1901

1901   Grambling State University. A request for assistance from the Farmers' Relief Association of Ruston, Louisiana, prompted Booker T. Washington of Tuskegee Institute to send Charles P. Adams to Louisiana to open the school that later became Grambling State University. The school's original mission was to teach all students willing to work how to farm and build houses. In 1905, when the school received a large donation, it moved to a two-hundred-acre campus. The school achieved university status and adopted its present name of Grambling State University in 1974.

JANUARY 16, 1901   Senator Hiram Revels Died. Hiram R. Revels, former United States Senator from Mississippi, died at Holly Springs. In 1870 he replaced Jefferson Davis and became the only black in the United States Congress. A former barber and preacher, he was a reluctant politician. Revels had also served as president of Alcorn College for Negroes in Mississippi.

MARCH 4, 1901   George White Left Congress. Representative George H. White left Congress. White had begun his work in the House of Representatives on March 15, 1897, after North Carolina had elected him in 1896. His state reelected him in 1898. In a moving valedictory address, White attacked Jim Crowism and predicted that the African American would return to the United States Congress. But more than twenty years passed before another African American served in Congress.

OCTOBER 1901   *Boston Guardian* Founded. William Monroe Trotter, a Phi Beta Kappa graduate of Harvard University, founded the *Boston Guardian*, a black newspaper that demanded full equality for blacks and spoke out against Booker T. Washington's policies on grounds that they were too accommodating. Trotter opened the *Guardian* offices in the

Congressman George White.

same building where William Lloyd Garrison had published *The Liberator*, and where Harriet Beecher Stowe's *Uncle Tom's Cabin* was printed. In editing the *Guardian*, Trotter abandoned a career as an insurance executive because, he said,

> "the conviction grew upon me that pursuit of business, money, civic, or literary position was like building a house upon sands; if race prejudice and persecution and public discrimination for mere color was to spread up from the South and result in a fixed caste of color . . . every colored American would be really a civil outcast, forever an alien, in the public life."

Trotter confronted Booker T. Washington to voice his differing views on July 30, 1903, at the Columbus Avenue African Zion Church in Boston. Trotter and his followers were arrested for heckling Washington; Trotter was sentenced to thirty days in jail. He explained that he had resorted to a public confrontation with Washington because the "Tuskegee kingpin" held a monopoly on the American media and opposing views could not be heard. The treatment of Trotter in Boston inspired W.E.B. Du Bois to become more active in the opposition to Washington. Trotter collaborated with Du Bois in the organization of the Niagara Movement, but declined a position of leadership in the NAACP because of his distrust of whites.

Yet Trotter continued his career as a civil rights activist. In 1906 he protested President Theodore Roosevelt's discharge of the black soldiers involved in the Brownsville, Texas, riot. In 1910 Trotter led a demonstration against a Boston performance of *The Clansman,* an anti-black play. In 1913 he accused President Woodrow Wilson of lying after Wilson had denied responsibility for segregation in the government cafeterias of Washington, D.C. Two years later, Trotter landed in jail for picketing the showing of the anti-black film *Birth of a Nation.*

In 1919, when the Paris Peace Conference convened, Trotter applied for a passport. He wanted to attend this world forum to present the grievances of American blacks. When the United States government denied his visa, Trotter obtained a job as a cook on a transatlantic ship and managed to reach Europe anyway. As a representative for the National Equal Rights League and for the Race Petitioners, Trotter supported the Japanese motion to include a prohibition against discrimination in the Covenant of the League of Nations. The Western Allies, which included the United States, opposed such a provision.

Trotter had been born in Boston in 1872. After earning a bachelor of arts degree from Harvard University he returned for his master's, which he received in 1895. In his final years, his money and energy dwindling, Trotter continued to agitate for equal rights. He died in 1934.

OCTOBER 16, 1901 Booker T. Washington Dined at White House. Booker T. Washington dined with President Theodore Roosevelt at the White House. But the meeting was bitterly criticized by many whites, especially Southerners, as a departure from racial etiquette. The previous year, Washington's autobiography, *Up from Slavery,* had been hailed by Southern and Northern whites for its non-vindictive attitude toward the South and its previous slave system. The book has become a classic in American letters, primarily because of Washington's prominence.

1902

FEBRUARY 1, 1902 Writer Langston Hughes Born. Langston Hughes was born to James Nathaniel and Carrie Mercer Langston Hughes in Joplin, Missouri. His grandfather, Charles Langston, was an abolitionist and a half-brother to educator and politician John Mercer Langston. Hughes received early schooling in Missouri and Ohio, and after spending a year in Mexico, he attended Columbia University and later Lincoln University. In 1926 Hughes published *The Weary Blues,* a collection of poems. He continued writing and published, among other works, *Not Without Laughter* (1930), *Shakespeare in Harlem* (1942), and his autobiography, *I Wonder as I Wander* (1956). In addition to poems, novels, and plays, Hughes wrote newspaper columns in which he had created the Harlem character Jesse B. Simple. Hughes died on May 22, 1967, in New York City.

1903

1903 *Giles v. Harris.* The case of *Giles v. Harris* made it to the U.S. Supreme Court after an Alabama district court ruled that it did not have jurisdiction to decide if the state's constitution was in violation of the Fourteenth or Fifteenth Amendment for requiring good character, understanding, and literacy in order to vote. The high court held that a federal district court could, in fact, hear the case, and it refused to

Booker T. Washington surveys the audience as President Theodore Roosevelt speaks.

order the registration of the plaintiff, Jackson W. Giles, as a voter.

1903 *The Souls of Black Folk* **Published.** W. E. B. Du Bois's *The Souls of Black Folk* was published. The book crystallized black opposition to the policies of Booker T. Washington which were viewed by many civil rights activists as too flexible.

JANUARY 7, 1903 Writer Zora Neale Hurston Born. Zora Neale Hurston was born to John and Lucy Ann Hurston in Eatonville, Florida. While attending Howard University, Hurston made a name for herself as one of the emerging writers of the Harlem Renaissance. Lorenzo Turner and Alain Locke served as mentors for Hurston. Her short stories appeared in *Opportunity* and her other works include *Jonah's Gourd Vine* (1934), *Mules and Men* (1935), *Their Eyes Were Watching God* (1937), *Tell My Horse* (1938), *Moses, Man of the Mountain* (1939), and *Seraph on the Suwanee* (1948). Her autobiography, *Dust Tracks on a Road*, was published in 1942.

Hurston died in Fort Pierce, Florida, on January 28, 1960.

MAY 30, 1903   Poet Countee Cullen Born.
Born Countee Porter, he was orphaned at an early age and adopted by Reverend Frederick Cullen, pastor of the Salem Methodist Church of New York. Cullen earned his bachelor's degree from New York University, where he was a Phi Beta Kappa scholar. In 1925, while still a student at NYU, he published his first volume of poetry, *Color,* which earned him the Harmon Foundation's first gold medal for literature in 1927. Cullen also received the Witter Bynner Poetry Prize. And in 1926, he received an M.A. degree from Harvard University and began a two-year sojourn in France sponsored by a Guggenheim Fellowship. When he returned to New York City, Cullen commenced his teaching career in the public school system. He continued to publish poetry and completed the novel *One Way to Heaven* in 1932. In 1947, one year after his death, a collection works chosen by Cullen himself was published under the title *On These I Stand.* Cullen died in New York City on January 10, 1946.

1904

1904   *Giles v. Teasley.* In *Giles v. Teasley,* the U.S. Supreme Court turned Jackson W. Giles away for the second time. A year earlier the Supreme Court had refused Giles's request for an order for Alabama to register him as a voter. With that, Giles tried to sue voting registrars in Alabama state courts, still contending that the state's voting requirements violated the Fifteenth Amendment. When the state court dismissed his case, Giles took it to the Alabama Supreme Court, which refused to make a decision on the constitutionality of the state's laws. The Alabama court also double denied Giles relief by ruling that, if the state's voting requirements violated the national constitution, then the registrars were invalid as registrars and could not register anyone at all. But if the state

Zora Neale Hurston. (Courtesy of Library of Congress.)

constitution was not in violation of the national one, then the registrars had acted within their authority and within the law, the court ruled. When this tangled decision was taken to the U.S. Supreme Court, it ruled, in 1904, that it could not hear the case because it had no lower court decision concerning the constitutionality of Alabama's laws to review.

1904   Girls' School Founded. The Daytona Normal and Industrial Institute for Girls was founded in 1904 by educator Mary McLeod Bethune. In 1923 the school merged with the Cookman-Collegiate Institute, forming Bethune-Cookman College. The school became a four-year college in 1942.

1904   *Rogers v. Alabama.* The U.S. Supreme Court, in *Rogers v Alabama,* decided that the exclusion of African Americans from juries was a violation of the equal protection clause. The case was brought to the high court by Dan Rogers, an African American who had been convicted of murder. His attorney argued that African Americans had been systematically excluded from his grand jury, and that the exclusion was a violation of the Fourteenth Amendment. The U.S. Supreme Court agreed and overturned Rogers's conviction by the Alabama Supreme Court. Associate justice Oliver Wendell Holmes wrote for the Court that prior Supreme Court decisions had already set a precedent that barred racial discrimination in grand jury selections.

1905

1905 Clyatt v. United States. The U.S. Supreme Court remanded *Clyatt v. United States* back to the lower court. The case was brought to the high court when Samuel Clyatt appealed his conviction for peonage after he had forced two blacks to return to Georgia to repay a debt. The two blacks, Will Gordon and Mose Ridley, argued that their Thirteenth Amendment rights had been violated in that the amendment prohibited slavery or involuntary servitude. The specific charge upon Clyatt, however, was "returning" two men to peonage. The high court ruled that an initial state of peonage was not evidenced and the case was sent back to Georgia courts for retrial.

1905 Politician Nelson Cornelius Nix, Sr., Born. Robert Nelson Cornelius Nix, Sr., was born to Nelson Nix, dean of South Carolina State College. Nix attended Townsend Harris High School in New York City prior to entering Lincoln University in Chester County, Pennsylvania, from which he graduated in 1912. Nix received his law degree from the University of Pennsylvania in 1924, and he later became the first African American to represent Pennsylvanians in the U.S. House of Representatives. He served in the eighty-fifth to the ninety-fifth Congress. Nix died in Philadelphia on June 22, 1987.

1905 Atlanta Life Insurance Founded. Alonzo F. Herndon founded the Atlanta Life Insurance Company as the largest black-owned business in the United States. The company

later lost that distinction to the North Carolina Mutual Insurance Company of Durham, founded in 1898 by John Merrick, C. C. Spaulding, and others.

1905 *Chicago Defender* Published. Robert S. Abbott began publication of the militant *Chicago Defender.* It became one of the most widely read, influential black newspapers in the country. Abbott was the son of a slave butler and a field woman who purchased their son's freedom. After his father's death, Abbott's mother married John Sengstacke, an editor, educator, and clergyman. Young Abbott worked on his stepfather's newssheet. He received his education at Hampton Institute, where he came under the influence of General Samuel C. Armstrong, the man who had also molded Booker T. Washington. In Chicago, Abbott began his newspaper with a staff composed of former barbers and servants as well as a few recently educated blacks. He attracted journalists, Willard Motley among them, and he published the early poems of Gwendolyn Brooks. Abbott's scathing attacks on Southern racism coupled with his appeals for Northern migration enhanced the *Chicago Defender's* prestige.

JULY 11–13, 1905 Niagara Movement. A group of black intellectuals from across the nation met near Niagara Falls and adopted resolutions demanding full equality for American blacks. The meeting has become known as the beginning of the Niagara Movement. W. E. B. Du Bois and William Monroe Trotter spearheaded the movement.

1906

FEBRUARY 9, 1906 Paul Dunbar Died. Paul Laurence Dunbar, the black poet who was instrumental in making black dialect an accepted literary form, died of tuberculosis in Dayton, Ohio, at thirty-four years of age. Dunbar had been born in Dayton on June 27, 1872, to the former slaves Joshua and Matilda Dunbar. His father had escaped slavery and fled to Canada. But he returned during the Civil War to fight with the Massachusetts 55th Regiment.

Although Paul Dunbar was senior class poet at Dayton's Central High School and the editor of the school newspaper and yearbook, his first career was operating an elevator for four dollars a week. By 1893 he had compiled a book of his verse and was selling it to passengers on his elevator. Two years later he published *Majors and Minors,* which received a favorable review by William Dean Howells in *Harper's Weekly.* That review brought Dunbar national recognition. The following year, his *Lyrics of Lowly Life* appeared. Many of these earlier works were published by Orville and Wilbur Wright, who were experimenting with printing newspapers on a homemade press.

In the last ten years of his life, Dunbar produced eleven volumes of verse, three novels, and five collections of short stories. Critics generally agree that Dunbar's best works are his poems, particularly those written in dialect. Despite his Midwestern origins, Dunbar's poems deal nostalgically with the pathos and humor of the old South. William Dean Howells considered Dunbar the first African American to ably express an aesthetic appreciation of black life through verse. Dunbar's biographer, Benjamin Brawley, observed that Dunbar

> "soared above race and touched the heart universal. . . . In a world of discord, he dared to sing his song about nights bright with stars, about the secret of the wind and the sea, and the answer one finds beyond the years. Above the dross and strife of the day, he asserted the right to live and love and be happy. That is why he was so greatly beloved and why he will never grow old."

APRIL 13, 1906 Brownsville, Texas, Riots.
White civilians and black soldiers clashed at Brownsville, Texas, apparently after black sol-

Author and poet Paul Laurence Dunbar. (Courtesy of Library of Congress.)

diers had retaliated racial slurs and taunting by whites. The violence that erupted resulted in the deaths of at least three white men, and the soldiers were consequently dishonorably discharged by President Theodore Roosevelt. The president's handling of the matter convinced many blacks that they could not look to him for help in the wake of increasing anti-black assaults. When Congress met in December of 1906, a group of Northerners, led by Senator Joseph B. Foraker of Ohio, argued that a full investigation and trial should have preceded the president's action. An investigation was launched by the Senate in January of 1907, but the Senate Committee's majority report upheld the soldiers' dishonorable discharges. In 1909, however, Senator Foraker won approval to allow the reenlistment of some of the soldiers.

JUNE 1906 John Hope at Morehouse College. John Hope assumed the presidency of Morehouse College. Hope, one of the most militant of early black educators, was the school's first African American president and was the catalyst behind many of the programs that resulted in the institution's reputation. Hope was born on June 2, 1868, in Augusta, Georgia, to prosperous parents, a white father, James Hope, and mulatto mother, Mary Frances (Fanny). His relatively secure childhood was shaken by his father's death in 1876 and the subsequent loss of much of the family's wealth.

That same year, Hope witnessed a violent racial clash in Atlanta. This incident, with the Atlanta riot of 1906, probably influenced his militancy. Hope denounced Booker T. Washington's "Atlanta Compromise" address, and he was the only black college president to join the militant Niagara Movement. Likewise, Hope was the only college administrator to attend the founding meeting of the NAACP in 1909. Ten years later Hope became a founder of the South's first biracial reform group, the Commission on Interracial Cooperation; this group was the forerunner of the Southern Regional Council. Hope assumed leadership of the Commission in 1932. He also served as president of Atlanta University from 1929 until his death in 1936.

SEPTEMBER 22–24, 1906 Atlanta Race Riot. A major race riot in Atlanta, Georgia, left twelve dead. The practically all-white media and attempts to disfranchise blacks had coupled to build racial tensions in the city. On September 22, newspapers reported four successive assaults on white women by black men. Many of the city's whites, joined by ruralites who were in town for Saturday shopping, formed mobs bent on retaliation. Blacks who sought to arm themselves in defense were quickly arrested. The state of panic existed for several days. The Atlanta Civic League, an interracial organization dedicated to racial harmony, was formed in the wake of the riot.

DECEMBER 4, 1906 Alpha Phi Alpha Established. The first African American fraternity, Alpha Phi Alpha, was established by Henry Callis, Charles Chapman, Eugene Jones, George Kelley, Nathaniel Murray, Robert Ogle, and Vertner Tandy at Cornell University in Ithaca,

New York. The purpose of the organization was education and the "mutual uplift of its members." Kelley was the first president of the organization. Its first general convention was held on December 28, 1908, in Washington, D.C.

1907

1907 First Black to Receive Rhodes Scholarship. Alain Locke, a prominent African American intellectual, received a Rhodes Scholarship; no other African American won this academic honor for more than half a century. Locke was born in Philadelphia in 1886. He obtained his Ph.D. from Harvard University in 1918. As a Rhodes Scholar, Locke studied at England's Oxford University from 1907 to 1910. He continued his studies at the University of Berlin from 1910 to 1911, and he became a professor of philosophy at Howard University in 1912, a position he held until his retirement in 1953. Locke published *Race Contacts and Interracial Relations* in 1916. His fame as a literary and art critic and interpreter of black culture rests largely on his anthology, *The New Negro* (1925), a seminal work about the Harlem Renaissance. Locke died in 1954, prior to completing *The Negro in American Culture.* This work was completed by Margaret Just Butcher and published in 1956.

1907 Miles College Founded. Miles College was an outgrowth of a high school that was founded in Booker City, Alabama, in 1902 by the Colored Methodist Episcopal Church, now the Christian Methodist Episcopal Church. Miles became a college and moved to its present site in Birmingham, Alabama, in 1907. The college is named after Bishop William H. Miles, a former slave who was active in the missions of the African Methodist denominations. Miles College was one of the first four-year colleges open to black students. The school's first bachelor's degree was awarded in 1911.

1908

1908   Berea College Forced to Segregate. The Kentucky legislature passed a law that made illegal the teaching of black and white students in the same institution. Berea College had been an integrated institution for more than fifty-five years but was required, by this new law, to segregate. Berea sued on grounds that it was a private institution and therefore, not required by the law to comply. But the U.S. Supreme Court upheld its *Plessy v. Ferguson* decision of 1896 which mandated separate but equal facilities.

AUGUST 14–19, 1908   Illinois Race Riot. A racial disturbance occurred in Springfield, Illinois. The shock of the riot prompted concerned whites to call the conference that led to the founding of the NAACP.

1909

FEBRUARY 12, 1909   NAACP Founded. The National Association for the Advancement of Colored People (NAACP) was founded in New York City. White progressives and black intellectuals were the group's first leaders, among them were Jane Addams, John Dewey, W. E. B. Du Bois, Mary White Ovington, and Oswald Garrison Villard. Boston's Moorfield Storey was named president.

APRIL 6, 1909   Matthew Henson Atop the World. Matthew H. Henson, a black servant, accompanied Commodore Robert E. Peary to the North Pole. Henson was the son of free-born parents in Charles County, Maryland. He had received a modest education, worked as a cabin boy, then later as a stock boy in a Washington, D.C., clothing store. There he met Peary and was hired as his servant. After sharing with Peary the feat of discovering the North Pole, Henson worked as a messenger in the New York Customs House. In 1912 he wrote

Explorer Matthew Henson.

his autobiography, *A Negro Explorer at the North Pole.* In 1945 he received a medal for "outstanding service to the government of the United States in the field of science," and the Geographical Society of Chicago awarded him with a gold medal in 1948. Presidents Harry Truman and Dwight Eisenhower also honored him. Henson died in March of 1955; a bronze plaque recognizing Henson as co-discoverer of the North Pole hangs in the Maryland State House.

December 1909   *Amsterdam News* Published. James H. Anderson established the *Amsterdam News* as an information outlet with a black perspective. In 1936 the paper changed hands, and the former crusading format was replaced by a milder, less progressive voice. By the 1960s it had the largest readership of any African American paper in the country.

1910

1910   *The Crisis* Published. The NAACP began the publishing of its official organ, *The Crisis.* W. E. B. Du Bois was its first editor.

1910   Population Counted. According to the U.S. Bureau of Census 9,827,763 blacks, 265,683 Native Americans, and 81,731,957 whites were living in the nation.

JANUARY 15, 1910   President Appointed Black Judge. President William Taft nominated Robert Herberton Terrell to be a judge of the Municipal Court of the District of Columbia. With the help of Booker T. Washington, Terrell was able to secure the position even though the Senate protested the appointment of a black to the post. Nine years earlier, Washington had been instrumental in Terrell's appointment as justice of the peace in the District of Columbia. But Terrell was not a wholehearted follower of Washington. He openly criticized Washington's condonation of the dishonorable discharge, in 1906, of the 25th black infantry after the Brownsville, Texas, riot. Terrell pushed for the civil rights that he believed in through the Grand United Order of Old Fellows of the District of Columbia, of which he was the grand master. Terrell and others established a chapter of the Sigma Pi Phi fraternity in the District of Columbia.

Terrell was born to Harris and Louisa Ann Terrell in Charlottesville, Virginia, on November 27, 1957. He had attended a District of Columbia school and the Groton Academy in Groton, Massachusetts, for his early education. In June of 1884 he graduated magna cum laude from Harvard College, and Howard University Law School granted him an LL.B. degree in 1889. Terrell married Mary E. Church on October 28, 1891; they had two daughters. On December 20, 1925, Terrell died at his home in Washington, D.C. He was buried in Harmony Cemetery in Washington.

APRIL 1910   National Urban League Established. The National Urban League (NUL) was established in New York City to assist Southern blacks who emigrated to the North. It soon became a social relief organization for black urban dwellers in the North, West, and South.

SEPTEMBER 27, 1910   W. C. Handy Published *Memphis Blues.* A revolution in the music world occurred when W. C. Handy published his blues composition, *Memphis Blues.*

1911

1911   *Bailey v. Alabama.* The U.S. Supreme Court, in *Bailey v. Alabama,* weakened state statutes that supported peonage, a contractual form of involuntary servitude incurred by debt. After Reconstruction, many blacks in the South were desperate for money and fell into such contracts to work. The defendant, Alonzo Bailey, had been convicted by an Alabama state court for violating his contract because he left his job before his contract was up, still owing money to his employer. In such cases, Alabama law presumed an intent to defraud, and the defendant was prohibited from testifying otherwise. The high court, however, found that the law breached the U.S. Constitution's presumption of innocence by disallowing a defendant to testify and make a case. State statutes that supported peonage were also found in violation of the Thirteenth Amendment and federal anti-peonage laws.

1912

1912   *The Autobiography of an Ex-Colored Man* Published. James Weldon Johnson anonymously published *The Autobiography of an Ex-Colored Man.* The novel describes Johnson's discovery of his heritage.

1913

MARCH 10, 1913   Harriet Tubman Died. Harriet Tubman, often referred to as "the Moses of

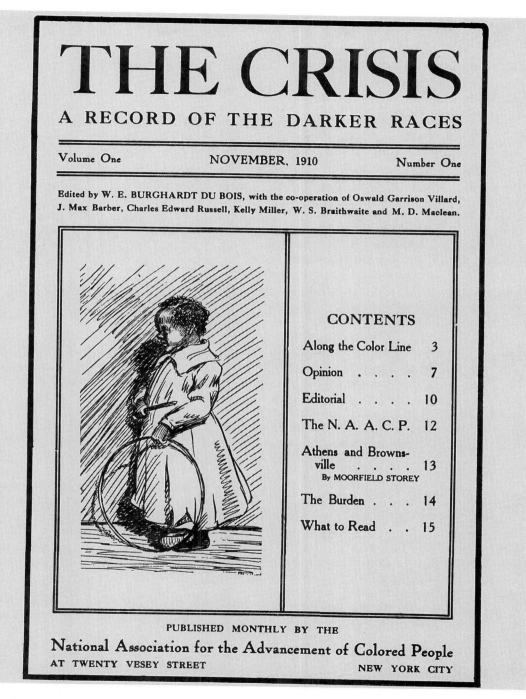

THE CRISIS

A RECORD OF THE DARKER RACES

Volume One   NOVEMBER, 1910   Number One

Edited by W. E. BURGHARDT DU BOIS, with the co-operation of Oswald Garrison Villard, J. Max Barber, Charles Edward Russell, Kelly Miller, W. S. Braithwaite and M. D. Maclean.

CONTENTS

PUBLISHED MONTHLY BY THE

National Association for the Advancement of Colored People

AT TWENTY VESEY STREET   NEW YORK CITY

Cover of the first issue of *The Crisis*.

her people," died in Auburn, New York. A leading black female abolitionist, Tubman was born in Dorchester County, Maryland, in 1823 and had escaped from slavery in July of 1849. She returned to Maryland and Virginia at least twenty times and is credited with freeing more than three hundred slaves.

While working as a field hand as a young girl, Tubman was injured when an overseer threw a weight at another slave but hit Tubman in the head. The blow caused Tubman to suffer from "sleeping seizures" for the rest of her life. In 1844 she married a free black, John Tubman, but she remained a slave. In 1849 her master died and rumors emerged that his slaves were to be sold in the Deep South. With two of her brothers, Tubman escaped. Fearing punishment or death, the brothers returned to the plantation, but Tubman, using the North Star for direction, marched on until she reached Philadelphia. In 1850, Tubman returned to Maryland for a sister and a brother, and in the following year she led a party of eleven blacks from the South into Canada. She left her husband, who had married another woman, behind. In 1857 Tubman made one of her last trips into Maryland to rescue her parents and three additional brothers and sisters. The family then settled in Auburn, New York. The family home, purchased from the abolitionist senator William H. Seward, was later turned into a home for elderly and indigent blacks. After serving in the Civil War as a nurse and a spy, Tubman devoted her energy and earnings to this home.

1914

1914　African American Joined Foreign Legion. Eugene Jacques Bullard joined the Foreign Legion. Bullard was born in Columbus, Georgia, in 1894. He had attempted to become a pilot in the states but failed. For France, however, he flew his way into the Lafayette

Escadrille and gained notoriety as one of the Lafayette Flying Four. Bullard died in 1961.

1915

1915　Blacks Migrated North. The war-time migration of Southern blacks to Northern industrial centers began. Millions of blacks left the South in search of economic and social security.

APRIL 7, 1915　Singer Billie Holiday Born. Born Eleanor Fagan in Baltimore, Massachusetts, she got the nickname Billie for her tomboyish nature. Holiday's parents separated when she was an infant, and her mother left her with relatives in Boston. When she was ten years old, Holiday was raped by a forty-year-old neighbor; the man was imprisoned and Holiday was sent to a Catholic correctional home. At thirteen she joined her mother in New York City, where her lifestyle worsened. She started smoking marijuana and was in and out of jail for prostitution.

Meanwhile, her interest in music was beginning to blossom. When Holiday was eighteen she began singing professionally in Lower Manhattan for ten dollars a week. She was encouraged and promoted by the famed jazzman John Hammond, who arranged for her to make her recording debut with Benny Goodman in November of 1933. Her fame grew when she made a series of recordings, most of them with pianist Teddy Wilson. She worked as a vocalist with Count Basie and Artie Shaw and toured during the 1940s and 1950s as a solo performer.

Unfortunately, Holiday's personal life was beginning to unravel. She developed a serious addiction to heroin which landed her in prison for one year. Upon release, her performances were restricted as she was denied a cabaret performer's license. And although she enjoyed several successful tours in Europe, her voice began to fail. Her final appearance was at the Phoenix Theater in New York City in early 1959. On July 17 of that year, Holiday died, a result of serious heart, lung, and liver diseases.

MAY 8, 1915 Bishop Henry Turner Died. Black Pan-African leader and A.M.E. churchman Bishop Henry McNeal Turner died in Windsor, Ontario. Turner was born free in Abbeville, South Carolina, in 1833. At an early age he was hired out to work in the field with slaves. Turner's first teachings came from a white playmate. Making his way to Baltimore at age fifteen, Turner worked as a messenger and a handyman at a medical school, where he had access to books and magazines. He educated himself there until an Episcopal bishop consented to teach him. This was one of the influences that led Turner into the church, where he became an A.M.E minister.

Bishop Henry McNeal Turner.

During the Civil War, President Abraham Lincoln appointed Turner as Chaplain of the 54th Massachusetts Negro Regiment. After the war, he worked with the Freedmen's Bureau in Georgia and became actively involved in Republican politics. Turner served in the Georgia constitutional convention of 1868 and was elected to the state legislature. Turner vehemently opposed the successful attempt of white Georgia lawmakers to expel the black Reconstruction legislators. These and other experiences convinced him that the black man had no future in the United States.

Turner became a colonizationist and Pan-Africanist. He was one of the sponsors of an ill-fated expedition of approximately two hundred blacks to Liberia in 1878. In spite of the failure of this venture, Turner continued his support of colonization. Prior to his death in 1915, Turner also served as director of the A.M.E. publishing house, editor of denominational periodicals, and chancellor of Morris Brown College, an A.M.E. school in Atlanta.

JUNE 21, 1915 *Guinn v. United States*. The U.S. Supreme Court, in *Guinn v. United States*, outlawed the grandfather clauses used by Southern states to disenfranchise blacks. The clauses,

originally found in Louisiana, restricted the ballot to descendants of voters that were qualified to vote as of January 1, 1867—before Reconstruction.

SEPTEMBER 9, 1915 Black History Association Founded. Professor Carter G. Woodson founded the Association for the Study of Negro Life and History (ASNLH). The group stood virtually alone for a time in attempting to properly portray the role of the African American in U.S. history. Woodson, the son of former slaves, held a doctorate from Harvard University. He is sometimes called "the father of modern black historiography," having edited for many years the *Journal of Negro History*, other publications of the ASNLH, and having published a number of his own works on African Americans.

NOVEMBER 14, 1915 Film Boycotted. The NAACP led the black outcry against the showing of D. W. Griffith's controversial film, *Birth of a Nation*. The film, based on the writings of Thomas Dixon, was the most technologically advanced motion picture produced at that time. The NAACP claimed that the film told a

Historian Carter G. Woodson. (AP/Wide World Photos.)

distorted story of emancipation, Reconstruction, and black immorality, and glorified anti-black organizations such as the Ku Klux Klan. The film portrayed African Americans as either docile servants or insolent monsters and sympathized with its Southern white protagonists. The film sparked the first national black social protest that combined legislative lobbying in the Massachusetts state House, picketing in Boston streets, and protests. The movement was later joined by several black West Coast businessmen who financed all-black movies to counter racist, mainstream cinema.

NOVEMBER 14, 1915 Booker T. Washington Died. Booker T. Washington, the most noted black American between Frederick Douglass and Martin Luther King, Jr., died at Tuskegee Institute. He was succeeded in the presidency by Robert Russa Moton of Hampton Institute. Moton was born in Virginia shortly after the Civil War. He was reared as a houseboy on a Virginia plantation, receiving secret instruction from his literate mother. Moton taught at Hampton Institute, his alma mater, before assuming the presidency at Tuskegee. He was one of the members of the Committee

on the Welfare of Negro Troops sponsored by the Federal Council of Churches during World War I. While continuing Washington's policies and practices at Tuskegee, Moton expanded the academic-classical curriculum at the institution. He also fought the efforts of racists who were attempting to prevent black control of the Tuskegee Veterans Hospital.

1916

1916 Black Film Production Company Formed. Between 1916 and 1922 a California group called the Lincoln Company formed to produce all-black films. Led by George and Noble Johnson, the company produced an average of one film per year with titles such as *The Realization of a Negro's Ambition* and *The Trooper of Troop K*. Inadequate distribution and a nationwide influenza epidemic stifled the company's success. Another all-black production company, led by the NAACP, met a similar fate.

1917

1917 Harry Burleigh Received Spingarn Medal. For excellence of creative music, Harry T. Burleigh was awarded the Spingarn Medal, the NAACP's highest honor. Burleigh was born in Erie, Pennsylvania, in 1866. Although he demonstrated an aptitude for music as a child, he did not receive formal training until 1892, when he began his studies at the National Conservatory of Music in New York. Burleigh majored in orchestral and vocal music. During his sophomore year, Burleigh studied under the famous Czech composer Antonin Dvorák, who took the young black student as a protégé. Two years after entering the conservatory, Burleigh was on his way to a career of singing. He became the first black soloist at St. George's Episcopal Church in New York and at the Temple Emanu-El. His European tours included a performance before King Edward VII in England. In his senior year, Burleigh became

Booker T. Washington on his horse. (Courtesy of Library of Congress.)

a voice instructor at the conservatory, a position he held for two years after his graduation.

Around 1900, Burleigh began to shift his attention from singing to composing. His first compositions were sentimental ballads, then he branched out into choral pieces, spirituals, and miscellaneous works. Among his better known compositions are *Six Plantation Melodies for Violin and Piano* (1901), *Southland Sketches* (1916), *The Prayer* (1915), *Little Mother of Mine* (1917), *Deep River* (1916), and *The Lovely Dark and Lonely One* (1935). Contem-

porary critics lauded Burleigh's imagination and his masterly musicianship. Of his spiritual compositions Burleigh wrote, "My desire was to preserve them in harmonies that belong to modern methods of tonal progression without robbing the melodies of their racial flavor." In addition to the Spingarn Medal, Burleigh was the recipient of honorary degrees from Atlanta University and Howard University.

1917 Residential Segregation Outlawed. The U.S. Supreme Court, in *Buchanan v. Warley,* unanimously decided that residential racial zoning laws were in violation of the Fourteenth Amendment. The NAACP helped William Warley take the case to the high court after a lower Kentucky court found him guilty of breach of contract because he refused to pay for a land lot he had purchased. Warley had refused to pay after finding that a local ordinance prohibited him from living on his own land.

APRIL 16, 1917   Blacks Fought in World War I. The United States entered World War I. About 370,000 African Americans served during this conflict, 1,400 of which were commissioned as officers. Three African American regiments received the Croix de Guerre for valor, and several individual blacks were decorated for bravery.

JULY 1–3, 1917   East St. Louis, Illinois, Riots. A serious race riot broke out in East St. Louis, Illinois. At least forty blacks were killed, and a small black child was reportedly shot down and then thrown into a burning building. Martial law was declared. The riot had apparently resulted from the employment of blacks in a factory that held a contract with the federal government. The Germans seized upon the incident in their campaign to attract African American sentiment in the World War.

JULY 28, 1917   New York Silent March. About 10,000 African Americans silently marched down New York City's Fifth Avenue in protest of racial oppression. The march, organized by the NAACP, was a response to the East St. Louis, Illinois, riot. The protestors asked the president, "Why not make America safe for Democracy?"

AUGUST 23, 1917   Houston Disturbed. A disturbance between black soldiers and white civilians erupted in Houston, Texas. Two blacks and seventeen whites were killed; thirteen blacks were later executed for participating in the violence.

NOVEMBER 5, 1917   Emmett Scott Appointed to Cabinet. Emmett J. Scott, former secretary to Booker T. Washington, was appointed special assistant to the Secretary of War. Specifically, Scott was to work for nondiscriminatory application of the Selective Service Act; to formulate plans to build up morale among blacks, soldiers, and civilians; and to investigate complaints of unfair treatment of blacks. He also disseminated news concerning black soldiers on the home front. In June of 1918, Scott called a conference of about thirty black newspaper publishers who pledged their support of the American war effort but denounced anti-black violence and discrimination at home. The coalition called for the recruitment of black Red Cross nurses and asked for the appointment of a black war correspondent.

1918

FEBRUARY 19–21, 1918   First Pan-African Congress. W. E. B. Du Bois led the first Pan-African Congress which was held in Paris while the Paris Peace Conference was convening. About sixty delegates, including West Indians, Africans, and American blacks, attended the meeting to determine how blacks of the world might benefit from the Paris Peace Conference. The democracy for which many of them fought in World War I, they said, should become a reality. While this Congress accomplished very little, it stimulated subsequent and more fruitful assemblages of blacks in later years.

JULY 13–OCTOBER 1, 1918   "Red Summer" of Violence. Major race riots occurred across the nation in what James Weldon Johnson called the "Red Summer." More than twenty-five riots left over one hundred people dead and more than one thousand wounded. Federal troops had to suppress the disorder in some

The "Fighting 369th" Regiment marches up New York City's Fifth Avenue after its return home. (Courtesy of the U.S. War Department.)

areas. Washington, D.C.; Chicago, Illinois; Longview, Texas; and Chester and Philadelphia, Pennsylvania were among the scenes of the disturbances.

JULY 29, 1918 Lynching Addressed. The National Liberty Congress of Colored Americans asked Congress to make lynching a federal crime.

DECEMBER 1918 Lynchings Tallied. Eighty-three lynchings were recorded during the year.

1919

1919 Archibald Grimké Recieved Spingarn Award. Founder of the National Association for the Advancement of Colored People (NAACP), Archibald Grimké received the Spingarn Award for his service as the U.S. consul to Santo Domingo. Grimké was born in Charleston, South Carolina, in 1849. He studied at Lincoln University, and in 1874 he graduated from the Harvard University Law

Civil rights activist W. E. B. Du Bois. (Courtesy of Library of Congress.)

School. Five years later Grimké marrried Sarah Stanley, and the couple had one child in 1880. Beginning in 1883 Grimké edited *The Hub,* a Boston weekly. Grimké was president of the American Negro Academy before becoming the consul to Santo Domingo in 1894. Grimké died February 25, 1930.

1919 *State v. Young.* The U.S. Supreme Court ruled that African Americans should be admitted to juries.

JULY 18, 1919   Race Riot Hit the Capital. Racial tension in the capital had been building

since June as a result of widespread rumors that black men were attacking white women. The violence erupted when two black men jostled a white woman on July 18. The woman's husband was a sailor and soon, sailors and marines were joined by other whites in an attack on the black population of Washington, D.C. Federal troops were used to tame the rioting, but President Woodrow Wilson was forced to call in more troops after an even more terrifying night of race-based violence on July 21.

OCTOBER 12, 1919   Navy Cross Recipient Dorie Miller Born. Dorie Miller was born on a small farm near Waco, Texas, to sharecropper parents. He enlisted in the navy when he was nineteen and was assigned to sea duty. On December 7, 1941, Miller was aboard the battleship *Arizona* when it was anchored at Pearl Harbor. This ship suffered tremendous damage when the Japanese attacked; Miller was knocked down by the blast. Unlike many crew members, however, Miller stayed aboard the ship and figured out how to fire a gun, a skill he had never been taught. After moving the mortally wounded captain to safety, Miller successfully fired at four Japanese planes. Three months later, he was awarded the Navy Cross and advanced to mess attendant first class. Miller died while serving aboard the *Liscome Bay* when she was sunk by a Japanese submarine on November 24, 1943.

Chapter 6

1920 TO 1949

1920

1920 *The Emancipation of Negro Music.* Robert Nathaniel Dett, a black composer, arranger, and conductor, was awarded the Bowdoin Prize by Harvard University for an essay titled *The Emancipation of Negro Music.* Dett was born in 1882 in the community of Drummondville, Quebec, which had been established by fugitive slaves before the Civil War.

Inspired as a child by black spirituals, Dett studied music at the American Conservatory of Music in Chicago, Columbia University, Harvard University, the Oberlin Conservatory, the Oliver Willis Halstead Conservatory in Lockport, New York, and at the University of Pennsylvania. During his early career, Dett performed as a concert pianist while teaching and engaging in further study. Dett taught at Lane College in Texas (1908-1911), Lincoln University in Missouri (1911-1913), Hampton Institute in Virginia (1913-1931), Sam Houston College in Texas (1935-1937), and at Bennett College in North Carolina (1937).

Under the leadership of Dett, the Hampton Institute choir became internationally known, performing at the Library of Congress, New York's Carnegie Hall, and Boston's Symphony Hall. In 1930 the choir toured seven European nations. Meanwhile, Dett took some time off to study with Arthur Foote in Boston and Nadia Boulanger at the American Conservatory at Fontainebleau.

Among Dett's notable compositions are *Magnolia* (1912), *Music in the Mine* (1916), *The Chariot Jubilee* (1921), *Enchantment* (1922), and *The Ordering of Moses* (1937). In addition to the Bowdoin Prize, Dett recieved the Francis Boot Prize for composition, the Palm and Ribbon Award of the Royal Belgian Band, the Harmon Foundation Award, and honorary degrees from Oberlin's Eastman School of Music and Harvard University. Dett died in 1943.

AUGUST 1–2, 1920 Universal Negro Improvement Association. The national convention of the Universal Negro Improvement Association (UNIA) met in New York City. Marcus Garvey, the founder, spoke to about 25,000 blacks during the rally at Madison Square Garden. Garvey-type black nationalism was reaching its zenith at the time.

Garvey had begun his organization in his native Jamaica in 1914. In 1916 he arrived in the United States to organize a New York chapter of UNIA. By the middle of 1919 thirty branches existed in the United States, principally in the Northern ghettoes. Garvey founded the newspaper *Negro World* to disseminate his ideas of race pride and to promote his back-to-Africa stance. His other organizations included the Universal Black Cross Nurses, the Universal African Motor Corps, the Black Star Steamship Line, and the Black Eagle Flying Corps.

In 1921 Garvey formally organized the Empire of Africa and appointed himself provisional president. He appealed, unsuccessfully, to the League of Nations for permission to settle a colony in Africa and negotiated towards that end with Liberia. After these failures, he began planning a military expedition to drive the white imperialists out of Africa. This campaign, however, was never launched. In 1923 Garvey was arrested for mail fraud in his attempts to raise money for his steamship line.

1921

1921 *Shuffle Along* **Produced.** Eubie Blake, with Noble Sissle, produced the historic musical *Shuffle Along.* Blake was born in Baltimore, Maryland, in 1883. He started practicing music at age six, and during his adolescent years he played music in department stores and "sporting" houses. In 1899, Blake composed his first ragtime piece, *The Charleston Rag.* Among his other compositions are *Chevy Chase* (1914), *Fitz Water* (1914), and *Bugle Call Rag* (1926). As late as 1970 Blake was still composing rags. He is often called "the leading exponent of the eastern school" of ragtime music.

1922

1922–1929 The Harlem Renaissance. The Harlem Renaissance emerged as a period of great achievement in African American art and literature. The movement embraced poets such as Claude McKay, Langston Hughes, Countee Cullen, and James Weldon Johnson; novelists Walter F. White, Wallace Thurman, Nella Larsen, and Zora Neale Hurston; sculptors Richmond Barthe and Augusta Savage; and painters Aaron Douglas, Alice Gafford, and Archibald Motley. The Harlem Renaissance artists were known for drawing critical atten-

Marcus Garvey, founder of the Universal Negro Improvement Association. (Courtesy of Consulate General of Jamaica.)

tion and popular sentiments from both blacks and whites.

During this period, James Weldon Johnson and Alain Locke edited *The Book of American Negro Poetry* (1925) and *The New Negro* (1925), respectively. Both were anthologies of the works of black writers. Claude McKay, the first important figure in the Harlem Renaissance, was noted for his *Harlem Shadows* (1922), a collection of bitter but eloquent poems on the condition of blacks in post-war America.

Among Countee Cullen's better-known works was his volume of poems titled *Color*. Its appearance in 1925 pushed the Harlem Renaissance to a new high.

Other notable works published during this period were poet Langston Hughes's *The Weary Blues* (1926), Walter White's *The Fire in the Flint* (1926), Nella Larsen's *Quicksand* (1928) and *Passing* (1929), and Wallace Thurman's *The Blacker the Berry* (1929).

JANUARY 8, 1922   Colonel Charles Young Died. Colonel Charles R. Young, one of the highest ranking blacks in the U.S. Army, died in Nigeria. Young, the son of a former slave-soldier in the Union Army, was born in Kentucky. He had entered West Point Academy in 1884 and served with distinction in Cuba, Haiti, and Mexico, but he always labored under the burdens of racial discrimination. During World War I, Young was called for a physical examination and made to retire because of poor health. This action was an apparent subterfuge to prevent Young's promotion to general. After protests by blacks, Young was recalled, but he was assigned to relatively obscure duty in Illinois and Liberia.

NOVEMBER 9, 1922   Actress, Singer Dorothy Dandridge Born. Dorothy Dandridge entered show business at a very young age, entertaining on road tours with her older sister Vivian. Dandridge performed at the Cotton Club when she was sixteen years old. She built a successful career as a nightclub singer while attempting to establish herself as a dramatic film actress. In 1954 Dandridge won the coveted title role in Otto Preminger's black production, *Carmen Jones.* Her performance earned her an Academy Award nomination, the first for an African American woman in a leading role.

Despite this success, Dandridge's film career came to a standstill in the conservative 1950s. Three years passed before her next film, *Island in the Sun,* was released. The film's theme of interracial romance was repeated in her next projects, *The Decks Ran Red* (1958), *Tamango* (1959), and *Malaga* (1962). Her last great role was Bess in *Porgy and Bess,* another black musical from Otto Preminger. Mainstream roles continued to elude Dandridge, whose race posed a dilemma to producers reluctant to cast her opposite white leading men.

In the early 1960s, Dandridge's life began to unravel personally and professionally. Her stormy marriage to restaurant owner Jack Dennison ended in divorce, and she later filed for bankruptcy and had to forfeit her Hollywood mansion. Dorothy Dandridge died in her apartment on September 8, 1965, apparently the result of an antidepressant drug overdose.

1923

SEPTEMBER 4, 1923   George Washington Carver Awarded Spingarn Medal. Tuskegee Institute's George Washington Carver received the Spingarn Medal, the NAACP's highest award, for his distinguished research in agricultural chemistry. In 1939, Carver had been awarded the Roosevelt Medal for distinguished achievement in science. Carver was born a slave in Diamond Grove, Missouri, in 1864. He attended an undergraduate school in Iowa and earned a master of science degree from Iowa State College. In 1896, Carver was appointed to the faculty of Tuskegee Institute, where he began a program of research in soil conservation and crop diversification. Carver's scientific fame rests largely in the four hundred different products he produced from the peanut, potato, and pecan. Carver was a Fellow of the Royal Academy of England, and a foundation and museum have been established in his honor at Tuskegee Institute, where he died in 1943.

OCTOBER 24, 1923   Black Migration Continued. Black migration to the North continued as the Department of Labor estimated that some half-million blacks left the South within the last year.

Chemist and educator George Washington Carver. (Courtesy of Library of Congress.)

NOVEMBER 20, 1923 Automatic Traffic Light Patented. Garrett A. Morgan, a black inventor, was awarded U.S. Patent no. 1,475,024 for developing a three-way, automatic traffic light. Earlier, Morgan had invented the gas mask used by American troops during World War I. Morgan was awarded a patent in 1914 for this "breathing device."

The black inventor was one of eleven children born to Sidney and Elizabeth Morgan. He was born in Paris, Tennessee, in 1875. In

1895 he moved to Cleveland, Ohio, where he produced, in 1901, a belt fastener for sewing machines. In 1914 Morgan won the First Grand Prize at the Second International Exposition of Sanitation and Safety for the invention of a smoke inhalator. This inhalator was used in a successful rescue of workers trapped in a tunnel under Lake Erie in 1916. The City of Cleveland awarded Morgan a gold medal following the rescue. The patent rights to the traffic light were sold by Morgan to the General Electric Company for $40,000. Morgan died in 1963.

1924

JULY 1, 1924 Roland Hayes Named Soloist. Roland Hayes, born in a Georgia cabin in 1887, was named a soloist with the Boston Symphony Orchestra. Earlier, he had received the NAACP's Spingarn Medal for his interpretations of black folk songs.

1925

JANUARY 10, 1925 Adelbert Roberts Elected to Illinois Legislature. Adelbert Roberts was elected to the Illinois state legislature—the first black to serve in a state assembly in at least twenty-five years.

MAY 8, 1925 Brotherhood of Sleeping Car Porters. The Brotherhood of Sleeping Car Porters, the trailblazing black labor union, was organized by A. Philip Randolph. Often called the dean of black leaders, Randolph had been reared in Florida. He was the son of a minister and a seamstress, both of whom were former slaves. Randolph attended Cookman Institute in Florida and City College in New York. His intellectual interests and his practical experiences in Harlem evoked an intense hatred of racial bias and a zeal for economic and social justice. He joined the Socialist Party and attempted to organize black students and workers. Randolph founded the *Messenger*, the socialist periodical that became one of the leading magazines in the history of black journalism. In later years he was prominent as an opponent of American intervention in foreign wars and of military segregation. Randolph was a presidential consultant in matters of civil rights, and he was a central figure in the 1941 March on Washington.

1926

1926   *Corrigan v. Buckley*. The U.S. Supreme Court, in *Corrigan v. Buckley*, held that racially restrictive covenants were not in violation of the Fifth or Fourteenth Amendments in relation to equal protection under the law. The case was heard by the high Court when Irene Corrigan attempted to sell property to an African American after having entered into a neighborhood agreement that excluded blacks from ever owning the property. Her neighbors sued to stop her and the Supreme Court ruled that it held no jurisdiction in the case. The decision was based on the fact that the amendments in question pertained to governmental actions, not to private actions or private contracts. Discriminatory contracts were, in effect, declared constitutional as long as no governmental actions were involved.

JUNE 30, 1926   NAACP Honored James Johnson. James Weldon Johnson was honored by the NAACP in New York City for his careers as executive secretary of the NAACP, member of the U.S. Consul, editor, and poet. Johnson was born in Florida in 1871 and was educated there. He continued his education at Atlanta University, New York City College, and Columbia University. Johnson began his professional life in Florida where he was a teacher, journalist, and lawyer before joining his broth-

Labor and civil rights leader Asa Philip Randolph. (Courtesy of the National Archives.)

er, Rosamond Johnson, in New York to write musical comedies.

Johnson is best known as a writer of prose and verse. His most notable works include *God's Trombones* (1927), *The Book of American Negro Poetry* (1925), *Black Manhattan* (1930), *The Autobiography of an Ex-Colored Man* (1912), and his autobiography, *Along This Way* (1933). Johnson's poem *Lift Every Voice and Sing*, when set to music by his brother, became known as the black national anthem. The song still retains that characterization among blacks today.

In New York, Johnson moved widely in interracial circles. These affiliations, with his success as a writer and diplomat and his moderate opposition to racial discrimination, made him a likely choice as the NAACP's first executive secretary. In this capacity, Johnson led the campaign to outlaw lynching in the United States, culminating in the Dyer Anti-lynching Bill of 1921 (which passed the House but died in the Senate). Before his death in 1938, Johnson also taught at Fisk University in Nashville, Tennessee.

James Weldon Johnson standing between Bob Cole and his brother Rosamond Johnson.

1927

1927 *Gong Lum v. Rice.* The U.S. Supreme Court, in *Gong Lum v. Rice,* upheld a Mississippi Supreme Court ruling that Chinese peoples could be classified as "colored" in the state, in effect, securing segregation of the Chinese. The case was heard by the high Court after Martha Gong Lum won a circuit-court suit against school trustees who were denying Lum's admittance to a white school because of her Asian background. The trustees had appealed to the state supreme court which reversed the decision.

MARCH 7, 1927 *Nixon v. Herndon.* The U.S. Supreme Court, in *Nixon v. Herndon,* struck down a Texas law that excluded blacks from the Democratic primaries in the state. Texas managed, however, to erect new defenses against black voting.

DECEMBER 1927 **Marcus Garvey Released from Jail.** Marcus Garvey, after having been convicted in 1925 for mail fraud, was released from the Atlanta Federal Penitentiary and deported as an undesirable alien. Garvey was unsuccessful in keeping his black nationalist movement alive while in prison.

1928

NOVEMBER 6, 1928   Oscar De Priest Elected to Congress. Illinois elected Oscar De Priest to serve in Congress. De Priest, the son of former slaves, was born in Alabama shortly after the Civil War. He was reared in Kansas, where he worked as a painter, but after moving to Chicago he became involved in real estate and politics, becoming Chicago's first black alderman. De Priest's activities with Republican ward politics was soon rewarded by local politicians with his nomination for Congress in 1928. When he first assumed office, some blacks considered him an unscrupulous politician and an accommodationist on racial matters. But by the end of three terms in office he had won a reputation for outspoken militancy. De Priest was the first black from a non-Southern state to sit in Congress and the only African American to serve in that body since George H. White's departure in 1901.

1929

1929   Colored Merchants Association Organized. Albon Holsey of the National Negro Business League organized the Colored Merchants Association in New York. The group planned to establish stores and buy their merchandise cooperatively. Blacks were urged to make their purchases from these merchants as a means for providing jobs for blacks, but the Depression forced the stores out of business within two years.

By 1931, the "Jobs-for-Negroes" movement began in earnest in St. Louis, Missouri. The St. Louis chapter of the National Urban League (NUL) launched a boycott against a white chain store whose trade was almost exclusively black but employed very few blacks. This movement spread to Chicago, Cleveland, New York City, Pittsburgh, and others. New York became the center of an intensive, sometimes bitter, campaign. The Citizens League for Fair Play launched a drive in 1933 to persuade white merchants to employ black sales clerks. They adopted as their motto: "Don't Buy Where You Can't Work." The campaign led to the employment of hundreds of blacks in Harlem stores and with public utility companies.

1929   Lynchings Declined. Lynchings were reportedly declining in the United States; ten were recorded for the year.

1929   Negro with an "N." The New York City Board of Education issued a directive that the word "Negro" should be spelled with a capital "N."

JANUARY 15, 1929   Martin Luther King, Jr., Born. Martin Luther King, Jr., was born in Atlanta, Georgia. King's parents were members of the city's black establishment, his father being one of the city's leading black ministers and his mother the daughter of a prominent preacher. King was educated at Morehouse College, Crozier Theological Seminary, and Boston University. He began his ministerial career as pastor of the Dexter Avenue Baptist Church in Montgomery, Alabama, in 1954.

OCTOBER 29, 1929   Stock Market Crashed. The New York Stock Exchange crashed, signaling the beginning of the Great Depression. During the Depression blacks complained that they were the last to be hired and the first to be fired.

Bojangles's funeral at the Abyssinian Baptist Church in New York City. (Courtesy of the National Archives.)

1930

1930 Bojangles Made Film Debut. Luther Robinson, also known as Bojangles, made his first film appearance in *Dixiana*. Previously, Robinson had made a name for himself dancing in traveling minstrel and vaudeville shows. By the time he started appearing in films, Robinson had developed complicated and rhythmic dances including his staircase dance that became famous when he taught Shirley Temple

how to do it on the screen in *The Little Colonel*. He also appeared with Temple in *The Littlest Rebel*, *Rebecca of Sunnybrook Farm*, and *Just Around the Corner*. Robinson's roles in these films, however, have been criticized as he played a happy-go-lucky childlike servant.

Robinson was born the son of Maxwell Robinson and his wife Maria in Richmond, Virginia, in 1878. Robinson and his siblings were raised by their grandmother after the death of their parents. He studied the "clog" and the "buck and wing," African American variation of the Irish gig. Robinson's first marriage was to Fannie Clay. After Clay and Robinson divorced, he married Elaine Plaines. On November 25, 1949, Robinson died of chronic heart condition at Columbia Presbyterian Medical Center in New York City. He was eulogized at the Abyssinian Baptist Church and buried at Cemetery of the Evergreens in New York City.

1930   *City of Richmond v. Deans.* In *City of Richmond v. Deans,* the U.S. Supreme Court upheld its 1917 *Buchanan v. Warley* decision that laws resting on racial distinctions are unconstitutional. Virginia's City of Richmond had taken J. B. Deans to the high Court after district and appeals courts protected Deans's right to own a home in a white neighborhood. The Supreme Court upheld the decision of the lower courts.

MARCH 31, 1930   NAACP Fought Judicial Nomination. President Herbert Hoover nominated known racist Judge John J. Parker of North Carolina to the U.S. Supreme Court. The NAACP launched a successful campaign against Parker's confirmation.

JUNE 7, 1930   "Negro" Capitalized by *Times*. Responding to black demands, the *New York Times* announced that the "N" in the word "Negro" would be henceforth capitalized in its pages.

JUNE 22, 1930   Mary McLeod Bethune Named Leader. African American educator, feminist leader, and civil rights spokesperson Mary McLeod Bethune was named one of America's fifty leading women by historian Ida Tarbell. Bethune was born in Maysville, South Carolina, in 1875. She studied at Scotia Seminary in North Carolina and at the Moody Bible Institute in Chicago. In 1904, Bethune founded the Bethune-Cookman College at Daytona Beach, Florida. A recipient of the Medal of Merit from the Republic of Haiti and the NAACP Spingarn

Award, Bethune was president of the National Council of Negro Women and the Association for the Study of Negro Life and History. She was a principal advisor as well as a friend to President and Mrs. Franklin Roosevelt.

1931

1931   *Aldridge v. United States.* The U.S. Supreme Court, in *Aldridge v. United States,* reversed the lower courts' decision in which an African American man was convicted for murdering a white police officer. The high Court's decision was largely based on the trial court's refusal to allow the defense to question the jurors on their racial biases. Chief Justice Charles Evans Hughes emphasized the necessity of determining a prospective juror's disqualifying state of mind in any type of case, stating that if prejudice would stand in the way of a juror's ability to render a fair verdict, "a gross injustice would be perpetrated in allowing him to sit."

APRIL 6, 1931   The Scottsboro Boys. Nine black youths went on trial for their lives in Scottsboro, Alabama, after being accused of raping two white women on a freight train. The case became a cause celebre with African American organizations, liberal whites, and the Communist Party all vying to defend the Scottsboro Boys. The defendants were hastily convicted, but by 1950 all were free on parole, appeal, or by escape.

AUGUST 4, 1931   Surgeon Daniel Williams Died. Pioneer heart surgeon and founder of the predominantly black Provident Hospital, Daniel Hale Williams, died in Chicago. Williams, of mixed blood, was born in Philadelphia. He received a medical education at the Chicago Medical College through the generosity of a former surgeon on General Ulysses S. Grant's staff. In 1913, Williams became the first black member of the American College of Surgeons. After withdrawing from Provident Hospital because of internal bickering, Williams became

Civil rights activist and educator Mary McLeod Bethune. (Courtesy of Library of Congress.)

Pioneer heart surgeon Daniel Hale Williams. (Bettmann Archive/Newsphotos, Inc.)

the only black doctor on the staff of Chicago's St. Luke Hospital. His withdrawal from Provident Hospital and his marriage to a white woman subjected him to bitter attacks from fellow blacks in the latter years of his life.

1932

1932–1940 Resurgence of Black Migration. Faced with agricultural distress and racial oppression in the South, blacks began a new wave of migration into the major industrial centers of the North. Most moved in search of economic and social opportunities.

NOVEMBER 1932 Franklin Roosevelt Elected President. Franklin Roosevelt was elected president of the United States, promising a New Deal to all in the Depression-ridden nation.

1934

1934 Elijah Muhammad Headed Black Muslims. Elijah Muhammad succeeded W. D.

Fard as the leader of the Black Muslim movement in the United States. Muhammad was born Elijah Poole in Sandersville, Georgia, in 1897. His father was a Baptist preacher, sawmill worker, and tenant farmer. Muhammad was a deeply religious and race conscious youth. While employed as a laborer in Georgia in 1923, a white employer cursed him and he decided to move to the North.

While living on relief in Detroit, Michigan, during the Depression, Muhammad came under the influence of Wallace Fard Muhammad (W. D. Fard), a mysterious silk peddler who had been teaching blacks that they were members of a superior race, descendants of Muslims from Afro-Asia. Fard claimed to be a messenger from Allah sent to reclaim his lost people and save them from the inferior race of "white devils" who had made their lives so miserable. Christianity, he asserted, was a false religion used by whites to keep blacks in subjection.

Elijah Poole soon became Fard's closest associate and when Fard mysteriously disappeared in 1934, Poole, now known as Elijah Muhammad, took control of the group as "The

Messenger of Allah to the Lost-Found Nation of Islam in the Wilderness of North America." Muhammad and his followers refused to bear arms for the United States during World War II, and Muhammad was convicted for encouraging resistance to the draft. He served three and a half years of a five-year sentence in a federal prison before he was released in 1946. Meanwhile, Muslim membership had dropped from a high of about 8,000 under Fard's leadership to 1,000.

NOVEMBER 7, 1934 Arthur Mitchell Elected to Congress. Democrat Arthur L. Mitchell defeated Republican Congressman Oscar De Priest of Chicago, becoming the pioneer black member of his party in Congress. Mitchell, like his predecessor De Priest, was born in Alabama to former slaves. He received his education at Tuskegee Institute, where he was Booker T. Washington's office boy, and at Talladega College in Alabama. Mitchell taught in rural Alabama and served as an assistant law clerk in Washington D.C. When he moved to Chicago, he became involved in Republican ward politics but joined the Democrats with the shifting black party preference in the Depression years. In Congress, Mitchell professed to be a moderate, thus drawing the ire of the black press and the NAACP. He did, however, sponsor the long and costly suit that led to the end of Jim Crowism in Pullman railroad cars. Mitchell served four terms in Congress.

1935

1935 *University of Maryland v. Murray.* In *University of Maryland v. Murray*, the University of Maryland failed to convince the Maryland Court of Appeals that Baltimore resident and Amherst College graduate Donald Gaines Murray should not be admitted to the college. The NAACP's Charles H. Houston and Thurgood Marshall represented Murray in front of the appellate court that maintained the lower court's decision to admit him. The decision was based on the state's failure to provide a separate law school for blacks, a violation of the Fourteenth Amendment's equal protection clause.

APRIL 1, 1935 *Grovey v. Townsend.* The U.S. Supreme Court, in *Grovey v. Townsend*, ruled that the Democratic party is a private organization and therefore, not subject to the Fourteenth and Fifteenth Amendments as they pertain to discrimination. R.R. Grovey had filed suit against Albert Townsend, a white official for the Democratic Party who refused Grovey's vote in the Democratic primary. Grovey was unsuccessful in Texas district and appellate courts before losing his case at the Supreme Court level.

JUNE 25, 1935 Joe Louis Began His Fighting Career. African Americans received an emotional boost when black boxer Joe Louis defeated Primo Carnera at Yankee Stadium in New York. Louis then began his great boxing career in earnest. Louis was born Joe Louis Barrow in Lafayette, Alabama, in 1914. Shortly thereafter, his family moved to Detroit, Michigan, where Louis attended Duffield Elementary School for a short time. After leaving school, he worked in an automobile plant and, in his leisure time, boxed. Louis became the heavyweight champion of the world in 1937 and held the title until 1949, interrupting his career to serve in World War II. But a series of unsuccessful marriages and business ventures left Louis nearly penniless after his retirement from the ring.

1936

1936 *Brown v. Mississippi.* The U.S. Supreme Court, in *Brown v. Mississippi*, increased federal supervision over civil rights. The defendants,

Professional boxer Joe Louis. (Courtesy of Library of Congress.)

Ed Brown and two other black men, had been convicted of murder after confessions were tortured out of them. The deputy sheriff admitted to hanging Brown from a tree and whipping the two others to get their confessions. The high Court reversed the convictions on grounds that confessions obtained through force violated the due process clause of the Fourteenth Amendment.

1936   Mary Bethune Appointed to Black Cabinet. President Franklin Roosevelt, in continuing to organize his unofficial black cabinet, appointed Mary McLeod Bethune as director of the Division of Negro Affairs of the National Youth Administration.

JULY 3, 1936   NAACP Honored John Hope. John Hope was honored in New York City by the NAACP for his achievements as an educational and civil rights leader. Hope was a founder of the Atlanta University Center which is comprised of Morehouse College, an undergraduate school for men; Spelman College, an undergraduate school for woman; and Atlanta

University, a co-educational graduate school founded in 1929. In later years, Clark College, Morris Brown, and a theological seminary joined the complex, making it the largest educational center in the world for blacks.

AUGUST 9, 1936   Jesse Owens Triumphed at Olympics. African Americans reacted warmly to the news that black track star Jesse Owens won four gold medals at the Summer Olympics held in Berlin. Owens' first-place victories embarrassed Adolph Hitler, who championed the theory of Aryan racial superiority. Owens had been born in Ohio in 1913. He started competing in track and field at Fairmount Junior High School in Cleveland, and he continued to compete throughout his years at Ohio State University. Owens was a student at Ohio State when he won the 100-meter dash, the 200-meter dash, the long jump, and anchored the victorious 400-meter relay at the 1936 Olympics. The Associated Press designated Owens "the outstanding track athlete of the first 50 years of the 20th century."

DECEMBER 8, 1936   *Gibbs v. Board of Education.* The NAACP filed suit against the Board of Education of Montgomery County, Maryland. The *Gibbs v. Board of Education* decision set the precedent for equalizing the salaries of black and white school teachers.

1937

1937   Bishop Isaac Lane Died. Isaac Lane, Bishop and patriarch of the Colored Methodist Episcopal Church and founder of Lane College in Tennessee, died. Lane was born a slave on a Tennessee plantation in 1834. While a slave, he was licensed to preach, but even after emancipation he had to supplement his income by

Jesse Owens on the victor's podium at the 1936 Olympics. (AP/Wide World Photos.)

NAACP office workers. (Courtesy of the National Association for the Advancement of Colored People.)

raising cotton and selling firewood. He founded Lane College in 1882.

1937 Poll Taxes Upheld. The U.S. Supreme Court upheld the disenfranchisement of indigents in its ruling of *Breedlove v. Suttles* by upholding the constitutionality of poll taxes. The case was heard after Georgia's poll tax was challenged on grounds that it offended the rule of equality because it required a yearly payment of one dollar to vote, but only from people between twenty-one and sixty years old. The Southern Conference for Human Welfare also opposed the tax, calling it "patently a device for disenfranchising Negroes." The high Court, however, supported the lower courts' decision that the poll tax did not violate any protection or privilege guaranteed by the Fourteenth, Fifteenth, or Nineteenth Amendment.

MARCH 26, 1937   First Black Federal Judge. William H. Hastie was confirmed as the first

African American federal judge. Hastie had entered government service as an assistant solicitor in the Department of the Interior in the early part of the New Deal era. His judicial appointment was supported by the NAACP and influential whites at Harvard Law School. His nomination was approved over the vigorous opposition of Southern senators who labeled him a leftist, primarily because of his support of civil rights activities. President-Franklin D. Roosevelt appointed him to his unofficial black cabinet as an aide to the Secretary of War. But in 1941, Hastie resigned in protest of the War Department's failure to act against segregation in the armed services.

MAY 17, 1937   Energy Secretary Hazel O'Leary Born. Hazel O'Leary was born in Newport News, Virginia. She received her bachelor's degree from Fisk College in 1959 and graduated from Rutgers University School of Law in 1966. She served as a utilities regulator under presidents Gerald Ford and Jimmy Carter and as executive vice president of the Northern States Power Co., where she functioned as a Washington lobbyist. A proponent of energy conservation and alternative energy sources, O'Leary was appointed Secretary of Energy by President Bill Clinton in 1993. She came under heavy scrutiny in the mid-1990s for using government money to pay a consulting firm to rank reporters by how favorably they treated her in their news coverage. She was also criticized for lavish spending on overseas travel. Though Vice President Al Gore came to her defense, noting that her trips had helped create new job opportunities in the United States, O'Leary resigned at the end of President Clinton's first term late in 1996.

MAY 25, 1937   Artist Henry Ossawa Tanner Died. African American artist Henry Ossawa Tanner died. Thirty-two years later, the Frederick Douglass Institute and the National Collection of Fine Arts co-sponsored the first American exhibition of Tanner's work. Opening in Washington, D.C., at the National Collection of Fine Arts, the ninety-piece exhibit traveled to seven American museums. Only a handful of black artists preceded Tanner, and this exhibit was the first one-man show by a black artist to tour the country's major museums.

The first of seven children born to Sarah Miller Tanner and Benjamin Tucker Tanner, a minister in the African Methodist Episcopal Church, he was raised in Philadelphia. At about the age of twelve Tanner saw a landscape painter at work in Fairmount Park in Philadelphia; he later wrote, "It set me on fire." Borrowing fifteen cents from his mother to buy supplies, he assiduously applied himself until the Pennsylvania Academy of Fine Arts in Philadelphia accepted him in 1880, when he was twenty-one. There, he studied with Thomas Eakins, the celebrated realist who taught him to manipulate light and shadow to express mood. An artist who depicted African Americans as individuals, not caricatures, Eakins proved to be an important role model for Tanner.

However, Tanner had trouble establishing his career in the states. In 1891 he set off for Paris to enroll in the Academie Julien, where he felt his success would not be inhibited by his race. However, his first entry in the Parisian Salon, *The Bagpipe Lesson,* was unsuccessful.

After contracting typhoid fever during his second year in France, Tanner returned to Philadelphia to convalesce, and he entered into what is generally called his black genre period. Influenced by a French tradition established by Jean-Francois Millet, Tanner addressed African American themes, often incorporating teaching themes. *The Banjo Lesson, The Knitting Lesson, The Reading Lesson,* and *The Sewing Lesson* were all produced during this period.

In the summer of 1893 Tanner delivered a paper titled *The American Negro in Art* before the World's Congress on Africa in conjunction with the World's Columbian Exposition in Chicago. Although the text has been lost, Tanner's later autobiography, *The World at Work* (1909), expressed his views on black genre painting. His genre period concluded the following year with *The Thankful Poor*. The work was lost for years but was rediscovered in 1970 and then exhibited for eleven years at the Philadelphia Museum of Art. Actor Bill Cosby and his wife purchased the piece in 1981 for $250,000.

Biblical themes dominated the rest of Tanner's professional life, which he spent primarily in his adoptive French home. His *Daniel in the Lion's Den* received an honorable mention from the Salon in 1896, and *The Raising of Lazarus* was awarded a medal at the 1897 exhibition. Purchased by the French government for the Luxembourg Gallery, the painting joined the tableaux of John Singer Sargent and James A. McNeil Whistler, the only other American artists whose works had been purchased by the French government. In 1923, the French government further honored the artist, electing him a Chevalier of the Legion of Honor.

Tanner, whose Pittsburgh homesite was designated a historical landmark by the Department of Interior in 1976, was the first black to be elected to the National Academy of Design. In 1991, the Philadelphia Museum of Art sponsored a major retrospective containing more than one hundred Tanner paintings, drawings, photographs, and memorabilia.

JUNE 22, 1937 Joe Louis Won Heavyweight Championship. African Americans rejoiced as boxer Joe Louis defeated James J. Braddock for the heavyweight championship of the world.

JULY 2, 1937 NAACP Honored Walter White. Atlanta-born writer and civil rights leader Walter F. White was honored by the NAACP for his work as the organization's executive secretary, his investigations into lynchings, and his lobbying for a federal anti-lynching law. White was successful in getting anti-lynching measures introduced in 1935 and 1940, but both attempts died in the Senate. Although White had blond hair and blue eyes, he was of African descent and identified with the black race, especially after the 1906 Atlanta race riot.

1938

AUGUST 15, 1938 Congresswoman Maxine Waters Born. Born in St. Louis, Missouri, Maxine Waters moved to Los Angeles after graduating from high school. She worked at a garment factory and the phone company and eventually attended California State University, where she earned a bachelor's degree in sociology. In 1976 Waters won a seat in the California State Assembly. In 1990 she went on to win a seat in the U.S. House of Representatives, where she actively promoted legislation to aid poor and minority neighborhoods. Waters served on the board of directors of *Essence* magazine and got involved in the National Women's Political Caucus. In 1996, she was the recipient of an *Essence* Award.

DECEMBER 12, 1938 *Missouri ex rel Gaines*. With the help of the NAACP, the *Missouri ex rel Gaines* case resulted in the U.S. Supreme Court's ruling that states must provide equal, even if separate, educational facilities for blacks within their boundaries. The plaintiff, Lloyd Gaines, mysteriously disappeared following the Court's decision.

1939

MARCH 1939 Concert Hall Closed Doors to Black Singer. The Daughters of the American Revolution (DAR) refused to allow Marian Anderson to sing in Washington D.C.'s Constitution Hall. Anderson, a black contralto from Philadelphia, had just completed a successful European tour. First Lady Eleanor Roosevelt resigned from the DAR in protest. The Secretary of Interior then provided the Lincoln Memorial for the Anderson concert which drew an audience of 75,000 on Easter Sunday, 1939.

Anderson was awarded the NAACP's Spingarn Medal later in the year.

OCTOBER 11, 1939 NAACP Legal Defense and Educational Fund. The NAACP Legal Defense and Educational Fund, pledging itself to an all-out war on discrimination, was organized. Charles H. Houston, an Amherst and Harvard-trained lawyer, spearheaded the effort to consolidate some of the nation's best legal talents in the fight against bias sanctioned by law.

1940

FEBRUARY 1940 *Native Son* **Published.** Richard Wright published *Native Son,* a novel reciting the effects of racial oppression on black Americans. The work became a best-seller.

MARCH 1940 "Mammy" Awarded an Oscar. Black actress Hattie McDaniel won an Academy Award for best performance by an actress in a supporting role for her performance as Mammy in *Gone with the Wind,* becoming the first black to win an Oscar. McDaniel also appeared in *The Little Colonel* and *Showboat.*

APRIL 1940 Virginia Adopted Black Composer's Anthem. The Virginia Legislature adopted black composer James A. Bland's *Carry Me Back to Ole Virginny* as the state song.

JUNE 10, 1940 Marcus Garvey Died. Civil rights leader and United Negro Improvement Association organizer Marcus Garvey died in London.

OCTOBER 16, 1940 Benjamin Davis Appointed Brigadier General. Benjamin O. Davis, Sr., was appointed brigadier general in the U.S. Army, becoming the highest ranking black officer in the armed services. Davis was born in Washington, D.C., in 1877, and he studied at Howard University. He entered the U.S. Army as a first lieutenant in 1898 and served with the 8th Infantry during the Spanish-American

Marian Anderson. (Courtesy of Library of Congress.)

War. Prior to World War II, Davis served in the Philippines, Liberia, and Wyoming. He also taught military science at Wilberforce University in Ohio and at Tuskegee Institute. In World War II he served in the European Theater of Operations as an advisor on the problems of black servicemen, and he helped implement the desegregation of armed forces facilities in Europe. When he retired in 1948, Davis was an assistant to the inspector general in Washington, D.C. His awards and decorations include the Distinguished Service Medal, the Bronze Star, the Croix de Guerre with Palm, and an honorary doctorate from Atlanta University. Davis's son, Benjamin, Jr., also had a distinguished military career.

1941

1941 Army Established Black Pilot School. The U.S. Army established a school for black pilots at Tuskegee, Alabama. Some blacks opposed the establishment of segregated Air Force facilities, but others seemed to view the move as a forward step since no training schools had hitherto existed. While the pilots began their

Author and essayist Richard Wright. (Courtesy of Library of Congress.)

work at Tuskegee, ground crews were prepared at Chanute Field in Illinois. By the end of the year, the 99th Pursuit Squadron was ready for action. About six hundred black pilots received their wings during World War II.

1941   President Addressed Discrimination. President Franklin Roosevelt met with black spokesmen and urged them to call off a march against employment discrimination and segregation in the national defense program. The march was scheduled for July 1. A. Philip Randolph, head of the Brotherhood of Sleeping Car Porters, refused and pledged that 100,000 blacks would march.

APRIL 28, 1941   Railroad Car Segregation. The U.S. Supreme Court ruled that separate railroad car facilities must be substantially equal. The case was brought to the high Court by black congressman Arthur L. Mitchell.

JUNE 25, 1941   President Attacked Discrimination. President Franklin Roosevelt issued Executive Order 8802, which forbade racial and religious discrimination in defense industries and government training programs. A.

Philip Randolph called off the march on Washington, D.C., that was planned in protest of the government's discriminatory policies.

JULY 19, 1941   Fair Employment Practices Committee. President Franklin Roosevelt established the Fair Employment Practices Committee to monitor discrimination against blacks in defense industries. Blacks hailed the committee and the preceding Executive Order 8802 of June 25 as revolutionary developments, perhaps the most significant executive action affecting them since the issuance of the Emancipation Proclamation. They were soon disappointed, however, when discrimination continued in spite of the committee. The committee became entangled in bureaucratic inefficiency and politics, and faced opposition in the South.

AUGUST 6, 1941   North Carolina Racial Conflict. The first in a series of serious racial disturbances involving white and black soldiers and civilians occurred aboard a bus in North Carolina.

DECEMBER 7, 1941   Japanese Attacked Pearl Harbor. President Franklin Roosevelt prepared to ask for a declaration of war as a result of the Japanese attack on Pearl Harbor. Doris "Dorie" Miller, a twenty-two-year-old black messman aboard the *USS Arizona,* downed four Japanese planes with a machine gun after having moved his wounded captain from the bridge to a place of greater safety. The next year, Admiral Chester W. Nimetz presented the Navy Cross to Miller. In 1943 the Waco, Texas, native was listed as missing in action and presumed dead.

1942

JUNE 1942   Congress of Racial Equality. Blacks and whites organized the Congress of Racial Equality (CORE) in Chicago. They commit-

Hattie McDaniel receives an Academy Award for her performance in *Gone with the Wind* in 1940. (AP/Wide World Photos.)

Brigadier General Benjamin O. Davis, Sr., pins a medal on his son, Benjamin, Jr. (Courtesy of the U.S. Army.)

ted themselves to direct, non-violent action, their first major effort being a sit-in against discrimination at a Chicago restaurant. The national CORE was founded in June of 1943.

JULY 20, 1942 Women's Army Auxiliary Corps. With the formation of the Women's Army Auxiliary Corps (WAC), black women were accepted with whites.

SEPTEMBER 29, 1942 *Booker T. Washington* Launched. Black captain Hugh Mulzac com-

manded the *Booker T. Washington* after its launch from Wilmington, Delaware.

NOVEMBER 3, 1942 William Dawson Elected to House. William L. Dawson, for two decades the dean of black congressmen, was elected to the U.S. House of Representatives by Chicago. Dawson was the son of an Alabama barber. He received his education at Fisk University and a Chicago law school. After serving in World War I, Dawson opened a law practice in Chicago and became interested in politics.

Admiral Chester Nimetz awards Dorie Miller the Navy Cross. (Courtesy of the U.S. Navy.)

He began as a precinct worker and soon won favor with the Thompson Republican machine. He won five terms (1933–1943) in the City Council as a Republican before switching to the Democrats with the New Deal tide. Dawson became an important member of the Kelly and Daley Democratic machines during World War II. He served as "ward boss" in five Chicago districts, precinct captain, committeeman, vice-chairman of the Cook County Democrats, and vice-chairman of the Democratic National Committee. Dawson won a reputation as a shrewd political strategist. Dawson did not run for reelection in 1970 and died a year later.

1943

JANUARY 5, 1943   George Washington Carver Died. George Washington Carver died in Tuskegee, Alabama. A museum and a foundation were established there in his honor.

MAY 12–AUGUST 2, 1943   Race Riots Killed Forty. A series of serious race riots occurred across the nation in which about forty people were killed. U.S. troops were called out in Mobile, Alabama, and Detroit, Michigan, where the clashes threatened defense production. Other incidents occurred in Beaumont, Texas, and in Harlem, New York.

1944

APRIL 3, 1944   *Smith v. Allwright.* The U.S. Supreme Court, in *Smith v. Allwright,* ruled that the white primary that excluded blacks from voting in the South was in violation of the Constitution. The decision paved the way for blacks to participate in Southern politics for the first time since Reconstruction. But many states responded by enacting legal vices to circumvent the ruling and continue black exclusion from voting.

APRIL 24, 1944   United Negro College Fund. The United Negro College Fund (UNCF) was founded to coordinate the fund-raising efforts of the private all-black institutions of higher learning in the nation. Many of these colleges were facing extinction due to inadequate finances.

AUGUST 1, 1944   Adam Powell, Jr., Elected to House. Harlem, New York, elected Adam Clayton Powell, Jr., a controversial twentieth century politician, to serve in the U.S. House of Representatives. Powell was the son of a Harlem minister and political leader. After being expelled from City College of New York, Powell went to Colgate University. After graduating, he became a minister and publisher and led Harlem ministers in a "Jobs-for-Negroes" campaign in the 1930s.

Powell had begun his political career in 1941 as the first black member of the New York City Council. He chaired the House Education and Labor Committee from 1960 to 1967. He became famous for his Powell amendments that aimed to deny federal funds for the construction of segregated schools. In 1967, however, he was temporarily denied his seat in the House due to Congressional ethics violations. Powell was reelected by Harlem in 1968, but he was defeated in 1970 by another black, Charles Rangel.

DECEMBER 13, 1944 Women's Naval Corp Accepted Blacks. Black women were permitted to enter the Women's Naval Corp (WAVES).

1945

MARCH 12, 1945 New York Addressed Job Discrimination. New York established the first state Fair Employment Practices Commission to guard against discrimination in the workplace.

JUNE 1945 United Nations Charter Approved. The United Nations Charter was approved in San Francisco. Several blacks, including Mary McLeod Bethune, W. E. B. Du Bois, Walter White, Ralph Bunche, and Mordecai Johnson attended the San Francisco conference.

SEPTEMBER 2, 1945 World War II Ended. The Japanese surrendered and World War II ended. More than one million blacks served in the conflict.

SEPTEMBER 18, 1945 School Integration Opposed. An anti-integration protest took place in the schools of Gary, Indiana; one thousand white students walked out of classes. This mas-

sive walk-out, unparalleled at the time, preceded the integration troubles of the next three decades.

1946

MAY 1, 1946 Black Appointed Governor of Virgin Islands. Former federal judge William H. Hastie was confirmed as governor of the Virgin Islands. Hastie became the only African American to govern a U.S. state or territory since Reconstruction.

MAY 1, 1946 Black Named Mother of the Year. Emma Clarissa Clement, a black woman and mother of Atlanta University president Rufus E. Clement, was named "American Mother of the Year" by the Golden Rule Foundation. She was the first African American woman to receive the honor.

JUNE 3, 1946 *Morgan v. Virginia*. The U.S. Supreme Court, in *Morgan v. Virginia*, prohibited segregation in interstate bus travel. The case originated when Irene Morgan, a black woman, was arrested and fined ten dollars for refusing to move to the back of a bus running from Gloucester County, Virginia, to Baltimore. She appealed her conviction. But the high Court's ruling in her favor had little immediate effect as buses in Southern states continued segregation practices.

JUNE 10, 1946 Boxer Jack Johnson Died. The first great African American boxing hero, Jack Johnson, died in Raleigh, North Carolina. Johnson, a former stevedore from Galveston, Texas, gained pugilistic fame when, in 1908, he became the first nationally prominent black champion.

AUGUST 10-SEPTEMBER 29, 1946 Race Riots. Nearly one hundred blacks were injured in the serious racial disturbances that broke out in Athens, Alabama, and Philadelphia, Pennsylvania.

Congressman Adam Clayton Powell, Jr., at a political rally. (AP/Wide World Photos.)

Soldiers of the 92nd Division in Italy during World War II. (Courtesy of the U.S. Army.)

DECEMBER 5, 1946 President Formed Civil Rights Committee. President Harry Truman appointed a national Committee on Civil Rights to investigate racial injustices and make recommendations.

1947

APRIL 9, 1947 Freedom Riders. Freedom riders were sent into the South by the Congress of Racial Equality (CORE) to test the U.S. Su-

preme Court's June 3, 1946, ban against segregation in interstate bus travel. CORE, organized in 1942, had pioneered the sit-in tactic at segregated restaurants, but gained national attention with the Freedom Rider demonstrations that began in May of 1961. These latter demonstrations eventually led to a firm anti-discrimination policy in interstate transportation.

APRIL 10, 1947 Jackie Robinson Admitted to Major League. Jackie Robinson, a Georgia-born athlete, joined the Brooklyn Dodgers.

Jackie Robinson. (Archive Photos, Inc.)

Robinson, the first black baseball player in the major leagues, became a hero in the eyes of many African Americans. He was also the first black player to enter the Baseball Hall of Fame.

JUNE 27, 1947 NAACP Honored Chemist Percy Julian. Percy Julian, black research chemist in the area of human reproduction, was honored in New York by the NAACP. Julian, the son of a Montgomery, Alabama, railway clerk, graduated from DePauw University and was a researcher at Harvard University and the

University of Vienna. He taught at Howard and DePauw before becoming an industrial chemist in Chicago. He later established his own company, Julian Laboratories, which manufactured soya products, hormones, and pharmaceuticals.

SEPTEMBER 1, 1947 Fisk University Headed by Charles Johnson. Charles Spurgeon Johnson began his administration as president of Fisk University, becoming the first black man to head the Nashville institution. Johnson was born in Bristol, Virginia, in 1893 and was educated at Virginia Union University and the University of Chicago. From 1917 to 1919 he directed the division of research for the Chicago Urban League while also investigating black migration for the Carnegie Foundation. Johnson served on the Chicago Committee on Race Relations from 1923 to 1929. When Johnson assumed the presidency of Fisk University, he had already become a sociologist and writer. He founded and edited the National Urban League's house organ, *Opportunity* magazine, in 1923 and sponsored literary contests for young black writers during the Harlem Renaissance. Johnson's major published works include *Shadow of the Plantation* (1934), *The Collapse of Cotton Tenancy* (1934), *The Negro College Graduate* (1938), and *Growing Up in the Black Belt* (1941). Johnson died in 1956.

OCTOBER 29, 1947 Presidential Committee Condemned Discrimination. The president's Committee on Civil Rights formally condemned racial injustice in the United States in its celebrated report titled *To Secure These Rights*. The biracial group also called for a positive program to eliminate segregation from American life.

1948

JANUARY 12, 1948 *Sipuel v. University of Oklahoma*. The U.S. Supreme Court, in *Sipuel*

Percy Julian in a laboratory. (AP/Wide World Photos.)

A segregated bus station in Durham, North Carolina. (Courtesy of Library of Congress.)

v. University of Oklahoma, ruled that a state must provide legal education for blacks at the same time it is offered to whites. The case stemmed from the application that Ada Sipuel filed in 1946 to attend the University of Oklahoma Law School. Sipuel sought relief in state and then federal courts after the university denied her admission. Despite the Supreme Court's decision, Sipuel did not enter the school immediately because of further legal proceedings. Meanwhile, it failed to establish a law school for blacks. Eventually, Sipuel did enter the university and became one of its first black law graduates.

MARCH 31, 1948   Military Segregation Protested. Black labor leader A. Philip Randolph told a Senate committee that he would counsel black youths to refuse military induction unless segregation and discrimination were prohibited in the selective service system. In June, Randolph formed the League for Non-Violent Civil Disobedience Against Military Segregation.

African American sailors were segregated from their white counterparts. (Courtesy of the National Archives.)

MAY 3, 1948 *Shelley v. Kraemer.* The U.S. Supreme Court, in *Shelley v. Kraemer* ruled that the courts could not enforce restrictive housing covenants. The case was brought to the Court by J. D. Shelley and his wife Ethel, who bought a home in St. Louis, Missouri, in 1945. The house sat on a tract whose owner had signed an agreement that prohibited black use or occupancy of the land. The agreement, made in 1911, provided that failure to comply with this restriction should result in the owner's loss of

title to the property. Other property owners on this same tract of land, Mr. and Mrs. Louis Kraemer among them, had filed suit against the Shelleys and won an order from the Missouri Supreme Court that forced the blacks out of their home and forfeited their title because of their violation of the agreement. In 1947, the Shelleys appealed to the U.S. Supreme Court.

JUNE 9, 1948 **Oliver Hill Elected to City Council.** A breakthrough in black office-holding occurred in the South when Oliver W. Hill

Ralph J. Bunche. (Courtesy of Library of Congress.)

was elected to the City Council in Richmond, Virginia.

JULY 14, 1948   Dixiecrats Opposed Civil Rights Measures. Several Southern delegates walked out of the National Democratic Convention after a strong civil rights plank was adopted. South Carolinians and Mississippians were in the vanguard of the movement that formed the Dixiecrat party.

JULY 26, 1948   President Addressed Military Segregation. President Harry Truman issued an executive order that called for equality of treatment and opportunity for all Americans in the armed forces. This order paved the way for the gradual elimination of discrimination in the armed services.

SEPTEMBER 13, 1948   Ralph Bunche Appointed Mediator. Black political scientist Ralph J. Bunche was confirmed by the United Nations Security Council as temporary UN mediator in Palestine. Bunche was born in a Detroit ghetto and reared by relatives in Los Angeles after his parents' deaths. He was educated at the University of California and at Harvard University. Bunche began a career as a teacher at Howard University. He began to identify with civil rights programs and became a staunch supporter of the NAACP. After receiving the 1951 Nobel Peace Prize, Bunche was elected president of the American Political Science Association and made a member of the Board of Overseers at Harvard University.

OCTOBER 1, 1948   Interracial Marriages Legalized. The Supreme Court of California ruled unconstitutional the state law that prohibited interracial marriages. Two decades later, the U.S. Supreme Court sanctioned interracial marriage in all states.

OCTOBER 24, 1948   NAACP President Kweisi Mfume Born. Born Fizzell Gray in Baltimore, Maryland, Kweisi Mfume was a wayward youth and fathered five children out of wedlock. But by 1976 he had earned a bachelor's degree from Morgan State University. He later received his master's degree from Johns Hopkins University. Mfume entered politics in 1978 when he was elected to the Baltimore City Council, where he became particularly interested in health issues. He was elected to the U.S. House of Representatives in 1987 and served on committees including the Congressional Black Caucus, in which he served as chairperson. Mfumi left Congress in 1995 to serve as president and CEO of the NAACP. He is a trustee of the Baltimore Museum of Art and the Morgan State University Board of Regents.

1949

OCTOBER 3, 1949   Black Radio Station Aired. The pioneer black-owned radio station, WERD, began operations in Atlanta, Georgia.

OCTOBER 15, 1949   William Hastie Appointed to Circuit Court. William H. Hastie, former district court judge and governor of the Virgin Islands, was appointed a judge in the Third U.S. Circuit Court of Appeals.

Part 5

THE CIVIL RIGHTS
AND BLACK POWER
MOVEMENTS
1950–1979

$$Chapter\ 7$$

1950 TO 1959

1950

APRIL 1, 1950 Hematologist Charles Drew Died. Charles R. Drew, the pioneer African American hematologist, who was often called the father of the blood bank, died in Burlington, North Carolina. Drew was born in Washington, D.C., in 1904. A football and track star at Amherst College, he studied medicine at McGill University in Canada. Drew began his research into the properties of blood plasma while holding a General Education Board Fellowship at Columbia University Medical School. During World War II, after discovering the method of preserving blood plasma for emergencies, he organized a blood-collection system for the British and American governments. Drew served as a faculty member at Howard University Medical School and was chief surgeon and chief of staff at Howard's Freedman's Hospital at the time of his death. Previously, Drew was the recipient of the NAACP's Spingarn Medal for outstanding contributions to human welfare.

APRIL 3, 1950 Historian Carter Woodson Died. Pioneer black historian and founder of the Association for the Study of Negro Life and History, Carter G. Woodson, died in Washington, D.C.

MAY 1, 1950 Poet Gwendolyn Brooks Awarded a Pulitzer. Gwendolyn Brooks was awarded the Pulitzer Prize for poetry, becoming the first African American to receive the honor. Brooks was born in Topeka, Kansas, in 1917 but was raised in Chicago, where she attended Wilson Junior College. Some of her earliest works appeared in the *Chicago Defender*. Brooks's later works appeared in *Harper's, Common Ground, Mademoiselle, Poetry,* and the *Yale Review.* Her first volume of poetry, *A Street in Bronzeville* (1945), won the Merit Award from *Mademoiselle.* Brooks's second volume of verse, *Annie Allen* (1949), captured the Pulitzer Prize.

JUNE 5, 1950 *McLaurin v Oklahoma.* The U.S. Supreme Court, in *McLaurin v. Oklahoma,* ruled that once a black student has been admitted to a previously all-white school, no further distinctions can be made on the basis of race. McLaurin had been segregated within the University of Oklahoma.

JUNE 5, 1950 *Sweatt v Painter.* The U.S. Supreme Court, in *Sweatt v. Painter,* ruled that equality in education involved more than identical physical facilities. The Law School of the University of Texas, the largest university in the South, was ordered to admit Heman Sweatt of Houston, but he never attended the school.

JUNE 27, 1950 Blacks Fought in Korean War. The United States intervened in the Korean conflict. Thousands of blacks were among those fighting in the war.

Members of the 2nd Infantry in a Korean fox hole. (Courtesy of the U.S. Department of the Army.)

SEPTEMBER 22, 1950 Ralph Bunche Awarded Nobel Peace Prize. Ralph J. Bunche was awarded the Nobel Peace Prize for mediating the Palestinian dispute.

1951

1951 NAACP Took School Segregation to Court. The NAACP argued cases in Kansas and South Carolina against the discriminatory effects of public school segregation.

1951 Ralph Bunche Appointed United Nations Undersecretary. Ralph J. Bunche, educator, diplomat, and Nobel Peace Prize winner, was appointed Undersecretary of the United Nations, the highest ranking American in the UN Secretariat.

APRIL 24, 1951 Southern Universities Desegregated. The University of North Carolina joined a growing list of major Southern and border-state universities in admitting black students.

MAY 10, 1951 Z. Alexander Looby Elected to City Council. Blacks continued to make po-

litical advances in the South with the election of attorney Z. Alexander Looby to the city council in Nashville, Tennessee.

MAY 24, 1951 Restaurant Segregation Outlawed. The municipal appeals court in Washington, D.C. outlawed segregation in District of Columbia restaurants. Black feminist leader Mary Church Terrell had been in the vanguard of the local anti-segregation movement.

JUNE 21, 1951 Black Soldier Honored. Private First Class William H. Thompson of Brooklyn, New York, posthumously received the Congressional Medal of Honor for heroism in Korea, the first such award to an African American since the Spanish-American War. Private Thompson died at his machine gun after having refused to withdraw in the face of overwhelming Communist forces.

JULY 12, 1951 National Guard Suppressed Illinois Riots. Governor Adlai Stevenson of Illinois ordered the National Guard to suppress a riot in Cicero, Illinois. More than three thousand whites were protesting the attempt of a black family to occupy a home in an all-white neighborhood.

OCTOBER 1, 1951 Last All-Black Regiment. The last all-black army unit, the 24th Infantry, was deactivated by Congress.

DECEMBER 25, 1951 NAACP Leader Assassinated. A new era of racist assassinations began with the bombing death, in Mims, Florida, of Florida NAACP leader Harry T. Moore.

1952

JANUARY 12, 1952 University of Tennessee Desegregated. The University of Tennessee became the latest major Southern university to admit black students.

DECEMBER 7, 1952 Racist Bombings Increased. The Southern Regional Council, an interracial civil rights reporting agency, announced that racist bombings were increasing in the nation. About forty had been reported since January of 1951.

DECEMBER 30, 1952 Lynchings Declined. Tuskegee Institute reported that no lynchings occurred during 1952, the first in the seventy-one years that the Institute had kept tabulations.

1953

APRIL 5, 1953 Fisk University Gained Honor Society. Fisk University received a chapter of Phi Beta Kappa, the prestigious scholastic honor society. In later years, Howard University and Morehouse College were awarded chapters.

JUNE 8, 1953 *District of Columbia v. John R. Thompson Co., Inc.* The U.S. Supreme Court, in *District of Columbia v. John R. Thompson Co., Inc.,* affirmed the opinions of lower courts that Washington, D.C., restaurants could not refuse to serve blacks. The Court ruled that well-behaved blacks must be served and upheld an 1873 law that made it a criminal act for proprietors of public eating places to refuse to serve any person solely because of race or color.

JUNE 19, 1953 Bus Boycott. Blacks protesting discriminatory treatment began a bus boycott in Baton Rouge, Louisiana.

AUGUST 4, 1953 Integrated Housing Sparked Riot. Another serious riot erupted in Illinois in protest of integrated housing. One thousand law enforcement officers were called into the Trumbull Park apartments in Chicago.

DECEMBER 2, 1953 Rufus Clement Elected to Board of Education. Black progress in Southern politics advanced with the election of Rufus E. Clement, president of Atlanta University, to the Atlanta Board of Education.

DECEMBER 31, 1953 Hulan Jack Elected Manhattan President. Hulan Jack, a native West Indian, was inaugurated president of the Borough of Manhattan, the highest municipal executive post to be held by an African American up to that time.

1954

MARCH 4, 1954 Black assistant secretary of labor Appointed. President Dwight Eisenhower named J. Ernest Wilkins Assistant Secretary of Labor. Wilkins, a Phi Beta Kappa member who earned a Ph.D. from the University of Chicago at age twenty, had the distinction of being the top-ranking black person in the executive branch of the federal government.

MAY 17, 1954 *Brown v. Board of Education.* The U.S. Supreme Court, in *Brown v. Board of Education of Topeka, Kansas,* ruled unanimously that racial segregation in public schools was unconstitutional. Declaring that separate educational facilities were inherently unequal, this historic decision overruled the 1896 *Plessy v. Ferguson* ruling that had codified the concept of separate but equal public facilities. The NAACP legal team, headed by chief council Thurgood Marshall, represented the plaintiffs in this case, marking its greatest victory in a series of recent judicial triumphs.

JULY 24, 1954 Activist Mary Church Terrell Died. Longtime leader of black-club women and civil rights activist Mary Church Terrell died in Washington, D.C. Born in Memphis, Tennessee, at the close of the Civil War, Terrell inherited a substantial fortune and received an Oberlin College education. Her husband, Robert Terrell, was a prominent educator, attorney, and judge. In 1896 she spearheaded the National Association of Colored Women (NACW). A feminist leader and close associate of a number of white feminist leaders, she worked toward racial integration.

SEPTEMBER 7–8, 1954 Public Schools Desegregated. Massive school desegregation began in the public schools of Washington, D.C., and Baltimore, Maryland. This was the first widespread school desegregation since the U.S. Supreme Court decision of May 17.

OCTOBER 27, 1954 First Black Air Force General. Benjamin O. Davis, Jr., commander of the 15th Air Force bombers in their attacks on Romanian oil fields during World War II, became the first black general in the U.S. Air Force. Davis, son of the Army's General Benjamin O. Davis, Sr., was born in Washington, D.C., in 1912. He was educated at Western Reserve University, the University of Chicago, and the U.S. Military Academy at West Point. In 1936 Davis became the fourth black to graduate from West Point. He received his wings from the Tuskegee Advanced Flying School in 1942 and became commander of the 99th Fighter Squadron at the Army Air Field at Tuskegee. He was ordered to North Africa in 1943. During and after World War II, Davis served in Italy, Japan, Formosa, Germany, and Korea, where he served as commander of the 51st Fighter-Interceptor Wing. Davis's awards and decorations include the Distinguished Service Medal, the Silver Star, the Legion of Merit, and the Distinguished Flying Cross.

OCTOBER 30, 1954 Armed Forces Desegregated. Desegregation of the U.S. armed forces

NAACP chief counsel Thurgood Marshall on the steps of the U.S. Supreme Court. (Bettmann Archive/Newsphotos, Inc.)

was completed as the Defense Department announced the final abolition of all-black units.

NOVEMBER 2, 1954 Charles Diggs Elected to Congress. Charles C. Diggs, Jr., was elected to the U.S. House of Representatives. Thirty-three-year-old Diggs was the first black congressman from Michigan. He joined congressmen William Dawson of Chicago, who was reelected in 1954 for a seventh term; and Adam Clayton Powell, Jr., of Harlem, who won his sixth term in 1954. Diggs's election marked the first time in the twentieth century in which three blacks were serving Congress. All three were Democrats.

1955

JANUARY 7, 1955 Marian Anderson Made Her Opera Debut. Black contralto Marian Anderson made her debut as Ulrica in Giuseppe Verdi's *Un Ballo in Maschera* (A Masked Ball), at the Metropolitan Opera House in New York City. She was the first black singer in the company's history.

MARCH 21, 1955 NAACP's Walter White Died. Walter F. White, the second African American to serve as executive secretary of the NAACP and the leader of the organization through many of its judicial triumphs, died in New York.

APRIL 11, 1955 Roy Wilkins Assumed NAACP Leadership. Roy Wilkins became the third executive secretary of the NAACP. Wilkins, a journalist, had been the editor of the NAACP's *The Crisis* magazine and assistant executive secretary of the organization.

Wilkins, a native of St. Louis, Missouri, was born in 1901. He studied at the University of Minnesota at Duluth and was editor of the school's *University Daily*. Racial violence during his college career influenced his decision to work actively against discrimination. Similar experiences in Kansas City, where Wilkins was managing editor of the *Kansas City Call*, further inspired him to seek a career fighting for equality. Wilkins joined the NAACP staff in 1931. He came to play a leading role in the organization, representing the interests of blacks in the Philadelphia transit strike of 1943. Wilkins also presided over the NAACP's efforts to bring about school integration in the *Brown v Board of Education* case which was heard by the U.S. Supreme Court in 1954.

MAY 18, 1955 Educator Mary McLeod Bethune Died. Noted black female educator and political leader, Mary McLeod Bethune, died in Daytona Beach, Florida. She was one of the founders of the Bethune-Cookman College.

MAY 21, 1955 Chuck Berry's *Maybellene* Recorded. Chuck Berry recorded *Maybellene*, and the song reached number one on the R&B charts by mid-September. Ten more top-ten Berry hits followed in the next six years, including *Roll Over Beethoven, Too Much Monkey Business, School Days, Rock and Roll Music,* and *Johnny B. Good.* Chuck Berry influenced the generation's musicians and listeners with his unique brand of guitar playing and showmanship. David Marsh of *Rolling Stone* magazine claimed, "Chuck Berry is to rock what Louis Armstrong was to jazz."

Among other awards, Berry received a Grammy Award for Lifetime Achievement in 1984; he was elected to the Rock and Roll Hall of Fame in 1986; and he received *Guitar Player* magazine's Lifetime Achievement Award in 1987.

MAY 31, 1955 School Desegregation Loosely Enforced. The U.S. Supreme Court decreed that its May 17, 1954, school desegregation decision should be implemented "with all deliberate speed." The vagueness of the phrase allowed school segregation to continue in the nation for several more decades.

AUGUST 28, 1955 Mississippi Lynching. Lynching was renewed in the South with the brutal slaying of fourteen-year-old Chicago youth Emmitt Till. He was killed in Money, Mississippi, after allegedly having made indecent advances toward a white woman.

NOVEMBER 7, 1955 Recreational Facilities Desegregated. The U.S. Supreme Court prohibited segregation in recreational facilities in a Baltimore, Maryland, case.

NOVEMBER 25, 1955 Interstate Travel Desegregated. The Interstate Commerce Com-

Roy Wilkins in conversation with President Lyndon Johnson. (Courtesy of NAACP.)

mission (ICC) prohibited segregation in public vehicles operating in interstate travel. The order also extended to waiting rooms.

DECEMBER 1955   Little Richard's *Tutti Frutti* Released. Little Richard's *Tutti Frutti* was released just before Christmas, and it reached number twenty-one on the charts by the end of the month. The pianist's frenetic style ignited the airwaves, and one hit followed another. *Long Tall Sally, Slippin' and Slidin', Lucille,* and *Good Golly Miss Molly* were all chart-toppers. *Rolling Stone*'s Gerri Hirshey commented that

"Little Richard bent gender, upset segregationist fault lines, and founded a tradition of rock dadaists devoted to the art of self-creation."

Born in December of 1932 in Macon, Georgia, Little Richard Penniman cultivated a cross-racial following with his piano and pompadour. Little Richard was booted from his devout Seventh Day Adventist home at the age of thirteen because of his homosexuality. He then left his eleven siblings behind and moved into a white family's home, whose Macon nightclub served as a venue for the performer. The

A segregated drinking fountain. (Courtesy of Library of Congress.)

gospel and piano training he had received in the church had given Little Richard an edge, and by 1951 he cut his first recordings, including *Every Hour, Why Did You Leave Me,* and *Get Rich Quick.*

At one point in his career, however, Little Richard foreswore rock and roll and devoted himself to Bible study at a Seventh Day Adventist seminary. He received a bachelor's degree from Oakwood College in Huntsville, Alabama, and was ordained a minister. But by the mid-1960s he was touring again, this time in England with a little-known band called The Beatles. Continuing to perform old, and with less success, new songs, Little Richard continued with his campy brand of rock and roll for another twelve years. A regular panel member on the TV game show *Hollywood Squares,* Richard has also appeared on the *Tonight Show* and the Grammy Awards. He was also cast in a major role in the movie *Down and Out in Beverly Hills.*

DECEMBER 1, 1955   Rosa Parks Arrested. Rosa Parks, a black seamstress in Montgomery, Ala-

Rosa Parks being fingerprinted in a Montgomery, Alabama, police station. (AP/Wide World Photos.)

bama, refused to surrender her seat as ordered by the bus's driver. She was arrested for violating Jim Crow ordinances, and the city's blacks began a city-wide bus boycott on December 5. Despite terrorist attacks on boycott leaders, legal harassment, massive arrests, and civil suits, the boycott continued until December 13, 1956, when the U.S. Supreme Court ruled that segregation on public buses in Montgomery was illegal. Another significant result of the boycott movement was the emergence of Martin Luther King, Jr., as a national leader.

DECEMBER 5, 1955 Blacks Appointed Vice Presidents of AFL-CIO. Two black labor leaders, A. Philip Randolph and Willard S. Townsend, were elected vice presidents of the AFL-CIO.

1956

JANUARY 30, 1956 Home of Martin Luther King, Jr., Bombed. The home of Martin Luther King, Jr., was bombed in Montgomery, Alabama.

FEBRUARY 3, 1956   University of Alabama Desegregated. The desegregation of major southern universities continued with the admission, under court order, of black coed Authurine Lucy into the University of Alabama. Lucy was suspended after a February 7 anti-black riot at the school, and she was expelled on February 29 for making "false and outrageous" statements about university officials.

APRIL 11, 1956   Singer Nat King Cole Attacked. Racial tensions in the South continued with the attack on popular black singer Nat King Cole in Birmingham, Alabama.

JUNE 30, 1956   Howard University President Retired. Mordecai Johnson retired as president of Howard University. Johnson was born in Paris, Tennessee, in 1890. He was educated at Morehouse College, the University of Chicago, the Rochester Theological Seminary, and Harvard University. Upon receipt of a Master of Sacred Theology degree from Harvard in 1923, Johnson attracted national attention for a speech titled *The Faith of the American Negro.* After teaching at Morehouse and Howard, he took his post as the first black president of Howard.

When Johnson assumed the presidency, in 1926, Howard consisted of a cluster of unaccredited departments, a situation that Johnson sought to improve. In 1928 Johnson secured a congressional allocation of annual appropriations for the support and development of Howard University. When Johnson retired, Howard had ten schools and colleges; was a fully accredited institution; had an enrollment of more than six thousand students; and its School of Medicine was producing about half of the black doctors in the United States. Johnson was succeeded by law professor and civil rights attorney James M. Nabrit, Jr.

AUGUST 30–SEPTEMBER 17, 1956   Violence Over School Desegregation. Anti-black protests and violence accompanied efforts to desegregate schools in Mansfield, Texas; Clinton, Tennessee; and Sturgis and Clay, Kentucky.

NOVEMBER 13, 1956   Montgomery Buses Desegregated. The U.S. Supreme Court upheld the decision of a lower court, outlawing the segregation of buses in Montgomery, Alabama.

DECEMBER 20–21, 1956   Montgomery Bus Boycott Ended. The Montgomery bus boycott ended with the U.S. Supreme Court's decision that outlawed the segregation of buses in Montgomery, Alabama.

DECEMBER 25–26, 1956   Home of Alabama Minister Bombed. The home of black minister and civil rights activist Fred L. Shuttlesworth was bombed in Birmingham, Alabama. The city's blacks responded with a massive defiance of bus segregation regulations. At least forty people were arrested.

DECEMBER 27, 1956   Tallahassee Buses Desegregated. Segregation was outlawed on buses in Tallahassee, Florida, after blacks had boycotted the vehicles for more than six months.

1957

FEBRUARY 14, 1957   First Southern Christian Leadership Conference. The Southern Christian Leadership Conference (SCLC) was organized in New Orleans, Louisiana. Atlanta, Georgia, was chosen as the SCLC's national headquarters, and Martin Luther King, Jr., was elected its first president.

MAY 17, 1957   Voting Rights Act Supported. More than fifteen thousand Americans, most of them black, gathered at the Lincoln Memorial in Washington, D.C., to support the proposed voting rights act. Martin Luther King, Jr., led the speakers in shouting "Give us the ballot!" The demonstration was the first large-scale black protest in Washington since World War II.

JUNE 1957   Gerrymandering Opposed. Blacks in Tuskegee, Alabama, began a boycott of

Federal troops escort students at Little Rock High School. (AP/Wide World Photos.)

white merchants in protest of the state legislature that had thwarted their quest for political power by gerrymandering, redividing the electoral districts of Tuskegee to make the black districts smaller. Charles G. Gomillion, a Tuskegee Institute sociologist, led the movement through the Tuskegee Civic Association.

AUGUST 29, 1957 Voting Rights Act Passed. The U.S. Congress passed the Voting Rights Act of 1957, the first major civil rights legislation since 1875.

SEPTEMBER 9, 1957 Violence Over School Desegregation. Violence aimed at preventing school desegregation continued in the South. One Nashville, Tennessee, school was bombed, and Reverend Fred L. Shuttlesworth was attacked in Birmingham, Alabama, while trying to enroll his children in school.

SEPTEMBER 24–25, 1957 School Desegregation Forced. After unsuccessfully trying to persuade Arkansas governor Orval Faubus to give up his efforts to block desegregation of

Central High School in Little Rock, President Dwight Eisenhower ordered federal troops into the city to halt interference with federal court orders to integrate. Faubus and a mob of whites gave way to the military power and permitted nine black children to attend a desegregated high school on September 25.

DECEMBER 5, 1957 Fair Housing Measure Passed. New York City took the lead in local efforts against housing discrimination by passing a Fair Housing Practice ordinance.

1958

JUNE 30, 1958 *NAACP v. Alabama.* Alabama's attempt to cripple the NAACP by imposing a $100,000 contempt fine against it was stymied by the U.S. Supreme Court. The fine had been imposed because of the NAACP's failure to produce its membership lists for an Alabama judge. In *NAACP v. Alabama,* the Court declared that it would not tolerate denial of constitutional rights through evasive application of obscure procedural rules.

Lunch counter sit-in.

AUGUST 19, 1958 Restaurant Segregation Protested. Members of the NAACP Youth Council began a new series of sit-ins at segregated restaurants. Lunch counters in Oklahoma City, Oklahoma, were the latest targets.

SEPTEMBER 20, 1958 Martin Luther King, Jr., Stabbed. Martin Luther King, Jr., was stabbed by a black woman while in Harlem, New York, autographing copies of *Stride Toward Freedom,* his story of the Montgomery bus boycott. King recovered from the serious wound.

1959

MARCH 11, 1959 *A Raisin in the Sun.* African-American playwright Lorraine Hansberry's *A Raisin in the Sun* became a Broadway hit. The play depicted black life in the ghetto. Lloyd Richard, a black, directed the play.

APRIL 25, 1959 Mississippi Black Lynched. Another Mississippi lynching was recorded with the death of Mack Parker of Poplarville.

Chapter 8
1960 to 1969

1960

1960   Black Muslim Population. The Black Muslims reportedly reached 100,000 members. Last year, the movement reported thirty temples and only about 12,000 members. (Because of the secrecy of the organization, membership can only be estimated.) The rapid rise in membership is partly attributed to the work of dynamic ministers like Malcolm X and increased media publicity.

FEBRUARY 1, 1960   Students Protested Restaurant Segregation. A wave of sit-ins at segregated lunch counters, led principally by black college students, began at Greensboro, North Carolina. Four students from North Carolina A & T College initiated the new movement.

In less than two weeks the drive spread to fifteen cities in five southern states, and within two years it engulfed the South. Sit-in participants met with physical violence and legal harassment including massive jailings. Most restaurants eventually desegregated voluntarily, under court order, or by legislation. The success of the sit-in technique encouraged blacks to use the method of nonviolent direct action in other areas where discrimination persisted. Martin Luther King, Jr., assumed leadership of the widened movement.

FEBRUARY 25, 1960   Sit-in at Alabama Courthouse. Black students from Alabama State University conducted a sit-in at the County Courthouse in Montgomery, Alabama. This was the first protest of its type in the capital of the Old Confederacy. Sheriff Mac Sim Butler and his deputies kept close watch on the demonstrators in the Courthouse's lunchroom while groups of white men, some armed with baseball bats, patrolled outside. Two days later, a black woman was injured by a white who struck her on the head with a club; no arrests were made in the incident. Alabama governor John Patterson responded, warning that there were not enough police officers in the country to prevent disturbances and offer protection if blacks "continued to provoke whites."

FEBRUARY 27, 1960   Sit-in Participants Attacked. Black and white demonstrators were attacked in Nashville, Tennessee. The violence occurred in two of the five stores where students had staged nonviolent lunch counter sit-ins. Police arrested about one hundred people, most of them black demonstrators. Seventy-six of those arrested declined payment of fines or bonds pending their trials. Their attorneys stated that the jailed protestors refused to support "the injustice and immoral practices that have been performed" in their arrest.

FEBRUARY 29, 1960   Martin Luther King, Jr., Urged Passive Resistance. Martin Luther King,

Meeting of Muslim men. (Courtesy of Library of Congress.)

Jr., spoke to a crowd of more than one thousand students in Montgomery, Alabama, following three days of racial tension sparked by student sit-ins. King urged continued passive resistance to segregation. The Alabama State University students pledged to withdraw from their college en masse if any were expelled for previous or future sit-ins.

MARCH 1, 1960   University Student Protestors Expelled. Blacks marched to the Old Confederate capitol building in Montgomery, Alabama, where they prayed and sang the *Star Spangled Banner* during a nonviolent demonstration against segregation. The next day, the State Board of Education expelled nine of the participating students from Alabama State University.

MARCH 4, 1960   Texas Sit-in Protestor Attacked. Lunch counter sit-ins reached the Southwest as about one hundred students from Texas Southern University conducted nonviolent protests in Houston. Three days later, four masked white men, apparently in retaliation, kidnaped a black man, Felton Turner, beat

him, and carved the letters "KKK" on his chest and stomach.

MARCH 6, 1960   Protest March to Alabama Capitol Blocked. State, county, and local police stopped a march of nearly one thousand blacks en route to a protest meeting at the Alabama state capitol. There were scattered fist fights between blacks and whites, but police prevented large-scale violence. Two days later, Montgomery police broke up another protest demonstration on the Alabama State University campus and arrested thirty-five students and at least one teacher. Thirty-three of the blacks were subsequently found guilty of disorderly conduct and fined $200 each.

MARCH 16, 1960   President Called for Biracial Talks. President Dwight Eisenhower stated during a press conference that he was "deeply sympathetic" with the effort of any group to enjoy constitutionally guaranteed rights. He did not endorse the lunch counter sit-in movement that was sweeping the South, but he did call for biracial conferences in "every city and every community of the South" in order to settle racial problems.

President Dwight Eisenhower meets with African American leaders, including Martin Luther King, Jr., and A. Philip Randolph. (Courtesy of the Dwight D. Eisenhower Library.)

APRIL 15–17, 1960 Student Non-Violent Coordinating Committee. The Student Non-Violent Coordinating Committee (SNCC) was founded in Raleigh, North Carolina. The group became the nationwide liaison for student sit-in activities.

APRIL 19, 1960 NAACP Attorney's Home Bombed. The home of Nashville, Tennessee's black city councilman Z. Alexander Looby was demolished by a dynamite bomb. The NAACP attorney and his family escaped injury. The bomb also damaged several homes in Looby's neighborhood and blew out hundreds of windows at the black Meharry Medical College; several medical students were injured by the flying glass. Looby had been chief counsel for more than one hundred students arrested in Nashville, Tennessee, sit-ins since demonstrations began there in February. After the bombing, more than two thousand blacks marched on the Nashville City Hall in protest of police failure to halt the racial violence. Reverend C.

T. Vivian accused Nashville mayor Ben West of encouraging the violence by permitting police to use their authority with partiality. West denied the accusation and claimed that he favored desegregation of lunch counters. But, he said, businessmen practicing segregation were acting within their rights.

MAY 6, 1960 Voting Rights Act of 1960 Signed. President Dwight Eisenhower signed the Voting Rights Act of 1960. The law was designed to bolster the Voting Rights Act of 1957 which granted protections to blacks trying to obtain suffrage. Under the new law, federal courts would be authorized to appoint voting referees who would be empowered to register blacks in areas where racial discrimination against voters had been proven. The referees could register all blacks who could establish their qualifications under state law, but who had been previously denied registration. But referees were appointed only after two conditions were met. First, the Justice Department was required to file suit under the Civil Rights Act of 1957 to obtain an order requiring the registration of such persons who had been unjustly disqualified by local registrars because of their race. Second, the Justice Department, upon winning the suit, had to ask the judge to declare that a pattern or practice of discrimination had blocked blacks from voting. The new law was invoked in the South for the first time on May 9.

JULY 31, 1960 Black Muslim Leader Called for All-black State. Elijah Muhammad, leader of the religious-nationalist Black Muslims, called for the establishment of an all-black state. Such a state, or group of states, later became a symbol and rallying cry for new supporters of black nationalism.

SEPTEMBER 8, 1960 New York Governor Praised Sit-in Protestors. In his address to the annual meeting of the National Urban League, New York governor Nelson A. Rockefeller called the lunch counter sit-ins an "inspiring example" for the nation. Rockefeller maintained that the sit-in demonstrators personified the moral force and made an "appeal to human conscience" that could solve civil rights problems.

OCTOBER 19, 1960 Martin Luther King, Jr., Arrested. Martin Luther King, Jr., and about fifty other blacks were arrested for sitting-in at an Atlanta, Georgia, department store restaurant. The arrest caused a Decatur, Georgia, judge to revoke King's previous parole for conviction on a traffic violation. King was then sentenced to serve four months in Georgia's maximum security prison. Robert F. Kennedy and his brother, presidential candidate John F. Kennedy, assisted the King family in obtaining his release.

NOVEMBER 10, 1960 Andrew Hatcher Named Presidential Press Secretary. Andrew Hatcher was named associate press secretary by President-elect John F. Kennedy. Hatcher was, for a time, the highest ranking black appointee in the executive branch of the federal government.

NOVEMBER 10, 1960 Louisiana Anti-school-integration Law Prohibited. U.S. District Judge J. Skelley Wright prohibited implementation of Louisiana's anti-school-integration laws. The same day, the New Orleans school board approved plans to admit five black children into two previously all-white schools. Three days later the Louisiana state legislature took control of New Orleans schools, fired the school superintendent, and ordered all schools closed on November 14. At the same time, Judge Wright issued a new order prohibiting interference by the state with the schools.

NOVEMBER 14, 1960 New Orleans Schools Integrated. Desegregation crept into the major industrial centers of the South with the admission of black children to schools in New Orleans. Amid the jeering of angry white parents, four black children enrolled in two schools on November 14. White protests, accompanied by

A. Philip Randolph Institute's Voter Registration Headquarters in Cincinnati, Ohio. (AP/Wide World Photos.)

a boycott, continued for much of the school year.

1961

JANUARY 11, 1961   University Student Suspension Sparked Riot. A riot resulted from the suspension of two recently admitted black students at the University of Georgia. The two were reinstated under court order on January 16.

JANUARY 27, 1961   Leontyne Price Made Opera Debut. Leontyne Price debuted with New York's Metropolitan Opera in *Il Trovatore,* and an unprecedented forty-two-minute standing ovation followed her performance. Price soon established herself as "the Stradivarius of singers," and when the New York company moved to its new quarters at Lincoln Center, director Rudolf Bing honored Price with an invitation to open the new opera house in the world premier of Samuel Barber's *Antony and Cleopatra.*

One season after her debut, she opened in the title role of Puccini's *The Girl of the Golden West* and launched a prolific recording career en route to becoming one of the world's leading sopranos and the first black singer to gain international stardom in opera. By 1969, Price had appeared in more than one hundred Metropolitan Opera productions.

Mary Violet Leontyne Price was born in Jackson, Mississippi, on February 10, 1927. At the age of nine she attended a concert by African American vocalist Marian Anderson and decided to devote her life to singing. After receiving her bachelor's degree in 1949, Price was awarded a four-year, full-tuition scholarship at the Juilliard School of Music in New York, where she studied voice with Florence Page Kimball.

After a two-year jaunt in a revival of George Gershwin's *Porgy and Bess,* the diva made her concert debut at New York's Town Hall, where she impressed audiences with her facility with modern compositions. Numerous NBC telecasts followed. The first telecast, Puccini's *Tosca,* distinguished Price as the first black singer to perform opera on television.

In 1957, conductor Kurt Herbert Adler, who had seen Price perform in *Tosca,* invited her to sing the role of Madame Lidoine in *Dialogues of the Carmelites* with the San Francisco Opera. That same year, the San Francisco Opera's lead soprano in *Aida* had an emergency appendectomy, and Adler asked the Mississippi soprano if she knew the opera. Price, whose perfect Verdi voice eventually came to define the role of *Aida,* recounted: "That was being in the right place at the right time."

Price has won thirteen Grammy Awards, and in 1965 she received the Presidential Medal of Freedom, the nation's highest civilian award. In 1980 she was awarded the Kennedy Center Honors for lifetime achievement in the arts, and five years later she received the first National Medal of the Arts. Price performed at the White House in 1978 and 1982, and she

opened the convention of the Daughters of the American Revolution (DAR) in Constitution Hall with a concert honoring Marian Anderson, who, in 1939, had been barred from appearing in Constitution Hall by the DAR because of her race.

FEBRUARY 11, 1961 Robert Weaver Assumed Federal Agency Control. Black housing expert Robert C. Weaver became administrator of the Housing and Home Finance Agency, the highest federal post held by an African American at that time. Weaver held a Ph.D. from Harvard University.

MAY 4, 1961 Youths Tested Desegregation Practices. A contingent of white and black youths sponsored by the Congress of Racial Equality (CORE) set out on a bus trip through the South to test desegregation practices. Despite court rulings and decrees set by the Interstate Commerce Commission (ICC), many southern states refused to sanction non-discriminatory transportation. The biracial group met with physical violence including beatings and arson, and legal harassment. In the fall, the ICC reaffirmed its order prohibiting discrimination in transportation. Such discrimination gradually disappeared on vehicles, but lingered in waiting rooms and other facilities, especially in the rural South.

AUGUST 9, 1961 Judge James Parsons Appointed to District Court. James B. Parsons was appointed by President John F. Kennedy as judge of the District Court of Northern Illinois, the first such appointment for an African American in the continental United States. Parsons, a fifty-year-old Chicago attorney, was serving as a judge on the Cook County Court at the time of his appointment.

SEPTEMBER 1, 1961 Peaceful School Desegregation Achieved. Four high schools were peacefully desegregated by ten black children in Atlanta, Georgia. The orderly desegregation in the Deep South's largest city won praise from President John F. Kennedy, who hoped it would set a new precedent. Previously, desegregation had been marked by violence.

SEPTEMBER 23, 1961 Thurgood Marshall Appointed to Circuit Court. The NAACP's chief counsel, Thurgood Marshall, was appointed judge of the Second Circuit Court of Appeals by President John F. Kennedy. The appellate court encompasses New York, Connecticut, and Vermont. Marshall, a native of Baltimore, Maryland, was fifty-three at the time, and had been with the NAACP for more than twenty years.

DECEMBER 12–16, 1961 Martin Luther King, Jr., Led Protest. Martin Luther King, Jr., and his forces launched an all-out attack against segregation and discrimination in Albany, Georgia. The effort was frustrated by mass arrests and political maneuverings, but the Albany debacle served to teach civil rights leaders lessons for future massive directaction assaults on segregation.

1962

1962 Fannie Lou Hamer Fired for Voting Attempt. Fannie Lou Hamer was fired from her job on a Mississippi cotton plantation in 1962 because she tried to vote. Upon violent threats that followed, Hamer moved from the state she had lived in for more than forty years and began her civil rights agenda, first by registering blacks to vote through the Student Non-Violent Coordinating Committee. In 1964 she helped form the Mississippi Freedom Democratic Party in a move to challenge Mississippi's Democratic Party which refused to send black delegates to the national presidential convention, though the state had a large black population. Four years later Hamer was a delegate to the Democratic National Convention.

In 1969, Hamer founded the Freedom Farms Corporation to help needy families raise food and fund their educational and business ventures.

JANUARY 18–28, 1962 University Closed Due to Student Protests. Louisiana's Southern University, the largest all-black state college in the South, closed as a result of student protests in opposition to the expulsion of sit-in demonstrators. These expulsions were used by administrators at publicly supported black colleges to meet the demands of state authorities to quell sit-in and related activities. The closing of the school became the precedent for handling student disturbances.

MAY 17, 1962 Historian E. Franklin Frazier Died. Sociologist and historian E. Franklin Frazier died in Washington, D.C. Frazier was the author of *Black Bourgeoisie,* the controversial book that argued middle-class blacks were isolating themselves from poverty-stricken blacks. Frazier, born in Baltimore, Maryland, on September 24, 1894, was a Howard University graduate. He received his Ph.D. from the University of Chicago in 1931 but returned to Howard three years later to begin a twenty-five-year affiliation with their sociology department. Eventually he was appointed chairman of the department. Before his retirement from Howard in 1959, he interrupted his tenure to teach at Columbia University and New York University, among others. He had traveled to Brazil and the West Indies as a Guggenheim fellow in the early 1940s, and he was made president of the American Sociological Society in 1948. For the United Nations Educational, Scientific and Cultural Organization (UNESCO), Frazier served as chairman of the committee of experts on race and chief of the organization's Applied Science Division in Paris.

A recognized authority on the black family, Frazier wrote *The Negro Family in the United States, The Negro in the United States, The Negro Church in America, The Free Negro*

Civil rights leader Fannie Lou Hamer. (Courtesy of Library of Congress.)

Family and Race, and *Culture Contacts in the Modern World.*

SEPTEMBER 9, 1962   Georgia Churches Burned. Two black churches were burned in Sasser, Georgia. Burnings and bombings of black churches, especially those used for civil rights meetings, became common during the decade.

SEPTEMBER 30, 1962   University of Mississippi Forced to Integrate. U.S. Supreme Court Justice Hugo Black ordered the admission of a black student, James H. Meredith, to the University of Mississippi. Governor Ross Barnett tried, unsuccessfully, to block Meredith's admission, and racial tension sparked a riot the day U.S. Marshals escorted Meredith onto the campus. Federalized National Guardsmen were used to restore order on the riot-torn campus. Meredith graduated from the school in 1963.

NOVEMBER 7–8, 1962   Blacks Elected to Office. Edward W. Brooke, an African American lawyer from Boston, was elected attorney general for Massachusetts, becoming the highest-ranking black official in New England. Black Atlanta lawyer Leroy R. Johnson was elected to

Georgia's Senate, making him the state's only black legislator since Reconstruction. And California's Augustus F. Hawkins became the first black to represent his state in the U.S. Congress.

NOVEMBER 20, 1962   Discrimination in Federally Financed Housing Prohibited. Racial discrimination in federally financed housing was prohibited by President John F. Kennedy. The order was applied principally to housing projects and apartments, but had little effect on homes that were not in commercially developed neighborhoods. Insured loans for home improvements from the Federal Housing Authority (FHA) were also excluded. In the event of violations, the government would first seek to obtain voluntary compliance. Administrative or court action leading to cancellation of loans or contracts would be taken in the event that voluntary compliance could not be obtained.

1963

APRIL 3, 1963   Discrimination Protest Resulted in Agreement and Rioting. Civil rights forces led by Martin Luther King, Jr., launched a drive against bias in Birmingham, Alabama. The city's police force, led by Commissioner Eugene "Bull" Connor, used high powered water hoses and dogs against demonstrators. The forceful repression and legal harassment, including massive arrests, aroused public opinion, especially in the North. President John F. Kennedy hoped to use this new public awareness to garner support for the civil rights proposals he had presented to Congress in March. The Birmingham protests continued until May 10, when an agreement was signed providing gradual desegregation of public accommodations. But the agreement was followed by bombings of homes and businesses of black leaders, causing further rioting.

JUNE–AUGUST 1963   Discrimination Protested Across the Nation. Civil rights demonstrations, protests, and boycotts occurred in

Protesters being hosed by the police in Birmingham, Alabama. (AP/Wide World Photos.)

almost every major urban area in the country. Boston, Massachusetts, and Harlem, New York, were scenes of protests of discrimination in the construction industry and de facto segregation in schools. Limited martial law was declared in July in Cambridge, Massachusetts, after black demonstrators and white segregationists clashed.

JUNE 11, 1963 University of Alabama Forced to Integrate. Two black students were admitted to the University of Alabama after an unsuccessful attempt by Governor George C.

Wallace to block their entrance. President John F. Kennedy ordered federalized National Guardsmen to insure enrollment of blacks to the University. In a televised address that night, the president made an impassioned plea for an end to discrimination through moral suasion and legislative action, but Congress continued to ignore Kennedy's civil rights proposals.

JUNE 12, 1963   Civil Rights Leader Medgar Evers Assassinated. Medgar W. Evers, NAACP field secretary in Mississippi and World War II

The police use dogs to break up racial demonstrations. (AP/Wide World Photos.)

Civil rights leader Medgar Evers. (AP/Wide World Photos.)

hero, became the latest victim of assassination resulting from civil rights activity. Evers was gunned down by a sniper in Jackson, Mississippi. His alleged assailant, a white segregationist, was initially acquitted by a hung jury.

AUGUST 17, 1963 NAACP Founder W. E. B. Du Bois Died. NAACP founder W. E. B. Du Bois died in Accra, Ghana. Du Bois, born on February 23, 1868, in Barrington, Massachusetts, was the first black to receive a Harvard University Ph.D. His dissertation, *The Suppression of the African Slave Trade to America,* was published in 1896 as the first volume in the Harvard Historical Studies Series. This work, along with *The Philadelphia Negro* (1899), *The Souls of Black Folk* (1903), and *The Atlanta University Publications* (1898-1914), established Du Bois's scholarly reputation. Du Bois, who became disillusioned with American racial attitudes and the democratic-capitalist system, had emigrated to Ghana in 1961.

AUGUST 28, 1963 Martin Luther King, Jr., Delivered "I Have a Dream." The largest single protest demonstration in U.S. history occurred at the Lincoln Memorial in Washing-

ton, D.C., where 250,000 blacks and whites gathered to lobby for passage of civil rights measures that had been presented to Congress. Martin Luther King, Jr., thrilled the crowd with his immortal "I Have a Dream" speech. President John F. Kennedy received a delegation of civil rights leaders at the White House and promised to push ahead for anti-discrimination legislation.

SEPTEMBER 15, 1963 Girls Died in Bombing of Black Church. Racial tensions were renewed in Birmingham, Alabama, when four black girls died in the bombing of the 16th Street Baptist Church. No serious disturbances followed the incident.

OCTOBER 22, 1963 Students Protested De Facto Segregation. A massive boycott involving nearly a quarter-million students was staged in Chicago, Illinois, to protest de facto school segregation.

NOVEMBER 22, 1963 Blacks Mourned Assassinated President. African Americans joined the world in mourning the assassination of President John F. Kennedy, whom many blacks believed had been killed because of his advocacy of civil rights. Kennedy's civil rights measures were still being debated in Congress when he died.

DECEMBER 7, 1963 Medals of Freedom Awarded to African Americans. Ralph J. Bunche and Marian Anderson were awarded Medals of Freedom, the highest civilian decoration. President Lyndon Johnson awarded the medals for their outstanding contributions to the ideals of freedom and democracy.

1964

1964 Civil Rights Activity Brought Violence to Mississippi. Reports from civil rights groups

March on Washington in 1963. (AP/Wide World Photos.)

indicated that three people were killed; three were wounded; eighty were physically assaulted; over one thousand were arrested; and thirty buildings were bombed in Mississippi during the course of the year's civil rights activity.

1964   Economic Opportunity Act Passed. The U.S. Congress passed the Economic Opportunity Act as part of the nation's "war on poverty." The legislation was later severely criticized by proponents and antagonists for its inefficiency. But many blacks benefited from it, especially through the Head Start program for pre-schoolers, the Upward Bound program for high school students, and the college work-study financial aid program.

JANUARY 21, 1964   Carl Rowan Appointed to Head Information Agency. Black journalist Carl T. Rowan of Minnesota was appointed director of the U.S. Information Agency. Rowan was the first of several blacks to receive high-ranking appointments by President Lyndon Johnson.

JANUARY 23, 1964   Poll Taxes Outlawed by Constitution. The Twenty-fourth Amendment to the Constitution was adopted, prohibiting the denial or abridgement of the right to vote by "reason of failure to pay any poll tax or other tax." The poll tax had been used by several Southern states as a means of discouraging black voters.

FEBRUARY 4, 1964   First Black Georgia Jurist Since Reconstruction. Veteran civil rights lawyer and political leader Austin T. Walden took the oath as a municipal judge in Atlanta, making him the first black jurist in Georgia since Reconstruction.

MARCH 12, 1964   Malcolm X Withdrew from Nation of Islam. Malcolm X, one of the most notable black Muslim ministers, announced his withdrawal from Elijah Muhammad's Nation of Islam. Born Malcolm Little in Omaha,

Nebraska, in 1925, his father was a Baptist minister from Georgia who had supported Marcus Garvey's "Back to Africa" movement in the early 1900s. His mother was West Indian. By the time Malcolm was thirteen, three of his uncles had been slain by whites; his father was murdered; and his mother was committed to a mental institution. A school drop-out, Malcolm made his living principally by illegal means, at one point ending up in a detention home for stealing. In February of 1946, Malcolm was sentenced to ten years in prison for burglary in Boston, where he eventually converted to Islam.

Upon his release from prison in August of 1952, Malcolm drew closer to the movement. In the summer of 1953 he became assistant minister of the Detroit temple, and in 1957 he founded *Muhammad Speaks,* a Muslim newspaper. By 1959 he had become one of the leading spokesmen for the Muslims. As Malcolm's charisma and media exposure brought him a larger following, Elijah Muhammad reportedly labeled him ambitious and dangerous. Following President John F. Kennedy's assassination in November of 1963, Malcolm referred to the killing as an example of "chickens coming home to roost." Muhammad immediately suspended Malcolm from his Muslim duties for that intemperate statement. This was the beginning of the end for Malcolm X as he left the movement on March 12, 1964, carrying only a few defectors with him.

APRIL 13, 1964   Sidney Poitier Won Academy Award. Sidney Poitier won an Academy Award for best actor for his role in *Lilies of the Field.* Poitier was the first African American actor to receive the coveted award.

JULY 2, 1964   Civil Rights Legislation Passed. The U.S. Congress passed a sweeping civil rights act, including provisions prohibiting discrimination in public accommodations and employment. The most important civil rights legislation since 1875, its passage was made certain after the Senate, for the first time in such a case, imposed cloture on June 10 to end a Southern-sponsored filibuster. President Lyndon Johnson signed the bill in the presence of civil rights leaders, among them Martin Luther King, Jr.

JULY 18–AUGUST 30, 1964   Race Riots Erupted in Major Cities. Serious racial disturbances occurred in a number of American cities, beginning in the Harlem section of New York City. The Harlem riot followed the shooting of a black teen by white police officers. Several other riots were also sparked by clashes between blacks and white police officers. Other areas that witnessed riots include Brooklyn and Rochester, New York; Jersey City, New Jersey; Chicago, Illinois; and Philadelphia, Pennsylvania. Injuries in the disturbances exceeded one hundred, property losses tallied up to millions of dollars, and National Guardsmen were needed to quell the unrest.

AUGUST 4, 1964   Civil Rights Workers Found Dead. The bodies of civil rights workers James E. Cheney, Michael Schwerner, and Andrew Goodman were discovered in a shallow grave on a farm outside Philadelphia, Mississippi. The Federal Bureau of Investigation accused nearly two dozen white segregationists of complicity in the murders. Included among them were law enforcement officers.

DECEMBER 1964   Prohibition of Discrimination Upheld. The U.S. Supreme Court upheld the constitutionality of the section of the Civil Rights Act of 1964 that prohibited discrimination in public accommodations.

DECEMBER 10, 1964   Martin Luther King, Jr., Awarded Nobel Peace Prize. Martin Luther King, Jr., the champion of non-violent resistance to racial oppression, was awarded the Nobel Peace Prize in Oslo, Norway. King, at age thirty-five, became the youngest man in history and the second African American to receive this prestigious honor.

Martin Luther King, Jr. (Courtesy of Library of Congress.)

1965

JANUARY 2–MARCH 25, 1965   Alabama Voter Registration Conflict. Civil rights forces led by Martin Luther King, Jr., opened a voter registration drive in Selma, Alabama. King was attacked as he registered at a formerly all-white hotel, but he was not seriously injured. After two weeks, on January 19, Dallas County law enforcement officers began arresting would-be black voters and their supporters. A federal

Selma-to-Montgomery march. (United Press International)

district court countered by issuing an order, on January 23, that prohibited interference with those seeking the right to vote.

The drive to register black voters in Alabama developed into a nationwide protest movement as local whites in Dallas County stiffened their resistance, and civil rights leaders intensified their efforts. More than seven hundred blacks, including Martin Luther King, Jr., were arrested on February 1.

On February 26, black demonstrator Jimmie L. Jackson died from wounds inflicted by state troopers in Marion, Alabama. On March 7, several hundred protestors were routed by billy clubs, tear gas, whips, and cattle prods as they attempted to march across the Edmund Pettus bridge in Selma, Alabama. President Lyndon Johnson, sympathizing with the demonstrators, denounced the incident. Reverend James Reeb, a white minister from Boston who assisted in the voting rights drive, died following an assault by three white men on March 11.

On March 17, a federal judge ordered Alabama officials not to interfere with a proposed march from Selma to Montgomery, the state capital. The march was designed to dramatize the denial of voting rights and drum up national support. The fifty-mile march, occurring between March 21–25, was protected by federal troops, and about fifty thousand people appeared before the Alabama state capitol to hear Martin Luther King, Jr., and others denounce Alabama leaders for interfering with voting rights. Alabama governor George C. Wallace received a petition from the crowd.

White civil rights supporter from Michigan, Viola Gregg Liuzzo, was murdered that night. Three Ku Klux Klansmen were later convicted of conspiracy to violate civil rights in Liuzzo's death.

FEBRUARY 21, 1965   Malcolm X Assassinated. Black nationalist and former member of the Nation of Islam hierarchy, Malcolm X was assassinated in New York City. Three African Americans were convicted of the murder in March of 1966.

Malcolm X, though a former convict, was largely self-educated and became known as a persuasive orator with a fiery tongue. In recent years, a cult has been built around his memory by young blacks. His *Autobiography of*

Black nationalist Malcolm X. (Courtesy of the Brooklyn Museum.)

Floyd McKissick.

Malcolm X, written in conjunction with Alex Haley, was published posthumously. The book has become a classic of twentieth-century black American literature. In 1992 film maker Spike Lee recounted the activist's life in a motion picture.

MAY 26, 1965   Voting Rights Extended. A new voting rights bill was passed by the U.S. Congress. The bill contained an anti-poll tax amendment designed to prevent states from using a tax to deny or abridge the right to vote. The bill also extended voting rights to those unable to read or write English but able to prove accomplishment of an eighth grade education in a school conducted under the American flag. Federal registrars could enroll voters who had been denied the suffrage by local officials.

JUNE 4, 1965   President Pledged Civil Rights Action. President Lyndon Johnson delivered a speech at Howard University's commencement, pledging an all-out effort to bring blacks into the mainstream of American society. He quoted the title of the civil rights anthem "We Shall Overcome" as a motto for action.

JUNE 9–15, 1965   Segregationist School Superintendent Protested. A united front of civil rights groups dissatisfied with the slow pace of school desegregation announced that a public school boycott would be held to protest the rehiring of Chicago school superintendent Benjamin C. Willis, whom blacks viewed as a segregationist. Willis had been given a new one-year contract on May 27.

A federally issued injunction against the boycott was ignored, and blacks in Chicago staged a round of demonstrations on June 10. The arrests began the next day, with entertainer Dick Gregory, nine clergymen, and James Farmer, the director of the Congress of Racial Equality (CORE), among the 225 who were arrested. Protests continued through June 15, when Mayor Richard Daley sanctioned a downtown march and agreed to negotiate with civil rights leaders.

JULY 13, 1965   Thurgood Marshall Appointed Solicitor General. Appeals court judge Thurgood Marshall was nominated as solicitor general of the United States by President Lyndon Johnson. This was the highest law enforce-

Aerial view of the 1965 Watts riot. (Bettmann Archive/Newsphotos, Inc.)

ment position yet to be held by an African American.

AUGUST 11–21, 1965   Rioting in Watts Section of Los Angeles. The most serious racial disturbance in American history to date erupted in the Watts section of Los Angeles, California. As in the riots of the previous year, a clash between blacks and white police officers triggered the disturbance. National Guardsmen assisted in quelling the disorder that left 34 dead and almost 900 injured. More than 3,500

people were arrested, and property losses neared $225 million. In the wake of the riot, federal, state, and local authorities sought ways to improve living conditions in the twenty-square-mile ghetto that housed 100,000 people. On August 20, President Lyndon Johnson denounced the Watts rioters and refused to accept "legitimate grievances" as an excuse for the disorder.

DECEMBER 3–10, 1965   Voter Registration Violence on Trial. On December 3, an Alabama federal court jury convicted Collie L. Wilkins of conspiracy to violate civil rights by killing, on March 25, voting rights activist Viola Gregg Liuzzo. On December 10, another Alabama jury acquitted the whites accused of the murder of Reverend James Reeb, a Boston minister who was slain at the same Selma, Alabama, demonstrations. The violence had erupted in Selma after voting rights activists pushed a major drive to register eligible blacks as voters.

1966

JANUARY 3, 1966   Floyd McKissick Installed CORE Leader. Floyd McKissick, a militant black civil rights leader from North Carolina, succeeded James Farmer as director of the Congress of Racial Equality (CORE). McKissick eventually came to guide CORE toward becoming an aggressive, mostly black group dedicated to black liberation even if by separatist routes. The forty-three-year-old attorney had served as CORE's national chairman since 1963. McKissick announced plans including a program of community organization to help disadvantaged blacks living under "feudalism."

JANUARY 10, 1966   Julian Bond Denied Seat in Georgia House. After having been duly elected, Julian Bond was denied his seat in Georgia's state legislature for openly opposing U.S. involvement in the Vietnam War. The vote against Bond in Georgia's House of Representatives was 184 to 12. The Atlanta native had, on January 6, told journalists that he supported a Student Non-Violent Coordinating Committee policy statement that advocated civil rights and social service alternatives to the draft. Many white Georgia legislators interpreted his statements as reflecting an un-American attitude. The seven other black members of the House voted to seat Bond.

JANUARY 13, 1966   Robert Weaver Appointed HUD Secretary. Robert C. Weaver, one of the nation's leading authorities on urban housing, was appointed the first secretary of the new Department of Housing and Urban Development (HUD). The appointment, by President Lyndon Johnson, made him the first African American to serve in a presidential cabinet and the highest ranking black in the executive branch of the government. Weaver had previously served as housing director for New York, been a member of President Franklin Roosevelt's unofficial black cabinet, and was the highest ranking black in President John F. Kennedy's administration.

JANUARY 25, 1966   Constance Motley Appointed Federal Judge. Former NAACP attorney Constance Baker Motley was appointed as a federal judge. The appointment, by President Lyndon Johnson, made her the second black woman to hold such a post. Marjorie Lawson had been appointed by President John F. Kennedy.

APRIL 12, 1966   First Black Umpire Hired. Emmett Ashford was hired by the American League, and became the first African American major league baseball umpire.

MAY 10, 1966   California Fair Housing Laws Disputed. The California Supreme Court ruled that the state constitutional amendment that nullified California fair-housing laws was in violation of the U.S. Constitution. The state amendment, known as Proposition 14, had been placed on the general election ballot in November of 1964 and was approved by a 2 to 1 margin. It provided that no state or local agency could interfere with a real estate owner's "absolute discretion" in the sale and rental of property. In effect it nulled California open-housing ordinances and sanctioned discrimination in selling or renting property.

But the state supreme court's 5 to 2 decision held that it was "beyond dispute" that the Fourteenth Amendment's equal protection clause secured "the right to acquire and possess property of every kind" without racial or religious discrimination. The court overruled a lower court's rejection of a complaint by Lincoln W. Mulkey against apartment owners in Orange County. The lower court had ruled that the California open housing acts on which Mulkey's petition was based had been rendered "null and void" by the passage of Proposition 14.

Six companion cases were also covered by the state court's order. Governor Edmund Brown, who had announced in March of 1966 that $200 million in federal urban-renewal funds had been withheld from California because of Proposition 14, promptly announced that the state court's decision would be appealed to the U.S. Supreme Court and that until then he would continue to enforce Proposition 14. State attorney general Thomas Lynch, however, said he would resume enforcement of the open-occupancy laws of 1959 and 1963 that had been invalidated by Proposition 14.

MAY 16, 1966 Stokely Carmichael Named Head of SNCC. West Indian-born Stokely Carmichael was named head of the Student Non-Violent Coordinating Committee. Carmichael transformed the SNCC into a more militant organization bent on achieving racial liberation, even if by employing a separatist route.

JUNE 6, 1966 "Pilgrim Against Fear" Shot. James H. Meredith, the black student who broke the color bar at the University of Mississippi in 1962, was shot during his self-proclaimed one-man pilgrimage "against fear" from Memphis, Tennessee, to Jackson, Mississippi. Meredith was not seriously injured. A white segregationist was arrested for the attack.

JUNE 7–26, 1966 March "Against Fear" Resumed. Civil rights leaders including Martin Luther King, Jr., and Stokely Carmichael resumed the march begun by James Meredith. Meredith had been shot shortly after embarking on his pilgrimage "against fear." The demonstration ended with a rally of fifteen thou-

Stokely Carmichael. (Courtesy of National Education Television.)

sand people at Jackson, Mississippi, where King, Carmichael, and Meredith addressed the crowd. It was during this march and rally that Carmichael and others began to freely employ the phrase "black power." The slogan was interpreted differently, but all agreed it denoted a more aggressive posture for its supporters.

JUNE 9, 1966 California Fair Housing Partially Reversed. The California Supreme Court partially reversed a May 10, 1966, decision that invalidated a state constitutional amendment that voided open-housing laws in the state. The new decision was based on a reconsideration of one of the seven cases covered by the earlier ruling. The court declared that the owner of a single-family home that was not financed by federal funds was not covered by state open-occupancy legislation and thus, the owner could refuse to sell or lease a home to blacks. The new ruling did not in any other way affect the earlier invalidation of the controversial constitutional amendment known as Proposition 14.

JULY 1–9, 1966 "Black Power" Endorsed by CORE. The national convention of the Congress of Racial Equality (CORE) endorsed the "black power" concept. Student Non-Violent Coordinating Committee leaders had already begun to adopt the slogan, while the Southern Christian Leadership Conference and the NAACP rejected the concept.

JULY 10, 1966 Martin Luther King, Jr., Addressed Chicago Crowd. Martin Luther King, Jr., addressed a predominately black crowd of forty-five thousand in Chicago, Illinois, and launched a drive to rid the nation's third largest city of discrimination.

JULY 12–15, 1966 Chicago Rioting Over Fire Hydrant Use. A dispute between police and black children over the use of a fire hydrant for recreation resulted in rioting in one of Chicago's black ghettoes. Two blacks were killed, many were injured, and 370 were arrested. Three days later Chicago mayor Richard Daley and Martin Luther King, Jr., announced new programs in recreation for Chicago blacks, a committee to study police-citizen relations, and a plan for closer cooperation between community residents and police.

JULY 18–23, 1966 Pub Incident Sparked Cleveland Race Riot. A serious racial disturbance occurred in Cleveland, Ohio, leaving 4 dead, 50 injured, 160 arrested, and widespread property damage. Shootings, fire bombings, and looting prevailed throughout Hough, a black ghetto on Cleveland's east side. The incident that touched off the riot took place in a neighborhood bar. One version claimed that the bar's white management had refused to serve water to blacks. Another held that a woman soliciting money for a friend's funeral had been ejected. Bands of blacks began roaming in the area after the incident. At least ten buildings were destroyed by fire.

AUGUST 5–6, 1966 Martin Luther King, Jr., Stoned. Martin Luther King, Jr., was stoned in Chicago while leading a demonstration against discrimination in the city. King was not seriously hurt, but he left the city shortly thereafter. The Chicago campaign had been only partially successful.

OCTOBER 1966 Black Panther Party Formed. The Black Panther Party was founded in Oakland, California. The two principal founders were Huey P. Newton, a native of Grove, Louisiana, and Bobby Seale of Dallas, Texas. Newton and Seale grew up in California and met in 1960 at Merritt Junior College in Oakland. Inspired by police brutality and other forms of racism, as well as the teachings of Malcolm X, the duo was active in the college's African American student association. They eventually withdrew and organized the Black Panther Party.

The Black Panther Party adopted a ten-point program demanding: full employment, restitution for past exploitation and oppression, education relevant to black needs and aspirations, release of all black political prisoners, decent housing, exemptions from military service, trial of blacks by all-black juries, an end to police brutality, and black political and economic power. The Panthers insisted on "power to the people." They advocated self-defense, called for a socialistic economy, provided food and educational programs for young children, and published their own newspaper. They drew wide admiration, if not a large following, from young blacks in the northern and West Coast ghettoes. As their numbers and influence increased, so did their clashes with law enforcement.

NOVEMBER 8, 1966   Edward Brooke Elected to Senate. Edward W. Brooke, the Massachusetts attorney general, was elected U.S. senator from Massachusetts. The Howard University graduate from Washington, D.C., thus became the first African American to sit in the U.S. Senate since Reconstruction.

1967

JANUARY 8, 1967   Julian Bond Regained Seat in Georgia House. Following a decision by the U.S. Supreme Court, Julian Bond was seated in the Georgia General Assembly. Bond had been elected, but he was denied the ability to sit after expressing his views against United States involvement in the Vietnam War.

JANUARY 9, 1967   Adam Clayton Powell, Jr., Lost House Seat. Adam Clayton Powell, Jr., was ousted as Chairman of the House Education and Labor Committee and denied his seat in the U.S. House of Representatives.

APRIL 4, 1967   Martin Luther King, Jr., Opposed Involvement in Vietnam. Martin Luther King, Jr., announced his unalterable opposition to the Vietnam War. King first spoke at a press conference at the Overseas Press Club in New York, and later that day at the Riverdale Church in Harlem, New York, where he suggested avoidance of military service "to all those who find the American course in Vietnam a dishonorable and unjust one." King compared the use of new weapons on Vietnamese peasants to the Nazis' testing of new medicines on Jews during World War II. He proposed that the United States take new initiatives to end the war "in order to atone for our sins and errors in Vietnam." Many of King's supporters disagreed with his strong anti-war stance.

MAY 1–OCTOBER 1, 1967   Most Serious Rioting to Date. The worst summer of racial disturbances to date occurred. More than forty riots were recorded as well as at least one hundred other smaller incidents. The most serious violence broke out in Newark, New Jersey, where twenty-six people died between July 12 and 17; and in Detroit, Michigan, where forty people died between July 23 and 30. New York City, Cleveland, Washington, D.C., Chicago, and Atlanta were also scenes of trouble. President Lyndon Johnson appointed a National Advisory Commission on Civil Disorders to investigate disturbances and make recommendations. The commission, commonly known as the Kerner Commission, conducted hearings and investigations and reported its findings to the president in March of 1968. The commission got its nickname as it was headed by Illinois governor Otto Kerner.

MAY 12, 1967   H. Rap Brown Became SNCC Head. H. Rap Brown, a militant black youth, was appointed the new chairman of the Student Non-Violent Coordinating Committee. Brown, who had numerous brushes with the law, disappeared in 1970 while awaiting trial on a charge of inciting a riot in Cambridge, Massachusetts.

JULY 1, 1967   Morehouse College President Resigned. Benjamin E. Mays retired as president of Morehouse College. Mays, the son of South Carolina tenant farmers, was educated at Bates College in Maine and at the University of Chicago. An ordained Baptist minister, Mays taught at Howard University and Morehouse College, among others, before becoming president of Morehouse in 1940. He expanded the programs begun by John Hope, and the college produced a number of black businessmen, professionals, and civil rights leaders.

Mays gained the reputation of a militant civil rights advocate, largely because of his membership on the NAACP board of directors and his forthright speeches and writings demanding racial equality. In April of 1968, Mays

Aerial view of a Detroit neighborhood in flames during the 1967 riot. (AP/Wide World Photos.)

delivered the eulogy at the funeral of Martin Luther King, Jr., blaming America's racist society for King's assassination. Mays was elected president of the Atlanta Board of Education in 1969. Mays was succeeded by Hugh M. Gloster, academic dean at the Hampton Institute and scholar of African American literature.

JULY 17, 1967 Saxophonist John Coltrane Died. John Coltrane died of liver cancer just months after cutting the album, *Expression.* Coltrane's music, which defied categorization and was a subject of controversy in its day, was instrumental in the development of modern jazz. The famed saxophonist was born on September 23, 1926, in North Carolina. By the late 1940s he had joined Dizzy Gillespie's orchestra, which he played with for four years, already beginning to experiment with technical innovation and composition.

In the 1950s modern jazz became a tremendously virile idiom, and, playing with the likes of Miles Davis and Thelonious Monk, Coltrane learned to deepen control of his instrument through tricks of phrasing and harmony. Exhausting every possibility for his horn in the course of a song, Coltrane's technique of

exploring all the avenues relied on rapid runs in which individual notes were virtually indistinguishable, a stylistic element that became known as "sheets of sound."

In 1960, with McCoy Tyner on piano, Elvin Jones on drums, and Jimmy Garrison on bass, Coltrane formed his own quartet. His most celebrated theme-and-variations piece, *My Favorite Things,* was produced during this period that was marked by experimentation with triple meter, pentatonic scales, and modal foundations. Coltrane's ever-increasingly complex ametric and improvisational experimentation made him one of the most famous living jazz legends by the mid-1960s, and he enjoyed celebrity that extended to Europe and Japan.

AUGUST 30, 1967 Thurgood Marshall Appointed to Supreme Court. Thurgood Marshall's appointment to the U.S. Supreme Court was confirmed by the Senate. He was the first black to serve in the nation's highest judicial court.

SEPTEMBER 2, 1967 Walter Washington Appointed Mayor. President Lyndon Johnson

Supreme Court Justice Thurgood Marshall. (Courtesy of Library of Congress.)

appointed Walter Washington as the first mayor of Washington, D.C. The fifty-five-year-old chairman of the New York City Housing Authority had officially been the commissioner of the newly reorganized municipal government of the District of Columbia, the nation's largest predominately black metropolis. One opponent of Washington's confirmation by the Senate was black militant Aketi Kimani, who stated, "any number of militant white men" could do a better job than "a house nigger" such as Washington.

NOVEMBER 1967   Blacks Elected as Mayors. The steady growth of the black population in the larger cities of the nation was reflected in the number of African Americans holding public offices. While blacks had substantial majorities in only a few cities, their numbers were large enough to, in conjunction with whites, elect African Americans in several localities. In 1967 Floyd McCree was elected mayor of Flint, Michigan; Carl B. Stokes was elected mayor of Cleveland, Ohio; and Richard B. Hatcher was elected mayor of Gary, Indiana.

1968

JANUARY 16, 1968   First Black Sheriff in South Since Reconstruction. Lucius Amerson began his tenure as sheriff of Macon County, Alabama, and the first black sheriff in the South since Reconstruction. Three newly appointed deputies, one white and two blacks, were sworn in with Amerson.

FEBRUARY 8, 1968   Students Protested Bowling Alley Discrimination. Three black students died and several others were wounded by South Carolina law enforcement officers during a disturbance on the campus of South Carolina State College at Orangeburg. Strong protesting had begun earlier in opposition of segregation at a local bowling alley. The National Guard was mobilized and the school was closed for two weeks after the protesting got out of control. Some of the students were jailed on charges of trespassing. The February 8 incident was preceded by an injury to a state trooper who was knocked down with a piece of wood. The Justice Department began an investigation two days later, and a suit was filed against the owners of the segregated bowling alley, charging them with violation of the Civil Rights Act of 1964. At the same time, action was filed against segregation and discrimination in Orangeburg hospital facilities. The courts upheld the anti-segregation complaints in both instances. But attempts to indict and prosecute the officers involved were unsuccessful.

MARCH 1968   Racism Found to be Perpetrator of Violence. The Kerner Commission reported that "white racism" was the principal cause of the disturbance that rocked the nation in 1967. The report also stated that the United States was headed toward two communities, "one white, one black, separate and unequal."

APRIL 4, 1968   Martin Luther King, Jr., Assassinated. Martin Luther King, Jr., was assassinated in Memphis, Tennessee. The assassination was followed by a week of racial rioting in at least 125 localities across the nation. Hundreds of thousands attended his funeral services on April 9, 1968, in Atlanta, Georgia. President Lyndon Johnson declared a day of national mourning.

APRIL 11, 1968 Fair Housing Act Passed. President Lyndon Johnson signed the Fair Housing Act, also known as the Civil Rights Act of 1968. The legislation prohibited racial discrimination in the sale and rental of most housing units in the country.

MAY 11, 1968 Poor Peoples Campaign. Ralph David Abernathy, successor to Martin Luther King, Jr., as head of the Southern Christian Leadership Conference, led a motley array of blacks, poor whites, Native Americans, and Mexican Americans to Washington, D.C., for a "poor peoples campaign." The drive, originally conceived by King, included lobbying and the erection of a campsite known as Resurrection City.

JUNE 25, 1968 Resurrection City Disbanded. Resurrection City, sponsored by the Southern Christian Leadership Conference, admitted failure and disbanded. Bad weather, insufficient discipline, and a preoccupied, unreceptive Congress limited the campaign's effectiveness.

JULY 23–24, 1968 Cleveland Race Riot. A serious racial disturbance in Cleveland, Ohio, left eleven people dead. A small band of armed black nationalists fought Cleveland police in the Glenville ghetto. This was followed by burning and looting, and resulted in an estimated $1.5 million in property damage. Three white police officers and eight blacks died during the riot.

AUGUST 29, 1968 Blacks Nominated in Presidential Primary. Channing Phillips's name was submitted in the Democratic nomination for president of the United States. But the African American minister from Washington, D.C., received only a handful of votes. Black

Georgia legislator Julian Bond's name was submitted in the Democratic nomination for vice president. He received several votes but withdrew his name as he was too young to occupy the office, according to the U.S. Constitution.

SEPTEMBER 8, 1968 Black Panther Convicted of Manslaughter. Black Panther leader Huey P. Newton was convicted of manslaughter in California. Militant black self-defense groups such as the Black Panthers in the North and the West Coast region, and the Deacons in the South were strengthening as result of the 1967 rioting in black ghettoes. The Panthers, an avowedly revolutionary group, drew the ire of law enforcement officers and others; several of its leaders were arrested, exiled, or killed.

NOVEMBER 5, 1968 Shirley Chisholm Elected to House. New York's Shirley Chisholm defeated James Farmer in the race for a seat in the U.S. House of Representatives, becoming the first black woman to serve in Congress.

NOVEMBER 5, 1968 Eighty Southern Blacks Elected into Office. Eighty blacks were elected to political offices in the South, bringing the total number of black elected officeholders in the eleven states that made up the Old Confederacy to nearly four hundred. Three years earlier, only seventeen blacks held political offices in these states. Most of the successful black candidates ran in districts with predominately black constituencies. In primaries as well as general elections, most black candidates lost when they challenged whites in predominately white districts.

To black Southerners, the highlight of the November general elections was the election, for the first time in the century, of blacks to the legislatures in North Carolina, Florida, and Tennessee. Greensboro lawyer Henry Frye won a seat in the North Carolina House, and Miami teacher Joe Lang Kershaw won a seat in the Florida House. James O. Patterson, Jr., of Memphis, Tennessee, and Avon Williams of Nashville, Tennessee, were elected to their state's senate.

Funeral of Martin Luther King, Jr., at Ebenezer Baptist Church. (Bettmann Archive/Newsphotos, Inc.)

One hundred and twenty-six blacks were serving the South as city councilmen, the most in any single type of office. Seventy-five blacks were school board members. According to figures from the Voter Educational Project of the Southern Regional Council, Alabama led the South with seventy-two black elected officials. Behind Alabama were: Arkansas with forty-five, Louisiana and Mississippi each with forty-three, Georgia with thirty-eight, Texas and North Carolina each with nineteen, and Florida with seventeen. More than three mil-

lion southern blacks were eligible to vote in these November elections.

DECEMBER 31, 1968 President Appointed Blacks Before Leaving Office. President Lyndon Johnson ended his last full year in office. Johnson had appointed more blacks to high-level federal positions than any previous president. Before leaving office, he appointed five black ambassadors, promoted Wade McCree from a district court to a court of appeals, appointed Hobart Taylor to the board of the

Shirley Chisholm on the steps of the Capitol.

Export-Import Bank, and named Andrew Brimmer a governor on the Federal Reserve Board.

1969

JANUARY–MARCH 1969 President Richard Nixon Took Office. President Richard Nixon, elected without substantial black support, made only three top-level appointments of blacks to the Washington bureaucracy. James Farmer was appointed assistant secretary of health, education and welfare; Arthur A. Fletcher was appointed assistant secretary of labor; and William H. Brown, III, was appointed chairman of the Equal Employment Opportunity Commission (EEOC). Nixon retained Walter Washington as mayor of Washington, D.C.

JANUARY 8, 1969 Brandeis University Students Made Demands. Sixty-five black students invaded Ford Hall at the predominantly white Brandeis University in Waltham, Massachusetts. The students barricaded themselves in and presented a non-negotiable list of demands. On the list were: an African studies department; year-round recruitment of black students by blacks; black directors for the Upward Bound and Transitional Year programs; the hiring of black professors; the establishment of an African American student center; and ten full scholarships for blacks. Morris B. Abram, the recently appointed president of the University, offered temporary amnesty to the blacks and agreed to communicate with the barricaded students.

JANUARY 25, 1969 Ku Klux Klan Leader Freed on Mistrial. A mistrial was declared in the Mississippi murder trial of Ku Klux Klan leader Samuel H. Bowers, Jr., one of thirteen men indicted for the 1966 fire-bomb slaying of black civil rights leader Vernon Dahmer. All were tried separately. Four defendants were convicted of murder, three of whom received life sentences, and the fourth was sentenced to serve ten years in prison. The Bowers trial was one of the five mistrials that resulted because juries were unable to reach verdicts. Bowers's May, 1968, trial for arson in connection with the Dahmer slaying had also resulted in a mistrial.

JANUARY 27, 1969 Housing Discrimination Prohibited. The U.S. Supreme Court ruled that cities, like states, cannot enact ordinances or charter provisions that have the effect of establishing discrimination in housing. The Court's decision involved a case filed by Nellie Hunter, a black housewife from Akron, Ohio. In 1965, Hunter had attempted to buy a home on Akron's all-white west side but was turned down by a real estate company because of her race. Hunter filed a complaint with Akron City Hall, requesting the protection of a 1964 ordinance that banned racial discrimination in housing. But city officials claimed that local real estate interests had successfully waged a drive to amend the charter. The amended charter now required a vote by the people in establishing fair-housing measures.

But the U.S. Supreme Court held that the Akron charter amendment "is no more permissible than denying racial minorities the vote on an equal basis with others." The city had unconstitutionally placed, the Court said, a "special burden" on its black residents by requiring that bans against housing discrimination be approved by the majority of the city's voters.

MARCH 10, 1969   Martin Luther King, Jr., Assassin Sentenced. James Earl Ray was sentenced to ninety-nine years in prison for the assassination of Martin Luther King, Jr.

JUNE 2, 1969   Minority Quotas in Federal Construction Projects. The U.S. Department of Labor issued guidelines that required contractors to hire specific numbers of minority workers onto federally assisted construction projects exceeding $500,000. The plan was first implemented in Philadelphia and thus, became known as the Philadelphia Plan. Secretary of Labor George P. Schultz called the Philadelphia Plan a "fair and realistic approach" toward eliminating racial discrimination in the construction industry. But he weakened the measure by adding that contractors who failed to meet the standards would not lose a federal contract if a "good faith effort" to recruit the required number of minority workers was demonstrated.

JULY 16, 1969   Philadelphia Plan Challenged. Laurence H. Silberman, solicitor for the U.S. Department of Labor, announced that the Philadelphia plan for minority hiring was legal under Executive Order No. 11246, which required equal employment clauses in all federal contracts. Silberman was responding to Republican minority leader Everett Dirksen of Illinois who thought it imposed a quota system in violation of the Civil Rights Act of 1964. Dirksen had asked President Richard Nixon, on July 8, to hold up the plan.

AUGUST 19, 1969   Black Panther Leader Arrested for Murder. The Federal Bureau of Investigation arrested Black Panther leader Bobby Seale for the torture-murder of Alex Rackley. Rackley was allegedly disloyal to the Panther organization and was burned to death on May 19 in New Haven, Connecticut. Francis J. McTernan, Seale's attorney, charged that the arrest was part of an organized campaign by the Justice Department to harass the Black Panthers. McTernan said his staff had information that the Justice Department had prepared a special file in connection with a program "of harassment against leaders of the Black Panther Party all over the country." Seale was arrested in California and later extradited for trial in Connecticut.

SEPTEMBER 1969   African American Studies at Harvard University. Harvard University moved to establish an African American studies program. An eight-person faculty committee on African and African American studies concluded, in January, that one was needed in addition to the already-established African studies program. The committee's report said, "We are dealing with 25 million of our own people with a special history, culture, and range of problems. It can hardly be doubted that the study of black men in America is a legitimate and urgent academic endeavor." Although the program was not the first of its kind, the prestigious university was viewed as lending impetus to the establishment of such programs at other universities.

OCTOBER 29, 1969 *Alexander v. Holmes.* The U.S. Supreme Court ruled unanimously that school districts must end racial segregation immediately and "operate now and hereafter only unitary schools." The Court rejected the Nixon administration's appeal for a delay in desegregating thirty Mississippi school districts. The new ruling indicated that the Court had abandoned its fourteen-year-old standard of allowing desegregation to proceed "with all deliberate speed." In the current decision, the high Court declared that "continued operations of segregated schools under a standard of all deliberate speed for desegregation is no longer constitutionally permissible." The case, known as *Alexander v. Holmes,* was the first major decision delivered by the Supreme Court under President Richard Nixon's appointee, Chief Justice Warren Burger.

OCTOBER 31, 1969 **Mississippi Schools Forced to Integrate.** The U.S. Court of Appeals for the Fifth Circuit moved to implement the U.S. Supreme Court's October 29 decision that mandated immediate school desegregation. Mississippi school districts were directed to file desegregation plans by November 5, 1969. Meanwhile, NAACP attorneys said they would file motions in some one hundred other school segregation cases pending in federal courts to press for immediate integration.

NOVEMBER 4, 1969 **Blacks Elected into Office.** Carl B. Stokes, the first black mayor of Cleveland, Ohio, was reelected. In other elections, Howard Lee was elected mayor of predominately white Chapel Hill, North Carolina. Veteran NAACP leader Charles Evers, brother of the slain Medgar Evers, was elected mayor of Fayette, Mississippi, a mostly black community. Blacks also took political control of the city of Tuskegee, Alabama.

DECEMBER 4–5, 1969 **Black Panther Leaders Killed.** Black Panther Party leaders Mark Clark and Fred Hampton were killed in a raid by Chicago police; four others were wounded. According to police reports, the pre-dawn raid was based on information that Hampton's apartment was being used to stockpile weapons. Police claimed that their knock on the door was answered by gunfire from a woman, and they contended that about two hundred shots were fired during the ten-minute altercation.

The next day, spokesmen for the Black Panthers dismissed the police accounts of the raid and claimed that Clark and Hampton were murdered in their beds by police. They purported to show that only police had fired shots in the apartment. State, federal, and congressional investigations were held, but neither Panther members nor police officers were brought to trial in the wake of the controversial encounter.

The incident served to heighten tensions between the Panthers and law enforcement, and the Panthers gained some additional sympathy among Americans for their objectives. Hampton had been the state party chairman for the Panthers, and Clark led the Peoria, Illinois, chapter.

Chapter 9

1970 to 1979

1970

JANUARY 1970   Blacks Elected to Serve Atlanta. Blacks gained a degree of political control over Atlanta, Georgia, as five African Americans were elected, or reelected, to the eighteen-member Board of Aldermen, or City Council. Also, three blacks were elected, or reelected, to the ten-member Board of Education. And attorney Maynard Jackson was elected vice mayor and president of the Board of Aldermen. Black educator Benjamin E. Mays was named head of the School Board.

JANUARY 2, 1970   FBI Reported on Militant Black Activities. Federal Bureau of Investigation's Director J. Edgar Hoover stated that black militant groups were "encouraged and inflamed from without" in violent attacks upon the government. In his report of FBI operations in 1969, Hoover also said that during the previous six months, there were more than one hundred attacks on police by "extremist, all-Negro, hate-type organizations, such as the Black Panther Party." He reported that 7 police officers were killed and 120 were injured in attacks by black militants.

JANUARY 3, 1970   Mississippi Governor Called for Peaceful Desegregation. Mississippi governor John Bell Williams announced in a state-wide telecast that he would help to build a private school system as a "workable alternative" to public school desegregation. Williams also urged white parents to peacefully accept the November 6, 1969, ruling of the Fifth Circuit Court of Appeals that ordered thirty Mississippi school districts to desegregate. The governor said it was "a time when reason must outweigh emotion, and calm must prevail over hysteria." Williams announced he would resubmit a proposal to the state legislature that authorized income-tax credits of up to $500 a year for those who donated to educational institutions. The legislature had previously rejected that request.

JANUARY 5, 1970   Families Fled Poverty-Stricken Areas. Bureau of the Census statistics confirmed earlier reports that nonwhite and white families were fleeing the poverty-stricken areas of their cities. The Bureau said that whites had been leaving the urban poverty areas for years, but the nonwhite migration seemed to have occurred chiefly since 1966. As factors behind the exodus, the Bureau cited crime, educational problems, land clearance resulting from urban renewal, and the increased availability of low-income housing outside of poverty areas. Between 1960 and 1968, minority families living in urban poverty areas declined by 9 percent. In 1968, 2.5 million whites and 1.6 million blacks lived in urban poverty areas.

JANUARY 5–7, 1970   Mississippi Blacks Attended Integrated Schools. Black children enrolled in formerly all-white public schools in three Mississippi districts under the watch of federal marshals. The officers were sent to prevent violence and look for signs of non-compliance as the government moved to implement the November 6, 1969, decision of the U.S. Fifth Circuit Court of Appeals that ordered thirty Mississippi school districts to desegregate. Three of those districts reopened classes for the second semester on January 5, 1970. The others followed between January 7 and 12.

The desegregation did not meet with violence, but many white parents picketed the newly desegregated schools while others boycotted the institutions. In Woodville, only 2 white children went to their school where 1,400 black pupils had registered. But in Yazoo City, white business leaders had asked parents to accept the arrangements, and nearly 1,500 white students attended the desegregated schools. Four thousand whites and 1,000 blacks in Petal went to classes together for the first time despite a peaceful sit-in by 300 white parents at an elementary school. The whites were protesting a desegregation plan that assigned their children to classrooms as far as thirteen miles away.

JANUARY 6, 1970   Tax Exemption for Private Schoolers Questioned. Secretary of health, education, and welfare Robert Finch expressed concern over the South's new private, all-white schools. He announced that there was a move within the Nixon administration to end the tax exemptions for private schools that had been established to avoid desegregation. Finch said he would request that the Treasury Department reconsider the policy of granting tax-exempt status to such private schools. He estimated that as many as four hundred private schools had opened in the South since the passage of the Civil Rights Act of 1964.

JANUARY 8, 1970   Martin Luther King, Jr., Assassin Retrial Denied. The Tennessee Supreme Court refused to consider a plea for a new trial for James Earl Ray, the white man serving a ninety-nine-year sentence for the murder of Martin Luther King, Jr. The court reasoned that there could be no legal basis for granting a new trial for the defendant who had pleaded guilty and fully understood what he was doing.

JANUARY 13, 1970   Private School Tax Exemption Halted. A three-judge federal district court in Washington, D.C., ordered the Internal Revenue Service to stop granting tax-exempt privileges to segregated private schools in Mississippi. The order did not affect the all-white private schools that had already been granted tax-exemptions. But the IRS was to stop granting tax-exempt status to schools with pending applications, or applications yet to be filed, unless the school could show it was enrolling blacks. The newly chartered, all-white private academies were being funded by white parents to avoid complying with the school desegregation taking place in Mississippi's public schools. Mississippi governor John Bell Williams asked the state legislature to grant financial assistance, in the form of state tax deductions, to those who donated money to the all-white schools. He claimed his program would "strengthen the hands of Mississippians" in facing the government's desegregation orders.

JANUARY 14, 1970   Supreme Court Hastened School Desegregation. The U.S. Supreme Court, in a brief, unsigned order, overruled a decision by the U.S. Fifth Circuit Court of Appeals that set September 1970 as the deadline for desegregation in Southern public schools. The high Court was acting on an NAACP appeal involving fourteen school districts in five Southern states, and its request of February 1, 1970, as the deadline for desegregation. The high Court's action affirmed this request, denying the Justice Department's request for approval of the September deadline.

JANUARY 15, 1970   Martin Luther King, Jr., Birthday Celebrated. Blacks and whites across the nation celebrated the forty-first anniversary of the birth of Martin Luther King, Jr. The movement to make the day a national holiday was gaining momentum, and several governors declared "Martin Luther King, Jr., Day" in their states. Among those who declared the holiday were: Kenneth Curtis of Maine, Frank Licht of Rhode Island, and Nelson Rockefeller of New York. Public schools were closed in Baltimore, Maryland; Kansas City, Missouri; New York; and Philadelphia, Pennsylvania, among others. In King's hometown of Atlanta, Georgia, four hundred people listened as the city's new mayor, Sam Massell, eulogized King at a memorial service. Following the service, King's widow, Coretta Scott King, dedicated Atlanta's new Martin Luther King, Jr., Memorial Center that comprised King's birthplace, church, and crypt.

JANUARY 19, 1970   Pleas for Desegregation Delays Denied. Florida governor Claude Kirk, Jr., personally told the U.S. Supreme Court that his state was "financially and physically unable" to meet the Court's January 14, 1970, order for immediate school desegregation. Kirk announced that he had instructed his school districts to change their school calendars during mid-term. The governor asked the Court for a re-hearing and requested a delay in the February 1 school desegregation deadline. Kirk said that Florida was ready to comply with the orders but was unable to do so under the time constraint. Attorneys for two Louisiana school districts also appeared before the Court with similar pleas. The Supreme Court listened to the arguments, then ordered the desegregation to proceed as scheduled.

JANUARY 20, 1970   Integration of California Schools Ordered. Federal district judge Manuel Real in Los Angeles ordered the Pasadena, California, school district to submit a desegregation plan for its public schools by February 16. The plan, covering all schools in the subur-ban Los Angeles district, was to take effect in September. The Pasadena case was the first federal government suit against a non-southern school district to be acted upon. The judge ruled that the plan submitted by the school officials should not produce any school with a majority of nonwhite students. Judge Real also ordered that the plan should cover new teaching assignments, hiring and promotional practices, and the construction of new school buildings.

JANUARY 21, 1970   Black Panthers' Deaths Found Justified. A coroner's jury in Chicago, Illinois, concluded that the deaths of Black Panther Party leaders Fred Hampton and Mark Clark, were justifiable. The two were slain during a police raid on Hampton's apartment on December 4, 1969. Seven other Panthers were arrested following the raid. A special inquest was assembled on January 6 after Panther leaders charged that Hampton was murdered in his bed. Chicago detectives who participated in the pre-dawn raid testified that one or more persons in Hampton's apartment opened fire on the police. The attorneys representing the families of the two slain Panthers did not call any witnesses during the hearing. They indicated that they did not want to reveal their plans for the defense of the seven Panthers who faced possible trial for attempted murder. The foreman of the six-man jury said the verdict was reached "solely on the evidence presented." A Cook County grand jury was also investigating the incident.

JANUARY 24, 1970   Army Race Tensions Documented. In a report released in Saigon, South Vietnam, army investigators found that "all indications point toward an increase in racial tension" on military bases throughout the world. The investigation was ordered by U.S. Army Chief of Staff General William C. Westmoreland, and it was presented to the Joint Chiefs of Staff in Washington, D.C., in the fall of 1969. Congressmen and military commanders in the U.S. and abroad also received the report that

Brigadier General Frederice Davison and Captain Murray consult in a Vietnamese jungle. (AP/Wide World Photos.)

said, "Negro soldiers seem to have lost faith in the Army system," and predicted increased racial problems unless "aggressive command action, firm but impartial discipline, and good leadership can prevent physical confrontation of racial groups." The study concluded that the army had "a race problem because our country has a race problem." Yet there were conditions within the army that possibly contributed to unrest among black soldiers. For instance, according to the report, the number of black junior officers was decreasing although there were more black non-commissioned officers of lower rank. The report also found that on European bases, where one out of eight soldiers was black, a disproportionate one out of four non-judicial punishments was imposed on a black soldier.

JANUARY 27, 1970 Supreme Court Nominee Opposed. In the first day of confirmation hearings on his nomination to the U.S. Supreme Court, Judge G. Harold Carswell of Florida told the U.S. Senate's Judiciary Committee: "I am not a racist. I have no notions, secretive or otherwise, of racial superiority." Carswell was responding to senators' questions about a white supremacy speech he made during a political campaign in Georgia in 1948. Carswell said that "the force of twenty-two years of history" had changed him as well as the South.

On January 21, the NAACP had urged the Senate to reject Carswell because of his pro-segregation record. NAACP board chairman Bishop Stephen G. Spottswood noted that the NAACP and 124 other organizations had opposed Carswell's appointment to the U.S. Court of Appeals for the Fifth Circuit in May of 1969.

Two days later, Southern Christian Leadership Conference president Ralph David Abernathy announced that he had sent a telegram to Senate leaders opposing Carswell. Abernathy said the rejection of Carswell "would provide some reassurances to the black community that there is still some understanding and support among government officials for our needs." The Senate later rejected the Carswell nomination.

JANUARY 29, 1970 President Addressed Lack of Black Confidence. President Richard Nixon expressed concern over his administration's failure to gain the confidence of the nation's black citizens. The president said he could improve his standing among blacks by using phrases and slogans, but that he eschewed such tactics because it would only serve to widen the gap between the government and African Americans. Nixon said he was more concerned with deeds than words, and that approval of his legislative proposals against crime and for increased job opportunities would serve to end the performance gap and inspire trust in his administration.

FEBRUARY 1, 1970 Schools Ignored Court-Ordered Desegregation. School officials in twenty Alabama, Georgia, and Mississippi districts defied federal court orders that called for total school desegregation, refusing to implement federally designed desegregation plans. Some administrators closed their schools temporarily, while others supported boycotts by white parents and students. Others closed schools to await further appeals for delays.

Two Alabama districts ignored the Court's orders entirely. In Bessemer, Alabama, school officials flatly stated they would not comply with the desegregation orders. Black lawyers filed suit the same day, requesting that the Bessemer school board be found in contempt of court. In Burke County, Georgia, the schools reopened under a "freedom of choice" arrangement, even though the courts had previously invalidated such a scheme.

Of the forty districts under the Court's orders to desegregate, only a few obeyed, including three in Louisiana, two in Mississippi, and one in Florida. Panama City, Florida, was one of the few districts to fully comply; about 1,000 of its 17,500 students were transferred to new schools to achieve a more racially balanced system. The February 1 deadline for desegregation had been set by the U.S. Supreme Court on January 14, 1969.

FEBRUARY 26, 1970 Percent age of Blacks in National Guard Dropped. According to a *New York Times* report, efforts to increase black enlistments in the National Guard were largely unsuccessful. A survey conducted by the Guard revealed that there were 5,487 blacks in the air and army units at the end of 1969, out of a total enlistment of nearly 500,000 men. This 1.15 percent of black guardsmen was a drop from 1.18 percent in 1968. Congress refused a request in 1969 for $6.5 million to recruit blacks into the Guard; the Defense Department did not renew the request in 1970.

FEBRUARY 28, 1970 President's Confidential Memo Exposed. A confidential memorandum to the president from Daniel P. Moynihan, domestic advisor to President Richard Nixon, was made public. The memo proposed that "the time may have come when the issue of race could benefit from a period of benign neglect." Moynihan, a liberal Democrat, explained later that he had meant that blacks could fare better if extremists on both sides of the political spectrum would lower their voices. He asserted that his memorandum had been written with a twofold purpose: to bring the president up to date on the progress of blacks in the last decade, and to suggest ways in which these gains could be consolidated in the future.

MARCH 3, 1970 Violence over School Integration. A mob of angry whites with ax handles and baseball bats stormed buses transporting black children to a formerly all-white school in Lamar, South Carolina. About one hundred South Carolina state police officers dispersed them with riot clubs and tear gas after the crowd of approximately two hundred whites had rushed the buses and smashed the windows at Lamar High School. Thirty-nine black students were aboard the buses. Several children were injured by flying glass and the effects of tear gas. None were arrested, but state and federal officials later moved to apprehend the mob's leaders.

MARCH 5, 1970 Black Leaders Responded to "Benign Neglect." Twenty black civil rights leaders, authors, legislators, and educators issued a statement describing Daniel Moynihan's "benign neglect" memorandum to President Richard Nixon as "symptomatic of a calculated, aggressive, and systematic" effort by the Nixon administration to "wipe out" nearly two decades of civil rights progress. The signers included Professor Nathan Hare, Michigan congressman John Conyers, Jr., and civil rights leader Bayard Rustin.

MARCH 13, 1970   Voting Rights Act Extended. The U.S. Senate voted to extend the Voting Rights Act of 1965 for five additional years, making 1975 its expiration. Among the provisions of the act were a ban on literacy tests as a voting qualification and permission to vote in presidential elections if residency had been established in a locality a month before election day.

MARCH 14, 1970   Philadelphia Plan Upheld. Philadelphia's District Court Judge Charles R. Weiner upheld the constitutionality of the Labor Department's controversial Philadelphia plan which sought to increase minority employment in the construction industry. Judge Weiner rejected a request for an injunction against the plan that was requested in a suit filed by the Contractors Association of Eastern Pennsylvania on January 6, 1970. Judge Weiner said the pilot job program did not in any way violate the Civil Rights Act of 1964 which forbade racial quotas in employment. The Philadelphia Plan did not violate the act, the judge said, because it "does not require the contractor to hire a definite percentage of a minority group." The contractors had only to make "good faith" efforts to hire a certain number of blacks and other minorities. And, he reasoned that "it is fundamental that civil rights without economic rights are mere shadows."

MAY 12–14, 1970   Blacks Slain by Police. Six black men died on May 12 as a result of racial rioting in Augusta, Georgia. On May 14, two black youths were killed during a racial disturbance at Jackson State College in Jack-

son, Mississippi. All died at the hands of local police.

MAY 29, 1970   Black Panther's Murder Conviction Reversed. The conviction of Black Panther Party leader Huey P. Newton for manslaughter was reversed by a California Court of Appeals. Newton had been convicted on September 8, 1968, for the fatal shooting of an Oakland, California, police officer. Newton was also implicated in the wounding of another officer and the kidnaping of a black motorist. In his 1968 trial, Newton was defended by Charles A. Garry. A major contention of the defense was that Newton laid unconscious from a gunshot wound at the time the Oakland police officer was shot. The California court found procedural errors in the original trial and ordered the reversal of his conviction.

JUNE 1970   Eight Blacks Served in House of Representatives. African American politician Charles Rangel, of Harlem, New York, defeated incumbent Adam Clayton Powell, Jr., for his long-held seat in the U.S. House of Representatives. Eight African Americans sat in the House during 1970, including William L. Dawson; Charles C. Diggs, Jr., of Michigan; Augustus F. Hawkins of California; Robert C. Nix of Pennsylvania; Shirley Chisholm of New York; Louis Stokes of Ohio; and John Conyers of Michigan.

JUNE 29, 1970   President Accused of Anti-Black Policies. The chairman of the NAACP's board of directors, Bishop Stephen Gill Spottswood, charged the Nixon administration with being "anti-Negro" and accused it of implementing a "calculated policy to work against the needs and aspirations of the largest minority of its citizens." In his keynote address at the NAACP annual convention in Cincinnati, Ohio, Spottswood indicted the administration for retreating on school desegregation and nominating conservative Southerners Clement Haynsworth and G. Harrold Carswell to the U.S. Supreme Court. Spottswood also con-

The NAACP's Stephen Spottswood. (Courtesy of Stephen Spottswood.)

demned the exposed memo to the president that called for "benign neglect" of race issues. The statement marked a significant break between the largest and oldest black civil rights organization and the national administration. Because of this, and the NAACP's reputation as a moderate organization, the administration quickly responded, calling the charges "unfair" and "disheartening," and pointing to positive contributions such as the administration's support of the extension of the Voting Rights Act of 1965.

JULY 1, 1970   Newark Elected Black Mayor. Kenneth Gibson, a city engineer, became the mayor of Newark, New Jersey. At the time, Gibson was the only African American mayor of a large eastern city. But there were more than five hundred black officeholders in other elected positions.

JULY 7-31, 1970   Curfews Imposed to Curb Rioting. Racial rioting broke out in several Northern cities. On July 7, a curfew was imposed in Asbury Park, New Jersey, following four days of violence; forty-three people were

shot during the rioting. The curfew was lifted on July 10, and calm was restored in the New Jersey resort town after Mayor Joseph Mattice agreed to consider a list of demands presented to him by a coalition of black organizations. William Hamm, a spokesperson for the black community leaders, presented the list of twenty-two demands that included requests for better housing, more jobs, and increased efforts at halting narcotics traffic. In New Bedford, Massachusetts, a curfew was imposed on July 12, following four nights of racial disturbances. Hartford, Connecticut, following three days of rioting by African Americans and Puerto Ricans, imposed a curfew on July 31.

JULY 10, 1970   Private Segregated Schools Lost Tax Exemptions. The Internal Revenue Service announced that the tax-exempt status of private schools practicing racial discrimination in their admissions policies would be revoked. The action came as the government sought to respond to the growing number of all-white private schools in the South. Most of the schools had sprung up in the wake of desegregation of the public schools.

JULY 29, 1970   Alabama Ordered to Adopt Anti-discrimination Policies. U.S. District Court Judge Frank M. Johnson, Jr., ordered seven Alabama state agencies to end discrimination against blacks in their hiring practices and give immediate job consideration to sixty-two black applicants who were denied positions earlier. The federal judge directed state authorities to take steps to eliminate future racial discrimination in hiring practices, and he ordered them to submit a report to the court within thirty days, detailing the steps taken to comply with his order. In reviewing the case, which was filed by the Justice Department in 1968, Johnson noted that Alabama was the only remaining state that refused to adopt a resolution that formally prohibited racial discrimination and provided for a system of redress in such cases. Johnson also directed the seven agencies to hire blacks and to appoint them in positions other than custodial, domestic, or general labor, when such applicants were listed as qualified and eligible.

AUGUST 1970 Black Panther Released from Jail. Huey P. Newton, one of the founders and leader of the Black Panther Party, was released on a $50,000 bond after serving more than two years in a California prison. Newton was serving time for a manslaughter conviction in the death of an Oakland, California, police officer. The California Court of Appeals had reversed the conviction on the grounds that the trial judge erred in instructing the jury and opened the way for Newton's release pending a new trial. Newton's attorney, Charles Garry, charged that the bail was excessive, but acquiesced. Newton was greeted by a crowd of about three hundred upon his release. He shouted, "The people have the power! All power to the people!"

AUGUST 1, 1970 Blacks in Vietnam War. The U.S. Department of Defense reported that the percentage of black soldiers killed in Vietnam had declined substantially during the first three months in 1970. The Pentagon report said that, for the first time, the percentage of black soldiers killed in action in Southeast Asia had fallen below the percentage of blacks among the American forces there. The government's data showed that as of March 31, 1970, blacks serving in Indo-China represented about 10 percent of the total American military presence in the area. During the same three months, black fatalities accounted for 8.5 percent of the combat deaths there. This was a drop from 9.5 percent in 1969. The Defense Department cited no specific effort in decreasing the casualty rates among black servicemen in Vietnam.

AUGUST 7, 1970 California Convicts Killed in Escape Attempt. Four people died during a courthouse shootout in San Rafael, California, when three black convicts attempted to escape. Two of the convicts, a judge, and another black

youth aiding the convicts were killed. Angela Davis, an African American and former professor at the University of California at Los Angeles, was implicated in the incident and fled the state in order to avoid arrest.

AUGUST 13, 1970 Chicago Officer Shot in Black Neighborhood. Chicago detective James A. Alfonso, a member of the city police's gang intelligence unit, was shot while on the city's south side in an unmarked police car. The next day, Chicago police said that they had arrested four members of the "Main 21," the ruling body of the Black P. Stone Nation, a confederation of sixty black street gangs based on the old Blackstone Rangers. One of those held, twenty-three-year-old Charles E. Bey, identified himself as vice president of the "nation" and a member of the "Main 21." Some Chicago blacks contended that the recent wave of violence grew out of a widespread pattern of police brutality, including incidents in which police had slain blacks, most notably, members of the Black Panther Party. Thirty-year-old Alfonso was the fourth Chicago police officer slain in the city's black neighborhoods since mid-June; he died from his wounds four days later.

AUGUST 19, 1970 Philadelphia Plan Enforced. The Nixon administration announced its plans to terminate a contract with Edgeley Air Products, Inc., of Levittown, Pennsylvania, for failing to comply with the Philadelphia Plan which was designed to train and employ minority workers on construction jobs. This was the government's first enforcement action against a contractor charged with violation of a job agreement. Secretary of Health, Education, and Welfare Elliott L. Richardson notified Edgeley Air Products, Inc., that his Office for Civil Rights intended to cancel the contract and bar the company from future federal contracts on grounds of noncompliance. Leonard Nucero, the president of Edgeley, denied that the company practiced discrimination and said the company would appeal termination of the contract.

AUGUST 26, 1970   Tax Exemptions for Segregated Schools Challenged. A federal court in Washington, D.C., refused the Nixon administration's request to dismiss a pending suit against federal tax exemptions for private, all-white academies in the South. The court also denied the request of the civil rights groups that brought the suit for all such academies to have their tax-exempt status revoked immediately. The administration's lawyer told the court that the Internal Revenue Service would no longer grant tax-exempt status to private schools practicing racial discrimination in admissions policies, but that the government had relied on the word of the schools in determining whether they were willing to desegregate.

AUGUST 27, 1970   Nebraska Officer Killed in a Trap. David L. Rice, minister of information for the National Committee to Combat Fascism, surrendered to police in Omaha, Nebraska, in connection with the August 17 death of local police officer Larry D. Minard. Twenty-nine-year-old Minard was one of eight officers who had been called to a vacant house in Omaha's predominantly black north side district to investigate a report of a woman in distress. He was killed when he touched a satchel that was filled with an explosive and rigged as a booby trap; the seven other policemen were injured. Rice was charged with illegal possession of explosives.

AUGUST 29, 1970   Cemetery Forced to Intern Black Body. Poindexter E. Williams, a black soldier killed in Vietnam during a mortar barrage, was buried in a formerly all-white cemetery in Fort Pierce, Florida. The cemetery had refused to bury the soldier since August 20, but a federal judge ordered the cemetery to accept Williams's body. Williams was buried in a grave site donated to his family by a white woman. Other whites, citing the Caucasians-only clause in lot purchase contracts, opposed the burial, and some plot owners in the Hillcrest Memorial Gardens threatened to remove their relatives' remains.

AUGUST 29–31, 1970   Officer Died in Black Panther Raid. In Philadelphia, one police officer was killed and six others were wounded in a series of gun battles between police and black militant organizations, including the Black Panthers. Police Commissioner Frank L. Rizzo blamed the incidents on the Black Panther Party and a group called The Revolutionaries that, he said, plotted to murder police officers. The altercation resulted from an early morning raid at the Panther Information Center on Philadelphia's north side. Police said they were searching for a suspect in connection with an earlier shooting.

AUGUST 31, 1970   Integrated Southern Schools Opened. More than two hundred school districts across the South that had resisted the 1954 U.S. Supreme Court order that mandated segregation finally reopened peacefully with desegregated classrooms. Nearly 300,000 black children from Virginia to Louisiana began classes with whites as threats of school boycotts by white parents failed to materialize. Despite the massive compliance, 175 other districts continued to hold out, most of which were involved in litigation on the issue of student busing. Others were involved in negotiations with government officials aimed at ending segregated school systems.

Chief Justice of the Supreme Court, Warren E. Burger, announced that the Court would consider the remaining school desegregation problems when the new court term began on October 12. Many blacks and whites had raised questions concerning the legality of busing, the concept of racial balance, and the definition of a unitary school system.

AUGUST 31, 1970   Black Panther Convicted of Conspiracy to Murder. Black Panther Lonnie McLucas was convicted of conspiracy to murder in his trial for the 1969 slaying of a New York party member. Twenty-four-year-old McLucas was the first of eight Black Panthers, including national chairman Bobby Seale, to stand trial for conspiracy to murder Alex Rackley, whose body was found near Middlefield, Connecticut, in May of 1969. The state had charged in the original indictments that Rackley was slain because he had been suspected by the party of being a police informant. McLucas's attorney, Theodore I. Kossoff, contended that the order for Rackley's murder originated from George Sams, Jr., the Panther member whom the defense alleged was responsible for the torture and murder of Rackley. McLucas was acquitted on three other charges: conspiracy to kidnap, kidnaping resulting in death, and binding with intent to commit a crime. He faced a maximum sentence of fifteen years in prison; the three charges on which McLucas was acquitted all carried heavier penalties

AUGUST 31, 1970 Desegregation Pressures Resulted in Resignations. John S. Martin, superintendent of public schools in Jackson, Mississippi, resigned, citing the federal courts and the pressure of school desegregation as reasons. According to the *New York Times,* Martin joined at least two hundred other school superintendents in the South who had resigned in the past two years because of the problems resulting from desegregation in their districts. William Dunn, superintendent of schools in Louisiana, predicted the federal government's latest attempt to desegregate schools in the South would lead to a wave of resignations from experienced educators. The rate of turnover among superintendents in Alabama, Louisiana, and Georgia since 1968 was nearly forty percent, almost double the rate in any previous two-year period. Louisiana led the South in the rate of turnovers. In two years, there had been thirty-nine turnovers among the sixty-six district superintendents.

SEPTEMBER 1, 1970 Officers Indicted for Civil Rights Violations. A federal grand jury in Augusta, Georgia, indicted two white police officers on charges of violating the civil rights of two black men who were shot May 12 during a night of racial rioting that left six blacks dead

and sixty others injured. Officer William S. Dennis was charged with the fatal shooting of John W. Stokes, and officer Louis C. Dinkins was accused of wounding Louis N. Williams. The grand jury had begun its inquiry into the shootings on August 24 and found cause for indictment in only one of the six deaths. After the biracial jury handed down the indictments, the decision was denounced by Georgia governor Lester Maddox. The "national government, from the president on down," he said, "is only worrying about agitators."

SEPTEMBER 1, 1970 Trucking Company Ordered to Equally Employ. The Justice Department announced that a federal judge in Cleveland, Ohio, had issued a consent decree requiring Roadway Express Company, the nation's third largest trucking concern, to implement an equal employment program. The order ended the department's first efforts to prohibit job discrimination throughout the company's nationwide operation. Judge Thomas D. Lambros had specifically prohibited Roadway from engaging in any act or practice that had the purpose of denying blacks equal employment opportunities in hiring, upgrading, and promotions. The decree also ordered Roadway, which had freight terminals in twenty-eight states, to offer job opportunities on a first-available-vacancy basis to 105 individuals with seniority and other benefits for forty-five of them. The Justice Department had filed suit against Roadway in May 1968, charging that blacks had been discriminated against in job placement and other opportunities.

SEPTEMBER 2, 1970 Black Muslim Refused Military Exemption. In Baltimore, Maryland, U.S. District Court Judge Frank A. Kaufman rejected the appeal of William H. Murphy, Jr., a member of the Nation of Islam. Murphy contended that he should be exempted from military service as a conscientious objector of war, but Kaufman ruled that the Nation of Islam represented a political, rather than a religious, objection to war.

SEPTEMBER 3, 1970 Colleges Requested Federal Financial Support. Representatives of nine black colleges charged the Nixon administration with failure to support black higher education. The educators met in Detroit, Michigan, under the leadership of president Lucius H. Pitts of Miles College, and called for increased government and private funds to strengthen the more than one hundred black colleges and universities. Vivian Henderson, president of Clark College in Atlanta, Georgia, accused the Nixon administration of an "utter lack of sensitivity" to the needs of black colleges and said that this fed "the flames that already roar in the hearts of many black students." About two billion dollars was cited by Vernon Jordan, head of the United Negro College Fund, as the minimum amount necessary to maintain black colleges. White House press secretary Ronald L. Ziegler, in a letter to Pitts, reminded the educators of a July 23 pledge by the administration to increase support for their colleges.

SEPTEMBER 5–7, 1970 Revolutionary People's Constitutional Convention. The Black Panther Party and members of the Women's and Gay Liberation movements held the first session of their Revolutionary People's Constitutional Convention, in Philadelphia. Despite tensions over the August 29 slaying of a Philadelphia police officer and the subsequent arrest of fourteen people at three Black Panther offices, the three-day conference was conducted in a peaceful manner. The Panther Party had organized the convention in order to rewrite the U.S. Constitution, which, according to the group, did not go far enough in protecting the rights of the oppressed. About 6,000 participated in the meeting. Among the Panther's delegation were co-founder Huey P. Newton and Panther Chief of Staff David Hilliard. The second session of the convention was slated for November 4, 1970, in Washington, D.C.

SEPTEMBER 9, 1970 Desegregation Attempts Brought Mixed Results. Another round of school desegregation in the South was marked by stiffening white resistance to federal court orders and confusion over new student assignments. More disruptions were recorded with this batch of school reopenings than had occurred when most of the South's schools desegregated peacefully on August 31. White parents in Mobile, Alabama, resisted desegregation efforts by boycotting their newly assigned schools and enrolling their children in their formerly segregated schools. The school superintendent in Bogalusa, Louisiana, closed the public schools on September 14 after police used tear gas to end a fight between black and white students at a recently desegregated school. Police Chief Thomas Mixon, Jr., estimated six hundred high school students were involved in the two-hour altercation in which fourteen students were arrested.

On September 10, the NAACP charged that the Mobile school board had discriminated against black children in the inner city by its deployment of 225 school buses. The board replied that it did not have the time or the funds to buy more buses to handle inner city children. On September 14, the Justice Department accused the same school board of repeated violations of desegregation orders. Federal Judge Daniel H. Thomas commanded the board to cease circumventing the school orders.

There was little resistance in the large Charlotte-Mecklenburg, North Carolina, school system as it reopened under a court-ordered desegregation plan that required extensive busing of children. The plan had aroused community opposition in Charlotte, yet school officials said 80 percent of the high school students reported to their classes.

SEPTEMBER 11, 1970 Segregated School's Tax Exemptions Revoked. The Internal Revenue Service revoked the tax-exempt classification of five all-white private academies in Mississippi after the schools refused to enroll black children. The cancellations brought the total to sixteen all-white academies in the South that lost their tax-exempt status since the IRS prohibited tax deductions for segregated schools.

SEPTEMBER 12, 1970　California Desegregation Circumvented. California governor Ronald Reagan signed into law a bill prohibiting the busing of students "for any purpose or any reason without the written permission of the parent or guardian." The law was to take effect in November. The California branch of the NAACP announced it would test the constitutionality of the measure in court.

SEPTEMBER 13, 1970　Black Panther Party Expanded. Exiled Black Panther Party leader Eldridge Cleaver presided over the opening of the party's first international section in Algiers. The Algerian government, which had broken diplomatic ties with the United States in 1967, had formally accorded the Panther party the status of a liberation movement.

SEPTEMBER 14–15, 1970　Black Panthers Discovered Undercover Police. One black youth was killed and twenty-one others were injured during a day-long gun battle between police and blacks in a New Orleans, Louisiana, housing project. The incident began when two black policemen were discovered by the National Committee to Combat Fascism, a branch of the Black Panther Party. The undercover officers had successfully infiltrated the organization, but, on September 14, they were discovered and beaten. The officers escaped when the NCCF turned them over to a crowd of about one hundred blacks for a "people's trial." Later, police returned to the project to investigate reports of a burning automobile. Officers and fire fighters were fired upon and the melee broke out in full force. Fourteen blacks, most of them from the NCCF, were arrested during the disturbance and charged with attempted murder.

SEPTEMBER 18, 1970　Convicted Black Panther Sentenced. Lonnie McLucas, the first of eight Black Panther Party members to stand

Black Panther Eldridge Cleaver. (Courtesy of Library of Congress.)

trial for the slaying of Alex Rackley, was sentenced to twelve to fifteen years in prison by a New Haven, Connecticut, court. McLucas was convicted of conspiracy to murder in the Rackley case on August 31, 1970. Superior Court Judge Harold M. Mulvey assessed the maximum term allowed under Connecticut law for the crime of conspiracy to murder. McLucas immediately filed notice of appeal.

SEPTEMBER 28, 1970　Activist Convicted for Riot Participation. Black activist Cleveland L. Sellers, Jr., was convicted by a biracial jury in Orangeburg, South Carolina, for participating in a riot on the campus of South Carolina State College in 1968. Three black students had been killed by state highway patrolmen in the incident. Sellers, a former national program secretary for the Student Non-Violent Coordinating Committee, was sentenced the maximum one year in prison and a $250 fine. Sellers was released on a $5,000 appeal bond by State Circuit Court Judge John Grimball, who said he could leave the state to attend college. Two days earlier, Grimball had ordered a directed verdict of acquittal of two other riot charges against Sellers, citing that the prosecution had failed to prove Sellers incited the Orangeburg student riot in which twenty-seven blacks were wounded, including Sellers, and three students were slain.

SEPTEMBER 28, 1970 Northern School Illegally Segregated. For the first time, a Health, Education, and Welfare hearing examiner ruled that a Northern school district was illegally segregating its pupils according to race. The Ferndale, Michigan, school district was deprived of $275,000 in federal aid because of its segregated elementary schools.

SEPTEMBER 30, 1970 Top Corporations Devoid of Blacks. The Race Relations Information Center in Nashville, Tennessee, reported that there were only three black executives among the 3,182 senior officers of the top fifty American corporate firms. These were Robert C. Weaver of the Metropolitan Life Insurance Co., Clifton R. Wharton, Jr., of the Equitable Life Assurance Society, and Thomas A. Wood of the Chase Manhattan Bank. All three held the position of corporate director.

OCTOBER 1, 1970 School Desegregation Circumvented. J. Stanley Pottinger, the director of the Office of Civil Rights of the Department of Health, Education and Welfare, reported that federal school monitors in the South found extensive school segregation. Pottinger said his office had investigated 120 desegregated school districts since the fall term began and found patterns of segregation in at least half of them. Throughout the summer of 1970, segregation by classrooms received much attention from the Senate Select Committee on Equal Educational Opportunity. Pottinger announced that the Nixon administration intended to move against the new form of segregation, but only after it solicited the advice of educators. He promised to develop guidelines by the spring semester of 1971.

OCTOBER 1, 1970 Segregationist Statute Struck Down. A federal court in Buffalo, New York,

ruled unconstitutional a New York statute that made it illegal for appointed school boards to reshuffle pupil assignment plans to achieve racial balance without the consent of parents. The law, enacted in May of 1969, was challenged by a group of black and white parents. School administrators in the South had hailed it as a means of forestalling school desegregation. But the court found the law in violation of the Fourteenth Amendment in that it served to continue segregation and it involved discrimination by a state institution.

OCTOBER 1, 1970 Funding to Black Colleges Increased. Elliot L. Richardson, Secretary of Health, Education, and Welfare, announced a 30 percent, or $30 million, increase in federal aid to predominantly black colleges. This increased the total aid from HEW to $129 million a year. Richardson noted the increase was a response to recent appeals by black educators for more aid. But blacks complained that matching provisions of the fund grants, and early deadlines for applications, made it difficult for most African American institutions to qualify.

OCTOBER 5, 1970 Schools Desegregated to Receive Tax Exemption. The Internal Revenue Service reported that nine all-white private academies in Mississippi agreed to admit black students. In the same announcement, the IRS said it had removed fourteen other all-white academies from its list of schools eligible for tax-exempt status. This brought the number of suspension to thirty-eight.

OCTOBER 5–NOVEMBER 8, 1970 Violence over Desegregation. Violent racial clashes connected with school desegregation occurred in three cities in the North and South. Four white boys and one black youth were shot and wounded in two apparently related incidents on October 5 and 7 outside a desegregated high school in Pontiac, Michigan. A second black student was struck down by a car near Pontiac Central High

School on October 7 as white and black students continued in their two-day battle with rocks and bottles. Tensions had run high in Pontiac following a recent court decision ordering desegregation of Pontiac's public schools.

Public schools in Trenton, New Jersey, were closed October 29 and 30, due to racial disorders that were sparked by the school board's decision to implement a student busing plan that called for the cross-town busing of fifty-five black and one hundred white students to achieve racial balance. The trouble started on October 29 when fighting began between one hundred black and white students in a predominantly Italian section of the city. Fighting spread into the downtown area when bands of black youths surged into the district hurling bottles at police officers and breaking windows. More than two hundred people were arrested during the three days of disorder. On November 1, the board voted to reopen the schools, and the dusk-to-dawn curfew that had been imposed on the city was relaxed.

Blacks in Henderson, North Carolina, had been engaged in a long protest over a decision by school officials to reopen an all-black school in the community. They charged that the board of education was trying to evade desegregation by reopening the school. Four days of sporadic sniper fire and burnings erupted in Henderson in the aftermath of the dispute. The National Guard was called to help restore order, and police jailed 101 people between November 5 and 8. By November 9, the school board agreed to close the school and bus its black pupils to desegregated schools. The National Guard remained on duty.

OCTOBER 12, 1970   Breakdown in Civil Rights Enforcement Reported. The U.S. Commission on Civil Rights reported a major breakdown in the enforcement of the nation's legal mandates prohibiting racial discrimination. The Commission urged President Richard Nixon to use "courageous moral leadership" and estab-

lish committees to oversee enforcement of court decrees, executive orders, and legislation relating to civil rights. Reverend Theodore M. Hesburgh, the chairman of the commission, said the findings were based on a six-month study of the executive departments and agencies charged with enforcing the nation's civil rights laws. The report, entitled *The Federal Civil Rights Enforcement Effort,* asserted that the credibility of the government's total civil rights efforts had been "seriously undermined." Hesburgh warned that "unless we get serious about this, the country is on a collision course."

OCTOBER 12–14, 1970   School Busing and Racial Balance Hearings. The U.S. Supreme Court heard arguments on student busing and racial balance in Southern schools. The arguments were heard by the Court as part of appeals filed by attorneys representing school districts in Charlotte, North Carolina, and Mobile, Alabama. Attorneys for the NAACP Legal Defense and Educational Fund, Inc., argued on October 13 that each black child possessed the constitutional right to be enrolled in a school that was not recognizably black. The lawyers contended that any desegregation plan that did not eliminate every all-black school should be deemed inadequate. NAACP lawyers further argued that the *Brown v. Board of Education* decision of 1954 would be undermined if the Court would permit some Southern school districts to maintain recognizably black schools.

Solicitor General Ervin N. Griswold, representing the Justice Department, rebutted the NAACP argument. He contended that the NAACP's petition amounted to a demand for racial balance in the schools, something that the Constitution did not require. Lawyers for the school districts told the Court, on October 13, that the *Brown v. Board of Education* decision was being violated by court-ordered desegregation plans that assigned children to schools by race. They asserted that the busing of school children to increase the incidence of desegregation was unconstitutional. The Court promised a ruling during its present term.

OCTOBER 13, 1970   Activist Angela Davis Arrested. Angela Davis, a twenty-six-year-old black former professor at the University of California at Los Angeles, was apprehended by Federal Bureau of Investigations agents in a New York City motel. Davis, who was the object of a two-month nationwide search for her alleged role in the murder of a California judge, was arraigned the next day. She was charged, in federal court, with unlawful flight to avoid prosecution on the California charges. The federal charge was later suspended when the California warrants charging Davis with the capital offenses arrived in New York. Federal authorities announced that it was customary in such cases for the state warrants to take precedence. Davis's attorney, John J. Abt, refused to waive extradition to California. Since Davis was being held for capital offenses, no bail was permitted. Thirty-six-year-old David R. Poindexter, Jr., had been arrested with Davis and charged with harboring a fugitive. He was released on October 16 on a $100,000 bond.

OCTOBER 19, 1970   Civil Rights Enforcement on Trial. The NAACP and the Washington law firm of Rauh and Silard filed suit against the Department of Health, Education, and Welfare, charging it with "general and calculated default" in its enforcement of federal school desegregation guidelines. The suit accused the federal agency of laxity in applying the cut-off of federal school funds to force recalcitrant school districts to comply with the law. It was the second time in two weeks that the government's enforcement of civil rights had been questioned. The U.S. Commission on Civil Rights reported on October 12, 1970, that there had been a "major breakdown" in the enforcement of the nation's laws that forbade racial discrimination. HEW secretary Elliot L. Richardson replied that his department was "committed faithfully to carry out both the letter and the spirit of the 1964 Civil Rights Act."

OCTOBER 19, 1970   Panther's Conspiracy to Riot Charge Dropped. U.S. District Court Judge Julius J. Hoffman dismissed the government's conspiracy charges against Bobby Seale, chairman of the Black Panther Party. Attorney William J. Bauer had asserted that "it would be inappropriate to try Seale alone on a conspiracy charge." Seale was one of eight defendants charged with conspiracy to cross state lines with intent to riot at the 1968 Democratic National Convention in Chicago. Hoffman severed Seale's case after the Black Panther leader had bitterly denounced the manner in which the jurist handled the trial. Seale's co-defendants, all whites, were subsequently acquitted on the conspiracy to riot charges. But Seale still faced a four-year prison term on contempt of court charges in Chicago and charges of kidnaping and murder in connection with the slaying of a New York Black Panther Party member.

OCTOBER 24-25, 1970   Northern Racial Disturbances. Violent clashes between blacks and police officers continued in Northern ghettoes. The attacks began the evening of October 24, shortly after a white-owned grocery store across from the all-black Pyramid Housing Project was burned. Several carloads of armed blacks riddled the police station in Cairo, Illinois, with hundreds of rounds of gunfire, three times in six hours. No officers were wounded, and the attackers were repelled after each assault. It was the first outbreak in racially tense Cairo since September of 1969. Cairo Mayor A.B. Thomas called the incident an "armed insurrection."

In Detroit, on October 24, black police officer Edward Smith was killed and another officer was wounded in an altercation with members of the National Committee to Combat Fascism. The disturbance was triggered by an incident involving the sale of Black Panther Party literature on a Detroit street corner. The NCCF claimed that two policemen beat two youths distributing the literature, and that police fired the first shots in the melee. According to police accounts, the policemen were felled by shotgun blasts from the NCCF's headquarters. Fifteen blacks were arrested after a day-long confrontation around the offices. Seven men and eight women were charged with murder and conspiracy.

OCTOBER 28, 1970 NCCF Leaders Ordered to Stand Trial. Edward A. Poindexter and David L. Rice, leaders of the National Committee to Combat Fascism, were ordered to stand trial in Omaha, Nebraska, on murder charges in connection with the August 17, 1970, slaying of an Omaha police officer. The two blacks, who had been in custody since August, remained in jail without bond.

NOVEMBER 20–22, 1970 Prison Riot over Segregation. More than five hundred inmates reportedly took part in a racial disturbance at the 16,000-acre Cumming Prison farm, ninety miles southeast of Little Rock, Arkansas. The fighting was sparked by inmates' demands for separate quarters for blacks and whites. Commissioner of corrections, Robert Sawer, reported that state troopers were called in after the violence reached riot proportions; some of the prisoners had armed themselves with knives, pipes, and broomstick handles. Prison guards broke up the fighting with tear gas.

DECEMBER 1970 Military Discrimination Abroad. Captain Curtis R. Smothers and six other black army officers petitioned Secretary of the Army Stanley R. Resar for a court of inquiry and an investigation of alleged racial bias against black soldiers in West Germany. The seven black servicemen complained of widespread housing discrimination and charged that the bias was going unchallenged because the United States government failed to press the West Germans to enforce the laws against discrimination. According to the blacks, "only an open court of inquiry convened by the Secretary of the Army could adequately determine the facts, assess the feasibility of alternative

solutions, and inquire into factors motivating the long-standing noncompliance with applicable laws and regulations." Smothers, also a military circuit judge in West Germany, was joined in the petition by Major Washington C. Hill, Lieutenant Edwin Dorn, Sergeant Willie Payne and three Specialists, 4th Class: Gregory Jones, Bobby Metcalf, and James Wilder.

Pentagon officials returned to Washington, D.C., on March 13, 1971, after having discussed the December petition with Smothers in West Germany. Smothers was then summoned to Washington for further discussions. This was seen by some as an attempt to persuade Smothers to withdraw his petition. But on June 3, 1971, the black members of the U.S. House of Representatives announced they were sending a staff member to Germany, Greece, Italy, and Turkey to investigate complaints of racism and discrimination in the armed forces abroad. Representative Shirley Chisholm, chairman of the Black Caucus's Military Affairs Committee, later reported that racial tension between Germans and black enlisted men was critical.

DECEMBER 11, 1970 Civil Rights Act Enforced. The Justice Department filed suit in a federal district court in Alabama, charging the United States Steel Corporation, the United Steelworkers of America, the AFL-CIO, and twelve union locals with violations of the Civil Rights Act of 1964 which prohibits discrimination in employment. Three days later, the chairman of the board of U.S. Steel Corporation announced that the Justice Department had demanded that the company allocate fifty percent of its office and clerical jobs in its Fairfield, Alabama, plant to blacks within the next five years. The company was also to ensure that blacks make up forty percent of all promoted to management positions in the next five years.

DECEMBER 11, 1970 None Found Guilty of Students' Deaths. A federal grand jury concluded its deliberations without returning any indictments in the investigation into the killing of two black youths at Jackson State College, on May 14, 1970. The jury also failed to submit a report.

DECEMBER 27, 1970 Soviets Invited to Angela Davis Trial. The U.S. State Department invited fourteen leading Soviet scientists to attend the forthcoming murder trial of former University of California professor and avowed Communist, Angela Davis, to ensure that she would receive a fair trial. The invitation was personally sanctioned by President Richard Nixon. The offer was an apparent response to a cablegram sent by the fourteen scientists to the president asking him "to safeguard the life of Angela Davis and give her an opportunity of continuing her scientific work." According to U.S. officials, the government's quick response was due to the high regard in which the scientists were held by professional colleagues in America. Among the fourteen scientists were: Igor P. Tamm, a Nobel- Prize-winning physicist, and Pyotr L. Kapitsa, the dean of Soviet physicists. This was the first time Soviet personalities were invited to observe American judicial proceedings.

DECEMBER 30, 1970 HUD Ordered to Promote Fair Housing. The U.S. Court of Appeals for the Third Circuit ordered the Department of Housing and Urban Development to "affirmatively promote fair housing" in considering applications for support of housing projects. The case involved HUD mortgage insurance and rent supplements in a predominantly black neighborhood in Philadelphia, Pennsylvania.

The court ruled that HUD had to determine, through public hearings or by other means, whether its projects would increase or maintain segregation. According to the court, HUD could not support such housing unless it was determined that the need for urban renewal or increased minority housing clearly outweighed "the disadvantages of increasing or perpetuating racial concentration." The court reasoned that after the passage of the 1964 and 1968 civil rights acts, HUD could no longer "remain blind to the very real effect that racial concentration has had in the development of urban blight." Edwin D. Wolf, executive director of the Philadelphia office of the Lawyers Committee for Civil Rights, called the ruling a landmark decision that could have an impact comparable to the Supreme Court's 1954 school desegregation decision.

1971

JANUARY 1, 1971 Floyd Elected Mayor of Princeton Township. James A. Floyd was named mayor of Princeton Township, an affluent, predominantly white suburban community in west central New Jersey. Floyd became the first black mayor in the township's history. He was selected unanimously by the five-member Township Committee, Princeton's governing body. In December 1970, the same committee had named Frederick M. Porter, a black police lieutenant, as chief of police.

JANUARY 4, 1971 GM Elected Black Director. The Reverend Leon Howard Sullivan, a forty-eight-year-old Philadelphia black minister, was elected to the board of directors of the General Motors Corporation (GM). Sullivan, pastor of Zion Baptist—Philadelphia's largest Protestant church—was the founder of Opportunities Industrialization Centers of America, a job-training program for blacks and other minorities, and a director of the Girard Trust Bank in Philadelphia. His election to the GM Board was interpreted as a move to placate demands that the company, the world's largest industrial corporation, give the public and minority groups a voice in corporate decision-making. At GM's annual stockholders meeting in May 1970, a reform group, the Project on Corporate Responsibility, had criticized GM for not having a black director on its board.

JANUARY 5, 1971 Angela Davis Charged with Crimes. Angela Davis was arraigned on charges of murder, kidnapping, and criminal conspiracy in a Marin County, California, court for her alleged participation in the August 7, 1970, incident at the San Rafael Courthouse which resulted in the deaths of four men. Flanked by her attorney, Howard Moore, a black Atlantan, Davis declared her innocence and said she was the target of a political frame-up.

JANUARY 5, 1971   Bethlehem Steel Charged with Discrimination. A federal labor panel charged the Bethlehem Steel Corporation, the second largest steel producer in the United States, with discriminating against blacks through its seniority system. A report compiled by the panel was sent to Secretary of Labor James D. Hodgson, who would decide what sanctions, if any, to impose on the firm. The three-member federal panel reached a unanimous decision against Bethlehem but disagreed on what corrective measures should be taken. In a statement that accompanied the report, Bethlehem denied the charge but agreed to set new hiring, promotion, and training quotas for blacks while studying the government's report. The action against Bethlehem was the second taken against one of the nation's major steel corporations. On December 11, 1970, the Justice Department had filed a suit against the U.S. Steel Corporation, accusing it of bias against blacks at its Fairfield, Alabama, steelworks.

JANUARY 6, 1971   Police Brutality on the Rise. FBI Director J. Edgar Hoover issued his annual report in which he stated that the number of racial incidents in schools had declined during the year, but attacks on police by blacks had increased. The FBI chief said racial disorders in secondary schools declined from 299 in the first months of the 1969–70 year to 160 in the corresponding period of the new term. Hoover warned, however, that "the number of incidents of racial disorder that did occur in our cities and in secondary schools, along with the many unwarranted attacks on police, strongly indicated that we are far from the realization of racial harmony in the nation." Hoover said there was a marked increase in attacks on police officers by persons identifying themselves as

Black Panthers. He said such persons were responsible for the deaths of six police officers and the wounding of twenty-two others and that in the previous two years, five police officers were killed and forty-two wounded under such circumstances.

JANUARY 11, 1971   Muhammad Ali Draft Evasion Reconsidered. The U.S. Supreme Court agreed to review the 1967 draft evasion conviction of former heavyweight boxing champion Muhammad Ali. The action assured that Ali, who won the championship under the name Cassius Clay, would be free to fight the recognized title holder, Joe Frazier, in March. (Frazier defeated Ali on March 8 in New York). Ali was convicted when the courts rejected his contention that he should be exempted from the draft because of his religious status as a Black Muslim minister. The current appeal was based largely on the Supreme Court's ruling in 1969 that conscientious objectors could base their claims on philosophical or moral objections rather than strictly religious grounds.

JANUARY 14, 1971   Voting Rights Protected. The U.S. Supreme Court ruled that Southern states must obtain federal approval before making any changes in their election laws that might affect the rights of black voters as provided by the 1965 Voting Rights Act. The order came in a case brought by two black voters and six defeated black candidates in the 1969 municipal elections in Canton, Mississippi. The plaintiffs contended that the city, in shifting polling places, annexing neighborhoods with white majorities, and changing to at-large elections of aldermen, had discouraged and diluted the black vote. The Supreme Court returned the case to the district court to decide if the election should be reheld.

JANUARY 14, 1971   School Desegregation in North Too Slow. Secretary of Health, Education, and Welfare Elliot L. Richardson announced in Washington that the Nixon administration would soon turn its attention to the task of increasing the rate of school desegregation in the North. The report cited a survey showing the percentage of blacks attending desegregated schools in the North and West rose from 27.6 percent to 27.7 percent in the period since 1968. This compared with a two-year increase from 18.4 percent to 38.1 percent in the South. The administration concluded that a Northern drive was necessary because there were now more desegregated school systems in the South than in the North.

JANUARY 14, 1971   Court Allowed Compensation for Discrimination. The Oregon Court of Appeals ruled that mental anguish was one of the effects of racial discrimination and could be compensated by a cash award. The court sustained the contention of Beverley A. Williams, a young black woman, who said she was discriminated against when Margaret C. Joyce refused to rent her an apartment in Portland. Williams's charge was earlier upheld by the Oregon state Bureau of Labor, which assessed Joyce $200 for humiliating Williams and $140 to pay for her moving expenses, but the cash award for humiliation was overthrown by the state circuit court on appeal by Joyce. The Court of Appeals, in setting aside the circuit court's ruling, said that compensation for humiliation was proper.

JANUARY 16, 1971   Suburban Segregation Continued. Preliminary studies of the 1970 Bureau of the Census indicated very little racial integration of American suburbs during the 1960s, according to a *Washington Post* report. Specialists at the Census Bureau predicted that early trends showing little suburban integration would hold true even as more detailed analyses were completed. Meyer Zitter, assistant chief of the Bureau's population division, estimated that about 15 percent of the nation's blacks lived within metropolitan areas and outside the central cities. The figure for whites was nearly 40 percent. Census officials said that if the preliminary reports were sustained, it would again illustrate that whites were fleeing the

inner cities to the suburbs. During the 1960s, there was a reported net loss of about 2.5 million whites from the inner city areas and an increase of about three million blacks. Two-thirds of the rise in the number of black inner-city dwellers was attributable to births. These preliminary reports came at a time when the Nixon administration was still shaping its policies regarding suburban desegregation.

JANUARY 17, 1971   Chicago Gang Members Acquitted. A jury in Chicago acquitted seven members of the Black P. Stone Nation, a confederation of sixty black street gangs, of murder in the August 17, 1970, sniper slaying of a Chicago detective. All were acquitted of charges of murder and conspiracy to commit murder in the death of Detective James A. Alfonso, Jr. The acquittal came three days after the biracial jury had begun deliberations. Those freed were Edward Bey, Lamar Bell, Tony Carter, Dennis Griffin, Ronald Florence, William Throup, and Elton Wriks. The alleged involvement of the black gangs in the murder had exacerbated tensions between the black community and Chicago police. Concomitantly, Chicago black leaders, including the the Reverend Jesse Jackson, had criticized the black gangs for terrorizing black communities.

JANUARY 20, 1971   North Carolina Ruled on Busing. The North Carolina Supreme Court sustained the state's policy of providing school buses for urban children involved in desegregation programs. As long as state funds were used to transport children from rural areas to their schools, the court reasoned, city dwelling children must have the same rights. The ruling struck down a lower court's prohibition on the use of state funds for busing. In effect, the court's decision gave the state legislature the choice of continuing busing for all children who required it or discontinuing the practice altogether. An assistant state attorney general expressed the view that the court's decision could not be appealed because it did not involve any constitutional issue.

FEBRUARY 1, 1971 Georgia State Board of Regents Named First Black Vice-Chancellor. Howard Jordan, Jr., the president of Savannah State College in Georgia, assumed duties as vice-chancellor of the Georgia State Board of Regents, becoming the first black so named. Jordan had served as president of Savannah State College since 1963. His new duties involved handling administrative matters for all state-run colleges and universities in Georgia.

FEBRUARY 1, 1971 New Orleans Court Ordered Fair Services. The U.S. Court of Appeals for the Fifth Circuit in New Orleans ruled that local governments must provide such public services as road paving and sewers on a racially equal basis. The suit was filed by black residents of Shaw, Mississippi. According to the court, no compelling interests "could possibly justify the gross disparities in services between black and white areas of town."

FEBRUARY 4–5, 1971 Lawsuit Called Civil Service Exams Discriminatory. Eight black federal employees charged in a suit filed in the U.S. Court in Washington, D.C., that the Federal Service Entrance Examination, the principal test that must be passed by qualified college graduates for civil service posts, was culturally and racially discriminatory. The eight plaintiffs, employees of the Department of Housing and Urban Development's (HUD) Chicago regional office, alleged that the examination violated the equal opportunity guarantees of the Fifth Amendment. They also charged that it violated, among other things, the 1964 Civil Rights Act. The suit asked the court to prevent the use of the examination until its alleged discriminatory aspects were eliminated, and that the use of other testing procedures be stopped until a determination could be made of their relation to specific job requirements. According to the plaintiffs, about 49 percent of the 100,000 applicants who took the test in 1969 finished with scores above seventy (the passing percentile) with a disproportionately low percentage of blacks and other minority group members passing.

In another development involving blacks and examinations, Edward F. Bell, president of the National Bar Association (NBA), a predominantly black lawyers' group, asked other lawyers' organizations on February 5 to ascertain whether bar examinations should be abolished as racially discriminatory. Bell said recent studies seemed to indicate that bar examinations discriminated against black law school graduates. The Detroit attorney cited lawsuits that were filed in several states by law students seeking to abolish the bar examinations because they did not test a graduate's legal knowledge.

FEBRUARY 5, 1971 Georgia School District Sued. The Justice Department filed a suit in the U.S. District Court in Atlanta charging Georgia's Clayton County school board with maintaining a dual public school system. The Clayton system was described by the department as one of fifty remaining recalcitrant school districts in the South. According to the suit, Clayton officials assigned the district's 1,479 black and 25,220 white pupils and their teachers to different sets of schools. The department requested a court order demanding that the county submit a desegregation plan immediately.

Judge Oren Harris of the U.S. District Court for the Eastern District of Arkansas issued an ultimatum to the officials of the Watson Chapel, Arkansas, School District No. 24, warning them that they faced stiff jail terms if they continued to defy a court-ordered desegregation ruling. Harris said a fine of $350 a day would also be levied for each day they remained in contempt of court by ignoring the school order. Watson Chapel District, which included part of Pine Bluff, Arkansas, as well as the town of Watson Chapel, had about 4,000 students, almost half of them black. Judge Harris had ordered all children in grades one through four to attend three elementary schools, all of which would retain a substantial white majority.

The Justice Department, also on February 5, charged the Henry County, Virginia, school district with failing to execute a desegregation arrangement that it had earlier agreed to implement. In a suit filed in the federal district court in Danville, Virginia, the department accused the Henry County system of continuing to assign its high school pupils on a freedom-of-choice plan in violation of the 1964 Civil Rights Act. Henry County, according to the suit, had used the freedom-of-choice scheme to assign nearly 800 black pupils to an all-black high school.

FEBRUARY 6–9, 1971 Protests Led to Violence in North Carolina. National Guardsmen patrolled the streets of Wilmington, North Carolina, in the wake of four days of racial violence in which two people were killed. The unrest was linked to a boycott of Wilmington's high school by black students. Blacks were protesting the city's desegregation plans. The first of the two slayings took place on February 6 when a black youth was killed by a police officer who said the boy pointed a shotgun at him. Blacks in Wilmington asserted the youth was shot as he helped move furniture from a home threatened by a nearby fire. The second victim was a white man who was shot later outside of a black church which was being used as headquarters by the boycotting blacks. The white man was armed with a pistol. Local officers, aided by the 600 National Guardsmen, restored order on February 8 but remained on alert.

FEBRUARY 10, 1971 Blacks Disapproved of Nixon. A Gallup Poll reported that American blacks continued to disapprove of the way President Richard Nixon was handling his job by a 2:1 ratio, the same ratio recorded in surveys the previous spring.

FEBRUARY 11, 1971 White Students Protested Desegregation. Scores of white high school students walked out of their school near Pine Bluff, Arkansas, to protest a court-ordered desegregation plan. They were greeted by their parents and other adult supporters. The mostly peaceful demonstration was the only incident on the day the school district began operating under the desegregation order. Watson Chapel School District No. 24 reluctantly implemented the plan after a federal judge warned the school board members that they faced stiff jail terms and fines if they continued to defy his orders.

FEBRUARY 16, 1971 Whites Charged in Riots. Twenty-two whites were indicted by a county grand jury in Darlington, South Carolina, on riot charges in connection with a March 1970 incident in which a mob of angry whites overturned two school buses transporting black children to desegregated schools in nearby Lamar. Charges against twenty-one other whites, including a state legislator, were dropped by the grand jury.

FEBRUARY 17, 1971 Black Sheriff Charged with Beating Black Prisoner. Lucius D. Amerson, sheriff of Macon County, Alabama, and the state's first black sheriff since Reconstruction, and one of his black deputies were arrested on a federal indictment accusing them of beating a black prisoner. Amerson and his deputy, Richard Coleman, Jr., posted bonds of $1,000 each on the charge of violating the civil rights of Wilbert D. Harris while acting under the cover of the law. Harris was arrested in Tuskegee, the county-seat of Macon County, in August 1970 and charged with driving while intoxicated. The prisoner reportedly used a pistol to disarm two deputies and was also accused of firing at Amerson. Harris was subdued and charged with assault with intent to murder. The alleged beating by Amerson and Coleman reportedly took place after Harris was subdued. Conviction on the federal charge carried a penalty of up to a year in prison and a $1,000 fine.

FEBRUARY 17, 1971   Commission Called for Aid to Black Colleges. The Carnegie Commission on Higher Education called for a tripling of federal aid to the nation's 105 black colleges and universities. In a report entitled "From Isolation to Mainstream: Problems of the Colleges Founded for Negroes," the Commission also urged increased funds from states, corporations, and foundations to allow black colleges to double their current enrollment of 150,000. The commission, headed by Dr. Clark Kerr, said that the black colleges were faced with special difficulties at a time of major transition as they emerged from their historic isolation into the mainstream of U.S. education. The report pointed out that at a time when other institutions were enlarging black enrollment and developing black studies programs, the black colleges had to compete for students, faculty, and financial resources. In addition, black colleges had to meet the special expenses of remedial training for poorly prepared students and financial aid for the 70 percent of their students who required some type of scholarly assistance.

MARCH 3, 1971   Black Migration to North Leveled Off. The Bureau of the Census announced that, contrary to earlier reports, the rate of black migration from the South to the North during the 1960s had remained unchanged from the pace of the two previous decades. Earlier statistics had indicated that the number of Southern blacks moving North had dropped sharply during the 1960s to about half the levels of the prior twenty years. The new figures from the 1970 census showed that the migration pace through the 1960s was nearly the same as the high levels of the 1940s and 1950s. According to the Bureau's analysts, more than three-fourths of the 1.4 million blacks who left the South during the decade settled in five large industrial centers. New York had a Southern black influx of 396,000; California, 272,000; New Jersey, Michigan, and Illinois each gained about 120,000. The analysts said there were indications that the migration rate

would continue to be high and might increase in the 1970s. The Bureau also reported an increased movement of whites to the South. This dual movement of blacks to the North and whites to the South was reportedly a continuation of a long-term trend toward distribution of the black population throughout the United States. According to the Bureau's report, the South still contained 53 percent of the nation's blacks, compared to 77 percent in 1940. Since 1940, the percentage of blacks in the Northeast and North Central states had risen from about 11 percent to 20 percent. Bureau analysts said that each of the eleven states of the Confederacy had lost residents. Mississippi and Alabama led with 279,000 and 231,000 respectively. Secretary of Commerce Maurice H. Stans speculated that the continued black Northern migration was due in part to the higher welfare benefits of the Northern states. He added, however, that he assumed that greater job opportunities in the North would be the primary motivating factor. The Bureau statistics showed that there were about 22,672,570 blacks in the United States or about 11.2 percent of the population. In 1960, the figures were 18,871,831 or about 10.6 percent.

MARCH 8, 1971   Supreme Court Condemned Racially-Biased Job Testing. The U.S. Supreme Court ruled that employers could not use job tests that had the effect of screening out blacks if the tests were not related to ability to do the work. According to the Court, the employment bias section of the 1964 Civil Rights Act involved the consequences of employment practices, not simply whether the practices were motivated by racial bias. The Court imposed limits on the use of general educational and aptitude tests and said that "any tests used must measure the person for the job and not the person in the abstract." The case stemmed from the application for promotion by thirteen black workers at the Duke Power Company's generating plant in Draper, North Carolina. The NAACP, the Justice Department, and the federal Equal Employment Opportunity Commission had sought the ruling.

MARCH 8, 1971   FBI Targeted Black Activist Groups. FBI files stolen from a Bureau office in Media, Pennsylvania, and released to the public revealed several documents relating to black activist groups. One of the FBI memoranda was a November 4, 1970, dispatch from Director J. Edgar Hoover ordering an investigation of all groups organized to project the demands of black students. The dispatch said that increased campus disorders involving black students posed a definite threat to the nation's stability and security and indicated a need for an increase in both the quality and quantity of intelligence information on black student unions and similar groups. The memorandum went on to say that such groups were targets for influence and control by the Black Panther party and other extremist organizations. (Black student unions and other such groups had sprung up on mostly predominantly white campuses during the past five years. Their origins stemmed from the increased enrollment of black students at such schools and the bias which they allegedly encountered on the campuses. Sometimes their organized protests bordered on violence.) The memoranda also contained a report of a 1970 convention of the National Association of Black Students at Wayne State University in Detroit, reports of surveillance of black student activities at Swarthmore College in Pennsylvania, of the Philadelphia Black Panthers, and the National Black Economic Conference held in Philadelphia during 1970. Muhammad Kenyatta, who headed the Philadelphia conference and was mentioned prominently in several of the FBI documents, stated on March 24 that he had received copies of the memoranda relating to him before they were published. He would not identify his sources. On March 23, Attorney General John Mitchell denounced the thefts and the publication of the records. He warned that the information could endanger the lives of people engaged in investigative activities on behalf of the United States.

MARCH 11, 1971   National Urban League Director Died. Whitney M. Young, Jr., executive director of the National Urban League, died in Nigeria. Young and a group of other Americans, white and black, were in Lagos attending an African American conference designed to bridge the gap between Africans and Americans. Young drowned while swimming with a party that included former U.S. Attorney General Ramsey Clark. Young left his position as Dean of the School of Social Work at Atlanta University in 1961 to become head of the nation's leading black economic and social reform agency. He made the organization more effective and increased its influence. During the height of the civil rights era, Young became, with Martin Luther King, Jr., Roy Wilkins, and James Farmer, one of the movement's "Big Four" leaders. President Nixon expressed personal sorrow at the news of Young's death, commenting, "I have lost a friend, Black America has lost a gifted and commanding champion of its just cause."

MARCH 23, 1971   Black Congressional Delegate Elected. The Reverend Walter E. Fauntroy, a Baptist minister and a Democrat, was elected the District of Columbia's first non-voting Congressional delegate in this century. Fauntroy captured 58 percent of the vote to defeat Attorney John A. Nevins, a white Republican, Julius W. Hobson, a black independent, and three minor independent candidates. Fauntroy's salary of $42,500 per year would equal that of other members of the House of Representatives and he would be permitted to sit on the House District Committee, vote in other committees, but could not vote on the House floor. The black members of Congress immediately selected Fauntroy as the thirteenth member of the so-called Black Caucus.

MARCH 24, 1971   Suburban Zoning Laws Challenged. The NAACP filed a suit challenging the legality of zoning laws that prohibited the construction of apartment buildings in suburban communities. It was the first time the

Civil rights activist Whitney Young, Jr. (Courtesy of the National Urban League.)

NAACP had gone to court against suburban zoning laws. The action was taken in the federal court in Brooklyn, New York, against the town of Oyster Bay, New York. The NAACP charged that the town's zoning laws had "foreclosed black and other non-white minorities from obtaining housing in the town," with results that "intensify and harden patterns of racial ghetto living" in the city of New York. Roy Wilkins, executive secretary of the NAACP, said black workers employed in Oyster Bay often could not find suitable housing. He said forty-five new industries had located in Oyster Bay since 1965, but that workers earning less than $17,000 a year could not afford to buy houses in the town because of the minimum lot sizes prescribed by the zoning laws.

MARCH 24, 1971 Southern School Desegregation Report. The Southern Regional Council issued a report in Atlanta which said that for the first time desegregation in the South's public schools was the rule rather than the exception. This transformation had occurred, the Council said, despite the proliferation of all-white private academies in the region and the continued operation of some all-black schools.

At the same time, the Council accused the Nixon administration of "playing a deceptive game of numbers" by using misleading figures about the extent of actual desegregation. Despite the recent gains, the Council asserted that the South was "a far cry from the final dismantling of the dual [school] system." Desegregation in 1970 and in 1971, according to the Council, was less successful than the administration asserted in its figures, but "more successful than policies of [the] government gave it any right to be." The Council's report was entitled "The South and Her Children: School Desegregation, 1970–71."

MARCH 25, 1971 Black Caucus Met with Nixon. President Richard Nixon met with a group of black members of the U.S. House of Representatives to receive a list of sixty grievances presented on behalf of African Americans. The so-called Black Caucus asked for reforms in welfare, job discrimination and job placement, social justice, school desegregation, etc. The President appointed five White House staff members to work on the list of recommendations. The meeting, first proposed in 1969, was set up soon after the black members of the House boycotted the President's State of the Union Address in January. The group charged that the President's failure to meet with them up until that time constituted a flagrant disregard for the opinions of African Americans.

MARCH 31, 1971 More Black Recruits Sought by Navy. Admiral Elmo R. Zumwalt, Jr., Chief of Naval Operations, announced the formation of a six-man team (including three admirals) to oversee a five-year program to recruit more black officers and enlisted men for the navy. The aim of the recruiting drive was to bring the numbers of black navy personnel up to the level of the nearly twelve percent black representation in the total U.S. population. Black recruiters were added to the staffs of the thirty-seven recruiting stations across the nation. New Navy Reserve Officer Training Corps units were added at Savannah State College in Georgia and Southern University at Baton Rouge, Louisiana. These were to supplement the sole existing black Navy ROTC unit at Prairie View A&M College in Texas. The navy said it would also increase the number of black midshipmen at the Naval Academy at Annapolis, Maryland. On June 2, 1971, Samuel L. Gravely, Jr., was named the first black admiral in the navy. Vice Admiral Raymond Peet performed the ritual known as "frocking" which promoted Gravely from captain to admiral. Gravely became director of naval communications in Washington, D.C.

APRIL 6–13, 1971 Blacks Won in Municipal Elections. Warren Widener, a Berkeley, California, city councilman, was elected mayor of the city. Widener defeated Wilmount Sweeney, described as a moderate black, by fifty-six votes. Widener was considered to be aligned with the so-called radical coalition, which sought to take political control of the town. Two black lawyers, also called radical, D'rmy Bailey and Ird T. Simmons, were elected to the city council. Bailey said a description of their politics as radical was misleading and suggested instead the term "progressive." The election results pointed to a radical-moderate control of the city council. In other spring municipal elections, James E. Williams, Sr., was elected the first black mayor of East St. Louis, Illinois, on April 6, and John Franklin, a Chattanooga, Tennessee, educator and businessman, was elected the first black commissioner in the city's history on April 13.

APRIL 12, 1971 David R. Poindexter Acquitted. A federal jury in New York City acquitted David R. Poindexter of harboring and concealing the identity of black militant Angela Davis while she was the target of a nationwide police search. Poindexter was arrested in New York on October 13, 1970, along with Davis, who was at that time one of the FBI's ten most wanted fugitives. She was being sought in connection with the murder of a California judge during a courtroom shootout on August 7,

1970. During the trial, the prosecution presented more than forty witnesses in an effort to prove that Poindexter had moved through several cities with Davis under assumed names and must have known that she was being sought under federal warrant. The defense summoned no witnesses, relying on the argument that the prosecution had failed to prove its case beyond a reasonable doubt. Following the verdict, Poindexter commented that his trial "was a minor skirmish in a big war. The major battle is in California over Angela."

APRIL 13, 1971 Tax Privileges Suspended for All-White School. The Internal Revenue Service announced that the Fayette Academy in Somerville, Tennessee, was notified that contributions for its operation were no longer tax deductible because it had failed to adopt non-discriminatory admissions policies. The action was the first time the IRS had suspended tax privileges for an all-white private school outside of Mississippi.

APRIL 15, 1971 Florida Students Protested Enrollment Practices. Approximately 2,000 black and white students gathered at the home of the president of the University of Florida at Gainesville protesting what they called the school's "racist" policies and demanding the resignation of President Stephen C. O'Connell. Earlier the same day, sixty-seven blacks, members of the school's Black Student Union, were arrested during a sit-in outside O'Connell's office. The blacks and their white allies called for increased black enrollment at the university by recruiting five hundred new students. There were at the time about three hundred blacks out of a 22,000 total enrollment. In a television address to the students, President O'Connell said, "We have made remarkable racial progress," but he rejected the black recruitment demands calling them "a racial quota" and "racism in reverse." Nearly one hundred black students subsequently withdrew from the university in further protest of the school's policies.

APRIL 16, 1971   Cleveland's First Black Mayor Announced Plans. Carl B. Stokes, the first black mayor of Cleveland, Ohio, announced that he was leaving office at the end of his current term in 1971. He said he would help develop a "people's lobby" to bring pressure on the two major political parties toward "responsive" presidential candidates in 1972 and toward a reordering of the nation's priorities. Stokes was first elected in 1967 as the first black mayor of a major American city, and was reelected in 1969.

APRIL 19, 1971   Black Illegitimacy Rate Dropped. The U.S. Bureau of the Census released a study compiled from federal and private sources which revealed that black women, on the average, had fewer illegitimate births in the late 1960s than they did in the earlier part of the decade. Meanwhile, the white illegitimacy rate was climbing. According to the report, the black illegitimacy rate, which was ten times higher than the white rate in 1961, had dropped to about seven times in 1968, the last year considered in the study. The raw figures for 1968 alone were 184,000 black and 155,000 white illegitimate births. The report, entitled "Fertility Indicators: 1970," was developed by Campbell Gibson of the Census Bureau.

APRIL 20, 1971   Busing Declared Constitutional. The U.S. Supreme Court, in a series of unanimous decisions, told the Charlotte-Mecklenburg County, North Carolina, joint school system and all the other school districts of the nation that busing children as a means of dismantling a racially dual school system was constitutional. The rulings ended the final legal efforts by Southern school boards to prevent the busing of students to achieve more desegregation in schools. Chief Justice Warren E. Burger wrote the opinions of the Court in the four cases on which it ruled. In addition to upholding the school desegregation plan, which included busing for the Charlotte-Mecklenburg district, the Court struck down an anti-busing law enacted by the North Carolina Legislature, ordered school officials in Mobile, Alabama, to use all available techniques to correct segregation in their schools, and overruled a Georgia Supreme Court order that had said certain desegregation efforts in the city of Athens were unconstitutional. The High Court reasoned that "desegregation plans cannot be limited to the walk-in school." The justices held that busing school children was proper unless "the time or distance is so great as to risk either the health of the children or significantly impinge on the educational process." The Court added that at times busing was an indispensable method of eliminating the last vestiges of racial segregation. The Court made it clear, however, that the rulings did not apply to *de facto* segregation caused by neighborhood housing patterns, as is found most often in the North. The landmark decision has become known to history as *Swann v. Charlotte-Mecklenburg.*

APRIL 23, 1971   Philadelphia Plan Upheld. The U.S. Court of Appeals for the Third Circuit upheld the legality of the Nixon administration's pilot job plan for minorities, known as the Philadelphia Plan. The plan, devised by the Labor Department in 1969, required contractors bidding on federal or federally-assisted projects to hire a fixed number of minority group members by a certain date. A number of groups, foremost among them building and construction organizations, had sought in a number of courts to stop the plan on the grounds that it was unconstitutional. In this case, the Court of Appeals was asked by the Contractors Association of Eastern Pennsylvania to declare the plan illegal. They contended that the plan denied the group equal protection of the law and violated the 1964 Civil Rights Act because it required racial quotas. The court reasoned that the plan did not violate the 1964 Civil Rights Act because the contractors were not, in fact, required to hire a definite percentage of a minority group.

APRIL 28, 1971   Number of Black Elected Officials Grew. The Joint Center for Political

Studies in Washington reported that the number of black elected officials in the U.S. rose 22 percent during 1970. Despite these gains, however, black public officials still represented only about .3 percent of all officeholders in the nation. The center's director, Frank D. Reeves, commented that the 22 percent rise showed that "blacks are gaining clout more and more in the nation's electoral systems." The report also revealed that 1,860 blacks held office as of April 1971. By comparison, in 1967 only 475 blacks held elective offices. Nearly three-fifths of the blacks in office were Southerners. According to the report, 711 blacks held office in the eleven states of the old Confederacy, a 26 percent rise above the 1970 figure of 563.

MAY 4, 1971   Blacks Won in Primary Elections. In another spring primary election, Richard B. Hatcher was renominated to a second four-year term as mayor of Gary, Indiana. Hatcher won 59 percent of the vote cast and was heavily favored to win the general election over the Republican nominee, Theodore Nering. In the primary Hatcher, who was first elected mayor in 1967, defeated Dr. Alexander Williams, the Lake County Coroner, and John Armento, the president of the city council.

MAY 4, 1971   Black Panther Released from Custody. U.S. District Judge William P. Gray ordered David Hilliard, chief of staff of the Black Panther Party, released from federal custody after the government refused to divulge wiretap logs of conversations involving Hilliard. Hilliard was charged with threatening the life of President Richard Nixon during an anti-war speech in November 1969. When U.S. Attorney James Browning told the court that he was not authorized to make the wiretap logs available to Hilliard's lawyers, Judge Gray ordered the indictment dismissed and the case dropped.

MAY 5, 1971   Riots Broke Out in New York City. A riot involving mostly black youths occurred in the Brownsville section of New York City. Hundreds of youths set scores of fires and fought police. One police officer was shot and fourteen others were injured during the melee. Police arrested twenty-five people on charges of larceny or malicious mischief. At the height of the rioting, marauding bands of young people looted stores and battled police with rocks, bricks, and bottles. The rioting began after thousands of angry Brownsville (Brooklyn) residents closed off dozens of streets in their neighborhood with abandoned cars and trash piles to protest state budget cuts affecting welfare assistance, anti-narcotics programs, Medicaid, educational facilities, and the food stamp program. The legislation was signed by Governor Nelson A. Rockefeller on April 15. Organizers of the peaceful protest disavowed the actions of the rioting youths, and the disturbance was brought under control by late evening.

MAY 5, 1971   Labor Department Announced Racial Quotas. The U.S. Labor Department announced that it would impose mandatory racial hiring quotas on federally sponsored construction projects under way in San Francisco, St. Louis, and Atlanta. The established plans for the three cities varied slightly in their formats. Overall, however, they required contractors bidding on federal or federally-sponsored projects to agree to hire a fixed percentage of minority group members by a certain date. Washington and Philadelphia were the only other two cities to have such job plans.

MAY 10, 1971   Nixon Administration Showed Progress. The U.S. Commission on Civil Rights reported that the Nixon administration had shown some signs of progress in enforcing civil rights laws but considerable strides needed to be made. The new commission report came seven months after a harsh indictment of the administration was issued, asserting that there had been a major breakdown in the enforcement of the civil rights laws. The commission singled out for praise George P. Shultz, director of the Office of Management and Budget and Leonard Garment, a presidential counselor, for what it termed their efforts at "active intervention" in seeking compliance with civil rights laws. The report also cited other signs of progress:

1. President Nixon, in his fiscal 1972 budget recommendations, had sought more funds for the Office of Federal Contract Compliance and the Equal Employment Opportunity Commission.

2. The Army, among other departments, had set up a program to establish goals for minority employment in its own offices.

3. The Justice Department had announced that it would add six lawyers to its office to coordinate efforts to enforce Title VI of the 1964 Civil Rights Law, which forbade discrimination in federally assisted programs.

MAY 13, 1971 African American Colonels Nominated for Promotion. The U.S. Army announced that it had nominated three black colonels for promotion to the rank of brigadier general. The three black officers were among eighty colonels approved by President Nixon for promotion to the one-star rank. The three officers promoted were Colonels Alvin W. Dillard, James F. Hamlet, and Roscoe C. Cartwright. Their nominations would bring the number of black army generals to four. The air force also had one black general, while the navy nominated its first black admiral on April 28, 1971.

MAY 14, 1971 Busing Recommended for Texas. The Department of Health, Education and Welfare (HEW), complying with the Supreme Court's ruling upholding school busing to achieve greater desegregation, recommended extensive crosstown busing as part of a plan to desegregate the public schools in Austin, Texas. The desegregation proposal was the first made by the government since the Supreme Court in *Swann v. Charlotte-Mecklenburg* (April 1971) rejected the administration's objections to busing and declared the method constitutional as a means of dismantling dual school

systems. Austin, the sixth largest city in Texas, had about 56,000 students in fifty-six elementary schools, nineteen junior high schools and eight high schools. About 15 percent of the students were black and about 20 percent Mexican-American. The city had two high schools and seven elementary schools with virtually all-black enrollments.

MAY 17, 1971 Sheriff Acquitted of Brutality Charges. An all-white jury in Opelika, Alabama, acquitted black Macon County Sheriff Lucius D. Amerson and his deputy, Richard Coleman, Jr., of a federal charge that they had beaten a prisoner in their custody. Amerson commented that the verdict reaffirmed his belief that he could receive a fair trial at the hands of an all-white jury in the South.

MAY 18, 1971 Nixon Responded to Black Caucus. In a 115-page report, President Richard Nixon told the Black Caucus of the House of Representatives that his administration would continue to support "jobs, income, and tangible benefits, the pledges that this society has made to the disadvantaged in the past decade." The president was responding to a list of sixty grievances the black congressmen had asked him to consider in a meeting on March 25, 1971. The president announced that he agreed with the caucus's welfare reform proposals but limited his guaranteed annual income figure to $2,400, compared to the $6,500 a year figure proposed by the blacks. In almost all of the recommendations, the president differed with the caucus in amounts and scope of reform programs. For instance, the black legislators suggested one million summer jobs for youths; the president promised 500,000 jobs, with some 300,000 more being made available through private sectors. The Black Caucus received the report through the office of its chairman, Representative Charles C. Diggs, Jr., from Michigan. After studying the report, the caucus issued a seventy-six-page reaction that expressed its disappointment. The legislators called the president's message "a mere codification of slim

The Black Caucus at a news conference on May 24, 1971.

efforts" rather than "massive immediate aid for minorities and the poor." In the end, the blacks charged, the administration "lacked a sense of understanding, urgency and commitment in dealing with the critical problems facing black Americans." It was pointed out that only one of the sixty demands was fully agreed on by both sides—the formation of a task force to study the problems of black soldiers and veterans.

MAY 21–26, 1971   Racial Violence in Chattanooga, Tennessee. Racial violence erupted

in Chattanooga, Tennessee, after a black musician failed to perform at a rock concert in the city auditorium. When some of the black youths did not get refunds for their admission fees, they began vandalizing the building. The disorder later spread into the streets. On May 24, Governor Winfield Dunn ordered 2,000 National Guardsmen into the city after local police were unable to contain the arson and sniping which was centered in the black neighborhoods located on the outskirts of the downtown area. On May 25 a young black man was killed by police who said they fired after the man hurled bricks at them. Black witnesses said the victim, Leon Anderson, was apparently drunk, and they charged that police shot him without provocation. The incident increased tensions but did not lead to heightened violence. On May 26 a rigid dusk-to-dawn curfew was lifted in the city and Governor Dunn announced that guardsmen would be gradually withdrawn.

MAY 25, 1971   Charges Against Black Panthers Dismissed. Judge Harold H. Mulvey of the Connecticut State Court in New Haven dismissed all charges against Black Panther Party members Bobby Seale and Ericka Huggins. The two were on trial for six months for the murder of former Black Panther member Alex Rackley in May 1969. Judge Mulvey ordered the charges dropped after the jury in the case told him it was hopelessly deadlocked. The judge declared a mistrial and announced that the massive publicity about the case had made it too difficult to select an unbiased jury to try the pair again. Seale was chairman and co-founder of the Black Panther Party, and Huggins was a party member from Connecticut. Throughout the trial the state, led by state attorney Arnold Markle, sought to prove that Seale had ordered a group of party members to murder Rackley after he was accused of treason against the party. The state's principal witness, George Sams, Jr., testified that Seale had given him the orders. Seale's defense counsel, Charles R. Gary, countered consistently that Sams ordered Rackley's death. Sams, a member of the party, had already pleaded guilty to second-degree murder in the case. The dismissal of charges brought to an end another chapter of violence and legal proceedings connected with the Black Panther Party.

MAY 25, 1971   Shooting Sparked Racial Tension. Racial tension was sparked anew in Mississippi as Jo Etha Collier, an eighteen-year-old black girl, was shot dead in Drew, Mississippi. Collier was felled by a bullet from a passing car as she stood with other young blacks on a street corner in her hometown. The incident occurred less than an hour after the girl graduated from desegregated Drew High School and was designated the student with the best school spirit. Three white men were arrested and charged with the killing on May 26. On June 14, Wayne and Wesley Parks of Drew, Mississippi, and Allen Wilkerson of Memphis, Tennessee, were arraigned on charges of murder before circuit court Judge Arthur B. Clark in Indianola, Mississippi. The three pleaded innocent. The swift arrests, arraignments, and the sympathetic attitude of local white officials served to help calm tensions in the community.

MAY 30, 1971   Gun Battle Injured Three. Three police officers were injured in a gun battle in Cairo, Illinois, one of the most racially tense cities in America. Cairo mayor Albert B. Thomas blamed the shootings on the United Front, a predominantly black organization that had led a boycott of the town's white merchants. The United Front declined to comment on the incident.

JUNE 4, 1971   Labor Department Imposed Racial Quotas. Arthur A. Fletcher, assistant secretary of labor, announced that the Labor Department was withdrawing its support of Chicago's voluntary equal hiring plan for federal construction projects and would impose mandatory racial quotas on federally assisted projects throughout the city. Chicago's voluntary plan failed after being in operation for eighteen months. The plan called for the hiring and training of some 4,000 minority group members. But by June 4, 1971, only 885 blacks and Hispanic-Americans were enrolled for training, and only a few had obtained membership in the city's construction unions. The Labor Department said it would replace the Chicago plan with the now-standard formula known as the Philadelphia Plan, under which a certain number of minority group members should be employed on federal projects exceeding $500,000.

Black Panther leader Bobby Seale (left) and his deputy, Huey Newton. (AP/Wide World Photos.)

JUNE 4–22, 1971   Racial Violence in Columbus, Georgia. Racial tensions in Columbus, Georgia, the state's second largest city, erupted into violence. The trouble began on May 31, 1971, when seven members of the African American Police League, including its executive director, were fired from the police department for picketing police headquarters and removing the American flag shoulder patches from their uniforms. The blacks were protesting alleged racial discrimination in the police department. Police department officials accused the blacks of conduct unbecoming to an officer and said they ripped the flags from their uniforms. The officers said they gently removed the emblems. On June 3, the Muscogee County Grand Jury announced that complaints of discrimination against black officers were unfounded. The jury said it found no basis for charges of the use of unnecessary force in the arrests of blacks but instead criticized both the African American Police League, which made the charges of discrimination and police brutality, and the Fraternal Order of Police, a union.

On June 19, Hosea Williams, national program director for the Southern Christian Leadership Conference (SCLC) and chairman of the Georgia statewide Black Leadership Coalition, led more than five hundred blacks on a fifteen-block march in Columbus then issued a five-point ultimatum to city and county officials. The coalition demanded the reinstatement of thirteen black policemen, promotion of the thirty-eight blacks still on the force, desegregation of jail facilities, a biracial citizens police review board, and increased hiring of black police officers. On June 21 Columbus mayor J. R. Allen declared a state of emergency following a weekend of racial strife. A total of twenty-six fires attributed to arsonists were set in the city, and a black man was fatally wounded by police. The city council gave the mayor broad powers to order a curfew, shut down stores selling alcoholic beverages, stop the sale of firearms, and curtail gasoline sales.

Meanwhile, the African American Police League called for a city-wide boycott of white businesses.

JUNE 7, 1971   Supreme Court Ruled Against Reapportionment. The U.S. Supreme Court ruled that states are not required to carve out separate legislative districts for urban blacks or any other racial or ethnic group. The Court held in an apportionment case from Indiana that core-city blacks may be lumped with more populous suburban white voters into one large district that is represented by a number of legislators elected at large. The 5-3 ruling upset a federal district court's finding that Indianapolis blacks were the victims of racial gerrymandering and were entitled to their own district with state legislators elected by and responsible to them. The five-man judicial majority, led by Justice Byron R. White, said there was no evidence that Indianapolis blacks did not have an equal say in choosing legislative candidates or that they were not allowed to register or vote. The majority reasoned that "the mere fact that one interest group or another concerned with the outcome of Marion County elections have found themselves outvoted and without legislative seats of its own provides no basis for invoking constitutional remedies." No explanation was given of the different result that was reached on May 31 when the Court ordered Hinds County, Mississippi, which included the capital city of Jackson, to be divided into single-member districts so that black voters would have a chance to elect their own representatives. Had the Supreme Court established the Jackson principle consistently, blacks and other inner-city residents would have been assured of larger representation in state legislatures.

JUNE 11, 1971   Legislators Discussed Black Representation. Black legislators from nine Southern states met in closed sessions in Atlanta to talk about black representation in reapportioned legislatures. The major problem concerning the group centered around recent decisions of the U.S. Supreme Court, which black lawmakers felt pointed in opposite directions. In one decision, the Supreme Court ruled that one-representative legislative districts are allowable in Mississippi. In another decision, the Court declared that multi-member districts are allowable in Indiana. The black legislators said that they were confused and concerned about what the Supreme Court intended, and concluded that they had a better chance for election in the South if they were candidates in districts where more than one representative is elected. There were forty black legislators in the eleven Southern states. Only Arkansas was without a black lawmaker.

JUNE 11, 1971 Nixon Addressed Housing Discrimination. President Richard Nixon promised to enforce federal laws prohibiting racial discrimination in housing but said the government would not force introduction of low cost housing for blacks or whites into suburban communities that did not want it. The president's fifteen-page report sharply distinguished between economic segregation and racial segregation, and the government's authority to deal with each situation. Nixon said that his administration would seek to carry out all requirements of federal law and judicial decisions involving housing but that it would take no action to go beyond them. "Racial discrimination in housing is illegal and will not be tolerated," the President affirmed, but the issue of public housing projects for the poor was another matter. Although predominantly white and affluent suburbs would be encouraged to accept them, the ultimate decision about the location of the housing projects would be made at the local level.

JUNE 12, 1971 Evers Began Campaign for Governorship. Charles Evers, the black mayor of Fayette, Mississippi, began his campaign for governor on the eighth anniversary of his brother Medgar's death. Surrounded by ten armed black men acting as security guards, Evers returned to his hometown of Decatur, Mississippi, to campaign as an independent. Evers was the first black to seek the governorship since Recon-

struction. He told a crowd of three hundred supporters at the Newton County Courthouse that it was time for members of both races to work together for common goals.

JUNE 12, 1971 Black Panther's Case Decided. David Hilliard, Chief of Staff of the Black Panther Party, was found guilty of assault but innocent of attempted murder in connection with a 1968 shootout with police. Hilliard contended that he was not involved in the Panther-police altercation on April 6, 1968. That gun battle resulted in the death of Panther Party member Bobby Hutton, the wounding of two police officers, and criminal charges against Panther Minister of Information Eldridge Cleaver, who later jumped bail and fled to Algeria. Hilliard was charged with two counts of attempted murder and another dual count of assault on a police officer. The trial was held in the Alameda County Superior Court in Oakland, California, before Judge William J. Hayes. Frank Vukota prosecuted Hilliard, who was defended by Attorney Vincent Hallinan.

JUNE 13, 1971 Race Riots Continued at Sheppard Air Force Base. The latest in a series of race riots on military bases occurred at Sheppard Air Force Base, Texas. A midnight battle between white and black airmen left twenty injured. According to a military spokesman, the two-and-one-half hour fight started when one black airman and one white airman clashed in the base's club. The fight then escalated among young trainees and was eventually halted by base police. Major General Jerry Page, the base commander, said no arrests would be made until an investigation of the incident was completed.

JUNE 14, 1971 School Survey Revealed Alarming Trend. Owen B. Kiernan, executive secretary of the National Association of Secondary School Principals, told the U.S. Senate's Equal Educational Opportunity Committee that a survey of eleven Southern and two border states had revealed that more than twelve hundred black school principals lost their jobs to whites after public school desegregation began in the South. Dr. Kiernan claimed that the problem of the elimination, displacement, and demotion of black public school principals had reached such serious proportions that it required the intervention of the federal government.

JUNE 14, 1971   St. Louis Suburb Charged with Housing Discrimination. The Justice Department announced the filing of a suit in St. Louis against Black Jack, Missouri, a St. Louis suburb, charging the town with illegally blocking a desegregated housing development. The action came on the heels of President Nixon's policy statement on housing issued on June 11, 1971. The issue arose when a nonprofit corporation made detailed plans in late 1969 to build a housing development for people of limited income. It was widely known that the project would be desegregated. The federal suit charged that the residents of Black Jack incorporated their community to gain zoning power and then used that power to block construction of the project. This action, the suit said, violated federal civil rights laws and the U.S. Constitution.

JUNE 14, 1971   Supreme Court Ruled on Public Swimming Pools. The U.S. Supreme Court ruled 5 to 4 that officials may close swimming pools and other public facilities to avoid desegregating them. The closings are not unconstitutional since blacks and whites are treated equally, Justice Hugo L. Black reasoned in the Court's rare recent setback for blacks. The ruling went against blacks in Jackson, Mississippi, who tried to force the city to reopen public swimming pools. They were closed after a district court ruled they could not remain segregated. In announcing the majority opinion, Justice Black cautioned that the decision did not signal approval of any subterfuge for desegregation. "We want no one to get any hope that there has been any retreat," he said. In one of three dissenting opinions, Justice Thurgood Marshall reasoned that the city's

actions were unconstitutional and that "the fact that the color of [a black's] skin is used to prevent others from swimming in public pools is irrelevant."

JUNE 15, 1971   Jordan Named Director of National Urban League. Vernon E. Jordan, Jr., former Atlanta attorney and executive director of the United Negro College Fund (UNCF), was named executive director of the National Urban League (NUL). Jordan succeeded Whitney Young, Jr., who drowned on March 11, 1971, in Lagos, Nigeria. Jordan was director of the Voter Education Project (VEP) of the Southern Regional Council in Atlanta until 1969. As head of the VEP, he helped organize massive voter registration campaigns across the South to help blacks win political power. In January 1970, Jordan became head of the UNCF, which raises funds for more than thirty black colleges across the country.

JUNE 16, 1971   Report Warned Black Public Colleges. The Race Relations Information Center (RRIC) of Nashville, Tennessee, announced that predominantly black public colleges were in "imminent danger of losing their identity through integration, merger, reduced status, or outright abolition." In a report entitled "The Black Public Colleges—Integration and Disintegration," the RRIC said "the prevailing pattern is one of racially separate and qualitatively unequal higher education." The 1970–71 academic year marked the first time in their history that the nation's thirty-three state-supported black colleges enrolled more than 100,000 students. During the past decade, enrollment at the institutions increased 75 percent. The report said the figures suggested thriving institutions, but that in reality, the death knell of the black state-supported colleges had already been sounded. There were originally thirty-five public colleges created for blacks, two of which had become predominantly white. Those two, Maryland State College and West Virginia's Bluefield State College, were joined by two more, West Virginia State and Missouri's Lincoln University. The RRIC said three other institutions—Delaware State, Maryland's Bowie State, and Kentucky State— could soon follow suit. Of the twenty-six remaining schools, fourteen were in direct competition with a predominantly white college. The RRIC speculated that most of these would eventually lose their identity, perhaps even be completely abolished.

JUNE 17, 1971   Court Ordered Desegregation of Southern Schools. The U.S. Fifth Circuit Court of Appeals ordered complete desegregation in eighty-one Southern school districts. The court reversed a U.S. District Court decision of April 22, 1970, which exempted some districts (mostly in Georgia) from full desegregation compliance on the grounds that such compliance would produce educationally unsound school systems. The Appeals Court said that the District Court must apply the Singleton decree to the eighty-one school districts in the areas of faculty and staff desegregation, school construction, site selection, and school attendance outside the system. The decree, issued in 1970 by the Fifth Circuit Court in the case of *Singleton v. Jackson*, required that the faculty of each school have approximately the same racial ratio as the entire school system, and that decisions regarding school construction and selection of school sites be made without evidence of racial discrimination. The New Orleans-based court also said the eighty-one school systems must comply with the U.S. Supreme Court's decision in *Swann v. Charlotte-Mecklenburg*, which held that busing could be used as a tool to dismantle a dual school system. The eighty-one school districts have been under federal court jurisdiction since December 1969. The latest appellate ruling in the case stemmed from the intervention by Charley Ridley, Jr., a black student from Gray, Georgia, in the blanket desegregation suit filed against Georgia and the State Board of Education in 1969.

JUNE 17, 1971   Racial Violence in Jacksonville, Florida. Jacksonville police officers armed with riot equipment dispersed a crowd of 400 black youths in a second night of racial violence in that Florida city. Three youths were arrested and charged with looting. Several police officers were slightly injured by rocks and bottles during the melee. Sheriff's Captain E. W. Hartley said police went into the black neighborhood to protect its many elderly black residents in the wake of the rock and bottle hurling. Deputies reported that two supermarkets in the black business district were looted and set afire, but there was no gunfire. Black youths were angered by an earlier slaying of a young black man by Jacksonville police.

JUNE 17, 1971   NAACP's Roy Wilkins Criticized Nixon. NAACP executive secretary Roy Wilkins called the Nixon administration's policy on housing discrimination a "timid tightrope walking act of the greatest kind." Wilkins challenged President Nixon to exert more positive federal power to help blacks move to the suburbs in search of employment. "The issue of the 1970s now appears to be whether the black population will be able to move into the suburbs in pursuit of jobs that are moving to the suburbs," Wilkins declared. "The fifteen-page statement issued last week by the White House had done nothing to solve that problem." President Nixon had announced on June 11 that he would enforce federal laws preventing racial discrimination in housing but would not force communities to accept low-cost housing for blacks or whites. According to an *Atlanta Constitution* report, Wilkins also said that "Mr. Nixon ought to stop going around saying he does not want to enforce integration of the suburbs, because he is using the language and nomenclature of those who simply do not want Negroes in the suburbs." Wilkins made his criticisms of the President at a panel discussion called "The Status of Civil Rights in 1971" at the annual meeting of the black National Newspapers Publishers Association in Atlanta.

JUNE 18, 1971 School Desegregation Study Released. The Department of Health, Education, and Welfare (HEW) completed and released the most detailed study of school desegregation in the nation's history. According to the report, the only significant gains in school desegregation in the nation's largest school districts during the past two years have occurred in the South. The 38 Southern school districts among the country's largest districts accounted for almost all of the desegregation gains in urban areas while 26 of the 63 districts in Northern and Western states showed a decrease in desegregation. The figures reflected the amount of desegregation based on the number of black children in predominately white schools, the statistical yardstick favored by most civil rights groups. Of the 756,000 black pupils who moved from largely black into predominately white schools during the past two years, a total of 690,000 lived in the South. The national desegregation comparison was the result of an eight-month survey conducted by HEW. The preliminary results of the study were revealed on January 14, 1971.

JUNE 22, 1971 Southern Schools Ordered to Desegregate. The Department of Health, Education and Welfare (HEW) announced that letters were forwarded to thirty-nine school districts in eleven Southern and border states suggesting that they must further desegregate by the fall of 1971. HEW was attempting to bring all school districts in line with the Supreme Court's ruling in the *Swann* case in North Carolina. Recent action was taken in Nashville, Tennessee; Norfolk, Virginia; and Austin, Texas. The latest action included such diverse localities as Wilmington, Delaware; Paducah, Kentucky; Gulfport, Mississippi; Fayetteville, North Carolina; Amarillo, Texas; and Martinsville, Virginia. HEW told the districts that they must prove that the presence of heavily black schools is not discriminatory.

JUNE 23, 1971 Desegregation Plan Approved in Mississippi. School officials and civil rights leaders in Jackson, Mississippi, the largest school district in the state, agreed on a plan for desegregating the city's elementary schools through busing and educational parks. Both parties, in the first such compromise they had ever reached, agreed that the plan would remain in effect for three years without a court challenge. Dr. Harry S. Kirshman, acting superintendent of schools, announced that the agreement would affect about 18,000 to 19,000 elementary school children, with approximately 8,000 to 9,000 being bused to classes. The educational park concept is built on clusters of modules around a common center. Each module is to accommodate the equivalent of four traditional classrooms with 30-1 pupil-teacher ratios. Black enrollments in the schools would range from 41 to 70 percent.

JUNE 25, 1971 Bomb-Making Operation Uncovered. Agents from the Bureau of Alcohol, Tobacco, and Firearms arrested three black men in Columbus, Georgia, and charged them with possessing firebombs in the racially tense city. The agents said they confiscated enough material at the People's Panther Party headquarters to make more than fifty firebombs. Two of the three arrested men were soldiers stationed at nearby Fort Benning, and the third was a former army private. The agents arrested William Craig Garr, Jesse Reed, Jr., and Anthony L. Brewer less than a week after the outburst of new racial disorders, which included firebombings. Garr was identified as the president of the People's Panther Party, an organization described by a federal official as a training group for the Black Panther Party. Meanwhile, white police officers in Columbus presented a petition to Mayor J. R. Allen urging him not to give in to black demands. The petition was prompted by black charges of racial discrimination in the city's police department and a subsequent announcement by the mayor that the department would be investigated. Earlier, black police officers had told the mayor, in response to his plea to them to help cool the black community, that they would protect the black community from the white police.

JUNE 28, 1971 Ali's Draft Evasion Conviction Overturned.

The U.S. Supreme Court overturned the 1967 draft evasion conviction of former heavyweight boxing champion Muhammad Ali. In an unanimous 8-0 opinion (Justice Thurgood Marshall did not participate), the Court ruled that the Justice Department had erred in contending that Ali's objection to military service was based on political rather than religious beliefs. The Court said it was "indisputably clear . . . that the Department was simply wrong as a matter of law in advising that Ali's beliefs were not religiously based and were not sincerely held." Ali, who is a Black Muslim, exclaimed "Thanks to Allah!" when he learned of the Court's decree. "I thank the Supreme Court for recognizing the sincerity of my belief in myself and my convictions," he said.

JUNE 28–JULY 8, 1971 School Desegregation Plans Continued

Court action and out-of-court settlements continued in an effort to desegregate the nation's schools. On June 28, a federal district judge in Nashville, Tennessee, approved a cross-town busing plan designed to desegregate the Nashville-Davidson County public school system. Judge L. C. Morton adopted, with modifications, a plan drawn up by the Department of Health, Education, and Welfare which required the daily busing of about 47,000 students, an increase of approximately 13,500 over those bused in 1970–71. The number of black children required to ride buses would almost double while the number of whites to be transported would increase by only one-third. The Nashville-Davidson County school system had an enrollment of about 95,000 pupils. Judge Morton ordered the plan implemented in September 1971. On July 8, the NAACP's Legal Defense Fund and the Mobile, Alabama, school board agreed upon a school desegregation plan that would allow at least ten of Mobile's public schools to retain virtually all-black student bodies until the fall of 1972. Attorneys for the blacks said they accepted the school board's suggested course of action only to avoid another year of litigation before a federal district judge they regarded as hostile to desegregation.

JUNE 30–AUGUST 8, 1971 Black Panthers on Trial.

Throughout the summer of 1971, members of the Black Panther Party were continuously engaged in legal disputes of various kinds. On June 30, a jury in Detroit acquitted twelve party members of charges that they murdered a police officer and of conspiracy to murder in a gun battle with police at the party's local headquarters in October 1970. Three party members, however, were convicted of felonious assault in the case. This trio, Erone D. Desansser, Benjamin Fandrus, and David Johnson, faced a maximum penalty of four years imprisonment. The Detroit jury, consisting of ten blacks and two whites, returned its verdict after four and a half days of deliberations. On July 2, David Hilliard, the Black Panther Party's Chief of Staff, was sentenced to a one-to-ten year prison term by an Oakland, California, judge for assault in connection with a gun battle with police in April 1968. Hilliard, who was convicted on June 12, was denied a retrial and remanded to custody. On August 6, a biracial jury of ten blacks and two whites acquitted twelve Black Panther Party members of the attempted murder of five New Orleans police officers in a gun battle at a local housing project in September 1970. The bi-racial jury, which received its instructions from a black judge, Israel M. Augustine, reached its verdict after only thirty minutes of deliberation. If convicted, the blacks could have faced terms of twenty years in prison on each of the five counts. During the trial, nine of the black defendants participated in an uprising involving thirty-four inmates at the Orleans Parish Prison, where they were held. The uprising was staged to protest what the blacks called the prison's "corrupt judicial system." The protest, which was held on July 26, ended after almost eight hours as the inmates released two black guards they had been holding hostage. On August 8, Superior Court Judge Harold B. Hove declared a mistrial in the second manslaughter trial of Huey P. Newton, co-founder of the Black Panther Party, in Oakland, California. A lone white housewife held out for the acquittal of Newton, who had been charged in connection with the killing of an Oakland police officer in October 1969.

JULY 5–6, 1971 American Bar Association Criticized. Members of the National Conference of Black Lawyers and the Black American Law Students Association distributed leaflets accusing the American Bar Association of excluding blacks from its major policy making organs and of emphasizing the "order" side of the law and order issue. The leaflets also called for an end to bar exams which allegedly excluded blacks. Similarly, Judge Edward F. Bell, president of the black National Bar Association (NBA), speaking before his group's annual convention, urged the abolition of bar exams, claiming that they did not reflect the potential for a successful practice and that they discriminated against minority applicants.

JULY 5–9, 1971 Nixon Policies Acknowledged by NAACP Chairman. Bishop Stephen G. Spottswood, board chairman of the NAACP, remarked during the group's 62nd Annual Convention in Minneapolis that the Nixon administration had taken steps during 1971 to dispel the image that it was anti-black. Without being very specific, Spottswood said that the president had taken certain steps and announced certain policies which had "earned cautious and limited approval among African Americans." A year before, at the NAACP's convention, Spottswood portrayed the Nixon administration as anti-black. Some NAACP leaders apparently disagreed with Bishop Spottswood's new assessment of the Nixon policies. NAACP Labor Director Herbert Hill characterized the administration's racial policy as criminal negligence, a posture even worse

than benign neglect. Hill specifically accused the administration of failure to enforce laws forbidding discrimination by federal contractors which resulted, in his view, in a high unemployment rate among blacks. Similarly, NAACP Executive Secretary Roy Wilkins told the delegates that President Nixon could increase his influence among black voters in the 1972 elections if he made more jobs available to black voters.

JULY 6, 1971 Trumpeter Louis Armstrong Died. Louis Armstrong, the legendary jazz trumpeter, died in New York. Seventy-one-year-old "Satchmo" Armstrong had reshaped the development of American music by introducing the black folk music of New Orleans into mainstream American culture. His distinctive abrasive voice and innovative solos were trademarks of his long career which began in small Southern nightclubs at the close of the World War I. President Nixon eulogized Armstrong as "one of the architects of the American art form."

JULY 7, 1971 Negro League Veteran Honored. Professional baseball commissioner Bowie Kuhn announced that veteran player Satchel Paige, who pitched for twenty-five years in the Negro Leagues and the Major Leagues, would be given full membership in the Baseball Hall of Fame at Cooperstown, New York. Originally, it was intended that Paige and other black players be honored in a separate division of the Hall of Fame which was established for players in the old Negro Leagues. In response to criticism by baseball fans of the separate division of the shrine, the decision was made to give Paige full honors.

JULY 11, 1971 Education Appropriation Bill Signed. President Nixon signed a five-billion dollar education appropriation bill, the largest of its kind in history. Among the features of the bill was a provision which prohibited the use of any of the funds to force school districts considered already desegregated under the Civil Rights

Louis Armstrong entertaining the crowds on the streets of London, England. (AP/Wide World Photos.)

Act of 1964 to bus students, abolish schools, or to set attendance zones against parents' wishes or as a stipulation for receiving federal funds.

JULY 13, 1971   Conference Attacked Nixon's Housing Policies. A coalition of 126 civil rights groups held a Leadership Conference on Civil Rights in Washington, D.C. The coalition attacked President Nixon's housing policies as insufficient to the needs of minorities and the poor. The President's policy, which was outlined on June 11, 1971, was "disastrous and chaotic," according to the group's spokesperson, Bayard Rustin. The coalition urged the federal administration to require localities to provide for low-income housing needs or risk losing all federal aid. The civil rights groups also urged the Justice Department to take action against any local zoning laws erected to block housing for low and moderate income families.

JULY 18–20, 1971   School Desegregation Plan Nixed. U.S. District Judge Jack Roberts refused to accept a Department of Health, Education, and Welfare (HEW) school desegregation plan for Austin, Texas, schools which would have required extensive cross-town bus-

ing. Instead, the judge accepted a desegregation plan filed by the local school board which established learning centers in fine arts, avocations, and social and natural sciences which would be open to elementary pupils of all races for a portion of the school day. Students could be bused, if necessary, to these learning centers. The plan also assigned black junior high school students to schools which were not "identifiably Negro." In a related matter, on July 20 HEW officials announced that they had told sixty-four school districts in Southern and border states that they would have to alter their school desegregation plans for the fall of 1971 so as to achieve greater racial desegregation. An HEW representative said that most of the sixty-four districts were in small and rural areas and that each contained one or more all-black schools.

JULY 21, 1971   Boycott Began in Passaic, New Jersey. Blacks in Passaic, New Jersey, began a long boycott against downtown merchants protesting alleged police brutality. The boycott grew out of a series of incidents of police harassment and brutality which culminated in an incident on the night of July 20 between police and eight blacks. During the altercation a black man was beaten and shots were fired. The Reverend Calvin McKinney, leader of the black Urban Crisis Council, protested that the town's all-white City Council ignored black pleas for protection against police harassment. The FBI did, however, agree to investigate the charges.

JULY 26, 1971   Blacks Faired Poorly in Census Results. Federal analysts studying the 1970 Census returns concluded that despite a decade of general progress, African Americans remained far behind whites in terms of economic prosperity, social gains, and educational advancement. The study, compiled by the Bureau of the Census and the U.S. Bureau of Labor Statistics and entitled "The Social and Economic Status of Negroes in the United States, 1970," found that 28.9 of every one hundred black families were headed by women. Many analysts saw this proportion of female-headed households as an important indicator of black social progress. (That view was disputed immediately by Dr. Robert B. Hill, a research analyst for the National Urban League, as he appeared before the League's annual convention.) The percentage of fatherless white families in the 1960s remained at about 9 percent. Other statistics showed that blacks increased their median income by 50 percent during the 1960s, but that their incomes were still only three-fifths of that earned by whites, and that about half of the all-black occupied housing units in rural areas were substandard in 1970 as compared with only 8 percent of white rural housing.

JULY 27, 1971   Military Cracked Down on Racial Offenders. Frank W. Render, second deputy assistant secretary of defense, announced that almost a dozen military officers were relieved of command, transferred to new assignments, or reprimanded for failing to adequately enforce the Defense Department's guidelines for racial equality in the armed services. The unidentified officers were said to rank from general down to company grade.

JULY 28, 1971   Jordan Criticized Nixon Administration. Vernon E. Jordan, Jr., executive director designate of the National Urban League, told the closing session of his group's annual convention in Detroit that the Nixon administration had compiled a "record of ambiguity" toward African Americans. He accused the administration of allowing federal civil rights laws to "languish in dusty books." The remarks were a part of Jordan's first major address to the Urban League since he was named its director, succeeding the late Whitney M. Young, Jr.

AUGUST 2, 1971   Jesse Jackson Criticized Postal Service. The Reverend Jesse Jackson of Chicago, leader of the Operation Breadbasket unit of the Southern Christian Leadership Conference (SCLC), accused the newly reorganized U.S. Postal Service of discriminating against blacks. Jackson, speaking to postal workers in Washington, D.C., said the Postal Service had begun laying off a number of workers as part of its reorganization plan and that since the majority of the black postal employees were in the lower job categories, they were the first to be fired. The black civil rights leader also accused the Postal Service of discrimination for placing new offices in all-white suburban areas where blacks could not obtain services or jobs.

AUGUST 3–11, 1971   Nixon Opposed Busing. President Nixon disowned a school desegregation plan drawn up by the Department of Health, Education, and Welfare (HEW) which would have required extensive crosstown busing in Austin, Texas. The President also took the occasion to reaffirm his strong opposition to any busing designed to achieve a racial balance in the schools. The president further directed HEW secretary Elliott L. Richardson to aid individual school districts as they attempted to "hold busing to the minimum required by the law." The president, however, reasserted the duty of his administration to enforce orders of the federal courts, including those calling for busing to achieve desegregation. On August 11, the White House announced that President

Nixon had warned administrative officials that they risked losing their jobs if they pushed for extensive busing as a means of desegregating the nation's schools.

AUGUST 3–12, 1971   Illegal Busing in Texas. In an August 3 announcement, the U.S. Commission on Civil Rights (USCCR) charged that air force officials in southwest Texas were seeking to continue the illegal busing of school children on a military base to a predominantly white school nearby. The busing permitted 850 children to bypass the closer San Felipe school district that was largely Mexican-American in order to attend the mostly white Del Rio schools. In July, the Texas Education Agency had advised the Del Rio district that it could no longer accept the air force children because of a federal court ruling that the transfers were illegally perpetuating segregation. The air force, denying that it was seeking to perpetuate segregation, contended that the San Felipe school district did not have sufficient educational facilities to handle the 850 children from Laughlin Air Force Base and hence the plea for continued busing. On August 12, the USCCR maintained that President Nixon's directives to keep busing for racial desegregation to a minimum would undermine efforts to desegregate the nation's schools. The transportation of students, according to the commission's unanimous report, was essential to eliminating segregation.

AUGUST 4, 1971   Legal Reforms Sought by Judges. The nation's black federal, state, and municipal judges attending the 46th annual meeting of the black National Bar Association (NBA) in Atlanta announced the formation of a judicial court through which they would work for legal reform. Judge Edward Bell of Detroit, president of the NBA, said the new council would seek to return to the idea that the courts belong to all of the people, poor as well as rich, black as well as white. The judges also pointed out the absence of black federal judges in the South. At the time of the meeting, there were 285 black judges in the country, representing slightly more than 1 per cent of 20,000 jurists in the nation.

AUGUST 12, 1971   Desegregation Delay Denied. The U.S. Court of Appeals for the Ninth District declined to grant a delay in the implementation of a citywide elementary school desegregation program scheduled to take effect in San Francisco on September 8, 1971. The desegregation program involved the transfer of 48,000 children and had been ordered into effect on April 28, 1971, by U.S. District Judge Stanley A. Weigel.

AUGUST 16, 1971   Desegregation Plan Unfeasible. The school board of Richmond, Virginia, told Federal District Court Judge Robert R. Merhige, Jr., that it was unable to reduce the large number of black students attending its public schools without a merger with the Henrico and Chesterfield county school systems. The board asked the court to order such a merger. The Richmond officials reported to the judge that they were not able to fully comply with his previous desegregation orders which involved widespread crosstown busing. This feature of the desegregation plan had been offset because too many white families had moved to the suburbs. The plight of the Richmond school board was typical of that of many urban school districts trying to desegregate with large black populations in the inner cities and predominantly white populations in the suburbs. Suburban residents expressed strong opposition to the school board's proposal and demonstrated outside the home of Judge Merhige, who was protected by U.S. marshals.

AUGUST 18, 1971   Police Officer Killed in Gun Battle. A Jackson, Mississippi, police officer was killed in a gun battle that broke out when local police raided the headquarters of the Republic of New Africa (RNA) to serve three of its members with fugitive warrants. Another Jackson police officer and a FBI agent were wounded during a twenty-minute exchange of gunfire. On August 23, 1971, eleven members of the black separatist group were accused of murdering Lieutenant W. L. Skinner. Previously, the eleven were charged with treason for allegedly engaging in armed insurrection against the state of Mississippi. Among those arrested was Imari A. Obadele, president of the RNA. Obadele expressed regret over Skinner's death but criticized the Jackson Police Department and the FBI for raiding the office. He declared that his group would receive any warrant peacefully, provided one or two black lawyers were present.

AUGUST 18, 1971   Wallace Refused to Desegregate. Governor George C. Wallace of Alabama ordered two of his state's school boards to ignore federal court-ordered desegregation plans. Wallace directed the school boards in Calhoun County and the city of Oxford to disregard the orders of a federal judge that an all-black school in Hobson City be paired with two predominantly white schools in Oxford. Governor Wallace contended that his actions were consistent with President Richard Nixon's anti-busing declaration of August 3. The governor's actions followed by only two days a declaration from federal district Judge Sam C. Pointer, Jr., that such action was legally meaningless. Mississippi Governor John Bell Williams was one of those, however, who announced immediate support for Wallace's anti-desegregation tactics. Wallace, Williams said, had "drawn a line in the dust and I stand fully with him."

AUGUST 18–SEPTEMBER 8, 1971   Desegregation Problems Continued in South. As the fall school term approached, additional legal skirmishes concerning desegregation took place across the South. On August 18, the Justice Department filed a brief with Associate Supreme Court Justice Hugo Black which supported the Corpus Christi, Texas, school board's request for a stay of a federal court order to desegregate the school district. The court-approved plan had called for massive busing of students.

On September 2, Supreme Court Justice Potter Stewart refused to stay a court order requiring extensive busing to achieve desegregation in the Nashville-Davidson County, Tennessee, school system.

On September 4, Supreme Court Chief Justice Warren E. Burger refused to halt the busing of students to achieve desegregation in Arlington, Virginia. And on September 8, the Mobile, Alabama, school board implemented a plan which called for the massive busing of students to desegregate schools.

AUGUST 20, 1971   Reapportionment Plan Rejected. U.S. Attorney General John Mitchell rejected a plan for reapportioning the legislative districts of Louisiana, contending that the plan would discriminate against blacks.

AUGUST 23, 1971   Black Panthers Evaluated by Government. The Internal Security Committee of the U.S. House of Representatives issued a report declaring that while the Black Panther Party posed a physical danger to the nation's law enforcement officers, the group was totally incapable of overthrowing the U.S. government by violent means. The four Republican members of the committee, John M. Ashbrook of Ohio, John G. Schmitz of California, Fletcher Thompson of Georgia, and Roger H. Zion of Indiana, objected to the panel's findings, contending that the majority view did not give "a clear understanding of the Black Panther Party as a subversive criminal group using the facade of politics as a cover for crimes of violence and extortion."

AUGUST 24, 1971   Law Enforcement Officials Indicted. Fourteen law enforcement officials, including Illinois state attorney Edward U. Hanrahan, chief prosecutor for Chicago, were named in a long-suppressed indictment handed down in Chicago on charges of conspiracy to obstruct justice by trying to suppress or thwart criminal prosecutions of eight police officers who participated in the December 4, 1969, raid of an apartment rented by a Black Panther Party member. The indictment was made public on orders issued by the Illinois Supreme Court. Judge Joseph A. Power of the Illinois Criminal Court had kept the indictment sealed since April 1971, when it was first prepared. Power had refused to accept the indictment, contending that the grand jury had not heard all the pertinent witnesses and that it was pressured into returning true bills. Among others named in the indictment were an assistant state attorney, the police superintendent of Chicago, eight police officers who took part in the controversial raid, and four other officers who later conducted departmental investigations into the affair.

AUGUST 26, 1971 Black College Enrollment Increased. The Office of Civil Rights of the Department of Health, Education, and Welfare (HEW) reported that black student enrollment in the nation's colleges and universities had increased at a rate five times greater than white student enrollment since 1968. Black enrollment grew from 303,397 in 1968 to 379,138 in the fall of 1970, a 24 percent increase. According to the HEW report, 44 percent of all black undergraduates were enrolled in colleges with black minorities. The largest increase in black enrollment, 47 percent since 1968, came in the eleven states comprising the Deep South. Nevertheless, blacks still represented only 6 percent of the undergraduates in the nation.

AUGUST 26, 1971 Federal Court Refused Nixon Administration's Request. A federal court in Washington, D.C., refused a request by the administration of President Nixon to dismiss a suit pending against federal tax exemptions for private all-white academies in the South. The court also denied a request by civil rights groups who brought the suit that urged all such academies have their tax-exempt status revoked immediately. The administration's law-

yer told the court that the Internal Revenue Service would no longer grant tax exempt status to private schools practicing a policy of racial discrimination in admissions, but that for now the government had relied on the word of the schools in determining whether they were willing to desegregate.

AUGUST 30–SEPTEMBER 8, 1971 North and West Resisted Desegregation. As the nation's schools reopened for their fall terms, the stiffest resistance to court-ordered racial desegregation in public education was seen in the North and West. In Pontiac, Michigan, eight white students and one black pupil were injured on September 8 as fights erupted during protests against a school busing plan. On August 30, 1971, arsonists in Pontiac had set firebombs that destroyed ten school buses to be used for implementing desegregation plans. The protests in Pontiac were among the most violent seen in the country. White parents carrying American flags marched in front of the school bus depot on September 8, daring bus drivers to run them down.

In San Francisco, Chinese-American spokesmen announced that they intended to resist a court-ordered busing plan scheduled to be implemented on September 13, 1971. The Chinese Americans acted in response to Supreme Court Justice William O. Douglas's rejection of their anti-busing appeal on August 29, 1971. Under the plan, upheld by the courts, approximately 6,500 Chinese Americans were to be included among 48,000 students to be bused in order to achieve further school desegregation.

In Boston, Massachusetts, parents of about three hundred children who were assigned to a new racially desegregated school refused to enroll their children there on September 8. Instead, the children were returned to their previous neighborhood schools. A similar defiance of court-ordered desegregation occurred in Evansville, Indiana. By contrast, most newly desegregated schools reopened quietly in the South, although many were faced with new busing plans.

AUGUST 31, 1971   Chief Justice Clarified Court's Decision. Warren E. Burger, Chief Justice of the U.S. Supreme Court, announced that he was afraid that federal judges were misinterpreting the high Court's decision on busing that was delivered on April 20, 1971. Burger feared that judges were assuming that the order required racial balance in every school. In an unusually long ten-page opinion denying a stay of enforcement of a court-ordered busing plan for the schools in Winston-Salem (Forsyth County), North Carolina, Burger said the unanimous court ruling in April did not require a fixed racial balance or quota in order to legally desegregate schools. A school district's racial balance could be used as a point of beginning to determine "whether in fact any violation [of law] existed." On the same day, Secretary of Health, Education, and Welfare Elliott L. Richardson reported that he agreed with President Nixon's announced policy of limiting school busing to achieve racial desegregation. Richardson denied that he had considered resigning after the president repudiated a school desegregation plan that his department had drawn up for the Austin, Texas, school district, a plan which required extensive crosstown busing.

SEPTEMBER 13, 1971   Attica Strike Ended. More than one thousand state troopers, prison guards, and sheriff's deputies stormed the Attica State Prison in New York, ending a five-day strike by inmates. Forty-three people, including nine guards held as hostages, were killed in the most disastrous prison tragedy in U.S. history. Most of the slain prisoners were black. The troubles at Attica were sparked by a misunderstanding between two inmates who were playing touch football and a guard who believed they were fighting. Rumors spread through the prison that the inmates, one black and one white, were beaten by guards.

SEPTEMBER 13, 1971   Students Protested Desegregation. Approximately 45 percent of the school children in San Francisco, California, refused to attend classes as a new school desegregation plan calling for the busing of 48,000 children was put into effect.

SEPTEMBER 22, 1971   Wallace Signed Bill. Alabama Governor George C. Wallace signed a bill passed by the Alabama legislature which permitted parents to send their children to their neighborhood schools if they felt that busing to achieve desegregation would be harmful to their children.

SEPTEMBER 23, 1971   Justice John M. Harlan Retired. Associate Supreme Court Justice John M. Harlan, citing reasons of health, retired from the bench after sixteen years of service. Harlan had participated in many historic decisions concerning civil rights and legal protections for minorities and the poor.

SEPTEMBER 25, 1971   Justice Hugo L. Black Died. Associate Justice Hugo L. Black, who retired from the U.S. Supreme Court after thirty-four years of service on September 13, 1971, died on September 25. During his last years on the Court, Justice Black was accused of inconsistency and turning his back on blacks, yet the justice, a native Alabamian and one-time Ku Klux Klansman, replied: "I haven't changed a jot or a tittle." Black was eulogized by the popular black news magazine *Jet* as "a real American."

SEPTEMBER 26, 1971   Labor Study Results Released. The U.S. Bureau of Labor Statistics released a study which showed that 27.9 percent of the blacks employed across the country held white collar jobs during 1970. In 1960, 16.1 percent of the white collar jobs were held by blacks.

OCTOBER 1971   Civil Rights Leader Returned to U.S. Ralph David Abernathy, president of the Southern Christian Leadership Conference

(SCLC), returned to the country from a European tour which took him, among other places, to the Soviet Union and East Germany. Abernathy preached to approximately seven thousand people in the Russian Orthodox Cathedral. In East Germany, the veteran civil rights leader was awarded the Peace Medal of the German Democratic Republic.

OCTOBER 1971   Rehnquist and Powell Nominated to Supreme Court. President Richard M. Nixon nominated William Rehnquist of Phoenix, Arizona, and Lewis F. Powell of Richmond, Virginia, to the U.S. Supreme Court. Both nominations were opposed by many blacks. Black judge George W. Crockett of the Detroit Recorders Court assailed the president for his refusal to consult black lawyers on the appointments. The chief criticisms coming from blacks were that Rehnquist was a "rational reactionary" and that Powell was associated with private clubs and law firms in Virginia which discriminated against African Americans. Both nominees denied anti-black attitudes and practices. Rehnquist, at the time, employed a black secretary in his office where he was an assistant U.S. attorney. The U.S. Senate subsequently confirmed both appointees with a minimum of difficulty.

OCTOBER 1971   Senator's Statement Raised Controversy. A lively controversy arose among black and white politicians after Senator Edmund Muskie from Maine, a likely candidate for the Democratic nomination for president in 1972, stated that a black vice-presidential candidate, regrettably, would be a handicap to the Democratic ticket. (Muskie himself was the Democratic vice-presidential candidate in 1968.) Vice President Spiro Agnew, former Assistant Secretary of Labor Arthur Fletcher, both Republicans, and Democratic National Committeeman Hobart Taylor, Jr., were among those disagreeing with Muskie. Former Georgia governor Lester Maddox claimed he would vote for a qualified black vice-presidential candidate, but Alabama Governor George C. Wallace,

himself a presidential candidate, said that Muskie's position was "probably right."

OCTOBER 6, 1971   First Legal Interracial Marriage in North Carolina. A black man and a white woman were married officially for the first time in North Carolina. Lorraine Mary Turner and John A. Wilkinson took their vows in Durham County, North Carolina.

OCTOBER 9, 1971   Ford Foundation Aided Black Colleges. The Ford Foundation in New York announced a six-year, $100-million program to aid private, black colleges in providing individual study awards to various minority students. About twenty of the nation's better-known private, black colleges, including Hampton and Tuskegee Institutes, Benedict College, Fisk University, and the six schools comprising the Atlanta University Center complex of black institutions, were chosen to receive awards averaging as much as $300,000 annually. In a closely related matter, Morris Brown College announced that it might withdraw from the famous Atlanta University Center and reject the Ford funds. Morris Brown officials objected to a proviso in the Atlanta grants which called for a reorganization of the Atlanta University Center, so as to effect closer cooperation.

OCTOBER 15, 1971   Racial Violence in Memphis, Tennessee. Elton Hayes, a seventeen-year-old black youth, was killed by police officers in Memphis, Tennessee. The slaying of Hayes was followed by five days of racial violence in Memphis. Nine local law enforcement officers, including a black police lieutenant, were later charged with the brutal murder of the youth.

NOVEMBER 1971   Alonzo G. Moron Died. Alonzo G. Moron, the first black president of Hampton Institute in Virginia, died in San Juan, Puerto Rico. Moron had recently served as deputy director of the Department of Housing and Urban Development in San Juan.

NOVEMBER 2, 1971 Election Results. In general elections across the country, blacks were elected mayors in four additional American cities and were named to various other local and state offices. In Englewood, New Jersey, the Reverend Walter S. Taylor was elected the city's first black mayor. Gilbert H. Bradley, Jr., was elected mayor of Kalamazoo, Michigan. In Benton Harbor, Michigan, Charles Joseph became the town's first black mayor. Richard B. Hatcher was easily reelected to a four-year term as mayor of Gary, Indiana. Two blacks, Henry Owens and Saundra Graham, were elected to the city council in Cambridge, Massachusetts, and a third black, Charles Pierce, was selected to the city's school board.

In Mississippi, Fayette's black mayor Charles Evers was defeated in his bid for governor, but state representative Robert Clark, the only black legislator in Mississippi, was returned to his seat. Blacks also won seven county supervisor posts, one circuit court clerk's position, and about twenty other county offices. Almost three hundred blacks campaigned for offices in Mississippi during the November elections.

Also in the elections, former heavyweight boxing champion Jersey Joe Walcott was elected sheriff of Camden, New Jersey. Blacks were elected to city councils in Indianapolis, Indiana; Davenport, Iowa; Burlington, Iowa; Memphis, Tennessee; and Miami, Florida. In Memphis, black councilman Fred Davis was elected chairman of the thirteen-member city council. In Miami, the Reverend Edward Graham managed to retain his seat on the city council, although black mayoral candidate Tom Washington was defeated.

Defeated in the Mississippi state legislature race were veteran civil rights leaders Fanny Lou Hamer and Aaron Henry. Voters in Cleveland, Ohio, rejected a second black mayor in Arnold R. Pinkney's candidacy. Although Thomas I. Atkins, a black city councilman in Boston, was defeated in his bid for mayor, he was appointed secretary of the Department of Communications and Development, the highest position held by an African American in Massachusetts state government.

NOVEMBER 16, 1971 Nixon Administration Criticized Again. The U.S. Commission on Civil Rights again criticized the administration of President Richard M. Nixon, charging that it had failed to adequately enforce civil rights laws and regulations.

DECEMBER 1971 Anti-Busing Law Ruled Unconstitutional. U.S. District Court Judge Sam C. Pointer declared an Alabama anti-busing law unconstitutional. The judge ruled that the stature "is but a freedom-of-choice option dressed in slightly different colors," and such options, he said, were illegal.

DECEMBER 1971 Two Civil Rights Leaders Died. Two veteran champions of civil rights died before the close of the year. Arthur B. Spingarn, the NAACP's president since 1940, succumbed at his home in New York at age ninety-three. Spingarn, a white civil rights lawyer, once headed the NAACP's National Legal Committee. The NAACP's annual meritorious award, the Spingarn medal, was named in honor of the long-time civil rights leader. NAACP executive secretary Roy Wilkins eulogized Spingarn as one who had challenged the sanctioned institutions of Jim Crow and characterized his death as "a great loss to the Negroes in particular and the liberal social movement in general." Ralph J. Bunche, undersecretary general of the United Nations, Nobel Peace Prize winner, scholar, and civil rights activist, died at age sixty-seven in New York. Bunche, who was a familiar figure in international councils as well as on civil rights battlefields and was a key figure in Martin Luther King, Jr.'s march from Selma to Montgomery in 1965, was eulogized by United Nations Secretary General U Thant as "an international institution in his own right."

DECEMBER 15, 1971   Huey Newton Freed. Huey P. Newton, co-founder of the Black Panther Party, was declared free after manslaughter charges against him were dismissed. Newton was imprisoned for nearly two years for the 1967 death of an Oakland, California, police officer, and was tried three times on the manslaughter charge. His latest trial ended in a hung jury when the jury reported that it was "utterly unable to reach a verdict."

1972

JANUARY 3, 1972   Alabama Districts Reapportioned. A U.S. District Court in Montgomery, Alabama, ordered the implementation of a new reapportionment plan that would split the Alabama legislature into single-member districts. The decision could put as many as twenty additional blacks in the Alabama state legislature. There were, at the time, only two black members of the Alabama legislature. The new districts would represent the decennial population count based upon the enumerated districts of the U.S. Census.

JANUARY 10, 1972   Judge Ordered School Merger. U.S. District Court Judge Robert R. Merhige, Jr., ordered the merger of the predominately black schools of Richmond, Virginia, with those of two suburban counties with nearly all-white enrollments to promote school desegregation. Judge Merhige directed that the new metropolitan school district be formed as the only possible solution to end segregated education based upon separate housing patterns. The order required the merger of the 70-percent-black Richmond city schools with the 90-percent-white schools of Henrico and Chesterfield counties.

JANUARY 25, 1972   Shirley Chisholm Announced Presidential Aspirations. Representative Shirley Chisholm from New York, the first black woman ever to serve in the U.S. Congress, announced that she would seek the Democratic presidential nomination. Representative Chisholm said that her candidacy would help repudiate the notion that the American people would not vote for a qualified black or female candidate.

JANUARY 27, 1972   Mahalia Jackson Died. Mahalia Jackson, one of the world's foremost gospel singers, died at age sixty in Evergreen Park, Illinois. Jackson was largely responsible for spreading gospel music from black churches in the Deep South to concert halls throughout the world. Her 1946 recording of "Move On Up a Little Higher" sold at least one million copies. President Nixon eulogized Jackson as "an artist without peers."

FEBRUARY 11, 1972   Black Group Opposed Desegregation. About fifty members of the Congress of Racial Equality (CORE) went to the office of black Democratic Congressman Augustus Hawkins of California demanding that black opponents of busing to achieve school desegregation be given a voice in national black meetings. Victor A. Solomon, leader of the CORE contingent, said his group advocated separate but "really equal" schools under community control. The NAACP and other black organizations had supported busing as a necessary tool to achieve school desegregation.

MARCH 24, 1972   Z. Alexander Looby Died. Z. Alexander Looby, one of the first blacks elected to the Nashville, Tennessee, city council (1951–1971) and a veteran civil rights activist, died at age seventy-two in Nashville.

MARCH 27, 1972   Soledad Brothers Acquitted. An all-white jury in San Francisco, California acquitted Fleeta Drumgo and John Cluchette—the so-called Soledad Brothers—in the slaying of a Soledad Prison guard in 1970. Black Communist Angela Davis was charged with plotting to free Drumgo, Cluchette,

Gospel singer Mahalia Jackson. (Courtesy of Library of Congress.)

and the late George Jackson, her alleged lover, in the famous Marin County Courthouse shootout on August 7, 1970. In the Soledad Brothers trial, the prosecution was unable to produce witnesses who actually saw any fatal blows delivered or who had seen the defendants toss a guard over a third floor tier. The defendants had denied that they were present at the scene of the slaying.

APRIL 4, 1972   Adam Clayton Powell, Jr., Died. Adam Clayton Powell, Jr., U.S. Representative from Harlem for more than twenty years (1945–1969) and one-time chairman of the influential House Education and Labor Committee (1960–67), died at age sixty-three in Miami, Florida. Powell was surrounded with controversy in death, as in life, as two women fought over the disposition of his body and his estate. On April 10, Powell's body was cremated and the ashes scattered over the island of Bimini in the Bahamas.

MAY 19, 1972   Southern Black Teachers Lost Jobs. The National Education Association (NEA) reported that over 30,000 black teachers had lost their jobs in seventeen Southern and border states because of segregation and discrimination since 1954. Twenty-one percent of teachers in these states were black in 1954, but by 1970 that percentage had dropped to nineteen. The percentage of job losses among blacks was lowest in Alabama and highest in Kentucky, Missouri, and Delaware.

MAY 19, 1972   "Black Agenda" Issued. The National Black Political Convention issued a 58-page "Black Agenda" that had been adopted at its founding meeting in March in Gary, Indiana. Although a special committee had modified provisions on school busing and on black attitudes toward Israel, these statements continued to arouse opposition. Partly because of these provisions, the NAACP, as well as other black organizations and individuals, criticized that part of the report that called for the dismantling of Israel and which condemned that nation's expansionist policy. The school provision that provoked controversy called busing racist and suicidal. The Israeli statement embraced the condemnations of Israel contained in numerous resolutions of the Organization of African Unity and the United Nations Commission on Human Rights, while the school provision criticized the Nixon administration's busing policies and demanded that blacks retain control of any busing program. Despite the modifications, however, the NAACP announced its continued opposition and withdrawal on May 16. NAACP assistant executive director John A. Morsell called the Israeli and busing statements "particularly outrageous."

MAY 21, 1972   School Desegregation Study Released. Professor David J. Armor, a white Harvard University professor, released a study of school desegregation programs in six Northern cities in which he concluded that there was no improvement in either academic achievement among black students or racial cooperation. While no significant academic differences were found among black students who had been bused for desegregation purposes and those who remained in black ghetto schools, the desegregated students tended to reveal declines in educational and career aspirations and in self-esteem. Professor Armor did, however, recommend the continuation of voluntary programs of busing to achieve desegregation, because those bused students tended to get better opportunities for higher education. The study was conducted in Boston, Massachusetts; White Plains, New York; Ann Arbor, Michigan; Riverdale, California; and Hartford and New Haven, Connecticut.

MAY 23, 1972   National Congress of Parents and Teachers Met. The annual convention of the National Congress of Parents and Teachers adopted a resolution requesting governmental and educational authorities "to search for solutions that would by rational means reduce racial isolation through transportation." The resolution passed by a vote of 303-296. The National Congress has 8.5 million members.

MAY 24, 1972   Senate Passed Desegregation Bill. The U.S. Senate passed and sent to the House of Representatives a final version of an omnibus higher education and desegregation aid bill with an anti-busing provision. The bill would delay all new court-ordered busing until appeals had been exhausted or until January 1974. Federal funds could not be used to finance busing to achieve desegregation unless specifically requested by local authorities. Federal officials would be prohibited from encouraging or ordering school districts to spend state or local funds for busing in cases where such busing endangered the health or education of students involved, unless constitutionally required. The bill further appropriated $2 billion over a two-year period to aid school districts in the process of desegregating. Although the Nixon administration had criticized the bill as inadequate, HEW Secretary Elliott Richardson announced that it embodied the heart of the president's higher education initiative. On

June 8, 1972, the U.S. House of Representatives approved the bill and sent it to President Richard Nixon for his signature. Nixon signed the bill into law on June 23.

JUNE 2, 1972   H. Rap Brown Sentenced to Prison. H. Rap Brown, former leader of the Student Non-Violent Coordinating Committee (SNCC), was sentenced to five years in prison and fined $2,000 for a 1968 conviction on a federal weapons charge by U.S. District Court Judge Lansing L. Mitchell in New Orleans. Brown was flown to New Orleans from New York City, where he had been held since his capture by New York police during an alleged robbery attempt in October 1971. Brown was wounded by police in that altercation and his attorneys protested against the trip to New Orleans, claiming that it endangered their client's health.

JUNE 3, 1972   Black Panther Cleared of Perjury Charges. U.S. District Court Judge Alfonso J. Zirpoli of San Francisco ordered David Hilliard, chief of staff of the Black Panther Party, cleared of perjury charges after the Justice Department refused to disclose wiretap evidence requested by the jury. Hilliard was accused of filing a false declaration of poverty in 1971. At the time of his latest trial he was serving a prison sentence for assaulting a police officer.

JUNE 4, 1972   Angela Davis Acquitted. Black Communist Angela Davis was acquitted on all charges of murder, kidnapping, and conspiracy by a Superior Court jury in San Jose, California. An all-white jury deliberated for thirteen hours before announcing their verdict. Davis reacted to the acquittal by at first proclaiming that the "only fair trial would have been no trial," but later added that the verdict was a victory for the people. Praise for the verdict was generally heard in the black and white liberal communities of the nation and overseas, including Moscow.

JUNE 6, 1972 Senator James Eastland Nominated for Sixth Term. U.S. Senator James O. Eastland, a Democrat from Mississippi, was renominated for a sixth term with 70 percent of the vote over two challengers, including James H. Meredith, the first black to enroll at the University of Mississippi. Eastland had earned a reputation for supporting anti-black policies.

JUNE 6, 1972 School Merger Order Overruled. The Fourth U.S. Circuit Court of Appeals in Richmond, Virginia, overruled a federal district court order that called for the merger of the school districts of Richmond and two suburban countries, which would have involved the busing of thousands of children to achieve desegregation. The court held that U.S. District Court Judge Robert R. Merhige, Jr., had excessively interpreted the Fourteenth Amendment when he earlier ordered the "metropolitan desegregation" plan into effect. The Richmond Board of Education announced that it would appeal the court's 5-1 ruling to the U.S. Supreme Court where, along with a similar case from Denver, Colorado, it was expected to bring a new crucial ruling in the annals of school desegregation. The appeal to the Fourth Circuit Court was sponsored by the U.S. Department of Justice. The NAACP, the National Education Association (NEA), and the American Civil Liberties Union (ACLU) opposed the appeal to the circuit court.

JUNE 12, 1972 Discriminatory Clubs Allowed Liquor Licenses. The U.S. Supreme Court ruled in a 6-3 decision that a state could grant a liquor license to a private club that practiced racial discrimination. The Court ruled against the petition of K. Leroy Irvis, black majority leader of the Pennsylvania House of Representatives. Irvis had been denied service in the restaurant of the lodge of the Loyal Order of Moose in Harrisburg, Pennsylvania. Justice William H. Rehnquist wrote that the authority to grant liquor licenses did not "sufficiently implicate the state in the discriminatory guest policies" of private clubs. Justices Douglas, Brennan, and Marshall dissented from the majority view.

JUNE 14, 1972 Massive Busing Program Ordered in Detroit. U.S. District Court Judge Stephen J. Roth ordered a massive busing program to desegregate the city and suburban schools in the Detroit, Michigan, area. It was the most extensive desegregation plan ever ordered by a federal court. Under the plan, 310,000 of 780,000 students in Detroit and fifty-three suburban school districts would be bused to achieve desegregation. The Detroit schools had, at the time, 290,000 students, 65 percent black, while 29 of the 53 suburban districts had all-white enrollments and the rest were predominately white. On June 22, President Nixon voiced complete disagreement with the court's decision and reiterated his appeal for congressional action on a strong anti-busing law. The President called the Detroit order "perhaps the most flagrant example that we have of all the busing decisions, moving against all the principles that I, at least, believe should be applied in this area." On July 21, the Sixth U.S. Circuit Court of Appeals issued an order delaying the implementation of Judge Roth's order until it could hear the merits of the case on August 24, 1972.

JUNE 26, 1972 McGovern Endorsed by Black Democrats. A bloc of black delegates to the Democratic National Convention, led by Representative Walter E. Fauntroy from Washington, D.C., endorsed the presidential candidacy of South Dakota Senator George McGovern. Fauntroy announced that ninety-six previously uncommitted black delegates would now vote for McGovern. McGovern predicted that the black bloc might be enough to give him the nomination on the first ballot. A later recount by all parties confirmed that the black bloc really numbered only about sixty votes, not enough to assure McGovern a first ballot victory. Senator McGovern had won favor among blacks for his support of parts of the programs of the Black Congressional Caucus, the Black

National Convention, and his pledge to appoint blacks to high-ranking positions in any administration which he should head.

JUNE 29, 1972 Death Penalty Ruled Unconstitutional. The U.S. Supreme Court, in a 5-4 decision, ruled that the death penalty as it was usually enforced violated the Eighth Amendment prohibition against cruel and unusual punishment. The high Court order overturned the conviction of two Georgia blacks, Henry Furman, a convicted murderer, and Lucius Jackson, a convicted rapist, and a Texas black, Elmer Branch, also a convicted rapist. All of the victims in the crimes were white. Of the 600 men and women awaiting execution at the time of the ruling, 329 were black, while 14 belonged to other minority groups. Justice William O. Douglas wrote that the disproportionate number of minority and poor felons sentenced to death were victims of unconstitutional discrimination.

JULY 3–7, 1972 NAACP Condemned Nixon Administration. During its annual convention held in Detroit, Michigan, the NAACP again criticized the Nixon administration for its attitude towards black people. The 2,632 delegates passed an emergency resolution condemning the administration for its school busing policies. On July 6, NAACP Labor Director Herbert Hill reiterated his criticism of the administration's record on black employment. Black officials in the Nixon administration, including Assistant Secretary of Housing and Urban Development Samuel Jackson, defended the Nixon program and claimed support for the President even among NAACP board of directors.

JULY 6, 1972 Baker Assigned to Africa. James E. Baker, a career foreign service officer, was appointed economic and commercial officer at the U.S. embassy in Pretoria, South Africa, becoming the first African American diplomat to gain a permanent assignment in that nation. The Department of State expressed confidence

that Baker would be accepted in South Africa without restrictions, despite that nation's racist apartheid policy.

JULY 12, 1972 McGovern Won Nomination. South Dakota Senator George S. McGovern, with widespread support from black delegates, won the Democratic presidential nomination on the first ballot in Miami Beach, Florida. Representative Shirley Chisholm from New York, the first black woman ever to seek a presidential nomination, received 151 of the more than 2,000 votes cast.

AUGUST 2, 1972 Desegregation Orders Countermanded. The U.S. Circuit Court of Appeals for the Fifth District countermanded desegregation orders of lower courts for the school districts in Austin and Corpus Christi, Texas. In Austin, the lower court had rejected plans for crosstown busing of students, but the appellate court counselled against the total rejection of the busing tool and ordered new plans from all of the concerned parties. In the Corpus Christi case, the appeals court overturned a crosstown busing plan, instructing the lower court to examine all neighborhood-oriented tools before resorting to busing to achieve desegregation.

AUGUST 3–8, 1972 Primary Election Results. In fall primary elections, state senator James O. Patterson, Jr., was nominated for a congressional seat in the new Fourth Congressional District (Memphis) of Tennessee. Patterson thus became the first black to win a major party congressional nomination in the state's history. In Georgia, a former aide to Dr. Martin Luther King, Jr., Hosea Williams of Dekalb County, placed a distant third in the Democratic race for U.S. senator and, in the same state, another former aide to King, Andrew Young of Atlanta, won the Democratic nomination from the Fifth Congressional District. Five blacks were also elected to the ten-person city council in Selma, Alabama, the scene of violent voting rights demonstrations in the 1960s. This group, elected from predominately black wards rather than at-large, were the first of their race to win seats on the local council.

AUGUST 25–OCTOBER 28, 1972   Black Leaders Campaigned for Presidential Nominees. Black civil rights and political leaders campaigned in behalf of the presidential nominees of both parties. On August 25, Georgia State Representative Julian Bond told an audience at Columbia University in New York that African Americans ought to "come together to drive Richard Nixon from the White House." Bond predicted that Nixon's opponent, Senator George McGovern from South Dakota, would capture 90 percent of the nation's black vote. On October 28, Floyd McKissick, former national director of the Congress of Racial Equality (CORE) and developer of the new town of Soul City in North Carolina, told an Atlanta audience that he supported the reelection of President Nixon because blacks should belong to both political parties and because Nixon had done more for blacks than Senator McGovern. Veteran Atlanta civil rights leader William Holmes Borders, another Nixon supporter, cited the administration's aid to Howard University in Washington, D.C., Tuskegee Institute in Alabama, sickle-cell anemia research, and job retraining programs as evidence of the President's concern for blacks.

AUGUST 26, 1972   More Buses Ordered for Nashville Schools. U.S. District Court Judge L. Clure Morton ordered the Nashville, Tennessee, school board to obtain thirty additional school buses in order to meet the court's desegregation requirements. Nashville's mayor and city council had hesitated to release the necessary funds for the new buses. Judge Morton, however, told city officials that they must acquire the additional buses immediately so that his year-old busing order could be made effective.

AUGUST 26, 1972   Busing Advocate Resigned. Dr. Thomas A. Shaheen, an advocate of busing to achieve racial desegregation in the public schools, resigned under board pressure as superintendent of schools of San Francisco. Shaheen directed the first massive busing plan to achieve desegregation in a major Northern or Western city in September 1971, when more than half of San Francisco's 40,000 elementary school children were ordered to be bused by the federal courts. Shaheen predicted that troubled times were ahead for proponents of desegregation in American education. He was succeeded by Dr. Stephen Morena, assistant chancellor of the San Francisco Community College District.

AUGUST 26, 1972   Alabama Certified First Black Senate Candidate. John LeFlore, a veteran civil rights leader and journalist in Mobile, Alabama, was officially certified as the first black candidate for the U.S. Senate in Alabama since the Reconstruction era. LeFlore was certified by Alabama Secretary of State Mabel Amos under the banner of the mostly black National Democratic Party of Alabama (NDPA). Other candidates in the senate race were Democratic incumbent John Sparkman and Republican W. M. Blount, former Postmaster General of the United States.

AUGUST 30, 1972   Whites Freed from Prison. Three Meridian, Mississippi whites were freed from a federal prison after serving slightly more than two years of their three-year sentences on charges of slaying three civil rights activists in Neshoba County, Mississippi, in 1964. Jimmy Arledge, Jimmie Snowden, and Horace Doyle Barnette were convicted in 1967 on conspiracy charges following the deaths of Andrew Goodman, Michael Schwerner, and James E. Chaney near Philadelphia, Mississippi. Chief Deputy U.S. Marshal Charles T. Sutherland said the convicted trio were approved for release in the spring of 1972 after receiving time off of their sentences for good behavior.

SEPTEMBER 1, 1972   Black Parents Demanded Protection for Children. A group of black parents asked for federal protection for their children attending desegregated schools in Oklahoma City, Oklahoma. The blacks vowed not to return their children to the schools—scenes of continued outbursts of racial violence—without protection. The parents presented their requests to the local school board and to the offices of the U.S. Attorney and U.S. Marshal. They suggested that federal officers board school buses and patrol the schools.

NOVEMBER 2, 1972   Tensions Flared in Georgia. Racial tensions flared in Lavonia, Georgia, after a black man was slain in a gunbattle with police. Police Chief Joe Foster said Ollis Hunter was killed after he opened fire on officers attempting to serve him with a peace warrant at his home. Lavonia patrol officer Freddie Smith was wounded in the exchange of gunfire. Blacks contended that the slaying of Hunter could have been avoided. Almost immediately, the town's black population began a boycott of downtown merchants, demanding, among other things, better streets in their communities, more black school bus drivers and police officers, and the firing of Chief Foster. Mayor Herman Ayers and the city council took the demands under advisement. On December 8, 1972, a gunman rode through the black residential area of Lavonia, firing shotgun blasts into two homes, two restaurants, and a church. Police said one of the homes belonged to the head of the local chapter of the Southern Christian Leadership Conference. There were no injuries in the incident and no immediate arrests.

NOVEMBER 7, 1972   Nixon Reelected. Richard M. Nixon was reelected president of the United States by one of the largest majorities in the nation's history. As in 1968, the President failed to win substantial support from black voters. Preliminary estimates gave Nixon only about 30 percent of the black votes cast in the election.

The fall elections also saw the selection of two additional black women for seats in the U.S. Congress and the election of the first black

representative from the South since Reconstruction days. The new black congresswomen were Yvonne Braithwaite Burke from California and Barbara Jordan from Texas. Andrew Young, formerly a top aide to the late Dr. Martin Luther King, Jr., was elected congressman from Georgia's Fifth District (Atlanta).

NOVEMBER 11, 1972   Gridiron Club Elected First Black Member. Black syndicated columnist Carl T. Rowan was elected to membership in the Gridiron Club, a prestigious organization of Washington journalists. Rowan became the first black member of the club, which was established in 1885.

NOVEMBER 14, 1972   Blacks Arrested After Sit-In. Thirteen blacks, members of the Dallas, Texas, chapter of the Southern Christian Leadership Conference, were arrested on charges of disrupting a public meeting after they staged a sit-in demonstration in the chambers of the Dallas City Council. George Holland, spokesperson for the SCLC group, read a list of demands which included the resignation of Dallas Mayor Wes Wise, Police Chief Frank Dyson, and City Attorney Alex Bickley; the arrest of three officers who were recently cited but exonerated in the slaying of local blacks; and a percentage of city jobs commensurate with that of the city's black population. Police officers arrested the group before Holland could finish reading his demands.

NOVEMBER 15, 1972   Black Soldier Acquitted. Private Billy Dean Smith, a black soldier, was acquitted by a military court in San Francisco of the "fragging" slaying of two officers in South Vietnam. Smith later stated at a news conference, which was attended by black Communist Angela Davis, that "the system of military justice is still riddled with injustice." Smith said the only fair trial in his case would have been "no trial at all."

NOVEMBER 15, 1972   Black Lawyers Protested Examinations. The black National Bar

Association (NBA) announced that it will co-sponsor a federal court suit protesting the failure of all black applicants in the last semi-annual Georgia Bar examination. Atlanta City Councilman Marvin S. Arrington, deputy regional director of the NBA, said that none of the fifty-five black applicants received a passing grade and charged that "there is conscious and invidious discrimination" on the part of the bar examiners in Georgia. He pledged to call on the U.S. Department of Justice and Georgia Governor Jimmy Carter to conduct investigations into allegations of discrimination. Georgia Bar Examination Board Chairman Trammell Vickery denied that discrimination existed against black applicants and cited the fact that applicants are not identified by race.

NOVEMBER 16, 1972 Civil Rights Commission Chair Resigned. The Reverend Theodore Hesburgh, chairman of the U.S. Civil Rights Commission (USCCR) since 1969 and a member since its inception in 1958, resigned. Hesburgh, president of Notre Dame University, had led the USCCR in a constant stream of criticism of the Nixon administration's commitment to civil rights progress. Maurice Mitchell, chancellor of the University of Denver, also announced his resignation. Mitchell had charged that President Nixon ignored the commission and its work.

NOVEMBER 16, 1972 College Students Killed in Altercation. Two black students at Southern University in Baton Rouge, Louisiana, were killed during a confrontation between black students and law enforcement officers. High-ranking police officials had denied in their first statements following the shooting that their men had fired the fatal shots. Some suggested that there might have been accidental firings. Spokespersons for the students charged intentional shooting by law enforcement units. Louisiana Governor Edwin Edwards immediately requested State Attorney General William J. Guste, Jr., to investigate the incidents. Guste subsequently appointed a biracial committee

consisting of police officers, university administrators, students, elected officials, and private citizens. Some blacks expressed distrust of the official committee and vowed to assemble a group of their own to look into the altercation.

Southern University, one of the nation's largest all-black colleges, had been the scene of student protests in recent years. The students had generally charged the school's administration, backed by the power of the state government, with being unresponsive to academic and social change.

NOVEMBER 17, 1972 Funds Withheld from Segregated School Districts. U.S. District Court Judge John H. Pratt ruled in Washington, D.C. that efforts made by the Department of Health, Education, and Welfare (HEW) to obtain voluntary compliance with the 1964 Civil Rights Act had been largely unsuccessful and that HEW should withhold funds from school districts still practicing segregation. U.S. Attorneys announced that they would appeal the ruling, claiming that there appeared to be serious errors in the judge's decision. They did not specify the errors.

NOVEMBER 18, 1972 Southern Cotton Farming Investigated. Fayette, Mississippi, Mayor Charles Evers called for a federal investigation into problems faced by small Southern cotton farmers. The black mayor told Secretary of Agriculture Earl Butz in a telegram that many farmers, black and white, had come to him with their problems.

NOVEMBER 18, 1972 Contempt-of-Court Sentence Limited in Chicago 7 Trial. U.S. District Court Judge Edward T. Ginouz set a limit on the contempt-of-court sentence that may be ordered for the "Chicago 7" defendants and their lawyers and ordered contempt charges against Black Panther leader Bobby Seale entirely dropped. The contempt charges arose from the actions of the defendants and the lawyers in the courtroom of Judge Julius J. Hoffman, who heard the case after distur-

bances during the 1968 Democratic National
Convention in Chicago. The charges against
Seale were dropped at the government's request. An appeals court had ruled earlier that if
Seale were prosecuted, the government would
have to reveal the contents of electronic surveillance logs. The prosecution refused, claiming
such disclosures would endanger the national
security.

**NOVEMBER 22, 1972 Election Divided by
Race.** The Louis Harris Poll, a major survey of
public opinion, announced that the sharpest
division in the 1972 presidential election was
according to race, with blacks voting 79-21
percent for Senator George McGovern while
whites voted 67-33 percent in favor of President Nixon. The survey went on to say that in
terms of their political inclinations and in their
outlook on American issues, blacks and whites
have rarely been so far apart. The survey cited
such examples as the blacks' overwhelming
preference for racially desegregated schools (78-
12 percent) as against a plurality of 46-43
percent among whites. While roughly 50 percent of the black population endorsed busing to
achieve school desegregation, only 14 percent
of the nation's whites approved of this method
to dismantle separate schools. Also, nearly 80
percent of the nation's blacks, versus 46 percent
of whites, supported increased federal assistance for poverty-stricken Americans. The Harris
Survey reflected racial attitudes as of Thanks-
giving Day, 1972.

**NOVEMBER 27, 1972 H. Rap Brown Trial
Began.** H. Rap Brown, former secretary of the
Student Non-Violent Coordinating Committee (SNCC), went on trial on charges of robbery, attempted murder, and possession of an
illegal weapon. There was speculation, however, that the trial might be further delayed by
legal arguments over the effect of a magazine
article dealing with one of the arresting officers.
Brown was arrested after a New York robbery
on October 16, 1971. The trial finally got under
way after Brown's lawyers, William Kuntsler

H. Rap Brown speaking to reporters. (Bettmann Archive/
Newsphotos, Inc.)

and Howard Moore, Jr., both famed civil liberties attorneys, failed in an effort to have the case
transferred to the federal courts.

**NOVEMBER 29, 1972 Blacks Opposed Nomi-
nation.** President Nixon nominated Peter J.
Brennan, president of the Building and Construction Trades Councils of New York, to be
his new secretary of labor. Many blacks voiced
opposition to the nomination, claiming that
Brennan was a representative of a segment of
organized labor which had been desegregated
minimally and generally at government insistence.

**DECEMBER 4, 1972 Baraka Spoke to Relig-
ious Groups.** Black poet Imamu Amiri Baraka
(born LeRoi Jones) told the representatives at
the triennial general assembly of the National
Council of Churches that the nation's major
religious organizations must support the revolution of the poor or cease to exist. Baraka, an
influential resident of Newark, New Jersey,
called for the destruction of capitalism, claiming it was part of a cruelly primitive social
system that subjected the poor to misery in this
country and abroad. Observers of the American
Jewish Committee, Rabbi A. James Ruden and

the Reverend Gerald Strober, voiced their disappointment at Baraka's appearance and accused him of anti-white racism and anti-Semitism. Many other delegates stood to applaud the black poet.

DECEMBER 7, 1972 Cary Elected President of National Council of Churches. The Reverend W. Sterling Cary, the administrative officer for approximately ninety United Church of Christ congregations in New York City, was unanimously elected president of the National Council of Churches at the group's annual meeting in Dallas, Texas. Cary, the first African American to head the group, was originally a Baptist minister before he began preaching at Presbyterian, Congregational, and interdenominational churches in a ministerial career spanning twenty-four years. The newly elected president of the liberal religious group told his fellow delegates at Dallas that American churches preach but do not practice integration. He said that as president of the National Council of Churches he would promote efforts to achieve decent housing for the poor, better employment opportunities for racial minorities, and an overhaul of the welfare system.

DECEMBER 9, 1972 Kerr Nominated to Head Newark Police Department. Lieutenant Edward Kerr, a black police officer with fifteen years of service, was nominated director of the Newark Police Department, the largest in the state of New Jersey. Kerr, a native of Willacoochee, Georgia, and a student at Rutgers University, was slated to succeed John Redden, a white police officer who resigned after becoming embroiled in a controversy over whether a black-sponsored housing project ought to be built in a white community. The white members of Newark's biracial city council asked black mayor Kenneth Gibson not to accept Redden's resignation. Gibson refused to heed their plea.

DECEMBER 11, 1972 James Brown Arrested. Soul singer James Brown was arrested and charged with disorderly conduct in Knoxville,

Writer Amiri Baraka. (Bettmann Archive/Newsphotos, Inc.)

Tennessee. The arrest of Brown, an idol of rock and soul fans and a political supporter of President Nixon, sparked a heated controversy in which lawyers for the singer threatened to sue the city of Knoxville for one million dollars. Brown said he was talking with a group of children about drugs and the importance of school attendance when he was arrested by Knoxville police. The police charged Brown with disorderly conduct by creating a scene and failing to move on. On December 12, Knoxville mayor Kyle Testerman said the arrest of Brown apparently resulted from a misunderstanding and promised to meet with Brown's attorney, Albert G. Ingram, in an effort to resolve differences brought about by the incident. Following his meeting with the mayor on December 18, Ingram announced that the matter still had not been satisfactorily resolved.

DECEMBER 14, 1972 "White Ghetto" Residents Authorized to Sue. The U.S. Supreme Court, in a unanimous opinion, ruled that the Civil Rights Act of 1964 authorized the residents of "white ghettos" to file lawsuits aimed at ending racial discrimination in their own apartment developments. The opinion, which was written by Justice William O. Douglas, said residents of both races who lived in discriminatory housing developments could sue because they may suffer specific individual injury when deprived of the social, professional, and business benefits available in integrated communities. The decision was rendered in a San Francisco case involving an apartment complex formerly owned by the Metropolitan Life Insurance Company. The NAACP applauded the Court's decision because it said it lacked the personnel and resources to fight widespread housing discrimination.

DECEMBER 14, 1972 Angela Davis Formed Legal Aid Group. Black Communist Angela Davis announced plans to form a national defense organization to help "black and brown political prisoners of the government."At a Harlem news conference, Davis said that the new group would provide legal aid to the oppressed.

DECEMBER 15, 1972 Racial Violence in Pensacola, Florida. Fifty special sheriff's deputies and police officers patrolled the Escambra High School in Pensacola, Florida, after a day of fighting between black and white students that left several people injured and forty-seven arrested. The thirty-eight whites and nine blacks were subsequently released when school officials dropped trespassing charges against them. The fighting apparently began in the school's cafeteria and spread to other parts of the large school. The deputies who broke up the melee said they seized bicycle chains, belts, and knives used as weapons by the students.

DECEMBER 17, 1972 George Wiley Resigned. George Wiley, black director of the National Welfare Rights Organization (NWRO) since its founding in 1965, announced his resignation in Washington, D.C. Wiley said he was leaving the NWRO, the nation's leading group of welfare recipients, to form a broader-based organization to help the nation's poor.

DECEMBER 21, 1972 Horace Mann Bond Died. Horace Mann Bond, former dean of the School of Education at Atlanta University and former president of Georgia's Fort Valley State College and Pennsylvania's Lincoln University, died in Atlanta. The seventy-year-old educator was a pioneer in black scholarship, publishing distinguished books and articles in the fields of black education and history. He was the father of Georgia State Representative Julian Bond, whose name was placed before the 1968 Democratic National Convention as a vice-presidential candidate. The *Atlanta Constitution* eulogized the black scholar as one who had "a full and fruitful life of achievement."

1973

JANUARY 4, 1973 FBI Report Under Suspicion. U.S. Attorney General Richard Kleindienst announced that the Civil Rights Division of the Justice Department would have to conduct a careful examination of an FBI report on the killings of two students at black Southern University in Baton Rouge, Louisiana, before deciding whether to call a federal grand jury into the case. The two black youths were slain by law enforcement officers on the Southern campus during student protests on November 16, 1972.

JANUARY 29, 1973 Connecticut Judge Ordered Quota. U.S. District Court Judge Jon O. Newman ordered the city of Bridgeport, Connecticut, to hire blacks and Puerto Ricans to fill 50 percent of the vacancies on the police force until the two minority groups constituted at least 15 percent of the force. The judge's order was designed to correct racial imbalances in Bridgeport's law enforcement.

MAY 29, 1973 Thomas Bradley Elected Mayor of L.A. Thomas Bradley, a veteran Los Angeles city councilman, was elected mayor of the city of Los Angeles, California. Bradley defeated incumbent mayor Sam Yorty, who was seeking a fourth four-year term. The new black mayor, who lost to Yorty in 1969, won about 56 percent of the votes cast. Yorty's campaign rhetoric had pictured Bradley as a left-wing radical. Bradley assessed his victory as a rejection of racism in the election.

JULY 1, 1973 New Superintendent Assumed Duties. Alonzo A. Crim, former superintendent of schools in Compton, California, assumed his duties as the first black superintendent of the public schools in Atlanta, Georgia, one of the Deep South's largest predominantly black school systems. Crim's selection resulted from a compromise desegregation plan worked out between local black and white business and political leaders in which the blacks agreed to desist from further pressures for busing to achieve desegregation and the whites agreed to the hiring of a black superintendent and other black school administrators. The plan, reminiscent of the famous Atlanta Compromise of 1895, in which Booker T. Washington urged blacks to shun social equality for economic advancement, was denounced by the national NAACP leadership in New York. They felt the agreement set a bad precedent and would hamper future efforts to achieve massive desegregation of the nation's schools. Although local NAACP leaders who assented to the pact argued that massive desegregation was impossible in Atlanta, a city with a 55 percent black population and an 80 percent black school-age population, they were suspended and eventually expelled from office for their support of the desegregation agreement.

JULY 2, 1973 All-Black Radio Station Began Operating. The National Black Network (NBN), the nation's first radio news network owned and operated by African Americans, began operations with hourly newscasts to forty affiliated stations. Although based in New York City, the NBN planned to provide news stories of interest to blacks everywhere.

JULY 29, 1973 Census Report Released. The Bureau of the Census released a report of six northern urban areas that showed that southern-born black males living in those areas were more likely to be employed and living with their wives than northern-born blacks living in the same areas. The study, which was based upon data from the 1970 Census, reported that about 65 percent of the black men born in New York City were employed. The figure rose to 78 percent for southern-born blacks who migrated north before 1965 and to 85 percent for those who moved north since 1965. The study also revealed that 70 percent of southern-born black men were living with their wives as compared with 51 percent of the blacks born in Illinois. Robert Hill, the National Urban League's research director, said the report refuted the widely held view that southern blacks migrated to the North to obtain higher welfare benefits.

AUGUST 15, 1973 National Black Feminist Organization Founded. The National Black Feminist Organization (NBFO) was founded in New York City with chapters in several other localities, including Chicago, Cleveland, and San Francisco. Eleanor Holmes Norton, a member of the New York City Human Rights Commission and a founder of the feminist group, accused the nation of expecting black women to suppress their aspirations in deference to black males. Another founder, Margaret Sloan, said the new group would remind "the black liberation movement that there can't be liberation for half a race."

AUGUST 15, 1973 Abernathy Agreed to Stay. Ralph David Abernathy announced that he would remain as president of the Southern Christian Leadership Conference (SCLC) after the civil rights group's board of directors refused to accept his resignation during the SCLC's sixteenth annual convention in Indianapolis, Indiana. The board, however, agreed to try to remedy some of the complaints which led Abernathy, successor to Martin Luther King, Jr., to offer his resignation. These complaints included inadequate financing and insufficient staff. The board pledged increased fund-raising efforts, the hiring of more full-time staff, and the creation of five regional offices to assist in administrative functions.

SEPTEMBER 1973 Southern Colleges Elected Presidents. Henry C. Ponder, vice president of academic affairs at Alabama A&M College, assumed the presidency of Benedict College in Columbia, South Carolina. W. Clyde Williams, acting president of Miles College in Birmingham, Alabama, since 1971, was inaugurated as the tenth president of the historically black institution.

OCTOBER 1973 Republic of New Africa Members Convicted. Seven members of the Republic of New Africa (RNA), including its president, Imari A. Obadele, were convicted in the U.S. District Court in Biloxi, Mississippi, on charges resulting from a shootout at RNA headquarters in Jackson, Mississippi, in 1971. Two women and five men were charged with illegal possession of weapons and assault on a federal officer. Two of the defendants, Wayne M. James and Thomas E. Norman, were already serving life sentences for convictions in state courts. In the federal trial Obadele received a twelve-year sentence; the other defendants received sentences ranging from three to twelve years. Attorneys for the RNA indicated they would file a motion for a rehearing of the cases.

OCTOBER 1973 Threatt Assumed Presidency at Morris Brown College. Robert Threatt, president of the Georgia Association of Educators, assumed duties as president of Morris Brown College in Atlanta, Georgia. Threatt succeeded John A. Middleton, a black member of the Atlanta Board of Education, who resigned because of the school's deteriorating financial condition, a situation which appeared to worsen as the school withdrew from the Atlanta University Center complex of black colleges. Threatt, a graduate of Morris Brown

and the University of Oklahoma, was also a professor of education at Fort Valley State College in Georgia prior to becoming, at forty-six years of age, the youngest president in the history of Morris Brown.

OCTOBER 1973 Willie Mays Retired. As the 1973 professional baseball season closed, black centerfielder Willie Mays ended his long, outstanding career. Mays won national acclaim for his fielding heroics and for his powerful bat during nearly twenty years of play with the New York and San Francisco Giants and the New York Mets of the National Baseball League. Upon his retirement, New York City honored Mays in special ceremonies at Shea Stadium on September 25. Mayor John Lindsay issued a proclamation of celebration as 55,000 fans cheered the star. Alabama-born Mays was also presented with a honorary LL.D degree from his home state's Miles College during the ceremonies.

OCTOBER 1973 Reggie Jackson Won MVP Award. Reggie Jackson of the world champion Oakland Athletics was unanimously selected as the World Series's Most Valuable Player (MVP). Four other black players had won the MVP award in previous years: Roberto Clemente of the Pittsburgh Pirates in 1971; Brooks Robinson of the Baltimore Orioles in 1970; Bob Gibson of the St. Louis Cardinals in 1967 and 1964; and Frank Robinson of the Baltimore Orioles in 1966.

OCTOBER 1973 Jesse W. Lewis Died. Jesse W. Lewis, a founder and former director of Industrial Bank in Washington, D.C., died in Washington. Industrial Bank was one of the nation's first black financial institutions, having been founded during the Great Depression of the 1930s.

Lewis was born in 1902 in Richmond, Virginia, and was educated at Shaw University in North Carolina and New York University. He began his career as a teacher at Howard University, where he taught for nineteen years.

In 1934, Lewis joined Jesse H. Mitchell and other black financial leaders to form the Industrial Bank. He was also a lawyer, a real estate broker, and a trustee of Virginia Union University.

OCTOBER 10, 1973 Georgia Elected First Black Mayor. Richmond Hill, a sixty-eight-year-old mortician and mayor pro tempore of Greenville, Georgia, was elected mayor of his city and became the first black mayor in Georgia's history. Hill, who had previously worked as a farmer and then a businessman, defeated a white opponent in a town with a population of about fifteen hundred, 40 percent of whom were black.

OCTOBER 14, 1973 B.B. King Honored. The famed African American blues singer B. B. King was awarded an honorary doctor of humanities degree from Tougaloo College in Mississippi, making him the first blues musician ever to receive an honorary doctorate for his contributions to the music world. George A. Owens, president of the college, conferred the degree during the celebration of the 104th anniversary of the founding of Tougaloo, the state's most prestigious private black college.

OCTOBER 16, 1973 Atlanta Elected First Black Mayor. Maynard H. Jackson, a thirty-five-year-old attorney and vice mayor of the city of Atlanta, was elected mayor of the Deep South's largest city. Jackson defeated incumbent mayor Sam Massell in a campaign marred by Massell's injection of the race issue. Jackson ousted the city's first Jewish mayor to become the city's first black mayor.

Jackson, the son of a minister and a college professor, was educated at Morehouse College and North Carolina Central University Law School. He had run unsuccessfully for the U.S. Senate in 1968 before being elected vice mayor in 1969. Jackson's election signaled a swing of political power from white to black in Atlanta as African Americans achieved equality on the eighteen-member city council and a slight majority on the nine-member school board. Slightly more than 50 percent of the population of Atlanta was black at the time of Jackson's election, but whites held a slight edge in voter registration. Although opposed by many whites for his forthright opposition to alleged police brutality in Atlanta, Jackson appealed to voters of both races and captured at least 20 percent of the white vote cast in the election.

OCTOBER 26, 1973 Jordan Criticized Nixon Administration. Vernon Jordan, Executive Director of the National Urban League, told an audience at Clark College in Atlanta that the Nixon Administration left unfinished the economic improvement of African Americans after a decade of advancement in civil rights. Jordan said the steady flow of congressional action, executive orders, and federal court decisions in the 1960s did for blacks what the New Deal had done for whites and organized labor, but the Nixon Administration allowed this "Second Reconstruction" to expire uncompleted. Jordan's remarks reiterated a continuing theme among African American leadership: criticism of President Nixon's failure to recognize the legitimate needs of black citizens.

NOVEMBER 1973 George Washington Carver Honored. George Washington Carver, the famed black scientist from Tuskegee Institute who won acclaim for developing hundreds of uses for the peanut, was elected to the Hall of Fame of Great Americans at New York University. Carver's bust was placed in the Hall of Fame along with one hundred other great Americans, including Tuskegee's founder Booker T. Washington, who was elected in 1945. Candidates for election to the Hall of Fame must have been deceased for at least twenty-five years and must have been American citizens who made significant contributions to the nation. Carver's selection was sponsored in the Hall of Fame by black educator Benjamin E. Mays, an elector since 1958.

NOVEMBER 6, 1973 Detroit's First Black Mayor Elected. Michigan State Senator Coleman Young was elected mayor of Detroit, Michi-

Vernon Jordan. (Courtesy of the National Urban League.)

gan. With only about 10 percent of the white blue-collar votes going for him, Young won with an overwhelming vote in black precincts and some support from white middle-income voters. He defeated white former police commissioner John F. Nichols, becoming the Motor City's first black mayor. Young, a native of Tuscaloosa, Alabama, would preside over the nation's fifth largest city, but one plagued with crime.

Black political power in Detroit was also measurably increased by the election of state representative James Bradley as the first black city clerk, the second highest elective position in the city, and by the fact that four of the nine city councilmen were black.

By the end of 1973, blacks would hold mayoral positions in almost 100 of the nation's 18,000 local governments, including such major cities as Los Angeles, Newark, Cincinnati, Atlanta, and Washington, D.C.

NOVEMBER 9, 1973 Committee Formed to Select Portraits. An eight-member biracial committee which included Georgia's Secretary of State Ben Fortson and Clarence A. Bacote, veteran professor of history at Atlanta Univer-

sity, met at the request of Georgia governor Jimmy Carter to select the portraits of three outstanding black Georgians to be displayed in the rotunda of the Georgia State Capitol in Atlanta. It was agreed almost immediately that the portrait of slain civil rights leader Martin Luther King, Jr., would be one of those selected. Tennessee had previously honored blacks by placing the portraits of blues musician W. C. Handy and Memphis political leader and writer George Washington Lee in its capitol building at Nashville.

NOVEMBER 26, 1973 Segregated Establishments Sued. The U.S. Department of Justice filed fifteen civil rights suits to desegregate twenty-four bars, liquor stores, and pool halls in seven Southern states—Arkansas, Florida, Georgia, Louisiana, South Carolina, Tennessee, and Texas. The civil suits charged the owners and operators of the establishments with violating the public accommodations section of the 1964 Civil Rights Act. A Justice Department representative said it was the largest number of civil rights suits filed in one day within memory.

DECEMBER 2, 1973 Quota Systems Ordered in San Francisco. Two U.S. District Court judges, in separate decisions, ordered the city of San Francisco to implement quota systems for the employment of minorities in its police and fire departments. Judge Robert F. Peckham directed the police department to hire three minority persons (defined by Peckham as African, Asian, and Hispanic Americans) for every two whites at the patrolman's level until minority representation reached 30 percent. The department was also instructed to adopt a one-to-one ratio in appointments to the rank of sergeant until 30 percent of those officers were from minorities. The judge outlawed a hiring and promotion test which had been used by the city's Civil Service Commission. He found the test to be discriminatory and ordered that any future tests be submitted to him for approval. In the second decision, Judge William T.

Sweigert ordered the San Francisco Fire Department to fill half of its more than two hundred vacancies with members of racial minorities.

DECEMBER 3, 1973   Contempt Convictions Maintained. The U.S. Supreme Court refused to overturn the contempt conviction of eighty-one Columbus, Georgia, blacks who were convicted of violating a city ordinance prohibiting the gathering of more than twelve people in a group. The blacks were part of a larger movement formed to protest local police hiring practices in June 1971.

DECEMBER 4, 1973   Memphis Desegregation Plan Upheld. The U.S. Court of Appeals for the Sixth Circuit upheld a desegregation plan for the Memphis, Tennessee, school system. Although the plan involved some crosstown busing, the NAACP opposed it because it allowed too many all-black schools. In rejecting the NAACP's contentions, the court said there was a "necessity of tolerating some one-race schools because minority groups concentrate in urban areas." The Appeals Court also agreed with a lower court that the city of Memphis had acted improperly by cutting its transportation budget in an attempt to circumvent an order for busing to achieve desegregation.

DECEMBER 19, 1973   Department of Health, Education, and Welfare Reprimanded. U.S. District Court Judge Frank Gray, Jr., ruled that the Department of Health, Education, and Welfare's (HEW) refusal to consider applications for transportation aid had impeded a court-ordered busing plan for the public schools in Nashville, Tennessee. Gray called the action illegal and ordered HEW to review within thirty days its earlier refusal to grant the city of Nashville funds to purchase buses to transport about half of its 95,000 students.

DECEMBER 20, 1973   Department of Labor Presented Plan. The Department of Labor announced that it had prepared and presented a plan to increase the employment of minorities on federally aided construction projects in the Chicago area. The plan set goals and timetables and provided penalties, including contract cancellations and ineligibility for future contracts, if companies failed to demonstrate good faith efforts to comply. The labor department imposed its plan in Chicago after voluntary efforts to end bias failed.

1974

JANUARY 7, 1974   Maryland Agreed to Hire More Blacks. The Department of Justice announced that it had obtained a consent decree whereby the state of Maryland agreed to hire more blacks and women for the state police and assign them on a nondiscriminatory basis. The state police stipulated that they would set a goal for the force to become 16 percent black within a five-year period and that it would no longer use a pre-employment test that had been adjudged discriminatory to blacks and women. The Maryland agreement was made in response to a suit filed by the Justice Department on January 4, 1974.

JANUARY 11, 1974   NASA Ordered to Change Hiring Practices. U.S. Senator William Proxmire, a Wisconsin Democrat and chairman of the congressional appropriations subcommittee which oversees funds for the National Aeronautics and Space Administration (NASA), ordered the space agency to double the fiscal 1975 budget of its equal employment office and to report to his subcommittee every three months on progress in hiring minorities and women. Proxmire's action was prompted by reports that NASA, as of mid-1973, had the lowest percentage of minority and female employees of any federal agency, and that two-thirds of these workers were in lower-level jobs. NASA officials also admitted that the agency had failed to act against project contractors who had not met minority employment goals.

JANUARY 11, 1974   Black Population Increased. The Bureau of the Census reported that as of July 1, 1973, the black population in the United States had increased to 23.8 million, up 1.2 million from the 1970 census. The Bureau also reported a continuing pattern of black youthfulness, in comparison to the general population. According to the latest statistics, the median age of blacks was 22.9 years; the median age for the total population was 28.4 years.

JANUARY 15, 1974   Supreme Court Ruled Against Injunctions. The U.S. Supreme Court, in a six to three decision, ruled that a group of seventeen blacks and two whites from Cairo, Illinois, could not obtain injunctions against local judges and prosecutors who, the plaintiffs claimed, were engaged in a pattern of setting excessive bail and harsher punishments for blacks than whites. The Court held that the complaints did not constitute a real case of controversy, hence they did not meet the necessary test for receiving relief from the federal courts. Five members of the six-justice majority also ruled that the plaintiffs would not have been entitled to injunctions even if they had been able to prove discrimination, for such a procedure would be tantamount to "an on-going audit of state criminal proceedings" in violation of the principle of federalism—federal-state harmony. The majority opinion was supported by Justices Burger, White, Powell, Stewart, Rehnquist, and Blackmun. In a dissent, Justice William O. Douglas said that the record of the case demonstrated "a more pervasive scheme for suppression of blacks and their civil rights than I have ever seen." The majority's decision, Douglas added, "will please the white superstructure, but it does violence to the conception of even-handed justice envisioned by the Constitution." Cairo had been the scene of angry clashes between blacks and whites since 1969.

JANUARY 17, 1974   Topeka Schools Investigated. The Department of Health, Education, and Welfare (HEW) reported that racial discrimination still existed in the Topeka, Kansas,

school system. The Board of Education of Topeka was a defendant in the landmark Supreme Court decision, *Brown v. Board of Education*, which outlawed school segregation in 1954. HEW said that it found a substantial number of schools which had disproportionate minority enrollments and that attendance zone transfers had impeded desegregation. Most of the black junior high and elementary pupils, HEW discovered, attended schools where the facilities were generally inferior to those at predominantly white schools. The department began its investigation of Topeka's schools in December 1973 after being named a party in a new suit against the city. As a result of its inquiry, HEW ordered Topeka school officials to submit corrective plans.

JANUARY 20, 1974   Intelligence Test Study Released. Dr. Peggy Sandy, a University of Pennsylvania anthropologist, released a study that indicated that whites scored higher than nonwhites on intelligence tests because of environmental factors rather than genetic differences between races. The study was conducted in the Pittsburgh public school system and financed by a grant from the Department of Health, Education, and Welfare (HEW). Sandy concluded that test score differences were a function, among other factors, of middle-class social integration and that her study, combined with data from other investigations, suggested that I.Q. differences between racial groups were exclusively a matter of environment while differences within racial groups were determined by both genetics and environment. These findings ran counter to the theories of Dr. William Shockley, a Nobel Prize-winning physicist at Stanford University who had held that intelligence was largely inherited and that the disadvantaged social position of American blacks was caused more by heredity than environment. Shockley's views had become increasingly controversial by late 1973, when he was prevented from speaking on several college campuses by protesters who contended that giving him a public forum would lend dignity to racist theories.

JANUARY 21, 1974 Knoxville Desegregation Plan Upheld. The U.S. Supreme Court upheld a lower court ruling approving a school desegregation plan for Knoxville, Tennessee. Under the approved plan, 59 percent of the city's black students would be placed in nine schools where the black enrollment would be 64 percent or more. Justices Powell and White dissented. Justice Marshall did not participate.

JANUARY 24, 1974 City of Boston Sued. The U.S. Department of Justice filed a suit in the federal court in Boston accusing the city of Boston of discrimination in the hiring of black and Hispanic applicants as firemen. The Justice Department cited that out of twenty-one hundred firemen in Boston, only sixteen were black and three were Hispanic, although these minorities constituted 16 percent and 4 percent of the city's population, respectively. These facts demonstrated, the department said, that the city had failed or refused to hire minorities on an equal basis with whites and had employed tests and other qualifications that had "not been shown to be required by the needs of the fire department or predictive of successful job performance." The suit asked the district court to order city officials to begin an active recruiting program and to hire enough black and Spanish-surnamed firemen to compensate for individuals who had taken fire department examinations but had been unfairly denied positions. In a closely related matter, the Justice Department also reported that a job-bias suit against Montgomery, Alabama, was resolved by a consent decree filed on October 3, 1972. This action, the department said, substantially expanded job opportunities for blacks in Montgomery's city government.

JANUARY 28, 1974 Junior High School Desegregation Plan Announced. U.S. District Court Judge Jack B. Weinstein of New York City ordered federal, state, and local housing authorities, along with the city departments of police, parks, and transportation, to cooperate with city school officials in formulating plans to desegregate a junior high school in Brooklyn. As of 1973, the school in question had an enrollment of 43 percent black, 39 percent Hispanic, and only 18 percent white. In his order, Weinstein told housing officials to develop a joint plan to undo the racial imbalance in the public housing near the school. He said all levels of government had failed to take appropriate and available steps to counter trends toward segregation in both housing and education and ruled that "federal complicity in encouraging segregated schooling through its housing programs" was unconstitutional. In his order, Weinstein directed housing authorities to include in their plan advertisements and inducements directed at the white middle class so as to stabilize the district's population. He also directed the city's department of transportation to develop busing plans for the immediate balancing of the school's enrollment. The police department was ordered to submit plans for the adequate protection of children in the area and the parks department, whose facilities were used frequently by the school, was directed to develop a desegregation plan. Weinstein set a March 1, 1974, deadline for submission and a September deadline for implementation of the joint desegregation program. The ruling, said to be the first decision of its kind, resulted from a suit filed by attorneys for the NAACP.

JANUARY 31, 1974 Georgia Power Company Ruling. A federal court in Atlanta ordered the Georgia Power Company, the state's largest utility corporation, to pay retroactive wages and pension benefits amounting to almost 2.1 million dollars to black employees who had been denied equal job rights. The ruling also required the company to increase black employment to 17 percent of the total work force within five years. At the time of the court's decision, 9.3 percent of the company's 8,278 workers were black. The ruling resulted from a suit filed by the U.S. Department of Justice in 1969.

FEBRUARY 4, 1974   Election Statistics Reported. The Voter Education Project (VEP) reported that 363 blacks had won elective offices in the South in the 1973 off-year elections. Of these victories, 253 were in elections for local councils and commissions, sixty-three were for school boards, nineteen were new black mayors, fourteen were election commissioners, and two were selected to state legislatures. The VEP, a privately funded political study group, reported from its headquarters in Atlanta.

FEBRUARY 13, 1974   American Colleges Criticized. The American Association of University Professors (AAUP) issued a statement condemning both students and faculties at American colleges who prevented research and debate on the race-intelligence issue that recently had been brought into focus by Stanford University's William Shockley. The AAUP accused some of its own members of "undermining the integrity of the academic community by attempting to suppress unpopular opinions." Nevertheless, on February 18 the student-controlled Political Union at Yale University cancelled a scheduled debate between Shockley and Roy Innis, national director of the Congress of Racial Equality (CORE), after protest from various student groups.

FEBRUARY 15, 1974   Prison Escapees Tied to Symbionese Liberation Army. The *San Francisco Chronicle* reported that two black escaped convicts had been identified as leaders of the Symbionese Liberation Army (SLA). The head of the interracial group of radical revolutionaries, which received notoriety for their alleged kidnapping of newspaper heiress Patricia Hearst, was said to be Donald D. DeFreeze, age thirty. DeFreeze, who called himself Field Marshall Cinque on tapes sent to the Hearst family, was listed as an escapee from the minimum security area of the Soledad State Prison in California

on March 5, 1973. The other black SLA leader was identified as Thero M. Wheeler, age twenty-nine, an escapee from the medical facility at Vacaville State Prison in August 1973. The report traced Wheeler and DeFreeze's association with the SLA to their memberships in the Black Cultural Association (BCA) at Vacaville State Prison. The BCA was described as an inmate group which sponsored cultural activities, educational programs, and pre-release preparation projects for prisoners. Russell Little, Jo Ann Little, and William Wolfe, all white, reportedly gained control of the BCA while working as tutors at the prison. DeFreeze was listed as a teacher of a BCA course entitled "Insight" which was designed to increase the racial consciousness of black inmates.

MARCH 15–17, 1974   National Black Political Convention Met. The second National Black Political Convention met in Little Rock, Arkansas. The seventeen hundred delegates approved several resolutions, including (1) the creation of a black united fund of about $10 million to further convention agenda items, local organization within the United States, and to develop projects to aid African nations; (2) the condemnation of black congressmen who had voted for military aid to Israel while ignoring the plight of Palestinian refugees; and (3) support of African liberation movements. The delegates rejected a resolution calling Israel a major instrument of an American-supported "world strategy of monopoly," and another that sought to establish an all-black political party. Opponents of the latter resolution argued that the convention had not done enough local organizational work to effectively build such a party. The convention was seriously split, as it had been in 1972, between those arguing for a black separatist approach to political organization and those who favored a continuation of ties with existing political structures. Black elected officials, such as Mayor Richard B. Hatcher of Gary, Indiana, and Democrat Congressman Ronald V. Dellums of California, led those who urged the convention to remain an inclusive organization, embracing and tolerating different ideologies. Black separatist spokesmen, lead by Newark's Imamu Amiri Baraka, accused the more conservative delegates of espousing neocolonialism and opportunism. Baraka said blacks should build an anti-capitalist revolutionary ideology and operate as a separate political force. NAACP leaders again boycotted the convention and drew the ire of the co-chairman Mayor Hatcher. Many black elected officials, including veteran Congressman Charles C. Diggs of Michigan (co-chairman of the 1972 convention), were also criticized for being conspicuously absent.

MARCH 17, 1974   Oklahoma State Prison Ordered to Desegregate. U.S. District Court Judge Luther L. Bohanon ordered an end to racial segregation at the Oklahoma State Prison at McAlester, Oklahoma. Observing that he had "no idea of the deep cruelty inmates were subjected to," the judge also ordered prison officials to stop mistreating convicts. Bohanon found that since the riots that had occurred at the prison in the summer of 1973, inmates were not provided with proper food, bedding, or heat, and that they were subjected to arbitrary punishments with chemical mace and tear gas. The judge noted that black inmates had received worse treatment than whites.

MARCH 31, 1974   Agreement Reached in Jackson, Mississippi. The U.S. Department of Justice announced that it had reached an agreement with the city of Jackson, Mississippi, calling for an increase in the number of blacks on municipal jobs and granting back pay up to $1,000 for blacks currently employed who had been denied promotion opportunities. The five-year plan set a goal of a 40 percent black work force, approximately the same percentage of blacks as in the city's population. At the time of the agreement, about eight hundred of Jackson's three thousand municipal workers were black, most of these serving in the lowest-paying job classifications. Both the police and fire departments were affected by the accord.

APRIL 1974   Virginia School Board Ordered to Rehire Black Teachers. The U.S. Circuit Court of Appeals for the Fourth District ordered the Nansemond County, Virginia School Board to rehire 56 black teachers who the court said were arbitrarily discriminated against in the administration of a national teaching test. The appellate court directed the U.S. District Court in Norfolk to reexamine the circumstances surrounding the dismissal of the teachers, a practice which was begun in 1971. The court also enjoined the school board from any further discrimination.

APRIL. 8, 1974   Hank Aaron Broke Babe Ruth's Record. Atlanta Braves baseball star Henry (Hank) Aaron hit his 715th career home run, thus becoming the all-time leading home run slugger. Aaron broke the record, previously held by the immortal Babe Ruth, at Atlanta Stadium. The Braves star had tied Ruth's record on April 4, 1974, in Cincinnati. The record-breaking pitch was thrown by a Los Angeles Dodgers pitcher, Al Downing.

APRIL 8, 1974   Denver Schools Ordered to Desegregate. U.S. Circuit Court Judge William E. Doyle ordered the desegregation of 70,000 students in the Denver public school system during the 1974–75 school year. The desegregation was to be accomplished mostly through the redrawing of attendance boundaries or zones and the pairing of black, white, and Mexican-American pupils so that they might share classrooms on a half-day basis. The order further provided that elementary schools would have between 40 percent and 70 percent white enrollment and that white enrollment in high schools would be between 50 and 60 percent. Judge Doyle rejected the school board's plan to close twelve of the public schools. He saw his move as a tactic to avoid adoption of a desegregation plan. He also ordered the merger of two high schools and the introduction of bilingual programs in schools with large numbers of Mexican-American pupils. The U.S.

Hank Aaron presenting a baseball to U.S. Army officer Joseph Kingston.

Supreme Court had first ordered a desegregation plan to be drawn up by Denver in 1973.

APRIL 8, 1974 Chicago Theological Seminary Named President. The Reverend C. Shelby Rooks was named the first black president of the predominantly white Chicago Theological Seminary, an affiliate of the United Church of Christ. Rooks, age forty-nine, was executive director of the Fund for Theological Education in Princeton, New Jersey, at the time of his new appointment.

APRIL 15, 1974 Steel Companies Agreed to End Discrimination. The U.S. Departments of Labor and Justice and the Equal Employment Opportunities Commission (EEOC) announced that nine major steel companies had agreed to a five-year plan for ending job discrimination against women and minorities, and would grant back pay of more than $30 million to the victims of such bias. The companies directly involved were the Allegheny-Ludlum Industries, Inc., Amco Steel Corporation, Bethlehem Steel Corporation, Jones and

Laughlin Steel Corporation, National Steel Corporation, Republic Steel Corporation, United States Steel Corporation, Wheeling-Pittsburgh Steel Corporation, and Youngstown Sheet and Steel Company. Together, they employed 347,000 employees in 249 plants at the time of the agreement. The steel companies vowed to restore more than $30 million in back pay to 34,000 black and Spanish-surnamed male employees and to 5,599 women who were adjudged to be victims of job bias. The back pay settlements ranged from $250 to $3,000 per person, depending upon length of service.

APRIL 18, 1974 Nationwide School Desegregation Reviewed. Peter Holmes, civil rights director of the Department of Health, Education, and Welfare (HEW), reviewed the progress of school desegregation in the nation on the eve of the 20th anniversary of the historic *Brown v. Board of Education* decision and the 10th anniversary of the enactment of the Civil Rights Act of 1964. Holmes told a group of Washington journalists that there were virtually no blacks in school with white students in the eleven southern states in 1964. By 1968, he noted, a total of 18.4 percent of the black pupils in the South were in majority white schools. This rose to 39.1 percent in 1970 and 44.4 percent in 1972. Perhaps of greater significance, Holmes said, was the fact that the black pupils in all-black schools decreased in the South from 68 percent in 1968 to 14.1 percent in 1970, and to 9.2 percent in 1972. On the other hand, Holmes noted that while current school year figures were not available, there was likely to be an increase in segregation in northern metropolitan school districts.

APRIL 20, 1974 Black Studies Curricula Reviewed. The *New York Times* reported a sixth anniversary assessment of black studies in predominantly white colleges and universities. Since the student protests in the 1960s, which helped to give impetus to black studies as a legitimate academic enterprise, 1,272 institutions of higher learning had offered at least one course in the

area. Although the tumult that surrounded the initiation of black studies movement had ceased, the controversy over the validity, viability, and aims of the programs continued. One of the more vocal critics of the programs was been Professor Martin Kilson, a black political scientist at Harvard University who called them "distinctly anti-intellectual and anti-achievement in orientation." Others saw them differently. Professor Barbara A. Wheeler of the City University of New York supported black studies as different from traditional studies in that they are organized around the black experience rather than around the subject matter, allowing the black student to see the impact of the event on his own life. Professors Elias Blake, head of the Institute for Services to Education; Henry Cobb, dean of Southern University at Baton Rouge; and Tobe Johnson, director of undergraduate African American studies programs for the Atlanta University Center, completed an analysis of twenty-nine black studies programs for the U.S. Office of Education just prior to the *Times* report. Blake told the *Times* that the ideological questions had been settled, saying, "God knows we need more study on black Americans. The issue is how do you build a good program." The Blake-Cobb-Johnson team found that only carefully structured programs were likely to survive in an era when colleges were undergoing financial retrenchment.

APRIL 22, 1974 Number of Elected Black Officials Released. The Joint Center for Political Studies, a privately funded research organization, reported from Washington that 2,991 blacks held political office in forty-five states and the District of Columbia, a gain of more than 300 between 1972 and 1973 and a jump of more than 1,000 from 1969. The center noted that most of the gains during 1973 had resulted from municipal elections. For example, 1,080 out of the latest total were city councilmen, and 108 were mayors. Michigan led in the number of black elected officials with 194, followed by Mississippi with 191. Other states with 150 or more black officeholders included New York, New Jersey, Illinois, Alabama, Arkansas, and Louisiana.

APRIL 25, 1974   San Francisco Police Investigation Ruled Unconstitutional. U.S. District Court Judge Alfonso J. Zirpoli in San Francisco ruled that the San Francisco police had violated the constitutional rights of six hundred black men they had stopped for questioning in their investigation of the so-called "Zebra" killings ("Operation Zebra" was the police code used in the dragnet officers conducted in their probe of the random slayings of twelve whites). Zirpoli issued an injunction prohibiting their profile of the Zebra killer, a slim-built young black man, as the sole basis for stopping men for questioning. The suit was filed by the American Civil Liberties Union.

APRIL 26, 1974   Mississippi Voting Act Rejected. The U.S. Department of Justice rejected a Mississippi act eliminating party primaries and replacing them by a single open primary in which no candidate could be elected with less than a majority vote. The Justice Department said that such a system would discriminate against independent candidates, and thus against blacks, since most of the successful black candidates in recent general elections had run as independents. The Mississippi legislature was seeking to repeal current statutes which required a majority vote to win the separate party primaries but which allowed independents to run in the general election and win with only a plurality. Under the Voting Rights Act of 1965, states like Mississippi, where a pattern of voter discrimination had been found, were required to submit changes affecting the suffrage to the justice department for approval.

MAY 1, 1974   ACLU and NAACP Appeals Rejected. U.S. District Court Judge Albert Henderson in Atlanta ruled that the city's school system had done all it could to desegregate public education. Attorneys for the American Civil Liberties Union (ACLU) and the NAACP had argued for increased desegregation in the

system, which only had an 18 percent white enrollment. The ACLU argued for more desegregation through a merger of the Atlanta city schools with surrounding suburban systems. The NAACP wanted more desegregation within the bounds of the current Atlanta system. Judge Henderson rejected both appeals and allowed previous court decisions approving the Atlanta Compromise school desegregation plan to stand. That controversial program required a minimum of school integration. Attorneys for the ACLU and NAACP filed notices of appeal to the 5th Circuit Court of Appeals in New Orleans.

MAY 7–14, 1974   Primary Election Results. In primary elections held in the spring, southern blacks continued to increase their numbers in major posts in state governments and blacks continued to hold the mayor's office in major American cities. Fourteen blacks were assured election to the Alabama House of Representatives in the May 7 primary. Two blacks were assured election to the Alabama State Senate, with the possibility of one other also being selected. In North Carolina, three blacks won state house seats and one a post in the state senate in the May 7 primary. A black was elected to a municipal judgeship in Nashville, Tennessee. Another was elected a constable in Cleveland, and still another won an alderman's seat in Ripley, Tennessee. Three blacks led in contests for seats in the Texas legislature. Kenneth A. Gibson won an easy victory in his second bid for mayor of Newark, New Jersey, on May 24. Gibson, the first black mayor of a major northeastern city, claimed that his victory showed that "Newark had come up from its past." He noted that the racial issue which divided the city during the 1970 mayoral election was not a major factor in the current campaign. Gibson won the support of about 65 percent of the 118,000 registered voters in defeating State Senator Anthony Imperiale. Also, in the May 7 Alabama primary, Alabama governor George Wallace made a direct appeal for black votes for the first time. Estimates of the number he actually received ranged from about 10 percent to as much as 30 percent. Wallace won important backing from several black Alabama politicians, including Mayor Johnny Ford of Tuskegee. Despite criticism from fellow blacks throughout the nation, Ford stood by his support for Governor Wallace. The young mayor justified his actions on the fact that Wallace had been responsive to the economic problems of Tuskegee and had aided the city in receiving state and federal grants. In connection with the spring elections, a joint report issued by the Voter Education Project in Atlanta, the Joint Center for Political Studies, and the Lawyers Committee for Civil Rights Under Law in Washington, showed that implementation of the 1965 Voting Rights Act led to a 169 percent increase in the number of black elected officials in the South between 1969 and 1974 alone. According to the report, there were 299 black elected officials in the six Southern states covered by the act—Alabama, Georgia, Louisiana, Mississippi, South Carolina, and Virginia—in 1969. By 1974, the number had risen to 815, a 169 percent increase.

MAY 8, 1974   Voter Registration Bill Defeated. Southern Democratic Congressmen, reportedly concerned about a major increase in black registered voters, joined with Republicans to defeat a bill (by a vote of 204 to 197) which would have allowed voters to register for federal elections by postcard.

MAY 16, 1974   Four Indicted in "Zebra" Killings. Four young black men were indicted in the random "Zebra" killings of whites which left the city of San Francisco tense for five months. Indicted on various charges of murder, robbery, and assault with a deadly weapon were Manuel Moore, J. C. Simon, Larry C. Green, and Jessie Cooks. All but Cooks were arrested during a massive manhunt by police on May 1, known as "Operation Zebra." Cooks was already serving a prison term for murder. Twelve murders and six assaults were attributed by police to the Zebra killers. During "Operation

Zebra," San Francisco police blanketed the city stopping and searching young black males. A federal judge subsequently ruled the searches unconstitutional.

MAY 16, 1974   Bill Approved to Limit Court-Ordered Busing. The U.S. Senate approved a bill to limit court-ordered busing to achieve school desegregation but allowed judges to issue such orders as they saw fit. The principal new limitation provided that pupils should not be bused beyond the next nearest school to their homes. The legislation also required the consideration of alternatives to achieve desegregation before any busing could be required. These included such things as construction of new schools, revision of attendance zones, and permission for students to transfer to schools in which their race was a minority. The bill also stated that the new limitations were not intended to inhibit the courts from ordering busing if such measures were necessary to enforce the equal rights provisions of the U.S. Constitution.

MAY 17, 1974   Harvard Psychiatrist Addresses Homicide Among Blacks. In a speech at Emory University in Atlanta, Dr. Alvin Poussaint, a black psychiatrist affiliated with the Harvard School of Medicine, gave a major assessment of the growing incidence of homicide among blacks. Poussaint said that 23 percent of the deaths among black males aged seventeen to twenty-five were the result of homicide, and that the matter should be treated as a health problem. Among the causes of homicide among blacks, according to Poussaint, is "black racism" or low self-esteem, which is evidenced by the use of racial epithets before a homicide is committed and by an inner battle by black men to preserve their self-respect in a racist society. Another contributing factor is the devaluation of African American life. Because of this, Poussaint said, some police officers do not follow up on solving crimes in black neighborhoods and the media fail to give much attention to homicide unless it involves whites. Poussaint contended that the American black community was in a state of despair and demoralization, partly because of its failure to realize some of the dreams of the civil rights era and partly because of governmental corruption. When such corruption goes unpunished, he said, a "jungle mentality is created and people begin to believe that they can do whatever they can get away with." Reduction of crime among blacks, Poussaint suggested, required the development of new values and psychological as well as political approaches. He called for the regulation of violence depicted in the media, particularly as portrayed in black exploitation films; the establishment of homicide prevention centers to help potential criminals before they commit murder; the control of handguns; increased black employment, particularly among black youths; and the promotion of black pride or black consciousness programs. Although the matter was defined by Poussaint as a black health problem, he concluded that it would take interracial cooperation to solve it. Poussaint is the author of *Why Blacks Kill Blacks* (1972).

MAY 17, 1974 Anniversary of *Brown v. Board of Education* Observed. The twentieth anniversary of the historic Supreme Court decision *Brown v. Board of Education*, which outlawed school segregation, was observed in the nation. In assessing the impact of the decision, the editors of the *Atlanta Constitution*, the South's leading daily newspaper, admitted that even after a generation, racial prejudice and discrimination had not been eliminated. This fact gave credence, in the editor's opinion, to the view that one cannot legislate morals. Yet, the *Constitution* said, "there is no denying that tremendous progress has been made in race relations in our country since 1954. . . . The progress, the vast changes in education, in employment, in housing, in politics, was the result of a struggle for civil rights that was given a decisive impetus on the day the Supreme Court ruled in the case of *Brown v. Board of Education of Topeka* in 1954." The noted black syndicated columnist Carl Rowan, in his as-

sessment of *Brown* twenty years later, found that "we are still a racist society," and that the historic school decision did not deliver justice to the black plaintiffs of 1954, or even to their children. "Some of the litigants in that 1954 decision," he said, "never saw a day of desegregated education. They saw evasion, circumvention, massive resistance and a generation of litigation." One of the plaintiffs, Linda Brown Smith (the "Brown" in the famous 1954 case) was now a grown woman with children of her own. In Atlanta, at an April 1974 meeting of the Association of Social and Behavioral Scientists (ASBS), a mostly black professional group, she recalled her family's motivations for permitting her to become a plaintiff. The family was incensed by the fact that their children had to wait in often inclement weather to be taken to black schools in Topeka when a white school was within walking distance from their home. Ironically, Smith said she now opposed crosstown busing to achieve racial desegregation in the schools.

MAY 18, 1974 Hooks Encouraged White Participation in NAACP. Benjamin L. Hooks, the only black member of the Federal Communications Commission (FCC), called for increased participation by whites in the NAACP. Although Hooks acknowledged that there was a difference between being born black and being born white, in that those "born black live in the valleys while those born white live on the mountain tops," he also said "We made a mistake when we close the doors on our white brothers." Hooks also urged more blacks to join the organization as he spoke to the 38th Annual NAACP Freedom Banquet held in Port Huron, Michigan. Hooks was appointed to the FCC by President Nixon in 1972. Other blacks, including the late Harlem congressman Adam Clayton Powell, Jr., had repeatedly asked the NAACP to purge itself of white influence.

MAY 22, 1974 Montgomery Judge Ordered New Desegregation Plan. U.S. District Court Judge Frank M. Johnson, Jr., in Montgomery,

Alabama, rejected crosstown busing as a remedy for the desegregation of some predominantly black schools in Montgomery County and instead ordered a new desegregation plan, one which allowed, with some exceptions, elementary school children to attend neighborhood schools. He endorsed the creation of a biracial committee to help the school board carry out the program.

MAY 24, 1974 Duke Ellington Died. Edward Kennedy "Duke" Ellington, one of America's greatest musician-composers, died in New York at age seventy-four.

Described as a musical genius, Ellington began playing the piano at age seven, composed his first song at seventeen, and began playing professionally at eighteen. He wrote more than a thousand compositions, including "Take the A Train," "Don't Get Around Much Anymore," "Satin Doll," and "Caravan." In later years he composed several orchestral pieces, tone poems, jazz masses, film, television, and ballet scores, and several operas. His orchestra was one of the few of the big bands to thrive after the 1940s. Some of the members of his orchestra remained with him for more than forty years.

Among Ellington's numerous awards were the NAACP's Spingarn Medal, the French Legion of Merit (France's highest honor), and America's highest civilian honor, the Medal of Freedom, bestowed upon him in 1970 by President Richard M. Nixon. The president had told Ellington in February 1974 that "There'll never be another you."

The NAACP responded to Ellington's death by noting: "Few composers have attained the greatness of stature that was the Duke's at the time of his death. Prolific, versatile, and popular, the Duke claimed the hearts of a wide range of followers, black and white, rich and poor. He was indomitable." Although sometimes criticized for not taking on an active role in the civil rights movement, Ellington himself claimed that "protest and pride in the Negro

have been the most significant themes in what we've done." His composition of "My People" was a musical salute to African Americans.

MAY 25, 1974 Jury Visited Site of Police Slayings. A federal grand jury paid a personal visit to Southern University at Baton Rouge, Louisiana, to inspect the site where two students, Denver Smith and Leonard Brown, were shot to death on November 16, 1972. The jury was investigating the slaying of the youths by law enforcement officers during a student demonstration to determine whether or not their civil rights had been violated.

MAY 27, 1974 Demonstrators Protest Atlanta's Police Chief. About a thousand orderly demonstrators marched through downtown Atlanta, Georgia, demanding the ouster of the city's controversial police chief, John Inman. The marchers were led by veteran protester Hosea Williams, formerly a top aide to slain civil rights leader Martin Luther King, Jr. Many Atlanta blacks had labelled the white police chief a racist and had long sought his removal. Atlanta's black mayor, Maynard Jackson, attempted to fire Inman on May 3, 1974, for administrative inefficiency and insubordination but was prohibited from doing so by a Dekalb County Superior Court judge. The marchers reaffirmed their support of the efforts to oust Inman.

JUNE 4, 1974 James Meredith Nominated for Congress. James Meredith, the first officially recognized black student to attend the University of Mississippi, led a field of five candidates for the Democratic congressional nomination in the Fourth District of Mississippi. Meredith, a forty-three-year-old businessman, had previously run for the U.S. Senate in 1972 and the Jackson City Council in 1973. Forty-four percent of the population of the fourth district was black at the time of the election. Meredith assessed his primary victory as a milestone in the black struggle for self-determination and full freedom, boasting that he had won the nomination without "white folks' money" and without "white folks' niggers, white folks' colored people, and white folks' Negroes."

JUNE 6, 1974 Nixon Made Racial and Ethnic Slurs. The *Washington Star-News* reported that President Richard Nixon called the U.S. Supreme Court's only black justice, Thurgood Marshall, a "jackass" in a tape recording of a White House conference with then-counsel John W. Dean III on February 28, 1973. In the same conversation, the President reportedly made other racial and ethnic slurs, particularly against Jews. The tape recording was one of many released to the public during the Watergate scandal.

JUNE 16, 1974 General Assembly of the Presbyterian Church Elected First Black Moderator. The Reverend Lawrence W. Bottoms, a Decatur, Georgia, minister, was elected as the first black moderator of the General Assembly of the Presbyterian Church of the United States at its 114th general meeting in Louisville, Kentucky. Bottoms, a sixty-six-year-old native of Selma, Alabama, had long experience as a pastor and leader of Georgia's black Presbyterians. A strong supporter of racial integration and toleration, Bottoms's election placed him at the head of that portion of the Presbyterian Church that broke with its national body to defend slavery before the Civil War.

JUNE 17, 1974 Martin Luther King, Jr., Portrait Defaced. A tour guide in the Georgia State Capitol in Atlanta reported that the portrait of slain civil rights leader Martin Luther King, Jr., was defaced with a red ink pen. Although the portrait was only slightly damaged, it was removed immediately and placed with the artist, Paul Mandus, for repairs. Two days later, Georgia Governor Jimmy Carter announced that a black woman who had a history of mental illness had marred the King portrait. The woman told state officials that she scribbled on the painting to show her respect for King. The incident was reminiscent of the

stabbing King had suffered at the hands of a knife-wielding black woman in 1958. The King portrait was the first of a black Georgian to hang at the state capitol.

JUNE 21, 1974 University Desegregation Plans Accepted. The U.S. Department of Health, Education, and Welfare (HEW) accepted university system desegregation plans from nine states, eight of them in the South. The HEW action stemmed from an order issued in February 1973, by U.S. District Court Judge John H. Pratt in Washington, D.C., which required the department to increase efforts to assure that the states were in compliance with the Civil Rights Act of 1964. States winning approval of their desegregation plans were Arkansas, Florida, Georgia, Maryland, North Carolina, Oklahoma, Pennsylvania, and Virginia. The HEW rejected Mississippi's plan and announced that it would initiate a lawsuit against that state. Louisiana refused to submit a plan and was promptly sued by the HEW. Louisiana officials had protested attempts by federal authorities to force a merger of the state's black and white universities.

At the time, black educators and civil rights leaders across the country had become increasingly divided over the question of desegregation in higher education. Many blacks feared losses of jobs, social status, and aspects of their cultural heritage through desegregation plans that involved merger. Black students, particularly those in state-supported institutions, formed a nation-wide coalition called "Save Black Schools" to protest school mergers or other actions that might destroy the racial identification of their colleges. On the other hand, many civil rights leaders continued to clamor for desegregation at all costs.

In approving the new desegregation plans, HEW Civil Rights Director Peter E. Holmes remarked, "We have seen the development of consciousness, a sensitivity and an awareness to the problems of predominantly black institutions and minority students that was absent in these states in previous years."

JUNE 21, 1974   James Earl Ray Reconsidered. U.S. District Court Judge Robert McRae, Jr., began a preliminary hearing in Memphis, Tennessee, to determine whether or not James Earl Ray, the confessed assassin of Dr. Martin Luther King, Jr., should receive a new trial. Ray was sentenced in 1969 to a term of ninety-nine years for the slaying of King on April 4, 1968. He was serving his time in the Tennessee State Prison at Nashville. Ray had sought a new trial on the grounds that he was pressured into pleading guilty by his original attorneys, Percy Foreman and Arthur Haynes, Sr., because of their alleged financial relationships with William Bradford Huie, author of one of the first books to be published about King's death. Ray's new attorney, Robert Livingston, had also charged that his client was innocent of King's murder and that two professional assassins hired by four wealthy, socially prominent Americans had killed the Nobel Prize-winning civil rights leader.

JUNE 21, 1974   Boston Schools Ordered to Desegregate. U.S. District Court Judge W. Arthur Garrity, Jr., ruled in Boston, Massachusetts, that the Boston public school system was unconstitutionally segregated and ordered the implementation of a desegregation plan, including the busing of several thousand school children in the fall of 1974. The order prohibited enrollments of 50 percent or more non-whites in any school. There were 95,000 pupils attending Boston public schools at the time of the decision. The Boston edict stemmed from a suit filed on behalf of black parents by the NAACP in the spring of 1972. The blacks contended that Boston operated a dual school system and asked the court to dismantle it.

JUNE 22, 1974   Humphrey Introduced Bill to Honor Minority Leaders. Senator Hubert H. Humphrey, a Minnesota Democrat, introduced a bill in congress providing for the placing in

the U.S. Capitol of the portraits and statues of individuals from minority groups who had made significant contributions to the nation's history. Humphrey said that the statues and paintings now existing in the Capitol building "do not properly reflect the ethnic, cultural, and racial diversity of the people of the United States who have made outstanding contributions to our country."

JUNE 22, 1974   Navy Found No Basis in Racial Charges. The U.S. Navy reported that its investigation showed no basis for accusations of racial discrimination made by a group of black sailors who refused to return to the aircraft carrier USS *Midway* when it left the Yokosuka Naval Base near Tokyo, Japan, the previous week. Eight of the fifty-five sailors involved called for the U.S. Congress to investigate conditions aboard the ship and demanded replacement of the ship's captain, Richard J. Schutte. They complained of torture in the brig, long duty hours, and dangerous work, which they said they were forced to perform. Naval officials reported that twenty-two of the absentees had returned to their base by June 22 and that the remaining thirty-three were listed as unauthorized absentees. The navy reasoned that since the complaint of racial bias was found to be unsubstantiated, the men were being misled by private organizations trying to exploit them for their own purposes. There was no further elaboration. The *Midway* incident was one in a series of racially-related events involving black armed forces personnel. Although naval officials had announced new and far-reaching policies to combat bias as early as 1971, this branch of the service continued to experience racial problems.

JUNE 26, 1974   Demonstration Led to Violence in Atlanta. Atlanta police officers armed with clubs broke up a march of about 250 blacks and arrested fourteen people, including the demonstration's leader, Hosea Williams, president of the local chapter of the Southern Christian Leadership Conference (SCLC). Seven people, including three police officers, were injured in the disturbance. The violent conflict, the first in Atlanta since the riots of the 1960s, came as the marchers sought to protest the killing by police of a seventeen-year-old black youth the previous weekend and to continue their demand that the city's police chief, John Inman, be removed from office. The blacks arrested were charged with parading without permits.

The controversial police chief defended the force used against the marchers, but the city's black mayor, Maynard Jackson, described it as excessive. The latest incident occurred as the Georgia Supreme Court was considering whether the city of Atlanta could legally fire Inman, who was viewed by many of the city's whites as a staunch defender of law and order, but by many blacks as a racist.

JUNE 29, 1974 Conspiracy Suspected in King Assassination. Robert Livingston, the Memphis, Tennessee, attorney handling the legal appeals of James Earl Ray, the convicted assassin of Martin Luther King, Jr., told newsmen he was convinced that a conspiracy existed in the slaying of the civil rights leader. The attorney said he was contacted on March 22, 1974, by an intermediary for the gunmen actually hired to kill King. The intermediary and two other men were prepared to testify before a grand jury that they were hired to kill King by four prominent black and white men, according to Livingston. The theory of a conspiracy in the assassination of the famed civil rights leader had been previously discounted by law enforcement officials. They continued to insist that James Earl Ray acted alone.

JUNE 30, 1974 Mother of Martin Luther King, Jr., Killed. A young black man interrupted the worship services at Ebenezer Baptist Church in Atlanta with gunfire, killing church deacon Edward Boykin and Alberta King, mother of slain civil rights leader Martin Luther King, Jr. Another worshipper, Mrs. Jimmie

Mitchel, was wounded. The alleged gunman, identified as Marcus Chenault of Dayton, Ohio, was subdued by other worshippers, including Derek King, grandson of the slain woman. Chenault told Atlanta police that he had orders from "his god" to go to Atlanta and kill the Reverend Martin Luther King, Sr., father of the Nobel Prize-winning civil rights leader. Instead, he allegedly fired upon Mrs. King and others as the sixty-nine-year-old matriarch of the King family played "The Lord's Prayer" on a church organ.

The accused slayer was described as an Ohio State University dropout who became deeply involved in a small religious cult that claimed that blacks were descendants of the original Jews. Chenault was said to have taken the name "Servant Jacob" and discarded his original name. The cult reportedly believed that black Christian ministers deceived African Americans and hence were the cause of many of the social and economic woes of blacks.

Mrs. Martin Luther King, Sr., was born Alberta Williams, the daughter of the Reverend Adam Daniel Williams, one of the founders of the historic Ebenezer Baptist Church. Her husband, a powerful religious and political figure in Atlanta for more than twenty-five years, succeeded Williams as pastor of the church. Dr. Martin Luther King, Jr., was serving as co-pastor of the church at the time of his assassination in April 1968. Another son, the Reverend A. D. Williams King, drowned in 1969.

Reacting to the tragedy, Atlanta Mayor Maynard H. Jackson compared the deaths of the King family to those of the family of the late President John F. Kennedy, stating "Never have I seen a family suffer so much for so long and yet give such brilliant leadership."

JUNE 30, 1974 Alabama Improved Hiring Practices. The *Atlanta Journal-Constitution* reported that the state of Alabama was moving toward total compliance with a federal court order issued in 1972 which required that racial discrimination in hiring be eliminated. When the suit was filed in 1970, only a few blacks were on the state's payroll, most of these in janitorial and other low-paying jobs. As of June 30, 3,000 of the state work force of 21,000 were black. At that rate of hiring, the state was about four years away from reaching the court-assigned goal of a 25 percent black work force. At the upper levels, a black executive assistant had been hired by the head of the Public Service Commission and the Attorney General had selected several black assistants. Alabama Governor George C. Wallace, according to the report, had named several blacks to positions on various governmental boards, commissions, and committees but had not hired a single black to an administrative position. The report quoted an unidentified black leader as saying that Alabama "will someday have the most model race relations program of any state in the Union."

JULY 1, 1974 United Negro College Fund Received Large Donation. The *Atlanta University Center Digest* reported that the largest single gift ever donated by a black organization was received by the United Negro College Fund (UNCF). UNCF executive director Christopher F. Edley announced that the $132,000 gift came from the Links, Inc., a national black women's social organization. At the time, the Links had more than 130 chapters in thirty-five states across the nation. Helen G. Edmonds, a North Carolina Central University history professor and president of the Links, said that her organization "recognized the absolute importance of higher education to black people at this point in history and [agreed] wholeheartedly with the UNCF slogan, 'A Mind Is a Terrible Thing to Waste.'"

JULY 3, 1974 Funeral for Alberta King Held. More than six hundred mourners, including First Lady Betty Ford, Mrs. Nelson Rockefeller, Georgia governor Jimmy Carter, and Atlanta mayor Maynard H. Jackson, attended funeral services for Alberta King, mother of the slain civil rights leader, in Atlanta, Georgia.

Mrs. King was murdered by a gunman on June 30, 1974.

JULY 4, 1974 Davis and Abernathy Led Protests in Raleigh. Several thousand protesters, led by black Communist Angela Davis and SCLC president Ralph David Abernathy, marched on the North Carolina state capitol in Raleigh to call for an end to the death penalty in that state. The march, which was organized by the National Alliance Against Racist and Political Repression, was called by its organizers "a rebirth of the civil rights movement of the 1960s, but on a higher level." During the march, twelve picketers representing the American Nazi Party, the Ku Klux Klan, and similar groups stood alongside the route holding signs urging segregation forever as well as support for Governor George Wallace of Alabama as president of the United States. Raleigh police kept the two groups apart amid jeering and shouting. There were no major incidents or arrests. The crowd of four to five thousand protesters were invited to the city by its black mayor, Clarence Lightner.

JULY 5, 1974 Blacks Protest Police Shooting. Approximately 200 blacks marched about seven miles along Highway 41 in Talbot County, Georgia, to protest the shooting of a young black man by the white police chief of Woodland. Willie Gene Carraker, a twenty-five-year-old black resident of Woodland, died from gunshot wounds on June 29, 1974. The black man's family accused Police Chief Doug Watson of aggravated assault and murder in the slaying of Carraker. These charges were subsequently dismissed by a local Justice of the Peace. In the march on July 5th, black protesters, led by SCLC field secretary Tyrone Brooks, demanded the prosecution and removal of the chief. During the demonstration Brooks told the crowd: "We are sick and tired of white folks shooting down our young men every weekend. We are sick and tired of being treated like second class citizens." Woodland city attorney

George R. Jacobs defended the dismissal of charges against Chief Watson and advised that the matter be considered by the county grand jury in November, or by a specially called grand jury.

JULY 6, 1974 United Methodist Church Abolished Last All-Black Districts. The *Atlanta Constitution* reported that the United Methodist Church had abolished districts that were racially segregated. According to the report, the last all-black districts, ones in Mississippi and South Carolina, were abolished in June 1974. At the same time, Methodist officials announced that 37 of its 530 districts in the United States were now headed by ethnic minority persons, including 34 blacks.

JULY 7, 1974 Blacks Recognized in *Time* Magazine. In a special supplement to *Time* magazine, fifteen blacks were among two hundred people named who seem destined to provide the country with a new generation of leadership. *Time* said the principal criterion for inclusion on its list was that the persons selected have the capability to achieve significant civic or social impact. Eligibility was restricted to individuals forty-five years old and younger. The blacks named included: State Senator Julian Bond of Georgia; Congresswoman Yvonne Braithwaite Burke of California; Congressman Ronald V. Dellums of California; Marian Wright Edelman of the Children's Defense Fund; Mayor Kenneth A. Gibson of Newark, New Jersey; Earl G. Graves, founder of *Black Enterprise* magazine; Mayor Richard Hatcher of Gary, Indiana; Mayor Maynard Jackson of Atlanta, Georgia; Congresswoman Barbara C. Jordan of Texas; Vernon E. Jordan of the Urban League; John Lewis of the Voter Education Project; Eleanor Holmes Norton, Chairman of the New York City Commission on Human Rights; Congressman Charles Rangel of New York; Bill Russell, coach of the Seattle Supersonics; and Congressman Andrew Young of Georgia.

AUGUST 1974 Beverly Johnson Appeared on *Vogue*'s Cover. Beverly Johnson became the first black model to adorn the cover of *Vogue* magazine. Johnson had won a full academic scholarship to Boston's Northeastern University but left after her freshman year to pursue modeling as a career. She became one of the world's top high fashion models as well as an outspoken and career-minded woman. When a radio host commented that she was the biggest black model in the business, she replied: "No, I'm not. I'm the biggest model—period."

AUGUST 19, 1974 Congressional Hiring Practices Investigated. The Joint Committee on Congressional Operations, which handles hiring requests for members of Congress, began an investigation to determine whether one senator and nineteen congressmen were duped or actually had been practicing racial or religious discrimination in seeking staff personnel. The *Fort Worth Star Telegram* reported on August 18, 1974, that it had obtained copies of the hiring forms with varying discriminatory requests from Senator William Scott from Virginia and members of the House of Representatives. Senator Lee Metcalf from Montana, chairman of the Joint Committee, said that some of the request forms contained such notations as "no minorities," "white only," "no Catholics," or "no Blacks." While most of the congressmen disclaimed responsibility for the biased forms, Senator Metcalf said it was "possible that (discriminatory) limitations expressed were those of the staff persons placing the request or a misunderstanding by the office staff."

AUGUST 23, 1974 Franklin W. Morton Elected to VFW Post. Franklin W. Morton was elected chief legal advisor for the Veterans of Foreign Wars (VFW). He was the first black person to hold a national leadership position in the organization.

AUGUST 25, 1974 Former HUD Secretary Criticized Federal Policies. Robert C. Weav-

Beverly Johnson on the cover of *Vogue*. (Courtesy of *Vogue*.)

er, former Secretary of Housing and Urban Development (HUD) and the first black to serve in a presidential cabinet, said during a news conference in Atlanta that the federal government had a laissez-faire attitude that threatened efforts for equal opportunity in housing. Weaver said the attitude was based on the revenue-sharing policy of allowing federal funds to be allocated at the local level and the lack of responsibility for social issues on the federal level. He said: "Federal funds (for housing) without strings attached are used for other things. . . . Sophisticated and concerned people must be watchful and vigilant to see that there is equitable participation and involvement in access to housing. . . . The federal government can make an impact." Weaver, president of the National Committee Against Discrimination in Housing (NCADH), made his remarks as he prepared to address the Southern Regional Conference of the NCADH.

AUGUST 29, 1974 Unemployment and Poverty Statistics. The U.S. Department of Labor announced that in 1973 the unemployment rate in poverty areas of metropolitan centers was almost twice that in the non-metropolitan poverty areas, 9 percent as opposed to 4.7 percent. The report also revealed that 70 percent of the blacks living in poverty areas were in metropolitan centers. The total unemployment for blacks in all poverty areas was 10.8 percent as opposed to 4.6 percent for whites. The labor department defined a poverty area as a census tract in which at least one-fifth of the residents had income at or below $4,540 (based upon a non-rural family of four).

SEPTEMBER 7, 1974 National Black Network Announced Expansion. Owners of the National Black Network (NBN), the nation's first all-black radio network, announced plans to expand its coverage with a black news service. The twenty-four-hour-a-day service was expected to be fully operational by March 1, 1975, employ twenty-five reporters, and use

the resources of the networks' affiliates in sixty-eight major cities.

SEPTEMBER 7, 1974 Casper Weinberger Criticized. Public officials and spokesmen for civil rights groups criticized Secretary of Health, Education, and Welfare Casper Weinberger's latest pronouncement on school desegregation. During an interview on September 6, Weinberger said that the cutoff of federal funds for education, which had been used in the past to coerce recalcitrant southern school districts into compliance, would serve to increase segregation in the North. Secretary Weinberger denied that his department was hesitating on the question of desegregation, but admitted that "we are dealing with a very fierce public opposition to desegregation." Ruby Hurley, Southeastern Regional Director of the NAACP, disagreed with Weinberger's assessment that a cutoff of funds would be counterproductive and compared the conciliatory approach to northern school desegregation with the more forceful tactics in the South. According to Hurley, "Public school systems are often poor even without federal money. Officials who run segregated school systems will think twice if they are faced with a cutoff. . . . If you wait for people to change their minds on a problem like this without leverage, you'll wait a long time. . . . It's a lot easier to clean up somebody else's back yard than your own."

Atlanta School Superintendent Alonzo Crim responded to Weinberger's statement by declaring: "The law should be applied with equal force in all parts of the country . . . quite often segregation is intensified by these delays."

Margie Hames, an attorney for the American Civil Liberties Union who had handled many desegregation cases, expressed the belief that "segregation in the South was more open and easy for us to deal with. I don't think the North has accepted the fact yet that they have more subtle forms of segregation." In defense of Weinberger, Peter Holmes, director of HEW's office for civil rights enforcement, pointed out that the cutoff of funds and other legal actions are more complex in the North than in the South since segregation was not legalized in the North.

SEPTEMBER 9–OCTOBER 31, 1974 Boston Busing Program Drew Opposition.

The city of Boston, Massachusetts, began a program of busing to achieve school desegregation which sparked boycotts and demonstrations reminiscent of the early, vehement opposition to school integration in the South. In June 1974, U.S. District Court Judge W. Arthur Garrity had ordered the busing of about 18,200 of the city's 94,000 public school pupils as part of a plan to dismantle Boston's dual school system. Opposition arose immediately.

On September 9, 1974, Senator Edward M. Kennedy was heckled and splattered with a tomato as he tried to address an angry group of anti-busing demonstrators. The crowd, estimated at between eight and ten thousand, shouted insults, called for the impeachment of the senator, and sang "God Bless America" when Kennedy stepped to a microphone. After preventing Senator Kennedy from speaking at the John F. Kennedy Memorial Building, the demonstrators—most of them white women—marched to the federal building. They stopped in front of the office of Judge Garrity and shouted, "Garrity must go." Kennedy, an advocate of peaceful school integration, said he was disappointed that he had not been able to speak but assessed this treatment as milder than that he received at the hands of anti-war demonstrators.

On September 11, 1974, Boston school superintendent William Leary said that everything possible had been done in the time allowed to prepare for desegregation. Yet, he added, "I know there will be problems. I ask the public for patience." Boston mayor Kevin White, on the eve of the scheduled desegregation, appealed for calm but warned that swift and sure punishment would be measured out to those who resorted to violence. When the de-

segregation began on September 12, many white and black parents kept their children at home. Black children attending some of the schools, particularly in the white neighborhoods of South Boston, Hyde Park, and Dorchester, were subjected to jeers from angry white parents.

On September 16, a crowd of white teenagers and mothers clashed with police officers at South Boston High School. Twenty-two people were arrested during the confrontation. Police ordered the closing of bars and liquor stores in the area for the next two days.

Violence continued in Boston for the next several weeks. Four white students were injured in skirmishes with black students at the Washington Irving Junior High School in Roslindale on September 18. None of them required hospitalization. After the incident, forty black children walked out of the school. Police made no arrests. Eleven people, including three teachers, were injured on October 2 at the racially tense South Boston High School. A number of weapons were confiscated during the incident in which two black girls who allegedly pulled a knife on a police officer were arrested. Fighting broke out during an assembly of ninth graders at the Hart Deah Annex of South Boston High School on October 21. After this incident thirty of the forty white pupils walked out of the school; most of the 130 black pupils remained.

On October 26, Matt Koehl, national commander of the American Nazi Party, demonstrated in front of the Boston federal building, protesting Judge Garrity's desegregation orders. He bore a sign reading, "White Power." Koehl was arrested and charged with impeding access to a federal building. Three days later, three other Nazi Party members were charged with attempting to incite a riot as they distributed anti-black literature in south Boston. Those charges were later reduced to disorderly conduct. John W. Roberts, director of the Civil Liberties Union of Massachusetts, decried the arrests, saying that the state charges were a violation of the Nazis' constitutional rights. In a final decree, issued on October 30, 1974, Judge Garrity told the Boston school committee to complete the total desegregation of its schools by the fall of 1975. The final order authorized Boston school officials to use any known desegregation techniques, including busing (although this was to be minimized), changing school districts, and voluntary transfers. The judge promised a new order at a later date dealing with minority recruitment and hiring of school teachers and administrators.

The traumatic experience of desegregating schools in Boston highlighted the growing manifestation of white opposition to massive school desegregation in the North. It also struck many observers as a sign of retrogression in American race relations.

SEPTEMBER 12, 1974 Chenault Convicted in Murder of King's Mother. Marcus Wayne Chenault of Dayton, Ohio, was convicted and sentenced to death for the murder of Alberta King, mother of the slain civil rights leader, and Deacon Edward Boykin during a worship service at the Ebenezer Baptist Church in Atlanta on June 30, 1974. Chenault was identified as the gunman who interrupted that service with bullets. The Fulton County Court jury rejected Chenault's plea of insanity in delivering their verdict.

SEPTEMBER 17, 1974 Funding for Busing Prohibited. The U.S. Senate approved amendments to a $39.9 billion appropriations bill to prohibit the use of federal funds for busing to achieve school desegregation. According to the anti-busing amendment, which was approved by a vote of 45-42, federal funds could not be used for transporting students to achieve racial balance in schools. The practical effect of the bill, however, would be minimal, since very little federal money is used for such purposes.

SEPTEMBER 21, 1974 Voting Trends. White voters are reluctant to vote for black candidates for mayor in cities where blacks constitute a majority of the population, according to a study

appearing in the September issue of *Psychology Today*. In comparing recent mayoral elections in Los Angeles (a white majority city) with Detroit and Atlanta (black majority cities), the article's author, Professor Howard Schuman of the University of Michigan Institute for Social Research, found that Los Angeles was the only major city where close to a majority of whites voted for a black candidate (Thomas Bradley) in preference to a white candidate (Sam Yorty). Los Angeles, Schuman said, apparently separated the question of the candidate's own race from the issue of which race would control the city. By contrast, in Atlanta and Detroit, where whites were becoming the minority population, the elections became "full scale battles over which race would run the city."

In a previous study, Schuman had found that about 60 percent of the whites surveyed in fifteen cities said they would be willing to vote for a qualified black mayoral candidate of their own party. Yet, he pointed out, successful black mayoral candidates like Maynard Jackson of Atlanta and Coleman Young of Detroit received far less than half of the white vote.

Schuman concluded that while whites are becoming more liberal, they are still opposed to basic, structural changes in society. At the same time, he observed, blacks are becoming more open in their criticism of whites and are more distrustful of whites than in the past.

Schuman's study is entitled "Are Whites Really More Liberal?"

SEPTEMBER 27, 1974 "Bumping" Sanctioned in Civil Rights Case. U.S. District Judge Albert V. Bryan, Jr., in Richmond, Virginia, ordered the American Tobacco Company and Local 182 of the Tobacco Workers' International Union to allow blacks and females to "bump" white employees with less seniority. Having found Local 182 and the American Tobacco Company's two Richmond plants guilty of racial and sexual discrimination in violation of the Civil Rights Act of 1964, Judge Bryan directed the company to freeze hiring and promoting white male supervisors and adjust retirement and pension plans in order to halt discrimination. Any white employees who were displaced would be allowed to retain their present rates in the lower classifications. Litigation in the case began in March 1973. It is believed to be the first instance in which a court has sanctioned "bumping" in a civil rights case. At the time of the decision, the tobacco company employed more than 1,000 production workers at its two plants in Richmond. Of that number, 239 were black and 441 were female.

SEPTEMBER 28, 1974 Southern Black Population Decreased. The *Atlanta Inquirer* reported a study by the Southern Regional Council (SRC) which showed that the South, the historic home of African Americans, was going through a "whitening" process despite increasing black concentrations in the urban areas of the region. All Southern states, except Texas, were losing more blacks than were being replaced by the birthrate and the migration of young blacks from the North. According to the study, the black exodus from the South continued at such a steady pace that the region's black population, as shown in the 1970 Census, was down to 20 percent—the same percentage recorded in 1790. The loss of black populations was particularly acute in the rural areas. In Georgia, two-thirds of the state's 152 counties were losing blacks; in Mississippi, 90 percent of the counties had declining black populations. A similar story was told for Alabama, South Carolina, and Arkansas, all of which had 80 percent or more of their counties losing blacks. Conversely, 51 percent of the population of Atlanta was black. Augusta, Georgia, had a 50 percent black population, and New Orleans, Charleston, and Savannah boasted black populations of 45 percent or more. In sum, the study reported, there were ten metropolitan areas in the 11 southern states where the black population was 40 percent or more.

The SRC report's authors, Jack Tucker of Atlanta University and Everett S. Lee of the University of Georgia, concluded that the growth of the black population lagged behind that of whites, such that year by year, "the South becomes increasingly white. Losses of black population are frequent and heavy in rural counties, so Southern blacks are increasingly concentrated in metropolitan areas. And within the metropolitan areas, blacks are clustered in central cities with relatively few making their way into the more affluent suburbs."

"Generally," the report says, "people move from one area to another for one of two reasons, either the attractiveness of destination outweighs that of origin or there are so many negative features at the point of origin that any place seems better." Migration thus becomes a movement of the upper socio-economic classes to seek better opportunities and of the lower economic classes to escape oppression that can no longer be endured.

OCTOBER 3, 1974 Frank Robinson Became Baseball's First Black Manager. Frank Robinson, the only man in baseball history to be named Most Valuable Player in both the American and National Leagues, was named baseball's first black manager by the Cleveland Indians. During a press conference held to announce the appointment, Robinson said: "To say that this is a proud day for me would be an understatement. . . . If I had one wish in the world today, that wish would be to have Jackie Robinson here to see this happen. . . . I don't think I could have stood the pressure or have gone through what Jackie had to." Jackie Robinson (no relation to Frank) became the major league's first black baseball player in 1947. He died in 1972. Frank Robinson, as a professional player, had accumulated nearly 3,000 hits, including 574 home runs, before breaking the 105-year-old managerial color-line.

OCTOBER 3, 1974 Composer Scott Joplin Honored. A bronze plaque was placed upon the then-unnoticed and unattended grave of ragtime composer Scott Joplin, who died in 1917. Joplin began composing ragtime in 1899 with "The Maple Leaf Rag." Ragtime music, however, was largely ignored until it regained popularity through the soundtrack of a 1974 film, *The Sting*. The plaque on Joplin's grave, located in St. Michael's Cemetary in Queens, was purchased by the American Society of Composers, Authors, and Publishers (ASCAP).

OCTOBER 4, 1974   Research Money for Blacks Diminished. Money for research dealing with blacks has diminished, according to an assessment given by Professor Charles Hamilton of Columbia University. Although Hamilton decried the lack of money, saying "It may affect our budgets, but never our integrity or our legitimacy." Hamilton, co-author of the widely acclaimed book, *Black Power*, spoke to more than four hundred black professors and students at the W.E.B. Du Bois Conference on the American Black in Atlanta.

OCTOBER 12, 1974   Publisher Frank L. Stanley Died. Frank L. Stanley, Sr., owner and publisher of the *Louisville Defender* and veteran civil rights activist, died in Louisville, Kentucky, at age sixty-eight. Stanley, the son of a butcher, was born in Chicago. At the age of six, his family moved to Louisville. He attended Atlanta University, where he was an all-American quarterback and captain of the football and basketball teams, and the University of Cincinnati. He received honorary doctorate degrees from several universities, including the University of Kentucky. In 1933, Stanley went to work for the *Louisville Defender* as a reporter. Three years later he became editor, general manager, and a part owner. During the years that he published the *Defender*, it received more than thirty-five awards in journalism, including the President's Special Service Award of the National Newspaper Publishers' Association (NNPA) in 1970 and the coveted Russwurm Award in 1974. He was a co-founder of the NNPA and was elected its president on five separate occasions.

Stanley drafted the legislation which led to the desegregation of state universities in Kentucky by its General Assembly in 1950.

Ragtime composer Scott Joplin. (Bettmann Archive/Newsphotos, Inc.)

Ten years later he wrote the bill that created the Kentucky Commission on Human Rights, and was one of the original members of that body. His influence on race relations in Kentucky was noted by the *Louisville Courier Journal* on the occasion of the 25th anniversary of the *Defender* in 1950. "Much of the credit," the newspaper said editorially, "for the even and amiable pace Kentucky has maintained in its working out of race relations problems must be given the *Defender*." Stanley was the force behind the *Defender*'s role in that achievement.

OCTOBER 16, 1974   Black Businesses Addressed at Convention. Dr. Berkeley G. Burrell, president of the National Business League (NBL), told the 74th Annual Convention of the NBL in Atlanta that black businessmen must develop hard strategies in this time of economic turmoil. "If we do not come out of this 74th convention with a sound assessment of the situation and a unified front of committed allies to guarantee the continued survival of the black community and its economic resources," Burrell said, "a severe blow will be dealt to the potential economic independence of our people." The whole range of minority businesses, from the black capitalists to the Nation of Islam, were represented at the convention.

OCTOBER 26, 1974 Arson Suspected in Georgia Fires. Fire swept through three black-owned businesses in the heart of downtown Sparta, Georgia. Police suspected arson in the blazes, which destroyed a furniture store and damaged an adjacent warehouse and barber shop. Police also reported some attempted burglaries during the three-hour fight to bring the fires under control. On October 30, 1974, the *Atlanta Constitution* reported that the records of the furniture store burned on October 24 had been subpoenaed by a federal grand jury investigating the affairs of Hancock County's foremost black political leader, John McCown. Local investigators, however, were unable to say whether the subpoenaed records were destroyed in the fire.

OCTOBER 26, 1974 Black Insurance Companies Showed Trend. The *Atlanta Inquirer* quoted a report from the Department of Commerce that cited a trend of larger black insurance companies purchasing or merging with smaller ones to keep them from passing out of the hands of blacks. Overall, the number of black insurance companies had declined to thirty-nine, but the assets of these firms had increased within the past five years by $73 million.

OCTOBER 29, 1974 King's Assassin Denied Charges. James Earl Ray, convicted assassin of Dr. Martin Luther King, Jr., insisted during a federal court hearing in Memphis, Tennessee, that he did not slay the Nobel Peace Prize-winning civil rights leader. Ray admitted that he had purchased the gun that killed King and that he rented the room in the building from which the shot was fired, but said he did not pull the trigger. Ray referred to a mysterious individual as the possible slayer in a conspiracy to murder the civil rights leader. Prosecuting attorneys faced difficulties in their efforts to elicit further details from Ray because of a

ruling from presiding judge Robert McRae that only questions about what he told his previous lawyers and not about what he failed to tell them could be admitted. Ray was seeking his freedom or a new trial on the grounds that his original lawyers misled him into a guilty plea at the time of his 1968 trial. Those lawyers, Ray now contended, conspired with author William Bradford Huie for such a plea so that Huie could write a financially profitable book on King's assassination.

OCTOBER 29, 1974 Muhammad Ali Regained Title. Muhammad Ali regained the heavyweight boxing championship by defeating George Foreman in Kinshasa, Zaire. Ali, a thirty-two-year-old Black Muslim, knocked out the title holder, Foreman, in the eighth round of a scheduled fifteen-round match. Ali was stripped of his title in 1967 after being convicted of draft evasion. Four years later that conviction was overturned by the U.S. Supreme Court. The Zaire title fight was the richest contest in history, with both Ali and Foreman earning $5 million each.

OCTOBER 30, 1974 Election Abuses Reported in Georgia. A biracial group of citizens in Sparta, Georgia, requested that the state elections board send officials to observe the conduct of the November general elections in Hancock County. A committee of three persons sent to Hancock County under court order for the August primary elections reported widespread election abuses. That report, however, was ignored by the Hancock County grand jury in its September presentments. In the report on the August elections, the committee had said that the balloting was conducted in a tense and undesirable atmosphere caused partially by the presence of armed men in the polling places. Hancock County is the only county in Georgia with a black-run government. It has often been the scene of racial and political strife.

OCTOBER 31, 1974 Record Number of Blacks Sought Public Office. The Voter Education

Muhammad Ali with the heavyweight boxing championship belt. (Photo by Carl Nesfield.)

Project (VEP) in Atlanta reported the record number of 118 blacks were seeking major public office in the November general elections in nine southern states. Seven blacks were seeking congressional seats, fourteen were candidates for state senate seats, and the remaining ninety-seven blacks were candidates for state houses. The VEP predicted that at least thirty-one of the candidates for state legislative seats would be successful. In 1962, when the VEP first began monitoring and promoting black politi-

cal participation in the South, there were no black members in any southern legislature. The black political progress continued despite "repulsive national political scandals and severe economic problems," according to VEP executive director John Lewis. "The black gains in state legislative posts in 1974, and the possible addition of at least one black member of Congress from the South will be yet another milestone in a steady progression of black political gains in the past few years," Lewis concluded.

NOVEMBER 2, 1974   Huey Newton Sought for Murder. Huey P. Newton, co-founder of the Black Panther Party, was being sought for murder. Newton was accused of shooting seventeen-year-old Kathleen Smith in the head during a dispute on an Oakland street on August 6, 1974. She never regained consciousness. The results of the police investigation as to the cause of the dispute were not released. Newton jumped a bail of $55,000 and disappeared on August 23, 1974. The accusation of murder was the latest in a long history of altercations between Newton and the law.

NOVEMBER 5–6, 1974   Hosea Williams Acquitted. Controversial Atlanta civil rights activist Hosea Williams, who has had numerous encounters with the law, was acquitted on charges of simple battery on a police officer and of carrying a concealed and unlicensed pistol by two separate Fulton County Criminal Court juries. Williams was accused of grabbing the genitals of Officer A.L. Bradfield during a demonstration at the Martin Luther King, Jr., Nursing Home on September 15, 1972, and of carrying a pistol into the Atlanta Hartsfield International Airport on March 9, 1974. Williams's attorneys claimed that he was the victim of political harassment. Williams himself responded to the verdicts by declaring: "I carry only the love of God in my heart."

NOVEMBER 15, 1974   "Dixie" Removed from Marching Band's Repertoire. Robert Dancz, associate professor of music and director of the marching band at the University of Georgia, announced that the University of Georgia Redcoat Band would not play "Dixie" at future university football games. In a campus referendum held several days before Dancz's statement, students had approved the playing of the song by a margin of 3,467 to 1,270. Despite this vote, however, Dancz said that his band would under no circumstances play the song. It "brought out the worst in some people," he said, and "black people feel like it is a slap in the face. This isn't the same school it was twenty years ago and not many southern schools play 'Dixie' anymore." Dancz also said that playing the Civil War melody exposed his band members to physical danger.

DECEMBER 8, 1974 Discrimination Claims Rejected in Grand Rapids, Michigan. The Sixth U.S. Court of Appeals in Cincinnati upheld a lower court ruling that the Grand Rapids, Michigan, schools were not segregated. The appealate court said that "a review of the evidence and statistics in this case makes it clear not only that Grand Rapids was not guilty of acts of intentional segregation, but that much progress has been made toward elimination of the de facto segregation resulting from housing patterns." The court rejected the contentions of black plaintiffs that discriminatory acts of other individuals and governmental agencies were sufficient to support a finding of *de jure* segregation.

DECEMBER 21, 1974 Five Black Women Honored. Five black women were named among the forty most highly respected women in the United States, according to a poll appearing in the January 1975 edition of *Good Housekeeping* magazine. Those honored were California Congresswoman Yvonne Braithwaite Burke, New York Congresswoman Shirley Chisholm, Texas Congresswoman Barbara Jordan, civil rights activist Coretta Scott King, and actress Cicely Tyson. The blacks were selected from a slate of forty-seven prominent women presented to the readers of *Good Housekeeping* in the sixth

annual Most Admired Women's Poll. In the poll, King, whose name has been among the winners since 1970, ranked 19th, the highest position among the five black women selected. The total number of black women named for 1974 was three more than in 1973.

1975

JANUARY 1, 1975 Dillard University's New President. Samuel DuBois Cook assumed the presidency of Dillard University in New Orleans, Louisiana. Cook earned his bachelor's degree from Morehouse College and his master's and doctorate degrees from Ohio State University. Previously, he had taught at Atlanta University and Duke University and served as a consultant to the U.S. Office of Education and the Ford Foundation. Cook was also a former president of the Southern Political Science Association and, at the time of his appointment, was serving as a trustee of the Martin Luther King, Jr., Center for Social Change. Cook succeeded Broadus Butler as president of the 105-year-old predominantly African American college.

JANUARY 2–26, 1975 CIA and FBI Practices Questioned. Several reports appeared in the nation's newspapers revealing a history of Central Intelligence Agency (CIA) and Federal Bureau of Investigation (FBI) spying on African American individuals and organizations. The *New York Times* reported on January 2 that the CIA had been collecting data on singer Eartha Kitt since 1956. According to the CIA files, Kitt had danced, at the age of twenty, with a group whose leader allegedly had "served as a sponsor or endorser of a number of Communist-front activities"; she was involved in "escapades overseas and her loose morals were said to be the talk of Paris" in 1956; she had "a very nasty disposition" and was "a spoiled child, very crude," with "a vile tongue"; and she "often bragged that she had very little Negro blood." The CIA file also revealed that in 1960 Kitt signed an advertisement in support of the civil rights activities of the late Martin Luther King, Jr., which was also endorsed by "a number of persons identified in the past with the Communist party." However, the CIA report concluded that there was no evidence of any foreign intelligence connections on the part of Kitt. The detailed investigation of Kitt, according to the *Times*, was also possibly related to remarks that she made during a White House luncheon in January 1968. At that time, Kitt shouted that the nation's youth were in rebellion because they were being "snatched off to be shot in Vietnam." Both President and Mrs. Lyndon B. Johnson were reportedly upset by the singer's remarks.

In response to the investigation of Kitt, the *Atlanta Constitution*, on January 6, 1975, published an editorial that stated that "nobody in today's world should deny our government the right to protect itself and us by keeping a close eye on potential threats, foreign or domestic. The question is, who should do it and under what kind of controls and guidelines? The pursuit of national security should not lead us to a place where we jettison the Bill of Rights." Kitt responded, "I don't understand this at all. I think it's disgusting. . . . I've always lived a very clean life and I have nothing to be afraid of and I have nothing to hide."

On January 25, the *Washington Post* reported that the FBI had wiretapped the conversations of Martin Luther King, Jr., and other civil rights leaders during the 1964 Democratic National Convention in Atlantic City, New Jersey. The reports from the wiretaps, according to the *Post*, were delivered to President Lyndon B. Johnson.

These reports of government spying on African Americans came in the wake of the Watergate scandals and newer accusations that governmental agencies had illegally invaded the privacy of American citizens.

JANUARY 3, 1975 Swope Parkway National Bank Closed. The Swope Parkway National

Bank, the only black-operated bank in Kansas City, was declared insolvent by the Federal Deposit Insurance Corporation (FDIC). Officials, however, said that the bank, with total assets of $10.6 million, would be reopened on January 4 as the Deposit Insurance National Bank under FDIC receivership. The Deposit Insurance Bank stood ready to assume all of Swope's "insured and fully secure deposits." An FDIC spokesman said these moves were being taken "in recognition of both the practical and symbolic importance of the Swope Parkway National Bank to [Kansas City's] black community."

JANUARY 5, 1975 Vaughn Began Study of "Soul Food." Professor Moses W. Vaughn of the University of Maryland-Eastern Shore announced that he was studying the nutritive value of some types of soul food—the popular name for a number of items, including chitterlings, pigs' ears, pig knuckles and feet, hog maws, neck bones and pigs' tails, said to be particularly favored by African Americans. Vaughn said the study was expected to fill a gap in nutritional knowledge, for even the official Department of Agriculture handbook contained no mention of soul food pork products. Yet, according to Vaughn, consumer research organizations and the Agriculture Department had received numerous requests for information about these foods. Vaughn received a $175,000 federal grant for his two-year study.

JANUARY 8, 1975 Racial Discrimination at Television Stations. The Federal Communications Commission (FCC) denied the Alabama Educational Television Commission renewals of licenses for all eight of its television stations because of racial discrimination. The FCC said that the Alabama Commission had, between 1967 and 1970, failed to meet the high standards it expected broadcast stations to maintain. It found that the Alabama Commission had followed a racially discriminatory policy in its overall programming practices and through its "pervasive neglect" of Alabama's African American population. Furthermore, it had failed to adequately meet the needs of the public it served. Still, the FCC said the commission could continue to operate the television stations on an interim basis pending a final determination of its future. The denial of license renewal was one of the FCC's most severe and most rarely used actions.

JANUARY 8, 1975 Students Return to Classes. Students returned to school in South Boston, Massachusetts, for the first time in four weeks as more than four hundred police officers kept watch on the arrival and departure of school buses. Four schools in the South Boston area had been closed since December 11, 1974, when a white student was stabbed at South Boston High School. As the students returned to school, officials announced a first day attendance of 876 out of a total of 3,000 pupils enrolled in the four affected buildings. Meanwhile, the Boston School Committee appeared before U.S. District Court Judge W. Arthur Garrity, Jr., with a new desegregation plan. The new plan, which omitted busing, was the means by which the committee hoped to avoid punishment for contempt of court for three of its five members.

JANUARY 10, 1975 Unemployment in Atlanta. A crowd of three thousand people, most of them young African Americans, crashed into the glass doors at the Atlanta Civic Center Auditorium in their rush to apply for 225 new public-service jobs. The job seekers had gathered in the pre-dawn hours in search of employment. In December 1974, the unemployment rate in Atlanta had been 7.5 percent, but the jobless rate among African Americans was 9.2 percent. The spectacle at the Civic Center Auditorium pointed out again the growing economic desperation of African Americans during the current recession.

JANUARY 11, 1975 Mississippi Highway Patrol Misconduct. A committee of the Gover-

nor's Minority Affairs Council of Mississippi reported that it was investigating reports that highway patrol officers had beaten African Americans. The council, composed of fifteen African American citizens, met with Governor Bill Waller to inform him of its plan for the investigation.

JANUARY 12–15, 1975 King's Life Remembered. Celebrations were held throughout the nation commemorating the forty-sixth birthday of slain civil rights leader Martin Luther King, Jr. Much of the activity was focused in King's hometown, Atlanta, Georgia.

On January 12, King's widow, Coretta Scott King, gave a major new assessment of the current civil rights struggle. Excerpts from her statement follow:

"What we are seeing in the South is a transformation. . . . You don't have the tension in the South that you had 10-15 years ago. The battleground is definitely in the North now . . . Detroit, Chicago, New York—most of these cities are sitting on a powder keg because of neglect. Urban America is where it is going to happen in the 70's and 80's. The problems in the major cities across the country are the problems of America in miniature. Every city is beset by problems of poverty, crime and housing. . . . Blacks always suffer more than any other group. . . .

"[The Nixon administration was] totally unresponsive to the basic human needs of blacks and whites. . . . [In the Ford administration] the only thing is the climate is a little less oppressive. . . . I think that the people were so relieved to get rid of Nixon that they set Ford up as a kind of savior. I don't think that he's really a leader. . . .

"In some instances we still have to march but not as much as we once did. . . . I think the movement has reached a more sophisticated state. Marches, picketing and boycotting are part of it, but we are at the stage now where we have some political power. We are the balance of power in many areas. . . .

"We do have a lot to work on but I do believe Martin Luther King left us a great legacy and told us how we can achieve the American dream—a just and peaceful society."

King made her remarks during an interview with Walt Smith of United Press International.

Also in connection with the birthday celebration, a summit meeting of national civil rights and political leaders was held in Atlanta on January 13. The meeting, called to discuss the Voting Rights Act of 1965 and its possible extension or renewal, was sponsored by the Martin Luther King, Jr., Center for Social Change. Participants included United States Senators Hugh Scott, a Michigan Republican, and Birch Bayh, an Indiana Democrat; U.S. Representatives Ronald Dellums of California and Andrew Young of Georgia (both African Americans); former U.S. Attorney General Nicholas Katzenbach; National Urban League director Vernon E. Jordan; veteran civil rights leader Bayard Rustin, executive director of the A. Philip Randolph Institute; John Lewis, executive director of the Voter Education Project; Georgia State Senator Julian Bond; and Atlanta Mayor Maynard Jackson.

In his remarks at the conference, Senator Bayh said that other minorities needed the extension of the Voting Rights Act to foster their causes, because there was substantial evidence that the protections provided by the act could aid Mexican Americans especially. The Nixon administration, according to Bayh, tried to "gut" the Voting Rights extension bill in 1970, but he didn't anticipate that the Ford administration would try to do the same.

Former Attorney General Katzenbach expressed the opinion that the Voting Rights Act freed Southern white politicians from campaigns of "race, race, race" and enabled them to seek office without reference to race. It also

enabled African Americans to seek national office for the first time in forty years, he said.

In his remarks, Rustin said that the issues of the turbulent 1960s were African American issues—equality under the law and the end of segregation. But today the issues were broader and included African Americans, other minorities, and women and were economic and political in nature. The agenda, he said, had now changed from getting the rights whites had to the things whites wanted—"a job, a house, a decent education."

On January 15, an ecumenical service was held at the Ebenezer Baptist Church where King pastored, with the Reverend Theodore Hesburgh, president of Notre Dame University and former chairman of the U.S. Commission on Civil Rights, as the principal speaker. Other activities in King's hometown during the day included the dedication of the civil rights leader's birthplace as a national historic site and a "people's march" in the downtown area of the city.

JANUARY 15, 1975 Lewis Awarded Peace Prize. John Lewis, executive director of the Voter Education Project (VEP), was awarded the Martin Luther King, Jr., Non-violent Peace Prize for 1975. The award is the highest prize of the Martin Luther King, Jr., Center for Social Change. The presentation was made by Coretta Scott King, widow of the slain civil rights leader, who said of Lewis:

"We feel that this man exemplifies the life, the teachings, and the contributions of Martin Luther King, Jr., and certainly has brought about in his efforts the kind of non-violent social changes in our society that have moved us forward and will continue to move us toward the dream. . . . This young man is a very humble man, a deeply committed man, and a man whom I respect, admire, and love very deeply."

Lewis began his civil rights career as a member, and later executive secretary, of the

Student Non-Violent Coordinating Committee (SNCC). He participated in the first Freedom Rides in 1961 and was a principal speaker at the March on Washington in 1963. He was a leader of the Selma-to-Montgomery Voting Rights Marches. It was during the first of these marches in 1965 that Lewis received a fractured skull after Alabama law enforcement officers charged the crowd of peaceful demonstrators. As head of the VEP, Lewis directed programs to advance, through nonpartisan action, minority political participation.

In receiving the award, Lewis said, "I am deeply moved and I hope that in the days, months, and years to come I will be worthy of this honor. As Dr. King said so many times, 'We've come a distance, but we still have a distance to go.'"

JANUARY 16, 1975 Ali Athlete of the Year. Muhammad Ali, heavyweight boxing champion, was named the Associated Press' Athlete of the Year for 1974. In winning the award, as a result of a nationwide poll of sportswriters and sportscasters, Ali edged out another African American, baseball's Hank Aaron, by a margin of 162 to 110. Ali became only the third fighter to win the AP award since it was initiated in 1931. Joe Louis, an African American, won it in 1937 after he had knocked out heavyweight Jim Braddock for the title, and Ingemar Johansson of Sweden was selected in 1959 after he defeated Floyd Patterson for the heavyweight championship.

The AP award signaled a new acceptance of Ali by Americans. The champion had incurred widespread disfavor and was forced to take a three and one half year retirement from the ring when he refused induction into the Armed Forces in 1968. Ali began his comeback in 1971 after the United States Supreme Court overturned his conviction for draft evasion. His comeback fight was a third round knockout over Jerry Quarry in Atlanta, Georgia.

JANUARY 16–FEBRUARY 22, 1975 Demonstrations in DeKalb County, Georgia. African Americans in DeKalb County, Georgia, staged a number of demonstrations protesting what they called "the racist" DeKalb school system. On January 15 (the anniversary of the birthday of Dr. Martin Luther King, Jr.), sixty black parents and pupils picketed at the Columbia High School in Decatur. They accused the school system of, among other things, dishonoring the memory of Martin Luther King, Jr., by refusing to declare a holiday on his birthday. However, Joe Renfroe, an assistant superintendent of schools, said that special programs, rather than a holiday, would "make all students more aware of [King's] contributions better than closing down which we do not do for the birthdays of other great men."

On February 20, about one hundred African American students at Columbia High School were arrested after they refused to obey an order from school authorities to leave the campus. The arrested students were part of a group of 170 African Americans who had been suspended the previous week for staging a sit-down and walkout because the school failed to hold an assembly during Black History Week.

On February 22, more than one hundred black students and parents marched from Columbia High School to the DeKalb County Courthouse in the continuing protest. According to one parent: "Our children have been coming home all this time telling us how bad the situation is and some of the things that the school officials up there do to them. . . . We see what they've been telling us is true."

Also on February 22, Columbia High School readmitted nearly all of the black students suspended during earlier demonstrations. DeKalb County, whose seat is the city of Decatur, is a part of the Metropolitan Atlanta area.

JANUARY 17, 1975 Ownership of African American Newspapers. Stanley Scott, President Ford's chief African American White

House aide, said during a seminar on mass communications at the John F. Kennedy Center in Atlanta, Georgia, that "fast buck operators" were threatening America's remaining black newspapers. He said wealthy whites were "buying out black-owned newspapers and franchising them like McDonald's hamburgers." The "black press should survive," Scott added, because the "majority white press" did not cover adequately all aspects of life in black communities. "I believe in integration," Scott continued, "but I think we should maintain and save some of our old institutions too." Scott estimated that of the 500 black-oriented newspapers in the country, "only about 30 or 35 are still black-owned." One of those was the *Atlanta Daily World*, a pioneer black daily, published by Scott's family.

JANUARY 22, 1975   School Desegregation Laws.
In its latest report, the United States Commission on Civil Rights said that President Gerald Ford must exert leadership to insure "vigorous and effective enforcement" of school desegregation laws. The commission was also, as in the past, highly critical of the civil rights enforcement of several governmental agencies. Noting the continued resistance to school desegregation in Boston, Massachusetts, and elsewhere, the commission said: "We are at a dangerous crossroads in connection with school desegregation. . . . We cannot afford—because of organized resistance in Boston or any other community—to turn back." It called for "extraordinary actions," including appointment by the President of a federal official who would have the responsibility of making certain federal agencies fully enforce civil rights laws.

In the new report, the commission charged that the Department of Health, Education, and Welfare (HEW), the Internal Revenue Service (IRS), and the Veterans Administration (VA) had failed to use existing federal laws to guarantee equal educational opportunities for racial minorities, non-English speaking people, and women.

The HEW, according to the commission, had "diminished its overall effectiveness and credibility" by interminable negotiations with segregated school districts, rather than cutting off their federal funds. It had also failed to tell school districts what they must do to comply with civil rights laws, including the degree of busing required to desegregate schools.

The IRS, the commission contended, had taken little action to make sure that private schools that received exemptions from federal taxes were operated without racial bias.

The VA, which was responsible for enforcing anti-bias laws regarding profit-making schools, apprenticeship programs, and on-the-job training programs, remained deficient in several areas, according to the commission. The VA, for example, had refused to examine possible discrimination in the hiring of faculty at certain schools.

The latest Civil Rights Commission document was the third in a series of reports assailing the degree of civil rights enforcement under the Nixon and Ford administrations.

JANUARY 22, 1975   Voter Statistics Assessed.
The Voter Education Project (VEP) rendered an assessment of the political progress of blacks in the 1974 general elections. Georgia, according to the VEP, led the South in the number of blacks elected and reelected to public office. In elections from coroner to congressman, Georgia had 101 blacks elected out of the 525 successful black candidates in the region. Among the new black officeholders in Georgia were John White, the first African American to represent Dougherty County in the state legislature, and Henry Dodson and J. O. Wyatt, the first black commissioners of Fulton County (of which Atlanta is the county seat).

Elsewhere, Harold Ford was elected to the U.S. Congress from Memphis, Tennessee; forty-six blacks were elected to state legislatures in Alabama, Georgia, and South Carolina; and blacks were elected to 226 city councils and commissions. In the end, however, VEP

Executive Director John Lewis said "the election of 525 blacks in a single year is a small but important step in the long march toward equity of representation in Southern politics."

JANUARY 24, 1975   Death of Brewer. J. Mason Brewer, possibly the best known writer of African-American folklore in the United States, died in Commerce, Texas, at age seventy-eight.

Brewer wrote some of his stories and poems in black dialect so ancient that it was difficult for most people to read. Others were written in standard English. Prior to his death, Brewer had served as a vice president of the American Folklore Society and a member of the Texas Institute of Letters and the Texas Folklore Society. He was a lecturer at Yale University, the University of Southern California, and the University of Texas, and a Distinguished Visiting Professor at East Texas State University. The late J. Frank Dobie, himself a distinguished folklorist, once called Brewer "the best storyteller of Negro folklore anywhere in the world."

JANUARY 25, 1975   Mitchell Died. Nannie Mitchell, founder of the *St. Louis Argus* and a veteran black business and civic leader, died in St. Louis, Missouri, at age eighty-eight.

In 1905, Mitchell, along with her late husband William and her brother-in-law, J. E. Mitchell, founded the We Shall Rise Insurance Company in St. Louis and began publishing a newsletter to be distributed to black churches in the area. This newsletter eventually became the *Argus,* a newspaper that was published weekly starting in 1915.

JANUARY 25–FEBRUARY 15, 1975   Wallace Began Third Term. George C. Wallace, a perennial symbol of resistance to civil rights for blacks, began his third term as governor of Alabama. At this inauguration, Wallace observed that social changes had been effected so smoothly in Alabama that other states might

want to emulate it. Fifteen black state legislators and the state's first black cabinet officer, Jesse Lewis, witnessed the ceremonies. Wallace had received more black support than ever before in his recent successful reelection campaign and his subsequent recognition by black organizations had been the source of considerable controversy in the black communities of the nation. John Lewis, Director of the Voter Education Project (VEP), who was assaulted during the famous Selma to Montgomery March, is one of those who opposed black support for Wallace. In an interview with Boyd Lewis of the *Atlanta Inquirer,* John Lewis said: "Black people giving Wallace an award is like the Anti-Defamation League giving a posthumous award to Hitler." Lewis also observed that "George Wallace, in spite of his condition, remains a symbol of the most brutal forms of violence inflicted against poor and black people in Alabama. . . . There is no way you can erase that from the psyche of black people. . . . As we celebrate Black History Week, we must not forget. . . . I am troubled by this newly found admiration of a man like Governor Wallace."

JANUARY 29, 1975   African Americans Appointed in Atlanta. Atlanta Mayor Maynard H. Jackson appointed the first full-time black municipal traffic judge and the first black municipal court solicitor in the city's history. Edward L. Baety, a thirty-year-old attorney who graduated from Morris Brown College and Harvard University, was named judge. Mary Welcome, a thirty-one-year-old attorney who graduated from the Howard University Law School, was named municipal court solicitor.

JANUARY 29, 1975   Johnson Convicted of IRS Fraud. Former Georgia State Senator Leroy R. Johnson was convicted in the United States District Court in Atlanta of submitting a false statement to the Internal Revenue Service (IRS) in connection with his 1969 and 1970 income tax returns. Johnson was acquitted of two other charges of willfully evading some $40,000 in taxes for 1969 and 1970. Johnson's lawyers announced that they would appeal the verdict. Johnson was the first African American elected to a Southern state legislature since Reconstruction days when he won a seat in the Georgia legislature in 1962. During his twelve years in the state legislature, he became one of the most powerful black politicians in Georgia and the South. Johnson was defeated for reelection in 1974, after an unsuccessful campaign for mayor of Atlanta, with the tax charges against him still pending.

FEBRUARY 1975   First On Tour Performance of the Free Southern Theater. The Free Southern Theater presented the play *If the Opportunity Scratches, Itch It,* in Eutau, Alabama. It was the first time ever that live theater, other than high school plays, was performed in this predominantly black farm community in central Alabama. The occasion also marked the first time since 1969 that the Free Southern Theater had taken a show on tour, although this was its original purpose when it was established in 1962 as a cultural arm of the Student Non-Violent Coordinating Committee (SNCC). The Free Southern Theater was viewed by some as the beginning of a modern renaissance of black culture that grew out of the civil rights and black consciousness movements of the 1960s and 1970s. The idea of a theater to dramatize the concept of black liberation had spread rapidly across the country, and most cities with a sizeable black population had some form of organized cultural activity. They included: The Fire Company in Birmingham, Alabama; the New African Company; the National Center of Afro-American Artists and the Museum of Afro-American History in Boston, Massachusetts; the Ku Mba Workshop in Chicago, Illinois; the Karamu House Theater in Cleveland, Ohio; the Rapa House in Detroit, Michigan; Opera South in Jackson, Mississippi; Bodaciouis Buggerilla; the Mafandi Institute and the Performing Arts Society in Los Angeles, California; the Black Theater Troupe and Umba Ujaama in Phoenix, Arizona; and the Kahero Cultural Gallery of Richmond, Virginia.

The aim of all of this activity was to allow blacks, who felt that they had been generally left out or misrepresented in America's cultural media, to interpret their own history, thought, ideas, strengths, weaknesses, and aspirations. In addition to theater, blacks were engaged in community writing, dancing, directing, designing, sculpturing, singing, and photography.

In interviews with the *New York Times* in February 1975, Kenneth E. Snipes, executive director of the Karamu House Theater, and Gilbert Moses, one of the founders of the New Orleans-based Free Southern Theater, assessed the new movement. According to Snipes: "Blacks have more needs for certain kinds of programs to provide them with a sense of self-worth, more of the things that are appreciative of black people. There is a need to appreciate black people, to appreciate the role of blacks in the history of this country, to appreciate the work of the black playwright or what the black dancer is doing today to eventually attain self-worth and self-esteem." Moses added that "it was more important that we develop our own artists, our own image. It had to happen."

FEBRUARY 1, 1975   Study on Learning Released. The results of a study of the public schools of Philadelphia, Pennsylvania, showed that whether the race of the pupil and teacher was the same appeared unrelated to learning. The report also concluded that counseling and remedial education—given current rates of expenditure—had no particular value in increasing learning. The report said that optimal learning growth at the elementary level occurred in classes that were about half black and half white. In junior high schools, the achievement among blacks increased as the percentage of blacks increased. On the other hand, white junior high school students experienced a decline in learning in schools that were more than half black. The study, sponsored by the Federal Reserve Bank of Philadelphia, was co-authored by Anita Summers and Barbara L. Wolfe.

FEBRUARY 2, 1975 Improved Business for Minority-Owned Companies. Sam Beard, head of the Development Council, announced in New York that minority-owned companies were moving into the economic mainstream and doing business with the industrial giants of the nation. According to Beard, "There was almost no history of minority business ownership prior to the Sixties," but in the last three years, his nonprofit organization had arranged 1,003 contracts totaling $141 million between minority-owned businesses and major corporations. Included among the Council projects were the financing of a health center in South Jamaica, a section of Queens, New York, where thirty black doctors had tried unsuccessfully for eighteen months to raise money for a medical facility to treat the community of 150,000; the funding of Soul City, the multi-racial town under construction in North Carolina; assistance to the Black Feet Indian Writing Company in Montana, which supplied pens to Atlantic-Richfield Company; and assistance to the black-owned Baldwin Ice Cream Company of Chicago, which sold food to United Airlines. The Council, according to Director Beard, was not a charity organization. Instead, he said, "We're building long-lasting business relationships that will feed hundreds of thousands of dollars back into minority communities and create jobs."

FEBRUARY 3, 1975 Demonstrators Arrested. Georgia State Representative Hosea Williams, head of the Atlanta chapter of the Southern Christian Leadership Conference, and three other men, including Socialist Workers Party presidential candidate Peter Camejo, were arrested during a demonstration in Atlanta outside of a hotel where President Gerald Ford was speaking. Williams and fifty other demonstrators demanded to see the president to ask for jobs for the poor. A presidential aide told them that Ford's schedule did not permit such a meeting. Amid jeering from hotel guests, the demonstrators were arrested and charged with trespassing and disorderly conduct.

FEBRUARY 4, 1975 OIC Held Convention. The Opportunities Industrialization Centers (OIC) held its eleventh annual convention in Atlanta, Georgia. The OIC, a black self-help organization, was founded in Philadelphia, Pennsylvania, by the Reverend Leon Howard Sullivan, the pastor of Philadelphia's Zion Baptist Church. Sullivan first received national attention in 1963 when, after increasing his church's membership from six hundred to five thousand, he established a day care center, a federal credit union, a community center, an employment agency, adult education reading classes, several athletic teams, choral groups, and a family counseling service. For these and other things, Sullivan was cited by *Life* magazine as one of one hundred outstanding young adults in the United States in 1963. During this same period he was named one of the ten outstanding young men of Philadelphia, won the city of Philadelphia Good Citizenship Award, the Silver Beaver Award of the Boy Scouts of America, the West Virginia State College Outstanding Alumnus Award, the Freedom Foundation Award, and the Russwurm Award.

In 1964, at the age of forty-one, Sullivan established the first OIC in an abandoned jailhouse in Philadelphia. Starting with almost nothing, Sullivan built OIC into a $4.5 million per year enterprise that trained and found jobs for more than 200,000 people. A comparison of the OIC's expenditures with the number of people it had successfully trained over the previous ten years showed that the organization was able to put trainees through its programs at an average cost of only $1,500 each. Secretary of Health, Education, and Welfare Caspar Weinberger stated that the OIC was more effective in training people and finding jobs for them than the vocational education programs in the nation's high schools.

During the eleventh annual convention, President Gerald Ford addressed the delegates and praised the work and enthusiasm of Sulli-

Reverend Leon Sullivan. (Schomburg Center for Research in Black Culture.)

van. The OIC head responded: "Mr. President, we are glad you came. It is time someone came to us to give the poor, and those who work with the poor, some encouragement and some hope. It is refreshing to know that now, at last somebody in the White House seems to care."

Also on February 4, the OIC presented a State Government Award to Alabama Governor George Wallace. In presenting the honor, Connie Harper, the black executive director of the Central Alabama OIC, kissed the handicapped former segregationist on the cheek. A week later, however, Tyrone Brooks, public information officer for the Southern Christian Leadership Conference, resigned from the Board of Directors of the Atlanta OIC in protest of the award to Wallace. Brooks called the presentation "an insult to all of black Atlanta and black America."

FEBRUARY 12, 1975 Desegregation of Fort Valley State College. United States District Court Judge Wilbur Owens, Jr., in Macon, Georgia, approved the Georgia State Board of Regents' plan for the desegregation of predominantly black Fort Valley State College.

The thrust of the plan called for upgrading academic programs, especially in agriculture, in order to attract more whites to Fort Valley State. Special education courses and a master's degree program in education were also parts of the plan. The suit against Fort Valley was filed in 1972 by a group of white citizens of the town who objected to a black state school existing in their midst while their children attended other state schools.

In his ruling, Judge Owens said: "there is no magic way whereby this college can be transformed overnight." Yet, he continued, "the court feels the plan is real and it is designed to do what is necessary. The court believes the plan is evidence of an intention to attempt to do what the court says."

Black faculty members and students at Fort Valley announced that they would probably appeal the judge's ruling. Some of them had joined the case with a contention that the desegregation suit was in reality an attempt by whites to take control of the school. Thomas M. Jackson, attorney for the blacks, said some provisions of the plan were commendable, but that the "concept is most suspect that a college must be controlled or operated by whites in order to attract white students." One of the attorneys for the Board of Regents told Judge Owens that there was no justification for Jackson's fears. In his ruling, Owens himself noted that "there are some who will say the plan will result in the demise of this college but the court feels that those fears are unfounded. . . . If the plan is carried out by everyone involved the end result will be that students who attend—be they black, white or any other race—will get a good college education that they need, want, and ought to have!"

Even before Judge Owens' ruling, some white faculty members were transferred to the school from other colleges and some white students had enrolled. About 25 percent of the faculty and student body were white at the time of the decision.

The issues involved in the desegregation of Fort Valley State College were similar to those that have faced a number of predominantly black colleges in the past decade. Federal law had dictated the dismantling of dual school systems. In most instances white-controlled state boards of regents or trustees had recommended the closing, merger, or transformation of predominantly black colleges as a principal means of accomplishing these objectives. Blacks, while generally not opposed to the principle of desegregation, had often contended that the plans for achieving it would destroy essential elements of their cultural heritage and place them at an unfair disadvantage in competition for positions in the newly desegregated schools.

FEBRUARY 13, 1975 Singleton Received Award. Dr. Peter T. Singleton, Jr., of Atlanta, Georgia, was awarded the Commendation for Excellence in Clinical Medicine and Human Relations at the Walter Reed General Hospital and Medical Center in Washington, D.C. The young black cardiologist graduated from Morehouse College and the Howard University Medical School.

FEBRUARY 15, 1975 Judgement for Reverse Discrimination Awarded. Alameda County, California, Superior Court Judge Lyle Cook ordered the city of Berkeley to promote eight white firemen who were passed over in favor of minority race candidates. Judge Cook ruled that the city's affirmative action program, introduced in 1972, was unconstitutional because it amounted to discrimination in reverse. According to the 1972 act, persons of minority races should be represented in the fire department in proportion to their population in the city. Whites, however, complained that they were discriminated against because non-whites were hired and promoted ahead of them on the basis of quota rather than merit. Judge Cook agreed that ignoring competitive examinations to hire and promote minority persons violated the Berkeley Charter, the Civil Rights Act of 1964, and the Fourteenth Amendment of the United States Constitution.

FEBRUARY 16, 1975 Black History Exhibit Slated to Tour Country. The Anacostia Neighborhood Museum, a branch of the Smithsonian Institute, announced that a traveling exhibit on black history would tour the country as part of the bicentennial celebration. The exhibit would include forty-six illustrated panels, along with artifacts and a written text. Among the characters and events in the exhibit were York, William Clark's slave; Mary Fields, a colorful Western pioneer; Benjamin "Pap" Singleton, an early black migrationist; Bill Pickett, a pioneer black cowboy; and Mary Ellen Pleasant, a pioneer civil rights leader.

York was a strapping, six-foot interpreter for the Lewis and Clark expedition of 1804–1806. His fluency in French and Indian dialects as well as English made him indispensable to the exploration. He was, in fact, seen as the leader of the expedition by the Indians. Because of his services, York was granted his freedom in 1805.

"Black Mary" Fields was born in slavery but migrated to Montana after emancipation. She became a friend and confidante of the nuns of Cascade, a restaurant owner, and a mail woman. She often walked through the snow when it was too deep for horses to ensure that the mail got through.

Benjamin "Pap" Singleton, one of the earliest "Black Moses," led an exodus of blacks from the South to the West in 1879. Between 1870 and 1890, a number of these Western migrations took place as blacks sought to escape racial oppression in the Post-Reconstruction South. Men like Singleton organized "colonies" to help the blacks move West, where they often faced legal and extra-legal moves to keep them out of the frontier territories. Once in the West, blacks founded all-black towns and worked on the railroads and in cattle drives. It is estimated that there were at least 8,000 black cowboys during this pioneer era.

Among the most famous of the black cowboys was Bill Pickett, "the Dusky Demon" of the rodeo circuit. Pickett lost his life at age seventy-one, when he tried to make a comeback to the rodeo by roping and taming a wild horse.

Mary Ellen Pleasant was born a slave in Georgia but also became a migrant to the West. She was one of San Francisco's first civil rights leaders and allegedly helped to finance the raid of John Brown at Harpers Ferry, Virginia, in 1859.

FEBRUARY 25, 1975 Elijah Muhammad Died. Elijah Muhammad, leader of the Black Muslims, died in Chicago at age seventy-seven. Muhammad was born Elijah Poole near Sandersville, Georgia, in 1897. He moved to Detroit in the 1930s and met W. D. Fard, founder of the Temple of Islam (Black Muslims). Muhammad himself erected a temple in Detroit, then, in 1934, moved to Chicago. Subsequently, seventy-nine temples were erected in seventy cities. Jesse Jackson eulogized Muhammad as "the single most powerful black man in this country. . . . His leadership extended far beyond his membership. He was the father of black self-consciousness during our 'colored' and Negro days." Muhammad was succeeded by his son, Wallace D. Muhammad.

During the height of the civil rights movement, Muhammad and his followers provoked the ire of white and black leadership alike for their preaching of racial separatism, racial pride, and self-defense. The increasing popularity of those teachings among blacks, however, was demonstrated in the scope of philosophies represented in the eulogies for Muhammad. Civil rights leaders, including Jackson and Tyrone Brooks of the Southern Christian Leadership Conference (SCLC), joined Julian Bond of Georgia and traditional black Baptist ministers in extolling the virtues of the Black Muslim patriarch.

FEBRUARY 25, 1975 Georgia's Governor Pushed Affirmative Action Plan. Georgia

Muslim leader Elijah Muhammad. (Bettmann Archive/ Newsphotos, Inc.)

Governor George Busbee urged his state legislature to pass a bill dictating increased state employment for blacks and women. Busbee told leaders of the House and Senate that an affirmative action plan was needed to prevent mandatory hiring quotas imposed by the federal government. In May 1974 the Equal Employment Opportunities Commission had accused eleven state departments and agencies of racial and sexual discriminatory hiring practices. The federal government had earlier imposed hiring quotas on the states of Alabama and Mississippi.

FEBRUARY 28, 1975 James Earl Ray's Motion Denied. United States District Court Judge Robert M. McRae, Jr., in Memphis, Tennessee, denied James Earl Ray's motion to withdraw his guilty plea and face a new trial on the charge that he murdered Dr. Martin Luther King, Jr., in 1968. McRae said Ray's original plea of guilty was "cooly and deliberately" submitted and that he found no violation of Ray's constitutional rights that would warrant a reversal of the plea and a full trial in state court. McRae rejected Ray's contention that he came to believe he had no choice but to plead guilty because of his former attorney's actions and rejected Ray's allegations that famed criminal lawyer Percy Foreman of Houston, Texas, and attorney Arthur Hanes, Sr., of Birmingham, Alabama, failed to take adequate steps to prepare a defense because they were more interested in promoting their royalties on the Ray story under contracts with Alabama author William Bradford Huie. McRae ruled groundless Ray's argument that Foreman, specifically, coerced him into the guilty plea. The judge said there was no impermissible pressure from the attorney. "On the contrary, the matter was discussed on numerous separate occasions over almost one month, at the least." Ray "carefully considered and partially amended the lengthy stipulation of facts that formed the basis for accepting his guilty plea . . . and entered the plea in an open court where he spoke to correct the record as he thought appropriate," according to Judge McRae. Robert I. Livingston, one of Ray's new attorneys, announced an immediate appeal to the U.S. Court of Appeals for the Sixth Circuit.

MARCH 2, 1975 Ashe Defeated Okker. Arthur Ashe, the nation's leading black tennis player, won the singles finals of the World Championship Tennis Green Group Tournament in Rotterdam. He defeated Tom Okker of the Netherlands 3–6, 6–2, 6–4, in a ninety-five minute match at the Ahoy Sports Palace.

MARCH 14, 1975 School Desegregation Enforced. United States District Court Judge John H. Pratt in Washington, D.C. ordered the Department of Health, Education, and Welfare (HEW) to quickly enforce school desegregation laws in 125 school districts in sixteen states where voluntary desegregation was in effect. The judge told HEW to begin proceedings against the school systems within two months and said that in the future only seven months would be granted for systems to formulate voluntary school desegregation plans. HEW had found within the past fifteen months that the school districts included in the order were substantially disproportionate in their racial

composition. The affected districts were located in Arkansas, Delaware, Florida, Kentucky, Louisiana, Maryland, Mississippi, Missouri, North Carolina, Oklahoma, South Carolina, Tennessee, Texas, Virginia, and West Virginia. The ruling came as a result of a suit filed by the NAACP's Legal Defense Fund in 1971. Failure of any district to comply with HEW requirements could mean a cut off of federal funds.

MARCH 17, 1975 Documents Released in Kenyatta Suit. The American Civil Liberties Union (ACLU) released documents indicating that the FBI had fabricated a threatening letter in order to persuade a black civil rights worker to leave Mississippi in 1969. A month after Muhammad Kenyatta received the letter, he returned with his family to Pennsylvania. The ACLU said that Kenyatta (formerly Donald W. Jackson) had come under the scrutiny of Cointelpro, the FBI's counter-intelligence unit, which the bureau operated between 1956 and 1971 in an effort to disrupt groups it considered subversive. The letter in question, allegedly written by a group of Tougaloo (Mississippi) college students, warned Kenyatta to leave Mississippi or "we shall consider contacting local authorities regarding some of your activities or take other measures available to us which would have a more direct effect and which would not be as cordial as this note." The ACLU obtained the FBI documents in connection with a suit filed against the Bureau by Kenyatta, alleging a violation of his constitutional rights.

MARCH 17, 1975 Jackson Threatens Boycott of Bowl Games. The Reverend Jesse Jackson of Chicago, Illinois, head of People United to Save Humanity (Operation PUSH), said during a press conference in New York City that the National Collegiate Athletic Association (NCAA) was racist and warned that a black boycott of the college football bowl games may be the next target of civil rights groups. Jackson remarked that "the NCAA is not fair. . . . The colleges don't have black head coaches. They will select an assistant grudgingly but they don't consider the black man to be head coach or athletic director. . . . We found that the selection committees for various bowl games are almost totally white. This is a situation we intend to change."

Earlier, Jackson had met with Michael Burke, president of Madison Square Garden in New York City, and Peter Carlesimo of Fordham University on the issue of giving black colleges a role in the National Invitational Basketball Tournament (NIT). Jackson's organization had threatened to picket the NIT unless changes were made. Under an agreement reached with Burke and Carlesimo, two athletic directors from black colleges would be elected to the NIT Selection Committee (Jackson suggested the names of Earl Banks of Morgan State University and Eddie Robinson of Grambling University), at least one black institution would be invited to compete in future NIT events, and the New York branch of Operation PUSH would play a supportive role in the promotion of future tournaments. Jackson said that the pressure on the NIT was part of a national program to break down racial barriers that extended beyond the playing field.

MARCH 20, 1975 African American Women Qualified for Top Government Offices. The April issue of *Redbook* magazine listed four black women among the forty-four American women qualified for top governmental positions, including cabinet officers, in the United States. The blacks included U.S. Representative Barbara Jordan of Texas, who was suggested as eminently qualified to be Attorney General of the United States; Coretta Scott King, listed as qualified to be chairperson of the Equal Employment Opportunity Commission; Eleanor Holmes Norton, Commissioner of Human Rights for New York City, listed as qualified to be Secretary of Housing and Urban Development; and C. Delores Tucker, Secretary of State of Pennsylvania, seen as qualified to be Ambassador to the United Nations. The

list of qualified women was drawn up by Frances "Sissy" Farentold, chairperson of the National Women's Political Caucus, because she became convinced that women's abilities were underestimated when selections for high level jobs were made.

MARCH 20, 1975 Boy of the Year. Kenneth Ivory, a seventeen-year-old black youth from Milwaukee, Wisconsin, was named national Boy of the Year in a White House ceremony attended by President Gerald R. Ford. Ivory, a senior at Lincoln High School in Milwaukee, was president of his student body and captain of the football, baseball, and basketball teams at the time of his selection as Boy of the Year.

MARCH 24, 1975 Ali Defeated Wepner. Heavyweight boxing champion Muhammad Ali defeated Chuck Wepner in the final round of a 15-round title fight to retain his crown. Wepner went down in the last round from a right to the head and referee Tony Perez stopped the fight at the count of eight.

MARCH 28, 1975 Evidence of Spying. The *Washington Star* reported new evidence of governmental spying on black individuals and organizations. These included investigations of Marion Barry, a former Student Non-Violent Coordinating Committee (SNCC) activist and ex-president of the Board of Education of Washington, D.C.; Walter Fauntroy, Washington, D.C.'s delegate to the U.S. House of Representatives; the Reverend David Eaton, pastor of Washington's All Souls Unitarian Church; and Absalom Frederick Jordan, chairman of the Black United Front. According to the *Star*, Barry's file read, "subject referred . . . by FBI due to activities in SNCC, active in civil rights movement. Dislikes police."

APRIL 1, 1975 Black Christian Nationalist Church Convention. The Black Christian Nationalist (BCN) Church opened its Third Biennial National Convention in Atlanta, Georgia. The BCN was a movement dedicated to changing the condition of black people by changing their life-styles. According to the creed of the BCN, "Jesus, the Black Messiah, was a revolutionary leader, sent by God to rebuild the Black Nation, Israel, and to liberate Black people from powerlessness and from the oppression, brutality and exploitation of the white gentile world." The national chairman of the BCN, Jaramazi Abebe Agyeman (formerly the Reverend Albert Cleage), was lauded by Atlanta Mayor Maynard Jackson as "a master teacher." Coleman Young, mayor of Detroit, Michigan, where the BCN was founded, presented Agyeman with a certificate from his city council. Young said that the "BCN is a force to be reckoned with not only in Detroit but in the nation."

APRIL 1, 1975   Poppy Cannon White Died. Poppy Cannon White, widow of the late NAACP Executive Secretary Walter Francis White, died by jumping off the terrace of her apartment in New York City. Walter White, whose marriage to the white author in 1947 created a mild controversy within the ranks of the NAACP, died in 1955. The NAACP issued an official statement of sorrow, however, upon the death of White.

APRIL 2, 1975   Demonstrators' Charges Dismissed. Judge Dennis Jones of the DeKalb County, Georgia, Juvenile Court dismissed charges against eighty black students arrested during a demonstration in February 1975 at the Columbia High School in Decatur. Judge Jones did not specify his reasons for dismissing the charges. Assistant School Superintendent Joe Renfroe, who had brought charges against the blacks, said he was shocked by the judge's ruling, contending that the demonstrating blacks had disrupted the instructional and academic process at Columbia. Defense Attorney Roger Mills praised the judge's decision, calling it "amazing." The blacks were originally charged with juvenile delinquency by violation of public disturbance statutes during a series of protests aimed at what they called the racist administration of DeKalb County schools.

APRIL 8, 1975   African American Golfer Joins the Pros. One of the last remaining barriers in professional sports fell as Lee Elder, a black golfer, began competition in the famed Masters Tournament at Augusta, Georgia. Elder was invited to participate in the prestigious Masters after winning the Monsanto Open in 1974. The black golfer was officially welcomed to Georgia by the state's governor, George Busbee. Elder was later disqualified in the preliminary rounds of the tournament.

APRIL 9, 1975   Conviction and Sentence Upheld. The Georgia Supreme Court upheld the murder conviction and death sentence of Marcus Wayne Chenault for the slaying of Alberta King, mother of Martin Luther King, Jr., and Deacon Edward Boykin at the Ebenezer Baptist Church in Atlanta on June 30, 1974. Chenault was convicted by a Fulton County Court jury on September 12, 1974. Like the jury that convicted him, the state supreme court rejected Chenault's plea of insanity.

APRIL 12, 1975   Death of Josephine Baker. Josephine Baker, one of the most popular American singers in France during the 1920s and 1930s, died in Paris at age sixty-nine.

Baker began dancing and singing as a small child. She left her hometown of St. Louis, Missouri, with a dance troupe at age fifteen and began regular performances at the Music Hall and the Plantation Club in Harlem. After Broadway rejected her as being "too ugly," she went to Paris, where in 1925 she became an instant success in the all-black Blackbird Revue at the Champs-Elysees theater. In the 1920s and 1930s, Baker also starred in the Folies-Bergere and the Casino de Paris. She became a French citizen in 1937. During the Second World War, Baker won the Croix de guerre and Resistance Medal for her dangerous assignments with French intelligence units.

Baker announced numerous retirements but kept coming out of them in order to raise money for the orphan home that she set up in the French countryside for children of all races and nationalities. Two days before her death, she celebrated the fiftieth anniversary of her first appearance in Paris with a gala performance of *Josephine*. Princess Grace of Monaco was one of the celebrities in the audience. French President Valéry Giscard d'Estaing sent a congratulatory telegram. During this performance, Baker said, "I have two loves, Paris and my own country." She collapsed two days later, prior to going on stage. Baker once said "the day I no longer go on stage will be the day I die."

APRIL 14, 1975   Motions Made in Little Case. Preliminary legal motions were presented in the Beaufort County, North Carolina, Superior Court in the celebrated murder case of Joann Little, a twenty-year-old black woman charged with murder after a Beaufort County Jail guard, Clarence Alligood, was found dead in her cell on August 27, 1974. Little pleaded self-defense on the grounds that the seminude Alligood had attempted to rape her. In the preliminary legal skirmishes, Little's attorneys, Jerry Paul and Karen Galloway, sought a change of venue and a delay of the trial. They argued that racist feelings and pretrial publicity had made it impossible for Little to get a fair trial in Beaufort County.

The Little case became a cause célèbre when civil rights groups and feminist organizations rallied to the young black woman's defense, claiming that the case typified the abuses that the Southern criminal justice system had long heaped upon blacks and women. By early April, thousands of dollars had been raised on behalf of the defense effort. Also, Representative Shirley Chisholm from New York asked U.S. Attorney General Edward Levy to intervene in the case on Little's behalf. Representative Chisholm said: "There are very few black people of either sex called to serve on juries in

Singer and dancer Josephine Baker. (Courtesy of Library of Congress.)

these eastern North Carolina counties. So this can really hurt Joann, who lives in a region where many, many Caucasian people hold the worst sort of prejudices against black women."

APRIL 15, 1975   First African American Assistant Football Coach at Georgia Tech. The Georgia Institute of Technology (Georgia Tech) announced that it had hired the first black assistant football coach in its history. Bill McCullough of Atlanta, a graduate of Fort Valley State College and Georgia State University, resigned from his position as Education Program Coordinator with the Georgia Department of Public Safety to accept the position at Tech.

APRIL 23, 1975   Demonstrators Arrested. Thirteen people, including self-avowed Communist and Black Panther Party leader Ron Carter, were arrested during a demonstration outside the office of Georgia State Labor Commissioner Sam Caldwell. The protest centered on demands for an extension of unemployment benefits, a minimum $75 per week payment, and a reduction of red tape in connection with unemployment aids. The arrests came after the demonstrators refused to clear the halls outside of Caldwell's office. Labor department officials had told the protesters that they could picket on the sidewalk outside the building.

APRIL 23, 1975 Students Clashed. Racial fighting erupted at the Boca Raton High School in Boca Raton, Florida. Three students and a police officer were injured. Two white students were arrested on charges of disorderly conduct. Police said the melee began about seven a.m. when several buses carrying black students from Delray Beach arrived at the school. The blacks discovered a racial slur on the wall, became incensed, and the fight was on. The school, located in a resort area for millionaires, was first desegregated in 1971. At the time of the racial incident, it had 225 black and 1,050 white students.

MAY 1, 1975 Stamp Honored Poet. A new ten-cent commemorative stamp honoring the African American poet Paul Laurence Dunbar went on sale. Dunbar, the son of ex-slaves, was born June 27, 1872, in Dayton, Ohio, and the first-day issue of the stamp was sold there.

Dunbar, best known for his humorous poems in black dialect, published several volumes of verse, three novels, and five collections of short stories. He died in 1906.

Coincidental with the issuance of the Dunbar stamp, the United States Postal Service opened a special exhibit called "Black Americans on U.S. Postage Stamps" at the Museum of African Art in Washington, D.C. At the conclusion of the special showing in Washington, the exhibit toured various post offices throughout the nation.

JUNE 5, 1975 Little Files Suit Against Alleged Rapist. Attorneys for Joann Little, accused of murdering a North Carolina jail guard, announced that they were filing a $1 million damage suit against the estate of the man whom Little accused of attempting to rape her in a Beaufort County jail, where she stabbed him to death. The suit claimed that the de-

ceased guard, Clarence Alligood, acting under the color of North Carolina law, inflicted cruel and unusual punishment on Little and invaded her privacy in the alleged sexual attack. Little was being held in the Beaufort County Jail on a charge of breaking and entering at the time of the alleged assault. The suit, sponsored by the Southern Poverty Law Center in Montgomery, Alabama, also asked the Federal District Court in New Bern, North Carolina, to protect all female inmates from sexual abuse by male attendants at the Beaufort County Jail. The class action portion of the suit claimed that women prisoners were largely supervised by males who could see them as they bathed, undressed, or used restroom facilities; that women inmates were "confined in such a manner that male trustees, jailers, and other male persons given free run of the jail expose[d] their genitalia . . . and ma[d]e vulgar and obscene remarks and gestures against the will and beyond the control" of the female inmates; that bail bondsmen were allowed access to the women's cells to conduct bonding business and at times had "made lewd and vulgar sexual propositions" to the female prisoners; and that prior to the slaying of Alligood, the women inmates were under twenty-four-hour surveillance by closed-circuit television cameras that anyone in the jailer's office could watch. Little's suit was filed as she awaited trial for the murder of Alligood.

JUNE 6, 1975 Reports Suggested Spying by the FBI. News reports of FBI spying on black individuals and organizations appeared in the *Atlanta Constitution.* According to the newspaper, the FBI had spied on the Afro-American Patrolmen's League since its founding in Chicago in 1968. The report quoted the Patrolmen's League founder, Renault Robinson, as saying that the FBI shared its information with Army intelligence units and with the intelligence division of the Chicago Police Department. The Afro-American's Patrolmen's League was organized to voice the particular racial grievances of black police officers in the United States.

JUNE 10, 1975 Black-Owned Companies Used by Harvard. Harvard University announced that it had negotiated an agreement under which 20 percent of the university's $228 million in group life insurance was to be insured by the North Carolina Mutual Life Insurance Company and the Atlanta Life Insurance Company, the two largest black-owned insurance companies in the nation. The total amount involved in the deals was approximately $45 million, with one half going to each company. A spokesman for Harvard, Walter J. Leonard, said "the agreement is a mutually beneficial one. . . . Our joint venture will not only enhance North Carolina Mutual Life Insurance Company's and the Atlanta Life Insurance Company's images as growing and strong companies, but it will, simultaneously, radiate Harvard's concern for the development and growth of stable and strong black business enterprises."

JUNE 12, 1975 Mistrial in Evers' Trial. Judge Dan M. Russell of the United States District Court in Jackson, Mississippi, declared a mistrial in the tax evasion trial of Fayette, Mississippi, mayor Charles Evers after an Internal Revenue Service (IRS) agent suggested from the witness stand that Evers might have pocketed campaign contributions. The questionable remarks were made by IRS agent William Jack Sykes when asked about possible sources of taxable income that Evers allegedly failed to report. Sykes said, "Well, he did run for Congress." Defense attorney Michael Fawer objected to the agent's remarks on the ground that the government's attorneys had agreed not to bring up the 1968 campaign as a source of more than $161,000 in taxable income that Evers allegedly concealed between 1968 and 1970. Although he declared a mistrial, Judge Russell refused to agree to a defense motion to dismiss the indictment against Evers.

JUNE 14, 1975 Voting Rights of Minorities Affected by Reapportionment Plan. The United States Department of Justice announced in Washington that it had asked a federal court in Mississippi to order that state to adopt a new reapportionment plan for its legislature that would meet federal standards prior to the 1975 elections. The justice department asked the court specifically to prohibit the use of a reapportionment plan drawn up by the Mississippi legislature during its 1975 session and to forbid the implementation of any plan that was not cleared in advance as having met federal standards. The Voting Rights Act of 1965 required that such advanced clearance be obtained either from the U.S. Attorney General or the U.S. District Court in Washington and that any political change in an affected Southern state must meet the test of whether it would have the intent or effect of diminishing the voting rights of minorities.

JUNE 22, 1975 Mayor Bradley Gave Interview. In an interview on the second anniversary of his electoral victory in Los Angeles, California, Mayor Tom Bradley said that race was not a factor in his administration. Excerpts from Bradley's statements follow:

> "I don't think that race is a significant factor in my administration. In part this is because I have tried to serve all the people of the city in the best way I know how. We've tried to bring in the advice of all segments of the city: the business community, homeowner groups, and just grassroots citizens. That kind of [openness] has created the atmosphere of acceptability that has made possible the view of my service without regard to color. I have not run across a single incident of bigotry. In fact, the usual expression I hear is: 'Well, I didn't vote for you, but I think you're doing an excellent job and commend you and I'd like to help.'"

Bradley's remarks were in response to a question from Paul Finch of the Associated Press.

JULY 3–AUGUST 25, 1975 NAACP Filed Suit for Desegregation Efforts. On July 3, attorneys for the NAACP, the NAACP Legal Defense and Educational Fund (LDEF), and the Center for National Policy Review (CNPR) filed a suit in the United States District Court in Washington, D.C., to compel the federal government to require Northern and Western states to end school segregation or to face the termination of their school aid, as had been done in the South. The suit was filed on behalf of the children of eighteen families in eight Northern and Western school districts and as a class action representing the interests of minority children in thirty-three states outside of the South. The suit charged that Secretary of Health, Education, and Welfare (HEW) Caspar W. Weinberger had not performed his legal obligation to be certain that no federally funded school system segregated students and teachers by race or national origin. The complaint also charged that HEW had failed to act even when evidence came to its attention suggesting segregation, and that protest proceedings tended to drag on indefinitely. The suit asked that HEW make findings of noncompliance, seek voluntary compliance on a prompt basis, and then cut off federal aid if all else failed.

On August 13, 1975, officials at HEW responded to the suit by calling for a meeting in Cleveland, Ohio, to plan stepped-up enforcement of school desegregation in Northern districts.

JULY 24–28, 1975 Voting Rights Act Extended. On July 24, the United States Senate voted 77-12 to extend the Voting Rights Act of 1965 for an additional seven years. On July 28, the U.S. House of Representatives voted 346-56 to approve the same measure.

The Voting Rights Act of 1965 allowed federal registrars and the Department of Justice to enable thousands of blacks to register and vote in the South. The new law was even supported by a few Southern senators and scores of representatives from the region. Some of the Southerners had failed earlier in an attempt to extend the coverage of the law from the South to the entire nation.

JULY 30, 1975 Judge Ordered Desegregation. United States District Court Judge James F. Gordon ordered the full desegregation of the Louisville, Kentucky, public schools. The judge's order called for the busing of 22,600 pupils to achieve the desegregation. Judge Gordon's ruling climaxed four years of litigation by civil rights groups. The order affected a city-county system of 140,000 pupils, including about 20,000 blacks. Judge Gordon said that all of the Louisville-Jefferson County schools were to be desegregated and each should have a black enrollment of at least 12 percent. No school could be more than 40 percent black. Gordon also warned those "who would resort to public disorder and violence" to oppose the desegregation to "think twice."

AUGUST 6–15, 1975 Continuing Racial Violence in Boston. Racial violence continued in Boston, Massachusetts, the scene of sporadic incidents ever since busing to achieve school desegregation was ordered in the city in 1974. On August 6, racial fighting erupted at the Charles Street Jail and 150 police officers were called in to put down the disturbance involving seventy-five to one hundred inmates. Martin Whitkin of the Sheriff's Office said the trouble apparently started in the lunchroom with a fight between a white man and several blacks, then escalated into a full-scale brawl throughout the jail.

On August 10, black and white swimmers threw rocks and bricks at one another on South Boston's Carson Beach. About five hundred blacks were at the beach in the predominantly white section of the city in response to a request by black leaders who urged them to "reassert the rights of all Boston residents to use all public facilities." There were no reports of injuries.

On August 13, police patrols were increased in the predominantly black Roxbury section of the city after young blacks had made sporadic attacks on passing whites for three days.

On August 15, three people were slightly injured during incidents of stone throwing in the city. A sixteen-year-old black youth was arrested during the melee in the Roxbury section. Meanwhile, U.S. Senator Edward Brooke of Massachusetts joined local leaders in an attempt to ease racial tensions. Brooke said, "I think the polarization in the community is unfortunate, but it seems to be building."

AUGUST 8, 1975 Cannonball Adderly Died. Julian "Cannonball" Adderley, called a "prophet of contemporary jazz," died in Gary, Indiana. Adderley was born in Tampa, Florida, in 1928, the son of a jazz cornetist. Known primarily as an alto saxophonist, Adderley also played tenor sax, trumpet, clarinet, and flute. He studied brass and reed instruments in a Tallahassee, Florida, high school from 1944 until 1948 and formed his first jazz group there with the school's band director as advisor. Because of his hearty appetite, fellow students nicknamed him "Cannibal," which later became "Cannonball." From 1948 until 1956, Adderley was music director at the Dillard High School in Fort Lauderdale, Florida. At the same time, he directed his own jazz group in southern Florida. He served for three years as a member of the 36th Army Dance Band and later studied at the Naval School of Music in Washington, D.C. Adderley's first big break came in New York in 1955 when he appeared with Oscar Pettiford. The next year he signed his first recording contract with EmArcy Records. Adderley later recorded for Capitol Records and other companies and became famous for such albums as *Black Messiah, Country Preacher, Fiddler on the Roof, Walk Tall,* and *Quiet Nights.* His last album was *Phoenix.* Until 1957, Adderley toured with his brother, Nat, a cornetist. In 1957, he joined the Miles Davis group. After a tour with George Shear-

ing, he formed his own quintet, including his brother Nat, in 1959. Charles Suber, publisher of *Down Beat* magazine, which named Adderley New Alto Star of the Year in 1959, described the "Cannonball" as "a helluva musician. . . . He was one of the best alto players in recent years." During his eulogy of Adderley before 2,000 mourners in Tallahassee, Florida, the Reverend Jesse Jackson, director of People United to Save Humanity (PUSH), said the "Cannonball" had "his greatness and his fame, but he did not use it, abuse it, or lose it. He expanded it. . . . When he blew his saxophone you felt a little ease in the troubled world and the savage beast had to hold his peace."

AUGUST 10, 1975   Editor Emory O. Jackson Died. Emory O. Jackson, editor of the *Birmingham World,* was laid to rest in Birmingham, Alabama. Jackson was born on September 8, 1908, in Buena Vista, Georgia. He moved with his parents to Birmingham in 1919. He graduated from Morehouse College in 1932, after which he taught school in Dothan and Jefferson counties, Alabama. After serving in World War II, Jackson became managing editor of the *Birmingham World* —a position he held from 1943 until his death. Jackson was one of the founders of the Alabama Conference of NAACP Branches and was a leader of several other political and civil rights organizations. In his eulogy of Jackson, the Reverend Samuel Pettagrue of the Sardis Baptist Church of Birmingham proclaimed that "the presses in heaven have stopped. A new edition was on the street and its headline read: 'The paper's top foreign correspondent, Emory O. Jackson, after serving sixty-seven years away has returned home to serve out his assignment eternally.'" In another eulogy, Benjamin E. Mays, president of the Atlanta, Georgia, Board of Education and president-emeritus of Morehouse College, said the late editor was "born a free man. He walked like one; talked like one and looked like one."

AUGUST 15, 1975 Little Acquitted. A jury of six whites and six blacks in Raleigh, North

Carolina, acquitted Joann Little, a twenty-one-year-old black woman, of the August 27, 1974, murder of white guard Clarence Alligood. The murder case became a *cause célèbre* for feminist and civil rights groups after Little claimed she stabbed Alligood while defending herself against a sexual attack.

AUGUST 16, 1975 Busing of Students Denied. United States District Court Judge Robert DeMascio rejected the busing of students to achieve school desegregation in Detroit, Michigan. He ordered the Detroit Board of Education to seek an alternate plan to better balance the races in the schools. C. L. Golightly, president of the city's school board, called the judge's decision "a victory for the school children of Detroit." Lawrence Washington of the Detroit branch of the NAACP expressed disappointment, commenting, "We're right back where we started five years ago."

SEPTEMBER 1, 1975 First African American Four-Star General. Lieutenant General Daniel "Chappie" James, Jr., became the first African American to be promoted to the rank of four star general in the U.S. Armed Forces. The Pentagon announced that James, a veteran of nearly two hundred combat missions in Korea and Vietnam, was also appointed chief of the North American Air Defense Command (NORAD).

James, age fifty-five, was born in Pensacola, Florida, and graduated from Tuskegee Institute. He was one of the original black pilots in the U.S. Army Air Corps, predecessor to the present-day Air Force. He achieved a great deal of notoriety for his speeches on Americanism and patriotism. With the appointment of James, there were twenty-one black generals and admirals in the army, air force, and navy out of a total of about twelve hundred in the U.S. Armed Services.

NOVEMBER 19, 1975 Bugs and Wiretaps Unjustified. James B. Adams, associate deputy director of the FBI, told the United States Senate's Intelligence Committee that there was no legal justification for the twenty-five separate attempts by the Bureau in the 1960s to discredit the late Dr. Martin Luther King, Jr., as a civil rights leader. The FBI, he continued, was led to investigate King because of the possibility that Communist influences were being brought to bear on him and the civil rights movement. No such evidence, however, was ever uncovered. During its spying on King, the FBI installed a total of sixteen electronic bugs and eight wiretaps in an attempt to collect damaging evidence against the civil rights leader and even sent his wife an anonymous letter and tape recording that King reportedly interpreted as a suggestion for suicide.

NOVEMBER 19, 1975 Cleaver Faces Murder Charges. Former Black Panther Party leader Eldridge Cleaver arrived in California in federal custody to face charges of attempted murder. Cleaver, age forty, was to be charged in connection with a shootout with Oakland police on April 6, 1968, in which Panther Bobby Hutton, age seventeen, was killed and a police officer was wounded. Cleaver had earlier ended his seven years of exile abroad to have his day in court. After having lived in Cuba, Guinea, Algeria, North Korea, and France, Cleaver said his voluntary return was prompted by his belief that the United States had changed to the extent that he could now receive a fair trial. Cleaver's *Soul on Ice,* revealing intimate details of his life in the ghetto and imprisonment, had become a minor classic in revolutionary literature.

NOVEMBER 21, 1975 Calhoun Appointed by President Ford. John Calhoun, age thirty-eight and a former foreign service officer and deputy special assistant to President Gerald R. Ford, was appointed special assistant to the president for minority affairs. Calhoun succeeded Stanley Scott, another black man, who resigned. Calhoun, at the time of his new appointment, had been a member of the White House staff since 1973.

"Chappie" James in the cockpit of his aircraft. (AP/Wide World Photos.)

1976

JANUARY 20, 1976   Congress Approved Work Honoring King. The U.S. House of Representatives voted by voice vote to authorize an appropriation of $25,000 for the creation of a bust of the late Martin Luther King, Jr., and to install it in the Capitol. King would be the first black person ever so honored, if the bill was passed by the U.S. Senate. The House measure noted King's contribution to the civil rights movement and his winning of the Nobel Peace Prize. The House's Administration Committee had said that the tribute was appropriate "because of Dr. King's prominence in American history and because of all the black Americans who have done so much to contribute to this country's greatness, [yet] not one is now honored among the 681 works of art in the Capitol."

JANUARY 21–MAY 31, 1976   School Desegregation Led to Violence.   Racial violence erupted in Boston, Massachusetts, amid protests by whites against court-ordered school desegregation.

On January 21, black and white students at Hyde Park High School fought with fists and chairs. Across the city in East Boston, approximately three hundred whites tried to block a major Boston Harbor tunnel during the morning rush hour. Five people, including a Boston police officer and the mother of a student, received minor injuries at Hyde Park. Seventeen people were arrested in the two incidents.

On February 15, about two thousand people fought the police near South Boston High School, "the focus of opposition to federal court ordered desegregation." Between forty and fifty police officers were injured in the mob attack. There "was no estimate of the number of civilians injured." Thirteen people, three of them juveniles, were arrested. Boston Police Commissioner Robert J. Di Grazia called the twenty-minute melee (during a so-called "Father's March") "an obvious conspiracy" by "an element of hoodlums."

On May 30, a fire was set next to the replica of the *Beaver,* a two-masted sailing ship, which was moored at a bridge that led into South Boston. Although the ship was unharmed, $75,000 worth of damage was done to an adjoining gift shop and ticket office. The Fire Department said the blaze was "of suspicious origin." The next day United States Attorney General Edward H. Levi announced that the Department of Justice would not intervene in an appeal of the Boston desegregation orders to the Supreme Court. Some whites had urged the administration of President Gerald Ford to side with them in their anti-busing stance before the high court, while civil rights leaders had urged the federal government to stay out of the Boston desegregation controversy.

At the time of this violence and controversy, Boston was in the second year of a school desegregation program ordered by U.S. District Court Judge W. Arthur Garrity. The program had been periodically marred by fighting in schools as well as scattered attacks on blacks in white neighborhoods and of whites in black sections of the historic city.

JANUARY 23, 1976 Paul Robeson Died. Paul Robeson, athlete, actor, singer, and civil rights activist, died in Philadelphia, Pennsylvania, at age seventy-seven.

Robeson was born on April 9, 1898, in Princeton, New Jersey, to William, a minister, and Maria Louisa Bustill Robeson. William Robeson was a former slave from North Carolina who worked his way through Lincoln University in Pennsylvania. In 1915, young Paul entered Rutgers University after earning an academic scholarship in a statewide competition. When he joined the football team, where he became an all-American, Robeson was once nearly mangled on the playing field by white bigots. The scholar-athlete graduated with Phi Beta Kappa honors in 1919.

Robeson scorned his father's wishes that he follow him into the ministry, but after a brief career in law, he grudgingly accepted his wife Eslanda's urging to use his rich baritone voice in singing and acting. She helped persuade her husband to accept a role in *Simon the Cyrenian* at the Harlem YMCA in 1920. "Even then," Robeson later recalled, "I never meant to [become an actor]. I just said yes to get her to quit pestering me."

The Harlem performance, however, did launch the remarkable stage career of Robeson. In 1922, he made his first Broadway appearance as Jim in *Taboo.* He also made his debut in London in the same year in *Taboo,* which was retitled *The Voodoo.*

Upon his return to New York in late 1922, Robeson joined the Provincetown Players, a Greenwich Village group that included dramatist Eugene O'Neill, and took the role of Jim Harris in O'Neill's *All God's Chillun Got Wings.* This led to another successful appearance as Brutus Jones in *The Emperor Jones,*

Singer and human rights activist Paul Robeson.

another play by O'Neill that had been especially revived for Robeson.

The Provincetown Players also sponsored Robeson's first major concert in 1925, which consisted of a collection of spirituals. Between 1925 and 1928, he had a triumphant performance in *The Emperor Jones* and a heralded portrayal of Joe in *Show Boat*, in which he sang "Ol' Man River," both in London, England, as well as in an appearance as Crown in George Gershwin's *Porgy and Bess* on Broadway.

Between 1928 and 1939, Robeson lived mostly abroad, particularly in London, where he found fewer color barriers than in the United States. One of his most spectacular successes in London occurred in 1930 when he played the lead in Shakespeare's *Othello*. To many, the *New York Times* stated, Robeson's performance was "an unforgettable experience." Following these latest triumphs, Robeson toured the major cities of Europe both as a recitalist and an actor.

Robeson's political consciousness was first jolted in 1928 when writer George Bernard Shaw asked him what he thought of socialism. Robeson later recalled, "I hadn't any-

thing to say. I'd never really thought about Socialism." In 1934, Robeson visited the Soviet Union where he was warmly received. He was also impressed "by the absence of racial prejudice among Soviet citizens" (in Germany, Robeson was subjected to racial slurs by a Nazi soldier). Later, Robeson began to publicly express a belief "in the principles of scientific Socialism" and his "deep conviction that for all mankind a Socialist society represents an advance to a higher stage of life."

In the late 1930s, Robeson sang for the Republican troops and for members of the International Brigades who were fighting the fascist dictator Francisco Franco in Spain. That experience led him to see "the connection between the problems of all oppressed people and the necessity of the artist to participate fully" in the struggle for human rights. It also convinced him to return to the United States to continue his work.

On October 19, 1943, Robeson became the first black actor to play the title role of *Othello* (with a white supporting cast, including Jose Ferrer and Uta Hagen) before a Broadway audience. The next year, the NAACP bestowed upon him its highest award, the Spingarn Medal.

Meanwhile, Robeson increased his political activity. He led a delegation to national baseball commissioner Kenesaw Mountain Landis that urged him to remove the racial bias in baseball. Robeson called on President Harry S Truman to extend civil rights to blacks in the South. He was also a co-founder and chairman of the Progressive party, which nominated former Vice President Henry A. Wallace for President in 1948. Then, at a World Peace Conference in Paris in 1949, Robeson declared, "It is unthinkable that American Negroes will go to war on behalf of those who have oppressed us for generations against a country [the Soviet Union] which in one generation has raised our people to the full dignity of mankind." Although Robeson later asserted that this statement had been taken "slightly out of context," adding that he had really spoken for two thousand students "from the colonial world" who had requested him to express their desire for peace, his words stirred widespread opposition in the United States. In August 1949, veterans' groups and right wing extremists attacked crowds who were arriving for one of his concerts in Peekskill, New York. Subsequently, professional concert halls were closed to him and commercial bookings grew scarce. Robeson's income reportedly dropped from $100,000 in 1947 to $6,000 in 1952.

Beginning in 1948, Robeson was called before Congressional committees on several occasions in which he was usually asked if he was a member of the Communist party. He always refused to answer, invoking his Fifth Amendment rights. The *New York Times*, however, reported that Robeson maintained "privately . . . that he was not a member." Nevertheless, in 1950 the United States State Department canceled his passport on "the ground that he had refused to sign the then-required non-Communist oath" for travelling abroad. Robeson had contended that "the Government had no right to base his freedom of travel on his political beliefs or a lack of them." He sued the State Department over the issue, and in 1958, the United States Supreme Court, in a related case, ruled that Congress "had not authorized the department to withhold passports because of applicants' 'beliefs and association[s]'."

Once Robeson received his passport, he departed immediately for Great Britain, declaring, "I don't want any overtones of suggestion that I am deserting the country of my birth. If I have a concert in New York, I will go there and return to London." He did return permanently to the United States in 1963, where he lived quietly, first in a Harlem apartment and then with his sister, Marian Forsythe, in Philadelphia, Pennsylvania.

Despite his difficulties with Congress, the State Department, and many American organizations and individuals, Robeson became a

hero to much of black America and to countless numbers of other peoples throughout the world. On his sixtieth birthday in 1958, he was given a thunderous ovation by a sold-out house at Carnegie Hall in New York City. It was his first New York recital in eleven years, and on the same day, birthday celebrations were held in many nations abroad, including India. There Prime Minister Jawaharlal Nehru called Robeson "one of the greatest artists of our generation [who] reminds us that art and human dignity are above differences of race, nationality, and color." In 1973, on his seventy-fifth birthday, another tribute in his honor was held at Carnegie Hall. Although the ailing actor-singer could not attend, he sent a recorded message to the crowd, which included many theatrical personalities.

Upon the occasion of Robeson's death, the official Soviet news agency Tass commented: "The persistent struggle for black civil rights and for stronger world peace won him recognition not only in the United States but also outside of it."

JANUARY 27, 1976 National Urban League Issued Report. The National Urban League (NUL), in its annual "The State of Black America" Report, contended that "many of the gains blacks made over the past decade were either wiped out or badly eroded in 1975 and the portents for the future are not encouraging." The League warned that "the absence of overt discontent in the cities" did not mean that the problems did not continue to exist and that the future of the nation was "bound-up in how it deals with these problems."

As examples of how blacks lost ground in 1975, the NUL cited the following:

1. There was a further decline in middle-income black families, continuing a trend from 1973–1974 that saw these families decrease from one-fourth to one-fifth of the total population for all black families.

2. The average black family income was only fifty-eight percent of that of average white

family income, representing a decline from sixty-one percent in 1969.

3. The black unemployment rate remained virtually unchanged at 14.1 percent for the first three quarters of 1975.

4. In 1975, Congress failed to enact any substantial legislation that would "foster full employment."

5. The outbreaks of racial violence in Boston, Massachusetts, a city "long regarded, if incorrectly as the fountainhead of liberalism in this country, served notice that racism has no geographical limits and continues to exist in the American body politic."

In concluding the review, Vernon Jordan, executive director of the NUL, commented that "all across the board, black people lost out in 1975."

In order to alleviate the distress among blacks that the League cited, it recommended "a full employment policy that assures decent jobs for all; an income maintenance system that alleviates economic hardship and replaces the present welfare system; and housing, health, and education programs that go beyond rhetoric to bring our nation closer to a prosperity that includes all of its citizens."

JANUARY 28, 1976   President of Clark College Died. Vivian W. Henderson, president of Clark College in Georgia, died during heart surgery in Atlanta, at age fifty-two.

Henderson, a native of Bristol, Virginia, was born on February 10, 1923. He received a bachelor's degree from North Carolina College in Durham (later North Carolina Central University), and M.A. and Ph.D. degrees in economics from the University of Iowa. In 1948, Henderson began his teaching career in Texas at Prairie View A & M College, but returned to his alma mater, North Carolina College, the following year as a professor of economics. In 1952, Henderson moved to a similar position at Fisk University in Tennessee where he eventually became chairman of the Department of

Economics. Henderson was named president of Clark College in 1965.

In addition to his roles as a teacher and an administrator, Henderson achieved distinction as one of the nation's most foremost African-American scholars in economics. He was the author of *The Economic Status of Negroes* (1963), co-author of *The Advancing South: Manpower Prospects and Problems* (1959), and contributing author of *Principles of Economics* (1959). He also contributed to *Race, Regions and Jobs,* edited by Arthur Ross and Herbert Hill in 1967. His work, according to the *Atlanta Journal,* "is considered to have had an important impact in convincing industry and business of the buying power of the black American community."

Outside the academic world, Henderson was a member of the boards of directors of the Atlanta Community Chest (later the United Way), the Atlanta chapter of the American Civil Liberties Union, the Atlanta Urban League, the Ford Foundation, the National Sharecroppers Fund, the Institute for Services to Education, the Martin Luther King, Jr. Center for Non-Violent Social Change, and the Voter Education Project (VEP), among others. He was also chairman of the board of the Southern Regional Council (SRC) and chairman of the Georgia advisory committee of the U.S. Commission on Civil Rights (CCR).

Henderson's governmental activities included serving as a member of the advisory committee of the Atlanta Charter Commission, co-chairman for education of the Georgia Goals Commission, advisor to former President Lyndon Johnson, and member of the Manpower Advisory Committee of the U.S. Department of Labor.

Former Atlanta mayor Ivan Allen, Jr., called Henderson's death "a great loss to the city. . . . He left a vital and lasting impact. . . ." Atlanta mayor Maynard H. Jackson added that the educator was a man "never too busy to accept the call to service."

JANUARY 30, 1976   Death of Alabama Representative. John L. LeFlore, black legislator and civil rights activist, died of an apparent heart attack in Mobile, Alabama. He was serving his first term as a member of the Alabama House of Representatives.

Prior to being elected to the legislature, LeFlore had spent thirty-eight years as a civil rights activist, much of it as executive secretary of the Mobile Branch of the NAACP. He helped lead the successful challenge to Alabama's Democratic White Primary in 1944. LeFlore was also a member of the Alabama Advisory Council to the United States Civil Rights Commission.

JANUARY 31, 1976   School Desegregation in Detroit. A plan that involved a limited amount of busing to achieve school desegregation was initiated in the Detroit, Michigan, school system—the nation's fifth largest. The implementation of the desegregation plan climaxed a court battle that began in 1970. The NAACP filed suit against the Detroit system in 1970 after the Michigan legislature overruled the city's first desegregation plan. In 1972, a federal district court ordered the integration of the primarily black schools of Detroit with those of surrounding, predominantly white suburbs. But in an important decision in July 1974, the United States Supreme Court struck down the provision relating to suburbs and ordered the district court to draw up a plan relating to Detroit only.

The Detroit plan, which was ordered by U.S. District Court Judge Robert De Mascio, permitted a total of 21,800 pupils in kindergarten through the eighth grade to be bused. Another 4,700 were transferred to schools within walking distance. In addition, 1,500 ninth and tenth graders were transferred to other schools, but they had to provide their own transportation.

In sum, approximately 160 schools exchanged pupils in order to achieve enrollments of about half black and half white. The city's remaining 140 schools remained all black.

The NAACP opposed the Detroit plan on the grounds that it did not go far enough, but urged compliance with the court order.

FEBRUARY 5–26, 1976   Racial Violence at a Florida High School. Racial violence erupted in Pensacola, Florida, over the issue of whether athletic teams at a local high school would be called "Rebels" or "Raiders."

On February 5, fifteen hundred people rioted at the Escambia High School. Four white students were wounded by gunfire, six others were also injured, and at least nine people were arrested. One of these was a twenty-three-year-old black man who was suspected in the shootings. Subsequently, crosses were burned on the lawns of school board members, a bullet was fired through a window of a home owned by a black school board member, and the homes of a human relations council member and a state legislator were burned by arsonists. Blacks began a boycott of the school.

On February 9, one hundred of the six hundred blacks enrolled in Escambia High School attended classes, but they were met with taunts from whites. Nearly one thousand white students also remained out of class "apparently in anticipation of violence." The school had a total enrollment of 2,523 students. The only incident of the day, however, was the arrest of a fifteen-year-old white youth who was brandishing a foot-long chain "equipped with a bolt-type grip."

On February 21, the home of Teresa Hunt, a member of the Pensacola-Escambia Human Relations Commission and the county school board Citizens Advisory Committee, was set afire with diesel fuel. Four nights later, the home of State Representative R. W. Peaden, a block away from Hunt's residence, was destroyed when a flammable liquid was poured on its floors and ignited. Both Hunt and Peaden had been involved in the controversy over the school name.

The Escambia Chapter of the Southern Christian Leadership Conference (SCLC) continued to urge black parents to keep their children away from the school, warning that they would be unsafe there. The chapter's president, F. L. Henderson, remarked, "We'd rather see a child held back in school than see them in the morgue." He asked Florida Governor Reuben Askew to provide "as much protection as within his power" for black students.

The controversy over the school's nickname first arose in 1973 when black students, who had been attending the school since 1969, protested both the name and the flying of the Confederate flag at athletic events and other functions. They said both symbols were a direct insult to them. After several protests, some of which were accompanied by violence, a U.S. District Court, on July 24, 1973, permanently enjoined the use of the rebel name, the flag, "and related symbols on the grounds that they were 'racially irritating.'" Students then chose the name "Raiders" to represent the school. But after an appeal by a group of white students and school board members, a U.S. Court of Appeals overturned the injunction and returned the matter to the school board "to make its own decision on the name." On February 4, 1976, an election was scheduled at Escambia High to allow students to choose between "Raiders" and "Rebels". The riot erupted the next day.

MARCH 20, 1976 Convicted Murderers Released. Rubin "Hurricane" Carter and John Artis were released from prison in New Jersey after serving nine years for murder. Carter, a former middleweight boxer, and Artis, his "casual friend," had been convicted in 1967 for allegedly participating in the fatal shootings of three people in a Patterson, New Jersey, tavern on June 17, 1966. The shootings occurred at a time of heightened racial tensions in the city and the two black men were convicted largely on the testimony of two ex-convicts who claimed "they had seen the defendants at the murder scene with guns." But the defendants maintained their innocence and many blacks

believed they were being prosecuted and persecuted because of their race.

In September 1974, the *New York Times* reported that Alfred Bello and Arthur Bradley, the former convicts, had recanted their testimony and claimed that "they had been pressured to lie" by Passaic County (of which Patterson is the county seat) detectives.

On March 17, the Supreme Court of New Jersey unanimously reversed the convictions of Carter and Artis because "evidence beneficial to the defense had been withheld" at the original trial. This evidence "included secret promises by detectives" to Bello and Bradley "that they would be aided in unrelated criminal cases if they testified for the prosecution."

On March 20, pending new trials, Carter was released on $20,000 bail and Artis was set free on $15,000 bail. Some of the bail money was provided by heavyweight boxing champion Muhammad Ali, a supporter of the campaign by the Carter-Artis Defense Committee to win a new trial for the men.

APRIL 3, 1976 New President at Dillard University. Samuel DuBois Cook, former professor of political science at Duke University in North Carolina, was inaugurated as the sixth president of Dillard University, a historic black institution located in New Orleans, Louisiana.

Cook, a native of Griffin, Georgia, received a bachelor's degree from Morehouse College and master's and doctorate degrees from Ohio State University. He had previously taught political science at the Atlanta and Southern Universities, the University of Illinois, and the University of California at Los Angeles.

At Duke University, Cook won an Outstanding Professor Award. He also received a Citation of Achievement from Duke University, a honorary Doctor of Laws degree from his alma mater, Morehouse College, and was a member of Phi Beta Kappa.

JUNE 16, 1976 A.M.E. Church General Conference in Atlanta. The Reverend Richard

Allen Chapelle of Jacksonville, Florida, was elected general conference secretary of the African Methodist Episcopal (A.M.E.) Church during the Fortieth Quadrennial General Conference of the Church in Atlanta, Georgia. Chapelle succeeded the Reverend Russell S. Brown of Chicago who at seventy-eight was at the age of retirement. More than thirty thousand participants, representing more than one million members of the denomination from eighteen districts in the United States, Africa, Central America, and the Caribbean, attended the meeting.

JUNE 25, 1976 Racial Discrimination in Private Schools. The United States Supreme Court voted 7-2 to prohibit private schools from excluding blacks on the basis of their race. The private school case stemmed from a suit filed by the parents of two black children who were turned away from the Fairfax-Brewster School and Bobbe's Private School, both in the Virginia suburbs of Washington, D.C. The two schools had denied that they discriminated and said they had not had previous black applicants. They contended, however, that they had a right to discriminate if they so chose.

The Council for American Private Education, which represented about 90 percent of the nation's private school enrollment, and the Department of Justice supported the black children in their suit, but the Southern Independent Schools Association, which represented 395 schools, and President Gerald R. Ford opposed judicial relief for the blacks. President Ford did say that he personally disapproved of discrimination against blacks by such schools. According to the Court, racial discrimination by private schools was a "classic violation" of the Civil Rights Act of 1866 that prohibited, among other things, discrimination in the enforcement of contracts. The Court continued: "It may be assumed that parents have a First Amendment right to send their children to educational institutions that promote the belief that racial segregation is desirable, and that the

children have an equal right to attend such institutions. . . . But it does not follow that the practice of excluding racial minorities from such institutions is also protected by the same principle."

In reacting to the ruling, Andrew Lipscombe, an attorney for the Fairfax-Brewster, Virginia, schools, said: "Parents are not going to be able to have the associations for their children that they wish, even in private situations which in small, private schools are intimate."

The Court's majority opinion was written by Justice Potter Stewart. In their dissents, Justices Byron R. White and William H. Rehnquist said the Act of 1866 prohibited only discrimination imposed by state law; hence the majority had gone too far in outlawing bias in the private schools.

JUNE 25, 1976 Reverse Discrimination Ruling. The United States Supreme Court ruled unanimously that victims of so-called reverse discrimination have the same rights as blacks to sue in federal courts if they have been terminated from their jobs. The high Court said that the Civil Rights Act of 1964 was "not limited to discrimination against members of any particular race."

The Court ruled in a case from Houston, Texas, where two white employees of the Santa Fe Trail Transportation Company had been fired because they allegedly misappropriated ten cases of antifreeze. A black employee who was also charged in the incident was not terminated. The whites charged that their employer had discriminated against them on the basis of race and that their labor union had acquiesced in the bias by failing to represent one of them properly. The Supreme Court agreed with the petitioners and returned the matter to a lower court.

JULY 15, 1976 Carter Accepted Nomination for President. Jimmy Carter, former governor of Georgia, accepted the Democratic nomination for president of the United States at the close of his party's national convention in New York City. The convention ended with the singing of the anthem of the Civil Rights Movement, "We Shall Overcome," and a benediction by Martin Luther King, Sr., father of slain civil rights leader Martin Luther King, Jr., and one of Carter's strongest supporters during the presidential primary campaigns.

JULY 26, 1976   Integration of Dayton, Ohio, Schools. The United States Court of Appeals for the Sixth Circuit ruled that each of the sixty-eight public schools of Dayton, Ohio, "must reflect roughly the same black-white population as the entire state school system." The order would require a black-white student population in each school that "reflects within 15 percent" the racial composition of each school district. The Dayton Board of Education said it would appeal the ruling to the United States Supreme Court.

AUGUST 28, 1976   Death of Former Ethiopian Emperor. Haile Selassie, former emperor of Ethiopia and also known as "King of Kings," "The Conquering Lion of Judah," and "Elect of God," died of prostrate gland problems in Addis Ababa, Ethiopia, at the age of eighty-three.

Selassie had been a hero for many African Americans since 1936 when he made an impassioned plea and took a firm stance for Ethiopian self-determination before the League of Nations following the invasion of his country by fascist Italy. Selassie last visited the United States in 1969 and laid a wreath on the grave of slain civil rights leader Martin Luther King, Jr. Five years later, the emperor was deposed in a military coup after ruling the African nation (one of human civilization's oldest countries) for fifty-seven years. Selassie was "the world's longest serving monarch."

SEPTEMBER 10, 1976   Former President of Howard University Died. Mordecai Wyatt Johnson, former president of historically black

Howard University, died in Washington, D.C., at age eighty-six.

Johnson was born on January 12, 1890, the son of a Baptist minister. He received undergraduate degrees from both Atlanta Baptist College (now Morehouse College) in 1911 and the University of Chicago in 1913, a Bachelor of Divinity degree from Rochester (New York) Theological Seminary in 1920, and a Master of Sacred Theology degree from Howard University in 1932.

After serving nine years as pastor of the First Baptist Church of Charleston, West Virginia, Johnson assumed the presidency of Howard University in 1926 and held the position until 1960. Under his leadership Howard grew from a mostly black school to an international university in its student body, faculty, and scope of its academic programs. During this period, the student population increased by 250 percent, seventeen new buildings were constructed, and the annual budget increased from $700,000 to $6 million.

Johnson also gained a reputation as a champion of human rights and a spellbinding orator. After addressing the North Atlantic Treaty Organization (NATO) in June 1959, the French newspaper *Le Monde* reported that the "650 delegates heard the most courageous exposé that one might be able to hear at such a meeting," and the *New York Post* remarked that "many were moved (by the address), some with annoyance, but at its end, the applause lasted for five minutes."

In commenting on Johnson's death, the current president of Howard University, James Cheek, said that "love and dedication to Howard University will long be remembered by thousands of persons whose lives he touched throughout the world."

SEPTEMBER 19, 1976   Director of Player Personnel Named. William "Bill" Lucas, a former baseball player for the Milwaukee and Atlanta Braves of the National Baseball League, was named director of player personnel by the Atlanta Braves club. The position is the highest ever held by an African American in professional baseball.

After leaving the playing field in 1964, Lucas joined the Braves' executive staff in sales and promotions. The following year he worked in public relations, and then, in 1962, was named assistant farm director and director of player development.

Of his new appointment, Lucas said that it held no special meaning. Wayne Embry, also an African American, held a similar position for the Milwaukee Bucks of the National Basketball Association. Another prominent black baseball figure, Hank Aaron, also formerly of the Atlanta Braves, led a campaign to get more blacks into "front office" jobs in baseball and other professional sports.

SEPTEMBER 20, 1976 Death of Davage. Matthew Simpson Davage, former president of Clark College in Georgia, died in New Orleans, Louisiana, at age ninety-seven.

Davage was born in 1879 in Shreveport, Louisiana. He earned a B.A. degree from New Orleans University (now Dillard University) in 1900 and immediately joined the faculty there as an instructor in mathematics. He remained on the faculty until 1905 and, at the same time, pursued graduate studies at the University of Chicago.

Between 1905 and 1915, Davage was business manager of the *Southwestern Christian Advocate,* a Methodist publication. In 1915, he returned to education as president of the George R. Smith College at Sedalia, Missouri. After only one year at Sedalia, he assumed the presidency of the Haven Institute at Meridian, Mississippi, which he quickly left to assume the presidency of Samuel Huston College (now Huston-Tillotson College) in Austin, Texas. In the spring of 1920, Davage was elected president of Rust College in Holly Springs, Mississippi, where he became the first black to

head the fifty-four-year-old historically black institution. In 1924, he became the sixteenth president of Clark University, as it was then called. Davage was the second black person to head the institution, the first having been his predecessor, William Henry Crogman.

During his seventeen-year tenure at Clark, Davage presided over the removal of the institution from southeast Atlanta to its present location near the city's other black institutions of higher education, and he helped to provide new financial strength and vitality for the school, even during the Depression years.

In 1939, Davage became one of the first blacks to speak before the all-white Atlanta Rotary Club. Because of the Jim Crow laws and customs of the time, he could not eat lunch with the Rotarians and had to wait in an adjoining room until the meal was finished. Then he gave a speech entitled "The Negro's Place in Atlanta's Life." In it, he said, "Some day we may hope, the thinking people of both races will translate that mutual respect and trust into some concrete work. . . . They may meet and work on the same critics trying to say they are seeking to tear down a social order."

SEPTEMBER 28, 1976 Ali Retained Title. Muhammad Ali won a hard-fought bout to retain his world heavyweight championship title in New York City. Forty-two thousand people paid a total of $3.5 million (a record for a title fight at that time) to see Ali defeat challenger Ken Norton in a unanimous fifteen-round decision. Ali employed his usual wiggling style, known as the "rope-a-dope," while Norton was only able to land several solid blows with both hands. The previous largest gate in a heavyweight title fight was $2.6 million, when Gene Tunney fought Jack Dempsey in Chicago in 1927.

OCTOBER 4, 1976 Secretary of Agriculture Resigned. President Gerald R. Ford accepted the resignation of Secretary of Agriculture Earl L. Butz, who had made uncomplimentary remarks about African Americans. The President said it was "one of the saddest decisions" of his presidency.

Butz, in a private conversation following the Republican National Convention in August 1976, had accused blacks of laziness and shiftlessness. The "off-color" remarks were traced to the secretary in September 1976.

African-American civil rights leaders and Democratic presidential candidate Jimmy Carter, among others, had roundly criticized Butz for his racial slurs and Ford for not immediately firing him.

OCTOBER 25, 1976 Governor Wallace Pardoned Norris. Clarence "Willie" Norris, the last of the "Scottsboro Boys," was pardoned for a 1931 rape conviction. The order was signed in Montgomery, Alabama, by Governor George C. Wallace.

Norris, age sixty-four, was among eight black men convicted of raping two white women near Scottsboro, Alabama, and sentenced to death in 1931. The original conviction was later overturned by the U.S. Supreme Court, and a subsequent guilty verdict was set aside after one of the alleged victims recanted her previous testimony. Although the eight were also convicted at a third trial, all but Norris, who escaped while on parole in 1946, had already been pardoned.

The NAACP, along with the Communist Party and other organizations, had waged celebrated protests as well as legal actions on behalf of the Scottsboro Boys over the years and announced after the pardon that it was interpreting it "as a total absolution for Norris. . . . [He] has been absolved of any wrongdoing. We will interpret this as applying to the others." All of the other Scottsboro Boys were, however, presumed to be dead at the time of Norris's release.

NOVEMBER 15, 1976 African Americans Accepted by Plains Baptist Church. The congregation of all-white Plains Baptist Church in

The Scottsboro Boys. (Bettmann Archive/Newsphotos, Inc.)

Plains, Georgia, voted 120–66 to admit black worshipers as members. The church's racially exclusionary policy had been under attack since October of that year when Clennon King, a fifty-six-year-old black minister from Albany, Georgia, announced that he would seek to join the congregation. The Plains Baptist Church had at various times included among its membership President-elect Jimmy Carter, his wife, Rosalyn, and his mother, Lillian. After the motion to admit blacks was approved, Carter admitted being proud of my church, God's church."

DECEMBER 8, 1976 Court Rejected Desegregation Plan. The United States Supreme Court, in a 7–2 decision, ruled against a sweeping desegregation plan for the city of Austin, Texas. The Court sent the case back to the U.S. Court of Appeals for the Fifth District to review in light of its decision last June that government acts are not unconstitutional simply because "they have [a] disproportionate effect on blacks."

The Court also contended that "school desegregation plans should be tailored to correct only the amount of segregation caused intentionally by school officials." They argued that the courts cannot impose "sweeping orders" designed to correct all school segregation that may result "from racial and ethnic housing patterns." The dissenting Justices, William J. Brennan and Thurgood Marshall, believed the appellate court had "decided the case correctly."

DECEMBER 16, 1976 African American Nominated to U.S. Ambassador to the United Nations. President-elect Jimmy Carter announced the nomination of Georgia Congressman Andrew Jackson Young as U.S. Ambassador to the United Nations. The nomination marked the first time an African American had ever been asked to lead the American delegation at the world peace organization. The position also carries cabinet-level status in the United States government.

Young, the first black congressman from Georgia since 1871, was serving his second term in Washington at the time of the nomination.

DECEMBER 23, 1976 Carter Made Cabinet Nominations. President-elect Jimmy Carter completed the nominations for his cabinet. The cabinet nominees included two blacks, Georgia Congressman Andrew Young as U.S. Ambassador to the United Nations and Washington, D.C., attorney Patricia Roberts Harris as Secretary of Housing and Urban Development (HUD).

1977

JANUARY 17, 1977 Steele Named Attorney General of Iowa. Shirley Creenard Steele, a black attorney, was appointed Assistant Attorney General for the state of Iowa. Steele, a native of Salisbury, North Carolina, graduated from Livingstone College in North Carolina in 1974 and received a Doctor of Jurisprudence degree from the Drake University School of Law in Iowa.

U.N. Ambassador Andrew Young.

In her new position, Steele would be responsible for representing the state in civil rights legislation and criminal appeals. She is the first black woman ever to serve in such a position in Iowa's history.

JANUARY 19, 1977 Secretary of the Army Appointed. Clifford Alexander, Jr., a forty-three-year-old black attorney, was named Secretary of the Army by President-elect Jimmy Carter.

Alexander, who served one year as a private in the Army during 1958 and 1959, was Chairman of the Equal Employment Opportunities Commission (EEOC) under President Richard M. Nixon but resigned in the middle of a five-year term because of policy disagreements with the Republican administration. He had also served as an assistant district attorney in New York City and a White House aide under Presidents John F. Kennedy and Richard Nixon.

Alexander practiced law in Washington, D.C. for more than six years and ran an unsuccessful mayoral campaign in that city in 1975. Alexander's appointment marked the first time in United States history that a black American had served as Secretary of the Army.

JANUARY 20, 1977   Carter Sworn In. Jimmy Carter, former governor of Georgia, took the oath of office of the President of the United States at the Capitol in Washington, D.C. A black woman from his native state was overheard in the crowd murmuring, "Yes, Lord!" Black voters had supported Carter overwhelmingly in his campaign for the nation's highest executive office.

JANUARY 26, 1977   Indiana Court Asked to Reexamine Busing Plan. The United States Supreme Court, in a 6–3 decision, returned a plan involving the busing of black students to surrounding predominantly white school districts in Indianapolis, Indiana, to a lower federal court for reexamination. The effect of the high court's ruling was to nullify the busing plan to achieve further desegregation, which the lower court had already ordered.

JANUARY 27, 1977   Drew Days Selected. U.S. Attorney General Griffin Bell selected Drew Days, a thirty-six-year-old black lawyer, to be assistant attorney general in charge of civil rights in the U.S. Department of Justice.

Days, a Florida native, graduated from the Yale University Law School in 1966. In 1970, he took a position as an attorney with the NAACP Legal Defense Fund (LDF), which handles legal matters for the parent organization. The appointment made Days the first black person ever to oversee civil rights enforcement and also the first black assistant attorney general in American history.

JANUARY 30, 1977   Young Sworn In. Andrew Jackson Young, an African American congressman from Georgia, took the oath of office as United States Ambassador to the United Nations (UN), the highest diplomatic post ever held by a black American. The appointment also carried cabinet rank in the administration of President Jimmy Carter.

Young was born in New Orleans, Louisiana on March 12, 1932, the son of a dentist and a school teacher. He received a bachelor's degree from Howard University in 1951 and a Bachelor of Divinity degree at the Hartford Theological Seminary in Connecticut in 1951. Young was then ordained a minister in the United Church of Christ. His early pastorates were in Marion, Alabama, and Thomasville and Beachton, Georgia. After a brief period of service at the National Council of Churches, Young joined the staff of the Southern Christian Leadership Conference (SCLC).

In 1964, Martin Luther King, Jr. named Young executive director of the SCLC, and in 1967 he became its executive vice president. In these roles, Young was one of the principal negotiators "with recalcitrant white leaders" who were just "beginning to understand the moral and political power of nonviolent protest."

Young entered national politics in 1970 when he ran unsuccessfully for Congress from Georgia's Fifth District. Two years later, the majority white district in the Atlanta area had undergone reapportionment. Young was then elected as the first black Georgia congressman since the Reconstruction era. Although whites retained a slight voting edge in his district, Young was returned to Congress in 1974 and 1976.

In commenting on the appointment of Young, President Carter said the congressman "did not want or ask for this job. It was only with the greatest reluctance on his part that he finally agreed to accept [it] for me and for our country." Young himself remarked: "Through many dangers, toils and snares we have already come, the faith that brought us safe thus far will lead us safely on."

FEBRUARY 3, 1977   "Roots" Concluding Segment Aired. The "Roots" miniseries, based on Alex Haley's novel of the same title in which he traced his ancestry to Africa and slavery, ended eight nights of presentations on the ABC television network. The Sunday night finale achieved the highest single ratings ever amassed by a television production. The previous top television presentation had been the epic Civil War drama, *Gone with the Wind.* During the eight nights of programming, "Roots" was watched by more than 130 million viewers.

FEBRUARY 17, 1977 Violations of Civil Rights Laws Alleged. The Department of Health, Education, and Welfare (HEW) announced that it was cutting off funds to the public schools of Chicago, Illinois, because of alleged violations of civil rights laws. The alleged violations included an "inadequate bilingual program and too many black teachers in schools with overwhelming black student populations." The order was to become final within twenty days unless the school district appealed or made "appropriate changes to comply with the law." It was estimated that $100 million of the district's annual budget of $600 million came from the federal government.

HEW Secretary Joseph A. Califano, Jr., in his first formal statement on civil rights, stated: "We have no desire ever to cut off funds to any school district or other educational institutions. But the way to insure compliance with civil rights laws is to make clear that we will order funds cut off if we must."

MARCH 2, 1977 Lowrey Succeeded Abernathy. Joseph E. Lowery, chairman of the board of the Southern Christian Leadership Conference (SCLC), was named acting president of the civil rights organization. He succeeded the Reverend Ralph David Abernathy, who resigned to run for a congressional seat in Georgia's fifth district. Lowery was appointed to serve until the SCLC convention in August, when he or some other person would be confirmed as permanent president.

MARCH 3, 1977 Death of Civil Rights Leader. Lester Kendel Jackson, minister and civil rights leader, died in Chicago, Illinois.

Jackson, the son of tenant farmers, was born in Fort Gaines, Georgia, in 1895. He earned a Bachelor of Divinity degree at the Virginia Theological Seminary and a Doctor of Divinity from Union Theological Seminary in New York. Jackson pastored Baptist churches in Hollins, Lynchburg, and Danville, Virginia; Passaic and Long Branch, New Jersey; and Gary, Indiana. At the time of his death, he was the pastor of the St. Paul Baptist Church in Gary. All totaled, he spent fifty-five years of life in the Christian ministry.

Jackson also served as executive secretary of the Hunter Branch YMCA in Lynchburg, Va., professor of religious education, educational secretary and general manager, and trustee of Virginia Theological Seminary. In addition, he was a member of the Board of Directors of the National Council of Churches in the United States.

Jackson was a leader of civil rights protests in both Long Branch, New Jersey, and Gary, Indiana. His activities in Long Branch resulted in a court decision that permitted blacks to bathe on local beaches, and his work in Gary led to the hiring of hundreds of blacks by banks, savings and loan associations, and public utilities companies.

In September 1973, more than 250 people, including the Reverend Martin Luther King, Sr., father of slain civil rights leader Martin Luther King, Jr., attended a tribute for Jackson in Gary. Jackson called that occasion the "most joyful moment" in his life.

MARCH 9, 1977 Black Muslims Took Hostages. A group of armed Black Muslims took hostages at three sites in Washington, D.C., slaying one man. The attacks occurred at the offices of the Jewish organization B'nai B'rith, an Islamic center, and the Washington City Hall. At city hall, Maurice Williams, a twenty-two-year-old radio reporter, was killed and at least eleven others were wounded. Washington's Mayor Walter Washington barricaded himself inside his office.

The gunmen demanded that the premiere of the film *Mohammad, Messenger of God* be cancelled because they said it "ridiculed the Prophet." United Artists immediately cancelled showings of the film in New York City. Another gunman, however, said the attacks were a reprisal for the slaying in Washington four years ago of seven Hanafi Muslims. The Hanafis were allegedly killed by members of a rival Muslim sect.

MARCH 14, 1977 Haley Honored by Senate. The United States Senate adopted a resolution praising Alex Haley, the author of *Roots,* for "his exceptional achievement." The unanimous resolution, sponsored by Senator John Glenn from Ohio, said the historical novel and its television adaptation had "contributed to the cause of a better racial understanding in the United States."

MARCH 15, 1977 President of Florida A & M Resigned. B.L. Perry, Jr., resigned as president of Florida A & M University, one of the nation's largest historically black institutions of higher education. Perry, who left because of personal reasons, was an alumnus of Florida A & M. Before departing, he told faculty and students that the university "must remain as an institution, changed of course by the social and legal evolutions it institutionalized, as a force for providing higher education to a discernible segment of the population, and providing hope and inspiration to thousands who look upon it as a model for pursuing pluralistic ideals in a multi-ethnic, multi-cultural, and multi-racial society." Perry had been president of Florida A & M since 1968.

MARCH 31–APRIL 18, 1977 Demonstration at Rust College. On March 31, Rust College, a black school in Holly Springs, Mississippi, was closed and all of its eight hundred students were ordered off campus following a demonstration and fire on campus. The fire, of unknown origins, caused an estimated $500,000 damage to the college's administration building.

Students blamed the school's president W.A. McMillan for the disturbance. Some said that he exercised "strict discipline," had failed to communicate with them, had alienated them, and "forced them to action." George Dupont, a

sophomore student, called the president "a stubborn dictator, deceitful, unreaching. We want him out. . . . He runs this place like a penal institution."

The damaged building, a replica of Independence Hall in Philadelphia, was constructed on the small, church-related liberal arts campus in 1947.

On April 18, Rust College reopened to students and faculty. In a statement, W.A. McMillan, who had been asked by twenty of his faculty members to resign, stated: "I am disappointed, but not discouraged. Rust has a heritage that a disruption or a fire cannot destroy. We will heal our wounds and get to the business of making Christian higher education better than ever at Rust College."

APRIL 2, 1977 Desegregation of Southern Universities. U.S. District Court Judge John Pratt ruled in Washington, D.C., that the Department of Health, Education, and Welfare (HEW) had violated civil rights laws by failing to order "adequate racial desegregation" in the higher educational institutions of six Southern states. The judge ordered HEW to solicit new desegregation plans from Florida, Georgia, North Carolina, Arkansas, Oklahoma, and Virginia, but he warned that the plans "must preserve the status of their historically black colleges."

Under Pratt's order, HEW was given ninety days to set guidelines for which the states must comply. The states would then have sixty days to submit detailed plans on the "best way to balance the proportion of black and white students in schools that receive federal aid." HEW would then have an additional 120 days to accept or reject the states' plans.

In 1972, Pratt had found Louisiana, Maryland, Mississippi, and Pennsylvania, in addition to the aforementioned states, guilty of violating the Civil Rights Act of 1964. They were not included in the most recent order, however, because they were involved in civil rights suits elsewhere.

APRIL 14, 1977 U.S. Court of Appeals Judge Died. William H. Hastie, the first black person appointed to a United States Court of Appeals, died after collapsing on a golf course in Philadelphia, Pennsylvania, at the age of seventy-one.

Hastie, the son of a federal clerk, was born in Knoxville, Tennessee. He graduated *magna cum laude* from Amherst College in 1925 and taught junior high school in New York before enrolling in Harvard Law School. He was admitted to the bar in 1930.

Between 1939 and 1946, Hastie was dean of the law school of Howard University. While at Howard, President Franklin D. Roosevelt asked him to join his "Black Cabinet" (a group of African-American advisors) as a civilian aide to Secretary of War Henry Stinson. In 1943 Hastie resigned from the War Department in protest against what he called the "reactionary policies and discriminatory practices" of the Air Force. At that time, he said "the simple fact is that the air command does not want Negro pilots flying in and out of various fields, eating, sleeping, and mingling with other personnel. . . ." These and other actions led some persons to regard him "as one of the pioneers in the civil rights movement in the United States."

After leaving the War Department, Hastie further served the federal government as the first black on the District Court of the Virgin Islands and later governor of the United States possession from 1946 to 1949. In 1949, President Harry S. Truman elevated Hastie to a position of justice of the United States Court of Appeals for the Third Circuit. He retired from that court as chief judge in 1971 but retained the position of senior judge until his death.

Upon learning of Justice Hastie's death, the U.S. Supreme Court's Chief Justice Warren Burger called it "a great loss to the judiciary and to the country."

MAY 3, 1977 West Point Honored Lieutenant Flipper. Nearly forty years after his death,

Judge William Hastie. (AP/Wide World Photos.)

West Point's first African American graduate was honored with a commemorative bust. In a ceremony attended by Flipper's relatives, two of the academy's four regiments marched in review. Superintendent Lieutenant-General Sidney B. Berry called Flipper "one of the most honored citizens of the nation, a credit to all of its people and its rich diversity." Flipper had been exonerated by the military in the previous year.

MAY 5, 1977 Students Demanded Resignation of College President. About 150 students continued their demands calling for the resignation of Prince Jackson, Jr., as president of predominantly black Savannah State College in Georgia. The students' grievances included decreased alumni financial support because of "several scandals involving college staff members," alleged diversion of scholarship monies to other purposes, and alleged illegal diversion of student government association funds to "pay a deficit in the athletic program." President Jackson did not make an immediate public response to the students' allegations.

Savannah State was one of several historically black colleges that experienced student

Ethel Waters. (AP/Wide World Photos.)

protests recently over questionable internal practices.

MAY 16, 1977   Ali Defeated Evangelista to Retain Title. Muhammad Ali retained his world heavyweight boxing championship with a unanimous decision over twenty-two year old Alfredo Evangelista after fifteen rounds in Landover, Maryland. Evangelista, a native of Uruguay who had been heralded as "the Spanish Rocky," never caught Ali with a solid punch during the entire fight. He fought a mostly defensive contest. Ali received $2.75 million for the victory, $200,000 of which had been used to buy tickets for disadvantaged youths to attend the fight.

It was the ninth time in his second reign as champion that Ali had defended his title. He had been beaten only twice, by Joe Frazier and Ken Norton, in 56 career bouts.

MAY 19, 1977   Festival Honored Haley. A three-day statewide festival honoring Alex Haley, the Pulitzer Prize-winning author of the novel *Roots,* began in Henning, Tennessee, the author's hometown. Haley said that he was inspired by his grandmother's tales of his fami-

ly's struggles in slavery and freedom. By the spring of 1977, *Roots* had sold more than 1.6 million copies in the first six months after publication and was translated into 22 languages.

JUNE 1, 1977   Magazine Published Photographs of African Slaves. The oldest known identified photographs of African slaves in the United States were published in the June issue of *American Heritage Magazine.* The photographs were discovered eighteen months previously in an otherwise empty cabinet in an attic of the Peabody Museum at Harvard University by Elinor Reichlin. The daguerreotypes were taken in Columbia, South Carolina, in 1850 "for scientific study," by J.T. Zealy, whom Reichlin traced as a photographer in Columbia until 1880.

Professor Stephen Williams, director of the Peabody Museum, asserted that the photographs were "the oldest examples of rare pictures of American slaves born in Africa." At least four of the seven subjects shown in several poses were identified on the prints by first name, African nation or tribe of origin, and by slave owner. Among them was a man named Alfred, identified as a Foulah, a West African tribe, and owned by an I. Lomas of Columbia, South Carolina, and Jack and Renty from Guinea and the Congo, respectively, owned by a B.F. Taylor, also of Columbia. Nude photos of African women were not released by the Peabody Museum.

AUGUST 1, 1977   Blake Assumed Presidency of Clark College. Elias Blake, Jr., forty-seven-year-old president of the Institute for Services to Education (ISE), became the new president of Clark College in Atlanta, Georgia. Blake succeeded Vivian W. Henderson, who died during heart surgery on January 28, 1976.

Blake, a native Georgian, received bachelor and master's degrees from Paine College in Augusta, Georgia, in 1951 and Howard University in 1954, respectively, and a doctorate from the University of Illinois in 1960. He came to Clark College from the Institute for Services to Education in Washington, D.C., where he was a consultant to governmental and private educational agencies.

AUGUST 1, 1977 Singer Ethel Waters Died. Ethel Waters, African American singer and actress, died of apparent heart failure in Chatsworth, California, at age seventy-six.

Waters was born on October 31, 1900, in Chester, Pennsylvania. She first appeared on stage at age seventeen and later toured with jazz groups where she became "a leading theater and cafe personality." But after a religious conversion, Waters gave up singing in nightclubs and turned to spirituals.

After her talents were more widely recognized, Waters made her Broadway debut in *Plantation Revue of 1924.* In this production, she scored one of the greatest song hits ever when she introduced the piece "Dinah." From Broadway she began making motion pictures and was cast in *As Thousands Cheer, At Home Abroad,* and *Rhapsody in Black.* In 1950, Waters was nominated for an Academy Award for her role in *Pinky.* Her last motion picture was *The Sound and the Fury* in 1958. By this time, however, Waters began appearing on such television programs as "The Tennessee Ernie Ford Show," "Daniel Boone," and "Route 66."

In her later life, Waters turned increasingly to singing, becoming noted particularly for blues renditions of "Am I Blue" and "Stormy Weather" as well as black spirituals. She was, according to an article in the *Atlanta Constitution,* "the first woman ever to sing 'St. Louis Blues'" and thrilled millions around the world with her rendition of "His Eye Is on the Sparrow" with the Billy Graham Evangelical Crusade. She had been singing with the Crusade for fifteen years at the time her death. Waters's autobiography, also entitled *His Eye Is on the Sparrow,* was published in 1951 and became a best seller.

In the 1960s, stricken with diabetes and heart problems, it was revealed that Waters had lost much of her wealth and was subsisting on social security. She admitted her financial difficulties but said "if half the people that owed me money paid it back, I'd be a rich woman." Yet she refused to make television commercials in order to earn more money. Instead, she exclaimed "I couldn't be happier because I'm at peace with the Lord."

In an editorial published after Waters's death, the *Atlanta Constitution* commented that "few American entertainment figures have had careers as varied and memorable as Ethel Waters."

AUGUST 1, 1977 Talladega College Named New President. Joseph N. Gayles, Jr., program director of the medical education program at Morehouse College, assumed the presidency of Talladega College in Alabama. Gayles succeeded Herman Long, who died in office in 1976.

Gayles, a *summa cum laude* graduate of Louisiana's Dillard University, received a Ph.D. degree in chemical physics from Brown University in Rhode Island. He was previously a professor of chemistry at Morehouse College.

SEPTEMBER 1, 1977 Atlanta University Named New President. Cleveland L. Dennard, president of the Washington Technical Institute in Washington, D.C., assumed the presidency of historically black Atlanta University in Georgia.

Dennard, a native of Sebring, Florida, was educated at Florida A & M University, the University of Colorado, and the University of Tennessee, from which he earned a Ed.D. degree. Prior to becoming president of the Washington Technical Institute in 1967 he had been principal of the George Washington Carver Vocational School in Atlanta (1960–1965), and Deputy Commissioner for Manpower and Program Management in the New York City Human Resource Administration (1965–1967). Dennard had also lectured in sixteen foreign countries under the auspices of the United States Information Agency (USIA).

SEPTEMBER 5–7, 1977 Labor Day Picnic Turned Bloody. On September 5, Kenneth Wilson, a seventeen-year-old white youth wearing a Nazi armband, shot into a crowd of about two hundred blacks attending a Labor Day church picnic in Charlotte, North Carolina, before killing himself. One black man, Roosevelt Davis, aged twenty-nine, was killed in the attack. On September 7, a second victim, Jo Ann Terry, a twenty-eight-old widow, died of wounds received two days earlier. Two other black victims survived the assault.

SEPTEMBER 6, 1977 Federal Racial Quotas Rejected by Virginia. Governor Mills E. Godwin announced that the state of Virginia would not comply with federal racial quotas ordered by the Department of Health, Education, and Welfare (HEW) to desegregate its colleges and universities. In a letter to HEW, Governor Godwin stated: "All our accomplishments to date signal one thing—Virginia's intention to provide access, for all of its citizens regardless of race, to higher education which is as diverse and as excellent as it can possibly be." But he said the state would not surrender its "administrative responsibilities to the federal government."

Alabama, Florida, Georgia, North Carolina, Oklahoma, and Virginia were under orders to submit revised desegregation plans to HEW by the week of September 5. Louisiana had previously refused to submit any plan to HEW and Mississippi had submitted an unacceptable one. Both states were still in federal courts for their actions.

Virginia, which did not fully comply with the HEW desegregation guidelines, faced the possible loss of an estimated $40 million in federal funds.

SEPTEMBER 8, 1977 Study Listed Homicide as Leading Cause of Death. A study by scholars at the Case Western University in Cleveland, Ohio, confirmed that homicide was "the leading cause of death nationally among black men aged 25–34." Although the research team focused their study on Cleveland, they also used a federal government report entitled "Homicide Trends in the United States" to draw nationwide conclusions. In Cleveland, however, between 1958 and 1962, 20 blacks died of homicide for every white, and from 1963 to 1974, 12 blacks for every white. Nationwide, in 1975, 1,913 blacks between the ages of 24 and 34 died of accidental causes; 3,256 from disease; 439 from suicide; and 2,506 from homicide. The study was published in the September 1977 issue of the *New England Journal of Medicine*.

SEPTEMBER 9, 1977 Ford Named Miss Black America. Claire Ford, an eighteen-year-old student at Memphis State University, was crowned Miss Black America for 1977 in Santa Monica, California. Mary Denise Bentley, Miss Indiana, was the first runner-up.

Ford, who entered the pageant as Miss Tennessee, won $10,000 in prize money, an acting role in the television miniseries "Roots: The Next Generation," and screen tests at both NBC and Universal Studios. Ford later revealed that she wanted to become a lawyer.

SEPTEMBER 11, 1977 Emmy Awards Honored "Roots." The epic television mini-series "Roots," based on Alex Haley's novel about his family in Africa and America, swept the nineteenth annual Emmy Award presentations in Los Angeles, California. Among the top Emmys awarded were: Outstanding Lead Actor for a Single Appearance in a Drama or Comedy Series: Lou Gossett, Jr., who portrayed the smooth survivor "Fiddler;" Outstanding Writing in a Drama Series: Ernest Kinoy and William Blinn; Outstanding Directing in a Drama Series: David Greene; and Outstanding Single Performance by a Supporting Actor and Actress in a Drama or Comedy Series: Edward Asner and Olivia Cole, respectively. The drama also garnered the Outstanding Limited Series award.

"Roots," the most successful mini-series in television history, was broadcast over eight nights on the ABC television network in January and February 1977.

OCTOBER 3, 1977 Attempt to Impeach Young Filed. Ten members of the United States House of Representatives signed a resolution calling for the impeachment of Andrew J. Young, the first African American ambassador to the United Nations (UN). Most of the charges stemmed from public statements made by Young before and since his appointment to this position. The document cited twenty actions by Young that warranted his impeachment, including his depiction of Great Britain and Sweden as racist nations. The resolution also accused Young of failing to oppose the admission of Vietnam to the United Nations and of "seeking to transfer the governing power in the anti-communist nation of Rhodesia to the pro-Marxist guerilla coalition."

OCTOBER 18, 1977 Jackson Sets Baseball Record. Reggie Jackson, African American outfielder for the New York Yankees of the American Baseball League, hit three home runs in a single World Series game, the first time in history that such a feat had been accomplished. The Yankees went on to defeat the Los Angeles Dodgers of the National Baseball League 8–4 and to capture the 1977 World Series title.

Dodgers manager Tommy Lasorda called Jackson's achievement "the greatest performance that I've ever seen in a World Series." Jackson himself commented, "It's a nice feeling, but I'm beat. I know there's a God in heaven."

OCTOBER 29, 1977 Ali Remained the Champion. Muhammad Ali retained the World Heavyweight Boxing Championship with a unanimous decision in fifteen rounds, over challenger Earnie Shavers. The pattern of the fight was "one of Shavers stalking and looking to throw the big right hand that had enabled him to knock out fifty-two of his first sixty opponents, while Ali looked for ways to nullify the challenger's power." Ali, using "jabs, hooks and flurries of punches with both hands to the head," was the most successful. At the end of the New York City fight, Shavers cried, "they robbed me! They robbed me!"

NOVEMBER 13, 1977 Carter Appointed Four African Americans as U.S. Attorneys. The Associated Press reported that since taking office in January 1977, President Jimmy Carter had appointed four blacks as United States attorneys (chief prosecutors). They were: G. William Hunter of San Francisco, California; Hubert H. Bryant of Tulsa, Oklahoma; James R. Burgess, Jr., of East St. Louis, Illinois; and Henry M. Michaux of Greensboro, North Carolina. During the administrations of Presidents Richard M. Nixon and Gerald R. Ford, there was only one black U.S. attorney, Frederick Coleman in Cleveland, Ohio.

NOVEMBER 18, 1977 Former Klansman Convicted of Murder. Robert Edward Chambliss, a seventy-three-year-old former Ku Klux Klansman, was convicted of first degree murder in the 1963 dynamite bombing of the Sixteenth Baptist Church in Birmingham, Alabama. The blast killed four young black girls who were attending Sunday school. Chambliss was convicted specifically for the death of eleven-year-old Carol Denise McNair. He was immediately sentenced to a term of life imprisonment.

NOVEMBER 30, 1977 Enrollment Rose at Black Colleges and Universities. The *Atlanta Constitution* reported increased enrollments in many of the nation's historically black colleges and universities. The ten black colleges with the largest enrollments in 1977 were: 1) Howard University, Washington, D.C. (9,752); 2) Texas Southern University, Houston (9,552); 3) Southern University, Baton Rouge (9,002); 4) Jackson State University, Mississippi (7,844); 5) Norfolk State College, Virginia (7,263); 6) Morgan State College, Baltimore (6,424);

7) Florida A & M, Tallahassee (5,837); 8) North Carolina A & T State University, Greensboro (5,515); 9) Tennessee State University, Nashville (5,348); 10) Prairie View A & M University, Texas (5,146).

DECEMBER 10, 1977　Congresswoman Jordan Announced Intentions. Barbara Jordan, African American congresswoman from Texas, announced that she would not seek reelection. She denied rumors of poor health and said she would not seek a seat on the federal bench. She did say "the longer you stay in Congress, the harder it is to leave. . . . I didn't want to wake up one fine sunny morning and say there is nothing else to do."

Jordan had gone to Congress from Houston's eighteenth district in 1972 after serving in the Texas State Senate, where she became president pro tempore (the first African American to preside over that body). During the impeachment hearings for President Richard Nixon in 1974, Jordan caught the attention of the nation with an eloquent condemnation of the president's involvement in the Watergate burglary scandal and an equally eloquent defense of the Constitution of the United States. At the 1976 Democratic National Convention held in New York City, she "electrified what had previously been a dull gathering, speaking with a precise, clipped delivery."

1978

JANUARY 13, 1978　Humphrey Died. Hubert Horatio Humphrey, who served as senator from Minnesota, vice president of the United States under Lyndon Johnson, and a key leader in the fight for passage of civil rights legislation in the 1960s, died of cancer in Waverly, Minnesota, at age sixty-one.

Commenting on Humphrey's death, African American civil rights activist John Lewis said, "in this century, we lost two great Americans. . . . One was Dr. Martin Luther King, Jr.,

the other was Hubert Humphrey, who was the champion for the rights of all people. His life should be an inspiration to us all."

JANUARY 15, 1978　Payton Named MVP. Walter Payton, African American running back for the Chicago Bears, was named the National Football League's Most Valuable Player for 1977. Payton received 57 of 87 votes cast by sportswriters and broadcasters, three from each league city. Quarterbacks Bob Griese of the Miami Dolphins and Craig Morton of the Denver Broncos were the runner ups with ten votes each.

Payton, a graduate of Jackson State University in Mississippi, led the League in rushing with 1,852 yards during the 1977 season, his third year in the NFL (a League record). He ran for 275 yards in one game (November 20 against the Minnesota Vikings), which surpassed the record set by African American O. J. Simpson. Payton also exceeded Simpson's record of 332 carries with 339 of his own. Finally, Payton's 1,852 yards rushing was third only to Simpson's 2,003 and the African American Jim Brown's 1,863 during a season.

JANUARY 17, 1978　National Urban League Released Third Report. In its third "State of Black America" report, the National Urban League (NUL) stated that 1977 was "a year of continued depression, with unacceptably high unemployment and a widening income gap" for African Americans.

In remarks accompanying the presentation of the report, NUL director Vernon Jordan said the group was "disappointed" in President Jimmy Carter. He added, "the administration must face up to two basic realities. First— more, much more, is needed by way of federal actions to assist poor people and the cities. . . . Second, it must recognize that the priority of balancing the budget by 1981 cannot be reconciled with more pressing priorities."

FEBRUARY 15, 1978　Ali Defeated by Spinks. Leon Spinks, a black former Marine, defeated

Muhammad Ali for the heavyweight boxing championship of the world. The championship was given to Spinks, age twenty-four, after fifteen rounds on a split decision by ring officials. The thirty-six-year-old Ali bled from the mouth during most of the fight. Both men were former Olympic light heavyweight champions—Spinks in 1976 at Montreal and Ali in 1960 in Rome.

Spinks's victory represented one of the biggest upsets in world heavyweight title history since Ali, an 8–1 underdog himself at the time, dethroned the late Sonny Liston in 1964. It also ranked alongside Jim Braddock's upset over Max Baer in 1935, Jersey Joe Walcott's defeat of Ezzard Charles in 1951, and Ingemar Johansson's win over Floyd Patterson in 1959. Spinks received $350,000 for his victory; Ali made $3.5 million in defeat.

FEBRUARY 25, 1978   Four-Star General Died. Daniel "Chappie" James, the only four-star black general in the U.S. Armed Forces, died of a heart attack in Colorado Springs, Colorado, at age fifty-eight.

James, a graduate of Tuskegee Institute, grew up in Pensacola, Florida, during a period of rigid racial segregation. His mother, Lillie A. James, who founded her own school for black youths, encouraged him to dream of higher things. James emerged from pushing a coal dolly in a Pensacola gas plant to one of the nation's most influential military leaders. Of his mother's influence, James once stated: "My mother used to say, 'Don't stand there banging on the door of opportunity, then, when someone opens it, you say, 'Wait a minute, I got to get my bags.' You be prepared with your bags of knowledge, your patriotism, your honor, and when somebody opens that door, you charge in."

James, who served in three wars with the Air Force, retired on January 26, 1978. He wrote on a portrait of himself that now hangs in the Pentagon: "I fought three wars and three more wouldn't be too many to defend my country. . . . I love America and as she has weaknesses or ills, I'll hold her hand."

FEBRUARY 27, 1978   Court Ruled on Aiding School Busing. The United States Supreme Court ruled that the federal government does not have to help pay the costs of court-ordered busing to achieve racially desegregated public schools. The justices rejected without comment an appeal by Kentucky Governor Julian M. Carroll, who sought permission to ask for federal help in paying for the busing of school children in Louisville and surrounding Jefferson County, Kentucky. A school desegregation plan, which was in effect in the area, required the busing of approximately 23,000 students daily.

In his appeal, Governor Carroll had said that "the drain on state and local funds [was] quite real and devastating." Thus, he challenged the constitutionality of three federal laws that prohibited federal funding of busing to achieve desegregation.

MARCH 3, 1978   Man Pleaded Guilty in Involuntary Servitude Case. Riaz Hussain Shah, a horticulturist who formerly taught at Miami-Dade Community College, pleaded guilty in federal court in Miami, Florida, to "holding a person in involuntary servitude." Shah admitted that he and his wife, Isharad Majed Shah, an anesthesiologist, bought a ten-year-old African girl from her mother and employed the child "for at least two years as a house slave." During most of her enslavement, the girl, Rose Iftony, had only one dress to wear, ate rice from a tin plate, and drank from a broken glass.

Iftony was ten years old in 1974 when she arrived in the United States from Sierra Leone, where the Shahs paid her mother $200 and promised to educate her. Both of the Shahs, at the time, were registered aliens from Pakistan.

FBI agent Joseph Bell called the girl's bondage "the first classic case of slavery in this century [that] the FBI knows of. . . . That's what used to happen before the Civil War."

MARCH 3, 1978 New President of Atlanta University. Cleveland Leon Dennard was inaugurated as the eighth president of historically black Atlanta University. The new president of the 112-year old institution formerly served as president of the Washington Technical Institute in the District of Columbia.

MARCH 5, 1978 Death Row Inmate Study Released. A study of death row inmates financed by the Southern Poverty Law Center showed that very few blacks and no whites received the death penalty for the killing of blacks. In the three southern states surveyed, Florida, Georgia, and Texas, 45 percent of the death row inmates were blacks who killed whites, while only 5 percent were blacks who killed blacks. 50 percent were whites who killed whites. There were no white inmates on death row who killed blacks.

Morris Dees, director of the Poverty Law Center (based in Montgomery, Alabama), claimed that the study "proved that blacks still make up a far greater proportion of the death row population than are represented in the general population. . . . But the real clincher is that death is reserved for those who kill whites."

The death penalty study was conducted by William J. Bowers, a Northwestern University professor, who published *Executions in America* in 1974.

MARCH 14, 1978 Catholic Schools Saw Minority Enrollment Increase. The National Catholic Educational Association reported that while the overall attendance in Roman Catholic parochial schools dropped in 1977, the percentage of minority students increased sharply. The exact percentage of minority students enrolled in both Catholic elementary and secondary schools over the six year period, 1971 to 1977, increased from 10.8 percent to 16 percent. Among black students in elementary schools alone, the increase was from 5.1 to 7.6

percent. The figures were contained in the Catholic Educational Association's 1978 edition of "Catholic Schools in America."

MARCH 15, 1978 African American Boy Honored by President Carter. President Jimmy Carter presented Anthony Owens, a seventeen-year-old African-American youth from Austin, Texas, with a plaque naming him Boy of the Year. Owens won the distinction in a competition sponsored by Boys' Clubs of America.

MARCH 17, 1978 CIA Activities Publicized. The *Atlanta Constitution,* quoting from the *New York Times,* reported that the Central Intelligence Agency (CIA) recruited African Americans to spy on members of the Black Panther Party in the United States and Africa in the late 1960s and early 1970s. The *Times* based its information on "sources with firsthand knowledge of the operation." The activities of the black agents included "following and photographing" suspected Black Panther Party members in the United States and infiltration of Panther groups in Africa. One agent even "managed to gain access to the personal overseas living quarters of Eldridge Cleaver, the exiled Panther leader who set up a headquarters in Algeria in the late 1960s."

The CIA had said "repeatedly that the goal of the agency's domestic spying program was to determine whether anti-war activists and black extremists were being financed and directed by Communist governments," but "one longtime operative with direct knowledge of the spying said . . . that there was an additional goal in the case of the Black Panthers living abroad: to 'neutralize' them; to try and get them in trouble with local authorities wherever they could."

The *Times* sources further revealed that the CIA conducted at least two major operations or programs involving the use of African Americans at the time that the Black Panther Party was "attracting wide public attention" in the 1960s and 1970s. One of the programs, directed by the CIA Office of Security, was operated in the Washington, D.C., area with the code name "Merrimac." In this operation, black agents attended rallies and even funerals, "in hopes of identifying members of the Black Panther Party." In the second program, centered in North and East Africa, "carefully recruited" African American agents were sent to Algeria, Kenya, and Tanzania, "among other places, to keep close watch on American black radicals."

Details of the clandestine activities against the Panthers were considered among the CIA's "most sensitive and closest held information," according to the *Times* sources, "because of fears that disclosures about the program would arouse a public backlash."

MARCH 22, 1978   Federal Funds Detained. Joseph A. Califano, Jr., secretary of Health, Education, and Welfare (HEW), announced that he would withhold some federal funds for public universities in North Carolina because that state had "failed to submit an acceptable plan to eliminate the vestiges of segregation." At the same time, the HEW secretary "initiated formal administrative action" that could result in a withdrawal of all federal funds for the sixteen universities in North Carolina, which were once legally segregated. At the time of this action, eleven of the schools were still predominantly white (91.2 percent) and five predominantly black (91.6 percent).

On February 3, 1978, HEW had rejected North Carolina's plan to desegregate its universities but accepted a proposal for its 57 community colleges. North Carolina was one of six Southern states under a federal court order to submit an acceptable plan to HEW by February 3. It was the only one of the six states that did not fully comply.

MARCH 24, 1978   Singer Bill Kenny Died. Bill Kenny, "whose tenor voice helped make the original Ink Spots one of the world's best known singing groups in the 1940s," died of a respiratory ailment in New Westminster, British Columbia, at age sixty-three.

Kenny, together with Charles Fuqua, Orville Jones, and Ivory Watson, formed the Ink Spots in 1939. He was the last survivor of the group and continued performing almost up to his death.

APRIL 15, 1978   Ward Awarded by Northwestern University. Horace T. Ward, the first black person to sit on the Fulton County (Georgia) Superior Court, was presented the 1978 Northwestern University Alumni Merit Award for "outstanding contributions to his profession" in Evanston, Illinois.

After receiving undergraduate and graduate degrees from Morehouse College and Atlanta University and serving a three year stint in the United States Army, Ward earned a Doctor of Jurisprudence degree from Northwestern in 1959. He enrolled at Northwestern only after having been denied admission, possibly because of his race, to the School of Law at the University of Georgia.

In 1964, Ward became one of the first blacks elected to the Georgia State Senate since Reconstruction. He was reelected to the Senate four times, ending his service there in 1974. He also served as a deputy city attorney for Atlanta (1969–1970) and assistant attorney for Fulton County (of which Atlanta is the county seat).

In 1974, Georgia Governor Jimmy Carter appointed Ward to the Civil Court of Fulton County and three years later Governor George Busbee elevated him to the Fulton Superior Court, where he became one of eleven judges of the Atlanta circuit.

Ward was an active civil rights attorney during the height of the civil rights movement in Georgia. He participated in bus desegregation cases in Augusta; the Martin Luther King, Jr., case in Dekalb County; and the desegregation of the University of Georgia at Athens.

APRIL 17, 1978   Pulitzer Prize Awarded. James Alan McPherson, Jr., African American author, was awarded a Pulitzer Prize in fiction for his volume of short stories, *Elbow Room.* The book characterized "various aspects of the black experience."

McPherson, a thirty-four year old native of Savannah, Georgia, received a bachelor's degree from Morris Brown College in 1965, and an LL.B. degree from the Harvard University Law School in 1968. A year later he earned a master's of fine arts degree from the University of Iowa. McPherson taught writing in the college of law at Iowa before joining the faculty at the University of California at Santa Cruz from 1969 until 1970.

The new Pulitzer Prize winner had also been a contributing editor of *Atlantic Monthly* magazine and a contributor to *Black Insights, Cutting Edges,* and *New Black Voices.* He also wrote *Hue and Cry,* a collection of short stories and edited *Railroad: Trains and Train People in American Culture* in 1969 and 1976, respectively.

In 1970, McPherson won the National Institute of Arts and Letters literature prize, and in 1972 and 1973 he was awarded Guggenheim fellowships.

At the time of his receipt of the Pulitzer Prize, McPherson was an associate professor of English at the University of Virginia.

The Pulitzer Prize, considered by many "the most prestigious award that can be bestowed in the literary arts and journalism," carried a stipend of $1,000 and was administered by the trustees of Columbia University.

APRIL 24, 1978 Morehouse Given Accreditation for Medical School. The Liaison Committee on Medical Education, the official accrediting agency for medical schools in the United States, announced provisional accreditation for the School of Medicine at Morehouse College in Atlanta. The decision paved the way for the opening of the first new predominantly black medical school in the United States in one hundred years. The other two black medical schools are Meharry Medical College in

Nashville, Tennessee, and Howard University in Washington, D.C.

In September 1978, the new medical school planned to enroll a class of twenty-four students in a two-year program. By 1983, the institution planned to begin graduating four-year medical students. Until that time, under an arrangement with four other medical schools, Emory University (also in Atlanta), the Medical College of Georgia in Augusta, Meharry and Howard, Morehouse students would go elsewhere for their final two years of training.

Discussions about a possible medical school at Morehouse College began in the 1960s, but it was not until February, 1973, when the institution received a federal grant of almost $100,000 to study the feasibility of such a school, that "intensive efforts" got under the way.

Medical officials had consistently pointed out the "great need" for more black doctors in the United States. Of the 370,000 physicians in the United States in 1976, only 6,600, or 1.8 percent, were black.

In response to the news of provisional accreditation, Dr. Louis Sullivan, dean of the medical school, remarked: "As we look to the future, we are confident that, with continued broad support from both public and private sources, we will train those primary-care physicians needed for our underserved rural areas and inner cities in Georgia, the Southeast and the nation."

MAY 9, 1978 Kaunda Honored with Peace Prize. The Martin Luther King, Jr., Center for Non-Violent Social Change announced that Kenneth D. Kaunda, president of the Republic of Zambia, would receive the annual Martin Luther King, Jr., Nonviolent Peace Prize. The announcement was made in Atlanta by Coretta Scott King.

Kaunda led his country's transition from colonial rule under the British to self-determination in 1964 without resorting to violence.

Prior to achieving independence, Zambia had been known as Northern Rhodesia. Since independence, Kaunda, who was imprisoned several times by British authorities, was the only president to serve the country.

Mrs. King said that Kaunda was chosen for the peace prize because he exemplified her husband's "ideals in searching for peaceful and meaningful methods of bringing about social and political justice. . . . Kenneth Kaunda's leadership in preparing his people for self-government and in resisting the forces of violence and hatred is truly a model for all countries to follow."

MAY 29–JUNE 3, 1978   FBI Pushed to Release Information. On May 29, Joseph Lowery, president of the Southern Christian Leadership Conference (SCLC) urged the FBI to release "all the facts" in the Bureau's "attempt to discredit Dr. Martin Luther King, Jr., during the 1960s." At the same time, while refusing "to comment specifically on the alleged FBI excesses," King's widow, Coretta Scott King, said "J. Edgar Hoover's monstrous acts refuse to leave the stage. He is dead, but his despicable legacy lives on."

Lowery's comments came in response to a recent report that "a prominent black leader worked with the FBI in its undercover campaign to replace King as head of the civil rights movement." He said the new report was "another in a long line of FBI attempts to smear black leadership. . . . This is a terrible shadow to be holding over the head of black leadership. . . . I find it incredible [that] any prominent black leader would cooperate to destroy the movement." Lowery added that civil rights leaders had always "had reason to believe" that FBI informants were working within the movement.

On June 3, the *Atlanta Daily World* published an article that reported "claims that Roy Wilkins, former head of the National Association for the Advancement of Colored People (NAACP) was the black collaborator

who sided with the Federal Bureau of Investigation in an attempt to discredit the late Dr. M. L. King, Jr." Lowery gave a "blistering" response to these new allegations. Excerpts from Lowery's statement follows:

"Black folks in particular and the nation in general must see through this vicious effort to shift a portion of the blame for attacks on Dr. King to the black community. . . .

"We (SCLC) in no way condone nor place any credence in attempts to vilify Roy Wilkins, whose distinguished career in civil rights speaks for itself. We condemn the continued attempts of the FBI to discredit black leaders and impede the civil rights movement. . . .

"The fact that Wilkins had conversations with the FBI in no way indicates that he collaborated with them to discredit Dr. King and the movement. The failure of the FBI to substantiate the fantastic claim that a black leader collaborated with them is evidence that the FBI's intent is to discredit, divide, and destroy. . . .

"[Referring to an FBI memo which described the so-called collaborator as 'young and ambitious,' and since the collaboration was alleged to have taken place in 1964] I hardly consider a man in his mid-60s [as Wilkins was in 1964] as 'young and ambitious'. . . .

"We're all aware . . . that in the mid-60's Mr. Hoover had a fierce determination to discredit Dr. King and thereby weaken the civil rights movement by establishing the Communist influence or by any other means."

JUNE 3, 1978   Hurley Honored. Several hundred people gathered at a hotel in Atlanta, Georgia, to pay tribute to Ruby Hurley, southeastern regional director of the NAACP, on the occasion of her retirement after more than three decades of service to the nation's "oldest, largest, and most respected" civil rights organization.

Hurley, a native of Washington, D.C., joined the NAACP after heading a committee "that sought to establish singer Marian Anderson's right to sing" at Constitution Hall in the capital in 1939. Because of white opposition, the famed opera star had to perform her concert at the Lincoln Memorial instead. In 1943, Hurley joined the NAACP as national youth director. In her eight years as youth director, the NAACP's membership tripled to 92 college chapters and 178 youth councils, enrolling 25,000 members.

Following her success in the youth division, Hurley was sent into the Deep South to coordinate membership campaigns and reactivate dormant branches. Out of these activities, the southeastern regional office, embracing the states of Alabama, Florida, Georgia, Mississippi, North Carolina, South Carolina, and Tennessee, was established. It became the largest region of the entire NAACP.

Hurley began her work in the South in 1951, the same year that a Christmas night bomb killed Harry T. Moore, the NAACP's Florida coordinator, and his wife, Harriett. Hate and violence, then, became her constant companions for the next twenty-seven years.

In an interview with the *Atlanta Constitution* on May 30, 1978, Hurley, who said she "never found time to sit down and worry about the obscene telephone calls, threats against her life, and 'never say die' pro-segregation politicians," recalled her life's work and commented on present and future trends. For example, Hurley recalled her attempts to gather information about the murder of black teenager Emmett Till in 1955 by posing as a field hand at several Mississippi plantations:

"I must have been crazy. Young people talk about what they would have done if they were living during those times. . . . But they wouldn't have done anything. They couldn't have done any more than their elders. . . .

"I started worrying about black young people when I heard them saying they're black and they're proud. But just being black is no reason to be proud. . . . My feeling is that if you're going to be proud, you ought to have some knowledge (about the history of the black race) to build a basis to be proud. You won't have to go bragging that you're black and proud. . . .

"As long as there are black people and white people, there will be conflicts. . . .

"There is still a lot of work to be done, and I'm too old to do it. I can't keep up with the pace and maintain sanity anymore. I'll leave that to someone else."

JUNE 9, 1978 African American Enrollment Rose. The Bureau of the Census reported that the number of black youths attending colleges and universities in the United States rose from 282,000 in 1966 to 1,062,000 in 1976, an increase of 275 percent. The number of black women in college rose more than four fold, while the number of black men tripled. In 1976, the number of black women college students exceeded the number of black men by 84,000. Despite the increases, the proportion of blacks aged eighteen to twenty-four years of age enrolled in colleges was only 20 percent in 1976, considerably less than the 27 percent of whites in the same age group. At the time, 74 percent of blacks completed high school by their mid-twenties, compared to 86 percent of whites. In addition, of those blacks who enrolled in college, only about 39 percent actually graduated as compared to 57 percent of whites. The new enrollment statistics, however, raised the black percentage of all college students to 10.7 percent, up from 4.6 percent in 1966. At the time, blacks made up 11.6 percent of the population of the United States.

JUNE 25, 1978 Founder and Councilman Died. Abraham Lincoln Davis, a founder of the Southern Christian Leadership Conference (SCLC) and the first black city councilman in New Orleans, Louisiana, died there at age sixty-three.

Davis, pastor of the New Zion Baptist Church in New Orleans for forty-three years, met there with Martin Luther King, Jr., and other civil rights activists in 1957 to organize the SCLC. King was chosen the group's first president and Davis vice president. Davis was elected to the New Orleans City Council in January 1975.

JUNE 28, 1978   Court Ruled on Reverse Discrimination. The Supreme Court, in a 5–4 decision, ordered that white student Allan P. Bakke be admitted to the Medical College of the University of California at Davis, indicating that the refusal to admit Bakke was tantamount to reverse discrimination and that the use of racial or ethnic quotas was an improper means of achieving racial balance. The Court held that the college's affirmative action program was invalid since it had the effect of discriminating against qualified white applicants, although the Court perceived the goal of attaining a diverse student body constitutional and permissible.

JULY 1, 1978   Alarming Suicide Rate Noted. The *Atlanta Inquirer,* quoting a study by Beverly Howze, a University of Michigan psychologist, reported that suicides among blacks had increased by 97 percent since the mid-1950s. In Wayne County, Michigan (of which Detroit is the county seat), the focus of the Howze study, the increase was 187 percent, compared with less than 23 percent for whites. The greater proportion of black suicides, as for white ones, was among black youth aged 15 to 34. The new statistics represented "a complete reversal for the black race . . . which has a history of rarely resorting to suicide," Howze claimed.

As a result of her study among 300 black and 41 white teenagers in the Detroit area, Howze found "an alarming pattern of alienation and self-destructiveness. . . . While these traits were strongest among black youths in the low income group, they were also evident among . . . young people in general. . . . Many showed feelings of very low self esteem and self confidence. They admit difficulty in dealing with day to day stress and frustration, yet they are extremely hesitant to ask for help—even from their own families. Blacks, particularly black males, insist on handling their problems alone."

The study also revealed "striking differences between blacks and whites and between males and females. White males were more capable of admitting varied feelings, like sadness and frustration. Females mentioned seeking consolation from a parent or close friend. But the black males were the most likely to close themselves off. 'I wouldn't feel anything, only emptiness' they would claim."

JULY 3, 1978   Court Upheld Quotas. The United States Supreme Court upheld a plan that used race and sex quotas to end job discrimination. The Court denied, without comment, an appeal protesting a quota system adopted by the Bell Telephone System.

AUGUST 19, 1978   Miss Black America Crowned. Lydia Monice Jackson, a nineteen-year-old music student from Willingboro, New Jersey, was crowned Miss Black America for 1979 in Philadelphia, Pennsylvania. The lyric soprano was selected over twenty-nine other young women from twenty-seven states, the District of Columbia, and Puerto Rico.

AUGUST 20, 1978   Black Golfer Triumphed. Lee Elder, one of the few black professional golfers in the United States, won the Westchester Golf Classic in Harrison, New York. The triumph resulted in a purse of $300,000. The forty-four-year-old Elder won with a 274, ten under par on the 6,603-yard Westchester County Club course. In the previous month, he had won the less prestigious Milwaukee Open. Elder called the Westchester victory "a little more significant to me personally" than his historic feat of four years ago, when he became the first black to compete in the Masters Tournament held in Augusta, Georgia.

AUGUST 20, 1978   Documents Published in Detroit. The *Detroit Free Press* published de-

Protesters march against the Bakke decision. (AP/Wide World Photos.)

tails of documents obtained by the American Civil Liberties Union (ACLU) that showed that the FBI passed along information about two Freedom Rider buses to a Birmingham, Alabama, police sergeant who was "a known Ku Klux Klan agent" in 1961. The actual documents consisted of approximately three thousand pages of letters, memoranda, and teletype.

The documents indicated that the FBI knew that Sgt. Thomas Cook of the Birmingham Police Department's intelligence unit was passing the information that the Bureau gave him to the "top leadership" of the Ku Klux Klan. The papers also showed that the chief of the FBI office in Birmingham called Cook to inform him of the progress the buses were "making through the racially tense" South and when they arrived at terminals in Birmingham. They further revealed a plan under which the Birmingham police agreed to get to the terminals fifteen or twenty minutes after the arrival of the buses in order to give Klansmen enough time to attack Freedom Riders.

The documents were released to ACLU attorneys for Walter Bergman, aged seventy-eight, a former professor at Wayne State University in Detroit who had filed suit against the FBI alleging that he was partially paralyzed from a beating he suffered at the hands of Ku Klux Klansmen when they intercepted a Freedom Riders' bus in Anniston, Alabama (fifty miles east of Birmingham). On the same day, a similar Klan assault occurred in Birmingham. In commenting on the documents, Howard Simon, executive director of the Michigan ACLU, said that they showed that the FBI's "failure to provide protection provoked" the assaults on the Freedom Riders.

AUGUST 20, 1978 Georgia Minister Interrupted Service. The Reverend Clennon King, a black Albany, Georgia, minister, interrupted worship services at the Americus Fellowship Baptist Church, where President Jimmy Carter and his eighty-year-old mother Lillian were among the worshipers. The outburst was a continuation of King's efforts to agitate the president on the question of desegregation of churches. He had previously tried to join the all-white Plains Baptist Church, where the president and his mother previously attended services. Mrs. Carter had withdrawn from that church after its deacons reaffirmed a decision to continue prohibiting black membership.

In his outburst, King accused the president of preventing him from building a new church across from the all-white, Plains Maranatha Baptist Church that "was formed by a group which split from Plains Baptist." He asserted that he loved "the president and he loves me, but he is listening to the wrong Negroes." Although Secret Service agents surrounded King, he was not removed from the church. Of the incident, President Carter said "I hope he gets his church. . . . I didn't know anything about it."

SEPTEMBER 1, 1978 Survey Sought Solutions to Racial Discrimination. The *Atlanta University Center Digest* reported that 74 percent of blacks participating in a national survey favored integration, but only 29 percent of them felt that it was the best method for overcoming racial discrimination. A larger proportion, 45 percent, felt that although integration was "desirable, blacks should have an equal voice in the control of schools and housing first."

The poll, conducted by Lee Slurzberg Research, Inc., for the National Urban League, questioned more than two thousand black men and women in the spring of 1978. Other results of the poll showed: 1) Employment/economic development were the principal black concerns. Seventy-seven percent cited it "as a priority issue and 46 percent mentioned it as their first priority"; 2) Education/youth were cited second in importance. Sixty-four percent called it a priority issue and 20 percent mentioned it as their first priority; 3) Seventy-seven percent of blacks felt that American society had "serious problems" and 36 percent called for "sweeping changes." Only 20 percent felt that "the American way of life was superior to that of any other country." This attitude was greatest among blacks fifty-five and older, those living in the South, and those with less than a high school education.

SEPTEMBER 7, 1978 Harassment Reported at Military Base. The Southern Christian Leadership Conference (SCLC) office in Jacksonville, Florida, reported that within the preceding week it had received twenty-two complaints from black soldiers of abusive treatment at Fort Stewart-Hunter near Savannah, Georgia. The head of the Jacksonville SCLC office said white officers and non-commissioned officers were harassing blacks, who were being "inflamed by harsh treatment and harsh words." Black soldiers said the whites used the derisive epithet "nigger" and other such inflammatory words.

The Fort Stewart-Hunter incidents followed an announcement in August 1978 by Army Chief of Staff Bernard Rogers that a year-long study would be launched to find out why a greater percentage of black soldiers were being punished and dishonorably discharged

Soldiers in training at Camp Lejeune, North Carolina. (Courtesy of the U.S. Defense Department.)

than white soldiers. In a letter sent to commanders of major army installations across the country, Rogers described the situation as a "disturbing trend" that was worsening. Rogers based his comments on a recent army equal opportunity report which showed that blacks received 54 percent of all dishonorable discharges during the fiscal year 1976 and nearly 57 percent of such discharges during the 1977 fiscal year. Those figures were about twice the rate of dishonorable discharges for white sol-

diers. In addition, blacks were charged with more serious offenses than white soldiers.

SEPTEMBER 9, 1978   Busing and School Desegregation. United States Supreme Court Justice Lewis F. Powell refused a new request by opponents of busing to achieve school desegregation to delay a wide-spread busing plan scheduled to take effect the following week in Los Angeles, California. A similar request had been denied earlier the same day by Justice William H. Rehnquist. The desegregation plan

Charles Diggs. (Courtesy of the NAACP.)

had been previously upheld by the California State Supreme Court.

SEPTEMBER 12, 1978 Morton Sworn in as Treasurer. President Jimmy Carter appointed Azie Taylor Morton treasurer of the U.S., making her the first African American to hold that post. Morton was born in Dale, Texas. In 1956 she graduated cum laude from Huston-Tillotson College in Austin, Texas. Morton, a Texas Democrat, worked on President Kennedy's Committee on Equal Employment Opportunity from 1961 to 1963. Morton served as deputy convention manager of the 1976 Democratic National Convention in 1976. As treasurer, Morton also served as national director for the U.S. Savings Bonds Program.

SEPTEMBER 15, 1978 Ali Regained Title. Muhammad Ali regained the World Boxing Association's (WBA) heavyweight boxing championship in a unanimous decision over Leon Spinks, age twenty-five, in New Orleans. The thirty-six-year-old Ali thus became the first heavyweight boxer to win the championship three times. A crowd of seventy thousand witnessed the match in the Louisiana Superdome.

OCTOBER 7, 1978 Congressman Convicted of Fraud. Democratic Congressman Charles Diggs of Michigan was convicted in a federal district court in Washington, D.C., of using the mail to defraud and file false payroll vouchers. The latter charge stemmed from "a scheme to require his staff members to give him money from their padded pay raises so he could pay off huge personal debts."

Diggs, a veteran black congressman and a founder of the Congressional Black Caucus (CBC), had just been overwhelmingly reelected by his Detroit, Michigan, constituents the prior week.

NOVEMBER 17, 1978 FBI Agents Testified. Two agents of the Federal Bureau of Investigation (FBI), Charles D. Brennan and George C. Moore, testified before the Select Committee on Assassinations of the U.S. House of Representatives that the Bureau's eleven-year surveillance of Dr. Martin Luther King, Jr., "was based solely" on the late FBI Director J. Edgar Hoover's "hatred of the civil rights leader." The two agents added that "neither the surveillance ordered under the guise of communist influences on King nor that supposedly linking King's efforts with radical violent groups could be justified." However, the two witnesses did not link the FBI directly to the murder of King.

Another FBI agent, Arthur Murtaugh, had told the U.S. Senate's Select Committee of Intelligence in 1975 that another agent, James J. Rose, who worked with him in the Bureau's Atlanta office, was "overjoyed" when he heard of King's murder. Murtaugh added, "I never heard anyone say anything favorable about Dr. King in . . . 10 years. . . . It just defies reason to say that the same people who have engaged in a 10-year vendetta against Dr. King should investigate his murder." But the Bureau did just that, and within twenty-four hours after King's assassination the FBI concluded "that there was no conspiracy and its investigation was basically in search of the fugitive [James Earl] Ray," according to Murtaugh.

In a syndicated column published in the *Atlanta Constitution* on September 11, 1978, Jesse L. Jackson, one of the civil rights leaders who was with King when the fatal bullet struck him on April 4, 1968, said "circumstantial evidence" suggested that the FBI was "deeply implicated" in King's assassination.

1979

AUGUST 15, 1979   Young Resigned from UN Post. Andrew J. Young, the African American United States Ambassador to the United Nations, resigned, asserting that he "could not promise to muzzle himself and stay out of controversies that might prove politically [embarrassing] to President [Jimmy] Carter." The president accepted the ambassador's resignation with regret. Young indicated that he didn't "feel a bit sorry for a thing I have done. I have tried to interpret to our country some of the mood of the rest of the world. Unfortunately, but by birth, I come from the ranks of those who had known and identified with some level of oppression in the world. . . . By choice," Young said, "I continued to identify with what would be called in biblical terms the least of

these my brethren. . . . I could not say that given the same situation, I wouldn't do it again, almost exactly the same way."

Because of his unorthodox approaches to diplomacy, Young's brief career as the first black UN ambassador was marked by continued controversy. He had made American relations with African nations a priority of his mission while at the same time condemning such leading Western democracies as Great Britain and Sweden as racist. His downfall occurred after he held an unauthorized meeting in July 1979 with a representative of the Palestine Liberation Organization (PLO), a group that the United States government considered a terrorist organization. Young was also accused of first failing to inform the State Department about the talks and then of giving "only a partial and inaccurate version of events when he was asked."

Following the disclosure of Young's unauthorized meeting with the PLO representative, many influential Americans, including Robert C. Byrd, majority leader of the United States Senate, called for his removal from office. Yet African American civil rights leader Jesse Jackson defended the former ambassador and accused President Carter of sacrificing "Africa, the third world, and black Americans," adding, "I think it's tragic."

Part 6

TOWARD A BLACK AGENDA
1980–1996

Chapter 10

1980 TO 1989

1980

MAY 18, 1980   Rioting in Miami. At least fifteen people died after two nights of racial rioting in Miami, Florida. The disturbances were the worst in the nation since the black ghettos of Watts and Detroit erupted in the late 1960s. The Miami riot began in the wake of a controversial verdict in a case of alleged police brutality.

The violence began on May 17 after the announcement that not guilty verdicts had been returned in Tampa, Florida, against four white deputy sheriffs from Dade County (of which Miami is the county seat). The four former deputies were charged with beating Arthur McDuffie, a black insurance executive, to death and then covering up the beating to make it appear that McDuffie had died in a motorcycle accident. The all-male, all-white jury was empaneled in Tampa because Dade Circuit Court Judge Lenore Nesbitt had ruled that the case was "a racial time bomb" in Miami. In the wake of the rioting, U.S. Attorney Atlee Wampler III said that evidence already assembled by the FBI in the McDuffie case would be presented to a federal grand jury in Miami on May 20, 1980.

During the riot, snipers shot at cars, civilians, and police. Three Miami police officers were wounded by gunfire on May 18. At least two of the rioters were shot dead by police. Florida Governor Bob Graham called up eleven hundred National Guardsmen, three hundred highway patrol officers, four helicopters, and an armored personnel carrier to assist local law enforcement authorities. At least 216 people were injured in the rioting and widespread looting and property damage were reported.

The disturbances occurred in a section of northwest Miami known as "Liberty City." Black leaders in the area said they had seen the violence building for months and blamed the unrest on a long series of accusations of police brutality against blacks, none of which resulted in significant action against the accused white officers; the conviction and suspension of leading black officials on corruption charges; and a new wave of Cuban refugees, sharpening the economic competition that had left blacks on the margin of the city's economy since the first black workers went to Miami in the 1920s to work in the city's new resort hotels.

As the riot progressed, Miami Mayor Maurice Feree received a set of eleven demands from a grassroots black organization. Feree said he thought at least nine of the demands, including hiring and promoting blacks, could be readily met. He also said he would consider granting amnesty to all of those accused of looting but could not agree with the demand to fire state attorney Janet Reno, the prosecutor in the McDuffie case.

OCTOBER 26, 1980 African American Bishops Spoke Out. The ten black Roman Catholic bishops in the United States issued a pastoral letter proclaiming that "the black Catholic community has come of age within the Church and must seize the initiative to 'share the gift of our blackness with the church in the United States.'" The fifteen-thousand-word letter, entitled "What We Have Seen and Heard," was the first collaboration by the bishops, and it emphasized both the strengths blacks brought to the church as well as the "stain" of racism that they claimed still existed in Catholic structures.

At the time that the letter was written, there were an estimated one million black Roman Catholics in the nation, less than 2 percent of the country's approximately fifty-two million Catholics. Within the church hierarchy, in addition to the ten black bishops, there were approximately three hundred black priests and seven hundred black religious women.

DECEMBER 22, 1980 Samuel Pierce Named to HUD Post. President-elect Ronald Reagan named Samuel Riley Pierce, Jr., an African American lawyer, secretary of Housing and Urban Development (HUD). He was the only minority person selected to join the new president's cabinet.

Pierce was born on September 6, 1922, in Glen Cove, Long Island, New York. He played football at Cornell University and graduated with Phi Beta Kappa honors. After service in World War II, Pierce obtained a law degree from Cornell and began working as an assistant district attorney in New York City. In later years, he was appointed, on two separate occasions, to court vacancies in Manhattan borough by then-Governor Nelson Rockefeller, yet in 1959 he was defeated in a bid for election to a Manhattan judgeship.

Pierce entered governmental service at the federal level in 1955 when President Dwight Eisenhower named him an assistant to the undersecretary of labor. He was the first African American appointed to this position. In 1970, President Richard M. Nixon made him the first black to serve as a general counsel to the Treasury Department. At the time of his appointment to the Reagan cabinet, however, Pierce had left government and was serving as a partner in a prestigious New York law firm.

Of Pierce's cabinet appointment, Barbara Penn Wright, Pierce's wife and a physician with the Metropolitan Life Insurance Company, remarked, "He's never been adverse to accepting a challenge. And he's always been able to handle them."

1981

APRIL 15, 1981 Bradley Won Third Term. Thomas (Tom) Bradley was reelected to a third term as mayor of Los Angeles, California. Bradley, a sixty-three-year-old African American, defeated his perennial opponent, former mayor Sam Yorty, by a margin of 64 to 32 percent to gain four more years as mayor of the nation's third largest city.

AUGUST 1, 1981 Payton Took Helm of Tuskegee Institute. Benjamin F. Payton assumed the office of president of Tuskegee Institute. Payton succeeded Luther H. Foster, who retired after twenty-eight years as president of the historic and predominantly black university founded by Booker T. Washington in 1881.

Payton was program officer for education and public policy at the Ford Foundation at the time of his appointment to Tuskegee. He had previously taught and directed the Community Service Project at Howard University, directed the Commission on Religion and Race and the Department of Social Justice at the National Council of Churches in the U.S.A., and was a president of Benedict College in South Carolina.

NOVEMBER 16, 1981 Flemming Lost Chairmanship of Civil Rights Commission. Presi-

President-elect Ronald Reagan and Samuel Pierce. (Courtesy of The White House.)

dent Ronald Reagan fired Arthur S. Flemming, the seventy-six-year-old chairman of the United States Commission on Civil Rights (CCR). Sources told United Press International (UPI) that the White House was "angered by the Commission's and Flemming's strong advocacy of affirmative action, voting rights, and . . . busing to achieve school desegregation." This was the first time in the twenty-four-year history of the commission that "an incoming administration [had] changed [the CCR's] membership, a restraint underlining a biparti-

san commitment to civil rights." Flemming, a former secretary of Health, Education, and Welfare (HEW) in the administration of President Dwight D. Eisenhower, was appointed to the commission in 1974 by President Richard M. Nixon. He had recently said that the Reagan administration's views on school desegregation were "in conflict with the Constitution."

Reagan appointed Clarence Pendleton, Jr., a fifty-year-old black Californian, to replace Flemming as chairman of the CCR. Pendleton, considered a conservative Republican, had supported Reagan in the 1980 elections. He had previously been chairman of the San Diego Transit Corporation and head of the San Diego Urban League. Pendleton became the first black chairman of the Civil Rights Commission.

1982

FEBRUARY 17, 1982   Pianist Monk Died. Pianist Thelonious Sphere Monk died after suffering a massive stroke. An important pioneer in the development of bop, Monk played a vital role in the jazz revolution of the early 1940s. At first, the pianist—a gifted technician and composer—was appreciated only by a small circle of New York's brightest. His angular melodies, harmonies marked by jarring surprises, unusual treatment of notes, and the absence of notes conspired to limit his initial appeal. Before his death in 1982, however, he was generally recognized as one of the founding fathers of modern jazz, and he is considered by some to be the most important jazz composer since Duke Ellington.

Born October 10, 1917, in Rocky Mount, North Carolina, Monk moved with his family to New York City in the early 1920s. At the age of eleven, weekly piano lessons supplemented Monk's rigorous gospel training, and he accompanied the Baptist choir in which his mother sang. Two years later, Monk was already playing in a trio at a local bar and grill, and he eventually won so many of the weekly Apollo Theater amateur contests that he was banned from entering any more. At age sixteen he left school to travel with an evangelical faith healer and preacher, and he returned the following year, well schooled in rhythm and blues accompaniment, to form his first group. With the exception of some brief work with the Lucky Millander Band and Coleman Hawkins, Monk was generally the leader of his own small groups.

In the early 1940s, Monk found himself in the midst of a new wave of jazz music.

Bebop, a faster and more complex style than its swing predecessor, was spontaneously generated late at night in jam sessions at jazz clubs, most notably at Minton's, where Monk reigned as house pianist. In fact, *Keyboard* claimed "Monk was at the eye of what would become the bebop hurricane." Monk's own music, however, was developing a unique style, and by the early 1950s the iconoclastic composer had penned the classics *Blue Monk, Round Midnight,* and *Epistrophy.*

In 1951, Monk's career—already faltering—was dealt a serious blow as the result of questionable charges of narcotics possession that landed him in jail for sixty days and, more importantly, caused the New York State Liquor Authority to rescind his cabaret card. Without the card, Monk was prevented from playing local club dates and relied on the support of his patron and friend, the Baroness Nica de Koenigswarter.

Within a few years his luck changed: Monk gave a series of concerts in Paris in 1954, cut *Pure Monk,* his first solo album, and signed with the Riverside label. An eight-month engagement at New York's Five Spot in 1957 established Monk as a cult icon and there he met jazz newcomer John Coltrane. In the following couple of years, the improvisational genius made several recordings for Riverside, including *Brilliant Corners, Thelonious Himself,* and *Monk with Coltrane.*

These recordings were so successful that in 1962 Columbia Records offered Monk a lucrative contract, and in 1964 *Time* magazine featured his picture on its cover, a rare distinction for a jazz musician. In the following decade, living up to the *New York Post*'s description of him as "one of jazz's great eccentrics," Monk retreated from the public eye, making only a few solo and trio recordings for Black Lion in London and giving occasional concerts. After suffering a massive stroke on February 17, 1982, Monk died. Monk's son, T. S. Monk, Jr., a drummer, recorded with Blue Note; his recording, *Take One,* was a tribute to his father and other bop composers.

FEBRUARY 21, 1982   African Americans Given Preferences at DEA. United States District Court Judge Aubrey E. Robinson, Jr., of the District of Columbia, ruled that the federal Drug Enforcement Administration (DEA) must give black special agents preference in promotions and pay them for the period during which they suffered from a discriminatory promotions policy. The order required a payment of about $2 million to be shared among the hundreds of black DEA agents, according to their attorney. The ruling also meant that one black agent for every two whites would have to be promoted to the sixth highest pay grade, or a higher federal pay grade. Those ranks carried salaries of $33,586 to $47,500 at the time.

Judge Robinson had ruled in 1981 that the drug agency discriminated against black agents with respect to salary, entry grades, work assignments, evaluations, discipline, and promotion during the period 1972 to 1981. The new order set the amount of back pay and provided a remedy for "eliminating the effect of the discrimination in the future." The judge said the preferential promotions for blacks must continue either for five years or "until the percentage of blacks in the six highest pay grades reached 10 percent."

FEBRUARY 27, 1982   Talent Agent Convicted of Murder. Wayne Williams, a twenty-three-year-old black entertainment talent scout, was convicted of murder in the slaying of Jimmy Ray Payne, age twenty-one, and Nathaniel Cater, age twenty-seven, in Atlanta, Georgia. Payne and Cater were two of the twenty-eight young blacks, mostly males, who were slain in Atlanta in a twenty-two month period beginning in 1979. Most of the victims were strangled. The serial murders became known as the "Atlanta child murder cases," since most of the victims were under twenty-one years of age.

The case began on July 27, 1979, when the first two bodies were found, but it was July 1980 before the police publicly linked the two cases. By that time, eleven black children had disappeared or were found slain. The police action came after an organization of parents, the Committee to Stop Children's Murder (STOP), led by the mother of one of the victims, was formed in May 1980 to show linkages in the cases.

During the twenty-two months when black children's bodies were being found periodically in the metropolitan Atlanta area, President Ronald Reagan committed $1.5 million in federal funds and scores of FBI agents to the case. Heavyweight boxing champion Muhammad Ali pledged $400,000, and hundreds of thousands in additional dollars were donated by other athletes and celebrities or raised in benefit concerts. The state of Georgia and citizens throughout the nation gave thousands of dollars to help with the investigation or for a reward fund. Some of the donations went to STOP or directly to the mothers of the slain youths.

The Guardian Angels, a group of New York City citizens who patrolled the subways of their city to deter crime, went to Atlanta to teach local youths how to defend themselves. A vigilante group of blacks armed with baseball bats in the Techwood housing projects formed a "Bat Patrol" to protect black children. In addition, psychics, writers, civil rights activists, and others offered theories on the motives and identities of the killer or killers. Many were convinced that Ku Klux Klansmen or other white supremacist groups were responsible for the murders. And since most of the victims were young black males, the theory that a homosexual committed the crimes also emerged.

On May 22, 1981, law enforcement officers on stake out along the Chattahoochee River in north Atlanta heard a loud splash. Shortly thereafter, other officers questioned and detained Wayne Williams after he was noticed driving slowly with his headlights dimmed across the James Jackson Parkway Bridge over the Chattahoochee. Two days later, the body of twenty-seven-year-old Nathaniel Cater was found floating in the river. On June 21, 1981, Williams was arrested and charged with the murders of Cater and Jimmy Ray Payne.

Williams, who took the stand in his own defense during the trial, vigorously denied that he had committed the murders. He and his attorneys refuted suggestions of a homosexual motive and denied any acquaintance with most of the seven victims in whose company prosecution witnesses had placed him. The prosecution, however, had also presented fibers taken from clothing and other fabrics and bloodstains found in Williams's car as evidence. On February 27, 1982, after eleven hours of deliberations, a majority black jury found Williams guilty of two counts of murder. The presiding judge, Clarence Cooper, also an African American, sentenced Williams to two consecutive life terms in prison. The defense promised an immediate appeal.

The "Atlanta child murder cases" involved one of the largest searches for a killer in the nation's history, and Wayne Williams was convicted as America's first black major serial murderer.

MARCH 17, 1982   First Black Chief of Police in Charleston. Reuben M. Greenberg, a thirty-two-year-old deputy director of the Florida Division of Criminal Justice Standards and Training, was named the first black police chief of Charleston, South Carolina, by Mayor Joseph Riley. The South Carolina Criminal Justice Academy also announced that Greenberg's appointment made him "the first black police chief in modern South Carolina history."

MARCH 20, 1982   New Orleans Mayor Reelected. Ernest "Dutch" Morial was reelected mayor of New Orleans, Louisiana. The city's first African American chief executive defeated Ron Raucheux, a white legislator, 71,231 votes

(56 percent) to 55,814 votes (44 percent) with 75 percent of the vote counted. Although New Orleans had a majority black population at the time of the election, more whites were registered to vote than blacks. Morial was expected to need about fifteen percent of the white vote to win.

MARCH 23, 1982   Houston's First Black Police Commissioner. The City Council of Houston, Texas, confirmed Lee P. Brown as the city's first black police commissioner. Brown, age forty-four, had recently been the second black police commissioner in Atlanta, Georgia. During his tenure in Atlanta, the city was the site of the murders of twenty-eight young black people over a period of twenty-two months. The murders were linked in 1980 and in the following year, Wayne Williams, a young black man, was accused of the serial slayings. He was convicted and sentenced to two consecutive life terms in prison less than one month before Brown resigned from the police department. Although Brown was variously praised and criticized for his department's handling of the "Atlanta child murder cases," he denied that his resignation was connected with the infamous case. Brown, a former head of the police department in Portland, Oregon, said it was simply time for him to seek a new challenge. Brown was the first person chosen from outside the department to head Houston's police force. The department was frequently under criticism by some of the city's blacks for alleged brutality.

MAY 6, 1982   Glickman Elected in Pasadena. Loretta Glickman, a thirty-six-year-old African-American investment counselor, was elected mayor of Pasadena, California, by the city's board of directors. Glickman, who had also been a teacher and singer, was the first black woman to become mayor of a major city in the United States. In response to her election, Glickman said that Pasadena was a place "where dreams can and do come true."

JUNE 23, 1982 Young Elected President of Mayor's Association. Coleman Young, the first African American mayor of Detroit, Michigan, was elected president of the U.S. Conference of Mayors at its fiftieth annual meeting in Minneapolis, Minnesota, succeeding Helen Booalis of Lincoln, Nebraska. Young announced immediately after his selection that he would ask mayors to return soon for a special meeting to recommend ways to strengthen their local economies.

JUNE 30, 1982 Court Handed Down Judgement on Voluntary Integration. The United States Supreme Court, in a 5–4 decision, overturned an initiative from the state of Washington that prohibited the voluntary assignment of students to schools beyond their neighborhoods. In an opinion written by Justice Harry Blackmun, the Court said the statewide vote in the state of Washington violated the equal protection guarantee of the U.S. Constitution because it imposed an "unfair burden" on minority groups, who were to "be dealt with at the state level, which is more remote than the local school board." The high Court also said the initiative burdened "all future attempts to integrate Washington schools in districts throughout the state by lodging decision-making authority over the question at a new and remote level of government." Justices Lewis F. Powell, Jr., William H. Rehnquist, Sandra Day O'Connor, and Chief Justice Warren Burger dissented. Justice Powell considered the ruling an "unprecedented intrusion into the structure of a state government" by depriving "the state of Washington of all opportunity to address the unsolved questions resulting from extensive mandatory busing."

The case stemmed from a voluntary plan that the Seattle school board adopted in 1977. It involved the busing of some seven thousand students. In 1978, the state's voters approved Initiative 350 to end the busing. A lower federal court, in a suit filed by the school board, upheld the plan and declared the refer-endum unconstitutional. Thus, the case reached the Supreme Court on further appeal by opponents of busing.

JULY 5, 1982 Boycotts Protected by Constitution. The United States Supreme Court ruled that "nonviolent boycotts, organized to achieve constitutional rights goals," are protected by the First Amendment guarantees of free speech. The decision reversed a ruling by the supreme court of Mississippi that held that the NAACP and ninety-one black citizens were liable for business losses caused by a boycott of local merchants in Port Gibson, Mississippi, which began in 1966.

The Port Gibson boycott was launched by blacks to achieve desegregation in schools and public facilities, to encourage the hiring of black police officers, and to improve lighting, sewers, and the paving of streets in black neighborhoods. The Mississippi court, however, citing evidence of coercion and violence during the boycott, declared the protest "an illegal conspiracy" and ordered its end.

Yet the U.S. Supreme Court, in an opinion written by Justice John Paul Stevens, ruled that "the presence of some illegal threats and violence" did not mean that all of the business losses, in the seven-year period, were attributable to the "illegal" aspects of the boycotts.

AUGUST 21, 1982 Death of Conductor. Calvin Simmons, the thirty-two-year-old African American conductor of the Oakland (California) Symphony Orchestra, was presumed drowned in Lake Placid, New York. Witnesses said he never surfaced after his boat capsized in about twenty-three feet of water on Connery Pond. Simmons was considered one of the nation's most promising young black Conductors.

OCTOBER 27, 1982 U.S. Court of Appeals Judge Died. Richard T. Rives, senior judge of the United States Court of Appeals for the Eleventh Circuit, died of an apparent heart attack in Montgomery, Alabama, at age eighty-seven.

Rives had served on the U.S. Court of Appeals for the Fifth Circuit since 1951 and served as that court's chief judge from 1959 to 1966. He became senior judge of the eleventh circuit court after it was split from the fifth circuit at the time of his death.

Rives and Judge Frank M. Johnson rendered the historic decision in 1955 that declared discrimination on Montgomery, Alabama, buses unconstitutional. The ruling was later upheld by the United States Supreme Court.

NOVEMBER 5, 1982   King's Daughter Accepted Honor for Him. Bernice King, daughter of slain civil rights leader Martin Luther King, Jr., accepted a posthumous award for her father from the United Nations General Assembly in New York City. The award recognized the late civil rights leader's work against apartheid in South Africa. In 1965, King had called for an international boycott against South Africa. He predicted that "the day is fast approaching when people of good will all over the world will rise up in nonviolent solidarity with freedom fighters in Africa."

DECEMBER 4, 1982   Walker Won Heisman Trophy. Herschel Walker, African American running back for the University of Georgia, won the Heisman Trophy, football's highest collegiate award, in New York City. Walker, a native of Wrightsville, Georgia, became the seventh person to capture the Heisman in his junior year. He had previously been named to the football writers All-America team on three occasions.

In the balloting for the Heisman, Walker received 525 first place votes, followed by Stanford University (California) quarterback John Elway with 139 first place votes, and Southern Methodist University (Texas) running back Eric Dickerson with 31 first place votes.

DECEMBER 16, 1982   Affirmative Action Plan Approved. The United States Court of Ap-

peals for the Fifth Circuit ordered approval of a system of promotions on the New Orleans police force that would make it half black at every level. Under the ruling, blacks would be promoted to forty-four new positions immediately, then blacks and whites would be promoted on a one-to-one ratio. In addition, the police department was ordered to recruit more blacks, make it more difficult for a black police cadet to fail, set up $300,000 as a back-pay fund, and pay the fees of the plaintiffs' lawyers.

The suit that resulted in this ruling was filed by thirteen black New Orleans police officers in 1973. They claimed that the city, its Civil Service Commission, and various officials discriminated against them. The suit was dismissed for failure to prosecute in 1978, but was later reopened.

DECEMBER 16, 1982   Wallace Appointed African American to Commissioner Post. James C. White, a thirty-four-year-old accountant, was named commissioner of the Department of Revenue for the state of Alabama. White, a resident of Birmingham, was appointed to the position by Governor George C. Wallace, formerly a staunch segregationist.

White, a native of Montgomery, Alabama, earned a Bachelor's degree in accounting from Dillard University in Louisiana. In May 1973, he co-founded Banks, Finley, White, and Company Certified Public Accountants, "the largest minority CPA firm in the nation."

White's appointment as revenue commissioner made him the highest-ranking black in the executive branch of Alabama government and one of the few blacks to hold such a position in the nation.

DECEMBER 28–29, 1982   Racial Violence Claimed Lives in Miami. A new wave of racial violence erupted in Miami, Florida, after a Hispanic police officer, Luis Alvarez, shot and killed twenty-one-year-old Nevell Johnson, a suspected black looter. The altercations in the Overtown section of the city left two people dead and twenty-seven wounded. Dozens of businesses were destroyed or damaged. Forty-three people were arrested in the area.

During the melee, up to two hundred people participated in rampages throughout the Overtown section, but the disturbances did not reach the proportions of racial rioting in Miami's Liberty City area in 1980, when eighteen people died during three days of violence.

1983

JANUARY 1983   Gumbel Named Co-host of Morning Television. Bryant Gumbel began co-hosting the "Today" show with Jane Pauley on NBC. Gumbel was born Sept. 29, 1948, to Rhea and Richard Gumbel in New Orleans, Louisiana. Bates College in Lewiston, Maine, awarded him a liberal arts degree in 1970. He worked as a sports writer and editor-in-chief for *Black Sports Magazine* before entering broadcasting. In 1972 Gumbel became the weekend sportscaster for KNBC. Gumbel retired from the "Today" show January 3, 1997.

JANUARY 6, 1983   Desegregation in Chicago Schools. United States District Court Judge Milton Shadur upheld the constitutionality of a new desegregation plan for the public schools of Chicago, Illinois. The plan pledged that by September 1983, no school would be more than 70 percent white. It relied largely on "magnet schools" and voluntary transfers, with 180 programs from which students of all races and ethnic groups could choose. At the time of the ruling, only 16.3 percent of white students were in the public schools of Chicago and more than 100,000 of 435,000 students were in desegregated settings.

JANUARY 15, 1983   Dual Honorees of Peace Prize. Martin Luther King, Sr., and Richard Attenborough, the British film maker who produced and directed the epic motion picture *Gandhi,* were named co-recipients of the Martin Luther King, Jr., Non-Violent Peace Prize.

Television personality Bryant Gumbel. (AP/Wide World Photos.)

The awards were presented by Coretta Scott King, president of the Martin Luther King, Jr., Center for Non-Violent Social Change and widow of the slain civil rights leader, at ceremonies marking the 15th annual observance of King Jr.'s birthday in Atlanta, Georgia. Each man was given a medal inscribed with a quote from a King, Jr., speech: "Now the judgment of God is upon us, and we must all live together as brothers or we will all perish together as fools." They were also presented checks for $1,000.

Upon receipt of his award, Attenborough recalled that in the Gandhi Museum in New Delhi there was one picture in "the great hall," the picture of Martin Luther King, Jr. "That is fitting," he said, because "no one—and there are many who claim to—followed his teachings more closely than Dr. King. . . . I feel more touched now than I can ever remember on any occasion in my life." King, Sr., thanked his family for helping him through the deaths of his two sons and his wife and thanked "God for what He left me."

JANUARY 19, 1983   Report Detailed Conditions for African Americans. In its annual report on the "State of Black America," the National Urban League (NUL) claimed that blacks ended 1982 "in worse shape than in 1981" and expressed concern that "an economic recovery would bypass many minority Americans." The League added that blacks had continued to be hurt by the severity of the economic recession and by federal cut backs in domestic social service programs. "Vital survival programs were slashed at the same time that the black economy was plunged even deeper into depression. The result was to drive already disadvantaged people to the wall," according to John Jacob, president of the NUL. Jacob also contended that many black Americans would not benefit from an economic up turn. "We've never fully participated in post recession recoveries," Jacob said. He also noted that black employment was concentrated in automobile and other heavy industries that were hit hard by the recession, and he predicted that those industries would never employ as many people as in the past. "A major question facing the nation in 1983 is whether the inevitable restructuring of the American economy will include black people," Jacob asserted.

Jacob also claimed that President Ronald Reagan didn't understand the effects his economic policies were "having on the nation's poor. . . . He is looking at the world through rose-colored glasses, both of which are painted black."

The NUL maintained that federal programs serving the poor had been cut by $10 billion in 1972. As a result, welfare rolls had fallen by one million people, the federal school lunch program was serving about one million fewer children, one million people weren't getting federal food stamps any longer, and 200,000 infants and pregnant women weren't receiving federal nutrition aid.

The NUL recommended that Congress pass "a broad job-training and job creation program" and that it resist efforts by President Ronald Reagan to decrease money for several federal civil rights enforcement agencies. It also

urged the Reagan administration not to reduce Social Security benefits in "an attempt to bolster the nation's financially beleaguered retirement system." The League report concluded: "We are not recommending a 'welfare state,' but certainly some better way has to be found to take care of our people than we presently practice."

The administration of President Reagan continued to reject suggestions by the NUL and other civil rights groups and leaders that its policies were unfair or insensitive to the concerns of minorities. Yet criticisms continued from these as well as other sources. The *Atlanta Constitution,* in an editorial on December 15, 1982, had made sharp and specific attacks on the Reagan administration's civil rights policies.

JANUARY 25, 1983 Desegregation in Nashville. The United States Supreme Court refused to hear a challenge to a busing plan to achieve school desegregation in Nashville, Tennessee. The plan required elementary school pupils to be bused rather than attend neighborhood schools. It had been opposed by the Department of Justice, which contended that "busing does not work." After the Court's action, Assistant Attorney General William Bradford Reynolds remarked that the decision "in no way indicates that the legal issue of mandatory busing is closed. . . . We see no reason for a change of this administration's position of advancing alternatives to mandatory transportation to remedy intentional school segregation." But the decision pleased Avon N. Williams, Jr., a civil rights lawyer who had fought segregation in Nashville's schools for over twenty-five years. Williams stated: "I think all right-thinking people were or should have been shocked that the Justice Department, for the first time in several decades, intervened on the side of segregation and discrimination."

FEBRUARY 12, 1983 Death of Composer. Eubie Blake, African-American ragtime pianist-composer, died of natural causes in Brooklyn, New York, after having celebrated his one-hundreth birthday on February 7.

Blake, the son of former slaves, was born in Baltimore, Maryland. At the age of four, he wandered into a music store while his mother was shopping and began to play a pump organ. A salesman convinced his mother that the boy had "a God-given talent" and she purchased the $75 instrument. Blake learned about ragtime by tagging after black funeral processions, where he heard melodies played as dirges on the way to the cemetery and "ragged" on the way back. In his biography, *Eubie Blake* by Al Rose, he recalled the processions and exclaimed, "Oh how they'd swing."

Like most young black musicians of his time, Blake began his career as a pianist playing in a local bordello. He was fifteen at the time and his mother, Emily Blake, a deeply religious woman, was mortified when she found out. His father, however, convinced her to allow him to continue to play, especially since he contributed a portion of his earnings to the family.

Blake wrote his first composition, *Charleston Rag*, in 1899 (although it was not notated until 1915). Yet Blake observed in his memoirs that "it ain't until modern times that I ever really looked at it as a piece of music." His biographer Rose also observed that Blake "considered most of what he composed a mere point of departure for his personal improvisations. The music on the paper wasn't designed to be played literally. In fact, it would change in each rendition."

After 1915, Blake collaborated with bandleader Noble Sissle, who served not only as a lyricist but also a business agent. Then, in 1921, Blake composed *Shuffle Along*, one of the first black musicals to appear on Broadway. It played for 504 performances and helped launch the careers of Josephine Baker, Florence Mills, and Paul Robeson, among others. The song *Love Will Find a Way* made musical history depicting blacks as people with a full range of emotions. *Shuffle Along* was such a success that

police had to make 63rd Street in New York into a one-way thoroughfare in order to handle the crowds. After Broadway, the show toured the country in three companies.

Another of Blake's shows, *Blackbirds* (with lyrics by Andy Razaf), became a big hit in 1930. It featured John Bubbles, Buck Washington, and Ethel Waters and such famous tunes as *Memories of You* and *You're Lucky to Me*.

Blake's popularity began to wane during the Great Depression of the 1930s, and he himself fell into a state of dejection and depression following the death of his wife of twenty-eight years, Avis, in 1939. He emerged to play in USO camps and military hospitals during World War II. In 1945, Blake married Marion Tyler, a former show girl and secretary, who helped him put his personal life and business affairs back in order. But it was not until the 1960s, with the increased awareness of Scott Joplin and ragtime (furthered by the emergence of the black consciousness and black studies movements), that Blake became known to new generations of music lovers. In 1969, Columbia Records signed him to a massive recording project. At the time, Blake was the oldest living exponent of ragtime, and scores of fans hummed *I'm Just Wild About Harry*, the hit tune from *Shuffle Along*, and the song that also became the theme song for Harry Truman's 1948 presidential campaign.

FEBRUARY 16, 1983 Police Officer Indicted for Manslaughter. Luis Alvarez, a police officer in Miami, Florida, was indicted by the Dade County (of which Miami is the county seat) grand jury for manslaughter in the shooting death of Nevell Johnson, Jr., a twenty-one-year-old black man, on December 28, 1982. The killing of Johnson had sparked two days of racial rioting in the Overtown section of Miami.

Garth Reeves, editor of the *Miami Times*, a black newspaper, said the indictment of Alvarez would probably satisfy "the black communities, although he [Alvarez] had expected a harsher charge." He added: "For so long, police killings have gone unindicted. So this is a small victory of sorts."

FEBRUARY 23, 1983 African American Won Chicago Democratic Primary for Mayor. Former African American congressman Harold Washington won the Democratic primary election for mayor of Chicago, Illinois. Washington defeated incumbent Mayor Jane Byrne by 32,810 votes in a race that drew a record 1.2 million voters.

Washington's election came after a bitter and racially divisive campaign. While the African American candidate appealed to whites for their votes, he built the foundation of his quest on turning out a solid bloc of black voters. Washington repeatedly told them that "it's our turn. . . . We don't need to apologize for it, and we're not going to waste a lot of time explaining it. . . . It's our turn—that's all." In the end, Washington garnered about 85 percent of the votes cast by blacks.

The new Democratic nominee was born in Chicago, the son of an attorney and a Democratic precinct captain. He attended Roosevelt College in Chicago and the Northwestern University Law School. Before his election to the U.S. Congress, Washington was a city prosecutor, an arbitrator for the Illinois Industrial Commission, a state legislator, and a Democratic precinct captain in Chicago. The sixty-year-old-nominee had also served in the Army Air Corps during World War II.

FEBRUARY 23, 1983 Largest Contract in Football Signed. Herschel Walker, the African American collegiate football player who received the Heisman Trophy in December 1982, signed the biggest contract in football history with the New Jersey Generals of the United States Football League. The value of the three-year contract was estimated at more than $8 million. Walker, a resident of Wrightsville, Georgia, passed up his senior year at the University of Georgia in order to join the Generals.

Harold Washington in his office.

MARCH 4, 1983 Freedom Medal Given to King's Widow. Coretta Scott King, president of the Martin Luther King, Jr., Center for Non-Violent Social Change, was awarded the Franklin D. Roosevelt Freedom Medal at Hyde Park, New York. King was cited for epitomizing the late president's four freedoms: worship, speech, from want, and from fear.

APRIL 4, 1983 Widespread Desegregation in St. Louis County. Twenty-two school districts in St. Louis County, Missouri, agreed to a desegregation plan to begin the nation's first widespread voluntary school busing between a major city and its suburbs. The accord came just before a deadline imposed by United States District Judge William L. Hungate in an eleven-year-old desegregation suit.

Under the plan, all transfers would be voluntary. Predominantly white suburban school districts agreed to accept black students from the city of St. Louis until "their racial balance was at least 15 percent, but no more than 25 percent, black." In order to achieve the ratios, fifteen thousand black students would have to be bused to suburban schools in the fall of 1983. White suburban students would be encouraged to attend "magnet schools" in the city and city schools would be improved. Teachers were also to be reassigned to achieve more racial balance.

APRIL 7, 1983 Journalist Offered Thoughts on King's Meaning. As the nation marked the fifteenth anniversary of the assassination of Dr. Martin Luther King, Jr., with memorial services across the country, Hodding Carter III, one of the nation's leading journalists and a correspondent for the PBS network, gave a broad assessment of King's meaning for America, then and now, in the April 7, 1983, edition of the *Wall Street Journal.*

APRIL 12, 1983 Washington Elected Mayor of Chicago. Former African American congressman Harold Washington defeated Republican lawyer Bernard Epton to become the first black mayor of Chicago, Illinois. Washington, a Democrat, captured 636,136 votes (51.5 percent) to 595,694 (48.2 percent) for Epton, totaling 96 percent of 2,914 precincts. Washington's victory was made possible by a very heavy turnout of black voters, strong Hispanic support, and some support from middle class whites, although the election had been marked by serious racial divisions. On March 27, for example, an angry white crowd forced Washington to curtail a campaign appearance at a Catholic church in a white area of the city. The group waved signs in support of candidate Epton, who later denounced the incident.

APRIL 19–20, 1983 Protest of Confederate Flag. On April 19, about one hundred black students prayed and sang in front of the administration building at the University of Mississippi at Oxford in a protest against the use of the Confederate flag as a symbol of the university. During the previous night, several hundred white students had waved the flag and sang the Confederate battle song, "Dixie," in front of a black fraternity house on the campus. Charles Griffin, a black student, told reporters that the whites also yelled "nigger night" and "save the flag."

In the fall of 1982, some black students at the university had called for the banning of the rebel flag, the display of the Colonel Reb cartoon mascot, and the singing of "Dixie" at athletic games. John Hawkins, the first black varsity cheerleader at the university, refused to wave the flag as he lead cheers at football games. The protesting blacks said the Confederate symbols were both racist and offensive.

On April 20, Porter Fortune, chancellor of the University of Mississippi, announced that the Confederate flag would no longer be used as a school symbol. But black students complained because the statement did not ban individuals from continuing to wave the flag on campus or at athletic contests, nor did it prohibit the use of the Colonel Reb mascot or the singing of "Dixie." A group of white students cheered the chancellor's announcement and waved Confederate flags.

MAY 12, 1983 Gossett Won Oscar. Louis Gossett, Jr., won an Academy Award as best supporting actor for his role as a Marine Corps drill sergeant in the film *An Officer and a Gentleman.* He became the third black actor or actress to win an Oscar in the fifty-five-year history of the awards. The first black person to win the coveted honor was Hattie McDaniel, who was named best supporting actress for her work in *Gone with the Wind* in 1940. Sidney Poitier was named best actor for his lead role in the 1963 film *Lillies of the Field.*

Gossett, age forty-four, had won an Emmy Award in 1977 for his role as Fiddler in the ABC miniseries "Roots." As Gossett received his Oscar, blacks demonstrated outside the Hollywood Music Center calling the Academy Awards a racist affair. In reaction to the protest, Gossett commented: "You shouldn't call anything racist if [it is] improving." He expressed the hope that his award would "catch on like measles" and lead to the creation of more roles for black actors and actresses in Hollywood.

MAY 24, 1983   Tax Exemption and Discrimination. The United States Supreme Court, in an 8–1 decision, ruled that the federal government cannot grant tax exemptions to private schools that practice racial discrimination. Chief Justice Warren Burger, writing for the majority, stated that "it would be wholly incompatible with the concepts underlying tax exemption to grant the benefit of tax exempt status to racially discriminatory educational entities." Justice William H. Rehnquist was the lone dissenter.

The Court's ruling upheld a policy of non-exemption for discriminatory private schools that the Internal Revenue Service (IRS) had adopted in 1971, but which the administration of President Ronald Reagan had tried to abandon in 1982. Under the original policy, Bob Jones University in Greenville, South Carolina, lost its tax-exempt status in 1975 because it prohibited interracial dating or marriage among its students, and the Goldsboro Christian Schools of Goldsboro, North Carolina, which refused to admit blacks, also lost its tax-exempt status for 1969 through 1972. Both schools subsequently sued the IRS, but lost in both federal district and appellate courts. Both cases reached the Supreme Court on appeal from a lower court.

JUNE 17, 1983   Trout Promoted to Bishop. Nelson W. Trout, the sixty-two-year-old professor and director of minority studies at Trinity Lutheran Seminary in Columbus, Ohio, was elected Bishop of the American Lutheran Church's South Pacific District (located in California), becoming the first black person ever elected to full-time office among North American Lutheran Church bodies.

The members of the Lutheran Church in the United States have been historically concentrated among Scandinavian and Germanic ethnic groups in the East and Midwest and had little success in attracting large members of blacks to the denomination. Election of blacks to positions of "prominence in predominately-white denominations has been a way of

returning the church's focus to black concerns," according to the *National Leader,* a black-oriented news digest. Trout himself said of his election, "It's the one exception that defies the rule. It does not mean that the rapture has come or anything like that. It means that at a certain time and place the Lord was in our midst and He blessed us."

JUNE 22, 1983   Racial Classification Law Repealed. The state senate of Louisiana repealed the last of the nation's racial classification laws. The unanimous senate action followed a 90–4 vote for repeal in the Louisiana House of Representatives on June 9, 1983. The racial classification law had defined a black person as anyone with one-thirty-secondth "Negro" blood.

The repeal effort gained impetus after an unsuccessful effort was made by Susan Guilliory Phipps of Sulphur, Louisiana, to have the racial designation on her birth certificate changed from black to white. A state court judge, however, had ruled that Phipps had not proved "beyond doubt" that she was not at least one-thirty-second black.

AUGUST 13, 1983   Reagan Vetoed Funds for Desegregation Program. President Ronald Reagan vetoed a bill that allocated $20 million to implement a school desegregation program in Chicago. The desegregation had been ordered by United States District Court Judge Milton I. Shadur on June 30, 1983. In that order, the judge said that the federal government should allocate more than $14 million for desegregating Chicago's schools in 1983–1984 and set aside $250 million more for possible distribution in the next five years. Pending resolution of the case, Shadur also ordered that $55 million allocated for other education programs across the nation be frozen. But in July 1983, he freed $6.5 million of the amount.

In his veto message, President Reagan said: "The Chicago court's ostensible purpose in issuing this order was to provide a source of funds for the implementation of its decree. . . .

Congress hoped by the passage of this legislation to induce the court to release the funds that were impounded by the court. But I believe that the better course is to seek swift reversal of the district court's order." The president added that the government would pay the money mandated by the court if the decision was upheld, but he claimed that it was "inappropriate . . . for a court to withhold millions of dollars worth of unrelated and necessary education programs to enforce its orders."

AUGUST 20, 1983   Black Voter Registration Survey. A *Chicago Sun Times* survey revealed that more than 600,000 new black voters were expected to register in nine southern states—Alabama, Arkansas, Georgia, Louisiana, Mississippi, North Carolina, South Carolina, Tennessee, and Virginia—in time for the 1984 presidential election. The survey's projections were derived from interviews with election officials in six states, who based their estimates on "current and anticipated registration trends." In the other three states—Alabama, Arkansas, and Tennessee—the figures were provided by independent black organizations. By August 1983, 190,000 new black voters had already been added to voter rolls in the southern states.

The new black voters were expected to have a "potent" and "perhaps decisive" impact not only in the upcoming presidential contest, but also in many local elections. One potential presidential candidate, Jesse Jackson, a black minister and civil rights leader, had set a goal of two million new black voters in the South by 1984. The attainment of this goal was viewed as "a key to his decision" whether or not to pursue the Democratic presidential nomination.

AUGUST 21, 1983   Migration Patterns Shifted. The Bureau of the Census reported that "the traditional migration of blacks from the South to the urban centers of the North and West ended" in the 1970s. "Between 1975 and 1980, about 415,000 blacks moved to the South, whereas (in the more recent period) only about 220,000 left, thereby reversing the longstanding black exodus from the South."

In 1980, 53 percent of the nation's blacks lived in the South—the same proportion as in 1970, yet approximately 60 percent of the nation's black population lived in central cities—an increase of approximately 13 percent. The new demographic data was contained in a report entitled "America's Black Population: 1970 to 1982." It was based on data from the Census Bureau, the U.S. Labor Department, and other governmental agencies.

The Census Bureau's report also noted that: 1) The number of blacks in the civilian labor force increased by 2.7 million or 31 percent between 1972 and 1982, and the number of employed blacks grew by 1.4 million, or 19 percent. However, the number of blacks who were unemployed rose 140 percent, from 900,000 in 1972 to 2.1 million in 1982. The unemployment rate for blacks continued at more than double the rate for whites. In 1972, when the unemployment rate for whites was 5 percent, the unemployment rate for blacks was 10.3 percent. In 1982, the unemployment rates for both blacks and whites were the highest for any period since the second World War. 2) The median income for black married couples increased 6.9 percent between 1971 and 1981. Such families, however, made up only 55 percent of all black families in 1982, compared with 64 percent in 1972. 3) For all black families, median income, after adjustment for inflation, declined by 8.3 percent since 1971, with a 5.2 percent drop occurring between 1980 and 1981. This decline was attributed to the increase in the number of single-parent black families headed by females. In 1982, these families totaled 2.6 million—up 32 percent from 1972. Female-headed households made up 41 percent of all black families and 70 percent of all poor black families. 4) The poverty rate for blacks remained steady at 34 percent, though there were one million more poor blacks in 1980 than in 1970—nine million compared with eight million.

AUGUST 23, 1983 Thomas Expressed Concerns Over Desegregation. Clarence Thomas, the black chairman of the Equal Employment Opportunity Commission, told a group of faculty and staff at Clark College in Atlanta, Georgia, that black colleges had become "the victim" in the effort to desegregate the nation's colleges. He added that the "threat" to black colleges stemmed "from a misguided philosophy of desegregation that focuses on numbers rather than quality education for blacks. . . . If the goal of desegregation is to have every black student sit next to a white student then there is no room in education for black colleges," he said. "If the goal is for quality education," Thomas asserted, "then there is plenty of room."

Thomas also said that as the former assistant secretary for civil rights in the Department of Education, he became "terrified by the prospective effects of desegregation on black colleges," but added "they were not the ones doing the discriminating."

AUGUST 24, 1983 Lowery Opens Twenty-Sixth Annual Convention of SCLC. The Southern Christian Leadership Conference (SCLC) opened its twenty-sixth annual convention in Washington, D.C. In one of the opening addresses, the Reverend Joseph E. Lowery, president of the SCLC, asserted: "We are being told still that America cannot afford freedom and justice for all of our citizens. . . . Two decades of hard-fought progress are in danger of erosion through budget cuts. . . . Federal agencies have callously abdicated their mandated responsibility to enforce anti-discrimination laws. . . . Those rights we fought for dearly are being eroded."

The SCLC was founded in 1957 by Dr. Martin Luther King, Jr., and other southern civil rights leaders. The focus of the 1983 convention was "Jobs, Peace, and Freedom."

SEPTEMBER 1, 1983 Fort Valley State College's New President. Luther Burse, former interim president of Cheyney State College in Pennsylvania, assumed the presidency of Fort Valley State College in Georgia.

Burse was born June 3, 1937, in Hopkinsville, Kentucky. He received a bachelor's degree from Kentucky State University in 1958 and a master's degree from the University of Maryland in 1969. He was also a research assistant at the University of Maryland from 1966 to 1969.

Prior to accepting the presidency of Fort Valley State, Burse had also taught at Elizabeth City State University in North Carolina (1960–1966), served as coordinator of graduate studies in the division of Applied and Behavioral Sciences (1969–1981), and was interim president of Cheyney State from 1981 to 1982.

SEPTEMBER 17, 1983 Vanessa Williams Crowned Miss America. Vanessa Williams, a twenty-year-old African American woman from Millwood, New York, was crowned Miss America for 1984. It was the first time in the history of the sixty-year-old pageant that a black woman had won the title. Indeed, for half of the pageant's history, black females were barred from entering the competition.

Williams, a junior at Syracuse University, entered the pageant as Miss New York. She cried as she walked down the runway after receiving the crown.

OCTOBER 1983 Conference on the Study and Teaching of Afro-American History. Hundreds of scholars, teachers, and students attended a major conference on the Study and Teaching of Afro-American History at Purdue University in West Lafayette, Indiana. The meeting, which assessed the latest studies and trends in African American life and history, was sponsored by the American Historical Association and directed by Darlene Clark Hine, a Purdue University history professor.

In one of the keynote addresses at the conference, John Hope Franklin, professor of history at Duke University and one of the premiere scholars in African American history, described a fourth generation of practitioners of African American historical scholarship. He said the approaches of the recent generation of scholars, "the largest and perhaps the best trained [ever] were greatly stimulated by the drive for equality [during the 1950s and 1960s]." He also said that they had kept the subject "alive and vibrant."

Another keynote speaker, African American labor historian William H. Harris (also the president of Paine College in Augusta, Georgia), suggested that scholars needed to do "more work" on the black working class. He also indicated that "the quest for a change in perspective" by historians would "improve overall the range of history and the level of our understanding of the numerous black experiences that have been lived in America."

OCTOBER 27, 1983 Civil Rights Activist Honored. John Lewis, civil rights activist, was presented the Martin Luther King, Jr., Award for his contributions to voter education and registration by the Voter Education Project (VEP), at ceremonies commemorating the organization's twenty-first anniversary in Atlanta, Georgia. During its twenty-one year history, the VEP had helped register at least four million black voters across the South.

Lewis, who was beaten unconscious four times and arrested at least forty times during the civil rights movement of the 1960s, served as executive director of the Voter Education Project from 1970 to 1977. In accepting the VEP's highest honor Lewis said, "it means a great deal to me, but this isn't so much an honor for me as it is for the thousands of people who have worked in the voter registration movement. . . . I think we're on the way to a biracial democracy in the South."

NOVEMBER 2, 1983 Reagan Signed Bill Honoring King. President Ronald Reagan signed a bill at the White House establishing a federal holiday in honor of slain civil rights leader Martin Luther King, Jr. The president also

paid personal tribute to King, saying his words and deeds had "stirred our nation to the very depths of its soul." Reagan continued: "Dr. King made equality of rights his life's work. . . . Often he was beaten, imprisoned, but he never stopped teaching nonviolence. . . . If American history grows from two centuries to 20, Americans and others will still remember King's 'I Have a Dream' speech." The president warned, however, that "traces of bigotry still mar America. . . . So each year on Martin Luther King Day, let us not only recall Dr. King, but rededicate ourselves to the commandments he believed in and sought to live every day. 'Thou shalt love thy God with all thy heart and thou shall love thy neighbor as thyself.'"

Many Americans, including soul singer Stevie Wonder (who composed and recorded a birthday song honoring King) and Coretta Scott King, the slain civil rights leader's widow, had lobbied for the holiday (which was to begin on the third Monday in January 1986) since King's assassination in 1968. At the White House ceremonies at which the president signed the holiday bill, Mrs. King remarked: "Thank God for the blessing of his [King's] life and his leadership and his commitment. What manner of man was this? May we make ourselves worthy to carry on his dream and create the [beloved] community."

NOVEMBER 11, 1983 U.S. Commission on Civil Rights Extended. Representatives from the United States Congress and the Reagan administration reached an agreement to extend the life of the United States Commission on Civil Rights (CCR). Under the new accord, the six-member body would be reorganized into an eight-member one. The president and Congress would each name four members to serve staggered six-year terms and can only be removed "for cause, thus eliminating the possibility of firings for political reasons."

Earlier, President Reagan had tried to replace but eventually fired three Democratic members of the Commission "who did not share his administration's views in opposing busing to achieve school desegregation and broad affirmative action relief in job-discrimination cases." Many congressmen complained that Reagan was attempting to destroy "the commission's independence and integrity." Congress refused to appropriate funds for the extension of the Commission on September 30, 1983.

Under the agreement of November 11, two Democratic commissioners, Mary Frances Berry (an African American) and Blandina C. Ramirez (a Hispanic), were reappointed by Congress. The two women were among the three commissioners released by Reagan.

The CCR, an advisory group, investigated reports of discrimination and recommended steps for Congress and the president to take in remedying it. It was established in 1957.

NOVEMBER 24, 1983 Television Viewing Survey Released. An A.C. Nielson survey reported that blacks spent more time watching television (35 percent) than whites, and "that their prime-time choices" were different. The top ranked television program among whites was the CBS news program "60 Minutes," which ranked eighteenth among black viewers. The top rated program among blacks was the drama "Dynasty," which ranked sixth among whites. Television programs with largely black casts, "The A Team," "Gimme a Break," and "The Jeffersons" ranked second, third, and fourth among blacks; among white viewers they were 23rd, 64th, and 24th, respectively.

1984

JANUARY 2, 1984 Goode Began Mayorship. W. Wilson Goode, the forty-five-year-old son of North Carolina sharecroppers, was inaugurated as mayor of Philadelphia, Pennsylvania. Goode became the first African American chief executive in the city's 301-year history. At the time of his inauguration, about 40 percent of Philadelphia's 1.6 million people were black.

In an eight-minute inaugural address, Goode, who served in the cabinet of former mayor William Green, said that his election "might have been thought an impossible dream" for a black person, "but in America dreams can come true."

JANUARY 4, 1984 Navy Lieutenant's Release Celebrated at the White House. Robert O. Goodman, Jr., a black Navy lieutenant, was welcomed by President Ronald Reagan and others at the White House after having been freed from captivity in Syria. The release was negotiated by the African American Democratic presidential candidate Jesse L. Jackson. At the White House, Reagan declared, "this is a homecoming, and a very happy and welcomed one. . . . We are very proud of him."

Goodman had served a month as a prisoner in Syria after an A-6E Intruder jet, on which he was serving as bombardier-navigator, was shot down during an American air strike against Syrian anti-aircraft positions in Lebanon on December 4, 1983. The pilot of the plane, Mark Lange, was killed in the attack.

Goodman's release was made possible by "a moral appeal" that candidate Jackson, also a national civil rights leader, made to Syrian President Hafez Assad. Jackson's intervention into the realms of American foreign policy had been the subject of both praise and criticism, yet President Reagan said following Goodman's release, "you don't quarrel with success."

JANUARY 6, 1984 African American Named Pennsylvania Chief Justice. Robert N. C. Nix, Jr., was inaugurated as chief justice of the Pennsylvania Supreme Court, becoming the first African American to sit on a state supreme court bench since the Reconstruction era.

Nix was born on July 13, 1928, the grandson of a college dean and the son of Robert N. C. Nix, Sr., Pennsylvania's first black Democratic congressman. He received a bachelor's degree from Villanova University in Pennsylvania and a law degree from the University of Pennsylvania.

After serving as deputy attorney general of Pennsylvania in 1956–1957, Nix spent ten years in private practice. In 1968, he returned to public life to serve on the Philadelphia Court of Common Pleas. He was elected to the Pennsylvania Supreme Court in 1971.

Nix hoped that his appointment as chief justice would "inspire confidence in the legal system," and saw it as a reaffirmation of those principles upon which "American democracy was founded."

JANUARY 6, 1984 Mays Honored by South Carolina Hall of Fame. Benjamin E. Mays, former president of Morehouse College and the Atlanta, Georgia, school board, was inducted into the South Carolina Hall of Fame. Mays, age eighty-nine, a native of South Carolina and the son of former slaves, was cited for his long career in education and civil rights.

Since Mays was hospitalized with pneumonia, the plaque recognizing his induction was presented to him in Atlanta by former president Jimmy Carter, a longtime friend. Carter called Mays "a credit to Georgia and South Carolina, he's a credit to the Southland and he's a credit to the United States of America and to the world." In his response, Mays commented: "I was born a little stubborn on the race issue. . . . I felt that no man had a right to look down on another man. Every man, whether he's on the right of you, the left of you, certainly in back of you—it makes no difference—is still a man."

JANUARY 16, 1984 Jackson Honored at American Music Awards. The American Music Awards presented the Award of Merit to African American pop singer Michael Jackson at its eleventh annual ceremonies. The award recognized Jackson's "outstanding contributions over a long period of time to the musical entertainment of the American public." Previous Afri-

can American winners of the award included Berry Gordy, Jr., founder of Motown Records, and singers Ella Fitzgerald and Stevie Wonder.

JANUARY 22, 1984 Allen Named MVP at Twenty-Eighth Super Bowl. Marcus Allen, African American running back for the Los Angeles Raiders, was named Most Valuable Player (MVP) of the twenty-eighth annual Super Bowl in Tampa, Florida. Allen gained a record 191 yards rushing on 20 carries and scored two touchdowns, one on a five-yard run, the other on a seventy-four-yard run. The Raiders defeated the Washington Redskins 38–9.

FEBRUARY 2, 1984 Klansman Sentenced to Death for Murder. Mobile County Circuit Court Judge Braxton Kittrell sentenced Ku Klux Klansman Henry Hays to death for the 1981 strangulation murder of Michael Donald, a nineteen-year-old black youth whose body was found hanging from a tree in downtown Mobile, Alabama. Hays, age twenty-nine, was convicted of capital murder by a jury of eleven whites and one black on December 10, 1983.

In sentencing Hays to death by electric chair, Judge Kittrell ignored the recommendation of the jury for a life sentence in prison. But Mobile County District Attorney Chris Galanos said there was only "one chance in a million" that the death penalty would stand up on appeal since Donald (who was beaten, slashed across the throat, and found hanging across the street from Hays's house) had been killed four months before Alabama law permitted judges to give a stiffer penalty than that recommended by jurors.

FEBRUARY 7, 1984 African American Awarded Damages. United States District Court Judge Richard Enslen in Kalamazoo, Michigan, awarded a judgement of $50,000 to Walter Bergman, an eighty-four-year-old former Freedom Rider who was beaten by Ku Klux Klansmen at an Alabama bus station in 1961.

On May 31, 1983, Judge Enslen had decided that there was a "preponderance of evidence" to indicate that the FBI knew the Klan planned to attack Bergman and other Freedom Riders as they rode through Anniston and Birmingham, Alabama, during the height of the civil rights movement. The Bureau, he added, "had specific information" that the Klan "would be given free reign" by police in the two cities "to attack the Freedom Riders." Thus, he ruled, it could be sued for damages.

At the time of Judge Enslen's decision, Bergman, a former Wayne State University professor from Grand Rapids, was confined to a wheelchair from injuries suffered in the 1961 attack. He had asked for $2 million from the FBI for himself and the estate of his late wife, Frances.

FEBRUARY 28, 1984   Court Ruled on Grove College Suit. The United States Supreme Court, in a 6–3 decision, ruled that federal law prohibiting racial or sexual discrimination by schools and colleges extends only to the affected program or unit, not to the entire institution.

The case came to the high Court from Grove College in Pennsylvania, which had refused to sign a required "assurance of compliance" with Title IX of the Education Amendments of 1972. The federal government then began proceedings to disqualify the college from receiving federal scholarship aid. The college and four of its students brought suit in a U.S. District Court in Pennsylvania, challenging the government's actions. Although the district court sided with the college, the U.S. Court of Appeals for the Third Circuit ruled that despite the limited nature of the federal assistance received by Grove College, the law applied to the entire institution. The Supreme Court's majority disagreed. Justices Lewis Powell and Sandra Day O'Connor wrote that the case presented "an unedifying example of overzealousness on the part of the federal government" in its previous interpretation of Title IX.

While the administration of President Ronald Reagan applauded the decision, many congressmen and women's rights and civil rights

groups reacted with alarm. For a while the issue presented by Title IX of the Education Amendments of 1972 focused on sex discrimination, the broader provisions of the landmark Title VI of the omnibus Civil Rights Act of 1964 contained almost identical language. Thus, these groups feared its application too might be restricted by the Supreme Court's decision in the Grove College case.

MARCH 15, 1984   SAT Scores of African Americans Improved. The College Board, promoters of the Scholastic Aptitude Test (SAT), reported that the average SAT scores for blacks had risen twenty-two points since 1976. While the national SAT verbal average decreased six points between 1976 and 1983, the average for blacks increased by seven points verbally and fifteen points in mathematics during the period. The report said that the black SAT score increases had occurred "in all regions of the country." But among blacks students who took the SAT in 1983, those enrolled in private schools had average scores forty-three points higher in verbal and twenty-four points higher in mathematics than those in public schools. The new results of black SAT scores, overall, represented a reversal of a trend of falling test performances.

The new statistics on black SAT performances were included in a report entitled, "Profiles, College Bound Seniors," published by the College Board in New York City.

MARCH 28, 1984   Death of Educator and Civil Rights Activist. Benjamin Elijah Mays, educator and civil rights spokesperson, died of heart failure in Atlanta, Georgia, at age eighty-nine.

Mays was born August 1, 1894, in Epworth, South Carolina, the youngest of eight children of Hezekiah and Louvenia Carter Mays, former slaves and tenant farmers. After graduating as valedictorian from the high school department of South Carolina State College in Orangeburg, he entered Virginia Union College in Richmond, where he earned an "A" average. A year later Mays transferred to Bates College in Lewiston, Maine, from which he graduated with honors in 1920. While a graduate student at the University of Chicago, Mays taught mathematics at Morehouse College in Atlanta, Georgia. He completed a doctorate degree at Chicago in 1935. In the interval, Mays had also pastored the Shiloh Baptist Church in Atlanta (1921–1924), taught English at South Carolina State College (1925), served as executive secretary of the Tampa, Florida, Urban League (1926–1928), served as national student secretary of the Young Men's Christian Association (YMCA) (1928–1930), directed a study of black churches under the auspices of the Institute of Social and Religious Research (1930–1932), and began a career as dean of the School of Religion at Howard University in Washington, D.C. (1934–1940).

In 1940, Mays was elected president of Morehouse College (a prestigious all-black, all-male institution), which was faltering in a weakened Depression economy and which had lost much of its student body to war-time employment. One of his earliest students was young Martin Luther King, Jr., who came to the school in 1944 from the eleventh grade of high school. King soon became a protégé of the college president.

Through his skills as an orator and a fund-raiser, Mays restored the viability and prestige of Morehouse College and when he retired in 1967, the school had just been awarded a chapter of Phi Beta Kappa, the country's oldest and most prestigious academic honors society. Only two other black institutions of higher education in the nation, Fisk and Howard Universities, had previously earned such a distinction.

Following his retirement as president of Morehouse, Mays won a seat on the Atlanta Board of Education in 1969. The next year he was elected the first black president of the city's school board and was subsequently reelected six times over the next twelve years. During Mays's tenure as head of the school board, a group of black and white leaders adopted the so-called Atlanta Compromise Plan for school desegregation. With the approval of federal court judges, the blacks agreed to abandon pressures for cross-town and cross-jurisdictional busing to achieve further school desegregation, while whites consented to black administrative control of the school system. As a result of the pact, Alonzo Crim became the first black superintendent of the Atlanta Public Schools in 1973.

Mays began his civil rights activities as early as 1942 when he filed a successful suit challenging separate black and white dining cars on railroads. Between 1950 and 1970, he wrote hundreds of essays in magazines and newspapers (including a column in the *Pittsburgh Courier*), scholarly articles, and books denouncing segregation and discrimination and pleading for racial justice and racial harmony. Among these were *A Gospel for the Social Awakening* (1950), *Seeking to Be Christian in Race Relations* (1957), *Disturbed About Man* (1969), and his autobiography, *Born to Rebel* (1971). He gave an invocation and remarks at the historic March on Washington in 1963 and preached the principal eulogy at the funeral of Martin Luther King, Jr., in 1968. During that sermon Mays said, "God called the grandson of slaves and said to him, 'Martin Luther, speak to America about war and peace, speak to America about social justice, speak to America about racial discrimination, about its obligation to the poor.'"

In commenting on Mays's death, Charlie Moreland, president of the Morehouse College Alumni Association, remembered one of Mays's favorite quotations: "It must be born in mind that not reaching your goal is not tragic. The tragedy lies in not having a goal to reach."

APRIL 2, 1984 Thompson First Black Coach to Win NCAA Title. John Robert Thompson, Jr., head basketball coach at Georgetown University (Washington, D.C.), became the first African American to coach a team to the National Collegiate Athletic Association (NCAA) basketball title.

APRIL 26, 1984 Bandleader Died. William "Count" Basie, African American band leader, died of cancer in Hollywood, Florida, at the age of seventy-nine.

Basie grew up in Red Bank, New Jersey, and began taking twenty-five-cent music lessons at age eight. Despite his protests, Basie's mother insisted that he was "going to learn how to play the piano if it kills you."

Basie began playing professionally with Walter Page's Blue Devils group in Kansas City, Missouri, in the late 1920s and later joined Benny Moten's band in 1929. When Moten died six years later, Basie took over and began the Count Basie Band. The group was not really "discovered" until 1935 when John Hammond, a jazz impresario who had brought Billie Holiday to prominence, saw Basie's ten-piece band in Kansas City. He was so impressed that he urged Basie to increase the size of his ensemble and booked its first national tour.

It was also in Kansas City that Basie acquired the famous nickname "Count." A radio announcer discussing the "royal family" of jazz, which included "Duke of Ellington" and "King of Oliver," struck upon the idea of a "Count of Basie," yet Basie never really liked the title. He said in 1982, "I wanted to be called Buck or Hoot or even Arkansas Fats," all silent-film heroes. By 1936, Basie and his band had garnered a reputation far beyond Kansas City and it traveled widely throughout the country, with its residency at the Roseland Ballroom in New York City. It "delivered several seminal improvisers to the world of jazz." Most notable were Buck Clayton, Herschel Evans, and Lester Young, "whose logical flow of melody became the standard for horn players of subsequent generations."

The Basie band began recording in 1937 and such tunes as "One O'Clock Jump" became

"studies in call-and-response phrasing in which the saxophones often trade simple blues riffs with the brass." The group's early albums included *Basie's Back in Town, Blues by Basie,* and *Super Chief.*

The Basie band began to pare down in the 1950s, collaborating with blues singer "Big" Joe Williams in what "was widely considered a creative peak" for both Basie and Williams.

The demeanor of Basie, who was influenced by the legendary "Fats" Waller, was perhaps best described by Whitney Balliett, a jazz critic, in his book *Night Creature* (1980). Balliett said the band leader "pilots his ship from the keyboard with an occasional raised finger, an almost imperceptible nod, a sudden widely opened eye, a left-hand chord, a lifted chin, a smile, and plays background and solo piano that is the quintessence of swinging and taste and good cheer, even when almost nothing happens around it."

Basie's last performance was on March 19, 1984, at the Hollywood Palladium in California. He was completing more than fifty years as a jazz artist.

In commenting on Basie's death, blues singer Joe Williams said "we have just lost a national treasure but the happiness that his music gave us will live."

JUNE 12, 1984 Court Ruled on Seniority Plans. The United States Supreme Court, in a 6–3 decision, ruled that employers may not eliminate seniority plans that favor white men in order to protect "affirmative action gains by minorities and women when hard times hit." The Court also ruled that special preferences to remedy past discriminations were available only to persons who could prove they had been victimized by such bias, and not to "a class of people such as all blacks in an employer's work force." The decision arose from a Memphis, Tennessee, case when the city protected blacks from possible layoffs or demotions during an economic crisis in 1961. The Court's action

Bandleader William "Count" Basie. (Courtesy Columbia Records.)

was seen as a major defeat for civil rights advocates.

JULY 17, 1984 Study Noted Disparity. The Center for the Study of Social Policy, a Washington, D.C., research group, released a study that revealed that "the gap between the average incomes of whites and blacks" was as wide in 1984 as it was in 1960. The group blamed the disparity on the increase in the proportion of black families headed by females, from one-fifth to nearly one-half, and a sharp drop in the number of jobs held by black men.

In 1984, 14 percent of white families with children were headed by women, whereas 47 percent of black families fell in that category, an increase of 8 percent since 1950 and 21 percent since 1960. In 1984, only 55 percent of black men over the age of sixteen were employed, compared to 74 percent in 1960. As a consequence, the Center's study disclosed the median income of black families in 1981 was 56 percent of the whites' median, compared to 51 percent in 1960, but "the difference of one percentage point is statistically insignificant."

The report concluded: "Despite the fact that black Americans have made some gains since the civil rights movement, the economic gap between blacks and whites remains wide and is not diminishing. On measures of income, poverty, and unemployment, wide disparities between blacks and whites have not lessened or have even worsened since 1960."

JULY 27, 1984 Death of C. L. Franklin. C. L. Franklin, minister and civil rights leader, died in Detroit, Michigan, at the age of sixty-nine. Franklin, who was the father of soul singer Aretha Franklin, had been in a coma for five years after having been shot by robbers in his home.

Franklin was pastor of the New Bethel Baptist Church in Detroit for thirty-eight years and recorded more than twenty albums of his sermons, including *The Eagle Stirred Its Nest*. On some of his recordings, he was joined by the New Bethel Baptist Church Choir and his daughter Aretha.

Just months before the famous March on Washington in 1963, Franklin led a civil rights march in Detroit that attracted thousands of people. Jesse Jackson, one of the nation's most prominent civil rights leaders and also a minister, eulogized Franklin as "the high priest of soul preaching."

AUGUST 4–11, 1984 African American Athletes Won Gold. At the Summer Olympic Games held in Los Angeles, California, several African American athletes captured the coveted gold medal, indicating first-place finishes.

On August 4, Carl Lewis won the finals of the prestigious 100-meter dash in track and field. Lewis defeated Sam Graddy by finishing in 9.99 seconds. Graddy won the silver medal for his second place finish in 10.19 seconds. Lewis's winning margin of two-tenths of a second was the largest in Olympic history for the event. It was also the first gold medal in track and field for the United States in the 1984 Olympics and the first for the United States in the 100-meter since 1968, when Jim Hines set a world record of 9.95 in the high altitude of Mexico City. Still, Lewis's 9.99 represented the fastest 100 meters ever run at sea level in the Olympics.

On August 5, Evelyn Ashford set an Olympic record of 10.97 seconds while winning the women's 100-meter finals, and Edwin Moses won the 400-meter intermediate hurdles in 49.75 seconds.

On August 11, Carl Lewis completed his sweep of four gold medals by running the last leg of the U.S. 400-meter relay team. He went 100 meters in 8.94 seconds, enabling the Americans to set the first track and field record of the 1984 Games, 37.83 seconds. Earlier, Lewis had won gold medals in the 100-meter dash, the 200-meter dash, and the long jump.

Lewis's feats in the 1984 Olympics equaled those of Jesse Owens, the African

Track athlete Carl Lewis. (AP/Wide World Photos.)

American who won four gold medals in the same events in the 1936 Olympics in Berlin, Germany. Of his achievements, Lewis told news reporters, "it is an honor. Two years ago, everyone in the world said it couldn't be done. Even a year ago, I said I couldn't do it." He added, "I was looking for Ruth Owens [Jesse Owens's widow]. Jesse has been such an inspiration to me. I wanted to dedicate one medal to her."

NOVEMBER 6, 1984   Reagan Recaptured Presidency. Ronald Reagan was reelected president of the United States by the biggest margin in recent history. Reagan captured at least 58 percent of the more than fifty million votes cast, while his Democratic challenger, former vice president Walter Mondale, received approximately 41 percent. Reagan's landslide victory was comparable to that of Franklin D. Roosevelt's over Alf Landon in 1936; Lyndon B. Johnson's defeat of Barry Goldwater in 1964; and Richard Nixon's defeat of George McGovern in 1972. Reagan, who was frequently attacked by civil rights leaders during his first term for alleged insensitivity toward black issues, received only 20 percent of the African American

vote by most estimates, including media exit polls.

NOVEMBER 11, 1984   Martin Luther King, Sr., Died. Martin Luther King, Sr., minister, civil rights activist, and father of slain civil rights leader, Martin Luther King, Jr., died following a heart attack in Atlanta, Georgia, at age eighty-four.

King, Sr., was born Michael Luther King to a sharecropper and cleaning woman in Stockbridge, Georgia, on December 19, 1899. He changed his name "to honor" the famous German theologian Martin Luther in 1934.

King moved to Atlanta and became a minister at age seventeen. He also attended Morehouse College, from which he graduated in 1930. A year later King succeeded his deceased father-in-law, the Reverend Adam Daniel Williams, as pastor of the Ebenezer Baptist Church, one of Atlanta's largest black congregations. He remained as pastor or co-pastor of the church until 1975.

Even before King assumed the pastorate at Ebenezer Baptist Church, he had become active in political and racial affairs in Atlanta. He was one of the black leaders who "successfully lobbied" for the construction of the Booker T. Washington High School, the first secondary school for blacks in the city, in 1924. In 1936, King was a leader in a voting rights march to Atlanta's City Hall and participated in protests against segregated cafeterias in the city and helped negotiate an agreement for their desegregation in 1961.

The elder King accumulated considerable wealth as well as political and social influence. He was a director of Citizens Trust Company, the city's black bank, and a member of the board of directors or trustees of SCLC, Morehouse College, the Morehouse School of Religion, and the Carrie Steele-Pitts Orphans Home. In 1972, he was named "Clergyman of the Year" by the Atlanta Chapter of the National Conference of Christians and Jews. A year before his death, King was awarded the

Martin Luther King, Jr., Non-Violent Peace Prize.

Although King lost his famous son to an assassin's bullet in 1968 and his wife to another assassin in 1974, he continued to insist: "I don't hate. . . . There is no time for that, and no reason either. Nothing that a man does takes him lower than when he allows himself to fall so low as to hate anyone."

In commenting on King's death, Marvin Arrington, the black president of the Atlanta City Council, remarked, "we've lost one of our patriarchs."

NOVEMBER 14, 1984 Rosa Parks Honored. The Wonder Woman Foundation presented its first "Eleanor Roosevelt Woman of Courage Award" to Rosa Parks, the black woman who sparked the famous Montgomery, Alabama, bus boycott in 1955. Parks, age seventy-one, recalled her experience in accepting the award in New York. She said, "I am not going to move," when a bus driver told her to give up her seat to a white man. Parks added, "I stand before you full of new courage and determination not to retire, as long as I feel I can be of some assistance to troubled people. . . ."

The Wonder Woman Awards were established in 1981 to highlight the fortieth anniversary of "Wonder Woman," the comic book heroine created by William Moulton Marston.

DECEMBER 15, 1984 Davis Honored in Denmark. Miles Davis, the fifty-eight-year-old African American jazz trumpeter, was awarded the Sonning prize for musical excellence in Copenhagen, Denmark. He was also presented with $9,000 in cash. Davis has played a major role in the transition from the hard, aggressive stance of bop to a softer, more subtle sound in jazz. In 1956 success came to the performer with the release of his first record, *Miles Ahead.* Other landmark recordings included *Porgy and Bess* and *Sketches of Spain.* By the late 1960s Davis's musical explorations took him into the realm of electronic instruments, a sound that

can be heard in the album *Bitches Brew.* In decades to follow, Davis's rhythmic and harmonic experimentation served to diversify the musician's audience and increase his popularity.

DECEMBER 31, 1984 Telethon Raised $14 Million. The United Negro College Fund (UNCF), a coordinating fund-raising organization for most of the nation's private black colleges and universities, announced that it had raised more than $14.1 million in pledges during a national telethon. The event, the first of its kind carried on national television, was hosted by singer Lou Rawls and had a goal of $15 million.

1985

1985 Octavia E. Butler Won Science Fiction's Highest Literary Honors. Butler, a graduate of Pasadena City College, won the Nebula Award, the Hugo Award, and the Locus Award for her novella, *Bloodchild.* Butler, a member of Science Fiction Writers of America, had served as a contributor for several science fiction journals and had attended numerous workshops. She was the 1995 recipient of the MacArthur Foundation's "Genius Grant." Her writing focused on the impact of race and gender on future societies. Other works by the author include *Patternmaster, Mind of My Soul,* and *Kindred.*

JANUARY 7, 1985 Brock Elected to Hall of Fame. Lou Brock, African American outfielder for the St. Louis Cardinals of the National Baseball League, was elected to the Baseball Hall of Fame at Cooperstown, New York. Brock received 315 of the 395 ballots cast (79.5 percent) by members of the Baseball Writers' Association of America. He was only the fifteenth ballplayer to be elected in his first year of eligibility.

Brock played in the major leagues from 1961 until 1975. He began his career with the Chicago Cubs, but spent most of it with the St.

Louis Cardinals. At the time of his election to the Hall of Fame, Brock still lead all players in the number of bases stolen with 938; held the National League record of 118 bases stolen in one season (1974); and held the highest batting average for World Series games (.391) in 21 games.

JANUARY 7, 1985   Court Upheld Affirmative Action Plan. The United States Supreme Court, in a 6–3 decision, upheld the use of affirmative action plans by states that grant special employment preferences to minorities. The Court rejected arguments by fifteen prison guards in New York who contended that their chances of being promoted to captain were unlawfully diminished when state officials added points to promotion test scores of blacks and Hispanics. The guards sued the New York Civil Service Commission in 1982 after eight minority guards, whose promotion test scores had been upgraded, were added to a list of candidates for the rank of captain. At the time, there were no minority officers holding permanent positions as captain in any prison in the state of New York.

JANUARY 11, 1985   First African American on Mississippi's Supreme Court. Reuben V. Anderson was appointed to the Mississippi Supreme Court, becoming the first black person ever to sit on the bench of that state's highest court. Anderson, who was previously a state Circuit Court Judge, was named to the court by Mississippi Governor Bill Allain to fill the unexpired term of Justice Francis S. Bowling, who retired on January 1. Bowling's term ran to the fall of 1986.

Anderson, an attorney practicing in Mississippi starting in 1967, recalled that he never thought of the possibility of sitting on Mississippi's highest court. "When I first started practicing law," Anderson said, "I had to take my diploma with me wherever I went. Judges would not allow black lawyers to practice in a

lot of courts in this state. . . . Back then many court houses had separate facilities for blacks and whites. . . . It makes you proud, so proud that Mississippi has come so far."

JANUARY 23, 1985   National Urban League Assessed 1984. The National Urban League (NUL) said that 1984 was a year of "survival and hope" for African Americans, despite attempts by the administration of President Ronald Reagan "to be a Rambo-like destroyer of civil rights gains."

In 1984, the NUL reported that most black children lived in poverty; black unemployment had declined to 15 percent but was still three points above the black average since 1975 and more than double the white rate; and although black family incomes rose, the gap between black and white incomes had "grown wider for every type of family except those with two earners." The statistics and observations were included in the NUL's eleventh annual "State of Black America" report.

In commenting on the report, John Jacob, president of the NUL, said that President Ronald Reagan's citation of Martin Luther King, Jr.'s, call for "a colorblind society" in 1963 was "obscene" and used "as a justification for trimming 'measures like affirmative action [that] move us toward a racially neutral society by opening opportunities that help black people enter the mainstream.'"

FEBRUARY 26, 1985   African American Artists Took Home Grammys. Several African American entertainers received awards during the presentations of the 1984 Grammys, the highest honors for recording artists. Tina Turner, the "Queen of Rhythm and Blues," won three Grammys, including Record of the Year and Song of the Year for "What's Love Got to Do With It?" Three Grammys also went to Prince for Best Rock Performance by a Group and Best Original Film Score for *Purple Rain*. For his songwriting efforts, Prince won Best New

Rhythm and Blues Song for "I Feel for You." Lionel Richie's "Can't Slow Down" was named Album of the Year. Jazz trumpeter Wynton Marsalis, the Pointer Sisters, and Shirley Caesar also won two Grammys each. Marsalis won in the jazz and classical categories, the Pointer Sisters in pop, and Caesar in gospel. Michael Jackson won an award for his video *Making Michael Jackson's 'Thriller,'* and the late Count Basie was awarded a Grammy for his orchestra's *88 Basie Street.*

MARCH 21, 1985   1984 Elections Increased Number of Black Mayors. The Joint Center for Political Studies (JCPS), a Washington, D.C., research firm, reported that the 1984 elections increased the number of black mayors serving in the United States to 286. Thirty-one new black mayors were elected in 1984 in such cities as Battle Creek, Michigan; Gainesville, Georgia; Union Springs, Alabama; Pasco, Washington; Peekskill, New York; and Portsmouth and South Boston, Virginia. The increases in black mayors during 1984 was the largest "one-year increase yet recorded." Since 1975, the number of black mayors in the country had more than doubled from 135 to 286.

MAY 5, 1985   Apollo Theater Reopened. The historic Apollo Theater in the Harlem section of New York City reopened to celebrate its fiftieth anniversary. The theater, which was once the premiere showplace for America's black entertainers, had been closed for fifteen months and had undergone more than $10 million in refurbishments. More than fifteen hundred people attended the reopening celebrations while another two thousand stood outside.

The Apollo opened on 125th street in Harlem in 1916 as an unnamed storefront and began offering showcase talent in 1935. Its earliest performers included comedians Jackie "Moms" Mabley and "Pigmeat" Markham. At the reopening ceremonies, many of the biggest names in black entertainment returned for an appearance, including comedian Bill Cosby, and singers and dancers Patti LaBelle, Gregory Hines, Wilson Pickett, Little Richard, Stevie Wonder, and the Four Tops.

During the ceremonies, Percy Sutton, the chairman of the Inner City Broadcasting Company who was "the prime mover behind the renovation," said, "this theater is legendary to the thousands of performers who appeared on its stage, to the millions of people who attended its shows, and to the entertainment industry, which has been influenced by the innovations that occurred on the stage for five decades."

JULY 30, 1985   U.S. General Accounting Office Agreed to Compensate Black Employees. The United States General Accounting Office (GAO) agreed to pay $3.5 million in back pay to about three hundred present and former black employees who were denied promotions because of racial discrimination. Under the terms of the arrangement, thirty-two black evaluators would be promoted immediately and the GAO would then change its "competitive selection programs, including the preparation of an affirmative action plan to increase the percentage of minority people in upper-level positions."

The settlement resulted from class action suits filed by two GAO employees from Washington, D.C., and San Francisco, California, in 1980 and 1983, respectively, which claimed that whites were favored over blacks in promotion to supervisory positions from 1976 through 1983. In 1984 the Equal Employment Opportunity Commission (EEOC) found that the GAO's use of two different promotion systems had, indeed, "resulted in racial discrimination against many of its black employees."

NOVEMBER 7, 1985   More Black-Owned Businesses. The Bureau of the Census reported that the number of black-owned businesses in

Apollo Theater on 125th Street in the 1930s. (Courtesy of the National Archives.)

the United States had increased forty-seven percent over a five year period. In 1982, there were 339,231 black-owned firms, compared to 231,203 in 1977.

The majority of black-owned companies were service and retail businesses with gross receipts totaling $12.4 billion in 1982. That was an increase of nearly forty-four percent from $8.6 billion five years earlier.

The largest segment of black firms were "miscellaneous retail businesses," 53,981, with total receipts in 1982 of $993 million. Black

automotive dealers and service stations accounted for the largest dollar volume, however, $1.3 billion for 3,448 firms in 1982.

Small, sole proprietorships firms totaling 322,975 accounted for more than ninety-five percent of all black businesses in 1982, while corporations made up only 1.8 percent.

NOVEMBER 19, 1985   Death of Black Actor. Veteran African American actor Lincoln Theodore Andrew Perry, better known as Stepin Fetchit, died of pneumonia and congestive heart failure in Woodland Hills, California. He was eighty-three years old.

Perry, a native of Key West, Florida, began his acting career in the 1930s, appearing in such films as *Steamboat Round the Bend,* and was best known for his roles as "a shuffling, head-scratching" servant. He took his stage name from a race horse on which he had won some money in Oklahoma before leaving for Hollywood in the 1920s. Perry was the first black performer to appear on film with such movie stars as Will Rogers and Shirley Temple.

Perry's film characters were viewed by many blacks as negative stereotypes of their race, but Perry himself often bristled at such criticism and defended his "contributions." He once said that "when I came into motion picture, it was as an individual. . . . I had no manager, and no one had the idea of making a Negro a star. . . . I became the first Negro entertainer to become a millionaire. . . . All the things that Bill Cosby and Sidney Poitier have done wouldn't be possible if I hadn't broken that law [the race barrier]. I set up thrones for them to come and sit on."

After the CBS television documentary entitled "Of Black America" characterized him as a "stupid, lazy, eye-rolling stereotype" in the 1960s, Perry sued the network for $3 million, alleging that he had been held "up to hatred, contempt, [and] ridicule." A federal judge dismissed the suit in 1974.

1986

JANUARY 16, 1986   Capitol Building Statue. A bronze bust of Dr. Martin Luther King, Jr., was placed in the United States Capitol building. The statue was the first of any black American to stand in the halls of Congress. The bust, which depicts King in a meditative mood with a slightly bowed head, was created by John Wilson, a black artist at Boston University. After being displayed in the rotunda of

the Capitol building for six months, the bust was to be moved to Statuary Hall to stand beside the statues of other famous Americans on display there.

The bust was unveiled by King's widow, Coretta Scott King. Among those who spoke at the ceremonies were Senator Charles Mathias from Maryland who said, "today, Martin Luther King, Jr., takes his rightful place among the heroes of this nation." Representative Mary Rose Oakar from Ohio added: "No other American of my generation affected the course of American history more than Dr. King."

JANUARY 18, 1986   March in Raleigh. A group of whites marched in downtown Raleigh, North Carolina, to honor the birthday of Confederate General Robert E. Lee and to protest the first federal holiday honoring Dr. Martin Luther King, Jr. Glenn Miller, leader of the White Patriots Party and a former Ku Klux Klansman, said that he was "nauseated and sickened" by the national tribute to King. Miller added, "we're down here to tell the world that we will never accept a birthday honoring a black communist. Never!"

The Raleigh demonstration was one of several protests and acts of vandalism directed at the first annual King holiday. During the week, vandals in Buffalo, New York, painted a bust of King displayed in a city park white, while several municipalities and states refused to recognize the holiday altogether.

JANUARY 20, 1986   First National Holiday to Honor King. The nation celebrated the first national holiday in honor of slain civil rights leader Dr. Martin Luther King, Jr. In Atlanta, Georgia (King's birthplace), Vice President George Bush attended a wreath laying ceremony at King's crypt and an ecumenical service at Ebenezer Baptist Church, where King pastored at the time of his death. Other political leaders attending the services were Senators Bill Bradley from New Jersey, Bob Dole from Kansas, and Mack Mattingly and Sam Nunn, both from Georgia. Housing and Urban Development Secretary Samuel Pierce, Representative Newt Gingrich from Georgia, and Georgia Governor Joe Frank Harris were also in the audience, as was Rosa Parks, whose refusal to give up her bus seat to a white man sparked the famous Montgomery, Alabama, bus boycott in 1955.

The celebrations also included the first national Martin Luther King, Jr., Holiday Parade held in Atlanta. Atlanta Police Chief Morris Redding stated that the parade yielded "probably the largest turnout we've ever had" for such an event in the city.

The Martin Luther King, Jr., national holiday was the first such honor ever extended to an African American in United States history.

JANUARY 20, 1986   Tutu Won Peace Prize. The 1986 Martin Luther King, Jr., Non-Violent Peace Prize was awarded to Bishop Desmond Tutu, a leader in the struggle against apartheid in South Africa. The award was presented on behalf of the King Center for Non-Violent Social Change by its president and King's widow, Coretta Scott King. She said that Tutu, like King, possessed "faith that dissipates despair." Also, like King, Tutu repeatedly encouraged those "who are denied fundamental human, civil, and political rights never to doubt that they will one day be free."

In his acceptance speech, Tutu, winner of the 1984 Nobel Peace Prize, said he trembled as he stood "in the shadow of so great a person" as King. He added, "I receive [the award] on behalf of those languishing in jail, sentenced to terms of life imprisonment because they have the audacity to say, 'All we want for ourselves is what white people want for themselves.'"

JANUARY 28, 1986   Space Shuttle Exploded. Ronald McNair, an African American astronaut, died aboard the *Challenger* space shuttle shortly after its lift-off from Cape Canaveral, Florida. McNair, a thirty-five-year-old physi-

cist, was the nation's second black astronaut. He was one of a crew of seven aboard the *Challenger* when it exploded in the skies.

In one of the eulogies for McNair, actress Cicely Tyson remarked, "Ron and his crewmates touched . . . us. . . . They touched the other side of the sky for us."

FEBRUARY 8, 1986   Black Banker Died. Lorimer Douglas Milton, one of the nation's leading black bankers, died in Atlanta, Georgia, at age eighty-seven.

Milton was born on September 3, 1898, in Prince William County, Virginia, to Samuel Douglas and Samuella Anderson Milton. He was raised in Washington, D.C., and attended Brown University in Massachusetts on an ROTC scholarship. After receiving bachelor's and master's degrees in business from Brown in the 1920s, he began a long teaching career at Morehouse College and Atlanta University in Georgia. He retired as director of the Graduate School of Business Administration at Atlanta University in 1955.

In 1921 Milton began working in the Citizens Trust Bank of Atlanta, one of the nation's oldest and largest black financial institutions. He was elected president of the bank in 1930 and served in that position until 1971. At the time of Milton's retirement, Citizens Trust Bank had assets totaling $30 million and had established "a reputation for having opened the doors of the credit market to blacks."

Milton had served on a number of federal banking committees, including the advisory board of the Commodity Credit Corporation, which had responsibility for financing the government's farm price-support program. He also served on the president's Committee for the White House Conference on Education in 1955; the Federal Advisory Council's Social Security Board; and the National Commission of Economic Development in 1963. In addition, Milton was a former chairman of the board of trustees of Howard University.

Astronauts from NASA's Space Shuttle program (left to right): Col. Guion S. Bluford, Jr., Dr. Ronald McNair, Col. Frederick D. Gregory, and Lt. Col. Charles F. Bolden, Jr. (Courtesy of NASA.)

MARCH 2, 1986 New Mayor of New Orleans. City Councilman Sidney Barthelemy defeated state senator William Jefferson to become the second black mayor of New Orleans, Louisiana. Barthelemy garnered 93,054 votes (58 percent) to Jefferson's 67,668 (42 percent) votes to succeed Ernest "Dutch" Morial, New Orleans's first black mayor. Barthelemy, age forty-three, told his supporters after his victory, "this is like a dream! . . . Let us close ranks and fight the real problems."

In the New Orleans municipal elections held on March 2, two African Americans were also elected to the city council, giving blacks a majority on the seven-member body for the first time in that city's history.

JUNE 30, 1986 Armed Service Statistics. A U.S. Department of Defense survey revealed that more than 400,000 African Americans were serving in the armed services during 1986.

JULY 2, 1986 Court Upheld Affirmative Action Programs. The United States Supreme Court, in two separate rulings, upheld affirmative action programs in hiring and promotions.

In one case, the justices approved by a vote of 6–3 a plan from Cleveland, Ohio, that reserved about half of the promotions in its fire department for "qualified minority candidates." In the other ruling, the Court declared by a margin of 5–4 that a union representing sheet metal workers in New York state and New Jersey must double its non-white membership.

In the majority opinion, Justice William Brennan wrote, "We . . . hold that [federal law] does not prohibit a court from ordering in appropriate circumstances, affirmative race-conscious relief as a remedy for past discrimination."

SEPTEMBER 30, 1986 Perkins Named to Ambassadorship. Edward Perkins, a veteran diplomat, was named United States Ambassador to the Republic of South Africa, becoming the first African American ever to serve in that position. At the time of the appointment, the U.S. Senate was considering whether or not to override President Ronald Reagan's veto of "harsh" economic sanctions against the white-minority government of South Africa. However, a "senior White House official" told news reporters that the "nomination was not made with the expectation of winning any converts in the Senate."

Perkins was currently serving as United States Ambassador to Liberia when President Reagan appointed him to the South African post.

OCTOBER 15, 1986   Reagan's Approval Rate Among Blacks. A special Gallup Poll commissioned by the Joint Center for Political Studies in Washington, D.C., revealed that President Ronald Reagan's approval rating among blacks tripled between 1984 and 1986. The approval rate climbed from only eight percent in 1984 to 25 percent in 1986. In 1984, 82 percent of African Americans polled disapproved of the president's performance. By 1986, however, the negative rating had dropped to 66 percent. The highest approval rates for Reagan (30 percent or better) came from blacks who were male, blue-collar workers, political independents, urban southerners, and individuals younger than thirty years of age. The poll was based on a national survey of 868 blacks.

OCTOBER 18, 1986   NAACP Dedicated New Headquarters. The NAACP, one of the oldest and most prominent of the nation's civil rights organizations, dedicated its new national headquarters in Baltimore, Maryland. The group, which was founded in 1909 "to fight discrimination and injustice," moved to Baltimore from its original headquarters in New York City, partially because "it could not afford the high rent and taxes." Baltimore was chosen for the new headquarters largely because of "its majority black population and long history in promoting civil rights."

OCTOBER 23, 1986   Cadet Targeted at The Citadel. Five white students dressed in Ku Klux Klan-type attire broke into the room of Kevin Nesmith, a black cadet at The Citadel in South Carolina. The five students taunted Nesmith and left a charred paper cross in his room. Nesmith said that he slept through most of the incident.

On November 14, Nesmith resigned from the South Carolina military college because he felt he had been "made the [villain]" in the hazing incident, but added "the [villains] remain at Citadel." Nesmith also said that "anger and frustration built up, and I felt mentally drained and no longer wanted to subject myself to this humiliation."

The five white cadets who cursed Nesmith in the October incident were suspended from the college, but the suspensions were "stayed on the condition they not get into any more serious trouble during the school year." They were also restricted to campus for the remainder of the school year and "given additional marching tours." But some black leaders in the state contended that the five should have been expelled. The NAACP filed an $800,000 lawsuit against The Citadel, alleging that Nesmith's civil rights had been violated and that the school historically had "tolerated and sanctioned" racial bigotry. On November 17, civil rights leader Jessie Jackson met with Nesmith and later requested a congressional investigation of race relations at the college.

On November 16, the South Carolina Human Affairs Commission issued a report stating that a "minimal black representation" on the campus created "an environment lacking in ethnic diversity and cultural sensitivity." They recommended, among other things, that the school increase its black enrollment from 6 percent to 10 percent in two years and incorporate "mandatory human relations and cultural sensitivity classes" into the leadership training curriculum.

DECEMBER 10, 1986   Segregation Suit Dismissed. United States District Court Judge R. Allan Edgar dismissed a school segregation suit against the board of education of Chattanooga, Tennessee, which was first filed in 1960. Edgar commented: "Based upon their conduct for many years, there is no indication that the defendants [the school board] will take any steps to reinstitute vestiges of segregation." He ruled that the board had finally met the court order "to racially integrate students and faculty."

At the time of Edgar's ruling, there were nearly 23,700 students, 51.26 percent of them black, enrolled in Chattanooga's public schools. Most recently, the school board had reassigned 185 teachers in order that the faculty at each school in the system match approximately the 60–40 white-to-black teacher ratio system wide.

The desegregation suit, filed by black real estate agent James Mapp, was "the longest to linger" in the federal court in Chattanooga. But Mapp, whose home was bombed in 1970, said, "I think the past effects of state-imposed racial discrimination and segregation have not been completely done away with." He cited several local schools that were still either "almost 100 percent black or white."

DECEMBER 20–23, 1986   Racial Violence in Queens. One black man was killed and two others injured after a gang of white youths attacked them in the predominately white Howard Beach section of Queens, New York. Michael Griffith, a twenty-three-year-old construction worker from Brooklyn, was hit by a car and killed on a highway while attempting to escape his attackers. Another black man, Cedric Sandeford, age thirty-seven, was beaten with a baseball bat. The three blacks were attacked outside a pizza parlor after being taunted with racial slurs.

The three blacks, whose car had experienced mechanical problems, had gone into the pizza parlor to call for help when they were confronted by a gang of whites yelling racial epithets and asking "What are you doing in this neighborhood," according to a statement by New York Police Commissioner Benjamin Ward. New York Mayor Edward Koch posted a $10,000 reward "for information leading to the arrests of the assailants."

On December 23, three white teenagers were ordered held without bond on second-degree murder charges in connection with the

attack. Meanwhile, a group of blacks in the Jamaica section of Queens, chanting "Howard Beach! Howard Beach!" chased and beat a white teenager who was walking to a bus stop. Mayor Koch condemned the apparent retaliation.

The Howard Beach incident was another in a series of ugly racial confrontations that had occurred in various parts of the country that year. The first major encounter took place in Raleigh, North Carolina, on the eve of the first national holiday honoring Dr. Martin Luther King, Jr.

1987

JANUARY 2, 1987   Barry Begins Third Term. Marion Barry, Jr., was inaugurated for an unprecedented third term as mayor of Washington, D.C. In his inaugural address, the former black civil rights activist asserted: "Nobody's going to turn us around from educating every person who wants to learn, employing every person who wants to work, housing every person who needs shelter, helping every person who needs new hope."

JANUARY 14, 1987   National Urban League Released Annual Report. The National Urban League (NUL) said that black Americans were "besieged by a resurgence of violent racism, economic depression, and a national climate of selfishness marked by a retreat from civil rights" during 1986. In its annual "The State of Black America" report, the NUL noted that 15 percent of the black work force was unemployed and that black family income "over the past dozen years" had decreased by $1,500 "while economic need increased."

In presenting the report, NUL president John Jacob said, "we can't forget that for six years and more, Americans have been told that racism is a thing of the past. That poverty is caused by habits of the poor. . . . The result is a national climate of selfishness and a failure of government to take a positive role in ending racism and disadvantage."

The League's recommendations for solving the maladies that it identified included a "broad-based" attack on violent racism and a call for congressional action to toughen and tighten civil rights laws.

Larry Speakes, spokesman for the administration of President Ronald Reagan (which was harshly criticized in the report), said although he had not read the document, "certainly we would share a concern with the Urban League over any increase or, for that matter, a single incident of racial intolerance or racial violence that would occur in this country."

JANUARY 17, 1987 Counter-Demonstrators Arrested. Ku Klux Klansmen and other white supremacists threw rocks and bottles at a group of ninety civil rights marchers in Forsyth County, Georgia. The four hundred counter-demonstrators also shouted racial slurs at the protestors, who had gathered on a state road about two miles outside of the city of Cumming. There were no serious injuries, but eight of the supremacists were arrested on charges including disorderly conduct, trespassing, and carrying a concealed weapon.

The aborted march was led by Dean Carter, a white martial arts instructor from Hall County, Georgia, and veteran civil rights leader Hosea Williams. Most of the marchers were blacks from Atlanta, thirty miles south of Forsyth County. Williams, an Atlanta city councilman, commented: "In thirty years in the civil rights movement, I've never seen it worse than this," as he responded to the violence. He also added, "in 1987, who would believe this kind of racial violence in America?"

The march had been planned after the cancellation of a previous "brotherhood walk" that Carter had organized, partially to honor the memory of assassinated civil rights leader Martin Luther King, Jr. The event was canceled after the organizers were threatened.

JANUARY 24, 1987 Demonstration Against Racism. More than twenty thousand people marched for "brotherhood" and against racism in Forsyth County, Georgia. The biracial demonstrators were protected by three thousand state and local police officers and National Guardsmen. There were a few minor injuries and sixty people, mostly white counter-demonstrators, were arrested. It was "the largest civil rights demonstration in two decades."

The march was organized after a similar, smaller protest a week earlier had been broken up by white counter-demonstrators who threw rocks and bottles. That "brotherhood" march, also designed to honor the memory of slain civil rights leader Martin Luther King, Jr., was led by veteran civil rights activist and Atlanta City Councilman Hosea Williams and Dean Carter, a white marital arts instructor. Coretta Scott King, widow of the assassinated civil rights leader, was among the leaders of the January 24th march, as was Williams, Carter, and civil rights leaders Benjamin Hooks of the NAACP and Joseph Lowery of the SCLC.

All of the speakers during the demonstration denounced the racist attack on the earlier protesters and called for a renewal of the commitment to racial justice. Hosea Williams, a leader of the January 17th march, called the January 24th march "the greatest."

JANUARY 31, 1987 Protest in Louisville. About one thousand people rallied in Louisville, Kentucky, to protest the burning of a picture of slain civil rights leader Martin Luther King, Jr., by Ku Klux Klansmen and what they called a resurgence of racism and racist violence in the United States.

FEBRUARY 19–20, 1987 Looting Followed Death at Hands of Police. On February 19, about two hundred blacks ran through the streets throwing rocks and setting fires in Tampa, Florida. The disturbances began one night after a twenty-three-year old black man died after police had tried to subdue him by using a "choke hold,"which entails applying pressure to the carotid artery.

On February 20, isolated incidents involving rock and bottle throwing by black youths continued, but there were no injuries. Two people were arrested. Meanwhile, black leaders and other volunteers walked the streets urging residents to remain calm.

Before the most recent incidents, another black man had been killed by police, and other incidents involving blacks and law enforcement officers had occurred in December 1986, including the arrest of the New York Mets's star pitcher Dwight Gooden. Gooden had been charged with "battering police officers." A report released on February 19, 1987, by City Attorney Michael Fogarty, however, placed some of the blame for the Gooden incident on the police. The report also called on the city of Tampa to recruit more black police officers. At the time of these latest altercations, only 65 members of Tampa's 790 member police force were black, and the paucity of black police officers had been a constant complaint of local black leaders.

FEBRUARY 26, 1987 Death of Civil Rights Activist. Edgar Daniel "E.D." Nixon, "one of the fathers of the civil rights movement," died after prostate surgery in Montgomery, Alabama, at the age of eighty-seven.

Nixon was born July 12, 1899, in Montgomery. He received only about sixteen months of formal education. Between 1923 and 1964, he worked as a Pullman porter on a Birmingham-to-Cincinnati train and was a long-time member of the Brotherhood of Sleeping Car Porters. In 1949, Nixon was elected president of the Alabama state NAACP.

At the time that a Montgomery seamstress, Rosa Parks, refused to give up her seat on a segregated Montgomery bus to a white man, Nixon was still active in the state and local NAACP and was, according to another local NAACP official, "the most militant man in town." Parks was also secretary of the local

NAACP at the time and a close acquaintance of Nixon's. After Parks's arrest, she called Nixon, but he was unable to learn more about the situation because Montgomery police told him he was an "unauthorized person."

Following his rebuff by the Montgomery police, Nixon phoned Clifford Durr, a white Montgomery lawyer sympathetic to blacks. Durr was able to obtain the specific charge against Parks, "failing to obey a bus driver," and urged Nixon to seek the services of NAACP lawyer Fred D. Gray. Durr further advised that the defense should be based on the unconstitutionality of the state law requiring segregation on city buses, rather than the Montgomery city ordinance relating to retaining and giving up seats. Such a defense, he suggested, could best provide "a test case" for bus segregation laws.

In addition to contacting Durr and Gray immediately after Parks's arrest, Nixon is also credited with posting bail for the seamstress; informing Martin Luther King, Jr., of the arrest; proposing the Montgomery bus boycott; and helping to choose King as president of the Montgomery Improvement Association, which directed the successful 381-day boycott. Nixon is quoted as once having told a friend, referring to King, "I don't know just how, but one day I'm going to hook him to the stars." He made the remark after hearing King preach.

Nixon is also credited with avoiding a potential major division at the beginning of the boycott by declining to aspire to the leadership of the movement. This move may also have helped keep one of his rivals, Rufus Lewis, a local funeral director, from seeking the presidency of the Improvement Association, opening the way for King, who had few partisan ties, to lead the boycott. Finally, it was also Nixon who publicly browbeated recalcitrant blacks and chided fearful ones into action. After some black ministers urged that the boycott be keep secret, Nixon asked, "What the heck you taking about? How you going to have a mass meeting, going to boycott a city bus line, without the white folk knowing it? You ought to make up your mind right now that you either admit you are a grown man or concede to the fact that you are a bunch of scared boys." He also told a crowd at a mass meeting, "Before you brothers and sisters get comfortable in your seats, I want to say if anybody here is afraid, he better take his hat and go home. We've worn aprons long enough. It's time for us to take them off." According to the Reverend Ralph David Abernathy, also one of the leaders of the Montgomery boycott, Nixon "wouldn't take any mess."

Nixon's home, which had a bomb tossed in its driveway during the height of the protests, is now an Alabama state historical landmark. Nixon himself was feted at a testimonial dinner in Atlanta, Georgia, in 1985. At that time, he remarked: "Fifty thousand people rose up and rocked the cradle of the Confederacy until we could sit where we wanted to on a bus. . . . A whole lot of things came about because we rocked the cradle."

MARCH 19, 1987 Atlanta Politicians Accused of Drug Use and Sale. Alice Bond, estranged wife of former Georgia senator and civil rights activist Julian Bond, told police in Atlanta, Georgia, that her husband and other prominent Atlantans were either users or suppliers of cocaine. Andrew Jackson Young, the black mayor of Atlanta, was also drawn into the matter when his name appeared as one of those individuals allegedly named by Bond, and when he made a telephone call "to counsel" her after her allegations were revealed. The accusations led to investigations by the Atlanta police, the FBI, and the U.S. attorney for the northern district of Georgia. No formal charges, however, were lodged against Senator Bond, and after a lengthy federal grand jury investigation U.S. Attorney Robert Barr announced that there was "insufficient evidence" to prosecute Mayor Young for obstruction of justice.

APRIL 16, 1987 Newspaper Found Guilty of Retaliation. A United States District Court

jury in New York City found that the *New York Daily News,* considered the nation's largest general newspaper, was guilty of retaliation against copy editor Causewell Vaughan, reporters Steven Duncan and David Hardy, and editor Joan Shepard because they complained of unfair treatment. The four black journalists had filed suit against the *Daily News* claiming they had been denied salaries comparable to their white colleagues and were given fewer promotions. At the time of the trial, only 6.5 percent of the nation's journalists were members of minority groups. In praising the jury's verdict in the *Daily News* case, Albert Fitzpatrick, president of the National Association of Black Journalists (NABJ), commented that "blacks are under-represented in all areas of the media."

AUGUST 24, 1987 March Organizer Died. Bayard Rustin, the African American civil rights activist who directed the 1963 March on Washington, died in New York City at the age of seventy-seven. In addition to being chief organizer of the 1963 march, Rustin was also responsible for "many of the tactics and much of the strategy" used by Martin Luther King, Jr., and other leaders of the civil rights movement. During the 1960s and 1970s he was often criticized by "more radical blacks" because he advocated better education as the best means for blacks to gain racial equality and because he was an apostle of non-violent protest. Yet Rustin continued to oppose nationalist and separatist ideas among African Americans.

Rustin's pacifist ideology extended at least back to World War II when he spent more than two years in jail as a conscientious objector. In the 1960s, he became an early vocal opponent of American involvement in the war in Vietnam.

At the time of his death, Rustin was co-chairman of the A. Philip Randolph Institute, a social-reform lobbying group and had recently traveled to Cambodia and Haiti investigating "violence and injustice."

Bayard Rustin. (Courtesy of A. Philip Randolph Institute.)

In its tribute to Rustin published on August 26, 1987, the *Atlanta Constitution* said that he "devoted his life to the fight for human rights, freedom and justice, not just in [the United States], but around the world. . . . His commitments to human rights and peace were neither trendy nor shallow. . . . America is indebted to Bayard Rustin. It is a better nation because of him."

SEPTEMBER 13, 1987 Supreme Court Justice Spoke Out. Thurgood Marshall, at that time the only African American ever to sit on the United States Supreme Court, said in a televised interview that President Ronald Reagan ranked at "the bottom" among presidents in "protecting and advancing civil rights." "Honestly," Marshall said, "I think he's down with [Herbert] Hoover and that group—[Woodrow] Wilson—when we [blacks] really didn't have a chance." Marshall went on to say that Reagan, "as the 'gatekeeper' of fairness and justice in America, had neglected his job. . . . I don't care whether he's the president, the governor, the mayor, the sheriff, whoever calls the shots determines whether we have integration, segregation, or decency. . . . That starts exactly with

the president." Marshall's remarks were broadcast on television stations affiliated with the Ganett Broadcasting Company.

Marshall's off-the-bench criticisms were rare both for him and for any justice of the United States Supreme Court. When excerpts were published in newspapers prior to the actual telecast, President Reagan's advisor for domestic affairs, Gary Bauer, called them "outrageous." He said President Reagan's policies had permitted blacks and other minorities to "enter the economic mainstream of the country." He specifically cited the president's endorsement of the 1986 tax reform act, which he claimed removed the federal tax burden from millions of poor people, and the president's proposals to help low income families buy public housing and to receive cash vouchers to pay for their children's tuition at better schools.

Justice Marshall's criticisms echoed those of other African American leaders who had complained for several years that the president had "tried to undercut minority hiring programs, school busing to achieve integration, the Voting Rights Act, and other efforts to prevent discrimination and advance the social and economic conditions of minorities." The Justice Department, for example, had joined several cases in federal courts to argue against affirmative action in employment, contending that employers should exercise total "color blindness" in hiring and promotions. The government also took the side of the Norfolk, Virginia, School Board in a case challenging the use of busing to achieve racial desegregation in public schools.

While domestic advisor Bauer had defended "a colorblind approach," saying "if people are looking for us to meet certain quotas all the time, they're going to be very disappointed," B.J. Cooper, a White House deputy press secretary, countered that Reagan's critics overlooked "the administration's crackdown on cases of racial violence and its commitment to enforce fair employment and fair housing laws." He claimed that the administration had prosecuted 55 cases of racial violence involving 137 defendants, including 75 Ku Klux Klansmen, since Reagan took office. "That compares," Cooper added, "with 22 cases involving 52 defendants, of whom 35 were Klansmen, in the previous Democratic administration of President Jimmy Carter."

SEPTEMBER 24, 1987 Alcohol Use Alarmed Council. Members attending the annual convention of the National Black Alcoholism Council, Inc. (NBAC) in Atlanta, Georgia, declared that alcoholism was a serious threat to the continued welfare of black America. Although figures varied, it was estimated that between ten million and twenty-four million Americans were alcoholics in 1987. However, a recent government study showed that blacks were twice as likely to die from cirrhosis than whites and that esophageal cancer among blacks was ten times higher than among whites.

Maxine Womble, chairwoman of the nine-year-old NBAC, said that the impact of alcoholism among blacks could be seen in "the large number of single-parent households, the prevalence of poverty, youth gangs, violence," high dropout rates from schools, teenaged pregnancies, and "black-on-black crime." Some studies, for example, suggested that alcohol and drugs were involved in between 50 percent and 70 percent of the black homicides in the United States. "A lot of what we're doing is about images and education," Mrs. Womble said. "People in these [black] communities must realize only they can save themselves."

SEPTEMBER 24, 1987 Congressional Black Caucus Issued Report. The Congressional Black Caucus (CBC) issued a report that charged that black elected officials were "victims" of harassment by various prosecutorial branches of government and the white-controlled media in disproportionate numbers. The report concluded that while the number of black elected officials had almost doubled between 1977 and 1987 and "some of the names in the drama . . . changed . . . the circumstances remain[ed] es-

sentially unchanged." The CBC contended that while black officials were rightfully scrutinized, their "scrutiny . . . too often issue[d] from ignoble motives; it [was] designed not to protect the public interests but to prevent the public's interest from being represented by persons of the public's choosing."

An appendix to the report listed seventy-eight cases of "harassment" against black elected officials, but almost half of the cases occurred before 1977 and several did not involve investigations by government or the press. For example, Lloyd Edwards, who ran for president of the St. James Parish in Louisiana in 1983, and Katie Jackson Booker, who ran for mayor of Ditmoor, Illinois, in 1985, were not included because of cross-burnings on their lawns.

The report included, however, at least a dozen cases of black politicians who were either brought before grand juries and never indicted or who were indicted and later acquitted since 1977. These included Kenneth Gibson, the former mayor of Newark, New Jersey, whom the study said was indicted in 1982 on 146 counts of "conspiracy misuse of funds and misconduct" and was acquitted of all the charges; Mayor Marion Barry of Washington, D.C., who was the target of an investigation of cocaine use and whose administration was probed extensively by the FBI and the U.S. Attorney's Office for alleged corruption in the letting of contracts to minority businesses; and that of Mayor Andrew Young of Atlanta, Georgia, who appeared before a federal grand jury investigating whether he "tampered" with a witness during a probe into allegations of drug abuse by several well-known Atlanta citizens. Of Young, the report said, "for him even to have become the subject of an investigation, was widely perceived as a totally inappropriate and abusive use of prosecutorial discretion by the U.S. Attorney."

The CBC report also claimed that the harassment of black officials occurred through audits and investigations by the Internal Revenue Service (IRS); electronic surveillance, burglaries, and covert disruptive activity by various intelligence agencies; and grand jury investigations and indictments by criminal justice agencies.

However, John Russell, a spokesman for the U.S. Department of Justice, labeled the CBC report "nonsense." He said, "I don't think those allegations can be substantiated in any way." Jackie Greene, regional director for the National Association of Black Journalists and director of editorial services at *USA Today* in Washington declared, "I think that black politicians should be held to the same scrutiny that any other politician faces by the media. . . . For the most part that is being done."

The CBC report was written by Mary Sawyer, a professor of religion at Iowa State University, who wrote a similar report in 1977, and was published by Voter Registration Action Inc. in Washington, D.C.

OCTOBER 27, 1987   Author and Teacher Died.
John Oliver Killens, author and teacher, died in New York City. Killens was born in Macon, Georgia, but left the South at age seventeen and lived most of his life in the North. Like many other blacks who left the South in the first half of the twentieth century, Killens was "reluctant to return" to his native region. His first extended visit to his hometown occurred in 1986, when he spent two weeks as a lecturer and writer-in-residence.

Killens' major novels included *Youngblood* (1954), *And Then We Heard the Thunder* (1963), and *The Cotillion, or One Good Bull Is Half the Herd* (1971). *Youngblood* was a story of "powerful courage" among ordinary black folks in a small Georgia town, while *The Cotillion* was a "hilarious satire [of] social-climbing" black Northerners.

Some critics contended that Killens's later works "lacked the power" of his first two novels, *Youngblood* and *And Then We Heard the Thunder*. But at least one reviewer, Tina McElroy Ansa, asserted that if literary historians are looking for the quality of "power . . . they

should also look to the man. There, they will find the power they seek. The power of his teaching, the power of his courage, the power of his generosity, the power of his gentleness, the power of his example, the power of his life."

Killens was known to have inspired a generation of young black writers, including Wesley Brown, Nikki Giovanni, Richard Perry, Janet Tolliver, and Brenda Wilkinson. His own philosophy was that "the responsibility of the writer is to take the facts and deepen them into eternal truth. Every time I sit down to the typewriter, put pen to paper," he once said, "I'm out to change the world."

Killens was an original member of the Harlem Writers Guild and worked on Paul Robeson's newspaper, *Freedom*. He held fund raisers during the civil rights movement for Dr. Martin Luther King, Jr., and traveled to Africa, China, and the Soviet Union. During his tenure on the faculty of Columbia University, Killens achieved a reputation for opening his home at night to students "for talk, food, and sometimes, shelter."

NOVEMBER 3, 1987   Municipal Elections Involved African American Candidates. Baltimore, Maryland, elected its first black mayor; the black mayor of Philadelphia, Pennsylvania, was reelected; and the black mayor of Charlotte, North Carolina, was defeated.

In Baltimore, Kurt Schmoke, an attorney, prosecutor, and Rhodes Scholar, gained 100,923 votes (78.5 percent) to defeat his Republican challenger Samuel Culotta, who had 27,636 votes.

In Philadelphia, Mayor W. Wilson Goode, the city's first black mayor, gained 331,659 votes (51.1 percent) to defeat former mayor Frank Rizzo who had 317,331 votes (48 percent) with 99.13 percent of the vote counted. Goode scored heavily among blacks who made up 40 percent of the 1.6 million residents of the nation's fifth largest city, despite lingering opposition to his decision to bomb a house occupied by MOVE, a radical black group in 1985. The sixty-seven-year-old Rizzo continued to labor under accusations that he was a racist and had permitted police brutality against blacks while he served as police commissioner and later as mayor.

In Charlotte, Sue Myrick, a white Republican and former city councilwoman, defeated mayor Harvey Gantt, the first black mayor of the city, 47,311 to 46,296. Myrick had accused Gantt of failing to solve the city's traffic congestion problems. Her campaign was also aided by the support of North Carolina Governor Jim Martin. Sixty-four percent of the registered voters in Charlotte were white at the time of the election.

NOVEMBER 25, 1987 Death of Chicago's Mayor. Harold Washington, the first African American mayor of Chicago, Illinois, died of an apparent heart attack at Northwestern Memorial Hospital. Washington was six months into his second term as mayor when he collapsed while working in his City Hall office.

Washington was first elected mayor of Chicago in 1983 after "a bitter, racially-charged election." He had once said he wanted to serve the city for twenty years. Washington won reelection in April 1987 after campaigning on a theme of "uniting the city's diverse racial and ethnic groups." His first term was marred by racial divisiveness among black and white aldermen and by white, ethnic opposition to his policies on the city council.

President Ronald Reagan led those expressing grief at Washington's death. The president observed that "Harold Washington will truly be missed, not only by the people of Chicago but also by many across the country for whom he provided leadership on urban issues." Massachusetts Senator Edward Kennedy called Washington's death "a tragedy for Chicago and for civil rights. . . . He was an outstanding congressman and an outstanding mayor, and the civil rights movement in America has lost one of its greatest and most respected leaders."

Representative William Gray from Pennsylvania, the most powerful black in Congress, said Washington's death was "a real great tragedy." Finally, Richard Daley, Cook County state's attorney and the son of the legendary Chicago Mayor Richard J. Daley remarked, "Mayor Washington had a deep love for his city, which has suffered a tremendous loss with his passing. His name will loom forever large in the history of Chicago, and rightfully so."

DECEMBER 1, 1987 Writer and Activist Died. James Baldwin, African American writer and civil rights activist, died of cancer in St. Paul de Venece, France, at age sixty-three. Baldwin had moved to France in 1948 to escape what he felt was "the stifling racial bigotry" of the United States.

Baldwin, the son of "an autocratic preacher who hated his son," was born in the Harlem section of New York City in 1924. He began writing while a student at the DeWitt Clinton High School in the Bronx and by his early twenties was publishing essays and reviews in such publications as the *Nation*, the *New Leader*, *Commentary*, and *Partisan Review*. Baldwin also began socializing with a circle of New York writers and intellectuals, including William Barrett, Irving Howe, and Lionel Trilling.

A prolific author, Baldwin published his three most important collections of essays— *Notes of a Native Son* (1955), *Nobody Knows My Name* (1961), and *The Fire Next Time* (1963) during the height of the civil rights movement. Some critics, the *New York Times* reported, "said his language was sometimes too elliptical, his indictments sometimes too sweeping. But then [his] prose, with its apocalyptic tone—a legacy of his early exposure to religious fundamentalism—and its passionate yet distanced sense of advocacy, seemed perfect for a period in which blacks in the South lived under continued threats of racial violence and in which civil rights workers faced brutal beatings and even death."

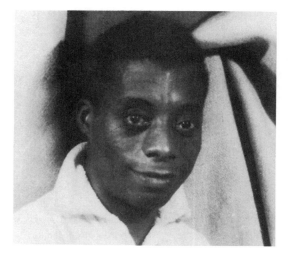

Author James Baldwin.

Other important works by Baldwin included *Go Tell it On the Mountain* (1953), his first book and novel; *Giovanni's Room* (1956) and *Another Country* (1962), which contains a frank discussion of homosexuality; and the drama *Blues for Mister Charlie* (1964). In the preface to *Blues for Mister Charlie,* Baldwin noted that the work had been inspired "very distantly" by the murder of Emmett Till, a black youth in Mississippi in 1955. He wrote:

"What is ghastly and really almost hopeless in our racial situation now is that the crimes we have committed are so great and so unspeakable that the acceptance of this knowledge would lead, literally, to madness. The human being, then, in order to protect himself, closes his eyes, compulsively repeats his crimes, and enters a spiritual darkness which no one can describe."

During the civil rights movement, Baldwin not only wrote about the struggle, but helped raise money for it and organized protest marches. He was also an early opponent of the United States's involvement in the Vietnam War and a critic of discrimination against homosexuals. Baldwin's writings and activism were recognized by many groups both in this country

and abroad. Perhaps the most distinguished of these was the Legion of Honor, France's highest national award, which was presented to him in 1986.

Among those eulogizing Baldwin was a fellow African American novelist, Ralph Ellison, who commented, "America has lost one its most gifted writers." Henry Louis Gates Jr., a literary critic and professor at Cornell University, said Baldwin "educated an entire generation of Americans about the civil rights struggle and the sensibility of Afro-Americans as we faced and conquered the final barriers in our long quest for civil rights."

DECEMBER 15, 1987 Death of Civil Rights Activist. Septima Poinsetta Clark, African American civil rights activist, died on John's Island, South Carolina, at age eighty-nine.

Clark was born to a former slave in Charleston, South Carolina, in 1898. She received a bachelor's degree from Benedict College in her native state and a master's from Hampton Institute in Virginia. Clark began her teaching career in a public school on John's Island in 1916. In 1918, she transferred to Avery Institute in Charleston and in that same year Clark led a drive to collect 20,000 signatures on a petition to have black teachers hired by the Charleston County School District. The law barring their employment was changed in 1920. When Clark moved to Columbia in 1927, she aided a campaign to equalize salaries for black and white teachers.

After returning to Charleston several years later, Clark was dismissed from her teaching job for being a member of the National Association for the Advancement of Colored People (NAACP) in 1955.

In the late 1950s, Clark worked at the Highlander Folk School in Tennessee, where she developed a program to teach illiterate blacks so that they could pass literacy tests and qualify to vote. She later became a director of the school, a supervisor of teacher training for the Southern Christian Leadership Conference

(SCLC), and a national lecturer for voting and civil rights.

In recognition of her contributions to the civil rights movement, Martin Luther King, Jr. selected Clark to accompany him to Norway in 1964 when he was presented the Nobel Peace Prize. In 1974, she was elected to the Charleston County School Board. Five years later, President Jimmy Carter presented to Clark a Living Legacy Award. In 1982, she received the Order of the Palmetto, South Carolina's highest civilian award.

Clark told the story of much of her life in her autobiographies, *Echo in My Soul* (1962) and *Ready from Within: Septima Clark and the Civil Rights Movement* (1987). The latter won an American Book Award.

Upon learning of Septima Clark's death, South Carolina Governor Carroll A. Campbell, Jr., said "the state has lost not only a leading civil rights activist but a legendary educator and humanitarian."

1988

JANUARY 6, 1988 Jackson, Mississippi, Honored King The city council of Jackson, Mississippi, voted unanimously to declare a local holiday in honor of the late Dr. Martin Luther King, Jr. The vote in Jackson raised to seven the number of Mississippi localities commemorating the birth of the slain civil rights leader.

The action of the Jackson City Council followed that of the governing body of Clarksdale, a Mississippi Delta town, by just one day and also followed "disparaging remarks" that New York City mayor Ed Koch had made about the South in general, only a few days earlier. Koch, in noting a recent racial attack in New York, said such an incident was "something he expected to see in the Deep South," but not in his region. Several Mississippi mayors wrote Koch in protest. After the Jackson vote, Councilman Louis Armstrong declared, "I think this will send a clearer message to the Mayor Koches of the world that Mississippi has changed." E. C. Foster, the black president of the Jackson City Council who introduced the motion to honor King, added, "Dr. King had those values most Americans shared."

JANUARY 18, 1988 King Honored Nationally. Political, civil rights, and religious leaders throughout the nation led commemorations of the third national holiday in honor of civil rights leader Dr. Martin Luther King, Jr. They generally urged Americans to renew King's struggle against injustice and intolerance of any kind.

In Phoenix, Arizona, thousands marched through the downtown area demanding that the King holiday be restored. In 1987, Governor Evan Meacham had repealed the state's observance of the holiday. This action was the first of many that led to an effort to remove him from office. During the demonstration, Phoenix Mayor Terry Goddard observed that "it is time to stop having the rest of the country think of us as the site of a three-ring circus."

In Los Angeles, California, celebrities and politicians led a group of singers, marching bands, and floats down a boulevard named for King to Exposition Park.

In Boston, Massachusetts, Senator Edward Kennedy, commented that it was a "national disgrace that social justice [was] in retreat." He added, "bankrupt national policies have spawned a national environment that encourages discrimination and repudiates opportunity."

In Gretna, Florida, Governor Bob Martinez led 250 marchers in a driving rain through the streets of a poverty-ridden black neighborhood. The Republican governor told the crowd that he had felt the efforts of King's work himself. Martinez recalled that he had been told years ago that he could never become mayor of Tampa because he was both Roman Catholic and Hispanic.

At Yokota Air Base in Japan, 150 black airmen and civilians gathered on a baseball field to re-enact King's famous "I Have a Dream" speech. Jackie Chambers, a secretary at the base, recited the oration. During the ceremony Chambers stated that King "gave me the opportunity to get an education, and he's always given me the opportunity to progress." Sergeant Earl Richard, a native of New Orleans, Louisiana, commented, "I think he made a difference in everybody's life, no matter who you are, if you are an American."

In Philadelphia, Pennsylvania, Rosa Parks, whom King once called "the great fuse" of the civil rights movement for her role in the Montgomery, Alabama, bus boycott of 1955, was given a replica of the Liberty Bell during ceremonies honoring King in that city.

Finally, in Memphis, Tennessee, a wreath was laid at the steps of the Lorraine Motel where King was mortally wounded in 1968. Blues musicians played "When the Saints Go Marching In," and Jacqueline Smith, a motel resident who refused to leave to make way for the construction of a civil rights museum on the site, was generously applauded when she simply said "Happy birthday, Dr. King."

JANUARY 18, 1988   King Birthday Celebrated with Ecumenical Service. Hundreds of Americans, black and white, attended the 20th annual ecumenical services honoring the birthday of slain civil rights leader Martin Luther King, Jr., at the Ebenezer Baptist Church in Atlanta, Georgia. The services were held on the third observance of the national holiday in honor of King. Among those in attendance were two Democratic presidential candidates, the Reverend Jesse L. Jackson and Senator Paul Simon from Illinois; National Security Advisor Lieutenant General Colin Powell; Senators Lowell Weicker, Jr., from Connecticut and Sam Nunn from Georgia; Congressmen John Lewis and Newt Gingrich, both from Georgia; comedian Dick Gregory; and Martin Luther King III, a Fulton County, Georgia, commis-

sioner, and son of the martyred civil rights leader.

One of the speakers at the services, Ebenezer's pastor, Joseph L. Roberts, called King a visionary and "our general of peace," and urged the crowd to continue King's work. Senator Weicker told the congregation that King's death would not be in vain if Americans remembered the ideals for which King stood. Weicker asserted: "Martin Luther King, Jr., did not wait for the multitude. He talked and wrote and marched through the intimidation, through the violence. . . . And in the end, even his death was an ally, and his example lives as powerfully as the man." Another speaker, the Rev. Joseph Lowery, president of the Southern Christian Leadership Conference (SCLC), cautioned that "the holiday cannot lose sight of the holy day and close the curtain before the crowning victory is won. . . . The holy day reminds us that the holiday honors an individual but also a struggle and a people who are on fire for justice and liberty."

Later in the day, more than 200,000 people from throughout the United States and abroad stood in a drizzle in downtown Atlanta to watch the third annual Martin Luther King, Jr., National Holiday Parade. Floats and banners in the procession included "Free South Africa," "Prejudice Is a Handicap," "Civil Rights/ Gay Rights. Same Struggle, Same Fight," and "Stop the Death Penalty."

The Atlanta Constitution conducted an informal poll of children along the parade route, asking "Who was Martin Luther King, Jr.?" A third grader, Michael Paisant of Duluth, Georgia, responded typically, "he was a peacemaker."

JANUARY 23, 1988   Maximum Sentence Given to Teen for Racial Assault. Jon Lester, a white teenager, was sentenced in New York City to a prison term of ten to thirty years for his part in the beating death of a black man in the Howard Beach section of Queens in December 1986. The assault of three black men in the predominantly white neighborhood inflamed racial tensions in the city and led to several days of protest demonstrations. Lester was the first of three convicted white teenagers to be sentenced.

Lester's attorney, Bryan Levinson, said after the sentencing that his client should not have been sentenced "so harshly because this was a reckless act, not an intentional act." However, Justice Thomas Demakos, who sentenced the youth to the maximum term under the law, commented that Lester showed "no remorse, no suggestion of guilt," but instead demonstrated a "pretty close to craven indifference to life." The judge also added that the three black victims were attacked "just because they [were] black. . . . Make no mistake. . . . There are no ifs, ands, or buts about it: This was racial violence." The Reverend Al Sharpton, the civil rights activist who had led demonstrations against the assault, said "the stiff sentencing vindicated those who pressed for appointment of a special prosecutor to investigate the case." Sharpton also contended that Lester's sentence was "an affirmation that racism and racist violence will not have a place in our society."

JANUARY 31, 1988   Confederate Flag Still Flown in Alabama. The *Atlanta Journal-Constitution* reported the results of a poll showing that 75 percent of Alabama's white residents favored the continued flying of the Confederate flag over the state capitol at Montgomery.

In December 1987, the Alabama NAACP announced a campaign to remove the flag from the statehouse, and the organization's state director, Thomas Reed, said he would climb the flagpole and tear it down. Yet Alabama governor Guy Hunt assured that the flag would remain unless a majority of Alabamians wanted it removed.

The poll also revealed that 63 percent of the four hundred people queried believed that the Confederate flag should fly over state office buildings. But among whites, 75 percent wanted the flag to continue to fly, while 53 percent of blacks said the flag should be removed.

In 1988, Alabama and South Carolina were the only two southern states that continued to officially fly the Confederate flag. Mississippi and Georgia incorporated the Confederate symbol into their state flags. Some blacks in these states have periodically protested the use of the Confederate symbol by public agencies and institutions. They contended that its identification with the pro-slavery states in the American Civil War made it a racist emblem.

JANUARY 31, 1988   First Black Quarterback Won Super Bowl MVP Award. Doug Williams, the African American quarterback of the Washington Redskins, was named the Most Valuable Player of Super Bowl XXII. Williams, the first black quarterback ever to start in a Super Bowl, completed 18 of 29 passes totaling 340 yards and four touchdowns. The Redskins defeated the Denver Broncos of the American Football Conference, 42-10.

Of Williams's achievements, Redskins coach Joe Gibbs commented: "I think it's a great success story. . . . He's had some tough experiences in life, and in football. He saw the downs, but he's the type of man who has overcome them." Redskins owner Jack Kent Cooke added, "this is a tribute not only to a black quarterback, but to a very great quarterback." Williams, a graduate of predominantly black Grambling University in Louisiana, remarked, "I didn't come here with the Washington Redskins as a black quarterback. I came here as a quarterback with the Washington Redskins to play a football game."

FEBRUARY 11, 1988   Second Defendant in Racial Assault Sentenced. New York State Supreme Court Justice Thomas Demakos sentenced Jason Ladone, age seventeen, to five to fifteen years in prison for his part in the December 20, 1986, death of Michael Griffith, a twenty-three-year-old black man, in the Howard Beach section of Queens, New York City. In imposing the light sentence for manslaughter and assault, Demakos rejected the defense's appeal for mercy because of Ladone's age. The judge said that on the night of the incident, the otherwise exemplary Ladone had become a "violent person." Ladone was the only defendant in the Howard Beach assaults to plead for mercy and the only one to apologize to the victim's mother, Jean Griffith. He told Mrs. Griffith, "I am sorry . . . for your senseless loss."

FEBRUARY 19, 1988 Racial Demonstration Held at Amherst. Several hundred students at the University of Massachusetts at Amherst held a demonstration against racism at the institution. Shouting "Hey, hey, ho, ho, racism has got to go," the students supported an agreement reached between minorities and the school's administration after a six-day takeover of a campus building. The demonstrators also called for a two-day moratorium, beginning March 22, on attending classes. The moratorium was aimed at denouncing racism, sexism, and an alleged attack against three Puerto Rican students on February 17.

Racial tensions on the Amherst campus had increased after at least two hundred black, American Indian, and Hispanic students took over the New Africa House on February 12 to protest alleged assaults and racial slurs by white students. The occupation of the building ended on February 17 after an agreement was reached that stipulated that Chancellor Joseph Duffey would expel students who repeatedly committed acts of racial violence and that he would also promote multicultural education.

About 7 percent of the university's 18,000 undergraduates were African Americans at the time of the incidents.

FEBRUARY 20, 1988 Harvard Dean Warned Students to Avoid Racial Incidents. Alfred Jewett, the dean of Harvard University in Cambridge, Massachusetts, warned students on his campus that anyone involved in racial incidents would be subject to expulsion and other disciplinary measures. Jewett's warning was pub-

lished in the student newspaper, the Harvard *Crimson*, a week after a group of students took over a building at the University of Massachusetts at Amherst, to protest campus racism.

FEBRUARY 20, 1988 Boston University Requested Release of King Conversation Tapes. Attorneys for Boston University asked a Suffolk Superior Court judge to order Coretta Scott King to release tapes of conversations between her late husband, Dr. Martin Luther King, Jr., and others that were secretly recorded by federal investigators. The motion also asked for release of correspondence between King and his colleagues.

This action was the latest round in a legal battle between the school and Mrs. King over an estimated 83,000 documents relating to her husband that were held at Boston University. Mrs. King had filed suit earlier, contending that the documents belonged in the Martin Luther King, Jr., Center for Non-Violent Social Change in Atlanta, Georgia. She further claimed that the university had "mishandled or lost some of the papers."

The tapes sought in the suit included those reportedly sent anonymously to Mrs. King in the 1970s, after the FBI had bugged hotel rooms where Martin Luther King, Jr., was staying. Some of these tapes implicating King in alleged extramarital sexual activities were made available also to President Lyndon Johnson, members of Congress, and news reporters.

FEBRUARY 25, 1988 Community Service Sentence Handed Out for Racial Assault. Associate Judge Stuart Nudelman of the Cook County (Illinois) Circuit Court sentenced James Kalafut, a twenty-one-year-old white man, to two hundred hours of community service for his role in an assault on three blacks in the Gage Park neighborhood in 1987. Kalafut, who had stated that he had been "taught to hate black people," was also ordered to report to the judge's chambers once a month for a year.

Edward McClellan, executive secretary of the NAACP's south side Chicago branch, responded to the sentencing by declaring that Judge Nudelman had "opened up a completely new approach to dealing with an old American problem: racism."

The sharp increase in the number of racist attacks on blacks in the 1980s led many African American leaders to link the civil rights policies of President Ronald Reagan to such incidents, contending that the Reagan administration was hostile to civil rights advances.

FEBRUARY 27, 1988 Affirmative Action Plan Ruled Unconstitutional. A U.S. Court of Appeals in Washington, D.C., in a 2-1 decision, ruled that "an affirmative action plan aimed at increasing the number of black firefighters" in the District of Columbia was unconstitutional. The court said that "preferential treatment" for black firefighter applicants was not needed because blacks had not been discriminated against. The Washington, D.C., city government had set aside six out of every ten new positions in the fire department for black applicants. In 1984, when blacks first complained about tests being used to "screen applicants for entry-level" firefighter jobs, only 38 percent of the members of the D.C. fire department were black. Only 26 percent of the higher ranking officers were black at the time. The population of the city was 70 percent black. Judge Kenneth Starr wrote in the majority opinion, however, that it "was undisputed that the fire department [had] consistently hired from the entire Washington metropolitan area," where the black population was only 29.3 percent.

MARCH 1, 1988 Prediction of Race Division Reported a Reality. Experts on race and urban affairs, some of whom worked with the Kerner Commission in producing the 1968 Report of the President's Commission on Civil Disorders, announced that the prediction of the Commission twenty years ago that the United States was moving toward two societies—one white and affluent, the other black and impoverished—was becoming a reality.

A new report, published after a seven-month study following widespread racial rioting in the summer of 1987, proclaimed that "segregation by race still sharply divides American cities in both housing and schools for blacks, and especially in schools for Hispanics." It also contended that the nation was being torn apart "by quiet riots": unemployment, poverty, crime, and housing and school segregation. It claimed that "less than one percent of the federal budget is spent for education, down from two percent in 1980" and that "the gap between rich and poor has widened, and there is a growing underclass."

One of the former members of the original Kerner Commission, former senator Fred Harris of Oklahoma, and the co-chairman of the new panel, former Justice Department official Roger Wilkins, offered comments on the new report at a news conference in Washington, D.C., as the new study was presented. Harris said that "twenty years later, poverty is worse, more people are poor. . . . It is harder to get out of poverty now." Wilkins added that the "quiet riots" of 1987 were caused "by racism in American culture" and economic discrimination. The original fourteen-hundred-page Kerner Report had also said that "white racism" was largely responsible for the "explosive mixture" of "poverty and frustration" in the black communities that erupted in violence. Both Harris and Wilkins blamed the administration of President Ronald Reagan for "cutting back funds on social programs and not taking a stronger stand for equal rights in employment and housing."

The new report concluded its findings with this statement: "We know what should be done. . . . Jobs are the greatest need. Full employment is the best anti-poverty program."

MARCH 5, 1988 Dukakis Won Wisconsin Presidential Primary. Governor Michael Dukakis of Massachusetts moved closer to winning the

Democratic nomination for president of the United States after a "decisive victory" over his African American rival, the Reverend Jesse Jackson, in the Wisconsin primary. As a result of the balloting, Dukakis took 43 of the state's 81 Democratic delegates, while Jackson captured 27 and Senator Albert Gore from Tennessee won 11. Before the Wisconsin primary, Dukakis led Jackson in delegates only by a margin of 691 to 682.

Although Wisconsin had a black population of only 3 percent at the time of the balloting, Jackson was expected to run very well among white blue collar workers and white liberals in the state. Yet, in the end, while Jackson won nearly all of the black vote, he lost the white blue collar vote to Dukakis and garnered only about 25 percent of the total white vote, according to exit polls conducted by the media.

MARCH 12, 1988   Jackson Won South Carolina Presidential Primary. The Reverend Jesse L. Jackson, African American candidate for the Democratic party's presidential nomination, won precinct caucuses in the state of South Carolina. In the caucus election, Jackson acquired approximately 55 percent of the delegates; 20 percent were uncommitted, 17 percent went to Tennessee senator Albert Gore, 6 percent to Massachusetts governor Michael Dukakis, and two other candidates shared the remaining 2 percent. Kevin Gray, Jackson's campaign manager in South Carolina, estimated that his candidate would eventually be awarded about 25 of the 44 national convention delegates at stake in the South Carolina balloting. Although Jackson was a resident of Chicago, Illinois, he was a native of Greenville, South Carolina, had "the status of a favorite son" as well as the almost solid support of the South's second largest black population, and had a campaign organization that worked hard with the state's 4,000 black churches to turn out the vote. Before the South Carolina caucuses, according to figures from the Associated Press, Jackson

trailed Governor Dukakis in the delegate count 459.5 to 400.5.

MARCH 15, 1988   Civil Rights Activist C. B. King Died. Chevene Bowers "C. B." King, the first black person to run for governor of Georgia since the Reconstruction era, died of cancer in San Diego, California, at age sixty-four.

King, who was also an attorney and civil rights activist, represented Martin Luther King, Jr., Ralph David Abernathy, and other civil rights leaders as well as student sit-in demonstrators during the tumultuous civil rights movement in Albany, Georgia, in 1962. He was beaten on the steps of the Dougherty County courthouse (of which Albany is the county seat) during the demonstrations.

Prior to running for governor in 1970, King had also ran unsuccessfully for Congress in 1964. In the governor's race, he received 70,424 votes (8.82 percent) in the Democratic primary. The victorious candidate for governor was Democrat Jimmy Carter, who was later elected president of the United States. Reacting bitterly to his defeat, King blamed it on "little black political puppets who have exploited politics for their own selfish ends" and on blacks who still had "social and psychological hangups" about voting for a candidate of their own race.

MARCH 15, 1988   Eugene Marino Named First Black Archbishop. Pope John Paul II appointed Eugene Antonio Marino, a black Josephite priest, as the archbishop of Atlanta, Georgia. It was the first time that an African American was named an archbishop in the American Roman Catholic Church.

Marino, age fifty-three and a native of Biloxi, Mississippi, studied at St. Joseph's Seminary in Washington, D.C., from 1956 to 1962 and earned a master's degree in religious education from Fordham University. From 1962 to 1968, he taught in and directed training activities in the archdiocese of Washington, D.C. On July 13, 1971, Marino was elected to a four-

Presidential candidate Jesse Jackson. (Bettmann Archive/Newsphotos, Inc.)

year term as vicar general of the Josephite Fathers. Prior to being named archbishop of Atlanta, Marino was the auxiliary bishop of Washington, D.C., and secretary of the National Conference of Catholic Bishops. He was one of only twelve black bishops in the United States at the time of his appointment as archbishop.

In 1985, Marino was one of the ten black bishops who called on the National Conference of Catholic Bishops to create "a preferential option for black Americans" to help

forestall "potential explosive racial strife in our country" which was "as immediate a threat as a nuclear holocaust."

Marino's appointment made him the spiritual leader of 156,000 Roman Catholics in sixty-nine counties in north Georgia, comprising the Archdiocese of Atlanta, of which ten thousand are blacks (most of whom were members of seven churches, including three predominantly black ones, in the city of Atlanta). In the United States, 1.3 million of the Church's 52 million members were black in 1988.

MARCH 16, 1988   Reagan Vetoed Civil Rights Bill. President Ronald Reagan vetoed a civil rights bill that was designed to reverse a 1984 U.S. Supreme Court decision and restore the impact of four federal laws that prohibited discrimination on the basis of race, age, handicap, or sex. The high Court's ruling had limited "the liability for discrimination only to offending programs or activities that receive federal funds, not to an entire institution or entity."

Reagan objected to the bill, which passed 75-14 in the U.S. Senate and 315-98 in the House of Representatives, because he felt it "proposed unwarranted federal intervention in the affairs of corporations and institutions with religious affiliations." But supporters of the bill contended that its provisions adequately exempted small businesses, church institutions, and farmers. Nevertheless, Reagan said the bill failed "to eliminate invidious discrimination and to ensure equality of opportunity for all Americans while preserving their basic freedoms from governmental interference and control." Instead, he offered an alternative—a slight expansion on a previous version that had been rejected in both houses of the Congress—which he said would "protect civil rights and at the same time preserve the independence of state and local governments, the freedom of religion, and the right of America's citizens to order their lives and businesses without extensive federal intrusion."

Massachusetts senator Edward M. Kennedy, one of the sponsors of the legislation, called Reagan's veto "shameful."

MARCH 16, 1988   Jesse Jackson Won Estimated 460.5 Delegates in Ilinois. After finishing second in the Democratic presidential primary in Illinois on March 15, African American presidential candidate Jesse Jackson had an estimated 460.5 delegates. Jackson's total placed him four delegates behind the Democratic frontrunner, Massachusetts Governor Michael Dukakis, who had 464.5 delegates at the time.

A total of 2,082 votes were required to capture the Democratic nomination.

With almost half of the Democratic delegates chosen by March 16, Jackson had obtained more popular votes than any other Democratic contender and had combined the largest number of first and second place finishes in the balloting held in thirty states thus far.

MARCH 20, 1988   U.S. House Voted to Overturn Supreme Court Civil Rights Ruling. The U.S. House of Representatives voted 315-98 to overturn a U.S. Supreme Court ruling that limited four laws banning discrimination based on age, race, sex, or handicap. The same measure had been approved by the U.S. Senate on January 28, by a vote of 75-14.

The legislation, known as the Civil Rights Restoration Act, requires that any institution or entity receiving federal funds, including school systems, corporations, and health facilities, must comply with civil rights statutes. It allows limited exemptions for small businesses and for institutions controlled by religious organizations.

The Supreme Court, in a 1984 case involving Grove City College in Pennsylvania, had ruled that only a program or activity receiving federal funds was subject to the federal antibias laws. Although the case focused on a 1972 law that prohibited sex discrimination in education, the Court's decision also applied to three other civil rights laws that contained the same language at issue in the Grove City College case. After the decision, federal agencies had dropped or limited hundreds of civil rights cases.

In October 1987, a federal court of appeals rejected a lawsuit by a group in Alabama, which had been joined by the federal government against the state school system. That court held that only the "allegedly discriminatory program could be sued."

MARCH 20, 1988   Tyson Defended World Heavyweight Title. Mike Tyson knocked out challenger Tony Tubbs to retain the world heavyweight boxing championship in Tokyo, Japan. The thirty-year-old Tubbs collapsed in the second round of the scheduled fifteen-round fight in the Tokyo Dome; his cornermen asked referee Arthur Mercante to stop the fight. Tyson improved his record to 34 wins (30 by knockout) with no losses. The twenty-one-year-old Tyson was guaranteed $5 million for defending his title.

MARCH 22, 1988 Civil Rights Restoration Act Favored by Congress. The U.S. Congress overrode President Ronald Reagan's veto of the Civil Rights Restoration Act. The vote in the Senate was 73-24 and in the House of Representatives 292-133. The new law was designed to reverse a decision of the U.S. Supreme Court in 1984 which had limited the enforcement of previous civil rights acts. In that decision, the Court, in a case involving Grove City College in Pennsylvania, had ruled that some earlier civil rights laws "did not cover entire school systems, businesses, local governments or other entities, but only the programs receiving federal aid." The new law specifically extended coverage to entire institutions, although exemptions were provided for small businesses, churches, farmers who received price supports, and welfare recipients. President Reagan had objected on the grounds that the exemptions were inadequate and that religious freedoms were being threatened.

After the veto was overridden, Republican senator Lowell Weicker from Connecticut, one of the sponsors of the measure, exclaimed: "[This] is as important a day as any of us have ever experienced or will experience in the near future. It has the potential of being a restatement . . . of our national commitment to equal opportunity for all."

MARCH 25, 1988 Advancement of Minorities Needed for Future Prosperity. The *Chronicle of Higher Education* reported that a study by the American Council on Education and the Education Commission of the United States had concluded that America must renew its commitment to the advancement of minority groups or jeopardize the future prosperity of the nation. The Council and Commission report stated that "America is moving backward—not forward—in its efforts to achieve the full participation of minority citizens in the life and prosperity of the nation."

The report, entitled "One Third of a Nation," also documented that "in education, employment, income, health, longevity, and other basic measures of individual and social well-being, gaps persist—and in some cases are widening—between members of minority groups and the majority population. . . . If we allow these disparities to continue, the United States inevitably will suffer a compromised quality of life and a lower standard of living. . . . In brief, we find ourselves unable to fulfill the promise of the American dream."

"One Third of a Nation" emerged from a project established in 1987 by the American Council on Education and the Education Commission of the United States because of concern over a series of racial incidents on college and university campuses and the declining proportion of minority students in college. The report noted specifically that in 1986, 31.1 percent of the nation's blacks and 27.3 percent of its Hispanics had incomes below the poverty level—nearly three times the rate for whites. Also, in 1986, 20.1 percent of whites over age twenty-five had completed at least four years of college. For blacks, the completion rate was only 10.9 percent and for Hispanics, only 8.4 percent. In the same year, blacks were twice as likely to be unemployed than were whites.

As a result of its findings, the report recommended, among other things, that colleges and universities, particularly: 1) recruit minority students more aggressively; 2) create an academic atmosphere that nourishes and encourages minority students to stay enrolled and to succeed; 3) create a campus culture that values the diversity minorities bring to institutional life—one that responds powerfully and forthrightly to the recrudescences of racism that have occurred too often on campus in recent years; 4) place special emphasis on inspiring and recruiting minority candidates for faculty and administrative positions; and 5) work with educators at the primary and secondary levels to improve the education, training, and preparation of minority students.

MARCH 31, 1988 Toni Morrison Awarded Pulitzer Prize. African American novelist Toni Morrison won a Pulitzer Prize for Fiction for her book *Beloved*. The novel depicts the agonizing reminiscences of a former slave in post-Civil War Ohio. Morrison's work had provoked a controversy in the fall of 1987 when it failed to win the prestigious National Book Award. In January 1988, forty-eight black writers had written an open letter to the *New York Times Book Review* protesting that failure as well as the fact that Morrison had never won the even more prestigious Pulitzer.

Responding to the announcement of the award, Morrison said, "I think I know what I feel. . . . I had no doubt about the value of the book and that it was really worth serious recognition. But I had some dark thoughts about whether the book's merits would be allowed to be the only consideration of the Pulitzer committee. The book had begun to take on a responsibility, an extra-literary responsibility, that it was never designed for."

An excerpt from a review of *Beloved* by author and critic Margaret Atwood in the *New York Times*, September 13, 1987, follows:

"In *Beloved*, Ms. Morrison turns away from the contemporary scene that has been her concern of late. The new novel is set after the end of the Civil War, during the period of the so-called Reconstruction, when a great deal of random violence was let loose upon blacks, both the slaves freed by emancipation and others who had been given or bought their freedom earlier. But there are flashbacks to a more distant period, when slavery was still a going concern in the

South and the seeds for the bizarre and calamitous events of the novel were sown. The setting is similarly divided: the countryside near Cincinnati, where the central characters have ended up, and a slave-holding plantation in Kentucky, ironically named Sweet Home, from which they fled 18 years before the novel begins. . . .*Beloved* is written in an antiminimalist prose that is by turns rich, graceful, eccentric, rough, lyrical, sinuous, colloquial, and very much to the point."

MAY 11, 1988 Multiple Organ Recipient Died. Tabatha Foster, a three-year-old African American child, died after having been the longest survivor among American children who had received multiple organ transplants. Tabatha had survived nearly seven months after she received the organs of a baby killed in an automobile accident in October 1987. Other children who were recipients of multiple organ transplants had survived no longer than three days.

JUNE 5, 1988 CCR Chairman Pendleton Died. Clarence M. Pendleton, Jr., chairman of the U.S. Civil Rights Commission (CCR), died of an apparent heart attack in San Diego, California, at age fifty-seven.

Pendleton was born on November 10, 1930, in Louisville, Kentucky, but grew up in Washington, D.C., where his father was the first swimming coach at Howard University and an assistant director of the District of Columbia's recreation department. He received a bachelor of science degree from Howard in 1954 and worked briefly for the D.C. recreation department before joining the U.S. Army. After his release from the Army in 1957, Pendleton returned to Howard and became an instructor of physical education.

In 1970, Pendleton became a director of the urban affairs department of the National Recreation and Parks Association. Two years later he moved to San Diego to take a position as director of the Model Cities program there. By 1975, Pendleton had become head of the San Diego Urban League. He was the only one of more than 150 officers in the League to support the presidential candidacy of former California governor Ronald Reagan.

By 1980, Pendleton had abandoned what he called his "bleeding-heart liberalism" and switched to the Republican party. On November 16, 1981, President Reagan appointed him chairman of the CCR. As CCR chairman, Pendleton followed Reagan's desires and led the commission toward a "color-blind" approach to matters of civil rights. He opposed busing to achieve school desegregation and called affirmative action a "bankrupt policy." Civil rights leaders, some political leaders, and even some members of the CCR itself expressed shock at the stances that the commission's first black chairman took. Congress responded by cutting the CCR's budget from $11.6 million in 1985 to only $7.5 million in 1986. These cuts caused a considerable slowing of activity at the CCR.

After Pendleton's death, William Bradford Reynolds, assistant attorney general for civil rights, called him "a man who felt very deeply that the individuals in America should deal with one another as brothers and sisters totally without regard to race and background."

JUNE 17, 1988 Thomas Reed Indicted in Bribery. Alabama state representative Thomas Reed, who also served as president of the state's NAACP, was indicted by a federal grand jury on charges of accepting more than $15,000 in cash and restaurant equipment to secure the early release of a convicted murderer, Anthony Chesser. According to the indictment, Chesser's family paid Reed to use his position as a member of the Legislature's Joint Prison Committee to get "the state Department of Corrections to place Chesser in a work release program and get the Board of Pardons and Paroles to move up his date for parole consideration by 5½ years." At the time, Chesser was serving a 40-year

sentence in a 1984 conviction for murdering his wife.

Reed, age sixty, was one of fourteen black state legislators arrested February 2, 1988, when they tried to remove the Confederate flag from the Alabama state capitol at Montgomery. Reed, who was also a member of the Board of Trustees of Tuskegee University, refused to comment on his indictment except to reiterate his innocence.

JULY 1, 1988 William Harris Named Texas Southern University President. William H. Harris, a forty-four-year-old black historian, assumed the presidency of Texas Southern University in Houston. Harris, a native of Fitzgerald, Georgia, had previously been president of Paine College in Georgia, and a professor of history and associate dean of the graduate school at Indiana University in Bloomington. At the time of his selection to the Texas Southern presidency, Harris was also completing a three-year term as president of the Association for the Study of Afro-American Life and History (ASALH).

At his inaugural ceremonies, which were attended by the new president's ninety-eight-year-old grandmother, Mary Graham, Harris commented, "we now begin to speak in one voice, play by one score and the theme of that voice and score will be academic excellence."

JULY 11, 1988 African American Influence Felt in Democratic Party. The *Atlanta Constitution* reported results of a poll that revealed that if African American presidential candidate Jesse Jackson was not offered the vice presidential nomination or did not signal his support for the presidential ticket, more than a third of the delegates to the Democratic National Convention indicated that they would be less likely to support the party in the 1988 presidential election. The poll showed a strong potential for disunity among Democratic party delegates as they headed to the National Convention in Atlanta, Georgia, on July 18. Another important result of the poll was that 20 percent of the delegates polled thought Jackson was "pulling the party too far to the left." Among delegates pledged to Massachusetts governor Michael Dukakis, 24 percent expressed that sentiment, compared with only 5 percent of the Jackson delegates.

The poll was conducted from June 15 to July 7, 1988. It included interviews with 1,921 delegates and alternates pledged to Governor Dukakis, 935 pledged to the Reverend Jackson, and 447 who were "either uncommitted or technically committed" to other candidates who had dropped out of the presidential race.

JULY 13, 1988   Jackson Passed Over as Vice-presidential Running Mate. As the date for the 1988 Democratic National Convention approached, Massachusetts governor Michael Dukakis had secured enough delegate votes to win his party's nomination over his closest rival, African American candidate Jesse Jackson. However, there were serious concerns within the Democratic party over whether Jackson and his forces would attempt to disrupt the convention and/or enthusiastically support the party nominees in the November general elections.

One of the major disputes between the Jackson and Dukakis camps was over Dukakis's selection of Lloyd Bentsen, U.S. senator from Texas, as his choice as a vice-presidential running mate. Jackson complained earlier that Dukakis "had not engaged him in their private meetings on substantial issues, such as the platform," his role in the fall campaign, and the vice-presidency, yet indicated that he would not be adverse to a vice-presidential nomination. The Jackson campaign was most angered, however, by the fact that Jackson had learned from news reporters that Dukakis had chosen Bentsen as his running mate a full hour before the governor called with the information. Although the Dukakis campaign insisted that "the slight had not been deliberate" and apologized for having caused Jackson any embarrass-

ment, Ronald Brown, Jackson's campaign manager, said he was shocked by his client's treatment.

The Bentsen incident refueled speculation in the media and in the Democratic Party as to exactly what it would take to mollify or pacify Jackson and his supporters. In an article published in the *Atlanta Constitution* on July 13 entitled "A Letter to My Delegates on the Road to Atlanta," Jackson said it was "not what . . . Jesse wants . . . [but] a question of what we have built."

JULY 19, 1988   Jesse Jackson Delivered "Keep Hope Alive" Speech. Using the theme "Keep Hope Alive," Jesse Jackson, African American Democratic presidential candidate, addressed 11,000 people at the Democratic National Convention in Atlanta, Georgia, on the eve of the balloting for the presidential nomination. The speech, in which Jackson said "America must never surrender to a high moral challenge," electrified the audience.

JULY 20, 1988   Dukakis Defeated Jackson for Democratic Presidential Nomination. The quest of Jesse L. Jackson for the Democratic nomination for president of the United States ended in Atlanta, Georgia. Delegates at the Democratic National Convention there gave the party's nomination to Massachusetts governor Michael Dukakis. Dukakis won the votes of 2,876.25 delegates; Jackson emerged second in the contest with 1,218.5 delegate votes. Five other candidates divided nine votes. The number needed for nomination was 2,082.

Jackson began his second attempt to win the Democratic nomination shortly after he failed to capture the position in 1984. He remained a visible spokesman for the civil rights of blacks, other minorities, and women, by using his organizations Operation PUSH and the Rainbow Coalition as bases and adding the causes of labor and depressed farmers to his agenda.

Unlike his race in 1984, when several major black leaders publicly opposed his candidacy, Jackson won their support or at least neutrality in his latest quest. He was also able to persuade more whites to back his candidacy. He campaigned as a populist, championing the cause of the downtrodden, those in "the outhouse" who were not fully sharing in the nation's opportunities, political, social, and economic.

In the primary elections and caucuses prior to the convention, Jackson won the votes of 92 percent of blacks and 12 percent of whites. Four years earlier he had captured 77 percent of the black vote, but only 5 percent of the white vote.

Jackson's achievements in the 1988 campaign established him as the most formidable black candidate ever to seek the American presidency.

JULY 31, 1988 Willie Stargell Inducted into Baseball Hall of Fame. Willie Stargell, a former African American baseball star with the Pittsburgh Pirates of the National League, was inducted into the Baseball Hall of Fame in ceremonies at Cooperstown, New York. Stargell got 82.4 percent of the vote by being named on 352 of 427 ballots cast by the Baseball Writers Association of America. (In order to be elected, a player must be named on 75 percent of the ballots). Stargell, age forty-seven, became the first player to be selected on his first attempt since Lou Brock, another African American, accomplished the feat in 1985.

Stargell's best seasons as a baseball player were in 1971, when he scored 48 home runs, batted in 125 runs, and had a total batting average of .295; and 1973, when he hit 44 home runs, batted in 119 runs, and ended with a batting average of .299. Stargell played in the 1971 and 1979 World Series and was named the Most Valuable Player in the 1979 Series.

AUGUST 2, 1988 Civil Rights Activist Joseph Hankerson Died. Joseph "Big Lester" Hankerson, black civil rights activist, died of a heart attack in Atlanta, Georgia, at age sixtythree. Hankerson, a leader of the civil rights

movement in Savannah, Georgia, often marched at the side of Martin Luther King, Jr., during the 1960s.

Joseph E. Lowery, president of the Southern Christian Leadership Conference (SCLC), called Hankerson "one of the earliest among the valiant field workers who was a heart and soul of the [civil rights] movement. They did the harsh and dangerous groundwork that made it possible for the captains and generals to claim the victory." Another veteran civil rights activist, Hosea Williams, remarked, "Big Lester was a true unsung hero. . . . He contributed as much to the street movement as Dr. King did in the suite movement. He didn't go to jail as many times as I, but no one took more beatings and no one shed more blood."

AUGUST 11, 1988 NUC President M. Carl Holman died. M. Carl Holman, president of the National Urban Coalition, died of cancer in Washington, D.C., at age sixty-nine.

Holman was born June 27, 1919, in Minter, Mississippi. He grew up in St. Louis, Missouri, and was a *magna cum laude* graduate of Lincoln University. He earned master's degrees at the University of Chicago in 1944 and Yale University in 1954. After receiving his Chicago degree, Holman taught English at Hampton Institute and his alma mater, Lincoln University. Beginning in 1949, he began a long career in Georgia as a professor of English at Clark College.

While in Georgia, Holman was an advisor to the student sit-in movement in Atlanta and helped to escort and protect Charlayne Hunter and Hamilton Holmes, when the two black students desegregated the University of Georgia in 1961. He was also editor of the *Atlanta Inquirer,* a black weekly newspaper that was founded as a voice for civil rights demonstrators.

In 1962, Holman left Clark College to become information officer and later deputy staff director of the U.S. Civil Rights Commission (CCR) from 1962 to 1968. He then became a vice-president of the National Urban Coalition, a study and advocacy group on urban issues and policies. Holman was named president of the Coalition in 1971.

AUGUST 14, 1988   Absence of Black Men Felt in Society. Participants at the annual convention of the American Psychological Association in Atlanta, Georgia, concluded that "the increasing absence of black men in the work force, on college campuses and as heads of households" was a problem that threatened "the 'fabric of American society.'" Statistics quoted at the meeting to substantiate the point included: 1) the leading cause of death among black males between the ages of 15 and 24 is homicide; 2) a black man has a 1 in 21 chance of being murdered, 6 times greater than that of other Americans; 3) the average life expectancy of 65 years for black men is less than what it was for white men more than 40 years ago; 4) black men represent 6 percent of the country's population but more than 40 percent of the prison population; 5) a black man is more than twice as likely to be unemployed as a white man; and 6) black men are increasingly absent from the home, with almost 60 percent of all births to black women occurring out of wedlock.

AUGUST 27, 1988   March on Washington Commemorated. More than 55,000 Americans marched in Washington, D.C., to commemorate the twenty-fifth anniversary of the historic March on Washington of 1963. The original march had drawn 250,000 people to push for passage of the Civil Rights Bill of 1964. The leaders of the new march included Democratic presidential candidates Jesse Jackson and Michael Dukakis, Benjamin Hooks of the NAACP, Coretta Scott King, widow of slain civil rights leader Martin Luther King, Jr., and Joseph E. Lowery, president of the Southern Christian Leadership Conference (SCLC). The themes of the gathering were a tribute to King, and his memorable "I Have a Dream" speech at the 1963 march, as well as a protest against the civil rights policies of the adminis-

tration of President Ronald Reagan. In addressing the latter topic, the SCLC's Lowery told the crowd, "we fought too long, we prayed too hard, we wept too bitterly, we bled too profusely, we died too young to let anybody ever turn back the clock on racial justice. We ain't going back."

SEPTEMBER 1, 1988   FBI Announced Affirmative Action Program. William S. Sessions, director of the FBI, announced that he had approved a five-year affirmative action program to hire and promote more minority employees in the Bureau. The program included the hiring of an advertising agency, assignment of some of the "most capable people" to serve as recruiters, improvements in career development and training programs, internal audits of promotion procedures, equal opportunity programs, and complaint processes. Sessions also said that "from the beginning, I have tried to make the FBI's policy against racism and discrimination crystal clear to every member of the FBI, both by policy statements . . . and by personally addressing employees."

As Sessions issued his declaration, there were only 417 blacks and 439 Hispanics among the 9,597 agents in the FBI. Of the Hispanic agents, 311 had filed a class action suit contending that the FBI discriminated in the promotion, discipline, and assignment of Hispanics, while a black agent, Donald Rochon of the Philadelphia, Pennsylvania, office, had filed a racial harassment charge with the Equal Employment Opportunity Commission (EEOC). In July 1988, Gary Miller, a white agent in the Chicago, Illinois, office, acknowledged that he and some white colleagues had harassed Rochon. The EEOC also upheld many of Rochon's complaints of actions against him while he served in the FBI's Omaha, Nebraska, office in 1983–1984 and in Chicago from 1984 to 1986.

SEPTEMBER 6, 1988   Desegregation Order Refused. City officials in Yonkers, New York, paid a fine of $192,000 for contempt of court for refusing to carry out a federal judge's order to desegregate the city's housing.

SEPTEMBER 12, 1988   Mississippi Judicial Elections Ruled Discriminatory. U.S. District Court judge William H. Barbour, Jr., ruled in Jackson, Mississippi, that Mississippi judges were elected in a discriminatory manner. The order divided some of the state's judicial districts into subdistricts where the black majority would be 60 percent to 65 percent. This division was designed to overcome what the judge said was the white majority's bloc votes, which usually defeat the minority's preferred candidate. As a result of the ruling, eight judicial subdistricts with large black majorities were created. At the time of the ruling, there were only three blacks among the 111 trial and appellate judges in Mississippi, although blacks constituted 35 percent of the state's population. In 1985, the Fund for Modern Courts, a Washington, D.C., research group, had reported that there were only 238 blacks among the 7,500 elected judges in the United States. At that time, blacks constituted 12 percent of the American population.

SEPTEMBER 13, 1988   Housing Discrimination Law Strengthened. President Ronald Reagan signed a bill strengthening enforcement of the open housing law Congress passed in the wake of the assassination of Martin Luther King, Jr., in 1968. The law, which was passed overwhelmingly by both the U.S. House of Representatives and the Senate, authorized the federal government, for the first time, to seek fines of up to $100,000 against individuals or organizations found to have engaged in a pattern of housing discrimination. Under the open housing provisions of the Civil Rights Act of 1968, the government could only mediate housing discrimination disputes. The act also extended anti-discrimination protection in housing to the handicapped and families with children.

President Reagan called the new housing law the most important civil rights legislation in twenty years. He said that discrimination was "particularly tragic when it means a family is refused housing near good schools, a good job, or simply in a better neighborhood to raise children."

SEPTEMBER 26, 1988   Grand Jury Concluded Investigation of Brawley Abduction. The *New York Times* reported that a seven-month New York state grand jury investigation had concluded that Tawana Brawley, a sixteen-year-old African American, had fabricated her story of abduction and sexual abuse by a gang of white men in Wyspingers Falls, New York, on November 24, 1987. Brawley, who disappeared from her home four days earlier, was found nude in a garbage bag with feces and racial slurs covering her body.

Within days of Brawley's disappearance, her case became a focal point of protests and racial tensions throughout the state. Leaders of the protest and advisors to Brawley included the Reverend Al Sharpton, a community activist, and New York lawyers C. Vernon Mason and Alton H. Maddox, Jr. The three counseled the Brawley family not to cooperate with law enforcement authorities, whom they accused of perpetrating a cover-up in the case. Furthermore, the group contended that law enforcement officials were involved in the alleged attack on Brawley.

Nevertheless, the grand jury's final report found "no evidence of any abduction, racial or sexual attack, or any other crime against Miss Brawley."

SEPTEMBER 26, 1988   Ben Johnson Stripped of Olympic Gold Medal. The International Olympic Committee (IOC) took Canadian Ben Johnson's gold medal in the 100-meter dash away after he tested positive for performance-enhancing anabolic steroids. The medal, which he won in the Summer Olympic Games at Seoul, South Korea, on September 24, was then presented to the second place finisher in the 100-meter, African American Carl Lewis.

OCTOBER 3, 1988   Michael Jackson Reportedly Highest Paid Entertainer. *Forbes Magazine* reported that Michael Jackson, a thirty-year-old African American, had become the world's highest paid entertainer, earning an estimated $60 million during 1988. Jackson was ranked ninth in *Forbes'* Top 40 list of wealthiest celebrities in 1987. Jackson had made about $40 million from a recent worldwide tour. The rest of his earnings came from sales of his album *Bad,* his autobiography *Moonwalk,* music publishing, and endorsements and commercials he made for the Pepsi Cola Bottling company.

In 1987, the wealthiest entertainer was another African American, comedian Bill Cosby. Cosby had an income of $84 million in 1986–87. Other African Americans on the 1988 list were actor-comedian Eddie Murphy, talk show host Oprah Winfrey, and professional boxers Mike Tyson, Sugar Ray Leonard, and Michael Spinks.

OCTOBER 26, 1988   Fuller Products Company Founder S. B. Fuller Died. S. B. Fuller, founder and president of Fuller Products Company and a "dean of black entrepreneurs," died of kidney failure in Blue Island, Illinois, at age eighty-three.

Fuller, a native of Ouachita Parish, Louisiana, left school after the sixth grade and lived in poverty until his mother, who died when he was seventeen, convinced him to become a door-to-door salesman. He sold cosmetics and built a national enterprise with more than five thousand salesmen. In the 1960s, Fuller expanded his company into newspapers, appliance and department stores, and farming and beef cattle production. He is credited with teaching business acumen to John H. Johnson, publisher of the highly successful Johnson Publishing Company, and George Johnson, one of the nation's leading cosmetic manufacturers, both of Chicago, Illinois.

NOVEMBER 4, 1988   Bill Cosby Donated $20 Million to Spelman College. Comedian and television star Bill Cosby announced his intention to donate $20 million to Spelman College, an institution for African American women in Atlanta, Georgia. The contribution represented the largest individual gift in the 107-year history of the college and the largest such gift ever made by an African American. In announcing the donation, Cosby told a group of two thousand people attending an inaugural reception for Spelman's new president, Johnnetta Cole, that "Mrs. Cosby and I wanted this woman to know how much we love this school." He also urged other blacks to do more in supporting historically black colleges. "I think we all understand that schools need money, but I think we accepted that white folks were going to keep them alive."

College officials indicated that Cosby's money would be used to construct a new academic building, establish endowed academic chairs in the fine arts, humanities, and social sciences, and strengthen the school's $42 million endowment.

NOVEMBER 4, 1988   Martin Luther King, Jr., Federal Building Dedicated in Georgia. Dedication of the Martin Luther King, Jr., Federal Building was held in Atlanta, Georgia. U.S. Congressman John Lewis and members of the slain civil rights leader's family participated in the ceremonies. Lewis had sponsored the bill in Congress to rename the building for King, the first federal building in the nation to bear his name.

NOVEMBER 16, 1988   Toni Morrison Won Elmer Holmes Bobst Award. Toni Morrison, African American novelist, won a 1988 Elmer Holmes Bobst Award in Arts and Letters for her "powerful and haunting" book, *Beloved.* Like Morrison's other works, *Beloved* draws heavily on the black oral tradition. The Bobst Awards, sponsored by New York University, include medals and $2,000 cash prizes. Previously Morrison had won a National Book Critics Award for *Song of Solomon,* and the coveted Pulitzer Prize for *Beloved.*

NOVEMBER 24, 1988   Housing Discrimination Reported in Suburbs. Two University of Chicago researchers reported that blacks still encounter major barriers to integrated housing in the nation's suburbs. In a report entitled "Suburbanization and Segregation in U.S. Metropolitan Areas," Douglas S. Massey and Nancy A. Denton found that Asians and Hispanics had greater contact with other races as they moved out of larger American cities than did blacks. They concluded that "two decades after the Civil Rights Act of 1968, which, in theory, banned racial discrimination in the sale and rental of housing, blacks have still not achieved equal access to housing in American cities and suburbs." The study was published in the November 1988 issue of the *American Journal of Sociology.*

DECEMBER 19, 1988   Internal Navy Report Showed "Subtle Bias" Against Minorities. An internal report on equal opportunity released by the U.S. Navy found "widespread but subtle bias against black and Hispanic sailors and other minorities in its ranks." Among the shortcomings cited in the report were "failure to direct recruiting ads to minority-dominated areas; enlist highly qualified blacks; instill a sense of racial and ethnic equality in training; and guide minorities equitably into technical fields." The study also found that black and Hispanic sailors were promoted less quickly than whites, though rates of promotion varied from grade to grade.

In response to the report, Admiral Carlisle Trost, chief of naval operations, instructed naval officers "to maintain a climate in the Navy that provides the opportunity for our people to perform and achieve realistic goals."

DECEMBER 20, 1988   Black News Anchorman Max Robinson Died. Max Robinson, the first black news anchorman on American network television, died of complications relating to AIDS in Washington, D.C., at age forty-nine. Robinson, who had worked as a news anchor at WTPO-TV in Washington, became a co-anchor with Peter Jennings and Frank Reynolds on the ABC-TV Network's "Evening News" in 1978.

Carl Bernstein, chief of the ABC News bureau in Chicago, said Robinson was "deliberately excluded from any decision-making related to the newscast." In a speech at Smith College in February 1981, Robinson accused ABC of racism. Two years later, after the death of Reynolds, Jennings was named sole anchor of the "Evening News" and Robinson was "relegated to weekend anchor stints and news briefs." The next year he left ABC and joined WMAQ-TV in Chicago, Illinois. In June 1985, Robinson entered a hospital suffering from "emotional and physical exhaustion." He never returned to full-time news reporting.

In commenting on Robinson's death, Roone Arledge, president of ABC News, said, "he made an important contribution to ABC News for which we will always be grateful."

DECEMBER 28, 1988   Ethnic Designation Terms Debated. Widespread discussion began in African American communities throughout the United States over the proper ethnic designation for Americans of African origins. Former Democratic presidential candidate Jesse L. Jackson, leaders of the NAACP, and others had agreed during a conference in Chicago that "African American" was the preferable term and should replace "black," which gained prominence during the civil rights movement of the 1960s. Jackson said the term African American "[places] us in our proper historical context." The Reverend B. Herbert Martin, head of the Human Relations Commission in Chicago, and others disagreed. Martin said a change in nomenclature from "black to African American amounted to little more than semantics."

DECEMBER 28, 1988 School Choice Plan Approved. The School Committee of Boston, Massachusetts, voted 10-1 to allow parents to choose a public school for their children closer to home. In 1974, U.S. District Court Judge W. Arthur Garrity, Jr., had imposed a desegregation plan on the city of Boston that gave parents "little choice as to which schools" their children would attend. Garrity's latest orders in the case, however, required "only that a racial balance be maintained," which freed the School Committee to devise a plan of its own.

The new plan, which was subject to final approval by the state board of education, divided the Boston public school system into three zones of 14,000 students each, and parents could choose any school within the zone, "provided it did not upset the school's racial balance." A lottery would determine assignments in "oversubscribed" schools.

1989

JANUARY 1989 Brimmer Named President of the Association for the Study of Afro American Life and History. Andrew F. Brimmer, former African-American governor of the Federal Reserve Board, was installed as president of the Association for the Study of Afro-American Life and History (ASALH). Brimmer, who had also served as president of the nation's oldest black history organization in 1969, returned to the leadership of the group at a time when it was just beginning to recover from severe financial difficulties. Administrative problems and a declining membership had seriously curtailed the association's ability to provide programs and deliver services in the 1980s. These financial straits had led to suspension of its two principal publications, the *Journal of Negro History* and the *Negro History Bulletin*. Just prior to Brimmer's installation, the *Journal*

of Negro History, the oldest and most prestigious of black scholarly journals, was revived through the assistance of Morehouse College, the base of its editorial operations. Leroy Keith, Jr., the newly inaugurated president of the college, had made the pledge to resurrect the periodical soon after taking office. Upon assuming the leadership of ASALH anew, Brimmer pledged to make a similar effort on behalf of the entire association and those it served.

JANUARY 14, 1989 Coretta Scott King Resigned as President of Martin Luther King, Jr., Center. Coretta Scott King announced her resignation as president of the Martin Luther King, Jr., Center for Nonviolent Social Change in Atlanta, Georgia, having been president of the Center since its founding in 1974. She also announced that her successor would be her twenty-seven-year-old son, Dexter Scott King, whom she described as "uniquely qualified to assume the civil rights mantle." Mrs. King, however, said that she would remain as chief executive officer and spokesperson for the center.

JANUARY 15, 1989 Reagan Defended Civil Rights Policies. On the eve of his departure from office, President Ronald Reagan criticized civil rights leaders for allegedly exaggerating the degree of racism in America. The president suggested that black leaders were striving "to keep their cause alive and to maintain their own prominence." In an interview with the CBS television network news program "60 Minutes," Reagan specifically said: "Sometimes I wonder if they really want what they say they want . . . because some of those leaders are doing very well leading organizations based on keeping alive the feeling that they're victims of prejudice."

During his eight years in office, Reagan had been constantly attacked by black leaders for allegedly seeking to thwart progress in civil rights. But in the interview, Reagan defended his position on civil rights. He pointed out that as governor of California he had "appointed more blacks to executive and policy-making positions in government than all the previous governors of California put together." Reagan regretted that he was seen as being "on the other side" of the struggle for civil rights.

JANUARY 16, 1989　Bush Praised Accomplishments of King. President-elect George Bush praised the life and work of slain civil rights leader Martin Luther King, Jr., and promised to make King's "dream of racial equality" his mission in the White House. In a speech to the American Bicentennial Presidential Inaugural Afro-American Committee in Washington, D.C., Bush said that King had "lived a hero's life. He dreamed a hero's dreams. And he left a hero's indelible mark on the mind and imagination of a great nation. . . . So today we remember the man; we pay tribute to his achievements, and we pledge once more our nation's sacred honor in continuing pursuit of his dream."

In his remarks, Bush characterized King as a "'great gift' from God to the nation," adding, "What becomes of Martin Luther King's dreams is up to us. We must not fail him. We must not fail ourselves. And we must not fail the nation he loved so much and gave his life for. I understand that five days before becoming president of the United States of America."

Bush concluded his comments by vowing to pursue equality, freedom, justice, and peace so "that bigotry and indifference to the disadvantaged will find no safe home on our shores, in our public life, in our neighborhoods or in our home, and that Reverend King's dream for his children and for ours will be fulfilled . . . This must be our mission together. It will, I promise, be my mission as president of the United States."

The administration of Bush's predecessor, Ronald Reagan, in which the president-elect served as vice president, had faced constant criticism from black leaders for alleged insensitivity to civil rights issues. A few days before Bush's speech, one such leader, the Reverend Jesse L. Jackson, had offered that Reagan "may be the worst civil rights president we've had in recent memory."

JANUARY 23, 1989　*City of Richmond v. J. A. Coson Co.* The U.S. Supreme Court, in a 6-3 decision, ruled unconstitutional a program in Richmond, Virginia, which required contractors in city construction projects to set aside at least 30 percent of the value of the project for companies at least half-minority owned. The high Court said the quota was "an unlawful form of reverse discrimination." Justice Sandra Day O'Connor said local and state government could no longer rest on the "amorphous claim" that quotas were necessary remedies for past racial discrimination, adding "it is sheer speculation" to claim that if past discrimination had not occurred, there would be more minority firms. Justice O'Connor further commented: "The dearth of minority firms might have a number of explanations. For example, whites and blacks may simply make different 'entrepreneurial choices.'" In any event, she wrote, if quotas were not "realistically tied to any injury suffered by anyone," they were not permitted by the equal protection clause of the Constitution's Fourteenth Amendment. Justice O'Connor concluded that it was "disingenuous" to include "Spanish-speaking, Oriental, Indian, Eskimo or Aleut persons" in the affirmative action program, because no member of that "random inclusion of racial groups" had ever suffered from discrimination in Richmond.

The *City of Richmond v. J. A. Coson Co.* case stemmed from a 1983 ordinance that required the 30 percent "set asides." At the time, although 60 percent of the population of Richmond was black, minority-owned business had received less than 0.6 percent of the $25 million awarded in city contracts over the preceding five years.

The high Court's ruling was one of the most far-reaching attacks on the notion of affirmative action since the *Regents of University of California v. Allan Bakke* decision in 1978.

JANUARY 24, 1989 Barbara Harris Elected First Female Bishop of Episcopal Church. The Episcopal Church approved the election of Barbara Harris, a fifty-eight-year-old African American, as the first female bishop in the "two-thousand-year tradition of apostolic succession, a line of bishops dating from Jesus and his apostles." Harris was assigned to the post of suffragan, or assistant bishop, in the Diocese of Boston.

Harris was first ordained an Episcopal priest in 1980, four years after the Church first approved women as priests. She had studied theology through correspondence courses and with tutors. Prior to her elevation to the bishopric, Harris was also the head of the Episcopal Church Publishing Company.

FEBRUARY 1, 1989 Black Population Projected to Increase. The Bureau of the Census projected that the black population of the United States would grow 50 percent by the year 2030, but the growth of the "other races" population (primarily Native Americans, Asians, and Pacific Islanders) was expected to "be the fastest of any of the racial groups." These groups had tripled in size in the past seventeen years, increasing from 2.6 million in 1970 to 7.9 million in 1987, and are expected to be 50 percent larger by the year 2000, "double the present size by 2015, and triple its size by the year 2040." By 2040, the "other races" population could reach almost 25 million larger than it was in 1987. On the other hand, the black population, which was 29.9 million in 1987 (7 million more than in 1970), was expected to change relatively little after 2030.

FEBRUARY 10, 1989 Ronald Brown Elected Chairman of Democratic National Committee. With his election as chairman of the Democratic National Committee, Ronald H. Brown became the first African American to lead a major American political party.

FEBRUARY 24, 1989 William Lucas Nominated Assistant Attorney General for Civil Rights. William Lucas, an African American attorney from Detroit, Michigan, was nominated assistant attorney general for civil rights by President George Bush. This appointment would also make him director of the Civil Rights Division of the Department of Justice.

Lucas, a 1962 graduate of the Fordham University School of Law, first joined the Justice Department in 1963 and represented the government in efforts to desegregate the public schools of Tuskegee, Alabama. He also served on the New York Police Department, was sheriff and executive of Wayne County, Michigan (of which Detroit is the county seat), and lost as the Republican candidate for governor of Michigan in 1986.

The nomination of Lucas was applauded by conservative groups. Patrick B. McGuigan, a leader of the Free Congress Foundation, "a conservative research organization" in Washington, D.C., called the selection "brilliant," adding that Lucas was "a fine, courageous man who, in his career, has been willing to put himself on the line." However, it also drew expressions of concern from national civil rights organizations, however, because Lucas had indicated "that he generally opposes quotas to advance the interests of minority groups" and because of his long absence from federal service. Elaine R. Jones, an attorney with the NAACP Legal Defense and Educational Fund, Inc., charged that "it doesn't appear at first glance that he has had any substantial experience in this area in 20 years."

FEBRUARY 25, 1989 Mike Tyson Retained Championship Title. Mike Tyson retained his heavyweight boxing championship with a knockout of British fighter Frank Bruno in the fifth round of a scheduled 15-round bout. Bruno had a record of 32-3 and was the number one contender for the title at the time of the fight. Tyson went into the contest with a record of 36-0, with 32 knockouts. The African American champion collected $8 million for the Las Vegas, Nevada, appearance, bringing his total career earnings to approximately $48 million. Bruno was paid approximately $4 million.

FEBRUARY 28, 1989   Acting Chicago Mayor Eugene Sawyer Lost in Primaries. Richard M. Daley, son of the legendary Chicago mayor Richard J. Daley, defeated acting mayor Eugene Sawyer for the Democratic nomination for that city's executive office. Daley, who is white, captured 57 percent of the vote, compared to 43 percent for Sawyer, who is black. The vote was marked by a sharp split along racial lines, but voter turnout in the black wards of the city was lower than usual.

As a result of the primary, the general election scheduled for April 11, 1989, was to be decided among three candidates: Republican Alderman Edward R. Vrdolyak, black independent Timothy C. Evans, and Daley. The winner of that election would serve the final two years of the late Harold Washington's term in office. Washington, Chicago's first black mayor, died of a heart attack in November 1987. His death led to the election of Sawyer as acting mayor by the Chicago City Council.

Political analysts quoted by the *Atlanta Constitution* attributed Sawyer's defeat to: 1) a lack of charisma; 2) his alienating many blacks because of his support for the position of acting mayor by many of the same white aldermen who had opposed Mayor Washington's policies; 3) the looming candidacy of Evans, who was endorsed by the "Harold Washington slate"; 4) an antiquated campaign based largely on grass roots support; and 5) the political experience of Daley, who had served eight years as a state senator before becoming chief prosecutor of Cook County, of which Chicago is the county seat.

MARCH 3, 1989   Atlanta Minority-Female Business Enterprise Declared Unconstitutional. The Georgia Supreme Court, in a unanimous decision, declared the Atlanta Minority-Female Business Enterprise (MFBE) program

unconstitutional. The Atlanta plan, one of the nation's oldest affirmative action programs, had set a 35 percent minority participation goal in all city contracts. It had been applauded nationally as a model device for insuring fair representation of minority and female businesses in public works. However, the Georgia Supreme Court contended that the plan "was too broadly drawn and failed to consider alternatives to the yearly goal." The Georgia decision was also based on a recent ruling by the U.S. Supreme Court that struck down an affirmative action program in the city of Richmond, Virginia.

MARCH 6, 1989   Supreme Court Ruled Against Two Affirmative Action Programs. The U.S. Supreme Court ruled against affirmative action programs in Florida and Michigan.

In the Florida case, the Court heard an appeal of a ruling from the U.S. Court of Appeals for the Eleventh Circuit which had upheld a set-aside plan for minorities in Dade County, Florida. Under the plan, which was adopted in 1979, in order to qualify for federal funds for a mass transit project, the county had to set aside 5 percent of construction contracts for minorities. But after a low bid on a construction project by the H. K. Porter Co. was rejected because the county did not meet the 5 percent goal, Porter sued. In light of its recent ruling in an affirmative action case from Richmond, Virginia, however, the Supreme Court vacated the decision of the appeals court and ordered it to reexamine the case of *Porter v. Metropolitan Dade County.*

In the Michigan case, the Court affirmed without a written opinion a ruling by the U.S. Court of Appeals for the Sixth Circuit which declared a Michigan law unconstitutional. That act, adopted in 1981, provided that 7 percent of state contracting expenditures should go to minority-owned businesses and an additional 5 percent to businesses owned by women. Although the state argued in its appeal of *Milliken v. Michigan Road Builders* that the set-aside percentages were carefully selected "to redress discriminatory practices by state agencies," the Supreme Court still ruled against it.

MARCH 6, 1989 Sculptor Richmond Barthe Died. Richmond Barthe, a major twentieth-century sculptor, died at his home in Pasadena, California. Born in 1901 in Bay St. Louis, Mississippi, Barthe was educated at the Art Institute of Chicago. A member of the National Academy of Arts and Letters, his work was exhibited at several major American museums, including the Metropolitan Museum of Art in New York City. Some of his notable works include *Singing Slave, Maurice Evans,* and *Henry O. Tanner.*

MARCH 7, 1989 Republican Party Chairman Lee Atwater Resigned College Board Post. Lee Atwater, chairman of the Republican National Committee, resigned as a member of the board of trustees of predominantly black Howard University in Washington, D.C. The resignation came as several hundred African American students continued a sit-in that began as a protest against Atwater's selection to the board.

During the demonstrations, which began on March 3, 1989, students took over the school's administration building. Although city police stormed the captured building on March 7, they left without removing or arresting any protestors at the request of Howard president James A. Cheek.

In announcing his resignation, Atwater remarked, "The opposition of some students to my service on the board appears to me to be counterproductive to Howard University and is a distraction to the work that I want to do in fulfilling George Bush's and my efforts to provide equal opportunity to all Americans . . . I would never forgive myself if someone was hurt in one of these episodes."

Although Atwater's appointment to the Howard University Board of Trustees had been seen by some political analysts "as symbolic of his drive to broaden the Republican Party's appeal to blacks," others, including Democratic

party and civil rights leaders, had accused the Republican leader of orchestrating "subtly racist appeals" during the 1988 presidential campaign. One Republican television ad, for example, featured Willie Horton, a convicted black rapist, in the party's attack on crime. Regina Davis, a twenty-year-old business management major at Howard, applauded Atwater's resignation, saying, "If you're going to appoint someone, they should have the same views as the people they're going to represent."

But Atwater's resignation did not bring an immediate end to the protests, as students continued to press their demands for better housing and security, improvements in student services, and the appointment of more African Americans to Howard's board of trustees.

MARCH 8, 1989 Drop in African American Voter Participation Reported. The Bureau of the Census reported that 52 percent of the 19.7 million voting-age blacks went to the polls in the 1988 presidential election, as compared to 56 percent in 1984. White voter turnout also dropped from 61 percent to 59 percent, while the rate for Hispanics fell from 33 percent to 29 percent. Black voter participation was higher in the North and West (56 percent) than in the South (48 percent). Among whites, 60 percent voted in the North and West, and 56 percent in the South.

MARCH 10, 1989 Louis Wade Sullivan Confirmed as Health and Human Services Secretary. Louis Wade Sullivan, president of the Morehouse School of Medicine in Atlanta, was confirmed as Secretary of Health and Human Services (HHS) by the U.S. Senate. The confirmation came more than two months after President George Bush had nominated Sullivan for the position. Sullivan's nomination first ran into trouble on December 18, 1988, after the black physician told an *Atlanta Journal-Constitution* reporter that while opposing federal funding for abortions, he supported a woman's right to have one. This view was incompatible with the president's outright opposition to abortion except in cases of rape or incest, or to save the pregnant woman's life. The same position had been taken by several Republican senators and other leaders of the president's party.

On December 21, 1988, Sullivan had begun to back away from his pro-choice position. In a letter to the editors of the *Atlanta Constitution,* he wrote that he was "opposed to abortion, except in cases of rape, incest, and where the life of the mother is threatened. I am opposed to federal funding for abortions, except when the life of the mother is endangered. My position is entirely consistent with President-elect [George] Bush's position." Still, some pro-life activists were skeptical.

While Sullivan attempted to convince influential Republican senators in Washington of his correct position on the abortion question, President Bush announced on January 25, 1989, that Sullivan would carry out his abortion policies if confirmed by the senate. On February 22, Sullivan confessed to the Senate Finance Committee that he had "misspoke" earlier when he said he supported a woman's right to an abortion. Sullivan's confirmation occurred the following month.

Sullivan was born on November 3, 1933, in Atlanta, Georgia, the son of Walter and Lubirda Elizabeth Priester Wade Sullivan. He graduated *magna cum laude* from Morehouse College in 1954 and earned a doctor of medicine degree (*cum laude*), from the Boston University Medical School. A respected hematologist, Sullivan taught at the Harvard Medical School (1963–64), the New Jersey College of Medicine (1964–66), and the Boston University Medical School before he was named dean of the new Morehouse School of Medicine in 1974. The next year, he became both dean and president of this institution. During his fifteen-year tenure at Morehouse, the school emerged from being a two-year institution housed in two trailers, to a fully accredited, four-year institution comprised of three buildings.

MARCH 10, 1989   James A. Goodman Named Executive Vice-president of Morehouse Medical School. James A. Goodman, executive vice president of the Morehouse Medical School, was named president of the predominately black institution. The school's board of trustees selected Goodman, age fifty-five, who had served as an administrator there since 1980, to succeed Louis W. Sullivan, the school's first president. On the same day, Sullivan was sworn in as secretary of the Department of Health and Human Services (HHS).

Goodman, who earned an undergraduate degree from Morehouse College and post-graduate degrees from the Atlanta University School of Social Work and the University of Minnesota, had previously served as a director of the Office of International Training for the Agency for International Development (AID) in the U.S. State Department. Goodman's teaching experience included tenures at the School of Social Work at the University of Minnesota and at the National Academy of Science's Institute of Medicine. At the time of Goodman's appointment, the Morehouse Medical School had an annual budget of $18 million and an enrollment of 144 students.

MARCH 15, 1989   Life Expectancy of African Americans Shown to Decline. The federal government issued a report that showed that the life expectancy of African Americans was continuing to decline. Major causes of premature deaths among blacks included homicide and acquired immunodeficiency syndrome (AIDS). Blacks were also twice as likely to die in infancy as whites, because "pregnant black women receive early prenatal care far less than whites," and black children were disproportionately afflicted with influenza and pneumonia. The report also indicated that black men, "frequently the victims of drug-related violence," died at a 50 percent higher rate than white men in 1986, the last year for which comprehensive statistics were available. Also, a white child born in 1986 had a life expectancy of 75.4 years, an increase from 75.3 the previous year, while a black child, born at the same time, could expect to die at 69.4 years, down from 69.5 in 1985 and 69.7 in 1984.

In the period from 1970 to 1986, the AIDS infection rate rose 51 percent among blacks, with a 74 percent increase among black women. In the same period, infant mortality among all groups was cut in half—from 20 deaths per 1,000 births in 1970 to 10.4 per 1,000 births in 1986, but in 1986 alone, the mortality rate for black infants was 18 deaths per 1,000 births compared with 8.9 per 1,000 births for whites.

Responding to the report, the African American secretary of Health and Human Services (HHS), Louis W. Sullivan, said that "there is a disparity between the health of our white and black populations," and the nation needed to focus more attention "in such critical areas as prevention of AIDS, unintentional injuries, homicide, and suicide."

MARCH 16, 1989 Senate Voted to Begin Impeachment Proceedings Against District Judge. The U.S. Senate voted to try U.S. District Court Judge Alcee Hastings, the first African American to be appointed to the federal bench in Florida, on all seventeen articles of impeachment adopted by the U.S. House of Representatives. The senators voted 92-1 to try Hastings on fifteen articles, charging fraud, corruption, and perjury in a 1981 bribery conspiracy case for which he was acquitted in 1983. In voting against the articles, Senator Howard M. Metzenbaum from Ohio said that he felt they had placed Hastings in double jeopardy—the principle in American law that a person cannot be tried twice for the same offense—because of the previous acquittal. But Metzenbaum joined fellow senators in a unanimous vote for an article alleging "a pattern of misconduct and its harmful effect on the judiciary."

The senate also created a special twelve-member committee to hear testimony and col-

lect evidence before it debated and voted on whether to convict Hastings.

MARCH 18, 1989 Blacks Owned Thirty-Seven Banks in 1989. The *Atlanta Journal-Constitution* reported that there were 37 black-owned banks in the United States in 1989. Four of the institutions, including the number-one ranked IndeCorp, were located in Chicago, Illinois. The other Chicago banks, Seeway National, Highland Community, and Community Bank of Lawndale, were among the top twenty in total assets as ranked by *Black Enterprise* magazine.

MARCH 22, 1989 Shoeshine Stand Law Declared Unconstitutional. U.S. District Court Judge John Pratt declared that an eighty-four-year-old law prohibiting shoeshine stands on the streets of Washington, D.C., was unconstitutional. The case was brought to court on behalf of Ego Brown, a thirty-six-year-old black shoeshine vendor who had offered employment to homeless men until the city closed down his business in 1985. The suit was sponsored by the Landmark Legal Foundation Center for Civil Rights, which was based in Washington, D.C. The Landmark Center claimed that it provided an alternative to the NAACP. Its director, Clint Bolick, charged that "the other major civil rights organizations are more worried about imposing racial quotas than protecting individual rights." The Brown case was the center's first legal victory.

APRIL 1, 1989 First African American Named National League President. Bill White, a six-time All Star first baseman, was elected president of baseball's National League, becoming the first African American ever to head a major professional sports league in the United States.

White played baseball with the St. Louis Cardinals, the Philadelphia Phillies, and the New York and San Francisco Giants between 1956 and 1969. At the time of his appointment, White was a television announcer for the

New York Yankees of the American League and a broadcaster with CBS Radio.

Atlanta Braves vice president Hank Aaron, who had been campaigning for more blacks in executive positions in baseball, applauded White's selection. He characterized White as "a baseball man. He knows baseball. There will be nothing that will be a surprise for him." White himself commented, "You just do the job whether you're red, yellow, purple, or whatever."

APRIL 3, 1989   Student Demonstration Occurred at Morris Brown College. Twenty students occupied and barricaded the administration building at predominantly black Morris Brown College in Atlanta, Georgia. The demonstrators' demands included "a more lenient delinquent fees policy, a Pan-African studies program, better campus services [including a new cafeteria vendor] and [after a recent dormitory fire], an upgraded physical plant." The Morris Brown demonstration followed by one month a similar campus takeover at historically black Howard University in Washington, D.C., and by a week a black student takeover at predominantly white Wayne State University in Detroit, Michigan.

The campus demonstrations were reminiscent of similar protests on both black and white campuses during the 1960s, yet the young college students differed in both tone and manner from the radicals of earlier generations. For example, there was less damage to property in the current protests and little personal rage toward college administrators. At Morris Brown College, the students called their takeover "an act of love." The demonstrators did acknowledge, however, linkages to the 1960s through their quotations of both Martin Luther King, Jr., and Malcolm X, and their references to similar actions in the earlier period. Yet some observers saw the current demonstrators as having too much reverence for the radicalism of the 1960s "without a full understanding of the time in which the leaders worked."

Werner Sollors, a professor of Afro-American Studies at Howard University and author of a biography of black poet Amiri Baraka (one of the heroes of today's radicals), believed that the current campus protestors were "totally misreading the historical context of [the earlier movements], so what they're doing now seems pretty wacky."

APRIL 6, 1989   African Americans Spent More Income on Housing. The Bureau of the Census reported that African Americans spent a larger share of their income on housing in 1985 than all other American ethnic groups. The median monthly housing cost for black households was $311 compared with $355 for all households. Because their incomes were lower, black households spent a median of 27 percent of their income for housing costs, compared with 21 percent for all U.S. households. Housing costs for homeowners include mortgage payments, real estate taxes, property insurance, utilities, fuel, and garbage collection. Renter costs were based on contract rent and the estimated cost of utilities and fuels, if these were paid in addition to rent.

The Census Bureau also reported that: 1) black householders occupied 9.9 million housing units in 1985; 44 percent were homeowners compared with 64 percent of all households; 2) 16 percent of black householders lived in public or subsidized housing compared with 5 percent of all householders; and 3) there were five million black householders in single, detached homes. The median size of their unit was 1,337 square feet, or 487 square feet per person. The national average was 633 square feet per person.

APRIL 29, 1989   Civil Rights Commission Criticized for "Ineffectiveness." Bobby Doctor, a member of the staff of the U.S. Commission on Civil Rights (CCR), told a state CCR meeting in Atlanta, Georgia, that "federal agencies have gone to sleep on the question of civil rights enforcement." He also "attributed the ineffectiveness" of the Commission on Civil

Rights "during the last decade to the anti-civil rights posture" of the administration of President Ronald Reagan.

The CCR, which was established in 1957, is responsible for monitoring such federal agencies as the Department of Housing and Urban Development (HUD) for possible discrimination in education, employment, housing, and other areas. According to Doctor, "for the past seven years we have not done that." He added that during the last decade, the budget of the CCR had been cut by at least 50 percent and seven of its ten regional offices were closed. "The agency has been teetering on the brink of annihilation," he added.

By not strongly enforcing civil rights compliance in federal agencies, Doctor accused the CCR of contributing to a national climate that condoned "hate activity" against minorities and such discriminatory practices as redlining, and other improper mortgage lending activities.

MAY 22, 1989   Oprah Winfrey Received Doctorate from Morehouse College. Oprah Winfrey, African American national talk-show television host, received a doctor of humane letters degree from Morehouse College in Atlanta, Georgia, and gave the all-male college a gift of one million dollars. She requested that the money be used to establish a scholarship fund to educate at least one hundred black men in the coming decades. Morehouse, one of the country's most prestigious black colleges, was the alma mater of slain civil rights leader Martin Luther King, Jr.

Winfrey's gift represented a growing trend among black entertainers and athletes to lend their support to America's financially impoverished black colleges. Other recent donations included $800,000 to Meharry Medical College, $325,000 to Howard University, $1.3 million to Fisk University, and $20 million to Spelman College by comedian Bill Cosby; $500,000 to Tuskegee University by singer Lionel Richie; and $600,000 to the United

Negro College Fund (UNCF) by singer Michael Jackson.

MAY 23, 1989   Educational Reform Demanded by Committee on Policy for Racial Justice. The Committee on Policy for Racial Justice, a group of prominent African American scholars, called for smaller, more personal schools, significant parental involvement, and other steps that they said would help black children achieve greater academic success. Sara Lawrence Lightfoot, professor of education at Harvard University and a member of the committee, said, "We believe it is the school's responsibility to overcome social barriers that limit academic progress." She added: "What we demand is this: that the schools shift their focus from the supposed deficiencies of the black child and the alleged inadequacies of black family life to the elimination of the barriers that stand in the way of academic success."

The committee's report (much of which was contained in its publication, *Vision of a Better Way: A Black Appraisal of Public Schooling*) also called upon black communities to make the improvement of public schools their main objective in the next decade. It further noted that the black middle class and such black institutions as churches and fraternal organizations had a special responsibility to set expectations and support academic development among black children.

The committee's recommendations and suggestions included expanded funding for Head Start and Chapter I, the federal government's "major programs for at-risk and disadvantaged students, closer ties between schools and social services, recruitment of more black teachers, and an expanded curriculum that recognizes the realities of black children's lives."

MAY 24, 1989   Congressional Black Caucus met with Bush. President George Bush met with seventeen members of the Congressional Black Caucus (CBC). It was the first time since 1981 that the Caucus, which had been critical of the civil rights policies of former president Ronald Reagan, was invited to the White House. Representative Ronald V. Dellums from California, who led the delegation, said that President Bush indicated that he was "ready to open up" and meet regularly with the CBC. Representative John Lewis from Georgia remarked, "There certainly is a new level of sensitivity at the White House."

MAY 31, 1989 Cito Gaston Named Toronto Blue Jays Manager. Clarence (Cito) Gaston was named manager of the Toronto Blue Jays of baseball's American League. Gaston became only the fifth African American manager. (Frank Robinson, Larry Doby, Maury Wills, and Hal McRae preceded him.)

Gaston began his major league career in 1967 with the Atlanta Braves of the National League. In 1968 Gaston was traded to the San Diego Padres. He played six years with the Padres and was selected to the National League All-Star team in 1970. In that year, Gaston hit 29 home runs, batted in 93 runs, and had a batting average of .318. He returned to Atlanta in 1974 before being traded to the Pittsburgh Pirates in 1977. After being dropped by the Pirates in 1979, Gaston played two years in the Dominican League and the Mexican League before retiring. He emerged from retirement in 1981 as a minor league hitting instructor for the Atlanta Braves. He took a similar position with the Toronto Blue Jays in 1982, and the team improved its over-all batting average 36 points to .262.

Baseball commissioner A. Bartlett Giammati, who had been a champion of equal opportunity for blacks in professional sports, applauded the choice of Gaston. Gaston said of his selection, "The organization doesn't see any colors . . . I don't see any colors. I'm black, I'll always be black. When I stand here and look at you, I just see you as a person."

JUNE 5, 1989 U.S. Supreme Court Ruled on Minority Bias Case. The U.S. Supreme Court,

in a 5-4 decision, ruled that "when minorities allege that statistics show they are victims of bias, employers only have the burden of producing evidence that there is a legitimate reason for apparently neutral racial practices." Justice Byron White wrote that "the plaintiff bears the burden of disproving an employer's assertion that the adverse employment action or practice was based solely on a legitimate neutral consideration." He also added that an absence of minorities in skilled jobs is not necessarily evidence of bias if the absence reflected "a dearth of qualified non-white applications for reasons that are not [the employer's] fault." In one of the dissenting opinions, Justice John Paul Stevens charged that the ruling retreated from eighteen years of court decisions "aimed at helping minorities victimized by discrimination that may be unintentional."

The case came to the Supreme Court from Alaska where a lower court had ruled in favor of Filipinos, Alaska natives, and Asians who claimed that they had been discriminated against by the Wards Cove Packing Co. and Castle and Cooke, Inc., owners of Alaskan salmon canneries.

JUNE 5, 1989 *Brown v. Board of Education.* The U.S. Court of Appeals for the Tenth Circuit refused to close the landmark desegregation case, *Brown v. Board of Education.* The court said that the school board of Topeka, Kansas, had still failed to fully carry out the Supreme Court's order of May 17, 1954. The appeals court ruling reversed a decision by a lower court that could have closed the case "that paved the way for nationwide school desegregation." In its decision, the appellate court concluded that "Topeka has not sufficiently countered the effects of both the momentum of its pre-Brown segregation and its subsequent acts in the 1960s."

The Brown case had been reopened in 1979 when a group of parents, including one of the original plaintiffs, Linda Brown Buckner, complained that the school system was not desegregated.

JUNE 7, 1989   First African American Elected Presbyterian Church Moderator. Joan Salmon Campbell, a fifty-year-old African American from Philadelphia, Pennsylvania, was elected moderator of the Presbyterian Church, U.S.A. She became the sixth female and the first black woman to head the church. The moderator presides at assembly sessions and travels around the nation and the world promoting the programs of the 3 million member church.

Campbell had campaigned for the position of moderator on a platform of liberality and diversity. She said, "We must be liberal enough to include the rich diversity of God's family within our membership in its varied cultures, races, lifestyles, theological perspectives and economic status without restraint due to age, sex, or physical capacity."

JUNE 12, 1989   Reverse Discrimination Suit Stemmed from Affirmative Action Case. The U.S. Supreme Court, in a 5-4 decision, ruled that workers "who are adversely affected by court-approved affirmative action plans may file lawsuits alleging discrimination."

The high Court's ruling came in a case from Birmingham, Alabama, which had adopted an affirmative action plan, with federal court approval, in 1981 after blacks had filed suit "charging that the city had engaged in discriminatory hiring and promotions." However, white fire fighters challenged the plan, claiming that it denied them promotions because of their race. The Supreme Court agreed with the U.S. Court of Appeals for the Eleventh Circuit that, contrary to previous appellate court findings that prohibited "secondary attacks on court-approved affirmative action plans," the white fire fighters did have a right to sue. Chief Justice William Rehnquist wrote, "A voluntary settlement . . . between one group of employees and their employer cannot possibly settle, vol-

untarily or otherwise, the conflicting claims of another group of employees who do not join in the agreement." Justices Harry Blackmun, William Brennan, Thurgood Marshall, and John Paul Stevens dissented. Justice Stevens called the majority opinion "unfathomable" and said it would "subject large employers who seek to comply with the law by remedying past discrimination to a never-ending stream of litigation and potential liability."

JUNE 12, 1989   Supreme Court Ruled on Discrimination Suit. The U.S. Supreme Court, in a 5-3 decision, ruled that "the three-hundred-day period that federal law allows for filing job discrimination lawsuits begins when . . . seniority plans [are] adopted." In a dissent, justices Thurgood Marshall, Harry Blackmun, and William Brennan agreed with civil rights lawyers that such an interpretation was unfair because employees were often unaware of the discriminatory effect that a seniority system may have on them for months or years. Justice Sandra Day O'Connor did not participate in the case and did not offer an explanation.

The case came to the high Court from Aurora, Illinois, where three women filed suit in 1982 claiming that a change in the seniority system at the American Telephone and Telegraph Co. there caused them to lose seniority. However, federal courts in Chicago had held that the litigation (*Lorance v. AT&T Technologies, Inc.*) was filed too late. The U.S. Supreme Court agreed with the lower courts.

JUNE 15, 1989   *Patterson v. McClean Credit Union.* The U.S. Supreme Court unanimously reaffirmed a 1976 decision "that interpreted an 1866 civil rights law to permit lawsuits to remedy some forms of private discrimination." But the Court also ruled 5-4 that the 1866 law may "no longer serve as the bases for lawsuits alleging racial harassment in the workplace." Civil rights attorneys said this latter ruling, written by Justice Anthony Kennedy, would make it almost impossible "to stop racial harassment by supervisors or co-workers." Barry Goldstein, an attorney with the NAACP Legal Defense and Educational Fund, said the decision left "no effective legal remedy for racial harrassment in the workplace."

The Supreme Court's ruling came in the case of a black bank teller in North Carolina who had alleged that her supervisor at the McLean Credit Union had failed to promote her and then fired her on account of her race. A federal district court in North Carolina and a federal appeals court in Richmond, Virginia, had said that she could not sue alleging harassment. While the Supreme Court's decision ended the harassment phase of the litigation, it sent the case back to the appeals court for another hearing on whether the woman could "prove that the company's reason for not promoting her was invalid."

JUNE 20, 1989 African American Population Largest in New York. The Bureau of the Census reported that New York State had the largest number of African American residents in 1985 while California had the fastest growing black population. New York had a black population of 2.7 million, followed by California with 2.1 million. Fourteen other states had black populations of one million or more. These included Texas, Illinois, Georgia, Florida, North Carolina, Louisiana, Michigan, and Ohio.

The state with the largest proportion of blacks in its population was Mississippi with 36 percent, followed by South Carolina, 31 percent, and Louisiana, 30 percent. During the period 1980–1985, only West Virginia and the District of Columbia had declines in their black populations.

The bureau's report also revealed that four out of every five blacks lived in metropolitan areas in 1985. Four metropolitan areas had black populations of one million or more. These included New York (metropolitan New York also includes Long Island and portions of Connecticut and New Jersey, 3.2 million), Chicago (1.6 million), Los Angeles (1.2 million) and

Philadelphia (1.1 million). The fastest growing metropolitan area in black residents was Atlanta, up 15.6 percent to 608,000 from 1980 to 1985, followed by Houston, up 13.6 percent to 641,000 in the same period.

The new calculations of the African American population were the first detailed estimates of minorities by state since the 1980 census. They also showed that blacks remained the nation's largest minority at 28.9 million, or 11.8 of the estimated U.S. population.

JUNE 26, 1989 Atlanta University and Clark College Merged. Two of the nation's oldest black institutions of higher education, Atlanta University and Clark College, merged. The new institution, Clark-Atlanta University, was created in response to severe financial problems at Atlanta University and a shortage of classroom space and research facilities at Clark College. Atlanta University was founded in 1867; Clark College was founded two years later.

The new university was expected to focus its activities on science and technology, foreign service careers, and teachers for rural areas, according to Thomas W. Cole, Jr., Clark-Atlanta University's new president. The university also hoped to offer six doctoral programs to "assist in curbing the shortage of blacks" holding doctorate degrees. In 1989, Clark-Atlanta University and Howard University in Washington, D.C., were the only two comprehensive historically black institutions in the nation that offered academic studies from undergraduate through graduate levels.

JUNE 26, 1989 Civil Rights Activist Moreland Griffith Smith Died. Moreland Griffith Smith, a retired architect and civil rights activist, died of heart failure in Atlanta, Georgia. Smith was born December 15, 1906, to Charles M. and Jennie Moreland Smith in Adrian, Michigan. He received a bachelor's degree from Auburn University in Alabama, a master's degree in architecture from the Massachusetts

Institute of Technology, and studied at the Ecole des Beaux-Arts in Fontainebleau, France.

In 1954, Smith went to the office of his friend, William "Tacky" Gayle, mayor of Montgomery, Alabama, to discuss what he termed "a simple matter of fairness"—the issue of seating for blacks on city buses. The meeting occurred before Rosa Parks refused to give up her seat on one such bus and the launching of the famed Montgomery bus boycott. Two issues had already surfaced: Blacks were forced to stand on buses when "the white section" was nearly empty, and they had to pay their fares up front, exit, and reenter through the back door (sometimes the bus driver would pull away before they could do so). Smith urged Mayor Gayle to end both of these practices.

Because of his support for the demands of blacks regarding seating on buses, Smith was berated numerous times by whites. Among his detractors was Governor George C. Wallace, who allegedly tried to keep Smith from getting architectural jobs in the area. One bank, in fact, declined to extend a line of credit to Smith's architectural firm. Yet he "stubbornly" served on local civil rights committees and was a trustee at Tuskegee Institute. Smith hired many black architects and proposed some for membership in the American Institute of Architecture (AIA). These activities led to social ostracism among Montgomery's white community for Smith and his wife, Marjorie. In 1965, Smith lost the lucrative architectural business he had founded and built up over the years, and subsequently moved to Atlanta.

In 1987, the Atlanta chapter of the AIA honored Moreland Smith "for his conviction and courage during the tumultuous early years of the Civil Rights Movement."

JULY 10, 1989   Denver Nuggets Purchased by African American Businessmen. African American businessmen Bertram Lee of Boston, Massachusetts, and Peter Bynoe of Chicago, Illinois, purchased the Denver Nuggets of the National Basketball Association for $65

million. They became the first blacks ever to own a professional sports franchise.

After the purchase, Lee commented, "Do we overestimate the significance of a barrier coming down? A barrier that presumably had to do with other than people's abilities or their financial wherewithal? No, I don't think so. I think the analogy about Jackie Robinson is something that is very special to me. If breaking the color barrier in ownership is sort of put up there with that, I'm honored by it."

JULY 21, 1989   Mike Tyson Retained Heavyweight Title. African American heavyweight boxing champion Mike Tyson knocked out Carl "The Truth" Williams in the first minute and a half of the first round to retain his world title. It was the fifth fastest title bout in boxing history. Although Williams was on his feet at the count of seven (knockouts are usually declared at the count of ten), referee Randy Neumann declared him out in the Atlantic City, New Jersey, contest.

JULY 23, 1989   *Brown v. Board of Education of Topeka, Kansas.* A federal appeals court in Denver, Colorado, without explanation, withdrew its June 5, 1989, ruling that the historic case of *Brown v. Board of Education of Topeka, Kansas,* be continued.

AUGUST 1, 1989   Nomination of William Lucas for U.S. Assistant Attorney General Rejected. The Judiciary Committee of the U.S. Senate voted 7-7 on whether to recommend the February 24, 1989, nomination of William Lucas, an African American attorney, as U.S. assistant attorney general, to the full senate. The tie vote meant a rejection of the nomination. Had Lucas been confirmed, he would have headed the civil rights division of the U.S. Justice Department. Some legislators and civil rights leaders opposed the nomination, citing Lucas's "inexperience," his opposition to racial quotas in employment and contracts, and his support of recent Supreme Court decisions severely limiting affirmative action programs.

AUGUST 7, 1989 Texas Congressman Mickey Leland Killed in Airplane Crash. On August 7, an airplane with African American congressman Mickey Leland aboard crashed en route to the Fugnido refugee camp in Ethiopia. Six days later, the bodies of Leland and fifteen others were discovered. Other Americans aboard the ill-fated aircraft included Hugh A. Johnson, Jr., a staff member of the U.S. House Select Committee on Hunger, Patrice Y. Johnson, Leland's chief of staff, and Joyce Williams, a member of the staff of California representative Ronald V. Dellums.

Leland, age forty-four, represented Texas and served as chairman of the House Select Committee on Hunger at the time of his death. He had made six previous trips to Africa to investigate and underscore famine conditions, particularly in war-torn Ethiopia.

After the congressman's body was discovered, Thomas S. Foley, speaker of the U.S. House of Representatives, said "there will be a determination on the part of members of the House to work for those goals that Mickey Leland sought to achieve, the alleviation of hunger and suffering here and in Africa and elsewhere in the world."

AUGUST 8, 1989 Dexter Scott King Resigned as President of Martin Luther King, Jr., Center. Dexter Scott King, son of slain civil rights leader Martin Luther King, Jr., resigned as president of the Martin Luther King, Jr., Center for Non-Violent Social Change in Atlanta, Georgia. He had held the position for only four months. Sources for the *Atlanta Constitution* blamed a power struggle involving young King, his mother, Coretta Scott King, his aunt, Christine Farris King, and his top aide, Barbara Williams-Skinner for the resignation. The King Center itself had no comment at the time of King's resignation.

AUGUST 8, 1989 Holt Street Baptist Church Minister Died. A. W. Wilson, minister and civil rights activist, died in Montgomery, Alabama, at age eighty-seven. Wilson was the pastor of the Holt Street Baptist Church in Montgomery for fifty years. The church was the site of the first mass meeting of organizers of the famous Montgomery Bus Boycott in 1955. Many other rallies were also held at the church during the civil rights movement in Montgomery.

AUGUST 9, 1989 Bush Addressed National Urban League Convention. President George Bush told delegates to the 79th Annual Convention of the National Urban League (NUL) in Washington, D.C., that his administration would not "tolerate discrimination, bigotry or bias of any kind—period." He added, "Your problems are my problems. . . . The 'great gulf' between black and white America has narrowed, but it has not closed." President Bush also said that "race hate" still existed and as long as bigotry persisted, "our work is not over."

NUL president John E. Jacob said it was "significant" that Bush came to the meeting and made a vow to fight racial bias. It was, he thought, a first step in changing the "national atmosphere" of the preceding eight years. The previous administration of President Ronald Reagan was frequently criticized by the NUL and other civil rights groups for insensitivity to black issues and actually trying to roll back progress in civil rights. Reagan never addressed a NUL Convention and rarely appeared before any civil rights group. Former president Jimmy Carter spoke to the NUL in 1977.

AUGUST 10, 1989 Colin Powell named Chairman of U.S. Joint Chiefs of Staff. Army General Colin L. Powell was named chairman of the U.S. Joint Chiefs of Staff, the highest military position in the country. Powell, age fifty-two, became the first African American to occupy the position and the youngest man to lead the Joint Chiefs.

Powell, the son of West Indian immigrants, was born in the Harlem section of New York City on April 5, 1937. He received a

Gen. Colin Powell at a West Point graduation. (AP/Wide World Photos.)

bachelor's degree from the City College of New York in 1958 and an M.B.A. from George Washington University in 1971. In 1975–76, he attended the National War College.

Powell was commissioned a second lieutenant in the army in 1958 and was promoted to full general in 1989. He was also a staff officer at the Pentagon (1974–75); brigade commander, 101st Airborne Division, (1976–77); senior military assistant to the deputy secretary of defense (1977–81); deputy commander of Fort Carson, Colorado (1981–82); deputy commander at Fort Leavenworth, Kansas (1982–83); senior military assistant to the secretary of defense (1983–86); commander, Fifth Corps U.S. Army, Europe (1986–87); and deputy assistant and assistant to the president for national security affairs (1987–89). Prior to being named chairman of the Joint Chiefs, he was commander in chief, Forces Command, Fort McPherson, Georgia.

After the Iran-Contra diplomat scandal in 1987, Powell, then a lieutenant-general and national security advisor to President Ronald Reagan, restored order to the National Security Council (NSC). John Poindexter, a previous NSC advisor, had been implicated in the arms deal with Iran, with some of the profits allegedly illegally sent to rebels (Contras) in Nicaragua. After becoming chairman of the Joint Chiefs, Powell directed the American invasion of Panama, which led to the arrest of its leader, Manuel Antonio Noriega, on drug trafficking charges.

Former secretary of defense Caspar Weinberger, under whom Powell served in the Pentagon, once described the general as "the quintessential soldier. He has a remarkable understanding of the great issues of our times, the problems in world affairs, and how our government operates."

AUGUST 21, 1989   Bomb Exploded in NAACP Offices. Fifteen people, including a four-month-old baby girl, were injured when a parcel exploded in the offices of the Southeast regional NAACP in Atlanta, Georgia. The injuries, mostly eye irritations and congestion, resulted from a tear-gas bomb but were not considered serious.

John Lewis, an African American congressman from Georgia who was giving a speech nearby when the incident occurred, called the attack "another form of harassment and intimidation that seeks to have a chilling effect on individuals and organizations who may want to do something about racism." He added, "I thought it was over."

AUGUST 22, 1989   Black Panther Co-founder Newton Killed. Huey P. Newton, a co-founder of the Black Panther Party, was shot to death in Oakland, California. He was forty-seven years old.

Since the demise of his racial activism in the 1960s, Newton continued to have numerous encounters with law enforcement and the criminal justice system. In 1974, he was charged with pistol-whipping his tailor, possession of a handgun, and murdering a seventeen-year-old prostitute. Before his murder trial, Newton fled to Cuba but returned to face the charges in 1977. He was tried twice on the murder charge, but both trials ended in mistrials with the juries deadlocked in favor of acquittal. The charges were later dismissed in 1979. In 1978, Newton was convicted of possession of a handgun, but was acquitted on the charge of assaulting his tailor after the alleged victim refused to testify against him. Newton served nine months in California's San Quentin Prison on the gun charge in 1987. In March of 1989, Newton was sentenced to six months in jail after pleading no contest to charges of misappropriating $15,000 in public monies which had been given for a school the Black Panther Party had operated in the early 1980s.

At the time of his death, Newton, who had earned a Ph.D. degree in social philosophy from the University of California at Santa Cruz in 1980, was attempting to rehabilitate himself from alcohol and drug abuse.

After Newton's death, Charles Garry, his attorney, called Newton the founder of "the renaissance of the black liberation movement." He said the Panther leader had "a very sweet side, a humane side, a dignified side, a man who was theoretically in favor of a better world."

AUGUST 23, 1989   African American Youth Killed in Racial Assault. Yusef Hawkins, a sixteen-year-old African American youth, was shot to death in the predominantly white Bensonhurst section of Brooklyn, New York. Hawkins and three friends had answered an advertisement for a used car when at least thirty whites wielding baseball bats, golf clubs, and at least one pistol attacked them. The whites allegedly thought that Hawkins and his companions had to come into the area to visit a white girl. Police quickly arrested six white youths in connection with the assault.

Following the Bensonhurst incident, the Reverend Al Sharpton and other local civil rights activists led two days of confrontational demonstrations though the largely Italian American neighborhood. The furor was the largest and bitterest in New York since 1986, when a black man was killed while fleeing a white mob in the Howard Beach section of Queens.

AUGUST 26, 1989   "Silent March" Reenacted. About 30,000 people—many of the men dressed in black, and women and children in white—staged a reenactment of the NAACP's famous "Silent March" of 1917 in Washington, D.C. The 1917 march down Fifth Avenue in New York City was held to protest lynching and racial segregation. The 1989 march sought to persuade the U.S. Congress to reverse recent decisions of the U.S. Supreme Court, which civil rights groups and others believed had weakened affirmative action laws and minority "set aside" programs. Many of the demonstrators wore signs reading "What the court has torn asunder, let Congress set right."

One of the speakers at a rally at the U.S. capitol, Joseph Lowery, president of the South-

ern Christian Leadership Conference (SCLC), told the crowd, "We declare here today in no uncertain terms that the path of progress has been filled with pain and suffering and sacrifice, and that we're fed up and fired up . . . We don't intend to sit by and watch the meager gains washed away by a flood tide of insidious insensitivity nor invidious individualism . . . In other words, we ain't going back."

AUGUST 28, 1989   Protest Riot Occurred in New Jersey. Forty businesses and twenty cars were damaged in Vineland, New Jersey, after two hundred blacks rioted in protest of the slaying of Samuel Williams, a twenty-six-year-old black man, by police on August 27. Twenty-three people were arrested in the city of 54,000, located forty miles southeast of Philadelphia, Pennsylvania.

Williams, who was being sought by police on drug and weapon charges, allegedly attacked officers with a rod as they attempted to arrest him. No drugs or weapons were found on Williams's body. The state attorney general's office took over the investigation.

AUGUST 30, 1989   Mourners Attended Funeral for Slain Youth. More than three hundred mourners attended funeral services for Yusef Hawkins, an African American youth slain in New York City. Another one thousand persons who could not enter the church stood outside singing and listening to the eulogy. Hawkins had been shot to death on August 23 in the predominantly white Bensonhurst section of Brooklyn.

The Reverend Al Sharpton, a civil rights activist who lead protests immediately following the killing, said in one of the eulogies, "We're not going to let you down. . . . They're going to pay this time, Yusef. It's time for us to change our ways. We can run a man for the White House, but we can't walk a child through Bensonhurst." Another speaker, Minister Louis Farrakhan, a leader of the Nation of Islam, proclaimed: "We say, as the Jews say, never again, never again, never again . . . As long as white children can get away with killing black children, and white law enforcement does not know how to make examples of its own . . . then justice is far off." The church's pastor, the Reverend Curtis Wells, exhorted, "Let freedom ring from Howard Beach, Mr. Mayor" (addressing New York mayor Edward Koch) . . . "Let freedom ring from Bensonhurst. We're not going to take it anymore. We're going to walk where we want to walk." Mayor Koch, New York governor Mario M. Cuomo, and Republican mayoral candidate Rudolph W. Giuliani were heckled outside the church, and Koch left the ceremonies through a side door. Others attending the funeral included African American mayoral candidate David Dinkins and black filmmaker Spike Lee.

AUGUST 31, 1989   Thousands Joined Protest March in Brooklyn. More than seven thousand people chanting "No more!" and "Whose street? Our street!" marched through the downtown section of Brooklyn, New York, in further protests of the killing of sixteen-year-old Yusef Hawkins. Hawkins, a black youth, was shot and killed in Brooklyn on August 23.

The march turned violent after reaching the Brooklyn Bridge, where police had set up barricades. The marchers ran through the barricade, shouting "Take the bridge, take the bridge!" Hand-to-hand battles erupted between demonstrators and police. The rioters also threw bottles and rocks at police officers, who freely wielded their nightsticks. At least twenty-three police officers were injured, only one seriously. There were no immediate reports of injuries to civilians.

SEPTEMBER 3, 1989   Labor Day Festivities Ended in Violence. Four people were injured (two by gunfire) and at least 160 were arrested during a confrontation between police and black college students in Virginia Beach, Virginia. An estimated ten thousand people, mostly black collegians from Eastern colleges and universi-

ties, had gone to the resort city for Labor Day frolicking. The police department said that more than one hundred businesses were looted in the riot. Some students who witnessed the melee said law enforcement authorities overreacted to their activities.

SEPTEMBER 8, 1989   Justice Marshall Criticized Supreme Court Rulings. U.S. Supreme Court Justice Thurgood Marshall told a group of federal judges meeting at Bolton Landing, New York, that a recent series of high Court decisions had "put at risk not only the civil rights of minorities but the civil rights of all citizens." The Supreme Court's only black justice was referring to several rulings during the 1989 term of the Court that struck severe blows to the notions of affirmative action programs and minority "set aside" laws. In a rare criticism of colleagues on the high bench, Marshall also said "it is difficult to characterize last term's decisions as the product of anything other than a deliberate retrenching of the civil rights agenda." But he warned, "We forget at our peril [that] civil rights and liberty rights [are] inexorably intertwined."

SEPTEMBER 11, 1989   Scholastic Aptitude Test Condemned for Bias Against Minorities. *USA Today* reported new criticisms of the Scholastic Aptitude Test (SAT) for alleged bias against blacks and other minorities. The complaints against the SAT, the nation's best known college admission test, were contained in a book by John Weiss, Barbara Beckwith, and Bob Schaeffer entitled *Standing Up to the SAT*. The authors emphasized that the SAT employed vocabulary that unfairly penalized low income and minority students because they were unfamiliar with them. The *USA Today* report cited terms like regatta, melodeon, and heirloom as examples of such words. But Donald Stewart, the African American president of the College Board, which conceived, developed, and owns the SAT, said "it's reverse racism that holds certain assumptions about a race or a gender and what they should know. . . . That's an insult. . . . If there is a bias in the test, it's the same bias we have in American education."

SEPTEMBER 11, 1989 Occurrence of Racism Encounters Reported in Poll. After recent racial tensions and violence, including the killing of young blacks in predominantly white neighborhoods in New York City, a *USA Today* poll found that 60 percent of America's blacks encounter racism at least occasionally. Higher-income African Americans reported that they experienced racism more than poor blacks. Blacks who reside in southern states reported less racism than blacks in other regions of the country. Another finding was that 71 percent of the blacks surveyed would like to live in integrated neighborhoods, although 53 percent live in largely black areas.

USA Today also asked a number of prominent African Americans to offer solutions to the nation's racial problems. Eleanor Holmes Norton, a professor of law at Georgetown University and former chairperson of the Equal Employment Opportunity Commission (EEOC), suggested that "there needs to be a continuing public, conciliatory dialogue between racial and cultural groups so that those who continue to harbor racial prejudice feel isolated. We need to talk these things out, not act them out. . . . Black-white relations between average Americans are not hostile—they simply are not close enough. The kind of integrated society that has been hypothesized simply has not yet been achieved." Tony Brown, executive producer and host of PBS's "Tony Brown's Journal," remarked: "It doesn't surprise me that southern blacks find less racism. If blacks had marched in Bensonhurst and Howard Beach 30 years ago instead of Selma [Alabama], then the whites in Bensonhurst and Howard Beach would be as sensitive today to racism as whites in Selma are. . . . What blacks must do is through our achievements, through our own unity, through faith in ourselves, through sharing our resources, we must make these gains that will destroy the environmental supports [of racism]." Charles

Moody, Sr., vice president for minority affairs at the University of Michigan and founder of the National Alliance of Black School Educators, suggested that "the first thing that people have to do is come to grips with the fact that racism does exist and not be so quick to try to rationalize it away or justify it, but to accept the fact that it's there and begin to do something about it. . . . I think people as individuals can do something about it by looking at themselves and trying to change that part of the institution or community that they have control over."

SEPTEMBER 16, 1989 African American Crowned Miss America. Debbye Turner, a twenty-three-year-old black veterinary student at the University of Missouri, was crowned Miss America at the 68th Annual Miss America pageant in Atlantic City, New Jersey. Turner, a born-again Christian, became the third African American woman to hold the beauty and talent title. Of this achievement, Turner stated: "Being black is the very least of who I am. I had nothing to do with it, and that's not a landmark. I just came that way."

SEPTEMBER 16, 1989 Michael Jackson Listed as World's Highest Paid Entertainer. *Forbes* magazine estimated that African American pop singer Michael Jackson would make $65 million in 1989 and would remain "the world's highest paid entertainer." The magazine placed his total earnings for 1988–89 at $125 million.

Other African Americans on the *Forbes* list of the highest paid entertainers for 1988–9 were actor-comedian Bill Cosby ($95 million); boxer Mike Tyson ($71 million); actor-comedian Eddie Murphy ($57 million); talk-show hostess and actress Oprah Winfrey ($55 million); boxer Sugar Ray Leonard ($42 million); and recording artist Prince ($36 million).

SEPTEMBER 19, 1989 Fraternity Members Involved in Racial Harassment. Gerald Turner, chancellor of the University of Mississippi, apologized to officials at predominantly black Rust College after members of a fraternity at his university dumped two naked white pledges, whose bodies were painted with racial slurs, on the Rust campus. The two naked pledges of the Beta Theta Pi fraternity with "KKK" and "We Hate Niggers" painted on their chests ran into the Rust College security office in Holly Springs while escaping pursuing students. In addition to his own apology, Chancellor Turner had directed officers of the Beta Theta Pi fraternity to also extend an apology to Rust College. The black private school is located about twenty-five miles from the University of Mississippi campus at Oxford.

SEPTEMBER 20, 1989 House Voted to Subpoena HUD Secretary Pierce The employment and housing subcommittee of the Government Operations Committee of the House of Representatives voted unanimously to subpoena former Housing and Urban Development (HUD) secretary Samuel R. Pierce, Jr., to testify about alleged influence-peddling and mismanagement at the department he headed for eight years during the administration of President Ronald Reagan. The subpoena was issued after Pierce demanded a third delay on the eve of his scheduled voluntary testimony on September 15. Pierce's attorney, Paul L. Perito, said the former secretary—who had appeared voluntarily before the subcommittee in May—was willing to testify but needed two additional weeks for preparation. But Representative Ted Weiss from New York, a member of the subcommittee, charged that "rather than coming forth and clearing the record . . . he is toying with the subcommittee in order to evade or avoid his responsibility." The subcommittee ordered Pierce to make his first appearance on September 26.

The former HUD secretary, who served from 1981 to 1989, was the only African American appointed to the cabinet of former President Reagan.

SEPTEMBER 20, 1989 Colin Powell Nominated Chairman of Joint Chiefs of Staff. The Armed Services Committee of the U.S. Senate voted unanimously to approve the nomination of General Colin L. Powell as chairman of the Joint Chiefs of Staff. The vote cleared the way for Powell to become the first African American to lead the joint military forces of the United States.

SEPTEMBER 20, 1989 Two National Magazines Targeted African American Readers. The *Atlanta Constitution* reported that two new national magazines targeted for African American audiences were beginning publication. *Sazz*, a women's fashion magazine, was founded by Mary Anne Holley, and *Emerge*, a national news monthly, was founded by Wilmer Ames. The New York City-based magazines were the first national black-oriented periodicals to surface since the mid-1980s, according to Samir Husni, a journalism professor at the University of Mississippi who specializes in new magazines. Both publications arose at a time, however, when the magazine industry in general was facing declining circulations, and black magazines in particular were "facing a tough battle for advertising dollars." Both were aimed at "upscale black readers," i.e., higher income and college-educated blacks.

Prior to the appearances of *Sazz* and *Emerge*, several other recent attempts at publishing national black magazines had failed. These included *Elan, Elancee, Excell, Modern Black Man (MBM), Spice,* and *Black Teen.* The most successful black magazines continued to be *Ebony, Jet, Ebony Man,* and *Essence,* geared toward women; and *Black Enterprise,* aimed at the black entrepreneur. All of these are produced by Chicago's Johnson Publishing Co. *Ebony* was founded in 1945 and had a circulation of 1.8 million in 1989; *Jet,* a news weekly, was founded in 1951 and reported a circulation of 892,000 in 1989. Both *Essence* and *Black Enterprise* were founded in 1970, and had circulations of 850,000 and 230,000, respectively, in 1989; and *Ebony Man,* which first appeared in 1985, had gained a circulation of 205,000 by 1989.

SEPTEMBER 24, 1989 Clark-Atlanta University Named Cole President. Thomas W. Cole, Jr., former president of West Virginia State College, was inaugurated as the first president of Clark-Atlanta University. The new institution resulted from a merger of historically black Clark College and Atlanta University on June 26, 1989. Cole had formerly been a professor of chemistry and served as provost at Atlanta University.

OCTOBER 2, 1989 Supreme Court Affirmed Jury Selection Decision in Civil Cases. The U.S. Supreme Court affirmed a decision of the U.S. Court of Appeals for the Eleventh Circuit that prohibited attorneys in civil cases from striking jurors because of their race. Although the Supreme Court had barred criminal prosecutors from using their preemptory challenges in a racially discriminatory fashion in 1986, the Eleventh Circuit was one of the first courts in the nation to extend the rule to civil cases.

The case reached the Supreme Court from Richmond County, Georgia, (of which Augusta is the county seat) where a black man sued a white deputy sheriff who had "accidentally" shot him while arresting him on suspicion of drugs. In 1982, an all-white jury found in favor of the defendants, deputy sheriff Frank Tiller and former sheriff J. D. Dykes. However the plaintiff, Willie Fludd, contended that the jury selection process was biased and appealed the decision.

OCTOBER 3, 1989 Maynard Jackson Reelected Atlanta Mayor. Maynard Holbrook Jackson was elected to a new term as mayor of Atlanta, Georgia. Jackson scored a landslide victory over city councilman and veteran civil rights activist Hosea Williams to return to City Hall. Jackson won 82 percent of the votes to less than 20 percent for Williams. Jackson's victory had become all but certain after a more formidable candidate, Michael Lomax, the African American chairman of the Fulton County Commission, withdrew from the race on Au-

gust 8, 1989. When polls consistently showed that Lomax would also lose decisively to Jackson, the commissioner withdrew rather than jeopardize his seat on the county body.

Jackson was first elected mayor of Atlanta in 1973, becoming the first African American to be elected mayor of a major Southern city since the Reconstruction era. He served two terms until 1982, when he became ineligible for another successive reelection. Between terms in the mayor's office, Jackson had served as a corporate attorney in Chicago and Atlanta.

OCTOBER 3, 1989 Art Shell Named Head Coach of Los Angeles Raiders. Art Shell, former lineman for the Oakland Raiders of the National Football League (NFL) and a member of the Professional Football's Hall of Fame, was named head coach of the Los Angeles Raiders. The appointment made Shell, age forty-two, the first black head coach in the NFL since Fritz Pollard was a player-coach for the Hammond (Indiana) Pros in 1923–25.

Shell's selection came just one day before the fifteenth anniversary of the appointment of Frank Robinson as the first black manager in major league baseball. Robinson was first hired by the Cleveland Indians. The first black head coach in professional basketball, which has had more blacks in this position than any other professional sport, was Bill Russell of the Boston Celtics, who served in 1966–67.

Shell called his appointment "an historic event," but did not believe that "the color of my skin entered into [the] decision."

OCTOBER 6, 1989 Racial Discrimination Suit Filed Against Restaurant Chain. Two former employees of Shoney's restaurants—one black, one white—filed a lawsuit in the Federal Court for the Northern District of Georgia, alleging that the restaurant chain practiced racial discrimination. The suit claimed that the managers of Shoney's franchises in the metropolitan Atlanta area discriminated by limiting the type and number of jobs offered to blacks as well as their chances of promotion. It also alleged that the company retaliated against non-black employees "who [refused] to implement their racist policies."

The black plaintiff, Jackie Montgomery, claimed she was forbidden to work in a Shoney's dining room because of the restaurant's policy that "blacks should not be allowed out front," particularly in facilities located in predominantly white neighborhoods. The white plaintiff, Cylinda Adams, asserted that she complained to several supervisors about the alleged racism and was fired because of it.

The Atlanta suit was filed only four months after a similar allegation was brought before the courts in Florida and only two months after Shoney's executives signed an affirmative action agreement with the Southern Christian Leadership Conference (SCLC). In that accord, Shoney's promised to provide $90 million in jobs and minority business participation over the next three years. The agreement also included recruitment and training of blacks in managerial positions, and pledged to provide scholarships to African American students interested in the food service industry. Shoney's chief executive officer, J. Mitchell Boyd, had said that there was "no real connection" between the lawsuit filed in Pensacola, Florida, in June and the firm's agreement with SCLC.

OCTOBER 10, 1989   School Board in Georgia Voted for Desegregated Bus Routes. The school board of White County, Georgia, voted unanimously to begin new desegregated bus routes, thus ending nine years of segregated busing in the area. The school board members claimed that they had only recently been made aware of the segregated routes. The board's chairman, Bob Owens, said in a public apology, "Our community has taken pride as a leader in public integration. For a black bus route to be scheduled into two predominantly black communities and to be operated for an extended period of time is . . . unacceptable."

The dual busing system came to the board's attention after Jimmy Bolinger, the school system's new director of transportation, reported that nine of the twenty-three school routes were overcrowded with white students; meanwhile Andy Allen, the county's only black school bus driver, complained that she crossed the county to pick up black children, yet her bus was only half full.

OCTOBER 11, 1989   Court of Appeals Ruled in Favor of Desegregating School System. The U.S. Court of Appeals for the Eleventh Circuit ruled that the Dekalb County, Georgia, school board must dismantle its segregated neighborhood school system and consider "forced busing" of students to achieve greater desegregation. The Court of Appeals also declared that Dekalb County must consider "drastic gerrymandering" or redrawing of school attendance zones and "dramatically expanded magnet schools" to expand its desegregation.

The court overturned a June 1988 decision by U.S. District Court judge William C. O'Kelley, that ruled the Dekalb school board had done all that it could to desegregate its schools. O'Kelley agreed with the board's argument that housing patterns were the primary cause of any remaining school segregation. The appeals court disagreed and ruled that the Dekalb school system "may not shirk its constitutional duties by pointing to demographic shifts. . . . [The] system has a continuing constitutional duty to achieve the greatest possible degree of desegregation and to prevent segregation."

OCTOBER 11, 1989   Survey Reported African Americans More Likely to Be Committed to Psychiatric Hospitals. The Institute for Southern Study released a report that stated that African Americans are nearly three times as likely as whites to be committed against their will to the seventy-two public psychiatric hospitals in nine southern states. The survey found that commitment rates for blacks and whites differed most in Florida, where blacks were 4.8 times as likely as whites to be committed. In

Georgia, blacks were twice as likely as whites to be committed. Blacks in Mississippi and South Carolina were committed 1.8 times as often as whites.

Eric Bates, who supervised the study for the institute's *Southern Exposure* magazine, said there was "no simple answer why blacks are committed more than whites, but racism clearly plays a part."

OCTOBER 11, 1989 Educator J. Rupert Picott Died. J. Rupert Picott, educator and lobbyist, died of cancer in Washington, D.C., at age sixty-nine. Picott, a native of Suffolk, Virginia, received his undergraduate training from Virginia Union University in Richmond, a master's degree in education from Temple University in Philadelphia, and a doctorate in education from Harvard University. In the 1940s, he became executive secretary of the black Virginia Teachers Association. After the decision of the U.S. Supreme Court in *Brown v. Board of Education* in 1954, when some school systems in Virginia attempted to fire some of their black teachers in the wake of desegregation, Picott moved to protect the jobs of the blacks. He became best known as executive director of the Association for the Study of Afro-American Life and History (ASALH), where he served between 1969 and 1985. In this position, Picott lobbied for the promotion of the study and celebration of African American history and succeeded in getting both state and federal governments to proclaim February as Black History Month.

OCTOBER 11–12, 1989 Violence Erupted at Alabama High School. The principal and a student of Minor High School in Adamsville, Alabama, were stabbed during a fight between black and white students.

Principal Judson Jones, who received a two-inch knife wound to his stomach in the altercation, said tensions had escalated for several days, with several fights between blacks and whites in the previous week. In an effort to bring peace, he had called for additional police officers to patrol the grounds of the school and ordered all black students into the cafeteria and all whites into the gymnasium as they entered the school on October 11. But when Jones took a group of white students to the cafeteria to meet with the blacks, a fight erupted that quickly spread to other areas of the building.

Seven students were arrested at the school on October 11 on charges ranging from disorderly conduct to attempted murder. On October 12, two additional students were incarcerated on charges of possessing alcohol and weapons.

William James, a black senior at Minor High School, told newspaper reporters that the school's problems were not new. "There's always been racial trouble here. . . . They didn't want us here anyway."

These racial disturbances in Alabama were a part of the growing number of such encounters on high school and college campuses throughout the year.

OCTOBER 12, 1989 NAACP and Justice Department Threatened Restaurant Owner with Discrimination Suit. A North Augusta, South Carolina, restaurant owner, Rose Salter, announced that she would begin serving African Americans in her establishment. Salter's declaration was made during a hearing before the South Carolina Alcoholic Beverage Control (ABC) Commission, which was considering revoking the liquor license of the Buffalo Room Restaurant and Lounge for barring six black government and NAACP officials from the premises in early September. As a result of the incident, both the NAACP and the Justice Department threatened to file suit against the restaurant's proprietors for illegal discrimination. During the investigation, it was revealed that the Buffalo Room had discriminated against blacks for the past twelve years.

OCTOBER 12, 1989 Civil Rights Leaders Condemned Abernathy's Memoirs. Several of the nation's civil rights leaders sent a telegram to the Reverend Ralph David Abernathy, former president of the Southern Christian Leadership Conference (SCLC), urging him to repudiate sections of his published memoirs that claimed that the late Dr. Martin Luther King, Jr., spent part of the last night of his life with two different women. The accusations were made in Abernathy's autobiography, *And The Walls Came Tumbling Down,* which had been released earlier in the month.

The civil rights leaders told Abernathy in a "message of pain and love" that "as friends and beneficiaries of the King dream, we are shocked and appalled by some of the statements in your new book." One of the signers of the telegram, John Hurst Adams, president of the National Congress of Black Churches, charged that the book was "riddled with gross inaccuracies and painful distortions." Another signer, NAACP executive secretary Benjamin Hooks, called the book "criminally irresponsible." Hooks took particular issue with Abernathy's account of an alleged encounter between King and a woman on the eve of the assassination. While Abernathy placed King in the woman's home at 1 a.m., Hooks recalled that he was with the civil rights leader at the Mason Temple in Memphis, where he had delivered his final sermon, at that hour.

Others who endorsed the message to Abernathy included U.S. representatives Ronald V. Dellums, William H. Gray III, John Lewis, Floyd H. Flake, Alan D. Wheat, Walter D. Fauntroy, former representative Parren Mitchell, Southern Christian Leadership Conference president Joseph L. Lowery, Operation PUSH leader Reverend Jesse L. Jackson, and Atlanta mayor Andrew J. Young.

In his response, Abernathy asserted: "In including some of the things in the book, I have had to agonize, balancing my need to tell a complete and honest story with what I know to be my responsibility to respect the privacy and dignity of the living and the dead. . . . I can only

say that I have written nothing in malice and omitted nothing out of cowardice."

OCTOBER 18, 1989 Allen Resigned as Civil Rights Commission Chairman. The White House revealed that President George Bush had accepted the resignation of William Barclay Allen as chairman of the U.S. Commission on Civil Rights. During his tenure, Allen, a California professor, had created repeated controversies that led to criticism of his leadership both inside and outside the commission. A recent controversy arose when he gave a speech entitled "Blacks? Animals? Homosexuals? What Is a Minority?" to the California Coalition for Traditional Values.

OCTOBER 20, 1989 Judge Hastings Impeached by Senate. Alcee L. Hastings, a black U.S. District Court judge from Florida, was convicted by the U.S. Senate on eight articles of impeachment relating to conspiracy and perjury. He became the sixth federal official in American history to be removed from office by impeachment. The vote to convict Hastings was 69-26.

Originally, Hastings was charged with seventeen articles of impeachment by the U.S. House of Representatives, but the Senate acquitted him on three of the articles and took no action on the six others.

Hastings, age fifty-three, was appointed to the federal bench in 1979 by President Jimmy Carter. He was the first African American to serve in this position in Florida. After the verdict, Hastings remarked, "I don't accept this as a reading of Al Hastings the man. I didn't commit a crime. . . . There may be something about me—my outspokenness and what have you—that allows that maybe it's best that I'm out of this particular arena." He announced that he would later seek the Democratic nomination for governor of Florida.

OCTOBER 23, 1989 Farrakhan Delivered "Savior's Day Message." Louis Farrakhan, minister of the Nation of Islam, delivered his "Savior's Day Message" before a crowd of twelve thousand people in Washington, D.C. Speaking on the theme "Stop the Killing," Farrakhan said the black people of Washington, D.C., were "brought to nothing in this society by their former slavemasters . . . and [were] being kept as nothing by the cruel hand of the government."

OCTOBER 24, 1989 Ralph Abernathy's Autobiography Disputed. In a news conference in Washington, D.C., Abjua Abi Naantaanbuu, a civil rights activist from Memphis, Tennessee, and Bernard Lee, a veteran civil rights activist, disputed allegations made by Ralph David Abernathy in his autobiography, *And the Walls Came Tumbling Down,* that Dr. Martin Luther King, Jr., may have engaged in extramarital affairs on the night before his assassination in 1968. Naantaanbuu and Lee, who were present when the alleged infidelity occurred, accused Abernathy of being drunk and asleep at the time.

The news conference was sponsored by the Coalition of Friends and Beneficiaries of the Martin Luther King, Jr., Dream, which had taken strong exception to Abernathy's published views ever since they appeared earlier in the year. Members of the Coalition of Friends included civil rights leaders Dick Gregory, Benjamin Hooks, John Lewis, Jesse Jackson, Joseph Lowery, and Andrew Young.

OCTOBER 24, 1989 Restaurant's Liquor License Revoked for Discrimination Practices. Despite the pledge of a North Augusta, South Carolina, restaurant to end its barring of black customers, the South Carolina Alcoholic Beverage Commission revoked its liquor license. The Commission said the action to end discrimination was "very fragile and will likely continue only so long as official scrutiny is close at hand."

The Buffalo Room Restaurant and Lounge had been under scrutiny by federal and state governments and the NAACP since several

blacks were turned away by its owners on September 5. Within weeks of this incident, the owners, Bruce and Rose Salter, announced that they would serve all people.

NOVEMBER 5, 1989 Monument Dedicated to Martyrs of Civil Rights Movement. Thousands attended the dedication of a monument to martyrs of the Civil Rights Movement in downtown Montgomery, Alabama. Among those in the audience were civil rights activist Julian Bond, Mrs. Ethel Kennedy, widow of slain senator Robert F. Kennedy, and Carolyn Goodman, mother of Andrew Goodman, one of three young civil rights workers slain by Ku Klux Klansmen in Philadelphia, Mississippi, in 1964. Forty names of martyred civil rights activists were inscribed in a great curving circle of black granite built by the Southern Poverty Law Center. Among those honored, in addition to Goodman, were James Chaney and Mickey Schwerner, who were killed with him; Medgar Evers, a Jackson, Mississippi, NAACP leader assassinated in 1966; Emmett Till, a fourteen-year-old black youth murdered in 1955 for speaking to a white woman in Money, Mississippi; Jimmie Lee Jackson, a young black student slain in a civil rights demonstration in Marion, Alabama, in 1965; and Martin Luther King, Jr., the last name on the stone. Some of King's words spoken at the March on Washington in 1963 were inscribed at the back of the monument by sculptress Maya Lin, with water flowing over them: "We will not be satisfied until justice rolls down like waters, and righteousness like a mighty stream."

NOVEMBER 7, 1989 African American Dinkins Elected Mayor of New York. David Dinkins, the sixty-two-year-old president of the borough of Manhattan, was elected mayor of New York City, becoming the first African American to occupy that office. Dinkins, a Democrat, won a narrow victory over the Republican challenger, Rudolph W. Giuliani, and two other candidates. Dinkins captured approximately 898,000 votes to Giuliani's 856,450.

After defeating Democratic mayor Edward I. Koch in the primary election on September 12, Dinkins ran a moderate campaign designed to "soothe, not excite." His campaign theme was an appeal to the city's ethnic diversity, which he termed "a gorgeous mosaic." Some analysts, however, including the *New York Times,* claimed that Dinkins's solutions to New York's problems were "often simple." For example, Dinkins's answer to the city's massive crime problem was to "double community patrol officers and put a cop on every subway train."

Despite the city's recent racial troubles, sparked by the killings of black men in predominately white neighborhoods, Dinkins was able to build a biracial coalition that carried him to victory. At the time of the election, only 25.2 percent of New York City's eight million people were black.

Dinkins's mayoral campaign was also threatened by accusations of personal "financial laxity" and his friendship with former Democratic presidential candidate Jesse L. Jackson. Voters apparently overlooked his "fumbling on questions about his personal finances," while Jackson failed to return to New York after the primary election.

Dinkins, a former marine, entered local politics in the 1950s as a Democratic precinct leader. In 1965, he was elected to the state senate. Dinkins also served as city clerk in New York City before running for president of the borough of Manhattan in 1977. In his first two campaigns for this office, Dinkins lost by wide margins, but finally secured the office in 1985.

NOVEMBER 7, 1989   L. Douglas Wilder Elected Virginia's First African American Governor. L. Douglas Wilder, lieutenant governor of Virginia, was elected the state's first African American governor. The fifty-eight-year-old Wilder, a Democrat, won a narrow victory over his Republican rival, J. Marshall Coleman. Of the more than 1.7 million votes cast, Wilder's margin of victory was only 7,000 votes. He

New York City mayor David Dinkins. (AP/Wide World Photos.)

garnered 888,475 ballots to 881,484 for Coleman (with all but two Virginia precincts counted). In addition to becoming Virginia's first black governor, the victory made Wilder the first black elected governor in American history.

Following his victory, Wilder sought to downplay any expectations that he would seek to become a major spokesman for African Americans, stating, "I don't see a confrontation with anybody. I'm not an activist. I'm not running for president."

NOVEMBER 7, 1989   African Americans Elected Mayors of Major Cities. Several African Americans were elected or reelected mayors in major American cities during general elections. They included Michael White in Cleveland, Ohio; Coleman Young in Detroit, Michigan; Chester Jenkins in Durham, North Carolina; John Daniels in New Haven, Connecticut; and Norm Rice in Seattle, Washington.

In Cleveland, White, a city councilman, became the city's second black mayor. He defeated a fellow African American, city council president George Forbes, 89,829 to 68,167. In Detroit, Young won an unprecedented fifth

L. Douglas Wilder being sworn in as governor of Virginia. (AP/Wide World Photos.)

term, defeating business executive Tom Barrow (a nephew of boxing champion Joe Louis), 138,175 to 107,195. In Durham, Jenkins won the mayor's office over Nelson Strawbridge, 19,381 to 17,118. In New Haven, Daniels captured 19,302 votes (69 percent) in his win over two opponents to become the city's first black mayor. In Seattle, Rice, a Democrat, defeated a Republican, Doug Jewett, by a margin of 93,901 to 67,575 to become the first black mayor of a city with only a 9.5 percent black population.

NOVEMBER 8–20, 1989 Historic Political Victories Assessed. Political leaders, political analysts, journalists, and other commentators assessed the historic victories of L. Douglas Wilder as the nation's first elected black governor in Virginia, and the election of David Dinkins as New York City's first African American mayor.

After Dinkins won the Democratic primary in September 1989, syndicated columnist Carl Rowan suggested that Dinkins's victory was "desperately needed proof that resurgent racism in America can be stopped wherever political, business and other leaders ask the people to walk away from the dark side of man's animal impulses."

In an editorial on November 9, the *Wall Street Journal* said, "There's irony in the failure of Republican candidates to learn the lessons of the Reagan presidency: David Dinkins . . . and Virginia's Doug Wilder . . . ran as 'moderate' Democrats, promising to hold the line on taxes and spending." The newspaper also reported that Wilder "kept [civil rights leader Jesse] Jackson at arm's length during a year-long campaign that stressed his mainstream appeal to white voters. Wilder appealed for economic development, not economic empowerment, and talked about racial issues only under duress."

Cynthia Tucker, an African American columnist for the *Atlanta Journal-Constitution*, wrote that "Mr. Wilder has apparently overcome the color question with a strong pro-choice position. . . . And, [he] has now provided a guidebook to other candidates of color who wish to serve beyond their traditional constituencies."

NOVEMBER 10, 1989 Rhythm and Blues Foundation Presented First Achievement Awards. The Rhythm and Blues Foundation presented its first career achievement awards at the Smithsonian Institution in Washington, D.C. The impetus for the awards came from Howell Begle, a Washington attorney, life-long soul music fan, and admirer of blues singer Ruth Brown. After Begle discovered that Brown and dozens of other rhythm and blues artists had fallen into financial difficulties in the mid-1960s, he established the Rhythm and Blues Foundation to assist them, and later appointed blues singer Ray Charles chairman of the organization. The group eventually amassed an endowment of one and one half million dollars, donated mostly by Atlantic Records Company.

Several of the honorees performed for the audience, including Percy Sledge, whose "When a Man Loves a Woman," was the first soul recording to rise to the top of the pop music charts; Mary Wells, known for her recordings of "My Guy" and "You Beat Me to the Punch;" Charles Brown, who sang "Driftin' Blues" and "Black Night;" and Ruth Brown, often called "Miss Rhythm." In her remarks, Brown recalled the distressing segregated South. "Charles Brown nearly went to jail for me in Mississippi because they wouldn't let me use the bathroom at a gas station. . . . How many buses did we ride together? How many back doors did we go through together?"

Each winner of the Rhythm and Blues Award received a check for $15,000 in order to "right some past wrongs" as well as recognize lifetime achievement.

NOVEMBER 15, 1989 Federal Building Renamed to Honor Leland. President George Bush signed into law a bill to redesignate the Federal building located at 1990 Smith Street in Houston, Texas, as the George Thomas "Mickey" Leland Federal Building in honor of the late African American congressman from Texas who died in a plane crash in Africa on August 7, 1989. The bill was introduced by Democratic representative Jack Brooks from Texas.

NOVEMBER 17, 1989 Gloria Naylor Received Lillian Smith Award. African American writer Gloria Naylor won a Lillian Smith Award for 1989. The award was presented for her third novel, *Mama Day,* which centers on cultural conflict in an all-black sea island community off the coast of South Carolina. The Smith awards were named for the late Georgia civil rights activist, who was also the author of *Strange Fruit.* They "recognize and encourage outstanding writing about the South." In 1983, Naylor won an American Book Award for *The Women of Brewster Place.*

NOVEMBER 17, 1989 Black Leadership Forum Met with Bush. President George Bush met at the White House with leaders of the national Black Leadership Forum (BLF). The blacks told Bush that racism was rising in some areas of the country, particularly on college campuses. They urged him to set "a goal of bringing blacks to 'parity' with the rest of the population" in education, housing, and employment by the year 2000. President Bush made no commitments to the group and expressed surprise "to hear that there was [still] overt racism and he hoped it wasn't true." One of the leaders present, Dorothy Height, president of the National Council of Negro Women (NCNW), remarked, "I think the most significant thing was that [Bush] listened, that he showed a genuine interest." Other members of the BLF present at the meeting included Benjamin Hooks, executive director of the NAACP, Joseph Lowery, president of the Southern Christian Leadership Conference (SCLC), and Coretta Scott King.

NOVEMBER 17, 1989 Dinkins and Wilder Victories Analyzed. Ron Walters, a professor of political science at Howard University, observed that "the key to victory for [David Dinkins and L. Douglas Wilder] was that, in terms of both style and substance, they ran mainstream campaigns tailored to the political realities of their respective jurisdictions. . . . But the new crossover black politics creates an ultimate iro-

Choreographer Alvin Ailey. (AP/Wide World Photos.)

ny for the black voter. Historically the black voter has laid the basis for the emergence of black politicians and has taken heart in their upward mobility. The danger is that the higher they go, the more restrained they will be in pursuing a black political agenda."

Hodding Carter III, a national political commentator, warned that "no one should minimize the distance yet to travel before the mountaintop is achieved. There is no excuse for complacency. But there is also no excuse for refusing to celebrate when, as with last week's election results, real cause for celebration is provided."

NOVEMBER 30, 1989 Racial Protest Occurred at University of Alabama. About two hundred people gathered to protest racism at the Tuscaloosa campus of the University of Alabama and the school's financial investments in the Republic of South Africa. The protest was sparked by an incident that took place during a football game on October 14, when Kimberly Ashely, the university's black homecoming queen, was subjected to jeers by spectators. The protestors also took offense at the prominent display of Confederate flags. University officials contended that less than one percent of its total investments were in South Africa.

DECEMBER 1, 1989 Alvin Ailey Died in New York City. Alvin Ailey, African-American dancer and choreographer, died of a blood disorder in New York City at age fifty-eight.

Ailey was born in the rural town of Rogers, Texas, where he faced discrimination at a very early age. Yet by the time of his death, Ailey had received New York's Handel Medallion and the Samuel H. Scripps American Dance Festival Award for lifetime contributions to modern dance. In 1988, he received Kennedy Center honors in Washington, D.C., for lifetime achievement in the performing arts.

He founded the Alvin Ailey American Dance Theater in 1958 and choreographed seventy-nine ballets. In 1961, Ailey created his best known work, "Revelations," which was based on his childhood experiences in black Baptist churches. The dance became his company's rousing signature piece.

Ailey also had a penchant for honoring the works of others whom he admired or with whose causes he sympathized. For example, he choreographed "For Bird with Love" as a tribute to jazz saxophonist Charlie "Bird" Parker, whose career was shortened by drug abuse. While Ailey refused to allow his company to perform in the Republic of South Africa, he choreographed, in collaboration with jazz drummer Max Roach, "Survivors," in honor of South African anti-apartheid activists Nelson and Winnie Mandela.

Although Ailey retired from performing twenty years before his death, he created "a choreographic style distinctly his own—a combination of modern, ballet, jazz, and ethnic [dance]." Professor Richard Long, author of *The Black Tradition in American Dance,* called Ailey "the best-known American dancer in the world."

DECEMBER 6, 1989 African American Culture Scholar Nathan Huggins Died. Nathan I. Huggins, a leading scholar of African American culture, died of cancer in Boston, Massachusetts, at the age of sixty-two. Huggins was the author of works on black anti-slavery leader Frederick Douglass and on the Harlem Renaissance, the black cultural movement of the 1920s. Since 1980, he had been professor of history and Afro-American Studies and director of the W. E. B. Du Bois Institute for Afro-American Research at Harvard University.

DECEMBER 7, 1989 Percy Snow Awarded Vince Lombardi Trophy. Percy Snow, African American linebacker for the Michigan State University Spartans, was awarded the Vince Lombardi trophy in Houston, Texas. The Lombardi trophy, named for the legendary coach of the Green Bay Packers, is awarded every year to the nation's top collegiate lineman. On December 5, Snow had also won a Dick Butkus Award for his outstanding feats as a linebacker. At the time, Snow held the Michigan State record of 164 tackles.

DECEMBER 9, 1989 Craig Washington Elected Texas Representative. Craig A. Washington, a Houston, Texas, attorney, was elected to the U.S. House of Representatives from the predominately black Eighteenth Congressional District. Washington defeated Houston city councilman Anthony Hall to take the seat

formerly held by Mickey Leland, who died in a plane crash in Ethiopia on August 7, 1989.

DECEMBER 11, 1989 Convictions Reversed in Racial Murder Trial. A state appeals court in New York reversed the convictions of three white men who were found guilty in the 1986 death of Michael Griffith, a black man, in the Howard Beach section of Queens, New York. The unanimous ruling found that Thomas A. Demakos, the trial judge, had made two errors in his charge to the jury. He had, the higher court said, supplied the jury with verdict sheets that contained the charges against the defendants (which improperly described some of the alleged crimes) and he had improperly refused to instruct the jury on disorderly conduct, a lesser offense than the ones with which the defendants were charged.

The three defendants, William Bollander, Thomas Farino, and James Povinelli, all aged nineteen, were convicted in 1988 of second degree riot charges for their part in the racial attack on December 20, 1986.

DECEMBER 16–19, 1989 Mail Bombs Used in Racial Attacks. On December 16, a mail bomb exploded in the home of Robert S. Vance, a judge on the U.S. Court of Appeals for the Eleventh Circuit, in Birmingham, Alabama. The Eleventh Circuit had handled many civil rights cases, including some covering school desegregation, over the past decade. On December 18, a mail bomb exploded in the office of Robert E. Robinson, an attorney in Savannah, Georgia, who had represented the NAACP and other clients in civil rights cases. The bombs, which were sent to Vance and Robinson in parcels addressed to them, killed both men instantly. The FBI announced on December 18 that it suspected white supremacists in the mail bombings. Earl Shinhoster, southeast regional director of the NAACP, whose office was the target of an earlier mailed tear-gas bomb, called the attacks "a very serious situation."

DECEMBER 18–20, 1989   FBI Investigated Mail Bombs. On December 19, a mail bomb was found and defused at the U.S. Court of Appeals for the Eleventh Circuit in Atlanta, Georgia. The Appeals Court had handled many of the South's civil rights suits over the past decade. That same day, a mail bomb found outside the headquarters of the Jacksonville, Florida, chapter of the NAACP did not explode. The FBI announced that the packages were mailed from Georgia, as were the bombs that killed federal judge Robert Vance and Savannah, Georgia, attorney Robert Robinson on December 16 and 18. The FBI also said it suspected the same person (or persons) was responsible for all of the incidents.

DECEMBER 21, 1989   Federal Housing Law Violated. A U.S. administrative law judge in Atlanta, Georgia, ordered Gordon C. Blackwell, a real estate broker, to pay $75,000 to a black couple whom he had discriminated against in the sale of a house. Judge Alan W. Heifetz also found that Blackwell, a sixty-six-year-old resident of Sandy Springs, Georgia, had flouted the civil rights of Terryl and Janella Herron by refusing to close the sale of a Stone Mountain, Georgia, home. He also ordered the broker to complete the sale of the house.

The case was the first in the nation under the recently enacted federal law, which "provides quicker and harsher penalties if bias is proved." Gordon H. Mansfield, assistant secretary for fair housing at the Department of Housing and Urban Development (HUD), said the case was "a landmark in civil rights enforcement . . . making housing discrimination expensive as well as unlawful."

DECEMBER 24, 1989   First African American Mayor of New Orleans Died. Ernest Nathan "Dutch" Morial, the first black mayor of New Orleans, Louisiana, died of an apparent heart attack in New Orleans at age sixty.

Morial was born in New Orleans on October 9, 1929, to Walter and Leonie Morial. He became the first black law school graduate of Louisiana State University in 1954.

Morial's public service career began in 1960 when he was elected president of the NAACP chapter in New Orleans. He worked with civil rights activist A. P. Tureard in filing suits against segregation in public facilities and institutions in the city. In 1965, Morial became the first black assistant U.S. attorney in Louisiana, and in 1967 the first black legislator since the Reconstruction era. He also served as a member of the State House of Representatives from 1967 to 1970, and became the first black elected to Louisiana's 4th Circuit Court of Appeals in 1973.

In 1977, on the strength of a huge black vote, Morial became New Orleans' first black mayor. As mayor for two terms, he faced rampant floods in 1978, a police strike that crippled the city's annual Mardi Gras festival in 1979, and a financially plagued World's exposition in 1984. Morial left office in 1986 following an unsuccessful attempt to amend the city charter to allow the mayor to serve a third four-year term. Nationally, Morial had been a president of the National Conference of Mayors, a member of the Democratic National Committee (DNC), and one of the key black advisors to Democratic presidential candidate Michael S. Dukakis in 1988.

After Morial's death, his predecessor, former mayor Moon Landrieu, remarked: "Dutch was the first black individual to achieve high public office in this state. . . . That alone I think is a very significant achievement."

Chapter 11

1990 TO 1996

1990

JANUARY 9, 1990 Economic Aid Program Recommended. The National Urban League (NUL) said that in order "to close the economic gap" between black and white Americans, a $50 billion aid program, similar to the one that rebuilt Europe after World War II (the Marshall Plan) was needed. In the 15th Annual "The State of Black America" Report, the NUL contended that the fiscal and social policies of the administration of former president Ronald Reagan had helped "stall the efforts of blacks to achieve greater economic parity" with whites in the 1980s. The report added, however, that the "greater openness" of the administration of President George Bush had "inspired new confidence in the federal government's ability to complete our unfinished revolution for democracy and human rights."

JANUARY 10, 1990 African American Named Brigadier General. Marcelite J. Harris, a forty-six-year-old native of Houston, Texas, was named brigadier general in the U.S. Air Force. She was the first African American woman to hold this rank in that branch of the Armed Services.

Harris earned a bachelor's degree in business management from the University of Maryland. She was the Air Force's first female aircraft maintenance officer. In 1975 Harris

was named personnel staff officer at Air Force Headquarters in Washington, D.C., where she also served as a White House aide to former president Jimmy Carter.

JANUARY 10, 1990 Black Population Increased in Southern U.S. The Bureau of the Census reported that the proportion of blacks living in the Southern region of the United States increased from 1980 to 1988, the first such rise in this century. Fifty-six percent of all blacks resided in the South in 1988, compared with 52 percent in 1980. The proportion had been declining since the beginning of the century when it was at 90 percent.

The Northeast was the only region in the 1980s to show a significant decline in the proportion of its black population, dropping from 19 percent to 17 percent. The proportion for the Midwest (19 percent) and West (8 percent), according to the Bureau, did not change significantly.

The number of blacks living in the South in 1988 totaled 16.4 million, an increase of 2.8 million since 1980.

JANUARY 13, 1990 Lawrence Wilder Inaugurated Virginia Governor. Lawrence Douglas Wilder was inaugurated as governor of Virginia, making him the first African American elected chief executive of a state in American history. The only other black to occupy a governor's office was P. B. S. Pinchback, who served as acting governor of Louisiana for a month at the end of 1872.

Wilder, the grandson of slaves, was born in Richmond, Virginia, in 1931, the seventh of eight children of Robert and Beulah Wilder. He received a bachelor's degree in chemistry from Virginia Union University in 1951 and a law degree from the Howard University School of Law in 1959. Returning immediately to his Church Hill neighborhood in Richmond to open a law practice, Wilder "soon developed a reputation for flamboyance, driving convertibles and breezing into court, all smiles and trendy clothes, to take on difficult criminal cases."

Wilder's political career began in 1970, when he was elected to the Virginia state senate. There he spearheaded a campaign to make the birthday of Martin Luther King, Jr., a state holiday. The best he could achieve, however, was the addition of King's name to a holiday for Confederate generals Robert E. Lee and Thomas "Stonewall" Jackson. Although he had not been an active participant in the Civil Rights Movement of the 1960s, Wilder began his tenure in the senate with "a blistering attack" on the state song "Carry Me Back to Old Virginny." He and other blacks objected to "the sentimental [melody] about a slave pining for the plantation," which included such lyrics as "There's where this old darky's heart am long'd to go" and "There's where I labor'd so hard for old massa." Although the song was not removed, its playing at public functions was greatly diminished.

Wilder remained in the state senate until 1986, when he was lieutenant-governor. At the time, he was the only black serving in that position in the country, but gained increasing popularity in the state for his opposition to a sales tax increase. When Wilder began his campaign for governor, he changed his position against the expansion of the death penalty to support for its more frequent use. He also went from a vague position on a woman's right to an abortion to an enthusiastic supporter of that

right, after polls showed that some two-thirds of Virginians supported a woman's right to choose. Following his election, several analysts credited Wilder's strong pro-choice position for providing him the margin of his slim victory.

When Wilder took the oath of office as governor, he declared, "I am a son of Virginia. . . . We mark today not a victory of party or the accomplishments of an individual but the triumph of an idea, an idea as old as America, as old as the God who looks out for us all. It is the idea expressed so eloquently from this great commonwealth by those who gave shape to the greatest nation ever known. . . . The idea that all men and women are created equal, that they are endowed by their Creator with certain inalienable rights: the right to life, liberty, and the pursuit of happiness. . . ."

FEBRUARY 3, 1990   Angela Davis Addressed Spelman Crowd. Angela Davis, professor of ethnic and women's studies at San Francisco State University, told a crowd of 1,500 people at Spelman College in Atlanta that "we're moving to an era of intense activism, something that is going to make the '60s look like a tea party."

Davis was a controversial figure in the 1960s and 1970s as an activist who took more radical stances on issues than did leaders of the Civil Rights Movement, like Martin Luther King, Jr., and Roy Wilkins, of SCLC and the NAACP, respectively. In 1972, at the age of twenty-eight, Davis was tried and later acquitted of aiding three black men who killed a judge during a shootout at the Marin County, California, courthouse. In 1980, she was the vice-presidential candidate of the American Communist Party.

In the 1980s, Davis, the late Malcolm X, and other black "radicals" of the 1960s and 1970s have had a resurgence of influence among young African Americans, particularly on college campuses, as folk heroines and heroes. Their calls for "liberation by any means necessary" seemed to have new relevance to the problems of blacks in the current decades, in the eyes of the students.

FEBRUARY 4–7, 1990 Protesters Arrested in Selma, Alabama. Four black protesters were arrested after a melee in the mayor's office in Selma, Alabama, on February 4. The blacks were protesting the earlier dismissal of Norward Roussell as the first black superintendent of the city's schools. The Selma Board of Education had said that Roussell's managerial skills were questionable. Among those arrested on February 4 were, Rose Sanders and Carlos Williams, local attorneys, and Perry Varner, a Dallas County commissioner.

On February 6, the Selma Board of Education offered to rehire Superintendent Roussell at least temporarily and asked the five black members of the board to return to their posts. The five blacks had resigned in December 1989 after a racially divided school board voted against extending Roussell's contract. F. D. Reese, the black high school principal who had been named interim school superintendent on February 4, said he would relinquish the job to Roussell.

On February 7, despite the temporary reinstatement of Roussell as superintendent of Selma's schools, hundreds of demonstrators protested at City Hall. They demanded a permanent reinstatement for Roussell and charged that Rose Sanders, an attorney arrested in a previous protest on February 4, had been brutalized by police. Meanwhile, the town's schools, which were 70 percent black, remained closed.

Since December 1989, when the six white school board members rebuffed the five black ones and voted to oust Roussell as superintendent, black students had also boycotted several of the city's schools.

FEBRUARY 5, 1990 $10 Million Suit Filed Against Abernathy and His Publisher. Abjuda Abi Naantaabuu, a Memphis, Tennessee, woman who Ralph David Abernathy implied had an extramarital affair with Dr. Martin Luther King,

Jr., filed a $10 million suit against Abernathy and Harper and Row, the publisher of his autobiography, *And the Walls Came Tumbling Down.* The suit, which Naantaabuu brought to the U.S. District Court in New York City, charged that the defendants "falsely and maliciously . . . caused the readers of [the] book to believe that she had engaged in adulterous behavior and sexual relations with Dr. Martin Luther King on the last night of his life." King, Abernathy, and other civil rights activists had dinner at Naantaabuu's home the night before he was assassinated in Memphis on April 4, 1968.

FEBRUARY 11, 1990 Nelson R. Mandela Released from Prison. Nelson R. Mandela, the major symbol of the struggle for human rights in the Republic of South Africa, was released from prison after serving twenty-seven years. Mandela's release was ordered by Frederick W. de Klerk, the new president of South Africa. It was applauded by political and human rights leaders around the world, including the United States.

In 1986, the U.S. Congress had passed the Anti-Apartheid Act, which imposed economic sanctions on the white minority government of South Africa. (President Ronald Reagan had vetoed the measure earlier.) The act stipulated that the sanctions could only be lifted after South Africa had freed all political prisoners (of which Mandela was considered the principal one); legalized the African National Congress (ANC) and other anti-apartheid groups; engaged in good faith negotiations on the nation's political future; lifted the state of emergency; and made substantial progress on dismantling apartheid, South Africa's system of racial segregation. President de Klerk lifted a thirty-year-old ban on the ANC on February 2, 1990.

Randall Robinson, executive director of Trans-Africa, the leading anti-apartheid group in the United States, expressed the great de-

Nelson Mandela and Randall Robinson. (AP/Wide World Photos.)

light of most African Americans upon the news of Mandela's release, but he warned that sanctions must remain in place and that "it would be a mistake . . . at this juncture for President Bush to invite President de Klerk to visit the U.S."

FEBRUARY 11, 1990   "Buster" Douglas Defeated Mike Tyson. James "Buster" Douglas knocked out Mike Tyson in the tenth round of a Tokyo, Japan, match to take the world's heavyweight boxing championship in a major upset. Douglas, a twenty-four-year-old African American from Columbus, Ohio, went into the contest against the champion with a 18-2-1 record, including fourteen knockouts.

FEBRUARY 21–24, 1990   Sit-ins and Marches Staged at Tennessee State University. Students at historically black Tennessee State University in Nashville staged sit-ins and marches protesting poor conditions at the school. Targets of the protest were university president Otis Floyd and the state Board of Regents, the governing body for Tennessee's institutions of higher education. Several students were arrested for violating school rules or criminal laws

during the demonstrations. Some of them, including Jeff Carr, the student body president, rejected offers of amnesty.

FEBRUARY 23, 1990   Arthur A. Fletcher Named Chairman of Commission on Civil Rights. President George Bush named African American businessman Arthur A. Fletcher chairman of the U.S. Commission on Civil Rights (CCR).

Fletcher, age sixty-five, had served with Bush when the president was U.S. ambassador to the United Nations in 1971. Fletcher was an assistant secretary of labor in the administration of President Richard M. Nixon and deputy assistant for urban affairs for President Gerald R. Ford. In 1978, he lost a contest for mayor of Washington, D.C., to Democrat Marion Barry.

Fletcher succeeded William Barclay Allen, who, as chairman of the CCR, had been embroiled in several controversies, even with fellow commissioners. After he delivered a speech in 1989 titled "Blacks? Animals? Homosexuals? What is a Minority?" the commission, by a vote of 6-1, condemned Allen's speech as "thoughtless, disgusting and unnecessarily inflammatory." Allen and his predecessor, the late Clarence Pendleton, had also drawn the ire of some congresspersons and civil rights leaders for failing to aggressively champion civil rights enforcement. But the appointment of Fletcher drew praises. Benjamin Hooks, executive director of the NAACP, for example, described Fletcher as "a fair-minded, down-the-middle-of-the-road kind of person."

MARCH 2, 1990   African American Population Increased. The Bureau of the Census estimated the African American population at 30.6 million as of January 1, 1989, an increase of 462,000 from a year earlier. The total represented a growth of 1.5 percent during the year for blacks, which doubled the white increase of 0.8 percent. The annual growth rate of blacks had exceeded that of whites since 1950, according to the Bureau. Most of the gain for both groups came from "natural increase."

At the beginning of 1989, blacks made up 12.3 percent of the nation's population of 247.6 million. Whites comprised 84 percent of the total and other races (including Asians, Native Americans, Aleuts, Eskimos, and Pacific Islanders) made up three percent. The number of Hispanics rose by 3.4 percent and totaled 20.2 million or eight percent of the national total.

MARCH 3, 1990   United Negro College Fund Receive $50 Million. Walter H. Annenberg, former publisher of *TV Guide,* made a fifty-million-dollar pledge to the United Negro College Fund (UNCF). His gift was the largest single donation ever offered to the group, which serves as a coordinating fund-raising agency for more than forty private black colleges in the United States. Annenberg called black colleges "a major force for positive change.... As a society we cannot afford to waste our most valuable resources—our citizens.... Unless young blacks are brought into the mainstream of economic life, they will continue to be on the curbstone. The key to this problem is education." President George Bush applauded the gesture, remarking, "I think that generosity is a challenge ... that will bring on well-deserved support from others. It's most generous and one of the most brilliant points of light I can think of." In 1989, the UNCF had raised a total of $45.8 million for distribution to its member institutions.

MARCH 3, 1990   First African American Selected as Miss USA. Carole Gist, a twenty-year-old African American from Detroit, Michigan, was crowned Miss USA in Wichita, Kansas. Gist, a student at Northwood Institute, became the first black American to gain the beauty title. (Three blacks have held the older title of Miss America.) Of her selection, Gist said "there is so much more to me than my blackness, the color of my skin.... Never give up on your dreams." The new Miss USA received prizes totalling about $220,000, including $88,000 in cash.

MARCH 12, 1990   African American Leaders Lobbied for Economic Aid for African Nations. A group of African American leaders met with Secretary of State James A. Baker III in Washington, D.C., for discussions involving the redistribution of foreign aid "from emerging East European democracies to needy African nations struggling for freedom." The group specifically requested an increase in aid to Namibia, from $7.8 million budgeted for 1991 to $25 million in 1990 and 1991, and a grant of $25 million to the African National Congress (ANC) "for its struggle to end apartheid in South Africa."

One of the blacks present at the meeting, Randall Robinson, head of TransAfrica, a lobbying group for U.S. foreign policy towards Africa, said there were "sharp disagreements" with Baker over increased aid to Namibia, as well as "continued covert aid" to rebels in Angola. Other blacks who attended the meeting included civil rights leader Jesse Jackson and Coretta Scott King, widow of slain civil rights leader Martin Luther King, Jr.

MARCH 19, 1990   Minister Harold Bearden Died. Harold Irwin Bearden, minister and civil leader, died after suffering a stroke in Atlanta, Georgia, at age seventy-nine. Bearden was born in Atlanta on May 8, 1910, to Lloyd and Mary Da Costa Bearden. He obtained an A.B. degree at Morris Brown College and a B.D. degree from Turner Theological Seminary (both in Georgia). Bearden was ordained a deacon in the African Methodist Episcopal (A.M.E.) Church in 1930 and an elder in 1931. He pastored the Big Bethel A.M.E. Church, one of the oldest and largest congregations in Atlanta, from 1951 to 1964.

From 1960 to 1962, Bearden was an acting presiding elder of the A.M.E. Church and in 1964, he was consecrated a bishop in Cincinnati, Ohio. Bearden's first assignments upon elevation to the bishopric were in Central and West Africa. While there, he was elected president of the board of trustees of Monrovia College in Liberia. Upon his return to the United States, Bearden had church district assignments in Ohio and Texas before being named bishop of the Sixth Episcopal District in his native Georgia in 1976. He was president of the A.M.E. Council of Bishops in 1973–4.

Bearden served as bishop in the Sixth Episcopal District of Georgia until 1980 and continued to serve on special assignments for his church until his retirement in 1984.

While Bearden was president of the Atlanta chapter of the NAACP in 1958–59, a suit was filed to desegregate the Atlanta public schools and a federal court ordered desegregation on the city's buses. Bearden was one of several black ministers who were arrested in 1957 for defying Georgia's bus segregation laws. He continuously used his Sunday radio broadcasts to chide both segregationists and black accommodationists about Jim Crow practices in Atlanta and the nation, and he supported student sit-in demonstrations in the city in the 1960s.

Bearden served as a director of the Atlanta University Center consortium of black colleges and was a chairman of the boards of trustees at both of his alma maters, Morris Brown College and Turner Theological Seminary. The state senate of Georgia named him an outstanding citizen in 1978.

In one of the eulogies for Bearden, Jesse Hill, president of the Atlanta Life Insurance Company and a trustee of the Big Bethel Church, said, "When the history of the turbulent '60s and the bi-racial progress of Atlanta is written, the name of bishop Harold I. Bearden, then the dynamic, fearless pastor of Big Bethel A.M.E. Church, has to be placed up front." John Hurst Adams, the current senior bishop of the A.M.E.'s Sixth Episcopal district, remembers Bearden as "a major influence in the life of the community. He was active in community development, the civil rights movement, and all aspects in the advancement of the community and especially aspects of African American community unity."

MARCH 30, 1990   Catholic Educator Thea Bowman Died. Thea Bowman, Catholic educator died of cancer in Jackson, Mississippi, at age fifty-two.

Bowman was the only African-American member of the Franciscan Sisters of Perpetual Adoration. She served as director of intercultural awareness for its Jackson diocese and was a member of the faculty of the Institute of Black Catholic Studies at Xavier University in New Orleans, Louisiana.

In 1988, Bowman recorded an album, *Sister Thea: Songs of My People,* which consisted of fifteen black spirituals. The recording made the nun a popular figure at conventions and on college campuses across the nation. In that same year, she was featured on the CBS-TV news program "60 Minutes," which led to plans for a movie about her life and work.

She was widely honored for her educational work as well as her pioneering efforts to encourage black Catholics "to express their cultural roots inside the church." In 1989, she received the U.S. Catholic Award from *U.S. Catholic Magazine* "for furthering the cause of women in the Roman Catholic Church." In addition, the Sister Thea Bowman Black Catholic Educational Foundation was established in 1989 "to provide financial support for black students in Catholic primary and elementary schools and Catholic colleges and universities."

Upon her death, Joseph Houck, bishop of the Diocese of Jackson, said, "She was an outstanding woman. She was proud of her heritage and totally dedicated to the vision of Jesus Christ for love and growth of all people."

APRIL 4, 1990   Jazz Great Sarah Vaughan Died. Sarah Vaughan, African American jazz singer known affectionately as "the Divine One," died of cancer in San Fernando Valley, California, at age sixty-six.

Vaughan was born on March 27, 1924, in Newark, New Jersey, to Asbury, a carpenter and amateur guitarist, and Ada Vaughan, a laundry worker and choir singer. Sarah joined a Baptist church choir as a child and the gospel influence remained with her throughout her career. She occasionally included a version of "The Lord's Prayer" in her performances.

Ada Vaughan had wanted her daughter to pursue a career in classical music, and sent her to weekly organ and piano lessons, but young Sarah soon turned to a different path. At age eighteen, she won a talent contest at the Apollo Theatre in Harlem, New York, with a rendition of "Body and Soul." She was soon singing and playing piano with the Earl Hines Band and later toured with Billy Eckstine.

Vaughan began a solo career in the 1940s. Between 1940 and her death, she performed before jazz audiences throughout the nation and recorded at least three Top 10 pop singles, including "Broken-Hearted Melody," which sold more than a million records. Other notable recordings included "Misty," *The Divine Sarah Vaughan, Gershwin Live,* and *Lover Man.*

Although Vaughan "did not swing as effortlessly as Ella Fitzgerald," according to Bo Emerson, music critic of the *Atlanta Constitution,* "nor bring to bear Billie Holiday's intensity, the physical pleasure of [her] voice set her apart from most vocalists in any discipline." "She had the kind of voice that comes along once in a hundred years, once in a lifetime, maybe once in a thousand years," remarked jazz saxophonist and "elder statesman" Benny Carter.

At the 1989 Grammy Award ceremonies, Vaughan received a Lifetime Achievement Award.

APRIL 12, 1990   President Bush Given High Marks by African Americans. A *New York Times*/CBS Network News Poll revealed that African Americans had given George Bush "the highest level of sustained approval" of any Republican president in thirty years. Fifty-six percent of black Americans in the poll supported the way the president was doing his job. The survey was conducted by telephone from March 30 to April 2, 1990, and involved 403 blacks.

APRIL 17, 1990   Civil Rights Leader Ralph David Abernathy Died. Ralph David Abernathy, minister and civil rights leader, died of heart problems in Atlanta, Georgia, at age sixty-four.

Abernathy was born on March 11, 1926, in Linden, Alabama, to William L., a farmer and deacon, and Louiverney Valentine Abernathy. He was the tenth of twelve children. After his discharge from the U.S. Army in 1945, Abernathy enrolled in the Alabama State College in Montgomery, where he became both student body and class president. Abernathy led successful student protests against poor food in the cafeteria and inadequate living conditions for male students. He received a bachelor's degree from Alabama State in 1950. While attending graduate school at Atlanta University, Abernathy heard Martin Luther King, Jr., speak at the Ebenezer Baptist Church in Atlanta and developed an acquaintance with the young minister.

Prior to his involvement in the Civil Rights Movement of the 1950s and 1960s, Abernathy was a dean at Alabama State College and a part-time pastor of a church in Demopolis, Alabama. In 1948, he was named pastor of Montgomery's black First Baptist Church.

When King went to Montgomery in 1954 to assume the pastorate of the Dexter Avenue Baptist Church, he received a warm welcome from Abernathy and their friendship was strengthened. King planned to spend two or three years getting himself established in the city before becoming active in civic affairs, while Abernathy wanted to return to his graduate studies in order to obtain, in his words, "the same kind of academic credibility" that his friend King had. Their plans were disrupted by the arrest of Rosa Parks and the subsequent Montgomery bus boycott of 1955–1956. Both men were thrust into the leadership of the protest—King as the major figure and Abernathy as his number one lieutenant.

For thirteen years, Abernathy remained King's closest aide, confidante, and supporter as they engaged in the civil rights struggles of Montgomery, Albany, Birmingham, Selma, Chicago, Memphis, and dozens of other cities, towns, and hamlets. After an assassin's bullet struck King on the balcony of the Lorraine Hotel on the evening of April 4, 1968, Abernathy cradled his fallen comrade in his arms and remained with him through his death and autopsy. He gave one of the principal eulogies at King's funeral ceremonies, on what he called "one of the darkest days in American history." Abernathy then succeeded King as president of the Southern Christian Leadership Conference (SCLC).

In his own right, Abernathy also led the "Poor People's Campaign" for jobs and freedom in Washington after King's death in 1968. He ran for Congress from Georgia's Fifth District in 1978 but received only 3,614 votes. Abernathy addressed the United Nations in 1971 and was a president of the World Peace Council. In 1980, he was one of the few national black leaders to endorse the Republican presidential candidate Ronald Reagan over President Jimmy Carter. Abernathy considered Carter's presidency ineffectual and felt that Reagan would revive the economy and develop jobs for blacks. In 1984, he broke with some of his colleagues in the Civil Rights Movement, including former United Nations ambassador Andrew Young, and endorsed another civil rights veteran, Jesse L. Jackson, for president.

APRIL 27, 1990 Jury Deadlocked in Harold Ford Case. A federal court jury in Memphis, Tennessee, announced that it was unable to reach a verdict in the two-and-one-half month trial of Harold Ford, a black U.S. representative. The forty-four-year-old Tennessee Democrat had been charged with nineteen counts of bank fraud, mail fraud, and conspira-

cy. He was specifically accused of taking more than one million dollars in "political payoffs disguised as loans" from bankers C. H. and Jake Butcher of Knoxville, Tennessee. Ford had consistently maintained his innocence and suggested that the charges against him were racially motivated.

MAY 4, 1990 Andrew J. Young Addressed Rainbow Coalition. Andrew J. Young, former U.S. ambassador to the United Nations and mayor of Atlanta, Georgia, addressed the annual convention of the Rainbow Coalition in Atlanta. The coalition was founded by former African American Democratic presidential candidate Jesse L. Jackson. In the 1984 Democratic presidential contest, Young publicly opposed Jackson's candidacy and supported his rival, former vice-president Walter Mondale. In 1988 Young, citing his role as mayor of the host city of the Democratic National Convention, remained neutral. He once called Jackson's presidential ambitions "dangerous." But at the Rainbow Coalition Convention on May 4, 1990, Young drew applause when he described Jackson as the "only person in the Democratic Party who has dared to challenge" the administration of President George Bush. He also said that Jackson had "had the fire in his belly, the dream in his heart. He had the gleam and vision in his eyes." For his part, Jackson said, "Young can win and deserves to win" his current quest for the Democratic nomination as governor of Georgia.

MAY 12, 1990 Race Relations Workshop Held with Klansmen. Joseph E. Lowery, president of the Southern Christian Leadership Conference (SCLC), held a workshop on race relations with four Ku Klux Klansmen in Birmingham, Alabama. The four were among a group of five Klansmen who had been sentenced to participate in the two-hour meeting for their participation in a racial melee in Decatur, Alabama, in 1979. Four people were wounded in an exchange of gunfire between blacks and whites after more than one hundred Klansmen tried to block a civil rights march. After the workshop, Roger Handley, a former grand dragon of the Alabama Ku Klux Klan, called the affair "a waste of two hours." Lowery, who preached patriotism, love, and brotherhood to the white supremacists, however, called it "heartwarming."

MAY 12, 1990 Governor Wilder Ordered State Agencies to Divest Investments in South Africa. Virginia governor L. Douglas Wilder ordered all of his state's agencies and institutions to divest themselves of business investments in companies not "substantively free" of economic activity in South Africa. Virginia officials estimated that such holdings amounted to more than $750 million. A large amount of this money was invested by the agency, which paid pensions to retired state employees.

In announcing his actions, Governor Wilder said that Virginians should support the efforts of South African blacks to break the chains of apartheid with the same vigor and enthusiasm that greeted the aspirations to freedom by people in China and Eastern Europe. He added: "If we are to participate in the extension to all peoples of the freedoms and liberties which we hold dear, we must take concrete actions which reflect our support." Wilder made his declarations in a commencement address at the predominantly black Norfolk State University.

MAY 13, 1990 George Stallings Ordained as Bishop. George Augustus Stallings was ordained the first bishop of the African American Catholic Church. The forty-one-year-old black priest broke away from the Roman Catholic Church in June 1989 after declaring that the Church failed to meet the needs of its African American parishioners. On July 4, 1989, he was suspended for "founding an independent black congregation."

At the ordination of Bishop Stallings, African dancers and gospel singers performed before an audience of 1,000 people. Stallings

"knelt on a decorated stage filled with elaborate banners, drummers, and icons" as six white bishops from the Independent Old Catholic Churches of California (which broke away from Rome in the 1870s) declared him "a suitable candidate for the office of bishop in the Church of God."

At the time of Stallings' assumption of his new post, his African American Catholic Congregation had expanded from Washington, D.C., to Baltimore, Maryland, Norfolk, Virginia, and Philadelphia, Pennsylvania.

MAY 16, 1990 Sammy Davis, Jr., Died of Cancer. Sammy Davis, Jr., African American entertainer and America's "Ambassador of Goodwill," died of cancer in Beverly Hills, California, at age sixty-four. He was born on December 8, 1925, in the Harlem section of New York City.

Davis was the consummate star, the epitome of versatility. He began performing at age three with his father, Sam, Sr., and his uncle, Will Mastin, in vaudeville. In his adult years, Davis's talents as a dancer, singer, and actor were revered on the stage, film, television, and in nightclubs. He made his Broadway debut in 1956 in the musical *Mr. Wonderful* and won a Tony nomination for his starring role as a cosmopolitan boxer in *Golden Boy.*

Davis's major recordings included "The Way You Look Tonight" (1946); "Hey There" (1954); "That Old Black Magic" (1955); "The Shelter of Your Arms" (1964); "I've Got to Be Me" (1969); and "The Candy Man" (1972).

In his recordings, as in his films, Davis often worked with his friends Frank Sinatra and Dean Martin. His first movie role was as a child in *Rufus Jones for President* (1933) with singer Ethel Waters. Davis also had major roles in *Anna Lucasta* (1958); *Porgy and Bess* (1959); *Oceans Eleven* (1960); *Robin and the Seven Hoods* (1964); and *Sweet Charity* (1969). Davis's last film appearance was in 1989 with dancer Gregory Hines in *Tap.*

Between 1956 and 1980, Davis appeared on almost every variety show and comedy series on network television; in 1966, he starred in his own television series, one of the first ever hosted by a black person.

Davis supported the Civil Rights Movement of the 1960s by singing at fund raisers, especially for Dr. Martin Luther King, Jr., and was with King at the end of the famous Selma to Montgomery voting rights march in Alabama. He also helped raise money for the defense of Angela Davis, who was imprisoned for conspiracy to commit murder in the late 1960s. The entertainer was also the target of controversy; after being invited to an inaugural activity for President John F. Kennedy in 1961, he was later asked not to attend the affair because of fear that his presence there with his then-wife, Swedish actress Mai Britt, would "inflame Southerners." Davis also made headlines in 1972 at a function for President Richard M. Nixon during the Republican National Convention. He startled the president and many African Americans, particularly, when he came up behind Nixon and gave him a big hug while flashing a wide, "cattish" grin.

The rise of Davis from demeaning, stereotypical roles in vaudeville and his early films to the highest place in the annals of American entertainment is documented in his autobiographies *Yes I Can* (1965) and *Why Me* (1989). At the time of his death, Davis had become, in the words of NAACP executive director Benjamin Hooks, "an American treasure that the whole world loved."

MAY 18, 1990 Defendant Convicted in Hawkins Murder Trial. Joseph Fama, a nineteen-year-old New York City youth, was convicted of second degree murder in the 1989 slaying of Yusuf Hawkins, a sixteen-year-old black youth, in the Bensonhurst section of the city. The mob attack that led to Hawkins's death in an all-white neighborhood had been the focus of racial tension in the nation's largest city for more than six months. It was also

frequently cited by some blacks as evidence of a resurgent racism in the United States.

MAY 18, 1990 Consolidated Bank and Trust Company Expanded. Consolidated Bank and Trust Company, the nation's oldest black-owned commercial bank, expanded, in a move that allowed it to purchase the assets of two failed Virginia lending institutions. In an agreement with the Federal Deposit Insurance Corporation (FDIC), the Richmond-based Consolidated paid a $315,000 premium to add the assets of the black-owned People's Savings and Loan Association and Community Federal Savings & Loan Association to its portfolio. It also assumed all loans and deposits of the two S&Ls. The 107-year-old People's of Hampton and Community Federal, a 23-year-old Newport News, Virginia, financial institution, had combined assets of $30 million. The transaction boosted Consolidated's total assets to $93.5 million—up from $62 million. The bank was the 12th largest on a listing of black-owned banks by *Black Enterprise* magazine.

MAY 25, 1990 Judge Ruled Hood-wearing Law Unconstitutional. A Gwinnett County, Georgia, state court judge ruled that a thirty-nine-year-old law that prohibited members of the Ku Klux Klan from wearing hooded masks in public was unconstitutional. Judge Howard E. Cook said that the state law was "overly broad" and violated the rights to "free speech, association, and [equal] protection" of the Klansmen. Although the Klan may "represent . . . hateful ideas, such ideas are still entitled to . . . protection," Judge Cook declared. Georgia state officials and civil rights leaders said they were "shocked" by the judge's decision and filed notice of appeal to the state Supreme Court "20 minutes after [the decision] was filed."

JUNE 3, 1990 Bobby Rush Named Deputy Chairman of Illinois Democratic Party. Bobby Rush, former leader of the militant Black Panther Party in Chicago, became deputy chair-

Ku Klux Klan members march down Pennsylvania Avenue in Washington, D.C. (Courtesy of Library of Congress.)

man of the Illinois Democratic Party. A South Side alderman since 1983, Rush had quietly gained political clout in the city where he once decreed, "The power structure has genocide in their minds," and noted that the solution was revolution.

Rush rode into city council in 1983 on the coattails of the popular Harold Washington, the first black mayor of the Windy City. He made an unsuccessful bid for alderman in 1974 shortly after leaving the Panther Party. Born in Albany, Georgia, he moved to Chicago

with his family in 1954 when he was seven years old.

JUNE 6, 1990   Gantt Nominated for Senate Seat. Harvey Gantt, the former African American mayor of Charlotte, North Carolina, won his state's Democratic nomination for the U.S. Senate. Gantt gained 272,576 votes (57 percent) to defeat Michael Easley, a county district attorney. Easley received 206,397 votes (43 percent) with 99 percent of the state's precincts reporting. Gantt, a forty-seven-year-old architect, was the first black in North Carolina to receive the Democratic nomination for U.S. senator. In 1963, he became the first black student to enroll in Clemson University in South Carolina and was the first black mayor of Charlotte. Of his nomination Gantt remarked, "There's a new day in North Carolina. This is a day where people are judged by what they can do and not by the color of their skin."

JUNE 11, 1990 Two Teens Sent to Prison for Hawkins Murder. Judge Thaddeus Owens sentenced two nineteen-year-old white youths to prison for the August 23, 1989, shooting death of Yusuf K. Hawkins, a sixteen-year-old black youth, in New York City. Joseph Fama, who prosecutors and police authorities said actually shot Hawkins, was sentenced to thirty-two-and-two-thirds years to life in prison. He had been convicted of second-degree murder, inciting a riot, unlawful imprisonment, weapons possessions, and other crimes. Keith Mondello received a sentence of five-and-one-third to sixteen years in prison and a two-thousand-dollar fine. He was acquitted of murder and manslaughter, but convicted of inciting a riot, unlawful imprisonment, and discrimination. Mondello was identified as the ringleader of the mob that attacked Hawkins and three other blacks in the Bensonhurst neighborhood of New York City in 1989.

The family of the slain Hawkins and other blacks applauded Fama's sentence, but some threw rocks and bottles in Brooklyn when they heard that Mondello had been acquitted of the more serious charges.

JUNE 12, 1990 Mitchell Won South Carolina Democratic Gubernatorial Primary. Theo Mitchell, a black state senator, won the Democratic primary contest for governor of South Carolina. Mitchell gained 107,473 votes (61 percent) to 69,766 votes (39 percent) for Ernest Parsailaigue, a freshman senator (with 92 percent of precincts reporting).

JUNE 13, 1990 Mayor Barry Announced He Would Run Again. Marion S. Barry, Jr., mayor of Washington, D.C., announced he would not seek a fourth term. At that time, Barry, a former civil rights activist, was on trial in a federal district court in Washington. He was arrested on January 18, 1990, in a drug sting at a local hotel. The mayor had pleaded innocent to three felony counts of lying to a grand jury about his alleged drug use, ten misdemeanor cocaine possession charges, and one misdemeanor cocaine conspiracy charge.

JUNE 17, 1990 National Collegiate Black Caucus Sponsored Rally. About 850 people, mostly students, attended a march and rally sponsored by the National Collegiate Black Caucus (NCBC) in Washington, D.C. The organizers had expected a crowd of more than 5,000.

The demonstration was organized to coordinate the concerns of black collegians throughout the nation. In the past decade, black college students on both predominantly black and predominantly white campuses had demonstrated against racism and for a greater infusion of African and African American studies into college and university curricula. The students at the Washington rally were also concerned about inadequate housing on their campuses and insufficient financial aid.

JUNE 18, 1990 Kenny Leon Named Artistic Director of Alliance Theater Company. Kenny Leon, a thirty-four-year-old actor, was named artistic director of the Alliance Theater Company in Atlanta, Georgia. The appointment made him the second black artistic director of a major American theater. (Yale Repertory Theatre's, Lloyd Richards, who was the first.) Leon was associate artistic director at the Alliance Theater, where he gained popularity for his direction of such productions as *Fences*, *Gal Baby*, and *Joe Turner's Come and Gone*.

JUNE 20, 1990 Increase Reported for Black High School Graduates. The U.S. Department of Commerce reported that the percentage of black high school graduates increased between 1978 and 1988 and now approaches the percentage rate for whites. The report, based on national census data, indicated that in 1988, 75 percent of blacks and 82 percent of whites, aged eighteen to twenty-four, graduated from high school, compared with 68 percent for blacks and 83 percent for whites in 1978. There was apparently no change in the graduation or dropout rate for Hispanics during the same period.

JUNE 20–30, 1990 Mandela Visited United States to Promote South African Sanctions. Nelson Mandela, deputy president of the African National Congress (ANC) and the major symbol of the struggle for freedom in the Republic of South Africa, conducted a major tour of the United States. The ten-day foray was designed to convince Americans to maintain sanctions against the white-minority government in South Africa until its racial apartheid system was dismantled, and to raise money to assist the ANC's campaign for majority rule.

On June 20, Mandela was feted to a ticker tape parade in downtown New York City, where approximately 750,000 people lined the parade routes to greet him. He told crowds that apartheid in his country was "doomed," and that with the aid of supporters in the United States, "we have made the government listen, and we have broken the walls of the South African jails."

On June 22, the South African freedom fighter addressed the United Nations (UN). He cautioned that "nothing which has happened in South Africa calls for a revision of the position that this organization has taken in the struggle against apartheid." During the almost three decades that Mandela was in prison, the UN consistently adopted resolutions opposing South African apartheid and the many speeches by delegates and others against the system usually ended in the refrain, "Free Mandela."

Mandela was in Boston, Massachusetts, on June 23, where his hosts included Jacqueline Kennedy Onassis, widow of slain president John F. Kennedy, and the late president's brother, Massachusetts senator Edward "Ted" Kennedy. Mandela told audiences, "We lower our banners in memory of Crispus Attucks [an African American], the first victim to fall in your Revolutionary War," and "given the illustrious history of this city, it is only natural that we consider ourselves as visiting our second home." He also looked forward to a South Africa that was "free from all forms of racism and sexism. We do not seek to dominate whites in our country. We intend to live true to this principal to the end of our day."

On June 25, Mandela arrived in Washington, D.C., where he was greeted by, among others, Randall Robinson, head of TransAfrica, the principal anti-apartheid organization in the United States.

The South African leader met President George Bush on June 26. While Bush hailed Mandela's freedom and again denounced the apartheid system, he asked that "all elements in South African society . . . renounce the use of violence in armed struggle, break free from the cycle of repression and violent reaction that breeds nothing but more fear and suffering." In making his plea, Bush quoted slain civil rights leader Martin Luther King, Jr.: "Let us not seek to satisfy our thirst for freedom by drinking from the cup of bitterness and hatred." In his response, Mandela said Bush's remarks resulted from him not getting "a proper briefing from us." He added that when a government prohibits free political activity, "the people have no alternative but to resort to violence." The two met for three hours, after which Mandela said they had reached substantial agreement on most issues.

Before leaving the capital, Mandela addressed a joint session of the U.S. Congress on June 26. He invoked the names of Frederick Douglass, Thomas Jefferson, Joe Louis, and other American heroes, and repeated his plea for a continuation of sanctions against the white-minority government in South Africa. He received several thunderous standing ovations.

On June 27, Mandela visited Atlanta, Georgia, "the capital of the Civil Rights Movement," where he laid a wreath at King's tomb, received honorary degrees from about a third of the nation's historically black colleges, and addressed a rally of more than 50,000 people. In his brief remarks to the mostly black crowd, Mandela made frequent references to King, and said, "We are . . . conscious that here in the southern part of the country, you have experienced the degradation of racial segregation. We continue to be inspired by the knowledge that in the face of your own difficulties, you are in the forefront of the anti-apartheid movement in this country." Then, drawing upon King's famous "I Have a Dream" oration, Mandela declared, "Let Freedom ring. Let us all acclaim now, 'Let freedom ring in South Africa. Let freedom ring wherever people's rights are trampled upon.'"

On June 28, Mandela made brief visits to Miami Beach, Florida, where he spoke to the annual convention of the American Federation of State, County, and Municipal Employees (AFSCME), and to Detroit, Michigan, where he addressed a rally of 50,000 people. In Miami, he repeated his call for continued sanctions against South Africa and thanked the American labor unions which had refused to handle materials destined for South Africa and lent financial support to his struggle. About 250 anti-Castro Cubans and Cuban Americans protested Mandela's visit, however, because he had expressed gratitude for the Cuban dictator's support of the anti-apartheid movement and refused to denounce him during an appearance on an ABC-TV "Nightline" segment. A crowd of 2,000 demonstrators, mostly black, chanted to the beat of an African drum and waved colorful flags in support of Mandela. There were only a few minor clashes between the two groups.

In Detroit, Mandela met Rosa Parks, the Alabama seamstress who sparked the famed Montgomery bus boycott. While visiting the Ford Rouge plant, one of the oldest automobile factories in the country, he told members of the United Auto Workers, another anti-apartheid union, that he was their "comrade . . . your flesh and blood." Later that evening, Mandela and his entourage were honored at a rally held at Tiger Stadium.

June 29–30, Mandela ended his American tour in California, with stops in Los Angeles and Oakland. He spoke to 80,000 people at the Los Angeles Memorial Coliseum, after declaring that he was on the "last leg of an exhausting but exhilarating tour." He also said, "Our masses in action are like a raging torrent. We are on freedom road, and nothing is going to stop us from reaching our destination."

As he prepared to leave the United States, Mandela indicated that he would probably return in October 1990 to receive a $100,000 award from the Gandhi Memorial International Foundation in New York and to meet with several Native American leaders. He declared that he was "very disturbed" about the condition of the Native American.

While some Americans either expressed grave concern or opposition to Mandela's views, particularly his refusal to denounce Colonel Muammar al-Qaddafi, Libya's "pro-terrorist" leader, Yassar Arafat, leader of the Palestine Liberation Organization (PLO), and Cuban dictator Fidel Castro, and his unwillingness to abandon the use of violence in his struggle, the South African leader was very warmly received by most Americans on his tour. In New York, eighteen-year-old Tanera Ford remarked, "I'm glad to see so many black people here. . . . To have all these people together for something positive, it just makes me feel great." In Atlanta, Joseph E. Lowery, president of the SCLC, told Mandela, "We reject the constant nagging that you have experienced about denouncing violence." Finally, in Detroit, Quirita Quates, a young dancer, said the South African anti-apartheid leader was "just the greatest man in the world."

JUNE 25, 1990 NUL Founder Moon Died.

Mollie Lewis Moon, the founder of the National Urban League Guild (NULG), died from an apparent heart attack in Long Island City, Queens, New York, at age eighty-two. Moon founded the NULG in 1942 to raise money for Urban League programs "for racial equality and amity." Under her leadership, the guild grew to eighty units, with thirty thousand volunteers in the United States. A major guild event, over which Moon presided for almost half a century, was the annual Beaux Arts Ball. It began at the old Savoy Ballroom in the Harlem section of New York City in 1942, but moved downtown in 1948. In that year, Winthrop Rockefeller, a New York financier and philanthropist, arranged for the ball to be held in the Rainbow Room atop Rockefeller Center. Moon later recalled that the invitations for the event were sent out in both her name and that of Rockefeller. "Nobody was going to buck the landlord," she said, "that's how we broke the color barrier."

On April 23, 1990, which marked the beginning of National Volunteer Week, David Dinkins, the new black mayor of New York City, presented an award for "dedicated and innovative volunteerism" to Moon on behalf of President George Bush.

JUNE 27, 1990 Oscar Prater Named President of Fort Valley State College.

Oscar L. Prater, vice president for administrative services at Hampton University in Virginia, was named president of Fort Valley State College in Georgia. Prater, a fifty-one-year-old African American, succeeded Luther Burse, who left office in August 1988.

The Sylacauga, Alabama, native did his undergraduate work at Talladega College (Alabama) and received a doctoral degree from the College of William and Mary in Virginia. At Hampton University, he had been a professor

of mathematics and an administrator for eleven years. Prater was also active in community affairs in both Hampton and Williamsburg, Virginia, particularly in the Head Start program for disadvantaged youth.

AUGUST 17, 1990 Pearl Bailey Died of Heart Attack.

Pearl Bailey, a renowned cabaret singer and actress, died of an apparent heart attack in Philadelphia, where she was recovering from knee surgery. She was seventy-two. Bailey, who had a history of heart ailments, collapsed in her home and was rushed to Thomas Jefferson Hospital where she died. She was buried in Rolling Meadow, in suburban West Chester, Pennsylvania.

Bailey was born on March 29, 1918, in Newport News, Virginia, of black and Creek Indian ancestry. She began her professional career in vaudeville. Her greatest triumph came when she starred with Cab Calloway in the all-black version of the Broadway hit "Hello Dolly." Bailey's success came partly because she adeptly used her talent to transcend the racial stereotypes that hindered many other black performers of her time. She went on to become a legend known as the "Ambassador of Love."

An entertainer noted for her distinctive style, she often punctuated her performances with mischievous witticisms. "If I just sang a song, it would mean nothing," she once said.

SEPTEMBER 11, 1990 Victory Declared for Newcomers to District of Columbia Elections.

Sharon Pratt Dixon, Eleanor Holmes Norton, and civil rights activist Jesse Jackson, all newcomers to District of Columbia politics, were victorious at the polls. Dixon won the Democratic mayoral nomination, Norton won her bid to the House of Representatives, and Jackson won his bid to become the District's "statehood senator"—a newly created office devised by the Washington city council to help lobby Congress for the district's statehood.

Dixon distinguished herself early in the campaign when she called for Mayor Marion

Barry's resignation. She vowed to use a shovel, not a broom, to clean up after the scandal that plagued Barry's administration. Dixon also promised to cut 2,000 senior municipal jobs.

Norton, the former chairperson of the Equal Employment Opportunity Commission (EEOC), won a narrow victory. She had to overcome a late disclosure that she had failed to file city income taxes since 1982. Norton succeeded former representative Walter Fauntroy.

Jackson's victory proved he could win elective office and gave him a platform to lobby for D.C. statehood.

OCTOBER 1990 Boycott Requested of National Bar Association Convention in Miami. The Dade County, Florida, affiliate of the National Bar Association (NBA), a group that primarily represents African American lawyers, called for a boycott against Miami as a convention and meeting site. The NBA was reacting to treatment city officials gave to South African anti-apartheid leaders Nelson and Winnie Mandela during their June visit. The group also condemned the rampant job discrimination in South Florida's hotel and tourism industry, which they said was dominated by Hispanics who formed labor unions that shut blacks out of entry-level jobs in hotels and restaurants.

Asking all business, professional, religious, labor, and civil associations to join the boycott, one of the NBA's first acts was to call off plans to host its annual convention in the Miami. More than 2,000 members had been expected to attend. The organization was angry that city officials didn't give the Mandelas an official welcome when they arrived during their tour of major U.S. cities. Miami officials had denounced Mandela for his praise of Fidel Castro, Yassar Arafat, and Muammar al-Qaddafi. Convention delegate expenditures totaled more than $405 million in 1989.

OCTOBER 1990 Former Football Player Brady Keys, Jr., Invested in Steel Industry. Brady

Keys, Jr., age fifty-two, a former professional football player who established the first major black-owned fast food franchise, ventured deeper into the steel industry. The former Pittsburgh Steelers defensive back invested the proceeds from the sale of twelve Detroit-based Burger King restaurants into a new steel company. He formed the Keys Industrial Group with Stoneworth Group executives, Harry Farmer and William Moorehead III.

Upon his retirement from football, Keys first built his reputation with the Keys Group Company, owner of fast food franchises, with annual sales of $18.6 million. In 1988 he was franchisee of the year.

He then bought HCE Enterprises, a fabricated steel company, renamed it RMK Steel, secured several government contracts, and built sales from $100,000 to $3 million in its first eight months. The company has since been sold for three times its original purchase price.

OCTOBER 1990 Nielsen Media Research Improved Minorities Research. Nielsen Media Research, the leading provider of television information services, improved its data collection and reporting on TV viewing by minorities.

The improvements came after criticism by black media representatives who alleged that Nielsen avoided predominantly black areas, which minimized the potential impact African American viewers could have on ratings.

Byron E. Lewis, president of Uniworld Group Inc., a black-owned advertising firm headquartered in New York City, said the problem affected African Americans financially. He noted that advertisers who target black audiences are less likely to advertise if the programs have low ratings.

Nielsen expanded its monthly National Audience Demographic Report to include black households and approximately 20 black demographic categories. It also includes additional marketing information, such as market penetration estimates.

OCTOBER 16, 1990 Jazz Great Art Blakely Died. Art Blakely, drummer and jazz band leader, died in New York City. He was seventy-one. A powerful and influential jazz talent, Blakely was the leader of a constantly evolving ensemble known as the Jazz Messengers. The group, which Blakely founded with Horace Silver, was a virtual conservatory of up-and-coming musicians, including Freddie Hubbard, Wayne Shorter, Branford and Wynton Marsalis, Donald Byrd, and McCoy Tyner. His group also included such notable musicians as Keith Jarrett, Chuck Mangione, Chick Corea, Terence Blanchard, Jackie McLean, and Donald Harrison.

OCTOBER 19, 1990 Harold Washington Party Barred from November Election Ballot. The Illinois Supreme Court upheld a lower-court decision to bar the Harold Washington Party from Cook County's November election ballot. The four Democratic judges voted against including the primarily black party, while the three Republicans voted for its inclusion. Democrats had been concerned about losing votes to the party, named in honor of the late Democratic mayor of Chicago, while Republicans anticipated gaining a majority of votes as a result. The Washington Party subsequently urged its supporters either to boycott the election or to vote Republican in protest of the Democratic opposition.

OCTOBER 22, 1990 Bush Vetoed Civil Rights Bill. President George Bush vetoed the Civil Rights Bill of 1990, saying the document "employs a maze of highly legalistic language to introduce the destructive force of quotas" in the workplace. Two days later an attempt to override the veto in the Senate fell one vote short of the necessary two-thirds majority.

OCTOBER 26, 1990 African-American Marketing & Media Association Founded. The African-American Marketing & Media Asso-

ciation was formed to improve advertising to black audiences and alter what it viewed as stereotyping. Clarence O. Smith, the association chairperson and president and co-founder of Essence Communications, publisher of *Essence* magazine, said the organization would also help find more work for members.

NOVEMBER 1990 Hilmon Sorey Named CEO of Largest Minority-owned Dairy. Chicago business executive Hilmon Sorey, Jr., purchased 51 percent of Hawthorn-Mellody and became president and chief executive officer of the nation's largest minority-owned dairy. The fifty-two-year-old company projected sales of more than $100 million and expected to achieve a modest profit after showing a $500,000 loss the previous year. The Schaumburg, Illinois-based dairy has production and distribution facilities in Whitewater, Wisconsin. Sorey was previously president of Hilmon S. Sorey & Associates, a Chicago-based management consultant firm.

NOVEMBER 1990 Merger Made Atlanta Life One of the Largest Black-owned Insurance Companies. The Atlanta Life Insurance Company, in its third major acquisition in five years, purchased 100 percent of the stock of the Chicago Metropolitan Life Assurance Company for $750,000. This made Atlanta Life one of the largest black-owned insurance companies, boosting the company's net worth to more than $231 million.

NOVEMBER 5, 1990 Freedom National Bank Closed after Federal Regulation Controversy. The Freedom National Bank closed its doors amid controversy over federal regulation standards. Established in New York City's Harlem section in 1964, Freedom National quickly became a symbol of African American pride. With total assets of $120.6 million in 1990, it was ranked among the nation's top five African American banks by *Black Enterprise* magazine. The financial institution was a depository for many prominent African American celebrities and was the bank for numerous African American organizations and businesses.

Representative Charles B. Rangel of New York, citing unfair treatment, called for a probe by the House Banking Committee. He charged that regulators used a double standard in procedures used to close the financial institution. Several major customers stood to lose a significant amount of uninsured deposits unless the Federal Deposit Insurance Corporation (FDIC) agreed to repay at least 50 percent of all deposit accounts in excess of the insured limit of $100,000. The United Negro College Fund and the Fort Greene Senior Citizen Council were among the larger depositors. The two organizations had more than $11 million in uninsured deposits in Freedom National.

NOVEMBER 6, 1990   Continued Debated in Arizona over Martin Luther King, Jr., Holiday. Debate increased over the enactment of a Martin Luther King, Jr., holiday in Arizona. Voters in that state defeated a referendum on the issue, proposing a paid holiday for state employees, by a narrow 17,226 margin. Only two other states, Montana and New Hampshire, had not yet observed a state holiday marking King's birthday.

The National Football League had threatened to move the 1993 Super Bowl from Phoenix unless the state adopted the holiday—an act that would cost the state more than $200 million in lost revenues. The defeated legislation also led to the cancellation of a golf tournament memorializing the slain civil rights leader as well as numerous other conventions and special events.

The referendum was intended to help voters decide whether to overturn Governor Evan Mecham's 1987 decision to cancel the holiday. Since that decision, the state had lost about 58 conventions and about an estimated $30 million in financial revenues.

NOVEMBER 27, 1990   Charles Johnson Honored with National Book Award. Charles

Johnson, the author of *Middle Passage,* a novel about a freed slave and his adventures, won the 1990 National Book Award for fiction. He was the first African American male to win the award since Ralph Ellison won it in 1954 for *Invisible Man.*

DECEMBER 1990   African Americans Concerned over Involvement in Operation Desert Shield. President George Bush promised an infusion of more than 500,000 troops to Saudi Arabia to assure an early end to Operation Desert Shield—a mission to liberate oil-rich Kuwait from the unyielding Iraqi leader Saddam Hussein.

A *Wall Street Journal* poll revealed that most whites but only 41 percent of the nation's black Americans supported Operation Desert Shield. Blacks also expressed concern over the disproportionate number of African Americans in the military—many of whom were on the front line—and the belief that far too many minorities served in low-level military positions with far too few in leadership roles. A noted exception was the nation's top soldier, General Colin L. Powell, an African American who served as chair of the Joint Chiefs of Staff.

Speculation about the quality of African American life after Operation Desert Shield increased throughout the ordeal. The public television forum "Frontline" addressed the issue in a segment titled "Black America's War," a one-day town meeting in Philadelphia. Moderated by Harvard law professor Charles Ogletree, the program featured the Reverend Jesse Jackson; Lt. Gen. Frank Petersen, the first black general in the U.S. Marine Corps; Pulitzer prize-winning author Roger Wilkins; Major Elwood Driver, a retired Army Air Corps officer; and journalist Hodding Carter III as panelists.

DECEMBER 12–18, 1990   Education Department Announced Prohibition on Minority Funding. The Education Department announced a prohibition on colleges that received federal funds from setting aside scholarships for minorities—a ban that would affect millions of dollars in minority aid programs. Michael L. Williams, the department's assistant secretary for civil rights, called "race exclusive" scholarships discriminatory and therefore in violation of Title VI of the 1964 Civil Rights Act, which prohibits discrimination on the grounds of race, color, or national origin in any program or activity receiving federal financial assistance.

On December 18, the Education Department partially reversed the policy, now allowing federally funded colleges to award minority scholarships if the money comes from private donations or from federal programs designed to aid minority students. Robert H. Atwell, president of the American Council on Education, said the reversal, "was not a clarification, it was not a retraction, it was a confusion."

1991

JANUARY 1991   First Black Editor of *Times Picayune*. Keith Woods became the first African American city editor of the *New Orleans Times Picayune*. His duties included directing news coverage in the city and supervising editors and reporters. Woods previously served as assistant city editor.

JANUARY 1991   *Brotherman* Comic Created. *Brotherman,* the comic super hero created by brothers David, Jason, and Guy Sims, became a hit with African American youths in 1991. The Simses created *Brotherman* to provide a positive African American image for comic book readers. The first issue sold more than 8,000 copies.

JANUARY 9, 1991   Economic Measures Urged by National Urban League. In its *16th Annual Report of Black America,* the National Urban League urged President George Bush to introduce measures to stimulate the economy. The organization contended that black Americans were in a permanent recession and would bear

the brunt of hard economic times unless preventative measures were taken.

JANUARY 11, 1991   Calendar Promoted Positive Black Male Images. Troy Chapman, a black third-year student at Harvard University, produced a calendar featuring black male students at the Harvard Law School. He stated that the calendar would promote more positive images of black men to serve as role models for black youths.

JANUARY 11, 1991   Pastoral Letter Addressed Racism. The United Church of Christ issued a pastoral letter contending that racism was a deepening problem in America. The document also stated that poverty was worse for non-white Americans and that racially motivated violence had increased since the birth of the civil rights movement thirty years earlier.

JANUARY 17, 1991   Half of Blacks Opposed Gulf War. A *New York Times*/CBS survey suggested that 50 percent of the black population supported Operation Desert Storm, the war to free Kuwait from Iraq, compared to 80 percent of whites. Critics charged that blacks were being placed in front-line battle positions at a higher rate than their white counterparts.

Several black leaders, including representative Charles Rangell of New York, expressed concern over the high number of blacks serving in the Persian Gulf. Rangell asked how President Bush could order African Americans into battle after rejecting the civil rights bill, and similar comments were made by National Urban League president John Jacob and Atlanta mayor Maynard Jackson.

About 104,000 of the 400,000 troops serving in the Persian Gulf were black. According to the Department of Defense, blacks accounted for 30 percent of the Army, 21 percent of the Navy, 17 percent of the Marines, and 14 percent of the Air Force personnel stationed in the Gulf. African Americans accounted for 11 percent of all American citizens over sixteen years old.

Critics contended that a high number of fatalities among black soldiers would have grave implications for the black community. A high death rate among black soldiers would create many one-parent households, and some families would lose both parents. Many skilled positions in America's workforce that were held by blacks who were called up from the reserves would be lost, further diluting black representation in critical areas of the government and the private sector.

Martin Binkin, a military analyst with the Brookings Institute in Washington, D.C., estimated that up to 35 percent of all qualified black men between the ages of 19 and 24 have served in the military, compared to 17 percent of all qualified white men.

JANUARY 24, 1991   AIDS Called Major Threat to Blacks. The U.S. Centers for Disease Control called the AIDS epidemic a major health threat to African Americans. In New Jersey and New York, AIDS was the leading cause of death among African Americans between the ages of fifteen and forty-four. Recognizing the need for a major reevaluation of sexual behavior among blacks, African American leaders called for safer sex practices. They also noted that drug addicts using infected needles are at high risk.

JANUARY 24, 1991   Operation PUSH Laid Off Staff. Operation PUSH, the Chicago-based civil rights group formed by the Reverend Jesse Jackson, laid off staff members because of financial problems, which had worsened since Jackson left Chicago to pursue a political career in Washington, D.C.

JANUARY 29, 1991   "Black" Deemed Preferred Term of Racial Identity. The Joint Center for Political and Economic Studies reported that most black Americans prefer to be called black, despite the growing use of the term African American.

Seventy-two percent of those polled preferred the designation black. Fifteen percent preferred African American, three percent preferred Afro-American, and two percent preferred Negro.

FEBRUARY 1991   Apollo Performing Arts Theater Deal Completed in Japan. Inner City Broadcasting Corp., the owner of Harlem's famed Apollo Theater, struck a deal to redesign a performing arts theater in metropolitan Tokyo; under the arrangement, Nichii Company Ltd. paid $150,000 to use the Apollo name for its theater. Inner City thus became one of a few minority-owned American companies with a business interest in Japan. The project grew out of a 1986 cultural exchange program designed to help educate Japanese citizens about African Americans. The New York-based Inner City owns several radio stations and a cable company.

FEBRUARY 9, 1991   Gospel Music Great James Cleveland Died. James Cleveland, a Baptist clergyman and major figure in gospel music, died in Los Angeles, California, at the age of sixty.

Cleveland was a pianist, composer, arranger, impresario, and leader of the James Cleveland Singers. He was also the founder of the Gospel Music Workshop of America. During his career Cleveland served as mentor to Aretha Franklin, Billy Preston, and many other soul singers who began their career in gospel music.

Cleveland wrote more than 400 gospel songs, including "Grace Is Sufficient," "Everything Will Be All Right," "He's Using Me," "The Man Jesus," "Peace Be Still," and "The Love of God." He recorded scores of albums that sold millions of copies and won three Grammy Awards; he was the first gospel singer to have a star on Hollywood's Walk of Fame.

FEBRUARY 20, 1991   Jesse Jackson Honored by U.S. Postal Service. The likeness of civil rights leader Jesse Jackson appeared on U.S. Postal cancellations in celebration of Black History Month. Jackson was the second living personality to be chosen for this honor.

FEBRUARY 26, 1991 All-male Academy Approved in Detroit. The Detroit Board of Education approved an all-male academy for African American students. The approval came after intense debate over whether black boys should be segregated from black girls and white students.

Opponents contended that the academy constitutes a return to school segregation akin to that practiced in the rural South before the landmark *Brown v. Board of Education* Supreme Court decision in 1954.

Others believed that the academy and others like it help African Americans who need the most support, particularly young males. Supporters cited a high dropout rate among black males and the absence of positive male role models as reasons to establish such academies.

FEBRUARY 26, 1991 President Bush Praised Black Military Heroes. President George Bush acknowledged Black History Month during a White House ceremony where he called the country's military the "greatest equal opportunity employer." He praised past and present black military heroes, including General Colin Powell, chairman of the Joint Chiefs of Staff, and Lieutenant General Calvin Waller, deputy commander of Persian Gulf forces.

MARCH 1991 Bernette G. Ford Named Head of Cartwheel Books. Bernette G. Ford was named head of Cartwheel Books, a new imprint of Scholastic Books. The imprint, which was designed to target very young readers, was scheduled to release 25 titles in its first fall season. Ford was the only African American to head a children's book division at a major American trade publishing company.

MARCH 3–5, 1991 Rodney King Beaten by Los Angeles Police. In Los Angeles, motorist Rodney King was severely beaten by several white police officers after being stopped for a speeding violation. The beating was videotaped by George Holliday, who witnessed the incident from his apartment balcony. The two-minute-long videotape revealed that the officers continued beating King with nightsticks even after he was put in restraints and appeared to be incapacitated. Police officers on the scene said that King had subjected them to a high-speed chase and had resisted arrest.

The incident immediately became an international issue after the videotape was shown on network news programs. Following the beating, King spent two days in a hospital recovering from his injuries before being booked on charges of evading police officers.

MARCH 7, 1991 Negro Leaguer James Bell Died. James "Cool Papa" Bell, a Hall of Fame baseball player who once dazzled spectators with his base-running exploits in the Negro Leagues, died at St. Louis University Hospital after a brief illness. He was eighty-seven years old.

Considered to be the fastest player in the old Negro Leagues, Bell often played two and three games a day for twenty-nine summers and twenty-one winters. He is believed to have been the highest paid player, having earned $90 a month.

Bell was sixteen years old when he began his career as a centerfielder who hit and threw lefthanded. He played for the Homestead Grays, the St. Louis Stars, the Chicago American Giants, the Pittsburgh Crawfords, and the Kansas City Monarchs.

He once hit twenty-one home runs in a single season, but Bell's specialty was punching the ball and running. He claimed that with a runner on first and the first baseman holding the bag, he could single through the hole nine times out of ten. He could circle the bases in thirteen seconds.

Bell batted .407 in 1946, his final season, but he was denied access to the major leagues, retiring a year before Jackie Robinson broke major league baseball's color line. After retirement, several major league teams called him with offers; one offered an $8,000 contract. Bell rejected it, however, realizing that his legs were no longer as good as they once were and wanting to keep his image intact.

After retiring from baseball, Bell worked as a custodian at the St. Louis City Hall. He later worked as a night watchman.

MARCH 14, 1991   Police Officers Indicted in Rodney King Beating. Four Los Angeles police officers—Stacey C. Koon, Theodore J. Briseno, Laurence M. Powell, and Timothy E. Wind—received indictments from a grand jury for their roles in the beating of motorist Rodney King on March 3, 1991. The four were formally charged with one count of assault with a deadly weapon and one count of unnecessary assault or beating by a police officer.

MARCH 20, 1991   Ban on Minority Scholarships Terminated. Education Secretary Lamar Alexander lifted the ban on federally funded minority scholarships, advising colleges to continue granting race-specific financial aid.

MARCH 25, 1991   Whoopi Goldberg Awarded Oscar. The Academy of Motion Picture Arts and Science awarded comedienne and actress Whoopi Goldberg an Oscar for her supporting actress role in the movie *Ghost*. She became the second African American female ever to win an Oscar. The late Hattie McDaniel won an Oscar fifty-three years earlier for her best supporting role in the Civil War epic *Gone with the Wind*.

Goldberg's performance in *Ghost* also garnered a Golden Globe Award and the Excellence Award at the Sixth Annual Women in Film Festival. In 1990, the NAACP named her Black Entertainer of the Year. Goldberg's previous honors included the NAACP's Image Award and an Academy Award nomination for her performance in *The Color Purple*.

Goldberg was born Caryn Johnson in New York's Chelsea section. Other films she made include *Jumpin' Jack Flash, Burglar, Fatal*

Beauty, Clara's Heart, The Long Walk Home, and Soap Dish.

APRIL 1991   Judy A. Smith Named Deputy White House Press Secretary. Judy A. Smith, a spokesperson for U.S. attorney Jay B. Stephens, was named deputy White House press secretary. Her duties included assisting White House press secretary Martin Fitzwater with daily press briefings and scheduling interviews with White House staff members.

APRIL 4–8, 1991   L.A. Police Chief Suspended from Duty. Los Angeles police chief Darryl F. Gates was suspended with pay for sixty days by the Los Angeles Police Commission for "allegations of mismanagement and/or neglect of duty" in connection with the March 3 beating of motorist Rodney King. While Los Angeles mayor Tom Bradley had called for Gates's resignation two days earlier, the Police Commission's ruling was overruled by the L.A. City Council on April 5. Chief Gates returned to work on April 8.

APRIL 8, 1991   "The Muslim Program" Published. *The Final Call* published "The Muslim Program." Their program includes desires for "a full and complete freedom" and "justice applied equally to all, regardless of creed or class or color."

APRIL 15, 1991   Survey Revealed Americans Support of Affirmative Action. The National Opinion Research Center (NORC), an affiliate of the University of Chicago, revealed in its annual national survey that Americans supported affirmative action but opposed reverse discrimination. It found that 71 percent of the white males and 70 percent of the white females polled believed it was very likely or somewhat likely that an equally qualified or less qualified black person would be hired or promoted before a white person.

The survey also asked the white respondents whether they thought the government should have a special obligation to help im-

Los Angeles police officer Theodore Briseno defends his actions in the assault on motorist Rodney King. (AP/Wide World Photos.)

prove the living standards of African Americans, or whether there should be no special treatment. Only 15 percent of the white men polled said they believed there was a special obligation for government help, and 53 percent opposed special treatment. Only 16 percent of the white female respondents said there should be a special obligation, while 49 percent opposed special treatment.

APRIL 23, 1991   Study Revealed African American and Hispanic Students Behind in Grades and Test Scores. A study by the Philadelphia School District revealed that African American and Hispanic students were lagging far behind white and Asian students in grades and test scores.

The school board released the findings in an eighty-one-page fact sheet that contained "baseline" figures for the district's five-year academic achievement goals.

The data showed that during the 1989–90 school year, African American and Hispanic students earned only half as many A's as white and Asian students; received twice as many F's; and scored below average on standardized tests about twice as often as whites and Asians.

"You can't read the document without having concern for African American and Latino students," Superintendent Constance E. Clayton, an African American, told the board. Some educators and parents, however, contended that the statistics were not useful because they were not broken down on a school-by-school basis.

To remedy the problem, the school board wanted to make several changes by 1994, including cutting academic-performance gaps that separate African American and Hispanic students from white and Asian students by 10 percent; increasing the attendance rate by five percent; increasing the number of students passing from elementary to middle school and from middle to high school by 10 percent; decreasing the number of students who drop out of high school; and decreasing student suspensions.

APRIL 28, 1991 Former CORE Chairman Floyd McKissick Died. Floyd McKissick, a former national chairman of the Congress of Racial Equality (CORE), died in Durham, North Carolina. He was sixty-nine years old.

McKissick's long career as a civil rights activist began after he had difficulty entering the all-white University of North Carolina Law School. He was admitted under a federal appeals court order after he enlisted the legal services of Thurgood Marshall, an NAACP lawyer.

McKissick began practicing law in Durham, where he specialized in civil rights, criminal defense, and personal injury cases. He served as national chairman for the Congress of Racial Equality (CORE) from 1963 to 1966, when he succeeded James Farmer as director, In 1990, McKissick served as a North Carolina district state judge.

MAY 5, 1991 Rosa Vernell Became First Female Candidate for Priesthood. Rosa Vernell, a former Roman Catholic nun who joined the African American Catholic congregation organized by Father George Augustus Stallings, Jr., became the first female candidate for priesthood.

MAY 12, 1991 Hampton Awarded Honorary Degree to Bush. President George Bush received an honorary degree at Hampton University, a historically black institution in Hampton, Virginia. He was greeted with silent protest by students who disapproved of his civil rights policies. Bush avoided discussion of civil rights in his commencement speech.

JUNE 1, 1991 Temptations Singer Died of Drug Overdose. David Ruffin, a former lead singer with the Temptations, died of an apparent drug overdose at the Hospital of the University of Pennsylvania in Philadelphia. Ruffin, who was fifty, had been the baritone voice behind such Temptations hits as "My Girl," "Since I Lost My Baby," and "Ain't Too Proud to Beg."

On the evening of his death, Ruffin was seen carrying a briefcase with about $40,000 in cash and British travelers checks. A close friend, Linster "Butch" Murrell, owner of a limousine service, said that Ruffin went to an alleged crack house. The limousine driver later took him to the hospital where he was pronounced dead on arrival.

Only three weeks before his death, Ruffin had returned to Philadelphia after a successful tour of England with two other former Temptations, Eddie Kendrick and Dennis Edwards.

Born January 18, 1941, in Meridian, Mississippi, Ruffin joined the Temptations in the early 1960s and was one of the group's three lead singers. The others were Kendrick and Paul Williams. In 1985, Ruffin made a brief comeback when he and Kendrick recorded an album with Daryl Hall and John Oates. The album, "Live at the Apollo with David Ruffin and Eddie Kendrick," went gold.

JUNE 5, 1991   Resurrection of Vetoed Civil Rights Bill of 1990 Attempted. Congressional Democrats attempted to resurrect the vetoed Civil Rights Bill of 1990 with alterations that included provisions for discrimination against women. Provisions in the Civil Rights Bill and the Women's Equality Employment Act of 1991 made it easier for minorities and women to sue employers who did not maintain a work force that resembled the labor pool.

JUNE 23, 1991   Four White Supremacists Ordered to Stand Trial for Cross Burning. White supremacist Tom Metzger, leader of the White Aryan Resistance, and three other men were ordered to stand trial for burning a cross in a racially mixed suburb near Los Angeles. The incident occurred in 1983.

JUNE 27, 1991   Thurgood Marshall Retired from Supreme Court. Supreme Court Justice Thurgood Marshall announced his retirement, decrying the conservative direction that the nation's highest court was taking. The eighty-three-year-old Marshall, the first black to serve on the Supreme Court, contended that "power, not reason, is the new currency of this Court's decision-making." Failing health and a rigorous court schedule prompted him to retire after serving on the Court for twenty-four years.

Marshall was born in Baltimore, Maryland, in 1908. He attended Lincoln University with the hopes of becoming a dentist. After graduating in 1930, Marshall decided to change his career path by enrolling in Howard University Law School, where he graduated at the top of his class in 1933. He entered private practice and a year later became counsel for the Baltimore branch of the NAACP; in 1938, Marshall was appointed chief legal officer of the organization. He later served as director-counsel of the NAACP Legal Defense Fund. In this capacity, Marshall played a crucial role in the fight to dismantle segregation in the United States, leading the legal team that argued before the Supreme Court in the landmark case *Brown v. Board of Education of Topeka, Kansas* in 1954, in which the high Court ruled unanimously that racial segregation in American public schools was unconstitutional.

In 1961, President John F. Kennedy appointed Marshall judge of the Second Circuit Court of Appeals, making him the second black jurist to serve on a federal appeals court. Marshall made history in 1965 when President Lyndon B. Johnson named him solicitor general of the United States, and again in 1967 when President Johnson appointed him to the Supreme Court.

Marshall, a man of fierce pride, understood his role in American history. As a liberal member of the Supreme Court, he was often the influencing factor that kept his fellow justices mindful of the less fortunate. During his tenure on the Court, Marshall earned a reputation for his outspoken interpretations of the First Amendment to the Constitution and for his passionate attacks on discrimination. Among the Supreme Court decisions Marshall authored are *Amalgamated Food Employees Union v. Logan Valley Plaza* (1968) and *Dunn v. Blumstein* (1972).

Marshall "brought a diversity of viewpoints to the Court," noted J. Clay Smith, Jr., professor of constitutional law at the Howard University Law School. "Justice Marshall provided the Court the point of view of the poor in this country—black and white. I'm sure his experience and knowledge of poverty and segregation influenced the Justices, conservative and liberal alike."

JUNE 30, 1991   National Civil Rights Museum Established on King Assassination Site. The Lorraine Motel in Memphis, Tennessee, where Martin Luther King, Jr., was assassinated in 1968, was converted into the National Civil Rights Museum. It was scheduled to open on July 4.

Members of the United Klans of America burn a cross in Mississippi. (AP/Wide World Photos.)

JULY 1991   Minority Students Discriminated Against in Public Schools. A General Accounting Office (GAO) study revealed that "a disproportionate number of minority students in the nation's public elementary and secondary schools are in lower-ability classes and special education programs."

Richard J. Wenning, senior evaluator for the GAO's human resources department, said that the findings suggested that schools were discriminately tracking black students, and that large numbers of African American and other minority students were being placed in racially identifiable classes.

The GAO's study coincided with findings of a Rand Corporation study that reported 25 percent of all black males in urban high schools were classified as learning disabled and were kept in classes for the handicapped. The Rand study was conducted in late 1990 by social scientist Paul Hill. "Public schools," Hill said, "have low expectations when it comes to black males."

A GAO spokesperson said that congressional members were becoming increasingly concerned over student resegregation, believing it could promote discrimination.

The GAO's research suggested that "schools often assign students to ability-grouped classes for academic subjects with no regrouping to reflect differential ability in various subjects. As a result, ability-grouped students remain with the same classmates throughout the day."

JULY 1, 1991   Clarence Thomas Nominated for Supreme Court Vancancy. President George Bush nominated Judge Clarence Thomas of the U.S. District of Columbia Court of Appeals to fill the Supreme Court vacancy created by the retirement of Thurgood Marshall.

Many African Americans rejected Judge Thomas because of his stance on affirmative action programs. He was a strong opponent of such programs during his tenure as head of the Equal Employment Opportunity Commission (EEOC). Ironically, Thomas attended the Yale University Law School under a program designed to admit minorities.

Bush's appointment was also considered controversial because some politicians and groups were reluctant to criticize an African American nominee, but did not want a person who was as opposed to abortion or affirmative action as Thomas was believed to be.

Such groups as the National Urban League and the NAACP were reluctant to reject the forty-three-year-old Thomas. In a printed statement, the Urban League commented: "We welcome the appointment of an African American jurist to fill the vacant seat left by Justice Marshall. Obviously, Judge Thomas is no Justice Marshall. But if he were, this administration would not have appointed him. We are hopeful that Judge Thomas's background of poverty and minority status will lead him to greater identification with those in America who today are victimized by poverty and discrimination. And we expect the Senate,

in its confirmation hearings, to explore whether he is indeed likely to do so."

JULY 9, 1991   Independent Commission Criticized LAPD Behavior. An independent commission that was appointed following the Rodney King beating released a searing report condemning the Los Angeles Police Department. The report, which was compiled over a three-month period, stated that L.A.P.D. officers "are encouraged to command and confront, not to communicate," and contended that racist and sexist behavior was rampant throughout the department.

The commission's panel offered many recommendations, including a "major overhaul" of the police department's procedures for disciplining officers and for handling citizens' complaints, and replacement of the current Police Commission. The panel also recommended that Chief Darryl F. Gates retire after a replacement was hired.

JULY 12, 1991   *Boyz N the Hood* Film Opened. John Singleton's box office hit *Boyz N the Hood* opened, starring rap artist Ice Cube, Cuba Gooding, Jr., Larry Fishburne, and Morris Chestnut. The plot revolves around a black father's struggle to raise his teenage son in the midst of drugs and gang violence in south central Los Angeles. Despite the film's anti-drug, anti-violence message, its opening sparked violence in several cities across the United States. The film ultimately grossed more than $57 million.

JULY 20, 1991   Rape Charge Filed Against Mike Tyson. An eighteen-year-old contestant in the Miss Black America pageant filed a complaint with the Indianapolis Police Department charging that former heavyweight champion Mike Tyson raped her in his hotel room the night before. A sexual assault lawsuit was filed for $21 million.

AUGUST 1991   Study Showed Higher Employment Discrimination for Blacks. A study by the Urban Institute entitled "Opportunities Denied, Opportunities Diminished in Hiring" revealed that blacks were three times more likely to be discriminated against than whites when applying for jobs. The findings came when Congress and President George Bush were vigorously debating changes in civil rights laws.

Ten pairs of black and white men aged nineteen to twenty-four with the same job qualifications acted as testers for the study. They responded to advertisements for 476 entry-level job listings in Chicago and Washington, D.C. The black applicants were denied jobs that were offered to equally qualified white males. Twenty percent of the black job seekers failed to advance after they were hired.

AUGUST 1991   Negro Leagues Baseball Museum Plan Announced. Plans were announced for a Negro Leagues Baseball Museum in Kansas City, Missouri, as a tribute to the men who played the game at a time when the major leagues excluded them. The museum was to be part of a black culture complex, the first phase of which was expected to open in early 1994. Proceeds from the museum will be used to cover pension, health, and other benefits for surviving members of the Negro Leagues.

Although the Major League Baseball Hall of Fame in Cooperstown, New York, now inducts former star Negro League players, the new museum would do much more, said W. Lloyd Johnson, executive director of the Negro Baseball Leagues. "There's no commitment to black baseball by the Hall of Fame. It honors the cream of the crop and people don't visit the Hall of Fame to see the stars of the Negro Leagues. We want to honor all the Negro League players and the men and women who made the enterprise work."

AUGUST 10, 1991   Number of Affluent African Americans Increased. A Population Reference Bureau study found that more black Americans moved into the upper-middle-class income bracket in the 1980s, while one-third of blacks remained locked in deprivation.

The number of affluent black families was 266,000, or one in seventeen, in 1967. In 1989, the latest year for statistics, there were more than one million black families among the ranks of the affluent, or one in seven. By comparison, one in three white families was affluent by the same measure in 1989.

SEPTEMBER 1991   Benjamin Franklin Award Given for *Brown Eyes, Brown Skin*. The Publishers Marketing Association awarded Just Us Books the 1991 Benjamin Franklin Award for children's picture books. The Orange, New Jersey, publisher won the award for the book *Brown Eyes, Brown Skin,* a story promoting pride and self-awareness, written by Cheryl Hudson and Bernette G. Ford. Founded in 1988 by Wade and Cheryl Hudson, Just Us Books also publishes a bimonthly newspaper, *Harambee,* for young school children.

SEPTEMBER 1991   "Hammerman" Cartoon Debuted. ABC-TV introduced "Hammerman," a Saturday morning cartoon series about a black man who found magic dancing shoes. A depiction of rap artist M. C. Hammer, Hammerman was a hero who rescued troubled people. When trouble came, he snuck away to don his magic shoes.

SEPTEMBER 1991   L. Douglas Wilder Announced Candidacy for Presidency. Virginia governor L. Douglas Wilder announced his candidacy for the presidency. Some political observers believed that Wilder, who became the nation's first elected African American governor in 1989, could be a serious candidate.

SEPTEMBER 9, 1991   Mike Tyson Indicted for Rape. A Marion County, Indiana, grand jury indicted boxer Mike Tyson for allegedly raping an eighteen-year-old Miss Black America contestant. He was charged with rape and deviate sexual conduct. Tyson had been in Indianapolis in July to promote the pageant.

SEPTEMBER 10–27, 1991 Nomination Hearings Started for Clarence Thomas. Judiciary Committee hearings for Judge Clarence Thomas began. Since his nomination to the Supreme Court on July 1, more African American and women's rights leaders were speaking out in opposition, fearing that Thomas, a conservative who opposed abortion and affirmative action, would not serve the best interests of the country.

SEPTEMBER 28, 1991 Jazz Great Miles Davis Died. Miles Davis, the jazz legend who helped to define the genre, died of pneumonia, respiratory failure, and stroke at St. John's Hospital and Health Center in Santa Monica, California. He was sixty-five.

A risk-taking innovator who was forever evolving as a musician, Davis was perhaps the best jazz trumpeter in modern times. He had an unmistakably distinct sound—sometimes haunting, sometimes melancholy, and virtually free of vibrato. Davis played for his own ear and often performed with his back to the audience. He constantly created more distinctive musical styles than any other musician in jazz history. Davis also influenced some of the best musicians, from saxophonists John Coltrane and Wayne Shorter to keyboardist Herbie Hancock and trumpeter Wynton Marsalis.

Davis played bebop with Charlie Parker's ensemble in the mid-1940s. In the 1950s, he formed his own group, introducing such forms as "cool jazz," hard bop, and jazz-rock, and he experimented with new forms of electrified jazz and funk. Some of Davis's most notable albums include *The Miles Davis Chronicles, Birth of the Cool, Sketches of Spain, Kind of Blue, Blue Sorcerer, In a Silent Way, Bitches Brew, On the Corner, Star People,* and *Tutu.*

OCTOBER 6–15, 1991 Anita Hill Testified at Nomination Hearings for Clarence Thomas. Anita Hill, a law professor at the University of Oklahoma who once worked with Su-

Clarence Thomas testifies before the Senate Judiciary Committee. (AP/Wide World Photos.)

preme Court nominee Clarence Thomas at the U.S. Department of Education and the Equal Employment Opportunity Commission (EEOC), testified before the Senate Judiciary Committee and accused Thomas of making sexual advances toward her years earlier. Hill's appearance, which was televised nationally October 11–14, prompted stiff debate. Many viewers wondered why she had waited several years before coming forward with her allegations and questioned the appropriateness of the issue in selecting a Supreme Court justice, while others criticized the Senate Judiciary Committee's initial reluctance to pursue Hill's allegations and questioned Thomas's suitability as a justice.

The hearings brought out the twin issues of race and gender. Hill became a symbol for all working women, and for African American women her testimony resurrected an age-old dilemma: whether to maintain loyalty to race or have an allegiance to gender.

Thomas was later confirmed for the Supreme Court.

OCTOBER 11, 1991 Comedian Redd Foxx Died of Heart Attack. Redd Foxx, well-known

Anita Hill testifies before the Senate Judiciary Committee during the Clarence Thomas hearings.

comedian and actor, died of a heart attack during a brief rehearsal for the television sitcom *The Royal Family.*

Born John Elroy Sanford in St. Louis on December 9, 1924, Foxx began his career performing in various musical groups, including the Bon-Bons, beginning in 1939. He performed as a stand-up comedian and recorded numerous comedy albums during a fifty-year span that began in 1941. Foxx's early comedy routines often featured "blue" material in which he told sex-oriented jokes and used profanity. He performed with comedian Slappy White for predominantly black audiences from 1947 through 1951.

Foxx's career began to accelerate in the 1970s. He made television history as the star of *Sanford & Son,* which ran from 1972 to 1977 and is still in syndication. He also starred in his own *Redd Foxx Comedy Hour, Redd Foxx Show,* and *The Royal Family.* His movie credits included *Cotton Comes to Harlem, Norman . . . Is That You,* and *Harlem Nights.*

Foxx won a Golden Globe Award for his performance as best television actor in a musical comedy and received three Emmy

Award nominations for best actor in a comedy series.

OCTOBER 15, 1991   March Against White Supremacists Held. About 300 people marched against bigotry in North Attleboro, Massachusetts, after hearing reports that white supremacists were active in the area.

OCTOBER 25, 1991   CUNY Chairmanship of Jeffries Jeopardized. The board of the City University of New York (CUNY) planned to vote on whether to retain Dr. Leonard Jeffries, Jr., as chairman of the Afro-American Studies Department in light of anti-Semitic remarks that had been attributed to him. Trustees attempted to block Jeffries's reappointment and hoped to enlist Governor Mario Cuomo, Senator Alphonse D'Amato, and other politicians who had been critical of Jeffries.

CUNY chancellor Dr. W. Ann Reynolds lobbied to allow Jeffries to remain as chairman of the department under restrictions, that included a one-year probation.

NOVEMBER 7, 1991   "Magic" Johnson Announced Retirement. Earvin "Magic" Johnson, an all-star guard for the Los Angeles Lakers, shocked the nation by announcing his retirement from the National Basketball Association after he tested positive for the HIV virus. Johnson's announcement spurred public astonishment and reinforced for many Americans the importance of AIDS awareness.

Further, Johnson's announcement supported the fact that AIDS is a disease that can be transmitted through heterosexual sex. Some people believed that Johnson's announcement not only focused needed attention on the disease, but brought more sympathy to AIDS sufferers.

NOVEMBER 11, 1991   Marion Barry Began Prison Sentence. Former Washington, D.C., mayor Marion Barry began serving his six-month prison sentence for charges stemming from his 1990 conviction for perjury and co-caine possession. Barry, age fifty-five, served three terms as mayor of the District of Columbia. He faced a maximum penalty of $1.85 million in fines and twenty-six years in prison. Some blacks believed investigators pursued Barry because of his race and contended that the FBI was guilty of entrapment.

NOVEMBER 29, 1991   Author Frank Yerby Died. Frank Yerby, author of action romantic period fiction—a rare genre for black writers in the 1940s and 1950s—died in Madrid, Spain.

Yerby, who was born on September 5, 1916, lived the second half of his life in Europe, first living in France before settling permanently in Spain.

He published numerous short stories and novels that were set in the antebellum South. His first published short story, "Health Card," won a special O. Henry Memorial Award in 1944. Two years later, Yerby published his first novel, *The Foxes of Harrow*, which took place on a southern plantation before the Civil War. Some of Yerby's best-known works are *The Golden Hawk, A Woman Called Fancy,* and *The Saracen Blade.*

DECEMBER 1991   Nine People Trampled During Celebrity Basketball Game. Nine people were trampled to death during a celebrity basketball game featuring rap artists Heavy D and Michael Bivens at the City College of New York. The event created a frenzy among critics of rap music, who claimed there was a connection between rap music and violence.

DECEMBER 4, 1991   White Supremacist Tom Metzger Sentenced to Jail. Los Angeles Judge J. D. Smith sentenced white supremacist Tom Metzger to six months in jail, three years' probation, and 330 hours of community service working with minority groups for his part in a cross-burning incident eight years earlier. The co-defendants, Stanley Witek and Brad Kelley, were given similar sentences.

1992

1992   *Waiting to Exhale* Published. Terry McMillan (1951–) published her novel *Waiting to Exhale*. Within one week the work became a *New York Times* best-seller, and in 1995 it was made into a star-studded film. McMillan received a Matrix Award from New York Women in Communication in 1993. She had attended Los Angeles City College, Berkeley, and Columbia University, and went on to teach at the University of Wyoming and the University of Arizona. Before the success of *Waiting to Exhale*, she published *Mama* (1987) and *Disappearing Acts* (1989).

JANUARY 1992   James Brown Given Award of Merit. James Brown, the renowned "Godfather of Soul," joined Bing Crosby, Irving Berlin, Ella Fitzgerald, Stevie Wonder, Paul McCartney, and Elvis Presley as a recipient of the Award of Merit for his lifetime contribution to music.

Brown has put an imprint on virtually every black musical movement since the 1950s. He is credited with influencing soul, funk, disco, and rap either with his songwriting or with his trademark gravelly voice. Brown's performances are punctuated with screams, screeches, grunts, moans, and dramatic body movement. Many rap singers have copied his style or have used portions of his recordings, a technique known as "sampling," in their own performances.

Only the late Elvis Presley has appeared more often on the pop song charts. Brown has had ninety-four songs in the top 100 and more top-20 singles than any other musician in history.

JANUARY 1992   Public Enemy Released Song Honoring King. The rap group Public Enemy released its "By the Time I Get to Arizona" in celebration of Martin Luther King, Jr.'s, birthday. The recording generated national controversy because the accompanying video depicted the burning of an Arizona state trooper's car, rekindling sentiments about Arizona's failure to make King's birthday a state holiday. The record was the subject of an ABC-TV "Nightline" program. Chuck D, the leader of Public Enemy, appeared on the program.

JANUARY 1992 Madison Square Garden Hosted Rap Concert. In New York City, Madison Square Garden broke a five-year rap concert sabbatical by promoting one of the largest rap shows ever. The event was incident free. Rap artists believe the concert was a positive signal that large groups of teens can gather to hear music without incident.

JANUARY 1992 Tractor & Equipment Co. Purchased. Three African American and two white executives teamed to purchase Tractor & Equipment Co., a Midwestern tractor and heavy equipment sales and lease company, for $5.1 million. The African Americans obtained 52.5 percent of the company in the deal. The Hickory Hills, Illinois, company's clients included government agencies, private contractors, and corporations in the metropolitan Chicago area. Edward Lindsey was named chairman and chief executive officer.

JANUARY 2, 1992 First Philadelphia Black Mayor Tenure Ended. W. Wilson Goode's term as mayor of Philadelphia ended with the inauguration of Ed Rendell. Goode served eight years (1984–92) as the City of Brotherly Love's first black mayor.

During his tenure, there was enough new office construction to change the Philadelphia skyline. For the first time, buildings exceeded the height of the City Hall Building. Goode also helped promote African American business; before he left office, there were four black-owned shopping centers, three of which were built during his tenure.

While Goode brought more business and financial strength to the city, some critics believe that such positive contributions were overshadowed by his inability to handle the conflict with MOVE, a predominantly black "back to nature" group. MOVE members had held Goode responsible for the destruction of a square block of homes after he had authorized police to bomb a house on Osage Avenue, where MOVE members held police at bay in a day-long shootout in 1985.

JANUARY 3, 1992 Pioneer African American Naval Officer Died. James E. Hair, one of thirteen blacks who broke the U.S. Navy's color barrier by becoming officers in World War II, died at St. Luke's-Roosevelt Hospital Center in New York. Hair, who was seventy-six, died of an apparent heart attack.

A grandson of slaves, Hair faced a segregated Navy that relegated blacks to duties as cooks and stewards when he enlisted in 1942. When President Franklin D. Roosevelt challenged the segregation practice, the Navy reluctantly admitted thirteen blacks to its Great Lakes Training Station near Chicago. Segregated from the white candidates, the blacks were only given eight weeks of training instead of the customary sixteen, so they studied at night and quizzed one another thoroughly on Navy regulations. Dubbed the "Golden 13" in observance of the gold stripes they wanted to wear, they scored so high that skeptical Navy officers ordered them retested. The results were even higher, averaging 3.89 out of 4.00—the best class score ever recorded. They were commissioned as ensigns on March 17, 1944.

Hair was assigned to skipper USSYTB-215 tugboat. In 1945, as a first lieutenant, he became the first black officer on the USS *Mason*, a landing ship that sailed in Asia with a black crew.

JANUARY 10, 1992 Dennis Green Named Head Coach of Minnesota Vikings. Dennis Green became the second African American professional football coach when he was named to replace the retiring Jerry Burns of the Minnesota Vikings. The only other African American at that level in the National Football League was Art Shell, coach of the Los Angeles Raiders.

Green, age forty-two, was previously an offensive assistant with the San Francisco 49ers, and head coach at Stanford University and Northwestern University.

Green's appointment came three days after NFL commissioner Paul Tagliabue urged team owners to step up their efforts to hire blacks and other minority members for coaching and front office positions, recognizing that blacks already made up about 60 percent of the league's players and several were assistant coaches on winning teams.

JANUARY 17, 1992   Martin Luther King, Jr., Honored with National Holiday. President George Bush officially declared January 20 a national holiday commemorating the birth of slain civil-rights leader Martin Luther King, Jr. He signed a proclamation to that effect at the Martin Luther King, Jr., Center for Nonviolent Social Change in Atlanta, Georgia, where one of King's daughters, the Rev. Bernice King, delivered an angry speech, saying, "How dare we celebrate in the midst of a recession, when nobody is sure whether their jobs are secure? . . . How dare we celebrate when the ugly face of racism still peers out at us?"

JANUARY 20, 1992   Violence Occurred after Klan Rally. Civil-rights supporters and Ku Klux Klan members in Denver, Colorado, became violent following a Klan rally that took place on the national holiday honoring Martin Luther King, Jr.

JANUARY 29, 1992   Musician Willie Dixon Died. Willie Dixon, a musician considered one of the greatest traditional bluesmen, died in Burbank, California. He was seventy-six years old.

Dixon created lusty and sometimes humorous songs full of risque images and metaphors. He began recording in 1940 and wrote more than 300 songs, including such blues

standards as "Hoochie Coochie Man," "Little Red Rooster," "The Seventh Son," and "Bring It on Home." He also wrote "You Can't Judge a Book by Its Cover," "Built for Comfort," and "Wang Dang Doodle."

Although many of Dixon's songs were hits, they often were associated with other artists more so than with him. He wrote many of his best works for such artists as Howlin' Wolf, Bo Diddley, and Muddy Waters. Many of his songs also had an impact on the Rolling Stones, Led Zeppelin, the Grateful Dead, and the Yardbirds.

FEBRUARY 10, 1992   Author Alex Haley Died. Alex Haley, author of *Roots: The Saga of an American Family* and *The Autobiography of Malcolm X*, died of a heart attack in Seattle, Washington. He had been working on a literary project about his hometown of Henning, Tennessee.

The first African American to win literary fame for the delineation of his family history, Haley published *Roots* during America's bicentennial in 1976. In the book, he brought his family's history to life when he traced his ancestry back to its West African origins. Haley wrote the book after extensive genealogical research that spanned three continents. In 1977, however, Margaret Walker charged that *Roots* plagiarized her novel, *Jubilee,* and, later, Harold Courlander claimed that it plagiarized his novel, *The African.* Courlander received a settlement after several passages in *Roots* were found to be almost verbatim from *The African.* Haley claimed that researchers had given him this material without properly citing the source.

Roots won a Pulitzer Prize and, a year later, became the basis of one of television's most popular miniseries. The eight-part miniseries, which was viewed by more than 130 million people, provided a frank depiction of the country's formative years and the slavery era. It also reminded viewers that the birth of the nation was not without severe moral complications.

Haley was known for his exhaustive research and attention to detail, which are evident in both *Roots* and *The Autobiography of Malcolm X,* published in 1965 after a year of intense interviews with the Black Nationalist leader. It has since become the inspiration behind black filmmaker Spike Lee's biographical film of Malcolm X.

Haley also contributed stories, articles, and interviews to *Playboy, Harper's,* the *Atlantic Monthly,* and *Reader's Digest.*

FEBRUARY 15, 1992   Benjamin Hooks Retired as NAACP Executive Director. Benjamin Hooks, executive director of the National Association for the Advancement of Colored People (NAACP), announced his retirement from the organization he served for fifteen years. Hooks made the announcement in New York City at the winter meeting of the National Board. He succeeded the late Roy Wilkins.

During Hooks's tenure, the NAACP's membership grew to 500,000, making it one of the largest black institutions in the United States.

MARCH 1992   American Urban Radio Networks Formed. NBN Broadcasting Inc. and Sheridan Broadcasting Network, the nation's two largest black-owned radio network companies, merged to form the American Urban Radio Networks, the largest radio vehicle for black consumers. The merger began in October 1991 after both companies began to downsize and make other economic cutbacks. Sheridan chairman Ronald R. Davenport and NBN chairman Sydney L. Small were named co-chairs of the new firm. They said the deal was arranged without a financial exchange, but that the two companies merged to share profits.

APRIL 29, 1992   L.A. Police Officers Acquitted in King Beating. The four Los Angeles police officers who were captured on videotape beating motorist Rodney King were acquitted by an Alameda County, California, court jury. Their acquittal sparked the most severe riot in

Roots author Alex Haley. (Bettmann Archive/Newsphotos, Inc.)

U.S. history. Black youths brutally beat white motorists who drove through the riot-torn area. Rioters burned and looted stores and other businesses in predominantly black south central Los Angeles.

Some blacks were also upset over black-Korean relations in the city. Many of the stores destroyed were owned by Korean Americans. The black residents contended that the Korean merchants were impolite and treated black shoppers as if they would shoplift. They also cited an

The Ministers Coalition for Peace prays for an end to the Los Angeles riots. (AP/Wide World Photos.)

earlier incident in which a Korean shop owner shot and killed a girl who was suspected of shoplifting. Fearing for their lives and disappointed over the lack of police protection, some Korean shop owners armed themselves and fired at would-be looters. President George Bush called for calm and dispatched federal troops to the city. He said he would take whatever measures necessary to end the violence.

Blacks, whites, and Asians all believed that the police did not act swiftly enough to quell the rioting and blamed slow response for the property destruction, which was estimated in the billions of dollars. The Los Angeles coroner's office reported fifty-eight people were killed.

Rioting also broke out in several other major cities, including Atlanta, Seattle, and New York City, causing federal officials to fear a national crisis. San Francisco suffered more damage than any other city outside of Los Angeles. More than 100 downtown businesses were damaged, and more than 1,500 people were arrested.

Immediately after rioting broke out in Los Angeles, many workers in Manhattan left their offices fearing violence. Little happened, however; police officials said there were 13 serious incidents, 14 injured officers, and 116 people arrested.

MAY 2, 1992   Federal Troops Dispatched to South Central Los Angeles. Mayor Tom Bradley welcomed federal troops as the residents of south central Los Angeles began cleaning up the debris from three days of rioting. More than 2,000 people were injured, and the death total continued to climb. More than 20,000 federal troops, National Guard troops, federal agents, and police from neighboring cities were dispatched to the area. Property damage from the rioting was estimated at more than $550 million. Rioters destroyed 3,800 buildings and left 10,000 other structures burned, vandalized, or looted. President George Bush declared the riot-torn neighborhoods a disaster area, making Los Angeles eligible for federal disaster aid.

Former baseball commissioner Peter Ueberroth, who managed the city's preparations for the 1984 Summer Olympics, accepted Mayor Bradley's invitation to direct the city's rebuilding effort.

MAY 2, 1992   African American Entered Horse in Kentucky Derby. Dance Floor, a racehorse owned by rap artist M. C. Hammer and his family, finished third in the Kentucky Derby.

Hammer is believed to be the first African American to enter a horse in the Kentucky Derby, the first jewel of thoroughbred racing's Triple Crown.

MAY 3, 1992   City Leaders Called for Peace. Political and civil rights leaders in the nation's largest cities called for peace and began working on plans to quell future civil disturbances.

Newly elected Philadelphia mayor Ed Rendell went on tours of black neighborhoods, talking with community leaders, youths, and educators and pleading for calm in the city. He said the city would continue its plans for an Afro-American and African Cultural Festival that would feature a parade, food fair, and numerous other activities.

MAY 15, 1992   "Black Diamonds: An Oral History of Negro Baseball" Released. "Black Diamonds: An Oral History of Negro Baseball," featuring taped interviews with such noted Negro League baseball stars as Judy Johnson, James "Cool Papa" Bell, Roy Campanella, and Jimmy Crutchfield, was released. The series was a tribute to Negro League baseball players, many of whom were denied an opportunity to play in the major leagues.

JUNE 1992   Minority-Owned Bank Successful. Two months after it opened, the United Bank of Philadelphia was generating more than $5 million in deposits and $11 million in assets, with more than 3,800 depositors. The city's first African American-controlled commercial bank since 1956 became living proof that blacks could form a financial institution and succeed during tough economic times.

The bank had become a reality after it turned to the community for the support it needed. Emma C. Chappell, chairperson and chief executive officer, said the bank met some opposition when it tried to sell stock. "They said we couldn't sell stock for a minority bank. So, we created our own market and sold stock directly through the bank's board of directors."

United reached its $6 million goal. More than $2.8 million of it came from churches, sororities, fraternities, and individuals. The board itself contributed $600,000, and the balance came from high profile investors such as Mellon Bank and the Provident Mutual Life Insurance Company.

Chappell believed that United was a vital facility because Philadelphia's largest banks were not serving the black community. A recent study revealed that the city's six largest bank loaned more than $297.7 million to resident mortgage seekers. Only $8.9 million of that, however, went to people in predominantly black neighborhoods.

JUNE 30, 1992   Willie L. Williams Replaced Darryl Gates as LAPD Chief. Willie L. Williams, former police commissioner of Philadelphia, replaced controversial Los Angeles police chief Darryl Gates, becoming the city's first black police chief. Political infighting, community distrust, and low morale had plagued the department for the previous year. Conditions worsened in late April 1992, when four police officers were acquitted of using excessive force against motorist Rodney King. The verdict resulted in widespread violence.

JULY 13–16, 1992   African Americans Served Influential Roles in National Conventions. Greater numbers of African Americans served in influential and decision-making roles in the Democratic and Republican national conventions. The most significant gains were exhibited at the Democratic National Convention, where chairperson Ronald Brown's gavel started and ended activities in New York's Madison Square Garden.

For the first time, blacks dominated the administrative roles at the convention. Alexis M. Herman served as convention chief executive officer, overseeing a $35 million budget, Mario M. Cooper served as convention manager, and Frank Williams, Jr., was the convention's chief financial officer.

Twenty-three other blacks were named to key positions on convention committees. Some of those appointments went to such people as New York City mayor David Dinkins and Washington, D.C., delegate Eleanor Holmes Norton, both of whom served as vice chairs of the Platform Committee, and Representative Louis Stokes of Ohio and Seattle mayor Norman Rice, both of whom were vice chairs of the Rules Committee.

JULY 26, 1992   First Black M.B.A. Graduate from Harvard Died. H. Naylor Fitzhugh, the first black person to earn a master's degree from the Harvard School of Business Administration, died after suffering from a long illness. He was eighty-two.

The Washington, D.C., native became a pioneer in black consumer marketing. His teachings and philosophies inspired a generation of black professionals, and his methods of target marketing are well respected. Fitzhugh was often sought by major consumer marketers.

After a thirty-one-year tenure as marketing professor at Howard University, Fitzhugh left to join the Pepsi Cola Co. in 1965, where he served as vice president of special markets for nine years.

JULY 28, 1992   "Cop Killer" Song Removed from Album. Rap artist Ice-T removed the song "Cop Killer" from his *Body Count* album, a move critics decried as a precedent for the censorship of rap. Criticism fell to the producer, Time Warner, which was accused of bowing to pressure from politicians and special interest groups after initially vowing to support Ice-T's First Amendment rights.

AUGUST 1992   Clifton Toulson Selected to Head S.B.A. Office in Philadelphia. Clifton Toulson was named director of the Philadelphia district office of the U.S. Small Business Administration. Toulson's duties included responsibility for the headquarters office in King of Prussia, Pennsylvania, three satellite offices, and a business-loan portfolio of $200 million.

He said he would promote more bank involvement with small businesses and contended that heightened interest in small business investments would benefit minority-owned companies.

SEPTEMBER 1992   Minority Enterprise Growth Assistance Plan Announced. The U.S. Department of Commerce declared plans to open Minority Enterprise Growth Assistance centers to provide specialized management and technical support to expanding minority-owned companies. The first center was planned for Chicago, Illinois.

SEPTEMBER 12, 1992   *Endeavor* Blasted off with First African American Female Astronaut. Mae C. Jemison, a physician and scientist, was one of seven astronauts aboard the space shuttle *Endeavor* as it blasted off for a seven-day mission—the fiftieth mission in the shuttle program. Jemison, age thirty-five, was the first African American woman in space. In honor of her accomplishment, a Detroit, Michigan, elementary science academy that opened in March was named after her.

OCTOBER 1992   First African American Manager Won World Series. Cito Gaston, manager of the Toronto Blue Jays since 1989, became the first African American manager to win a World Series championship. Toronto defeated the favored Atlanta Braves. The Toronto Blue Jays were the first non-U.S. team to compete in and win the World Series. (Toronto's two previous attempts for the championship were unsuccessful.)

OCTOBER 1992   John H. Johnson and Robert L. Johnson Honored by Executive Leadership Council. The Executive Leadership Council, an organization of African American business executives, honored magazine publisher John H. Johnson and Robert L. Johnson, the founder, chairman, and chief executive officer of Black Entertainment Television (BET). The Council honored John Johnson with its Heritage Award for his lifelong contributions and

Astronaut Mae C. Jemison in the cockpit. (Bettmann Archive/Newsphotos, Inc.)

dedication to the advancement of African Americans in business and communications. He began his publishing career in 1942 as editor and publisher of *Negro Digest* (later called *Black World*). He started with $500 and an idea for a monthly magazine with condensed articles. A year later, *Negro Digest* had a circulation of 50,000. Three years later, he published the first issue of *Ebony* magazine.

Robert Johnson was honored with the Council's Achievement Award for demonstrat-

ing outstanding leadership and commitment to the African American community. BET premiered on January 25, 1980, with initial programming airing only on Fridays from 11 P.M. to 2 A.M. "It's Bob Johnson's commitment and determination that brought Black Entertainment Television to the airways, making it the first and only African American-owned cable network in the United States," Council member James Jenkins said. "Johnson's success with Black Entertainment Television marks the first time in history that American viewers have had access to quality programming that reflects the needs, interests, and diverse lifestyles of Black America."

BET is now a 24-hour, seven-day-a-week operation, reaching more than 46 million households.

OCTOBER 5, 1992 Eddie Kendrick of the Temptations Died at Age 52. Eddie Kendrick, the melodic tenor behind most of the Temptations's biggest hits, died of lung cancer at age fifty-two, eleven months after losing a lung to that disease. He set the standard for falsetto singing and helped propel such Temptations hits as "Get Ready," "The Way You Do the Things You Do," and "Just My Imagination" to the top of the pop and R & B charts. With Kendrick as their lead singer, the Temptations became one of the nation's most popular and successful male groups. They garnered thirteen top-ten hits during his eleven years with the group. He left the group in the early 1970s for a solo career, and soon topped the music charts with the hit "Keep On Trucking." Kendrick rejoined the Temptations in 1982 for a short reunion tour.

Fellow Temptations singer David Ruffin died in June 1, 1991, of an apparent drug overdose.

OCTOBER 6, 1992 Students Protested Racial Assault. Alarmed by an earlier attack on a black student, minority students at the University of Massachusetts protested and asked school officials to designate Columbus Day as a time to study discrimination against non-white societies. Students occupied offices of a building during a visit by South African clergyman and Nobel Prize-winner Desmond Tutu. The protest culminated two weeks of racial turmoil that began on September 25 with an attack on a black dormitory assistant by a white man who allegedly punched him and shouted racial insults. The assistant later found feces dumped outside his room and racial epithets written on his door.

OCTOBER 11, 1992 Prince Negotiated Album Deal with Warner Brothers Prince, a musician known for sensual rock songs and provocative outfits, negotiated a deal with Warner Bros. Records to guarantee him the highest royalty ever paid to a recording artist; additionally, Prince was made a company vice president. Under the deal, Prince, who is also a composer and producer for other artists, could earn a $10 million advance for each of his next six albums, if the previous album sells more than five million copies.

OCTOBER 15, 1992 *Oakland Tribune* Sold. The name and certain assets of the 118-year-old *Oakland Tribune,* the nation's only major black-owned daily newspaper, were sold to the Alameda Newspaper Group—part of the Singleton newspaper empire that owns four small dailies in California's East Bay area.

The newspaper became a symbol of racial pride when Robert C. Maynard, a well-respected columnist with the *Washington Post,* and his wife, Nancy Hicks, a noted journalist with the *Boston Globe,* bought the *Tribune* from the Gannett Company. The purchase offered hope for African American success in mainstream publishing; when Maynard and Hicks bought the newspaper, African Americans represented less than 10 percent of the staffs of the nation's newspapers.

Despite cost-effective measures and a restructuring of debt, the *Tribune* struggled

under Maynard's tutelage. High production costs and the inability to upgrade the presses to remain competitive with other newspapers in the San Francisco Bay/San Jose region were major hindrances. Maynard attempted to make the newspaper competitive with a special regionalized East Bay section that catered to that region's residents, but he continually had to battle financial woes.

Maynard, who died a year later, announced the sale would not include the newspaper's presses and its landmark building. The *Tribune* maintained a daily circulation of 121,500 and 120,930 Sundays.

OCTOBER 20, 1992 Laree Sugg Joined Ladies Professional Golfers Association Tour. Laree Sugg, a UCLA senior majoring in English, attempted to become the first African American woman on the Ladies Professional Golfers Association (LPGA) tour since Renee Powell in 1980. She had been invited to participate in the LPGA qualifying school. Sugg helped UCLA win the NCAA tournament in 1991 when she sank a birdie on the first hole of a sudden-death playoff against San Jose State University.

OCTOBER 22, 1992 Webster Commission Report on L.A. Riots Released. The 222-page Webster Commission report on the Los Angeles riots blasted former police chief Darryl F. Gates for improper handling of the conflict. It also recommended solutions for avoiding future disturbances.

Headed by FBI and CIA chief William Webster, the Webster Commission blamed Chief Gates for failing to provide an effective plan and meaningful training to control the disorder sparked by the controversial verdicts in the Rodney King trial. It also said political infighting paralyzed officials when unity was crucial. "Gates had a responsibility to protect citizens," Webster said. "There was too little help and it came too late."

Gates, who retired in June, took a job as a radio talk show host. Angry over the report, he responded: "We should've blown a few heads off. Maybe that would have stopped it," according to a news report in *USA Today*. Gates insisted that he had a good plan that was poorly executed.

The committee interviewed more than 400 residents, police, and city officials before issuing recommendations. They were expected to serve as a blueprint for riot response in other areas of the country. Some of the recommendations included increasing police patrols; shoring up outdated emergency communications systems, including 911; developing a riot response plan before controversial riot-related trials end; and improving coordination and cooperation among officials.

The Webster Commission report prompted response in other areas such as Dallas, where police chief William Rathburn called for a national riot police squad similar to those in France and other countries.

Fifty-three people died during the riot, making it the most deadly riot in U.S. history.

OCTOBER 22, 1992   First Black Member of U.S. Golf Association Executive Committee Selected. John Merchant, a Bridgeport, Connecticut, lawyer, was selected as the first black member of the U.S. Golf Association's executive committee. Merchant's appointment occurred at a time when African Americans were becoming increasingly visible on the professional circuit. Some private country clubs, however, still restricted African Americans and other minorities from becoming members.

OCTOBER 27, 1992   Don Baylor Named Colorado Rockies Manager. Don Baylor was named manager of the Colorado Rockies, a 1993 National League expansion team. Baylor, who had played for six American League teams during his nineteen-year playing career, became the sixth African American to manage a team at the major league level. Frank Robinson, Larry Doby, Maury Wills, Hal McRae, and Cito Gaston preceded him.

OCTOBER 28, 1992   Bill Cosby Attempted to Purchase NBC. Bill Cosby, an outspoken critic of the image of blacks on television, made a bid to purchase the National Broadcasting Company (NBC).

Cosby, who at the time had an estimated net worth of $300 million, was believed to be one of six candidates to buy the financially struggling NBC. Losing in the ratings war against rivals CBS and ABC, NBC was believed to be on the trading block for $3.5 billion.

Cosby said he would make the deal in an arrangement involving two close friends in the industry, and that he would not plan to run the network. In earlier years Cosby helped bring the network from the number-three to the number-one spot with his groundbreaking series *The Cosby Show*, which debuted in 1984. The situation comedy about middle-class African American life shot to the top of the ratings and held that position for a record number of years. It featured Cosby as an obstetrician and Phylicia Rashad portraying his wife, an attorney.

He later became host of the syndicated game show *You Bet Your Life*, a remake of the game show that was hosted by the late Groucho Marx in the 1960s, and executive producer for NBC's struggling *Here and Now* sitcom featuring Malcolm Jamal Warner, a star from *The Cosby Show*.

OCTOBER 29, 1992   African American Literature Author Melvin Dixon Died. Melvin Dixon, a novelist, poet, and author of a textbook on African American literature, died in his Stamford, Connecticut, home from complications related to AIDS. He was forty-two.

An English professor at Queens College in New York, Dixon was noted for his translation of French literature to English. His translations included the *Selected Poems of Leopold Senghor*, by the longtime president of Senegal.

The Senghor translation was published by the University Press of Virginia in 1990.

Dixon's own writings included *Trouble in the Water*, his first novel, which won the Minority Fiction Award in 1989. He also wrote a volume of poetry called *Change of Territory* and a second novel, *Vanishing Rooms*.

OCTOBER 29, 1992 Lemrick Nelson Acquitted in Murder Trial. The New York State Supreme Court acquitted Lemrick Nelson, age seventeen, of the August 19, 1991, stabbing death of an Australian rabbinical student during a riot in a Brooklyn neighborhood shared by blacks and Jews.

Nelson was accused of murdering Yankel Rosenbaum, age twenty-nine, of Melbourne, Australia, during the melee that erupted in the Crown Heights community after Gavin Cao, a seven-year-old black child, was killed by a car that belonged in a motorcade escorting the Lubavitch Grand Rebbe, leader of the ultraconservative Jewish sect based in Crown Heights. Witnesses said the car went out of control before striking the child.

Shortly after the accident, Rosenbaum, a bystander, was surrounded by more than a dozen black youths and was beaten and stabbed. Only Nelson was charged with the murder; police said they discovered a bloody knife on Nelson and that Rosenbaum had identified the youth as his assailant before he died. The police also stated that Nelson later confessed to the crime. Nelson's lawyer contended that his client was framed by corrupt police.

Both deaths created a stir throughout New York City. About 200 people marched on City Hall. New York mayor David Dinkins pleaded for calm and later announced a $10,000 reward for information leading to the conviction of Rosenbaum's murderer.

OCTOBER 30, 1992 Singer James Walker Died. James Walker, a lead singer with the Dixie Hummingbirds, one of the country's best-known gospel quartets, died in his home in Philadelphia. The charismatic tenor, who was known by family and friends as "Walker," was sixty-six. He was buried in Northwood Cemetery in West Oak Lane, Pennsylvania.

Born in Mileston, Mississippi, he joined the twenty-six-year-old Dixie Hummingbirds quartet in 1954, after a stint in the Navy and work with other singing groups. Walker eventually became one of the Hummingbirds' most powerful singers and songwriters, composing more than seventy of the group's songs.

NOVEMBER 1992 Reginald F. Lewis International Law Center Established at Harvard. The Harvard Law School established the Reginald F. Lewis International Law Center, thanks to a $3 million grant from the Reginald F. Lewis Foundation.

The Lewis Foundation is a charitable organization endowed by the personal contributions of Reginald Lewis, chief executive officer of the New York-based TLC Beatrice International Holdings Inc.

Lewis, an African American business executive and financier and Harvard graduate, made the largest gift in the 175-year history of the school. Dean Robert C. Clark said the unprecedented gift would help sustain the law school's preeminence in the decades ahead. The Lewis Center will house the school's Graduate Legal Studies Program and the school's international library collection. Portions of the grant will also create a faculty committee chaired by professor Christopher Edley and the Reginald F. Lewis Fund for International Study and Research.

NOVEMBER 3, 1992 Bill Clinton Elected President. William "Bill" Clinton rode a tide of discontentment to a lopsided election victory over President George Bush. Clinton was elected by winning in several key states, including New Jersey, Michigan, New York, Illinois, and California. Much of his support came from black voters and discontented middle-class whites who suffered the brunt of a long-lasting recession that left thousands of workers hitting the unemployment lines.

A Harris Poll study revealed that Clinton received 78 percent of the black vote. Among white voters, Bush received 41 percent of the vote, while Clinton received 39 percent.

Some political analysts suggested black support came partly because he managed to bring together coalitions—such as gays, women's rights activists, and African Americans—who had decided they needed a change from the previous presidential administration and Republican leadership. Many political analysts believed that president-elect Clinton would fill key Cabinet, Supreme Court, and other federal agency positions with women, African Americans, and members of other underrepresented groups.

Clinton launched a multifaceted approach to winning voters. He was the first presidential candidate to visit the riot-torn ruins of South Central Los Angeles: he actually arrived before that section of the city was under police control. He promised that his administration would pay more attention to urban problems. Clinton became the first presidential candidate to appear on the youthful music television station MTV and on "Arsenio," a syndicated talk show written, produced, and hosted by African American Arsenio Hall. Clinton visited urban areas that were heavily populated by African Americans and addressed many of their concerns.

Many African Americans hoped that Clinton's election would bring more domestic programs to help spur the economy, help balance minority affairs, and prompt the appointment of a liberal to the U.S. Supreme Court. The president-elect's transition team was expected to include several women and blacks, including former Urban League leader Vernon Jordan. Others included Texas academic and former Democratic representative Barbara Jordan; former Democratic house majority whip and appropriations expert William Gray III,

who resigned to head the United Negro College Fund; Marian Wright Edelman, founding president of the Children's Defense Fund; and Jocelyn Elders, an African American who ran the human resources department in Arkansas.

NOVEMBER 3, 1992 Mosely, Page, and Rush Won Elections.

Carol Moseley Braun, age forty-five, became the nation's first black female senator when she defeated Republican Richard Williamson, a Chicago lawyer. She became the first African American in the U.S. Senate since Republican Edward Brooke of Massachusetts lost his seat in 1979. She was the third black to serve in the Senate and the second to come from Illinois. (Hiram R. Revels, also from Illinois, was elected in 1870 to fill the seat once occupied by Confederate president Jefferson Davis and was the first African American in the Senate.)

Braun won with 55 percent of the vote. Prior to her primary victory over incumbent Alan J. Dixon, Braun was not considered a serious threat. Her upset victory, however, set her on the path to an easy win over the Republican candidate. Braun drew support from an interracial majority. She appealed to a significant number of young voters and those who strongly believed that Clarence Thomas should not have been confirmed to the U.S. Supreme Court. She even drew some Republican defectors, surveys revealed.

Alan Page, a National Football League Hall of Fame defensive lineman, was elected to a six-year term on the Minnesota Supreme Court, becoming the first African American to hold an elective statewide office in that state. Page won with 62 percent of the vote after fighting to get on the ballot following a dispute with state officials.

Bobby Rush, a former Black Panther party leader who later served as deputy chairman of the Illinois Democratic Party and as a Chicago alderman, was elected to Congress.

Reports by the Senate Historian, House Historian, Congressional Black Caucus, Con-

Carol Moseley Braun at the 1992 Democratic National Convention. (AP/Wide World Photos.)

gressional Hispanic Caucus, and *Congressional Quarterly* revealed that there were now more minorities in Congress. A record number of minorities ran for Congress in 1992 and won, making the House and the Senate more reflective of the nation's population than ever before in history. Early campaign returns revealed that sixty-seven of ninety-seven minority candidates claimed victory; that the twenty-six-member Black Caucus would add seventeen members; and that the fourteen-member Hispanic Caucus would add seven members. Be-

cause several minorities retired, the result would be forty blacks in both houses and nineteen Hispanics in the House. At least one Asian American would go to the House, raising the total to six in both houses. The lone Native American, Colorado's Ben Nighthorse Campbell, won a seat in the Senate.

NOVEMBER 4, 1992 Pearl Stewart Named Editor of *Oakland Tribune*. Pearl Stewart, a longtime journalist in the San Francisco Bay area, was named editor of the *Oakland Tribune*.

Upon assuming her new position on December 1, Stewart became the first African American woman to head a major metropolitan daily newspaper. She was named by officers of the Alameda Newspaper Group, the *Tribune's* new owners who bought the newspaper from Robert Maynard, the first African American to own a major metropolitan daily.

Maynard, who had bought the newspaper from the Gannett Company, sold the *Tribune's* name, circulation, and advertising client lists in October 1992.

NOVEMBER 6, 1992 Vernon Jordan Selected to Head Bill Clinton's Transition Team. President-elect Bill Clinton selected Vernon Jordan, former president of the National Urban League (NUL) and the United Negro College Fund (UNCF), to head his transition team with Warren M. Christopher, who served as a senior policy adviser in the Clinton campaign.

Jordan, age fifty-seven, became a major figure in Washington during the 1970s and 1980s. He served as head of the Urban League from 1972 to 1981, the year he became a partner in the law firm Akin, Gump, Hauer & Feld.

Active in the civil rights movement since the early 1960s, Jordan served on the board of directors for many corporations, including American Express, Bankers Trust, Union Carbide, J. C. Penney, Xerox Corporation, Corning, Dow Jones, Revlon, and RJR Nabisco.

NOVEMBER 9, 1992 Murder Conviction for Klan Leader Upheld. The U.S. Supreme Court upheld the murder conviction and death sentence of Ku Klux Klan leader Henry Hays, who argued that his sentence for the 1981 murder of nineteen-year-old Michael Donald was cruel and unjust. Hays's accomplice in the murder was out on parole.

NOVEMBER 9, 1992 Johnson Publishing Company Celebrated Fiftieth Anniversary. The Johnson Publishing Company, publishers of *Jet, Ebony,* and *EM* magazines, celebrated its fiftieth anniversary.

Founded by John H. Johnson, the company set out to publish magazines that filled a void not met by white publications. The Johnson Publishing Company became a model for other black-owned companies.

The company and its founder have been credited with helping change the way blacks view themselves. Through his magazines, Johnson helped blacks build self-esteem, learn about others, follow black news, and realize that African Americans could enjoy a satisfying life-style and obtain top professional goals.

Johnson got the idea for his first publication, *Negro Digest,* while working with a black-owned insurance company and compiling a weekly digest for the company's president. Johnson eventually realized that black news should reach more blacks. Unable to convince friends to support his dream, he took out a $500 loan secured by his mother's furniture. He then sent a letter to 20,000 people on the insurance company's mailing list. Johnson asked each person if they liked the idea, then asked them to send him $2. Three thousand people responded, and *Negro Digest* was born.

The key to the company's growth was *Ebony* magazine. Founded in 1945, it was modeled after *Life* magazine. By 1996, *Ebony* was the largest circulating magazine published for blacks, boasting a readership of over 1.9 million.

NOVEMBER 16, 1992 Detroit Police Officers Charged with Murder. Two Detroit, Michigan, police officers—Walter Budzyn and Larry Nevers—were formally charged with murder and one other with manslaughter in the death of Malice Green, a black motorist. A fourth officer was charged in the assault. Three other officers, who had been suspended, were not charged. Three of the officers, including those charged with murder, were white; the manslaughter charge was lodged against a black officer.

Malice Green, a thirty-five-year-old Detroit resident, died of head wounds after being beaten by officers on November 5. The incident occurred near a suspected drug house. The Green death sparked an outcry in Detroit as parallels were drawn between it and the March 1991 police beating of Los Angeles motorist Rodney King, which led to several days of civil unrest in the spring of 1992 after the accused officers were aquitted. In Detroit, however, both the African American mayor, Coleman Young, and the African American police chief, Stanley Knox, quickly denounced the beating and immediately suspended the officers involved.

NOVEMBER 18, 1992 *Malcolm X* **Film Opened.** The epic motion picture *Malcolm X,* starring Oscar-winning actor Denzel Washington, opened nationwide. The $34 million film was produced by African American filmmaker Spike Lee and based on author Alex Haley's biography of the slain civil rights leader.

The film on the life of the controversial Muslim minister and human rights activist was made over a period of two years and was itself wrought with controversy. Hollywood studios initially seemed reluctant to support the story of the black activist who has become best known for his declaration that African Americans must defend themselves and achieve racial equality "by any means necessary." They also balked at Lee's proposed length for the movie (more than three hours) and the cost. Lee, however, argued successfully that no less than the recently released film on President John F. Kennedy—a difficult subject like Malcolm X—required more time. Additionally, African American entertainers, sports figures, and others came to his rescue when money for the project ran low.

In the course of filming Malcolm's "life-changing" 1964 pilgrimage, Lee became the first Hollywood filmmaker to be granted permission to film the annual gathering in the Saudi Arabian city of Mecca—Islam's holiest

city. The movie was also filmed in New York, Egypt, and the Republic of South Africa.

Despite some criticism about odd omissions and changes (such as ignoring the importance of Malcolm's supportive sister Ella, who had, among other things, helped finance his pilgrimage to Mecca), *Malcolm X* was widely praised as an epic motion picture comparable to such films as *Lawrence of Arabia* and *Gandhi.*

The screening of *Malcolm X* became a literal *cause célèbre* among many African Americans and particularly young blacks, who have raised the stature of Malcolm in recent years to a point where he rivals Martin Luther King, Jr., in their esteem. His fiery orations, including his rejection of non-violence as a way of life in the human rights struggle, have been adopted as the credo for many disaffected blacks in the 1990s.

1993

JANUARY 1993   Barrett Became First Black Female Sheriff. In Fulton County, Georgia, Jackie Barrett was sworn in as the nation's first black female sheriff.

JANUARY 1993   Alabama Lawmakers Won Suit Against Confederate Flag. In Alabama, black legislators celebrated a courtroom victory that ended Governor Guy Hunt's practice of flying a Confederate flag over the state capitol in Montgomery. According to a circuit court judge, an 1895 law said that the only acceptable flags were the U.S. flag and the state flag.

The legislators had decided to take the issue to court because they felt the Confederate flag was an offensive symbol of racial oppression and hatred. Various Alabama business groups agreed and spoke out against the governor, too, insisting that displaying the rebel banner hurt the state's image.

JANUARY 1, 1993   Jamaican Immigrant Burned by White Racists. A black man vacationing near Tampa, Florida, was kidnapped by three white men, robbed, drenched with gasoline, and set on fire. His attackers left behind a misspelled note reading, "One les nigger, one more to go. KKK."

Thirty-one-year-old Christopher Wilson, a Jamaican immigrant from New York City, had gone out early New Year's morning to buy a newspaper. As he stopped at a shopping center, he was confronted by three men and forced at gunpoint to drive to a remote area. There he was taunted with racial slurs, assaulted, and left for dead. But he managed to make his way to a nearby home where a resident hosed him down with water. When police arrived, Wilson was in so much pain that he begged them to shoot him.

Although he suffered severe burns over forty percent of his body, Wilson survived and was able to identify one of the men police later arrested, twenty-six-year-old Mark Kohut. Also arrested were Charles Rourk, age thirty-three, and Jeff Ray Pellett, age seventeen. Authorities described all three men as drifters who had met each other through a day-labor service. They were charged with carjacking (a federal crime), attempted murder, robbery, and kidnapping, for which they faced up to twenty-five years in prison. And since the case was officially classified as a hate crime because the attackers had referred to race as a motive, they faced even more jail time for violating Wilson's civil rights.

JANUARY 6, 1993   Dizzy Gillespie Died. Jazz trumpeter Dizzy Gillespie, who helped create the revolutionary bebop style as well as Afro-Cuban jazz, died of pancreatic cancer in a New Jersey hospital at the age of seventy-five. His trademark bulging cheeks, bent horn, and fun-loving showmanship had entertained audiences throughout the world for over fifty years.

JANUARY 18, 1993   States Recognized King's Birthday. For the first time since Martin Luther King, Jr., Day became an official federal holiday, all fifty states marked its observance, even longtime holdouts New Hampshire and Arizona.

JANUARY 19, 1993   Reginald Lewis Died. Reginald Lewis, the chairman of TLC Beatrice International Holdings, Inc., the nation's largest black-owned business, died of a cerebral hemorrhage in New York City. The fifty-year-old executive had been diagnosed with brain cancer about two months earlier.

Lewis's background in Baltimore, Maryland, was a modest one. He left there to earn a degree in economics from Virginia State University and a law degree from Harvard University in 1968. He then joined a New York City law firm and specialized in corporate and securities (stocks and bonds) law.

In 1973, Lewis established his own law firm. Ten years later he set up an investment company, TLC Group L.P. Its first big deal was to buy the McCall Pattern Company, producer of sewing patterns. In 1987, Lewis sought the multinational food distribution company Beatrice for $985 million. It was the largest deal of its kind in history.

Despite his status as the country's most prominent black businessman, Lewis always downplayed the importance of race in his career. He preferred to be judged by his performance, and he refused to consider race as a crutch or an obstacle. "It's understandable that [my race] is something people focus on," he once remarked. "But what I focus on and what others focus on are two different things. . . . I focus on doing a first-rate job on a consistent basis."

Lewis's success eventually brought him a personal fortune of some $400 million. Although he carefully guarded his own and his family's privacy, he was well known for his generous donations to civic and charitable causes, including a $1 million gift to Howard University and a $3 million gift to Harvard Law School.

JANUARY 20, 1993 Angelou Read Poem at Clinton Inauguration. At President Bill Clinton's inauguration, renowned black poet Maya Angelou read the special verse she had been asked to compose for the occasion. (She was the first poet asked to participate in an inauguration since Robert Frost was part of John F. Kennedy's inauguration in 1961.) Entitled "On the Pulse of Morning," her poem reflected the optimism many people felt at the thought of the country's "new beginnings" under a different administration.

JANUARY 21, 1993 O'Leary Appointed Secretary of Energy. President Bill Clinton appointed Hazel O'Leary as secretary of the Department of Energy in 1993. Although she was instrumental in dismantling the nation's nuclear weaponry complex and in helping energy producers finance nuclear waste storage programs, O'Leary came under attack for questionable spending of government money. She resigned from her post in late 1996.

JANUARY 21, 1993 Espy Appointed Secretary of Agriculture. President Bill Clinton appointed Michael Espy as secretary of agriculture in 1993. Espy had served as congressman from Mississippi in the U.S. House of Representatives since 1986, working on committees such as the House Agricultural Committee, the Sub-Committee on Cotton, Rice, and Sugar, and the Sub-Committee on Conservation, Credit, and Rural Development. Espy resigned as secretary in December of 1994 because of a federal ethics investigation of accusations that he had accepted gifts from companies regulated by the Department of Agriculture.

JANUARY 24, 1993 Thurgood Marshall Died. Just days after illness forced him to cancel plans to swear in new vice-president Al Gore, retired Supreme Court justice Thurgood Marshall died of a heart attack in Bethesda, Maryland. An outspoken opponent of the conservative direction the country had taken since 1980, the eighty-four-year-old jurist had once vowed that he would not die until the Democrats were in the White House again.

On the Wednesday after Marshall's death, nearly twenty thousand people filed past his coffin in the Great Hall of the Supreme Court. There they paid their respects to the man known as "Mr. Civil Rights" in recognition of his lifelong commitment to achieving justice for all, especially the poor and minorities. The next day, four thousand civil rights leaders, members of Congress, and others (including the president and the vice-president and their wives) gathered at Washington's National Cathedral for a memorial service. Marshall was buried on Friday at a private ceremony at Arlington National Cemetery.

JANUARY 25, 1993 Bert Andrews Died. Bert Andrews, a photographer whose work chronicled the history of black theater, died of cancer in New York City. He was sixty-three.

Andrews photographed many of Broadway's biggest stars, including James Earl Jones, Cicely Tyson, Denzel Washington, Billy Dee Williams, Lou Gossett Jr., Morgan Freeman, Phylicia Rashad, Raymond St. Jacques, and Diana Sands. He also took pictures of memorable scenes from the shows *Ma Rainey's Black Bottom*, *A Soldier's Play*, and *Bubbling Brown Sugar*, to name a few. Much of his work is on display at the Schomburg Center for Research in Black Culture in Harlem, New York, and in the 1990 book *In the Shadow of the Great White Way: Images from the Black Theater*.

JANUARY 26, 1993 FBI and Black Agents Settled Discrimination Dispute. After nearly two years of negotiations, a spokesman for the U.S. Justice Department announced that an agreement had been reached in a racial discrimination dispute between the Federal Bureau of Investigation (FBI) and its black agents.

Under the terms of the agreement, more than one hundred black special agents were scheduled for promotions, transfers, or new

Michael Espy testifying before Congress. (AP/Wide World Photos.)

training that had been denied to them as a result of racial bias in the overwhelmingly white federal agency. (At the time of the settlement, about ninety percent of FBI agents were white males; only about five percent were black.) The FBI also agreed to let a federal judge supervise its personnel practices for five years. In addition, the agency planned to hire outside consultants to study its procedures for promoting, evaluating, and disciplining special agents, and it pledged to change the way in which it chooses agents for assignments and training programs.

White agents opposed to the settlement later took steps to challenge it in federal court. They felt it was a "race conscious" agreement that violated the equal employee rights of non-black agents.

JANUARY 30, 1993 Thomas A. Dorsey Died. Thomas A. Dorsey, "the father of gospel music," died of Alzheimer's disease at his home in Chicago, Illinois. He was ninety-three.

FEBRUARY 3, 1993 Schott Fined for Racial Slurs. Major League Baseball owners fined

Cincinnati Reds owner Marge Schott $25,000 and suspended her from the game for one year for her alleged use of racial slurs.

Under the terms of the suspension, Schott was banned from watching games in the owner's box. She was also forbidden from running the team's day-to-day business but was allowed to be involved in major decisions. Her fellow owners also agreed to cut her suspension to only eight months if she behaved herself and if she attended a multicultural training program.

Many people, including Atlanta Braves vice-president Hank Aaron, were dissatisfied with this punishment. They felt it amounted to little more than a slap on the wrist for Schott. It was hoped that the other team owners would remove her from the game permanently.

FEBRUARY 6, 1993 Bowe Defeated Dokes in Boxing Match. In New York City, heavyweight boxing champion Riddick Bowe retained his title by taking only a little more than two minutes to defeat challenger Michael Dokes.

FEBRUARY 6, 1993 Arthur Ashe Died. Tennis great Arthur Ashe, the first and only black man to win the Wimbledon championship, died of AIDS-related pneumonia in New York City. He was forty-nine.

FEBRUARY 23, 1993 Black Burial Ground Designated Historic Landmark. The city of New York voted to make an eighteenth-century African American burial ground in Manhattan a historical landmark.

The site was first discovered in 1991 during construction of a federal office building. Scientists were eventually called in, and they took away the remains of over four hundred people and thousands of artifacts for closer inspection. Most of the blacks who had been buried there were believed to have died between 1710 and 1790.

In September 1993 the skeletal remains of the African Americans were turned over to

anthropologists at Howard University for further study. Once they have completed their work—which is not expected to be until 1999—the remains are scheduled to be returned to New York City and reburied. Plans are also under way for an African Burial Ground Museum and Research Center to be built near the site of the historic discovery.

FEBRUARY 25, 1993 Federal Trial Began in Rodney King Beating Case. In Los Angeles, California, opening arguments began in the federal trial of four white police officers charged with beating black motorist Rodney King.

In this second trial, Stacey Koon, Theodore Briseno, Laurence Powell, and Timothy Wind faced charges of violating King's civil rights. Their first trial on criminal charges related to the same incident ended with acquittals on all but one charge. The verdicts triggered days of deadly rioting in Los Angeles and elsewhere throughout the country.

The central issue in the federal case revolved around whether the officers had used excessive force and whether they intended to punish King. (If convicted, they faced up to $250,000 in fines and ten years in prison.) The federal trial was expected to follow along the same lines as the criminal trial with one difference—Rodney King himself was scheduled to take the stand for the first time and testify about his beating.

MARCH 1993 Jemison Resigned from NASA. Astronaut Mae Jemison, the first black woman in space, resigned from the National Aeronautics and Space Administration (NASA). Her immediate career plans included teaching at New Hampshire's Dartmouth University and establishing a technology firm in Houston, Texas, to improve communications and health care in western Africa. Later, it was announced that Jemison was also scheduled to appear in an episode of the highly popular and acclaimed syndicated television series *Star Trek: The Next Generation.*

Arthur Ashe with the Wimbledon trophy he won in 1975. (AP/Wide World Photos.)

MARCH 8, 1993 Billy Eckstine Died. Singer Billy Eckstine, popularly known as "Mr. B.," died in Pittsburgh, Pennsylvania, at the age of seventy-eight. During the late 1940s and early 1950s, his rich baritone voice made him one of America's top vocalists and among the first to become a crossover star with white audiences. With his coolly casual look—a shirt with a rolled collar and a jacket loosely draped from his shoulders—Eckstine was also pop music's first black male sex symbol.

Born William Clarence Eckstein in Pittsburgh in 1914, he grew up in Washington, D.C., and attended Howard University. He started singing when he was about seven and drifted into it professionally during the 1930s. His first performances were with various amateur shows and dance bands that toured throughout the East and Midwest.

In 1939, Eckstine joined Earl "Fatha" Hines's orchestra and taught himself to play the trombone and trumpet. But it was as a singer that he helped the band gain national fame with two hit records, "Jelly, Jelly" and "Stormy Monday Blues."

Eckstine left Hines in 1943 and spent a year as a solo act before pulling together his own band. It did much to popularize the new bebop style of jazz by featuring some of its greatest performers, including Miles Davis, Dizzy Gillespie, Charlie "Bird" Parker, Sarah Vaughan, Dexter Gordon, and Art Blakey.

During the late 1940s, Eckstine turned once again to a solo singing career. He then sang one hit romantic ballad after another. Among his biggest successes were "Fools Rush In," "Everything I Have Is Yours," "Prisoner of Love," "My Foolish Heart," "Body and Soul," "I Apologize," "Blue Moon," and "Passing Strangers." By singing such love songs when a white woman might be listening, Eckstine challenged one of the biggest taboos of a segregated society. "We weren't supposed to sing about love," he later recalled. "We were supposed to sing about work or blues."

Despite his popularity, Eckstine was rarely offered opportunities to work in movies or on television due to his race. And when he did make an appearance, he was told not to let his eyes rest on any of the white actresses watching him sing. So he spent the rest of his career entertaining enthusiastic audiences in major jazz clubs across the country.

MARCH 23, 1993 White Supremacist Sentenced to Probation. In Fort Worth, Texas, an all-white jury sentenced an admitted white supremacist to ten years' probation for the June 1991, drive-by shooting of a black man, Donald Thomas. Thomas was sitting in his pickup truck talking with some white neighbors when he was killed by shots fired from a car in which an eighteen-year-old white skinhead named Christopher W. Brosky was riding.

During Brosky's trial, it was revealed that he had helped plan the shotgun slaying of the thirty-two-year-old Thomas. Two seventeen-year-olds who were also involved, including the alleged triggerman, pleaded guilty and received prison terms. Brosky himself could have received life in prison for his part in the crime. But according to some jurors, his exceptionally light sentence came about as a result of a poorly worded note to the judge. What they had meant to recommend was that he serve five years in jail and then be put on probation for ten years. Instead, what they wrote was interpreted to mean only ten years' probation and no jail time.

The decision infuriated local blacks and sent thousands into the streets on March 28 to participate in what they called a "silent death march." A crowd estimated at more than five thousand people assembled in downtown Fort Worth and walked peacefully to the county courthouse, where they held a rally calling for justice for African American victims of crime.

APRIL 1, 1993 Denny's Settled Discrimination Case. The nationwide Denny's restaurant chain announced that it had reached a settlement with the U.S. Justice Department in a case of alleged racial discrimination against black customers.

The Justice Department had accused Denny's of treating black customers less favorably than white customers and of discouraging black customers from eating there. Restaurant officials denied the charges, but as part of the chain's settlement with the Justice Department, it agreed to hire a civil rights monitor and train its employees and managers to oppose racial discrimination. The company also pledged to let people know about its non-discrimination policy through advertisements in newspapers and on television and on notices appearing in the restaurants themselves.

Still waiting to be settled, however, was a lawsuit against the chain filed by an ex-employee claiming racial discrimination. And in March 1993, some black customers in California had filed a class-action lawsuit against Denny's. They charged that restaurant managers often refused to serve blacks and threatened them or threw them out. They also said they were routinely the target of racial slurs and insults. Finally, they claimed that managers required them to prepay for their meals or pay a cover charge, and that Denny's would not extend the chain's free birthday meal offer to them.

APRIL 4, 1993   Twentieth-fifth Anniversary of King's Death Observed. Across the United States, thousands of people observed the twenty-fifth anniversary of the death of Martin Luther King, Jr., with speeches, rallies, and other events. Memorial services were also held in Atlanta, Georgia, and Memphis, Tennessee.

APRIL 6, 1993   Bosley Elected First Black Mayor of St. Louis. In a surprise, come-from-behind victory over a better-known opponent who also happened to be his former high school counselor, Freeman Bosley, Jr., won election as the first black mayor of St. Louis, Missouri. A thirty-eight-year-old lawyer, he had been

serving as clerk of the circuit courts for the past eleven years.

APRIL 8, 1993   Marian Anderson Died. Singer Marian Anderson, whose 1939 concert at Washington, D.C.'s, Lincoln Memorial was a symbolic triumph over racial bigotry, died in Portland, Oregon, of complications from a stroke. She was ninety-six.

APRIL 9, 1993   Chavis Named Director of NAACP After a year-long search, the NAACP board of directors announced that they had chosen forty-five-year-old clergyman and activist Benjamin Chavis, Jr., to replace Benjamin L. Hooks as executive director of the nation's oldest civil rights group.

The energetic and progressive Chavis came to the NAACP from Cleveland, Ohio. He had worked there for the United Church of Christ's Commission for Racial Justice for twenty-five years, the last eight as its executive director. Originally from North Carolina, he received a bachelor's degree from the University of North Carolina, a master of divinity degree from Duke University, and a doctorate degree from Howard University.

A civil rights activist since joining the NAACP at the age of twelve, Chavis spent four years in prison during the late 1970s as a member of the so-called Wilmington Ten. This was a group of nine black men and one white woman who were convicted of firebombing a white-owned store in Wilmington, North Carolina, during a period of unrest over school desegregation. Chavis and the others had, in fact, been in town to protest but denied taking part in any bombing. The controversial case prompted Amnesty International to declare the Wilmington Ten political prisoners, making them the first to be identified as such in the United States. A federal appeals court eventually overturned the convictions after witnesses admitted they had lied while giving testimony.

Later, Chavis made a name for himself as one of the founders of the "environmental

CHRONOLOGY OF AFRICAN AMERICAN HISTORY

Benjamin Chavis. (AP/Wide World Photos.)

racism" movement. This group claims that unusually high amounts of toxic materials are stored in and near black communities.

As the new head of the NAACP, Chavis pledged to make the organization more aggressive and more in tune with young blacks and blacks in the inner cities. Describing himself as a Pan-Africanist, he also reached out to Africans all over the world by announcing plans to set up NAACP branches in Africa and the Caribbean. In addition, he promised to expand the membership of the NAACP to include other minorities.

APRIL 9, 1993 Ford Acquitted in Political Favors Case. In Memphis, Tennessee, U.S. representative Harold Ford—the state's first black member of Congress—was acquitted of charges that he accepted over $1 million in bank loans he never intended to repay from people seeking political favors from him. His first trial on the same charges ended in a mistrial in 1990.

APRIL 11, 1993 Janet Harmon Bragg Died. Janet Harmon Bragg, the first black woman in the United States to earn a full commercial

pilot's license, died at the age of eighty-six in a suburb of Chicago, Illinois.

A native of Georgia, Bragg graduated from Spelman College and did graduate work at Loyola University and the University of Chicago. She developed her interest in flying in 1930 while she was dating one of the country's first black flight instructors. She then took flying lessons and in 1933 bought the first of three airplanes she eventually owned.

Two years later, Bragg was one of the first nine blacks admitted to the Curtiss Wright Aeronautical University to study aircraft mechanics. After being denied the opportunity to try out for her commercial pilot's license in Alabama because of her race, she headed north to Illinois, where she was able to take and pass the test.

Bragg later formed the black Challenger Air Pilots Association and helped train Ethiopian soldiers during World War II. She continued to fly as a hobby throughout the 1950s, 1960s, and 1970s.

APRIL 12, 1993 University Basketball Coach Fired for Racial Slurs. Central Michigan University basketball coach Keith Dambrot, who is white, was fired for using a racial slur in front of his team and when referring to his black assistant coach.

At a team meeting during the season, Dambrot allegedly told his fifteen players— twelve of whom were black—that he wished "we had more niggers on this team." He later explained that he hadn't meant he needed more black players, just tougher team play in the midst of a losing season.

Some of the black members of the team defended their coach. They said they were not offended by what he had said and that he was not a racist. They insisted that his use of the word "nigger" had been misunderstood by outsiders. "If this were a black coach saying that, nothing would have been made of it," declared one. "It's just one of those things that's getting blown out of proportion."

APRIL 14, 1993 Attorney General Ordered Investigation of Jail Suicides. A spokeswoman for Attorney General Janet Reno confirmed that she had ordered the civil rights division of the U.S. Justice Department to look into a series of suspicious hanging deaths in Mississippi jails.

For nearly a year, civil rights activists had been calling for an investigation into the deaths of twenty-four black men over a six-year period. All had died by hanging while in police custody in various county jails. During the same period, twenty-three white prisoners had also been found hanged. Authorities ruled that all but one of the forty-seven deaths were suicides. Civil rights activists charged, however, that at least three black prisoners were actually lynched.

APRIL 17, 1993 Koon and Powell Convicted in Rodney King Federal Trial. In Los Angeles, California, a federal jury convicted white police officers Stacey Koon and Laurence Powell of violating the civil rights of black motorist Rodney King. Two other officers—Theodore Briseno and Timothy Wind—were acquitted.

While the verdicts in the officers' criminal trial a year earlier had sparked several days of deadly rioting, the verdicts in their federal trial were met with joy and relief. Los Angeles remained calm, as did other cities across the nation. Police and National Guard troops had been on alert for days in anticipation of violence as jurors worked to reach a decision.

On August 4, 1993, a judge handed down his sentences in the case. Both Koon and Powell received thirty months in prison, several years less than most observers had anticipated. The judge explained that he had chosen a lighter punishment because King's behavior had provoked police and because the two offi-

cers already had endured the loss of their jobs and a tremendous amount of notoriety. He also speculated that they faced the possibility of abuse in prison.

Blacks reacted to the sentences with anger and disbelief. They felt justice still had not been served in the case.

APRIL 28, 1993 Brown Nominated as "Drug Czar." President Bill Clinton nominated fifty-five-year-old Lee Brown as "drug czar"—the head of the U.S. Office of National Drug Control Policy, a cabinet-level position.

With a background in law enforcement, Brown had formerly served as head of the police departments in Atlanta, Georgia (1978–82), Houston, Texas (1982–90), and New York City (1990–92). He was the first black and the first police officer ever chosen to lead the country's war on drugs.

APRIL 30, 1993 First National Urban Peace and Justice Summit Held. In Kansas City, Missouri, the first National Urban Peace and Justice Summit began in an inner-city Baptist church. The unusual three-day meeting was deliberately scheduled to coincide with the first anniversary of the Los Angeles riots. It brought together over one hundred current and former gang members, community organizers, and religious leaders from twenty-six cities across the country. (About half the participants were African American, and the other half were Hispanic.) They discussed how to stop the violence in America's urban areas (including ways to expand the gang truce in Los Angeles that began after the riots), fostering neighborhood economic development, dealing with police brutality, and gaining political power.

APRIL 30, 1993 Guinier Nominated to Head Civil Rights Law Division. President Bill Clinton nominated University of Pennsylvania law professor Lani Guinier as assistant attorney general for civil rights, one of the most important posts in the Justice Department. If confirmed, she would be the first black woman to head the civil rights division.

MAY 6, 1993 Race Riot Erupts at Boston High School. Outside South Boston High School in Massachusetts, racial violence arose between black and white students. The problem began earlier in the day when about one hundred black and white students walked out of class to protest what they felt were inadequate security measures at the school. Classes were dismissed due to the peaceful demonstration. As black students got on buses to ride home, a crowd of white students began throwing rocks and bottles at them. The two groups exchanged racial slurs, and several people— including Boston's mayor, who had come to the school to talk to the students about security— received minor injuries.

During the mid-1970s, South Boston High School was the scene of the nation's most brutal battles against court-ordered busing to achieve desegregation.

MAY 6, 1993 Jury Awarded King Papers to Boston University. In a Boston courtroom, a jury ruled in favor of Boston University in a long-running dispute between the school and the family of Martin Luther King, Jr., over ownership of about one-third of the slain civil rights leader's personal papers.

On July 16, 1964, King had sent a letter to officials at Boston University (where he had received his doctorate degree) saying that he wanted to give his correspondence, manuscripts, and other papers and items of historical interest to the school's library. Later that year and the next, he did indeed hand over about 83,000 documents. Most dated back before 1961 and covered the birth of the civil rights movement.

In her lawsuit, King's widow, Coretta Scott King, claimed that her husband had changed his mind about the donation before his death but that he had never let the university know. She said that he had only sent his papers

up north temporarily because he thought they would be safer there than anywhere in the South. (At the time, his home and office were often the targets of firebombings.) According to Mrs. King, he really intended for them to be returned to him at some future date.

Describing herself and her family as deeply disappointed about the verdict, Coretta Scott King said she would consider filing an appeal. She had hoped to bring all of her husband's papers together in Atlanta, Georgia, at the Martin Luther King, Jr., Center for Nonviolent Social Change.

MAY 11, 1993 White Chattanooga Policemen not Charged in Black Motorist Death. In Chattanooga, Tennessee, a grand jury decided not to charge any white police officers in the choking death of a black motorist.

The incident occurred on February 5, 1993, when thirty-nine-year-old Larry Powell was pulled over by two police officers who suspected him of driving while drunk. Powell allegedly resisted arrest, and five other officers responded to a call for help from the two officers on the scene. In the scuffle that followed, the officers handcuffed Powell, put him face down on the ground, then gripped his neck with their hands and batons. A medical examiner testified that this choke hold caused Powell's death but that there was no evidence of abuse.

Outraged black leaders in Chattanooga, as well as Powell's widow, strongly condemned the grand jury's decision.

MAY 12, 1993 Miami Tourism Boycott Ended. After nearly three years, blacks in Miami, Florida, called off a tourism boycott that had cost the city an estimated $50 million. The boycott had begun shortly after local government officials snubbed South African anti-apartheid leader Nelson Mandela during his visit in June 1990. It ended when blacks in the Miami area felt they had finally convinced Hispanic and white business and government leaders to give them more economic and political power.

MAY 14, 1993 NAACP Began Founding First Hispanic Chapter. In Bronx, New York, the NAACP began organizing its first Hispanic chapter. The move was part of an effort by new executive director Ben Chavis to broaden the group's membership by reaching out to other minorities.

MAY 16, 1993 Marv Johnson Dies. Singer Marv Johnson, co-creator with Berry Gordy of the famous Motown sound, died two days after suffering a stroke during a concert in South Carolina. He was fifty-four.

Johnson was the first singer that Gordy recorded and managed. The two of them combined Johnson's background in gospel music with a churchy-sounding female chorus and a male bass to create a uniquely African American product that appealed to black as well as white audiences. The new sound debuted in 1959 with a song entitled "Come to Me" that Johnson recorded on the United Artists label. He had his first big hit a year later with "You Got What It Takes."

Several other hits followed over the next few years, but by the 1970s, Johnson's popularity declined. He continued to tour throughout the United States and Europe, however, often appearing with various Motown artists.

MAY 18, 1993 White Supremacists Arrested for Planning Bombing. In Toledo, Ohio, two members of a white supremacist group called the White Aryan Religion were arrested for planning to blow up a predominantly black public housing project on July 4.

Police said that Aaron Lee and Craig Lay, both twenty-two years old, had plotted to make several bombs and place them around a housing project on the city's east side. During a raid on Lay's house, authorities seized explosives, guns, drugs, and hate literature. They said it appeared that the White Aryan Religion

was a new group based in the Toledo area that may have also been responsible for some crimes in nearby Detroit, Michigan.

MAY 18, 1993 Dove Named U.S. Poet Laureate. Librarian of Congress James Billington named forty-year-old black poet Rita Dove as U.S. poet laureate. She was the first African American woman to serve in the ceremonial post. (Author Gwendolyn Brooks was a consultant on poetry to the Library of Congress before the poet laureate position was created.) The job of U.S. poet laureate—a term borrowed from the British—is to promote poetry through the library's literature programs and advise the library on literary matters.

MAY 18, 1993 Jury Ruled Black University Administrator Wrongfully Fired. In New York City, a jury ruled that Leonard Jeffries had been wrongfully dismissed from his job as chairman of City College's black studies department for criticizing Jews and whites. It then awarded him $400,000.

Jeffries had sued the college for $25 million for replacing him as department chairman. (He remained a member of the faculty, however.) He claimed school officials were upset about a controversial speech he gave in 1991. In that speech, he declared that Jews and the Mafia had conspired to depict blacks in a negative way in the movies and that Jews had financed the African slave trade. While his remarks created an uproar, they were not the reason for his firing, insisted school officials. They maintained that Jeffries was simply a poor administrator.

The jury sided with Jeffries, saying that his constitutional right to free speech had been violated. After the verdict, he vowed to continue his fight to regain his former job as department chairman.

MAY 22, 1993 Bowe Defeated Ferguson to Retain Boxing Title. In Washington, D.C., heavyweight boxing champion Riddick Bowe retained his title by defeating challenger Jesse Ferguson just seventeen seconds into the second round of their fight.

MAY 24, 1993   University Dropped Racial Charges Against White Student. The University of Pennsylvania dropped racial harassment charges against a white student who called a group of black women "water buffalo." The incident occurred near midnight on January 13, 1993. A white student named Eden Jacobowitz was trying to study in his dorm room when he was disturbed by members of a black sorority who were singing and making noises outside his window. He leaned out and shouted, "Shut up, you water buffalo!" The angry women, who said they also heard other racial and sexual slurs but could not tell where they came from, complained to campus police.

They tracked down Jacobowitz, who readily admitted that he had made the "water buffalo" comment. (Born in Israel and educated at a Jewish school, Jacobowitz said the words "water buffalo" had come to his mind because a Hebrew word meaning "water oxen" is used to insult thoughtless and disorderly people.) But he denied saying anything else and insisted that his remark had referred to the funny noises the women were making, not to their race.

University officials disagreed and ordered Jacobowitz to write a letter of apology to the women. They also told him he could be put on dormitory probation and that a note would be added to his student file indicating that he had violated the university's code of conduct on racial harassment. Jacobowitz refused to agree to these terms and instead demanded a hearing before a group of students and faculty.

Before the hearing could be held, however, the charges against him were dismissed when the women withdrew their complaints. They said their case had been undermined because they had never had the chance to tell their side of the story. Jacobowitz, on the other hand, had attracted national media attention with his version of what had happened.

MAY 24, 1993   Second African African American Summit Held. In the African city of Libreville, Gabon, the second African African American Summit opened. In attendance were more than one thousand black Americans (including prominent politicians, civil rights activists, religious leaders, corporate officials, and entertainers) and three thousand Africans, including twenty heads of state.

Organized by African American human rights activist Leon Howard Sullivan, the summit was intended to establish ties between blacks from all nations. Attendees were also scheduled to discuss ways of promoting economic development and improving health care and farming techniques in Africa.

MAY 24, 1993   Denny's Faced New Discrimination Allegations. A little more than a month after announcing it had reached a settlement with the U.S. Justice Department in a racial discrimination complaint, the Denny's restaurant chain faced still more allegations of bias against blacks.

In Baltimore, Maryland, six black Secret Service agents filed a lawsuit claiming that a Denny's in Annapolis, Maryland, had refused to serve them. They had been in town on April 1 with fifteen other agents preparing for a visit by the president. They stopped at a Denny's for breakfast and placed their orders. When no food was delivered, they ordered again several more times. After about an hour, they left the restaurant without having eaten. According to reports, a group of white agents at a nearby table was served promptly.

Denny's officials insisted the problem was related to poor service, not racial discrimination. They said they had fired the manager of the Annapolis restaurant for failing to report the agents' complaints. The company later agreed to work with the NAACP to visit Denny's restaurants at random throughout the country to make sure blacks were receiving fair treatment. The company also promised to hire more minorities, and the NAACP said it would help provide sensitivity training.

According to newspaper reports, at least ten other complaints had surfaced in five different states since Denny's had promised to make changes in its operations back in April. In June, the company hired black food executive Norman Hill to serve in the newly created job of vice president of human resources. His job was to help make sure Denny's anti-discrimination policies were followed at the chain's restaurants throughout the country.

MAY 28, 1993   Miami Policeman Acquitted of Murdering Black Motorcyclist. In Orlando, Florida, a racially-mixed jury acquitted a Miami police officer of manslaughter in the 1989 shooting death of a black motorcyclist.

On January 16, 1989, in the predominantly black Overtown section of Miami, Officer William Lozano shot and killed black motorcyclist Clement Lloyd. Lloyd then crashed, fatally injuring his passenger, Allan Blanchard. Lozano claimed the speeding motorcycle had tried to run him over and that he had fired his gun in self defense. The incident touched off three nights of racial violence in Overtown.

In December 1989, Lozano was convicted of manslaughter in both deaths and sentenced to seven years in prison. In 1991, however, an appeals court ordered a new trial for the policeman on the grounds that the Miami jury had been pressured into finding him guilty because of the threat of more racial violence.

Lozano's 1993 trial was held in Orlando, where authorities hoped it would be easier to find an impartial jury. They also hoped to avoid triggering another riot if he were acquitted.

In the hours after the verdict was announced, Miami remained relatively calm. Police reported only scattered instances of looting and rock- and bottle-throwing in two mostly black neighborhoods. However, outraged community leaders called on the U.S. Justice Department to file civil rights charges against Lozano, but experts considered that unlikely to happen.

MAY 30, 1993   Sun Ra Died. Sun Ra, an influential pianist and orchestra leader who experimented with jazz and many other forms of music, died at the age of seventy-nine. He had been ill since January 1993, after suffering a series of strokes.

Ra was born Herman Blount in Birmingham, Alabama, in 1914, but he later liked to claim he was born on the planet Saturn about five thousand years ago. As Sonny Blount, he played in Fletcher Henderson's jazz orchestra during the mid-1940s and also was active in experimental music circles in Chicago, Illinois.

Blount was already a well-known musician when he changed his name to Sun Ra during the 1950s. Along with the name change, he created a whole new identity for himself by drawing from the Bible, black spiritualism, science fiction, and Egyptian mythology. (Ra, in fact, was the name of the ancient Egyptian sun god.) Beginning in 1956, Sun Ra traveled with a multimedia group known as Arkestra that included musicians as well as exotically-costumed dancers.

Ra's career spanned over sixty years. During that time, he recorded more than two hundred albums, including *Saturn, Magic City, Savoy,* and *It's After the End of the World.* They encompassed a wide range of sounds and styles, including bop, gospel, blues, and electronic synthesizers.

Ra considered himself to be a bridge between different generations, and in February 1993, *Rolling Stone* magazine seemed to confirm that judgment when it called him "the missing link between Duke Ellington and Public Enemy." Yet he was not especially well known in his native country (he spent most of his later years in Europe) and never had the recognition and success that many bigger stars enjoyed.

JUNE 1993 *Menace II Society* **Was a Box-Office Hit.** *Menace II Society,* a film directed by twenty-one-year-old African American twin brothers Allen and Albert Hughes, was a surprise hit at theaters with earnings of more than $10 million in less than a month. The Hughes brothers and their critically acclaimed drama about urban violence had been nominated for awards at the 1993 Cannes Film Festival in France.

JUNE 1993   Prince Changed Name to a Sign. The often mysterious pop star Prince created a stir when he announced that he had changed his name to a sign that combined the symbols for male and female. The sign had served as the title of his most recent album, and it also appeared in his videos, on his clothing and guitar, and various places on stage with him. But since no spoken word existed for the sign and Prince himself did not provide a pronunciation, no one was sure exactly what he wanted to be called. He eventually came to be called "The Artist Formerly Known as Prince."

JUNE 1993   Cosby Made Second Attempt to Buy NBC. Black actor-comedian Bill Cosby was reported to be working on a second deal to buy the NBC television network. According to some sources, the deal involved several other unnamed Hollywood insiders besides Cosby.

JUNE 3, 1993   Guinier Nomination for Civil Rights Post Withdrawn. Acknowledging that he did not have enough support in the Senate to win a major confirmation battle, President Bill Clinton withdrew the controversial nomination of Lani Guinier to head the civil rights division of the U.S. Justice Department.

Opposition to the forty-three-year-old law professor had been growing steadily since Clinton announced her nomination in late April. Many people—mainly conservative Republicans—charged that her extensive writings about race and politics were too radical and seemed to support the idea of racial separatism. They

dubbed her the "Quota Queen" because of her call for racial quotas in electing and hiring public officials.

By late May, the White House had begun to hint that perhaps she should pull out of the running. Guinier refused, however, and insisted that her views deserved a fair hearing in the Senate, not just in the media. As pressure mounted, the president himself announced that he was withdrawing her name from consideration. He explained that he had not closely read her writings before choosing her for the civil rights job.

Afterwards, Guinier defended herself by saying that people had misinterpreted her writings. She insisted that she would have never pushed for quotas because of the racial discrimination her father suffered as the only black student at Harvard College in 1929.

Many others condemned Clinton's move, including members of the Congressional Black Caucus, civil rights organizations, and women's groups. They agreed with Guinier that she had been unfairly judged.

JUNE 7, 1993   Hearings Began in Jamaican Immigrant Burning Case. In Tampa, Florida, pre-trial hearings got under way for two men accused of kidnapping a black tourist from New York City on New Year's Day and setting him on fire.

Attorneys for Mark Kohut and Charles Rourk immediately asked for the trial to be moved out of town because of extensive local publicity about the case. A third man originally charged in the crime, Jeff Ray Pellett, was scheduled to testify against Kohut and Rourk as part of a plea bargain in which he admitted to helping with an armed carjacking and being an accomplice after a crime.

At first, the judge refused to change venues, but later agreed to move it to West Palm Beach. Jury selection began there on August 23, 1993. At the time the trial was scheduled to begin, victim Christopher Wilson was still recovering from the burns he received during the attack.

JUNE 7, 1993   Foreman Defeated in Boxing Comeback Attempt. In Las Vegas, Nevada, forty-four-year-old heavyweight boxer George Foreman's comeback attempt ended in defeat as he lost to twenty-four-year-old Tommy Morrison in a twelve-round unanimous decision.

Foreman had originally retired from the ring in 1977 and then began a comeback in 1987. In 1991, he became the oldest fighter ever to challenge for the heavyweight title when he took on Evander Holyfield.

JUNE 8, 1993   Black Teenager Convicted of Killing Texas State Trooper. In Austin, Texas, a nineteen-year-old black teenager named Ronald Ray was found guilty of killing a state trooper in 1992. The case was unusual in that Ray and his attorneys claimed that rap music had driven him to commit the crime and that he should not have to pay for it with his own life. (Since killing the trooper was a capital crime, Ray faced the possibility of receiving a death sentence).

Ray confessed to the murder but blamed it on years of listening to violent, anti-police "gangsta rap" that made him hate and fear law enforcement authorities. On the night of the incident, he had driven for about 120 miles while the music of California gangsta rapper Tupac Shakur played. He said he was very angry by the time Trooper Bill Davidson "pulled [him] over for nothing." (Actually, Davidson had pulled over Ray because he had a missing headlight.)

The power of gangsta rap to influence behavior also promised to be an issue in a related case. Davidson's widow filed a product liability lawsuit against Shakur and his record company, Time Warner, charging both of them with contributing to her husband's death.

JUNE 8, 1993   Judge Ordered U.S. Government to Release Haitian Refugees. A district court judge ordered the U.S. government to release more than 150 Haitian refugees who had been held at an American naval base in Cuba for as long as twenty months after testing positive for the AIDS virus.

Many black Americans had closely followed the problems of the Haitian men, women, and children ever since the Bush administration forbid them from entering the country. Prominent figures such as Jesse Jackson and, before his death, Arthur Ashe, had repeatedly condemned the government's actions as racist and inhumane. They described the crowded and dirty conditions at the naval base where the Haitians lived as little more than an "HIV prison camp."

JUNE 8, 1993   Scott Barrie Died. Scott Barrie, one of the first African American designers to gain fame in the world of fashion, died of brain cancer in Italy. He was fifty-two.

A native of Florida, Barrie—born Nelson Clyde—began creating clothes at the age of ten. He later studied at the Philadelphia Museum College of Art. After working for twenty years in New York City, he moved to Milan, Italy, in 1982. There Barrie worked for the fashion houses of Krizia and then Kinshido. He opened his own showroom in 1988. He specialized in a soft, fluid style of clothing, using jerseys and chiffon in designs that appealed mostly to young people.

JUNE 9, 1993   Jackson Announced He Would Not Re-seek Atlanta Mayoral Seat. Citing personal reasons that were believed to be related to his health, Mayor Maynard Jackson of Atlanta, Georgia, announced he would not seek reelection to a fourth term.

JUNE 9, 1993   Ford Motor Company Hit With Discrimination Suit. In Minneapolis, Minnesota, twelve African American managers employed by Ford Motor Company in eight different states filed a class-action lawsuit charging racial discrimination in promoting and paying blacks. The suit also claimed that supervisors had used racial slurs in front of several black managers.

The company had no immediate comment other than to say that it had aggressive anti-discrimination policies. The case was not expected to go to trial until 1995.

JUNE 18, 1993   White Detroit Policemen's Trial for Murder Began. In Detroit, Michigan, opening arguments began in the trial of three white police officers charged in the 1992 death of black motorist Malice Green.

According to witnesses who testified for the prosecution, officers Walter Budzyn and Larry Nevers approached Green while he was in his car, which was parked in front of a suspected drug house. They became angry when he refused to obey their orders to open up his clenched right fist, and began beating him with their heavy police flashlights. A third officer, Robert Lessnau, arrived while the beating was under way. He pulled Green from his car, threw him on the ground, and kicked him. The beating continued until the officers finally allowed a waiting ambulance crew to treat Green, who died on the way to the hospital. An autopsy later showed he had received at least fourteen blows to the head.

Budzyn and Nevers were charged with second-degree murder in Green's death, and Lessnau faced charges of assault with intent to do great bodily harm. All three men were fired from the police force after being charged.

Attorneys for the former officers based their defense on doubts about the true cause of Green's death. They did not deny that the policemen had beaten the black man, but they depicted Green as high on drugs and ready for a fight when the officers approached him. The defense attorneys claimed that he had alcohol and cocaine in his system when he died and that he had a diseased heart. They argued that those conditions played a bigger role in his death than the beating did.

On August 23, 1993, two separate juries found Budzyn and Nevers guilty of second-degree murder. They both faced up to life in prison but were allowed to go free on bond while waiting to be sentenced. Meanwhile, their attorneys vowed to appeal the convictions. Former officer Lessnau, who had allowed the judge rather than a jury to decide his case, was found not guilty of assault.

Most black Detroiters praised the verdicts but were angry that Budzyn and Nevers would remain free until their sentencing on October 12.

JUNE 19, 1993   James B. Parsons Died. James B. Parsons, who became the country's first black federal judge when President John F. Kennedy appointed him in 1961, died in Chicago, Illinois, at the age of eighty-one.

A native of Kansas City, Missouri, Parsons worked as a teacher during the 1930s and 1940s before earning his law degree at the University of Chicago in 1949. He then taught briefly at John Marshall Law School and was a lawyer for the city of Chicago. From 1951 until 1960, Parsons was an assistant U.S. attorney. He served with the old Superior Court of Cook County (Illinois) for a year before taking the federal judgeship. He remained in the position and was active in trial work until 1992, when he retired due to illness.

JUNE 20, 1993   Griffith Joyner Named to Presidential Fitness Council. President Bill Clinton appointed track star Florence Griffith Joyner co-chair of the President's Council on Fitness and Sports. She was scheduled to share the job with former basketball player and congressman Tom McMillen. Together, they replaced bodybuilder and actor Arnold Schwarzenegger, who had been appointed by President George Bush.

Griffith Joyner was a standout at the 1988 U.S. Olympic Trials, where she set a world record in the 100 meters. Later that year at the Olympic Games in Seoul, South Korea, she won three gold medals and set a world record in the 200 meters.

JUNE 22, 1993 Joe Louis Stamp Unveiled. In Detroit, Michigan, the U.S. Post Office unveiled a stamp honoring the late African American boxer Joe Louis on the fifty-fifth anniversary of his stunning defeat over Germany's Max Schmeling. Louis was the first fighter to be honored with a stamp.

JUNE 24, 1993 Young Opted Not to Re-seek Detroit Mayoral Seat. Saying he lacked the energy to continue leading the city, the long-time mayor of Detroit, Michigan, seventy-.n-Afear-old Coleman Young, announced that he would not seek re-election to a fifth term. He had served as mayor since 1973.

JUNE 24, 1993 Wilder Announced Plans to Seek Virginia Senate Seat. Virginia's L. Douglas Wilder, the country's first black elected governor, revealed that he intended to challenge fellow Democrat Charles Robb for Robb's seat in the U.S. Senate in the 1994 elections.

JUNE 25, 1993 Supreme Court Ruled Job Discrimination Must Be Proved. The U.S. Supreme Court ruled in a case involving job discrimination that workers do not automatically win bias suits by proving that their employers gave false reasons for firing them. According to legal experts, the new ruling meant that workers who suspected they were fired because of racial discrimination must *prove* the cause of the firing was really rooted in racial bias and not just the result of personal conflicts or other reasons.

JUNE 26, 1993 Roy Campanella Died. Former Brooklyn Dodgers catcher Roy "Campy" Campanella, who spent the last thirty-five years of his life in a wheelchair following a car accident that ended his career, died in Los Angeles, California, of a heart attack. He was seventy-one.

JUNE 26, 1993 Detroit Marchers Commemorated King Freedom Walk. In Detroit, Michigan, thousands of people assembled to commemorate the thirtieth anniversary of a freedom walk led by Martin Luther King, Jr. They celebrated the occasion with another march and a downtown rally calling for a renewed commitment to political activism, economic justice, and closer ties between people of African descent all over the world.

With a new generation of leaders in attendance—including NAACP executive director Ben Chavis and Martin Luther King III—marchers retraced the same route the slain civil rights leader took on June 23, 1963, along with 125,000 of his supporters. At the end of that historic march, King delivered for the first time a version of his famous "I Have a Dream" speech. The rest of the country heard the final version later that same summer in Washington, D.C.

JUNE 28, 1993 Supreme Court Ruled Against Race-Based Voting Districts. The U.S. Supreme Court declared that states may be violating white voters' rights by creating congressional districts that appear to be based only on race.

The ruling—which many legal experts called one of the most significant in a decade—cast doubt on key parts of the 1965 Voting Rights Act. This landmark civil rights law made it possible for blacks to gain more seats in the U.S. Congress as well as in state legislatures. It protected minority voters against discrimination and under-representation at the hands of whites who divided up voting districts in such a way that blacks never would be in the majority, a process known as "gerrymandering."

The new Supreme Court decision also cleared the way for white voters to sue states that go to extremes to create voting districts where black and/or Hispanic voters end up in the majority.

JUNE 30, 1993 Bradley Stepped Down as Los Angeles Mayor. In California, seventy-five-year-old Tom Bradley stepped down from office after serving as mayor of Los Angeles for twenty years. He had decided earlier not to run for re-election in the face of the city's serious financial problems, rising crime rate, and strained race relations.

A liberal black Democrat, Bradley had been in public service for fifty years at the time of his retirement, first as a policeman, then as a councilman, and finally as mayor. Taking his place was a conservative white Republican businessman, Richard Riordan.

JULY 19, 1993 Gaynelle Griffin Jones Nominated as U.S. Attorney in Texas. President Bill Clinton nominated Houston lawyer Gaynelle Griffin Jones to be the first black U.S. attorney in Texas.

JULY 22, 1993 Moseley-Braun Helped Defeat Confederate Insignia Patent. Senator Carol Moseley-Braun of Illinois led the charge in a 75-25 Senate vote that denied patent renewal of a Confederate flag insignia for the United Daughters of the Confederacy.

JULY 29, 1993 Texas Policemen Fired for Killing Black Car Passenger. In Corsicana, Texas, a black passenger of a car stopped for a traffic violation attempted to flee the police. He was captured and hog tied. Following his death from asphyxiation, two of the police officers were fired, though never charged with any criminal wrongdoing.

AUGUST 9, 1993 Pope Apologized for Church's Historical Support of Slavery. Pope John Paul II formally apologized for the Roman Catholic Church's historical support of the African slave trade. In his message, remarking on the millions of victims, he said, "The immensity of their suffering corresponds to the enormity of the crime committed against them."

AUGUST 14, 1993 First Black Miss South Africa Crowned. In Johannesburg, twenty-one-year-old Jacqui Mofokeng became the first black woman to be crowned Miss South Africa.

AUGUST 26, 1993 Black Men Forced Out of All-White Vidor, Texas. Following months of racial discrimination, including bomb threats, two black men left the all-white town of Vidor, Texas. The men were the first African Americans to move to Vidor after a U.S. court ruled that the east Texas town's public housing project be integrated.

AUGUST 28, 1993 Thirtieth Anniversary of March on Washington Marked. In Washington, D.C., more than 75,000 people celebrated the thirtieth anniversary of the March on Washington. The organizers of the celebration sparked considerable controversy by failing to invite Nation of Islam leader Louis Farrakhan to speak at the event.

SEPTEMBER 1993 U.S. Delegation Prevented U.S. Invasion of Haiti. After issuing a strong warning to the ruling military junta of Haiti to leave the country peacefully or face a U.S. invasion, President Bill Clinton decided to send a delegation to help smooth the island nation's return to democracy. Former president Jimmy Carter led the high-level group; he was joined by General Colin Powell and Senate Armed Services Committee chairman Sam Nunn. At the same time, a twenty-three-vessel armada was poised and ready for action off the coast of Haiti. A no-nonsense threat issued in military terms by Powell to General Raoul Cédras sealed the delegation's success.

SEPTEMBER 7, 1993 Rap Artist Charged with Murder. Rap artist Snoop Doggy Dogg and two companions were charged with the shooting murder of a man in Los Angeles, California, on August 25, 1993. The three defendants claimed that the victim, Philip Woldemariam, had threatened the rapper, and that they acted in self-defense.

SEPTEMBER 7, 1993   Elders Confirmed as U.S. Surgeon General. Joycelyn Elders won congressional confirmation, becoming the first African American surgeon general in U.S. history.

SEPTEMBER 19, 1993   Aiken Crowned Fifth Black Miss America. South Carolinan Kimberly Clarice Aiken became the first black woman from the South and the fifth African American to be crowned Miss America.

SEPTEMBER 22, 1993   *Black Bible Chronicles* Released. The *Black Bible Chronicles,* by journalist P. K. McCary, was released. A streetwise translation of the Bible from Genesis through Deuteronomy, McCary's book was inspired by the need to spread the word of God to young blacks in a new and down-to-earth manner.

SEPTEMBER 30, 1993   Powell Retired from Joint Chiefs of Staff. General Colin Powell retired from his position as chairman of the Joint Chiefs of Staff, ending his thirty-five-year military career. Upon his retirement he received his second Presidential Medal of Freedom; it was also revealed that he would receive some $6 million to write his autobiography.

Following the junta's departure, twenty thousand U.S. troops, as part of Operation Restore Democracy, landed in Haiti to keep the peace while Jean-Bertrand Aristide, the Haitian leader ousted by Cédras in 1991, returned to power. However, Aristide announced that his was to be only an interim presidency and that he would step down in February 1996.

OCTOBER 6, 1993   Jordan Announced Retirement from Basketball. Chicago Bulls superstar Michael Jordan announced his retirement from professional basketball after nine seasons and three consecutive NBA titles. Jordan's announcement stunned virtually the entire sports world, as did his entry, only months later, into baseball with the Birmingham Barons, the Class AA farm team of the Chicago White Sox.

When Jordan announced his early retirement, there was little he hadn't accomplished in basketball: he had led his team to an NBA championship, he had been voted league MVP several times, he had played continually to sellout crowds, and had dominated games and dazzled fans. But the luster of the sport had faded for him in 1993, a tragic year in which his father, James Jordan, became the victim of a random murder and the media alleged that the superstar was involved in heavy gambling. On October 6 he said, "There's nothing left for me to prove. . . . It's not worth it for me. It's not worth it for my teammates."

OCTOBER 7, 1993   Morrison Awarded 1993 Nobel Prize in Literature. Novelist Toni Morrison was named the winner of the 1993 Nobel Prize in Literature. She was the first African American to receive this highest of all literary honors.

OCTOBER 21–25, 1993   Civil Rights Leaders and Gangs Held Chicago Peace Summit. Thousands of gang members and dozens of African American civil rights leaders attended a United in/and for Peace gang summit in Chicago.

OCTOBER 22, 1993   White Racists Sentenced in Jamaican Immigrant Burning Case. In Tampa, Florida, white racists Mark Kohut and Charles Rourk were sentenced to life in prison for setting fire to Jamaican immigrant Christopher Wilson. Seventeen-year-old Jeff Ray Pellett, charged as an accessory in the hate crime, received a twenty-two-month jail sentence.

NOVEMBER 2, 1993   Belton Elected First Black and Female Minneapolis Mayor. Sharon Sayles Belton was elected the first black and the first female mayor of Minneapolis, Minnesota.

NOVEMBER 9, 1993   Wharton Resigned State Department Post. Deputy Secretary Clifton R. Wharton, Jr., the highest-ranking black in the State Department, resigned his position after a series of unfavorable press reports on his performance.

NOVEMBER 21, 1993   District of Columbia Denied Statehood. By a margin of more than one hundred votes, the U.S. House of Representatives defeated a bill proposing that the heavily black-populated District of Columbia become the nation's fifty-first state.

NOVEMBER 24, 1993   Albert Collins Died. Guitarist Albert Collins, a Grammy award winner and a member of the Blues Hall of Fame, died in Las Vegas at the age of 61.

DECEMBER 5, 1993   Stewart Resigned as Editor of *Oakland Tribune*. Pearl Stewart, the first African American woman editor of a major daily newspaper, resigned her position with the *Oakland Tribune* due to differences with the new management. A longtime symbol of racial pride, the formerly black-owned *Tribune* was sold to the Alameda Newspaper Group the previous year.

1994

JANUARY 25, 1994   Jackson Settled Child Molestation Suit. In an out-of-court settlement, singer Michael Jackson reportedly paid millions of dollars following charges of child sexual molestation, despite maintaining his innocence.

FEBRUARY 2, 1994   Brown Cleared of Bribery Charges. Commerce Secretary Ron Brown was cleared of charges that he accepted a $700,000 bribe in exchange for the lifting of a Vietnam trade embargo.

FEBRUARY 3, 1994   Farrakhan Suspended Nation of Islam Spokesman. Nation of Islam leader Louis Farrakhan suspended national spokesman Khalid Abdul Muhammad following a speech in which Muhammad labeled Pope John Paul II a "cracker" and Nelson Mandela "a fool." In May 1994 the spokesman was shot and wounded by another Nation of Islam member while delivering a speech at Riverside, California.

MARCH 1, 1994   Coleman Elected New National Baseball League President. Leonard Coleman was elected president of the National Baseball League, replacing fellow African American Bill White. A former marketing development director of major league baseball, Coleman now held the rank of the highest black executive in professional sports.

MARCH 5, 1994   Beckwith Sentenced for 1963 Murder of Medgar Evers. In Jackson, Mississippi, white supremacist Byron de la Beckwith was sentenced to life in prison for the 1963 assassination of NAACP field secretary Medgar Evers. In two previous trials, all-white juries were unable to reach a verdict. The case was reopened in 1989 following the discovery of new evidence and in February 1994 a jury of eight blacks and four whites found Beckwith guilty.

MARCH 10, 1994   Report Shows AIDS Cases Rose over 100 Percent in 1992–93. The Centers for Disease Control and Prevention in Atlanta reported that from 1992 to 1993 AIDS cases rose by 111 percent. Half of all new heterosexual cases involved African Americans.

APRIL 16, 1994   Ralph Ellison Died. Ralph Waldo Ellison died in New York at the age of eighty. Ellison won the National Book Award for his only published novel, *Invisible Man*, in 1952. He was the first black writer to win this award and his novel, about the alienation of blacks in a white society, has been hailed as an American masterpiece. Ellison was also honored during his lifetime by election to the National Institute of Arts and Letters and the American Academy of Arts and Letters. In

1969 he received the Medal of Freedom from President Richard M. Nixon.

APRIL 26, 1994 Supreme Court Ruled on Civil Rights Act of 1991. The Supreme Court ruled twice by an 8-1 margin that the Civil Rights Act of 1991 could not be applied retroactively. *Landgraf v. USI Film Products* and *River v. Roadway Express* were the two cases the court considered in rendering its decisions.

The 1991 Civil Rights Act allowed victims of work-place discrimination to file for compensatory and punitive damages in addition to back pay and lost benefits. It also allowed the right to a trial by jury. Then-president George Bush had signed the act into law.

APRIL 26–29, 1994 South African Blacks Voted for the First Time. South African blacks, for the first time in the history of the Republic of South Africa, participated in the election process. The milestone event, which promised to end nearly 350 years of minority rule by whites, was made possible following the momentous changes that began with Nelson Mandela's release from prison in 1990 by then-president Frederik Willem de Klerk. On May 10, African National Congress leader Mandela, following a landslide victory, was inaugurated as the first black president of South Africa.

MAY 2, 1994 Williams Convicted of Beating Denny During Los Angeles Riot. Damian Williams received a maximum ten-year sentence for his involvement in the beating of white trucker Reginald Denny during the 1992 Los Angeles Riot. Four other black men were acquitted of felony weapons charges stemming from the incident.

MAY 12, 1994 Top 100 African American Businesses Named. The *Atlanta Constitution* reported the results of *Black Enterprise Magazine*'s annual survey of the Top 100 African American businesses. The top-rated firm was the TLC Beatrice International Company, a New York food processor and distributor which in 1993 reported sales of $1.7 billion. Johnson Publishing Company of Chicago ranked second, with sales of $294 million. Other businesses in the top ten were: 3) Philadelphia Coca-Cola Bottling Co., $290 million; 4) H. J. Russell Construction Company of Atlanta, $290 million; 5) RMS Technologies of Menton, New Hersey, $115 million; 6) Anderson-Dubose food distributors of Solon, Ohio, $115 million; 7) Gold Line Refining Company of Houston, Texas, $108 million; 8) Threads 4 Life apparel makers of Commerce, California, $97 million; 9) Soft Sheen hair products company of Chicago, $97 million; and 10) Garden State Cable TV of Cherry Hill, New Jersey, $96 million.

MAY 14, 1994 Auburn Avenue Research Library Opened. The Auburn Avenue Research Library, part of the Atlanta-Fulton Public Library in Atlanta, Georgia, became the second public library in the nation to open with a focus exclusively on black history and culture (the first was New York Public Library's Schomburg Center for Research in Black Culture).

Opened at a cost of $10 million, the 50,000-square-foot library houses three buildings in one: a library research area containing general reference books and materials; a public section housing exhibit cases and a main reading room; and an archive that includes a core of library stacks running through the center of the building.

The library's core collection is the Negro History Collection, established at the original Auburn Avenue branch in 1934. The library's reference collection included 23,000 books, 2,000 periodical titles, 181 African American-related newsletters, and 1,600 vertical files augmenting these primary materials.

MAY 24, 1994 Denny's Settled Discrimination Lawsuit. Flagstar Cos., the parent company of Denny's restaurants, agreed to pay a settlement of more than $54 million to black customers who had filed a class-action discrimination lawsuit.

MAY 24, 1994 Hugh B. Price Named President of National Urban League. The National Urban League selected Hugh B. Price as its new president and chief executive officer. Price succeeded John E. Jacob, who had served the organization for the past twelve years.

JUNE 12–14, 1994   Chavis Hosted First African American Leadership Summit. NAACP Executive Director Benjamin F. Chavis, Jr., hosted the first African American Leadership Summit. Chavis received criticism for inviting controversial Nation of Islam leader Louis Farrakhan to the Baltimore conference.

JUNE 17, 1994   Simpson Led Police on Chase Before Surrendering. The nation watched with a mixture of fascination and horror as football hero Orenthal James "O.J." Simpson led police on a low-speed chase through Anaheim, California, before giving himself up for arrest for the June 12th murders of ex-wife Nicole Brown Simpson and her friend Ronald Lyle Goldman. The media had reported that Simpson had earlier left what appeared to be a suicide note and that he now carried a gun. Until Simpson reached his Brentwood estate, accompanied by friend Al Cowlings, it remained unclear whether the country would be witness to a televised suicide.

A possible motive for the crime remained clear from the beginning: Simpson, despite his until now largely untarnished public image, was known to be a jealous husband and wife-beater. Whether Simpson had the means to commit the murders remained to be seen. But on June 27, *Time* magazine featured an artificially darkened police mugshot of the football star, bringing home the fact that no other suspect existed and that race would, however unfortunately, play a key role in the trial and the minds of Americans.

A Heisman Trophy winner, Simpson began his professional football career with the Buffalo Bills in 1969. Three years later he won his first rushing title, after gaining over 1,200 yards in a single season. Then, in 1973, "The Juice" accelerated to superstar status. On opening day he rushed for 250 yards, becoming the first black to do so in a single game. Throughout the season, he chalked up 10 additional games in which he ran for more than 100 yards, an NFL record. Simpson concluded this remarkable season by amassing a total of 2,003 yards and eclipsing the record of 1,863 yards set earlier by Jim Brown. In 1979 Simpson was named the NFL Player of the Decade. Later honors included his entry into the College Football Hall of Fame (1983) and the Pro Football Hall of Fame (1985).

Following the conclusion of his pro football career, Simpson continued to make a name for himself as a sports commentator, actor, and TV commercial spokesman.

AUGUST 8, 1994   Barbara Jordan and Dorothy Height Awarded Medal of Freedom. In a ceremony held in Washington, D.C., President Bill Clinton awarded the nation's highest civilian honor, the Medal of Freedom, to nine people. Included in the group were Barbara Jordan, former representative from Texas, and civil rights activist Dorothy Height.

AUGUST 9, 1994   Justice Department to Investigated Espy. Attorney General Janet Reno called for the Justice Department to investigate Agriculture Secretary Mike Espy in connection with gifts he had allegedly accepted from Tyson Foods, Inc. Espy announced his resignation two months later, while the investigation was still in progress.

AUGUST 20, 1994   Chavis Fired as Head of NAACP. Benjamin F. Chavis, Jr., was fired by the board of the NAACP following allegations that he, acting as head of the organization, approved payments in excess of $300,000 in order to silence sexual discrimination charges against him.

AUGUST 22, 1994   Chevy Chase Federal Savings Bank Settled Discrimination Suit. The U.S. Justice Department announced that an $11-million-dollar settlement had been reached with Chevy Chase Federal Savings Bank. A discrimination suit contended that the bank had used bias in its lending practices against minorities and low-income people. The Justice Department claimed that the bank had violated the Fair Housing and Equal Opportunity Acts by engaging in "redlining," the practice of not providing services in known low-income areas.

In addition to the $11-million-dollar settlement, Chevy Chase Bank agreed to open three mortgage offices and one new branch office in areas of Washington, D.C., with majority black populations. The settlement also included recruitment of minorities for staffing, advertisement of mortgage services to agents representing minority areas, and the retraining of current staff on fair lending practices.

While the bank denied the Justice Department allegations, it opted to settle to avoid litigation that could prove to be more costly.

AUGUST 28, 1994   Tiger Woods Won U.S. Amateur Golf Championship. Eighteen-year-old Eldrick "Tiger" Woods became the first black player, and the youngest player ever, to win the U.S. Amateur Golf Championship. A year later, Woods won his second amateur golf title.

AUGUST 29, 1994   Tennessee Civil Rights Leader Williams Died. Avon Williams, a former Tennessee state senator, civil rights leader, and attorney, died in Nashville, Tennessee, at age seventy-two. In 1950, four years before the historic *Brown v. Board of Education* school desegregation decision, Williams sued to desegregate schools in Anderson County, Tennessee. He subsequently appeared before the U.S. Supreme Court seven times arguing public accommodations, school segregation, and

teacher dismissal cases. He was also active in other efforts to desegregate golf courses, lunch counters, and other public facilities in Tennessee.

AUGUST 30, 1994   Parks Attacked in Her Home. Eighty-one-year-old Rosa Parks, who helped launch the civil rights movement, was assaulted in her Detroit home and robbed of $50. The following day a suspect was arrested.

SEPTEMBER 18, 1994   Stamps Issued Honoring Jazz and Blues Greats. The U.S. Postal Service issued stamps honoring such jazz and blues greats as Billie Holiday, Gertrude "Ma" Rainey, Bessie Smith, Muddy Waters, and Howlin' Wolf.

SEPTEMBER 23, 1994   Morehouse President Resigned. Leroy Keith, Jr., resigned as president of Morehouse College amid charges that he had received a part of his salary and other benefits without the approval of the college's board of trustees. In his letter of resignation, Keith said the audit reports on his compensation were "filled with inaccuracies and misrepresentations." He had been president of the prestigious, all-male, African American institution since 1987.

OCTOBER 1–8, 1994   Mandela Visited U.S. During the first week of October, South African President Nelson Mandela visited the U.S. The highlights of his itinerary included speeches given to the United Nations General Assembly in New York and, as only the third foreign leader ever to do so, to a joint session of Congress in Washington, D.C.

OCTOBER 3, 1994   Espy Resigned as Secretary of Agriculture. Secretary of Agriculture Mike Espy announced his resignation, effective December 31, 1994, amid an ongoing Justice Department investigation into charges that Espy received gifts from businesses regulated by his department.

OCTOBER 14, 1994   Belafonte Awarded National Medal of Arts. President Bill Clinton

Performer Harry Belafonte. (Courtesy of Belafonte Enterprises, Inc.)

awarded the National Medal of Arts to actor and singer Harry Belafonte. A prominent civil rights crusader, Belafonte in 1959 became the first African American to have an hour-long television special. Born in New York City, he lived in Jamaica from 1935 to 1940. He received a Tony Award in 1954 for a supporting role in *John Murray Anderson's Almanac*. In 1966 Belafonte was the first African American to produce a major show for television. During President John F. Kennedy's administration, he became the first cultural adviser to the Peace Corps. In 1990 he was the first person to receive the Nelson Mandela Courage Award of TransAfrica Forum.

OCTOBER 21, 1994   Chavis Reached Settlement with NAACP. Reverend Benjamin F. Chavis, Jr., reached a settlement with the National Association for the Advancement of Colored People (NAACP). After serving the civil-rights organization as executive director for fifteen months, Chavis was dismissed after allegations were made that he used NAACP funds to settle a possible sex-discrimination lawsuit brought against him by a former employee, Mary Stansel. His suit against the

NAACP claimed that the organization did not use proper official procedures in his dismissal.

OCTOBER 26, 1994   Atlanta Appointed First Black Female Police Chief. Beverly Harvard was appointed chief of police in Atlanta and became the first African American woman to head a major U.S. police department. During her first year she distinguished herself by cracking down hard on corruption within the department, arresting six police officers on graft and related charges.

OCTOBER 31, 1994   NAACP Cuts Staff and Seeks Financial Aid. In the wake of Benjamin Chavis's firing and a near $4 million deficit, the NAACP laid off employees and sought financial assistance from numerous sources to sustain the organization.

NOVEMBER 1994   Lee Elected to Texas House Seat. Sheila Jackson Lee was elected to Congress from the historic Eighteenth District of Texas. The 1965 Voting Rights Act created the irregularly drawn district, which encompasses much of Houston. The renowned Barbara Jordan was the newly drawn district's first representative. In 1994 a federal court ruling declared that the district was racially drawn.

Democratic representative Lee, a former Houston city council member, won her campaign despite the nationwide trend for electing conservative Republicans to Congress. Democratic leader Richard Gephardt appointed the New York native and freshman congresswoman to the powerful House Steering Committee. Lee, a 1972 Yale honors graduate and municipal judge, received her law degree from the University of Virginia Law School in 1975.

In the Congress, Lee became an ardent spokesperson against the onslaught on affirmative action: "It is not time to close the door on affirmative action. It may be time to make it better, more efficient, to shore up the loose ends."

NOVEMBER 6, 1994 **Foreman Won Bout.** Retired heavyweight champ George Foreman re-entered the ring at age forty-five and proceeded to knock out twenty-six-year-old Michael Moorer.

NOVEMBER 8, 1994 **Republicans Gained Control of Congress After Forty Years.** For the first time in forty years, Republicans gained control of both houses in Congress. The historic shift, which promised to weaken the Clinton presidency, left Democrats and many black leaders dismayed.

NOVEMBER 8, 1994 **Watts Elected to U.S. House.** Julius Caesar Watts, Jr., defeated Oklahoma's Democratic incumbent in the race for a seat in the U.S. House of Representatives in 1994. This made him the first black Republican from a Southern state to win a seat in Congress since Reconstruction. Originally a Democrat, Watts had changed parties in 1989 as his positions on welfare reform and a balanced budget were more closely aligned with those of the Republican party.

NOVEMBER 12, 1994 **Wilma Rudolph Died.** Track star Wilma G. Rudolph died in Brentwood, Tennessee, at the age of fifty-four of a malignant brain tumor. Born with polio that left her paralyzed in the left leg and unable to walk well until age ten, Rudolph took part in the 1960 Olympic Games in Rome and became the first woman to win three Olympic gold medals in track and field. She ran in the 100-meter, 200-meter, and relay races, becoming also the first black woman winner of the 200-meter. Her autobiography *Wilma* was made into a television film in 1977. Rudolph was one of five athletes and the only track star honored in June 1993 at the first annual National Sports Awards held in Washington, D.C.

NOVEMBER 15, 1994 **Cochran Commands Blue Angels.** Captain Donnie Cochran assumed command of the United States Navy Flight Demonstration Squadron, the Blue An-

gels. Cochran was the first African American to hold this position. In June 1996 Cochran transferred from the Blue Angels to head the NROTC unit.

NOVEMBER 18, 1994 **Cab Calloway Died.** Big-band leader and scat singer Cab Calloway died in Hosckessin, Delaware, at the age of 86. Calloway began his rise to stardom at the Cotton Club in Harlem, filling in for Duke Ellington. He was one of the first performers to make use of scat singing—random use of nonsense syllables—when he forgot a song's lyrics. Audiences loved the sound, so he began to write songs with scat choruses. His legendary "Minnie the Moocher" song, which debuted at the Cotton Club, is one such composition. Its refrain—hi de hi de hi de ho—invites the audience to sing along in the old call-and-response style. A veteran performer who appeared in numerous films during the 1930s and 1940s, Calloway charmed a new generation of listeners much later in his career when he appeared in the 1980 film *The Blues Brothers* to perform the classic song "Minnie the Moocher."

DECEMBER 4, 1994 **Franklin Honored for Achievement in Performing Arts.** At the Kennedy Center Honors in Washington, D.C., singer Aretha Franklin was honored for lifetime achievement in the performing arts. The "Queen of Soul" was the first black woman selected for induction into the Rock 'n' Roll Hall of Fame and Museum. As a child she sang gospel in the church pastored by her father, a noted evangelist and singer, and later joined the quartet directed by James Cleveland. She turned to blues in the 1960s, and in 1967 two of her albums sold more than 1 million copies each. Franklin won four Grammy awards between 1967 and 1969.

DECEMBER 9, 1994 **Elders Asked to Resign as Surgeon General.** President Bill Clinton requested that Surgeon General Joycelyn Elders resign following remarks in which she implied that students should be taught how to

Wilma Ruldolph displaying the medals she won at the Olympics.

masturbate as part of their sex education in the schools.

DECEMBER 16, 1994 Brooks Honored by National Book Foundation. Gwendolyn Brooks received the National Book Foundation's Medal for Distinguished Contribution to American Letters for her poetry collection, *Annie Allen.* This same collection brought Brooks fame back in 1950, when she became the first African American to win a Pulitzer Prize for poetry. After the book's publication she became established as a major American poet, and in 1976 she was the first black woman to obtain membership in the National Institute of Arts and Letters. A sensitive interpreter of Northern ghetto life, Brooks began to write poetry at age seven. From 1969 on she has promoted the idea that African Americans must develop their own culture. She was poet laureate of Illinois for sixteen years and is poetry consultant to the Library of Congress.

DECEMBER 28, 1994 U.S. Park Service Barred from King's Birthplace. In opposition to the U.S. Park Service plan to build a visitor center across from Martin Luther King, Jr.'s, birthplace and tomb, the King family barred the agency from continuing its visitor's tours through the historic site. The King family wanted to create a multimedia museum instead of the planned visitor center. King's birthplace and tomb are owned by the Martin Luther King, Jr., Center for Nonviolent Social Change.

1995

JANUARY 12, 1995 Shabazz Arrested for Alledged Farrakhan Assassination Plot. In Minneapolis, police arrested Qubilah Shabazz, daughter of Malcolm X, for allegedly planning the assassination of Louis Farrakhan, leader of the Nation of Islam. The charges were dropped on May 1 after it was revealed that Shabazz may have been entrapped. Farrakhan and Betty

Shabazz, the widow of Malcolm X, accused the U.S. government entrapping Qubilah. The federal court dropped the charges on May 1 after Qubilah agreed to seek psychiatric treatment.

JANUARY 24, 1995 Simpson Trial Started. The "Trial of the Century," *The People of the State of California v. Orenthal James Simpson,* began with opening arguments before Judge Lance Ito. Lawyers for the prosecution included Marsha Clark and African American Christopher Darden.

The defense team included some of the most high-powered lawyers in the nation, among them Robert Shapiro, F. Lee Bailey, and Alan M. Dershowitz. Although Shapiro initially served as the lead attorney for the defense "dream team," flamboyant African American Johnnie L. Cochran, Jr., a close friend of Simpson, assumed this role as part of an overall defense strategy as the trial got underway.

The fifty-seven-year-old Cochran seemed tailor-made for the high-profile trial, having specialized in prosecuting police abuse cases as well as defending celebrities in trouble, including singer Michael Jackson, rapper Tupac Shakur, and former football player Jim Brown. And even before the trial was underway, Cochran demonstrated his confidence while hinting at a "race card" strategy—that of focusing attention away from Simpson and on L.A. detective Mark Fuhrman—that would become increasingly successful during the last months of the trial. In addition, Cochran proved instrumental in winning the first legal battle for Simpson when he met privately with District Attorney Gil Garcetti prior to the trial and then received a formal commitment that the D.A.'s office would not pursue the death penalty.

JANUARY 25, 1995 Chenault Named Vice Chairman of American Express. Kenneth Chenault was named vice chairman of American Express, elevating him to the highest ranks of African Americans working for mainstream

Defense attorneys Robert Shapiro and Johnny Cochran and defendant O. J. Simpson view evidence during the criminal trial. (Archive Photos, Inc.)

Fortune 500 companies in America. The position placed him "within one leap of the chairman's slot," according to *Black Enterprise*. The forty-three-year-old Chenault was also appointed the new head of American Express's Travel Related Services unit.

FEBRUARY 1, 1995 Holland Named Ben & Jerry's Chief Executive Officer. Fifty-four-year-old Robert J. Holland, Jr., was named chief executive officer by the owners of Ben & Jerry's ice cream following a well-publicized

essay contest for the position. Although Holland submitted a poem, rather than an essay, he became the first African American to be recruited for the position of CEO by a major mainstream company.

FEBRUARY 2, 1995 Foster Nominated to be New U.S. Surgeon General. In the wake of Joycelyn Elders's resignation, President Bill Clinton nominated Henry W. Foster, Jr., to serve as surgeon general. The professional record of Foster, former chairman of the department of obstetrics and gynecology at Meharry Medical College in Nashville, was closely examined by Republican members of Congress. The Senate rejected his confirmation on June 22 due especially to perceived inconsistencies in the number of abortions the surgeon said he had performed.

FEBRUARY 3, 1995 Fort Mose Designated a National Historic Site. Fort Mose, the first free African American community in the United States, was designated a national historic site. Fort Mose, also known as Gracia Real de Santa Teresa de Mose, was populated mostly by African slaves who had escaped bondage in Georgia and South Carolina. It was occupied from 1738 to 1740, when it was burned by the British. It was later reoccupied from 1752 to 1763. It is located about two miles south of St. Augustine, Florida.

FEBRUARY 9, 1995 Harris Became First Black American to Walk in Space. Bernard Harris, a doctor and astronaut aboard the space shuttle *Discovery*, became the first African American to walk in space.

FEBRUARY 17, 1995 Ferguson Convicted for Commuter Train Shooting Spree. African American Colin Ferguson was convicted and sentenced to life in prison for the murders of six people during a shooting spree on December 7, 1993. The shootings, in which nineteen others were wounded, took place on a Long Island Rail Road commuter train during rush hour. Serving as his own lawyer, Ferguson claimed that the gunman was white and had stolen his semi-automatic handgun while he was sleeping aboard the train.

FEBRUARY 18, 1995 Evers-Williams Elected NAACP Chair. The board of directors of the National Association for the Advancement of Colored People (NAACP) elected Myrlie Evers-Williams, the widow of slain civil rights leader Medgar Evers, chair of the venerable civil rights organization. Ever-Williams suc-

ceeded William Gibson, a Greenville, South Carolina, dentist, who had been the NAACP's chairman for ten years. Gibson had also been accused of "taking thousands of dollars from the civil rights group."

Evers-Williams, age sixty-one, had served as an administrator with the Claremont College system in California and a vice-president of community affairs for the Atlantic Richfield Oil Company in California. In 1970, she ran unsuccessfully for Congress from California, and in 1987 she was appointed a commissioner on the Board of Public Works in Los Angeles.

At the time of her election as chair, Evers-Williams had been a member of the NAACP for more than forty years and was the board's vice president.

MARCH 1995 Eric Clay Nominated to Appeals Judge Post. President Bill Clinton nominated attorney Eric Lee Clay to the U.S. Court of Appeals for the Sixth Circuit, which hears cases from Michigan, Ohio, Kentucky, and Tennessee. Clay, a 1969 Phi Beta Kappa graduate of the University of North Carolina, earned his law degree from Yale University Law School in 1972. From June 1972 to June 1973, the prominent Detroit attorney served as the law clerk for exiting Sixth Circuit Court of Appeals judge Damon Keith.

Since 1973, Clay had been an attorney and member of the Board of Directors of Lewis, White, and Clay, where he chaired the litigation department. He also represented the Museum of African American History and the NAACP Legal Defense Fund, and was a member of the State Bar of Michigan, American Bar Association, Detroit Bar Association, and National Association of Railroad Trial Counsel.

MARCH 4, 1995 King's Birthplace and Tomb Reopened. An agreement between the family of slain civil rights leader Martin Luther King, Jr., and the U.S. Park Service was reached. In 1994, the King family barred the agency from conducting free tours of the birthplace and tomb in opposition to the Park Service's plans to establish a visitor center across from the historic site, which is owned by the Martin Luther King, Jr., Center for Nonviolent Social Change. The family had wanted to charge admission to the birthplace and tomb to contribute to the budget deficit for the museum. In the newly reached agreement, the Park Service would provide a federal fund to offset the deficit and would be allowed to continue to conduct free tours.

MARCH 16, 1995 Mississippi House of Representatives Adopted Thirteenth Amendment. By a unanimous decision, the Mississippi House of Representatives adopted the thirteenth amendment—which abolished slavery—to the state constitution. The state Senate voted to approve the amendment on February 16, 1995. It had been disclosed earlier that the amendment had never been formally enacted. With the symbolic vote, Mississippi became the last of the states that existed in 1865 to adopt the legislation.

MARCH 24, 1995 Jordan Rejoined Bulls After Coming Out of Retirement. Following a seventeen-month retirement, newly unretired basketball star Michael Jordan faced a homecoming welcome as he rejoined his Chicago Bulls teammates against the Orlando Magic at United Center in Chicago. Rather than don his old jersey (No. 23), he chose No. 45, the same number he wore as a baseball player and as a junior high basketball player. Upon his much-celebrated return, which he announced on March 18, he stated: "I'm back for the love of the game. I tried to stay away but I couldn't."

According to several sources, the financial impact of Jordan's return to the game, though enormous, was impossible to calculate. One thing was certain, though: Jordan would maintain his rank atop the *Forbes* sports world's Super 40 as the highest paid professional athlete for the fourth straight year. The basketball star's salary and winnings totaled just $3.9 million for 1995. However, his endorsements boosted that figure by an additional $40 million.

MARCH 25, 1995 Tyson Released from Prison. Former heavyweight boxing champ Mike Tyson was released from the Indiana Youth Center in Plainfield on good behavior after serving more than half of his six-year sentence for a 1992 rape conviction. To the delight of his fans, he announced plans to resume his boxing career.

MARCH 26, 1995 Easy-E Died. Within two weeks after his revelation that he had contracted AIDS, rapper Eric "Eazy-E" Wright died from complications of the disease at the age of thirty-one. Considered the founder of the first "gangsta" rap group, N.W.A. (Niggaz With Attitude), Wright drew upon his experiences as a former L.A. drug dealer in his music. N.W.A.'s first album, *Straight Outta Compton*, sold more than two million copies and was followed up by *Niggaz4Life*, which became the first hardcore rap album to reach No. 1 on the charts. Following the breakup of N.W.A., Wright launched a solo career and his own record label, Ruthless Records, responsible for such acts as Blood of Abraham, Above the Law, MC Ren, Things in Harmony, and Hoes with Attitude.

MARCH 26, 1995 Keyes Announced Presidential Run. Radio talk show host and author Alan Keyes announced that he would seek the Republican nomination for president. A committed pro-life and pro-family spokesperson, Keyes served under President Ronald Reagan as an ambassador to the United Nations Economic and Social Council and also held the post of interim president at Alabama A&M University.

MARCH 30, 1995 Tribal Warfare Erupted in Rwanda. Some twenty thousand Rwandan refugees fled the violence in Burundi and began their journey to safety in neighboring Tanzania. Three weeks later, approximately two thousand refugees were massacred at a camp in Kibeho by

Rwandan troops. In April 1994 the presidents of Burundi and Rwanda had been assassinated upon their return from a conference in Tanzania. Tribal warfare soon erupted, leading to widespread famine, bloodshed, and exodus.

APRIL 6, 1995   Jackson Confirmed as Chair of Nuclear Regulatory Commission. The U.S. Senate confirmed Shirley Ann Jackson as chair of the Nuclear Regulatory Commission. A Rutgers University physicist, Jackson thus became the first black and the first woman to assume the post. She scored another first in 1973 when she became the first African American woman to receive a Ph.D. from Massachusetts Institute of Technology (MIT).

APRIL 12, 1995   Ownership Claim of King's Papers Upheld. The Supreme Judicial Court of Massachusetts upheld the earlier 1993 jury decision that favored Boston University's claim of ownership of a portion of Martin Luther King, Jr.'s papers. Coretta Scott King, widow of the slain civil rights leader, had contested the 1993 ruling, arguing that a jury should not have decided the case.

MAY 6, 1995   Kirk Elected Mayor of Dallas. Forty-year-old Ron Kirk, an attorney and former secretary of state of Texas, was elected mayor of Dallas. Capturing 62 percent of the vote and drawing more support from whites than either of his two major white opponents, Kirk became the first black mayor of any major city in the Lone Star State.

JUNE 12, 1995   Supreme Court Handed Down Decision in *Adarand Constructors v. Peña*. The U.S. Supreme Court ruled in *Adarand Constructors v. Peña* that Congress must obey the same tough standards as states with regard to minority aid. The decision led many to conclude that the future of federal affirmative action programs was in danger.

JUNE 12, 1995   Bristow Elected First Black President of the AMA. Lonnie R. Bristow became the first African American president in the 148-year history of the American Medical Association. The sixty-five-year-old physician from San Pablo, California, told *Jet*, "I think my being elected shows it is possible to accomplish things through hard work and education. . . . It's possible to accomplish things our parents would not dream of. Nothing's impossible." In 1985 Bristow was the first black elected to the AMA's Board of Trustees. During the annual meeting in which Bristow was named president, the AMA also elected its first black female to the Board of Trustees, thirty-eight-year-old Regina Benjamin of Bayou La Batre, Alabama.

JUNE 17, 1995   Drive Launched to Make Powell a Presidential Candidate. In Washington, D.C., a group of military veterans and black businessmen launched a petition drive to support Colin Powell as a 1996 presidential candidate. Ever since his retirement in 1993 as Chairman of the Joint Chiefs of Staff, Powell had been mentioned favorably by political analysts and others as a potentially strong candidate for the presidency. In a September 1993 *Baltimore Sun* article, Republican political consultant Charles Black said, "I don't think he has any negatives; it's more a matter of question marks. . . . I don't know where he stands on a lot of issues. He has to talk about his vision for the country, and as soon as he does that, people will criticize him."

JUNE 20, 1995   Southern Baptists Apologized for Supporting Slavery. During the annual conference of the Southern Baptist Convention in Atlanta, church members apologized to African Americans for the organization's historical support of slavery.

JUNE 29, 1995   Supreme Court Decided *Miller v. Johnson*. The U.S. Supreme Court ruled in *Miller v. Johnson* that Georgia voting districts created to ensure minority representation were unconstitutional. In another blow to affirmative action, the court stated that race could not be used as the main factor in the drawing of voting districts.

JUNE 1995   Harris Named Air Force Major General. A thirty-year veteran of the air force, Marcelite J. Harris was elevated to the rank of major general, the highest rank ever held by a black woman in the history of the armed services. Serving for four months as vice commander of the Oklahoma City Air Logistics Center, Harris was then promoted in October to director of maintenance for all air force bases, becoming the first woman ever to hold the position.

JULY 6, 1995   Brown Investigated for Allegedly Accepting Gifts. Commerce Secretary Ron Brown came under investigation for allegedly accepting money and gifts from a business partner and for falsifying financial documents.

JULY 20, 1995   University of California Ended Affirmative Action Hirings. In San Francisco, African American Ward Connerly led his fellow University of California Board of Regents members to end affirmative action in university hirings by January 1996. The board also voted to end similar practices regarding the admittance of students by 1997. Connerly, author of the anti-affirmative action proposal that prompted the voting, maintained that such race-based policies threatened to undermine black achievement.

JULY 24, 1995   Slayer of King's Mother Resentenced to Life in Prison. Fulton County, Georgia, district attorney Lewis Slaton announced that Marcus Wayne Chenault would not be executed for the slaying of Mrs. Alberta King, mother of Martin Luther King, Jr. Chenault had been sentenced to die, in Georgia's electric chair, on September 12, 1974, after having been convicted of the murder of Mrs. King and deacon Edward Boykin in the Ebenezer Baptist Church in Atlanta on June 3, 1974. The decision to rescind the death penalty for Chenault was apparently made with consent of the King family, who reportedly "never

wanted Chenault to be put to death." Chenault was resentenced to life in prison without parole.

AUGUST 19, 1995   Tyson Returned to Boxing after Prison Sentence. In Las Vegas, Mike Tyson, a recent convert to the Muslim religion, returned to the ring for the first time since his release from prison. His bout with Pete McNeeley lasted just eighty-nine seconds, ending after McNeeley's manager stepped into the ring following a second knockdown. Despite the short match, former heavyweight champ Tyson earned $25 million.

AUGUST 22, 1995   Reynolds Convicted in Sex Scandal. In Chicago, Representative Mel Reynolds of Illinois was convicted on charges of sexual assault, sexual abuse, child pornography, and obstruction of justice. The charges arose after Reynolds had sex with a teenage campaign volunteer. Reynolds was sentenced to five years in prison, forcing him to resign from his seat in Congress.

SEPTEMBER 4–15, 1995   UN Sponsors Women's Conference in China. In a conference sponsored by the United Nations, 45,000 women from around the world met in Beijing, China, to discuss and debate human rights issues affecting women worldwide. Three African American women were part of the official forty-five-member delegation from the United States, including J. Veronica Biggins, who served as vice chair of the U.S. delegation. Of the more than eight thousand Americans who attended the conference, an estimated one thousand were African American.

SEPTEMBER 12, 1995   Malvin R. Goode Died. Malvin R. Goode, the first African American television reporter, died in Pittsburgh at the age of eighty-seven. Goode was hired in 1962 by ABC News following a comment made by Jackie Robinson to an ABC vice president regarding the lack of blacks in prominent positions at the network. Among the major events Goode covered during his eleven-year career with ABC were the Poor People's March on Washington, the Cuban missile crisis, and the death of Martin Luther King, Jr. In 1971 Goode became the first black member of the National Association of Radio and Television News Directors.

SEPTEMBER 22, 1995 Powell Began Publicity Tour for Autobiography. In what many were calling a brilliant campaign to gain widespread public support with minimal political risk, Colin Powell embarked on a thirty-five-day publicity tour to promote his autobiography, *My American Journey.*

Throughout the tour, Powell refrained from committing to a presidential run although he continually fueled hopes that he would do so. However, even before the tour was complete, he stated: "As I speak around the country, I am constantly questioned about my future: specifically, am I going to run for President? I am flattered by my standing in public-opinion polls. To be a successful politician, however, requires a calling that I do not yet hear. I believe that I can serve my country in other ways, through charities, educational work or appointive posts."

OCTOBER 3, 1995 Simpson Declared not Guilty of Double Murder. Following an overnight wait so that all the principles in the O.J. Simpson trial could be reassembled, the entire nation watched as the jury rendered its verdict. Despite a mountain of testimony and evidence, the Simpson jurors deliberated for only three hours before reaching their decision—a unanimous verdict of not guilty. Simpson's reaction was one of immediate relief and thanks. The prosecution team, on the other hand, appeared numb with disbelief.

During the aftermath, virtually all legal analysts agreed that leading defense attorney Johnnie L. Cochran, Jr.'s genius had been to center the case on two points: 1) the assertion that Simpson—given the testimony of eyewitnesses—did not have enough time to commit

the murders, return to his residence, and then take a limousine ride to the airport and 2) the assertion that the racist remarks of police detective Mark Fuhrman were the clue to a much larger conspiracy by the L.A. police department to frame Simpson.

Prosecutor Marcia Clark, in her closing arguments, also labeled Fuhrman a racist and then attempted to redirect the jurors' attention to the overwhelming evidence, including DNA blood evidence, that linked Simpson, and no one else, to the murders. In the end, the jurors chose to believe the defense team's version of events and Simpson, imprisoned for 474 days, was declared a free man.

According to a *Washington Post* survey, eight out of ten blacks thought justice had been served while at least half of all whites thought that it had not. Once again, Los Angeles had become the stage to dramatize that a huge racial divide still separated many Americans.

As of December 1995, the Simpson case was still generating enormous interest, including some 36 book deals. One of these, the autobiography of Cochran that a publisher planned to place on bookstands in 1997, was estimated to be worth $4.2 million.

Although Simpson had been cleared in the criminal trial, in early 1996 he still faced a wrongful death civil suit filed on behalf of the family of Ronald Goldman and the estate of Nicole Brown Simpson.

OCTOBER 16, 1995 Million Man March. In a movement that generated enormous publicity during October, Nation of Islam leader Louis Farrakhan hosted the Million Man March on Capitol Hill in Washington, D.C. The March was conceived by Farrakhan and fellow organizer Benjamin Chavis, Jr., to ignite both a spiritual and social reawakening among black men. Despite naysayers and the controversies that have surrounded both Farrakhan and Chavis, the march was considered a success by those in attendance, many of whom made the pilgrimage not only to hear the numerous speak-

Louis Farrakhan speaking during the Million Man March. (AP/Wide World Photos.)

ers (Maya Angelou, Jesse Jackson, Rosa Parks, Kweisi Mfume, Marion Barry, and others), but to rejoice in black unity and a shared commitment to make a positive difference upon their return home.

Chavis later announced, during a sermon in Atlanta, that on the first anniversary of the Million Man March (October 16, 1996), a Million Family March would be held in the nation's capital and simultaneously across the country through satellite hookups.

OCTOBER 16, 1995   Winfrey Named to *Forbes*'s List of Richest Americans. In the October 16 issue of *Forbes* magazine, TV talk show host Oprah Winfrey was listed No. 399 on the list of "The 400 Richest People in America." The only black and the only entertainer to make the list, forty-one-year-old Winfrey was estimated to be worth $340 million. In 1986 Winfrey became the first black woman to host a nationally syndicated weekday talk show, *The Oprah Winfrey Show*. As owner of Harpo Productions and part-owner of her show's distributor, King World Productions, Winfrey is recognized as a sizeable force in the TV and film industry. A

formidable actress as well, she garnered Golden Globe and Academy Award nominations for her role as Sophia in *The Color Purple* and has plans to play the lead in a big screen adaptation of Toni Morrison's *Beloved,* to which she owns the film rights.

OCTOBER 1995   Clinton Honored Neglected Black West Point Cadet. In 1876 John Chestnut Whittaker entered the West Point Military Academy as one of the school's first black cadets. Four years later, shortly before graduation, Whittaker was mutilated, beaten, and left for dead by three white classmates. Although the black cadet survived the racially motivated attack, he was expelled from the academy after being accused of inflicting the injuries upon himself and then claiming the white cadets were responsible. Prevented from a military career, Whittaker began a law practice in Charleston, South Carolina, before becoming a principal in Oklahoma City and then a law professor at what is now South Carolina State University. Sixty-four years after his death in 1931, Whittaker was honored with a commission as second lieutenant by President Bill Clinton, who made the presentation to the cadet's granddaughter and great-grandson.

OCTOBER 28, 1995   Castro Visits Harlem. Cuban president Fidel Castro spoke to approximately 1,600 Harlem residents at the Abyssinian Baptist Church in Manhattan, New York. The predominately African American audience included New York Democratic congressional representatives Charles Rangel and Nydia Velasquez.

NOVEMBER 1, 1995   *Ebony* Celebrated Fiftieth Anniversary. *Ebony,* the largest black-owned magazine in the world, celebrated its fiftieth anniversary with a commemorative issue and a statement by the company founder and chairman. "It is important to remember," wrote John H. Johnson, "that when I founded *Ebony,* Black and White America were almost totally segregated, and nobody, or almost no-

Abyssinian Baptist Church, circa 1960. (AP/Wide World Photos.)

body, believed a Colin Powell could run the armed forces or the United States government or that a Michael Jordan could compete against White basketball players. . . . Today, as in 1945, I believe that the greater the obstacle, the greater the triumph and the greater the glory. It is in that spirit, and with that hope, that we rededicate ourselves to the spirit of the founding and the call of the future."

NOVEMBER 7, 1995 "Slappy" White Died. Slappy White, one of the first successful Afri-

can American stand-up comedians, died on this date. Born Melvin White in 1921 in Baltimore, Maryland, racial harmony was a theme often used in his routines. White emerged in the 1950s from the black nightclubs and began appearing before largely white audiences. In addition to his stand-up routines, White also appeared in movies and on television.

NOVEMBER 8, 1995 Powell Decided not to Pursue Presidential Run. After completing a lengthy tour to promote his book *An American*

Journey, Colin Powell announced he would not run for president or any other elected office. The retired general arrived at his decision after long consultations with friends and family. Powell did, however, affirm his commitment to work within the Republican party for the betterment of all Americans. According to numerous polls, if Powell had chosen to run, he would have posed a serious political threat to both Republican frontrunner Bob Dole and Democratic president Bill Clinton in the 1996 elections.

NOVEMBER 27, 1995 Pittsburgh Policemen Charged with Murder of Businessman. Following the October 12 death of Pittsburgh area businessman Jonny Gammage, two white police officers were charged with third-degree murder, while a third was charged with involuntary manslaughter. Gammage, a cousin of Pittsburgh Steelers player Ray Seals, suffocated after only seven minutes in police custody. He was arrested following a low-speed chase during which he ran three red lights and ignored signals by police to stop. Once stopped, Gammage allegedly charged the arresting officers and struggled violently before being subdued.

NOVEMBER 28, 1995 Savannah's First Black Mayor Elected. Floyd Adams, Jr., publisher of the *Weekly Herald* and veteran alderman, was elected the first African American mayor of Savannah, Georgia. Adams defeated incumbent mayor Susan Weiner by the slim margin of 15,912 to 15,660. Following his election, Adams promised "to move [the] city forward, to make progressive moves that will benefit everyone."

DECEMBER 1995 Black Woman Donated Life's Savings to Mississippi University. In one of the nation's most heartwarming stories of 1995, an eighty-seven-year-old Mississippi woman named Osceola McCarty brought attention to the virtues of hard work, thrift, and charity by donating $150,000, much of her life's savings, to the University of Southern Mississippi. The monetary gift was the largest ever made by an African American to a Mississippi university. McCarty was able to amass the large amount by saving the earnings from years of washing laundry by hand, all the while spending little on herself. "I want to give some child the opportunity I didn't have," she told *Ebony.* "I hope this money can help children, for years to come, make their dreams come true." Following the announcement of her gift, McCarty was invited to the University of Southern Mississippi, where she was made an honorary alumna, and to a Congressional Black Caucus dinner as the special guest of President Bill Clinton, who awarded her the Presidential Citizens Medal.

DECEMBER 2, 1995 Court Ruled That African Americans Could Not Sue for Slavery-Related Damages. The U.S. Court of Appeals for the Ninth Circuit ruled that African Americans could not sue the federal government for damages or an apology for racial discrimination and slavery. The unanimous opinion of the three-judge panel upheld several lower court rulings that had considered similar claims.

The suit, which had been filed by seven plaintiffs, sought more than $100 million in damages, along lines similar to the reparations the U.S. Congress had previously awarded to Japanese Americans interned during World War II. But the court ruled that the plaintiffs could not seek damages for the enslavement of their ancestors, could not require the judiciary to correct allegedly discriminatory acts by Congress, and failed to point to specific government actions that violated their rights. Judge Pamela Rymer, who wrote the majority opinion, also said that individuals who complained about historic or current societal discrimination lacked the standing and legal authority "to pursue claims in court arising out of the government's failure to do right as [they see] it."

In response to the decision, Samuel Patterson, chairman of "the Reparations Committee for African Americans," which sponsored the suit, declared that he was not surprised by it. He said: "You're not going to get anything from a pig but a grunt."

DECEMBER 9, 1995 Mfume Named President of NAACP. Democratic congressman Kweisi Mfume of Maryland, feeling he could better serve the interests of African Americans and the nation as a whole outside of Congress, accepted the presidency of the NAACP (Myrlie Evers-Williams remained the organization's chair). The position had been vacant since Benjamin Chavis, Jr., was fired in August 1994. Mfume pledged to restore the fiscal integrity and financial structure of the NAACP, which was $3.2 million in debt when Mfume assumed command.

DECEMBER 12, 1995 Jackson, Jr., Won House Seat. Democrat Jesse Jackson, Jr., was elected to the House of Representatives by defeating Republican Thomas Somer in Illinois's 2nd congressional district. Jackson had no previous political experience, but had campaigned on the ideas of economic development in his district. The son of civil rights activist Jesse Jackson captured 74 percent of the vote.

DECEMBER 12, 1995 Brown Resigned "Drug Czar" Post. After more than two years as the nation's top-ranking fighter in the war on drugs, Lee Brown submitted his resignation to President Bill Clinton. Brown declined to offer specific reasons for his departure, but did disclose that he was accepting a position at Rice University to teach criminology.

Anti-drug activists believed Brown had simply grown frustrated with the government's weak response to the increased drug use in the country. After Brown had taken office, President Clinton decided to cut Brown's staff by 75 percent, from 146 to 25. The budget of his office suffered a similar decrease.

DECEMBER 12, 1995 Brown Elected First Black San Francisco Mayor. Willie Brown, the former powerful California Assembly speaker, was elected by San Francisco residents to

become that city's first African American mayor. Brown easily defeated incumbent Frank Jordan for the position.

DECEMBER 22, 1995 Thelma "Butterfly" McQueen Died. Eighty-four-year-old actress Thelma "Butterfly" McQueen after suffering critical burns caused by a fire in her home near Augusta, Georgia. McQueen was perhaps best known for her role as the slave girl Prissy in the 1939 film *Gone with the Wind*. Unfortunately, like many black actresses of the period, she became typecast as a maid, a role she rebelled against strongly by the mid-1940s. For the next two decades she abandoned the big screen for the stage, but then returned to play several small movie roles during the 1970s and 1980s.

1996

JANUARY 11, 1996 Affirmative Action Programs Ended in Louisiana State Agencies. Republican governor Mike Foster of Louisiana announced that affirmative action programs in that state's government had ended.

JANUARY 15, 1996 President Clinton Addressed Crowd at King Celebration. The Ebenezer Baptist Church in Atlanta, Georgia, was the site of a Martin Luther King, Jr., Day celebration. President Bill Clinton spoke to a crowd of about 1,500 about his support for affirmative action programs.

JANUARY 15, 1996 Revelation Corporation Formed. The Revelation Corporation was formed by the leaders of five major black churches with the goal of increasing the buying-power of black consumers. E. Edward Jones of the National Baptist Convention of America Inc. was selected to head the organization, and John Lowery was named vice-president. The five churches involved in the program were the

National Baptist Convention of America, the African Methodist Episcopal Zion Church, the Christian Methodist Episcopal Church, the National Baptist Convention USA Inc., and the Progressive National Baptist Convention Inc.

JANUARY 17, 1996 Barbara Jordan Died. The first elected black state senator from Texas, Barbara Charline Jordan died of complications from leukemia. She had also suffered from multiple sclerosis for years.

Born on February 21, 1936, in Houston, Texas, the well-known speaker gained national attention when she asked for the impeachment of then-President Richard Nixon. She was also the first black woman to give the keynote address at the 1976 National Democratic Convention. President Bill Clinton awarded Jordan the highest civilian honor by presenting her with the Presidential Medal of Freedom in a ceremony on August 8, 1994.

JANUARY 26, 1996 Conductor Henry Lewis Died. Famed conductor Henry Jay Lewis died of a heart attack in New York City. Lewis was named conductor of the New Jersey Symphony Orchestra in 1968, the first black conductor of a major American orchestra. He was well known for attempting to make performances more available to the working class, often holding free outdoor concerts. Lewis was also the first African American to conduct New York City's Metropolitan Opera in 1972. He was born on October 16, 1932, in Los Angeles, California.

FEBRUARY 6, 1996 Supreme Court Upheld Districting Plan in Georgia. The U.S. Supreme Court upheld a 1995 redistricting plan constructed by three judges in Georgia that reduced the number of black-majority congressional districts from three to one based on the grounds that race could not be used as a "predominant factor" in establishing district boundaries. Despite pleas from a group of Georgia voters, the Court refused a request for an appeal of the decision on June 8.

FEBRUARY 8, 1996 Church Arson Investigation Started. The U.S. Department of Justice announced that a civil-rights investigation into the black church fires in Alabama and Tennessee had begun the previous December. Attorney General Janet Reno made the probe public after the National Association for the Advancement of Colored People (NAACP) had written her in January asking for such a study. Seventeen churches had been destroyed in southern states over the past year. The most notable fire was at the Inner City Baptist Church in Knoxville, Tennessee, where Green Bay Packers football star Reggie White was an associate pastor.

FEBRUARY 20, 1996 Kweisi Mfume Became NAACP Head. In Washington, D.C., Kweisi Mfume was sworn in as president and chief executive officer of the National Association for the Advancement of Colored People (NAACP). This came amidst serious financial and public relations troubles at the NAACP. Mfume's predecessor, Benjamin F. Chavis, Jr., was fired in 1994 for misuse of the organization's funds in connection with a threatened sexual-discrimination suit. Mfume promised "a new NAACP, reinvented and reinvigorated, standing at the threshold of change."

Mfume had resigned from his position as a U.S. House representative from Maryland on February 18. Fellow black Democrat Elijah E. Cummings defeated Kennth Dondner in special elections held to replace Mfume. Previously, Cummings was the pro tem speaker for the Maryland House of Delegates.

MARCH 13, 1996 Census Bureau Reported Increase in Black Population. The Census Bureau released its population projections through the year 2050. The black population was expected to make up 13.6 percent of the total population, marking an increase from the projected 1995 figure of 12 percent.

MARCH 19, 1996 Texas Admission Policy Rejected. A federal appeals court in Louisiana reversed an earlier decision and ruled that a race-based admissions policy at the University of Texas School of Law should not be allowed, even though the school's intention had been to enhance racial diversity. Four white students had sued the university in 1992 on the grounds of racial discrimination.

Judge Jerry E. Smith ruled that the school had not appropriately shown a justification for its racial preference policy. He further recommended that universities in general broaden their definition of diversity among their student bodies—this, in part, because one of the plaintiffs, Cheryl Hopwood, had faced great adversity through her life as a result of the death of her father when she was a child, and the births to Hopwood of a handicapped child and another child who later died. Smith believed the experiences of someone like Hopwood should be included in a school's expanded definition of diversity.

MARCH 20, 1996 High Court Said Undercounted Census Figures Could Stand. The U.S. Supreme Court unanimously ruled 1990 census figures could stand, despite that between 1.6 percent and 2 percent of the population had not been counted. Minority groups had sought an adjustment to the figures because the erroneous numbers represented 4.8 percent of the black population and 5.2 percent of the Hispanic population. The coalition of plaintiffs included such groups as the National Association for the Advancement of Colored People and the national League of Cities, from such cities as Chicago, Houston, Los Angeles, and New York.

After then-Commerce Secretary Robert Mosbacher refused to revise census figures in 1991, the groups filed suit, arguing that the miscount was an affront to minorities' constitutional right to equal protection, because census figures determined congressional seating and federal funding for social programs. Before the Supreme Court's ruling, Mosbacher's decision

had been upheld in 1993 by a district court, then overturned in 1994 by a circuit court of appeals.

Supreme Court chief justice William Rehnquist opined that Mosbacher's argument, which stated that determining congressional districts resulted more from a "distributive accuracy" and not a precise numerical count of the population, was reasonable.

MARCH 25, 1996 Jackson Led Protest at Academy Awards. The Reverend Jesse Jackson and 75 others marched outside the KABC-TV offices in Los Angeles during the Academy Awards ceremony to protest the lack of black nominees. Of the total 166 nominees, only one was black—Dianne Houston, who directed the film *Tuesday Morning Ride.*

APRIL 3, 1996 Commerce Secretary Ron Brown Killed in Plane Crash. U.S. commerce secretary Ron Brown and 34 others were killed in a U.S. Air Force jet when it crashed into a mountainside near Dubrovnik, Croatia. Brown, government officials, and business executives were touring Croatia and Bosnia-Herzegovina in attempts to obtain contracts for U.S. companies to help rebuild the infrastructures of both countries. The Air Force later blamed pilot error and the failure of Air Force commanders to properly make required safety evaluations before leaving the airport. Officials concluded that the bad weather that existed during the flight was not a significant factor in the crash.

Brown was born on August 1, 1941, in Washington, D.C., before moving to New York City. He was a successful lawyer before rising to national politics as Jesse Jackson's 1988 presidential campaign manager. A year later, he became chairman of the Democratic National Committee, the first African American to head a major national political party. He worked closely with then-Arkansas governor Bill Clinton's presidential campaign, and was named commerce secretary following Clinton's victory.

Ron Brown and Bill Clinton. (Bettmann Archive/Newsphotos, Inc.)

APRIL 3, 1996   Former Cleveland Mayor Carl Stokes Died. Former politician/newsman Carl Stokes died in Cleveland at the age of 68. Stokes was the first black to be elected mayor of a major city when he won the Cleveland mayoral election 1962. After serving two terms as mayor, Stokes left for New York and began a career as a news broadcaster for WNBC-TV. He also was the first African American elected to the Ohio House of Representatives, served eleven years as a municipal judge in Cleveland, and was named ambassador to the Seychelles in 1995. Stokes was born in Cleveland on June 21, 1927.

APRIL 9, 1996   African Americans Among 1996 Pulitzer Winners. George Walker and E. R. Shipp were two of twenty-two Pulitzer Prize recipients for 1996. Walker, the first African American musician to receive this honor in music in its eighty-year existence, accepted the prestigious award for *Lilacs*, which was composed for both voice and orchestra. Shipp, a columnist for *The Daily News* in New York, won the prize for commentary on race and welfare.

APRIL 17, 1996   Florida's Third District Held Unconstitutional. Federal judges ruled that Florida's black-majority Third District was unconstitutional because it used race as the major factor in determining the district's boundaries. Three judges ordered the state legislature to redraw the district's boundaries by May 22.

The plaintiffs in the case argued that the horse-shoe shaped district, which covered 250 miles and 14 counties, had been created primarily to intensify the representation of blacks.

The majority opinion held that the defendants had failed to show that the district had been "narrowly tailored to further a compelling governmental interest" and, therefore, violated the Fourteenth Amendment of the U.S. Constitution. The judges included an admonition that the ruling "should not be interpreted as 'turning back the clock' on the gains made by African American voters and other racial and ethnic voting minorities."

Representative Corrine Brown opposed the decision and stated that the Third District, located in northern Florida, was "the most integrated and diverse district" in the state.

APRIL 19, 1996   Ruling to End Texas University Affirmative Action Programs Deferred. A U.S. federal appeals court granted a stay that blocked the enforcement of a March 19 ruling that would have ended race-based admissions policies at Texas universities. On July 1, however, the Supreme Court let the March 19 ruling stand, not because it was endorsing the ruling but because the University of Texas School of Law had stopped using that admissions policy.

MAY 2, 1996   First African American Woman Confirmed as California Supreme Court Judge. California governor Pete Wilson's appointment of appellate court judge Janice Rogers Brown to the California Supreme Court was confirmed. Brown, daughter of Alabama sharecroppers, became the first African American woman to serve on the state's highest court. Although Justice Brown's nomination was unanimously confirmed, it was not without criticism. The State Bar Commission on Judicial Nominees Evaluation claimed that "Brown was unqualified because of limited experience as a lawyer and a judge." The Commission added she had a "tendency to inject her political and philosophical views into her court opinions." Wilson described his nominee as being "clearly the right choice at the right time. . . ." Justice Brown had also been characterized as more conservative than the other California Supreme Court justices.

Prior to her 1994 appellate court appointment, she served the state as Governor Wilson's legal affairs secretary, where she filed suit against the federal government seeking reimbursement of costs for providing public services to illegal immigrants. Previously, Brown served as California's deputy attorney general and deputy legislature counsel for the state Legislature Counsel Bureau. In 1974, she received her bachelor's degree from California State University and, in 1977, a law degree from the University of California at Los Angeles.

MAY 8, 1996   Court-Ordered Busing Ended in Cleveland. Federal judge Robert Krupansky lifted a seventeen-year desegregation order, which resulted in the end of court-ordered busing in Cleveland, Ohio. Student busing had been implemented in 1979 in an effort to integrate the city's public school system. Education officials asked to end busing because they felt integration had been successful and $10 million in busing costs could be saved.

The original ruling stemmed from a 1973 case involving black students who accused the school system of running segregated schools. The courts decided in favor of the students, and six years later Cleveland began busing students.

MAY 10, 1996   House of Representatives Passed Adoption Credit. The U.S. House of Representatives passed legislation that would provide families that adopted children with a $5,000 tax credit if their annual income was under $75,000. The law included a provision that would force adoption agencies to make interracial adoption easier by not allowing race or ethnicity to be such a determining factor when selecting possible adoptive families.

When the interracial provision was first brought forward, many Republicans were against the consideration of race during the adoption process. Democrats, however, opposed this stance and compromises were reached. These included: race could be used as a criterion only if at least two qualified families sought adoption of a child, and agencies could not delay an adoption with the intent of locating a qualified same-race family.

MAY 28, 1996   Commander Cochran Resigned from Blue Angels. Commander Donnie Cochran, the first black pilot to fly on the Navy's Blue Angels flight team, resigned following his concerns over his ability to continue to fly safely. Eight months earlier, Cochran participated in a flying demonstration with the Blue Angels when he missed an agreed upon landmark. Cochran became the team leader of the Blue Angels in 1994.

JUNE 10, 1996   Justice Thomas Spoke at Grade School Awards Ceremony. After much deliberation between members of the Landover (Maryland) School Board and officials at the Thomas G. Pullen Creative and Performing Arts School, Supreme Court justice Clarence Thomas addressed an eight-grade awards ceremony at the school.

Principal Kathy Kurtz had invited Thomas to speak, but on May 22 school superintendent Jerome Clark ordered her to rescind the invitation on the basis that Thomas's many rulings against affirmative action programs did "not represent the interests of my constituents." The Parent Teacher Association asked that Clark's request be denied; the school board agreed and Thomas was issued a second invitation.

Demonstrators for and against Justice Thomas held rallies in front of the school.

JUNE 12, 1996   President Clinton Spoke Against Black Church Fires. In Greeleyville, South Carolina, President Bill Clinton attended the dedication ceremony for the newly built sanctuary of the Mt. Zion African Methodist Episcopal Church. The previous sanctuary of the church had been destroyed by arson in 1995. Clinton, told the crowd, "We are not going back, we are not slipping back to those dark days (before the civil-rights movement)."

The southern United States had felt racial tension as arson claimed dozens of black churches over the previous seven years. The Federal Bureau of Investigations, in conjunction with the Bureau of Alcohol, Firearms, and Tobacco, led investigations into the suspicious fires. The departments concluded that no national conspiracy could be linked to the church fires.

JUNE 13, 1996   Race-based Districts Struck Down. The Supreme Court ruled against congressional districts in North Carolina and Texas in two separate cases that alleged that racial bias was used in determining district boundaries. Violation of the Fourteenth Amendment was stated as the reason for the unconstitutionality of the districts' formations. The Supreme Court considered *Bush v. Vera* and *Shaw v. Hunt* in handing down its rulings. Two months later, the Supreme Court refused to require North Carolina to redraw its Twelfth District boundaries.

JUNE 15, 1996   Singing Great Ella Fitzgerald Died. Popular jazz singer Ella Fitzgerald died in Beverly Hills, California, of undisclosed causes. In recent years, she had suffered from diabetes, which had resulted in the amputation of both her legs.

Born in Newport News, Virginia, on April 25, 1917, "the First Lady of Song" started her career with Chick Webb's band and had her first hit in 1938 with a song she wrote, "A-Tisket, A-Tasket." After Webb died in 1939, Fitzgerald began to concentrate on a style of singing known as scat and became well-known for the songs "Flying Home" and "Lady Be Good," which used the scat technique. Fitzgerald is credited with reviving the popularity of such composers as Ira and George Gershwin, Cole Porter, and Rodgers and Hart, by composing albums using their works. She won thirteen Grammy Awards in her career.

JUNE 24, 1996   Philadelphia Found Guilty of Excessive Force. A federal jury found the City of Philadelphia guilty of using excessive force in 1985, when the police used a bomb in an attempt to evict members of MOVE (a radical African American group) from their headquarters. The bomb killed eleven people, and destroyed 61 houses in the neighborhood. Police had tried unsuccessfully to remove the MOVE members from their homes after neighbors complained about excessive noise and garbage. The jury ordered that $1.5 million in damages be paid to survivor Ramona Africa and to families of the victims.

JULY 9, 1996   Connecticut Court Struck Down Segregation. The Connecticut Supreme Court ruled that racial segregation in public schools near Hartford violated the state constitution. The court allowed the state government the opportunity to integrate the schools.

JULY 9, 1996   Representatives McKinney and Bishop Won Primaries in Newly Formed Georgia Districts. Georgia's two newly formed congressional districts, the second and fourth, produced victories for two black representatives, Cynthia McKinney and Sanford D. Bishop, Jr. McKinney previously represented the state's Eleventh District, which was approximately 60% black. Bishop's former district was 59% black. In redrawing the congressional district boundaries, the black voting population was diminished from 60% to 30% in McKinney's Fourth District and from 59% to 35% in Bishop's Second District.

JULY 10, 1996   Statue Dedicated to Arthur Ashe. A statue of Arthur Ashe was dedicated in Richmond, Virginia, honoring the first black man to win the U.S. Open, Wimbledon, and Australian Open tennis tournaments. Ashe died in 1993 of complications from AIDS.

Controversy surrounded the placement of the statue. Ashe's widow, Jeanne Moutoussamy-Ashe, protested that the statue should not reside on a street were Confederate soldiers were honored. Many felt it would be an insult to Ashe, who was known for his stand against racial segregation. Plans have been made to move the statue to the front of the African American Sports Hall of Fame when it opens in the year 2000.

JULY 11, 1996   Dole Skipped NAACP Convention. Republican presidential hopeful Bob

Dole declined an invitation from National Association for the Advancement of Colored People (NAACP) president Kweise Mfume to speak at its convention, citing scheduling conflicts. But Dole claimed "the very liberal Democrat" Mfume was "trying to set me up" by inviting him, "probably" would not have been received warmly, and that in the future he would speak with audiences "I can relate to."

The NAACP turned down the Dole camp's offer to have presumed vice-presidential nominee Jack Kemp stand in for him. Prominent African American leader and fellow Republican Colin Powell was disappointed with Dole's decision. "I think it would have been useful for him to present his views to the NAACP." Dole later said he regretted skipping the NAACP event.

JULY 22, 1996 Jazz Musician Humphrey Died. Jazz trumpeter Percy Humphrey died in New Orleans, Louisiana, at age ninety. Humphrey was the grandson of Jim Humphrey, who taught many of the first generation of jazz musicians. Thge junior Humphrey, himself, began his musical career as a drummer, then changed to trumpet and became a member of the influential Eureka Brass band. In the 1950s he became the leader of this New Orleans group.

In 1961, Humphrey began playing at the then recently opened Preservation Hall in New Orleans, and continued regular performances there until March 1995. In the 1970s he also performed with the New Orleans Joymakers. He toured with the famed Preservation Hall Jazz Band into the 1980s. Humphrey contributed much to the history of jazz. He excelled at group improvisations and was skilled at scatting and other Louis Armstrong-style solos.

AUGUST 8, 1996 First Black and First Woman Mayor in Mississippi Town. Thelma Collins, a former Greenwood, Mississippi, schoolteacher, became the first African American and the first woman to serve as mayor of Ita Bena, Mississippi.

AUGUST 12, 1996 General Powell Addressed the Republican Convention. "Let us never step back from compassion," stated General Colin Powell, as he addressed the crowds at the Republican National Convention in Houston, Texas. The popular black Republican had been considered as a possible vice-presidential running mate with Bob Dole, but Powell wasn't interested. While his speech gathered loud cheers, there was some vocal discontent when he declared his support for abortion rights. Powell quickly answered the crowd by stating, "I was invited here by my party to share my views with you because we are a big enough party—and big enough people—to disagree on individual issues and still work together for our common goal: restoring the American Dream."

Other African Americans who spoke at the convention were House representatives J. C. Watts (Oklahoma) and Gary A. Franks (Connecticut) and antiabortion activist Kay C. James, who led the roll call leading to Dole's nomination.

AUGUST 21, 1996 Farrakhan Called Black Journalists "Slaves." At the annual meeting of the National Association of Black Journalists in Nashville, Tennessee, Nation of Islam leader Louis Farrakhan told members that black journalists were "slaves" to white newspaper owners. "White folk did not hire you to really represent what black people are really thinking, and you don't really tell what you think because you are too afraid," said Farrakhan. Many in the audience gave him standing ovations, though some objected to his view of black journalists.

AUGUST 23, 1996 Dole Spoke at Black Journalists Meeting. Republican presidential hopeful Bob Dole spoke at the National Association of Black Journalists convention in Nashville, Tennessee. This came only weeks after many blacks criticized him for not accepting an invitation to speak at the National Association for the Advancement of Colored People (NAACP) convention.

Dole told journalists, however, he regretted turning down the invitation and felt the Republican party had "missed opportunities" to win support of African Americans. He cited 1964 presidential nominee Barry Goldwater's opposition to the 1964 Civil Rights Act—as well as his own, as a House representative—as an example.

AUGUST 25, 1996   Tiger Woods Won U.S. Amateur Golf Tournament. For the third consecutive year, Tiger Woods won the U.S. Amateur Golf Tournament—becoming the first player to do so. Two days later, Woods announced that he would turn professional and consequently signed a deal with Nike, Inc., to endorse its products. The deal was reportedly worth $40 million, the largest endorsement ever make for a rookie golfer. Woods became the first black to win the U.S. Amateur title in 1994.

AUGUST 27, 1996   Actor Greg Morris Died. Greg Morris, who played Barney Collier on the popular 1960s television show *Mission Impossible,* died of cancer. The Cleveland native was one of the first black actors to star in a TV show.

AUGUST 27, 1996   Indianapolis Police Beat Black Motorist. Sixteen police officers in Indianapolis, Indiana, allegedly went on a drunken spree in which they used racial slurs and beat and arrested both a black motorist and a white man who tried to help the African American victim. The incident attracted national attention, as, perhaps, another example of police assault on unoffending African Americans. City authorities launched an investigation.

AUGUST 27, 1996   Jesse Jackson Addressed Democratic Conventioneers. Civil rights leader Jesse Jackson told attendees at the Democratic National Convention that Republicans were putting forward an image of a "big tent." "On the cover was General (Colin) Powell and (Republican vice-presidential nominee) Jack

Kemp. But clearly you cannot judge a book by its cover. For inside, the book was written by (speaker of the House) Newt Gingrich and (Moral Majority leader) Ralph Reed and (former presidential hopeful) Pat Buchanan." In endorsing President Bill Clinton for a second term, Jackson called on Democrats to accept diversity as "the measure of the party's strength . . . (and) character. We must find the bridge to keep our tent intact."

AUGUST 28, 1996   Kemp Gave Speech at Challengers Boys and Girls Club. Republican vice-presidential hopeful Jack Kemp addressed the Challengers Boys and Girls Club in south central Los Angeles, scene of racial riots in 1992. In an appeal for the black vote, Kemp promised that the Republican agenda would include scholarships for inner-city kids.

AUGUST 28, 1996   Judge Ruled Former Philadelphia Officials Didn't Have to Pay Damages in MOVE Case. U.S. District Court judge Louis Pollak ruled that the city of Philadelphia's former fire and police commissioners would not have to pay damages to relatives or survivors of a 1985 fire involving members of the radical African American group MOVE. Two months earlier, a jury had ordered former fire commissioner William Richmond and former police commissioner George Sambor to pay one dollar per week for the next eleven years to Ramona Africa, the only adult member of MOVE to survive the fire, and to relatives of other MOVE members. The jury had also awarded the plantiffs $1.5 million in punitive damages, to be paid by the city of Philadelphia.

Although the punitive damages against the city were not affected by Pollak's decision, Africa reacted angrily to his ruling. She said it "literally let [the former commissioners] get away with murder."

SEPTEMBER 7, 1996   Former CRC Chairman Flemming Died. Arthur Flemming, former chairman of the U.S. Civil Rights Commis-

Tiger Woods on the links. (AP/Wide World Photos.)

sion, died in Washington, D.C., at age ninety-one. After eight years on the job, he was fired by President Ronald Reagan in 1982 after the CRC issued a report that was harshly critical of the Reagan administration's record on desegregation and civil rights.

In 1994, President Bill Clinton awarded Flemming the Presidential Medal of Freedom, the nation's highest civilian honor. At the time of his death, Clinton remarked: "He transcended party, generation and race in search of consensus on some of the great issues of our day."

SEPTEMBER 30, 1996   Famed Photographer Died. Moneta J. Sleet, the first African American to win a Pulitzer Prize in photography, died in New York City, at age seventy. Sleet, a photographer for *Ebony* magazine, won the Pulitzer for feature photography in 1969 for his image of Coretta Scott King consoling her daughter, Bernice, in her lap, at the funeral of slain civil rights leader, Martin Luther King, Jr., in 1968.

Sleet studied photography at Kentucky State College. After serving in World War II, he helped establish the first photography department at Maryland State College. Then, he did further study at the School of Modern Photography in New York and earned a master's degree in journalism at New York University.

Following his studies, Sleet worked as a sportswriter for the *Amsterdam News* and as a photographer for *Our World* magazine, before joining *Ebony*, where he still worked at the time of his death.

Sleet's work has been exhibited at the Studio Museum in Harlem, the Metropolitan Museum of Art, and several other facilities. His awards included a Citation for Excellence from the Overseas Press Club of America as well as the National Urban League.

Sleet's notoriety stemmed principally from his photographic documentation of the marches, meetings, and rallies of the Civil Rights Movement of the 1960s. His images were described as "powerful and sensitive," which "showed genuine respect for his subjects."

NOVEMBER 12, 1996   Civil Rights Activists Reagon Murdered. Civil rights activist Cordell Hull Reagon was found murdered in Berkeley, California. Hull, age fifty-three, joined the Civil Rights Movement at the age of sixteen in 1959. He became known as "the baby of the movement." Reagon was arrested more than thirty times throughout the South as he fought against racial segregation and discrimination. He also led training workshops in nonviolence for hundreds of volunteers who went into the South to work for civil and voting rights for blacks.

In 1962, Reagon became one of the founders of the Freedom Singers, a group of men and women who sang freedom songs in a gospel-style to "rouse support" for the Civil Rights Movement. The quartet included Bernice Johnson of Albany, Georgia, who became Reagon's first wife. In the 1970s, he was active in protests against the Vietnam war, nuclear weapons, and environmental destruction. Before moving to Berkeley in 1988, he was an organizer for the Social Service Employees union and a member of Mobilization for Youth in New York. While in Berkeley, he founded the Urban Habitat and the Urban Justice organization to foster the protection of the environment.

DECEMBER 20, 1996   African Americans Nominated for Cabinet Posts. President Bill Clinton nominated two African Americans for positions in his Cabinet. Alexis Herman, director of the White House Office of Public Liaison, was selected as secretary of labor, and Rodney Slater, the federal highway administrator, was nominated for secretary of transportation.

Herman, a native of Mobile, Alabama, was a graduate of Xavier University in Louisiana. In 1977, she became the director of the Women's Bureau of the Labor Department. Since 1993, in her White House liaison post, she had been the president's chief emissary to the Congressional Black Caucus (CBC) and other African American groups. She also aided the president in the publicity campaign that he waged to win congressional approval of the 1994 crime bill.

Slater, who was born in Marianna, Arkansas, graduated from Eastern Michigan University. He was previously an assistant attorney general in Arkansas; executive assistant to then-Governor Clinton; and a member, then chairman, of the Arkansas State Highway Commis-sion. He was once named one of the Ten Outstanding Young Arkansans.

DECEMBER 27, 1996 Hugh Brown Elected to Bank Board. Hugh M. Brown, president and chief executive officer of BAMSI, Inc., an engineering and technical services firm in Titusville, Florida, was re-elected chairman of the Federal Reserve Bank of Atlanta. Brown had formerly served as deputy chairman of the bank before being elected chairman in January 1996.

DOCUMENTS OF HISTORY

MASSACHUSETTS BODY OF LIBERTIES OF 1641

There shall never be any bond slaverie, villinage or Captivitie amongst us, unless it be lawfull Captives taken in just warres, and such strangers as willingly sell themselves or are sold to us. And these shall have all the liberties and Christian usages which the law of God established in Israell concerning such persons doth morally require. This exempts none from servitude who shall be Judged thereto by Authoritie.

EXCERPTS TAKEN FROM VIRGINIA SLAVE LAWS, 1660–1669

I. On Running Away with Negroes (March 1660)

Be it enacted that in the case any English servant shall run away in company with any Negroes who are incapable of making satisfaction by addition of time . . . the English so running away in company with them shall serve for the time of the said Negroes absence as they are to do for their own by a former act.

II. On the Nativity Conditions of Slavery (December 1662)

Whereas some doubts have arisen whether children got by an Englishman upon a Negro woman should be slave or free, be it therefore enacted and declared by this present Grand Assembly, that all children born in this country shall be held bond or free only according to the condition of the mother; and that if any Christian shall commit fornication with a Negro man or woman, he or she so offending shall pay double the fines imposed by the former act.

III. On Baptism and Bondage (September 1667)

Whereas some doubts have risen whether children that are slaves by birth, and by the charity and piety of their owners made partakers of the blessed sacrament of baptism, should by virtue of their baptism be made free, it is enacted and declared by this Grand Assembly, and the authority thereof, that the conferring of baptism does not alter the condition of the person as to his bondage or freedom; that diverse masters, freed from this doubt may more carefully endeavor the propagation of Christianity by permitting children though slaves, or those of greater growth if capable, to be admitted to that sacrament.

IV. On Corporal Punishment (September 1668)

Whereas it has been questioned whether servants running away may be punished with corporal punishment by their master or magistrate, since the act already made gives the master satisfaction by prolonging their time by service, it is declared and enacted by this Assembly that moderate corporal punishment inflicted by master or magistrate upon a runaway servant shall not deprive the master of the satisfaction allowed by the law, the one being as necessary to reclaim them from persisting in that idle course as the other is just to repair the damages sustained by the master.

V. On the Killing of Slaves (October 1669)

Whereas the only law in force for the punishment of refractory servants resisting their master, mistress, or overseer cannot be inflicted upon Negroes, nor the obstinacy of many of them be suppressed by other than violent means, be it enacted and declared by this Grand Assembly if any slave resists his master (or other by his master's order correcting him) and by the extremity of the correction should chance to die, that his death shall not be accounted a felony, but the master (or that person appointed by the master to punish him) be acquitted from molestation, since it cannot be presumed that premeditated malice (which alone makes murder a felony) should induce any man to destroy his own estate.

THE GERMANTOWN MENNONITE RESOLUTION AGAINST SLAVERY (1688)

This is to the monthly meeting held at Richard Worrell's:

These are the reasons why we are against the traffic of men-body, as followeth: Is there any that would be done or handled at this manner? viz., to be sold or made a slave for all the time of his life? How fearful and faint-hearted are many at sea, when they see a strange vessel, being afraid it should be a Turk, and they should be taken, and sold for slaves into Turkey. Now, what is *this* better done, than Turks do? Yea, rather it is worse for them, which say they are Christians; for we hear that the most part of such negers are brought hither against their will and consent, and that many of them are stolen. Now, though they are black, we cannot conceive there is more liberty to have them slaves, as it is to have other white ones. There is a saying, that we should do to all men like as we will be done ourselves; making no difference of what generation, descent, or colour they are. And those who steal or rob men, and those who buy or purchase them, are they not all alike? Here is liberty of conscience, which is right and reasonable; here ought to be likewise liberty of the body, except of evil-doers, which is another case. But to bring men hither, or to rob and sell them against their will, we stand against. In Europe there are many oppressed for conscience-sake; and here there are those oppressed which are of a black colour. And we who know that men must not commit adultery—some do commit adultery *in* others, separating wives from their husbands, and giving them to others: and some sell the children of these poor creatures to other men. Ah! do consider well this thing, you who do it, if you would be done at this manner—and if it is done according to Christianity! You surpass Holland and Germany in this thing. This makes an ill report in all those countries of Europe, where they hear of (it), that the Quakers do here handel men as they handel there the cattle. And for that reason some have no mind or inclination to come hither. And who shall maintain this your cause, or plead for it? Truly, we cannot do so, except you shall inform us better hereof, viz.: that Christians have liberty to practice these things. Pray, what thing in the world can be done worse towards us, than if men should rob or steal us away, and sell us for slaves to strange countries; separating husbands from their wives and children. Being now this is not done in the manner we would be done at; therefore, we contradict, and are against this traffic of men-body. And we who profess that it is not lawful to steal, must, likewise, avoid to purchase such things as are stolen, but rather help to stop this robbing and stealing, if possible. And such men ought to be delivered out of the hands of the robbers, and set free as in Europe. Then is Pennsylvania to have a good report, instead, it hath now a bad one, for this sake, in other countries; especially whereas the Europeans are desirous to know in what manner *the Quaker* do rule in *their* province; and most of them do look upon us with an envious eye. But if this is done well, what shall we say is done evil?

If once these slaves (which they say are so wicked and stubborn men) should join themselves—fight for their freedom, and handel their masters and mistresses, as they did handel them before; will these masters and mistresses take the sword at hand and war against these poor slaves, like, as we are able to believe, some will not refuse to do? Or, have these poor negers not as much right to fight for their freedom, as you have to keep them slaves?

Now consider well this thing, if it is good or bad. And in case you find it to be good to handel these black in that manner, we desired and require you hereby lovingly, that you may inform us herein, which at this time never was done, viz., that Christians have such a liberty to do so. To the end we shall be satisfied on this point, and satisfy likewise our good friends and acquaintances in our native country, to whom it is a terror, or fearful thing, that men should be handled so in Pennsylvania.

This is from our meeting at Germantown, held ye 18th of the 2nd month, 1688, to be delivered to the monthly meeting at Richard Worrell's.

Garret Henderich,

Derick op de Graeff,

Francis Daniel Pastorius,

Abram op de Graeff.

PORTION OF THE PETITION TO MASSACHUSETTS LEGISLATURE BY BOSTON AFRICAN AMERICANS 1773

The endearing ties of husband and wife we are strangers to for we are no longer man and wife than our masters or mestesses thinks proper. . . Our Children are also taken from us by force and sent many miles from us wear we seldom or ever see them again there to be made slaves of for Life which sometimes is vere short by Reson of Being dragged from their mothers Breest. How can a slave perform the duties of a husband to a wife or part to his child? How can a husband leave master and work and cleave to his wife? How can the wife submit themselves o there husbands in all things? How can the child obey thear parents in all things?

THE DECLARATION OF INDEPENDENCE

When in the Course of human events, it becomes necessary for one people to dissolve the political bands which have connected them with another, and to assume among the Powers of the earth, the separate and equal station to which the Laws of Nature and of Nature's God entitle them, a decent respect to the opinions of mankind requires that they should declare the causes which impel them to the separation.

We hold these truths to be self-evident, that all men are created equal, that they are endowed by their Creator with certain unalienable Rights, that among these are Life, Liberty and the pursuit of Happiness. That to secure these rights, Governments are instituted among Men, deriving their just powers from the consent of the governed, That whenever any Form of Government becomes destructive of these ends, it is the Right of the People to alter or to abolish it, and to institute new Government, laying its foundation on such principles and organizing its powers in such form, as to them shall seem most likely to effect their Safety and Happiness. Prudence, indeed, will dictate that Governments long established should not be changed for light and transient causes; and accordingly all experience hath shown, that mankind are more disposed to suffer, while evils are sufferable, than to right themselves by abolishing the forms to which they are accustomed. But when a long train of abuses and usurpations, pursuing invariably the same Object evinces a design to reduce them under absolute Despotism, it is their right, it is their duty, to throw off such Government, and to provide new Guards for their future security.—Such has been the patient sufferance of these Colonies; and such is now the necessity which constrains them to alter their former Systems of Government. The history of the present King of Great Britain is a history of repeated injuries and usurpations, all having in direct object the establishment of an absolute Tyranny over these States. To prove this, let Facts be submitted to a candid world.

He has refused his Assent to Laws, the most wholesome and necessary for the public good.

He has forbidden his Governors to pass Laws of immediate and pressing importance, unless suspended in their operation till his Assent should be obtained; and when so suspended, he has utterly neglected to attend to them.

He has refused to pass other Laws for the accommodation of people, unless those people would relinquish the right of Representation in the Legislature, a right inestimable to them and formidable to tyrants only.

He has called together Legislative bodies at places unusual, uncomfortable, and distant from the depository of their Public Records, for the sole purpose of Fatiguing them into compliance with his measures.

He has dissolved Representative Houses repeatedly, for opposing with manly firmness his invasions on the rights of the people.

He has refused for a long time, after such dissolutions, to cause others to be elected; whereby the Legislative Powers, incapable of Annihilation, have returned to the People at large for their exercise; the state remaining in the meantime exposed to all the dangers of invasion from without, and convulsions within.

He has endeavoured to prevent the Population of these States; for that purpose obstructing the Laws of Naturalization of Foreigners; refusing to pass others to encourage their migration hither, and raising the conditions of new Appropriations of Lands.

He has obstructed the Administration of Justice, by refusing his Assent to Laws for establishing Judiciary Powers.

He has made Judges dependent on his Will alone, for the tenure of their offices, and the amount and payment of their salaries.

He has erected a multitude of New Offices, and sent hither swarms of Officers to harass our People, and eat out their substance.

He has kept among us, in times of peace, Standing Armies without the Consent of our legislature.

He has affected to render the Military independent of and superior to the Civil Power.

He has combined with others to subject us to a jurisdiction foreign to our constitution, and unacknowledged by our laws; giving his Assent to their acts of pretended legislation:

For quartering large bodies of armed troops among us:

For protecting them, by a mock Trial, from Punishment for any Murders which they should commit on the Inhabitants of these States:

For cutting off our Trade with all parts of the world:

For imposing taxes on us without our Consent:

For depriving us in many cases, of the benefits of Trial by Jury:

For transporting us beyond Seas to be tried for pretended offenses:

For abolishing the free System of English Laws in a neighboring Province, establishing therein in an Arbitrary government, and enlarging its Boundaries so as to render it at once an example and fit instrument for introducing the same absolute rule into these Colonies:

For taking away our Charters, abolishing our most valuable Laws, and altering fundamentally the Forms of our Governments:

For suspending our own Legislature, and declaring themselves invested with Power to legislate for us in all cases whatsoever.

He has abdicated Government here, by declaring us out of his Protection and waging War against us.

He has plundered our seas, ravaged our Coasts, burnt our towns, and destroyed the lives of our people.

He is at this time transporting large armies of foreign mercenaries to complete the works of death, desolation and tyranny, already begun with circumstances of Cruelty and perfidy scarcely paralleled in the most barbarous ages, and totally unworthy the Head of a civilized nation.

He has constrained our fellow Citizens taken Captive on the high Seas to bear Arms against their Country, to become the executioners of their friends and Brethren, or to fall themselves by their Hands.

He has excited domestic insurrections amongst us, and has endeavoured to bring on the inhabitants of our frontiers, the merciless Indian Savages, whose known rule of warfare, is an undistinguished destruction of all ages, sexes and conditions.

In every stage of these Oppressions We have Petitioned for Redress in the most humble terms: Our repeated Petitions have been answered only by repeated injury. A Prince, whose character is thus marked by every act which may define a Tyrant, is unfit to be the ruler of a free People.

Nor We have been wanting in attention to our British brethren. We have warned them from time to time of attempts by their legislature to extend an unwarrantable jurisdiction over us. We have reminded them of the circumstances of our emigration and settlement here. We have appealed to their native justice and magnanimity, and we have conjured them by the ties of our common kindred to disavow these usurpations, which would inevitably interrupt our connections and correspondence. They too have been deaf to the voice of justice and of consanguinity. We must, therefore, acquiesce in the necessity, which denounces our Separation, and hold them, as we hold the rest of mankind, Enemies in War, in Peace, Friends.

We, therefore, the Representatives of the United States of America, in General Congress, Assembled, appealing to the Supreme Judge of the world for the rectitude of our intentions, do, in the Name, and by Authority of the good People of these Colonies, solemnly publish and declare, That these United Colonies are, and of Right ought to be Free and Independent States; that they are Absolved from all Allegiance to the British Crown, and that all political connection between them and the State of Great Britain, is and ought to be totally dissolved; and that as Free and Independent States, they have full Power to levy War, conclude Peace, contract Alliances, establish Commerce, and to do all other Acts and Things which Independent States may of right do. And for the support of this Declaration, with a firm reliance on the Protection of Divine Providence, we mutually pledge to each other our Lives, our Fortunes and our sacred Honor.

THE DIARY OF COLONEL LANDON CARTER

Undated entry, 1775

some few thoughtless africans are sheltering themselves under the Royal stand(ard) offered to them

Wednesday, June 26, 1776

Last night after going to bed, Moses, my son's man, Joe, Billy, Postilion, John, Mulatto Peter, Tom, Panticove, Manuel and Lancaster Sam, ran away, to be sure, to Ld. Dunmarra, for they got privately into Beale's room before dark and took out my son's gun and one I had there, took out of his drawer in my passage all his ammunition furniture, Landon's bag of bullets and all the Powder, and went off in my Petty Auger. . . . These accursed villains have stolen Landon's silver buckles, George's shirts, Tom Parker's new waistcoat and breeches; and yet have not touched one thing of mine.

Saturday, June 29, 1776

At 7 in the morning after their departure some minute men at Mousquito Point saw the Petty Auger with ten stout men in her going very fast on the Middlesex shore. They pursued and fired at them, whereupon the negroes left the boat and took to the shore where they were followed by the minute men. By their firing they alarmed 11 King and Queen minute men who were waiting for the Roebuck's men, should any of them come ashore there. It is supposed that Moses and many of the negroes were killed.

Wednesday, July 3, 1776

Monday at Court we heard the K[ing] and Queen men below had killed a mulatto and two of the blacks out of the 8 of my people who ran away and the remaining 5 surrendered; how true it is I don't know.

Friday, July 5, 1776

Hearing so many contradictory stories about Moses and his gang I sent Beale off this morning to get fully informed either in Lancaster, Middlesex, or Gloster.

Tuesday, July 9, 1776

Beale returned but brought no account of Moses and his gang. . . . They had catched other people's negroes but not mine. Beale reported that the men who followed my people in the Petty Auger when they were driven ashore was the Towles Point guard in a boat of Burgess Ball.

Col. Carter things they could readily have overtaken the Petty Auger if they tried.< Another report from Guthrie, who I have a long time known to be an egregious liar, that some runaways told him that they saw some slaves who had run away from Dunmore, who told him that they saw Moses on the Island; who swore to them if he could get back he would return to his master; for Dunmore had deceived all the Poor Slaves and he never met so barbarous or so vile a fellow in all his life.

Saturday, July 13, 1776

. . . John Selden met Purcell coming up and bid tell me that Dunmore

last week sent off a load of negroes to one of the Islands which so alarmed the rest that the county of Gloster was disturbed with their howlings.

Monday, July 15, 1776

Last night John Beale came up. . . . He says that two French, who deserted from Dunmore's camp on the Island after our people had drove them off, declared we killed abundance of their men; and that no negroes were kept by Dunmore but were fine active fellows, but were all sent away to some of the West India Islands, and out of the strong and active scarce one in ten escaped death by distempers or ill usage except when a man was wanted in his vessels.

Thursday, February 13, 1777

. . . Yesterday J. Beale sent me word that 3 of my people, vizt., a young fellow Toney, Jacob, and a Johnny from B[eale's] P[lantation] had run away and gone on board the Man of war lying. . . . He was very sure that this war would bring us all to beggary.

Monday, February 24, 1777

There is a Story also brought down by a certain Rig Graham about Moses, my son's waiting man. . . . for Colo. Robt Lawson in the army told him that he knew Moses very well and saw him in Philadelphia. After this Graham told others that Moses was taken coming home to his Master who he had run away from; but they imprisoned him in Philadelphia. All this is said after many other stories, some of his waiting on Capt. Squires, who was with Dunmore at Gwins Island where he ran away. Some that he died there of the Smallpox or in Maryland at St. George's Island of the Contagious fever. Source: Jack P. Greene, ed., The Diary of Colonel Landon Carter of Sabine Hall, 1752B1778, II (Charlottesville, Va., 1965), pp. 960, 1051–1052, 1054–1057, 1075, 1084–1085.

THE OMITTED ANTI-SLAVERY CLAUSE TO THE DECLARATION OF INDEPENDENCE (1776)

He [King George III] has waged cruel war against human nature itself, violating its most sacred rights of life and liberty in the persons of a distant people who never offended him, captivating and carrying them into slavery in another hemisphere, or to incur miserable death in their transportation thither. This piratical warfare, the opprobium of *infidel* powers, is the warfare of the *Christian* king of Great Britain. Determined to keep open a market where MEN should be bought and sold, he has prostituted his negative for suppressing every legislative attempt to prohibit or restrain this execrable commerce.

THE CONSTITUTION OF THE UNITED STATES, ART. 1, SECTIONS 2 AND 9, ART. 4, SECTION 2 (1787)

They are not included, and were not intended to be included, under the word "citizens" in the constitution, and can therefore claim none of the rights and privileges which that instrument provides and secures. . . . On the contrary, they were at that time considered as a subordinate and inferior class of beings. . . .

Preamble

We the People of the United States, in order to form a more perfect Union, establish Justice, insure domestic Tranquility, provide for the common defense, promote the general Welfare, and secure the Blessings of Liberty to ourselves and our Posterity, do ordain and establish this Constitution for the United States of America.

Article I

Section 2. Representatives and direct Taxes shall be apportioned among the several States which may be included within this Union, according to their respective Numbers, which shall be determined by adding to the whole Number of free Persons, including those bound to Service for a Term of Years, and excluding Indians not taxed, three-fifths of all other Persons. The actual Enumeration shall be made within three Years after the first Meeting of the Congress of the United

States, and within every subsequent Term of Ten Years, in such manner as they shall by Law direct. . . .

Section 9. The Migration or Importation of such Persons as any of the States now existing shall think proper to admit, shall not be prohibited by the Congress prior to the Year one thousand eight hundred and eight, but a Tax or duty may be imposed on such Importation, not exceeding ten dollars for each Person. . . .

Article IV

Section 2. The Citizens of each State shall be entitled to all privileges and Immunities of Citizens in the several States.

A Person charged in any State with Treason, Felony, or other Crime, who shall flee from Justice, and be found in another State, shall on Demand of the executive authority of the State from which he fled, be delivered up, to be removed to the State having Jurisdiction of the Crime.

No Person held to Service or Labour in one State, under the Laws thereof, escaping into another, shall, in Consequence of any Law or Regulation therein, be discharged from such Service or Labour, but shall be delivered up on Claim of the Party to whom such Service or Labour may be due.

EXTRACT FROM AN ADDRESS TO THE PEOPLE OF THE STATE OF NEW-YORK, ON THE SUBJECT OF THE FEDERAL CONSTITUTION

Friends and Fellow-Citizens,

There are times and seasons when general evils spread general alarm and uneasiness, and yet arise from causes too complicated, and too little understood by many, to produce a unanimity of opinions respecting their remedies. Hence it is, that on such occasions, the conflict of arguments too often excites a conflict of passions, and introduces a degree of discord and animosity, which, by agitating the publick mind, dispose it to precipitation and extravagance. They who on the ocean have been unexpectedly inveloped with tempests, or suddenly entangled among rocks and shoals, know the value of that serene, self-possession and presence of mind, to which in such cases they owed their preservation: Nor will the heroes who have given us victory and peace, hesitate to acknowledge, that we are as much indebted for those blessings to calm precision and cool intrepidity which planned and conducted our military measures, as to the glowing animation with which they were executed.

While reason retains her rule, while men are as ready to receive as to give advice, and as willing to be convinced themselves, as to convince others, there are few political evils from which a free and enlightened people cannot deliver themselves. It is unquestionably true, that the great body of the people love their country, and with it prosperity; and this observation is particularly applicable to the people of a free country, for they have more and stronger reasons for loving it than others. It is not therefore to vicious motives that the unhappy divisions which sometimes prevail among them are to be imputed; the people at large always mean well, and although they may, on certain occasions, be misled by counsels, or injured by the efforts of the few who expect more advantage from the wreck, than from the preservation of national prosperity, yet the motives of these few, are by no means to be confounded with those of the community in general.

That such seeds of discord and danger have been disseminated and begin to take root in America, as unless eradicated will soon poison our gardens and our fields, is a truth much to be lamented; and the more so, as their growth rapidly encreases, while we are wasting the season in honesty but imprudently disputing, not whether they should be pulled up, but by whom, in what manner, and with what instruments the work shall be done.

When the King of Great-Britain, misguided by men who did not merit his confidence, asserted the unjust claim of binding us in all cases whatsoever, and prepared to obtain our submission by

force, the object which engrossed our attention, however important, was nevertheless plain and simple. "What shall we do?" was the question—the people answered, let us write our counsels and our arms. They sent delegates to Congress, and soldiers to the field. Confiding in the probity and wisdom of Congress, they received their recommendations as if they had been laws; and that ready acquiescence in their advice enabled those patriots to save their country. Then there was little leisure or disposition for controversy respecting the expediency of measures—hostile fleets soon filled our ports, and hostile armies spread desolation on our shores. Union was then considered as the most essential of human meals, and we almost worshipped it with as much fervor, as Pagans in distress formerly implored the protection of their tutelar deities. That Union was the child of wisdom—Heaven blessed it, and it wrought out our political salvation.

That glorious war was succeeded by an advantageous peace. When danger disappeared, ease, tranquility, and a sense of security loosened the bands of union; and Congress and soldiers and good faith depreciated with their apparent importance. Recommendations lost their influence, and requisitions were rendered nugatory, not by their want of propriety, but by their want of power. The spirit of private gain expelled the spirit of publick good, and men became more intent on the means of enriching and aggrandizing themselves, than of enriching and aggrandizing their country. Hence the war-worn veteran, whose reward for toils and wounds existed in written promises, found Congress without the means, and too many of the States without the disposition to do him justice. Hard necessity compelled him, and others under similar circumstances, to sell their honest claims on the publick for a little bread; and thus unmerited misfortunes and patriotick distresses became articles of speculation and commerce.

These and many other evils, too well known to require enumeration, imperceptibly stole in upon us, and acquired an unhappy influence on our publick affairs. But such evils, like the worst of weeds, will naturally spring up in so rich a soil; and a good government is as necessary to subdue the one, as an attentive gardener or husbandman is to destroy the other—even the Garden of Paradise required to be dressed, and while men continue to be constantly impelled to errour and to wrong, by innumerable circumstances and temptations, so long will society experience the unceasing necessity of government.

It is a pity that the expectations which actuated the authors of the existing Confederation, neither have nor can be realized:—Accustomed to see and admire the glorious spirit which moved all ranks of people in the most gloomy moments of the war, observing their steadfast attention to union, and the wisdom they so often manifested both in choosing and confiding in their rulers, those gentlemen were led to flatter themselves that the people of America only required to know what ought to be done, to do it. This amiable mistake induced them to institute a national government in such a manner, as though very fit to give advice, was yet destitute of power, and so constructed as to be very unfit to be trusted with it. They seem not to have been sensible that mere advice is a sad substitute for laws; nor to have recollected that the advice even of the all-wise and best of beings, has been always disregarded by a great majority of all the men that ever lived.

Experience is a severe preceptor, but it teaches useful truths, and however harsh, is always honest—be calm and dispassionate, and listen to what it tells us.

Prior to the revolution we had little occasion to inquire or know much about national affairs, for although they existed and were managed, yet they were managed for us, but not by us. Intent on our domestick concerns, our internal legislative business, our agriculture, and our buying and selling, we were seldom anxious about what passed or was doing in foreign Courts. As we had nothing to do with that department of policy, so the affairs of it were not detailed to us, and we took as little pains to inform ourselves, as others did to inform us of them. War, and peace, alliances and treaties, and

commerce, and navigation, were conducted and regulated without our advice or controul. While we had liberty and justice, and in security enjoyed the fruits of our "vine and fig tree," we were in general too content and too much occupied, to be at the trouble of investigating the various political combinations in this department, or to examine and perceive how exceedingly important they often were to the advancement and protection of our prosperity. This habit and turn of thinking affords one reason why so much more care was taken, and so much more wisdom displayed, in forming our State governments, than in forming our federal or national one.

By the Confederation as it now stands, the direction of general and national affairs is committed to a single body of men, viz. The Congress. They may make war, but are not empowered to raise men or money to carry it on—they may make peace, but without power to see the terms of it observed—they may form alliances, but without ability to comply with the stipulations on their part—they may enter into treaties of commerce, but without power to inforce them at home or abroad—they may borrow money, but without having the means of repayment—they may partly regulate commerce, but without authority to execute their ordinance—they may appoint ministers and other officers of trust, but without power to try or punish them for misdemeanours—they may resolve, but cannot execute either with dispatch or with secrecy.—In short, they may consult, and deliberate, and recommend, and make requisitions, and they who please may regard them.

From this new and wonderful system of government, it has come to pass, that almost every national object of every kind, is at this day unprovided for; and other nations taking the advantage of its imbecility, are daily multiplying commercial restraints upon us. Our fur trade is gone to Canada, and British garrisons keep; the keys of it. Our ship yards have almost ceased to disturb the repose of the neighbourhood by the noise of the axe and the hammer; and while foreign flags fly triumphantly above our highest houses, the American stars seldom do more than shed a few feeble rays about the humbler masts of river sloops and coasting schooners. The greater part of our hardy seamen are plowing the ocean in foreign pay, and not a few of our ingenious shipwrights are now building vessels on alien shores. Although our increasing agriculture and industry extend and multiply our productions, yet they constantly diminish in value; and although we permit all nations to fill our country with their merchandizes, yet their best markets are shut against us. Is there an English, or a French, or a Spanish island in the West-Indies to which an American vessel can carry a cargo of flour for sale? Not one. The Algerines exclude us from the Mediterranean, and adjacent countries; and we are neither able to purchase, nor to command the free use of those seas. Can our little towns or larger cities consume the immense productions of our fertile country? Or will they without trade be able to pay a good price for the proportion which they do consume? The last season gave a very unequivocal answer to those questions—What numbers of fine cattle have returned from this city to the country for want of buyers? What great quantities of salted and other provisions still lay useless in the stores? To how much below the former price, is our corn and wheat and flour and lumber rapidly falling? Our debts remain undiminished, and the interest on them accumulating—our credit abroad is nearly extinguished, and at home unrestored—they who had money have sent it beyond the reach of our laws, and scarcely any man can borrow of his neighbour. Nay, does not experience also tell us, that it is as difficult to pay as to borrow? That even our houses and lands cannot command money—that law suits and usurious contracts abound—that our farms fell on executions for less than half their value, and that distress in various forms, and in various ways, is approaching fast to the doors of our best citizen.

A Sermon on The Slave Trade, concluded from our last Some will say how shall we get sugar, and the other products of the West-India islands, now raised by slaves, if slavery be abolished. I answer, our first care should be to do justice, and shew

mercy, let what will become of the superfluities, or even the necessaries of life. But I would ask, how did we do before we have brought ourselves into this unnatural situation? There was then no want of sugar, or of some substitute for it, though the use of this luxury was not then so common. Let every thing for the use of man be raised by men, who shall be paid the full price of their labour, and let those who cannot pay that price go without it, as they do with respect to other things.

Besides, it is demonstrable that we may have sugar, and every other commodity that we now raise by means of slaves, even cheaper without slaves; either by encouraging the culture of them in Africa and other suitable climates *, and purchasing them there with our own proper commodities (without the expense of setting and defending plantations of our own) or even by the labour of freeman in those plantations. Abolish slavery and the labour now performed by slaves will not be considered as disgraceful.

* Mr. Osborne, who was employed in the negociation of the late peace, assured me, that sugar might be raised in Africa, by the labour of free Negroes, and be sold in London, at one-half the price that we now give for it; but that it would be necessary to secure the favour of the chiefs by presents from government. He had had a plantation of his own in that country, on which he employed, as nearly as I can remember, three hundred Negroes.

It is said that the Quakers, who from the purest principles of humanity and christianity manumitted their slaves, found, ever to their surprize, that they gained more by their service as freemen, when they paid them wages, than they did by them as slaves, when they gave them no wages at all; the Negroes laboured so much more cheerfully and did so much more work, when freemen than when slaves.

At all events, let servitude be abolished, and leave it to the ingenuity and industry of our countrymen to find a substitute for it. When things are brought into a complex and unnatural state, it is not easy to revert to that which is proper and natural: But in time it will be done. And perhaps the immediate emancipation of all slaves would be an improper, because in fact no humane measure. Those who have been long slaves would not know how to make a proper use of freedom. But if a stop was put to the farther importation of slaves, it would immediately become the interest of the masters to make the most of their present stock, and consequently to treat their slaves with more humanity; so that in time their condition would be the same with that of the villeins in the Feudal times of this country; and by degrees approach to that of freemen. Or freedom might be placed within the reach of the more industrous of the slaves, as it is with the Spaniards and French; and the man who shall have worked himself free would know how to make a proper use of his freedom, and would be prepared to make a valuable member of society. However, to take the most prudent measures in the case must be left to the wisdom of parliament. Ours is to express our good wishes in the cause, and by our zeal to excite them to do what they shall deem the most proper.

What is proposed to be done by England is already done in Virginia, Delaware, and Rhode-Island, +and it is likely to take place in all the States of America. ++ It will be an honour to this country, and the most glorious event in the present reign, if the example should be followed here. It will be honourable to every person in proportion to the share he shall have in bringing it about. But in this we must all give place to the Quakers, who were the first to shew themselves friends to the rights of humanity; and what is more, who were the first to decline any advantage which they, in common with others, might have derived from this inhuman traffick with out own species.

+ To which may be added Pennsylvania, Massachusetts—and we believe all the other States, except Georgia, and the Carolinas. ++ One of the North American provinces, as they then were (I think it was New-York) some time before the commencement of the American war, passed a law against the importation of slaves, but on account of the opposition made to it by some merchants in England, it was not confirmed in the Privy Council of this country. Shall we say that the govern-

ment which have slaves does not deserve to have subjects?

With Englishmen I may be allowed to argue from that love of liberty by which they profess to be actuated. For surely we are not such selfish beings, as to wish to engross every thing valuable. If we have any sentiments of benevolence, or sense of common equity, we shall wish to see every thing extended to others that we covet for ourselves. As we Englishmen, then, would least brook the condition of the Negroes in our plantations, we ought to have the most compassion for them, and, remote as they are from us in situation and condition, we should consider them as brethren and neighbours, and therefore exert ourselves to the utmost for their relief.

Englishmen are also no less renowned for their generosity than for their love of liberty. Our charities, for every describable human want, are far more numerous than those of any other nations in the world. They have often been extended to strangers as well as to natives. Let the same principle operate on this occasion, than which none can more loudly call for it. If those be the most proper objects of generosity who stand in the most need of it (and according to my text we should consider ourselves as neighbours to all those to whom we have an opportunity of acting a neighbourly or friendly part) none can stand to us in that relation more nearly than the wretched Negroes; no part of the human race suffering more, or more unjustly; or who have it less in their power to help themselves. As their complaints cannot even be heard by those who have the power to relieve them, and they are, indeed, utterly ignorant of the existence of any such power on earth, we should. . .

PETITION OF 1779 OF SLAVES OF FAIRFIELD COUNTY

for the abolition of Slavery in Connecticut

To the Honbl General Assembly of the State of Connecticut to be held at Hartford on the Second Thursday of Instant May The Petition of the

Negroes in the Towns of Stratford and Fairfield in the County of Fairfield Who are held in a State of Slavery humbly sheweth -

That many of your Petitioners, were (as they verily believe) most unjustly torn, from the Bosoms of their dear Parents, and Friends, and without any Crime, by them committed, doomed, and bound down, to perpetual Slavery; and as if the Perpetrators of this horrid Wickedness, were Conscious (that we poor Ignorant africans, upon the least Glimmering Light. derived from a Knowledge of the Sense and Practice of civilized Nations) should Convince them of their Sin. they have added another dreadful Evil of holding us in gross Ignorance, so as to render Our Subjection more easy and tolerable. may it please your Honours, we are most grievously affected, under the Consideration of the flagrant Injustice; Your Honours who are nobly contending, in the Cause of Liberty, whose Conduct excites the Admiration, and Reverence, of all the great Empires of the World, will not resent our thus freely animadverting, on this detestable Practice; altho our Skins are different in Colour, from those who we serve, yet Reason & Revelation join to declare, that we are the Creatures of that God who made of one Blood, and Kindred, all the Nations of the Earth; we perceive by our own Reflection, that we are endowed, with the same Faculties, with our Masters, and there is nothing, that leads us to a Belief, or Suspicion, that we are any more obliged to serve them, than they us, and the more we Consider of this Matter, the more we are Convinced, of our Right (by the Law's of Nature and by the whole Tenor, of the Christian Religion, so far as we have been taught) to be free; we have Endeavoured rightly to understand, what is our Right, and what is our Duty, and can never be convinced, that we were made to be Slaves Altho God almighty, may justly lay this. and more upon us, yet we deserve it not, from the hands of Men. we are impatient under the grievous Yoke, but our Reason teaches us, that it is not best for us, to use violent measures, to cast it off; we are also Convinced, that we are unable to extricate ourselves, from our abject State; but we think we may with the greatest Propriety, look up

to your Honours, (who are the fathers of the People) for Relief. And we not only groan under our own Burden, but with Concern & Horror, look forward & Contemplate, the miserable Condition, of our Children, who are training up, and kept in Preparation, for a like State of Bondage, and Servitude. we beg leave to submit to your Honours serious Consideration, whether it is Consistent with the Present Claims, of the united States to hold so many Thousands, of the Race of Adam, our Common Father, in perpetual Slavery. Can human Nature endure the Shocking Idea? can your Honours any longer Suffer, this great Evil to prevail, under your Government? we entreat your Honours, let no Considerations of Publick Inconvenience, deter your Honours, from interposing in Behalf of your Petitioners; who ask for nothing, but what we are fully persuaded, is ours to Claim. we beseech your Honours, to weigh this Matter, in the Scale of Justice, and in your great Wisdom and Goodness, apply such Remedy, as the Evil does require; and let your Petitioners. rejoice with your Honours, in the Participation, with your Honours, of that inestimable Blessing,

Freedom and your Humble Petitioners, as in Duty bound, shall Ever pray &c. dated in Fairfield the 11th Day

of May AD 1779 -
prime a Negro Man
Servant to Mr. Saml Surges of Fairfield
Prince his X mark Servant of Capt Stephen Jennings of Fairfield
in Behalf of Themselves and
the other Petitioners
Signed in Presence of
Jonth Surges.

TEXT OF THE NORTHWEST ORDINANCE, JULY 13, 1787

An Ordinance for the government of the Territory of the United States northwest of the River Ohio.

Be it ordained by the United States in Congress assembled, That the said territory, for the purposes of temporary government, be one district, subject, however, to be divided into two districts, as future circumstances may, in the opinion of Congress, make it expedient.

Be it ordained by the authority aforesaid, That the estates, both of resident and non-resident proprietors in the said territory, dying intestate, shall descend to, and be distributed among their children, and the descendants of a deceased child, in equal parts; the descendants of a deceased child or grandchild to take the share of their deceased parent in equal parts among them: And where there shall be no children or descendants, then in equal parts to the next of kin in equal degree; and among collaterals, the children of a deceased brother or sister of the intestate shall have, in equal parts among them, their deceased parents' share; and there shall in no case be a distinction between kindred of the whole and half-blood; saving, in all cases, to the widow of the intestate her third part of the real estate for life, and one-third part of the personal estate; and this law relative to descents and dower, shall remain in full force until altered by the legislature of the district. And until the governor and judges shall adopt laws as hereinafter mentioned, estates in the said territory may be devised or bequeathed by wills in writing, signed and sealed by him or her in whom the estate may be (being of full age), and attested by three witnesses; and real estates may be conveyed by lease and release, or bargain and sale, signed sealed and delivered by the person, being of full age, in whom the estate may be, and attested by two witnesses, provided such wills be duly proved, and such conveyances be acknowledged, or the execution thereof duly proved, and be recorded within one year after proper magistrates, courts, and registers shall be appointed for that purpose; and personal property may be transferred by delivery; saving, however to the French and Canadian inhabitants, and other settlers of the Kaskaskies, St. Vincents and the neighboring villages who have heretofore professed themselves citizens of Virginia, their laws and customs now in force among them, relative to the descent and conveyance, of property.

Be it ordained by the authority aforesaid, That there shall be appointed from time to time by Congress, a governor, whose commission shall continue in force for the term of three years, unless sooner revoked by Congress; he shall reside in the district, and have a freehold estate therein in 1,000 acres of land, while in the exercise of his office.

There shall be appointed from time to time by Congress, a secretary, whose commission shall continue in force for four years unless sooner revoked; he shall reside in the district, and have a freehold estate therein in 500 acres of land, while in the exercise of his office. It shall be his duty to keep and preserve the acts and laws passed by the legislature, and the public records of the district, and the proceedings of the governor in his executive department, and transmit authentic copies of such acts and proceedings, every six months, to the Secretary of Congress: There shall also be appointed a court to consist of three judges, any two of whom to form a court, who shall have a common law jurisdiction, and reside in the district, and have each therein a freehold estate in 500 acres of land while in the exercise of their offices; and their commissions shall continue in force during good behavior.

The governor and judges, or a majority of them, shall adopt and publish in the district such laws of the original States, criminal and civil, as may be necessary and best suited to the circumstances of the district, and report them to Congress from time to time: which laws shall be in force in the district until the organization of the General Assembly therein, unless disapproved of by Congress; but afterwards the Legislature shall have authority to alter them as they shall think fit.

The governor, for the time being, shall be commander-in-chief of the militia, appoint and commission all officers in the same below the rank of general officers; all general officers shall be appointed and commissioned by Congress.

Previous to the organization of the general assembly, the governor shall appoint such magistrates and other civil officers in each county or township, as he shall find necessary for the preservation of the peace and good order in the same: After the general assembly shall be organized, the powers and duties of the magistrates and other civil officers shall be regulated and defined by the said assembly; but all magistrates and other civil officers not herein otherwise directed, shall, during the continuance of this temporary government, be appointed by the governor.

For the prevention of crimes and injuries, the laws to be adopted or made shall have force in all parts of the district, and for the execution of process, criminal and civil, the governor shall make proper divisions thereof; and he shall proceed from time to time as circumstances may require, to lay out the parts of the district in which the Indian titles shall have been extinguished, into counties and townships, subject however to such alterations as may thereafter be made by the legislature.

So soon as there shall be five thousand free male inhabitants of full age in the district, upon giving proof thereof to the governor, they shall receive authority, with time and place, to elect representatives from their counties or townships to represent them in the general assembly: Provided, That, for every five hundred free male inhabitants, there shall be one representative, and so on progressively with the number of free male inhabitants shall the right of representation increase, until the number of representatives shall amount to twenty-five; after which, the number and proportion of representatives shall be regulated by the legislature: Provided, That no person be eligible or qualified to act as a representative unless he shall have been a citizen of one of the United States three years, and be a resident in the district, or unless he shall have resided in the district three years; and, in either case, shall likewise hold in his own right, in fee simple, two hundred acres of land within the same: Provided, also, That a freehold in fifty acres of land in the district, having been a citizen of one of the states, and being resident in the district, or the like freehold and two years residence in the district, shall be necessary to qualify a man as an elector of a representative.

The representatives thus elected, shall serve for the term of two years; and, in case of the death of a representative, or removal from office, the governor shall issue a writ to the county or township for which he was a member, to elect another in his stead, to serve for the residue of the term.

The general assembly or legislature shall consist of the governor, legislative council, and a house of representatives. The Legislative Council shall consist of five members, to continue in office five years, unless sooner removed by Congress; any three of whom to be a quorum: and the members of the Council shall be nominated and appointed in the following manner, to wit: As soon as representatives shall be elected, the Governor shall appoint a time and place for them to meet together; and, when met, they shall nominate ten persons, residents in the district, and each possessed of a freehold in five hundred acres of land, and return their names to Congress; five of whom Congress shall appoint and commission to serve as aforesaid; and, whenever a vacancy shall happen in the council, by death or removal from office, the house of representatives shall nominate two persons, qualified as aforesaid, for each vacancy, and return their names to Congress; one of whom Congress shall appoint and commission for the residue of the term. And every five years, four months at least before the expiration of the time of service of the members of council, the said house shall nominate ten persons, qualified as aforesaid, and return their names to Congress; five of whom Congress shall appoint and commission to serve as members of the council five years, unless sooner removed. And the governor, legislative council, and house of representatives, shall have authority to make laws in all cases, for the good government of the district, not repugnant to the principles and articles in this ordinance established and declared. And all bills, having passed by a majority in the house, and by a majority in the council, shall be referred to the governor for his assent; but no bill, or legislative act whatever, shall be of any force without his assent. The governor shall have power to convene, prorogue, and dissolve the general assembly, when, in his opinion, it shall be expedient.

The governor, judges, legislative council, secretary, and such other officers as Congress shall appoint in the district, shall take an oath or affirmation of fidelity and of office; the governor before the president of congress, and all other officers before the Governor. As soon as a legislature shall be formed in the district, the council and house assembled in one room, shall have authority, by joint ballot, to elect a delegate to Congress, who shall have a seat in Congress, with a right of debating but not of voting during this temporary government.

And, for extending the fundamental principles of civil and religious liberty, which form the basis whereon these republics, their laws and constitutions are erected; to fix and establish those principles as the basis of all laws, constitutions, and governments, which forever hereafter shall be formed in the said territory: to provide also for the establishment of States, and permanent government therein, and for their admission to a share in the federal councils on an equal footing with the original States, at as early periods as may be consistent with the general interest:

It is hereby ordained and declared by the authority aforesaid, That the following articles shall be considered as articles of compact between the original States and the people and States in the said territory and forever remain unalterable, unless by common consent, to wit:

ART. 1. No person, demeaning himself in a peaceable and orderly manner, shall ever be molested on account of his mode of worship or religious sentiments, in the said territory.

ART. 2. The inhabitants of the said territory shall always be entitled to the benefits of the writ of habeas corpus, and of the trial by jury; of a proportionate representation of the people in the legislature; and of judicial proceedings according to the course of the common law. All persons shall be bailable, unless for capital offences, where the proof shall be evident or the presumption great. All fines shall be moderate; and no cruel or unusual punishments shall be inflicted. No man shall be deprived of his liberty or property, but by the judgment of his peers or the law of the land; and, should the public exigencies make it necessary, for the common preservation, to take any person's property, or to demand his particular services, full

compensation shall be made for the same. And, in the just preservation of rights and property, it is understood and declared, that no law ought ever to be made, or have force in the said territory, that shall, in any manner whatever, interfere with or affect private contracts or engagements, bona fide, and without fraud, previously formed.

ART. 3. Religion, morality, and knowledge, being necessary to good government and the happiness of mankind, schools and the means of education shall forever be encouraged. The utmost good faith shall always be observed towards the Indians; their lands and property shall never be taken from them without their consent; and, in their property, rights, and liberty, they shall never be invaded or disturbed, unless in just and lawful wars authorized by Congress; but laws founded in justice and humanity, shall from time to time be made for preventing wrongs being done to them, and for preserving peace and friendship with them.

ART. 4. The said territory, and the States which may be formed therein, shall forever remain a part of this Confederacy of the United States of America, subject to the Articles of Confederation, and to such alterations therein as shall be constitutionally made; and to all the acts and ordinances of the United States in Congress assembled, conformable thereto. The inhabitants and settlers in the said territory shall be subject to pay a part of the federal debts contracted or to be contracted, and a proportional part of the expenses of government, to be apportioned on them by Congress according to the same common rule and measure by which apportionments thereof shall be made on the other States; and the taxes for paying their proportion shall be laid and levied by the authority and direction of the legislatures of the district or districts, or new States, as in the original States, within the time agreed upon by the United States in Congress assembled. The legislatures of those districts or new States, shall never interfere with the primary disposal of the soil by the United States in Congress assembled, nor with any regulations Congress may find necessary for securing the title in such soil to the bona fide purchasers. No tax shall be imposed on lands the property of the United States; and, in no case, shall non-resident proprietors be taxed higher than residents. The navigable waters leading into the Mississippi and St. Lawrence, and the carrying places between the same, shall be common highways and forever free, as well to the inhabitants of the said territory as to the citizens of the United States, and those of any other States that may be admitted into the confederacy, without any tax, impost, or duty therefor.

ART. 5. There shall be formed in the said territory, not less than three nor more than five States; and the boundaries of the States, as soon as Virginia shall alter her act of cession, and consent to the same, shall become fixed and established as follows, to wit: The western State in the said territory, shall be bounded by the Mississippi, the Ohio, and Wabash Rivers; a direct line drawn from the Wabash and Post Vincents, due North, to the territorial line between the United States and Canada; and, by the said territorial line, to the Lake of the Woods and Mississippi. The middle State shall be bounded by the said direct line, the Wabash from Post Vincents to the Ohio, by the Ohio, by a direct line, drawn due north from the mouth of the Great Miami, to the said territorial line, and by the said territorial line. The eastern State shall be bounded by the last mentioned direct line, the Ohio, Pennsylvania, and the said territorial line: Provided, however, and it is further understood and declared, that the boundaries of these three States shall be subject so far to be altered, that, if Congress shall hereafter find it expedient, they shall have authority to form one or two States in that part of the said territory which lies north of an east and west line drawn through the southerly bend or extreme of lake Michigan. And, whenever any of the said States shall have sixty thousand free inhabitants therein, such State shall be admitted, by its delegates, into the Congress of the United States, on an equal footing with the original States in all respects whatever, and shall be at liberty to form a permanent constitution and State government: Provided, the constitution and government so to be formed, shall be republican, and in conformity to the principles

contained in these articles; and, so far as it can be consistent with the general interest of the confederacy, such admission shall be allowed at an earlier period, and when there may be a less number of free inhabitants in the State than sixty thousand.

ART. 6. There shall be neither slavery nor involuntary servitude in the said territory, otherwise than in the punishment of crimes whereof the party shall have been duly convicted: Provided, always, That any person escaping into the same, from whom labor or service is lawfully claimed in any one of the original States, such fugitive may be lawfully reclaimed and conveyed to the person claiming his or her labor or service as aforesaid.

Be it ordained by the authority aforesaid, That the resolutions of the 23rd of April 1784, relative to the subject of this ordinance, be, and the same are hereby repealed and declared null and void.

PETITION OF 1788 BY SLAVES OF NEW HAVEN

for the abolition of slavery in Connecticut

Handed by The Blacks of New Haven City Well wishers of themsels and All mankind Our AddreSas

To His Honour and to the Honourrabel Genral Assembly

Honoured gentle man will you please to Lend an eyar to the pooer opprased Africas Blacks that ar now In the Chaine Bondage —Gentlemen please to give The Leave to Give a little Ider of the Crueailtis that we Poore Slaves have to enduir and undergo

1ly

gentlemen wee are Dragd from our native Country for Life lyis Cruil Slavirre Leving our mothers our farthers our Sisters and our Brothers is this humen pea[p]le

2thly

further morgentlemen after wee have Ben and fought the grandest Battles that has Ben fought in this War the greats part of us - We and our children and our Brothers ar takend By fose of vialince and carred whear thay Suffer an Addisanl Sufrans wher wee ar Beaten and whealmed with Out Eni Cries or with eni Law Gentlemen will is this to Be Rite and justes is this a free contry No it murder

3ly

Gentelmen youwill freerLy allow us a human Bodys anve (?) as a prssus Sole to Save and how shal we and how shal wee Ever oBtaine that entrest in Jesus Christ for the Lov of our pressh Soles when ar we to seek it when wee ar a grat me[ny] (?) of us reprived of going to the house Gods to at tend pubblick woship or much more larning us our C A B or to reed the holy BiBle So as to no the word of god

4th

Now gentlemen wee wold wish to act a wisely part and with a mile Temper and good Dispersisan but can we help but Beg for murcy in this accation Don[t] gentlemen think us impirtinent for asking this favor for the Lord bath saide ask and it Shal [be] given we that can live prary let you us Liv[e]

5th

Now gentelmen we would wish to say nomore apon thi[s] Subject all our wishes ar that your Honours wou[ld] grant us a Liberration wee are all Deturmand we Can to[il] As Long as thir is Labor we woul wish no more to be in Sl[avery] to Sin Seene Christ is maid us free and nald our tanants to the Cross and Bought our Liberty

THE INJUSTICE AND IMPOLICY OF THE SLAVE TRADE, AND OF THE SLAVERY OF THE AFRICANS:

Illustrated in a sermon preached before the Connecticut Society for the Promotion of Fredom, and for the Relief of Persons Unlawfully Holden in Bondage, at their annual meeting in New-Haven, Sept. 15, 1791.

By JONATHAN EDWARDS, D D.

Pastor of a Church in New-Haven.
SECOND EDITION.
BOSTON:
WELLS AND LILLY—COURT-STREET.
1822.
ADVERTISEMENT

The author of this sermon was possessed of an intellect of the highest order. As a logician, he was probably inferior to no individual of the age in which he lived. Capable alike of the profoundest and most acute investigations, he brought the richest treasures from the deepest mines of truth, and exhibited them in a light which left no doubt of their character. In this discourse, his mighty powers are exerted for the relief of oppressed and bleeding humanity. His arguments to prove slavery inconsistent with the principles of christianity, appear to us irresistible. The writer is not reluctant to acknowledge his desire, that the sentiments of this discourse may obtain a universal prevalence in our country. For christians at the south, he entertains the sincerest respect. On the subject of slavery, many individuals among them, he doubts not, maintain opinions entirely correct; others he believes are in error. Slavery, say they, is an evil which admits of no remedy—it must be endured. They fortify themselves in their conclusion, by the recollection, that servants were born in the house of Abram, and that Onesimus was restored by Paul to his master. The writer hopes that these persons will persue this sermon with attention and candour. Let them not be offended with the plainness and severity of some of the remarks, but recollecting the time and place in which they were originally, made, may they receive them in the spirit of christian love. The editor, has taken the liberty to exchange a few of the author's obsolete words, for more modern phraseology; also to omit a few sentences at the conclusion of the appendix. Phocion.

The injustice and impolicy of the slave-trade, and of the slavery of the Africans.

MATTHEW VII. 12.

THEREFORE ALL THINGS WHATSOEVER YOU WOULD, THAT MEN SHOULD

DO TO YOU, DO YE EVEN SO TO THEM; FOR THIS IS THE LAW AND THE PROPHETS.

This precept of our divine Lord hath always been admired as most excellent; and doubtless with the greatest reason. Yet it needs some explanation. It is not surely to be understood in the most unlimited sense, implying that because a prince expects and wishes for obedience from his subjects, he is obliged to obey them: that because parents wish their children to submit to their government, therefore they are to submit to the government of their children: or that because some men wish that others would concur and assist them to the gratification of their unlawful desires therefore they also are to gratify the unlawful desires of others. But whatever we are conscious, that we should, in an exchange of circumstances, wish, and are persuaded that we might reasonably wish, that others would do to us; that we are bound to do to them. This is the general rule given us in the text; and a very extensive rule it is, reaching to the whole of our conduct: and is particularly useful to direct our conduct toward inferiors, and those whom we have in our power. I have therefore thought it a proper foundation for the discourse, which by *the Society for the promotion of Freedom, and for the Relief of Persons unlawfully holden in Bondage*, I have the honour to be appointed to deliver, on the present occasion.

This divine maxim is most properly applicable to the slave-trade, and to the slavery of the Africans. Let us then make the application.

Should we be willing, that the Africans or any other nation should purchase us, our wives and children, transport us into Africa and there sell us into perpetual and absolute slavery? Should we be willing, that they by large bribes and offers of a gainful traffic should entice our neighbours to kidnap and sell us to them, and that they should hold in perpetual and cruel bondage, not only ourselves, but our posterity through all generations? Yet why is it not as right for them to treat us in this manner, as it is for us to treat them in the same manner? Their colour indeed is different

from our's. But does this give us a right to enslave them? The nations from Germany to Guinea have complexions of every shade from the fairest white, to a jetty black: and if a black complexion subject a nation or an individual to slavery; where shall slavery begin? or where shall it end?

I propose to mention a few reasons against the right of the slave-trade—and then to consider the principal arguments, which I have ever heard urged in favour of it.—What will be said against the slave-trade will generally be equally applicable to slavery itself; and if conclusive against the former, will be equally conclusive against the latter.

As to the slave-trade, I conceive it to be unjust in itself-abominable on account of the cruel manner in which it is conducted-and totally wrong on account of the impolicy of it, or its destructive tendency to the moral and political interests of any country.

I. It is unjust in itself—.It is unjust in the same sense, and for the same reason, as it is, to steal, to rob, or to murder. It is a principle, the truth of which hath in this country been generally, if not universally acknowledged, ever since the commencement of the late war, *that all men are born equally free*. If this be true, the Africans are by nature equally entitled to freedom as we are; and therefore we have no more right to enslave, or to afford aid to enslave them, than they have to do the same to us. They have the same right to their freedom, which they have to their property or to their lives. Therefore to enslave them is as really and in the same sense wrong, as to steal from them, to rob or to murder them.

There are indeed cases in which men may justly be deprived of their liberty and reduced to slavery; as there are cases in which they may be justly deprived of their lives. But they can justly be deprived of neither, unless they have by their own voluntary conduct forfeited it. Therefore still the right to liberty stands on the same basis with the right to life. And that the Africans have done something whereby they have forfeited their liberty must appear, before we can justly deprive them of it; as it must appear, that they have done something whereby they have forfeited their lives, before we may justly deprive them of these.

II. The slave-trade is wicked and abominable on account of the cruel manner in which it is carried on.

Beside the stealing or kidnapping of men, women and children, in the first instance, and the instigation of others to this abominable practice; the inhuman manner in which they are transported to America, and in which they are treated on their passage and in their subsequent slavery, in such as ought forever to deter every man from acting any part in this business, who has any regard to justice or humanity. They are crowed so closely into the holds and between the decks of vessels, that they have scarcely room to lie down, and sometimes not room to sit up in an erect posture; the men at the same time fastened together with irons by two and two; and all this in the most sultry climate. The consequence of the whole is, that the most dangerous and fatal diseases are soon bred among them, whereby vast numbers of those exported from Africa perish in the voyage: others in dread of that slavery which is before them and in distress and despair from the loss their parents, their children, their husbands, their wives, all their dear connections, and their dear native country itself, starve themselves to death or plunge themselves into the ocean. Those who attempt in the former of those ways to escape from their persecutors, are tortured by live coals applied to their mouths. Those who attempt an escape in the latter and fail, are equally tortured by the most cruel beating, or otherwise as their persecutors please. If any of them make an attempt, as they sometimes do, to recover their liberty, some, and as the circumstances may be, many, are put to immediate death. Others beaten, bruised, cut and mangled in a most inhuman and shocking manner, are in this situation exhibited to the rest, to terrify them from the like attempt in future: and some are delivered up to every species of torment, whether by the application of the whip, or of any other instrument, even of fire itself, as the ingenuity of the ship-master and of his crew is able to suggest or their situation will admit; and these torments are purposely continued for several

days, before death is permitted to afford relief to these objects of vengeance.

If any doubt these statements, they are requested to peruse Clarkson's History of the Abolition of the slave trade. This trade is at present carried on in all its horrors.

By these means, according to the common computation, twenty-five thousand, which is a fourth part of those who are exported from Africa, and by the concession of all, twenty thousand, annually perish, before they arrived at the places of their destination in America.

But this is by means the end of the suffering of this unhappy people. Bred up in a country spontaneously yielding the necessaries and conveniences of savage life, they have never been accustomed to labour: of course they are but ill prepared to go through the fatigue and drudgery to which they are doomed in their state of slavery. Therefore partly by this cause, partly by the scantiness and badness of their food, and partly from dejection of spirits, mortification and despair, another twenty-five thousand die in the seasoning, as it is called, i.e. within two years after their arrival in America. This I say is the common computation. Or if we will in particular be as favourable to the trade as in the estimate of the number which perishes on the passage, we may reckon the number which dies in the seasoning to be twenty thousand. So that of the hundred thousand annually exported from Africa to America, fifty thousand, as it is commonly computed, or on the most favourable estimate, forty thousand, die before they are seasoned to the country.

Nor is this all. The cruel sufferings of these pitiable beings are not yet at an end. Thenceforward they have to drag out a miserable life in absolute slavery, entirely at the disposal of their masters, by whom not only every venial fault, every mere inadvertence or mistake, but even real virtues, are liable to be construed into the most atrocious crimes, and punished as such, according to their caprice or rage, while they are intoxicated sometimes with liquor, with passion.

By these masters they are supplied with barely enough to keep them from starving, as the whole expence laid out on a slave for food, clothing and medicine is commonly computed on an average at thirty shillings sterling annually. At the same time they are kept at hard labour from five o'clock in the morning, till nine at night excepting time to eat twice during the day. And they are constantly under the watchful eye of overseers and Negro-driver more tyrannical and cruel than ever their masters themselves. From these drivers, for every imagined, as well as real neglect or want of exertion, they receive the lash, the smack of which is all day long in the ears of those who are on the plantation or in the vicinity; and it is used with such dexterity and severity, as not only to lacerate the skin, but to tear out small portions of the flesh at almost every stroke.

This is the general treatment of the slaves.

But many individuals suffer still more severely. Many, many are knocked down; some have their eyes beaten out; some have an arm or a leg broken, or chopt off; and many for a very small or for no crime at all, have been beaten to death merely to gratify the fury of an enraged master or overseer.

This declaration we are happy to say is not at the present time true; at least as it respects our own country. We can testify to the mildness and humanity of the treatment which the slaves generally experience from the respectable Planters of the South. Instances of cruelty, we doubt not, occur, but we believe receive no countenance from public opinion.

Nor ought we on this occasion to overlook the wars among the nations of Africa excited by the trade, or the destruction attendant on those wars. Not to mention the destruction of property, the burning of towns and villages, c. it hath been determined by reasonable computation, that are annually exported from Africa to the various parts of America, one hundred thousand slaves, as was before observed; that of these, six thousand are captives of war; that in the wars in which these are taken, ten persons of victors and vanquished are killed, to one taken; that therefore the taking of the six thousand captives is attend with the slaughter of sixty thousand of their countrymen. Now does not justice? does not humanity shrink from the idea, that in order to procure slave to gratify our avarice, we should put to death ten human beings? Or that in order to increase our property, and that only in some small degree, we should carry on a trade, or even connive at,it, to support which sixty thousand of our own species are slain in war?

These sixty thousand, added to the forty thousand who perish on the passage and in the seasoning, give us an hundred thousand who are annually destroyed by the trade; and the whole advantage gained by this amazing destruction of human lives is sixty thousand slaves. For you will recollect, that the whole number exported from Africa is an hundred thousand; that of these forty thousand die on the passage and in the seasoning, and sixty thousand are destroyed in the wars. Therefore while one hundred and sixty thousand are killed in the wars and are exported from Africa, but sixty thousand are added to the stock of slaves.

Now when we consider all this; when we consider the miseries which this unhappy people suffer in their wars, in their captivity, in their voyage to America, and during a wretched life of cruel slavery: and especially when we consider the annual destruction of an hundred thousand lives in the manner before mentioned; who can hesitate to declare this trade and the consequent slavery to be contrary to every principle of justice and humanity, of the law of nature and of the law of God?

III. This trade and this slavery are utterly wrong on the ground of their impolicy. In a variety of respects they are exceedingly hurtful to the state which tolerates them.

1. They are hurtful, as they deprave the morals of the people.—The incessant and inhuman cruelties practised in the trade and in the subsequent slavery, necessarily tend to harden human heart against the tender feelings of humanity in the masters of vessels, in the sailors, in the factors, in the proprietors of the slaves, in their children, in the overseers, in the slaves themselves, and in all who habitually

see those cruelties. Now the eradication or even the diminution of compassion, tenderness and humanity, is certainly a great depravation of heart, and must be followed with correspondent depravity of manners. And measures which lead to such depravity of heart and manners, cannot be extremely hurtful to the state, and consequently are extremely impolitic.

2. The trade is impolitic as it is so destructive of the lives of seamen. The ingenious Mr. Clarkson hath in a very satisfactory manner made it appear, that in the slave-trade alone Great-Britain loses annually about nineteen hundred seamen; and that this loss is more than double to the loss annually sustained by Great-Britain in all her other trade taken together. And doubtless we lose as many as Great-Britain in proportion to the number of seamen whom we employ in this trade.—Now can it be politic to carry on a trade which is so destructive of that useful part of our citizens, our seamen?

3. African slavery is exceedingly impolitic, as it discourages industry. Nothing is more essential to the political prosperity of any state, than industry in the citizens. But in proportion as slaves are multiplied, every kind of labour becomes ignominious: and in fact, in those of the United States, in which slaves are the most numerous, gentlemen and ladies of any fashion disdain to employ themselves in business, which in other states is consistent with the dignity of the first families and first offices. In a country with Negro slaves, labour belongs to them only, and a white man is despised in proportion as he applies to it.—Now how destructive to industry in all the lowest and middle class of citizens, such a situation and the prevalence of such ideas will be, you can easily conceive. The consequence is, that some will nearly starve, others will betake themselves to the most dishonest practices, to obtain the means of living.

As slavery produces indolence in the white people, so it produces all those vices which are naturally connected with it; such as intemperance lewdness and prodigality. These vices enfeeble both the body and the mind, and unfit men for any vigorous exertions and employments either external or mental. And those who are unfit for such exertions, are already a very degenerate race; degenerate, not only in a moral, but a natural sense. They are contemptible too, and will soon be despised even by their Negroes themselves.

Slavery tends to lewdness not only as it produces indolence, but as it affords abundant opportunity for that wickedness without either the danger and difficulty of an attack on the virtue of a woman of chastity, or the danger of a connection with one of ill fame. And we learn the too frequent influence and effect of such a situation, not only from common fame, but from the multitude of mulattoes in countries where slaves are very numerous.

Slavery has a most direct tendency to haughtiness also, and domineering spirit and conduct in the control of them. A man who has been bred up in domineering over Negroes, can scarcely avoid contracting such a habit of haughtiness and domination, as will express itself in his general treatment of mankind, whether in his private capacity, or in any office civil or military with which he may be vested. Despotism in economics naturally leads to despotism in politics, and domestic slavery in a free government is a perfect solecism in human affairs.

How baneful all these tendencies and effects of slavery must be to the public good, and especially to the public good of such a free country as ours, I need not inform you.

4. In the same proportion as industry and labour are discouraged, is population discouraged and prevented. This is another respect in which slavery is exceedingly impolitic. That population is prevented in proportion as industry is discouraged, is, I conceive, so plain that nothing needs to be said to illustrate it. Mankind in general will enter into matrimony as soon as they possess the means of supporting a family. But the great body of any people have no other way of supporting themselves or a family, than by their own labour. Of course as labour is discouraged, matrimony is discouraged and population is prevented.—But the impolicy of whatever produeces these effects

will be acknowledge by all. The wealth, strength and glory of a state depend on the number of its virtuous citizens: and a state without citizens is at least a great an absurdity, as a king without subjects.

5. The impolicy of slavery still further appears from this, that it weakens the state, and in proportion to the degree in which it exist, exposes it to become an easy conquest.—The increase of free citizens is an increase of the strength of the state. But not so with regard to the increase of slaves. They not only add nothing to the strength of the state, but actually diminish it in proportion to their number. Every slave is naturally an enemy to the state in which he is holden in slavery, and wants nothing but an opportunity to assist in its overthrow. And an enemy within a state, is much more dangerous than one without it.

These observations concerning the prevention of population and weakening the state, are supported by facts which have fallen within our own observation. That the southern states, in which slaves are so numerous are in no measure so populous, according to the extent of territory, as the northern, is a fact of universal notoriety: and that during the late war, the southern states found themselves greatly weakened by their slaves, and therefore were so easily overrun by the British army, is equally notorious.

From the view we have now taken of this subject, we scruple not to infer, that to carry on the slave-trade and to introduce slaves into our country, is not only to be guilty of injustice, robbery and cruelty toward our fellow-men; but it is to injure ourselves and our country; and therefore it is altogether unjustifiable, wicked and abominable.

Having thus considered the injustice and ruinous tendency of the slave-trade, I proceed to attend to the principal arguments urged in favour of it.

1. It is said, that the Africans are the posterity of Ham, the son of Noah; that Canaan one of Ham's sons, was cursed by Noah to be a servant of servants; that by Canaan we are to understand Ham's posterity in general; that as his posterity are devoted by God to slavery, we have a right to

enslave them.—This is the argument: to which I answer:

It is indeed generally thought that Ham peopled Africa; but that the curse on Canaan extended to all the posterity of Ham is a mere imagination. The only reason given for it is, that Canaan was only one of Ham's sons; and that it seems reasonable, that the curse of Ham's conduct should fall on all his posterity, if on any. But this argument is insufficient. We might as clearly argue, that the judgments denounced on the house of David, on account of his sin in the matter of Uriah, must equally fall on all his posterity. Yet we know, that many of them lived and died in great posterity. So in every case in which judgments are predicted concerning any nation or family.

It is allowed in this argument, that the curse was to fall on the *posterity* of Ham, and not immediately on Ham himself; If otherwise, it is nothing to the purpose of the slave-trade, or of any slaves now in existence. It being allowed then, that this curse was to fall on Ham's posterity, he who had a right to curse the whole of that posterity, had the same right to curse a part of it only, and the posterity of Canaan equally as any other part; and a curse on Ham's posterity in the line of Canaan was as real a curse on Ham himself, as a curse on all his posterity would have been.

Therefore we have no ground to believe, that this curse respected any others, than the posterity of Canaan, who lived in the land of Canaan, which is well known to be remote from Africa. We have a particular account, that all the sons of Canaan settled in the land of Canaan; as may be seen in Gen. x. 15—20. "And Canaan begat Sidon his "first born, and Heth, and the Jebusite, and the "Emorite, and the Girgasite, and the Hivite, and "the Arkite, and the Sinite, and the Arvadite, and "the Zemorite, and the Hamathite; and afterward "were the families of the Canaanites spread abroad. "And the border of the Canaanites was from Sidon, "as thou goest to Gerar, unto Gaza; as thou goest "unto Sodom and Gomorrah, Admah, and Zeboim, "even unto Lashah."-Nor have we account that any of their posterity except the

Carthaginians afterward removed to any part of Africa: and none will pretend that these peopled Africa in general; especially considering, that they were subdued, destroyed and so far extirpated by the Romans.

This curse then of the posterity of Canaan, had no reference to the inhabitants of Guinea, or of Africa in general; but was fulfilled partly in Joshua's time, in the reduction and servitude of the Canaanites, and especially of the Gibeonites; partly by what the Phenicians suffered from the Chaldeans, Persians and Greeks; and finally by what the Carthagenians suffered from the Romans.

Therefore this curse gives us no right to enslave the Africans, as we do by the slave-trade, because it has no respect to the Africans whom we enslave.

Nor if it had respected them, would it have given any such right; because it was not an institution of slavery, but a mere prophecy of it. And from this prophecy we have no more ground to infer the right of slavery, than we have from the prophecy of the destruction of Jerusalem by Nebuchadnezzar, or by the Romans, to infer their right respectively to destroy it in the manner they did; or from other prophecies to infer the right of Judas to betray his master, or of the Jews to crucify him.

2. The right of slavery is inferred from the instance of Abraham, who had servants born in his house and bought with his money.—But it is by no means certain, that these were slaves, as our Negroes are. If they were, it is unaccountable, that he went out at the head of an army of them to fight his enemies. No West-India planter would easily be induced to venture himself in such a situation. It is far more probable, that similar to some of the vassals under the feudal constitution, the servants of Abraham were only in a good measure dependent on him, and protected by him. But if they were to all intents and purposes slaves, Abraham's holding of them will no more prove the right of slavery, than his going in to Hagar, will prove it right for any man to indulge in criminal intercourse with his domestic.

3. From the divine permission given the Israelites to buy servants of the nations round about them, it is argued, that we have a right to buy the Africans and hold them in slavery. See Lev. xxv. 44–47.

> Both thy bondmen and thy bondmaids, which thou shalt have, shall be of the heathen that are round about you; of them shall ye buy bondmen and bondmaids. Moreover, of the children of the strangers that do sojourn among you, of them shall ye buy, and of their families, that are with you, which they begat in your land; and they shall be your possession. And ye shall take them as an inheritance for your children after you, to inherit them for a possession; they shall be your bondmen for ever : but over your brethren the children of Israel ye shall not rule one over another with rigour.

But if this be at all to the purpose, it is a permission to every nation under heaven to buy slaves of the nations round about them; to us, to buy of our Indian neighbours; to them, to buy of us; to the French, to buy of the English, and to the English to buy of the French; and so through the world. If then this argument be valid, every man has an entire right to engage in this trade, and to buy and sell any other man of another nation, and any other man of another nation has an entire right to buy and sell him. Thus according to this construction, we have in Lev. xxv. 43, c. an institution of an universal slave-trade, by which every man may not only become a merchant, but may rightfully become the merchandise itself of this trade, and may be bought and sold like a beast.—Now this consequence will be given up as absurd, and therefore also the construction of scripture from which it follows, must be given up. Yet it is presumed, that there is no avoiding that construction or the absurdity flowing from it, but by admitting, that this permission to the Israelites to buy slaves has no respect to us, but was in the same manner peculiar to them, as the permission and command to subdue, destroy and extirpate the whole Canaanitish nation; and therefore no more gives countenance to African slavery, than the command to extirpate the Canaanites, gives countenance to the extirpation of any nation in these days, by an universal slaughter of men and women, young men and maidens, infants and sucklings.

4. It is further pleaded, that there were slaves in the time of the apostles; that they did not forbid the holding of those slaves, but gave directions to servants, doubtless referring to the servants of that day, to obey *their masters, and count them worthy of all honour* To this the answer is, that the apostles teach the genteral duties of servants who are righteously in the state of servitude, as many are or may be, by hire, by indenture, and by judgment of a civil court. But they do not say, whether the servants in general of that day were justly holden in slavery or not. In like manner they lay down the general rules of obedience to civil magistrates, without deciding concerning the characters of the magistrates of the Roman empire in the reign of Nero. And as the apostle Paul requires masters *to give their servants that which is just and equal,* (Col. iv. i.) so if any were enslaved unjustly, of course he in this text requires of the masters of such, to give them their freedom.—Thus the apostles treat the slavery of that day in the same manner that they treat the civil government; and say nothing more in favour of the former, than they say in favour of the latter.

Besides, this argument from the slavery prevailing in the days of the apostles, if it prove any thing, proves too much, and so confutes itself. It proves, that we may enslave all captives taken in war, of any nation, and in any the most unjust war, such as the wars of the Romans, which were generally undertaken from the motives of ambition or avarice. On the ground of this argument we had a right to enslave the prisoners, whom we, during the late war, took from the British army; and they had the same right to enslave those whom they took from us; and so with respect to all other nations.

5. It is strongly urged, that the Negroes brought from Africa are all captives of war, and therefore are justly bought and holden in slavery.—This is a principal argument always urged by the advocates for slavery; and in a solemn debate on this subject, it hath been strongly insisted on, very lately in the

British parliament. Therefore it requires our particular attention.

Captives in a war just on their part, cannot be justly enslaved; nor is this pretended. Therefore the captives who may be justly enslaved, must be taken in a war unjust on their part. But even on the supposition, that captives in such a war may be justly enslaved, it will not follow, that we can justly carry on the slave trade, as it is commonly carried on from the African coast. In this trade any slaves are purchased, who are offered for sale, whether justly or unjustly enslaved. No enquiry is made whether they were captives in any war; much less, whether they were captivated in a war unjust on their part.

By the most authentic accounts, it appears, that the wars in general in Africa are excited by the prospect of gain from the sale of the captives of the war. Therefore those taken by the assailants in such wars, cannot be justly enslaved. Beside these, many are kidnapped by those of neighbouring nations; some by their own neighbours; and some by their kings or his agents; others for debt or some trifling crime are condemned to perpetual slavery-But none of these are justly enslaved. And the traders make no enquiry concerning the mode or occasion of their first enslavement. They buy all that are offerred, provided they like them and the price.—So that the plea, that the African slaves are captives in war, is entirely insufficient to justify the slave trade as now carried on.

But this is not all; if it were ever so true, that all the Negroes exported from Africa were captives in war, and that they were taken in a war unjust on their part; still they could not be justly enslaved.— We have no right to enslave a private foe in a state of nature, after he is conquered. Suppose in a state of nature one man rises against another and endeavours to kill him; in this case the person assaulted has no right to kill the assailant, unless it be necessary to preserve his own life. But in wars between nations, one nation may no doubt secure itself against another, by other means than slavery of its captives. If a nation be victorious in the war, it may exact some towns or a district of country, by way of caution; or it may impose a fine to deter from future injuries. If the nation be not victorious, it will do no good to enslave the captives whom it has taken. It will provoke the victors, and foolishly excite vengeance which cannot be repelled.

Or if neither nation be decidedly victorious, to enslave the captives on either side can answer no good purpose, but must at least occasion the enslaving of the citizens of the other nation, who are now, or in future may be in a state of captivity. Such a practice therefore necessarily tends to evil and not good.

Besides; captives in war are generally common soldiers or common citizens; and they are generally ignorant of the true cause or causes of the war, and are by their superiours made to believe, that the war is entirely just on their part. Or if this be not the case, they may by force be compelled to serve in a war which they know to be unjust. In either of these cases they do not deserve to be condemned to perpetual slavery. To inflict perpetual slavery on these private soldiers and citizens is manifestly not to do, as we would wish that men should do to us. If we were taken in a war unjust on our part, we should not think it right to be condemned to perpetual slavery. No more right is it for us to condemn and hold in perpetual slavery others, who are in the same situation.

6. It is argued, that as the Africans in their own country, previously to the purchase of them by the African traders, are captives in war; if they were not bought up by those traders, they would be put to death: that therefore to purchase them and to subject them to slavery instead of death, is an act of mercy not only lawful, but meritorious.

If the case were indeed so as is now represented, the purchase of the Negroes would be no more meritorious, than the act of a man, who, if we were taken by the Algerines, should purchase us out of that slavery. This would indeed be an act of benevolence, if the purchaser should set us at liberty. But it is no act of benevolence to buy a man out of one state into another no better. Nay, the act of ransoming a man from death gives no right to

the ransomer to commit a crime or an act of injustice to the person ransomed. The person ransomed is doubtless obligated according to his ability to satisfy the ransomer for his expence and trouble. Yet the ransomer has no more right to enslave the other, than the man who saves the life of another who was about to be killed by a robber or an assassin, has a right to enslave him.—The liberty of a man for life is a far greater good, than the property paid for a Negro on the African coast. And to deprive a man of an immensely greater good, in order to recover one immensely, is an immense injury and crime.

7. As to the pretence, that to prohibit or lay aside this trade, would be hurtful to our commerce; it is sufficient to ask, whether on the supposition, that it were advantageous to the commerce of Great-Britain to send her ships to these states, and transport us into that perpetual slavery in the West Indies, it would be right that she should go into trade.

8. That to prohibit the slave trade would infringe on the property of those, who have expended large sums to carry on that trade, or of those who wish to purchase the slaves for their plantations, hath also been urged as an argument in favour of the trade.—But the same argument would prove, that if the skins and teeth of the Negroes were as valuable articles of commerce as furs and elephant's teeth, and a merchant were to lay out his property in this commerce, he ought by no means to be obstructed therein.

9. But others will carry on the trade, if we do not.—So others will rob, steal and murder, if we do not.

10. It is said, that some men are intended by nature to be slaves.—If this mean, that the author of nature has given some men a licence, to enslave others; this is denied and proof is demanded. If it mean, that God hath made some of capacities inferior to others, and that the last have a right to enslave the first; this argument will prove, that some of the citizens of every country, have a right to enslave other citizens of the same country; nay,

that some have a right to enslave their own brothers and sisters.—But if this argument mean, that God in his providence suffers some men to be enslaved, and that this proves, that from the beginning he intended they should be enslaved, and made them with this intention; the answer is, that in like manner he suffers some men to be murdered, and in this sense, he intended and made them to be murdered. Yet no man in his senses will hence argue the lawfulness of murder.

11. It is further pretended, that no other men, than Negroes, can endure labour in the hot climates of the West Indies and the southern states.—But does this appear to be fact? In all other climates, the labouring people are the most healthy. And I confess I have not yet seen evidence, but that those who have been accustomed to labour and are inured to those climates, can bear labour there also.—However, taking for granted the fact asserted in this objection, does it follow, that the inhabitants of those countries have a right to enslave the Africans to labour for them? No more surely than from the circumstance, that you are feeble and cannot labour, it follows, that you have a right to enslave your robust neighbour. As in all other cases, the feeble and those who choose not to labour, and yet wish to have their lands cultivated, are necessitated to hire the robust to labour for them; so no reason can be given, why the inhabitants of hot climates should not either perform their own labour, or hire those who can perform it, whether Negroes or others.

If our traders went to the coast of Africa to murder the inhabitants, or to rob them of their property, all would own that such murderous or piratical practices are wicked and abominable. Now it is as really wicked to rob a man of his liberty, as to rob him of his life; and it is much more wicked, than to rob him of his property. All men agree to condemn highway robbery. And the slave-trade is as much a greater wickedness than highway robbery, as liberty is more valuable than property. How strange is it then, that in the same nation highway robbery should be punished with death, and the slave-trade be encourage by national authority.

We all dread political slavery, or subjection to the arbitrary power of a king or of any man or men not deriving their authority from the people. Yet such a state is inconceivably preferable to the slavery of the Negroes. Suppose that in the late war we had been subdued by Great-Britain; we should have been taxed without our consent. But these taxes would have amounted to but a small part of our property. Whereas the Negroes are deprived of all their property; no part of their earnings is their own; the whole is their masters.—In a conquered state we should have been at liberty to dispose of ourselves and of our property in most cases, as we should choose. We should have been free to live in this or that town or place; in any part of the country, or to remove out of the country; to apply to this or that business; to labour or not; and excepting a sufficiency for the taxes, to dispose of the fruit of our labour to our own benefit, or that of our children, or of any other person. But the unhappy Negroes in slavery can do none of these things. They must do what they are commanded and as much as they are commanded, on pain of the lash. They must live where they are placed, and must confine themselves to that spot, on pain of death.

So that Great-Britain in her late attempt to enslave America, committed a very small crime indeed in comparison with the crime of those who enslave the Africans.

The arguments which have been urged against the slave-trade, are with little variation applicable to the holding of slaves. He who holds a slave, continues to deprive him of that liberty, which was taken from him on the coast of Africa. And if it were wrong to deprive him of it in the first instance, why not in the second? If this be true, no man hath a better right to retain his Negro in slavery, than he had to take him from from his native African shores. And every man who cannot show, that his Negro hath by his voluntary conduct forfeited his liberty, is obligated immediately to manumit him. Undoubtedly we should think so, were we holden in the same slavery in which the Negroes are: And our text required us to do to others, as we would that they should do to us.

To hold a slave, who has a right to his liberty, is not only a real crime, but a very great one. Many good christians have wondered how Abraham, the father of the faithful, could take Hagar to his bed; and how Sarah, celebrated as an holy woman, could consent to this transaction: Also, how David and Solomon could have so many wives and concubines, and yet be real saints. Let such inquire how it is possible, that our fathers and men now alive, universally reputed pious, should hold Negro slaves, and yet be the subjects of real piety? And whether to reduce a man, who hath the same right to liberty as any other man, to a state of absolute slavery, or to hold him in that state, be not as great a crime as concubinage or fornication. I presume it will not be denied, that to commit theft or robbery every day of a man's life, is as great a sin as to commit fornication in one instance. But to steal a man or to rob him of his liberty is a greater sin, than to steal his property, or to take it by violence. And to hold a man in a state of slavery, who has a right to his liberty, is to be every day guilty of robbing him of his liberty, or of manstealing. The consequence is inevitable, that other things being the same, to hold a Negro slave, unless he have forfeited his liberty, is a greater sin in the sight of God, than concubinage or fornication.

Does this conclusion seem strange to any of you? Let me entreat you to weigh it candidly before you reject it. You will not deny, that liberty is more valuable than property; and that it is a greater sin to deprive a man of his whole liberty during life, than to deprive him of his whole property; or that manstealing is a greater crime than robbery. Nor will you deny, that to hold in slavery a man who was stolen, is substantially the same crime as to steal him.

These principles being undeniable, I leave it to yourselves to draw the plain and necessary consequence. And if your consciences shall, in spite of all opposition, tell you, that while you hold your Negroes in slavery, you do wrong, exceedingly wrong; that you do not, as you would that men should do to you; that you commit sin in the sight of God; that you daily violate the plain rights of mankind, and that in a higher degree, than if you committed theft or robbery; let me beseech you not to stifle this conviction, but attend to it and act accordingly; lest you add to your former guilt, that of sinning against the light of truth, and of your own consciences.

To convince yourselves, that your information being the same, to hold a Negro slave is a greater sin than fornication, theft or robbery, you need only bring the matter home to yourselves. I am willing to appeal to your own consciences, whether you would not judge it to be a greater sin for a man to hold you or your child during life in such slavery, as that of the Negroes, than for him to indulge in one instance of licentious conduct or in one instance to steal or rob. Let conscience speak, and I will submit to its decision.

This question seems to be clearly decided by revelation. Exod. xxi. 16. "He that stealeth a man "and selleth him, or if he be found in his hand, "he shall surely be put to death." Thus death is, by the divine express declaration, the punishment due to the crime of man-stealing. But death is not the punishment declared by God to be due to fornication theft or robbery in common cases. Therefore we have the divine authority to assert, that manstealing is a greater crime than fornication, theft or robbery. Now to hold in slavery a man who has a right to liberty, is substantially the same crime as to deprive him of his liberty. And to deprive of liberty and reduce to slavery, a man who has a right to liberty, is man-stealing. For it is immaterial whether he be taken and reduced to slavery clandestinely or by open violence. Therefore if the Negroes have a right to liberty, to hold them in slavery is man-stealing, which we have seen is, by God himself, declared to be a greater crime than fornication, theft or robbery.

Perhaps, though this truth be clearly demonstrable both from reason and revelation, you scarcely dare receive it, because it seems to bear hardly on the characters of our pious fathers, who held slaves. But they did it ignorantly and in unbelief of the truth; as Abraham, Jacob, David and Solomon were ignorant, that polygamy or concubinage was wrong. As to domestic slavery our fathers lived in a *time of ignorance which God winked at; but now he commandeth all men every where to repent* of this wickedness, and to break *off this sin by righteousness, and this iniquity by shewing mercy to the poor, if it may be a lengthening out of their tranquillity.* You therefore to whom the present blaze of light as to this subject has reached, cannot sin at so cheap a rate as our fathers.

But methinks I hear some say, I have bought my Negro; I have paid a large sum for him; I cannot lose this sum, and therefore I cannot manumit him.—Alas! this is *hitting the nail on the head.* This brings into view the true cause which makes it so difficult to convince men of what is right in this case—You recollect the story of Amaziah's hiring an hundred thousand men of Israel, for an hundred talents, to assist him against the Edomites; and that when by the word of the Lord, he was forbidden to take those hired men with him to the war, he cried out, "But what shall we do for the hundred talents, "which I have given to the army of Israel?" In this case, the answer of God was, "The Lord is "able to give thee much more than this."—To apply this to the subject before us, God is able to give thee much more than thou shalt lose by manumitting thy slave.

You may plead, that you use your slave well; you are not cruel to him, but feed and clothe him comfortably, c. Still every day you rob him of a most valuable and important right. And a highway-man, who robs a man of his money in the most easy and complaisant manner, is still a robber; and murder may be effected in a manner the least cruel and tormenting; still it is murder.

Having now taken that view of our subject, which was proposed, we may in reflection see abundant reason to acquiesce in the institution of this society. If the slave-trade be unjust, and as gross a violation of the rights of mankind, as would be, if the Africans should transport us into perpetual slavery in Africa; to unite our influence against it, is a duty which we owe to mankind, to ourselves and to God too. It is but doing as we would that men should do to us.—Nor is it enough that we

have formed the society; we must do the duties of it. The first of these is to put an end to the slave-trade. The second is to relieve those who, contrary to the laws of the country, are holden in bondage. Another is to defend those in their remaining legal and natural rights, who are by law holden in bondage. Another and not the least important object of this society, I conceive to be, to increase and disperse the light of truth with respect to the subject of African slavery, and so prepare the way for its total abolition. For until men in general are convinced of the injustice of the trade and of the slavery itself, comparatively little can be done to effect the most important purposes of the institution.

It is not to be doubted, that the trade is even now carried on from this state. Vessels are from time to time fitted out for the coast of Africa, to transport the Negroes to the West-Indies and other parts. Nor will an end be put to this trade, without vigilance and strenuous exertion on the part of this society, or other friends of humanity, nor without a patient enduring of the opposition and odium of all who are concerned in it, of their friends and of all who are of the opinion that it is justifiable. Among these we are doubtless to reckon some of large property and considerable influence. And if the laws and customs of the country equally allowed of it, many, and perhaps as many as now plead for the right of the African slave-trade, would plead for the right of kidnapping us, the citizens of the United States, and of selling us into perpetual slavery.—If then we dare not incur the displeasure of such men, we may as well dissolve the society, and leave the slave-trade to be carried on, and the Negroes to be kidnapped, and though free in this state, to be sold into perpetual slavery in distant parts, at the pleasure of any man, who wishes to make gain by such abominable practices.

Though we must expect opposition, yet if we be steady and persevering, we need not fear, that we shall fail of success. The advantages, which the cause has already gained, are many and great. Thirty years ago scarcely a man in this country thought either the slave-trade or the slavery of Negroes to be wrong. But now how many and able advocates in private life, in our legislatures, in Congress, have appeared and have openly and irrefragably pleaded the rights of humanity in this as well as other instances? Nay the great body of the people from New-Hampshire to Virginia inclusively, have obtained such light, that in all those states the further importation of slaves is prohibited by law. And in Massachusetts and New-Hampshire, slavery is totally abolished.

Nor is the light concerning this subject confined to America. It hath appeared with great clearness in France, and produced remarkable effects in the National Assembly. It hath also shone in bright beams in Great-Britain. It flashes with splendour in the writings of Clarkson and in the proceedings of several societies formed to abolish the slave-trade. Nor hath it been possible to shut it out of the British parliament. This light is still increasing, and in time will effect a total revolution. And if we judge of the future by the past, within fifty years from this time, it will be as shameful for a man to hold a Negro slave, as to be guilty of common robbery or theft. But it is our duty to remove the obstacles which intercept the rays of this light, that it may reach not only public bodies, but every individual. And when it shall have obtained a general spread, shall have dispelled all darkness, and slavery shall be no more; it will be an honour to be recorded in history, as a society which was formed, and which exerted itself with vigour and fidelity, to bring about an event so necessary and conducive to the interests of humanity and virtue, to the support of the rights and to the advancement of the happiness of mankind.

APPENDIX

Some objections to the doctrine of the preceding sermon, have been mentioned to the author, since the delivery of it. Of these it may be proper to take some notice.

1. The slaves are in a better situation than that in which they were in their own country; especially as they have opportunity to know the Christian religion and to secure the saving blessings of it. Therefore it is not an injury, but a benefit to bring them into this country, even though their importation be accompanied and followed with slavery. It is also said, that the situation of many Negroes under their masters is much better, than it would be, were they free in this country; that they are much better fed and clothed, and are much happy; that therefore to hold them in slavery is so far from a crime, that it is a meritorious act.

With regard to these pleas, it is to be observed, that every man hath a right to judge concerning his own happiness, and to choose the means of obtaining or promoting it; and to deprive him of this right is the very injury of which we complain; it is to enslave him. Because we judge, that the Negroes are more happy in this country, in a state of slavery, than in the enjoyment of liberty in Africa, we have no more right to enslave them and bring them into this country, than we have to enslave any of our neighbours, who we judge would be more happy under their own. Let us make the case our own. Should we believe, that we were justly treated, if the Africans should carry us into perpetual slavery in Africa, on the ground that they judged, that we should be more happy in that state, than in our present situation?

As to the opportunity which the Negroes in this country are said to have, to become acquainted with Christianity; this with respect to many is granted: But what follows from it? it would be ridiculous to pretend, that this is the motive on which they act who import them, or they who buy and hold them in slavery. Or if this were the motive, it would not sanctify either the trade or the slavery. We are not at liberty to do evil, that good may come; to commit a crime more aggravated than theft or robbery, that we may make a proselyte to Christianity. Neither our Lord Jesus Christ, nor any one of his apostles has taught us this mode of propagating the faith.

2. It is said, that the doctrine of the preceding sermon imputes that as a crime to individuals, which is owing to the state of society. This is granted; and what follows? It is owing to the state of society, that our neighbours, the Indians roast their captives: and does it hence follow, that such

conduct is not to be imputed to the individual agents as a crime? It is owing to the state of society in Popish countries, that thousands worship the beast and his image: and is that worship therefore not to be imputed as a crime to those, who render it? Read the Revelation of St. John. The state of society is such, that drunkenness and adultery are very common in some countries; but will it follow, that those vices are innocent in those countries?

3. If I be ever so willing to manumit my slave, I cannot do it without being holden to maintain him, when he shall be sick or shall be old and decrepit. Therefore I have a right to hold him as a slave.—The same argument will prove, that you have a right to enslave your children or your parents: as you are equally holden to maintain them in sickness and in decrepit old age.—The argument implies, that in order to secure the money, which you are afraid the laws of your country will some time or other oblige you to pay; it is right for you to rob a free man of his liberty or be guilty of man-stealing. On the ground of this argument every town or parish obligated by law, to maintain its helpless poor, has a right to sell into perpetual slavery all the people, who may probably or even possibly occasion a public expence.

4. After all, it is not safe to manumit the Negroes: they would cut our throats; they would endanger the peace and government of the state. Or at least they would be so idle, that they would not provide themselves with necessaries: of course they must live by thievery and plundering.

This objection requires a different answer, as it respects the northern, and as it respects the southern states. As it respects the northern, in which slaves are so few, there is not the least foundation to imagine, that they would combine or make insurrection against the government; or that they would attempt to murder their masters. They are much more likely to kill their masters, in order to obtain their liberty, or to revenge the abuse they receive, while it is still continued, than to do it after the abuse hath ceased, and they are restored to their liberty. In this case, they would from a sense of gratitude, or at least from a conviction of the justice of their masters, feel a strong attachment, instead of a murderous disposition.

Nor is there the least danger, but that by a proper vigilance of the selectmen, and by a strict execution of the laws now existing, the Negroes might in a tolerable degree be kept from idleness and pilfering.

All this hath been verified by experiment. In Massachusetts, all the Negroes in the commonwealth were by their new constitution liberated in a day: and none of the ill consequences objected followed either to the commonwealth or to individuals.

With regard to the southern states, the case is different. The negroes in some parts of those states are a great majority of the whole, and therefore the evils objected would, in case of a general manumission at once, be more likely to take place. But in the first place there is no prospect, that the conviction of the truth exhibited in the preceding discourse, will at once, take place in the minds of all the holders of slaves. The utmost that can be expected, is that it will take place gradually in one after another, and that of course the slaves will be gradually manumitted. Therefore the evils of a general manumission at once, are dreaded without reason.

If in any state the slaves should be manumitted in considerable numbers at once, or so that the number of free Negroes should become large; various measures might be concerted to prevent the evils feared. One I beg leave to propose: That overseers of the free Negroes be appointed from among themselves, who shall be empowered to inspect the morals and management of the rest, and report to proper authority, those who are vicious, idle or incapable of managing their own affairs, and that such authority dispose of them under proper masters for a year or other term, as is done, perhaps in all the states, with regard to the poor white people in like manner vicious, idle or incapable of management. Such black overseers would naturally be ambitious to dischage the duties of their office; they would in many respects have much more influence than white men with their countrymen:

and other Negroes looking forward to the same honourable distinction, would endeavour to deserve it by their improvement and good conduct.

But after all, this whole objection, if it were ever so entirely founded on truth; if the freed Negroes would probably rise against their masters, or combine against government; rests on the same ground, as the apology of the robber, who murders the man whom he has robbed. Says the robber to himself, I have robbed this man, and now if I let him go he will kill me, or he will complain to authority and I shall be apprehended and hung. I must therefore kill him. There is no other way of safety for me.— The coincidence between this reasoning and that of the objection under consideration, must be manifest to all. And if this reasoning of the robber be inconclusive; if the robber have no right on that ground to kill the man whom he hath robbed; neither have the slave-holders any more right to continue to hold their slaves. If the robber ought to spare the life of the man robbed, take his own chance and esteem himself happy, if he can escape justice; so the slave-holders ought immediately to let their slaves go free, treat them with the utmost kindness, by such treatment endeavour to pacify them with respect to past injuries, and esteem themselves happy, if they can compromise the matter in this manner.

Some exceptionable sentences may perhaps be found in this Discourse. We cannot altogether agree with the Reverend Author in this passage. His reasoning will apply in its full force to slave-traders. The present slave-holders stand, we think, upon different ground. We however hope that these will soon be convinced, that it is an *immediate and imperious duty.* to adopt plans, and proceed with energy in the execution of them, which shall terminate in *universal emancipation.* Every master of slaves, enlightened on this subject, who does not act, (as far as the regulations of government will permit, and who does not exert his influence to change the law, where it opposes his design,) with reference to the accomplishment of this end, is, we believe, regarded by God as an enemy of the human race. We cannot, we would not, speak with

moderation of a principle which would bind down millions of our race, to ignorance and the chains of perpetual servitude.

In all countries in which the slaves are a majority of the inhabitants the masters lie in a great measure at the mercy of the slaves, and may most rationally expect sooner or later, to be cut off, or driven out by the slaves, or to be reduced to the same level and to be mingled with them into one common mass. This I think is by ancient and modern events demonstrated to be the natural and necessary course of human affairs. The hewers of wood and drawers of water among the Israelites, the Helots among the Lacedemonians, the slaves among the Romans, the villains and vassals in most of the kingdoms of Europe under the feudal system, have long since mixed with the common mass of the people, and shared the common privileges and honours of their respective countries. And in the French West-Indies the Mulattoes and free Negroes are already become so numerous and powerful a body, as to be allowed by the National Assembly to enjoy the common rights and honours of free men. These facts plainly show, what the whites in the West-Indies and the Southern States are to expect concerning their posterity, that it will infallibly be amalgamated with the slave population or else they must quit the country to the Africans whom they have hitherto holden in bondage.

We trust that evils like these will be known only in imagination. But what shall prevent them? Nothing but united and strenuous efforts in the execution of a plan similar to that which has been devised by the American Colonization Society.— Let this Association receive universal support.

FUGITIVE SLAVE ACT CH. 7, 1 STAT. 302 (1793)

Section 1. *Be it enacted by the Senate and House of Representatives of the United States of America in Congress assembled,* That whenever the executive authority of any state in the Union, or of either of the territories northwest or south of the river Ohio, shall demand any person as a fugitive from justice, of the executive authority of any such state or territory to which such person shall have fled, and shall moreover produce the copy of an indictment found, or an affidavit made before a magistrate of any state or territory as aforesaid, charging the person so demanded, with having committed treason, felony or other crime, certified as authentic by the governor or chief magistrate of the state or territory from whence the person so charged fled, it shall be the duty of the executive authority of the state or territory to which such person shall have fled, to cause him or her to be arrested and secured, and notice of the arrest to be given to the executive authority making such demand, or to the agent of such authority appointed to receive the fugitive, and to cause the fugitive to be delivered to such agent when he shall appear: But if no such agent shall appear within six months from the time of the arrest, the prisoner may be discharged. And all costs or expenses incurred to the state or territory making such demand, shall be paid by such state or territory.

Section 2. *And be it further enacted,* That any agent, appointed as aforesaid, who shall receive the fugitive into his custody, shall be empowered to transport him or her to the state or territory from which he or she shall have fled. And if any person or persons shall by force set at liberty, or rescue the fugitive from such agent while transporting, as aforesaid, the person or persons so offending shall, on conviction, be fined not exceeding five hundred dollars, and be imprisoned not exceeding one year.

Section 3. *And be it also enacted,* That when a person held to labour in any of the United States, or in either of the territories on the northwest or south of the river Ohio, under the laws thereof, shall escape into any other of the said states or territory, the person to whom such labour or service may be due, his agent or attorney, is hereby empowered to seize or arrest such fugitive from labour, and to take him or her before any judge of the circuit or district courts of the United States, residing or being within the state, or before any magistrate of a county, city or town corporate, wherein such seizure or arrest shall be made, and

upon proof to the satisfaction of such judge or magistrate, either by oral testimony or affidavit taken before and certified by a magistrate of any such state or territory, that the person so seized or arrested, doth, under the laws of the state or territory from which he or she fled, owe service or labour to the person claiming him or her, it shall be the duty of such judge or magistrate to give a certificate thereof to such claimant, his agent or attorney, which shall be sufficient warrant for removing the said fugitive from labour, to the state or territory from which he or she fled.

Section 4. *And be it further enacted,* That any person who shall knowingly and willing obstruct or hinder such claimant, his agent or attorney in so seizing or arresting such fugitive from labour, or shall rescue such fugitive from such claimant, his agent or attorney when so arrested pursuant to the authority herein given or declared; or shall harbor or conceal such person after notice that he or she was a fugitive from labour, as aforesaid shall, for either of the said offenses, forfeit and pay the sum of five hundred dollars. Which penalty may be recovered by and for the benefit of such claimant, by action of debt, in any court proper to try the same; saving moreover to the person claiming such labour or service, his right of action for or on account of the said injuries or either of them.

GEORGE WASHINGTON'S LAST WILL AND TESTAMENT (1799)

In the Name of God Amen

I, George Washington of Mount Vernon—a citizen of the United States,—and lately President of the same, do make, ordain and declare this Instrument; which is written with my own hand and every page thereof subscribed with my name, to be my last Will and Testament, revoking all other. . . . Upon the deceased of my wife, it is my Will and desire that all the Slaves which I hold in my *own right,* shall receive their freedom. . . . And whereas among those who will receive freedom according to this devise, there may be some, who from old age or bodily infirmities, and others who on account of their infancy, that will be unable to support themselves; it is my Will and desire that all who come under the first and second description shall be comfortably clothed and fed by my heirs while they live;—and that such of the latter description as have no parents living, or if living are unable, or unwilling to provide for them, shall be bound by the Court until they shall arrive at the age of twenty-five year;—and in cases where no record can be produced, whereby their ages can be ascertained, the judgment of the Court upon its own view of the subject, shall be adequate and final.—The Negros thus bound, are (by their Masters or Mistresses) to be taught to read and write; and to be brought up to some useful occupation, agreeably to the Laws of the Commonwealth of Virginia, providing for the support of Orphan and other poor Children.—And I do hereby expressly forbid the Sale, or transportation out of the said Commonwealth of any Slave I may die possessed of, under any pretence whatsoever.— And I do moreover most pointedly, and most solemnly enjoin it upon my Executors hereafter named, or the Survivors of them, to see that this clause respecting Slaves, and every part thereof be religiously fulfilled at the Epoch at which it is directed to take place; without evasion, neglect or delay, after the Crops which may then be on the ground are harvested, particularly as it respects the aged and infirm;—Seeing that a regular and permanent fund be established for their Support so long as there are subjects requiring it; not trusting to the uncertain provision to be made by individuals.—And to my Mulatto man William (calling himself William Lee) I give immediate freedom; or if he should prefer it (on account of the accidents which have befallen him, and which have rendered him incapable of walking or of any active employment) to remain in the situation he now is, it shall be optional in him to do so: In either case however, I allow him an annuity of thirty dollars during his natural life, which shall be independent of the victuals and cloaths he has been accustomed to receive, if he chooses the last alternative; but in full, with his freedom, if he prefers the first;— and this I give him as a testimony of my sense of his attachment to me,

and for his faithful services during the Revolutionary War.

ACT TO PROHIBIT THE IMPORTATION OF SLAVES CH.22, 2 STAT. 426 (1807)

An Act to prohibit the importation of Slaves into any port or place within the jurisdiction of the United States, from and after the first day of January, in the year of our Lord one thousand eight hundred and eight.

Be it enacted, that from and after the first day of January, one thousand eight hundred and eight, it shall not be lawful to import or bring into the United States or the territories thereof from any foreign kingdom, place, or country, any negro, mulatto, or person of colour, as a slave, or to be held to service or labour.

Section 2. That no citizen of the United States, or any other person, shall, from and after the first day of January, in the year of our Lord one thousand eight hundred and eight, for himself, or themselves, or any other person whatsoever, either as master, factor, or owner, build, fit, equip, load or to otherwise prepare any ship or vessel, in any port or place within the jurisdiction of the United States, nor shall cause any ship or vessel to sail from any port or place within the same, for the purpose of procuring any negro, mulatto, or person of colour, from any foreign kingdom, place, or country, to be transported to any port or place whatsoever within the jurisdiction of the United States, to be held, sold, or disposed of as slaves, or to be held to service or labour: and if any ship or vessel shall be so fitted out for the purpose aforesaid, or shall be caused to sail so as aforesaid, every such ship or vessel, her tackle, apparel, and furniture, shall be forfeited to the United States, and shall be liable to be seized, prosecuted, and condemned in any of the circuit courts or district courts, for the district where the said ship or vessel may be found or seized. . . .

Section 4. If any citizen or citizens of the United States, or any person resident within the jurisdiction of the same, shall, from after the first day of

January, one thousand eight hundred and eight, take on board, receive or transport from any of the coasts or kingdoms of Africa, or from any other foreign kingdom, place, or country, any negro, mulatto, or person of colour in any ship or vessel, for the purpose of selling them in any port or place within the jurisdiction of the United States as slaves, or be to held to service or labour, or shall be in any ways aiding or abetting therein, such citizen or citizens, or person, shall severally forfeit and pay five thousand dollars, one moiety thereof to the use of any person or persons who shall sue for and prosecute the same to effect. . . .

Section 6. That if any person or persons whatsoever, shall, from and after the first day of January, one thousand eight hundred and eight, purchase or sell any negro, mulatto, or person, of colour, for a slave, or to be held to service or labour, who shall have been imported, or brought from any foreign kingdom, place, or country, or from the dominions of any foreign state, immediately adjoining to the United States, after the last day of December, one thousand eight hundred and seven, knowing at the time of such purchase or sale, such negro, mulatto, or person of colour, was so brought within the jurisdiction of the United States, as aforesaid, such purchaser and seller shall severally forfeit and pay for every negro, mulatto, or person of colour, so purchased, or sold as aforesaid, eight hundred dollars. . . .

Section 7. That if any ship or vessel shall be found, from and after the first day of January, one thousand eight hundred and eight, in any river, port, bay, or harbor, or on the high seas, within the jurisdictional limits of the United States, or hovering on the coast thereof, having on board any negro, mulatto, or person of colour, for the purpose of selling them as slaves, or with intent to land the same, in any port or place within the jurisdiction of the United States, contrary to the prohibition of the act, every such ship or vessel, together with her tackle, apparel, and furniture, and the goods or effects which shall be found on board the same, shall be forfeited to the use of the United States, and may be seized, prosecuted, and condemned, in any court of the United States, having jurisdiction thereof. And it shall be lawful for the President of the United States, and he is hereby authorized, should he deem it expedient, to cause any of the armed vessels of the United States to be manned and employed to cruise on any part of the coast of the United States, or territories thereof, where he may judge attempts will be made to violate the provisions of this act, and to instruct and direct the commanders of armed vessels of the United States, to seize, take, and bring into any port of the United States all such ships or vessels, and moreover to seize, take, or bring into any port of the U.S. all ships or vessels of the U.S. wheresoever found on the high seas, contravening the provisions of this act, to be proceeded against according to law. . . .

THE FIRST ANNUAL REPORT OF THE AMERICAN SOCIETY FOR COLONIZING THE FREE PEOPLE OF COLOR, OF THE UNITED STATES; AND THE PROCEEDINGS OF THE SOCIETY AT THEIR ANNUAL MEETING IN THE CITY OF WASHINGTON, ON THE FIRST DAY OF JANUARY, 1818

WASHINGTON CITY:

PRINTED BY D. RAPINE, CAPITOL HILL.

1818.

The Constitution of the American Society, for Colonizing the Free People of Color of the United States.

Article I

—This Society shall be called, "The American Society for colonizing the free people of color of the United States."

Article II

—The object to which attention is to be exclusively directed, is to promote and execute a plan for colonizing (with their consent) the free people of color, residing in our country, in Africa, or such other place as Congress shall deem most expedient. And the Society shall act, to effect this object in co-operation with the general government, and such of the states as may adopt regulations upon the subject.

Article III

—Every citizen of the United States, who shall subscribe these articles, and be an annual contributor of one dollar to the funds of the Society, shall be a member. On paying a sum not less than thirty dollars, at one subscription, shall be a member for life.

Article IV

—The officers of this Society shall be, a President, thirteen Vice Presidents, a Secretary, a Treasurer, a Recorder, and a Board of Managers, composed of the above named officers, and twelve other members of the Society. They shall be annually elected by the members of the Society, at their annual meeting on the last Saturday of December, and continue to discharge their respective duties till others are appointed.

Article V

—It shall be the duty of the President to preside at all meetings of the Society, and of the Board of Managers, and to call meetings of the Society, and of the Board, when he thinks necessary, or when required by any three members of the board.

Article VI

—The Vice Presidents, according to seniority, shall discharge these duties in the absence of the President.

Article VII

—The Secretary shall take minutes of the proceedings, prepare and publish notices, and discharge such other duties, as the Board, or the President, or in his absence the Vice President, according to the seniority, (when the Board is not sitting) shall direct. And the Recorder shall record the proceedings and the names of the members, and discharge such other duties as may be required of him.

Article VIII

—The Treasurer shall receive and take charge of the funds of the Society, under such security as may be prescribed by the Board of Managers: keep the accounts and exhibit a statement of receipts and expenditures at every annual meeting, and discharge such other duties as may be required of him.

Article IX

—The Board of managers shall meet on the first Monday in January, the first Monday in April, the first Monday in July, and the first Monday in October, every year, and at such other times as the President may direct. They shall conduct the business of the Society, and take such measures for effecting its object as they shall think proper, or shall be directed at the meetings of the Society, and make an annual report of their proceedings. They shall also fill up all vacancies occurring during the year, and make such by-laws for their government, as they may deem necessary, provided the same are not repugnant to this constitution.

Article X

—Every Society which shall be formed in the United States to aid in the object of this association, and which shall co-operate with its funds for the purposes thereof, agreeably to the rules and regulations of this Society, shall be considered auxiliary thereto, and its officers shall be entitled to attend and vote at all meetings of the Society, and of the Board of Managers.

THE ANNUAL REPORT OF THE COLONIZATION SOCIETY

THE Society for Colonizing the Free People of Color held its first anniversary, on Thursday, the first day of January, 1818, in the Chamber of the House of Representatives; and it will be worthy of note, if on no other account, from the fame and talents of the individuals, whose influence and exertions have been blended to achieve the objects of the society. Nor can any subject more justly ennoble the efforts of genius, than the interests of an institution grasping so wide a field of patriotism and humanity. But to those patrons of it, by whose gracious endeavors it was begun and advanced, it must have been eminently gratifying to find, in the report of the proceedings of the past year, such abundant proofs of its prosperity and improvement. The concurrence of every part of the country to strengthen and establish it, leaves no doubt that the warmest wishes of the philanthrophist will be satisfied with the success of its issue. The succeeding publications, however, will best illustrate the views and resources of the Society.

The meeting was opened by the Hon. Bushrod Washington, with the following perspicuous and elegant address:

> It is with peculiar satisfaction that I meet the founders and patterns of the American Colonization Society, after the experience of a year has ascertained that their wise and benevolent purpose will be seconded by the voice of our common country.
>
> From every quarter of the United States, the aspirations of good men have been breathed to Heaven for the success of our future labors.
>
> The resolution of Virginia, soliciting the aid of the General Government, in effecting a similar object, which had passed the popular branch of her Legislature by a very large majority, before the organization of this Society, received, shortly after, the almost unanimous sanction of her Senate.
>
> Auxiliary Societies have been formed in many parts of the country, and the populous cities of New York, Philadelphia, and Baltimore, for the purpose of co-operating with the parent society established at the seat of the General Government; and many similar associations await only the measures which the President of the United States may be expected to take, in pursuance of the request of Virginia, to embody themselves, and to combine the resources of the Union, for the completion of our comprehensive and benevolent design.
>
> Among a small, but opulent society of slaveholders in Virginia, a subscription has been raised, by the zealous exertiens of a few individuals, of such magnitude, as to illustrate the extent of the funds which we may hope hereafter to command, and to induce a confident hope that our labours will be awarded by the willing contributions of a generous and enlightened people.
>
> Other public spirited individuals have forborne to make similar efforts, until the success of our preparatory measures shall have been clearly ascertained.
>
> The Society have engaged two agents to explore the western coast of Africa, and to collect such information as may assist the Government of the United States in selecting a suitable district on that continent for the proposed settlement. The performance of this preliminary duty has been confided to Samuel J. Mills, and Ebenezer Burgass, gentlemen possessing all the qualifications requisite for the important trust confided to them; and their report may reasonably be expected before the next annual meeting of the Society.
>
> The addition which has recently been make to our stock of knowledge of that continent, to which every eye is directed as the proper theatre of our future labours, is highly encouraging to that enlarged and beneficent plan, which associates the political emancipation and future comfort of an unfortunate class of men, with the civilization and happiness of an afflicted, oppressed, and degraded quarter of our globe.
>
> Amidst these encouraging prospects, I cannot forbear a momentary tribute of regret to the memory of a man, to whom Africa is indebted for a vindication of her capacity for moral and intellectual improvement, and the world for an illustrious example of disinterested benevolence. This event is the mere to be deplored, as the death of cap. Paul Cuffee occured after his usefulness has been

recently manifested, by the restoration of fifty of his countrymen to the land their forefathers; an act which must afford to every christian society fresh cause of gratitude to that God who inspired this generous African, to execute the counsels of universal benevolence.

An effort has been unfortunately made to prejudice the minds of the free people of color against this institution, which had its origin, it is believed, in an honest desire to promote their happiness. A suggestion has been made to them, which this society disclaims by the terms of its constitution, that they are to be constrained to migrate to the country which may be selected for the seat of our colony. No suspicion can be more unfounded. It is sanctioned by no declarations or acts of this Society, from which alone intentions can be candidly inferred.

As little can be apprehended by the proprietor, who will not voluntary avail himself of the opportunity, which this settlement will afford him, of emancipating his slaves, without injury to his country. The effect of this institution, if its prosperity shall equal our wishes, will be alike propitious to every interest of our domestic society; and should it lead, as we may fairly hope it will, to the slow, but gradual abolition of slavery, it will wipe from our political institutions the only blot which stains them; and in palliation of which, we shall not be at liberty to plead the excuse of moral necessity, until we shall have honestly exerted all the means which we possess for its extinction.

In the magnificent plans now carrying on for the improvement and happiness of mankind, in many parts of the world. We cannot but discern the interposition of that Almighty power, who alone could inspire and crown with success these great purposes. But, amongst them there is perhaps none upon which we may more confidently implore the blessing of Heaven, than that in which we are now associated. Whether we consider the grandeur of the object and the wide sphere of philanthrophy which it embraces; or whether we view the present state of its progress under the this society, and under the obstacles which might have been expected from the cupidity of many, we may discover in each, a certain pledge, that the same benignant hand which has made these preparatory arrangements, will crown our efforts with success. Having, therefore, these motives of piety to consecrate and strengthen the powerful considerations which a wise policy suggest, we may, I trust, confidently rely upon the liberal exertions of the public for the necessary means of effecting this highly interesting object.

The Secretary, E.B. Caldwell, Esq. then proceeded to read the annual report of the Board of Managers, as follows:

The Managers of the American Society for colonizing the free people of color of the United States, in submitting to the Society their first report, are encouraged to persevere in their efforts from an increased confidence as well in its practibility as in its importance. In a plan of such magnitude, involving the happiness of many millions; and the success of which, while it cannot fail to create a general interest might conflict with established prejudice, circumspection and delicacy become essential to its progress. The first step of the Board of Managers was to present a memorial to Congress at their last session, which, with the report of the committee to whom it was referred, is now laid before the society. The nature and novelty of the subject, not less than the mass of business which engaged the deliberations of that body, did not permit them to pursue the report. On the adjournment of Congress the Board adopted suitable measures to promote the view of the Society, without waiting the lapse of another session. No efficient and decisive measures could be adopted until it was ascertained where the most suitable situation could be procured on the west coast of Africa, for planting the proposed colony; and although the Managers collected much interesting and useful information, and such as gave them great encouragement to proceed, it could not supply the place of that which must be obtained from their own agents upon the spot. It was, therefore resolved, shortly after the rising of Congress, to appoint an agent to visit and explore a part of the west coast of Africa. Upon further deliberation, and considering the importance of the mission, the variety of objects to which the attention of a single agent would be directed—the danger of having the main object defeated by the casualties to which he might be exposed, as well as the importance of concert and co-operation in many difficulties which might occur, it was thought advisable to increase the number to two. The managers, accordingly, after having received the most satisfactory testimony of their zeal, ability, and other qualifications, appointed Mr. Samuel J. Mills and Mr. Ebenezer Burgess Agents of the Society for this purpose.

"It was supposed that much useful information might be procured in England and the enquiries of the agents much facilitated by calling there on their way to Africa. The members of the African institution in England have been many years engaged in the laudable work of meliorating the the condition of the long neglected and much abused Africans, and posses great influence in that country, and particularly in the colony of Sierra Leone. A letter was, therefore, addressed by the President to that body, in hopes that the high character of benevolence which characterizes the conductors of that institution, and the similarity of the objects of its pursuits, would lead them cordialy to co-operate in the great designs of this Society, and to give our agents all the aid in their power. This this report, for the information of the Society. The agents said from

the information of the Society. The agents sailed from this country the middle of November last.

"The raising of funds to meet the expenditure necessary for effecting this object, has occupied much of the attention and labors of the Board of Managers; and a still further increase of our resources will be essential to its completion. Nor do we fear that the American community will suffer an object of so much importance, and of so high a character of benevolence, to fail for the want of necessary pecuniary aid. We are happy to state that auxiliary Societies have been formed in Baltimore, Philadelphia, New York, Virginia, and Ohio, and the Board have received information of the intention of forming other societies in different parts of the country. The extension of these auxiliaries is of the first importance, as it is by their means the public mind must be enlightened on the great and important objects of the Society, and it is through them, in some measure, the necessary funds must be drawn for its support. In the prosecution of a plan which was likely to attract the public attention to subjects of deep interest and of great delicacy, it was expected that much jealousy would be excited, and many fears and prejudices would be awakened. Persons acting from the most opposite and contradictory views and principles, have been arrayed in opposition to the Society, from a mistaken apprehension of its tendency, as well as of the motives of its members. But, in the midst of these difficulties, which jealousy and prejudice have raised to impede our course, we are encouraged by the decided approbation of many of the most intelligent of our fellow-citizens, in different parts of the country, among those the most distinguished for whatever is great or good, and by almost all who have taken pains to investigate and examine the subject. The more the public mind becomes informed, the more decided and general will be its approbation; and we already number among our patrons many whose dispositions were at first neutral, if not unfriendly.

"The objectors to the Society are generally those who acknowledge the importance and utility of establishing the proposed colony, but suppose it impracticable; and they refer principally, 1st. To the difficulty of procuring a proper situation for the colony. 2d. The supposed repugnance of the colonists. 3d. The expense of emigration. The first objection is assuming a difficulty without proof, and will be best answered by the report of the agents, who have been sent to explore the country. The managers are enabled at present to state, that, from information derived from various sources, they are persuaded that a situation can be procured in Africa with the approbation, and secured from the hostility, of the neighboring nations, which will posses, such fertility of soil, and salubrity of climate, as to make it an inviting situation to the people of color in this country.

"2. The objection on the part of the coloured people, it is readily seen, springs from first impressions, and is the result entirely of ignorance and misapprehension? As these are reinoved, and their minds are informed upon the subject, the phantoms which their alarmed imaginations had conjured up, gradually disappear; and when they learn that the land of their fathers is not cursed by a perpetual and unvarying sterility, nor inhabited by the most sanguinary and ferocious savages, that instinctive principle which binds it to their affections, is soon seen to unfold itself; and though the Managers have learned with surprize and regret that their fears have been awakened in some places, by persons claiming their confidence as their peculiar and avowed defenders and benefactors, they still believe that the diffusion of juster opinions, founded on undoubted facts in relation to the state of things in Africa, and the advantages of a settlement there,

will make it very generally if not universally the place of their decided preference. The Managers are the more confirmed in this opinion from their knowledge of the approbation of many of the most intelligent among the people of color to the plan of the society, notwithstanding the alarms which had been created, and the misapprehensions which had been excited, and that many of those, who were at first violent in their opposition, have become as decidedly friendly, upon learning the real motives, intentions and objects of the society.

"The Managers have ascertained that there are numbers of the highest standing for intelligence and respectability among that class of people, who are warmly in favor of the plan, from a conviction that will, if accomplished, powerfully co-operate in placing the situation of their brethren here and in Africa, in that scale of happiness and respectability among the nations of the earth, from which they have long been degraded. Offers of service have been received from many worthy and influential individuals of their own color, and from a number of families from different parts of the U. States, to become the first settlers in the colony, whenever a suitable situation shall be procured. The Managers can with confidence state their belief, that they would have no difficulty in procuring individuals among them worthy of trust and confidence to explore the country if necessary, and to plant a colony of sufficient strength to secure its safety and prosperity. This being accomplished, there can be no difficulty in presenting its importance to their brethren, in such a manner and with such unquestionable testimony, as must command their fullest confidence. Without detailing the variety of information received by the Board on this subject, the Managers cannot omit the testimony of capt. Paul Cuffee, so well known in Africa, Europe, and America for his active and enlarged benevolence, and for his zeal and devotedness to the cause of the people of color. The opportunities of capt. Cuffee, of forming a correct opinion were superior perhaps to those of any man in America. His judgment was clear and strong, and the warm interest he took in whatever related to the happiness of that class of people is well known. The testimony of such a man is sufficient to outweigh all the unfounded predictions and idle surmises of those opposed to the plan of the Society. He had visited twice the coast of Africa, and became well acquainted with the country and its inhabitants. He states that upon his opinion alone, he could have taken to Africa at least two thousand people of color from Boston and its neighborhood. In the death of Paul Cuffee the Society has lost a most useful advocate, the people of color, a warm and disinterested friend, and Society a valuable member. His character alone ought to be sufficient to rescue the people to which he belonged from the unmerited aspersions which have been cast on them. The plan of the Society met with his entire approbation, its success was the subject of his ardent wishes, and the prospect of its usefulness to the native Africans and their descendants, in this country, was the solace of his declining years, and cheered the last moments of his existence.

"3 d. The objection urged on the score of expenditure in transporting so many persons to Africa, has been arrayed in all the imposing forms of figures and calculations. There is a material error in estimating the expence of removing each individual, by the same ratio which may be incurred in the removal of the first colonists, without making any allowance for the thousands that will be enabled to defray their own expences.

"The advantages of the progress of the colony must have been equally overlooked; as it may be expected soon to become sufficiently established and flourishing, to offer immediate employment to those who come among them, and who will be able to work and provide for their own subsistence. In addition to this, much may be expected from the augmented value of the land in proportion to its settlement.

"Our western countries present the best comment on this subject. An emigration to Africa, will be attended with less expence, and the emigrants will be exposed to less inconvenience, and to fewer difficulties, when the colony is established, than many of the emigrants to the western country now encounter-and yet we find thousands coming even from remote parts of Europe to the interior of America, without the means and advantages which thousands of people of color possess in this country, and that they often rise to respectability and independence, and even to wealth. "The Managers cannot pass the occasion, without noticing the death of the Reverend Doctor Finley, one of the Vice Presidents, during the past year. The deep interest which he took in the success of the Society, and the zeal he displayed in its formation, are well known to many present. In his last sickness, he was much gratified upon receiving information of the progress of the Society, and of its prospects of success. It gave consolation and comfort to his last moments. When we view the Society in this early stage of its proceedings, as animating the hopes and cheering the prospects of the dying christian who had been engaged in its service; when we view it as consecrated by the prayers of the pious, may we not be led with humble confidence to look to the good hand of an overruling Providence to guide its deliberations? May we not expect that the benedictions of millions yet unborn shall bless its anniversary?

On motion of Mr. Clay, a letter of Thomas Jefferson, late President of the United States, was read, which he understood was in the hands of some one present, and would show that the importance of such an institution had been long since duly appreciated, and had received the approbation of that illustrious individual.

Copy of a letter from Thomas Jefferson, late President of the United States, to John Lynd

MONTICELLO, JAN. 21, 1811.

SIR,

You have asked my opinion on the proposition of Ann Mifflin, to take measures for procuring, on the coast of Africa, an establishment to which the people of color of these States night, from time to time, be colonized, under the auspices of different governments. Having long ago made up my mind on this subject, I have no hesitation in saying, that I have ever thought that the most desirable measure which could be adopted for gradually drawing off this part of our population. Most advantageous for themselves as well as for us; going from a country possessing all the useful arts, they might be the means of transplanting them among the inhabitants of Africa; and would thus carry back to the country of their origin the seeds of civilization, which might render their sojournment here a blessing, in the end, to that country.

I received, in the last year of my entering into the administration of the general government, a letter from the governor of Virginia, consulting me, at the request of the legislature of the State, on the means of procuring some such asylum to which these people might be occasionally sent. I proposed to him the establishment of Sierra Leone, in which a private company in England had already colonized a number of negroes, and particularly the fugitives from these States during the revolutionary war: and at the same time suggested, if that could not be obtained, some of the Portuguese possessions in South America as most desirable.

The subsequent Legislature approving these ideas, I wrote the ensuing year (1802) to Mr. King, our minister in London, to endeavour to negotiate with the Sierra Leone company, and induce them to receive such of these people as might be colonized thither. He opened a correspondence with Mr. W—and Mr. Thornton, secretary of the company, on the subject; and in 1803 I received,

through Mr. King, the result; which was, that the colony was going on in but a languishing condition; that the funds of the company were likely to fail, as they received no return of profit to keep them up; that they were then in treaty with the government to take the establishment off their hands; but that in no event should they be willing to receive more of these people from the United States, as it was portion of settlers who had gone from the United States, who, by their idleness and turbulence, had kept the settlement in constant danger of dissolution, which could not have been prevented, but for the aid of the Marroon negroes, from the West Indies, who were more industrious and orderly than the others, and supported the authority of the government and its laws.

I think I learned, afterwards, that the British government had taken the colony into their own hands, and I believe it still exists.

The effort which I made with Portugal to obtain an establishment from them, within their colonies in South America, proved also abortive.

You inquired further whether I would use my endeavours to procure such an establishment secure against violence from other powers, and particularly the French. Certainly, I shall be willing to do any thing I can to give it effect and safety.

But I am but a private individual, and could only use endeavours with individuals. Whereas, the national government can address themselves at once to those of Europe to obtain the desired security, and will unquestionably be ready to exert its influence with those nations to effect an object so benevolent in itself, and so important to a great portion of its constituents. Indeed, nothing is more to be wished than that the United States, would themselves undertake to make such and establishment on the coast of Africa.

Exclusive of motives of humanity, the commercial advantages to be derived from it might defray all its expences; but for this, the national mind is not prepared. It may perhaps be doubted whether many of these people would voluntarily consent to such and exchange of situation, and but few of those who are advanced to a certain age in habits of slavery would be capable of governing themselves: this should not, however, discourage the experiment, nor the early trial of it. And propositions should be made with all the prudent caution and attention requisite to reconcile it to the interest, the safety, and prejudice of all parties.

Accept the assurance of my respects and esteem.

THOMAS JEFFERSON.

Mr. Mercer, then rose, and said he was happy to have it in his power to inform the Society, that the sentiments of our present Chief Magistrate were not less friendly to its benevolent object than those of his predecessor, whose letter had been just read. It was, said Mr. Mercer, through a very interesting correspondence between Mr. Monroe, then governor of Virginia with Mr. Jefferson, that the general assembly had first solicited the aid of the government of the United States, to procure and asylum for our free people of color. Nor was the sentiment which promoted this effort in the councils of Virginia, confined to a few individuals, distinguished for the extent of their political views, or by romantic feelings of benevolence. The resolution to which the address of the President had just called the attention of the Society, passed the popular branch of the legislature of Virginia with but nine dissenting voices out of one hundred and forty six, and a full quorum of the Senate, with but one. It was, in fact, but a repetition of certain resolutions, which had been unanimously adopted by the same legislature, tho' in secret session, at three antecedent periods, in the last seventeen years. It was truly the feeling and voice of Virginia.

Many thousand individuals in our native state, you well know, Mr. President, are restrained, said Mr. M. from manumitting their slaves, as you and I are, by the melancholy conviction, that they cannot yield to the suggestions of humanity, without manifest injury to their country.

The rapid increase of the free people of colour, by which their number was extended in the ten years proceeding the last census of the United States, from fifteen to thirty thousand, if it has not endangered our peace, has impaired the value of all the private property in a large section of our country. Upon our lowlands said Mr. Mercer, it seems as if some malediction had been shed. The habitations of our fathers have sunk into ruins; the fields which they tilled have become a wilderness. Such is the table land between the valleys of our great rivers. Those newly grown and almost impenetrable thickets which have succeeded a wretched cultivation, shelter and conceal a banditti, consisting of this degraded, idle, and vicious population, who sally forth from their coverts, beneath the obscurity of night, and plunder the rich proprietors of the valleys. They infest the suburbs of the towns and cities, where they become the depositories of stolen goods, and, schooled by necessity elude the vigilance of our defective police.

It has been suggested, said Mr. M. that resources will be wanted to give success to our enterprize. Let its commencement be but propitious, and it will eventually prosper to the extent of our most sanguine wishes. The great obstacle to be surmounted, will arise not from the sordid propensity of the slave-holder, but from the imperfect means within our reach of transporting and early providing for the numerous colonists who will present themselves to our charity or be tendered to our acceptance by their present masters.

The laws of Virginia now discourage, and very wisely, perhaps, the emancipation of slaves. But the very policy on which they are founded, will afford every facility to emancipation, when the colonization of the slave will be the consequence of his liberation.

I have Mr. President, offered these hasty remarks under the impression that some of the facts which they disclose may have been unknown to the Society. It has my most fervent prayers, and shall command my utmost efforts for its success, which requires, to insure it, nothing but our united, zealous, and preseverying exertions.

On motion of Mr. Clay,

Resolved, unanimously, That the thanks of the Society be presented to the Board of Managers, for the able and satisfactory manner in which they have discharged the duties assigned to them by the Society; and that they be requested to furnish a copy of the first report of their proceedings for publication.

Mr. Clay rose to submit a motion which he had hoped some other gentleman would have offered. It was a vote of thanks to the Board of Managers. He would not be restrained from proposing it by the official relation in which he stood to the Board, because, although he was ex-officio a member, he had really participated very little in its valuable labors, and therefore could not be justly reproached with proposing thanks to himself.

Whilst he was up, he would detain the Society for a few moments. It was proper again and again to repeat, that it was far from the intention of the Society to affect, in any manner, the tenure by which a certain species of property is held. He was himself a slave-holder; and he considered that kind of property as inviolable as any other in the country. He would resist as soon, and with as much firmness, encroachments upon it as he would encroachments upon any other property which he held. Nor was he disposed even to go as far as the gentleman who had just spoken,(Mr. Mercer) in saying that he would emancipate his slaves, if the means were provided of sending them from the country. It was also proper to repeat, that it was equally remote from the intention of the Society, that any sort of coertion should be employed in regard to the free people of color who were the objects of its proceedings. Whatever was proposed to be done was to be entirely voluntary on their part.

It has been said that the plan of the Society is impracticable and Utopian. Why? How have the descendents of Africa been brought to the shores of America? By the most nefarious traffic that ever disgraced the annals of man. It has been, it is true, the work of ages. May we not, by a gradual and persevering exertion, restore to Africa that portion of her race among us, that shall be liberated? He would not, he could not believe that man, in the pursuit of the vilest cupidity, in the prosecution of purposes of the most cruel injustice, which had constantly marked the African slave trade, could accomplish more than might be attained in a cause which was recommend by so many high, honorable, and animating considerations. Such was the cause in which this Society is engaged. The Christian, of whom unwearied constancy is the characteristic; the philanthropist; the statesman who looks only to the safety and the happiness of his own country; in short, all good men, will find motives for engaging their co-operation or their wishes in behalf of the society. Its object is not impracticable. Scarcely any thing—nothing is beyond the power of those who, in the pursuit of a just purpose, approved by good men, and sanctioned by Providence, boldly and resolutely determine to command success.

But the persons, the amclioration of whose condition is the object of the Society, will not, it is said, accept the proffered favor. Mr. C. believed at first, that, from want of information, very few of them would—not perhaps one in a hundred, in the interior. He was inclined to believe, however, that a number amply sufficient for the commencement of a colonial establishment would go. These would be drawn principally from the cities, which would act as a sort of depot from the country for the colony. Let five in a hundred only, of that portion of our population, be induced to migrate, and a number abundantly sufficient to begin with will be obtained. The first difficulties obviated, and all will be obviated. Let the colony be once firmly established and in prosperity, and all the obstacles will disappear. Why should they not go? Look at the earliest history of man; follow him through all his subsequent progress, and you find him continually migrating.

What is the motive of this unceasing change of abode? To better his condition. What brought our fathers voluntarily to these shores, then savage and forbidding, not less savage and forbidding perhaps than those of Africa itself? To render themselves more happy. This word happiness, Mr. C. said, comprised many items. It comprehended what was hardly less important than subsistence, political and social considerations. These the men of color never can enjoy here, but are what he would find in the contemplated colony. And can there be any thing, to a reflecting freeman, (and some among the class of persons to whom he alluded were doubtless capable of reflection) more humiliating, more dark and cheerless, than to see himself, and to trace in imagination his posterity, through all succeeding time, degraded and debased, aliens to the Society of which they are members, and cut off from all its higher blessing?

Further, several of the slave-holding states already had, and perhaps all of them would, prohibit entirely emancipation, without some such outlet was created. A sense of their own safety required the painful prohibition. Experience proved that persons turned loose who were neither freemen nor slaves, constituted a great moral evil threatening to contaminate all parts of society. Let the colony once be successfully planted, and legislative bodies, who have been grieved at the necessity of passing those prohibitory laws, which at a distance might appear to stain our codes, will hasten to remove the impediments to the exercise of benevolence and humanity. They will annex the condition that the emancipated shall leave the country; and he has placed a false estimate upon liberty who believes that there are many who would refuse the boon, when coupled even with such a condition.

But Mr. C. said, he would not longer digress from the object of his motion. He was persuaded he would meet the unanimous concurrence of the Society in the proposition that its thanks be tended to the Board of Managers for the able and satisfactory manner in which they had executed their duties.

On motion of Mr. Key,

Resolved, unanimously, That the thanks of the Society be presented to the President of the Society, for his aid and influence in promoting the objects of the Society; and that he be requested to furnish a copy of his address for publication.

On motion of Mr. Bayard,

Resolved, unanimously, That the thanks of this Society be presented to the members of those Auxiliary Societies that have been formed in vari-

ous parts of the United States, to forward the plan and to contribute to the funds of this institution.

On motion of Mr. Herbert,

Resolved, Unanimously, That the future annual meeting of this Society, be held on the last Saturday of December.

The Society then proceeded to the appointment of officers for the present year, when the following persons were elected:

The Hon.

Bushrod Washington was unanimously elected President.

VICE PRESIDENTS.

Hon. William H. Crawford, of Georgia.
Hon. Henry Clay, of Kentucky.
Hon. William Phillips, of Massachusetts,
Col. Henry Rutgers, of New York.
Hon. John E. Howard. . . .
Hon. Samuel Smith. . . .< of Maryland.
Hon. John C. Herbert, <
John Taylor, of Caroline, Esq. of Virginia.
Gen. Andrew Jackson, of Tennessee.
Robert Ralston, Esq. . . . .
Richard Rush, Esq. . . .< of Pennsylvania.
Gen. John Mason, District of Columbia.
Samuel Bayard, New Jersey.

MANAGERS.

Francis S. Key. . . . .
Benjamin G. Orr,
Walter Jones. . . . .
John Peter,
John Laird. . . . .
Edmund I. Lee,
Rev. Dr. James Laurie. . . . .
William Thornton,
Rev. Stephen B. Balch. . . . .
Wm. H. Fitzhugh,
Rev. Obadiah B. Brown. . . . .
Henry Carroll.
Elias B. Caldwell, Esq. Secretary.
John G. McDonald, Recording Secretary.
David English, Treasurer.
To Samuel J. Mills and Ebenezer Burgess

You have been appointed the agents of the "Board of Managers" of the American Society for Colonizing the free "people of color of the United States" for the purpose of visiting England and Africa, on a mission of inquiry.

The object which you will keep in view while engaged in this mission, is to obtain that information which will enable the Board to concert their future measures with a prospect of succeeding in their design. Your general conduct will be governed by the following instructions.

1. You will make the necessary preparation for leaving this country, and embrace the first favorable opportunity which shall present, for England.

2. Upon your arrival in London you will present your instructions and letters to such gentlemen as shall be named by the Board, and to others to whom you may have letters of introduction.

3. You will endeavor to procure information from those gentlemen relative to the state of the west coast of Africa, the best means of prosecuting your enquiries when you arrive there, and to obtain letters of introduction from the proper persons to the Governor of the Sierra Leone Colony, and to any other gentlemen on the coast who may probably aid you in your object.

4. When you have made the necessary preparations, which you are requested to do with the least possible delay, you will embark for the coast of Africa. You will make the Sierra Leone colony, with the approbation of the governor thereof, your principal station while you remain on the coast.

5. You will make yourselves acquainted with the Sierra Leone Colony, particularly of its history, progress, improvement and prospects, with a view to furnish such information as may be useful in forming a colony on the coast.

6. You will visit the coast above and below the colony of Sierra Leone, to as great an extent as shall be deemed expedient, and give a description of that part of the coast visited by you; and endeavor to procure as much information as possible of other parts of the coast, and of the interior. And we would particularly direct your attention to the climate, soil, and healthiness, of the country, and its fitness for agricultural improvements, as it is in contemplation to turn the attention of the new colonists mostly to agriculture. As connected with this object, you will procure all the information in your power as to the extent of the rivers on the coast, their sources and how far navigable, the mountains and general face of the country, and finally every thing that may be considered interesting and useful to the Society, to enable it to form an opinion as to the most eligible spot for the colony, and the prospect of success when established. It would be particularly desirable to ascertain the character of the different nations or tribes on the coast, and more especially of those in the neighborhood of the place you may recommend as a proper situation for the colony.

7. You will direct your attention particularly to the Sherbro country, which country it is expected you will visit. By means of native interpreters you will endeavor to consult with the native chiefs of the different tribes and explain to them the design which the board have in view. Should circumstances permit, you will obtain from them a pledge that they will promote the designs of the colony, should one be established, and that as far as they have the possession of the country, that a section of it shall be given up to the government of the United States, or the Society, at a fair price, should Congress or the Board hereafter make the request; for the purpose of colonizing the free people of color, as the Board propose.

8. After you shall have completed your inquires and as far as possible attained the object of your mission, you will return to America direct or by the way of England, as shall be deemed proper. It is desired that you would return direct to this country, unless the inducements to revisit England are strong

9. You will obtain as particular and accurate an account of the territories and their limits, claimed by the different European nations, on the west coast of Africa, as possible; together with the character of the different nations on the coast, and in the interior, and the boundaries of their territo-

ries. On your return you will present to the Board a full account of your expedition, and of the information procured by you, and improve every opportunity which may present to inform the Board of your progress.

10. You will keep an account of your expenses for the inspection of the Board.

In addition to these instructions you will be furnished with copies of the constitution of this Society, and of the memorial of the board of managers, which was addressed to the Congress of the United States, during their session of 1816 and 1817.

BUSHROD WASHINGTON,

President of the American Colonization Society.

E. B. CALDWELL, Secretary

Washington, Nov, 5th, 1817.

To Samuel J. Mills and Ebenezer Burgess

Gentlemen.—

The Board of Managers of the American Society for colonizing the free people of color of the United States, have appointed you their agents on a mission to explore a part of the west coast of Africa, for the purpose of ascertaining the best situation which can be procured for colonizing the free people of color of the United States. You will act in conjunction as much as possible; but should you be separated to forward the objects of the mission, or by a dispensation of Providence, you will act as if you had a separate commission, taking care, in case of acting separately, not to let your engagements interfere with each other. The situation to which you have been called, is one of great importance and responsibility, and will require from you the greatest diligence, skill and prudence, as the success of the benevolent designs of the Society may, in a great measure, depend upon your mission. General instructions will be given with this commission, but very much must be left to your own discretion and prudence, on which the Board place the greatest reliance. The objects of the Society are of that enlarge benevolence, affecting, as they believe, not only the temporal and

spiritual interests of thousands of our fellow-creatures in this country, but in Africa likewise, that they calculate upon the cordial aid and co-operation of the philanthropist of every clime and country, whose assistance you may need in the prosecution of your design; and they are the more sanguine in their calculations for this friendly support, from the attention which this class of the human family have received from the most distinguished individuals in Europe, and particularly in Great Brazen. But whilst we thus say "be ye wise as serpents, and harmless as doves," and recommend you to the benevolent and feeling stranger, your principal reliance will be on Him who has made of one blood all the nations of the earth, and in whose hands are the hearts of all the children of men, to turn them as he pleaseth. May he be your protector, and preserve you from "the arrow that flieth by day, and "the pestilence that walketh in darkness," and "the destruction that wasteth at noon day." May that "Saviour who is to receive Egypt as a ransom, and Ethiopia and Seba to himself"—who hath promised to "call his sons from far, and his daughters from the end of the earth," "make for you a way in the sea" and in "the wilderness," and "a path in the mighty waters," that all may issue to His honor and glory, and the spread of the Redeemer's kingdom.

BUSHROD WASHINGTON,

President of the American Colonization Society.

E. B. Caldwell, Sec'y.

To his Royal Highness the Duke of Gloucester, Patron and President of the African Institution

I have the honor to inform your Royal Highness that an association of number of persons, residing in various parts of the United States, has been recently formed at the city Washington, under the denomination of "The American Society for colonizing the free people of color of the United States." The object of this institution, indicated by its name, is to promote the colonizing of those persons, with their own consent. In the accomplishment of that object, it is necessary to determine upon a proper country wherein to plant the proposed colony. Africa, and particularly the western coast of it, has with this view, hitherto principally engaged the attention of the Society; and, in order to acquire all the information which it may be material to possess, in fixing its judgment on that important point, it has deputed to Europe and to Africa the bearers hereof, Samuel J. Mills and Ebenezer Burgess.

Aware that the African institution has been long occupied with Africa, and the people and descendants of Africa, the American Society has directed me to address your Royal Highness, as the Patron and President of the African institution, and respectfully to solicit any aid and assistance which it may be convenient to render to those deputies, in the business with which they are thus charged. These gentlemen will promptly afford any further explanations which your Royal Highness may require, relative to the nature and prospects of the American Society.

I am sure that it would be quite unnecessary to trespass further upon the time of your Royal Highness, in expatriating and insisting upon the benefits which may result from the successful establishment of the contemplated colony, to the colonists themselves, to their descendants, and to Africa. Restored to the land of their fathers, and carrying with them a knowledge of our religion, of letters, and of the arts, may they not powerfully cooperate with the benevolent and enlightened efforts of the African institution, in the introduction into African of christianity and civilization? If the exertions of the two institutions are directed in channels somewhat different, they both have the same common character of humanity and benevolence—the same common aim at meliorating the condition of the race of Africa. From this affinity in object, the American Society cherishes the hope of friendly intercourse and an interchange of good offices with the African institution.

I have the honor to be, with great respect, your Royal Highness's obedient servant.

BUSHROD WASHINGTON,

President of the American Colonization Society.

Address of the Synod of Tennessee, to the Society for the Colonization of the Free People of Color in the United States

To the Hon. Bushrod Washington Esq. President, c.

RESPECTED SIR,

Through you the Synod of Tennessee embraced with lively pleasure an early opportunity of congratulating the society formed at the capital of our nation, and consisting of so many of our distinguished statesmen and fellow citizens, for the colonization of the free people of color among us, who may accede to their plan. We congratulate you on the noble and important object for which you are associated, on the providential signs of our times which signally favor your efforts, and on the wide spread and growing impression upon the public mind, that your success is connected with the best interests, not only of the people of color, but of our country and mankind. If it is important that legal equality should accompany liberty, that Africa should receive the gospel, and that the evils of the slave trade should be overruled for her final enjoyment of the blessings of civilization and knowledge, liberty and religion, then it is important that your design should be encouraged. We wish you, therefore, to know, that within our bounds the public sentiment appears clearly and decidedly in your favor, and that the more vigorously and perseveringly you combine and extend your exertions on the plan you have adopted, the more you are likely to be crowned with the approbation of the people as well as with the higher rewards of doing good. As ministers and disciples of him who proclaims light to them that sit in darkness peace to a jaring world, liberty to the captives and the opening of the prison to them that are bound, we anticipate the glorious day, when men shall know the Lord from the least unto the greatest in all lands; when every one shall sit under his own vine and under his own figtree, having none to molest or to make him afraid; when the rod of the oppressor and the tears of the oppressed shall be known no more; but all men shall do unto others as they would be done unto in similar circumstances. This glorious change in the state of the world we expect will be brought about by the instrumentality of men under the blessing of God. While, then, the heralds of salvation go forth in the name and strength of their divine master to preach the gospel to every creature, we ardently wish that your exertions and the best influence of all philanthropists may be united, to meliorate the condition of human society, and especially of its most degraded classes, till liberty, religion and happiness shall be the enjoyment of the whole family of man.

Nashville Church, Oct. 3d, 1817.

A true copy from the Records of the Synod of Tennessee.

. . . .

CHARLES COFFIN,

Stated Clerk

Since the meeting of the Society, the following resolution has unanimously passed the Legislature of Maryland

BY THE HOUSE OF DELIGATES, January 26th, 1818.

Resolved, unanimously, That the governor be requested to communicate to the President of the United States and to our Senators and Representatives in Congress, the opinion of this General Assembly, that a wise and provident policy suggests the expediency, on the part of our national government, of procuring through negociation, by cession or purchase, a tract of country on the western coast of Africa, for the colonization of the free people of color of the United States.

By order.

LOUIS GASSAWAY,

Clerk

Copy of a letter from a respectable gentleman in Vincennes in the State of Indiana, to the Hon. Bushrod Washington, President of the Society for the Colonization of Blacks

SIR,

Having been informed through the medium of the newspapers of the formation of the society to which you do honour as president, but either not being informed of, or having forgotten the name of the society, I take the liberty to address this letter to you, requesting you to send it to the secretary or other proper officer, whose business it is to receive communications.

I feel a deep interest in your society, and highly approve the patriotic and benevolent motives which have induced its formation, and with every American citizen feel a pride in seeing the name of *Washington* at its head.

To aid its views I am prompted to send the following information. There are in this vicinity between fifty and a hundred free people of colour, who have by my means heard of your society, and are desirous of going to Africa, to help in forming a settlement or colony, should one be attempted. They live on the Wabash, on both sides; some in the Illinois territory, and some in Indiana. They are in general industrious and moral. Some of them have landed property and are good farmers; and some can read and write. They are sensible of the existing degraded condition in which they are placed by our laws, respecting the right of suffrage, and other disabilities.

If your society has formed a constitution, they wish to see it, as well as the consequent regulations, and they wish to be informed how soon any settlement or colony will be commenced.

Be pleased sir, to forward the constitution and other information to me, and I will communicate it to them. I will also aid the society in removing the people of colour from this, to the place of embarkation, and in any other manner in my power.

With best wishes for your success in your patriotic and humane labours, I have the honour to be sir,

Your devoted and obedient

Humble servant.

Vincenness, 16th Oct. 1807.

Extract of Letters written by Capt. Paul Cuffe to Mr. Mills. Westport, 8th mo. 6th inst. 1816.

ESTEEMED FRIEND,

I do not expect to send a vessel to Africa this ensuing winter, when I went last to Africa, I was somewhat disappointed in not having a special license from the British government.

My correspondent William Allen, of London, a member of the London African institution, wrote to me to come to London, and engage with them, and keep open a communication between England and Africa. I have informed him that my wish is for the good of the Africans generally. If we could open a circular rout from Africa to England, and thence to America, I feel disposed to be made use of in any way that appeared most advantageous, I have not had any returns.

The people I carried out to Africa, were well received and had land granted them, they much want at Sierra Leone, a good mill wright, a saw mill is necessary, also a rice mill for cleaning rice.

COPY OF CITATION.

Colony of Sierra Leone, 25th of March

Mr. Perry Locke. You are hereby summoned and required to appear at the ensuing general session of the peace, which will be held at the Court Hall in Freetown, on Wednesday the 10th day of April, at the hour of ten in the forenoon, there to serve as a grand juror: herein fail not at your peril.

W. D. GRANT,

Sheriff

Perry Locke was one of the passengers that I carried out, he made great complaint to me, because he was called upon, I told him he complained in America because he was deprived of these priviledges. And then he murmered because he was thus called upon; go and fill thy seat, do as well as thou canst. I mention this, that others may see, that they have equal rights in Africa.

. . . .

P. C.

Westport, 1st mo. 6th, 1817

RESPECTED FRIEND,

The population of Sierra Leone in 1811, was 2000, and about 1000 in the suburbs. Since that time they have not been numbered, but the colony according to my judgment, from 1811 to 1815, had much improved, the soil for cultivation is not very flattering, but it is advantageously

situated for a town, and ship navigation. The coast of Africa abounds with rivers, the great river Gambia, according to the best information given me is very fertile, as is the Island Burso at the mouth of said river, but they are said to be sickly to the northern constitutions. There is a river about 50 leagues south of Cape Sierra Leone, called the Sherborough, good navigation, and soil excellent.

Agreeable to information given me by a citizen of Sierra Leone, the citizen has ever been desirous that a settlement should be established at that place, with those people that may come from America, he is a man of good character. The great River Congo, near the equator, its powerful population and goodness of soil, I hope will not always be neglected. I much approve of a vessels being sent as thou has mentioned.

In 1815, I carried out to S. Leone, nine families, 38 in number, and in 1816, I have had so many applications, that I believe I might have had the greater part to have carried out of Boston and the vicinity. I should think about Christmas, would be the most healthy season for a vessel to arrive on the coast. As to the length of the voyage, it would depend on the extent of discoveries to be made. I think from twelve to eighteen months, provided the voyage should extend to the Cape of Goodhope and the Tristan Islands.

I should suppose that one vessel would be sufficient for visiting the coast; as to the force necessary, thou art the best judge. I think that the government of Great Britain, would not receive large numbers of every description of people of colour at their colony. Were the U. States to undertake to settle a colony in Africa, it would be best to have good characters until the colony was well established. The English would not probably admit a free trade at Sierra Leone, unless they made a neutral port of it.

I should suppose that all those people who are willing to go to Sierra Leone, would have no objection to settling a new colony, thirty eight in number went out with me, their expense was estimated at one hundred dollars per head; but were there a larger number, they could be carried out for sixty dollars—the expense of thirty of the above number was borne by Paul Cuffe, the others paid their own passages. In addition to the above expense, I furnished them with provisions to the amount of 1591 8s 3d sterling, all this was done without fee or reward, my hope is in a coming day.

PAUL CUFFE.

Baltimore, August 20th, 1817

DEAR SIR,

Ever since I received your letter of July 11th, requesting the communication of such ideas as had occured to me, concerning the proposed plan of colonizing the free blacks in the United States, with their own consent, and indeed from the time of our short interview at Washington, when you first mentioned the subject to me, I have kept it constantly in view, and revolved it much in my mind. Hitherto however, I have been prevented from putting my thoughts on paper, or even digesting and reducing them to method, by various interruptions, arising in part from accident, and in part from professional engagements, in the midst of which I am obliged at last to write. This may interfere very much with the order of my ideas, but will not I trust occasion any material omission. Nor do I apprehend much inconvenience from the delay: Since the preparitory measures for the first step in this great enterprise, the institution of a mission to the south western coast of Africa, to explore the ground, and seek out a suitable situation for the establishment of the colony, are not yet I believe entirely completed.

Although you confine your request to the communication of my ideas, concerning the manner and means of accomplishing this great design, it will not I trust be improper or unseasonable to throw out by way of preface and introduction, some hints on its usefulness and practicability, which have long engaged my attention, and are susceptible I think of very full proof. To many, and especially to you, this I know is quite unnecessary; but great numbers of your countrymen, including many persons of good sense, considerable influence and the best intentions, may have serious doubts on these two points, which is of great importance to remove, in order to gain their zealous co-operation. Towards the attainment of so desirable an object I wish to contribute my mite, for which this seems to be a fit occasion.

In reflecting on the utility of a plan for colonizing the free people of colour, with whom our country abounds, it is natural that we should be first struck by its tendency to confer a benefit on ourselves, by ridding us of a population for the most part idle and useless, and too often vicious and mischievous. These persons are condemned to a state of hopeless inferiority and degradation, by their colour; which is an indeliable mark of their origin and former condition and establishes an impassible barrier between them and the whites. This barrier is closed for ever, by our habits and our feelings which perhaps it would be more correct to call our prejudices, and which whether feelings or prejudices, or a mixture of both, make us recoil with horror from the idea of an intimate union with the free blacks and preclude the possibility of such a state of equality, between them and us, as alone could make us one people. Whatever justice humanity and kindness we may feel towards them, we cannot help considering them, and treating them, as our inferiors; not can they help viewing themselves in the same light, however hard and unjust they may be inclined to consider such a state of things. We cannot help associating them, in our feelings and conduct, nor can they help associating themselves, with the slaves; who have the same colour the same origin and the same manners, and with whom they or their parents have been recently in the same condition. Be their industry ever so great and their conduct ever so correct, whatever property they may acquire, or whatever respect we may feel for their characters, we never could consent, and they never could hope, to see the two races placed on a footing of perfect equality with each other: to see the free blacks or their descendants visit in our houses, form part of our circle of acquaintance, marry into our families, or participate in public honours and employments. This is strictly true of every part of our country, even those parts where slavery has long ceased to exist, and is held in abhorrence. There is no state in the union where a negro or mulatto can ever hope to be a member of congress, a judge, a militia officer, or even a justice of the peace: to sit down at the same table with the respectable whites, or to mix freely in their society. I may safely assert that Paul Cuffe, respectable intelligent and wealthy as he is, has no expectation or chance of ever being invited to dine with any gentleman in Boston, of marrying his daughter whatever may be her fortune or education to one of their sons, or of seeing his son obtain a wife among their daughters.

This circumstance, arising from the difference of colour and origin between the slaves and the free class, distinguishes the slavery of America from that of every other country, ancient or modern. Slavery existed among almost all the ancient nations. It now exists throughout Asia, Africa and America, and in every part of the Russian and Turkish dominions in Europe; that is in more that three fourths of the world. But the great body of the slaves, every where except in north and south America, are of the same race origin, colour and general character with the free people. So it was among the ancients. Mannumission therefore, by removing the slave from the condition of slavery, exempted him from its consequences, and opened his way to a full participation in all the benefits of freedom. He was raised to an equality with the free class, become incorporated into it with his family, and might by good fortune or good conduct soon wash out the stain, and obliterate the remembrance of his former degraded condition.

But in the United States this is impossible. You may manumit the slave, but you cannot make him a white man. He still remains a negro or a mulatto. The mark and the recollection of his origin and former state still adhere to him; the feelings produced by that condition, in his own mind and in the minds of the whites, still exist; he is associated by his colour, and by these recollections and feelings, with the class of slaves; and a barrier is thus raised between him and the whites, that is between him and the free class, which he can never hope to transcend. With the hope he gradually loses the desire. The debasement which was at first compulsory, has now become habitual and voluntary. The incitement to good conduct and exertion, which arises from the hope of raising himself or his family in the world, is a stranger to his breast. He looks forward to no distinction, aims at no excellence, and makes no effort beyond the supply of his daily wants; and the restraints of character being lost to him, he seeks regardless of the future to obtain that supply, by the means which cost him the least present trouble. The authority of the master being removed, and its place not being supplied by moral restraints or in incitements, he lives in idleness, and probably in vice, and obtains a precarious support by begging or theft. If he should avoid those extremes, and follow some regular course of industry, still the habits of thoughtless improvidence which he contracted while a slave himself or has caught from the slaves among whom he is forced to live, who of necessity are his companions and associates, prevent him from making any permanent provision for his support, by prudent foresight and economy, and in case of sickness, or of bodily disability from any other cause, send him to live as a pauper, at the expense of the community.

There are no doubt many honorable and some very distinguished exceptions; but I may safely appeal to the observation of every man, at all acquainted with the class of people in question, for the correctness of this picture.

Such a class must evidently be a burthen and a nuisance to the community; and every scheme which affords a prospect of removing so great an evil must deserve to be most favourably considered.

But it is not in themselves merely that the free people of colour are a nuisance and burthen. They contribute greatly to the corruption of the slaves, and to aggravate the evils of their condition, by rendering them idle discontented and disobedient. This also arises from the necessity under which the free black are, of remaining incorporated with the slaves, of associating habitually with them, and forming part of the same class in Society. The slave seeing his face companion live in idleness, or subsist however scantily or precariously by occasional and disultory employment, is apt to grow discontented with his own condition, and to regard as tyranny and injustice the authority which compels him to labour. Hence he is strongly incited to elude this authority by neglecting his work as much as possible, to withdraw himself from it altogether by flight, and sometimes to attempt direct resistance. This provokes or impels the master to a severity, which would not otherwise be thought necessary; and that severity, by rendering the slave still more discontented with his condition, and more hostile towards his master, by adding the sentiments of resentment and revenge to his original dissatisfaction, often renders him more idle and more worthless, and thus induce the real or supposed necessity of still greater harshness, on the part of the master. Such is the tendency of that comparison which the slave cannot easily avoid making, between his own situation and that of the free people of his own colour, who are his companions, and in every thing expect exemption from the authority of a master his equals: whose condition, though often much worse than his own, naturally appears better to him; and being continually under his observation, and in close contact with his feelings, is apt to chafe goad and irritate him incessantly. This effect indeed is not always produced, but such is the tendency of this state of things; and it operates more extensively, and with greater force, than is commonly supposed. But this effect, injurious as it must be to the character and conduct of the slaves, and consequently to their comfort and happiness, is far from being the worst that is produced by the existence of free blacks among us, a vast majority of the free blacks, as we have seen, are and must be an idle worthless and thievish race. It is with this part of

them that the slaves will necessarily associate, the most frequently and the most intimately. Free blacks of the better class, who gain a comfortable subsistence by regular industry, keep as much as possible aloof from the slaves, to whom in general they regard themselves as in some degree superior. Their association is confined as much as possible, to the better and more respectable class of slaves. But the idle and disorderly free blacks naturally seek the society of such slaves, as are disposed to be idle and disorderly too; whom they encourage to be more and more so, by their example, their conversation, and the shelter and means of concealment which they furnish. They encourage the slaves to theft, because they partake in its fruit. They receive secrete and dispose of the stolen goods; a part, and probably much the largest part, of which they often receive, as a reward for their services. They furnish places of meeting and hiding places in their house, for the idle and the vicious slaves; whose idleness and vice are thus increased and rendered more contagious. These hiding places and places of meeting are so many traps and snares, for the young and thoughtless slaves, who have not yet become vicious: so many schools in which they are taught, by precept and example, idleness lying debauchery drunkness and theft. The consequence of all this is very easily seen, and I am sure is severely felt in all places, where free people of colour exist in considerable numbers. That so many resist this contagion; that the free blacks themselves, as well as the slaves, do not become sill more generally profligate; is a strong and consoling proof that the race possesses a fund of good dispositions, and is capable in a proper situation and under proper management, of becoming a virtuous and happy people. To place them in a situation, to give them the benefit of such management, is the object of your noble enterprize; and surely no object is more entitled to approbation.

Great, however, as the benefits are, which we may thus promise ourselves, from the colonization of the free people of colour, by this tendency to prevent the discontent and corruption of our slaves, and to secure to them a better treatment by rendering them more worthy of it, there is another advantage infinitely greater, in every point of view, to which it may lead the way. It tends, and may powerfully tend, to rid us gradually and entirely, in the United States, of slaves and slavery: a great moral and political evil, of increasing virulence and extent from which much mischief is now felt and very great calamity in future in justly apprehended. It is in this point of view, I confess, that your scheme of colonization most strongly recommends itself, in my opinion, to attention and support. The alarming danger of cherishing in our bosom a distinct nation, which can never become incorporated with us, while it rapidly increases in numbers, and improves in intelligence; learning from us the arts of peace and war, the secret of its own strengths, and the talent of combining and directing its force; a nation which must ever be hostile to us, from feeling and interest, because it can never incorporate with us, nor participate in the advantages which we enjoy; the danger of such a nation in our bosom, need not be pointed our to any reflecting mind. It speaks not only to our understandings, but to our very senses: And however it may be derided by some or overlooked by others, who have not the ability or the time, or do not give themselves the trouble, to reflect on the estimate properly the force and extent of those great moral and physical causes, which prepare gradually and at length bring forth, the most terrible convalsions in civil society; it will not be viewed without deep and awful apprehension, by any who shall bring sound minds and some share of political knowledge and segacity, to the serious consideration of the subject. Such persons will give their most serious attention to any proposition, which has for its object the eradication of this terrible mischief, lurking in our vitals. I shall presently have occasion to advert a little to the manner in which your intended colony will conduce to this great end. It is therefore unnecessary to touch on it here. Indeed it is too obvious to required much explanation.

But independently of this view of the case, there is enough in the proposed measure to command our attention and support, on the score of benefit to ourselves.

No person who has seen the slave holding states, and those where slavery does not exist, and has compared ever so slightly their condition and situation, can have failed to be struck with the vast difference, in favour of the latter. This difference extends to every thing, except only the character and manners of most opulent and best educated people. These are very much the same every where. But in population, in the general diffusion of wealth and comfort, in public and private improvements, in the education manners and mode of life of the middle and labouring classes, in the face of the country, in roads bridges and inns, in schools, and churches, in the general advancement of improvement and prosperity, there is no companion. The change is seen the instant you cross the line, which separates the country where there are slaves, from that where there are none. Even in the same state, the parts where slaves most abound, are uniformly the worst cultivated the poorest, and the least populous; while wealth and improvement uniformly increase, as the number of slaves in the country diminishes. I might prove and illustrate this position by many examples, drawn from a comparison of different states, as Maryland and Pennsylvania, and between different countries on the same state, as Charles County and Frederick in Maryland; but it is unnecessary; because every body who has seen the different parts of the country, has seen struck by this difference.

Where does it arise? I answer from this; that in one division of country the land is cultivated by freemen, for their own benefit, and in the other almost entirely by slaves, for the benefit of their masters. It is the obvious interest of the first class of laboures, to produce as much and consume as little as possible; and of the second class to consume as much and produce as little as possible. What the slave consumes is for himself: what he produces is for his master. All the time that he can withdraw from labour is gained to himself: all that he spends in labour is devoted to his master. All that the free labourer, on the contrary, can produce is for himself: all that he can save is so much added to his own stock. All the time that he loses from labour is his own loss.

This, if it were all, would probably be quite sufficient, to account for the whole difference in question. But unfortunately it is far from being all. Another and a still injurious effect of slavery remains to be considered.

Where the labouring class is composed wholly or in a very considerable degree of slaves, and of slaves distinguished from the free class by colour features and origin, the ideas of labour and of slavery soon become connected, in the minds of the free class. This arises from that association of ideas, which forms on the characteristic features of the human mind, and with which every reflecting person is well acquainted. They who continually from their infancy see black slaves employed in labour, and forming by much the most numerous class of labourers, insensibly associate the ideas of labour and the slavery, and are almost irresistibly led to consider labour as a badge of slavery, and consequently as a degradation. To be idle, on the contrary, is in their view the mark of the privilege of freemen. The effect of this habitual feeling, upon that class of free whites which ought to labour, and consequently upon their condition, and the general condition of the country, will be readily perceived by those who reflect on such subjects. It is seen in the vast difference between the labouring class of whites in the southern and middle, and those of the northern and eastern states. Why are the latter incomparably more industrious, more thriving, more orderly, more comfortably situated, than the former? The effect is obvious, to all those who have travelled through the different parts of our country. What is the cause? It is found in the association between the idea of slavery, and the idea of labour; and in the feeling produced by this association, that labour the proper occupation of negro slaves, and especially agricultural labour, is degrading to a free white man.

Thus we see that where slavery exists the slave labours as little as possible, because all the time that he can withdraw from labour is saved to his own enjoyments; and consumes as much as possible, because what he consumes belongs to his master: while the free white man is insensibly but irresistibly led, to regard labour the occupation of slaves as a degradation, and to avoid it as much as he can. The effect of these combined and powerful causes, steadily and constantly operating in the same direction, may easily be conceived. It is seen in the striking difference which exists, between the slave-holding sections of our country, and those where slavery is not permitted.

It is therefore obvious that a vast benefit would be conferred on the country, and especially on the slave holding districts, if all the slave labourers could be gradually and imperceptibly withdrawn from cultivation, and their place supplied by free white labourers. I say gradually and imperceptibly; because if it were possible to withdraw suddenly and at once, so great a portion of the affective labour of the community, as is now supplied by slaves, it would be productive of the most disastrous consequences. It would create an immerse void, which could not be filled. It would impoverish a great part of the community, unhinge the whole frame of society in a large portion of our country, and probably end in the most destructive convulsions. But it is clearly impossible; and therefore we need not enlarge on the evils which it would produce.

But to accomplish this great and beneficial change, gradually and imperceptibly; to substitute a free white class of cultivators for the slaves, with the consent of the owners, by a slow but steady and certain operation; I hold to be as practicable as it would be beneficial: and I regard this scheme of colonization as the first step, it that great enterprize.

The considerations stated in the first part of this letter, have long since produced a thorough conviction in my mind, that the existence of a class of free people of colour in this country is highly injurious, to the whites the slaves and the free people of colour themselves: Consequently that all emancipation, to however small an extent, which permits the persons emancipated to remain in this country, is an evil, which must increase with the increase of the operation, and would become altogether intolerable, if extended to the whole, or even to a very large part, of the black population. I am therefore strongly opposed to emancipation, in every shape and degree, unless accompanied by colonization.

I may perhaps on some future occasion develope a plan, on which I have long meditated, for colonizing gradually and with the consent of their owners, and of themselves where free, the whole coloured population, slaves and all: but this is not the proper place for such an explanation, for which indeed I have not time now. But it is an essential part of the plan, and of every such plan, to prepare the way for its adoption and execution, by commencing a colony of blacks, in a suitable situation and under proper management. This is what your society propose to accomplish. Their project therefore, if rightly formed and well conducted will open the way for this more extensive and beneficial plan, of removing gradually and imperceptibly, but certainly, the whole coloured population from the country, and leaving its place to be imperceptibly supplied, as it would necessarily be, by a class of free white cultivators. In every part of the country this operation must necessarily be slow. In the southern and southern-western states it will be very long before it can be accomplished, and a very considerable time must probably elapse, before it can even commence. It will begin first, and be first completed, in the middle states; where the evils of slavery are most sensibly felt, the desire of getting rid of the slaves is already strong, and a greater facility exists of supplying their place, by white cultivators. From thence it will gradually extend to the south and south west; till by its steady constant and imperceptible operation, the evils of slavery shall be rooted out from every part of the United States, and the slaves themselves and their posterity shall be converted into a free civilized and great nation, in the country from which their progenitors were dragged, to be wretched themselves and a curse to the whites.

This great end is to be attained in no other way, than by a plan of universal colonization, founded on the consent of the slave holders, and of the colonists themselves. For such a plan that of the present colonization society opens and prepares the way, by exploring the ground, selecting a proper situation, and planting a colony, which may serve as a receptacle a nursery and a school for those that are to follow. It is in this point of view that I consider its benefits as the most extensive and important, though not the most immediate.

The advantages of this undertaking to which I have hitherto adverted, are confined to ourselves. They consist in ridding us to the free people of colour, and preparing the way for getting rid of the slaves and of slavery. In these points of view they are undoubtedly very great. But there are advantages to the free blacks themselves, to the slaves, and to the immense population of middle and southern Africa, which no less recommend this undertaking, to our cordial and zealous support.

To the free blacks themselves the benefits are the most obvious, and will be the most immediate. Here they are condemned to a state of hopeless inferiority, and consequent degradation. As they cannot emerge from this state, they lose by degree the hope and at last the desire of emerging. With this hope and desire they lose the most powerful incitements to industry, frugality, good conduct, and honourable exertion. For want of this incitement, this noble and ennobling emulation, they sink for the most part into a state of sloth wretchedness and profligacy. The few honorable exceptions serve merely to shew, of what the race is capable in a proper situation. Transplanted to a colony composed of themselves alone, they would enjoy real equality: in other words real freedom. They would become proprietors of land, master mechanics, ship owners, navigators and merchants, and by degrees school masters, justices of the peace, militia officers, ministers of religion, judges, and legislators. There would be no white population to remind them of, and to perpetuate, their original inferiority; but enjoying all the privileges of freedom, they would soon enjoy all its advantages, and all its dignity. The whites who might visit them as equals; for the purposes of a commerce mutually advantageous. They would soon feel the noble emulation to excel, which is the fruitful source of excellence, in all the various departments of life; and under the influence of this generous and powerful sentiment, united with the desire and hope of improving their condition, the most universal and active encitements to exertion among men, they would rise rapidly in the scale of existence, and soon become equal to the people of Europe or of European origin, so long their masters and oppressors. Of all this the most intelligent among them would soon become sensible. The others would learn it from them; and the prospect and hope of such blessings would have an immediate and most beneficial effect, on their condition and character. For it will be easy to adopt such regulations, as to exclude from this colony all but those who shall deserve by their conduct to be admitted: thus rendering the hope of admission a powerful incentive, to industry, honesty, and religion.

To the slaves the advantages, tho' not so obvious or immediate, are yet certain and great.

In the first place they would be greatly benefitted by the removal of the free blacks, who now corrupt them, and render them discontented: thus exposing them to harsher treatment, and greater privations. In the next place, this measure would open the way to their more frequent and easier manumission; for many persons who are now restrained from manumitting their slaves, by the conviction that they generally become a nuisance when manumitted in the country, would gladly give them freedom, if they were to be sent to a place where they might enjoy it, usefully to themselves and to Society. And lastly, as this species of manumission, attended by removal to a country where they might obtain all the advantages of freedom, would be a great blessing, and would soon be so considered by the slaves, the hope of deserving and obtaining it would be a great solace to their sufferings, and a powerful incitement to good conduct. It would thus tend to make them happier and better before it came, and to fit them better for usefulness and happiness afterwards.

Such a colony, too, would enlarge the range of civilization and commerce, and thus tend to the benefit of all civilized and commercial nations. In this benefit our own nation would most largely participate: because having founded the colony, and giving it constant supplies of new members, as well as its first and principal supply of necessaries and comforts, its first connections would be formed with us, and would naturally grow with its growth and our own, till they ripened into fixed habits of intercourse friendship and attachment.

The greatest benefit, however, to be hoped from this enterprize, that which in contemplation most delights the philanthropic mind, still remains to be unfolded. It is the benefit to Africa herself, from this return of her sons to her bosom, bearing with them arts knowledge and civilization, to which she has hitherto been a stranger. Cast your eyes my dear sir on this vast continent. Pass over the northern and north eastern parts, and the great desert, where sterility ferocious ignorance and fanaticism seem to hold exclusive and perpetual sway. Fix your attention on Soudan, and the widely extended regions to the South. You see there innumerable tribes and nations of blacks, mild and humane in their dispositions, sufficiently intelligent, robust active and vigorous, not averse from laborer or wholly ignorant of agriculture, and possessing some knowledge of the ruder arts, which minister to the first wants of civilized man. You see a soil generally fertile, a climate healthy for the natives, and a mighty river, which rolls its waters through vast regions inhabited by these tribes, and seems destined by an all wise and beneficient Providence, one day to connect them with each other, and all of them with the rest of the world, in the relations of commerce and friendly intercourse. What a field is here presented for the blessings of civilization and christianity, which colonies of civilized blacks afford the best and probably the only means of introducing!! These colonies, composed of blacks already instructed in the arts of civilized life, and the truths of the gospel; judiciously placed, well conducted, and constantly enlarged; will extend gradually into the interior, will from commercial and political connections with the native tribes in their vicinity, will extend those connections to tribes more and more remote, will incorporate many of the natives with the colonies, and in their turn make establishments and settlements among the natives, and thus diffuse all around the arts of civilization, and the benefits of literary moral and religious instruction.

That such must be the tendency of colonies of this description, if well placed well formed and well conducted, cannot I think be reasonably doubted. Such a colony has already been established, with satisfactory success, and flattering prospects. But it may be doubted perhaps whether the situation has been fortunably chosen, with respect to all the objects that ought to be kept in view; and it is still more questionable whether a sufficient supply of colonists, of proper discription, to give it the extent necessary for rendering it in any considerable degree beneficial, can be drawn from the sources on which it must rely. It is in the United States alone that such colonists can be found, in any considerable numbers. In the choice of a good situation too, on which so much depends, we have far more assistance from recent discoveries, and the extension of geographical knowledge in that quarter of the globe, than was possessed by the founders of that colony. We have the benefit of their experience, of their discoveries, and even of their errors; which we may be able to correct or avoid. Useful therefore and meritorious as their establishment certainly is, we may hope to render ours far more extensively beneficial.

An objection of some plausibility is frequently urged, against this scheme of colonizing the free people of colour, which it may be proper in this place to notice. These people it is said, especially the industrious and estimable part of them, will not go to the new colony. That many of them will decline to go at first, and some always, cannot be doubted. It is even probable, and may be safely admitted, that but few of them now think favourably of the project: for men, especially ignorant men, venture unwillingly upon great changes, the extent nature and consequences of which they are little capable of understanding. But it by no means follows that the same unwillingness or hesitation will continue, after the ground shall have been broken, the way opened, a settlement formed. In the first instant none will engage, but the most industrious intelligent and enterprizing, who are capable of discerning the advantages of the undertaking, and have resolution and energy enough to encounter its first hardships and risks. This is the case with all colonies, and especially those formed in distant unknown unsettled countries. Some resolute and adventurous spirits first embark; and they open and prepare the way for others. It is stated and believed, on evidence better known to you than to me, that a sufficient number of such persons stand ready at this time to commence the colony, as soon as the necessary previous arrangements can be made. I have no doubt of the fact, not only from information, but from general reasoning on the human character, and my knowledge of many individuals among the free blacks. When this first step is taken, and in most enterprizes the greatest difficulty lies in the first step; when a settlement of free blacks shall have actually been formed, the way opened, and the first difficulties surmounted; others will soon be disposed to follow. If successful and prosperous, as it certainly will be if properly conducted, its success will quickly become known to the free blacks, in every part of the country.

However distrustful of the whites, they will confide in the reports made to them by people of their own colour and class. The prosperity of the settlement, and the advantageous condition of the settlers, will soon be universally understood and believed; and indeed will be far more apt to be exaggerated than undervalued. The most ignorant and stupid of the free people of colour will speedily understand, or believe, that in the colony they may obtain a state of equality opulence and distinction, to which they can never aspire in this country. Hence the desire to join their friends and equals there, may be expected soon to become general among them: nor is it too much to hope and anticipate, that this desire will speedily grow into a passion; that the difficulty will be not to find colonists, but to select them; and that the hope of being received into the favored number, for whom it may be practicable to provide annually, will ere long become a most powerful and operative, incentive, to industry sobriety and general good conduct, among the whole class from which the selection will be annually made.

Having detained you thus long, my dear sir, much too long I am afraid, with these preliminary observations on the benefits which may be expected from this undertaking, I proceed now to the manner of carrying it into execution. I shall not however treat this branch of the subject in its whole extent, for which this is not the proper place; but shall confine myself to the objects more immediately in view at this time; the choice of a proper situation for the first settlement, and the circumstances to which the attention of the agent who is to be sent out for the purpose of exploring the ground, ought chiefly to be directed.

The first of these circumstances is salubrity; with a view to which the vicinity of low and marshy grounds, of swamps, and of rivers which are apt to overflow their banks, ought to be carefully avoided. High situations, open to the sea, or washed by rivers with high and steep banks, should be sought. Mountains in the vicinity, and in the direction from which the winds regularly blow, are much to be desired; and great attention should be paid to the abundance of brooks and springs, and to the quality of their water. On all these accounts an elevated and uneven surface ought to be prefered, though less fertile than the flat low grounds. Too much attention ought not to be paid, in the first settlements, either to great fertility, or the convenience of navigation. The first establishment should no doubt be within a convenient distance from a good port, but need not be close to it; nor ought to be so, unless the unmediate vicinity should be much more healthy, than such situations usually are. The settlement must be entirely agricultural at first, and will long perhaps always continue so, in a very great degree. Commerce there, as in our own country, must and will soon grow out of agriculture; but the first settlements ought to be made with a view to the latter, far more than to the former. Contiguity to a good market for agricultural productions, is indeed a very important incitement and aid to agricultural industry, and therefore a very important circumstance in the location of an agricultural colony; but it is far from being the most important, and care must be taken to prevent its being too much regarded.

Nor ought any thing in this respect to be sacrificed to great fertility; which is most frequently found in low flat and unwholesome situations. A good soil, well adapted to the cultivation of wheat, Indian corn or maize, and cotton, is all in this respect that ought to be desired: and such soils are found in places possession every advantage of good water, with a dry and pure atmosphere. Wheat and Indian corn are the best articles of food, and the soils that produce them are fit also for various other grains and vegetables, useful for food and of easy culture; especially the sweet potatoe and various kinds of pulse, which thrive well in hot climates. As an object of tillage, with a view to exportation, cotton is by far the best, because it thrives well in high and healthy situations, of a light soil, may be cultivated to advantage on small farms, and requires little labour which cannot be performed by women and children.

Attention should also be paid to suitable streams for the erection of grist mills, saw mills, and other water works, which will be almost indispensable to the colony in its infant state, and of great utility at a more advanced period. Fortunately such streams abound most, in the countries best adapted in other respects to agricultural settlements.

The character condition and disposition of the natives will also require very particular attention; it being of the greatest importance to gain and preserve their good will, so as to cultivate and cement a free and friendly intercourse with them, obtain from them assistance and supplies, and gradually communicate to them the knowledge and habits of civilized life. For this essential purpose we should not only avoid the neighourhood of fierce and warlike tribes, but that of very large and powerful ones; who will be much more unmanageable and dangerous than small ones, in many points of view.

It would also be best to select a situation as distant as possible from Sierra Leone. There would no doubt be some advantages, at first, in a close neighbourhood; but they would probably be soon overbalanced, by the jealousies and collisions which could hardly fail to take place, between two colonies established under different governments, and with different views and interests in many important points. This is an objection to Sherborough river; probably not insurmountable, but sufficient to turn the scale in favour of a more distant position, possessing in other respects equal or nearly equal advantages.

If indeed an arrangement could be made with the British government, for an union and incorporation of the two colonies, or rather for the reception of our colonists into their settlement, it might deserve serious consideration. There would no doubt be many advantages, at first, in sending them to a settlement already formed, where the first difficulties have been surmounted, and a regular government exists. But this is matter for future deliberation. We ought now to search out a fit place for ourselves; for it is doubtful whether an incorporation would be agreed to by the British government, and far from being certain that the best place has been chosen for their establishment. When these points shall have been ascertained, and we know what prospect there is of obtaining a suitable situation elsewhere, a negociation may be opened, if then thought advisable, for uniting the two colonies. There will always be one strong objection to the incorporation. The British colony will be for a long time retained in the colonial state, subject to a foreign and distant government; and when ripe for independence, will probably be compelled to seek it by force of arms. The nature and habitual policy of that government will almost necessarily lead to this result. Our colony, on the contrary, ought to be republican from the beginning, and formed and fashioned with a view to self-government and independence, with the consent of the mother country, at the earliest practicable period. It is thus only that it can be most useful to the colonists, to Africa, to us, and to the general cause of humanity.

It would, however be premature at present, to decide on the question of incorporation; and therefore with a view to this interesting part of the case, the agent should be instructed to investigate most carefully, the progress and present state of the Sierra Leone settlement, and to ascertain as exactly as possible all the circumstances of its locality, as relates to health, fertility, objects of culture suitable to its soil and climate, navigation, the nature of the country in its vicinity, the character situation and strength of the neighbouring tribes, and the facilities of communication with the remote and interior parts of the continent.

One very important circumstance, in the selection of a suitable place for our settlements, to which the attention of the agent ought to be particularly directed, still remains to be brought into view. I mean the facility of communication with the Niger, that mighty river, which seems destined to supply the link of connection, between the interior of Africa and the civilized world.

I take the question relative to the lower course and termination of the Niger to be now satisfactorily settled. The discoveries of Park in his last journey; compared and connected with the information derived from Mr. Maxwell and others, concerning the river Zayr, improperly called the Congo, from the name of a little district at its mouth, to say nothing of Sidi Hamets narrative as given to us by Captain Riley, which deserves great attention, authorize us I think to conclude, that these two rivers are the same: in other words that the Niger, after having traversed the interior of Africa four thousand miles, falls under the name of the Zayr into the Atlantic, south of the equator: thus laying open that vast continent to its inmost recesses, and bringing its immense population into contact with the rest of the world. There is some doubt and much contrariety of opinion on this point, and this is not the place for entering at large into the discussion. Fortunately a decision of the question, which cannot be absolutely decided till the course of the Niger shall be pursued to its termination, is not necessary for our present purpose; for whether this great body of waters, collected in a course of two thousand miles, be lost according to the opinion of some, in the sands marshes and lakes supposed to exist in the centre of Africa; or, as others have imagined, be discharged into the Mediterranean through the Nile, a river of a more elivated bed, and hardly a tenth part as large; or being arrested in its progress castward, toward the

Indian ocean, by the elevited country in which the Nile has its sources, is driven through the feebler barrier of the mountains on the south, and thrown off to the southern Atlantic; it is still the only avenue into the interior of Africa: and a noble avenue it is. At Bammakoo, where Park struck it in his last voyage, he states it to be a mile wide. From thence to Houssa, a distance of between six and seven hundred miles, its course has been satisfactorily ascertained. Throughout this great extent, in which it receives many large streams, and flows through a fertile country, its current though strong is smooth and even, uninterrupted by cateracts or shoals. As it advances eastward, it recedes more and more from the coast, and thus becomes more and more difficult of access. Settlements therefore on the Atlantic, formed with a view to commercial intercourse with the vast countries on the Niger, and those more distant to which it leads, must be placed as near as possible to its upper waters, where they first begin to be navigable for boats.

These waters probably approach much nearer the Atlantic than has hitherto been believed. We have seen that at Bammakoo, the highest point to which it has yet been traced, it is a mile wide: as large as the Susquehanna at its entrance into the Chesapeake bay. It must therefore be a very considerable stream, much higher up: that is much further to the southwest, and consequently much nearer to the Atlantic. It has its source in the western part of a chain of mountains, which runs from west to east, nearly parallel with that part of the coast of Africa which extends from Sierra Leone to the Bite of Benin. These mountains seperate it from the rivers which, rising on their southern side, fall into the Atlantic, in the neighbourhood of Sierra Leone. Their sources no doubt approach very near to those of the Niger: Probably no great distance divides its navigable waters from theirs. Such a river, with a good port at or near its mouth, and a fertile country on its banks, would present the proper situation for a colony, planted with a view to the civilization of Africa, by the commerce of the Niger.

The course of such a commerce would be, to ascend the Atlantic river as far as possible in boats,

with the commodities wanted for the interior consumption; and to establish at that point a place of deposit, from whence the merchandize would be sent over land to the Niger, and down it to the various markets below. The returns would go up the Niger to its highest navigable point, where a town would soon arise. From thence they would pass by land to the place of deposit on the other side of the mountain; and there be put into boats, for transportation down the river to the shipping port. If the Niger should be ascertained to continue its course to the ocean, an intercourse would gradually be extended down to its mouth, where a great commercial city would arise; and to this mart the return cargoes purchased above would gradually find their way, down the stream. Thus an immense circle of commerce would imperceptibly be formed, embracing the whole course of the Niger, and the vast countries which it waters and lays open, and connecting them all with each other, and with the whole commercial world. For a very considerable time this commerce would be confined to the countries far up the river, near to its source; where settlements would first be formed, and civilization would commence. As the communication between these first settlements and those on the Atlantic became more and more safe easy and expeditious, by means of intermediate settlements good roads and improved inland navigation, colonies and trade would extend further and further down the river. Other settlements would soon be commenced at its mouth. At last these two branches would meet and unite, in a commerce vast as the stream on which it would be borne, and as the continent which it civilize enlighten and adorn.

Ages indeed may be required, for the full attainment of these objects. Untoward events or unforeseen difficulties may retard or defeat them: But the prospect however remote or uncertain is still animating, and the hope of success seems sufficient to stimulate us to the utmost exertion. How vast and sublime a career does this undertaking open, to a generous ambition, aspiring to deathless fame by great and useful actions! Who can count the millions, that in future times shall know and bless the names of those, by whom this magnificent scheme of beneficence and philanthrophy has been conceived, and shall be carried into execution? Throughout the widely extended regions of middle and southern Africa, then filled with populous and polished nations, their memories shall be cherished and their praises sung; when other states, and even the flourishing and vigorous nation to which they belong, now in its flower of youth, shall have run their round of rise grandeur and decay, and like the founders of Palmyra Tyre Babylon Memphis and Thebes shall no longer be known, except by vague reports of their former greatness, or by some fragments of those works of art, the monuments of their taste their power or their pride, which they may leave behind.

It is in connection my dear sir with this great operation, that I consider your proposed colony of free blacks as most interesting and important. It ought to be the first step in this splendid career, and to be located with that view. In choosing a situation for it, therefore, the greatest regard ought to be had to its future connection with the Niger. To this end the agent ought to be instructed, to make the most careful enquiries concerning the sources of that river, and its highest or most southwestern point. He should also make every effort to obtain the most full and accurate information, concerning the rivers that rise in the mountains opposite to its sources, and take their course southwestardly to the ocean. Their size, the nature of the country through which they flow, the height to which they are navigable for ships and for boats, and the harbours at or near their mouths, should all be ascertained with the utmost care and accuracy. That river which combines in the greatest degree, the advantages of salubrity soil navigation and good neighbourhood, and at the same time brings us nearest to the navigable waters of the Niger, by a good pass over the intervening mountains, is I apprehend the proper place, in itself, for the establishment of our colony.

I say in itself: because a place combining all those advantages may still be very unfit for our purpose, if it lie within the claims of any European power,

or too near any of their settlements. It should therefore be a particular object of the agents attention, to ascertain the situation and extent of those claims, and the distance between any European settlements, and such place as may appear suited to our views. Enquiries concerning the territorial claims of European powers can best be made in London; but it is in Africa alone that such information, when obtained, can be applied to the object of the intended mission.

There is a river called in some maps the Mesurada which, as there laid down, extends its branches further northeast than any other, and enters the ocean about one hundred or one hundred and fifty miles southeast of the Sherborough. It deserves I think the particular attention of the agent, who should be instructed to make enquiries about it, with a view to all the circumstances which may render it proper for a settlement, and to visit it, should the result of this investigation offer encouragement.

The river Nunez or Noones also merits particular regard. It empties itself into the Atlantic in latitude 10 1 North, about one hundred and fifty miles Northwest from Sierra Leone. It has a very good harbour at its mouth, and carries from six to eight fathom of water about twenty miles up to a bar, over which there is however three fathom, or eighteen feet. After passing the bar the water continues from five to eight fathom deep, to a point about fifty miles up from the mouth. From thence to the falls about fifty miles higher up, it is said to admit vessels of one hundred and twenty tons. The country around and above the falls is represented as elevated fertile and healthy; abounding in game, well supplied with excellent timber, and watered by numerous streams large enough for mills. Indian corn, and all sorts of pulse and garden vegetables, are said to grow luxuriantly. Cattle abound so much, that an ox is sold for a dollar. The country below yields rice, Indian corn, and all the usual tropical productions. The natives were represented as peaceable and friendly, and the principal chief, who resides about ninety miles up the river, a little below the falls, and whose authority extends down to the mouth, and far into the interior, is said to be a man of sense and abilities, of a mild and humane character, and favorably disposed towards the whites, and especially the Americans. He speaks English perfectly well. This place would seem therefore to deserve the particular attention of the agent and the society. In addition to its other advantages its upper waters approach near to those of the river Grande; a very important and interesting feature of African Geography, as respect commercial intercourse with the interior, and the extention of civilization by means of colonies of civilized blacks.

These, my dear sir, are the hints that I thought I might venture to suggest to you, on this most interesting subject. I make no apology for the length of my letter. It might no doubt to be curtailed with advantage. But it might also, and with more ease, if not a better purpose, be very much enlarged: for I have touched briefly on less important topics, and altogether omitted some which belong properly to the subject, but did not seem to require immediate attention. Such as it is I submit it to your consideration, with the hope that it may be of some use, in the preparatory arrangements which you are engaged in making.

With the best wishes I am dear sir

Your most obedient servant,

ROB. G. HARPER.

Elias B. Caldwell Esq.

Secretary of the Colonization

Society of the United States.

EDITORIAL FROM THE FIRST EDITION OF *FREEDOM'S JOURNAL* (1827)

To Our Patrons

In presenting our first number to our Patrons, we feel all the diffidence of persons entering upon a new and untried line of business. But a moment's reflection upon the noble objects, which we have in view by the publication of this Journal; the expediency of its appearance at this time, when so many schemes are in action concerning our peo-ple—encourage us to come boldly before an enlightened public. For we believe, that a paper devoted to the dissemination of useful knowledge among our brethren, and to their moral and religious improvement, must meet with the cordial approbation of every friend to humanity.

The peculiarities of this Journal, renders it important that we should advertise to the world our motives by which we are actuated, and the objects which we contemplate.

We wish to plead our own cause. Too long have others spoken for us. Too long has the public been deceived by misrepresentations, in things which concern us dearly, though in the estimation of some mere trifles; for though there are many in society who exercise towards us benevolent feelings; still (with sorrow we confess it) there are others who make it their business to enlarge upon the least trifle, which tends to the discredit of any person of colour; and pronounce anathemas and denounce our whole body for the misconduct of this guilty one. We are aware that there are many instances of vice among us, but we avow that it is because no one has taught its subjects to be virtuous; many instances of poverty, because no sufficient efforts accommodated to minds contracted by slavery, and deprived of early education have been made, to teach them how to husband their hard earnings, and to secure to themselves comfort.

Education being an object of the highest importance to the welfare of society, we shall endeavor to present just and adequate views of it, and to urge upon our brethren the necessity and expediency of training their children, while young, to habits of industry, and thus forming them for becoming useful members of society. It is surely time that we should awake from this lethargy of years, and make a concentrated effort for the education of our youth. We form a spoke in the human wheel, and it is necessary that we should understand our pendency on the different parts, and theirs on us, in order to perform our part with propriety.

Though not desiring of dictating, we shall feel it our incumbent duty to dwell occasionally upon the general principles and rules of economy. The world has grown too enlightened, to estimate any man's character by his personal appearance. Though all men acknowledge the excellency of Franklin's maxims, yet comparatively few practice upon them. We may deplore when it is too late, the neglect of these self-evident truths, but it avails little to mourn. Ours will be the task of admonishing our brethren on these points.

The civil rights of a people being of the greatest value, it shall ever be our duty to vindicate our brethren, when oppressed; and to lay the case before the public. We shall also urge upon our brethren, (who are qualified by the laws of the different states) the expediency of using their elective franchise; and of making an independent use of the same. We wish them not to become the tools of party.

And as much time is frequently lost, and wrong principles instilled, by the perusal of works of trivial importance, we shall consider it a part of our duty to recommend to our young readers, such authors as will not only enlarge their stock of useful knowledge, but such as will also serve to stimulate them to higher attainments in science.

WE trust also, that through the columns of the FREEDOM'S JOURNAL, many practical pieces, having for their bases, the improvement of our brethren, will be presented to them, from the pens of many of our respected friends, who have kindly promised their assistance.

It is our earnest wish to make our Journal a medium of intercourse between our brethren in the different states of this great confederacy: that through its columns an expression of our sentiments, on many interesting subjects which concern us, may be offered to the public: that plans which apparently are beneficial may be candidly discussed and properly weighed; if worth, receive our cordial approbation; if not, our marked disapprobation.

Useful knowledge of every kind, and everything that relates to Africa, shall find a ready admission into our columns; and as that vast continent becomes daily more known, we trust that many things will come to light, proving that the natives of it are neither so ignorant nor stupid as they have generally been supposed to be.

And while these important subjects shall occupy the columns of the FREEDOM'S JOURNAL, we would not be unmindful of our brethren who are still in the iron fetters of bondage. They are our kindred by all the ties of nature; and though but little can be effected to us, still let our sympathies be poured forth and our prayers in their behalf, ascend to Him who is able to succor them.

From the press and the pulpit we have suffered much by being incorrectly represented. Men whom we equally love and admire have not hesitated to represent us disadvantageously, without becoming personally acquainted with the true state of things, nor discerning between virtue and vice among us. The virtuous part of our people feel themselves sorely aggrieved under the existing state of things—they are not appreciated.

Our vices and our degradation are ever arrayed against us, but our virtues are passed by unnoticed. And what is still more lamentable, our friends, to whom we concede all the principles of humanity and religion, from these very causes seem to have fallen into the current of popular feeling and are imperceptibly floating on the stream—actually living in the practice of prejudice, while they abjure it in theory, and feel it not in their hearts. Is it not very desirable that such should know more of our actual condition; and of our efforts and feelings, that in forming or advocating plans for our amelioration, they may do it more understanding? In the spirit of candor and humility we intend by a simple representation of facts to lay our case before the public, with a view to arrest the progress of prejudice, and to shield ourselves against the consequent evils. We wish to conciliate all and to irritate none, yet we must be firm and unwavering in our principles, and persevering in our efforts.

If ignorance, poverty and degradation have hitherto been our unhappy lot; has the Eternal decree gone forth, that our race alone are to remain in this state, while knowledge and civilization are shedding their enlivening rays over the rest of the human family? The recent travels of Denham and Clapperton in the interior of Africa, and the interesting narrative which they have published; the establishment of the republic of Haiti after years of sanguinary warfare; its subsequent progress in all the arts of civilization; and the advancement of liberal ideas in South America, where despotism has given place to free governments, and where many of our brethren now fill important civil and military stations, prove the contrary.

The interesting fact that there are FIVE HUNDRED THOUSAND free persons of color, one half of whom might peruse, and the whole be benefitted by the publication of the Journal; that no publication, as yet, has been devoted exclusively to their improvement—that many selections from approved standard authors, which are within the reach of few, may occasionally be made—and more important still, that this large body of our citizens have no public channel—all serve to prove the real necessity, at present, for the appearance of the FREEDOM'S JOURNAL.

It shall ever be our desire so to conduct the editorial department of our paper as to give offence to none of our patrons; as nothing is farther from us than to make it the advocate of any partial views, either in politics or religion. What few days we can number, have been devoted to the improvement of our brethren; and it is our earnest wish that the remainder may be spent in the same delightful service.

In conclusion, whatever concerns us as a people, will ever find a ready admission into the FREEDOM'S JOURNAL, interwoven with all the principal news of the day.

And while every thing in our power shall be performed to support the character of our Journal, we would respectfully invite our numerous friends to assist by their communications, and our coloured brethren to strengthen our hands by their subscriptions, as our labour is one of common cause, and worthy of their consideration and support. And we most earnestly solicit the latter, that if at any time we should seem to be zealous, or too pointed in the inculcation of any important lesson, they will remember, that they are equally interested in the cause in which we are engaged, and attribute our zeal to the peculiarities of our situation; and our earnest engagedness in their well-being.

EDITORIAL FROM THE FIRST EDITION OF *THE LIBERATOR* (1831)

During my recent tour for the purpose of exciting the minds of the people by a series of discourses on the subject of slavery, every place that I visited gave fresh evidence of the fact, that a greater revolution in public sentiment was to be effected in the free states—and particularly in New England—than at the south. I found contempt more bitter, opposition more active, detraction more relentless, prejudice more stubborn, and apathy more frozen, than among slave owners themselves. Of course, there were individual exceptions to the contrary. This state of things afflicted, but did not dishearten me. I determined, at every hazard, to lift up the standard of emancipation in the eyes of the nation, within sight of Bunker Hill and in the birth place of liberty. That standard is now unfurled; and long may it float, unhurt by the spoliations of time or the missiles of a desperate foe—yea, till every chain be broken, and every bondman set free! Let Southern oppressors tremble—let their secret abettors tremble—let their Northern apologists tremble—let all the enemies of the persecuted blacks tremble.

I am aware that many object to the severity of my language; but is there not cause for severity? I will be as harsh as truth, and as uncompromising as justice. On this subject, I do not wish to think, or speak, or write, with moderation. No! No! Tell a man whose house is on fire to give a moderate alarm; tell the mother to gradually extricate her babe from the fire into which it has fallen;—but urge me not to use moderation in a cause like the present. I am in earnest—I will not equivocate—I will not excuse—I will not retreat a single inch— AND I WILL BE HEARD. . . .

William Lloyd Garrison

EXCERPT FROM THE AMERICAN ANTI-SLAVERY SOCIETY'S *AMERICAN SLAVERY AS IT IS* (1839)

READER, YOU are empaneled as a juror to try a plain case and bring in an honest verdict. The question at issue is not one of law, but of act— "What is the actual condition of slaves in the United States?"

A plainer case never went to jury. Look at it. TWENTY SEVEN HUNDRED THOUSAND PERSONS in this country, men, women, and children, are in SLAVERY. Is slavery, as a condition for human beings, good, bad, or indifferent?

We submit the question without argument. You have common sense, and conscience, and a human heart—pronounce upon it. You have a wife, or a husband, a child, a father, a mother, a brother or a sister—make the case your own, make it theirs, and bring in your verdict.

The case of Human Rights against Slavery has been adjudicated in the court of conscience times innumerable. The same verdict has always been rendered—"Guilty;" the same sentence has always been pronounced "Let it be accursed;" and human nature, with her million echoes, has rung it round the world in every language under heaven. "Let it be accursed. . . ."

As slaveholders and their apologists are volunteer witnesses in their own cause, and are flooding the world with testimony that their slaves are kindly treated; that they are well fed, well clothed, well housed, well lodged, moderately worked, and bountifully provided with all things needful for their comfort, we propose—first, to disprove their assertions by the testimony of a multitude of impartial witnesses, and then to put slaveholders themselves through a course of cross-questioning which will draw their condemnation out of their own mouths.

We will prove that the slaves in the United States are treated with barbarous inhumanity; that they are overworked, underfed, wretchedly clad and lodged, and have insufficient sleep; that they are often made to wear round their necks iron collars armed with prongs, to drag heavy chains and weights at their feet while working in the field, and to wear yokes and bells, and iron horns; that they are often kept confined in the stocks day and night for weeks together, made to wear gags in their mouths for hours or days, have some of their front teeth torn out or broken off, that they may be easily detected when they run away; that they are frequently flogged with terrible severity, have red pepper rubbed into their lacerated flesh, and hot brine, spirits of turpentine etc., poured over the gashes to increase the torture; that they are often stripped naked, their backs and limbs cut with knives, bruised and mangled by scores and hundreds of blows with the paddle, and terribly torn by the claws of cats, drawn over them by their tormentors; that they are often hunted with bloodhounds and shot down like beasts, or torn in pieces by dogs; that they are often suspended by the arms and whipped and beaten till they faint, and when revived by restoratives, beaten again till they faint, and sometimes till they die; that their ears are often cut off, their eyes knocked out, their bones broken, their flesh branded with red hot irons; that they are maimed, mutilated and burned to death, over slow fires. All these things, and more, and worse, we shall *prove.* . . .

We shall show, not merely that such deeds are committed, but that they are frequent; not done in corners, but before the sun; not in one of the slave states, but in all of them; not perpetrated by brutal overseers and drivers merely, but by magistrates, by legislators, by professors of religion, by preachers of the gospel, by governors of states, by "gentlemen of property and standing," and by delicate females moving in the "highest circles of society."

We know, full well, the outcry that will be made by multitudes, at these declarations; the multiform cavils, the flat denials, the charges of "exaggeration" and "falsehood" so often bandied, the sneers of affected contempt at the credulity that can believe such things, and the rage and imprecations against those who give them currency. We know, too, the threadbare sophistries by which slaveholders and their apologists seek to evade such testimony. If they admit that such deeds are committed, they tell us that they are exceedingly rare, and therefore furnish no grounds for judging of the general treatment of slaves; that occasionally a brutal wretch in the *free* states barbarously butchers his wife, but that no one thinks of inferring from that, the general treatment of wives at the North and West.

They tell us, also, that the slaveholders of the South are proverbially hospitable, kind, and generous, and it is incredible that they can perpetrate such enormities upon human beings; further, that it is absurd to suppose that they would thus injure their own property, that self-interest would prompt them to treat their slaves with kindness, as none but fools and madmen wantonly destroy their own property; further, that Northern visitors at the South come back testifying to the kind treatment of the slaves, and that slaves themselves corroborate such representations. All these pleas, and scores of others, are build in every corner of the free States; and who that hath eyes to see, has not sickened at the blindness that saw not, at the palsy of heart that felt not, or at the cowardice and sycophancy that dared not expose such shallow fallacies. We are not to be turned from our purpose by such vapid babblings. In their appropriate places, we proposed to consider these objections and various others, and to show their emptiness and folly.

EDITORIAL FROM THE FIRST EDITION OF *THE NORTH STAR* (1847)

To Our Oppressed Countrymen

We solemnly dedicate the *North Star* to your cause, our long oppressed and plundered fellow countrymen. May God bless the offering to your good! It shall fearlessly assert your rights, faithfully proclaim your wrongs, and earnestly demand for you instant and even-handed justice. Giving no

quarter to slavery at the South, it will hold no truce with oppressors at the North. While it shall boldly advocate emancipation for our enslaved brethren, it will omit no opportunity to gain for the nominally free, complete enfranchisement. Every effort to injure or degrade you or your cause—originating wheresoever, or with whomsoever—shall find in it a constant, unswerving and inflexible foe.

We shall energetically assail the ramparts of Slavery and Prejudice, be they composed of church or state, and seek the destruction of every refuge of lies, under which tyranny may aim to conceal and protect itself. . . .

While our paper shall be mainly Anti-Slavery, its columns shall be freely opened to the candid and decorous discussions of all measures and topics of a moral and humane character, which may serve to enlighten, improve, and elevate mankind. Temperance, Peace, Capital Punishment, Education,—all subjects claiming the attention of the public mind may be freely and fully discussed here.

While advocating your rights, the *North Star* will strive to throw light on your duties: while it will not fail to make known your virtues, it will not shun to discover your faults. To be faithful to our foes it must be faithful to ourselves, in all things.

Remember that we are one, that our cause is one, and that we must help each other, if we would succeed. We have drunk to the dregs the bitter cup of slavery; we have worn the heavy yoke; we have sighed beneath our bonds, and writhed beneath the bloody lash;—cruel mementoes of our oneness are indelibly marked in our living flesh. We are one with you under the ban of prejudice and proscription—one with you under the slander of inferior—one with you in social and political disfranchisement. What you suffer, we suffer; what you endure, we endure. We are indissolubly united, and must fall or flourish together. . . .

We shall be the advocates of learning, from the very want of it, and shall most readily yield the deference due to men of education among us; but shall always bear in mind to accord most merit to those who have labored hardest, and overcome most, in the praiseworthy pursuit of knowledge, remembering "that the whole need not a physician, but they that are sick," and that "the strong ought to bear the infirmities of the weak."

Brethren, the first number of the paper is before you. It is dedicated to your cause. Through the kindness of our friends in England, we are in possession of an excellent printing press, types, and all other materials necessary for printing a paper. Shall this gift be blest to our good, or shall it result in our injury? It is for you to say. With your aid, cooperation and assistance, our enterprise will be entirely successful. We pledge ourselves that no effort on our part shall be wanting, and that no subscriber shall lose his subscription—" *The North Star* Shall live."

FUGITIVE SLAVE ACT CH. 60, 9 STAT. 462 (1850)

Section 5. That it shall be the duty of all marshals and deputy marshals to obey and execute all warrants and precepts issued under the provisions of this act, when to them directed; and should any marshal or deputy marshal refuse to receive such warrant, or other process, when tendered, or to use all proper means diligently to execute the same, he shall, on conviction thereof, be fined in the sum of one thousand dollars, to the use of such claimant, . . . and after arrest of such fugitive, by such marshal or his deputy, or whilst at any time in his custody under the provisions of this act, should such fugitive escape, whether with or without the assent of such marshal or his deputy, such marshal shall be liable, on his official bond, to be prosecuted for the benefit of such claimant, for the full value of the service or labor of said fugitive in the State, Territory, or District whence he escaped: and the better to enable the said commissioners, when thus appointed, to execute their duties faithfully and efficiently, in conformity with the requirements of the Constitution of the United States and of this act, they are hereby authorized and empowered, within their counties respectively, to appoint, . . . any one or more suitable per-

sons, from time to time, to execute all such warrants and other processes as may be issued by them in the lawful performance of their respective duties. . . .

Section 6. That when a person held to service or labor in any State or Territory of the United States, has heretofore or shall hereafter escape into another State or Territory of the United States, the person or persons to whom such service or labor may be due, . . . may pursue and reclaim such fugitive person, either by procuring a warrant from some one of the courts, judges, or commissioners aforesaid, of the proper circuit, district, or county, for the apprehension of such fugitive from service or labor, or by seizing and arresting such fugitive, where the same can be done without process, and by taking, or causing such person to be taken, forthwith before such court, judge, or commissioner, whose duty it shall be to hear and determine the case of such claimant in a summary manner; and upon satisfactory proof being made, by deposition of affidavit, in writing, to be taken and certified by such court, judge, or commissioner, or by other satisfactory testimony, duly taken and certified by some court, . . . and with proof, also by affidavit, of the identity of the person whose service or labor is claimed to be due as aforesaid, that the person so arrested does in fact owe service or labor to the person or persons claiming him or her, in the State or Territory from which such fugitive may have escaped as aforesaid, and that said person escaped, to make out and deliver to such claimant, his or her agent or attorney, a certificate setting forth the substantial facts as to the service or labor due from such fugitive to the claimant, and of his or her escape from the State or Territory in which he or she was arrested, with authority to such claimant, . . . to use such reasonable force and restraint as may be necessary, under the circumstances of the case, to take and remove such fugitive person back to the State or Territory whence he or she may have escaped as aforesaid.

Section 7. That any persons who shall knowingly and willingly obstruct, hinder, or prevent such claimant, his agent or attorney, or any person or persons lawfully assisting him, her, or them, from arresting such a fugitive from service or labor, either with or without process as aforesaid, or shall rescue, or attempt to rescue, such fugitive from service or labor, from the custody of such claimant, . . . or other person or persons lawfully assisting as aforesaid, when so arrested, . . . or shall aid, abet, or assist such person so owing service or labor as aforesaid, directly or indirectly, to escape from such claimant, . . . or shall harbor or conceal such fugitive, so as to prevent the discovery and arrest of such person, after notice or knowledge of the fact that such person was a fugitive from service or labor . . . shall, for either of said offenses, be subject to a fine not exceeding one thousand dollars, and imprisonment not exceeding six months . . . ; and shall moreover forfeit and pay, by way of civil damages to the party injured by such illegal conduct, the sum of one thousand dollars, for each fugitive so lost as aforesaid. . . .

Section 9. That, upon affidavit made by the claimant of such fugitive . . . that he has reason to apprehend that such fugitive will be rescued by force from his or their possession before he can be taken beyond the limits of the State in which the arrest is made, it shall be the duty of the officer making the arrest to retain such fugitive in his custody, and to remove him to the State whence he fled, and there to deliver him to said claimant, his agent, or attorney. And to this end, the officer aforesaid is hereby authorized and required to employ so many persons as he may deem necessary to overcome such force, and to retain them in his service so long as circumstances may require.

ACT TO SUPPRESS THE SLAVE TRADE IN THE DISTRICT OF COLUMBIA CH. 63, 9 STAT. 467 (1850)

Be it enacted, . . . That from and after January 1, 1851, it shall not be lawful to bring into the District of Columbia any slave whatsoever, for the purpose of being sold, or for the purpose of being placed in depot, to be subsequently transferred to any other State or place to be sold as merchandise. And if any slave shall be brought into the said District by its owner, or by the authority or consent of its owner, contrary to the provisions of this act, such slave shall thereupon become liberated and free.

FREDERICK DOUGLASS'S INDEPENDENCE DAY ADDRESS (1852)

Fellow Citizens

Pardon me, and allow me to ask, why am I called upon to speak here today? What have I or those I represent to do with your national independence? Are the great principles of political freedom and of natural justice, embodied in that Declaration of Independence, extended to us? And am I, therefore, called upon to bring our humble offering to the national altar, and to confess the benefits, and express devout gratitude for the blessings resulting from your independence to us?

Would to God, both for your sakes and ours, that an affirmative answer could be truthfully returned to these questions. Then would my task be light, and my burden easy and delightful. For who is there so cold that a nation's sympathy could not warm him? Who so obdurate and dead to the claims of gratitude, that would not thankfully acknowledge such priceless benefits? Who so stolid and selfish that would not give his voice to swell the hallelujahs of a nation's jubilee, when the chains of servitude had been torn from his limbs? I am not that man . . .

I am not included within the pale of this glorious anniversary! Your high independence only reveals the immeasurable distance between us. The blessings in which you this day rejoice are not enjoyed in common. The rich inheritance of justice, liberty, prosperity, and independence bequeathed by your fathers is shared by you, not by me. The sunlight that brought life and healing to you has brought stripes and death to me. This Fourth of July is *yours,* not *mine.* You may rejoice, I must mourn. To drag a man in fetters into the grand illuminated temple of liberty, and call upon him to join you in joyous anthems, were inhuman mockery and sacrilegious irony. Do you mean, citizens, to mock me, by asking me to speak today? . . .

Fellow citizens, above your national, tumultuous joy, I hear the mournful wail of millions, whose chains, heavy and grievous yesterday, are today rendered more intolerable by the jubilant shouts that reach them. If I do forget, if I do not remember those bleeding children of sorrow this day, "may my right hand forget her cunning, and may my tongue cleave to the roof of my mouth!" To forget them, to pass lightly over their wrongs, and to chime in with the popular theme, would be treason most scandalous and shocking, and would make me a reproach before God and the world. My subject, then, fellow citizens, is "American Slavery." I shall see this day and its popular characteristics from the slave's point of view. Standing here, identified with the American bondman, making his wrongs mine, I do not hesitate to declare, with all my soul, that the character and conduct of this nation never looked blacker to me than on this Fourth of July. Whether we turn to the declarations of the past, or to the professions of the present, the conduct of the nation seems equally hideous and revolting. America is false to the past, false to the present, and solemnly binds herself to be false to the future. Standing with God and the crushed and bleeding slave on this occasion, I will, in the name of humanity, which is outraged, in the name of Liberty, which is fettered, in the name of the Constitution and the Bible, which are disregarded and trampled upon, dare to call in question and to denounce, with all the emphasis I can command, everything that serves to perpetuate slavery—the great sin and shame of America! "I will not equivocate; I will not excuse"; I will use the severest language I can command, and yet not one word shall escape me that any man, whose judgment is not blinded by prejudice, or who is not at heart a slave-holder, shall not confess to be right and just.

But I fancy I hear some of my audience say it is just in this circumstances that you and your brother Abolitionists fail to make a favorable impression on the public mind. Would you argue more and denounce less, would you persuade more and rebuke less, your cause would be much more likely to succeed. But, I submit, where all is plain there is nothing to be argued. What point in the anti-slavery creed would you have me argue? On what branch of the subject do the people of this country need light? Must I undertake to prove that the slave is a man? That point is conceded already. Nobody doubts it. The slave-holders themselves acknowledge it in the enactment of laws for their government. They acknowledge it when they punish disobedience on the part of the slave. There are seventy-two crimes in the State of Virginia, which, if committed by a black man (no matter how ignorant he be), subject him to the punishment of death, while only two of these same crimes will subject a white man to like punishment. What is this but the acknowledgment that the slave is a moral, intellectual, and responsible being? The manhood of the slave is conceded. It is admitted in the fact that the Southern statute-books are covered with enactments, forbidding, under severe fines and penalties, the teaching of the slave to read and write. When you can point to any such laws in reference to the beasts of the field, then I may consent to argue the manhood of the slave. When the dogs in your streets, when the fowls of the air, when the cattle on your hills, when the fish of the sea, and the reptiles that crawl, shall be unable to distinguish the slave from a brute, then I will argue with you that the slave is a man!

For the present it is enough to affirm the equal manhood of the Negro race. Is it not astonishing that, while we are plowing, planting, and reaping, using all kinds of mechanical tools, erecting houses, constructing bridges, building ships, working in metals of brass, iron, copper, silver, and gold; that while we are reading, writing, and ciphering, acting as clerks, merchants, and secretaries, having among us lawyers, doctors, ministers, poets, authors, editors, orators, and teachers; that while we are engaged in all the enterprises common to other men—digging gold in California, capturing the whale in the Pacific, feeding sheep and cattle on the hillside, living, moving, acting, thinking, planning, living in families as husbands, wives, and children, and above all, confessing and worshipping the Christian God, and looking hopefully for life and immortality beyond the grave—we are called upon to prove that we are men?

Would you have me argue that man is entitled to liberty? That he is the rightful owner of his own body? You have already declared it. Must I argue the wrongfulness of slavery? Is that a question for republicans? Is it to be settled by the rules of logic and argumentation, as a matter beset with great difficulty, involving a doubtful application of the principle of justice, hard to understand? How should I look today in the presence of Americans, dividing and subdividing a discourse, to show that men have a natural right to freedom, speaking of it relatively and positively, negatively and affirmatively? To do so would be to make myself ridiculous, and to offer an insult to your understanding. There is not a man beneath the canopy of heaven who does not know that slavery is wrong *for him*.

What! Am I to argue that it is wrong to make men brutes, to rob them of their liberty, to work them without wages, to keep them ignorant of their relations to their fellow men, to beat them with sticks, to flay their flesh with the lash, to load their limbs with irons, to hunt them with dogs, to sell them at auction, to sunder their families, to knock out their teeth, to burn their flesh, to starve them into obedience and submission to their masters? Must I argue that a system thus marked with blood and stained with pollution is wrong? No; I will not. I have better employment for my time and strength than such arguments would imply.

What, then, remains to be argued? Is it that slavery is not divine; that God did not establish it; that our doctors of divinity are mistaken? There is blasphemy in the thought. That which is inhuman cannot be divine. Who can reason on such a proposition? They that can, may; I cannot. The time for such argument is past.

At a time like this, scorching irony, not convincing argument, is needed. Oh! had I the ability, and could I reach the nation's ear, I would today pour out a fiery stream of biting ridicule, blasting reproach, withering sarcasm, and stern rebuke. For it is not light that is needed, but fire; it is not the gentle shower, but thunder. We need the storm, the whirlwind, and the earthquake. The feeling of the nation must be quickened; the conscience of the nation must be startled; the hypocrisy of the nation must be exposed; and its crimes against God and man must be denounced.

What to the American slave is your Fourth of July? I answer, a day that reveals to him more than all other days of the year, the gross injustice and cruelty to which he is the constant victim. To him your celebration is a sham; your boasted liberty an unholy license; your national greatness, swelling vanity; your sounds of rejoicing are empty and heartless; your denunciation of tyrants, brass-fronted impudence; your shouts of liberty and equality, hollow mockery; your prayers and hymns, your sermons and thanksgivings, with all your religious parade and solemnity, are to him mere bombast, fraud, deception, impiety, and hypocrisy—a thin veil to cover up crimes which would disgrace a nation of savages. There is not a nation of the earth guilty of practices more shocking and bloody than are the people of these United States at this very hour.

Go where you may, search where you will, roam through all the monarchies and despotisms of the Old World, travel through South America, search out every abuse and when you have found the last, lay your facts by the side of the every-day practices of this nation, and you will say with me that, for revolting barbarity and shameless hypocrisy, America reigns without a rival.

MEMORIAL OF THIRTY THOUSAND DISFRANCHISED CITIZENS OF PHILADELPHIA, TO THE HONORABLE SENATE AND HOUSE OF REPRESENTATIVES.

PHILADELPHIA:

PRINTED FOR THE MEMORIALISTS,

At 22 South Third Street

1855

MEMORIAL

To the Honorable the Senate and House of Representatives of the Commonwealth of Pennsylvania, in General Assembly met. This Memorial of the "Colored Citizens" of this State, residents of the City of Philadelphia,

RESPECTFULLY SHEWETH,

THAT, after a disfranchisement of 17 years—after suffering all the injury, insult and outrage, consequent upon it,—our churches and other institutions pillaged and razed to the ground; our peaceful dwellings, erected by the labor of years, under the most discouraging and disadvantageous circumstances, invaded,—our persons assailed, cruelly-beaten, and in some cases, murdered with impunity, by ruthless ruffians, who boasted of their deeds of violence, alike regardless of the laws of God, of the land, and of common humanity; and, emboldened and encouraged by the acts of a convention, (miscalled Reform) that calmly and unjustifiably robbed us of those rights we had enjoyed under the Constitution for 47 years, thereby stamping us a race of vagabonds, paupers and criminals; for, by the articles of Confederation in 1778, none by paupers, vagabonds and fugitives from justice, were excluded from citizenship,—making our existence here one of mere toleration and sufferance, and leaving us a prey to every species of tyranny that may be practised upon a defenceless, unoffending people. Fresh in our recollections are the scenes, when mob-law ruled and triumphed over our city; when hundreds of harmless men, women and children were driven from their homes, to seek shelter and security on the banks of the Delaware, or on the meadows of the Schuykill, whose green and mossy beds were nightly occupied by these houseless wanderers—the victims of a prejudice, as heartless and relentless as it is mean and cowardly. Assaulted on the public streets, our wives, mothers and daughters insulted, and upon the slightest resistance, arrested and dragged before a magistrate, incapable of speaking our language correctly—whose only fitness for office consisted in his capacity to disgrace it. Forced from our places of business by a population incapable of comprehending the freedom of our institutions, and having no abiding interest in the welfare of our common country. They being candidates for those privileges of which we are debarred, gives them a power over us they too fatally use, and in imitation of that tyranny from which they have but recently escaped; they are ever ready to crus out the light of our souls, who, by disfranchisement, are reduced to a position beneath them. These are some of the evils of which your memorialists justly complain, and from their depressing effects our enfranchisement alone can redeem us. To attempt to enumerate all the wrongs inflicted upon us, would indeed be a Herculean task. These evils, these crimes, are the legitimate results of the monstrous doctrine promulgated by a Convention, that determined a man's rights by the curl of his hair—his citizenship by the color of his skin. But we trust that we shall find, at least before the legislative wisdom of this commonwealth, a tribunal worthy of the well-earned reputation of our native State, that will listen to the voice of truth and act in the spirit of justice. The Convention of 1838, by taking from us the right to voice, struck down that safeguard so indispensable to the protection, prosperity and happiness of every honest citizen; establishing a fearful precedent, by which any class of our citizens, white or colored, may be despoiled of their rights by an unprincipled majority; for by what other tenure hold you your privileges and claims to citizenship than those we present? Our relations to society are the same as all others; so all the rights, absolute and relative, belonging to all other citizens, from natural or acquired allegiance, or by general legislation. We are native Americans, and since allegiance is due from us, protection and equal rights are due from the Government. Here we take our position, and upon these principles demand our political privileges from this Commonwealth, which we are bound to aid and defend. Seventeen years continuations of this proscription does not palliate the wrong, but on the contrary augments the demand for its repeal. Against the concentrated injuries which the Reform Convention heaped upon us, we have remonstrated, memorialized, and petitioned in vain; we have waited patiently in the fond hope that the consciences of the people of this Commonwealth would be fully awakened to the magnitude and inhumanity of them. But, alas! in vain. To your Honorable bodies we now turn. In you, we expect to find the proper exponents of the declaration of the American Charter of Rights, and that independence of action which elucidates the true Republican character. We are citizens of the United States, as the articles of confederation between the States in 1778 indutiably show. The 4th of said articles declares, "The free inhabitants of each of those States—paupers, vagabonds, and fugitives from justice excepted, shall be entitled to all privileges and immunities of free citizens in the several States."

On the 25th of June, 1778, "the delegates from South Carolina moved the following amendment to the foregoing article, *in behalf of their own State.* In article 4th, between the words free inhabitants, insert the word *white.* Decided in the negative— ayes, two States; nays, eight States,—one State divided." Such was the righteous decision of the Convention prior to the adoption of the Constitution, and no change in that instrument has ever been made as to our right of citizenship. The Abolition Act of Pennsylvania, 1780, deliberately said, "That is was not for them to inquire why, in the creation of mankind, the inhabitants of the several parts of the earth are distinguished by a difference of feature and complexion," and had declared that all persons, of every nation and color should be "deemed, adjudged and holden to be freemen and free-women." The Constitution of 1790, adopting the same phraseology, says, "That every freeman having a residence and paying taxes, shall be an elector." Does our complexion exempt us from taxation? Certainly no. Taxation and representation, then, are among the fundamental principles of our Government. So long as the word white remains engrafted in the Constitution of this commonwealth, the practical conclusion is,

that we colored citizens shall not possess rights which belong to us, no matter how useful, virtuous and intelligent we may be. By retaining this discrimination, you violate a sacred principle without the plea or shadow of necessity. It was urged before the Convention in 1838, for the reforming of the Constitution, that expediency and conformity to the prejudices of the community required them to confine the elective franchise to the white population—that we were an inferior class and non-productive, and needed not those privileges which belong to other men. Expediency is always the pillar on which oppressors and tyrants lean. It is the vanguard in the army of iniquitous measures and practices. It is the support of every public wrong and the one argument against all public reform. If it were true that we are an inferior race, we would of necessity remain in that lower scale without the aid of legislative enactment. The very passage of such laws implies, our competency for intellectual and political equality, and declares louder than a million voices, that to confine use to degradation depends upon legislative enactments. We need not enlarge upon this humiliating topic. Enough has been said to show how abhorrent from all our notions of religious duty and rational behavior, is the conduct pursued against us, who are known only by our wrongs. The Constitution of 1790 did not recognize that intermediate state of being to which disfranchisement has reduced us. It said expressly the reverse; and declaring, as it did, that every freeman, complying with certain conditions, shall be a citizen in the broadest sense of the word, it said all that we now contend for, and demand at your hands. The phraseology of the Constitution was neither unadvised nor inconsiderate; there was very many free colored people in the Commonwealth at the time of its adoption. The meaning of the word, "freeman," was familiar to the intellectual and free-souled men who framed that instrument, and our existence and condition were formally brought before the Convention. The distinction which now degrades our Constitution may comport with the notions entertained by the oppressor, but it is abhorrent to the feelings of all honorable men, and cannot receive countence from them. The right to disfranchise citizens, guiltless of crime, is a modern device, spawned of a false democracy. Such was not the ideas of the heroes of the revolution, when our fathers stood in the same ranks of that army, which achieved for us all the liberties you *alone* enjoy. In the name of justice we ask what offence have we committed? Have we disgraced the State and abused the right of franchise, wherever we have possessed it, by the reception of bribes? Does there exist any act proving us recreant to these principles which adorn and beautify the citizen? No! We point you to the many honorable deeds accorded to our praise, and to the history of the past events of the revolution, whose pages are unsullied by the name of a sable traitor. By the act of 1791, giving the Supreme Court, the Attorney General and the Governor, authority to incorporate literary, charitable and religious associations, they are expressly limited to associations of *citizens;* and under that act, construed as it has been most cautiously in this very particular, we have had incorporated one hundred and eight Mutual Beneficial Societies, having 9,762 members; their annual income $29,600; permanent invested fund, $28,366; this amount is invested in various institutions among the *whites,* who derive a large per cent therefrom; 1,385 families were assisted by these societies during the year 1853; and the sums furnished amounted to $10,292.38; whole expenditure $27,347.02. It is evident from the above statement that these charitable institutions must materially relieve the distress of families, and maintain a large portion of our poor under privations and in circumstances which would otherwise throw them upon public relief. We have twenty-seven churches, with eight thousand members. Most of these congregations have Sunday schools taught by one hundred and eighty-three colored teachers, and attended by upwards of seventeen hundred scholars; we have also fifteen temperance societies, five public halls, three libraries, five literary associations, and twenty-seven private schools, sustained and taught by us.

By the following educational statistics and criminal reports, it will be seen that we compare favorably with the white population in intelligence, and morality.

The aggregate of pupils (whites) in the private and public schools in 1850, city and county of Philadelphia, were about 50,000—which is in proportion of 1 to every 10 of white population. Aggregate of colored pupils, 2,239—being 1 to every 10 of colored population. The colored population, therefore, are as assiduous in fitting their children to become good citizens as the other class, although they have not the same incentives. Another fact is important. By the census of 1840 there were in the State of Pennsylvania 1 in every 49 white adults that could not read or write, and by census of 1850, there were 1 in every 33; showing an increase (from whatever cause) of illiterate persons. And if rights are to be meted out according to educational preparation, the whites, as a whole, are not so fitted now to enjoy them as they were 10 years ago. Again, as to crimes among us: by a letter of Judge Kelly, written in answer to certain questions put to him, it is shown that for the three years up to 1854, the commitments of colored persons to the Philadelphia County Prison have gradually decreased, while those of the whites for the same period have markedly increased.

Your memorialists respectfully direct the attention of your Honorable bodies to the following opinions and facts set forth by the Hon. Joseph Hemphill, and others, of Pennsylvania, in speeches delivered in Congress, 1820, on the Missouri question.

HON. WILLIAM EUSTIS,

Late Governor of Massachusetts, and a Solider of the RevolutionExtracts from his Speech delivered in the Congress of the United States, Dec. 12, 1820, on the Missouri

The question to be determined, said Mr. *Eutis,* is, *whether* that article in the constitution of Missouri, requiring the legislature to provide by law "that free negroes and mulattoes shall not be admitted into the State," is, or is not, repugnant to that clause of the constitution of the United States which declares "that the citizens of each State shall be entitled to all the privileges and immunities of citizens in the several States." This is the question. Those who contend that the article is not repugnant to the constitution of the United States, take the position that free blacks and mulattoes are not citizens. *Now, I invite the gentlemen who maintain this, to go with me and examine this question to its root.*

The gentleman from Virginia says, that the term "We, the people," (in the preamble of our national constitution,) does not mean to include Indians, free negroes, or mulattoes. If it shall be made to appear that persons of this description, citizens at the time, were parties to, and formed an integral part of that compact, it follows that they are and must be included in it. To justify the inferences of gentlemen, the preamble should read, "We, the *white* people." But this was impossible; the members of the convention who formed the constitution, from the Middle and Northern States, could never have contend, knowing that there were in those States many thousands of people of color, who had rights under it. They were free—free from their masters. Yes, in the first instance they also became freemen of the State, and were admitted to all the rights and privileges of citizens. They enjoyed and exercised the rights of free citizens, and have continued to exercise them from the peace of 1783 to this day.

In Massachusetts they constituted, and were, in fact, an elementary part of the federal compact. They were as directly represented as the whites in the initiatory process; and from their votes, in common with those of the whites, emanated the convention of Massachusetts, by whom the federal constitution was received and ratified. Is not this proof? Is it not demonstration that they are entitled to, that they hold and exercise federal rights in common with our other citizens? If a doubt remains, it is answered by another important fact. They are also represented, not circuitously and indirectly, but *directly,* in this House. I very much doubt, Sir, if there be a member on this floor, from any one district in Massachusetts, whose election does not partake of the votes of these people.

Not only the rights, but the character of these men, do not appear to have been understood; nor is it to me at all extraordinary that gentlemen from other States, in which the condition, character, the moral faculties, and the rights of men of color differ so widely, should entertain opinions so varient from ours. In Massachusetts, sir, there are among them those who possess all the virtues which are deemed estimable in civil and social life. They have their public teachers of religion and morality—their schools and other institutions. On anniversaries, which they consider interesting to them, they have their public processions, in all which they conduct themselves with order and decorum. Now we ask only, that in a disposition to accommodate others, their avowed rights and privileges be not taken from them.

If their number be small, and they are feebly represented, we, to whom they are known, are proportionately bound to protect them. But their defence is not founded on their numbers; it rests on the immutable principles of justice. If there be only one family, or a solitary individual, who has rights guaranteed to him by the constitution, whatever may be his color or complexion, it is not in the power, nor can it be the inclination of Congress to deprive him of them. And I trust, sir, that the decision on this occasion will show that we will extend good faith even to the blacks.

Nat. Int., Jan. 2, 1831.

JOSEPH HEMPHILL, OF PENNSYLVANIA

Extracts from his Speech, delivered in Congress, December 11, 1820, on the Missouri Question.
ARE FREE BLACK PEOPLE CITIZENS OR NOT?

[Their condition at the time of forming the State Constitutions.] Mr. *Hemphill.* At this stage I beg the House to recollect, that previous to the adoption of the constitution of the United States, each State had the unquestionable right of saying who should compose its own citizens; and if, at the adoption of the constitution of the United States, free negroes and mulattoes were citizens of any

one State in the Union, the federal constitution gave to such citizens all the privileges and immunities of the citizens of the several States.

When our different constitutions were formed, this class of people lived among us; not in the character of foreigners—they were connected with no other nation; this was their native country, and as dear to them as to us, Thousands of them were free born, and they composed a part of the people in the several States; they were identified with the nation, and its wealth consisted in part of their labor. They had fought for their country, and were righteously included in the principles of the declaration of independence. This was their condition when the constitution of the United States was formed, and that high instrument does not cast the least shade of doubt upon any of their rights or privileges; I challenge gentlemen to examine it, with all the ability they are capable of, and see if it contains a single expression that deprives them of any privilege that is bestowed upon others.

[Their personal rights.]

They have a right to pursue their own happiness in as high degree as any other class of people. Their situation is similar to others in relation to the acquirement of property and the various pursuits of industry. They are entitled to the same rights of religion and protection, and are subject to the same punishments. They are enumerated in the census. They can be taxed, and made liable to militia duty. They are denied none of the privileges contained in the bill of rights. And although many of these advantages are allowed a strange during his temporary residence, yet in no instance is a free native black man treated as a foreigner.

When they enjoy all these rights, civil and religious, equally with the white people; and when they all flow from the same nation of them, I have a curiosity to learn upon what principle any right can be singled out as one of which they are to be deprived.

I appeal to the public transactions of this country, to the different constitutions and to the laws, for the correctness of this position; that whenever exceptions are intended to be made in regard to this class of people, that it requires express provisions for the purpose. It is said that they are not witnesses in some States; but it requires a particular law to render them incompetent to given testimony.

[Citizenship.]

As to citizenship—if being a native, and free born, and of parents belonging to no other nation or tribe, does not constitute a citizen in this country, I am at a loss to know in what manner citizenship is acquired by birth.

When a foreigner is naturalized he is only put in the place of a native freeman. This is the general idea of naturalization.

The word citizen, in its original sense, I believe only meant a free person of a city; it had no application here until after our independence; and then it had to be accommodated to the customary and peculiar character of our complex system. In our political acceptation of the word, it differs in theory and origin from allegiance; that was a feudal connection acknowledging the distinction of superior and inferior. It was a species of slaves tenure. But citizenship is rather in the notion of a compact, expressly or tacitly made; it is a political tie, and the mutual obligations are, allegiance and protection.

[Impressed Seamen.]

If our free black population should be impressed in a foreign port, how could we redress the wrong, if we have no political connection with them—if they do not belong to our political family? Previous to the revolution they were British subjects, and they were dissolved from any further connection with that nation at the same time with the white people; and it would be exceedingly strange, if from that moment they ceased to be connected with any political society. Cases are familiar where they assume, not only the appearance, but the reality of a citizenship. If they should engage in commerce, none of the regulations as to foreigners would be applicable to them. Can there exists any doubt as to their capacity of sustaining actions in the federal courts in the character of citizens?

[Citizens by the law of Congress of 1783.]

And in the Journal of Congress, 1783, we are furnished with the opinion of Congress on this subject in terms equally clear and explicit, when it was resolved (with the exception of two States, one of which was divided,) "that all charges of war, and all the expenditures that had been, or shall be incurred for the common defence and general welfare, c, shall be defrayed out of the common treasury, which shall be supplied by the several States, in proportion to the whole number of *white and* OTHER *free citizens,* and the inhabitants of every age, sex, and condition, c."

Here it is acknowledged expressly, that there were other free citizens besides *white* citizens. If this will not convince gentlemen that free negroes and mulattoes were, from early times, considered as citizens, and composed a part of the people who chose the delegates to frame the federal constitution, it will be in vain for me to urge the matter further.

MR. STRONG, OF NEW YORK

Extracts from his Speech, delivered in Congress, Dec. 9th, 1820, on the Missouri Question.

[Characteristics of a Citizen.]

Are our free negroes and mulattoes citizens? Facts and experience in politics and morals, are better than definitions. The characteristics of a citizen are, the right of passing freely, and unmolested, from town to town, and place to place, within the State, and of residing, at pleasure, in any part of the same. That these rights belong to every one entitled to the high privileges of a citizen, I think will not be denied. All free persons have this right, except aliens, lunatics, vagabonds, and criminals.

The federal constitution knows but two descriptions of freemen. These descriptions are citizens and aliens. Now Congress can naturalize only aliens, i.e., persons who owe allegiance to a foreign Government. But a slave has no country, and owes no allegiance, except to his master. How, then, is he an alien? If restored to his liberty, and made a freeman, what is his national character? It must be determined by the federal constitution, and without reference to policy: for it respects personal liberty. Is it that of citizen or alien? But it has been shown that he is not an alien; may we not, therefore, conclude, may, are we not bound to conclude, that he is a citizen of the United States.

Facts are better than theories. In many of the States they are recognized as citizens, and are, among other things, eligible to office, entitled to hold real estate, to vote, to sue, and to be sued. In some of the States, their fathers, with ours, fought the battles of the revolution. Vermont was admitted into the Union in 1791, and had then, and still has, free negroes and mulattoes, whose citizenship, by the citizens of that State, has never been doubted.

[Can prosecute in United States courts.]

I will refer again to the federal constitution. It is there declared, that the judicial power shall extend (among other cases) to controversies between citizens of different States. Now, any person in the State of Maryland who can prosecute a citizen of Virginia under this clause, must be a citizen of Maryland; and so of every other State. Is not this a sure criterion of citizenship? Who can then prosecute? Is there a *freeman* in the nation, not an alien, and domiciled in a State who cannot prosecute and be prosecuted in the federal courts? If there be one, it must be owing to some legal disability. Are *free* negroes and mulattoes, domiciled in a State, under any disability? The federal constitution interposes none, and I know no law or judicial decision that does. If they can prosecute in the federal courts, under this clause of the federal constitution, then they are citizens of the States.

HEZEKIAH NILES, OF BALTIMORE

This venerable gentlemen, in speaking of the Missouri question, says: "It is expressly provided *(Art. iv, Sec. 2, clause 1)* by the constitution of the United States, "that the citizens of each State shall be entitled to all the privileges and immunities of citizens in the several States." This is a very simple, plain, and imperative sentence. Free blacks and mulattoes are citizens in all the States, I believe, east of Delaware, as well as in the States northeast of the river Ohio, and they cannot be dispossessed of the right to locate themselves where they please.

The constitution of the United States equalizes the privileges of the citizens of the States, without respect to color or the country from whence they may be derived. This principle must be maintained. The few free blacks and mulattoes in the United States are not to be considered * * * * It is the disfranchisement of citizens who are citizens, and cannot be disfranchised. Shall we open the door to what may become the foulest proscriptions?

Nile's Register, Oct. 21, and Nov. 4, 1820, vol. xix pp. 113, 146.

We have no wish to go further into an argument of our rights as citizens, for we are fully aware that every member of your Honorable bodies is familiar with that question, as well as conscious of our value to the moral and pecuniary interests of our State. That we are a useful and productive class of citizens, the following facts will prove: We number 30,000 persons—residing in the city of Philadelphia—possessing at the present time of real and personal estate $2,685,693. We have paid for taxes, $9,766.42 during the last year; for house, water, and ground rent, $396,782.27. Here, then, is an addition to the wealth of the State, which requires something more than brute instinct to produce.

Return to us those rights of which we are deprived, and which you have so freely given to the sons of the men who fought against your independence, and you will have no class of citizens among you that will reflect more credit upon our state. Our loyalty—the most hardy hater of our race dare not gainsay—is proven by the readiness with which we hazarded our lives and property in those times "which tried the souls of men." We, if all other men, have the highest claims to the privilege of citizenship, since the first blood shed upon the altar of American Republicanism, and consecrated its soil to liberty and independence, was that of Crispus Attucks, a "colored man". In that trying

hour, the dubious twilight of our nation's history, when no reward seemed to await the heroes' struggles, when adversity, like a rigid sentinel, challenged the bold, the daring, and the brave; he, tinged with a complexion now scorned and despised, led on that little band of patriots whose deeds have given to Boston an immortality of fame, and fell the first martyr to the cause of justice, and the freedom of his native country. In every prominent battle of the revolution, and in the last war, our fathers stood shoulder to shoulder with yours,—at Bunker Hill, the battles of Lexington, Concord, Germantown, the storming of Red Bank, amid the horrors of Valley Forge, on the Banks of the Mobile, and on the Lakes with Perry. Of our services and sufferings in those eventful periods the following facts will clearly show:

The late Governor Eustis, of Massachusetts, the pride and boast of the democracy of the East— himself an active participant in the war, and, therefore, a most competent witness—Gov. Morrill, of New Hampshire, Judge Hemphill, of Pennsylvania, and other members of Congress, in the debate on the question of admitting Missouri as a Slave State into the Union, bore emphatic testimony to the efficiency and heroism of the black troops. Hon. Calvin Goodard, of Connecticut, states that, in the little circle of his residence, he was instrumental in securing, under the act of 1818, the pensions of nineteen colored soldiers. "I cannot," he says "refrain from mentioning one aged black man, Primus Babcock, who proudly presented to me an honorable discharge from service during the war, dated at the close of it, wholly in the handwriting of George Washington. Nor can I forget the expression of his feelings, when informed, after his discharge had been sent to the War Department, that it could not be returned. At his request it was written for, as he seemed inclined to spurn the pension, and reclaim the discharge." There is a touching anecdote related of Baron Steuben, on the occasion of the disbandonment of the American army. A black soldier, with his wounds unhealed, utterly destitute, stood on the wharf, just as a vessel bound for his distant home was getting under weigh. The poor fellow gazed at the vessel with tears in his eyes, and gave himself up in despair. The warm-hearted foreigner witnessed his emotion, and inquiring into the cause of it, took his last dollar from his purse, and gave it to him, with tears of sympathy trickling down his cheeks. Overwhelmed with gratitude, the poor wounded soldier hailed the sloop, and was received on board. As it moved out from the wharf, he cried back to his noble friend on shore, "God Almighty bless you, master Baron!"

"In Rhode Island," says Governor Eustis, in his able speech against slavery in Missouri, 12th of 12th month, 1820 "the blacks formed an entire regiment, and they discharged their duty with zeal and fidelity. The gallant defence of Red Bank, in which the black regiment bore a part, is among the proofs of their valor." In this contest, it will be recollected, that four hundred men met and repulsed, after a terrible and sanguinary struggle, fifteen hundred Hessian troops, headed by Count Donop. The glory of the defence of Red bank, which has been pronounced one of the most heroic actions of the war, belongs in reality to the black men; yet who now hears them spoken of in connection with it? Among the traits which distinguished the black regiment, was devotion to their officers. In the attack made upon the American lines near Crotan river, on the 13th of 5th month, 1781, Colonel Greene, the commander of the regiment, was cut down and mortally wounded; but the sabres of the enemy only reached him through the bodies of his faithful guard of blacks, who hovered over him to protect him, every one of whom was killed. The late Rev. Dr. Harris, of Dunbarton, New Hampshire, a revolutionary veteran, stated in a speech at Francestown, New Hampshire, some years ago, that on one occasion the regiment to which he was attached was commanded to defend an important position, which the enemy thrice assailed, and from which they were as often repulsed. "There was," said the venerable speaker, "a regiment of blacks in the same situation—a regiment of negroes fighting for our liberty and independence, not a white man

among them but the officers—in the same dangerous and responsible position. Had they been unfaithful, or given away before the enemy, all would have been lost. Three times in succession were they attached with most desperate fury by well- disciplined and veteran troops, and three times did they successfully repel the assault, and thus preserved the army. They fought thus through the war. They were brave and hardy troops.

In the debate of the New York Convention of 1821, for amending the Constitution of the State, on the question of extending the right of suffrage to the blacks, Dr. Clark, the delegate from Delaware County, and other members, made honorable mention of the services of the colored troops in the revolutionary army.

The late James Forten, of Philadelphia, well known as a colored man of wealth, intelligence, and philantrophy, enlisted in the American navy under Captain Decatur, of the Royal Louis, was taken prisoner during his second cruise, and, with nineteen other colored men, confined on board the horrible Jersey prison ship. All the vessels in the American service at that period were partly manned by blacks. The old citizens of Philadelphia to this day remember the fact, that when the troops of the North marched through the city, one or more colored companies were attached to nearly all the regiments.

Governor Eustis, in the speech before quoted, states that the free colored soldiers entered the ranks with the Whites. The time of those who were slaves were purchased of their masters, and they were induced to enter the service in consequence of a law of Congress by which, on condition of their serving in the ranks during the war, they were made freemen. This hope of liberty inspired them with courage to oppose their breasts to the Hessian bayonets at Red Bank, and enabled them to endure with fortitude the cold and famine of Valley Forge. The anecdote of the slave of General Sullivan, of New Hampshire, is well known. When his master told him that they were on the point of starting for the army, to fight for liberty, he shrewdly suggested that it would be a great satisfaction to know that he was indeed going to fight for his liberty. Struck with the reasonableness and justice of this suggestion, Gen. S. at once gave him his freedom.

The Hon. Tristram Burges, of Rhode Island, in a speech in Congress, 1st month, 1828, said:

> At the commencement of the revolutionary war, Rhode Island had a number of slaves. A regiment of them were enlisted into the Continental service, and no braver men met the enemy in battle; but not one of them was permitted to be a soldier until he had first been made a freeman.

The celebrated Charles Pinckney, of South Carolina, in his speech on the Missouri question, and in defence of the slave representation of the South, made the following admissions:

> They (the colored people) were in numerous instances the pioneers, and in all, the laborers of our armies. To their hands are owing the greatest part of the fortifications raised for the protection of our country. Fort Moultrie gave, at an early period of the inexperience and untried valour of our citizens, immortality to the American arms. And in the northern States numerous bodies of them were enrolled, and fought side by side with the whites at the battles of the Revolution.

Let us now look forward thirty or forty years, to the last war with Great Britain, and see whether the whites enjoyed a monopoly of patriotism at that time.

Said Martindale, of New York, in Congress, 22d of 1st month, 1828:

> Slaves, or negroes who had been slaves, were enlisted as soldiers in the war of the Revolution; and I myself saw a battalion of them, as fine martial-looking men as I ever saw, attached to the northern army, in the last war, on its march from Plattsburgh to Sackett's Harbor.

Hon. Charles Miner, of Pennsylvania, in Congress, 2nd month, 7th, 1828, said:

> The African race make excellent soldiers. Large numbers of them were with Perry, and helped to gain the brilliant victory of Lake Erie. A whole battalion of them were distinguished for their orderly appearance.

Dr. Clark, in the Convention which revised the Constitution of New York, in 1821, speaking of the colored inhabitants of the State, said:

> In your late war they contributed largely towards some of your most splendid victories. On Lake Erie and Champlain, where your fleets triumphed over a foe superior in numbers and engines of death, they were manned in a large proportion with men of color. And in this very house, in the fall of 1814, a bill passed, receiving the approbation of all the branches of your Government, authorizing the Governor to accept the services of a corps of 2,00 free people of color. Sir, these were times that tried men's souls. In these times it was no sporting matter to bear arms. These were times when a man who shouldered his musket did not know but he bared his bosom to receive a death wound from the enemy ere he laid it aside; and in these times these people were found as ready and as willing to volunteer in your service as any other. They were not compelled to go; they were not drafted. No; your pride had placed them beyond your compulsory power. But there was no necessity for its exercise; they were volunteers: yes, sir, volunteers to defend that very country from the inroads and ravages of a ruthless and vindictive foe, which had treated them with insult, degradation, and slavery.

On the capture of Washington by the British forces, it was judged expedient to fortify, without delay, the principal towns and cities exposed to similar attacks. The Vigilance Committee of Philadelphia waited upon three of the principal colored citizens, viz.: James Forten, Bishop Allen, and Absolom Jones, soliciting the aid of the people of color in erecting suitable defences for the city. Accordingly 2,500 colored men assembled in the

State House yard, and from thence marched to Gray's ferry, where they labored without intermission. Their labors were so faithful and efficient, that a vote of thanks was tendered them by the Committee. A battalion of colored troops was at the same time organized in the city, under an officer of the United States army; and they were on the point of marching to the frontier when peace was proclaimed.

Gen. Jackson's proclamations to the free colored inhabitants of Louisiana are well known. In his first, inviting them to take up arms, he said:

> As sons of freedom, you are now called on to defend our most inestimable blessings. As Americans, your country looks with confidence to her adopted children for a valorous support. As fathers, husbands, and brothers, you are summoned to rally around the standard of the Eagle, to defend all which is dear in existence.

The second proclamation is one of the highest compliments ever paid by a military chief to his soldiers:

To the Free People of Color

> Soldiers! When on the banks of the Mobile, I called you to take up arms, inviting you to partake the perils and glory of your white fellow citizens, I expected much from you, for I was not ignorant that you possessed qualities most formidable to an invading enemy. I knew with what fortitude you could endure hunger and thirst, and all the fatigues of a campaign. I knew well how you loved your native country, and that you, as well as ourselves, had to defend what man holds most dear—his parents, wife, children, and property. You have done more than I expected. In addition to the previous qualities I before knew you to possess, I found among you a noble enthusiasm, which leads to the performance of great things.

"Soldiers! The President of the United States shall hear how praiseworthy was your conduct in the hour of danger, and the Representatives of the Americans people will give you the praise your exploits entitle you to. Your General anticipates them in applauding your noble ardor.

Our right, then, to citizenship, is co-equal with the heroes of '76, and of the last war. The bones of our fathers have whitened every sanguinary field of the revolution— the blood trickling from their feet crimsoned the snows of Jersey.

With these facts before your Honorable bodies, showing our usefulness, fidelity and patriotism, and believing that you cannot but acknowledge that we are a peaceful, law-abiding people, we, therefore, ask you to interpose, in the fullness of your power, and remove that proscriptive clause from the Constitution, which so needlessly disgraces and alienates fifty-five thousand Pennsylvanian, whose property you tax, and at whose hands every service is required. We regret that our State should favor such a law—a State so distinguished for her early republican ardor, feeling, and attachment to justice. It was a most wanton and uncalled for persecution, and strengthens the prejudice already pervading the community against us, and makes Pennsylvania an ally in the unholy cause of oppression. In the name of the religion you profess, and the country you adore, we appeal to you for redress. The eyes of awakened nations, struggling for their rights, in the halls of legislation or on the field of battle, rest upon you. The spirits of your revolutionary sires, whose memories, venerated and revered, invite you, their unfettered and honored sons, to the performance of this act of justice. May that patriotism, which in the hour of need speaks a common language in a common cause, inspire you with a determination to restore to us those rights, purchased by our loyalty and by the blood of our fathers.

And your memorialists will ever pray.

Signed in behalf of the Colored Citizens of Philadelphia.

Jas. McCrummill,
Rev. Adam S. Driver,
Wm. P. Price,
N.W. Dupee,

Franklin Turner,
Wm. D. Forten,
Robt. B. Forten,
Committee.

DRED SCOTT V. SANDFORD 19 HOWARD 393 (1857)

The question is simply this: Can a negro, whose ancestors were imported into this country and sold as slaves, become a member of the political community formed and brought into existence by the constitution of the United States, and as such become entitled to all the rights, and privileges, and immunities, guaranteed by that instrument to the citizen?. . . .

The words "people of the United States" and "citizens" are synonymous terms, and mean the same thing. They both describe the political body who, according to our republican institutions, form the sovereignty, and who hold the power and conduct the government through their representatives. They are what we familiarly call the "sovereign people," and every citizen is one of this people, and a constituent member of this sovereignty. The question before us is, whether the class of persons described in the plea in abatement compose a portion of this people, and are constituent members of this sovereignty? We think they are not, and that they are not included, and were not intended to be included, under the word "citizens" in the constitution, and can therefore claim none of the rights and privileges which that instrument provides for and secures to citizens of the United States. On the contrary, they were at that time considered as a subordinate and inferior class of beings, who had been subjugated by the dominant race, and, whether emancipated or not, yet remained subject to their authority, and had no rights or privileges. . . .

It is not the province of the court to decide upon the justice or injustice, the policy or impolicy, of these laws. The decision of that question belonged to the political or law-making power; to those who formed the sovereignty and framed the constitution. The duty of the court is, to interpret the instrument they have framed, with the best lights we can obtain on the subject, and to administer it as we find it, according to its true intent and meaning when it was adopted.

In discussing this question, we must not confound the rights of citizenship which a State may confer within its own limits, and the rights of citizenship as member of the Union. It does not by any means follow, because he has all the rights and privileges of a citizen of a State, that he must be a citizen of the United States. He may have all of the rights and privileges of the citizen of a State, and yet not be entitled to the rights and privileges of a citizen in any other State. For, previous to the adoption of the constitution of the United States, every State had the undoubted right to confer on whomsoever it pleased the character of citizen, and to endow him with all its rights. But this character of course was confined to the boundaries of the State, and gave him no rights or privileges in other States beyond those secured to him by the laws of nations and the comity of States. Nor have the several States surrendered the power of conferring these rights and privileges by adopting the constitution of United States. . . .

It is very clear, therefore, that no State can, by any act or law of its own, passed since the adoption of the constitution, introduce a new member into the political community created by the constitution of the United States. It cannot make him a member of this community by making him a member of its own. And for the same reason it cannot introduce any person, or description of persons, who were not intended to be embraced in this new political family, which the constitution brought into existence, but were intended to be excluded from it.

The question then arises, whether the provisions of the constitution, in relation to the personal rights and privileges to which the citizen of a State should be entitled, embraced the negro African race, at that time in this country, or who might afterwards be imported, who had then or should afterwards be made free in any State; and to put it in the power of a single State to make him a citizen of the United States, and endue him with the full rights of citizenship in every other State without consent? Does the constitution of the United States act upon him whenever he shall be made free under the laws of a State, and raised there to the rank of a citizen, and immediately clothe him with all the privileges of a citizen in every other State, and in its own courts?

The court thinks the affirmative of these propositions cannot be maintained. And if it cannot, the plaintiff in error could not be a citizen of the State of Missouri, within the meaning of the constitution of the United States, and, consequently, was not entitled to sue in its courts.

It is true, every person, and every class and description of persons, who were at the time of the adoption of the constitution recognized as citizens in the several States, became also citizens of this new political body; but none other; it was formed by them, and for them and their posterity, but for no one else. And the personal rights and privileges guaranteed to citizens of this new sovereignty were intended to embrace those only who were then members of the several State communities, or who should afterwards by birthright or otherwise become members, according to the provisions of the constitution and the principles on which it was founded. . . .

In the opinion of the court, the legislation and histories of the times, and the language used in the declaration of independence, show, that neither the class of persons who had been imported as slaves, nor their descendants, whether they had become free or not, were then acknowledged as a part of the people, nor intended to be included in the general words used in that memorable instrument. . . .

. . . The government of the United States had no right to interfere for any other purpose but that protecting the rights of the owner, leaving it altogether with the several States to deal with this race, whether emancipated or not, as each State may think justice, humanity, and the interests and safety of society, require. . . .

The act of Congress, upon which the plaintiff relies, declares that slavery and involuntary servitude, except as a punishment for crime, shall be forever prohibited in all that part of the territory ceded by France, under the name of Louisiana, which lies north of thirty-six degrees thirty minutes north latitude and not included within the limits of Missouri. And the difficulty which meets us at the threshold of this part of the inquiry is whether Congress was authorized to pass this law under any of the powers granted to it by the Constitution; for, if the authority is not given by that instrument, it is the duty of this Court to declare it void and inoperative and incapable of conferring freedom upon anyone who is held as a slave under the laws of any one of the states. . . .

We do not mean . . . to question the power of Congress in this respect. The power to expand the territory of the United States by the admission of new states is plainly given; and in the construction of this power by all the departments of the government, it has been held to authorize the acquisition of territory, not fit for admission at the time, but to be admitted as soon as its population and situation would entitle it to admission. It is acquired to become a state and not to be held as a colony and governed by Congress with absolute Authority; and, as the propriety of admitting a new state is committed to the sound discretion of Congress, the power to acquire territory for that purpose, to be held by the United States until it is in a suitable condition to become a state upon an equal footing with the other states, must rest upon the same discretional. . . .

But the power of Congress over the person or property of a citizen can never be a mere discretionary power under our Constitution and form of government. The powers of the government and the rights and privileges of the citizen are regulated and plainly defined by the Constitution itself. . . .

These powers, and others, in relation to rights of person, which it is not necessary here to enumerate, are, in express and positive terms, denied to the general government; and the rights of private property have been guarded with equal care. Thus the rights of property are united with the rights of person and placed on the same ground by the Fifth Amendment to the Constitution, which provides that no person shall be deprived of life, liberty, and property without due process of law. And an act of Congress which deprives a citizen of the United States of his liberty of property, without due process of law, merely because he came himself or brought his property into a particular territory of the United States, and who had committed no offense against the law, could hardly be dignified with the name of due process of law. . . .

It seems, however, to be supposed that there is a difference between property in a slave and other property and that different rules may be applied to it in expounding Constitution of the United States. And the laws and usages of nations, and the writings of eminent jurists upon the relation of master and slave and their mutual rights and duties, and the powers which governments may exercise over it, have been dwelt upon in the argument.

But, in considering the question before us, it must be borne in mind that there is no law of nations standing between the people of the United States and their government and interfering with their relation to each other. The powers of the government and the rights of the citizen under it are positive and practical regulations plainly written down. The people of the United States have delegated to it certain enumerated powers and forbidden it to exercise others. It has no power over the person of property of a citizen but what the citizens of the United States have granted. And no laws or usages of other nations, or reasoning of statesmen of jurists upon the relations of master and slave, can enlarge the powers of the government or take from the citizens the rights they have reserved. And if the Constitution recognizes the right of property of the master in a slave, and makes no distinction between that description of property and other property owned by a citizen, no tribunal, acting under the authority of the United States, whether it be legislative, executive, or judicial, has a right to draw such a distinction or deny to it the benefit of the provisions and guaranties which have been provided for the protection of private property against the encroachments of the government.

Now, as we have already said in an earlier part of this opinion, upon a different point, the right of property in a slave is distinctly and expressly affirmed in the Constitution. The right to traffic in it, like an ordinary article of merchandise and property, was guaranteed to the citizens of the United States, in every state that might desire it, for twenty years. And the government in express terms is pledged to protect it in all future time if the slave escapes from his owner. That is done in plain words—too plain to be misunderstood. And no word can be found in the Constitution which gives Congress a greater power over slave property or which entitles property of that kind to less protection than property of any other description. The only power conferred is the power coupled with the duty of guarding and protecting the owner in his rights.

Upon these considerations it is the opinion of the court that the act of Congress which prohibited a citizen from holding and owning property of this kind in the territory of the United States north of the line therein mentioned is not warranted by the Constitution and is therefore void; and that neither Dred Scott himself, nor any of his family, were made free by being carried into this territory; even if they had been carried there by the owner with the intention of becoming a permanent resident. . . .

THE EMANCIPATION PROCLAMATION No. 17, 12 Stat. 1268 (1863)

By the President of the United States of America: A Proclamation

Whereas on the 22d day of September, A.D. 1862, a proclamation was issued by the President of the United States, containing, among other things, the following, to wit:

"That on the 1st day of January, A.D. 1863, all persons held as slaves within any State or designated part of a State the people whereof shall then be in rebellion against the United States shall be then, henceforward, and forever free; and the executive government of the United States, including the military and naval authority thereof, will recognize and maintain the freedom of such persons and will do no act or acts to repress such persons, or any of them, in any efforts they may make for their actual freedom."

"That the executive will on the 1st day of January aforesaid, by proclamation, designated the States and parts of States, if any, which the people thereof, respectively, shall then be in rebellion against the United States; and the fact that any State or the people thereof shall on that day be in good faith represented in the Congress of the United States by members chosen thereto at elections wherein a majority of the qualified voters of such States shall have participated shall, in the absence of strong countervailing testimony, be deemed conclusive evidence that such State and the people thereof are not then in rebellion against the United States.":

Now, therefore, I, Abraham Lincoln, President of the United States, by virtue of the power in me vested as Commander-in-Chief, of the Army and Navy of the United States in time of actual armed rebellion against the authority and government of the United States, and as a fit and necessary war measure for suppressing said rebellion, do, on this 1st day of January, A.D. 1863, and in accordance with my purpose so to do, publicly proclaimed for the full period of one hundred days from the first day above mentioned, order and designate as the States and parts of States wherein the people thereof, respectively, are this day in rebellion against the United States the following, to wit:

Arkansas, Texas, Louisiana (except the parishes of St. Bernard, Plaquemines, Jefferson, St. John, St. Charles, St. James, Ascension, Assumption, Terrebonne, Lafourche, St. Mary, St. Marti, and Orleans, including the city of New Orleans), Mississippi, Alabama, Florida, Georgia, South Carolina, North Carolina, and Virginia (except the forty-eight counties designated as West Virginia, and also the counties of Berkeley, Accomac, Northampton, Elizabeth City, York, Princess Anne, and Northfolk, including the cities of Norfolk and Portsmouth), and which excepted parts are for the

present left precisely as if this proclamation were not issued.

And by virtue of the power and for the purpose aforesaid, I do order and declare that all persons held as slaves within said designated States and parts of States are, and henceforward shall be, free; and that the Executive Government of the United States, including the military and naval authorities thereof, will recognize and maintain the freedom of said persons.

And I hereby enjoin upon the people so declared to be free to abstain from all violence, unless in necessary self-defense; and I recommend to them that, in all cases when allowed, they labor faithfully for reasonable wages.

And I further declare and make known that such persons of suitable condition will be received into the armed service of the United States to garrison forts, positions, stations, and other places, and to man vessels of all sorts in said service.

And upon this act, sincerely believed to be an act of justice, warranted by the Constitution upon military necessity, I invoke the considerate judgment of mankind and the gracious favor of Almighty God.

FREEDMEN'S BUREAU ACT CH. 90, 13 STAT. 507 (1865)

An Act to Establish a Bureau for the Relief of Freedmen and Refugees

Be it enacted, That there is hereby established in the War Department, to continue during the present war of rebellion, and for one year thereafter, a bureau of refugees, freedmen, and abandoned lands, to which shall be committed, as hereinafter provided, the supervision and management of all abandoned lands and the control of all subjects relating to refugees and freedmen from rebel states, or from any district of country within the territory embraced in the operations of the army, under such rules and regulations as may be prescribed by the head of the bureau and approved by the President. The said bureau shall be under the management and control of a commissioner to be appointed by the President, by and with the advice and consent of the Senate.

Section 2. That the Secretary of War may direct such issue of provisions, clothing, and fuel, as he may deem needful for the immediate and temporary shelter and supply of destitute and suffering refugees and freedmen and their wives and children, under such rules and regulations as he may direct.

Section 3. That the President may, by and with the advice and consent of the Senate, appoint an assistant commissioner for each of the states declared to be in insurrection, not exceeding ten in number, who shall, under the direction of the commissioner, aid in the execution of the provisions of this act. . . . And any military officer may be detailed and assigned to duty under this act without increase of pay of allowances. . . .

Section 4. That the commissioner, under the direction of the President, shall have authority to set apart, for the use of loyal refugees and freedmen, such tracts of land within the insurrectionary states as shall have been abandoned, or to which the United States shall have acquired title by confiscation or sale, or otherwise, and to every male citizen, whether refugee or freedman, as aforesaid, there shall be assigned not more than forty acres of such land, and the person to whom it was so assigned shall be protected in the use and enjoyment of the land for the term of three years at an annual rent not exceeding six per centum upon the value of such land, as it was appraised by the state authorities in the year eighteen hundred and sixty, for the purpose of taxation, and in case no such appraisal can be found, then the rental shall be based upon the estimated value of the land in said year, to be ascertained in such manner as the commissioner may by regulation prescribe. At the end of said term, or at any time during said term, the occupants of any parcels so assigned may purchase the land and receive such title thereto as the United States can convey, upon paying therefor the value of the land, as ascertained and fixed for the purpose of determining the annual rent aforesaid. . . .

AMENDMENT THIRTEEN TO THE UNITED STATES CONSTITUTION (1865)

Section 1. Neither slavery nor involuntary servitude, except as a punishment for crime whereof the party shall have been duly convicted, shall exist within the United States, or any place subject to their jurisdiction.

Section 2. Congress shall have power to enforce this article by appropriate legislation.

BLACK CODES OF MISSISSIPPI (1865)

An Act to Confer Civil Rights on Freedmen, and for other Purposes

Section 1. All freedmen, free negroes and mulatto es may sue and be sued, implead and be impleaded, in all the courts of law and equity of this State, and may acquire personal property, and choses in action, by descent or purchase, and may dispose of the same in the same manner and to the same extent that white persons may: Provided, That the provisions of this section shall not be so construed as to allow any freedman, free negro or mulatto to rent or lease any lands or tenements except in incorporated cities or towns, in which places the corporate authorities shall control the same.

Section 2. All freedmen, free negroes and mulattoes may intermarry with each other, in the same manner and under the same regulations that are provided by law for white persons: Provided, that the clerk of probate shall keep separate records of the same.

Section 3. All freedmen, free negroes or mullatoes who do now and have herebefore lived and cohabited together as husband and wife shall be taken and held in law as legally married, and the issue shall be taken and held as legitimate for all purposes; and it shall not be lawful for any freedman, free negro or mulatto to intermarry with any white person; nor for any person to intermarry with any freedman, free negro or mulatto; and any person who shall so intermarry shall be deemed guilty of felony, and on conviction thereof shall be confined in the State penitentiary for life; and those shall be deemed freedmen, free negroes and mulattoes who are of pure negro blood, and those descended from a negro to the third generation, inclusive, though one ancestor in each generation may have been a white person.

Section 4. In addition to cases in which freedmen, free negroes and mulattoes are now by law competent witnesses, freedmen, free negroes or mulattoes shall be competent in civil cases, when a party or parties to the suit, either plaintiff or plaintiffs, defendant or defendants; also in cases where freedmen, free negroes and mulattoes is or are either plaintiff or plaintiffs, defendant or defendants. They shall also be competent witnesses in all criminal prosecutions where the crime charged is alleged to have been committed by a white person upon or against the person or property of a freedman, free negro or mulatto: Provided, that in all cases said witnesses shall be examined in open court, on the stand; except, however, they may be examined before the grand jury, and shall in all cases be subject to the rules and tests of the common law as to competency and credibility.

Section 5. Every freedman, free negro and mulatto shall, on the second Monday of January, one thousand eight hundred and sixty-six, and annually thereafter, have a lawful home or employment, and shall have written evidence thereof as follows, to wit: if living in any incorporated city, town, or village, a license from the mayor thereof; and if living outside of an incorporated city, town, or village, from the member of the board of police of his beat, authorizing him or her to do irregular and job work; or a written contract, as provided in Section 6 in this act; which license may be revoked for cause at any time by the authority granting the same.

Section 6. All contracts for labor made with freedmen, free negroes and mulattoes for a longer period than one month shall be in writing, and a duplicate, attested and read to said freedman, free negro or mulatto by a beat, city or county officer, or two disinterested white persons of the county in which the labor is to be performed, of which each party shall have one: and said contracts shall be

taken and held as entire contracts, and if the laborer shall quit the service of the employer before the expiration of his term of service, without good cause, he shall forfeit his wages for that year up to the time of quitting.

Section 7. Every civil officer shall, and every person may, arrest and carry back to his or her legal employer any freedman, free negro, or mulatto who shall have quit the service of his or her employer before the expiration of his or her term of service without good cause; and said officer and person shall be entitled to receive for arresting and carrying back every deserting employee aforesaid the sum of five dollars, and ten cents per mile from the place of arrest to the place of delivery; and the same shall be paid by the employer, and held as a set off for so much against the wages of said deserting employee: Provided, that said arrested party, after being so returned, may appeal to the justice of the peace or member of the board of police of the county, who, on notice to the alleged employer, shall try summarily whether said appellant is legally employed by the alleged employer, and has good cause to quit said employer. Either party shall have the right of appeal to the county court, pending which the alleged deserter shall be remanded to the alleged employer or otherwise disposed of, as shall be right and just; and the decision of the county court shall be final.

Section 8. Upon affidavit made by the employer of any freedman, free negro or mulatto, or other credible person, before any justice of the peace or member of the board of police, that any freedman, free negro or mulatto legally employed by said employer has illegally deserted said employment, such justice of the peace or member of the board of police issue his warrant or warrants, returnable before himself or other such officer, to any sheriff, constable or special deputy, commanding him to arrest said deserter, and return him or her to said employer, and the like proceedings shall be had as provided in the preceding section; and it shall be lawful for any officer to whom such warrant shall be directed to execute said warrant in any county in this State; and that said warrant may be transmitted without endorsement to any like officer of another county, to be executed and returned as aforesaid; and the said employer shall pay the costs of said warrants and arrest and return, which shall be set off for so much against the wages of said deserter.

Section 9. If any person shall persuade or attempt to persuade, entice, or cause any freedman, free negro or mulatto to desert from the legal employment of any person before the expiration of his or her term of service, or shall knowingly employ any such deserting freedman, free negro or mulatto, or shall knowingly give or sell to any such deserting freedman, free negro or mulatto, any food, raiment, or other thing, he or she shall be guilty of a misdemeanor, and, upon conviction, shall be fined not less than twenty-five dollars and not more than two hundred dollars and costs; and if the said fine and costs shall not be immediately paid, the court shall sentence said convict to not exceeding two months imprisonment in the county jail, and he or she shall moreover be liable to the party injured in damages: Provided, if any person shall, or shall attempt to, persuade, entice, or cause any freedman, free negro or mulatto to desert from any legal employment of any person, with the view to employ said freedman, free negro or mullato without the limits of this State, such costs; and if said fine and costs shall not be immediately paid, the court shall sentence said convict to not exceeding six months imprisonment in the county jail.

Section 10. It shall be lawful for any freedman, free negro, or mulatto, to charge any white person, freedman, free negro or mulatto by affidavit, with any criminal offense against his or her person or property, and upon such affidavit the proper process shall be issued and executed as if said affidavit was made by a white person, and it shall be lawful for any freedman, free negro, or mulatto, in any action, suit or controversy pending, or about to be instituted in any court of law equity in this State, to make all needful and lawful affidavits as shall be necessary for the institution, prosecution or defense of such suit or controversy.

Section 11. The penal laws of this state, in all cases not otherwise specially provided for, shall apply and extend to all freedman, free negroes and mulattoes. . . .

An Act to Regulate the Relation of Master and Apprentice, as Relates to Freedmen, Free Negroes, and Mulattoes

Section 1. It shall be the duty of all sheriffs, justices of the peace, and other civil officers of the several counties in this State, to report to the probate courts of their respective counties semiannually, at the January and July terms of said courts, all freedmen, free negroes, and mulattoes, under the age of eighteen, in their respective counties, beats, or districts, who are orphans, or whose parent or parents have not the means or who refuse to provide for and support said minors; and thereupon it shall be the duty of said probate court to order the clerk of said court to apprentice said minors to some competent and suitable person on such terms as the court may direct, having a particular care to the interest of said minor: Provided, that the former owner of said minors shall have the preference when, in the opinion of the court, he or she shall be a suitable person for that purpose.

Section 2. The said court shall be fully satisfied that the person or persons to whom said minor shall be apprenticed shall be a suitable person to have the charge and care of said minor, and fully to protect the interest of said minor. The said court shall require the said master or mistress to execute bond and security, payable to the State of Mississippi, conditioned that he or she shall furnish said minor with sufficient food and clothing; to treat said minor humanely; furnish medical attention in case of sickness; teach, or cause to be taught, him or her to read and write, if under fifteen years old, and will conform to any law that may be hereafter passed for the regulation of the duties and relation of master and apprentice: Provided, that said apprentice shall be bound by indenture, in case of males, until they are twenty-one years old, and in case of females until they are eighteen years old.

Section 3. In the management and control of said apprentices, said master or mistress shall have the power to inflict such moderate corporeal chastisement as a father or guardian is allowed to infliction on his or her child or ward at common law: Provided, that in no case shall cruel or inhuman punishment be inflicted.

Section 4. If any apprentice shall leave the employment of his or her master or mistress, without his or her consent, said master or mistress may pursue and recapture said apprentice, and bring him or her before any justice of the peace of the county, whose duty it shall be to remand said apprentice to the service of his or her master or mistress; and in the event of a refusal on the part of said apprentice so to return, then said justice shall commit said apprentice to the jail of said county, on failure to give bond, to the next term of the county court; and it shall be the duty of said court at the first term thereafter to investigate said case, and if the court shall be of opinion that said apprentice left the employment of his or her master or mistress without good cause, to order him or her to be punished, as provided for the punishment of hired freedmen, as may be from time to time provided for by law for desertion, until he or she shall agree to return to the service of his or her master or mistress: Provided, that the court may grant continuances as in other cases: And provided further, that if the court shall believe that said apprentice had good cause to quit his said master or mistress, the court shall discharge said apprentice from said indenture, and also enter a judgment against the master or mistress for not more than one hundred dollars, for the use and benefit of said apprentice, to be collected on execution as in other cases.

Section 5. If any person entice away any apprentice from his or her master or mistress, or shall knowingly employ an apprentice, or furnish him or her food or clothing without the written consent of his or her master or mistress, or shall sell or give said apprentice spirits without such consent, said person so offending shall be guilty of a misdemeanor, and shall, upon conviction there of before the county court, be punished as provided for the punishment of persons enticing from their employer hired freedmen, free negroes or mulattoes.

Section 6. It shall be the duty of all civil officers of their respective counties to report any minors within their respective counties to said probate court who are subject to be apprenticed under the provisions of this act, from time to time as the facts may come to their knowledge, and it shall be the duty of said court from time to time as said minors shall be reported to them, or otherwise come to their knowledge, to apprentice said minors as hereinbefore provided.

Section 9. It shall be lawful for any freedman, free negro, or mulatto, having a minor child or children, to apprentice the said minor child or children, as provided for by this act.

Section 10. In all cases where the age of the freedman, free negro, or mulatto cannot be ascertained by record testimony, the judge of the county court shall fix the age. . . .

An Act to Amend the Vagrant Laws of the State

Section 1. All rogues and vagabonds, idle and dissipated persons, beggars, jugglers, or persons practicing unlawful games or plays, runaways, common drunkards, common night-walkers, pilferers, lewd, wanton, or lascivious persons, in speech or behavior, common railers and brawlers, persons who neglect their calling or employment, misspend what they earn, or do not provide for the support of themselves or their families, or dependents, and all other idle and disorderly persons, including all who neglect all lawful business, habitually misspend their time by frequenting houses of ill-fame, gaming-houses, or tippling shops, shall be deemed and considered vagrants, under the provisions of this act, and upon conviction thereof shall be fined not exceeding one hundred dollars, with all accruing costs, and be imprisoned, at the discretion of the court, not exceeding ten days.

Section 2. All freedmen, free negroes and mulattoes in this State, over the age of eighteen years, found on the second Monday in January, 1866, or thereafter, with no lawful employment or business, or found unlawfully assembling themselves together, either in the day or night time, and all white persons assembling themselves with freedmen, free negroes or mulattoes, or usually associating with freedmen, free negroes or mulattoes, on terms of equality, or living in adultery or fornication with a freed woman, freed negro or mulatto, shall be deemed vagrants, and on conviction thereof shall be fined in a sum not exceeding, in the case of a freedman, free negro or mulatto, fifty dollars, and a white man two hundred dollars, and imprisonment at the discretion of the court, the free negro not exceeding ten days, and the white man not exceeding six months.

Section 3. All justices of the peace, mayors, and aldermen of incorporated towns, counties, and cities of the several counties in this State shall have jurisdiction to try all questions of vagrancy in their respective towns, counties, and cities, and it is hereby made their duty, whenever they shall ascertain that any person or persons in their respective towns, and counties and cities are violating any of the provisions of this act, to have said party or parties arrested, and brought before them, and immediately investigate said charge, and, on conviction, punish said party or parties, as provided for herein. And it is hereby made the duty of all sheriffs, constables, town constables, and all such like officers, and city marshals, to report to some officer having jurisdiction all violations of any of the provisions of this act, and in case any officer shall fail or neglect any duty herein it shall be the duty of the county court to fine said officer, upon conviction, not exceeding one hundred dollars, to be paid into the county treasury for county purposes.

Section 4. Keepers of gaming houses, houses of prostitution, prostitutes, public or private, and all persons who derive their chief support in the employments that militate against good morals, or against law, shall be deemed and held to be vagrants.

Section 5. All fines and forfeitures collected by the provisions of this act shall be paid into the county treasury for general county purposes, and in case of any freedman, free negro or mulatto shall fail for five days after the imposition of any or forfeiture upon him or her for violation of any of the provisions of this act to pay the same, that it shall be, and is hereby, made the duty of the sheriff of the

proper county to hire out said freedman, free negro or mulatto, to any person who will, for the shortest period of service, pay said fine and forfeiture and all costs: Provided, a preference shall be given to the employer, if there be one, in which case the employer shall be entitled to deduct and retain the amount so paid from the wages of such freedman, free negro or mulatto, then due or to become due; and in case freedman, free negro or mulatto cannot hire out, he or she may be dealt with as a pauper.

Section 6. The same duties and liabilities existing among white persons of this State shall attach to freedmen, free negroes or mulattoes, to support their indigent families and all colored paupers; and that in order to secure a support for such indigent freedmen, free negroes, or mulattoes, it shall be lawful, and is hereby made the duty of the county police of each county in this State, to levy a poll or capitation tax on each and every freedman, free negro, or mulatto, between the ages of eighteen and sixty years, not to exceed the sum of one dollar annually to each person so taxed, which tax, when collected, shall be paid into the county treasurer's hands, and constitute a fund to be called the Freedman's Pauper Fund, which shall be applied by the commissioners of the poor for the maintenance of the poor of the freedmen, free negroes and mulattoes of this State, under such regulations as may be established by the boards of county police in the respective counties of this State.

Section 7. If any freedman, free negro, or mulatto shall fail or refuse to pay any tax levied according to the provisions of the sixth section of this act, it shall be *prima facie* evidence of vagrancy, and it shall be the duty of the sheriff to arrest such freedman, free negro, or mulatto, or such person refusing or neglecting to pay such tax, and proceed at once to hire for the shortest time such delinquent taxpayer to any one who will pay the said tax, with accruing costs, giving preference to the employer, if there be one.

Section 8. Any person feeling himself or herself aggrieved by judgment of any justice of the peace, mayor, or alderman in cases arising under this act, may within five days appeal to the next term of the county court of the proper county, upon giving bond and security in a sum not less than twenty-five dollars nor more than one hundred and fifty dollars, conditioned to appear and prosecute said appeal, and abide by the judgment of the county court; and said appeal shall be tried *de novo* in the county court, and the decision of the said court shall be final. . . .

CIVIL RIGHTS ACT CH. 31, 14 STAT. 27 (1866)

An Act to protect all Persons in the United States in their Civil Rights, and furnish the Means of their Vindication

Be it enacted . . . That all persons born in the United States and not subject to any foreign power, excluding Indians not taxed, are hereby declared to be citizens of the United States; and such citizens, of every race and color, without regard to any previous condition of slavery or involuntary servitude, except as a punishment for crime whereof the party shall have been duly convicted, shall have the same right in every State and Territory in the United States, to make and enforce contracts, to sue, be parties, and give evidence, to inherit, purchase, lease, sell, hold, and convey real and personal property, and to full and equal benefit of all laws and proceedings for the security of person and property, as is enjoyed by white citizens, and shall be subject to like punishment, pains, and penalties, and to none other, any law, statute, ordinance, regulation, or custom, to the contrary notwithstanding.

Section 2. *And be it further enacted,* That any person who, under color or any law, statute, ordinance, regulation, or custom, shall subject, or cause to be subjected, any inhabitant of any State or Territory to the deprivation of any right secured or protected by this act, or to different punishment, pains, or penalties on account of such person having at any time been held in a condition of slavery or involuntary servitude, except as a punishment for crime whereof the party shall have been duly convicted, or by reason of his color or race, than is prescribed for the punishment of

white persons, shall be deemed guilty of a misdemeanor, and, on conviction, shall be punished by fine not exceeding one thousand dollars, or imprisonment not exceeding one year, or both, in the discretion of the court. . . .

AN APPEAL TO CONGRESS FOR IMPARTIAL SUFFRAGE

by Frederick Douglass (January 1867)

A very limited statement of the argument for impartial suffrage, and for including the negro in the body politic, would require more space than can be reasonably asked here. It is supported by reasons as broad as the nature of man, and as numerous as the wants of society. Man is the only government-making animal in the world. His right to a participation in the production and operation of government is an inference from his nature, as direct and self-evident as is his right to acquire property or education.

It is no less a crime against the manhood of a man, to declare that he shall not share in the making and directing of the government under which he lives, than to say that he shall not acquire property and education. The fundamental and unanswerable argument in favor of the enfranchisement of the negro is found in the undisputed fact of his manhood. He is a man, and by every fact and argument by which any man can sustain his right to vote, the negro can sustain his right equally. It is plain that, if the right belongs to any, it belongs to all. The doctrine that some men have no rights that others are bound to respect, is a doctrine which we must banish as we have banished slavery, from which it emanated. If black men have no rights in the eyes of white men, of course the whites can have none in the eyes of the blacks. The result is a war of races, and the annihilation of all proper human relations.

But suffrage for the negro, while easily sustained upon abstract principles, demands consideration upon what are recognized as the urgent necessities of the case. It is a measure of relief,—a shield to break the force of a blow already descending with violence, and render it harmless. The work of destruction has already been set in motion all over the South. Peace to the country has literally meant war to the loyal men of the South, white and black; and negro suffrage is the measure to arrest and put an end to that dreadful strife.

Something then, not by way of argument, (for that has been done by Charles Sumner, Thaddeus Stevens, Wendell Phillips, Gerrit Smith, and other able men,) but rather of statement and appeal.

For better or for worse, (as in some of the old marriage ceremonies,) the negroes are evidently a permanent part of the American population. They are too numerous and useful to be colonized, and too enduring and self-perpetuating to disappear by natural causes. Here they are, four millions of them, and, for weal or for woe, here they must remain. Their history is parallel to that of the country; but while the history of the latter has been cheerful and bright with blessings, theirs has been heavy and dark with agonies and curses. What O'Connell said of the history of Ireland may with greater truth be said of the negro's. It may be "traced like a wounded man through a crowd, by the blood." Yet the negroes have marvellously survived all the exterminating forces of slavery, and have emerged at the end of two hundred and fifty years of bondage, not morose, misanthropic, and revengeful, but cheerful, hopeful, and forgiving. They now stand before Congress and the country, not complaining of the past, but simply asking for a better future. The spectacle of these dusky millions thus imploring, not demanding, is touching; and if American statesmen could be moved by a simple appeal to the nobler elements of human nature, if they had not fallen, seemingly, into the incurable habit of weighing and measuring every proposition of reform by some standard of profit and loss, doing wrong from choice, and right only from necessity or some urgent demand of human selfishness, it would be enough to plead for the negroes on the score of past services and sufferings. But no such appeal shall be relied on here. Hardships, services, sufferings, and sacrifices are all waived. It is true that they came to the relief of the country at the hour of its extremest need. It

is true that, in many of the rebellious States, they were almost the only reliable friends the nation had throughout the whole tremendous war. It is true that, notwithstanding their alleged ignorance, they were wiser than their masters, and knew enough to be loyal, while those masters only knew enough to be rebels and traitors. It is true that they fought side by side in the loyal cause with our gallant and patriotic white soldiers, and that, but for their help,—divided as the loyal States were,— the Rebels might have succeeded in breaking up the Union, thereby entailing border wars and troubles of unknown duration and incalculable calamity. All this and more is true of these loyal negroes. Many daring exploits will be told to their credit. Impartial history will paint them as men who deserved well of their country. It will tell how they forded and swam rivers, with what consummate address they evaded the sharp-eyed Rebel pickets, how they toiled in the darkness of night through the tangled marshes of briers and thorns, barefooted and weary, running the risk of losing their lives, to warn our generals of Rebel schemes to surprise and destroy our loyal army. It will tell how these poor people, whose rights we still despised, behaved to our wounded soldiers, when found cold, hungry, and bleeding on the deserted battle-field; how they assisted our escaping prisoners from Andersonville, Belle Isle, Castle Thunder, and elsewhere, sharing with them their wretched crusts, and otherwise affording them aid and comfort; how they promptly responded to the trumpet call for their services, fighting against a foe that denied them the rights of civilized warfare, and for a government which was without the courage to assert those rights and avenge their violation in their behalf; with what gallantry they flung themselves upon Rebel fortifications, meeting death as fearlessly as any other troops in the service. But upon none of these things is reliance placed.

These facts speak to the better dispositions of the human heart; but they seem of little weight with the opponents of impartial suffrage.

It is true that a strong plea for equal suffrage might be addressed to the national sense of honor. Something, too, might be said of national gratitude. A nation might well hesitate before the temptation to betray its allies. There is something immeasurably mean, to say nothing of the cruelty, in placing the loyal negroes of the South under the political power of their Rebel masters. To make peace with our enemies is all well enough; but to prefer our enemies and sacrifice our friends,—to exalt our enemies and cast down our friends,—to clothe our enemies, who sought the destruction of the government, with all political power, and leave our friends powerless in their hands,—is an act which need not be characterized here. We asked the negroes to espouse our cause, to be our friends, to fight for us, and against their masters; and now, after they have done all that we asked them to do, —helped us to conquer their masters, and thereby directed toward themselves the furious hate of the vanquished,—it is proposed in some quarters to turn them over to the political control of the common enemy of the government and of the negro. But of this let nothing be said in this place. Waiving humanity, national honor, the claims of gratitude, the precious satisfaction arising from deeds of charity and justice to the weak and defenceless,—the appeal for impartial suffrage addresses itself with great pertinency to the darkest, coldest, and flintiest side of the human heart, and would wring righteousness from the unfeeling calculations of human selfishness.

For in respect to this grand measure it is the good fortune of the negro that enlightened selfishness, not less than justice, fights on his side. National interest and national duty, if elsewhere separated, are firmly united here. The American people can, perhaps, afford to brave the censure of surrounding nations for the manifest injustice and meanness of excluding its faithful black soldiers from the ballot-box, but it cannot afford to allow the moral and mental energies of rapidly increasing millions to be consigned to hopeless degradation.

Strong as we are, we need the energy that slumbers in the black man's arm to make us stronger. We want no longer any heavy-footed, melancholy service from the negro. We want the cheerful activity of the quickened manhood of these sable

millions. Nor can we afford to endure the moral blight which the existence of a degraded and hated class must necessarily inflict upon any people among whom such a class may exist. Exclude the negroes as a class from political rights,—teach them that the high and manly privilege of suffrage is to be enjoyed by white citizens only,—that they may bear the burdens of the state, but that they are to have no part in its direction or its honors,—and you at once deprive them of one of the main incentives to manly character and patriotic devotion to the interests of the government; in a word, you stamp them as a degraded caste,—you teach them to despise themselves, and all others to despise them. Men are so constituted that they largely derive their ideas of their abilities and their possibilities from the settled judgments of their fellow-men, and especially from such as they read in the institutions under which they live. If these bless them, they are blest indeed; but if these blast them, they are blasted indeed.

Give the negro the elective franchise, and you give him at once a powerful motive for all noble exertion, and make him a man among men. A character is demanded of him, and here as elsewhere demand favors supply. It is nothing against this reasoning that all men who vote are not good men or good citizens. It is enough that the possession and exercise of the elective franchise is in itself an appeal to the nobler elements of manhood, and imposes education as essential to the safety of society.

To appreciate the full force of this argument, it must be observed, that disfranchisement in a republican government based upon the idea of human equality and universal suffrage, is a very different thing from disfranchisement in governments based upon the idea of the divine right of kings, or the entire subjugation of the masses. Masses of men can take care of themselves. Besides, the disabilities imposed upon all are necessarily without that bitter and stinging element of invidiousness which attaches to disfranchisement in a republic. What is common to all works no special sense of degradation to any. But in a country like ours, where men of all nations, kindred, and tongues are freely enfranchised, and allowed to vote, to say to the negro, You shall not vote, is to deal his manhood a staggering blow, and to burn into his soul a bitter and goading sense of wrong, or else work in him a stupid indifference to all the elements of a manly character. As a nation, we cannot afford to have amongst us either this indifference and stupidity, or that burning sense of wrong. These sable millions are too powerful to be allowed to remain either indifferent or discontented. Enfranchise them, and they become self-respecting and country-loving citizens. Disfranchise them, and the mark of Cain is set upon them less ercifully than upon the first murderer, for no man was to hurt him. But this mark of inferiority—all the more palpable because of a difference of color—not only dooms the negro to be a vagabond, but makes him the prey of insult and outrage everywhere. While nothing may be urged here as to the past services of the negro, it is quite within the line of this appeal to remind the nation of the possibility that a time may come when the services of the negro may be a second time required. History is said to repeat itself, and, if so, having wanted the negro once, we may want him again. Can that statesmanship be wise which would leave the negro good ground to hesitate, when the exigencies of the country required his prompt assistance? Can that be sound statesmanship which leaves millions of men in gloomy discontent, and possibly in a state of alienation in the day of national trouble? Was not the nation stronger when two hundred thousand sable soldiers were hurled against the Rebel fortifications, than it would have been without them? Arming the negro was an urgent military necessity three years ago,— are we sure that another quite as pressing may not await us? Casting aside all thought of justice and magnanimity, is it wise to impose upon the negro all the burdens involved in sustaining government against foes within and foes without, to make him equal sharer in all sacrifices for the public good, to tax him in peace and conscript him in war, and then coldly exclude him from the ballot-box?

Look across the sea. Is Ireland, in her present condition, fretful, discontented, compelled to support an establishment in which she does not believe, and which the vast majority of her people abhor, a source of power or of weakness to Great Britain?

Is not Austria wise in removing all ground of complaint against her on the part of Hungary? And does not the Emperor of Russia act wisely, as well as generously, when he not only breaks up the bondage of the serf, but extends him all the advantages of Russian citizenship? Is the present movement in England in favor of manhood suffrage—for the purpose of bringing four millions of British subjects into full sympathy and co-operation with the British government—a wise and humane movement, or otherwise? Is the existence of a rebellious element in our borders— which New Orleans, Memphis, and Texas show to be only disarmed, but at heart as malignant as ever, only waiting for an opportunity to reassert itself with fire and sword—a reason for leaving four millions of the nation's truest friends with just cause of complaint against the Federal government? If the doctrine that taxation should go hand in hand with representation can be appealed to in behalf of recent traitors and rebels, may it not properly be asserted in behalf of a people who have ever been loyal and faithful to the government? The answers to these questions are too obvious to require statement. Disguise it as we may, we are still a divided nation. The Rebel States have still an anti-national policy.

Massachusetts and South Carolina may draw tears from the eyes of our tender-hearted President by walking arm in arm into his Philadelphia Convention, but a citizen of Massachusetts is still an alien in the Palmetto State. There is that, all over the South, which frightens Yankee industry, capital, and skill from its borders. We have crushed the Rebellion, but not its hopes or its malign purposes. The South fought for perfect and permanent control over the Southern laborer. It was a war of the rich against the poor. They who waged it had no objection to the government, while they could use it as a means of confirming their power over the laborer. They fought the government, not because they hated the government as such, but because they found it, as they thought, in the way between them and their one grand purpose of rendering permanent and indestructible their authority and power over the Southern laborer. Though the battle is for the present lost, the hope of gaining this object still exists, and pervades the whole South with a feverish excitement. We have thus far only gained a Union without unity, marriage without love, victory without peace. The hope of gaining by politics what they lost by the sword, is the secret of all this Southern unrest; and that hope must be extinguished before national ideas and objects can take full possession of the Southern mind. There is but one safe and constitutional way to banish that mischievous hope from the South, and that is by lifting the laborer beyond the unfriendly political designs of his former master. Give the negro the elective franchise, and you at once destroy the purely sectional policy, and wheel the Southern States into line with national interests and national objects. The last and shrewdest turn of Southern politics is a recognition of the necessity of getting into Congress immediately, and at any price. The South will comply with any conditions but suffrage for the negro. It will swallow all the unconstitutional test oaths, repeal all the ordinances of Secession, repudiate the Rebel debt, promise to pay the debt incurred in conquering its people, pass all the constitutional amendments, if only it can have the negro left under its political control. The proposition is as modest as that made on the mountain: "All these things will I give unto thee if thou wilt fall down and worship me."

But why are the Southerners so willing to make these sacrifices?

The answer plainly is, they see in this policy the only hope of saving something of their old sectional peculiarities and power. Once firmly seated in Congress, their alliance with Northern Democrats re-established, their States restored to their former position inside the Union, they can easily find means of keeping the Federal government entirely too busy with other important matters to pay much attention to the local affairs of the Southern States. Under the potent shield of State Rights,

the game would be in their own hands. Does any sane man doubt for a moment that the men who followed Jefferson Davis through the late terrible Rebellion, often marching barefooted and hungry, naked and penniless, and who now only profess an enforced loyalty, would plunge this country into a foreign war to-day, if they could thereby gain their coveted independence, and their still more coveted mastery over the negroes? Plainly enough, the peace not less than the prosperity of this country is involved in the great measure of impartial suffrage. King Cotton is deposed, but only deposed, and is ready to-day to reassert all his ancient pretensions upon the first favorable opportunity. Foreign countries abound with his agents. They are able, vigilant, devoted. The young men of the South burn with the desire to regain what they call the lost cause; the women are noisily malignant towards the Federal government. In fact, all the elements of treason and rebellion are there under the thinnest disguise which necessity can impose.

What, then, is the work before Congress? It is to save the people of the South from themselves, and the nation from detriment on their account. Congress must supplant the evident sectional tendencies of the South by national dispositions and tendencies. It must cause national ideas and objects to take the lead and control the politics of those States. It must cease to recognize the old slave-masters as the only competent persons to rule the South. In a word, it must enfranchise the negro, and by means of the loyal negroes and the loyal white men of the South build up a national party there, and in time bridge the chasm between North and South, so that our country may have a common liberty and a common civilization. The new wine must be put into new bottles. The lamb may not be trusted with the wolf. Loyalty is hardly safe with traitors. Statesmen of America! beware what you do. The ploughshare of rebellion has gone through the land beam-deep. The soil is in readiness, and the seed-time has come. Nations, not less than individuals, reap as they sow. The dreadful calamities of the past few years came not by accident, nor unbidden, from the ground. You shudder to-day at the harvest of blood sown in the spring-time of the Republic by your patriot fathers. The principle of slavery, which they tolerated under the erroneous impression that it would soon die out, became at last the dominant principle and power at the South. It early mastered the Constitution, became superior to the Union, and enthroned itself above the law.

Freedom of speech and of the press it slowly but successfully banished from the South, dictated its own code of honor and manners to the nation, brandished the bludgeon and the bowie-knife over Congressional debate, sapped the foundations of loyalty, dried up the springs of patriotism, blotted out the testimonies of the fathers against oppression, padlocked the pulpit, expelled liberty from its literature, invented nonsensical theories about master-races and slave-races of men, and in due season produced a Rebellion fierce, foul, and bloody.

This evil principle again seeks admission into our body politic.

It comes now in shape of a denial of political rights to four million loyal colored people. The South does not now ask for slavery. It only asks for a large degraded caste, which shall have no political rights. This ends the case. Statesmen, beware what you do. The destiny of unborn and unnumbered generations is in your hands. Will you repeat the mistake of your fathers, who sinned ignorantly? or will you profit by the blood-bought wisdom all round you, and forever expel every vestige of the old abomination from our national borders? As you members of the

Thirty-ninth Congress decide, will the country be peaceful, united, and happy, or troubled, divided, and miserable.

AMENDMENT FOURTEEN TO THE UNITED STATES CONSTITUTION (1868)

Section 1. All persons born or naturalized in the United States, and subject to the jurisdiction thereof, are citizens of the United States and of the State wherein they reside. No state shall make or enforce any law which shall abridge the privileges or immunities of citizens of the United States; nor shall any State deprive any person of life, liberty, or property, without due process of law; nor deny to any person within its jurisdiction the equal protection of the laws.

Section 2. Representatives shall be apportioned among the several States according to their respective numbers, counting the whole number of persons in each State, excluding Indians not taxed. But when the right to vote at any election for the choice of electors for President and Vice President of the United States, Representatives in Congress, the Executive and Judicial officers of a State, or the members of the Legislature thereof, is denied to any of the male inhabitants of such State, being twenty-one years of age, and citizens of the United States, or in any way abridged, except for participation in rebellion, or other crime, the basis of representation therein shall be reduced in the proportion which the number of such male citizens shall bear to the whole number of male citizens twenty-one years of age in such State.

Section 3. No person shall be a Senator or Representative in Congress, or elector of President and Vice President, or hold any office, civil or military, under the United States, or under any State, who, having previously taken an oath, as a member of Congress, or as an office of the United States, or as a member of any State legislature, or as an executive or judicial officer of any State, to support the Constitution of the United States, shall have engaged in insurrection or rebellion against the same, or given aid or comfort to the enemies thereof. But Congress may by a vote of two-thirds of each House, remove such disability.

Section 4. The validity of the public debt of the United States, authorized by law, including debts incurred for payment of pensions and bounties for services in suppressing insurrection or rebellion shall not be questioned. But neither the United States nor any State shall assume or pay any debt or obligation incurred in aid of insurrection or rebellion against the United States, or any claim for the loss or emancipation of any slave; but all such debts, obligations and claims shall be held illegal and void.

Section 5. The Congress shall have power to enforce, by appropriate legislation, the provisions of this article.

AMENDMENT FIFTEEN TO THE UNITED STATES CONSTITUTION (1870)

Section 1. The right of citizens of the United States to vote shall not be denied or abridged by the United States or by any State on account of race, color, or previous conditions of servitude.

Section 2. The Congress shall have power to enforce this article by appropriate legislation.

KU KLUX KLAN ACT CH. 22, 17 STAT. 13 (1871)

Be it enacted, . . . that any person who, under color of any law, statute, ordinance, regulation, custom, or usage of any State, shall subject, or cause to be subjected, any person within the jurisdiction of the United States to the deprivation of any rights, privileges, or immunities secured by the Constitution of the United States; shall any such law, statute, ordinance, regulation, custom, or usage of the state to the contrary notwithstanding, be liable to the party injured in any action at law, suite in equity, or other proper proceeding for redress; such proceeding to be prosecuted in the several district or circuit courts of the United States, with and subject to the same rights of appeal, review upon error, and other remedies provided in like cases in such courts, under the provisions of the [Civil Rights Act of April 9, 1866] . . . and the other remedial laws of the United States which are in their nature applicable in such cases.

Section 2. That if two or more persons within any State or Territory of the United States shall conspire together to overthrow, or to put down, or to destroy by force the government of the United States, or to levy war against the United States or to oppose by force the authority of the government of the United States, or by force, intimidation, or threat to prevent . . . any person from accepting or holding any office or trust or place of confidence under the United States, or from discharging the duties thereof . . . or to injure him in his person or property on account of his lawful discharge of the duties of his office, or to injure his person while engaged in the lawful discharge of the duties of his office, or . . . to deter any party or witness in any court of the United States from attending such court, or from testifying in any matter pending in such court fully, freely, and truthfully, or to injure any party or witness in his person or property on account of his having so attended or testified, or by force, intimidation, or threat to influence the verdict, presentment, or indictment, of any juror or grand juror in any court of the United States, or to injure such juror in his person or property on account of any verdict, presentment, or indictment lawfully assented to by him, or on account of his being or having been such juror, or shall conspire together, or go in disguise upon the public highway or upon the premises of another for the purpose, either directly or indirectly, of depriving any person or any class of persons of the equal protection of the laws, or of equal privileges or immunities under the laws, or for the purpose of preventing or hindering the constituted authorities of any State from giving or securing to all persons within such State the equal protection of the laws, or shall conspire together for the purpose of in any manner impeding, hindering, obstructing, or defeating the due course of justice in any State or Territory, with the intent to deny to any citizen of the United States the due and equal protection of the laws, or to injure any person in his person or in his property for lawfully enforcing the right of any person or class of persons to the equal protection of the laws, or by force, intimidation, or threat to prevent any citizen of the United States lawfully entitled to vote from giving his support or advocacy in a lawful manner . . . or to injure any such citizen in his person or property on account of such support or advocacy, each and every person so offending shall be deemed guilty of a high crime. . . .

Section 3. That in all cases where insurrection, domestic violence, unlawful combinations, or conspiracies in any State shall so obstruct or hinder the execution of the laws thereof, and of the United States, as to deprive any portion or class of the people of such State of any of the rights, privileges, or immunities, or protection, named in the Constitution and secured by this act, and the constituted authorities of such State shall either be unable to protect, or shall from any cause fail in or refuse protection of the people in such rights, such facts will be deemed a denial by such State of the equal protection of the laws to which they are entitled under the Constitution of the United States; and in all such cases, or whenever any such insurrection, violence, unlawful combination, or conspiracy shall oppose or obstruct the laws of the United States or the due execution thereof, or impede or obstruct the due course of justice under the same, it shall be lawful for the President, and it shall be his duty to take such measures, by the employment of the militia or the land and naval forces of the United States, or either, or by other means, as he may deem necessary for the suppression of such insurrection, domestic violence, or combinations; and any person who shall be arrested under the provisions of this and the preceding section shall be delivered to the marshal of the proper district, to be dealt with according to law.

Section 4. That whenever in any State or part of a State the unlawful combinations named in the preceding section of this act shall be organized and armed, and so numerous and powerful as to be able, by violence, to either overthrow or set at defiance the constituted authorities of such State, and of the United States within such State, or when the constituted authorities are in complicity with, or shall connive at the unlawful purpose of, such powerful and armed combinations; and whenever, by reason of either or all of the causes aforesaid, the conviction of such offender and the preservation of the public safety shall become in such district impracticable, in every such case such combinations shall be deemed a rebellion, against the government of the United States, and during the continuation of such rebellion, and within the limits of the district which shall be so under the sway thereof, such limits to be prescribed by proc-

lamation, it shall be lawful for the President of the United States, when in his judgment the public safety shall require it, to suspend the privileges of the writ of habeas corpus, to the end that such rebellion may be overthrown. . . .

Section 6. That any person, or persons, having knowledge that any of the wrongs conspired to be done and mentioned in the second section of this act are about to be committed, and having power to prevent or aid in preventing the same, shall neglect or refuse so to do, and such wrongful act shall be committed, such person or persons shall be liable to the person injured, or his legal representatives, for all damages caused by any such wrongful act which such first-named person or persons by reasonable diligence could have prevented; and such damages may be recovered in an action on the case in the proper circuit court of the United States, and any number of persons guilty of such wrongful neglect or refusal may be joined as defendants in such action. . . .

CIVIL RIGHTS ACT OF 1875 CH. 114, 18 STAT. 335 (1875)

An Act to Protect All Citizens in Their Civil and Legal Rights.

Whereas it is essential to just governments we recognize the equality of all men before the law, and hold that it is the duty of government in its dealings with the people to mete out equal and exact justice to all, of whatever nativity, race, color, or persuasion, religious or political; and it being the appropriate object of legislation to enact great fundamental principles into law: Therefore, *Be it enacted,* That all persons within the jurisdiction of the United States shall be entitled to the full and equal enjoyment of the accommodations, advantages, facilities, and privileges of inns, public conveyances on land or water, theaters, and other places of public amusement; subject only to the conditions and limitations established by law, and applicable alike to citizens of every race and color, regardless of any previous condition of servitude.

Section 2. That any person who shall violate the foregoing section by denying to any citizen, except for reasons by law applicable to citizens of every race and color, and regardless of any previous condition of servitude, the full enjoyment of any of the accommodations, advantages, facilities, or privileges in said section enumerated, or by aiding or inciting such denial, shall for, every such offense, forfeit and pay the sum of five hundred dollars to the person aggrieved thereby . . . and shall also, for every such offense, be deemed guilty of a misdemeanor, and upon conviction thereof, shall be fined not less than five hundred nor more than one thousand dollars, or shall be imprisoned not less than thirty days nor more than one year. . . .

Section 4. That no citizen possessing all other qualifications which are or may be prescribed by law shall be disqualified for service as grand or petit juror in any court of the United States, or of any State, on account of race, color, or previous condition of servitude; and any officer or other person charged with any duty in the selection or summoning of jurors who shall exclude or fail to summon any citizen for the cause aforesaid shall, on conviction thereof, be deemed guilty of a misdemeanor, and be fined not more than five thousand dollars.

Section 5. That all cases arising under the provisions of this act . . . shall be renewable by the Supreme Court of the U.S., without regard to the sum in controversy. . . .

BOOKER T. WASHINGTON'S "ATLANTA COMPROMISE" SPEECH (1895)

Mr. President and Gentlemen of the Board of Directors and Citizens:

One-third of the population of the South is of the Negro race. No enterprise seeking the material, civil, or moral welfare of this section can disregard this element of our population and reach the highest success. I but convey to you, Mr. President and Directors, the sentiment of the masses of my race when I say that in no way have the value and manhood of the American Negro been more fit-

tingly and generously recognized than by the managers of this magnificent Exposition at every stage of its progress. It is a recognition that will do more to cement the friendship of the two races than any occurrence since the dawn of our freedom.

Not only this, but the opportunity here afforded will awaken among us a new era of industrial progress. Ignorant and inexperienced, it is not strange that in the first years of our new life we began at the top instead of at the bottom; that a seat in Congress or the State Legislature was more sought than real estate or industrial skill; that the political convention or stump speaking had more attractions than starting a dairy farm or truck garden.

A ship lost at sea for many days suddenly sighted a friendly vessel. From the mast of the unfortunate vessel was seen a signal: "Water, water; we die of thirst!" The answer from the friendly vessel at once came back: "Cast down your bucket where you are." A second time the signal, "Water, water; send us water!" ran up from the distressed vessel, and was answered: "Cast down your bucket where you are." And a third and fourth signal for water was answered: "Cast down your bucket where you are." The captain of the distressed vessel, at last heeding the injunction, cast down his bucket, and it came up full of fresh, sparkling water from the mouth of the Amazon River. To those of my race who depend on bettering their condition in a foreign land, or who underestimate the importance of cultivating friendly relations with the Southern white man, who is their next door neighbor, I would say: "Cast down your bucket where you are"—cast it down in making friends in every manly way of the people of all races by whom we are surrounded.

Cast it down in agriculture, mechanics, in commerce, in domestic service, and in the professions. And in this connection it is well to bear in mind that whatever other sins the South may be called to bear, when it comes to business, pure and simple, it is in the South that the Negro is given a man's chance in the commercial world, and in nothing is this Exposition more eloquent than in emphasizing this chance. Our greatest danger is, that in the great leap from slavery to freedom we may overlook the fact that the masses of us are to live by the productions of our hands, and fail to keep in mind that we shall prosper in proportion as we learn to dignify and glorify common labor, and put brains and skill into the common occupations of life; shall prosper in proportion as we learn to draw the line between the superficial and the substantial, the ornamental gewgaws of life and the useful. No race can prosper till it learns that there is as much dignity in tilling a field as in writing a poem. It is at the bottom of life we must begin, and not at the top. Nor should we permit our grievances to overshadow our opportunities.

To those of the white race who look to the incoming of those of foreign birth and strange tongue and habits for the prosperity of the South, were I permitted, I would repeat what I say to my own race, "Cast down your bucket where you are." Cast it down among the 8,000,000 Negroes whose habits you know, whose fidelity and love you have tested in days when to have proved treacherous meant the ruin of your firesides. Cast down your bucket among those people who have, without strikes and labor wars, tilled your fields, cleared your forests, builded your railroads and cities, and brought forth treasures from the bowels of the earth, and helped make possible this magnificent representation of the progress of the South. Casting down your bucket among my people, helping and encouraging them as you are doing on these grounds, and, with education of head, hand and heart, you will find that they will buy your surplus land, make blossom the waste place in your fields, and run your factories. While doing this, you can be sure in the future, as in the past, that you and your families will be surrounded by the most patient, faithful, law-abiding, and unresentful people that the world has seen. As we have proved our loyalty to you in the past, in nursing your children, watching by the sick bed of your mothers and fathers, and often following them with tear-dimmed eyes to their graves, so in the future, in our humble way, we shall stand by you with a devotion that no foreigner can approach, ready to

lay down our lives, if need be, in defense of yours, interlacing our industrial, commercial, civil, and religious life with yours in a way that shall make the interests of both races one. In all things that are purely social we can be as separate as the fingers, yet one as the hand in all things essential to mutual progress.

There is no defense or security for any of us except in the highest intelligence and development of all. If anywhere there are efforts tending to curtail the fullest growth of the Negro, let these efforts be turned into stimulating, encouraging, and making him the most useful and intelligent citizen. Effort or means so invested will pay a thousand percent interest. These efforts will be twice blessed—"blessing him that gives and him that takes."

There is no escape through law of man or God from the inevitable:

> The laws of changeless justice bind
> Oppressor with oppressed;
> And close as sin and suffering joined
> We march to fate abreast.

Nearly sixteen millions of hands will aid you in pulling the load upwards, or they will pull against you the load downwards. We shall constitute one-third and more of the ignorance and crime of the South, or one-third its intelligence and progress; we shall contribute one-third to the business and industrial prosperity of the South, or we shall prove a veritable body of death, stagnating, depressing, retarding every effort to advance the body politic.

Gentlemen of the Exposition, as we present to you humble effort at an exhibition of our progress, you must not expect over much. Starting thirty years ago with ownership here and there in a few quilts and pumpkins and chickens (gathered from miscellaneous sources), remember the path that has led from these to the invention and production of agricultural implements, buggies, steam engines, newspapers, books, statuary, carving, paintings, the management of drug stores and banks, has not been trodden without contact with thorns and thistles. While we take pride in what we exhibit as a result of our independent efforts, we do not for a moment forget that our part in this exhibition would fall far short of your expectations but for the constant help that has come to our educational life, not only from the Southern States, but especially from Northern philanthropists, who have made their gifts a constant stream of blessing and encouragement.

The wisest among my race understand that the agitation of questions of social equality is the extremist folly, and that progress in the enjoyment of all the privileges that will come to us must be the result of severe and constant struggle rather than of artificial forcing. No race that has anything to contribute to the markets of the world is long in any degree ostracized. It is important and right that all privileges of the law be ours, but it is vastly more important that we be prepared for the exercise of those privileges. The opportunity to earn a dollar in a factory just now is worth infinitely more than the opportunity to spend a dollar in an opera house.

In conclusion, may I repeat that nothing in thirty years has given us more hope and encouragement, and drawn us so near to you of the white race, as this opportunity offered by the Exposition; and here bending, as it were, over the altar that represents the results of the struggle of your race and mine, both starting practically empty-handed three decades ago, I pledge that, in your effort to work out the great and intricate problem which God has laid at the doors of the South, you shall have at all time the patient, sympathetic help of my race; only let this be constantly in mind that, while from representations in these buildings of the product of field, of forest, of mine, of factory, letters, and art, much good will come, yet far above and beyond material benefits will be that higher good, that let us pray God will come, in a blotting out of sectional differences and racial animosities and suspicions, in a determination to administer absolute justice, in a willing obedience among all classes to the mandates of law. This, coupled with our material prosperity, will bring into our beloved South a new heaven and a new earth.

LETTER OF CONGRATULATION FROM THE PRESIDENT OF THE UNITED STATES TO BOOKER T. WASHINGTON

Gray Gables, Buzzard's Bay, Mass.,

October 6, 1895.

Booker T. Washington, Esq.

My Dear Sir: I thank you for sending me a copy of your address delivered at the Atlanta Exposition.

I thank you with much enthusiasm for making the address. I have read it with intense interest, and I think the Exposition would be fully justified if it did not do more than furnish the opportunity for its delivery. Your words cannot fail to delight and encourage all who wish well for your race; and if our colored fellow citizens do not from your utterances gather new hope and form new deterinations to gain every valuable advantage offered them by their citizenship, it will be strange indeed.

Yours very truly,

Grover Cleveland.

PLESSY V. FERGUSON 163 US 537 (1896)

Justice Brown delivered the opinion of the Court.

This case turns upon the constitutionality of an act of the General Assembly of the state of Louisiana, passed in 1890, providing for separate railway carriages for the white and colored races. . . .

The constitutionality of this act is attacked upon the ground that it conflicts both with the Thirteenth Amendment of the Constitution, abolishing slavery, and the Fourteenth Amendment, which prohibits certain restrictive legislation on the part of the states.

1. That it does not conflict with the Thirteenth Amendment, which abolished slavery and involuntary servitude, except as a punishment for crime, is too clear for argument. Slavery implies involuntary servitude—a state of bondage; the ownership of mankind as a chattel, or at least the control of the labor and services of one man for the benefit of

another, and absence of a legal right to the disposal of his own person, property, and services. . . .

A statute which implies merely a legal distinction between the white and colored races—a distinction which is founded in the color of the two races, and which must always exist so long as white men are distinguished from the other race by color—has no tendency to destroy the legal equality of the two races, or reestablish a state of involuntary servitude. Indeed, we do not understand that the Thirteenth Amendment is strenuously relied upon by the plaintiff in error in this connection.

2. By the Fourteenth Amendment, all persons born or naturalized in the United States, and subject to the jurisdiction thereof, are made citizens of the United States and of the state wherein they reside; and the states are forbidden from making or enforcing any law which shall abridge the privileges or immunities of citizens of the United States, or shall deprive any person of life, liberty, or property without due process of law, or deny to any person within their jurisdiction the equal protection of the laws. . . .

The object of the amendment was undoubtedly to enforce the absolute equality of the two races before the law, but in the nature of things it could not have been intended to abolish distinctions based upon color, or to enforce social, as distinguished from political, equality, or a commingling of the two races upon terms unsatisfactory to either. Laws permitting, and even requiring, their separation in places where they are liable to be brought into contact do not necessarily imply the inferiority of either race to the other, and have been generally, if not universally, recognized as within the competency of the state legislatures in the exercise of their police power. The most common instance of this is connected with the establishment of separate schools for white and colored children, which has been held to be a valid exercise of the legislative power even by courts of states where the political rights of the colored race have been longest and most earnestly enforced. . . .

So far, then, as a conflict with the Fourteenth Amendment is concerned, the case reduces itself to the question whether the statute of Louisiana is a reasonable regulation, and with respect to this there must necessarily be a large discretion on the part of the legislature. In determining the question of reasonableness it is at liberty to act with reference to the established usages, customs, and traditions of the people, and with a view to the promotion of their comfort, and the preservation of the public peace and good order. Gauged by this standard, we cannot say that a law which authorizes or even requires the separation of the two races in public conveyances is unreasonable or more obnoxious to the Fourteenth Amendment than the acts of Congress requiring separate schools for colored children in the District of Columbia, the constitutionality of which does not seem to have been questioned, or the corresponding acts of state legislatures.

We consider the underlying fallacy of the plaintiff's argument to consist in the assumption that the enforced separation of the two races stamps the colored race with a badge of inferiority. If this be so, it is not by reason of anything found in the act, but solely the colored race chooses to put that construction upon it. The argument necessarily assumes that if, as has been more than once the case, and is not unlikely to be so again, the colored race should become the dominant power in the state legislature, and should enact a law in precisely similar terms, it would thereby relegate the white race to an inferior position. We imagine that the white race, at least, would not acquiesce in this assumption. The argument also assumes that social prejudices may be overcome by legislation and that equal rights cannot be secured to the Negro except by an enforced commingling of the two races. We cannot accept this proposition. If the two races are to meet upon terms of social equality, it must be the result of natural affinities, a mutual appreciation of each other's merits, and a voluntary consent of individuals. . . . Legislation is powerless to eradicate racial instincts or to abolish distinctions based upon physical differences, and the attempt to do so can only result in accentuating the difficulties of the present situation. If the civil and political rights of both races be equal, one cannot be inferior to the other civilly or politically. If one race be inferior to the other socially, the Constitution of the United States cannot put them upon the same plane.

It is true that the question of the proportion of colored blood necessary to constitute a colored person, as distinguished from a white person, is one upon with there is a difference of opinion in the different states, some holding that any visible admixture of black blood stamps the person as belonging to the colored race . . . others that it depends upon the preponderance of blood . . . and still others that the pre-dominance of white blood must only be in the proportion of three-fourths. . . . But these are questions to be determined under the laws of each state and are not properly put in issue in this case. Under the allegations of his petition it may undoubtedly become a question of importance whether, under the laws of Louisiana, the petitioner belongs to the white or colored race.

The judgment of the court below is therefore, *Affirmed.*

Justice Harlan Dissenting

In respect of civil rights, common to all citizens, the Constitution of the United Stats does not, I think, permit any public authority to know the race of those entitled to be protected in the enjoyment of such rights. Every true man has pride of race, and under appropriate circumstances with the rights of others, his equals before the law, are not to be affected, it is his privilege to express such pride and to take such action based upon it as to him seems proper. But I deny that any legislative body or judicial tribunal may have regard to the race of citizens when the civil rights of those citizens are involved. Indeed, such legislation, as that here in question, is inconsistent not only with that equality of rights which pertains to citizenship, national and state, but with the personal liberty enjoyed by everyone within the United States.

The Thirteenth Amendment does not permit the withholding or the deprivation of any right necessarily inhering in freedom. It not only struck down the institution of slavery as previously existing in the United States, but it prevents the imposition of any burdens or disabilities that constitute badges of slavery or servitude. It decreed universal civil freedom in this country. This Court has so adjudged. But that amendment having been found inadequate to the protection of the rights of those who had been in slavery, it was followed by the Fourteenth Amendment, which added greatly to the dignity and glory of the American citizenship, and to the security of personal liberty, by declaring that "all persons born or naturalized in the United States, and subject to the jurisdiction thereof, are citizens of the United States and of the state wherein they reside," and that "no state shall make or enforce any law which shall abridge the privileges or immunities of citizens of the United States; nor shall any state deprive any person of life, liberty, or property without due process of law, nor deny to any person within its jurisdiction the equal protection of the laws." These two amendments, if enforced according to their true intent and meaning, will protect all the civil rights that pertains to freedom and citizenship. Finally, and to the end that no citizen should be denied, on account of his race, the privilege of participating in the political control of his country, it was declared by the Fifteenth Amendment that "the right of citizens of the United States to vote shall not be denied or abridged by the United States or by any state on account of race, color, or previous condition of servitude."

These notable additions to the fundamental law were welcomed by the friends of liberty throughout the world. They removed the race line from our governmental systems.

It was said in argument that the statute of Louisiana does not discriminate against either race but prescribes a rule applicable alike to white and colored citizens. But this argument does not meet the difficulty. Everyone knows that the statute in question had its origin in the purpose, not so much to exclude white persons from railroad cars occupied by blacks, as to exclude colored people from coaches occupied by or assigned to white persons. Railroad corporations of Louisiana did not make discrimination among whites in the matter of accommodation for travelers. The thing to accomplish was, under the guise of giving equal accommodation for whites and blacks, to compel the latter to keep to themselves while traveling in railroad passenger coaches. No one would be wanting in candor as to assert the contrary. The fundamental objections, therefore, to the statute is that it interferes with the personal freedom of citizens. If a white man and a black man choose to occupy the same public conveyance on a public highway, it is their right to do so, and no government, proceeding alone on grounds of race, can prevent it without infringing the personal liberty of each.

It is one thing for railroad carriers to furnish, or to be required by law to furnish, equal accommodations for all whom they are under a legal duty to carry. It is quite another thing for government to forbid citizens of the white and black races from traveling in the same public conveyance, and to punish officers of railroad companies for permitting persons of the two races to occupy the same passenger coach. If a state can prescribe, as a rule of civil conduct, that whites and blacks shall not travel as passengers in the same railroad coach, why may it not so regulate the use of the streets of its cities and towns as to compel white citizens to keep on one side of a street and black citizens to keep on the other? Why may it not, upon like grounds, punish whites and blacks who ride together in streetcars or in open vehicles on a public road or street? Why may it not require sheriffs to assign whites to one side of a courtroom and blacks to other? And why may it not also prohibit the commingling of the two races in the galleries of legislative halls or in public assemblages convened for the consideration of the political questions of the day? Further, if this statute of Louisiana is consistent with the personal liberty of citizens, why may not the state require the separation in railroad coaches of native and naturalized citizens of the United States, or of Protestants and Roman Catholics?

The answer given as the argument to these questions was that regulations of the kind they suggest would be unreasonable and could not, therefore, stand before the law. Is it meant that the determination of questions of legislative power depends upon the inquiry whether the statute whose validity is questioned is, in the judgment of the courts, a reasonable one, taking all the circumstances into consideration? A statute may be unreasonable merely because a sound public forbade its enactment. But I do not understand that the courts have anything to do with the policy or expediency of legislation. The white race deems itself to be the dominant race in this country. And so it is, in prestige, in achievements, in education, in wealth, and in power. So, I doubt not, it will continue to be for all time, if it remains true to its great heritage and holds fast to the principles of constitutional liberty. But in view of the Constitution, in the eye of the law, there is in this country no superior, dominant, ruling class of citizens. There is no caste here. Our Constitution is color-blind and neither knows nor tolerates classes among citizens. In respect of civil rights all citizens are equal before the law. The humblest is the peer of the most powerful. The law regards man as a man and takes no account of his surroundings or of his color when his civil rights, as guaranteed by the supreme law of the land, are involved. It is, therefore, to be regretted that this high tribunal, the final expositor of the fundamental law of the land, has reached the conclusion that it is competent for a state to regulate the enjoyment by citizens of their civil rights solely upon the basis of race. . . .

The sure guarantee of the peace and security of each is the clear, distinct, unconditional recognition by our governments, national and state, of every right that inheres in civil freedom, and of the equality before the law of all citizens of the United States without regard to race. State enactments, regulating the enjoyment of civil rights, upon the basis of race, and cunningly devised legitimate results of the war, under the pretense of recognizing equality of rights, can have no other result than to render permanent peace impossible, and to keep alive a conflict of races, the continuance of which must do harm to all concerned. . . .

The arbitrary separation of citizens, on the basis of race, while they are on a public highway, is a badge of servitude wholly inconsistent with the civil freedom and the equality before he law established by the Constitution. It cannot be justified upon any legal grounds.

If evils will result from the commingling of the two races upon public highways established for the benefit of all, they will be infinitely less than those that will surely come from state legislation regulating the enjoyment of civil rights upon the basis of race. We boast of the freedom enjoyed by our people above all other peoples. But it is difficult to reconcile that boast with a state of the law which, practically, puts the brand of servitude and degradation upon a large class of our fellow-citizens, our equals before the law. The thin disguise of "equal" accommodations for passengers in railroad coaches will not mislead anyone, nor atone of the wrong this day done. . . .

I am of opinion that the statute of Louisiana is inconsistent with the personal liberty of citizens, white and black, in that state, and hostile to both the spirit and letter of the Constitution of the United States. If laws of like character should be enacted in the several states of the Union, the effect would be in the highest degree mischievous. Slavery, as an institution tolerated by law, would, it is true, have disappeared from our country, but there would remain a power in the states, by sinister legislation, to interfere with the full enjoyment of the blessings of freedom; to regulate civil rights, common to all citizens, upon the basis of race, and to place in a condition of legal inferiority a large body of American citizens, now constituting a part of the political community called the People of the United States, for whom, and by whom through representatives, our government is administered. Such a system is inconsistent with the guarantee given by the Constitution to each state of a republican form of government, and may be stricken down by congressional action, constitutional or laws of any state to the contrary notwithstanding.

For the reasons stated, I am constrained to withhold my assent from the opinion and judgment of the majority. . . .

OPEN LETTER TO PRESIDENT McKINLEY

BY

Colored People of Massachusetts.

"Not as Suppliants do we President Our Claims, but as American Citizens." The Colored People of Boston and vicinity, through the Colored National League, at a mass meeting held in the Charles Street church, Tuesday evening, October 3d, 1899, addressed an Open Letter to President Mckinley.

The reading of the letter by MR. Archibald H. Grimk, Chairman of the committee, was listened to with marked attention and interest, and at the conclusion of its reading the letter was adopted by the meeting with significant unanimity.

The letter was forwarded to President McKinley, signed by the officers of the meeting and others.

BOSTON, MASS., October 3, 1899. Hon. William McKinley,

President of the United States

Sir:—

We, colored people of Massachusetts in mass meeting assembled to consider our oppressions and the state of the country relative to the same, have resolved to address ourselves to you in an open letter, notwithstanding your extraordinary, your incomprehensible silence on the subject of our wrongs in your annual and other messages to Congress, as in your public utterances to the country at large. We address ourselves to you, sir not as suppliants, but as of right, as American citizens, whose servant you are, and to whom you are bound to listen, and for whom you are equally bound to speak, and upon occasion to act, as for any other body of your fellow-countrymen in like circumstances. We ask nothing for ourselves at your hands, as chief magistrate of the republic, to which all American citizens are not entitled. We ask for the enjoyment of life, liberty and the pursuit of happiness equally with other men. We ask for the free and full exercise of all the rights of American freemen, guaranteed to us by the Constitution and laws of the Union, which you were solemnly sworn to obey and execute. We ask you for what belongs to us by the high sanction of Constitution and law, and the Democratic genius of our institutions and civilization. These rights are everywhere throughout the South denied to us, violently wrested from us by mobs, by lawless legislatures, and nullifying conventions, combinations, and conspiracies, openly, defiantly, under your eyes, in your constructive and actual presence. And we demand, which is a part of our rights, protection, security in our life, our liberty, and in the pursuit of our individual and social happiness under a government, which we are bound to defend in war, and which is equally bound to furnish us in peace protection, at home and abroad.

We have suffered, sir,—God knows how much we have suffered!—since your accession to office, at the hands of a country professing to be Christian, but which is not Christian, from the hate and violence of a people claiming to be civilized, but who are not civilized, and you have seen our sufferings, witnessed from your high place our awful wrongs and miseries, and yet you have at no time and on no occasion opened your lips in our behalf. Why? we ask. Is it because we are black and weak and despised? Are you silent because without any fault of our own we were enslaved and held for more than two centuries in cruel bondage by your forefathers? Is it because we bear the marks of those sad generation of Anglo—Saxon brutality and wickedness, that you do not speak? Is it our fault that our involuntary servitude produced in us widespread ignorance poverty and degradation? Are we to be damned and destroyed by the whites because we have only grown the seeds which they planted? Are we to be damned by bitter laws and destroyed by the mad violence of mobs because we are what white men made us? And is there no help in the federal arm for us, or even one word of audible pity, protest and remonstrance in your own breast, Mr. President, or in that of a single member of your Cabinet? Black indeed we are, sir, but we are also men and American citizens.

From the year 1619 the Anglo-Saxon race in America began to sow in the mind of the negro race in America seeds of ignorance, poverty and social degradation, and continued to do so until the year 1863, when chattel slavery was abolished to save the union of these states. Then northern white men began, in order to form a more perfect union, to sow this self-same mind of the negro with quite different seeds,—seeds of knowledge and freedom; seeds garnered in the Declaration of Independence for the feeding of the nations of the earth, such as the natural equality of all men before the law, their inalienable right to life, liberty and the pursuit of happiness, and the derivation of the power of all just governments from the consent of the governed. These seeds of your own planting took root in the mind and heart of the negro, and the crop of quickening intelligence, desire for wealth, to rise in the social scale, to be as other men, to be equal with them in opportunities and the free play of his powers in the rivalry of life, was the direct and legitimate result.

The struggle of the negro to rise out of his ignorance, his poverty and his social degradation, in consequence of the growth of these new forces and ideas within him, to the full stature of his American citizenship, has been met everywhere in the South by the active ill-will and determined race-hatred and opposition of the white people of that section. Turn where he will, he encounters this cruel and implacable spirit. He dare not speak openly the thoughts which rise in his breast. He has wrongs such as have never in modern times been inflicted on a people and yet he must be dumb in the midst of a nation which prates loudly of democracy and humanity, boasts itself the champion of oppressed peoples abroad, while it looks on indifferent, apathetic, at appalling enormities and iniquities at home, where the victims are black and the criminals white. The suppression, the terror wrought at the South is so complete, so ever-present, so awful, that no negro's life or property is safe for a day who ventures to raise his voice to heaven in indignant protest and appeal against the deep damnation and despotism of such a social state. Even teachers and leaders of this poor, oppressed and patient people may not speak, lest their institutions of learning and industry, and their own lives pay for their temerity at the swift hands of savage mobs. But if the peace of Warsaw, the silence of death reign over our people and their leaders at the South, we of Massachusetts are free, and must and shall raise our voice to you and through you to the country, in solemn protest and warning against the fearful sin and peril of such explosive social conditions. We, sir, at this crisis and extremity in the life of our race in the South, and in this crisis and extremity of the republic as well, in the presence of the civilized world, cry to you to pause, if but for an hour, in pursuit of your national policy of "criminal aggression" abroad to consider the "criminal aggression" at home against humanity and American citizenship, which is in the full tide of successful conquest at the South, and the tremendous consequences to our civilization, and the durability of the Union itself, of this universal subversion of the supreme law of the land, of democratic institutions, and of the precious principle of the religion of Jesus in the social and civil life of the Southern people.

With one accord, with an anxiety that wrenched our hearts with cruel hopes and fears, the colored people of the United States turned to you when Wilmington, N.C., was held for two dreadful days and nights in the clutch of a bloody revolution; when negroes, guilty of no crime except the color of their skin and a desire to exercise the rights of their American citizenship, were butchered like dogs in the streets of that ill-fated town; and when government of the people by the people and for the people perished in your very presence by the hands of violent men during those bitter November days, for want of federal aid, which you would not and did not furnish, on the plea that you could not give what was not asked for by a coward and recreant governor. And we well understood at the time, sir, notwithstanding your plea of constitutional inability to cope with the rebellion in Wilmington, that where there is a will with constitutional lawyers and rulers there is always a way, and where there is no will there is no way. We well knew that you lacked the will, and, therefore, the way to meet that emergency.

It was the same thing with that terrible ebullition of the mob spirit at Phoenix, S. C., when black men were hunted and murdered, and white men shot and driven out of that place by a set of white savages, who cared not for the Constitution and the laws of the United States any more than they do for the constitution and the laws of an empire dead and buried a thousand years. We looked in vain for some word or some act from you. Neither word nor act of sympathy for the victims was forthcoming, or of detestation of an outrage so mad and barbarous as to evoke even from such an extreme Southern organ organ as is the *News and Courier,* of Charleston, S.C., hot and stern condemnation. Hoping against hope, we waited for your annual message to Congress in December last, knowing that the Constitution imposed upon you a duty to give, from time to time, to that body information of the state of the Union. That, at least, we said, the President will surely do; he will communicate officially the facts relative to the tragic, the appalling events, which had just occurred in the Carolinas to the Congress of the United States. But not one word did your message contain on this subject, although it discussed all sorts and conditions of subjects, from the so-called war for humanity against Spain to the celebration of the one hundredth anniversary of the founding of the national capital in 1900. Nothing escaped your eye, at home or abroad, nothing except the subversion of the Constitution and laws of the Union in the Southern States, and the Flagrant and monstrous crimes perpetrated upon a weak and submissive race in defiance of your authority, or in virtual connivance therewith. Yes, sir, we repeat, or in virtual connivance therewith.

And, when you made your Southern tour a little later, and we saw how cunningly you catered to Southern race prejudice and proscription; how you, the one single public man and magistrate of the country, who, by virtue of your exalted office, ought under no circumstances to recognize caste distinctions and discriminations among your fellow-citizens, received white men at the Capitol in Montgomery, Ala., and black men afterward in a negro church; how you preached patience, industry moderation to your long-suffering black fellow-citizens, and patriotism, jingoism and imperialism to your white ones; when we saw all these things, scales of illusion in respect to your object fell from our eyes. We felt that the President of the United States, in order to win the support of the South to his policy of "criminal aggression" in the far East, was ready and willing to shut his eyes, ears and lips to the "criminal aggression" of that section against the Constitution and the of the land, wherein they guarantee civil rights and citizenship to the negro, whose ultimate reduction to a condition of fixed and subject serfdom is the plain purpose of the Southern people and their laws.

When, several months subsequently, you returned to Georgia, the mob spirit, as if to evince its supreme contempt for your presence and the federal executive authority which you represent, boldly broke into a prison shed, where were confined helpless negro prisoners on a charge of incendiarism, and brutally murdered five of them. These men were American citizens, entitled to the rights of American citizens, protection and trial by due process of law. They were, in the eye of the law, innocent until convicted by a jury of their peers. Had they been in legal custody in Russia or Spain or Turkey they had not been slaughtered by a mob under like circumstances; for the Russian military power, or the Spanish or the Turkish, would have guarded those men in their helpless and defenceless condition from the fury of the populace who were seeking their blood. Sir, they were men; they were your brothers; they were God's children, for whom Jesus lived and died. They ought to have been sacred charges in the hands of any civilized or semi-civilized State people. But almost in your hearing, before your eyes (and you the chief magistrate of a country loudly boastful of its freedom, Christianity and civilization, they were atrociously murdered. Did you speak? did you open your lips to express horror of the awful crime and stern condemnation of the incredible villainy and complicity of the constituted authorities of Georgia in the commission of this monstrous outrage, which outbarbarized barbarism and stained through and through with indelible infamy before the world your country's justice, honor and humanity?

Still later considering the age, the circumstances and the nation in which the deed was done, Georgia committed a crime unmatched for moral depravity and sheer atrocity during the century. A negro, charged with murder and criminal assault, the first charge he is reported by the newspapers to have admitted, and the second to have denied, was taken one quiet Sunday morning from his captors, and burned to death with indescribable and hellish cruelty in the presence of cheering thousands of the so-called best people of Georgia, men, women and children, who had gone forth on the Christian Sabbath to the burning of a human being as to a country festival and holiday of innocent enjoyment and amusement. The downright ferocity and frightful savagery of that American mob at Newnan outdoes the holiday humor and thirst for blood of the tiger-like populace of Pagan Rome, gathered to witness Christian martyrs thrown to lions in their roaring arenas. The death of Hose was quickly followed by that of the negro preacher, Strickland, guiltless of crime, under circumstances and with a brutality of wickedness almost matching in horror and enormity the torture and murder of the first; and this last was succeeded by a third victim, who was literally lashed to death by the wild, beast-like spirit of a Georgia mob, for daring merely to utter his abhorrence of the Palmetto iniquity and slaughter of helpless prisoners.

Did you speak? Did you utter one word of reprobation of righteous indignation, either as magistrate or as man? Did you break the shameful silence of shameful months with so much as a whisper of a whisper against the deep damnation of such defiance of all law, human and divine; such revulsion of men into beasts, and relapses of communities into barbarism in the very center of the republic, and amid the sanctuary of the temple of American liberty itself? You did not, sir but your Attorney-General did, and he only the throw out to the public, to your meek and long-suffering colored fellow-citizens, the cold and cautious legal opinion that the case of Hose has no federal aspect! Mr. President, has it any moral or human aspect, seeing that Hose was a member of the negro race, whom your Supreme Court once declared has no rights in America which white men are bound to respect? Is this infamous dictum of that tribunal still the Supreme law of the land? We ask you, sir, since recent events in Arkansas, Mississippi, Alabama, Virginia and Louisiana, as well as in Georgia and the Carolinas, indeed throughout the South, and your own persistent silence, and the persistent silence of every member of your Cabinet on the subject of the wrongs of that race in those States, would appear together to imply as much.

Had, eighteen months ago, the Cuban revolution to throw off the yoke of Spain, or the attempt of Spain to subdue the Cuban rebellion, any federal aspect? We believe that you and the Congress of the United States thought that they had, and therefore used, finally, the armed force of the nation to expel Spain from that island. Why? Was it because "the people "the people of the Island of Cuba are, and of right ought to be free and independent?" You and the Congress said as much, and may we fervently pray, sir, in passing, that the freedom and independence of that brave people shall not much longer be denied them by our government? But to resume, there was another consideration which, in your judgment, gave to the Cuban question a federal aspect, which provoke at last the armed interposition of our government in the affairs of that island, and this was "the chronic condition of disturbance in Cuba so injurious and menacing to our interests and tranquillity, as well as shocking to our sentiments of humanity." Wherefore you presently fulfilled "a duty to humanity by ending a situation, the indefinite prolongation of which had become insufferable."

Mr. President, had that "chronic condition of disturbance in Cuba so injurious and menacing to our interest and tranquillity as well as shocking to our sentiments of humanity," which you wished to terminate and did terminate, a federal aspect, while that not less "chronic condition of disturbance" in the South, which is a thousand times more "injurious and menacing to our interests and tranquillity," as well as far more "shocking to our sentiments of humanity," or ought to be, none whatever? Is it better to be Cuban revolutionists

fighting for Cuban independence than American citizens striving to do their simple duty at home? Or is it better only in case those American citizens doing their simple duty at home happen to be negroes residing in the Southern States?

Are crying national transgressions and injustices more "injurious and menacing" to the Republic, as well as "shocking to its sentiments of humanity," when committed by a foreign state, in foreign territory, against a foreign people, than when they are committed by a portion of our own people at home? There were those of our citizens who did not think that the Cuban question possessed any federal aspect, while there were others who thought otherwise; and these, having the will and power eventually found a way to suppress a menacing danger to the country and a wrong against humanity at the same time. Where there is a will among constitutional lawyers and rulers, Mr. President, there is ever a way; but where there is no will, there is no way. Shall it be said that the federal government, with arms of Briareus, reaching to the utmost limits of the habitable globe for the protection of its citizens, for the liberation of alien islanders and the subjugation of others, is powerless to guarantee to certain of its citizens at home their inalienable right to life, liberty and the pursuit of happiness, because those citizens happen to be negroes residing in the Southern section of our country? Do the colored people of the United States deserve equal consideration with the Cuban people at the hands of your administration, and shall they, though late, receive it? If, sir, you have the disposition, as we know that you have the power, we are confident that you will be able to find a constitutional way to reach us in our extremity, and our enemies also, who are likewise enemies to great public interests and national tranquillity.

I. D. BARNETT,
President.
EDWARD E. BROWN,
Vice-President.
EDWARD H. WEST,
Secretary.
ARCHIBALD H. GRIMKE.

EDWIN G. WALKER
JAMES H. WOLFF.
EMERY T. MORRIS
WILLIAM O. ARMSTRONG.
THOMAS P. TAYLOR
AND OTHERS.

TRADE OF PUERTO RICO

SPEECH OF HON. GEORGE H. WHITE

Friday, February 23, 1900.

The House being in Committee of the Whole House on the state of the Union, and having under consideration the bill (H. R. 8245) to regulate the trade of Puerto Rico, and for other purposes—

Mr. WHITE said:

Mr. CHAIRMAN: Perhaps at no time in the history of our nation have there been more questions of moment before us for consideration than we have at this time. Our recent war with Spain and the result in acquisition of territory by reason of that war, and the necessary legislation for the overnment of these new possessions in order that they may not work any harm with us, to establish rules, laws, and customs, require the most thoughtful consideration of all of our statesmen. Not only the question that we have before us to-night as to the character of the the tariff to be imposed upon Puerto Rico, but the government that shall be established to perpetuate, elevate, and civilize and Christianize the Hawaiian Islands, the Philippine Island, and, in my opinion at no very distant day, the Cuban Island, also require our very best effort.

The weightiness of the consideration of these questions is increased by the peculiar circumstances surrounding these new possessions. Their relative geographical position, their climate, their distance from our shores, their close proximity to other foreign powers coupled with a heterogeneous composition of population of these islands, and their want in Christian and civil development, all tend to increase the consideration and make more complex the solution of their future government.

But these responsibilities are ours, taken of our own motion, and our plain duty with reference to these people must not be shirked, but met and disposed of honestly, patriotically, in the spirit of justice between man and man.

As a humble representative of this House, I would like to feel free to discuss and aid in the disposition of these questions in the same way that my 355 colleagues on this floor do.

Mr. Chairman, it would be great pleasure to me to know that fairness and justice would be meted out to all constituent parts of our beloved country alike in such a way as to leave no necessity for a defense of my race in this House against the attacks and unfair charges from any source. The very intimation of this fact with reference to the surroundings of the colored people of this country at this time, naturally causes the injury: Should not a nation be just to all of her citizens, protect them alike in all their rights, on every foot of her soil—in a word, show herself capable of governing all within her domain before she undertakes to exercise sovereign authority over those of a foreign land—with foreign notions and habits not at all in harmony with our American system of government? Or, to be more explicit, should not charity first begin at home?

There can be but one candid and fair answer to this inquiry, and that is in the affirmative. But, unfortunately for us, what should have been done has not been done, and to substantiate this assertion we have but to pause for a moment and make a brief survey of the manumitted Afro-American during the last thirty-five years. We have struggled on as best we could with theodds against us at every turn. Our constitutional rights have been trodden under foot; our right of franchise in most every one of the original slave States has been virtually taken away from us, and during the time of our freedom fully 50,000 of my race have been ignominiously murdered by mobs, not 1 per cent of whom have been made to answer for their crimes in the courts of justice, and even here in the nation's Capitol—in the Senate and House— Senators and Representative have undertaken the unholy task of extenuating and excusing these foul deeds, and in some instances they have gone so far as to justify them.

It was only a few days ago upon this floor that the gentlemen from Mississippi [Mr. Williams] depicted one of these horrible butcheries and held it up to the public in the following language: A man leaves his home—a farmer. He goes down to the little town of Canton to market and sell his crop. It is rumored in the neighborhood that he had brought money from the market town the week before and that it is in the house. That night six or seven negro men break in to that house, ravish his daughter and his wife, and then they manacle and tie them together, and not only them but the little children—one of them, I believe, four or five years of age—manacle them down in the center of that house and set it on fire and burn them all up, hoping that the fire had done away with all trace of the crime. One of the negroes happened to have a peculiar foot, which led to tracking him. That led to crimination and recrimination among the criminals and to a confession. It led to confessions from other others. The people arose and lynched those men, and while they were lynching them they burned one of them, a voice coming from the crowd that he ought to receive the punishment himself which he had meted out to this innocent, helpless woman, her helpless daughter, and her helpless little children.

This is entirely ex parte; nothing has been said of the other side. While I deprecate as much as any man can the fiend who commits an outrage upon any woman, and do not hesitate to say that he should be speedily tried and punished by the courts, yet I place but little credence in the statement of a mob hunting for an excuse for its crimes when the statement is made that the victim confessed with a rope perhaps around his neck. No court of justice anywhere in this broad land of ours would allow testimony under duress of this kind to be introduce against a defendant. A shoe track, a confession while being burned at the stake with the hope that life may be spared thereby, are very poor excuses for taking of a human life. A trial by jury is guaranteed to every one by the Constitution of the United States, and no one should be deprived of this guaranty, however grave the charge preferred against him.

In order to fasten public sentiment against the negro race and hold them up before the world in their entirety for being responsible for what some are pleased to call "the race crime"—rape—the gentleman from Georgia [Mr. Griggs] described in detail the other day the "fiendishness" of Sam Hose, late of his State, and I believe his district, and among other things he said:

But let me tell you of a case that happened in Georgia last year. A little family a few miles from the town of Newnan were at supper in their modest dining room. The father, the young mother, and the baby were seated at the table. Humble though it was, peace, happiness, and contentment reigned in that modest home. A monster in human form, an employee on the farm, crept into that happy little home and with an ax knocked out the brains of that father, snatched the child from its mother, threw it across the room out of his way, and then by force accomplished his foul purposed. *** I do not seek to justify that, but I do say that the man who would condemn those people unqualifiedly under these circumstances has water instead of blood to supply his circulation. Not the limpid water that flow from the mountain streams, Mr. Chairman, but the fetid water found in the cesspools of the cities.

The other side of this horrible story portrays a very different state of affairs. A white man, with no interest in Hose or his victim, declares upon oath that Hose did not commit this atrocious crime charged against him but was an employee of Cranford, and had importuned him for pay due him for labor. This incensed his employer, who rushed upon Hose with a gun. Hose seized an ax and killed Cranford instantly, in self-defense, and then fled to the woods with the greatest possible speed. I do not vouch for side of this story, but only refer to it to show the necessity for trying all persons charged with crime, as the law directs.

The gentleman might have gone further and described the butchery in his district of six colored persons arrested upon suspicion of being guilty of arson, and while they were crouching in a warehouse, manacled with irons, and guarded by officers of the law, these poor victims, perhaps guilty of no crime whatever, were horribly shot to death by irresponsibles, no one of whom has ever been brought to justice.

He might have depicted also, if he had been so inclined, the miserable butchery of men, women, and children in Wilmington, N.C., in November, 1898, who had committed no crime, nor were they even charged with crime. He might have taken the minds of his auditors to the horrible scene of the aged and infirm, male and female, women in bed from childbirth, driven from their homes to the woods, with no shelter save the protecting branches of the trees of the forest, where many died from exposure, privation, and disease contracted while exposed to the merciless weather. But this description would not have accomplished the purpose of riveting public sentiment upon every colored man of the South as a rapist from whose brutal assaults every white woman must be protected.

Along the same line the Senator from Alabama [Mr. MORGAN], in a recent speech, used this language:

In physical, mental, social, inventive, religious, and ruling power the African race holds the lowest place, as it has since the world has had a history, and it is no idle boast that the white race holds the highest place. To force this lowest stratum into a position of political equality with the highest is only to clog the progress of all mankind in its march, ever strenuous and in proper order, toward the highest planes of human aspiration.

Whoever has supposed or has endeavored to realize that free republican government has for its task the undoing of what the Creator has done in classifying and grading the races according to His will overestimates both the powers and the duties of its grand mission. It is a vain effort and is fatal to the spirit and success of free government to attempt to use its true principles as a means of disturbance of the natural conditions of the races of the human family and to re-establish them on the merely theoretical basis, which is not true, that, in political power, all men must be equal in order to secure the greatest happiness to the greatest number.

It is the experience of the younger men, arising out of the effort to work negro suffrage into our political system as a harmonious element, and not the prejudices or resentments of the former slaveholders, that have prompted This strong and decisive movement in the Southern States. It will never cease unless it is held down by military power. It is a social evil as well as political, and the cost of its suppression will not be counted by this and succeeding generations in connection with questions of material prosperity.

No great body of white people in the world could be expected to quietly accept a situation so distressing and demoralizing as is created by negro suffrage in the South. It is a thorn in the flesh and will irritate and rankle in the body politic until it is removed as a factor in government. It is not necessary to go into the details of history to establish the great fact that negro suffrage in Louisiana and the other Southern States has been one unbroken line of political, social, and industrial obstruction to progress and a constant disturbance of the peace in a vast region of the United States.

This language impliedly puts at naught and defies the fourteenth and fifteenth amendments to the Constitution of the United States, and from present indications it is only a matter of a short time when the abrogation of these constitutional provisions will be openly demanded.

It is easy for these gentlemen to taunt us with our inferiority, at the same time not mentioning the causes of this inferiority. It is rather hard to be accused of shiftlessness and idleness when theaccuser of his own motion closes the avenue for labor and industrial pursuits to us. It is hardly fair to accuse us of ignorance when it was made a crime under the former order of things to learn enough about letters to even read the Word of God.

While I offer no extenuation for any immorality that may exist among my people, it comes with rather poor grace from those who forced it upon us for two hundred and fifty years to taunt us with that shortcoming.

We are trying hard to relieve ourselves of the brand with which we were bound and over which we had no control, nothing daunted, however, like the skilled mariner who, having been overtaken by the winds and storms and thrown off his bearings, stops to examine the chart, the compass, and all implements of navigation, that he may be sure of the proper course to travel to reach his destination.

In our voyage of life struggle for a place whereon we can stand, speak think, and act as unrestricted Americans citizens, we have been and are now passing through political gales, storms of ostracism, torrents of proscription, waves and inundations of caste prejudice and hatred, and, like the mariner, it is proper that we should examine our surroundings, take our bearings, and devise ways and means by which we may pursue our struggle for a place as men and women as a part of this body politic.

Possibly at no time in the history of our freedom has the effort been made to mould public sentiment against us and our progress so strongly as it is now being done. The forces have been set in motion and we must have sufficient manhood and courage to overcome all resistance that obstructs our progress.

A race of people with the forbearance, physical development, and Christian manhood and womanhood which has characterized us during the past two hundred and eighty-five years will not down at the bidding of any man or set of men, and it would be well that all should learn this lesson now.

As slaves we were true to our rulers; true to every trust reposed in us. While the white fathers and sons went forth to battle against us and the nation to perpetuate our bonds the strong, brawny arms of the black man produced the food to sustain the wives, children, and aged parents of the Confederate soldier, and kept inviolable the virtue and care of those entrusted to his keeping, and nowhere will anyone dare say that he was unfaithful to the helpless and unprotected over whom he kept a guardian watch.

How does this statement of facts compare with the frequent charges made against colored men for outraging white females? Is it a futile attempt to prove that an ignorant slave was a better man and more to be trusted than an intelligent freeman? But of these brutal murders, let us revert to a few facts and figures.

Since January 1, 1898, to April 25, 1899, there were lynched in the United States 166 persons, and of this number 155 occurred in the South. Of the whole number lynched, there were 10 white and 156 colored. The thin disguise usually employed as an excuse for these inhuman outrages is the protection of the virtue among white women.

I have taken the pains to make some little investigation as to the charges against the 166 personskilled, and find as a result of my efforts that 32 were charged with murder, 17 were charged with assault, criminal or otherwise, 10 with arson, 2 with stealing, 1 with being impudent to white men, and I am ashamed to acknowledge it, but this latter took place in North Carolina. Seventy-two of the victims were murdered without any specific charge being preferred against them whatever. Continuing this record of carnage, I give the record of the number of lynchings, with causes, from April 24, 1899, to October 20, 1899, inclusive: Crime committed:

Murder . . .
Talked too much . . .
Barn burning . . .
Trespass . . .
Sheltering a murderer . . .
Defending a colored man . . .
Brother to murderer . . .
Suspected of murder . . .
Drowned a man . . .
Innocent . . .
Bad character . . .
Wounded a white man . . .
Mormonism . . .
Assault, criminal and otherwise . . . 16
Nothing . . .
Church burning . . .
No cause stated . . .

Put hand on white woman . . .
Shooting a man . . .
Entered a lady's room drunk . . .
Wanted to work . . .
Spoke against lynching . . .

—

Total . . . 63

Of the 63 lynched there were 1 Italian, 1 Cuban, 4 white men, and 57 negroes.

These facts and figures which I have detailed are reliable; still the same old, oft-repeated slander, like Banquo's ghost, will not down, but is always in evidence.

Perhaps I can not better answer the imputation of the gentleman from Texas [Mr. Burke] than by reading an editorial from the New York Press of February 2, 1900:

How "Usual" is the "Crime"

The time is passing when Southern members of Congressman defend the practice of lynching, as did Mr. BURKE of Texas, on Wednesday, on the ground of abhorrence of rape, the "usual crime." Statistics on the subject have been kept of late years. It has been shown as to last year both by the Chicago Tribune's and the figures presented by Booker T. Washington in a magazine article, that the "usual crime" was unusual by over 90 per cent. There were only 12 lynchings for rape out of 103 lynchings of all kinds. So when Southern politicians and Southern writers and speakers proceed, as they invariably do, to justify the practice of lynching on the ground that its terrors are necessary to restrain the brute instincts of the black, they are guilty of as serious a libel as was ever perpetrated by one race on another.

The ravishers among negroes are almost literally one in a million. The 10,000,000 blacks of the country furnish in one year a dozen criminals of this class. Comparative data would be troublesome to come at, for in the North the chastity of women is not paraded before the community upon its invasion and later at the polls by its men "protectors." Rape cases are swiftly and silently tried in Northern courts. Newspapers rarely, if ever, report

them, and consultation of the criminal statistics of every State would be necessary to establish the number. But it is doubtful if those statistics would make as good a showing for the white race. The refutation of this calumny is not merely a matter of abstract justice. The Democratic party rules States where it is in a minority, and at the same time maintains its full representation in the nation, both of that minority and the majority it has suppressed largely by virtue of this rape issue. The Northern sympathy which would redress these wrongs has been steadily and systematically alienated by the repetition of the story, with the "usual crime" as proof, that the negro race was rapidly devaluating to the missing-link stage. It has been the constant inculcation that every Southern family had a potential orang-outang in its woodshed in the shape of its "hired man."

There is no doubt whatever that this argument has had more to do with the astounding indifference of the North to the criminal invasion of the human rights of the blacks than any other one cause. That the nation, after spending more than 300,000 lives and three thousand millions in money to rescue the negro from slavery, should then abandon him to a state in many respects infinitely worse is explicable only on the theory that it has been persuaded of its mistake in the man. The attitude is the result simply of a conspiracy to make the man out a brute.

A sinful conspiracy it has been. Considering the motive of political maneuver, this systematic eprivation of the negro's good name is rather more discreditable to the people responsible than the old deprivation of his liberty, or the later deprivation of his political and civil rights. But to believe that it can long prevail is to despair of the Republic. It will come to be realized throughout this country before a great while that these sickening Southern horrors have not in nine cases out of ten the justification of a home destroyed. It will be generally known that the ordinary lynching is for murder, arson, theft, fun—anything but rape. Then there will be a Federal descent on all concerned in these demoniac pastimes which will be as much more "through" than the old Ku-Klux prosecutions as the crimes which inspired it are more inhuman than any perpetrated by the blood-stained klan. The few remaining Southern Republican members can not do a greater national service than by reiterating these facts to Congress and the country, as did Messrs. Linney and White in the recent debate.

Mr. chairman, in order to show the horrors which must inevitably follow where the laws are disregarded and the human butchers take the place of the courts, permit me to read from the white press again, The Roanoke Times, and allow me to again interject the information that these parties were all white:

The Terrors of Mob Law

From Newport News now comes the report that the lynching of young Watts in that city for an alleged criminal assault a few days ago was all a horrible mistake. From the statements now made it looks as if Watts were the victim of a woman's desire to hide her shame. The whole affair is most revolting, yet it is an instance of the most miserable effects of mob violence. Too often have communities allowed themselves to be wrought up and led into the commission of deeds that they could not but regret upon calm reflection. In the case of Watts, if the above statements are true, all of the facts would have come out and the lynching of an innocent man avoided. Of course there are times when men are so much worked upon by the horror of the crime committed that they can hardly be expected not to lose their heads, yet there are no cases in which the exercise of the law would not be a better course. The Watts instance is a striking example of the result of over-zealous law and order committees. We make this the occasion for relating a most remarkable incident which has recently come to our knowledge. Hon. W.W. Baker, member of the house of delegates from Chesterfield County, gives us the story, and in the interest of law and order authorizes us to use it. In the same spirit and for the same purpose we publish it. Some time ago a citizen of Chesterfield, upon the complaint of a married woman, was arrested on a charge of criminal assault. The

woman was heard to scream, and the man was seen to run from the house. There was no question as his identity, because he was well known to the community. The woman declared that he had assaulted her, and even went as far as to show finger prints upon her throat. There was great indignation in the community, and a party was organized to lynch the man, but, fortunately for him, a special grand jury was summoned and immediate steps taken to have the case regularly tried in court.

Mr. Baker was foreman of the grand jury, and although the evidence against the man seemed to be conclusive, he determined to do everything in his power to get at the facts. The woman told a straightforward story, and, as we have already said, exhibited finger marks on her throat, which she declared were inflicted by the prisoner. After her testimony was given, Mr. Baker impressed upon her the fact that this man's life was in her hands; that if he was guilty of the terrible crime of which she had charged him, he deserved to be hung, but that if he was not guilty she would be guilty of murder for swearing away his life. The woman finally broke down and confessed that she had told her story in order to conceal her own shame and the bruises on her throat were made by her indignant husband because of her infidelity. Of course the grand jury did not return a true bill, and the incident was closed.

This shows how dangerous mob law is. Human liberty and human life are precious, and the organic law of the land provides that whenever a man has been accused of a crime he shall have a fair trial before a jury of his peers and shall have the privilege of introducing testimony in his own behalf. It is the business of our courts to thoroughly investigate all such cases and ascertain the exact truth. But the mob does not pursue such a course. The mob acts upon impulse and often upon ex parte evidence and never gives the accused the opportunity of introducing testimony to prove his innocence. When the mob rules no man's life is safe, for the mob hangs men upon the mere suspicion.

In referring to the subject of lynching a few days ago on this floor to a privileged question of personal explanation in reply to some vile references made against me by the Raleigh (N.C.) News and Observer, I stated in defense of my race that this wretched crime was committed occasionally by both white men and black men. Thereupon this same paper, together with other lesser lights in the State, pounded upon me as a slanderer of white men in the South and especially in North Carolina. "Out of their own mouths shall ye know them."

I read from the columns of the same News and Observer that was issued but a few days after it jumped on me: [Fayetteville Observer.]

Sensation at Lumber Bridge—Magistrate who Tried Reuben Ross Charged with Rape

A big sensation was created in Lumber Bridge and throughout Robeson County this morning when it was known that M. L. Harley, J. P., had issued a warrant for the arrest of S. J. McLeod, J.P., charging him with criminal assault on a colored girl named Dora Patterson, at his home, in Lumber Bridge, day before yesterday.

Mr. McLeod is the magistrate who held the preliminary trial of Reuben Ross and committed him to jail for the crime for which he was hanged on last Friday.

I might add that McLeod's victim was not only colored, but a cripple, and that McLeod is a white man living in North Carolina.

Mr. Chairman, the sickening effect of these crimes is bad enough in degenerating and degrading the moral sensibilities of those who now play upon the arena of the nation, but this is nothing when compared with the degrading and morbid effect it must have upon the minds of children in communities where these murders are committed in open daylight with the flagrant defiance of all law, morals, the State and nation, and the actors are dubbed as the best citizens of the community.

I tremble with horror for the future of our nation when I think what must be the inevitable result if mob violence is not stamped out of existence and law once permitted to reign supreme.

If State laws are inadequate or indisposed to check this species of crime, then the duty of the National Government is plain, as is evidenced by section 1 of the fourteenth amendment to the Constitution of the United States, to wit:

All persons born or naturalized in the United States, and subject to the jurisdiction thereof, are citizens of the United States and of the State wherein they reside. No State shall make or enforce any law which shall abridge the privileges or immunities of citizens of the United States; nor shall any State deprive any person of life, liberty, or property, without due process of law; nor deny to any person within its jurisdiction the equal protection of the laws.

To the end that the National Government may have jurisdiction over this species of crime, I have prepared and introduced the following bill, now pending before the Committee on the Judiciary, to wit:

A bill for the protection of all citizens of the United States against mob violence, and the penalty for breaking such laws.

Be it enacted by the Senate and House of Representatives of the United States of America in Congress assembled   That all persons born or naturalized in the United States, and subject to the jurisdiction thereof, and being citizens of the United States, are entitled to and shall receive protection in their lives from being murdered, tortured, burned to death by any and all organized mobs commonly known as "lynching bees," whether said mob be spontaneously assembled or organized by premeditation for the purpose of taking the life or lives of any citizen or citizens in the United States aforesaid; and that whenever any citizen or citizens of the United States shall be murdered by mob violence in the manner hereinabove described, all parties participating, aiding, and abetting in such murder and lynching shall be guilty of treason against the Government of the United States, and shall be tried for that offense in the United States courts; full power and jurisdiction being hereby given to said United States courts and all its officers to issue process, arrest, try, and in all respects deal with such cases in the same manner now prescribed under existing laws for the trial of felonies in the United States courts.

Sec. 2. That any person or persons duly tried and convicted in any United States court as principal or principals, aiders, abettors, accessories before or after the fact, for the murder of any citizen or citizens of the United States by mob violence or lynching as described in section 1 hereof, shall be punished as is now prescribed by law for the punishment of persons convicted of treason against the United States Government.

Sec. 3. That all laws and parts of laws in conflict with this statute are hereby repealed.

I do not pretend to claim for this bill perfection, but I have prepared and introduced it to moot the question before the Congress of the United States with the hope that expediency will be set aside and justice allowed to prevail, and a measure prepared by the Committee on the Judiciary that will come within the jurisdiction of the Constitution of the United States, as above cited.

There remain now but two questions to be settled: First, perhaps, is it expedient for the American Congress to step aside from the consideration of economic questions, the all-absorbing idea of acquisition of new territory, and consider for a moment the rights of a portion of our citizens at home and the preservation of their lives? That question I leave for you to answer.

The second is: Has Congress power to enact a statute to meet these evils? In my opinion it has ample authority under the Constitution of the United States.

A right or immunity, whether created by the Constitution or only guaranteed by it, even with or without express delegation of power, may be protected by Congress. (Prigg vs. Commonwealth of Pennsylvania, 16 Peters, 536; Slaughterhouse Cases, 16 Wall., 36; 83 U.S., XXI, 394; Virginia vs. Rivers, 100 U.S., 370; United States vs. Reeves, 92 U.S., 214; Sturgis vs. Crowninshield, 4 heat. Rep., 122, 193.) But it has been argued that the act of Congress is unconstitutional because it does not fall within the scope of any enumerated powers of legislation confided to that body, and therefore is void.

Stripped of its artificial and technical structure, the argument comes to this, that although rights are exclusively secured by, or duties are exclusively imposed upon, the National Government, yet unless the power to enforce these rights or to execute these duties can be found among the express powers act of Congress and they must operate solely proprio vigor however defective may be their operation, nay, even although, in a practical sense, they may become a nullity from the want of a proper remedy to enforce them or to provide against their violation. If this be a true interpretation of the Constitution, it must in a great measure fail to attain many of its avowed and positive objects as a security of rights and a recognition of duties. Such a limited construction of the Constitution has never yet been adopted as correct, either in theory or practice.

No one has ever supposed that Congress could constitutionally, by its legislation, exercise powers or enact laws beyond the powers delegated to it by the Constitution. But it has on various occasions exercised powers which were necessary and proper as means to carry into effect rights expressly given and duties expressly enjoined thereby. The end being required, it has been deemed a just and necessary implication that the means to accomplish it are given also, or, in other words, that the power flows as a necessary means to accomplish the end. (United States Supreme Court Reports, 38–41, 618–619.)

By permission I will here reproduce a letter written by one of the ablest lawyers in the Commonwealth of Massachusetts, an ex-attorney-general of that State, to a friend of his in this city. I refer to the Hon. A.E. Pillsbury. His letter is as follows:

I am aware that this is a difficult subject to deal with, but is not to be dismissed offhand. The precise question is whether the United States has any power, under the fourteenth amendment or otherwise, to protect the lives of its own citizens against mob violence within the States which the

States do not prevent or punish or commonly make any attempt to prevent or punish. This question has never been directly decided. There are two grounds upon which I think it at least possible that Federal legislation for this purpose may be supported.

The first is found in the express rights and powers conferred by the fourteenth amendment. Strauder vs. West Virginia (100 United States, 303) holds that the fourteenth amendment confers, as a Federal right, immunity from hostile or unfriendly action of the States or their agencies. Ex parte Virginia (100 United States, 339) declares as of course that Congress has power to enforce the fourteenth amendment against State action however put forth, whether executive, legislative, or judicial; that such enforcement is no invasion of State sovereignty; and sustains the constitutionality of the section, civil-rights act of March 1, 1875, which punishes State officers for acts of omission, among others, for failing to summon colored citizens for jury duty. (See also Tennessee vs. Davis, ibid., 257.)

The Civil Rights Cases (109 U.S., 3), while holding unconstitutional the provision of the same act forbidding the denial of equal accommodations in railroad trains and places of entertainment, etc., on the ground that the law in this particular was not corrective of any hostile action of the State or its agencies, broadly declares that if State laws do not protect the citizen in all his Federal rights his remedy will be found in further corrective legislation, which Congress may adopt under the fourteenth amendment. See also the strong dissenting opinion of Mr. Justice Harlan.

The powers of Congress were by no means exhausted in the civil rights legislation. The fourteenth amendment creates and defines citizenship of the United States as a Federal right, and makes the primary change and citizenship of the States secondary and derivative.

It would be no greater stretch than the court has often indulged to hold that the amendment confers upon citizens of the United States within the States the right to the same protection, at least in their lives, that the Government owes them everywhere else, and that the United States may afford this protection against mob violence within the States or the inaction or indifference of the States and their agencies in refusing or omitting to prevent or punish the murder of colored citizens by mobs.

Suppose a State law against murder omits to provide any penalty against the murder of colored persons. It could hardly be denied that this would violate the equality clause of the fourteenth amendment and that Congress could interfere for their protection. Suppose a State law applies the penalty to all murders, but the State authorities openly and notoriously omit to enforce force it against the murders of colored persons. The resulting mischief is the same as if the law contains no penalty for the latter offense. The omission to enforce the penalty is as much the act of the as the omission to enact it. The open and notorious omission of the State to prevent or attempt to prevent lynching encourages and contributes to the doing of it. Can it be said that Congress, having power to correct the mischief in the former case, is powerless in the latter? Why has it not the power? For the sole reason, if any, that the general power of domestic regulation is reserved to the States.

But this is only a negative reason, and does not affirmatively exclude the exercise within the State of any power, expressed or implied, which the United States may possess. There is now another possible ground which had not appeared in the day of the Civil Rights case.

Siebold's case (100 U.S., 371, 394) broadly intimates, and Neagle's case (135 U.S., 1, 69) directly decides, that there is a "peace of the United States" throughout our jurisdiction; that the United States may preserve and enforce it by preventing an assault upon a Federal Officer within a State, even to the extent of killing the assailant, and that this is not an invasion of State sovereignty.

The same process of reasoning which leads to that conclusion is capable of leading to the conclusion that the United States has the same power of protecting its citizens as of its officers within the

States. It was only an implied power in the case of the officer. The power which the United States has and exercises to protect its citizens outside the States is only an implied power.

Under the "peace" doctrine there is at least ground to affirm that the murder of a citizen of the United States by a law-defined mob is an invasion of the peace of the United States; and under the four-teenth amendment that the default of a State and its officers in taking means to prevent or to punish such murders is a violation of the rights thereby secured: and that the United States may take measures to preserve the peace of the United States within the States, and may extend to its citizens the protection in their lives which the States deny by failing to furnish it. All reasonable presumptions, in legislation and in judicial con-struction, are to be made in favor of the protection of life.

It hardly need be said that the express provision of the fifteenth amendment against abridging the right of citizens of the United States to vote does not by implication authorize the States to kill citizens of the United States or suffer them to be killed without interference; or does the provision for Congressional legislation to enforce it exclude by implication the exercise of any other power which the United States may possess under the fourteenth amendment or otherwise.

I am not prepared to assert that this is impregnable for the constitutionality of such legislation; but there is enough in it to afford food for thought, and, in my opinion ground for the attempt. If Congress and the Executive deemed the protec-tion of our own citizens in their lives and liberties of as much importance as the conquest and subju-gation of the Filipinos, I think the Constitution would be found adequate to it.

It is quite possible that more difficulties may be found in working out the remedy than in estab-lishing the constitutional power; but if the power exists, I see no reason why the murder of a citizen of the United States by a mob should not be declared a crime against the United States and punished as such. The responsible officers of the county or other district in which such crimes occur might be punished by the United States for omis-sion to bring or attempt to bring the offenders to trial under the State laws. The occurrence of a lynching might be declared sufficient primary fact evidence of denial by the State and its officers of equal protection. A fine might be levied on the county or district in which the lynching occurs. The military powers might be brought to bear upon any such district or neighborhood for the prevention of further offenses, which provision by itself would go far to prevent them.

Any bill for the purpose must of course contain a certain provision for the empaneling of juries in the Federal courts in proceedings for the punish-ment of the offenses in question. It is also worth considering whether the equity powers of these courts may not be invoked. The rule that equity does not prevent or punish crimes may be reserved by statute, subject only to the constitutional guar-anty of jury trial. The liquor selling can be prevent-ed and punished by bill in equity, which is held constitutional in some of the States, and it is possible that mob violence directed against the lives of unoffending people may be.

If the Republican party leaders consider that any attempt at legislation of this character is inadmis-sible for political reasons, I can understand it though I do not agree to it. The legal proposition that the United States, having unquestioned pow-er to protect its citizens in their lives and their property in every other quarter of the world, has no power to protect them in their lives within sight of its own capital where the States openly, notorious-ly, and purposely fail to do it is so monstrous that it is not to be conceded until affirmed by final authority.

To admit that our nation, which is made up of several States, is unable to enforce law throughout its limits whenever the people therein are disposed to violate the same and that the State govern-ments, or rather the lack thereof, are superior to and ultimately independent of the General Gov-ernment, is to admit, if I mistake not, the sound-ness of the late contested platform of secession.

What is government if not enforcement rather than the enactment of law? And what is law if not the protection of the lives and peace of the people? If the United States has no government which can effect this throughout its jurisdiction, the will of any State to the contrary notwithstanding, what is the improvement of its Government over that of the Turks in Armenia?

In concluding these remarks, Mr. Chairman, I wish to disclaim any intention of harshness or the production of any friction between the races or the sections of this country. I have simply raised my voice against a growing and, as I regard it, one of the most dangerous evils in our country. I have simply raised my voice in behalf of people who have no one else to speak for them here from a racial point of view; in behalf of a patient and, in the main, inoffensive race, a race which has often been wronged but seldom retailed; in behalf of the people who—

Like birds, for others we have built the downy nest;

Like sheep for others we have worn the fleecy vest;

Like bees, for others we have collected the honeyed food;

Like the patient ox, we have labored for others' good.

[Prolonged applause.]

REMARKS OF HON. GEORGE H. WHITE

Monday, February 5 , 1900.

PERSONAL EXPLANATION.

Mr. WHITE. I rise to a question of personal privilege.

The SPEAKER. The gentleman will state it.

Mr. WHITE. I ask the Clerk to read the marked article which I send to the desk.

Mr. CUMMINGS. From what paper?

Mr. WHITE. From the News and Observer, published at Raleigh, N.C. The Clerk read as follows:

THE COLORED MEMBER

It is bad enough that North Carolina should have the only nigger Congressman. It is sufficiently humiliating to the white people of the Second district; a sad enough commentary upon the political conditions that have obtained in this State. What shall be said when that nigger Congressman gives utterance to the following on the floor of the House?—

"I have investigated the lynchings in the South and find that less than 15 per cent of them are due to the crime of rape. And I desire to announce here that if it were not for the assaults of white men upon black women, there would be less of the other class."

Thus does the Manleyism of 1898 show its head in 1900. Manley slandered white women in a scurrilous negro newspaper having a local circulation; White justifies assaults by negroes on white women by slandering white men in a speech in the Congress of the United States. WE are told that "the public galleries contained many colored people who applauded this utterance vigorously."

So far as this particular negro is personally concerned, he may be dismissed as beneath contempt. There is a far graver side to the matter. This negro is regarded as a leader; he both reflects the sentiments of his race, and his utterance react upon his followers with an effect that was made sufficiently plain by the "vigorous applause" with which his slander was greeted by the negroes in the gallery. As the blatant mouthing of a mere negro, White's utterances are not worth notice; as a fresh manifestation of negroism, of what the negro's attitude is toward the white man, now and always, its significance should not be allowed to escape us.

When a negro of some education and of more than ordinary intelligence among his race can so far forget himself as to use such language in a speech on the floor of Congress, what is to be expected of the more ignorant of his followers? If there were no other reason, this utterance of White's is sufficient to show the absolute necessity of permanent white rule in this State. It makes plain the fact that the negro has learned nothing from experience, and that he is utterly devoid of all sense of official responsibility and of public decency—nay, more that the negro in office regards himself as the enemy of the white man and is anxious to have his race share in that sentiment. Therefore he becomes a menace to the peace of the Commonwealth and a danger to the safety of both races.

The "inoffensive negro official" is largely a myth. The negro may be inoffensive as a private citizen, but with his induction into office he becomes a new individual. White is typical of his kind. Venomous, forward, slanderous of the whites, appealing to the worst passions of his own race, he emphasizes anew the need of making an end of him and his kind. That is what the white people of this State propose to do. They have had enough of Manleyism. They have more than enough of Negro Congressman WHITE. He must be made an impossibility for the future, and will be. The people of this State will not tolerate that sort of thing. This has been made sufficiently plain already. And after next August it will be so plain that even WHITE, PRITCHARD, BUTLER, and all advocates of Manleyism will be able to understand it.

Mr. WHITE. Mr. Speaker, I desire to give that vile, slanderous publication the widest possible circulation. I desire that it shall go out through the documents of this House that the world may see what the poor colored man in the Southland has to undergo from a certain class.

In making this statement it is proper, Mr. Speaker, that I should exonerate a very large percentage of the white people of North Carolina, my native State. No better people live anywhere on God's green earth than some of them. But, unfortunately, men of the type of him who wrote that article are now in the ascendency.

I desire to repudiate as slanderous and wholly untrue the utterances there attributed to me. I did the other day, while my colleague [Mr. Linney] was speaking, interject a remark to the effect that from an investigation which I made last summer, as stated in a paper which I read before a local organization of this city, I had found that less than

15 per cent of the lynchings in this country were for assaults committed upon women, not in the South, but in the entire United States. I repeat that utterance. I did not justify the commission of assaults by black men upon white women on the ground that white men did the same in regard to black women.

I said that there were assaults occasionally committed upon women and and that they were not all committed by black men upon white women, but were also committed by white men upon black women, as evidenced by the great numbers of mulattoes in the Southland. I said that then; I repeat it now; and if any man here or elsewhere desires to verify truthfulness of that statement, he has but to make a visit through the South, where I live.

I repudiate as much as any man can anyone, whether he be a white brute or a black brute, who commits an assault upon any woman, whether a white woman or a black woman. I think such a man ought to be hung—hung by the neck until dead. But it ought to be done by the courts, not by an infuriated mob such as the writer of that article would incite.

Mr. Speaker, this article is but an evidence of what we have got to contend with—an absolute perversion and slanderous misrepresentation of the truth—preparing for the election to be held in August. And the world is notified that those whom the Constitution of these United States, by the fourteenth and fifteenth amendments, has enfranchised are to be reduced once more to the condition of goods and chattels, if such men as the one who edits the News and Observer can have the control of affairs in North Carolina.

As I said before, I want to give the fullest publications to the utterances of this vile sheet; and I want my colleagues in this House, both Democrats and Republicans, with Populists thrown in, to judge my character and my conduct for the last three years on this floor and say whether or not it has conformed to the description given by this fellow who edits the News and Observer and pollutes the country and such literature has been read at the desk. [Applause.]

"LIFT EVERY VOICE AND SING" (1901)

Lift every voice and sing
Till earth and heaven ring,
Ring with the harmonies of Liberty;
Let our rejoicing rise
High as the listening skies,
Let it resound loud as the rolling sea.
Sing a song full of the faith that the dark past has taught us,
Sing a song full of the hope that the present has brought us,
Facing the rising sun of our new day begun
Let us march on till victory is won.

Stony the road we trod,
Bitter the chastening rod,
Felt in the days when hope unborn had died;
Yet with a steady beat,
Have not our weary feet
Come to the place for which our fathers sighed?
We have come over a way that with tears
have been
watered,
We have come, treading our path through
the blood
of the slaughtered
Out from the gloomy past,
Till now we stand at last
Where the white gleam of our bright star is cast.

God of our weary years,
God of our silent tears,
Thou who has brought us thus far on the way;
Thou who has by Thy might
Led us into the light,
Keep us forever in the path, we pray.
Lest our feet stray from the places, Our
God, where
We met Thee,
Lest, our heart's drunk with the wine of the world,

We forget Thee;
Shadowed beneath Thy hand,
May we forever stand.
True to our God,
True to our native land.

56TH CONGRESS, 2D SESSION. HOUSE OF REPRESENTATIVES. REPORT NO. 2981

Second Lieut. Henry Ossian Flipper

March 1, 1901. —Laid on the table and ordered to be printed. Mr. Parker, from the Committee on Military Affairs, submitted the following AD-VERSE REPORT. [To accompany H.R. 3598.] The Committee on Military Affairs, to whom was referred the bill (H.R. 3598) to enable the President to restore Second Lieut. Henry Ossian Flipper to duty, rank, and status in United States Army, having given the same full consideration, report said bill back to the House with the recommendation that it do not pass, but do lie upon the table. This is a bill to set aside a dismissal order of June 17, 1882, after court-martial, and restore to duty, rank, etc., as if he had remained in service.

Most careful consideration has been given this case to be sure that the dismissal was not caused by prejudice and fully justified by the facts. The record of the court-martial occupies many hundred pages. It fully proves the charges of which he was found guilty.

In 1881 he was acting commissary of subsistence at Fort Davis, Tex., under Colonel now General Shafter and in possession of public moneys to quite an amount.

About March 12, 1881 he was ordered to deposit these funds in some bank at San Antonio and did not do so.

In his petition for restoration he states this himself, as follows:

At this same interview the commanding officer suggested depositing the funds in some bank in San Antonio, Tex., and when called for to draw my personal check for them (R., Part I, 150 and

151). This I did not do, because I expected to be relieved at any moment, and the longer it was delayed made me more certain it would quickly be done.

Weekly accounts were rendered by him of commissary funds, and about July 2 he exhibited as part of the funds a false check on the San Antonio National Bank to his own order, dated May 20, 1881, for $1,440.43; so General Shafter swears. Lieutenant Flipper denies it, but gives no satisfactory explanation of drawing such check or showing it to Colonel Shafter. July 8 he was ordered to forward the funds to the chief commissary subsistence at San Antonio. He says he did not do so because he found himself short $200 or $300 for uncollected bills, and had to borrow the money for inspection. Thereupon, in weekly written statements of July 9, 16, and 23, he returned a false item, as follows:

In transit to chief commissary subsistence, San Antonio, Tex., $3,791.77.

His petition admits this, as follows:

At the inspection of July 8, 1881, I was ordered by Colonel Shafter to forward my funds to the chief commissary of subsistence at San Antonio, Tex. I did not do so because my funds were not complete by the $200 or $300 I had borrowed for that occasion. I did, however, submit to him the weekly statements dated July 9, 1881, the subject-matter of the second specification of the second charge with the statement therein: "In transit to chf. c.s., Dept. Texas, San Antonio, Texas, $3,791.77."

I had hoped, on July 9, to collect the bills due and forward the money before the next weekly statement of July 16. Failing to do this, I made the statement of that date, and for the same reason that of July 23. These statements are the subject-matter of the third and fourth specifications of the second charge.

He says he kept the funds in a trunk at his quarters, although there was a commissary safe in the post.

August 10 he told his commanding officer that he had sent the funds. This was false and he admits it.

On August 10, 1881 (R. Ex. 10), the crisis came and when questioned by Colonel Shafter I made the statement to him that I had sent the funds to the chief commissary of subsistence at San Antonio, Tex., Maj. M.P. Small, which is the subject-matter of the first specification of the second charge.

About August 13 it had been ascertained that the chief commissary had not received the money. Lieutenant Flipper was arrested, his quarters were searched, and after deducting checks, etc., his shortage was ascertained at $2,074.26. He says he had discovered the shortage about August 10, and supposed it was robbery, but said nothing of it. He then went to town, claimed to have borrowed the money, and made the amount good.

The court acquitted him of embezzlement, but found him guilty of fraud in these statements, which are admittedly untrue. The department commander disapproved the finding of not guilty of embezzlement and approved that of guilty of fraud.

At Washington the findings and sentence were approved, and President Arthur ordered his dismissal from the Army after reviewing the testimony.

Lieutenant Flipper waited eighteen years, and at last, at the Fifty-fifth Congress, second session, introduced a bill to restore him to the Army.

These facts are all from his own brief. His case is one of admitted falsehood, and the conviction was of fraud. His own oath alone denies the latter. The suggestion of robbery is the common refuge of embezzlers.

Under these circumstances we see no reason for a special bill to restore him to the Army by an exception to general law. No new facts are alleged. No new evidence is offered. Public policy demands the utmost care that legislation should not interfere with the army discipline that demands honor and truth in all its officers an honor and truth that were admittedly absent in this case.

It is to be noted that among Lieutenant Flipper's papers was found a list of assets drafted to show his accounts, in which the fraudulent check above referred to was included as cash.

We add from his brief a statement of the court martial record. It is not necessary to deal with the many other circumstances showing fraud that were developed in the evidence of General Shafter and others at the court-martial.

Appendix. Statement of the Record from Lieutenant Fliper's Petition

This case was heard at Fort Davis, Tex., beginning September 17, 1881, and terminating December 8, 1881, before a general court-martial, convened by Special Orders, No. 10S, Headquarters Department of Taxes, San Antonio, Tex., September 3, 1881, by Brig. Gen. C.C. Augur, and composed of eleven members. By the same order Capt. J.W. Clous, Twenty-fourth Infantry, was appointed judge-advocate of the court (R., Part 1, p. 1). Ten members of the court so detailed met at Fort Davis, Tex, September 17, 1881. one member having been excused by Special Orders, No. 112, dated September 10, 1881 (R., Part 1, 2). At the second day's session, September 19, 1881, the court of ten members, as it then stood, was accepted without challenge, and they and the judge-advocate were then duly sworn as required by law. A request was then made for a continuance, which was granted, till November 1, 1881 (R., Part 1, 4, 5, and Ex. 1), to which date the court then adjourned.

On October 18, 1881, General Augur, in Special Orders, No. 131, detailed; two additional members for the court (R., Part 1, 9). One of these being unable to attend, another member was detailed in his stead by Special Orders, No. 133, dated October 22, 1881 (R., Part 1, 15). Of the three additional officers detailed only one appeared, and be being thereupon challenged, was excused from sitting as a member of the court (R., Part 1, 15, and Ex. 1), and the trial proceeded November 1, 1881, by the court of ten members as accepted September 19, 1881.

The trial was held upon the following charges and specifications:

Charge I. - Embezzlement in violation of the sixtieth article of war.

Specification. —In this: That second Lieut. 11.0 Flipper, Tenth Calvary, did embezzle, knowingly and willfully misappropriate and misapply, public money of the United States, furnished and intended for the military service thereof, to wit: $3,791.77, more or less, which money came into his possession and was intrusted to him in the capacity of acting commissary of subsistence at the post of Fort Davis, Tex.

This at Fort Davis, Tex., between the 8th day of July, 1881, and the 13th day of August, 1881.

Charge II. -Conduct unbecoming an officer and a gentleman.

Specification 1. —In this: That Second Lieut. H. Q. Flipper, Tenth United States Cavalry, having been directed, at or near Fort Davis, Tex., on or about the 8th day of July, 1881, by his commanding officer Col. William R. Shafter, First United States Infantry, commanding the post of Fort Davis, Tex., to transmit certain funds, for which he, Lieutenant Flipper, was accountable as acting commissary of subsistence to the chief commissary of subsistence of the Department of Texas, and on being asked at or near Fort Davis, Tex., on or about August 10, 1881, by Colonel Shafter, if he had transmitted the said funds, part of which were in checks, did then, in substance and tenor, assure him, Colonel Shafter, that he had transmitted said funds, that he had endorsed the checks, making them payable to the order of said chief commissary of subsistence of the department, and sent the amount by mail: . . . . that he had taken the letter to the post-office himself, he, Lieutenant Flipper, well knowing the same to be false, in that the said funds had not been so transmitted and the check had not been so endorsed.

Specification 2. —In this: That Second Lieut H. Q. Flipper, Tenth United States Cavalry, being on duty as acting commissary of subsistence at the post of Fort Davis, Tex., did submit for the approval of the post commander, Col. William R. Shafter, First United States Infantry, his (Lieutenant Flipper's) "weekly statement of public funds," in words and figures to wit: . . . . Subsistence Department, United States Army, ... Fort Davis, Tex., July 9, 1881.

Sir: I have the honor to report my balance of subsistence funds on deposit and in hand at the close of the week ending Saturday, July 9, 1881, as follows: Deposited with assistant treasurer of the United States at _____ Deposited with the United States designated depository at _____ Deposited with _____ National Bank at _____ . . . . Deposited . . . . In transit to chief commissary of subsistence, San Antonio, Tex., since July 9, 1881 . . . . $3,791.77 In my personal possession, in office safe . . . . 150.77 . . . . _____ . . . . Total amount 3,941.94

Very respectfully, your obedient servant, Henry O. Flipper,

Second Lieutenant, Tenth Regiment of Cavalry, A.C.S.

The Chief Commissary Of Subsistence, Headquarters Department of Texas, San Antonio, Tex.

Which statement was false and known by him, Lieut. H. O. Flipper, Tenth Cavalry, to be false, in that the funds reported by him as in transit and amounting to $3,791.77, were not so in transit, but had been retained by him or applied to his own use or benefit.

This at Fort Davis, Tex., on or about the 9th day of July, 1881.

Specification 3. —In this: That Second Lieut. H. O. Flipper, Tenth United States Cavalry, being on duty as acting commissary of subsistence at the post of Fort Davis, Tex., did submit, for the approval of the post commander, Col. William R. Shafter, First United States Infantry, his, Lieutenant Flipper's, "weekly statement of public funds" in words and figures, to wit: Subsistence Department, United States Army, Fort Davis, Tex., July 16, 1881. Sir: I have the honor to report my balance of subsistence funds on deposit and in hand at the close of the week ending Saturday, July 16, 1881, as follows: Deposited with assistant

treasurer of the United States at _____ Deposited with the United States designated depository at _____ Deposited with _____ National Bank at _____ . . . . Deposited . . . . In transit to chief commissary of subsistence, Department of Texas . . . . $3,791.77 In my personal possession, in office safe . . . . 289.34 . . . . _____ . . . . Total amount 4,081.11

Very respectfully, your obedient servant, Henry O Flipper, Second Lieutenant, Tenth Regiment of Cavalry, A.C.S.

The Chief Commissary of Subsistence, Headquarters Department of Texas, San Antonio, Tex. Which statement was false, and known by him, Lieut. H. O. Flipper, Tenth Cavalry to be false, in that the funds reported by him as in transit and amounting to $3,791.77, were not so in transit, but had been retained by him or applied to his own use or benefit.

This at Fort Davis, Tex., on or about the 16th day of July, 1881.

Specification 4. —In this: That Second Lieut. H. O. Flipper, Tenth United States Cavalry, being on duty as acting commissary of subsistence at the post of Fort Davis, Tex., did submit, for the approval of the post commander, Col. William R. Shafter, First United States Infantry, his, Lieutenant Flipper's weekly statement of public funds" in words and figures to wit:

Subsistence Department, United States Army, Fort Davis, Tex., July 23, 1881. Sir: I have the honor to report my balance of subsistence funds on deposit and in hand at the close of the week ending Saturday, July 23, 1881, as follows: Deposited with the assistant treasurer of the United States at___ Deposited with the United States designated depository at . . . . _____ Deposited with the _____ National Bank at _____ . . . . Deposited . . . . In transit to chief commissary of subsistence, Department of Texas, San Antonio, Tex . . . . $3,791.77 In my personal possession, in office safe . . . . 479.30 Very respectfully, your obedient servant, HENRY O. FLIPPER, ... Second Lieutenant, Tenth Regiment of Cavalry, A.C.S.

The Chief Commissary of Subsistence, Headquarters Department of Texas, San Antonio, Tex. Which statement was false and known by him, Lieut. H.O. Flipper, Tenth Cavalry, to be false, in that the funds reported by him as in transit, and amounting to $3,791.77, were not so in transit, but had been retained by him or applied to his own use or benefit.

This at Fort Davis, Tex., on or about the 23d day of July, 1881.

Specification 5. —In this: That Second Lieut. H.O. Flipper, Tenth United States Cavalry, being acting commissary of subsistence at the post of Fort Davis, Tex., and in such capacity being required to make a weekly exhibit of the funds in his possession pertaining to the Government to his post commander, did exhibit to his commanding officer, Col. William R. Shafter, First United States Infantry, commanding post of Fort Davis, Tex., as part of the aforesaid funds, a check, in words and figures as follows: No. 9 . . . . San Antonio, Tex., May 20 , 1881. SAN ANTONIO NATIONAL BANK. [Designated depository of the United States.] Pay to Lieut. Henry O. Flipper, A.C.S., or order, fourteen hundred and forty and 43–100 dollars. Henry O. Flipper, $1,440.43 . . . . Second Lieutenant, Tenth Cavalry.

Which check was fraudulent and intended to deceive the said commanding officer, as he, Lieutenant Flipper, neither had nor ever had had personal funds in said bank and had no authority to draw said check.

This at Fort Davis, Tex., on or about the 2d day of July, 1881.

To all of these charges and specifications I made a plea of "not guilty."(R., Part 1, 37–38.)

The court found me "not guilty" of the first charge and its specification, and "guilty" of the second charge and its specifications, and sentenced me "to be dismissed from the service of the United States." (R., Part V., 209.)

On January 2, 1882, Brig. Gen. C.C. Augur, commanding the Department of Texas, disap-

proved the finding of "not guilty" as to the second charge and its specifications, and forwarded the proceedings for the action of the President, under the one hundred and sixth article of war. (R., Part V, 210.)

"The proceedings, findings, and sentence of the general court-martial in the foregoing case of Second Lieut. Henry O. Flipper, Tenth Cavalry, having been approved by the proper reviewing authority" in Washington, who is the Judge-Advocate General of the Army (Rev. Stat., sec. 1199), the disapproval of the finding of "not guilty" as to the first charge and its specification by the department commander was thereby set aside, and the finding of "not guilty," as made by the court, was approved. (General Court-Martial Orders, No. 39, June 17, 1882, Sec. 11.)

On June 14, 1882, the President, Chester A. Arthur, approved the sentence of dismissal. (R., Part V, 210.)

On June 30, 1882, I ceased to be an officer of the Army, by virtue of General Court-Martial Orders, No. 39, Headquarters of the Army, Adjutant-General's Office, Washington, June 17, 1882.

AMERICAN LIFE HISTORIES

Manuscripts from the Federal Writers Project 1936–1940

Life history of former slave, E. W. Evans, Brick Layer & Plasterer

"My parents were on the plantation of John H. Hill, a slave owner in Madison, Georgia. I wuz born on May 21, 1855. I wuz owned and kept by J. H. Hill until just befo' surrender. I wuz a small boy when Sherman left here at the fall of Atlanta. He come through Madison on his march to the sea and we chillun hung out on the front fence from early morning 'til late in the evening, watching the soldiers go by. It took most of the day.

"My master wuz a Senator from Georgia, 'lected on the Whig ticket. He served two terms in

Washington as Senator. His wife, our mistress, had charge of the slaves and plantation. She never seemed to like the idea of having slaves . Of course, I never heard her say she didn't want them but she wuz the one to free the slaves on the place befo' surrender. Since that I've felt she didn't want them in the first place.

The next week after Sherman passed through Madison, Miss Emily called the five wimmen that wuz on the place and tole them to stay 'round the house and attend to things as they had always done until their husbands come back. She said they were free and could go wherever they wanted to. See she decided this befo surrender and tole them they could keep up just as befo' until their husbands could look after a place for them to stay. She meant that they could rent from her if they wanted to. In that number of wimmen wuz my mother, Ellen, who worked as a seamstress for Mrs. Hill. The other wimmen wuz aunt Lizzie and aunt Dinah, the washer-wimmen, aunt Liza a seamstress to help my mother, and aunt Caroline the nurse for Miss Emily's chilluns.

"I never worked as a slave because I wuzn't ole 'nough. In 1864, when I wuz about nine years ole they sent me on a trial visit to the plantation to give me an idea of what I had to do some day.

The place I'm talkin' about, when I wuz sent for the tryout, wuz on the outskirts of town. It wuz a house where they sent chilluns out ole 'nough to work for a sort of trainin'. I guess you'd call it the trainin' period. When the chilluns wuz near ten years ole they had this week's trial to get them used to the work they'd have to do when they reached ten years. At the age of ten years they wuz then sent to the field to work. They'd chop, hoe, pick cotton and pull fodder, corn, or anything else to be done on the plantation. I stayed at the place a whole week and wuz brought home on Saturday. That week's work showed me what I wuz to do when I wuz ten years ole. Well, this wuz just befo Sherman's march from Atlanta to the sea and I never got a chance to go to the plantation to work agin, for Miss Emily freed all on her place and soon after that we wuz emancipated.

"The soldiers I mentioned while ago that passed with Sherman carried provisions, hams, shoulders, meal, flour and other food. They had their cooks and other servants. I 'member seeing a woman in that crowd of servants. She had a baby in her arms. She hollered at us Chillun and said, 'You chilluns git off dat fence and go learn yore ABC's.' I thought she wuz crazy telling us that for we had never been 'lowed to learn nothing at all like reading a writing. I learned but it wuz after surrender and I wuz over tens years ole.

"It wuz soon after the soldiers passed with Sherman that Miss Emily called in all the wimmen servants and told them they could take their chillun [?] to the cabin and stay there until after the war. My father, George, had gone with Josh Hill, a son of Miss Emily's to wait on him. She told my mother to take us to that cabin until a place could be made for us.

"I said I wuz born a slave but I wuz too young to know much about slavery. I wuz the property of the Hill family from 1855 to 1865, when freedom wuz declared and they said we wuz free.

"My master had four sons, three of them went to the army. Legree Hill, the youngest son, went to the war at the age of eighteen years. He wuz killed in the Kennesaw mountains. His mother seemed sad over his going because he was too young and ran off and went. A sharpshooter killed him. His father went for him. He wuz buried in the Yankee line, wrapped in a blanket. He had some of the money he had when he wuz killed, on him. He wuz dressed like a Yankee, in their uniform. Of course, nothing much wuz said about it, as I 'member, cause he wasn't supposed to be a Yankee at all. He wuz fighting against the Yankees. When he wuz so stirred up to go to the war he told his mother that he wanted to go because he wanted to bring Lincoln's head back and he wuz going after his head. He didn't get to come back. Another son, Clarence, a calvaryman, wuz the oldest son. He had two horses shot out from under him but he escaped himself.

"I left Madison and went to Athens, Georgia. I learned the trade of brick masonry and plasterin'. I moved to Athens on the second of April in 1877. I went there to work for a contractor, Nasus McGinty. I stayed in Athens from April, 1877, until August in 1880. I then moved to Atlanta. This wuz the beginning of life for me in Atlanta. I have been here ever since, working at my trade, except for short intervals I went out to work, out of town.

"I built this house in 1887 and moved in the same year on December 27. At first it had only two rooms but I've added to it until now we have ten or twelve rooms. My house now is somewhat larger than Colonel Hill's house where the family lived who owned us as slaves .

"I have worked at my trade until I got too old to work. Of course, now I do a little piddling 'round, nothin' much though, for you can see I'm a old man and can't do much.

"I helped build Stone Hall and the Work Shop on the Atlanta University campus. It is now used by the Morris Brown College since they changed to the Atlanta University System. I worked with Alex Hamilton and Son in the year 1888 in the building trade. I had a lot of building in College Park in the Military School. I wuz never idle, as there wuzn't so many brick layers and plasterers at that time. I kept quite busy. I did brick work on the Y. M. C. A. building, under Alex Hamilton. No, I don't recall any special handicap or discrimination in my building, except in the early eighties, when there wuz but few Negroes working as brick layers and plasters, I experienced somewhat a handicap being colored. This wuz when buildin' wuz low and I worked under a white contractor. No matter how good a Negro wuz he wuz the last to be hired and then he wuz given some minor job. I saw that even if a Negro wuz a better brick layer, all the white workers wuz given the first jobs and after they wuz all supplied, then the Negro workers got what wuz left.

"Most all of the brick layers that wuz active when I wuz young are dead now. [?] I wuz talking the other day to one of the old heads, West Todd, who wuz in my crowd in the early days and we could name only four of us living now.

"My wife wuz born in Cassville, after the war. She is seventy-five years old though. We wuz born about one hundred miles apart. She has been in Atlanta since a little girl. I bet she could give you a good story herself. We had nine children and seven of them live now. My baby is over 35 years old. He lives in the house with me and my wife. So you see I'm a old man, having a baby that old.

"My church life started in Atlanta. I joined the Friendship Baptist Church when I wuz twenty-seven years old. That has been fifty-seven years ago. I remember when they first started Spelman College in Friendship. That wuz a long time ago.

"I've seen Atlanta grow from a town of woods, pig and cow paths to a great city of paved streets, tall buildings and beautifully lighted streets. You wouldn't believe it but there wuz creeks and branches running along where the main part of town is now. There is a creek under the First National Bank Building and I 'member when they wuz building that bank they got a alligator out of the creek. It wuz small as I recall now, but 'magine that [was?] all along where the fine buildings is now, and to think I've lived to see all of this growth.

"I've witnessed some trying times here too. I saw the riot and the great fire that practically burned up a part of Atlanta. I saw the toll of the riot hatred, prejudice, and murder. I wuz working out on what is now Highland Avenue at the time. Soldiers had to be sent out and they wuz supposed to protect everyone but some of them didn't uphold the law. There wuz a gang of soldiers, and I say gang because that is just what I feel they wuz from the way they acted, dressed in uniform of Uncle Sam and sent out because they wuz supposed to keep the law and there they wuz breaking it. They wuz acting like ordinary, revengeful people, pouring out their hatred for the Negro. Those soldiers came down the streets shouting and singing:

'We are rough, we are tough, We are rough, we are tough We Kill niggers and never get enough.

That gang of soldiers went right on their marching and when they got to McGruder Street they killed a Negro. They patrolled Randolph Street and went on down Irwin. They seemed bent on showing their wrath against the Negro. That wuz a pitiful time. Negroes wuz shot down without any cause and they wuz scared to be seen on the street. We had no one, it seemed, on our side for there wuz the soldiers shouting and singing: 'We are rough, we are tough, we kill niggers and never get enough.' There they wuz really adding to the riot, more hatred, deaths, and not doing what they wuz supposed to do. At the time of the riot they claimed that only one white man wuz killed and thirteen Negroes. But it was rumored here - I don't know it to be true and don't know whether I ought to repeat it - but it was said the white undertaker shops wuz filled with victims of the riot and they wuz burying them at night so the Negroes wouldn't know how many wuz killed. We had no way of knowing whether this wuz true or not. There wu a man in South Atlanta, who, it is said, killed two or three white men before he wus captured. Really he wuzn't caught, for he barred hisself in a house and shot everyone who came near the house and the only way they got him wuz to burn the house and he wuz burned up in it.

"The same year that McKinley came through here as president, they burned a Negro, Hogue Smith. The Georgian newspaper wasn't called the Georgian then but the editor of what is now the Georgian ran a excursion down to Fairburn to see the burning of that Negro. That wuz something awful.

"Well, I'm glad I've lived to see a better understanding between the two races and I do believe in not many years to come there will be no more lynching of the Negroes and people just like us going to witness them like as though they were places of amusement. I know the mean, low, ignorant Negro is the one who really causes most of the trouble between the races but now that they are getting more civilized and the whites have come to realize they are trying to imitate them and make good citizens, they are spending large sums of money for their education and making them fit to live with."

Life history of Mary Thomas

As a child I remember hearing the old folks telling me of their terrible life which they led on the large farms of Maryland before the Emancipation.

My grandfather had been a chieftain's son and he remembered the time when he was a little fellow, playing with some other boys on the banks of the sea, and a band of men swooped down on them and carried them from their own people. My grandfather remembered the heavy gold bracelets and [armlets?] of his rank and those slave-stealers took the gold ornaments from him.

My grandfather had a black mark about an inch wide running down his forehead to the tip of his nose. This mark was the sign of his tribe. He was tall and very much respected by the other slaves and the slave-holder down in Maryland. He married, raised a family and grew old. Even in his old age he was a valuable piece of property, but soon he became useless in the fields and his master agreed to give him his freedom.

But the old man, my grandfather, asked for the freedom of his youngest son, who was my father. This the master refused to do at first but at the earnest insistence of my grandfather, he agreed . . . upon condition that the son, who was a great swimmer and diver, should dive into the Chesapeake Bay where a ship had sunk years before with a load of iron. If the son were successful in bringing to the surface this load of iron, then my grandfather and his son, my father, should go free.

My grandfather tied a rope around my father's waist and for over three months the two of them brought the pieces of iron to the shore for old master. They say that sometimes the son stayed under the water so long that my grandfather had to drag him up from the wreck and lay him on the and work over him like you'd work over a drowned person.

Day after day the two worked hard and finally there wasn't no more iron down there and they told the master so and he came down to the wreck and found out they was telling the truth . .but still he wouldn't let them go. The old man, yes, but not the son who was handy around the place, an' everything.

But my grandfather kept asking for his son and the old master said that if the tow of them brought up the sound timbers of the old wreck, then he would keep his word and let them go. So my grandfather and his son, my father, between them brought up all the sound [loose?] timber that was part of the wreck. It was cheaper to get this wood and iron from the wreck than to buy it, so the master wanted it.

The wreck had stayed down on the bottom of the Chesapeake Bay for over twenty years but nobody except my father had been able to dive that deep. So you see it was just like trading off some of the young slaves on the farm to be able to get the iron and wood.

When the two finished that chore, and it was a mighty big chore, too, they went up to the big house and asked for their freedom.

The master sent them back to their cabin and said that since the old man wasn't no good any more, and it just cost the master money to feed him, he could go whenever he pleased, but the son was going to stay on the farm and if he tried any foolishness, he would sell him south. Selling a slave south meant that the slave would be taken to one of the slave trader's jails and put on the block and be sold to some plantation way down south. And no worser thing could happen. Many a family was separated like that, mothers from their children, fathers from their children, wives from their husbands, and the old folks say that a pretty girl fetched (brought) a higher price and didn't have to work in the fields. These young girls, with no one to protect them, were used by their masters and bore children for them. These white masters were the ones who didn't respect our women and all the mixing up today in the south is the result of this power the law gave over our women.

Well, when the old man and his son knew it was no use, that their master did not intend to let them go, they began to plot an escape. They knew of the Underground Railroad, they knew that if they could get to Baltimore, they would meet friends who would see them to Philadelphia and there the Friends (Quakers) would either let them settle there or send them to other people who would get them safely over the border into Canada.

Well, one night my grandfather and my father made up their minds and my grandfather could read and write so he wrote hisself out a pass. Any slave who went off the farm had to have a pass signed by the master or he would be picked up by a sheriff and put in jail and be whipped. So my grandfather had this pass and got safely through to Baltimore. There they hid for several days and waited for an agent of the Underground Railroad.

One night they were dressed in some calico [?] homespun like a woman and rode to Philadelphia on the back seat of a wagon loaded with fish. In Philadelphia the town was being searched by slave-holders looking for runaway slaves , so the people where they were supposed to stay in Philadelphia hurried them across the river about ten miles.

The Line ran from Baltimore through Wilmington, Delaware, to Philadelphia and there branched off, some of the trails going westward and some leading into New York, with Canada the ultimate goal.)

My grandfather and my father stayed across the Delaware from Philadelphia, helping a farmer harvest his crops, and they built a cabin and soon other escaped slaves from among their former neighbors slipped into New Jersey where they were.

Finally there was almost a hundred escaped slaves in the one spot and because they were free at last and this place was a haven just like the Bible talked about, they decided to stay there and so they got together and called the place Free Haven.

My uncle says that he reached there by hiding in the woods all day and walking at night. So many people came from Maryland that they changed the name of the little village to Snow Hill, which was the name of the town nearest the farms from which all or most of the people had run away from. The post office people made them change the name again and now it is Lawnside, but I was born there sixty-four years ago and I still think of it as Free Haven.

EXECUTIVE ORDER NO. 8802, 3 C.F.R., 1938–1943 COMP. P. 957 (1941)

Whereas it is the policy of the United States to encourage full participation in the national defense program by all citizens of the United States, regardless of race, creed, color, or national origin, in the firm belief that the democratic way of life within the Nation can be defended successfully only with the help and support of all groups within its borders; and

Whereas there is evidence that available and needed workers have been barred from employment in industries engaged in defense production solely because of considerations of race, creed, color, or national origin, to the detriment of workers' morale and of national unity:

Now, Therefore, by virtue of the authority vested in me by the Constitution and the statues, and as a prerequisite to the successful conduct of our national defense production effort, I do hereby reaffirm the policy of the United States that there shall be no discrimination in the employment of workers in defense industries or Government because of race, creed, color, or national origin, and I do hereby declare that it is the duty of employers and of labor organizations, in furtherance of said policy and of this order, to provide for the full and equitable participation of all workers in defense industries, without discrimination because of race, creed, color, or national origin;

And it is hereby ordered as follows:

1. All departments and agencies of the Government of the United States concerned with vocational and training programs for defense production shall take special measures appropriate to assure that such programs are administered with-

out discrimination because of race, creed, color, or national origin;

2. All contracting agencies of the Government of the United States shall include in all defense contracts hereafter negotiated by them a provision obligating the contractor not to discriminate against any worker because of race, creed, color, or national origin;

3. There is established in the Office of Production Management a Committee on Fair Employment Practice, which shall consist of a chairman and four other members to be appointed by the President. The Chairman and members of the Committee shall serve as such without compensation but shall be entitled to actual and necessary transportation, subsistence and other expenses incidental to performance of their duties. The Committee shall receive and investigate complaints of discrimination in violation of the provisions of this order and shall take appropriate steps to redress grievances which it finds to be valid. The Committee shall also recommend to the several departments and agencies of the Government of the United States and to the President all measures which may be deemed by it necessary or proper to effectuate the provisions of this order.

EXECUTIVE ORDER NO. 9981, 3 C.F.R. 1943–1948 COMP. P.720 (1948)

Whereas it is essential that there be maintained in the armed services of the United States the highest standards of democracy, with equality of treatment and opportunity for all those who serve in our country's defense:

Now, therefore, by virtue of the authority vested in me as President of the United States, by the Constitution and the statutes of the United States, and as Commander-in-Chief of the armed services, it is hereby ordered as follows:

1. It is hereby declared to be the policy of the President that there shall be equality of treatment and opportunity for all persons in the armed services without regard to race, color, religion or

national origin. This policy shall be put into effect as rapidly as possible, having due regard to the time required to effectuate any necessary changes without impairing efficiency or morals.

2. There shall be created in the National Military Establishment an advisory committee to be known as the President's Committee on Equality of Treatment and Opportunity in the Armed Services, which shall be composed of seven members to be designated by the President.

3. The Committee is authorized on behalf of the President to examine into the rules, procedures and practices of the armed services in order to determine in what respect such rules, procedure and practices may be altered or improved with a view to carrying out the policy of this order. The Committee shall confer and advise with the Secretary of the Army, the Secretary of the Air Force, and shall make such recommendations to the President and to said Secretaries as in the judgment of the Committee will effectuate the policy hereof.

4. All executive departments and agencies of the Federal Government are authorized and directed to cooperate with the Committee in its work, and to furnish the Committee such information or the services of such persons as the Committee may require in the performance of its duties.

5. When requested by the Committee to do so, persons in the armed services or in any of the executive departments and agencies of the Federal Government shall testify before the Committee and shall make available for the use of the Committee such documents and other information as the Committee may require.

6. The Committee shall continue to exist until such time as the President shall terminate its existence by Executive order.

EXECUTIVE ORDER NO. 9981, 3 C.F.R. 1943–1948 COMP. P.720 (1948)

Whereas it is essential that there be maintained in the armed services of the United States the highest standards of democracy, with equality of treatment and opportunity for all those who serve in our country's defense:

Now, therefore, by virtue of the authority vested in me as President of the United States, by the Constitution and the statutes of the United States, and as Commander-in-Chief of the armed services, it is hereby ordered as follows:

1. It is hereby declared to be the policy of the President that there shall be equality of treatment and opportunity for all persons in the armed services without regard to race, color, religion or national origin. This policy shall be put into effect as rapidly as possible, having due regard to the time required to effectuate any necessary changes without impairing efficiency or morals.

2. There shall be created in the National Military Establishment an advisory committee to be known as the President's Committee on Equality of Treatment and Opportunity in the Armed Services, which shall be composed of seven members to be designated by the President.

3. The Committee is authorized on behalf of the President to examine into the rules, procedures and practices of the armed services in order to determine in what respect such rules, procedure and practices may be altered or improved with a view to carrying out the policy of this order. The Committee shall confer and advise with the Secretary of the Army, the Secretary of the Air Force, and shall make such recommendations to the President and to said Secretaries as in the judgment of the Committee will effectuate the policy hereof.

4. All executive departments and agencies of the Federal Government are authorized and directed to cooperate with the Committee in its work, and to furnish the Committee such information or the services of such persons as the Committee may require in the performance of its duties.

5. When requested by the Committee to do so, persons in the armed services or in any of the executive departments and agencies of the Federal Government shall testify before the Committee

and shall make available for the use of the Committee such documents and other information as the Committee may require.

6. The Committee shall continue to exist until such time as the President shall terminate its existence by Executive order.

BROWN V. BOARD OF EDUCATION OF TOPEKA 347 U.S. 483 (1945)

Chief Justice Warren delivered the opinion of the Court.

These cases come to us from the States of Kansas, South Carolina, Virginia and Delaware. They are premised on different facts and different local conditions, but a common legal question justifies their consideration together in this consolidated opinion.

In each of these cases, minors of the Negro race, through their legal representatives, seek the aid of the courts in obtaining admission to the public schools of their community on a nonsegregated basis. In each instance, they had been denied admission to schools attended by white children under laws requiring or permitting segregation according to race. This segregation was alleged to deprive the plaintiffs of the equal protection of the laws under the Fourteenth Amendment. In each of the cases other than the Delaware case, a three-judge federal district court denied relief to the plaintiffs on the so-called "separate but equal" doctrine announced by this Court in this Court in *Plessy v. Ferguson*. . . .

Under that doctrine, equality of treatment is accorded when the races are provided substantially equal facilities, even though these facilities be separate. In the Delaware case, the Supreme Court of Delaware adhered to that doctrine, but ordered that the plaintiffs be admitted to the white schools because of their superiority to the Negro schools.

The plaintiffs contend that segregated school public schools are not "equal" and cannot be made "equal," and that hence they are deprived of the equal protection of the laws. Because of the obvious importance of the question presented, the Court took jurisdiction. Argument was heard in the 1952 Term, and reargument was heard this Term on certain questions propounded by the Court.

Reargument was largely devoted to the circumstances surrounding the adoption of the Fourteenth Amendment in 1868. It covered exhaustively consideration of the Amendment in Congress, ratification by the states, then existing practices in racial segregation, and the views of proponents and opponents of the Amendment. This discussion and our own investigation convince us that, although these sources cast some light, it is not enough to resolve the problem with which we are faced. At best, they are inconclusive. The most avid proponents of the post-War Amendments undoubtedly intended them to remove all legal distinctive among "all persons born or naturalized in the United States." Their opponents, just as certainly, were antagonistic to both the letter and the spirit of the Amendments and wished them to have the most limited effect. What others in Congress and the state legislatures had in mind cannot be determined with any degree of certainty.

An additional reason for the inconclusive nature of the Amendment's history, with respect to segregated schools, is the status of public education at that time. In the South, the movement toward free common schools, supported by general taxation, had not yet taken hold. Education of white children was largely in the hands of private groups. Education of Negroes was almost nonexistent, and practically all of the race were illiterate. In fact, any education of Negroes was forbidden by law in some states. Today, in contrast, many Negroes have achieved outstanding success in the arts and sciences as well as in the business and professional world. It is true that public school education at the time of the Amendment had advanced further in the North, but the effect of the Amendment on Northern States was generally ignored the congressional debates. Even in the North, the conditions of public education did not approximate those existing today. The curriculum was usually rudimentary; ungraded schools were common in rural areas; the school term was but three months a year in many states; and compulsory school attendance was virtually unknown. As a consequence, it is not surprising that there should be so little in the history of the Fourteenth Amendment relating to its intended effect on public education.

In the first cases in this Court construing the Fourteenth Amendment, decided shortly after its adoption, the Court interpreted it as proscribing all state imposed discriminations against the Negro race. The doctrine of "separate but equal" did not make its appearance in this Court until 1896 in the case of *Plessy v. Ferguson*. . ., involving not education but transportation. American courts have since labored with the doctrine for over half a century. In this Court, there have been six cases involving the "separate but equal" doctrine in the field of public education. In *Cumming v. County Board of Education*. . . and *Gong Lum v. Rice*. . ., the validity of the doctrine itself was not challenged. In more recent cases, all on the graduate school level, inequality was found in that specific benefits enjoyed by white students were denied to Negro students of the same educational qualifications. In none of these cases [*Missouri ex rel. Gaines v. Canada, Sipuel v. University of Oklahoma, Sweatt v. Painter* and *McLaurin v. Oklahoma State Regents*] was it necessary to reexamine the doctrine to grant relief to the Negro plaintiff. And in *Sweatt v. Painter*. . ., the Court expressly reserved decision on the question whether *Plessy v. Ferguson* should be held inapplicable to public education.

In the instant cases, that question is directly presented. Here, unlike *Sweatt v. Painter,* there are findings below that the Negro and white schools involved have been equalized, or are being equalized, with respect to buildings, curricula, qualifications and salaries of teacher, and other "tangible" factors. Our decision, therefore, cannot turn on merely a comparison of these tangible factors in the Negro and white schools involved in each of the cases. We must look instead to the effect of segregation itself on public education.

In approaching this problem, we cannot turn the clock back to 1868 when the Amendment was adopted, or even to 1896 when *Plessy v. Ferguson* was written. We must consider public education in the light of its full development and its present place in American life throughout the Nation. Only in this way can it be determined if segregation in public schools deprives these plaintiffs of the equal protection of the laws.

Today, education is perhaps the most important function of state and local governments. Compulsory school attendance laws and the great expenditures for education both demonstrate our recognition of the importance of education to our democratic society. It is required in the performance of our most basic public responsibilities, even service in the armed forces. It is the very foundation of good citizenship. Today it is a principal instrument in awakening the child to cultural values, in preparing him for later professional training, and in helping him to adjust normally to his environment. In these days, it is doubtful that any child may reasonably be expected to succeed in life if he is denied the opportunity of an education. Such an opportunity, where the state has undertaken to provide it, is a right which must be made available to all on equal terms.

We come then to the question presented: Does segregation of children in public schools solely on the basis of race, even though the physical facilities and other "tangible" factors may be equal, deprive the children of the minority group of equal educational opportunities? We believe that it does.

In *Sweatt v. Painter* in finding that a segregated law school for Negroes could not provide them equal educational opportunities, this Court relied in large part on "those qualities which are incapable of objective measurement but which make for greatness in the law school." In *McLaurin v. Oklahoma State Regents* . . . the Court, in requiring that a Negro admitted to a white graduate school be treated like all other students, again resorted to intangible considerations: ". . .his ability to study, to engage in discussions and exchange views with other students, and, in general, to learn his profession." Such considerations apply with added force to children in grade and high schools. To separate them from others of similar age and qualifications solely because of their race generates a feeling of inferiority as to their status in the community that may affect their hearts and minds in a way unlikely ever to be undone. The effect of this separation on their educational opportunities was well stated by a finding in the Kansas case by a court which nevertheless felt compelled to rule against the Negro plaintiffs:

> Segregation of white and colored children in public school has a detrimental effect upon the colored children. The impact is greater when it has the sanction of the law; for the policy of separating the races is usually interpreted as denoting the inferiority of the negro group. A sense of inferiority affects the motivation of a child to learn. Segregation with the sanction of law, therefore, has a tendency to [retard] the educational and mental development of Negro children and to deprive them of some of the benefits they would receive in a racial[ly] integrated school systems.

Whatever may have been the extent of psychological knowledge at the time of *Plesssy v. Ferguson,* this finding is amply supported by modern authority. Any languages in *Plessy v. Ferguson* contrary to this finding is rejected.

We conclude that in the field of public education the doctrine of "separate but equal" has no place. Separate educational facilities are inherently unequal. Therefore, we hold that the plaintiffs and other similarly situated for whom the actions have brought are, by reason of the segregation complained of, deprived of the equal protection of the laws guaranteed by the Fourteenth Amendment. This disposition makes unnecessary any discussion whether such segregation also violates the Due Process Clause of the Fourteenth Amendment.

Because these are class actions, because of the wide applicability of this decision, and because of the great variety of local conditions, the formulation of decrees in these presents problems of considerable complexity. On reargument, the consideration of appropriate relief was necessarily subordinated to the primary question—the constitutionality of segregation in public education. We have now announced that such segregation is a denial of the equal protection of the laws. In order that we may have the full assistance of the parties in formulating decrees, the cases will be restored to the docket, and the parties are requested to present further argument on Questions 4 and 5 previously propounded by the Court for the reargument this Term. The Attorney General of the United States is again invited to participate. The Attorneys General of the states requiring or permitting segregation in public education will also be permitted to appear as amici curiae upon request to do so by September 15, 1954, and submission of briefs by October 1, 1954.

It is so ordered.

CIVIL RIGHTS ACT OF 1957, PUB.L. NO. 85–315, 71 STAT. 634 (1957)

An Act to provide means of further securing and protecting the civil rights of persons within the jurisdiction of the United States.

Part I—Establishment of the Commission on Civil Rights

Sec. 101. (a) There is created in the executive branch of the Government a Commission on Civil Rights (hereinafter called the "Commission").

(b)The Commission shall be composed of six members who shall be appointed by the President by and with the advice and consent of the Senate. Not more than three of the members shall at any one time be of the same political party.

(c) The President shall designate one of the members of the Commission as Chairman and one as Vice Chairman. The Vice Chairman shall act as Chairman in the absence or disability of the Chairman, or in the event of a vacancy in that office.

(d) Any vacancy in the Commission shall not affect its powers and shall be filled in the same manner, and subject to the same limitation with respect to party affiliations as the original appointment was made. . . .

Part IV—To Provide Means of Further Securing and Protecting the Right to Vote

Sec. 131. Section 2004 of the Revised Statutes (42 U.S.C. 1971), is amended as follows:

. . . No person, whether acting under cover of law or otherwise, shall intimidate, threaten, coerce, or attempt to intimidate, or coerce any other person for the purpose of interfering with the right of such other person to vote as he may choose, or of causing such other person to vote, for, or to vote as he may choose, or of causing such other person to vote for, or not to vote for, any candidate for the office of President, Vice President, presidential elector, Member of the Senate, or Member of the House of Representatives, Delegates or Commissioners from the Territories or possessions, at any general, special, or primary election held solely or in part for the purpose of selecting or electing any such candidate.

. . . Whenever any person has engaged or there are reasonable grounds to believe that any person is about to engage in any act or practice which would deprive any right or privilege secured by subsection (a) or (b), the Attorney General may institute for the United States, or in the name of the United States, a civil action or other proper proceeding for preventive relief, including an application for a permanent or temporary injunction, restraining order, or other order. In any proceeding hereunder the United States shall be liable for costs the same as a private person. . . .

EXECUTIVE ORDER NO. 10730, 3 C.F.R. 1954–1958 COMP. P. 388 (1957)

Whereas on September 23, 1957, I issued Proclamation No. 3204 reading in part as follows:

Whereas certain persons in the State of Arkansas, individually and in unlawful assemblages, combinations, and conspiracies, have wilfully obstructed the enforcement of orders of the United States District Court for the Eastern District of Arkansas with respect to matters relating to enrollment and attendance at public schools, particularly at Central High School, located in Little Rock School District, Little Rock, Arkansas; and

Whereas such wilful obstruction of justice hinders the execution of the laws of that State and of the United States, and makes it impracticable to enforce such laws by the ordinary course of judicial proceedings; and

Whereas such obstruction of justice constitutes a denial of the equal protection of the laws secured by the Constitution of the United States and impedes the course of justice under those laws;

Now, therefore, I, Dwight D. Eisenhower, President of the United States, under and by virtue of the authority vested in me by the Constitution and Statutes of the United States, including Chapter 15 of Title 10 of the United States Code, particularly sections 332, 333 and 334 thereof, do command all persons engaged in such obstruction of justice to cease and desist therefrom, and to disperse forthwith, and

Whereas the command contained in that Proclamation has not been obeyed and wilful obstruction of enforcement of said court orders still exists and threatens to continue:

Now, therefore, by virtue of the authority vested in me by the Constitution and Statutes of the United States, including Chapter 15 of Title 10, particularly sections 332, 333 and 334 thereof, and section 301 of Title 3 of the United States Code, it is hereby ordered as follows:

Section 1. I hereby authorize and direct the Secretary of Defense to order into the active military service of the United States as he may deem appropriate to carry out the purposes of this Order, any or all of the units of the National Guard of the United States and of the Air National Guard of the United States within the State of Arkansas to serve in the active military service of the United States for an indefinite period and until relieved by appropriate orders.

Section 2. The Secretary of Defense is authorized and directed to take all appropriate steps to enforce any orders of the United States District Court for the Eastern District of Arkansas for the removal of obstruction of justice in the State of Arkansas with respect to matters relating to enrollment and attendance at public schools in the Little Rock School District, Little Rock, Arkansas. In carrying out the provisions of this section, the Secretary of Defense is authorized to use the units, and members thereof, ordered into the active military service of the United States pursuant to Section 1 of this Order.

Section 3. In furtherance of the enforcement of the aforementioned orders of the United States District Court for the Eastern District of Arkansas, the Secretary of Defense is authorized to use such of the armed forces of the United States as he may deem necessary.

Section 4. The Secretary of Defense is authorized to delegate to the Secretary of the Army or the Secretary of the Air Force, or both, any of the authority conferred upon him by this Order.

CIVIL RIGHTS ACT OF 1960, PUB.L. NO. 86–449, 74 STAT. 86 (1960)

This act, signed by President Eisenhower on May 6, 1960, further defined civil rights violations and outlined penalties connected with such violations. It guaranteed the provision of criminal penalties in the event a suspect crosses state lines to avoid legal process for the actual or attempted bombing or burning of any vehicle or building, and provided penalties for persons who obstructed or interfered with any order of a federal court.

An Act to enforce constitutional rights, and for other purposes.

Title II

Sec. 201. Chapter 49 of title 18, United States Code, is amended by adding at the end thereof a new section as follows:

Section 1074. Flight to avoid prosecution for damaging or destroying any building or other real or personal property.

. . . Whoever moves or travels in interstate or foreign commerce with intent either (1) to avoid prosecution, or custody, or confinement after con-

viction, under the laws of the place from which he flees, for willfully attempting to or damaging or destroying by fire or explosive any building, structure, facility, vehicle, dwelling house, synagogue, church, religious center or educational institution, public or private, or (2) to avoid giving testimony in any criminal proceeding relating to any such offense shall be fined not more than $5,000 or imprisoned not more than five years, or both.

. . . Violations of this section may be prosecuted in the Federal judicial district in which the original crime was alleged to have been committed or in which the person was held in custody or confinement. . . .

Sec. 203. Chapter 39 of title 18 of the United States Code is amended by adding at the end thereof the following new section:

Section 837. Explosives; illegal use or possession; and, threats or false information concerning attempts to damage or destroy real or personal property by fire or explosives.

. . . Whoever transports or aids and abets another in transporting in interstate or foreign commerce any explosive, with the knowledge or intent that it will be used to damage or destroy any building or other real or personal property for the purpose of interfering with its use for educational, religious, charitable, residential, business, or civic objectives or of intimidating any person pursuing such objectives, shall be subject to imprisonment for not more than one year, or a fine of not more than $1,000 or both; and if personal injury results shall be subject to imprisonment for not more than ten years or a fine of not more than $10,000, or both; and if death results shall be subject to imprisonment for any term of years or for life, but the court may impose the death penalty if the jury so recommends.

. . . The possession of an explosive in such a manner as to evince an intent to use, or the use of, such explosive, to damage or destroy any building or other real or personal property used for educational, religious, charitable, residential, business, or civic objectives or to intimidate any person pursuing such objectives, creates rebuttable presumptions that the explosive was transported in interstate or foreign commerce or caused to be transported in interstate or foreign commerce by the person so possessing or using it, or by a person aiding or abetting the person so possessing or using it: Provided, however, that no person may be convicted under this section unless there is evidence independent of the presumptions that this section has been violated.

. . . Whoever, through the use of the mail, telephone, telegraph, or other instrument of commerce, willfully imparts or conveys, or causes to be imparted or conveyed, any threat, or false information knowing the same to be false, concerning an attempt or alleged attempt being made, or to be made, to damage or destroy any building or other real or personal property for the purpose of interfering with its use for educational, religious, charitable, residential, business, or civic objectives, or of intimidating any person pursuing such objectives, shall be subject to imprisonment for not more than one year or a fine of not more than $1,000, or both.

EXECUTIVE ORDER NO. 11053, 3 C.F.R. 1959–1963 COMP P.645 (1962)

Whereas on September 30, 1962, I issued Proclamation No. 3497 reading in part as follows:

Whereas the Governor of the State of Mississippi and certain law enforcement officers and other officials of that State, and other persons, individually and in unlawful opposing and obstructing the enforcement of orders entered by the United States District Court for the Southern District of Mississippi and the United States Court of Appeals for the Fifth Circuit; and

Whereas such unlawful assemblies, combinations, and conspiracies oppose and obstruct the execution of the laws of the United States, impede the course of justice under those laws and make it impracticable to enforce those laws in the State of Mississippi by the ordinary course of judicial proceedings; and

Whereas I have expressly called the attention of the Governor of Mississippi to the perilous situation that exists and to his duties in the premises, and have requested but have not received from him adequate assurances that the orders of the courts of the United States will be obeyed and that law and order will be maintained:

Now, therefore, I, John F. Kennedy, President of the United States, under and by virtue of the authority vested in me by the Constitution and laws of the United States, including Chapter 15 of Title 10 of the United States Code, particularly sections 332, 333 and 334 thereof, do command all persons engaged in such obstructions of justice to cease and desist therefrom to disperse and retire peaceably forth-with; and

Whereas the commands contained in that proclamation have not been obeyed and obstruction of enforcement of those court orders still exists and threatens to continue:

Now, therefore, by virtue of the authority vested in me by the Constitution and laws of the United States, including Chapter 15 of Title 10, particularly Sections 332, 333 and 334 thereof, and Section 301 of Title 3 of the United States Code, it is hereby ordered as follows:

Section 1. The Secretary of Defense is authorized and directed to take all appropriate steps to enforce all orders of the United States District Court for the Southern District of Mississippi and the United States Court of Appeals for the Fifth Circuit and to remove all obstructions of justice in the State of Mississippi.

Section 2. In furtherance of the enforcement of the aforementioned orders of the United States District Court for the Southern District of Mississippi and the United States Court of Appeals for the Fifth Circuit, the Secretary of Defense is authorized to use such of the armed forces of the United States as he may deem necessary.

Section 3. I hereby authorize the Secretary of Defense to call into the active military service of the United States, as he may deem appropriate to carry out the purposes of this order, any or all of the units of the Army National Guard and of the Air National Guard of the State of Mississippi to serve in the active military service of the United States for an indefinite period and until relieved by appropriate orders. In carrying out the provisions of Section 1, the Secretary of Defense is authorized to use the units, and members thereof, ordered into the active military service of the United States pursuant to this section.

Section 4. The Secretary of Defense is authorized to delegate to the Secretary of the Army or the Secretary of the Air Force, or both, any of the authority conferred upon him by this order.

THE BIRMINGHAM MANIFESTO (1963)

In 1963, a series of events in Birmingham, Alabama made known the plight of African Americans to the nation at large. Black citizens were arrested en masse during peaceful demonstrations—demonstrations which were crushed by police dogs and firehoses. The Manifesto, dated April 3, 1963, embodied the hope of the African-American community in Birmingham that law, order, and peace would somehow prevail.

The patience of an oppressed people cannot endure forever. The Negro citizens of Birmingham for the last several years have hoped in vain for some evidence. . . [of the] . . .resolution of our just grievances.

Birmingham is part of the United States and we are bona fide citizens. Yet the history of Birmingham reveals that very little of the democratic process touches the life of the Negro in Birmingham. We have been segregated racially, exploited economically, and dominated politically. Under the leadership of the Alabama Christian Movement for Human Rights, we sought relief by petition for the repeal of city ordinances requiring segregation and the institution of a merit hiring policy in city employment. We were rebuffed. We then turned to the system of the courts. We weathered set-back after set-back, with all of its costliness, finally winning the terminal, bus, parks and airport cases. The bus decision has been implemented begrudging and the parks decision

prompted the closing of all municipally-owned recreational facilities with the exception of the zoo and Legion Field. . . .

We have always been a peaceful people, bearing our oppression with superhuman effort. Yet we have been the victims of repeated violence, not only that inflicted by the hoodlum element but also that inflicted by the blatant misuse of police power. . . . For years, while our homes and churches were being bombed, we heard nothing but the rantings and ravings of racist city officials.

The Negro protest for equality and justice has been a voice crying in the wilderness. Most of Birmingham has remained silent, probably out of fear. In the meanwhile, our city has acquired the dubious reputation of being the worst big city in race relations in the United States. Last fall, for a flickering moment, it appeared that sincere community leaders from religion, business and industry discerned the inevitable confrontation in race relations approaching. Their concern for the city's image and commonwealth of all its citizens did not run deep enough. Solemn promises were made, pending a postponement of direct action, that we would be joined in a suit seeking the relief of segregation ordinances. Some merchants agreed to desegregate their restrooms as a good faith start, some actually complying, only to retreat shortly thereafter. We hold in our hands now, broken faith and broken promises. We believe in the American Dream of democracy, in the Jeffersonian doctrine that "all men are created equal and are endowed by their Creator with certain inalienable rights, among these being life, liberty and the pursuit of happiness."

Twice since September we have deferred our direct action thrust in order that a change in city government would not be made in the hysteria of a community crisis. We act today in full concert with our Hebraic-Christian traditions, the law of morality and the Constitution of our nation. The absence of justice and progress in Birmingham demands that we make a moral witness to give our community a chance to survive. We demonstrate our faith that we believe that the beloved community can come to Birmingham. We appeal to the citizenry of Birmingham, Negro and white, to join us in this witness for decency, morality, self-respect and human dignity. Your individual and corporate support can hasten the day of "liberty and justice for all." This is Birmingham's moment of truth in which every citizen can play his part in her larger destiny. . . .

AMENDMENT TWENTY-FOUR TO THE UNITED STATES CONSTITUTION (1964)

Section 1. The right of citizens of the United States to vote in any primary or other election for President or Vice President, for electors for President or Vice President, or for Senator or Representative in Congress, shall not be denied or abridged by the United States or any State by reason of failure to pay any poll tax or other tax.

Section 2. The congress shall have power to enforce this article by appropriate legislation.

CIVIL RIGHTS ACT OF 1964, PUB. L. NO. 88–352, 78 STAT. 241 (1964)

An Act to enforce the constitutional right to vote, to confer jurisdiction upon the district courts of the United States to provide injunctive relief against discrimination in public accommodations, to authorize the Attorney General to institute suits to protect constitutional rights in public facilities and public education, to extend the Commission on Civil Rights, to prevent discrimination in federally assisted programs, to establish a Commission on Equal Employment Opportunity, and for other purposes.

Title I—Voting Rights

Sec. 101. Section 2004 of the Revised Statutes (42 U.S.C. 1971). . .is further amended as follows: . . .

. . . "No Person acting under color of law shall—"

"(A) In determining whether any individual is qualified under State law or laws to vote in any Federal election, apply any standard, practice, or procedure different from the standards, practices, or procedures applied under such law or laws to other individuals within the same county, parish, or similar political subdivision who have been found by State officials to be qualified to vote;"

"(B) deny the right of any individual to vote in any Federal election because of an error or omission on any record or paper relating to any application, registration, or other act requisite to voting, if such error or omission is not material in determining whether such individual is qualified under State law to vote in such election; or"

"(C) employ any literacy test as a qualification for voting in any Federal election unless (i) such test is administered to each individual and is conducted wholly in writing, and (ii) a certified copy of the test and of the answers given by the individual is furnished to him within twenty-five days of the submission of his request made within the period of time during which records and papers are required to be retained and preserved pursuant to title III of the Civil Rights Act of 1960 (42 U.S.C. 1974–74e; 74 Stat. 88). . . ."

Sec. 201. (a) All persons shall be entitled to the full and equal enjoyment of the goods, services, facilities, privileges, advantages, and accommodations of any place of public accommodation, as defined in this section, without discrimination or segregation on the ground of race, color, religion, or national origin.

(b) Each of the following establishments which serves the public is a place of public accommodation within the meaning of this title if its operations affect commerce, or if discrimination or segregation by it is supported by State action:

(1) any inn, hotel, motel, or other establishment which provides lodging to transient guests, other than an establishment located within a building which contains not more than five rooms for rent or hire and which is actually occupied by the proprietor of such establishment as his residence;

(2) any restaurant, cafeteria, lunchroom, lunch counter, soda fountain, or other facility principally

engaged in selling food for consumption on the premises, including, but not limited to, any such facility located on the premises of any retail establishment; or any gasoline station;

(3) any motion picture house, theater, concert hall, sports arena, stadium or other place of exhibition or entertainment; and

(4) any establishment (A)(i) which is physically located within the premises of any establishment otherwise covered by this subsection, or (ii) within the premises of which is physically located any such covered establishment, and (B) which holds itself out as serving patrons of such covered establishment. . . .

(e) The provisions of this title shall not apply to a private club or other establishment not in fact open to the public, except to the extent that the facilities of such establishment are made available to the customers or patrons of an establishment within the scope of subsection (b).

Sec. 206. (a) Whenever the Attorney General has reasonable cause to believe that any person or group of persons is engaged in a pattern or practice of resistance to the full enjoyment of any of the rights secured by this title, and that the pattern or practice is of such a nature and is intended to deny the full exercise of the rights herein described, the Attorney General may bring a civil action in the appropriate district court of the United States. . . .

Title IV—Desegregation of Public Education

Sec. 407. (a) Whenever the Attorney General receives a complaint in writing—

(1) signed by a parent or group of parents to the effect that his or their minor children, as members of a class of persons similarly situated, are being deprived by a school board of the equal protection of the laws, or

(2) signed by an individual, or his parent, to the effect that he has been denied admission to or not permitted to continue in attendance at a public college by reason of race, color, religion, or nation-

al origin and the Attorney General believes the complaint is meritorious and certifies that the signer or signers of such complaint are unable, in his judgment, to initiate and maintain appropriate legal proceedings for relief and that the institution of an action will materially further the orderly achievement of desegregation in public education, the Attorney General is authorized, after giving notice of such complaint to the appropriate school board or college authority and after certifying that he is satisfied that such board or authority has had a reasonable time to adjust the conditions alleged in such complaint, to institute for or in the name of the United States a civil action in any appropriate district court of the United States against such parties and for such relief as may be appropriate. . . .

Title VI—Nondiscrimination In Federally-Assisted Programs

Sec. 601. No person in the United States shall, on the ground of race, color, or national origin, be excluded from participation in, be denied the benefits of, or be subjected to discrimination under any program or activity receiving Federal financial assistance. . . .

Title VII—Equal Employment Opportunity

Sec. 703. (a) It shall be an unlawful employment practice for an employer—

(1) to fail or refuse to hire or to discharge any individual, or otherwise to discriminate against any individual with respect to his compensation, terms, conditions, or privileges of employment, because of such individual's race, color, religion, sex, or national origin; or

(2) to limit, segregate, or classify his employees in any way which would deprive or tend to deprive any individual of employment opportunities or otherwise adversely affect his status as an employee, because of such individual's race, color, religion, sex, or national origin.

(b) It shall be an unlawful employment practice for an employment agency to fail or refuse to refer for employment, or otherwise to discriminate against, any individual because of his race, color, religion, sex, or national origin, or to classify or refer for employment any individual on the basis of his race, color, religion, sex, or national origin.

(c) It shall be an unlawful employment practice for a labor organization—

(1) to exclude or to expel from its membership, or otherwise to discriminate against, any individual because of his race, color, religion, sex, or national origin;

(2) to limit, segregate, or classify its membership, or to classify or fail or refuse to refer for employment any individual, in any way which would deprive or tend to deprive any individual of employment opportunities, or would limit such employment opportunities or otherwise adversely affect his status as an employee or as an applicant for employment, because of such individual's race, color, religion, sex, or national origin; or

(3) to cause or attempt to cause an employer to discriminate against an individual in violation of this section.

(d) It shall be an unlawful employment practice for any employer, labor organization, or joint labor-management committee controlling apprenticeship or other training or retraining, including on-the-job training programs to discriminate against any individual because of his race, color, religion, sex, or national origin in admission to, or employment in, any program established to provide apprenticeship or other training.

(e) Notwithstanding any other provision of this title, (1) it shall not be an unlawful employment practice for an employer to hire and employ employees, for an employment agency to classify, or refer for employment any individual, for a labor organization to classify its membership or to classify or refer for employment any individual, or for an employer, labor organization, or joint labor-management committee controlling apprenticeship or other training or retraining programs to admit or employ any individual in any such program, on the basis of his religion, sex, or national origin in those certain instances where religion,

sex, or national origin is a bona fide occupational qualification reasonably necessary to the normal operation of that particular business or enterprise. . . .

Sec. 705. (1) There is hereby created a Commission to be known as the Equal Employment Opportunity Commission, which shall be composed of five members, not more than three of whom shall be members of the same political party, who shall be appointed by the President by and with the advice and consent of the Senate. . . .

EXECUTIVE ORDER NO. 11246, 3 C.F.R., 1964–1965 COMP. P.339– 348 (1965)

Under and by virtue of the authority vested in me as President of the United States by the Constitution and statutes of the United States, it is ordered as follows:

Part I—Nondiscrimination in Government Employment

Section 101. It is the policy of the Government of the United States to provide equal opportunity in Federal employment for all qualified persons, to prohibit discrimination in employment because of race, creed, color, or national origin, and to promote the full realization of equal employment opportunity through a positive, continuing program in each executive department and agency. The policy of equal opportunity applies to every aspect of Federal employment policy and practice.

Section 102. The head of each executive department and agency shall establish and maintain a positive program of equal employment opportunity for all civilian employees and applicants for employment within his jurisdiction in accordance with the policy set forth in Section 101.

Section 103. The Civil Service Commission shall supervise and provide leadership and guidance in the conduct of equal employment opportunity programs for the civilian employees of and applications for employment within the executive departments and agencies and shall review agency program accomplishments periodically. In order to facilitate the achievement of a model program for equal employment opportunity in the Federal service, the Commission may consult from time to time with such individuals, groups, or organizations as may be of assistance in improving the Federal program and realizing the objectives of this part.

Section 104. The Civil Service Commission shall provide for the prompt, fair, and impartial consideration of all complaints of discrimination in Federal employment on the basis of race, creed, color, or national origin. Procedures for the consideration complaints shall include at least one impartial review within the executive department or agency and shall provide for appeal to the Civil Service Commission.

Section 105. The Civil Service Commission shall issue such regulations, orders, and instructions as it deems necessary and appropriate to carry out its responsibilities under this Part, and the head of each executive department and agency shall comply with the regulations, orders, and instructions issued by the Commission under this Part.

Part II—Nondiscrimination In Employment By Government Contractors And Subcontractors

Section 201. The Secretary of Labor shall be responsible for the administration of Parts II and III of this Order and shall adopt such rules and regulations and issue such orders as he deems necessary and appropriate to achieve the purposes thereof.

Section 202. Except in contracts exempted in accordance with Section 204 of this Order, all Government contracting agencies shall include in every Government contract hereafter entered into the following provisions:

"(1) The contractor will not discriminate against any employee or applicant for employment because of race, creed, color, or national origin. The contractor will take affirmative action to ensure

that applicants are employed, and that employees are treated during employment, without regard to their race, creed, color, or national origin. Such action shall include, but not be limited to the following: employment, upgrading, demotion, or transfer; recruitment or recruitment advertising; layoff or termination; rates of pay or other forms of compensation; and selection for training, including apprenticeship. The contractor agrees to post in conspicuous places, available to employees and applicants for employment, notices to be provided by the contracting officer setting forth the provisions of this nondiscrimination clause."

"(2) The contractor will, in all solicitations or advertisements for employees placed by or on behalf of the contractor, state that all qualified applicants will receive consideration for employment without regard to race, creed, color, or national origin. . . ."

Part III—Nondiscrimination Provisions In Federally Assisted Construction Contracts

Section 301. Each executive department and agency which administers a program involving Federal financial assistance shall require as a condition for approval of any grant, contract, loan, insurance, or guarantee thereunder, which may involve a construction contract, that the applicant for Federal assistance undertake and agree to incorporate, or cause to be incorporated, into all construction contracts paid for in whole or in part with funds obtained from the Federal Government or borrowed on the credit of the Federal Government pursuant to such grant, contract, loan, insurance, or guarantee, or undertaken pursuant to any Federal program involving such grant, contract, loan, insurance, or guarantee, the provisions prescribed for Government contracts by Section 202 of this Order or such modification thereof, preserving in substance the contractor's obligations thereunder, as may be approved by the Secretary of Labor, together with such additional provisions as the Secretary deems appropriate to establish and protect the interest of the United States in the enforcement of those obligations. . . .

VOTING RIGHTS ACT OF 1965 PUB.L. NO. 89–110, 79 STAT. 437 (1965)

An Act to enforce the Fifteenth Amendment to the Constitution of the United States, and for other purposes.

Section 2. No voting qualification or prerequisite to voting, or standard, practice, or procedure shall be imposed or applied by any State or political subdivision to deny or abridge the right of any citizen of the United States to vote on account of race or color.

Section 4. (a) To assure that the right of citizens of the United States to vote is not denied or abridged on account of race or color, no citizen shall be denied the right to vote in any Federal, State, or local election because of his failure to comply with any test or device in any State with respect to which the determinations have been made under subsection (b) or in any political subdivision with respect to which such determinations have been made as a separate unit, unless the United States District Court for the District of Columbia in an action for a declaratory judgment brought by such State or subdivision against the United States has determined that no such test or device has been used during the five years preceding the filing of the action for the purpose or with the effect of denying or abridging the right to vote on account of race or color: *Provided,* That no such declaratory judgment shall issue with respect to any plaintiff for a period of five years after the entry of a final judgment of any court of the United States, other than the denial of a declaratory judgment under this section, whether entered prior to or after the enactment of this Act, determining that denials or abridgments of the right to vote on account of race or color through the use of such tests or devices have occurred anywhere in the territory of such plaintiff. . . .

(d) For purposes of this section no State or political subdivision shall be determined to have engaged in the use of tests or devices for the purpose or with the effect of denying or abridging the right to vote on account of race or color if (1) incidents of such use have been few in number and have been promptly and effectively corrected by State or local action, (2) the continuing effect of such incidents has been eliminated, and (3) there is no reasonable probability of their recurrence in the future. . . .

Section 10. (a) The Congress finds that the requirement of the payment of a poll tax as a precondition to voting (i) precludes persons of limited means from voting or imposes unreasonable financial hardship upon such persons as a precondition to their exercise of the franchise, (ii) does not bear a reasonable relationship to any legitimate State interest in the conduct of elections, and (iii) in some areas has the purpose or effect of denying persons the right to vote because of race or color. Upon the basis of these findings, Congress declares that the constitutional right of citizens to vote is denied or abridged in some areas by the requirement of the payment of a poll tax as a precondition to voting. . . .

Section 11. (a) No person acting under color of law shall fail or refuse to permit any person to vote who is entitled to vote under any provision of this Act or is otherwise qualified to vote, or willfully fail or refuse to tabulate, count, and report such person's vote.

(b) No person, whether acting under color of law or otherwise, shall intimidate, threaten, or coerce, or attempt to intimidate, threaten or coerce any person for voting or attempting to vote, or intimidate, threaten, or coerce, or attempt to intimidate, threaten, or coerce any person for urging or aiding any person to vote or attempt to vote, or intimidate, threaten, or coerce any person for exercising any powers or duties under section 3 (a), 6, 8, 9, 10, or 12 (e). . . .

Section 14. (c) (1) The terms "vote" or "voting" shall include all action necessary to make a vote effective in any primary, special, or general election, including, but not limited to, registration, listing pursuant to this Act, or other action required by law prerequisite to voting, casting a ballot, and having such ballot counted properly and included in the appropriate totals of votes cast with respect to candidates for public or party office and propositions for which votes are received in an election. . . .

Sec. 17. Nothing in this Act shall be construed to deny, impair, or otherwise adversely affect the right to vote of any person registered to vote under the law of any state or political subdivision. . . .

THE BLACK PANTHER MANIFESTO (1966)

1. We want FREEDOM. We want power to determine the destiny of our Black Community.

We believe that black people will not be free until we are able to determine our destiny.

2. We want full employment for our people.

We believe that the federal government is responsible and obligated to give every many employment or a guaranteed income. We believe that if the white American businessman will not give full employment, then the means of production should be taken from the businessmen and placed in the community so that the people of the community can organize and employ all of its people and give a high standard of living.

3. We want end to the robberyby the CAPITALIST of our Black Community.

We believe that this racist government has robbed us and now we are demanding the overdue debt of forty acres and two mules. Forty acres and two mules was promised 100 years ago as restitution for slave labor and mass murder of black people. We will accept the payment in currency which will be distributed to our many communities. The Germans are now aiding the Jews in Israel for the genocide of the Jewish people. The Germans murdered six million Jews. The American racist has taken part in the slaughter or over fifty million black people, therefore, we feel that this is a modest demand that we make.

4. We want decent housing, fit for shelter of human beings.

We believe that if the white landlords will not give decent housing to our black community, then the housing and the land should be made into cooperatives so that our community, with government aid, can build and make decent housing for its people.

5. We want education for our people that exposes the true nature of this decadent American society. We want education that teaches us our true history and our role in the present-day society.

We believe in an educational system that will give to our people a knowledge of self. If a man does not have knowledge of himself and his position in society and the world, then he has little chance to relate to anything else.

6. We want all black men to be exempt from military service.

We believe that Black people should not be forced to fight in the military service to defend a racist government that does not protect us. We will not fight and kill other people of color in the world who, like black people, are being victimized by the white racist government of America. We will protect ourselves from the force and violence of the racist police and the racist military, by whatever means necessary,

7. We want an immediate end to POLICE BRUTALITY and MURDER of black people.

We believe we can end police brutality in our black community by organizing black self-defense groups that are dedicated to defending our black community from racist police oppression and brutality. The Second Amendment to the Constitution of the United States gives a right to bear arms. We therefore believe that all black people should arm themselves for self-defense.

8. We want freedom for all black men held in federal, state, county and city prisons and jails.

We believe that all black people should be released from the many jails and prisons because they have not received a fair and impartial trial.

9. We want all black people when brought to trial to be tried in court by a jury of their peer group or

people from their black communities, as defined by the constitution of the United States.

We believe that the courts should follow the United States Constitution so that black people will receive fair trials. The 14th Amendment of the U.S. Constitution gives a man a right to be tried by his peer group. A peer is a person from a similar economic, social, religious, geographical, environmental, historical and racial background. To do this the court will be forced to select a jury from the black community from which the black defendant came. We have been, and are being tried by all-white juries that have no understanding of the "average reasoning man" of the black community.

10. We want land, bread, housing, education, clothing, justice and peace. And as our major political objective, a United Nations-supervised plebiscite to be held throughout the black colony in which only black colonial subjects will be allowed to participate, for the purpose of determining the will of black people as to their national destiny.

When, in the course of human events, it becomes necessary for one people to dissolve the political bands which have connected them with another, and to assume, among the powers of the earth, the separate and equal station to which the laws of nature and nature's God entitle them, a decent respect to the opinions of mankind requires that they should declare the causes which impel them to the separation.

We hold these truths to be self-evident, that all men are created equal; that they are endowed by their Creator with certain inalienable rights; that among these are life, liberty, and the pursuit of happiness.

That, to secure these rights, governments are instituted among them, deriving their just powers from the consent of the governed; that, whenever any form of government becomes destructive of these ends, it is the right of the people to alter or to abolish it, and to institute a new government, laying its foundation on such principles, and or-ganizing its powers in such form, as to them shall seem most likely to effect their safety and happiness.

Prudence, indeed, will dictate that governments long established should not be changed for light and transient causes; and, accordingly, all experience hath shown, that mankind are more disposed to suffer, while evils are sufferable, than to right themselves by abolishing the forms to which they are accustomed. But, when a long train of abuses and usurpations, pursuing invariably the same object, evinces a design to reduce them under absolute despotism, it is their right, it is their duty, to throw off such government, and to provide new guards for their future security.

CIVIL RIGHTS ACT OF 1968 PUB.L. NO. 90–284, TITLES VIII & IX, 82 STAT. 284 (1968)

Title VIII—Fair Housing

Sec. 801. It is the policy of the United States to provide, within constitutional limitations, for fair housing throughout the United States.

Section 804. As made applicable by section 803 and except as exempted by sections 803(b) and 807, it shall be unlawful—

(a) to refuse to sell or rent after the making of a bona fide offer, or to refuse to negotiate for the sale or rental of, or otherwise make unavailable or deny, a dwelling to any person because of race, color, religion, or national origin.

(b) to discriminate against any person in the terms, conditions, or privileges of sale or rental of a dwelling, or in the provision of services or facilities in connection there-with, because of race, color, religion, or national origin.

(c) to make, print, or publish or cause to be made, printed, or published any notice, statement, or advertisement, with respect to the sale or rental of a dwelling that indicates any preference, limitation, or discrimination based on race, color, religion, or national origin, or an intention to make any such preference, limitation, or discrimination.

(d) to represent to any person because of race, color, religion, or national origin that any dwelling is not available for inspection, sale, or rental when such dwelling is in fact so available.

(e) for profit, to induce or attempt to induce any person to sell or rent any dwelling by representations regarding the entry or prospective entry into the neighborhood of a person or persons of a particular race, color, religion, or national origin.

Sec. 805. After December 31, 1968, it shall be unlawful for any bank, building and loan association, insurance company or other corporation, association, firm or enterprise whose business consists in whole or in part in the making of commercial real estate loans, to deny a loan or other financial assistance to a person applying therefor for the purpose of purchasing, constructing, improving, repairing, or maintaining a dwelling, or to discriminate against him in the fixing of the amount, interest rate, duration, or other terms or conditions of such loan or other financial assistance, because of the race, color, religion, or national origin of such person or of any person associated with him in connection with such loan or other financial assistance or the purposes of such loan or other financial assistance, or of the present or prospective owners, leases, tenants, or occupants of the dwelling or dwellings in relation to which such loan or other financial assistance is to be made or given. . . .

Title IX—Prevention of Intimidation in Fair Housing Cases

Section 901. Whoever, whether or not acting under color of law, by force or threat of force willfully injures, intimidates or interferes with, or attempts to injure, intimidate or interfere with—

(a) any person because of his race, color, religion or national origin and because he is or has been selling, purchasing, renting, financing, occupying, or contracting or negotiating for the sale, purchase, rental, financing or occupation of any dwelling, or applying for or participating in any service, organization, or facility relating to the business of selling or renting dwellings; or

(b) any person because he is or has been, or in order to intimidate such person or any other person or any class of persons from—

(1) participating, without discrimination on account of race, color, religion or national origin, in any of the activities, services, organizations or facilities described in subsection 901(a). . . .

PRESIDENT GEORGE BUSH'S MESSAGE TO THE SENATE RETURNING WITHOUT APPROVAL THE CIVIL RIGHTS ACT OF 1990 26

WEEKLY COMP. PRES.DOC. 1632–34 (OCT. 22, 1990)

To the Senate of the United States.

I am today returning without my approval [Separate Bill] 2104, the "Civil Rights Act of 1990." I deeply regret having to take this action with respect to a bill bearing such a title, especially since it contains certain provisions that I strongly endorse.

Discrimination, whether on the basis of race, national origin, sex, religion, or disability, is worse than wrong. It is a fundamental evil that tears at the fabric of our society, and one that all Americans should and must oppose. That requires rigorous enforcement of existing antidiscrimination laws. . . .

. . . Despite the use of the term "civil rights" in the title of S. 2104, the bill actually employs a maze of highly legalistic language to introduce the destructive force of quotas into our Nation's employment system. Primarily through provisions governing cases in which employment practices are alleged to have unintentionally caused the disproportionate exclusion of members of certain groups, S. 2104 creates powerful incentives for employers to adopt hiring and promotion quotas. These incentives are created by the bill's new and very technical rules of litigation, which will make it difficult for employers to defend legitimate employment practices. In many cases, a defense against unfounded allegations will be impossible. Among other problems, the plaintiff often need not even show that any of the employer's practices caused a significant statistical disparity. In other cases, the employer's defense is confined to an unduly narrow definition of "business necessity" that is significantly more restrictive than that established by the Supreme Court in *Griggs v. Duke Power Co.* and in two decades of subsequent decisions. Thus, unable to defend legitimate practices in court, employers will be driven to adopt quotas in order to avoid liability.

Proponents of S. 2104 assert that it is needed to overturn the Supreme Court's *Wards Cove Packing Co. v. Antonio* decision and restore the law that had existed since the Griggs case in 1971. S. 2104, however, does not in fact codify Griggs or the Court's subsequent decisions prior to Ward Cove. Instead, S. 2104 engages in a sweeping rewrite of two decades of Supreme Court jurisprudence, using language that appears in no decision of the Court and that is contrary to principles acknowledged even by the Justice Stevens' dissent in Wards Cove: "The opinion in Griggs made it clear that a neutral practice that operates to exclude minorities is nevertheless lawful if it serves a valid business purpose."

I am aware of the dispute among lawyers about the proper interpretation of certain critical language used in this portion of S. 2104. The very fact of this dispute suggests that the bill is not codifying the law developed by the Supreme Court in Griggs and subsequent cases. This debate, moreover, is a sure sign that S. 2104 will lead to years—perhaps decades—of uncertainty and expensive litigation. It is neither fair nor sensible to give the employers of our country a difficult choice between using quotas and seeking a clarification of the law through costly and very risky litigation.

D. 3205 contains several other unacceptable provisions as well. One section unfairly closes the courts, in many instances, to individuals victimized by agreements, to which they were not a party, involving the use of quotas. Another section radically alters the remedial provisions in Title VII of the Civil Rights Act of 1964, replacing measures designed to foster conciliation and settlement

with a new scheme modeled on a tort system widely acknowledged to be in a state of crisis. The bill also contains a number of provisions that will create unnecessary and inappropriate incentives for litigation. These include unfair retroactivity rules; attorneys fee provisions that will discourage settlements; unreasonable new statutes of limitation; and a "rule of construction" that will make it extremely difficult to know how courts can be expected to apply the law. In order to assist the Congress regarding legislation in this area, I enclose herewith a memorandum from the Attorney General explaining in detail the defects that make S. 2104 unacceptable.

Our goal and our promise has been equal opportunity and equal protection under the law. That is a bedrock principle from which we cannot retreat. The temptation to support a bill—any bill—simply because its title includes the words "civil rights" is very strong. This impulse is not entirely bad. Presumptions have too often run the other way, and our Nation's history on racial questions cautions against complacency. But when our efforts, however well intentioned, result in quotas, equal opportunity is not advanced but thwarted. The very commitment to justice and equality that is offered as the reason why this bill should be signed requires me to veto it. . . .

George Bush
The White House,
October 22, 1990.

CIVIL RIGHTS ACT OF 1991 PUB.L. NO. 102–166, 105 STAT 1071 (1991)

This act is designed to provide additional remedies to deter harassment and intentional discrimination in the workplace, to provide guidelines for the adjudication of cases arising under Title VII . . . and to expand the scope of civil rights legislation weakened by Supreme Court decisions, particularly the Court's ruling in *Wards Cove Packing Co. v. Antonio,* 490 US 642 (1989).

Sec. 2. Findings

The Congress finds that—

(1) additional remedies under Federal law are needed to deter unlawful harassment and intentional discrimination in the workplace;

(2) the decision of the Supreme Court in *Wards Cove Packing Co. v. Antonio,* 490 U.S. 642 (1989) has weakened the scope and effectiveness of Federal civil rights protections; and

(3) legislation is necessary to provide additional protections against unlawful discrimination in employment.

Sec. 3. Purposes.

The purposes of this Act are—

(1) to provide appropriate remedies for intentional discrimination and unlawful harassment in the workplace;

(2) to codify the concepts of "business necessity" and "job related" enunciated by the Supreme Court in *Griggs v. Duke Power Co.,* 401 U.S. 424 (1971), and in the other Supreme Court decisions prior to *Wards Cove Packing Co. v. Antonio,* 490 U.S. 642 (1989);

(3) to confirm statutory authority and provide statutory guidelines for the adjudication of disparate impact suits under title VII of the Civil Rights Act of 1964 (42 U.S.C. 2000e et seq.); and

(4) to respond to recent decisions of the Supreme Court by expanding the scope of relevant civil rights statutes in order to provide adequate protection to victims of discrimination.

Title I—Federal Civil Rights Remedies

Sec. 105. Burden of Proof in Disparate Impact Cases.

(a) Section 703 of the Civil Rights Act of 1964 (42 U.S.C. 2000e–2) is amended by adding at the end the following new subsection:

. . . An unlawful employment practice based on disparate impact is established under this title only if—

. . . A complaining party demonstrates that a respondent used a particular employment practice that causes a disparate impact on the basis of race, color, religion, sex, or national origin and the respondent fails to demonstrate that the challenged practice is job related for the position in question and consistent with business necessity. . . .

. . .With respect to demonstrating that a particular employment practice causes a disparate impact as described in subparagraph

(A)(i), the complaining party shall demonstrate that each particular challenged employment practice causes a disparate impact, except that if the complaining party can demonstrate to the court that the elements of a respondent's decisionmaking process are not capable of separation for analysis, the decisionmaking process may be analyzed as one employment practice.

. . . If the respondent demonstrates that a specific employment practice does not cause the disparate impact, the respondent shall not be required to demonstrate that such practice is required by business necessity. . . .

Sec. 106. Prohibition Against Discriminatory Use of Test Scores.

Section 703 of the Civil Rights Act of 1964 (42 U.S.C. 2000e–2) (as amended by section 105) is further amended by adding at the end of the following new subsection:

. . . It shall be an unlawful employment practice for a respondent, in connection with the selection or referral of applicants or candidates for employment or promotion, to adjust the scores of, use different cutoff scores for, or otherwise alter the results of, employment related tests on the basis of race, color, religion, sex, or national origin. . . .

Title II—Glass Ceiling

Sec. 202 Findings and Purpose.

(a) Findings—Congress finds that—

(1) despite a dramatically growing presence in the workplace, women and minorities remain underrepresented in management and decision-making positions in business;

(2) artificial barriers exist to the advancement of women and minorities in the workplace;

(3) United States corporations are increasingly relying on women and minorities to meet employment requirements and are increasingly aware of the advantages derived from a diverse work force;

(4) the "Glass Ceiling Initiative" undertaken by the Department of Labor, including the release of the report entitled "Report on the Glass Ceiling Initiative," has been instrumental in raising public awareness of—

(A) the underrepresentation of women and minorities at the management and decision-making levels in the United States work force;

(B) the underrepresentation of women and minorities in line functions in the United States work force;

(C) the lack of access for qualified women and minorities to credential-building developmental opportunities; and

(D) the desirability of eliminating artificial barriers to the advancement of women and minorities to such levels;

(f) the establishment of a commission to examine issues raised by the Glass Ceiling Initiative would help—

(A) focus greater attention on the importance of eliminating artificial barriers to the advancement of women and minorities to management and decision-making positions in business; and

(B) promote work force diversity. . . .

THE CHALLENGE TO OURSELVES (AN EXCERPT FROM THE MISSION STATEMENT FOR THE MILLION MAN MARCH, 1995)

By the National Million Man March/Day of Absence Organizing Committee

1. The Million Man March and Day of Absence are posed first in challenge to ourselves. We understand that the challenge to ourselves is the greatest challenge. For it is only by making demands on ourselves that we can make successful demands on society. In this regard we have raised

three basic themes: Atonement, Reconciliation and Responsibility. For it is through being at one with the Creator, each other and creation and reconciling our differences with each other, that we can stand up together in unity, strength and dignity and accept and bear the responsibility heaven and history have placed on us at this critical juncture in the life and struggle of our people.

Atonement

2. For us, atonement in the best spiritual and ethical sense is to recognize wrongs done and make amends, to be self-critical and self-corrective. It means turning inward and assessing the right and the wrong, recognizing shortcomings and committing oneself to correcting them.

3. Atonement means being always concerned about standing worthy before the Creator, before others and before the creation, being humble enough to admit mistakes and wrongs and bold enough to correct them.

4. We call then for a Holy Day of Atonement on this October 16, 1995, a day to meditate on and seek right relationships with the Creator, with each other and with nature.

5. We call also for a special remembering of the ancestors on this day and honoring them by a renewed commitment to speak truth, do justice, resist evil and always choose the good, as they taught us through word and deed.

6. To the extent that we have failed to do all we can in the way we can to make ourselves and our community the best of what it means to be African and human, we ask forgiveness from the Creator and each other. And therefore, we dare to atone.

7. And thus we commit and recommit ourselves on this day and afterwards to constantly strive to be better persons, live fuller and more meaningful lives, build strong, loving and egalitarian families and struggle to make our community, society and the world a better place in which to live.

Reconciliation

8. We call also for reconciliation, which is a companion practice of atonement. For it means,

for us, to bring oneself into harmony with the Creator, others and creation. 9. This means we call for all of us to settle disputes, overcome conflicts, put aside grudges and hatreds in our personal and social relationships. And in and between our organizations and institutions in the spirit of brotherhood and sisterhood, to reject and oppose communal, family and personal violence, and to strive to build and sustain loving, mutually respectful and reciprocal relations; in a word, to seek the good, find it, embrace it and build on it.

10. Reconciliation also means that we must strive for and achieve a principled and active unity for the common good. This we call operational unity, a unity in diversity, a unity without uniformity, a unity based on principle and practice.

11. We therefore commit and recommit ourselves to the principle and practice of reconciliation. For it is in and through reconciliation that we can embrace, stand together, organize our community and solve the problems in it, harness its energies for maximum development and struggle to end injustice and create the just and good society.

Responsibility

12. Finally, we challenge each Black man in particular, and the Black community in general, to renew and expand our commitment to responsibility in personal conduct, in family relations and in obligations to the community and to the struggle for a just society and a better world. And for us, to be responsible is to willingly and readily assume obligations and duties; to be accountable and dependable.

13. It means to stand up, stand together and stand in practice; to stand up in consciousness and commitment. To stand together in harmony and unity as men, as brothers, as women and sisters, as partners, as family and as community. And to stand in the practice of struggle, dedication, discipline, sacrifice and achievement; always building, doing good, resisting evil and constantly creating and embracing possibilities for fuller and more meaningful lives. We thus commit and recommit ourselves to take personal and collective responsi-

bility for our lives and the welfare and future of our families and our community. And we commit ourselves to stand up in knowledge and resolve. To stand together in principled and active unity and to stand in moral and liberating practice.

14. In raising the challenge of a new, renewed and expanded assumption of responsibility, we call on those Black men and women with greater means to shoulder greater responsibility. To invest in the community and transform it; and to avoid imitating the established order in its disdain for and blame of the poor and vulnerable.

15. Our obligation is to remember the ancient moral teaching that we should give food to the hungry, water to the thirsty, clothes to the naked and a boat to the boatless. that we should be a father for the orphan, a mother to the timid, a shelter for the battered, a staff of support for the aged, a companion and comforter of the ill, an aid to the poor, strength for the weak, a raft for the drowning and a ladder for those trapped in the pit of despair. In a word, we must love justice, hate wrongdoing, resist evil and always do the good.

NATIONAL AFRICAN AMERICAN HISTORY MONTH, 1996

By The President of The United States of America

A PROCLAMATION

Today's schoolchildren are fortunate to grow up in classrooms where they are taught to appreciate all of the many heroes of American history. While previous generations read textbooks that told only part of our Nation's story, materials have been developed in recent years that give our students a fuller picture — textured and deepened by new characters and themes. African American History Month provides a special opportunity for teachers and schools to celebrate this ongoing process and to focus on the many African Americans whose lives have shaped our common experience.

This year, our observance emphasizes black women and the strides made to bring their achievements to the fore. From Sojourner Truth's sermons, to Mary McLeod Bethune's speeches, to the contemporary novels of Nobel laureate Toni Morrison, the voices of African American women have called attention to the twin burdens of racism and sexism and have invited listeners to discover the richness of traditions kept alive in back kitchens and workrooms. In churches and communities, and more recently in universities and statehouses across America, these women have fought extraordinary battles for social, economic, and political empowerment. Barbara Jordan once wrote,

> 'We the people'; it is a very eloquent beginning. But when the Constitution of the United States was completed on the seventeenth of September, 1787, I was not included in that 'We the people.'

As we mourn the loss of this great American, let us honor her by seeking to further the progress made since those early days toward true equality and inclusion. During African American History Month and throughout the year, we must embrace the diverse strands of our story so that all children can see themselves in our Nation's past and know that they have a role to play in seizing the future's countless opportunities.

NOW, THEREFORE, I, WILLIAM J. CLINTON, President of the United States of America, by virtue of the authority vested in me by the Constitution and laws of the United States, do hereby proclaim February 1996, as National African American History Month. I call upon Government officials, educators in schools, colleges, universities, and libraries, and all the people of the United States to observe this month with appropriate ceremonies, activities, and programs that raise awareness of African American history and invite further inquiry into this area of study.

IN WITNESS WHEREOF, I have hereunto set my hand this thirtieth day of January, in the year of our Lord nineteen hundred and ninety-six, and of the Independence of theUnited States of America the two hundred and twentieth.

WILLIAM J. CLINTON

BIBLIOGRAPHICAL AIDS

MAJOR REPOSITORIES

The major collections of materials in African American history are the Amistad Collection at Tulane University, the Moorland Collection at Howard University, the Slaughter Collection at Atlanta University, the James Weldon Johnson Collection at Yale University, the Washington Collection and the Records and Research Center at Tuskegee University, the Schomburg Collection at the New York Public Library, and the Hampton University Library.

GENERAL BIBLIOGRAPHY

These are some of the sources used to compile and verify information in this book. Many are considered standard reference sources in African American history.

Adams, Russell L. *Great Negroes, Past and Present.* Chicago: Afro-American Publishing, 1963.

Adler, Mortimer J., Charles Van Doren, and George Ducas, eds. *The Negro in American History,* 3 vols. Chicago: Encyclopaedia Britannica, 1969.

The African American Experience: A History. Sharon Harley, Stephen Middleton, and Charlotte Stokes, consultants. Englewood Cliffs, N.J.: Prentice-Hall, 1992.

African American History in the Press, 1851–1899, 2 vols. Detroit: Gale Research, 1996.

Alexander, William T. *History of the Colored Race in America.* New York: Negro Universities Press, 1968.

Aptheker, Herbert, ed. *A Documentary History of the Negro People in the United States,* 6 vols. New York: Citadel Press, 1951–1993.

Bardolph, Richard. *The Negro Vanguard.* New York: Rinehart, 1959.

Bennett, Lerone, Jr. *Before the Mayflower: A History of Black America,* 5th ed. New York: Penguin Books, 1984.

Berry, Mary Frances, and John W. Blassingame. *Long Memory: The Black Experience in America.* New York: Oxford University Press, 1982.

Bond, Horace Mann. *The Education of the Negro in the American Social Order.* New York: Octagon Books, 1966.

Bone, Robert. *The Negro Novel in America.* New Haven: Yale University Press, 1965.

Brawley, Benjamin. *The Negro Genius: A New Appraisal of the Achievement of the American Negro in Literature and the Fine Arts.* New York: Dodd, Mead, 1937.

———. *The Negro in Literature and Art in the United States.* New York: Duffield, 1929.

———. *A Social History of the American Negro.* New York: The Macmillan Company, 1921.

Brotz, Howard, ed. *Negro Social and Political Thought, 1850–1920.* New York: Basic Books, 1966.

Christopher, Maurine. *Black Americans in Congress.* New York: Crowell, 1976.

Cowan, Tom and Jack Maguire. *Timelines of African-American History: 500 Years of Black Achievement.* New York: Roundtable Press/ Perigee, 1994.

Detweiler, Frederick G. *The Negro Press in the United States.* Chicago: University of Chicago Press, 1922.

Drimmer, Melvin, comp. *Black History: A Reappraisal.* Garden City, N.Y.: Doubleday, 1968.

Embree, Edwin R. *Brown America: The Story of a New Race.* New York: The Viking Press, 1931.

Fishel, Leslie H., Jr., and Benjamin Quarles. *The Negro American: A Documentary History.* New York: Morrow, 1968.

Foner, Eric, comp. *America's Black Past: A Reader in Afro-American History.* New York: Harper & Row, 1970.

Foner, Philip. *History of Black Americans,* 3 vols. Westport, Conn.: Greenwood Press, 1983.

Franklin, John Hope. *From Slavery to Freedom,* 6th ed. New York: Knopf, 1988.

———. *The Negro in Twentieth Century America: A Reader on the Struggle for Civil Rights.* New York: Vintage Books, 1967.

Franklin, Vincent P. *Black Self-Determination: A Cultural History of the Faith of the Fathers.* Westport, Conn.: L. Hill, 1984.

Ginzberg, Eli, and Alfred S. Eichner. *The Troublesome Presence: Amercian Democracy and the Negro.* New York: Free Press of Glencoe, 1964.

Gloster, Hugh Morris. *Negro Voices in American Fiction.* Chapel Hill: Univeristy of North Carolina Press, 1948.

Gossett, Thomas F. *Race: The History of an Idea in America.* Dallas: Southern Methodist University Press, 1963.

Greene, Lorenzo. *The Negro in Colonial New England.* New York: Antheneum, 1968.

Harding, Vincent. *There is a River: The Black Struggle for Freedom in America.* New York: Harcourt Brace Jovanovich, 1981.

Harper, Michael, and Robert B. Stepto, eds. *Chant of Saints: A Gathering of Afro-American Literature, Art, and Scholarship.* Urbana: Universitiy of Illinois Press, 1979.

Hayden, Robert Earl, David J. Burrows, and Frederick R. Lapides, comps. *Afro-American Literature: An Introduction.* New York: Harcourt Brace Jovanovich, 1971.

Hening, William Waller. *The Statutes at Large: Being a Collection of all the Laws of Virginia, from the First Session of the Legislature in the Year 1619.* Charlottesville: Published for the Jamestown Foundation of the Commonwealth of Virginia by the University Press of Virginia, 1969.

Hill, Levirn, ed. *Black American Colleges & Universities: Profiles of Two-Year, Four-Year & Professional Schools.* Detroit: Gale Research, 1994.

Hine, Darlene Clark, ed. *The State of Afro-American History: Past, Present, and Future.* Baton Rouge: Louisiana State University Press, 1986.

Hoover, Dwight W., comp. *Understanding Negro History.* Chicago: Quadrangle Books, 1969.

Hornsby, Alton, Jr. *The Black Almanac,* 2nd ed. Woodbury, N.Y.: Barron's Educational Series, 1977.

Hughes, Langston. *Famous Negro Heroes of America.* New York: Dodd, Mead, 1958.

Hughes, Langston, Milton Meltzer, and C. Eric Lincoln. *A Pictorial History of Black Americans,* 5th ed. New York: Crown Publishers, 1983.

Jones, LeRoi. *Blues People: Negro Music in White America.* New York: W. Morrow, 1963.

Johnson, Charles S. *The Negro in American Civilization: A Study of Negro Life and Race Relations in the Light of Social Research.* New York: H. Holt and Co., 1930.

Johnson, Edward A. *A School History of the Negro Race in America from 1619 to 1890.* Raleigh, N.C.: Edwards & Broughton, 1891.

Jordon, Winthrop D. *White over Black: American Attitudes Toward the Negro, 1550–1812.* Chapel Hill: University of North Carolina Press, 1968.

Katz, William Loren. *Eyewitness: The Negro in American History.* New York: Pitman, 1974.

Lewis, Samella S. *Art: African American.* New York: Harcourt Brace Jovanovich, 1978.

Locke, Alain L. *Negro Art: Past and Present* Washington, D.C.: Associates in Negro Folk Education, 1936.

Logan, Rayford W. *The Negro in the United States: A Brief History.* Princeton, N.J.: D. Van Nostrand, 1957.

Logan, Rayford W., and Michael Winston. *Dictionary of American Negro Biography.* New York: W. W. Norton, 1982.

Low, W. Augustus. *Encyclopedia of Black America.* New York: McGraw-Hill, 1981.

Lowery, Charles D., and John F. Marszalek. *Encyclopedia of African-American Civil Rights.* Westport, Conn.: Greenwood Press, 1992.

Mays, Benjamin E., and Joseph W. Nicholson. *The Negro's Church.* New York: Institute of Social and Religious Research, 1933.

McPherson, James M., et al. *Blacks in America: Bibliographical Essays.* Garden City, N.Y.: Doubleday, 1971.

Meier, August, and Elliott M. Rudwick. *Black History and the Historical Profession, 1915–1980.* Urbana: University of Illinois Press, 1986.

———. *From Plantation to Ghetto: An Interpretive History of American Negroes,* rev. ed. New York: Hill and Wang, 1970.

———, eds. *The Making of Black America: Essays in Negro Life and History.* New York: Atheneum, 1969.

Osofsky, Gilbert. *The Burden of Race: A Documentary History of Negro-White Relations in America.* New York: Harper & Row, 1967.

Parsons, Talcott, and Kenneth B. Clark, eds. *The Negro American.* Boston: Houghton, Mifflin, 1966.

Pennington, James W. C. *A Textbook of the Origin and History of the Colored People.* 1841. Detroit: Negro History Press, 1969.

Pride, Armistead S., et al. *The Black American and the Press.* Ed. Jack Lyle. Los Angeles: W. Ritchie Press, 1968.

Ragsdale, Bruce A., and Joel D. Treese. *Black Americans in Congress, 1870–1989.* Washington, D.C.: U.S. Government Printing Office, 1990.

Ruchames, Louis, ed. *Racial Thought in America: A Documentary History.* Amherst: University of Massachusetts Press, 1969.

Shade, William G., and Roy C. Herrenkohl, eds. *Seven on Black: Reflections on the Negro Experience in America.* Philadelphia: Lippincott, 1969.

Smith, Jesse Carney. *Black Firsts: 2,000 Years of Extraordinary Achievement.* Detroit: Gale Research, 1994.

Southern, Eileen. *The Music of Black Americans: A History.* New York: W. W. Norton, 1971.

Suggs, Henry Lewis, ed. *The Black Press in the South.* Westport, Conn.: Greenwood, Press, 1983.

Toppin, Edgar Allan. *A Biographical History of Blacks in America Since 1528.* New York: McKay, 1971.

————. *Blacks in America: Then and Now.* Boston: Christian Science Publishing Society, 1969.

Tovar, Federico Ribes. *A Chronological History of Puerto Rico.* New York: Plus Ultra Educational Publishers, 1973.

Trager, James. *The People's Chronology.* New York: Henry Holt, 1994.

Washington, Booker T. *The Story of the Negro: The Rise of the Race from Slavery,* 2 vols. New York: Doubleday, Page, 1909.

Washington, Joseph R. *Black Religion: The Negro and Christianity in the United States.* Boston: Beacon Press, 1964.

Weatherford, Willis, D. *The Negro from Africa to America.* New York: George H. Doran Co., 1924.

————. *Present Forces in Negro Progress.* New York: Associated Press, 1912.

Weinstein, Allen, and Frank Otto Gatell, eds. *The Segregation Era, 1863–1954: A Modern Reader.* New York: Oxford University Press, 1970.

Williams, George Washington. *A History of the Negro Race in America, 1619–1880.* New York: Arno Press, 1968.

————. *A History of the Negro Troops in the War and the Rebellion, 1861–1865.* New York: Harper & Brothers, 1888.

Woodson, Carter G. *The Education of the Negro Prior to 1861.* New York: Arno Press, 1968.

————. *The History of the Negro Church,* 2nd ed. Washington, D.C.: The Associated Publishers, 1945.

Woodson, Carter G., and Charles H. Wesley. *The Negro in Our History,* 10th ed. Washington, D.C.: Associated Publishers, 1962.

Work, Monroe N., comp. *A Bibliography of the Negro in Africa and America.* New York: The H. W. Wilson Company, 1928.

FURTHER READING

Special attention has been given to bibliographical references that may assist a reader in further research endeavors. The following suggested reading material is arranged by historical period.

1492–1618

Some of the better histories delineating African history, the slave trade, and slavery in the West Indies are: Maurice Delafosse, *The Negroes of Africa: History and Culture* (1931); Basil Davidson, *The Lost Cities of Africa* (revised edition, 1970); Melville J. Herskovits, *Myth of the Negro Past* (reprint, 1958); Roland F. Oliver, *Africa in the Iron Age* (1975); Daniel R. Mannix, *Black Cargoes: A History of the Atlantic Slave Trade, 1518–1865* (1962); Philip D. Curtin, *The Atlantic Slave Trade: A Census* (1969); and Eric Williams, *Capitalism and Slavery* (1944).

Other good sources include: Leo Wiener, *Africa and the Discovery of America* (3 vols., 1922); Ivan Van Sertima, *They Came before Columbus* (1976); Rayford W. Logan, "Estevanico, Negro Discoverer of the Southwest," *Phylon* (Fourth Quarter, 1940); Lowell J. Ragats, *The Fall of the Planter Class in the British Caribbean* (1928); Herbert S. Klein, *Slavery in the Americas* (1967); David Barry Gaspar, *Bondsmen and Rebels: A Study of Master-Slave Relations in Antigua* (1985); Franklin W. Knight, *The African Dimension in Latin American Societies* (1970); and Carl N. Degler, *Neither Black nor White: Slavery and Race Relations in Brazil and the United States* (1971).

1619–1860

The slave period in African American history is exhaustively treated. Some of the more useful of the older works include: Oscar and Mary Handlin, "Origins of the Southern Labor System," *William and Mary Quarterly* (1950); Carl Degler, "Slavery and the Genesis of American Race Prejudice," *Comparative Studies in Society and History* (1959); Winthrop D. Jordan, "The Influence of the West Indies on the Origins of New England Slavery," *William and Mary Quar-*

terly (1961); Eugene Sirmans, "The Legal Status of the Slave in South Carolina 1670–1740," and Winthrop D. Jordan, "Modern Tensions and the Origins of American Slavery," *Journal of Southern History* (1962).

A controversial essay best read in conjunction with the criticisms of Herbert Aptheker and C. Vann Woodward in the same issue is Eugene D. Genovese's "The Legacy of Slavery and the Roots of Black Nationalism," *Studies on the Left* (1966). See also Robert Twombly and Robert H. Moore, "Black Puritan: The Negro in Seventeenth-Century Massachusetts," *William and Mary Quarterly* (1967); Edward R. Turner, "Slavery in Colonial Pennsylvania," *Pennsylvania Magazine of History and Biography* (1911); Don B. Kates, "Abolition, Deportation, Integration: Attitudes Toward Slavery in the Early Republic," *Journal of Negro History* (1968); Ernest J. Clarke, "Aspects of the North Carolina Slave Code, 1715–1860," *North Carolina Historical Review* (1962); and Harold D. Woodman, "The Profitability of Slavery: An Historical Perennial," *Journal of Southern History* (1963).

Good reminiscences of former slaves include: Frederick Douglass, *My Bondage and My Freedom* (1955), an autobiographical reminiscence; John H. Moore, "Simon Gray, Riverman: A Slave Who Was Almost Free," *Mississippi Valley Historical Review* (1962); John B. Cade, ed., "Out of the Mouths of Ex-Slaves," *Journal of Negro History* (1935); E.O. Settle, "Social Attitudes During the Slave Regime: Household Servants Versus Field Hands," *Publications of the American Sociological Society* (1934); and J. Ralph Jones, ed., "Portraits of Georgia Slaves," *Georgia Review* (1967).

Other excellent sources of slave oral histories include Gilbert Osofsky, ed., *Puttin' On Ole Massa* (1969); Arna Bontemps, ed., *Great Slave Narratives* (1969); Benjamin Botkin, ed., *Lay My Burden Down* (1945), a comprehensive compilation of the reminiscences of former slaves; Frank Tannenbaum, *Slave and Citizen* (1946), a comparative work; and James Mellon, *Bullwhip*

Days: The Slaves Remember, An Oral History (1988).

For an excellent analysis of slave songs and folk beliefs, see Sterling Brown, "Negro Folk Expression: Spirituals, Secular Ballads, and Songs," *Phylon* (1953). Other noteworthy works about American slavery are Kenneth Scott, "The Slave Insurrection in New York in 1712," *New York Historical Society Quarterly* (1961); T.W. Clark, "The Negro Plot of 1741," *New York History* (1944); Ferene M. Szasz, "The New York Slave Revolt of 1741: A Re-examination," *New York History* (1967); Raymond and Alice Bauer, "Day to Day Resistance to Slavery," *Journal of Negro History* (1943); Marion D. Kilson, "Toward Freedom: An Analysis of Slave Revolts in the United States," *Phylon* (1964); and George M. Fredrickson and Christopher Lasch, "Resistance to Slavery," *Civil War History* (1967).

A controversial analysis of the famous South Carolina slave conspiracy was written by Richard Wade, "The Vesey Plot Reconsidered," *Journal of Southern History* (1964).

The best of the older books about American slavery include: Lorenzo Greene, *The Negro in Colonial New England* (1942); Ulrich B. Phillips, *American Negro Slavery* (1918), extensive scholarly research, though it reflects the racism of that epoch; Kenneth M. Stampp, *The Peculiar Institution* (1956), a major revisionist work; U.B. Phillips, *Life and Labor in the Old South* (1929); Stanley Elkins, *Slavery* (1959), a controversial historical-psychological study; Matthew T. Mellon, *Early American Views of Negro Slavery* (1934); Charles Sydnor, *Slavery in Mississippi* (1933); Edward J. McManus, *A History of Negro Slavery in New York* (1966); Joe Gray Taylor, *Negro Slavery in Louisiana* (1961); James C. Ballagh, *A History of Slavery in Virginia*; Guion G. Johnson, *Ante-Bellum North Carolina* (1937); Frank J. Klingberg, *An Appraisal of the Negro in Colonial South Carolina* (1941); Ralph B. Flanders, *Plantation Slavery in Georgia* (1933); Staughton Lynd, *Class Conflict, Slavery, and the United States Constitution* (1967); Frederic

Bancroft, *Slave Trading in the Old South* (1931); Richard C. Wade, *Slavery in the Cities* (1964); Eugene D. Genovese, *The Political Economy of Slavery* (1965); and Alfred H. Conrad and John R. Meyer, *The Economics of Slavery* (1964).

Abolitionists and abolitionism are well treated in Arthur Zilversmit, *The First Emancipation* (1967); Frederick Douglass, *The Life and Times of Frederick Douglass* (1881); and Miles M. Fisher, *Negro Slave Songs in the United States* (1953). Herbert Aptheker's *American Negro Slave Revolts* (1943) is one of the most controversial works on the subject.

Other works on abolitionists and abolitionism include Herbert Aptheker, ed., *One Continual Cry* (1965); Larry Gara, *The Liberty Line* (1961), a study of the Underground Railroad; Herbert Aptheker, *To Be Free* (1948); Martin Duberman, ed., *The Anti-Slavery Vanguard* (1965); Aileen Kraditor, *Means and Ends in American Abolitionism* (1969), a work weakened by the author's tendency to avoid controversy; Eugene H. Berwanger, *The Frontier against Slavery* (1967); Eric Foner, *Free Soil, Free Labor, Free Men* (1970); Henrietta Buckmaster, *Let My People Go: The Story of the Underground Railroad and the Growth of the Abolition Movement* (1941); David B. Davis, *The Problem of Slavery in Western Culture* (1958); Nicholas Halasz, *The Rattling Chains: Slave Unrest and Revolt in the American South* (1959), a novelistic treatment; Joseph C. Carroll, *Slave Insurrections in the United States, 1800–1860* (1938); Lorenzo J. Greene, "Mutiny on the Slave Ships," *Phylon* (1944), a fascinating but little studied subject; Ann Petry, *Harriett Tubman* (1955); Herbert Aptheker, *The Negro in the Abolitionist Movement* (1941); and David Walker, *Appeal in Four Articles* (1830), a militant anti-slavery pamphlet.

A study of Denmark Vesey's plot was conducted by John Lofton, *Insurrection in South Carolina* (1964); William Freehling's *Prelude to Civil War* (1966) is another account of the Vesey conspiracy; Herbert Aptheker's *Nat Turner's Slave Rebellion* (1966) is perhaps a bit exaggerated; Louis

Filler's *Crusade against Slavery* (1960) is an excellent study; see also Dwight Dumond's *Anti-Slavery* (1961) and Benjamin Quarles's *Black Abolitionists* (1969), a long overdue work.

Many authors have explored the contributions of Frederick Douglass, including Philip S. Foner, *The Life and Writings of Frederick Douglass* (4 vols., 1950–1955)and *Frederick Douglass* (1964); and Benjamin Quarles, *Frederick Douglass* (1948).

The better older works about antebellum free blacks are Charles S. Sydnor, "The Free Negro in Mississippi Before the Civil War," *American Historical Review* (1927); Horace Fitchett, "Origin and Growth of the Free Negro Population of Charleston, South Carolina," *Journal of Negro History* (1941); Dorothy B. Porter, "The Organized Educational Activities of Negro Literary Societies, 1818–1846," *Journal of Negro Education* (1936); Robert Ernst, "The Economic Status of New York City Negroes, 1850–1863," (1949); Lee Calligaro, "The Negro's Legal Status in Pre-Civil War New Jersey", *New Jersey History* (1967); Richard C. Wade, "The Negro in Cincinnati, 1800–1830," *Journal of Negro History* (1954); Benjamin Quarles, *The Negro in the American Revolution* (1961); Shirley Graham, *The Story of Phyllis Wheatley* (1949); William Nell, *The Colored Patriots of the American Revolution* (1855); William Wells Brown, *The Negro in the American Revolution* (1867); Howard H. Bell, "The Negro Emigration Movement, 1849–1854: A Phase of Negro Nationalism," *Phylon* (1959); and H.H. Bell, "Expressions of Negro Militancy in the North, 1840–1860," *Journal of Negro History* (1960).

Other sources on antebellum free blacks are H.H. Bell, "Negro Nationalism: A Factor in Emigration Projects, 1858–1861," *Journal of Negro History* (1962); Hollis R. Lynch, "Pan-Negro Nationalism in the New World Before 1862," *Boston University Papers on Africa* (1966); L. Mehlinger, "The Attitude of the Free Negro Toward African Colonization," *Journal of Negro History* (1916); H.N. Sherwood, "Paul Cuffe," *Journal of Negro History* (1923), the story of New

England's most noted free black man; Leon Litwack, *North of Slavery* (1961), the standard account on the subject; John Hope Franklin, *The Free Negro in North Carolina 1790–1860* (1943); John H. Russell, *The Free Negro in Virginia* (1913); Carter G. Woodson, *Free Negro Heads of Families in the United States in 1830* (1925); Emma Lou Thornbrough, *The Negro in Indiana before 1900* (1957); Charles H. Wesley, *Richard Allen* (1935), still the best biography of the founder of the A.M.E. Church; Philip J. Staudenraus, *The African Colonization Movement, 1816–1865* (1961); Roger W. Shugg, "Negro Voting in the Ante-Bellum South," *Journal of Negro History* (October 1936); John H. Russell, "Colored Freemen as Slave Owners in Virginia," *Journal of Negro History* (1916); and Carter G. Woodson, *Free Negro Owners of Slaves in the United States in 1830* (1925).

The role of free blacks in abolitionist activities appears in William Breser, "John B. Russwurm," *Journal of Negro History* (1928); Monroe Work, "The Life of Charles B. Ray," *Journal of Negro History* (1919); Dorothy Porter, "David Ruggles, An Apostle of Human Rights," *Journal of Negro History* (1943); Ray A. Billington, "James Forten, Forgotten Abolitionist," *Negro History Bulletin* (1949), an excellent though perhaps exaggerated account of this wealthy and influential black abolitionist; Larry Gara, "The Professional Fugitive in the Abolitionist Movement," *Wisconsin Magazine of History* (1965); Charles H. Wesley, "The Negro in the Organization of Abolition," *Phylon* (1941), "The Participation of Negroes in Anti-Slavery Political Parties, *Journal of Negro History* (1944), and "The Negro in New York in the Emancipation Movement, *Journal of Negro History* (1939); William and Jane H. Pease, "Anti-Slavery Ambivalence: Immediatism, Expediency, Race," *American Quarterly* (1965); Leon F. Litwack, "The Abolitionist Dilemma: The Anti-Slavery Movement and the Northern Negro," *New England Quarterly* (1961); Benjamin Quarles, "The Breach Between Garrison and Douglass," *Journal of Negro History* (1938); William and Jane H. Pease, "Boston Garrisonians

and the Problem of Frederick Douglass," *Canada Journal of History* (1967); and Eric Foner, "Politics and Prejudice: The Free Soil Party and the Negro, 1819–1852," *Journal of Negro History* (1965).

The outpouring of works examining the African-American slave community and the period of involuntary servitude in general has continued. Among the best of the more recent works are: Herbert S. Klein, *The Middle Passage: Comparative Studies in the Atlantic Slave Trade* (1978); Gerald W. Mullin, *Flight and Rebellion: Slave Resistance in Eighteenth-Century Virginia* (1972); T.H. Breen and Stephen Innes, *"Myne Owne Ground": Race and Freedom on Virginia's Eastern Shore, 1640–1676* (1980); Ira Berlin and Ronald Hoffman, *Slavery and Freedom in the Age of the American Revolution* (1983); Sidney Kaplan, *The Black Presence in the Era of the American Revolution, 1770–1800* (1973); David Brion Davis, *The Problem of Slavery in the Age of Revolution* (1975); Stavghton Lynd, *Class Conflict, Slavery and the United States Constitution* (1967); Lamont D. Thomas, *Rise to Be a People, A Biography of Paul Cuffe* (1986); Eugene Genovese, *Roll Jordan Roll: The World the Slaves Made* (1974); John Blassingame, *The Slave Community: Plantation Life in the Antebellum South* (1974); and Leslie Howard Owens, *This Species of Property: Slave Life and Culture in the Old South* (1976).

Additional valuable works include: Charles J. Joyner, *Down By the Riverside: A South Carolina Slave Community* (1984); Ann J. Lane, ed., *The Debate Over Slavery: Stanley Elkins and His Critics* (1971); William L. Van Deburg, *The Slave Drivers: Black Agricultural Labor Supervisors in the Ante-Bellum South* (1979); and Deborah Gray White, *Arn't I a Woman? Female Slaves in the Plantation South* (1985). Also, R.J.M. Blackett, *Building an Anti-Slavery Wall: Black Americans in the Atlantic Abolitionist Movement* (1983); Waldo E. Martin, Jr., *The Mind of Frederick Douglass* (1984); and Peter Wood, *Black Majority: Negroes in Colonial South Carolina from 1670 Through the Stono Rebellion* (1974). On free blacks, particularly, the best of the more recent works is Ira Berlin, *Slaves without Masters: The Free Negro in the Antebellum South* (1975).

Others of significant value are: Michael P. Johnson and James L. Roark, *No Chariot Let Down: Charleston's Free People of Color on the Eve of the Civil War* (1984); James Oliver Horton and Lois Horton, *Black Bostonians: Family Life and Community Struggle in the Ante-Bellum North* (1979); Robert Cottrol, *The Afro-Yankees: Providence's Black Community in the Antebellum Era* (1982); Suzanne Lebsock, *The Free Women of Petersburg: Status and Culture in a Southern Town* (1984); and Juliet E.K. Walker, *Free Frank: A Black Pioneer on the Ante-Bellum Frontier* (1984).

1861–1876

Significant older works about blacks during the Civil War include: Aptheker, "Negro Casualties in the Civil War," *Journal of Negro History* (1947); Edgar A. Toppin, "Humbly They Served: The Black Brigade in the Defense of Cincinnati," *Journal of Negro History* (1963); Richard H. Abbott, "Massachusetts and the Recruitment of Southern Negroes, 1863–1865," *Civil War History* (1986); N.W. Stephenson, "The Question of Arming the Slaves," *American Historical Review* (1913); Harvey Wish, "Slave Disloyalty Under the Confederacy," *Journal of Negro History* (1938); Charles H. Wesley, "The Employment of Negroes as Soldiers in the Confederate Army," *Journal of Negro History* (1919); Charles H. Wesley, "Lincoln's Plan for Colonizing the Emancipated Negro," *Journal of Negro History* (1919); Benjamin Quarles, *The Negro in the Civil War* (1953); Dudley Cornish, *The Sable Arm* (1956); James M. McPherson, *The Negro's Civil War* (1965); Thomas Wentworth Higginson, *Army Life in a Black Regiment* (1870), relating the experiences of a white officer with black troops; John Hope Franklin, *The Emancipation Proclamation* (1962) and *The Militant South* (1964); Benjamin Quarles, *Lincoln and the Negro* (1962); James M. McPherson, *The Struggle for Equality* (1964); Bell I. Wiley, *Southern Negroes, 1861–1865* (1953); V. Jacque Voegel, *Free but Not Equal* (1967); C.L. Wagandt, *The*

Mighty Revolution: Negro Emancipation in Maryland (1965); Charlotte L. Forten, *The Journal of Charlotte L. Forten* (1961), the diary of a black teacher in the South during the Civil War; and Irvin H. Lee, *Negro Medal of Honor Men* (1967).

Notable older works on the Reconstruction era include: Bernard Weisberger, "The Dark and Bloody Ground of Reconstruction Historiography," *Journal of Southern History* (1959); W.E.B. Du Bois, "Reconstruction and its Benefits," *American Historical Review* (1910); Joseph A. Barome, ed., "The Autobiography of Hiram Revels," *Midwest Journal* (1952–53); A.E. Perkins, "Oscar James Dunn," *Phylon* (1943); Robert H. Woody, "Jonathan Jasper Wright," *Journal of Negro History* (1933); Edward F. Sweat, "Francis L. Cardozo-Profile of Integrity in Reconstruction Politics," *Journal of Negro History* (1961); LaWanda Cox, "The Promise of Land for the Freedman," *Mississippi Valley Historical Review* (1958); Patrick W. Riddleberger, "The Radical's Abandonment of the Negro During Reconstruction, *Journal of Negro History* (1960); and Leslie H. Fishel, Northern Prejudice and Negro Suffrage, 1865–1900," *Journal of Negro History* (1954), "The Negro in Northern Politics, 1870–1900," *Mississippi Valley Historical Review* (1953), and "Repercussions of Reconstruction: The Northern Negro, 1870–1883," *Civil War History* (1968).

The pioneer revisionist work on the Reconstruction is W.E.B. Du Bois's *Black Reconstruction* (1935). Kenneth Stampp's *Era of Reconstruction* (1965) is a leading modern revisionist survey; other sources include John Hope Franklin, *Reconstruction After the Civil War* (1961); Lerone Bennett, *Black Power USA: The Human Side of Reconstruction, 1867–77* (1967), a slightly exaggerated account; LaWanda and John Cox, *Politics, Principle, and Prejudice* (1963), a revisionist study of national politics in the Reconstruction period; Henry L. Swint, *The Northern Teacher in the South* (1965); Robert Cruden, *The Negro in Reconstruction* (1965); Theodore Wilson, *The Black Codes of the South* (1965); Henderson Donald, *The Negro Freedman* (1952), not a wholly satisfactory work; Joel Williamson, *After Slavery* (1965), and Willie Lee Rose, *Rehearsal for Reconstruction: The Port Royal Experiment* (1964), both fine studies of South Carolina.

Further Reconstruction resources are: Joe M. Richardson, *The Negro in the Reconstruction of Florida* (1966); Vernon Lane Wharton, *The Negro in Mississippi, 1865–1890* (1947); A.A. Taylor, *The Negro in the Reconstruction of Virginia* (1926); Otis A. Singletary, *Negro Militia and Reconstruction* (1957); and Samuel Smith, *The Negro in Congress, 1870–1901* (1940). John M. Langston's *From the Virginia Plantation to the National Capitol* (1894) and John R. Lynch's *The Facts of Reconstruction* (1913) are both reminiscences of black Reconstruction politicians.

Add to the above resources Walter C. Fleming, *Documentary History of Reconstruction* (3 vols., 1906–1907); Harry Hyman, ed., *New Frontiers of the American Reconstruction* (1966); and James P. Shenton, ed., *The Reconstruction* (1963). E. Merton Coulter's *Negro Legislators in Georgia During the Reconstruction Period* (1968) and *The South During Reconstruction* (1948) both warrant caution for anti-Negro bias.

On the Freedman's Bureau, George Bentley's *A History of the Freedmen's Bureau* (1955) is the standard work, although not entirely satisfactory; others include William McFeeley, *Yankee Stepfather: General Oliver O. Howard and the Freedmen* (1968), a recent work that tells much about the workings of the Freedmen's Bureau as well as the life of its federal commissioner; Martin Abbott, *The Freedman's Bureau in South Carolina* (1967); and Walter L. Fleming, *The Freedmen's Savings Bank* (1927).

Among the more highly recommended of the recent works about the Civil War and Emancipation are: Hans L. Trefonsse, *Lincoln's Decision for Emancipation* (1975); Clarence L. Mohr, *On the Threshold for Freedom: Masters and Slaves in Civil War Georgia* (1985); C. Peter Ripley, *Slaves*

and Freedmen in Civil War Louisiana (1975); Roger L. Ransom and Richard Sutch, *One Kind of Freedom: The Economic Consequences of Emancipation* (1977); Eric Foner, *Nothing but Freedom* (1983); Ira Berlin, et al., *The Black Military Experience* (1982); Peter Kolchin, *First Freedom: The Responses of Alabama's Blacks to Emancipation and Reconstruction* (1972); Leon F. Litwack, *Been in the Storm So Long: The Aftermath of Slavery* (1979); Claude F. Oubre, *Forty Acres and a Mule: The Freedmen's Bureau and Black Land Ownership* (1978); Lawrence Levine, *Black Culture and Black Consciousness* (1977); Howard Rabinowitz, ed., *Southern Black Leaders of the Reconstruction Era* (1982); and Ronald E. Butchart, *Northern Schools, Southern Blacks and Reconstruction: Freedmen's Education, 1862–1875.*

1877–1900

Studies of black life in the post-Reconstruction era include: Clarence A. Bacote, "Negro Proscription and Proposed Solutions in Georgia, 1880–1908," *Journal of Southern History* (1959); John Hope Franklin, "The Negro Goes to School: The Genesis of Legal Segregation in Southern Schools," *South Atlantic Quarterly* (1959); Jack Abramowitz, "The Negro in the Populist Movement," *Journal of Negro History* (1953); Charles Crowe, "Tom Watson, Populists, and Blacks Reconsidered," *Journal of Negro History* (1970), perhaps the best summary on the subject; Edwin S. Redkey, "Bishop Turner's African Dream," *Journal of American History* (1967); C. Vann Woodward, *Origins of the New South* (1951); Thomas Clark and Albert Kirwan, *The South Since Appomattox* (1967); Charles Wynes, ed., *The Negro in the South Since 1865* (1965); George B. Tindall, *South Carolina Negroes, 1877–1900* (1952); Frenise Logan, *The Negro in North Carolina, 1876–1894* (1964); Albert D. Kirwan, *Revolt of the Rednecks* (1951), a good work on Mississippi politics; Stanley P. Hirshon, *Farewell to the Bloody Shirt* (1962); Vincent P. DeSantis, *Republicans Face the Southern Question* (1959); and Rayford Logan, *The Negro in American Life and Thought: The Nadir,* also titled *The*

Betrayal of the Negro, (1954), an excellent study of the entire period.

The standard account of the origins of segregation is C. Vann Woodward's *The Strange Career of Jim Crow* (third edition, 1966). More accounts of the period are: Horace Mann Bond, *Negro Education in Alabama* (1939); Louis R. Harlan, *Separate and Unequal* (1958); Henry Bullock, *A History of Negro Education in the South* (1967); Edwin S. Redkey, *Black Exodus* (1969); Charles E. Wynes, *Race Relations in Virginia, 1870–1902* (1961); Everett L. Jones, *The Negro Cowboys* (1965); Shirley Graham and George D. Liscomb, *Dr. George Washington Carver, Scientist* (1965); Arthur F. Raper, *The Tragedy of Lynching* (1933); and David M. Chalmers, *Hooded Americanism: The First Century of the Ku Klux Klan* (1965).

The best recent scholarship on the difficult period after Reconstruction includes: Charles L. Flynn, *White Land, Black Labor: Caste and Class in Late 19th Century Georgia* (1983); Arnold Taylor, *Travail and Triumph: Black Life and Culture in the South Since the Civil War* (1976); Paula Giddings, *When and Where I Enter . . . The Impact of Black Women on Race and Sex in America* (1984); Howard Rabonwitz, *Race Relations in the Urban South, 1865–1890* (1978); and H. Leon Prather, *"We Have Taken a City": The Wilmington Massacre and Coup of 1898* (1984).

1901–1917

Noteworthy among the earlier studies about the Booker T. Washington era in African American history are August Meier's works, "Booker T. Washington and the Negro Press," *Journal of Negro History* (1953), "Booker T. Washington and the Rise of the NAACP," *The Crisis* (1954) and "Toward a Reinterpretation of Booker T. Washington," *Journal of Southern History* (1957); Daniel Walden, "The Contemporary Opposition to the Political Ideas of Booker T. Washington," *Journal of Negro History* (1960); Donald J. Calesta, "Booker T. Washington: Another Look," *Journal of Negro History* (1964); and

Louis R. Harlan, "Booker T. Washington and the White Man's Burden," *American Historical Review* (1966).

Other sources on African Americans in the early twentieth century are: Vincent Harding, "W.E.B. Du Bois and the Black Messianic Tradition," *Freedomways* (1969); Mary L. Chaffee, "W.E.B. Du Bois' Concept of the Racial Problem in the United States," *Journal of Negro History* (1956); Elliott M. Rudwick, "The Niagara Movement," *Journal of Negro History* (1957); Thomas R. Cripps, "The Reaction of the Negro to the Motion Picture 'Birth of a Nation'," *Historian* (1963); Dewey W. Grantham, "The Progressive Movement and the Negro," *South Atlantic Quarterly* (1955); Kathleen Wohlgemuth, "Woodrow Wilson and Federal Segregation," *Journal of Negro History* (1959); Nancy J. Weiss, "The Negro and the New Freedom: Fighting Wilsonian Segregation," *Political Science Quarterly* (1969); Bernard Mandel, "Samuel Gompers and the Negro Workers, 1886–1914," *Journal of Negro History* (1955); Hugh Hawkins, ed., *Booker T. Washington and His Critics* (1962); August Meier, *Negro Thought in America, 1880–1915* (1963); Samuel R. Spencer, *Booker T. Washington and the Negro's Place in American Life* (1957); and Booker T. Washington's book-length works, *The Future of the American Negro* (1899), *Up from Slavery* (1900), *The Negro in the South* (1907), and *Selected Speeches* (1932).

Additional resources include: Francis Broderick, *W.E.B. Du Bois, Propagandist of the Negro Protest* (1961); Du Bois's autobiographies, *Dusk of Dawn* (1940) and *Autobiography of W.E.B. Du Bois* (1968), as well as his penetrating *The Souls of Black Folk* (1903); Kelly Miller, *Race Adjustment* (1908); Charles Kellogg, *NAACP* (1967); Langston Hughes, *Fight For Freedom: Story of the NAACP* (1962); Robert L. Jack, *History of the NAACP* (1943); Ray Stanndard Baker, *Following the Color Line* (1908); I.A. Newby, *Jim Crow's Defense: Anti-Negro Thought in America, 1900–1930* (1965); Charles Wesley, *Negro Labor in the United States 1850–1925* (1927); Elliott M.

Rudwick, *Race Riot at East St. Louis, July 2, 1917* (1964); Emmett J. Scott, *The American Negro in the World War* (1919); Ullin W. Leavell, *Philanthropy in Negro Education* (1930); and W.E.B. Du Bois, *Atlanta University Studies* (1898–1901).

Any examination of Booker T. Washington and his era must begin with Louis R. Harlan's *Booker T. Washington: The Making of a Black Leader, 1856–1901* (1972) and *Booker T. Washington: The Wizard of Tuskegee, 1901–1915* (1983). Other useful publications include: Arnold Rampersad, *The Art and Imagination of W.E.B. Du Bois* (1976); Alfred Moss, *The American Negro Academy: Voice of the Talented Tenth* (1981); and Walter B. Weare, *Black Business in the New South: A History of the North Carolina Mutual Insurance Company* (1975); Ann J. Lane, *The Brownsville Affair: National Crisis and Black Reaction* (1971); Willard B. Gatewood, *Black Americans and the White Man's Burden, 1898–1903* (1975); David M. Katzman, *Before the Ghetto: Black Detroit in the Nineteenth Century* (1973); Robert L. Zangrando, *The NAACP's Crusade against Lynching, 1909–1950* (1980); Nancy Weiss, *The National Urban League, 1910–1940* (1974); Alfreda M. Duster, ed., *Crusade For Justice: The Autobiography of Ida B. Wells* (1970); Stephen R. Fox, *Guardian of Boston: William Monroe Trotter* (1971), the story of one of Booker T. Washington's most militant antagonists; and Emma Lou Thornborough, *T. Thomas Fortune: Militant Journalist* (1972).

18–1932

e better of the older works on the Great gration include: Emmett J. Scott, ed., "Letof Negro Migrants", *Journal of Negro History* 19); Charles S. Johnson, "How Much Is the ration a Flight from Persecution?," *Opportunity* (1923); Gilbert Osofsky, *Harlem: The ing of a Ghetto* (1966) James Weldon Johnson, *Black Manhattan* (1930); Seth Scheiner, *o Mecca* (1965); Claude McKay, *Harlem: o Metropolis* (1940); Allan Spear, *Black Chi-* (1967); St. Clair Drake and Horace Cayton, *Metropolis* (1940), a classic study of black

Chicagoans; Emmett J. Scott, *Negro Migration during the War* (1920); Thomas J. Woofter, *The Negro Problem in Cities* (1928); Louise V Kennedy, *The Negro Peasant Turns Cityward* (1930); Claude V. Kiser, *Sea Island to City* (1932); Carter G. Woodson, *A Century of Negro Migration* (1918); and Arna Bontemps and Jack Conroy, *Anyplace but Here* (1966).

Other works on the period are: Robert Kerdin, ed., *Voice of the Negro* (1920); Edmund D. Cronon, *Black Moses* (1955), the standard biography of Marcus Garvey; Amy Garvey, *Garnet and Garocyism* (1968); Charles S. Johnson, *The Economic Status of Negroes* (1933); Arthur Fauset, *Black Gods of the Metropolis* (1944); John Hoshor, *God in a Rolls-Royce* (1936) and Sara Harris, *Father Divine: Holy Husband* (1953), both about Father Divine, leader of a pseudo-religious cult; Milton Meltzer and August Meier, *Time of Trial, Time of Hope: The Negro in America, 1919–1941* (1966); Roi Ottley, *The Lonely Warrior: The Life and Times of Robert S. Abbott* (1955), biography of the publisher of the militant newspaper, the *Chicago Defenders*; and Arthur I. Waskow, *From Race Riot to Sit-In* (1966), an account black protest from the riots of 1919 to the 1960s.

On the literature of this period, consult: Theodore Gross, eds., *Dark Symphony* (1968); John Henrik Clarke, ed., *American Negro Short Stories* (1966); Langston Hughes ed., *The Best Short Stories by Negro Writers* (1967); Abraham Chapman, ed., *Black Voices* (1968); Sterling Brown, *The Negro in American Fiction* (1937); Saunders Redding, *To Make a Poet Black* (1939); Stephen Bronz, *Roots of Negro Racial Consciousness* (1969); Mercer Cook and Stephen Henderson, *The Militant Black Writer in Africa and the United States* (1969); Alain Locke, ed., *The New Negro* (1925), an anthology of the works by the Harlem Renaissance writers; Blanche Ferguson, *Countee Cullen and the Negro Renaissance* (1966); James Weldon Johnson, *Along This Way* (1933), an autobiographical treatment, as is Langston Hughes's *The Big Sea* (1940); and Benjamin

Brawley, "The Negro Literary Renaissance," *The Southern Workman* (1927).

Among the most recommended newer studies about this era are: Robert V. Haynes, *A Night of Violence: The Houston Riot of 1917* (1976); William Tuttle, *Race Riot: Chicago in the Red Summer of 1919* (1970); Mary F. Berry, *Black Resistance, White Law: A History of Constitutional Racism in America* (1971); Theodore Draper, *The Rediscovery of Black Nationalism* (1970); Nathan I. Muggins, *Harlem Renaissance* (1971); James Richard Giles, *Claude McKay* (1976); Robert E. Hemenway, *Zora Neale Hurston: A Literary Biography* (1978); Russell J. Linnerman, ed., *Alain Locke: Reactions of a Modern Renaisance Man* (1983); Kenneth R. Manning, *Black Apollo of Science: The Life of Ernest Everett Just* (1983); Linda O. McMurry, *George Washington Carver: Scientist and Symbol* (1981); and Marcia M. Mathews, *Henry Ossawa Tanner: American Anist* (1969).

1933–1940

The African American in the New Deal era is still an inadequately treated subject. There are, however, some good studies. Among the older ones are James A. Harrell, "Negro Leadership in the Election Year 1936," *Journal of Southern History* (1968); John A. Salmond, "The CCC and the Negro," *Journal of American History* (1965); Leslie H. Fishel, "The Negro in the New Deal Era," *Wisconsin Magazine of History* (1964–65); Bernard Sternsher, ed., *The Negro in Depression and War* (1969); Arnold Hill, *The Negro and Economic Reconstruction* (1937); Abram Harris, *The Negro as Capitalist* (1936); Charles S. Johnson, et al., *The Collapse of Cotton Tenancy* (1938); and Charles S. Johnson, *Shadow of the Plantation* (1934).

John Dollar's *Caste and Class in a Southern Town* (1937), an in-depth study of black life and race relations in a Mississippi town, is considered by many to be a classic; Harold Gosnell's *Negro Politicians* (1935) is a standard account focusing on Chicago. Other notable sources are: Wilson Record, *The Negro and the Communist Party*

(1951); E. Franklin Frazier, *Negro Youth at the Crossroads* (1949); St. Clair Drake and Horace Cayton, *Black Metropolis* (cited above); James W. Ford, *Hunger and Terror in Harlem* (1935), the story of that year's Harlem riot; Roi Ottley, *New World A-Coming* (1943), treats FDR's Black Cabinet; Robert C. Weaver, *Negro Labor* (1946); Marian Anderson, *My Lord What a Morning* (1956), an autobiography of the well known contralto; and Catherine O. Peare, *Mary McLeod Bethune* (1961).

More recent works which have added to a better understanding of blacks during the New Deal era include: Raymond Walters, *Negroes and the Great Depression: The Problem of Economic Recovery*; Nancy Weiss, *Farewell to the Party of Lincoln: Black Politics in the Age of F.D.R.* (1983); Nell I. Painter, *The Narrating of Hosea Hudson: His Life as a Negro Communist in the South* (1979); Charles H. Martin, *The Angelo Herndon Case and Southern Justice* (1976); Mark Naison, *Communists in Harlem During the Depression* (1983) John H. Kirby, *Black Americans in the Roosevelt Liberalism and Race* (1980); William H. Harris, *Keeping the Faith: A. Philip Randolph, Milton P. Webster, and the Brotherhood of Sleeping Car Porters, 1925–1937* (1977); and Harvard Sitkoff, *A New Deal for Blacks: The Emergence of Civil Rights as a National Issue*.

1941–1945

The most noteworthy works about Africans Americans during the war years are Richard M. Dalfiume, "The Forgotten Years of the Negro Revolution," *Journal of American History* (1968); Dan T. Carter, *Scottsboro* (1969), the story of the multifaceted Alabama rape case; Alfred M. Lee, *Detroit Race Riot* (1943); Ulysses Lee, *The Employment of Negro Troops* (1966); Herbert Garfinkel, *When Negroes March* (1959), the story of A. Philip Randolph's proposed March on Washington; Rayford Logan, ed., *What the Negro Wants* (1944); Loren Miller's *The Petitioners* (1968), on the legal cases of the NAACP; Walter White's *A Rising Wind* (1945), a fine account of blacks on the fighting front; and Louis

Ruchames, *Race, Jobs and Politics: The Story of FEPC* (1953).

Other excellent sources include: Gunnar Myrdal, *An American Dilemma* (1944), a classic study of American race relations; Louis Kesselman, *The Social Politics of FEPC* (1953); B.R. Brazeal, *The Brotherhood of Sleeping Car Porters* (1946); Carl N. Degler, "The Negro in America—Where Myrdal Went Wrong," *New York Times Magazine* (1969); and Poppy Cannon, *A Gentle Knight* (1956), a biography of the NAACP leader Walter F. White written by his wife. Richard Wright's *Black Boy* (1945) is an autobiographical novel; see also John D. Silvera, *The Negro in World War II* (1946); Seymour J. Schorsfield, *The Negro in the Armed Forces* (1945); Earl Brown, "American Negroes and the War," *Harper's Magazine* (1942); John Temple Graves, "The Southern Negro and the War Crisis," *Virginia Quarterly Review* (1942); and Morris J. MacGregor, Jr., *Integration of the Armed Forces: 1940–1965* (1981).

1945–1954

The most useful early studies about the post-war years include: Elliott M. Rudwick, "How CORE Began," *Social Science Quarterly* (1969); Thurgood Marshall, "An Evaluation of Recent Efforts to Achieve Racial Integration Through Resort to the Courts," *Journal of Negro Education* (1952); L.D. Reddick, "The Negro Policy of the United States Army, 1775–1945," *Journal of Negro History* (1949); Walter F. White, *A Man Called White* (1948), the autobiography of the second executive secretary of the NAACP; Henry L. Moon, *Balance of Power: The Negro Vote* (1948), examining the role of the black vote in the election of 1948; Richard J. Stillman, *Integration of the Negro in the United States Armed Forces* (1968); Richard Dalfiume, *Desegregation of the U.S. Armed Forces* (1969); Harry S. Ashmore, *The Negro and the Schools* (1954); Abram Kardiner and Lionel Ovesey, *The Mark of Oppression* (1951), a classic study of the psychological effects of discrimination; J. Alvin Kugelmann, *Ralph J. Bunche, Fighter for Peace* (1952); Robert Penn Warren, *Who Speaks for the Negro?* (1954); Rayford W. Logan, *The Negro and the Post-War World* (1954); and Robert C. Weaver, *The Negro Ghetto* (1948).

Recent works about the post-war years in African American history include: Paul Burstein, *Discrimination, Jobs, and Politics: The Struggle for Equal Employment Opportunity in the United States Since the New Deal* (1985); Gerald Home, *Black and Red: W.E.B. Du Bois and the Afro-American Response to the Cold War, 1944–1963* (1986); William C. Berman, *The Politics of Civil Rights in the Truman Administration* (1970); Donald R. McCoy and Richard T. Ruetten, *Quest and Response: Minority Rights and the Truman Administration* (1973); and Jules Tygiel, *Baseball's Great Experiment: Jackie Robinson and His Legacy* (1984).

1954–1964

A flood of articles and books has appeared about the Civil Rights era; the better studies include: August Meier, "On the Significance of Martin Luther King," *New Politics* (1965); Edward A. Leonard, "Nonviolence and Violence in American Racial Protests, 1945–1967," *Rocky Mountain Social Science Journal* (1969); Lerone Bennett, "The South and the Negro: Martin Luther King, Jr.," *Ebony* (1957); Lerone Bennett, Jr., "Daisy Bates: First Lady of Little Rock," *Ebony* (1958), about the Little Rock NAACP leader who spearheaded school integration in her town; Benjamin Muse, *Ten Years of Prelude* (1964) and *The American Negro Revolution* (1968); Lerone Bennett, *What Manner of Man?* (1964), *Where Do We Go From Here?* (1967), and *The Trumpet of Conscience* (1969); James Peck, *Freedom Ride* (1962); James Farmer, *Freedom—When?* (1965); Waskow, *From Race Riot to Sit-In* (cited above); and Merill Proudfoot, *Diary of a Sit-In* (1962).

Howard Zinn's *The New Abolitionists* (1964) is mostly a story about the SNCC; Elizabeth Sutherland edited *Letters from Mississippi* (1965), which gives the views of civil rights workers in Mississippi. Also detailing civil rights work in Mississippi in 1964 are Len Holt's *The Summer That Didn't End* (1965) and Sally Belfrage's

Freedom Summer (1965). Other sources are: James Silver, *Mississippi, The Closed Society* (second edition, 1966); Louis Lomax, *The Negro Revolt* (1962); Charles Silberman, *Crisis in Black and White* (1964); Alan Westin, ed., *Freedom Now!* (1964); Lerone Bennett, *The Negro Mood* (1964); James Q. Wilson, *Negro Politics: The Search For Leadership* (1960); Jack Greenberg, *Race Relations and American Law* (1969), memoirs of an NAACP lawyer; and William Brink and Louis Harris, *The Negro Revolution in America* (1964).

More good sources on the Civil Rights era include: C. Eric Lincoln, *The Black Muslims in America* (1969); E.U. Essien-Udom, *Black Nationalism* (1962), also on the Muslims; E. Franklin Frazier, *Black Bourgeoisie* (1957), a classic on the black middle class; Robert F. Williams, *Negroes with Guns* (1962); Carl Rowan, *Go South to Sorrow* (1957); United States Commission on Civil Rights, *Freedom to the Free* (1963); Doris E. Saunders, *The Day They Marched* (1963), an illustrated account of the 1963 March on Washington; Vivian W. Henderson, *The Economic Status of Negroes* (1963); Robert Brisbane, *Black Activism: Black Revolution in the U.S., 1954–1970* (1984); Clayborne Carson, *In Struggle, SNCC and the Black Awakening of the 1960s* (1981); William H. Chafe, *Civilities and Civil Rights: Greensboro, North Carolina and the Black Struggle for Freedom* (1980); Roy Wilkins, *Standing Fast: The Autobiography of Roy Wilkins* (1982); Tony Freyer, *The Little Rock Crisis: A Constitutional Interpretation* (1984); Aldon D. Morris, *The Origins of the Civil Rights Movement: Black Communities Organizing for Change* (1984); and Theodore Cross, *The Black Power Imperative: Racial Inequality and the Politics of Nonviolence* (1984).

1964–1996

The renewed interest in African American history and the Black Revolution, as well as contemporary conditions, have produced a great outpouring of works. Some of the most useful studies are: Ulf Hannerz, "What Negroes Mean by Soul," *Trans-Action* (1968); Martin Kilson,

"Black Power: Anatomy of a Paradox," *Harvard Journal of Negro Affairs* (1968); A.J. Gregor, *Science and Society* (1963); Stokely Carmichael, "What We Want," *The New York Review of Books* (1966); Kenneth Clark, *Dark Ghetto* (1965); Thomas F. Pettigrew, *A Portrait of the Negro American* (1964); Alphonso Pincney, *Black Americans* (1969), a compact, interdisciplinary study; Karl E. and Alma F. Taeuber, *Negroes in Cities* (1965); Lee Rainwater and William Yancey, *The Moynihan Report and the Politics of Controversy* (1967); Ulf Hannerz, *Soulside* (1969); and Claude Brown, *Manchild in the Promised Land* (1965), a critically acclaimed autobiography of ghetto life.

Some noteworthy studies on urban race riots are: Paul Jacobs, *Prelude to Riot: A View of Urban America from the Bottom Up* (1967); Robert Conot, *Rivers of Blood, Years of Darkness* (1967), about the Watts Riot; Fred Shapiro and James Sullivan, *Race Riot* (1969); Ben W. Gilbert, *Ten Blocks from the White House* (1969), about the Washington, D.C. riot; John Hersey, *The Algiers Motel Incident* (1968), a novelistic treatment of one aspect of the 1967 Detroit riot; Louis H. Masottli and Don R. Bowen, eds., *Riots and Rebellion* (1969); William H. Grier and Price M. Cobbs, *Black Rage* (1968), a psychological study; Robert Fogelson, "From Resentment to Confrontation: The Police, the Negroes and the Outbreak of the 1960s Riots," *Political Science Quarterly* (1968); Nathan S. Caplan and Jeffrey M. Paige, "A Study of Ghetto Rioters," *Scientific American* (1968).

Alex Haley's *The Autobiography of Malcolm X* (1965) has become a classic. Other good sources are: George Brietman, *Malcolm X: The Man and His Times* (1969); Floyd Barbour, ed., *The Black Power Revolt* (1968), a documentary collection; Stokeley Carmichael and Charles Hamilton, *Black Power* (1967), a political definition of the controversial slogan by one of the originators of the concept; H. Rap Brown, *Die, Nigger, Die* (1969), a loosely autobiographical account written while Brown was in exile; Whitney M. Young, Jr., *Beyond Racism: Building an Open Society* (1969), views of the moderate head of the National

Urban League; Floyd McKissick, *Three-Fifths of a Man* (1969), views of the militant CORE leader; Nathan Wright, *Black Power and Urban Unrest* (1967); Lewis M. Killian, *Impossible Revolution? Black Power and the American Dream* (1968); and Eldridge Cleaver, *Soul on Ice* (1968), *Eldridge Cleaver* (1969), *Post-Prison Writings and Speeches* (1969), writings of the exiled Black Panther leader.

Other sources on the spirit of the times include: Harold Cruse, *The Crisis of the Negro Intellectual and Rebellion or Revolution* (1968); C. Eric Lincoln, ed., *Is Anybody Listening to Black America?* (1968), essays on the contemporary black mood; Gary T. Marx, *Protest and Prejudice* (revised edition, 1968); Robert Allen, *Black Awakening in Capitalist America* (1969); Elijah Muhammad, *Message to the Black Man in America* (1965), words from the head of the Muslim sect; Calvin Hernton, *Sex and Racism in America* (1967), an interesting, though slightly exaggerated work; Floyd B. Barbour, *The Black Power Revolt* (1968); Charles E. Fager, *White Reflections on Black Power* (1967); William Bradford Huie, *Three Lives for Mississippi* (1965), a well told story of the 1964 murders of civil rights workers Goodman, Cheney, and Schwerner; Fred Powledge, *Black Power, White Resistance: Notes on the New Civil War* (1967); *Report of the National Commission on Civil Disorders* (1968); Thomas F. Gossett, *Race: The History of An Idea in America* (1963); Vincent Harding, *Black Radicalism in America* (1970); Hanes Walton, *The Negro Pilgrimage in America* (1969); Hubert G. Locke, *The Detroit Riot of 1967* (1969); Robert H. Brisbane, *The Black Vanguard* (1970), traces the origins of the Negro "social revolution;" Lee Rainwater, *Behind Ghetto Walls* (1970).

Theodore Draper's *The Rediscovery of Black Nationalism* (1970) is not entirely satisfactory, but attempts to give a basic general treatment of the subject; Debbie Louis, *And We Are Not Saved: A History of the Movement as People* (1970), contains first-hand data from a young white CORE worker; C. Eric Lincoln, ed., *Martin Luther King, Jr.: A Profile* (1970) includes excerpts tak-

en from King's own writings as well as the assessments of others; James Boggs's *Racism and the Class Struggle* is a radical essay on the conditions of black Americans; and Peter Goldman's *Report from Black America* (1970) is a study of contemporary black public opinion.

New works on religion and racism include: Joseph C. Hough, *Black Power and White Protestants* (1968), Charles F. Sleeper, *Black Power and Christian Responsibility* (1969), and Robert S. Lecky and H. Elliott Wright, eds., *Black Manifesto: Religion, Racism, and Reparations* (1969).

Important critical studies of black capitalism include Robert L. Allen, *Black Awakening in Capitalist America* (1969) and Earl Ofari, *The Myth of Black Capitalism* (1970).

Recent noteworthy writings on the era which began in 1964 include: Donald Freed, *Agony in New Haven: The Trial of Bobby Seale, Ericka Huggins and the Black Panther Party* (1973); John Henry Cutter, *Ed Broome: Biography of a Senator* (1972); Edwin K. Norton, *Juror Number Four* (1973), the story of the trial of thirteen Black Panthers as seen by one of the jurors; Peter Goldman, *The Death and Life of Malcolm X* (1973); Stephen Henderson, *Understanding the New Black Poetry* (1972); Huey P. Newton, *Revolutionary Suicide* (1973).

Stephen B. Oates's *Let the Trumphet Sound: The Life of Martin Luther King, Jr.* (1982) is perhaps the best biography of the slain civil rights leader to date. Other sources on the period are: David J. Garrow, *Protest At Selma: Martin Luther King, Jr. and the Voting Rights Act of 1965* and *The FBI and Martin Luther King, Jr.* (1981); Richard Reeves, *The Reagan Detour* (1985); Adolph Reed, Jr., *The Jesse Jackson Phenomenon: The Crisis in Afro-American Politics* (1986); Barbara Reynolds, *Jesse Jackson, America's David* (1985); John A. Davis, ed., *Africa As Seen by American Negroes* (1958); Wallace Terry, *Bloods: An Oral History of the Vietnam War by Black Veterans* (1984); John Hope Franklin, *Racial Equality in America* (1976); and William J. Wilson, *The Declining Signifi-*

cance of Race: Blacks and Changing American Institutions (1978).

SELECTED RESOURCES ON THE WORLD WIDE WEB

The African American Mosaic: A Library of Congress Resource Guide for the Study of Black History and Culture
http://www.cweb.loc.gov/exhibits/
African.American/intro.html
A guide to the Library of Congress's African American collections.

African American Perspectives: Pamphlets from the Daniel A. P. Murray Collection 1818–1907
http: lcweb2.loc.gov/ammem/aap/
aaphome.html
A series of 351 rare pamphlets on African American history, life, and culture.

African-American Women On-line Archival Collections
Special Collections Library, Duke University
http://odyssey.lib.duke.edu/
On-line archival collections featuring scanned pages and texts of the writings of African-American women. Currently includes the memoirs of Elizabeth Johnson Harris (1867-1942), an 1857 letter from Vilet Lester, a slave on a North Carolina plantation, and several letters from Hannah Valentine and Lethe Jackson, slaves on the estate of David Campbell, a governor of Virginia.

A Chronology of U.S. Historical Documents
http://www.law.ou.edu/ushist.html

The University of Oklahoma's Law Center provides a chronology of U.S. historical documents, including many important to African American history, like Frederick Douglass's "Appeal to Congress for Impartial Suffrage."

The Faces of Science: African Americans in the Sciences.
Louisiana State University Libraries, Baton Rouge, Louisiana
http://www.lib.lsu.edu/lib/chem/display/
faces.html
Provides biographical information on African Americans in science.

The Gilder Lehrman Institute of American History
http://vi.uh.edu/pages/mintz/GILDER.HTM
Topics covered in the Gilder Lehrman Collection include exploration, expansion, Native Americans, slavery and abolitionism, freedoms and civil liberties, particularly the Bill of Rights and Reconstruction.

The Museum of Slavery in the Atlantic
http://squash.la.psu.edu/~plarson/smuseum/
homepage.html
Provides information regarding the history of slavery.

Nile of the New World
Lower Mississippi River Valley, National Park Service Southeast Region
http://www.cr.nps.gov/delta/index.htm
Provides information on the African American heritage, including slavery and the Underground Railroad.

Illustrations Credits

Illustrations appearing in the *Chronology of African American History* were received from the following sources:

A. Philip Randolph Institute 378

AP/Wide World Photos: i and ii (title and half title pages), 39, 86, 93, 124, 141, 147, 151, 154, 159, 168, 170, 176, 180, 181, 182, 183, 193, 203, 230, 238, 306, 321, 334, 339, 349, 365, 414, 425, 426, 428, 434, 453, 456, 459, 465, 468, 473, 478, 480, 483, 503, 509, 510, 521

Archive Photos, Inc. 153

Belafonte Enterprises, Inc. 499

Bettmann Archive/Newsphotos, Inc. 138, 164, 188, 196, 254, 255, 282, 296, 316, 339, 389, 464, 515

Brooklyn Museum 187

Carl Nesfield 284

Columbia Records 363

Consulate General of Jamaica 130

Denver Public Library-Wester Collection 92

Dwight D. Eisenhower Library 174

Fisk University 57

Granger Collection 34

Harper's Weekly 65, 74, 80, 81, 82, 83, 84, 96, 107

Library of Congress 1, 5, 6, 12, 14, 19, 21, 25, 28, 43, 48, 51, 53, 54, 56, 61, 65, 67, 69, 70, 77, 78, 85, 90, 108, 115, 117, 125, 128, 132, 138, 140, 145, 146, 155, 157, 159, 167, 173, 179, 185, 194, 211, 247, 300, 441

National Aeronautics and Space Administration 372

National Archives 89, 133, 136, 156, 322, 369

National Association for the Advancement of Colored People 142, 166, 337

National Education Television 190

National Portrait Gallery 30, 42

National Urban League 223, 260

New York Public Library 49

Schomburg Center for Research in Black Culture 30

Stephen Spottswood 206

United Negro College Fund 79

United Press International 186

U.S. Army 148, 152, 162

U.S. Defense Department 336

U.S. Navy 149

U.S. Senate Historical Office 87

U.S. War Department 127

Vogue 277

White House 343

SUBJECT INDEX

A

A. Philip Randolph Institute, *176*
Aaron, Hank, 265, *266*, 479
Abbott, Robert S., 116
Abda (slave), 10
Abernathy, Ralph David, 195, 203,
   243–44, 257–58, 275
   autobiography of, 422–23,
      424, 433
   death of, 437–38
Ableman v. Booth, 60
Abolition. *See* Slavery
Abolitionist societies, 23
Abolitionists
   Baptiste, George de, 42
   Barbadoes, James, 34
   Brown, William Wells, 44
   Douglass, Frederick, 50
   Douglass, Sarah Mapps, 37
   Jones, John, 41
   Malvin, John, 33
   Paul, Nathaniel, 44
   Pleasant, Mammy, 52
   Sanderson, Jeremiah Burke, 49
   Smith, Stephen, 41
   Tubman, Harriet, 52–53,
      120, 122
   Turner, Nat, 47
   Truth, Sojourner, 95
   Vassa, Gustavus, 13
   Walker, David, 46
   Wright, Theodore Sedgwick, 45
Abraham (slave), 31
Abyssinian Baptist Church, 509,
   510
Academy Awards, 145, 184, 353,
   452, 514

ACLU. *See* American Civil
   Liberties Union (ACLU)
Acquired immunodeficiency
   syndrome (AIDS), 450, 460,
   490, 495
Act of 1740, 31, 33
Act to Prohibit the Importation of
   Slaves, 557–58
Actors
   Belafonte, Harry, 498
   Bojangles, 136
   Dandridge, Dorothy, 131
   Fetchit, Stepin, 369
   Foxx, Redd, 459
   Goldberg, Whoopi, 452
   Gossett, Louis, Jr., 324, 353
   McDaniel, Hattie, 145
   McQueen, Thelma
      "Butterfly," 512
   Morris, Greg, 520
   Poitier, Sidney, 184
   Robeson, Paul, 307
   Waters, Ethel, 323
Adams, Floyd, Jr., 511
Adams, John (teacher), 37
Adams, John Quincy, 47, 48
Adamsville, Alabama, 422
Addams, Jane, 119
Adderley, Julian "Cannonball," 304
Address to People of State of New
   York on Constitution, 531–35
Adoption, 517
Affirmative action
   and Americans' support of,
      452–53
   in California, 507
   and FBI, 396
   in Georgia, 296, 403

in Louisiana, 348, 512
Supreme Court cases involving,
   362, 367, 372, 403–4,
   410, 506–7
in Washington, D.C., 387
AFL-CIO, 168
Africa, 11, 22, 35, 435
Africa, Ramona, 518
"African" (used as a term), 47
African African American
   Summit, 487
African American History
   Month, 674–75
African American Leadership
   Summit, 497
African-American Marketing &
   Media Association, 447
African American Police
   League, 231
African-American Sports Hall of
   Fame, 518
"African-American" vs.
   "black," 450
African Americans. *See also* Blacks
African Baptist Church, 44
African Burial Ground Museum
   and Research Center, 479
African Free School, 26, *29*
African Free School of New York
   City, 38
African Free Schools, 45, 47
African Lodge No. 459, 31
African Methodist Episcopal
   (A.M.E.) Church, 29, 33, 41,
   89, 312–13, 435
African Methodist Episcopal Zion
   Church, 513

Wallace, George C., 180, 241, 243, 268, 291, 294, 316
Ward, Horace T., 329
Washington (state), 347
Washington, Booker T., *108, 114, 125*
  and "Atlanta Compromise" speech, 107, 622–24
  died, 124
  dined at White House, 113
  The Souls of Black Folk opposed policies of, 114
  sponsored formation of National Negro Business League, 111
  and Trotter, William M., 112–13
  and universities, 93, 108
Washington, Craig A., 429
Washington, D.C.
  Act to Suppress the Slave Trade, 592
  affirmative action ruling for black firefighters in, 387
  Black Muslims took hostages in, 319
  elections in, 445
  King delivered "I Have a Dream" speech in, 182
  population increase reported in, 105
  segregation and desegregation, 162, 164
  schools for blacks in, 37
  "Silent March" reenactment in, 416
  slavery abolished in, 68
  as state, 495
  voting rights in, 78
Washington, Denzel, 475
Washington, George, 15, 16, 17, 22, 23, 24, 26
  last will and testament, 556–57
Washington, Harold, *352,* 352, 353, 381
Washington Technical Institute, 323
Washington, Walter, 194–95
Waters, Ethel, 323
Waters, Maxine, 144
Watts, Julius Caesar, Jr., 500
Wayland Seminary, 73
Weaver, Robert C., 177, 189, 276, 278
Webster Commission, 469
Weekly Advocate, 45
Weinberger, Casper W., 278, 303

Welcome, Mary, 291
Wells, Ebenezer, 15
Wells, Nelson, 73
Wepner, Chuck, 298
WERD (radio station), 157
Wesley, John, 15
West Indies, 5, 11
West Point Military Academy, 89, 92, 93
Western Freedmen's Aid Commission, 82
Wharton, Clifton R., Jr., 495
Wheatley, John, 22
Wheatley, Phillis, 15, 21–22, *23*
Wheeler, Thero M., 264
Whipple, Prince, 26
White Aryan Religion, 486
White Aryan Resistance, 455
White, Bill, 406–7
White County, Georgia, 421
White, George, *112,* 112
White, James C., 348
White, Melvin "Slappy," 510
White, Michael, 425
White, Poppy Cannon, 299
White supremacists, 375, 460, 461, 481, 486. *See also* Ku Klux Klan (KKK); Red Shirts
White, Walter, 144, 165
Whitefield, George, 15
Whitney, Eli, 33
Whittaker, J. C., 92–93, 509
Whittimore, B. Franklin, 83
Why Blacks Kill Blacks, 270
Widener, Warren, 224
Wilberforce School, 44
Wilberforce University, 58–59, 98
Wilberforce, William, 58
Wilder, L. Douglas, 425, *426,* 426, 427, 431–32, 439, 458, 492
Wiley College, 85
Wiley, George, 256
Wilkins, Collie L., 188–89
Wilkins, J. Ernest, 163
Wilkins, Roy, 165, *166,* 234
Williams, Avon, 498
Williams, Damian, 496
Williams, Daniel Hale, 137–38, *138*
Williams, Doug, 385
Williams, Frank, Jr., 466
Williams, Hosea, 284, 293
Williams, James E., Jr., 224
Williams, Poindexter E., 208
Williams, Vanessa, 356
Williams, W. Clyde, 258

Williams, Wayne, 345–46
Williams, Willie L., 466
Wills, 98
Wilmington, North Carolina, 220
Wilmot Proviso, 51
Wilson, A. W., 413
Wilson, Christopher, 476, 489, 494
Wilson, J. S., 63
Wilson, Woodrow, 128
Wind, Timothy, 479, 484
Windward Islands, 4
Winfrey, Oprah, 408, 509
Winthrop, John, 6–7
Wolofs, 4, 5
Women's Army Auxiliary Corps (WAC), 148
Women's Naval Corp (WAVES), 150
Women's Pennsylvania Branch of the American Freedmen's Aid Commission, 37
Wonder, Stevie, 461
Woodbrige, Ruggles, 29
Woods, Granville T., 97
Woods, Keith, 449
Woods, Tiger, 498, 520, *521*
Woodson, Carter G., 123, *124,* 161
World War I, 126
World War II, 150
Wright, Jonathan Jasper, 82, *83*
Wright, Richard, 145, *146*
Wright, Theodore Sedgwick, 45–46
Writers. *See also* Authors; Journalists; Poets
  Brooks, Gwendolyn, 502
  Brown, William Wells, 54–55
  Ellison, Ralph, 495
  Johnson, Charles, 448
  Marrant, John, 15
  Micheaux, Oscar, 96–97
  Morrison, Toni, 494

X

Ximenes (cardinal), 3

Y

Yerby, Frank, 461
Yonkers, New York, 396
York (slave), 36–37, 295
Young, Andrew J., 250, *317,* 318, 338, 325, 438
Young, Charles R., 131